Great Events from History

The Middle Ages

477 - 1453

Great Events from History

The Middle Ages

477 - 1453

Volume 2
c. 1150-May 29, 1453
Indexes

Editor
Brian A. Pavlac
King's College
Wilkes-Barre, Pennsylvania

Consulting Editors
Byron Cannon, *University of Utah*
David A. Crain, *South Dakota State University*
Jeffrey W. Dippmann, *Central Washington University*
Catherine Cymone Fourshey, *Susquehanna University*
Richard N. Frye, *Harvard University*
Katherine Anne Harper, *Loyola Marymount University*
Franklin Ng, *California State University, Fresno*
John A. Nichols, *Slippery Rock University*
Herbert Plutschow, *University of California at Los Angeles*

Salem Press
Pasadena, California   Hackensack, New Jersey

Editor in Chief: Dawn P. Dawson
Editorial Director: Christina J. Moose
Project Editor: Rowena Wildin
Developmental Editor: Leslie Ellen Jones
Copy Editor: Desiree Dreeuws
Assistant Editor: Andrea E. Miller
Editorial Assistant: Dana Garey
Photograph Editor: Philip Bader
Acquisitions Editor: Mark Rehn
Research Supervisor: Jeffry Jensen
Production Editor: Cynthia Beres
Graphics and Design: James Hutson
Layout: Eddie Murillo

Cover photos: PhotoDisc, Corbis

∞ The paper used in these volumes conforms to the American National Standard for Permanence of Paper for Printed Library Materials, Z39.48-1992 (R1997).

Some of the essays in this work originally appeared in the following Salem Press sets: *Great Events from History* (1972-1980, edited by Frank N. Magill), *Chronology of European History: 15,000 B.C. to 1997* (1997, edited by John Powell; associate editors, E. G. Weltin, José M. Sánchez, Thomas P. Neill, and Edward P. Keleher), *Great Events from History: North American Series, Revised Edition* (1997, edited by Frank N. Magill; associate editor, John L. Loos), *Great Events from History: Ancient and Medieval Series* (1972, edited by Frank N. Magill; associate editor, E. G. Weltin), and *Great Events from History: Modern European Series* (1973, edited by Frank N. Magill; associate editors, Thomas P. Neill and José M. Sánchez).

Library of Congress Cataloging-in-Publication Data

Great events from history. The Middle Ages, 477-1453 / editor, Brian A. Pavlac ; consulting editors, Byron Cannon, . . . [et al.].

p. cm.

Some of the essays were previously published in various works.

Includes bibliographical references and indexes.

ISBN 1-58765-167-X (set : alk. paper) — ISBN 1-58765-168-8 (v. 1 : alk. paper) — ISBN 1-58765-169-6 (v. 2 : alk. paper)

1. Middle Ages — History. 2. Civilization, Medieval. I. Title: Middle Ages, 477-1453. II. Pavlac, Brian Alexander, 1956- III. Cannon, Byron, 1940-

D119.G74 2004

909.07—dc22

2004016640

First Printing

PRINTED IN THE UNITED STATES OF AMERICA

Contents

Keyword List of Contents lv
List of Maps and Tables lxix
Maps lxxi

1101-1200 c.e. *(continued)*

c. 1150, Moors Transmit Classical Philosophy and Medicine to Europe 507
c. 1150, Refinements in Banking 511
1150, Venetian Merchants Dominate Trade with the East 513
c. 1150-1200, Development of Gothic Architecture 516
c. 1150-1200, Rise of the Hansa Merchant Union 519
1152, Frederick Barbarossa Is Elected King of Germany 522
1153, Jin Move Their Capital to Beijing 525
1154-1204, Angevin Empire Is Established 528
1155, Charter of Lorris Is Written 531
September 17, 1156, Austria Emerges as a National Entity 534
1156-1192, Minamoto Yoritomo Becomes Shogun 537
1167, Foundation of the Nemanjid Dynasty 540
1169-1172, Normans Invade Ireland 542
December 29, 1170, Murder of Thomas Becket 545
1175, Hōnen Shōnin Founds Pure Land Buddhism 547
c. 1175, Waldensian Excommunications Usher in Protestant Movement 549
c. 1180, Chrétien de Troyes Writes *Perceval* 552
c. 1181-1221, Lalibela Founds the Christian Capital of Ethiopia 554
1189-1192, Third Crusade 557
1190, Moses Maimonides Writes *The Guide of the Perplexed* 560
c. 1190-1279, Ma-Xia School of Painting Flourishes 562
1193, Turkish Raiders Destroy Buddhist University at Nalanda 565
1196-1258, Ch'oe Family Takes Power in Korea 567
c. 1200, Common-Law Tradition Emerges in England 569
c. 1200, Fairs of Champagne 571
c. 1200, Scientific Cattle Breeding Developed 574
c. 1200-1230, Manco Capac Founds the Inca State 576

1201-1300 c.e.

13th century, Ndiadiane N'diaye Founds the Wolof Empire 579
1204, Genghis Khan Founds Mongol Empire 581
1204, Knights of the Fourth Crusade Capture Constantinople 584
1206-1210, Quṭ al-Dīn Aybak Establishes the Delhi Sultanate 587
April 16, 1209, Founding of the Franciscans 589
1209-1229, Albigensian Crusade 593

1212, Children's Crusade 596
July 27, 1214, Battle of Bouvines 599
June 15, 1215, Signing of the Magna Carta 602
November 11-30, 1215, Fourth Lateran Council 605
1217-1221, Fifth Crusade 608
1219-1333, Hōjō Family Dominates Shoguns, Rules Japan 611
1221-1259, Mai Dunama Dibbalemi Expands Kanem Empire 614
1225, Tran Thai Tong Establishes Tran Dynasty 616
1225-1231, Jalāl al-Dīn Expands the Khwārizmian Empire 618
1227-1230, Frederick II Leads the Sixth Crusade 621
1228-1231, Teutonic Knights Bring Baltic Region Under Catholic Control 624
1230, Unification of Castile and León 627
1230's-1255, Reign of Sundiata of Mali 630
1233, Papal Inquisition 632
1236-1240, Reign of Raziya 636
July 15, 1240, Alexander Nevsky Defends Novgorod from Swedish Invaders 638
1248-1254, Failure of the Seventh Crusade 641
Late 13th century, Maoris Hunt Moa to Extinction 645
c. 1250, Improvements in Shipbuilding and Navigation 648
c. 1250-1300, Homosexuality Criminalized and Subject to Death Penalty 652
1258, Provisions of Oxford Are Established 655
1259, Mangrai Founds the Kingdom of Lan Na 657
September 3, 1260, Battle of Ain Jālūt 659
c. 1265-1273, Thomas Aquinas Compiles the *Summa Theologica* 662
1270-1285, Yekuno Amlak Founds the Solomonid Dynasty 665
1271-1295, Travels of Marco Polo 667
1273, Sufi Order of Mawlawīyah Is Established 671
1275, First Mechanical Clock 673
1275, Nestorian Archbishopric Is Founded in Beijing 676
c. 1275, The *Zohar* Is Transcribed 678
1285, Statute of Winchester 680
1290-1306, Jews Are Expelled from England, France, and Southern Italy 683
April, 1291, Fall of Acre 686
1295, Model Parliament 688
1295, Ramkhamhaeng Conquers the Mekong and Menam Valleys 690
1299, ʿAlāʾ-ud-Dīn Muḥammad Khaljī Conquers Gujarat 692

1301-1400 C.E.

July 27, 1302, Battle of Bapheus 695
November 18, 1302, Boniface VIII Issues the Bull *Unam Sanctam* 697
1305-1417, Avignon Papacy and the Great Schism 700
c. 1306-1320, Dante Writes *The Divine Comedy* 703
c. 1310-1350, William of Ockham Attacks Thomist Ideas 707
June 23-24, 1314, Battle of Bannockburn 709
November 15, 1315, Swiss Victory at Morgarten over Habsburg Forces 713
c. 1320, Origins of the Bubonic Plague 716

1323-1326, Champa Wins Independence from Dai Viet . . . 718
August 1, 1323-August 23, 1328, Peasants' Revolt in Flanders . . . 721
July 2, 1324, Lady Alice Kyteler Is Found Guilty of Witchcraft . . . 723
1324-1325, Mansa Mūsā's Pilgrimage to Mecca Sparks Interest in Mali Empire . . . 726
1325-1355, Travels of Ibn Baṭṭūṭah . . . 729
1325-1519, Aztecs Build Tenochtitlán . . . 731
1328-1350, Flowering of Late Medieval Physics . . . 734
November, 1330, Basarab Defeats the Hungarians . . . 737
1333, Kilwa Kisiwani Begins Economic and Historical Decline . . . 739
1336-1392, Yoshino Civil Wars . . . 741
1337-1453, Hundred Years' War . . . 744
1340, Al-ʿUmarī Writes a History of Africa . . . 748
August 26, 1346, Battle of Crécy . . . 750
1347, ʿAlāʾ-ud-Dīn Bahman Shāh Founds the Bahmanī Sultanate . . . 753
1347-1352, Invasion of the Black Death in Europe . . . 756
May 20, 1347-October 8, 1354, Cola di Rienzo Leads Popular Uprising in Rome . . . 759
1350, Ramathibodi I Creates First Thai Legal System . . . 762
c. 1350-1400, Petrarch and Boccaccio Recover Classical Texts . . . 764
January 10, 1356, and December 25, 1356, Golden Bull . . . 767
c. 1360-1440, Kan'ami and Zeami Perfect Nō Drama . . . 769
1366, Statute of Kilkenny . . . 772
1368, Establishment of the Ming Dynasty . . . 775
1368, Tibet Gains Independence from Mongols . . . 777
1373-1410, Jean Froissart Compiles His *Chronicles* . . . 780
1377, Ibn Khaldūn Completes His *Muqaddimah* . . . 783
1377-1378, Condemnation of John Wyclif . . . 786
c. 1380, Compilation of the Wise Sayings of Lal Ded . . . 789
September 8, 1380, Battle of Kulikovo . . . 791
May-June, 1381, Peasants' Revolt in England . . . 794
1381-1405, Tamerlane's Conquests . . . 797
1382-1395, Reign of Sthitimalla . . . 801
c. 1387, Chinese Create the Eight-Legged Essay . . . 803
1387-1400, Chaucer Writes *The Canterbury Tales* . . . 806
June 28, 1389, Turkish Conquest of Serbia . . . 809
c. 1392, Foundation of the Gelugpa Order . . . 812
July, 1392, Establishment of the Yi Dynasty . . . 815
1397, Publication of the Laws of Great Ming . . . 818
June 17, 1397, Kalmar Union Is Formed . . . 820
1399-1404, Tamerlane Builds the Bibi Khanum Mosque . . . 822
1400-1500, Foundation of the West African States of Benin . . . 824

1401-1453 C.E.

1403-1407, *Yonglo Dadian* Encyclopedia Is Compiled . . . 827
1405-1433, Zheng He's Naval Expeditions . . . 829
July 15, 1410, Battle of Tannenberg . . . 831
c. 1410-1440, Florentine School of Art Emerges . . . 834

1414-1418, Council of Constance . . . 837
July 6, 1415, Martyrdom of Jan Hus. . . . 841
1415-1460, Prince Henry the Navigator Promotes Portuguese Exploration. . . . 844
1428, Le Loi Establishes Later Le Dynasty . . . 847
May 4-8, 1429, Joan of Arc's Relief of Orléans. . . . 849
1440, Donation of Constantine Is Exposed . . . 852
1442-1456, János Hunyadi Defends Hungary Against the Ottomans . . . 854
1444-1446, Albanian Chieftains Unite Under Prince Skanderbeg . . . 858
c. 1450, Gutenberg Pioneers the Printing Press . . . 861
1453, English Are Driven from France . . . 864
May 29, 1453, Fall of Constantinople . . . 869

Time Line . . . 873
Glossary . . . 908
Bibliography . . . 924
Web Sites. . . . 948

Chronological List of Entries . . . III
Category Index . . . IX
Geographical Index . . . XXI
Personages Index . . . XXXI
Subject Index . . . XLIII

Keyword List of Contents

Abbess, Hildegard von Bingen Becomes (1136). 419
Acre, Fall of (April, 1291) 576
Adoption of *Nengo* System and Taika Reforms (645-646). 86
Advaita Vedānta, Śaṅkara Expounds (788-850) 170
Africa, Al-ʿUmarī Writes a History of (1340). 630
Africa, Islam Expands Throughout North (630-711). 75
Africa and Iberia, Expansion of Sunni Islam in North (11th century) 313
African Slaves, Zanj Revolt of (869-883) 227
African States of Benin, Foundation of the West (1400-1500). 692
Agricultural Settlements, Mogollons Establish (7th-13th centuries) 51
Agricultural Yields, Heavy Plow Helps Increase (c. 700-1000) 107
Ain Jālūt, Battle of (September 3, 1260). 554
al-Azhar Mosque, Building of (972) 286
Al-ʿUmarī Writes a History of Africa (1340) . . . 630
ʿAlāʾ-ud-Dīn Bahman Shāh Founds the Bahmanī Sultanate (1347) 634
ʿAlāʾ-ud-Dīn Muḥammad Khaljī Conquers Gujarat (1299) 583
Alaric II Drafts the *Breviarum Alarici* (February 2, 506). 14
Albanian Chieftains Unite Under Prince Skanderbeg (1444-1446) 720
Albigensian Crusade (1209-1229) 500
Alcuin Becomes Adviser to Charlemagne (781). . 165
Alexander Nevsky Defends Novgorod from Swedish Invaders (July 15, 1240) 537
Alfred Defeats the Danes (878) 234
Almoravid Empire, Almoravids Conquer Morocco and Establish the (1062-1147) 361
Almoravids Conquer Morocco and Establish the Almoravid Empire (1062-1147) 361
Almoravids Sack Kumbi (1076) 374
Alphabet, Development of Slavic (c. 850) 211
America, Bow and Arrow Spread into North (c. 700) 102
American City, Cahokia Becomes the First North (8th-14th centuries) 114
Amlak Founds the Solomonid Dynasty, Yekuno (1270-1285) 559
An Lushan, Rebellion of (755-763) 153
Andean Highlands, Tiwanaku Civilization Flourishes in (c. 500-1000) 9
Angevin Empire Is Established (1154-1204) 444
Aquinas Compiles the *Summa Theologica*, Thomas (c. 1265-1273). 556
Arabic Numerals Are Introduced into Europe (c. 1100) 388
Arc's Relief of Orléans, Joan of (May 4-8, 1429) 713
Archbishopric Is Founded in Beijing, Nestorian (1275) 568
Architecture, Great Zimbabwe Urbanism and (11th-15th centuries). 322
Arrow Spread into North America, Bow and (c. 700) 102
Art Emerges, Florentine School of (c. 1410-1440) 701
Asia, Papermaking Spreads to Korea, Japan, and Central (7th-8th centuries) 49
Asia, Uighur Turks Rule Central (840) 145
Asian Trade, Sogdians Dominate Central (6th-8th centuries) 12
Astronomical Observatory at Palenque, Maya Build (7th-early 8th centuries) 47
Austria Emerges as a National Entity (September 17, 1156). 448
Avicenna Writes His *Canon of Medicine* (c. 1010-1015) 338
Avignon Papacy and the Great Schism (1305-1417). 590
Awdaghust, Ghana Takes Control of (992-1054) 302
Aybak Establishes the Delhi Sultanate, Quṭ al-Dīn (1206-1210) 496
Azhar Mosque, Building of al- (972) 286
Aztecs Build Tenochtitlán (1325-1519) 616

Bahmanī Sultanate, ʿAlāʾ-ud-Dīn Bahman Shāh Founds the (1347) 634
Baltic Region Under Catholic Control, Teutonic Knights Bring (1228-1231). 525
Banking, Refinements in (c. 1150). 431

Bannockburn, Battle of (June 23-24, 1314) 598
Bapheus, Battle of (July 27, 1302) 586
Baptism of Clovis (496). 5
Baptism of Vladimir I (988) 299
Barbarossa Is Elected King of Germany, Frederick (1152) 439
Basarab Defeats the Hungarians (November, 1330) 621
Basil II, Reign of (976-1025). 290
Battle of Ain Jālūt (September 3, 1260) 554
Battle of Bannockburn (June 23-24, 1314). 598
Battle of Bapheus (July 27, 1302) 586
Battle of Bouvines (July 27, 1214). 504
Battle of Clontarf (April 23, 1014). 343
Battle of Crécy (August 26, 1346) 632
Battle of Hastings (October 14, 1066) 364
Battle of Kulikovo (September 8, 1380) 666
Battle of Manzikert (August 26, 1071). 368
Battle of Talas River (751) 149
Battle of Tannenberg (July 15, 1410) 699
Battle of Tours (October 11, 732) 138
Battle of Yarmūk (August 15-20, 636) 81
Bavaria, Magyars Invade Italy, Saxony, and (890's) 237
Bede Writes *Ecclesiastical History of the English People* (731) 136
Beginning of Bulgaria's Golden Age (893) 239
Beginning of the Harem System (780). 161
Beginning of the Rome-Constantinople Schism (1054) 359
Beijing, Jin Move Their Capital to (1153) 441
Beijing, Khitans Settle Near (936) 257
Benin, Foundation of the West African States of (1400-1500). 692
Bi Sheng Develops Movable Earthenware Type (c. 1045) 355
Bibi Khanum Mosque, Tamerlane Builds the (1399-1404). 690
Bingen Becomes Abbess, Hildegard von (1136). 419
Birth of Zhu Xi (1130) 414
Black Death in Europe, Invasion of the (1347-1352). 636
Boccaccio Recover Classical Texts, Petrarch and (c. 1350-1400) 643
Boethius, Imprisonment and Death of (524) 17
Bohemia, Jews Settle in (c. 960) 277
Boniface VIII Issues the Bull *Unam Sanctam* (November 18, 1302). 588
Book of Kells, Founding of Lindisfarne and Creation of the (635-800) 78
Book Printed, First (868). 224
Boris Converts to Christianity (864) 222
Borobuḍur, Building of (775-840) 159
Bouvines, Battle of (July 27, 1214) 504
Bow and Arrow Spread into North America (c. 700) 102
Breeding Developed, Scientific Cattle (c. 1200) 484
Breviarum Alarici, Alaric II Drafts the (February 2, 506). 14
Bubonic Plague, Origins of the (c. 1320) 603
Buddhism, Hōnen Shōnin Founds Pure Land (1175). 460
Buddhism, Suppression of (845). 207
Buddhism Arrives in Japan (538-552). 23
Buddhism Becomes Tibetan State Religion (791) 172
Buddhist University at Nalanda, Turkish Raiders Destroy (1193). 475
Building of al-Azhar Mosque (972) 286
Building of Borobuḍur (775-840) 159
Building of Chichén Itzá (c. 700-1000) 104
Building of Hagia Sophia (532-537) 21
Building of Romanesque Cathedrals (11th-12th centuries) 315
Building of the Dome of the Rock (685-691). 97
Building of the Grand Canal (605-610) 53
Bulgaria's Golden Age, Beginning of (893) 239
Bull, Golden (January 10, 1356, and December 25, 1356) 645
Bull *Unam Sanctam*, Boniface VIII Issues the (November 18, 1302) 588
Byzantine Empire, Silk Worms Are Smuggled to the (563). 25

Cālukya Dynasty, Foundation of the Western (973). 288
Cahokia Becomes the First North American City (8th-14th centuries) 114
Caliphate of Córdoba Falls (1031) 350
Canal, Building of the Grand (605-610). 53
Canon of Medicine, Avicenna Writes His (c. 1010-1015) 338
Canterbury Is Established, See of (596-597) 41
Canterbury Tales, Chaucer Writes *The* (1387-1400). 677

Canute Conquers England (1016) 345
Capac Founds the Inca State, Manco (c. 1200-1230) 486
Capet Is Elected to the French Throne, Hugh (987) 297
Cathedrals, Building of Romanesque (11th-12th centuries) 315
Catholic Control, Teutonic Knights Bring Baltic Region Under (1228-1231) 525
Cattle Breeding Developed, Scientific (c. 1200) 484
Central Asia, Papermaking Spreads to Korea, Japan, and (7th-8th centuries) 49
Central Asia, Uighur Turks Rule 145
Central Asian Trade, Sogdians Dominate (6th-8th centuries) 12
Champa, Le Dai Hanh Invades (982) 293
Champa Wins Independence from Dai Viet (1323-1326). 605
Champagne, Fairs of (c. 1200) 481
Chan Chan, Foundation of (After 850). 216
Chang'an, Tibetans Capture (763) 155
Charlemagne, Alcuin Becomes Adviser to (781) 165
Charter of Lorris Is Written (1155) 446
Chartres Revive Interest in the Classics, Scholars at (c. 1025) 348
Chaucer Writes *The Canterbury Tales* (1387-1400). 677
Chichén Itzá, Building of (c. 700-1000) 104
Children's Crusade (1212) 502
China, First Newspapers in (713-741) 127
China, Japan Sends Embassies to (607-839). 60
China, Paper Money First Used in (812). 194
China, Rice Is Introduced into (1012) 341
China, Sui Dynasty Reunifies (581). 32
Chinese Create the Eight-Legged Essay (c. 1387) 675
Chinese Society, Footbinding Develops in (c. 1000) 308
Ch'oe Family Takes Power in Korea (1196-1258) 477
Chrétien de Troyes Writes *Perceval* (c. 1180) 464
Christian Capital of Ethiopia, Lalibela Founds the (c. 1181-1221) 466
Christian Nubia and Muslim Egypt Sign Treaty (652-c. 1171) 88
Christianity, Boris Converts to (864). 222
Christianity Is Introduced into Germany (735) 140
Church of the Holy Sepulchre, Destruction of the (1009). 332
Cid Conquers Valencia, El (November, 1092-June 15, 1094) 380
Cistercian Order, Foundation of the (March 21, 1098) 385
City, Cahokia Becomes the First North American (8th-14th centuries) 114
Civil Service Model, Koreans Adopt the Tang (958-1076) 272
Civil Wars, Yoshino (1336-1392) 625
Classical Philosophy and Medicine to Europe, Moors Transmit (c. 1150). 428
Clock, First Mechanical (1275) 565
Clontarf, Battle of (April 23, 1014) 343
Clovis, Baptism of (496) 5
Coins Are Minted on the Swahili Coast (12th century). 400
Cola di Rienzo Leads Popular Uprising in Rome (May 20, 1347-October 8, 1354) 639
Collapse of the Huari and Tiwanaku Civilizations (c. 1000) 306
Common-Law Tradition Emerges in England (c. 1200) 480
Compilation of the *Engi Shiki* (927) 255
Compilation of the Wise Sayings of Lal Ded (c. 1380) 664
Condemnation of John Wyclif (1377-1378) 662
Confederation of Thai Tribes (c. 700-1253) 111
Confucianism Arrives in Japan (5th or 6th century) 1
Constance, Council of (1414-1418) 704
Constantine Is Exposed, Donation of (1440). . . . 716
Constantinople Schism, Beginning of the Rome (1054) 359
Constantinople, Fall of (May 29, 1453) 727
Constantinople, Knights of the Fourth Crusade Capture (1204) 493
Construction of the Kāilaśanātha Temple (c. 710) 120
Córdoba Falls, Caliphate of (1031) 350
Córdoba Flourishes in Spain, Court of (c. 950) 261
Coronation of Pépin the Short (754) 151
Council of Constance (1414-1418). 704
Court of Córdoba Flourishes in Spain (c. 950) 261
Courtly Love, Rise of (c. 1100) 394

Creation of the Kingdom of Sicily (1127-1130). . . . 412
Crécy, Battle of (August 26, 1346). . . . 632
Crusade, Albigensian (1209-1229). . . . 500
Crusade, Children's (1212). . . . 502
Crusade, Failure of the Seventh (1248-1254) 539
Crusade, Fifth (1217-1221) 511
Crusade, Frederick II Leads the Sixth (1227-1230). . . . 522
Crusade, Pope Urban II Calls the First (November 27, 1095). . . . 383
Crusade, Second (1147-1149) 426
Crusade, Third (1189-1192) 469
Crusade Capture Constantinople, Knights of the Fourth (1204) 493
Cult of Quetzalcóatl Spreads Through Mesoamerica (10th century) 244

Dai Viet, Champa Wins Independence from (1323-1326). . . . 605
Danes, Alfred Defeats the (878) 234
Dante Writes *The Divine Comedy* (c. 1306-1320) 593
Death Penalty, Homosexuality Criminalized and Subject to (c. 1250-1300) 547
Decimals and Negative Numbers, Invention of (595-665). . . . 39
Delhi Sultanate, Quṭ al-Dīn Aybak Establishes the (1206-1210). . . . 496
Desert Southwest, Hohokam Adapt to the (8th-15th centuries). . . . 116
Destruction of the Church of the Holy Sepulchre (1009). . . . 332
Development of Gothic Architecture (c. 1150-1200) 435
Development of Miracle and Mystery Plays (After 1000). . . . 324
Development of Slavic Alphabet (c. 850) 211
Development of the Ife Kingdom and Yoruba Culture (11th-15th centuries). . . . 320
Dharmapāla, Reign of (770-810). . . . 157
Dibbalemi Expands Kanem Empire, Mai Dunama (1221-1259). . . . 516
Divine Comedy, Dante Writes *The* (c. 1306-1320) 593
Doctorate, National University Awards First (606) 55
Dome of the Rock, Building of the (685-691). . . . 97
Domesday Survey (1086) 378
Donation of Constantine Is Exposed (1440) 716
Dunama Dibbalemi Expands Kanem Empire, Mai (1221-1259) 516

Ecclesiastical History of the English People, Bede Writes (731) 136
Egypt Sign Treaty, Christian Nubia and Muslim (652-c. 1171). . . . 88
Eight-Legged Essay, Chinese Create the (c. 1387) 675
El Cid Conquers Valencia (November, 1092-June 15, 1094) 380
El Tajín Is Built (c. 600-950) 44
Emergence of Mapungubwe (1075-c. 1220). . . . 372
Empress Wu, Reign of (690-705) 100
Encyclopedia Is Compiled, *Yonglo Dadian* (1403-1407). . . . 695
Engi Shiki, Compilation of the (927). . . . 255
England, Canute Conquers (1016) 345
England, France, and Southern Italy, Jews Are Expelled from (1290-1306). . . . 574
English Are Driven from France (1453) 725
English People, Bede Writes *Ecclesiastical History of the* (731). . . . 136
Establishment of the Ming Dynasty (1368) 652
Establishment of the Yi Dynasty (July, 1392) 684
Ethiopia, Lalibela Founds the Christian Capital of (c. 1181-1221) 466
Europe, Arabic Numerals Are Introduced into (c. 1100) 388
Europe, Invasion of the Black Death in (1347-1352). . . . 636
Europe, Prester John Myth Sweeps Across (c. 1145) 423
European-Native American Contact, First (11th-12th centuries) 317
European Universities Emerge (1100-1300). . . . 397
Excommunications Usher in Protestant Movement, Waldensian (c. 1175) 462
Expansion of Śrivijaya (682-1377) 95
Expansion of Sunni Islam in North Africa and Iberia (11th century) 313
Expansion of the Seljuk Turks (1040-1055) 353
Expelled from England, France, and Southern Italy, Jews Are (1290-1306) 574

Fāṭimid Dynasty and Revive Sunni Islam, Zīrids Break from (1048). . . . 357

Fāṭimids, Reign of the (969-1171) 283
Failure of the Seventh Crusade (1248-1254). . . . 539
Fairs of Champagne (c. 1200) 481
Fall of Acre (April, 1291) 576
Fall of Constantinople (May 29, 1453). 727
Fifth Crusade (1217-1221) 511
Firdusi Composes the *Shahnamah* (1010) 334
First Book Printed (868) 224
First Crusade, Pope Urban II Calls the (November 27, 1095). 383
First European-Native American Contact (11th-12th centuries) 317
First Hausa State Established (10th-11th centuries) 246
First Islamic Public Hospital (809). 192
First Mechanical Clock (1275). 565
First Newspapers in China (713-741) 127
Five Dynasties and Ten Kingdoms, Period of (907-960) 248
Florentine School of Art Emerges (c. 1410-1440) 701
Flowering of Late Medieval Physics (1328-1350). 618
Footbinding Develops in Chinese Society (c. 1000) 308
Foundation of Chan Chan (After 850) 216
Foundation of the Cistercian Order (March 21, 1098). 385
Foundation of the Gelugpa Order (c. 1392) 682
Foundation of the Jin Dynasty (1115) 408
Foundation of the Koryŏ Dynasty (918-936). . . . 252
Foundation of the Mount Athos Monasteries (963) 281
Foundation of the Nemanjid Dynasty (1167). 453
Foundation of the West African States of Benin (1400-1500) 692
Foundation of the Western Cālukya Dynasty (973). 288
Founding of Lindisfarne and Creation of the *Book of Kells* (635-800) 78
Founding of Nanzhao (729) 131
Founding of the Franciscans (April 16, 1209) 498
Founding of the Khmer Empire (802) 190
Founding of the Song Dynasty (960). 274
Founding of the Tang Dynasty (618) 66
Founding of Timbuktu (c. 1100) 390
Fourth Crusade Capture Constantinople, Knights of the (1204). 493
Fourth Lateran Council (November 11-30, 1215) 509
France, English Are Driven from (1453). 725
France, and Southern Italy, Jews Are Expelled from England, (1290-1306). 574
Franciscans, Founding of the (April 16, 1209) 498
Frederick Barbarossa Is Elected King of Germany (1152) 439
Frederick II Leads the Sixth Crusade (1227-1230). 522
French Throne, Hugh Capet Is Elected to the (987) 297
Froissart Compiles His *Chronicles*, Jean (1373-1410). 656
Fujiwara Family, Rise of the (858). 218

Gampo, Reign of Songtsen (627-650). 69
Gelugpa Order, Foundation of the (c. 1392) 682
Genghis Khan Founds Mongol Empire (1204). 491
Genji, Murasaki Shikibu Writes *The Tale of* (c. 1004) 329
Germany, Christianity Is Introduced into (735) 140
Germany, Frederick Barbarossa Is Elected King of (1152) 439
Ghana, Rise and Fall of (c. 750-1240) 147
Ghana Takes Control of Awdaghust (992-1054) 302
Ghazna, Reign of Maḥmūd of (998-1030) 304
Golden Bull (January 10, 1356, and December 25, 1356) 645
Gothic Architecture, Development of (c. 1150-1200) 435
Grand Canal, Building of the (605-610). 53
Great Zimbabwe Urbanism and Architecture (11th-15th centuries) 322
Gregory the Great, Reforms of Pope (590-604). . . 35
Guide of the Perplexed, Moses Maimonides Writes *The* (1190) 471
Gujarat, ʿAlāʾ-ud-Dīn Muḥammad Khaljī Conquers (1299) 583
Gunpowder and Guns, Invention of (Mid-9th century). 209
Guns, Invention of Gunpowder and (Mid-9th century). 209
Gutenberg Pioneers the Printing Press (c. 1450) 722
Gypsies Expelled from Persia (834) 198

Habsburg Forces, Swiss Victory at Morgarten over (November 15, 1315) 600
Hagia Sophia, Building of (532-537) 21
Hanoi, Nanzhao Captures (863) 220
Hansa Merchant Union, Rise of the (c. 1150-1200) 437
Harem System, Beginning of the (780) 161
Harṣa of Kanauj, Reign of (606-647) 57
Hārūn al-Rashīd, Reign of (786-809) 168
Hastings, Battle of (October 14, 1066). 364
Hausa State Established, First (10th-11th centuries) 246
Heavy Plow Helps Increase Agricultural Yields (c. 700-1000) 107
Heian Period (794-1185) 178
Henry the Navigator Promotes Portuguese Exploration, Prince (1415-1460) 709
Hildegard von Bingen Becomes Abbess (1136). 419
Hindi Becomes India's Dominant Language (c. 1000) 310
History of Africa, Al-ᶜUmarī Writes a (1340). 630
The History of al-Ṭabarī, Publication of (872-973) 229
Hohokam Adapt to the Desert Southwest (8th-15th centuries). 116
Hōjō Family Dominates Shoguns, Rules Japan (1219-1333). 514
Holy Sepulchre, Destruction of the Church of the (1009). 332
Homosexuality Criminalized and Subject to Death Penalty (c. 1250-1300) 547
Hōnen Shōnin Founds Pure Land Buddhism (1175). 460
Hospital, First Islamic Public (809) 192
Huari and Tiwanaku Civilizations, Collapse of the (c. 1000) 306
Hugh Capet Is Elected to the French Throne (987) 297
Hummay Founds Sefuwa Dynasty (c. 1075-1086) 370
Hundred Years' War (1337-1453) 627
Hungarians, Basarab Defeats the (November, 1330) 621
Hungary Against the Ottomans, János Hunyadi Defends (1442-1456) 718
Huns, Sāsānians and Turks Defeat the White (567-568). 28
Huns Raid India, White (484). 3
Hunyadi Defends Hungary Against the Ottomans, János (1442-1456) 718
Hus, Martyrdom of Jan (July 6, 1415) 706
Ḥusayn, Martyrdom of Prophet's Grandson (October 10, 680) 93

Iberia, Expansion of Sunni Islam in North Africa and (11th century). 313
Ibn Baṭṭūzah, Travels of (1325-1355) 614
Ibn Khaldūn Completes His *Muqaddimah* (1377). 659
Iconoclastic Controversy (726-843) 129
Ife Kingdom and Yoruba Culture, Development of the (11th-15th centuries). 320
Imprisonment and Death of Boethius (524) 17
Improvements in Shipbuilding and Navigation (c. 1250) 544
India, White Huns Raid (484). 3
India's Dominant Language, Hindi Becomes (c. 1000) 310
Indravarman I Conquers the Thai and the Mons (877-889). 232
Inquisition, Papal (1233) 532
Invasion of the Black Death in Europe (1347-1352). 636
Invention of Decimals and Negative Numbers (595-665). 39
Invention of Gunpowder and Guns (Mid-9th century) 209
Ireland, Normans Invade (1169-1172) 456
Islam, Qarakhanids Convert to (Early 10th century) 242
Islam, Songhai Kingdom Converts to (c. 1010) 336
Islam, Zīrids Break from Fāṭimid Dynasty and Revive Sunni (1048) 357
Islam Expands Throughout North Africa (630-711). 75
Islam Expands Throughout the Middle East (637-657). 84
Islam in North Africa and Iberia, Expansion of Sunni (11th century) 313
Islamic Public Hospital, First (809) 192
Islands, Settlement of the South Pacific (c. 700-1100) 109
Italy, Jews Are Expelled from England, France, and Southern (1290-1306) 574
Italy, Lombard Conquest of (568-571) 30
Italy, Saxony, and Bavaria, Magyars Invade (890's) 237

Jalāl al-Dīn Expands the Khwārizmian Empire (1225-1231) 520
János Hunyadi Defends Hungary Against the Ottomans (1442-1456) 718
Japan, Buddhism Arrives in (538-552) 23
Japan, Confucianism Arrives in (5th or 6th century) 1
Japan, Hōjō Family Dominates Shoguns, Rules (1219-1333) 514
Japan, and Central Asia, Papermaking Spreads to Korea, (7th-8th centuries) 49
Japan Sends Embassies to China (607-839) 60
Japanese Government, Taihō Laws Reform (701) 118
Jean Froissart Compiles His *Chronicles* (1373-1410) 656
Jews Are Expelled from England, France, and Southern Italy (1290-1306) 574
Jews Settle in Bohemia (c. 960) 277
Jin Dynasty, Foundation of the (1115) 408
Jin Move Their Capital to Beijing (1153) 441
Joan of Arc's Relief of Orléans (May 4-8, 1429) 713
John Myth Sweeps Across Europe, Prester (c. 1145) 423
Judaism, Khazars Convert to (740) 142
Justinian's Code Is Compiled (529-534) 19

Kāilaśanātha Temple, Construction of the (c. 710) 120
Kalmar Union Is Formed (June 17, 1397) 688
Kana Syllabary Is Developed (c. 800) 181
Kan'ami and Zeami Perfect Nō Drama (c. 1360-1440) 647
Kanauj, Reign of Harṣa of (606-647) 57
Kanem Empire, Mai Dunama Dibbalemi Expands (1221-1259) 516
Karakitai Empire Established (1130) 416
Kells, Founding of Lindisfarne and Creation of the *Book of* (635-800) 78
Khaldūn Completes His *Muqaddimah*, Ibn (1377) 659
Khaljī Conquers Gujarat, ʿAlāʾ-ud-Dīn Muḥammad (1299) 583
Khazars Convert to Judaism (740) 142
Khitans Settle Near Beijing (936) 257
Khmer Empire, Founding of the (802) 190
Khwārizmian Empire, Jalāl al-Dīn Expands the (1225-1231) 520
Kilkenny, Statute of (1366) 650
Kilwa Kisiwani Begins Economic and Historical Decline (1333) 623
Kilwa Kisiwani Founded, Trading Center of (12th century) 401
Kim Pu-sik Writes *Samguk Sagi* (1145) 421
Kisiwani Begins Economic and Historical Decline, Kilwa (1333) 623
Knights Bring Baltic Region Under Catholic Control, Teutonic (1228-1231) 525
Knights of the Fourth Crusade Capture Constantinople (1204) 493
Knights Templar Is Founded, Order of the (c. 1120) 410
Kojiki and *Nihon shoki*, Writing of (March 9, 712, and July 1, 720) 125
Korea, Ch'oe Family Takes Power in (1196-1258) 477
Korea, Silla Unification of (668-935) 91
Korea, Japan, and Central Asia, Papermaking Spreads to (7th-8th centuries) 49
Koreans Adopt the Tang Civil Service Model (958-1076) 272
Koryŏ Dynasty, Foundation of the (918-936) 252
Kulikovo, Battle of (September 8, 1380) 666
Kumbi, Almoravids Sack (1076) 374
Kyteler Is Found Guilty of Witchcraft, Lady Alice (July 2, 1324) 611

Lady Alice Kyteler Is Found Guilty of Witchcraft (July 2, 1324) 611
Lal Ded, Compilation of the Wise Sayings of (c. 1380) 664
Lalibela Founds the Christian Capital of Ethiopia (c. 1181-1221) 466
Lan Na, Mangrai Founds the Kingdom of (1259) 551
Language, Hindi Becomes India's Dominant (c. 1000) 310
Lateran Council, Fourth (November 11-30, 1215) 509
Law Tradition Emerges in England, Common (c. 1200) 480
Laws of Great Ming, Publication of the (1397) 686
Laws Reform Japanese Government, Taihō (701) 118
Le Dai Hanh Invades Champa (982) 293
Le Dynasty, Le Loi Establishes Later (1428) 711

Le Loi Establishes Later Le Dynasty (1428). . . . 711
Legal System, Ramathibodi I Creates First Thai (1350) 641
León, Unification of Castile and (1230) 527
Leprosy, Social and Political Impact of (12th-14th centuries) 405
Lindisfarne and Creation of the *Book of Kells*, Founding of (635-800). 78
Lindisfarne Monastery, Norse Raid (June 7, 793) 176
Lombard Conquest of Italy (568-571). 30
Lorris Is Written, Charter of (1155) 446

Ma-Xia School of Painting Flourishes (c. 1190-1279) 473
Madrasas, Rise of (c. 950-1100) 263
Magna Carta, Signing of the (June 15, 1215) 507
Magyars, Otto I Defeats the (August 10, 955) 268
Magyars Invade Italy, Saxony, and Bavaria (890's) 237
Mai Dunama Dibbalemi Expands Kanem Empire (1221-1259) 516
Maimonides Writes *The Guide of the Perplexed*, Moses (1190) 471
Mali, Reign of Sundiata of (1230's-1255) 530
Mali Empire, Mansa Mūsā's Pilgrimage to Mecca Sparks Interest in (1324-1325) 609
Manco Capac Founds the Inca State (c. 1200-1230) 486
Mangrai Founds the Kingdom of Lan Na (1259). 551
Mansa Mūsā's Pilgrimage to Mecca Sparks Interest in Mali Empire (1324-1325). 609
Manzikert, Battle of (August 26, 1071) 368
Maoris Hunt Moa to Extinction (Late 13th century). 542
Mapungubwe, Emergence of (1075-c. 1220) . . . 372
Marco Polo, Travels of (1271-1295). 561
Martyrdom of Jan Hus (July 6, 1415) 706
Martyrdom of Prophet's Grandson Ḥusayn (October 10, 680) 93
Mawlawīyah Is Established, Sufi Order of (1273). 563
Maya Build Astronomical Observatory at Palenque (7th-early 8th centuries) 47
Mecca Sparks Interest in Mali Empire, Mansa Mūsā's Pilgrimage to (1324-1325). 609
Mechanical Clock, First (1275) 565
Medicine, Avicenna Writes His *Canon of* (c. 1010-1015) 338
Mekong and Menam Valleys, Ramkhamhaeng Conquers the (1295) 581
Menam Valleys, Ramkhamhaeng Conquers the Mekong and (1295). 581
Merchant Union, Rise of the Hansa (c. 1150-1200) 437
Merchants Dominate Trade with the East, Venetian (1150) 433
Mesoamerica, Cult of Quetzalcóatl Spreads Through (10th century) 244
Middle East, Islam Expands Throughout the (637-657) 84
Migrations, Uighur (840-846) 203
Minamoto Yoritomo Becomes Shogun (1156-1192) 451
Ming Dynasty, Establishment of the (1368) 652
Miracle and Mystery Plays, Development of (After 1000). 324
Mississippian Mound-Building Culture Flourishes (c. 800-1350) 183
Moa to Extinction, Maoris Hunt (Late 13th century). 542
Model Parliament (1295). 579
Mogollons Establish Agricultural Settlements (7th-13th centuries) 51
Monastery, Norse Raid Lindisfarne (June 7, 793) 176
Money First Used in China, Paper (812). 194
Mongol Empire, Genghis Khan Founds (1204) 491
Mongols, Tibet Gains Independence from (1368) 654
Mons, Indravarman I Conquers the Thai and the (877-889). 232
Moors Transmit Classical Philosophy and Medicine to Europe (c. 1150) 428
Morgarten over Habsburg Forces, Swiss Victory at (November 15, 1315) 600
Morocco and Establish the Almoravid Empire, Almoravids Conquer (1062-1147) 361
Moses Maimonides Writes *The Guide of the Perplexed* (1190) 471
Mosque, Building of al-Azhar (972). 286
Mosque, Tamerlane Builds the Bibi Khanum (1399-1404). 690
Mound-Building Culture Flourishes, Mississippian (c. 800-1350) 183

Mount Athos Monasteries, Foundation of the (963) 281
Movable Earthenware Type, Bi Sheng Develops (c. 1045) 355
Muḥammad Receives Revelations (c. 610-632) 62
Muqaddimah, Ibn Khaldūn Completes His (1377) 659
Murasaki Shikibu Writes *The Tale of Genji* (c. 1004) 329
Murder of Thomas Becket (December 29, 1170) 458
Mūsā's Pilgrimage to Mecca Sparks Interest in Mali Empire, Mansa (1324-1325) 609
Muslim Egypt Sign Treaty, Christian Nubia and (652-c. 1171). 88
Mystery Plays, Development of Miracle and (After 1000). 324

Nalanda, Turkish Raiders Destroy Buddhist University at (1193) 475
Nanzhao, Founding of (729) 131
Nanzhao Captures Hanoi (863) 220
Nanzhao Subjugates Pyu (832). 197
Narasiṃhavarman I Mahāmalla, Reign of (630-668). 73
National University Awards First Doctorate (606) 55
Native American Contact, First European- (11th-12th centuries) 317
Naval Expeditions, Zheng He's (1405-1433). 697
Navigation, Improvements in Shipbuilding and (c. 1250) 544
Ndiadiane N'diaye Founds the Wolof Empire (13th century). 489
Negative Numbers, Invention of Decimals and (595-665). 39
Nemanjid Dynasty, Foundation of the (1167). 453
Nengo System and Taika Reforms, Adoption of (645-646) 86
Nestorian Archbishopric Is Founded in Beijing (1275) 568
Nevsky Defends Novgorod from Swedish Invaders, Alexander (July 15, 1240) 537
Newspapers in China, First (713-741) 127
Ngo Quyen, Reign of (939-944) 259
Nihon shoki, Writing of *Kojiki* and (March 9, 712, and July 1, 720) 125
Nō Drama, Kan'ami and Zeami Perfect (c. 1360-1440) 647
Normans Invade Ireland (1169-1172) 456
Norse Raid Lindisfarne Monastery (June 7, 793) 176
North Africa and Iberia, Expansion of Sunni Islam in (11th century) 313
North Africa, Islam Expands Throughout (630-711). 75
North America, Bow and Arrow Spread into (c. 700) 102
North American City, Cahokia Becomes the First (8th-14th centuries) 114
Nubia and Muslim Egypt Sign Treaty, Christian (652-c. 1171). 88
Numbers, Invention of Decimals and Negative (595-665). 39
Numerals Are Introduced into Europe, Arabic (c. 1100) 388

Observatory at Palenque, Maya Build Astronomical (7th-early 8th centuries) 47
Ockham Attacks Thomist Ideas, William of (c. 1310-1350) 596
Official Class Flowers Under Song Dynasty, Scholar- (960-1279) 279
Oğhuz Turks Migrate to Transoxiana (956) 270
Order of the Knights Templar Is Founded (c. 1120) 410
Origins of Swahili in Its Written Form (c. 1100) 392
Origins of the Bubonic Plague (c. 1320). 603
Orléans, Joan of Arc's Relief of (May 4-8, 1429) 713
Otto I Defeats the Magyars (August 10, 955). 268
Ottomans, János Hunyadi Defends Hungary Against the (1442-1456) 718
Oxford Are Established, Provisions of (1258). 549

Pacific Islands, Settlement of the South (c. 700-1100) 109
Painting Flourishes, Ma-Xia School of (c. 1190-1279) 473
Palenque, Maya Build Astronomical Observatory at (7th-early 8th centuries) 47
Pāṇḍya, Parāntaka I Conquers (915) 250
Papacy and the Great Schism, Avignon (1305-1417). 590

Papal Inquisition (1233) 532
Paper Money First Used in China (812) 194
Papermaking Spreads to Korea, Japan, and Central Asia (7th-8th centuries) 49
Parāntaka I Conquers Pāṇḍya (915) 250
Parliament, Model (1295) 579
Peasants' Revolt in England (May-June, 1381) 668
Peasants' Revolt in Flanders (August 1, 1323-August 23, 1328) 607
Pépin the Short, Coronation of (754). 151
Perceval, Chrétien de Troyes Writes (c. 1180) 464
Period of Five Dynasties and Ten Kingdoms (907-960) 248
Persia, Gypsies Expelled from (834). 198
Petrarch and Boccaccio Recover Classical Texts (c. 1350-1400) 643
Physics, Flowering of Late Medieval (1328-1350). 618
Pilgrimage of Xuanzang (629-645) 71
Pillow Book, Sei Shōnagon Completes *The* (c. 1001) 327
Plague, Origins of the Bubonic (c. 1320) 603
Plains Village Culture Flourishes (9th-15th centuries) 188
Plow Helps Increase Agricultural Yields, Heavy (c. 700-1000) 107
Political Impact of Leprosy, Social and (12th-14th centuries) 405
Pope Urban II Calls the First Crusade (November 27, 1095). 383
Portuguese Exploration, Prince Henry the Navigator Promotes (1415-1460). 709
Pratihāras, Rise of the (730) 133
Press, Gutenberg Pioneers the Printing (c. 1450) 722
Prester John Myth Sweeps Across Europe (c. 1145) 423
Prince Henry the Navigator Promotes Portuguese Exploration (1415-1460). 709
Printed, First Book (868). 224
Printing Press, Gutenberg Pioneers the (c. 1450) 722
Prophet's Grandson Ḥusayn, Martyrdom of (October 10, 680) 93
Protestant Movement, Waldensian Excommunications Usher in (c. 1175) 462
Provisions of Oxford Are Established (1258). 549
Publication of *The History of al-Ṭabarī* (872-973) 229
Publication of the Laws of Great Ming (1397). 686
Pulakeśin II, Reign of (c. 611-642) 64
Pure Land Buddhism, Hōnen Shōnin Founds (1175). 460
Pyu, Nanzhao Subjugates (832) 197

Qarakhanids Convert to Islam (Early 10th century) 242
Quṭ al-Dīn Aybak Establishes the Delhi Sultanate (1206-1210) 496
Quanzhen Daoism, Wang Chongyang Founds (12th century) 403
Quetzalcóatl Spreads Through Mesoamerica, Cult of (10th century). 244

Rājarāja I, Reign of (c. 985-1014) 295
Ramathibodi I Creates First Thai Legal System (1350) 641
Ramkhamhaeng Conquers the Mekong and Menam Valleys (1295) 581
Raziya, Reign of (1236-1240) 535
Rebellion of An Lushan (755-763). 153
Refinements in Banking (c. 1150) 431
Reforms, Wang Anshi Introduces Bureaucratic (1069-1072) 366
Reforms of Pope Gregory the Great (590-604) 35
Regency of Shōtoku Taishi (593-604). 37
Reign of Basil II (976-1025) 290
Reign of Dharmapāla (770-810) 157
Reign of Empress Wu (690-705). 100
Reign of Hārūn al-Rashīd (786-809). 168
Reign of Harṣa of Kanauj (606-647) 57
Reign of Maḥmūd of Ghazna (998-1030) 304
Reign of Narasiṃhavarman I Mahāmalla (630-668). 73
Reign of Ngo Quyen (939-944) 259
Reign of Pulakeśin II (c. 611-642) 64
Reign of Rājarāja I (c. 985-1014) 295
Reign of Raziya (1236-1240) 535
Reign of Songtsen Gampo (627-650) 69
Reign of Sthitimalla (1382-1395) 673
Reign of Sundiata of Mali (1230's-1255) 530
Reign of the Fāṭimids (969-1171) 283
Revelations, Muḥammad Receives (c. 610-632) 62

Revolt in England, Peasants' (May-June, 1381) 668
Revolt in Flanders, Peasants' (August 1, 1323-August 23, 1328) 607
Rice Is Introduced into China (1012) 341
Rienzo Leads Popular Uprising in Rome, Cola di (May 20, 1347-October 8, 1354). . . . 639
Rise and Fall of Ghana (c. 750-1240) 147
Rise of Courtly Love (c. 1100). 394
Rise of Madrasas (c. 950-1100) 263
Rise of Swahili Cultures (c. 500-1000) 7
Rise of the Fujiwara Family (858) 218
Rise of the Hansa Merchant Union (c. 1150-1200) 437
Rise of the Pratihāras (730) 133
Rise of the Sailendra Family (780). 163
Rise of the Samurai (792) 174
Rise of the Toutswe Kingdom (9th-14th centuries) 186
Romanesque Cathedrals, Building of (11th-12th centuries) 315
Rome-Constantinople Schism, Beginning of the (1054). 359

Sailendra Family, Rise of the (780) 163
Samguk Sagi, Kim Pu-sik Writes (1145). 421
Samurai, Rise of the (792) 174
Śaṅkara Expounds Advaita Vedānta (788-850) 170
Sāsānians and Turks Defeat the White Huns (567-568) 28
Saxony, and Bavaria, Magyars Invade Italy 237
Schism, Beginning of the Rome-Constantinople (1054) 359
Scholar-Official Class Flowers Under Song Dynasty (960-1279) 279
Scholars at Chartres Revive Interest in the Classics (c. 1025). 348
Scientific Cattle Breeding Developed (c. 1200) 484
Second Crusade (1147-1149) 426
See of Canterbury Is Established (596-597). 41
Sefuwa Dynasty, Hummay Founds (c. 1075-1086) 370
Sei Shōnagon Completes *The Pillow Book* (c. 1001) 327
Seljuk Dynasty Is Founded (1077). 375
Seljuk Turks, Expansion of the (1040-1055). . . . 353
Serbia, Turkish Conquest of (June 28, 1389) 679
Settlement of the South Pacific Islands (c. 700-1100) 109
Seventh Crusade, Failure of the (1248-1254) . . . 539
Shōnagon Completes *The Pillow Book*, Sei (c. 1001) 327
Shōnin Founds Pure Land Buddhism, Hōnen (1175). 460
Shōtoku Taishi, Regency of (593-604) 37
Shahnamah, Firdusi Composes the (1010). 334
Shipbuilding and Navigation, Improvements in (c. 1250) 544
Shogun, Minamoto Yoritomo Becomes (1156-1192). 451
Shoguns, Rules Japan, Hōjō Family Dominates (1219-1333). 514
Sicily, Creation of the Kingdom of (1127-1130). 412
Signing of the Magna Carta (June 15, 1215). . . . 507
Silk Worms Are Smuggled to Byzantine Empire (563) 25
Silla Unification of Korea (668-935) 91
Sixth Crusade, Frederick II Leads the (1227-1230). 522
Skanderbeg, Albanian Chieftains Unite Under Prince (1444-1446). 720
Slaves, Zanj Revolt of African (869-883) 227
Slavic Alphabet, Development of 211
Social and Political Impact of Leprosy (12th-14th centuries) 405
Sogdians Dominate Central Asian Trade (6th-8th centuries) 12
Solomonid Dynasty, Yekuno Amlak Founds the (1270-1285). 559
Song Dynasty, Founding of the (960) 274
Song Dynasty, Scholar-Official Class Flowers Under (960-1279). 279
Songhai Kingdom Converts to Islam (c. 1010) 336
Songtsen Gampo, Reign of (627-650). 69
South Pacific Islands, Settlement of the (c. 700-1100) 109
Southwest, Hohokam Adapt to the Desert (8th-15th centuries). 116
Spain, Court of Córdoba Flourishes in (c. 950) 261
Spain, Ṭārik Crosses into (April or May, 711). 123
Śrivijaya, Expansion of (682-1377) 95
Statute of Kilkenny (1366). 650
Statute of Winchester (1285). 572

Sthitimalla, Reign of (1382-1395) 673
Sufi Order of Mawlawīyah Is Established (1273). 563
Sui Dynasty Reunifies China (581) 32
Summa Theologica, Thomas Aquinas Compiles the (c. 1265-1273) 556
Sundiata of Mali, Reign of (1230's-1255) 530
Sunni Islam, Zīrids Break from Fāṭimid Dynasty and Revive (1048). 357
Sunni Islam in North Africa and Iberia, Expansion of (11th century) 313
Suppression of Buddhism (845) 207
Swahili Coast, Coins Are Minted on the (12th century). 400
Swahili Cultures, Rise of (c. 500-1000) 7
Swahili in Its Written Form, Origins of (c. 1100) 392
Swiss Victory at Morgarten over Habsburg Forces (November 15, 1315) 600
Syllabary Is Developed, *Kana* (c. 800). 181

Ṭabarī, Publication of *The History of al-* (872-973). 229
Taihō Laws Reform Japanese Government (701) 118
Tajín Is Built, El (c. 600-950) 44
Talas River, Battle of (751). 149
Tale of Genji, Murasaki Shikibu Writes *The* (c. 1004) 329
Tamerlane Builds the Bibi Khanum Mosque (1399-1404). 690
Tamerlane's Conquests (1381-1405). 670
Tang Civil Service Model, Koreans Adopt the (958-1076) 272
Tang Dynasty, Founding of the (618) 66
Tannenberg, Battle of (July 15, 1410)3 699
Ṭārik Crosses into Spain (April or May, 711). 123
Temple, Construction of the Kāilaśanātha (c. 710) 120
Ten Kingdoms, Period of Five Dynasties and (907-960) 248
Tenochtitlán, Aztecs Build (1325-1519) 616
Teutonic Knights Bring Baltic Region Under Catholic Control (1228-1231) 525
Thai and the Mons, Indravarman I Conquers the (877-889) 232
Thai Legal System, Ramathibodi I Creates First (1350) 641
Thai Tribes, Confederation of (c. 700-1253). . . . 111
Third Crusade (1189-1192) 469
Thomas Aquinas Compiles the *Summa Theologica* (c. 1265-1273) 556
Thomas Becket, Murder of (December 29, 1170) 458
Tibet Gains Independence from Mongols (1368). 654
Tibetan Empire Dissolves (838-842). 201
Tibetan State Religion, Buddhism Becomes (791) 172
Tibetans Capture Chang'an (763) 155
Timbuktu, Founding of (c. 1100). 390
Tiwanaku Civilization Flourishes in Andean Highlands (c. 500-1000) 9
Toltecs Build Tula (c. 950-1150). 266
Tours, Battle of (October 11, 732) 138
Toutswe Kingdom, Rise of the (9th-14th centuries) 186
Trade, Sogdians Dominate Central Asian (6th-8th centuries) 12
Trading Center of Kilwa Kisiwani Founded (12th century). 401
Tran Dynasty, Tran Thai Tong Establishes (1225). 518
Tran Thai Tong Establishes Tran Dynasty (1225). 518
Transoxiana, Oğhuz Turks Migrate to (956) 270
Travels of Ibn Baṭṭūṭah (1325-1355) 614
Travels of Marco Polo (1271-1295) 561
Treaty of Verdun (843) 205
Tula, Toltecs Build (c. 950-1150) 266
Turkish Conquest of Serbia (June 28, 1389) 679
Turkish Raiders Destroy Buddhist University at Nalanda (1193). 475
Turks Defeat the White Huns, Sāsānians and (567-568). 28
Turks Migrate to Transoxiana, Oğhuz (956) 270
Turks Rule Central Asia, Uighur (840) 145
Turks, Expansion of the Seljuk (1040-1055) 353

Uighur Migrations (840-846) 203
Uighur Turks Rule Central Asia (744-840) 145
Unification of Castile and León (1230) 527
Universities Emerge, European (1100-1300). 397
University at Nalanda, Turkish Raiders Destroy Buddhist (1193) 475

University Awards First Doctorate, National (606) 55
Urban II Calls the First Crusade, Pope (November 27, 1095) 383
Urbanism and Architecture, Great Zimbabwe (11th-15th centuries) 322

Vedānta, Śaṅkara Expounds Advaita (788-850) 170
Venetian Merchants Dominate Trade with the East (1150) 433
Verdun I, Treaty of (843) 205
Viet, Champa Wins Independence from Dai (1323-1326). 605
Viking Era (850-950). 213
Village Culture Flourishes, Plains (9th-15th centuries) 188
Vladimir I, Baptism of (988). 299

Waldensian Excommunications Usher in Protestant Movement (c. 1175). 462
Wang Anshi Introduces Bureaucratic Reforms (1069-1072). 366
Wang Chongyang Founds Quanzhen Daoism (12th century). 403
War, Hundred Years' (1337-1453) 627
Wars, Yoshino Civil (1336-1392) 625
West African States of Benin, Foundation of the (1400-1500). 692
White Huns, Sāsānians and Turks Defeat the (567-568). 28
White Huns Raid India (484) 3
William of Ockham Attacks Thomist Ideas (c. 1310-1350) 596
Winchester, Statute of (1285) 572
Wise Sayings of Lal Ded, Compilation of the (c. 1380) 664
Wolof Empire, Ndiadiane N'diaye Founds the (13th century). 489
Worms Are Smuggled to the Byzantine Empire, Silk (563) 25
Writing of *Kojiki* and *Nihon shoki* (March 9, 712, and July 1, 720) 125
Written Form, Origins of Swahili in Its (c. 1100) 392
Wu, Reign of Empress (690-705) 100
Wyclif, Condemnation of John (1377-1378) 662

Xuanzang, Pilgrimage of (629-645). 71

Yarmūk, Battle of (August 15-20, 636) 81
Yekuno Amlak Founds the Solomonid Dynasty (1270-1285). 559
Yi Dynasty, Establishment of the (July, 1392) 684
Yonglo Dadian Encyclopedia Is Compiled (1403-1407). 695
Yoritomo Becomes Shogun, Minamoto (1156-1192). 451
Yoruba Culture, Development of the Ife Kingdom and (11th-15th centuries) 320
Yoshino Civil Wars (1336-1392). 625

Zanj Revolt of African Slaves (869-883). 227
Zeami Perfect Nō Drama, Kan'ami and (c. 1360-1440) 647
Zheng He's Naval Expeditions (1405-1433). . . . 697
Zhu Xi, Birth of (1130). 414
Zimbabwe Urbanism and Architecture, Great (11th-15th centuries) 322
Zīrids Break from Fāṭimid Dynasty and Revive Sunni Islam (1048) 357
Zohar Is Transcribed, The (c. 1275) 570

List of Maps and Tables

Africa c. 1000-1500 (*map*). . . . . *lxxx*
African Expeditions Sponsored by
Prince Henry (*map*). 846
Americas to c. 1500 (*map*) . . . . *lxxxi*
Angevin Empire c. 1170 (*map*). 529
Arab Observes Frankish Medicine (*sidebar*). . . . 508

Battle of Bannockburn, 1314 (*map*) 712
Byzantine Empire at Justinian's Death,
565 C.E. (*map*) . . . . *lxxvi*

Carolingian Empire, 768-814 C.E. (*map*). . . . . *lxxvii*
Charter of Lorris: Key Provisions (*sidebar*) 532
Chaucer's English (*sidebar*) 807

Delhi Sultanate: Khaljī Dynasty (*table*) 693
Delhi Sultanate: Muʿizzī Slave Kings (*table*) . . . 588
Delhi Sultanate, 1236-1398 (*map*) 637

Eastern Hemisphere c. 800 C.E. (*map*) . . . . *lxxi*
Eastern Hemisphere c. 1000 (*map*) . . . . *lxxii*
Eastern Hemisphere, 1279 (*map*). . . . . *lxxiii*
Eastern Hemisphere, 1492 (*map*) . . . . *lxxiv*
England Before and After the Hundred
Years' War (*map*) 866
Europe at Clovis's Death, 511 C.E. (*map*) . . . . . *lxxv*
Europe in the Fourteenth Century (*map*) . . . . . *lxxix*

Flanders Peasants' Revolt, 1323-1328
(*map*) 722
Froissart on the Battle of Crécy (*sidebar*) 752

Great Schism, 1378-1417 (*map*) 702

Hanseatic League c. 1200 (*map*). 520
Hōjō Regents (*table*) 612
Holy Roman Empire c. 1190 (*map*) . . . . *lxxviii*
Hundred Years' War, 1337-1453 (*map*) 747

Inquisitor Denounces the Albigensians
(*sidebar*) 595

Jean de Venetteon the Plague and Anti-Semitism
(*sidebar*) 758

Kamakura Period (*table*) 539

Magna Carta: Key Provisions (*sidebar*) 604
Mamlūks c. 1300 (*map*) 660
Marco Polo's Journey, 1271-1295 (*map*). 668
Ming Dynasty (*table*). 776
Mongol Empire in 1260 (*map*). 582
Mongol Rulers (*table*) 581
Muromachi Emperors, 1336-1573 (*table*) 742

Nine Circles of Dante's Hell (*sidebar*). 705

Plague's Progress, c. 1333-1351 (*map*) 717

Sacrosancta, 1415 (*sidebar*) 838
Seventh Crusade, 1248-1254 (*map*) 643

Tamerlane's Empire c. 1400 (*map*). 798
Teutonic Knights' Lands, 13th Century
(*map*) 626

Unam Sanctam (extract) (*sidebar*) 698

Wat Tyler Meets King Richard (*sidebar*) 795

Yi Dynasty, 1392-1608 (*table*). 816

Zeami on the Art of Nō (*sidebar*) 770

Eastern Hemisphere c. 800 C.E.

Iceland
Atlantic Ocean
Celts
Anglo-Saxons
Asturias
Umayyad Caliphate
Lapps
Scandinavians
Finns
Balts
Slavs
Carolingian Emp.
Lombard duchies
Bulgars
Magyars
Bulgars
Khazars
Byzantine Emp.
Reindeer herders
Turkic nomads
Siberian hunter-gatherers
Kirghiz
Khitans
Uighers
Ainu
Parhae
Silla
Japan
Tibet
Tang Dynasty
Pacific Ocean
Abbasid Caliphate
Idrisid Caliphate
Aghlabid Emirate
Camel nomads
Makkura
Alwa
Aksum
Ghana
West African chiefdoms
Western Bantu farmers
Eastern Bantu herders/farmers
Pastoral nomads
San hunter-gatherers
Khoisan herders
Malagasay
Hindus & Buddhists
Rashtrakuta
Pallava
Pandya
Sinhalese
Burmese
Nanzhao
Pyu
Mon
Dvaravati
Thais
Champa
Chenla
Borneo
Celebes
Srivijaya
Sumatra
Mataram
Java
Timor
Papuans
Micronesia
Melanesia
Polynesia
Indian Ocean
Aboriginal hunter-gatherers

Eastern Hemisphere c. 1000

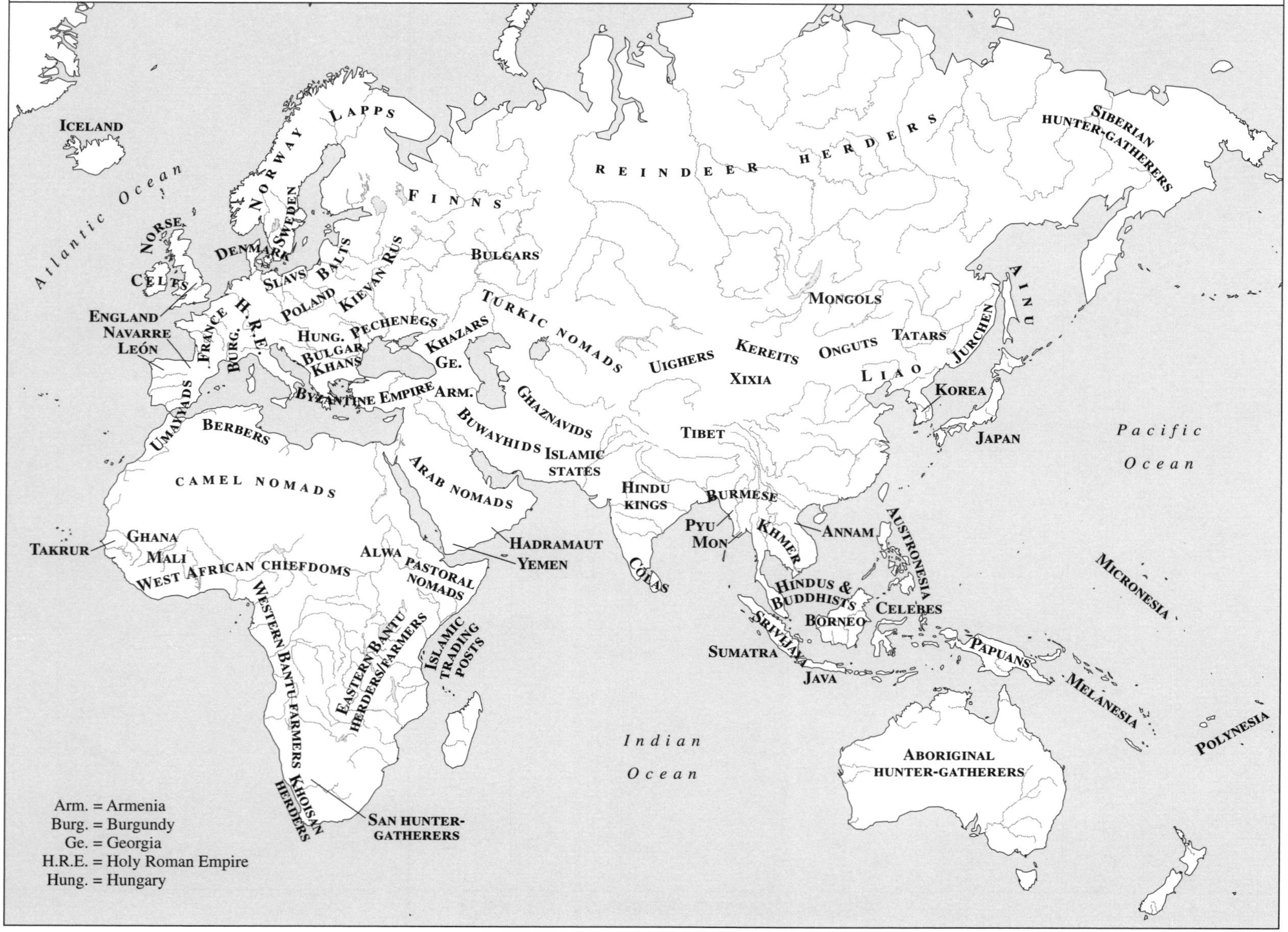
Iceland
Atlantic Ocean
Norse
Celts
England
Navarre
León
Norway
Lapps
Sweden
Denmark
Slavs
Balts
Finns
Kievan Rus
Poland
H.R.E.
France
Burg.
Hung.
Pechenegs
Bulgar Khans
Byzantine Empire
Khazars
Ge.
Arm.
Bulgars
Turkic nomads
Reindeer herders
Siberian hunter-gatherers
Mongols
Tatars
Jurchen
Ainu
Uighers
Kereits
Onguts
Xixia
Liao
Korea
Japan
Pacific Ocean
Umayyads
Berbers
Camel nomads
Ghaznavids
Buwayhids
Islamic states
Tibet
Arab nomads
Hadramaut
Yemen
Hindu kings
Burmese
Pyu
Mon
Khmer
Annam
Austronesia
Colas
Takrur
Ghana
Mali
West African chiefdoms
Alwa
Pastoral nomads
Western Bantu farmers
Eastern Bantu herders/farmers
Islamic trading posts
Khoisan herders
San hunter-gatherers
Hindus & Buddhists
Celebes
Borneo
Srivijaya
Sumatra
Java
Papuans
Micronesia
Melanesia
Polynesia
Indian Ocean
Aboriginal hunter-gatherers
Arm. = Armenia
Burg. = Burgundy
Ge. = Georgia
H.R.E. = Holy Roman Empire
Hung. = Hungary

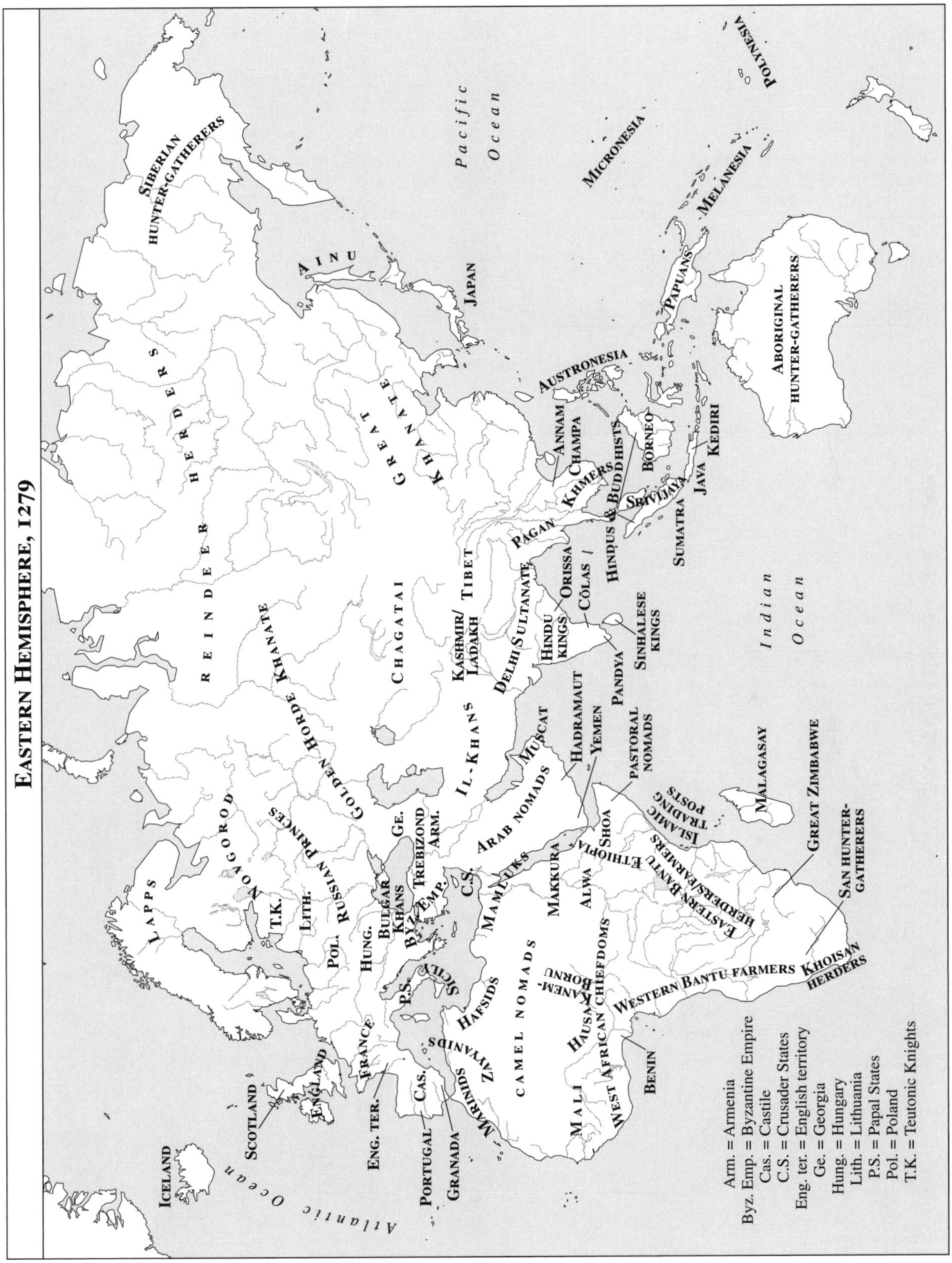
EASTERN HEMISPHERE, 1279
SIBERIAN HUNTER-GATHERERS
REINDEER HERDERS
GREAT KHANATE
AINU
JAPAN
Pacific Ocean
MICRONESIA
POLYNESIA
MELANESIA
PAPUANS
AUSTRONESIA
ABORIGINAL HUNTER-GATHERERS
ANNAM
CHAMPA
KHMERS
BORNEO
HINDUS & BUDDHISTS
SRIVIJAYA
KEDIRI
JAVA
SUMATRA
PAGAN
TIBET
ORISSA
CŌLAS
HINDU KINGS
SINHALESE KINGS
PANDYA
KASHMIR/ LADAKH
DELHI SULTANATE
Indian Ocean
CHAGATAI
GOLDEN HORDE KHANATE
IL-KHANS
MUSCAT
HADRAMAUT
YEMEN
PASTORAL NOMADS
MALAGASAY
ISLAMIC TRADING POSTS
GREAT ZIMBABWE
SAN HUNTER-GATHERERS
EASTERN BANTU HERDERS/FARMERS
ETHIOPIA
SHOA
ARAB NOMADS
NOVGOROD
RUSSIAN PRINCES
LAPPS
T.K.
LITH.
POL.
HUNG.
BULGAR KHANS
GE.
TREBIZOND
ARM.
BYZ. EMP.
C.S.
MAMLUKS
MAKKURA
ALWA
KANEM-BORNU
WEST AFRICAN CHIEFDOMS
WESTERN BANTU FARMERS
KHOISAN HERDERS
HAUSA
BENIN
MALI
CAMEL NOMADS
HAFSIDS
SICILY
P.S.
ZAYYANIDS
MARINIDS
FRANCE
ENG. TER.
CAS.
PORTUGAL
GRANADA
ENGLAND
SCOTLAND
ICELAND
Atlantic Ocean
Arm. = Armenia
Byz. Emp. = Byzantine Empire
Cas. = Castile
C.S. = Crusader States
Eng. ter. = English territory
Ge. = Georgia
Hung. = Hungary
Lith. = Lithuania
P.S. = Papal States
Pol. = Poland
T.K. = Teutonic Knights

Eastern Hemisphere, 1492

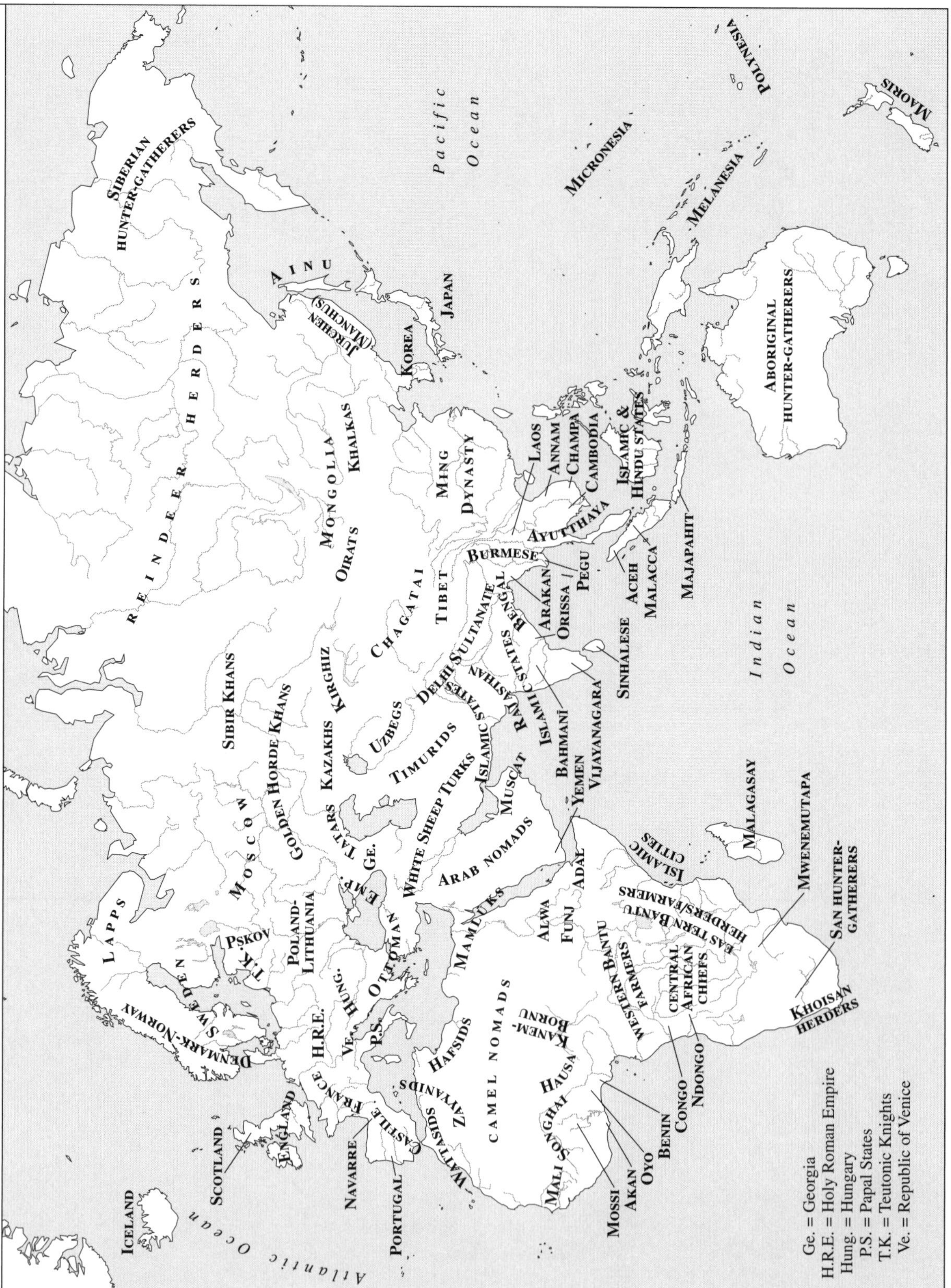

EUROPE AT CLOVIS'S DEATH, 511 C.E.

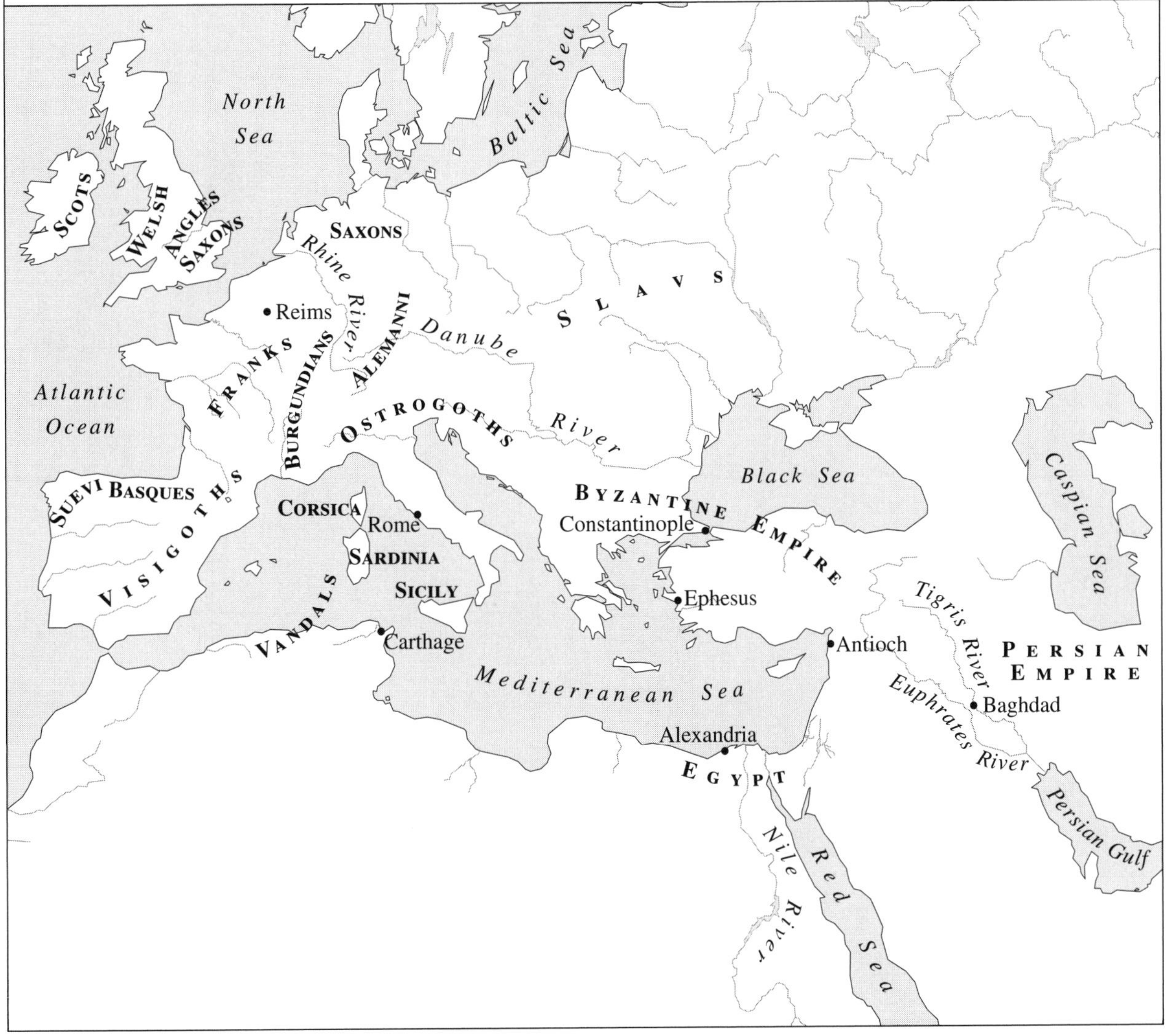
North Sea
Baltic Sea
SCOTS
WELSH
ANGLES
SAXONS
SAXONS
Rhine River
Reims
ALEMANNI
Danube River
SLAVS
FRANKS
BURGUNDIANS
Atlantic Ocean
OSTROGOTHS
Black Sea
Caspian Sea
SUEVI
BASQUES
VISIGOTHS
CORSICA
Rome
SARDINIA
SICILY
BYZANTINE EMPIRE
Constantinople
Ephesus
VANDALS
Carthage
Antioch
Tigris River
PERSIAN EMPIRE
Euphrates River
Baghdad
Mediterranean Sea
Alexandria
EGYPT
Nile River
Red Sea
Persian Gulf

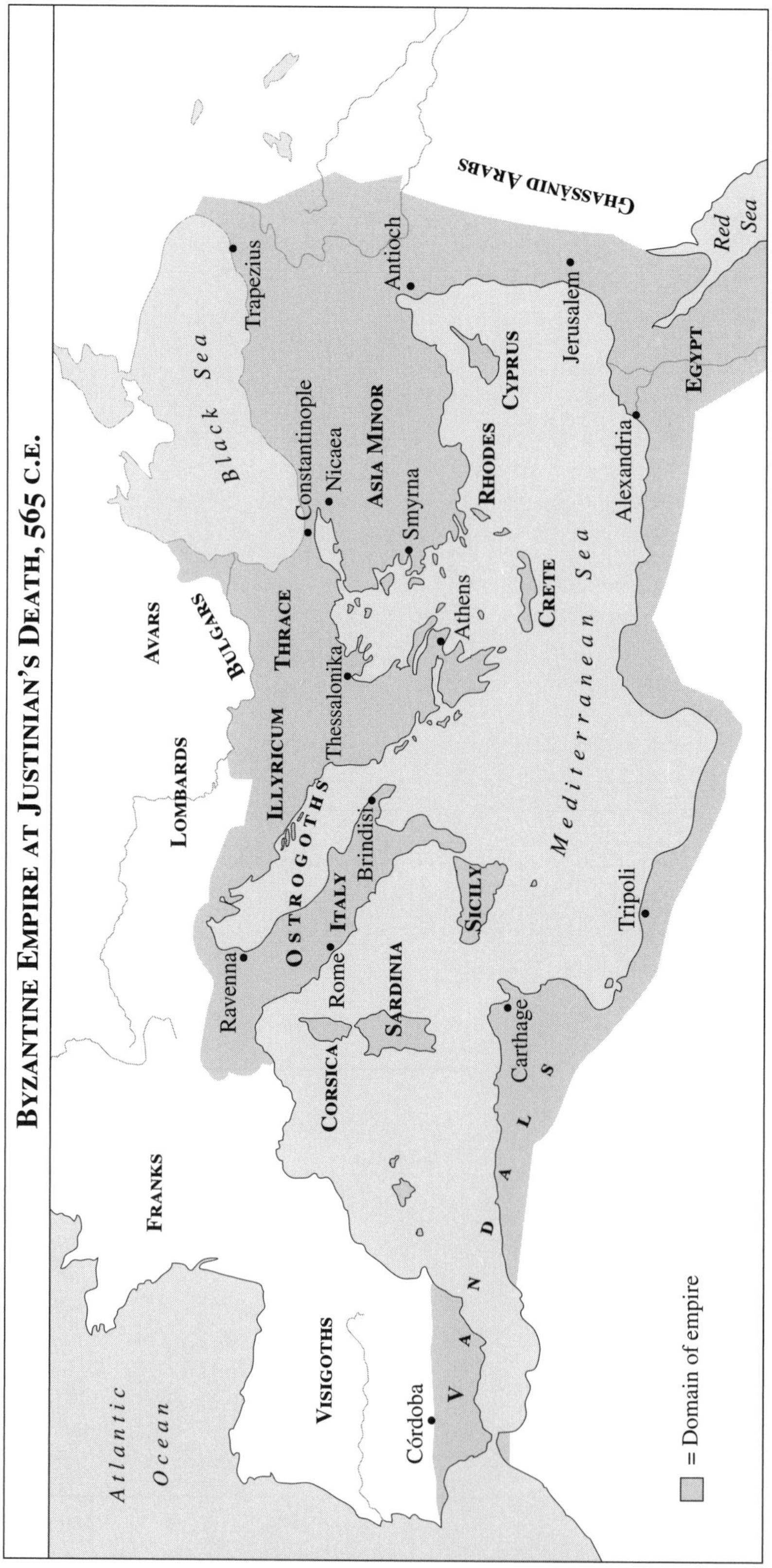
Byzantine Empire at Justinian's Death, 565 C.E.
Atlantic Ocean
Franks
Visigoths
Córdoba
V A N D A L S
Carthage
Corsica
Sardinia
Rome
Italy
Ravenna
O S T R O G O T H S
Lombards
Avars
Bulgars
Illyricum
Thrace
Sicily
Brindisi
Tripoli
Thessalonika
Athens
Crete
Rhodes
Mediterranean Sea
Constantinople
Nicaea
Smyrna
Asia Minor
Black Sea
Trapezius
Antioch
Cyprus
Jerusalem
Alexandria
Egypt
Red Sea
Ghassānid Arabs
= Domain of empire

CAROLINGIAN EMPIRE, 768-814 C.E.

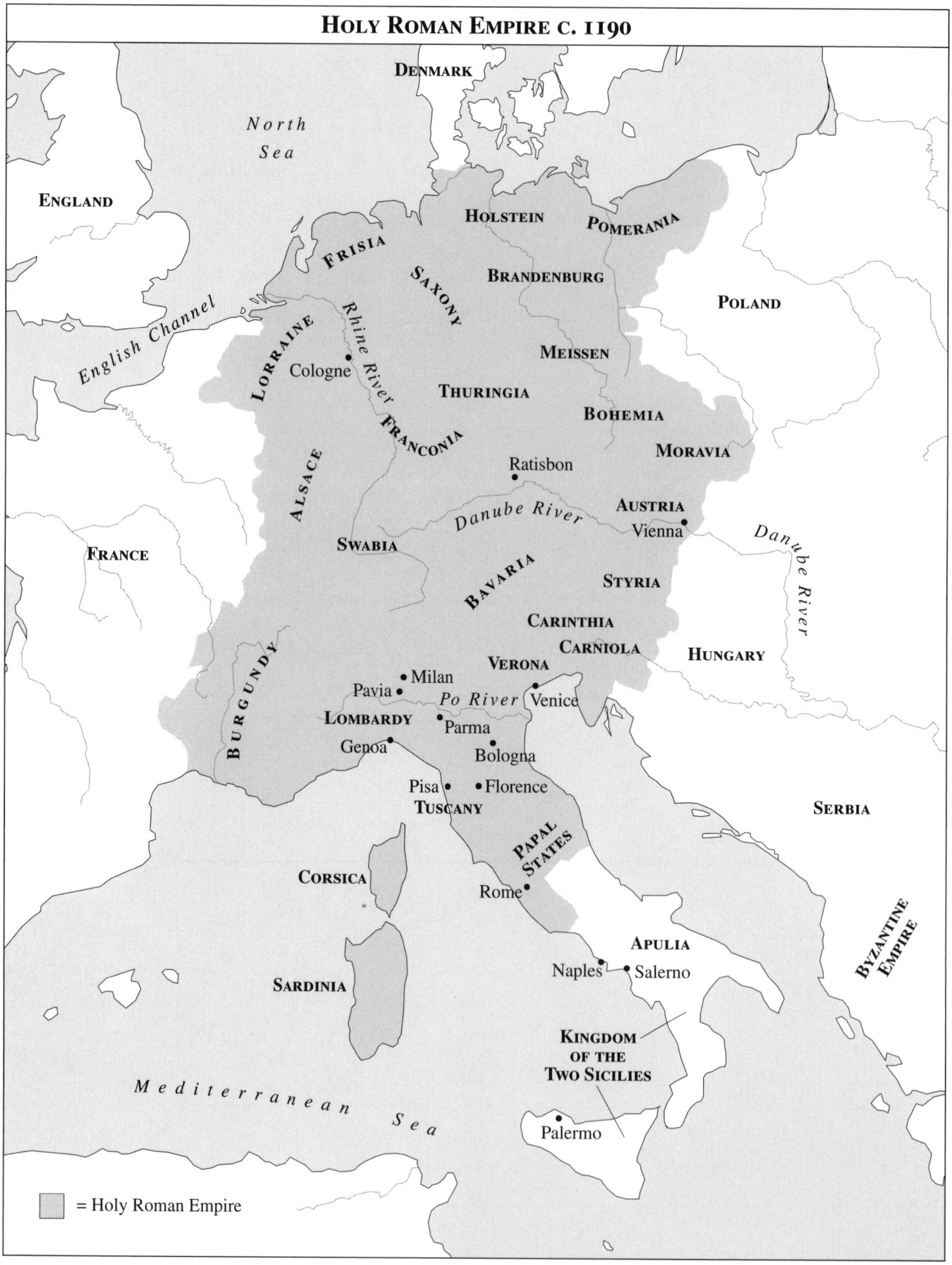
Holy Roman Empire c. 1190
Denmark
North Sea
England
Holstein
Pomerania
Frisia
Saxony
Brandenburg
Poland
English Channel
Lorraine
Rhine River
Cologne
Meissen
Thuringia
Bohemia
Franconia
Moravia
Alsace
Ratisbon
Austria
Danube River
Vienna
Danube River
France
Swabia
Bavaria
Styria
Carinthia
Carniola
Hungary
Burgundy
Verona
Milan
Pavia
Po River
Venice
Lombardy
Parma
Genoa
Bologna
Pisa
Florence
Tuscany
Serbia
Papal States
Corsica
Rome
Byzantine Empire
Apulia
Naples
Salerno
Sardinia
Kingdom of the Two Sicilies
Mediterranean Sea
Palermo
= Holy Roman Empire

Europe in the Fourteenth Century

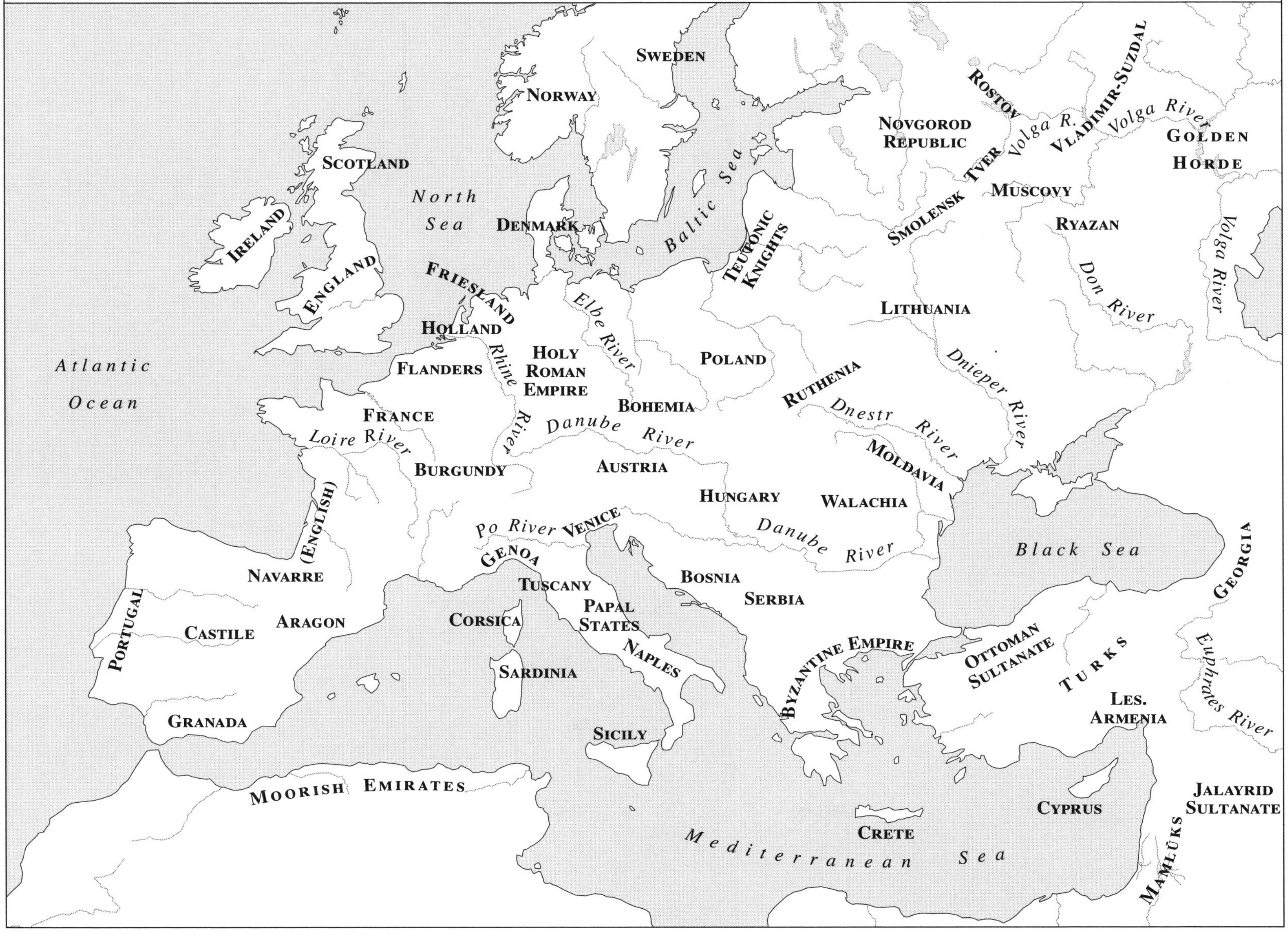

Africa c. 1000-1500

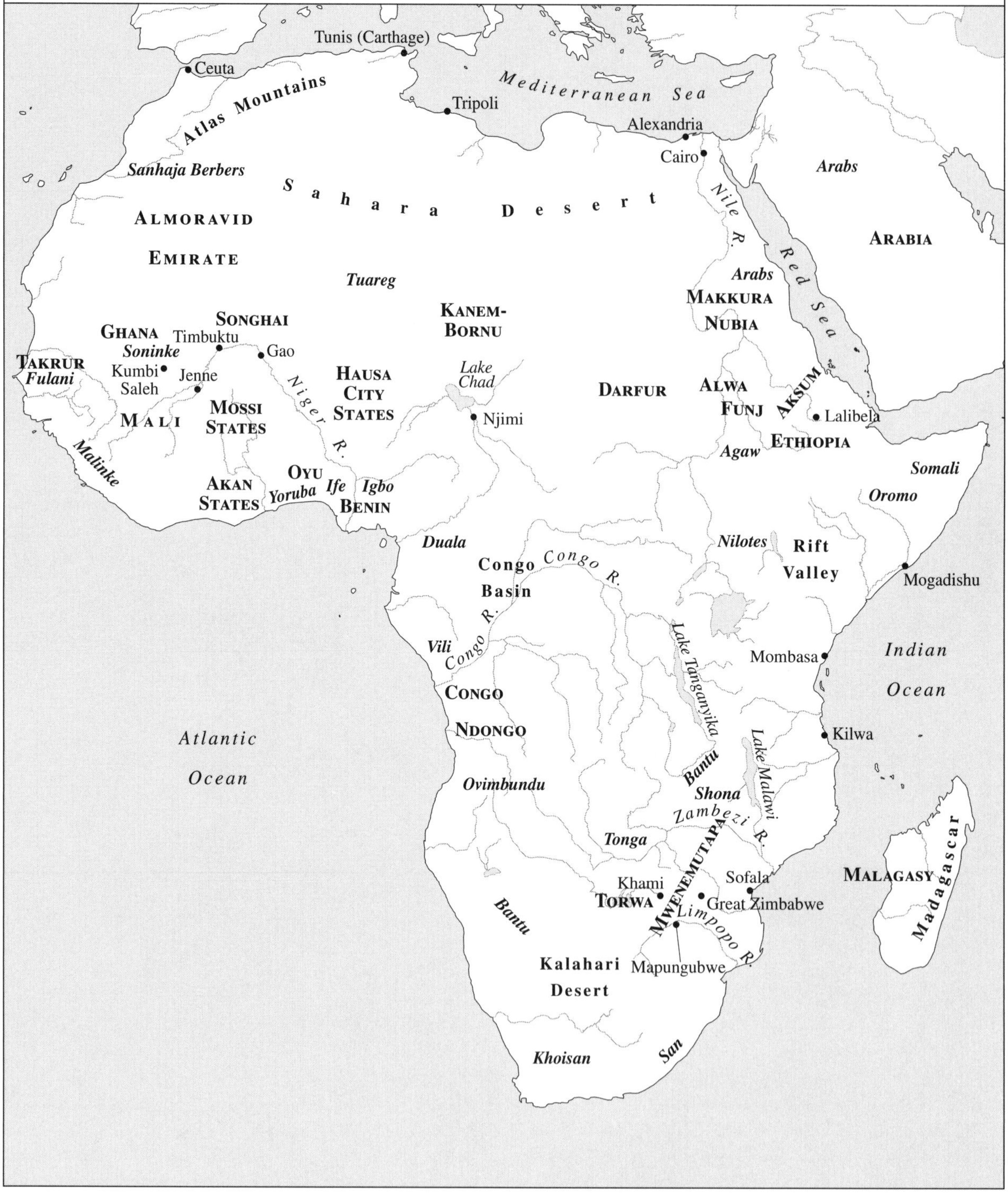

THE AMERICAS TO C. 1500

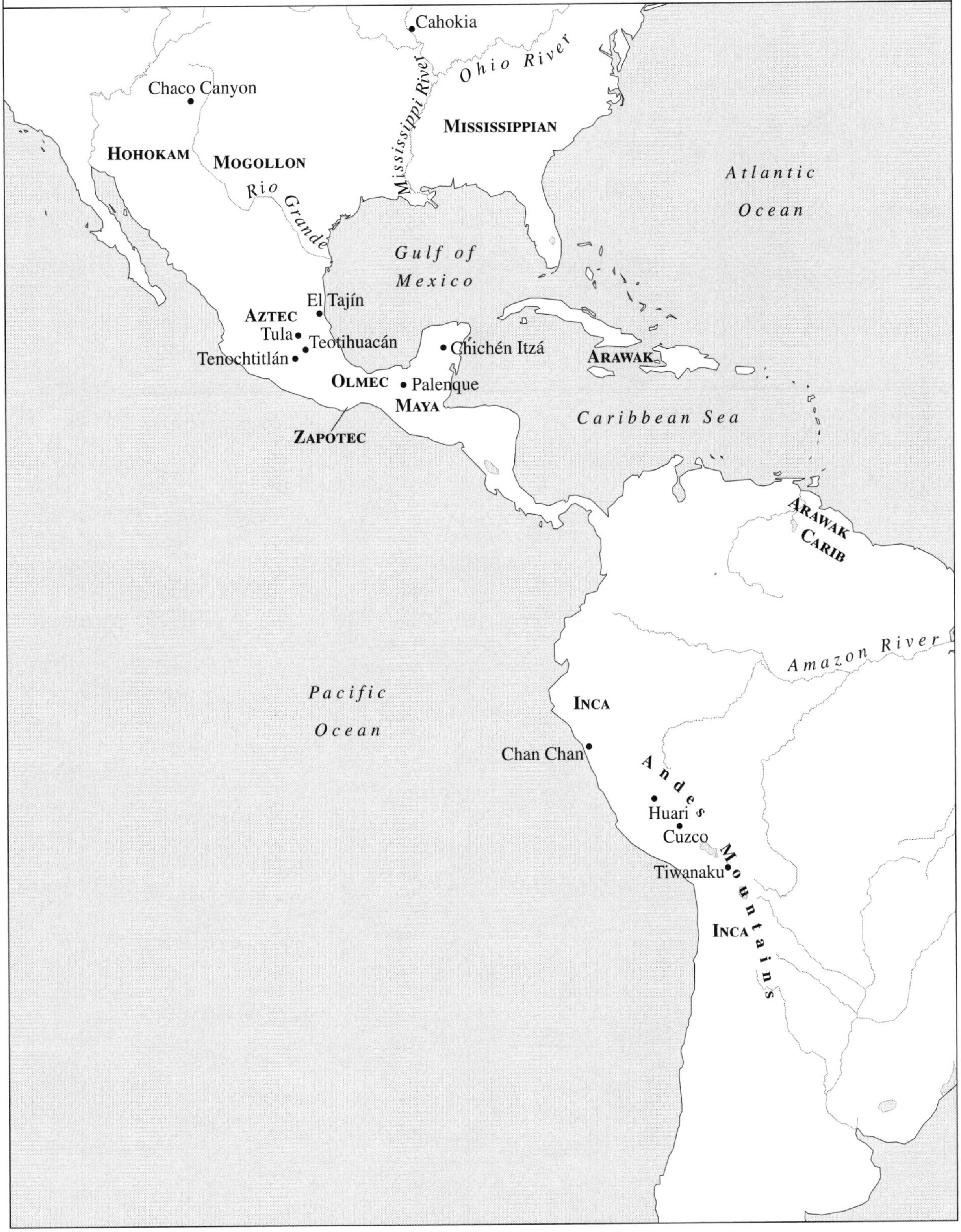
Cahokia
Ohio River
Chaco Canyon
Mississippi River
MISSISSIPPIAN
HOHOKAM
MOGOLLON
Rio Grande
Atlantic Ocean
Gulf of Mexico
El Tajín
AZTEC
Tula
Teotihuacán
Tenochtitlán
Chichén Itzá
ARAWAK
OLMEC
Palenque
MAYA
ZAPOTEC
Caribbean Sea
ARAWAK
CARIB
Amazon River
Pacific Ocean
INCA
Chan Chan
Andes Mountains
Huari
Cuzco
Tiwanaku
INCA

Great Events from History

The Middle Ages

477 - 1453

c. 1150
Moors Transmit Classical Philosophy and Medicine to Europe

The Moors brought classical philosophy and medicine to Europe from their stronghold in Spain, sharing Muslim scholarship and classical philosophies with the Latin West and profoundly influencing medieval European intellectual development.

Locale: Spain
Categories: Cultural and intellectual history; philosophy; education; health and medicine

Key Figures

Avicenna (980-1037), Persian physician and most famous philosopher-scientist of Islam
Avempace (c. 1095-1138), earliest known Moorish representative of Aristotelian-Neoplatonic tradition
Averroës (1126-1198), best-known Moorish philosopher and Aristotelian commentator
Ibn Tufayl (1109-1185), Moorish philosopher and physician
Adelard of Bath (fl. early twelfth century), English interpreter of Arabic works and Scholastic philosopher

Summary of Event

Contact between the Umayyad caliphs of Damascus (661-750) and Hellenic centers such as Antioch, Alexandria, and Edessa most likely resulted in the first translations of Greek scientific and philosophical documents into Arabic. The succeeding ʿAbbāsid sultans moved the capital to Baghdad and undertook a systematic attempt to obtain and translate the major Greek philosophical works. Their dissemination throughout the Islamic world had a profound impact on Muslim theologians, philosophers, medical doctors, and scientists. In Moorish Spain, classical learning was interpreted and expanded on by Muslim scholars before the blended Greco-Muslim philosophy and science were dispersed throughout Europe.

Interest in classical philosophy and medicine was initiated in Spain under its fifth Umayyad ruler, ʿAbd al-Raḥmān III al-Nāṣir (r. 912-961). Early Andalusian scholarship benefited from the rivalry existing between its flourishing court and the waning ʿAbbāsid court of Baghdad in terms of the collecting of fine books and patronizing of Muslim intellectuals. Despite lengthy periods during which philosophy was viewed with disfavor by the successive Moorish courts, a number of Andalusian scholars visited the East and returned with books and ideas, thus preserving a level of intellectual unity throughout the Muslim world.

The first significant writer in Spain on philosophical issues was Avempace (also known as Ibn Bajja of Saragossa), who drew acclaim and disciples by his work with Aristotelian and Neoplatonic ideas. His work and that of Ibn Tufayl stimulated on a vast scale the interest of Andalusian scholars in classical learning.

This interest came to fruition in the person of Averroës, acknowledged as the greatest Muslim commentator on Aristotle's works. Following his introduction to Caliph Abū Yaʿqūb Yūsuf by Ibn Tufayl, Averroës was appointed as *qadi* (judge) of Seville and instructed to comment on the works of Aristotle, which the caliph found difficult to understand. During his remarkable career, he was promoted to the position of chief *qadi* at Córdoba and royal physician to the Córdoban court. Among his works, which attempted to harmonize philosophy and theological dogma, is his great philosophical rebuttal of the eastern Muslim philosopher al-Ghazzālī (1058-1111), *Tahāfut at-tahāfut* (c. 1174-1180; *Incoherence of the Incoherence*, 1954). His work was to become highly regarded throughout the West, as evidenced by his inclusion among the masters of Hellenic thought in Raphael's masterpiece *School of Athens* (1513), a Vatican fresco.

Averroës's championing of genuine Aristotelianism dichotomized philosophical pursuits in the western Muslim world from those in the East, which primarily endorsed the quasi-mystical illumination (*ishraq*) philosophy supported by Avicenna. Yet Avicenna advanced Western knowledge in his own right, primarily by the dissemination of his medical treatises into Europe via Andalusia.

During the eighth century, a time when medicine in the Latin West was based largely on superstition, Muslim medicine was based on scientific method as inherited from classical works such as those by Hippocrates and Galen. Muslim medical literature was later translated into Latin and used in some European universities as late as the seventeenth century. A number of scholars agree that Muslim philosophers did little to expand most branches of Greek medical knowledge, serving instead as the preservers of Greek medical heritage. Noted exceptions are the work of Ibn al-Jazzar (d. 984) concern-

AN ARAB OBSERVES FRANKISH MEDICINE

In the twelfth century during the height of the Crusades, an Arab named Usāmah recorded his observations of the Franks—among whom, he asserts, he held one Frankish knight a dear friend. Nevertheless, he decries them as "animals possessing the virtues of courage and fighting, but nothing else":

A case illustrating their curious medicine is the following: The lord of al-Munaytirah wrote to my uncle asking him to dispatch a physician to treat certain sick persons among his people. My uncle sent him a Christian physician named Thabit [who related this story]:

"They brought before me a knight in whose leg an abscess had grown; and a woman afflicted with imbecility. To the knight I applied a small poultice until the abscess opened and became well; and the woman I put on diet and made her humour wet. Then a Frankish physician came to them and said, 'This man knows nothing about treating them.' He then said to the knight, 'Which wouldst thou prefer, living with one leg or dying with two?' The latter replied, 'Living with one leg.' The physician said, 'Bring me a strong knight and a sharp axe.' A knight came with the axe. And I was standing by. Then the physician laid the leg of the patient on a block of wood and bade the knight strike his leg with the axe and chop it off at one blow. Accordingly he struck it—while I was looking on—one blow, but the leg was not severed. He dealt another blow, upon which the marrow of the leg flowed out and the patient died on the spot. He [the Frankish physician] then examined the woman and said, 'This is a woman in whose head there is a devil which has possessed her. Shave off her hair.' Accordingly they shaved it off and the woman began once more to eat their ordinary diet—garlic and mustard. Her imbecility took a turn for the worse. The physician then said, 'The devil has penetrated through her head.' He therefore took a razor, made a deep cruciform incision on it, peeled off the skin at the middle of the incision until the bone of the skull was exposed and rubbed it with salt. The woman also expired instantly. Thereupon I asked them whether my services were needed any longer, and when they replied in the negative I returned home. . . ."

Source: Memoirs of Usamah, translated by P. K. Hitti (New York: Columbia University Press, 1929), quoted in *The Portable Medieval Reader* (New York: Penguin Books, 1977), edited by James Bruce Ross and Mary Martin McLaughlin, pp. 448-449.

ing the management and care of children and that of ʿArib bin Saʾid of Córdoba on gynecology, embryology, and pediatrics. Al-Rāzī (c. 864-c. 925) wrote a discourse describing the causes and treatment of smallpox. Al-Zahrawi (c. 940-1013) compiled a medical encyclopedia devoted, among other things, to midwifery, implying the existence of a thriving profession of trained nurses and midwives in Moorish Spain.

Muslim contributions to the fields of pharmacology and medical botany, however, greatly surpassed the work of the classicists. Advancing well beyond Dioscorides' *De materia medica* (first century B.C.E.), Muslims described identifications, modes of administration, and therapeutic qualities of more than one hundred plants known throughout the Muslim world. In addition, the increasing incidence of poisonings prompted an attempt by court physicians to expand their knowledge of toxicology. Galen's recipe for the theriac, the universal antidote, was translated and significantly modified before its introduction to the West in the thirteenth century.

While the Islamic world was translating and expanding classical works with great fervor, medieval Europe was for the most part ignorant of classical philosophy. Other than three dialogues of Plato, Aristotle's *Logic* (fourth century B.C.E.; English translation, 1812), and several mistranslated versions of Aristotle, examples of Greek works were unavailable to scholars. Limited contact between the Latin West and the Byzantine Empire, which preserved Greek manuscripts but little understood them and the dominant trend in medieval Europe to emphasize Christian theology over philosophy contributed to a general neglect of Greek knowledge north of Muslim Spain.

At the turn of the eleventh century, however, Greco-Muslim philosophy began its migration throughout the Latin West. Christian conquest of Muslim lands increased the level of interaction between European conquerors, merchants, pilgrims, and scholars and Muslim tributaries, spawning an effort to translate Arabic works into Latin in order to understand the past successes of Islam. Spain served as the major cultural and intellectual bridge between East and West and as the leading center for European scholars who wished to learn Arabic and engage in translation.

The first college of translators was established in Toledo by Don Raimundo, archbishop of that city from 1126 to 1151. Toledo was a natural center of translation and intellectual transmission because of the amicable coexistence there of Christians and Muslims and the existence of a large Jewish population, which was at home in both worlds and fluent in both Arabic and in Latin or Romance. A number of Toledo's Jews, including Moses Maimonides, were respected philosophers in their own right. Although many of Toledo's Christian translators used Jewish or Muslim intermediaries to translate into the vernacular before subsequent translation into Latin, others, such as Gerard of Cremona, learned Arabic in order to read the works and later render them directly into Latin. Gerard's translations eventually included virtually the entire field of science at that time.

Work in various disciplines, undertaken in Toledo under Church patronage by such scholars as Adelard of Bath and Peter the Venerable (c. 1091-1156), abbot of Cluny, revived classicism and increased acceptance of hitherto "heretical" disciplines in Western thought. As evidenced in the writings of Thomas Aquinas (1224 or 1225-1274), Dante (1265-1321), and Roger Bacon (c. 1220-c. 1292), the religion of Islam continued to be regarded as anathema in the Christian West, although Muslim learning was held in high esteem. The development of Christian Scholasticism is indebted in large part to the philosophical works of Ibn Tufayl and Averroës.

As Toledo's eminence as a translation center waned toward the end of the thirteenth century, Christian elites such as Alfonso X, king of Castile from 1252 to 1284, established new centers. In addition to translation, the Christian West made a concerted effort to obtain books, build libraries, and increase the number of Muslim and Jewish court scholars capable of elucidating classical learning. Throughout the Christian Reconquest, scholars of various religions and cultures maintained close collaboration. Ideas were transmitted with great speed, enabling a new work to make the journey from the Muslim East to Córdoba and on into Christian Europe in less than two years.

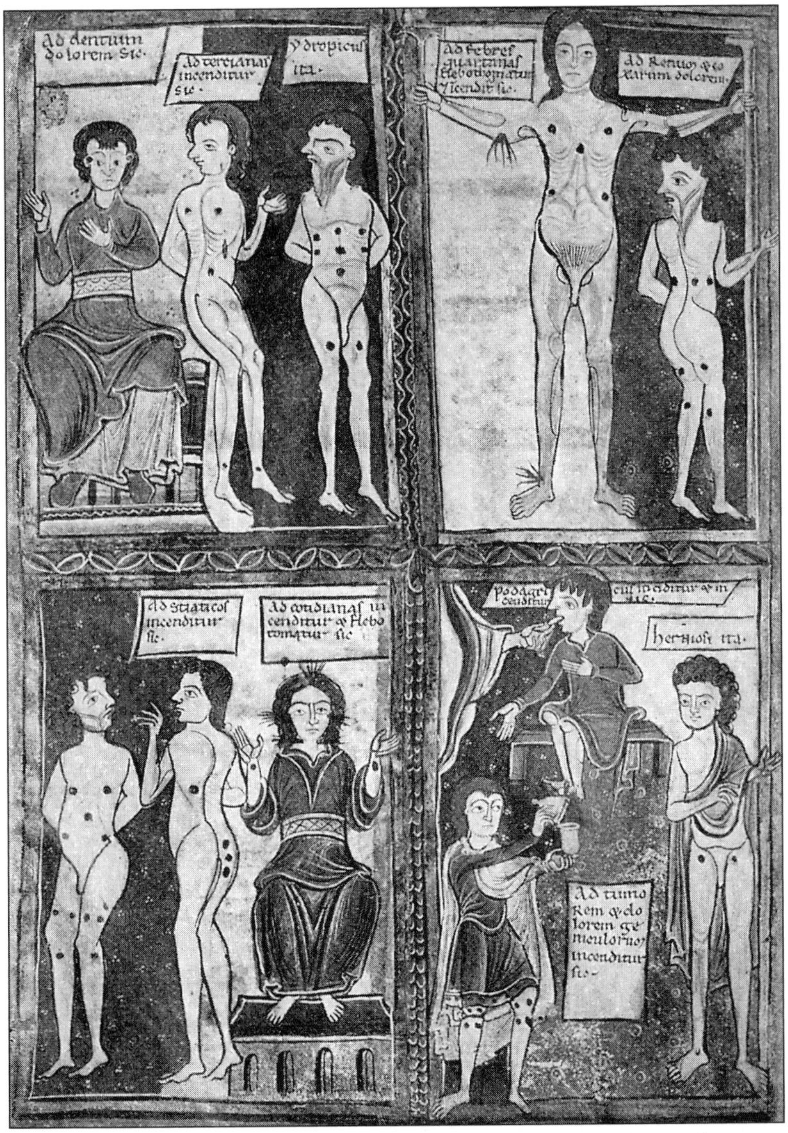

An Anglo-Saxon depiction of proper sites for cauterization, from a thirteenth century treatise on the topic. Cauterization was developed in Islamic hospitals during the ninth century and transmitted through Muslim Spain to the West. (Hulton|Archive by Getty Images)

Significance

Classical and Greco-Muslim ideas, new to Christian Europe and in many cases contradictory to the teachings of the Church, were hotly debated. It was not until 1251 that Aristotle was recognized as an acceptable subject for study in the University of Paris. Yet the process of debate and consequent intense study of the works inherited from Muslim philosophers slowly released medieval Europe from narrow modes of thought and encouraged appreciation of classical ideas. Such appreciation ultimately

Because Muslim doctors were not allowed to touch women patients, they could conduct their examinations only by interviewing them. (Hulton|Archive by Getty Images)

resulted in the European Renaissance, built on the foundation of classical achievements and a desire to emulate the all-embracing approach of classical thought.

—*Katherine S. Mansour*

FURTHER READING

Bakar, Osman. *The History and Philosophy of Islamic Science*. Cambridge, England: Islamic Texts Society, 1999. Discusses questions of methodology, doubt, spirituality and scientific knowledge, the philosophy of Islamic medicine, and how Islamic science influenced medieval Christian views of the natural world.

Chejne, Anwar G. *Muslim Spain: Its History and Culture*. St. Paul: University of Minnesota Press, 1974. Written as a text for graduate students, this work provides a well-written overview of the history, culture, and intellectual life of al-Andalus (Andalusia).

_______. "The Role of al-Andalus in the Movement of Ideas Between Islam and the West." In *Islam and the Medieval West*, edited by Khalil I. Semann. Albany: State University of New York Press, 1980. A defense of Muslim contributions to European culture and discussion of difficult-to-document contributions from Arabic literary genres.

Deitrich, Albert. "Islamic Sciences and the Medieval West: Pharmacology." In *Islam and the Medieval West*, edited by Khalil I. Semann. Albany: State University of New York Press, 1980. A detailed and well-documented discussion of the expansion of Greek knowledge of pharmacology by medieval Muslims.

Fletcher, Richard. "Christian-Muslim Understanding in the Later Middle Ages." *History Today* 53, no. 4 (April, 2003). A very brief but detailed discussion of the history of shared traditions—including intellectual—between Muslims and Christians in medieval Europe. Also explores how Muslims and Christians tried to move beyond a long history of hostilities between the two faiths.

_______. *Moorish Spain*. New York: Henry Holt, 1992. This work incorporates scholarship on al-Andalus and offers a concise treatment of the Moors in Spain. Chapter 4, "The Caliphate of Córdoba," considers the glories of the caliphate as well as its collapse.

García-Ballester, Luis. *Medicine in a Multicultural Society: Christian, Jewish and Muslim Practitioners in the Spanish Kingdoms, 1222-1610*. Aldershot, England: Ashgate, 2001. A look at medical practice and medical practitioners in the Spanish realm after the introduction of Moorish medical knowledge into the region. Includes an index.

Huff, Toby E. *The Rise of Early Modern Science: Islam, China, and the West*. 2d ed. New York: Cambridge University Press, 2003. Provides a strong cross-cultural background for the rise of science and medicine in Avicenna's time. Includes illustrations, a bibliography, and index.

Reilly, Bernard F. *The Contest of Christian and Muslim Spain: 1031-1157*. Cambridge, Mass.: Blackwell, 1995. Enlightening use of recently published primary sources to provide insight into the political and cultural changes in Iberia during this critical period.

SEE ALSO: April or May, 711: Ṭārik Crosses into Spain; c. 950: Court of Córdoba Flourishes in Spain; c. 1010-1015: Avicenna Writes His *Canon of Medicine*; 1031: Caliphate of Córdoba Falls; 1190: Moses Maimonides Writes *The Guide of the Perplexed*.

RELATED ARTICLES in *Great Lives from History: The Middle Ages, 477-1453*: Pietro d'Abano; ʿAbd al-Raḥmān III al-Nāṣir; Abū Ḥanīfah; Alfonso X; Alhazen; Averroës; Avicenna; Roger Bacon; al-Bīrūnī; Dante; Fakhr al-Dīn al-Rāzī; al-Ghazzālī; al-Ḥallāj; Judah ha-Levi; Moses Maimonides; al-Rāzī; Thomas Aquinas.

c. 1150
REFINEMENTS IN BANKING

The surge in trade during the eleventh and twelfth centuries in Europe created new and better methods of handling, using, and transferring money that eventually led to the development of banking houses.

LOCALE: Western Europe, principally present-day Italy
CATEGORY: Trade and commerce

SUMMARY OF EVENT

One of the most important aspects of the renaissance of trade during the eleventh and twelfth centuries was the stimulus it gave to new and improved methods of handling and employing money, which led to the development of full-fledged banking operations. Before the twelfth and thirteenth centuries, only the most rudimentary bookkeeping methods were employed. Credit had already been extended during the eleventh century, although usually limited to consumptive purposes; however, the twelfth century saw the Templars and Hospitalers introduce sophisticated instruments of foreign exchange or letters of credit that were freely employed among their far-flung houses.

The twelfth century also witnessed the emergence of professional moneylenders from the simple moneychangers at the great fairs held all over Europe. Seated behind their long benches, these nascent bankers at first traded in bullion and later in international coin. Selling drafts and changing money, these "bankers" roamed from fair to fair making fortunes exchanging money for a service charge. True banking was born when the moneychanger put out at interest coins that he was keeping for others in his strongbox and not on immediate demand by their owners. In addition, the twelfth century gave rise to the issuance of sound silver currency: the Venetian groat, the contemporary gold Florentine florin, and the later *gros tournois* and *gros parisis* of Louis IX. Issuance of such coinage necessitated the development of adequate banking procedures.

Moreover, the twelfth century economic experience caused the Church in the thirteenth century to relax its ban on usury, a ban that had been necessary in earlier centuries when loans were made primarily for immediate consumption rather than for investment. The Church reluctantly recognized the right of lenders to compensation for inconveniences suffered while their money was on loan or for lateness in repayment on the part of the borrowers. It is more proper to view these relaxations as bona-fide legal exceptions to the usury ban than loopholes surreptitiously contrived to circumvent the intent of canon law. Thomas Aquinas's determination of the just price by the seller's need, not by his greed, reflects the Church's adjustment of its economic thinking without sacrificing its basic Aristotelian indictment of the evils inherent in unchecked economic practices.

The twelfth century, as a result, caused the despised Jewish moneylender, whose high interest rates escaped Christian usury regulations, to give way to organized banking houses. Thanks to their profits from a revived overseas and overland trade and to their proximity to the Papacy, which had to transfer enormous sums of money from faraway places, merchants of Italian cities such as Venice, Genoa, Sienna, Florence, and Lucca—especially the houses of the Bardi, the Peruzzi, and the Frescobaldi—became prominent as the so-called Lombards in the European banking world.

These stationary institutions employed many of the sophisticated instruments of modern banking. Interest rates were roughly 15 percent for commercial and industrial loans, while small personal advances brought between 50 percent and 80 percent. Deposit banking allowed a merchant to leave his cash safely at home, where, for a service charge, the bank would transfer his funds to another merchant's account in the same way that a modern checking system transacts business. By 1200, Genoese banking establishments used merchants' money to make profitable loans and investments; the merchant customer, in turn, came to regard his deposited money as an interest-bearing savings account. To facilitate the transfer of money all over Europe, bankers developed ingenious new credit instruments such as the simple check and the bill of exchange. A signed check authorized banks of Europe to transfer funds from one person's account to pay off debts to a second or a third person.

Although the check remained the common instrument of exchange for domestic transfers between nationals, the bill of exchange was developed to expedite larger transactions over longer distances. This credit device originally consisted of a signed statement by a debtor swearing that he owed a certain sum of money to a foreign merchant. The letter of exchange stipulated that the merchant would settle his foreign debt by a specified date and with a fixed interest fee. By a series of paper transfers, a whole series of debts between individuals in different cities might be discharged by the sale and resale of one of these bills. Such transactions often involved few actual transfers of cash. The Papacy, as one of the greatest borrowers and lenders of the Middle Ages, naturally contributed much to the refinement of these instruments of international credit. Through checks and bills of exchange, it transferred, during the high Middle Ages, the great sums involved in Peter's Pence, ecclesiastical fines, and levies from the distant parts of Europe.

SIGNIFICANCE

The settling of accounts at the great international fairs of Europe, the Italian merchants' invention of bills of ex-

Fourteenth century Italian bankers. (Hulton|Archive by Getty Images)

change that allowed transfer of purchasing power over great distances without shipment of actual coins, and the Church's relaxation of its ban on usury contributed greatly to the creation and establishment of complex banking practices that would be continued in the Renaissance and into modern times, allowing for more efficient commerce and increased trade between nations.

—*Carl F. Rohne*

FURTHER READING

Ekelund, Robert B, Jr., et al., eds. *Sacred Trust: The Medieval Church as an Economic Firm*. New York: Oxford University Press, 1996. An examination of the Church as an economic institution and force, both as a participant in the market and through its policies on usury.

Hill, David, and Robert Cowie, eds. *Wics: The Early Mediaeval Trading Centres of Northern Europe*. Sheffield, England: Sheffield Academic Press, 2001. A collection of essays on the early medieval trading centers of northern Europe. Illustrations, maps, and bibliography.

Miskimin, Harry A. *Cash, Credit, and Crisis in Europe, 1300-1600*. London: Variorum Reprints, 1989. A collection of essays on economic conditions in Europe during the Middle Ages. Bibliography and index.

Nicholas, David. *Urban Europe, 1100-1700*. New York: Palgrave Macmillan, 2003. An examination of economic conditions and social life and customs in the cities of medieval and Renaissance Europe. Illustrations, maps, and index.

Pounds, Norman John Greville. *An Economic History of Medieval Europe*. 2d ed. New York: Longman, 1994. A study of the economic conditions in the Middle Ages in Europe. Bibliography and index.

Spufford, Peter. *Power and Profit: The Merchant in Medieval Europe*. London: Thames & Hudson, 2002. Spufford looks at the role of the merchant in the economic history of Europe in the Middle Ages. Bibliography and index.

SEE ALSO: 1150: Venetian Merchants Dominate Trade with the East; c. 1200: Fairs of Champagne.

RELATED ARTICLES in *Great Lives from History: The Middle Ages, 477-1453*: Louis IX; Thomas Aquinas.

1150
VENETIAN MERCHANTS DOMINATE TRADE WITH THE EAST

Venetian merchants came to control trade with the East, gaining commercial advantages as a result of the weakening and ultimate collapse of the Byzantine Empire.

LOCALE: Venice (now in Italy) and the Aegean Sea
CATEGORIES: Economics; trade and commerce; transportation

KEY FIGURES

Pietro II Orseolo (991-1009), doge of Venice
Robert Guiscard (c. 1015-1085), Norman noble who conquered southern Italy and became duke of Apulia and Calabria
Alexius I Comnenus (1048-1118), Byzantine emperor, r. 1081-1118
Urban II (c. 1042-1099), Roman Catholic pope, 1088-1099
John II Comnenus (1088-1143), Byzantine emperor, r. 1118-1143
Manuel I Comnenus (c. 1122-1180), Byzantine emperor, r. 1143-1180

SUMMARY OF EVENT

Venice, a city founded on a group of small islands in a lagoon at the northern end of the Adriatic, eventually became known as the Queen of the Adriatic as a result of its commercial and military control of this important body of water. From its earliest beginnings, Venice seemed destined to become an important maritime power. Geographically, Venice was located on the edge of both the Byzantine and Holy Roman Empires and became the gateway for trade for both empires.

Faced with very limited natural resources, the early Venetians earned their living fishing and participating in the fish and salt trade with the people on the Italian mainland. On rare occasions, Greek or Syrian merchants traveling to or from the nearby Byzantine cities of Ravenna and Aquilia might visit Venice, bringing with them trade goods from the East. When the Lombards, a Germanic tribe, took these cities in the eighth century, they quickly declined in importance. For a very brief time, the city of Comacchio rose to become the economic focus for the region before the Venetians took the city in 886.

Although being on the edge of the two greatest em-

The Piazzetta in Venice from a fourteenth century miniature from the Book of the Grand Khan *in the Bodleian Library, Oxford, England, showing the Polos setting out on their journey.* (Hulton|Archive by Getty Images)

fighting Slavic pirates operating from the Dalmatian coast, the Venetians earned the respect and favor of the Byzantine emperor. It did not take many years before the Dalmatian coastal cities came to recognize Venice as their nominal lord.

Each success in the Adriatic provided the Venetians with expanded opportunities in the eastern Mediterranean. By the late eleventh century, the Byzantines were losing control of their ports in southern Italy to the Normans of Robert Guiscard while simultaneously losing territories in the East to the Seljuk Turks. The Byzantine emperor, Alexius I Comnenus, appealed to Venice for naval aid against the Normans. It was in the Venetian self-interest to render the requested aid because the Normans wanted to control both shores of the lower Adriatic so they could plunder Venetian shipping. The Venetians quickly saw that they could both help themselves and earn some reward from the Byzantines. Although the Venetians already had the right to trade in the Byzantine Empire as the result of a commercial treaty signed in 992, they now saw the possibility of trade with reduced tariffs. The Venetians were successful in defending Byzantine interests in the area and were not disappointed in their expectations. The emperor Alexius granted the Venetians expanded trading rights and exemption from tolls in the Golden Bull of 1082.

Having temporarily halted the Norman advance on Byzantine possessions in eastern Europe, Alexius called on Pope Urban II in 1095 for military aid against the Seljuk Turks in the East. The pope preached the First Crusade to enlist Christian support for a holy war against the Islamic Seljuk Turks. Although Venice gained some trading rights and commercial concessions from Godfrey de Bouillon, leader of the kingdom of Jerusalem, most of the commercial activity in the area was in the hands of Venice's archrivals Genoa and Pisa. In the summer of 1123, Venice was able to deepen its relationship with the kingdom of Jerusalem when a Venetian fleet defeated a Muslim fleet at the Battle of Ascalon. This naval engagement ensured Christian control of the seacoast for the kingdom of Jerusalem for another generation.

pires of the time had its advantages for Venice, it also had its perils. Pietro II Orseolo succeeded in balancing the Venetian interests with those of the Byzantine and Holy Roman Empires without having Venice become subject to either power. The Venetians signed favorable trade treaties with both empires and were even able to sign commercial treaties with the Islamic states of North Africa. Building on their previous trade dominance in fish and salt with the mainland, the Venetians now became suppliers of incense, silks, spices, and other trade goods of the East.

Initially, Venetian trade with the Levant was in Slavic slaves and Italian lumber—two goods in ample supply. Although the slave trade would rise and fall in importance to Venice, the significance of lumber remained a mainstay of Venetian commerce. The Mediterranean-based powers all had a need for lumber, particularly for shipbuilding, and Venice was no exception. Because they possessed access to lumber, pitch, iron, and hemp, the Venetians were able to develop a very profitable shipbuilding industry and a powerful navy.

The Venetian Republic made it its business to police the Adriatic Sea to maintain its vital trade routes. By

Although the Byzantines regularly enlisted the aid of Venice against their enemies, they were never entirely happy about their relative relationship. Despite the successful Venetian efforts on behalf of the Byzantines against the Normans of southern Italy, the emperor Alexius began to show favor to Pisa in an effort to undermine Venice in the Adriatic and to play off one Italian maritime power against the other. In 1118, Alexius died and the new emperor John II Comnenus refused to renew the charter granting Venice commercial concessions. Although they hoped to sow the seeds of war among the competing Italian maritime states, the Byzantines overestimated their own importance to the Italians. Pisa and Genoa were more concerned at that time with their respective territorial claims to Corsica (which was certainly geographically more important to them) than with any Byzantine commercial prize in the East. To force the Byzantines to recognize their rights, the Venetians sacked a number of Greek islands and cities of the Aegean. Grudgingly, the Byzantines renewed their commercial ties with Venice.

Despite the Byzantine efforts to disrupt Venetian trade, the primary Venetian goal throughout this period was to maintain official trade relations with the Byzantine Empire rather than to resort to opportunistic plundering. The Venetians were more interested in maintaining the Byzantine Empire as a state than in seeing its collapse. There were, however, problems ahead for both peoples. The Greeks were increasingly irritated and unhappy because of Italian trade privileges in general and the Venetian concessions in particular. The Venetians were increasingly contemptuous of the Greeks because of their obvious political and military weaknesses.

In 1171, the Byzantine emperor Manuel I Comnenus ordered the arrest of all Venetians in the Byzantine Empire and the confiscation of their possessions and properties. The Venetians sent a fleet to the Aegean to plunder the Greek possessions to force the Byzantines to release their compatriots and restore their property. In this instance, the Venetians not only were unsuccessful but also returned to Venice carrying a plague that infected the city.

SIGNIFICANCE

When the Byzantines finally allowed the Venetians to renew their commercial concession, it was on a new, nonexclusive basis. The Venetians became just one of a number of Italian states given trade rights in the Byzantine Empire. By the end of the twelfth century, piracy became the rule rather than the exception, and the Byzantine Empire was now preyed on by the Genoese, Pisans, Muslims, Greeks, Saracens, Sicilian Normans, and the Venetians. From the Venetian perspective, the collapse of the Byzantine Empire was inevitable and imminent. Within this context, Venetian involvement in the Fourth Crusade and the overthrow of the Byzantine government becomes understandable.

—*Peter L. Viscusi*

FURTHER READING

Cheetham, Nicolas. *Mediaeval Greece.* New Haven, Conn.: Yale University Press, 1981. This history of Greece during the Middle Ages reflects contemporary scholarship and provides a clear account of the political, military, cultural, and religious turmoil in medieval Greece.

Lane, Frederic C. *Venice: A Maritime Republic.* Baltimore: The Johns Hopkins University Press, 1973. Written by one of the world's leading authorities, this is the classic reference work for a quick topical overview of the subject.

Mango, Cyril, ed. *The Oxford History of Byzantium.* New York: Oxford University Press, 2002. Among the topics covered in the fragmentation experienced by the Byzantine Empire in the Middle Ages. Bibliography and index.

Norwich, John Julius. *A History of Venice.* 1982. Reprint. New York: Vintage Books, 1989. The author, a noted British scholar, takes a detailed and chronological approach to Venetian history that is both interesting and colorful.

Treadgold, Warren T. *A History of the Byzantine State and Society.* Stanford, Calif.: Stanford University Press, 1997. Describes the Byzantine Empire throughout its history, including the period during which it interacted with Venice. Bibliography and index.

SEE ALSO: November 27, 1095: Pope Urban II Calls the First Crusade; c. 1150: Refinements in Banking; c. 1200: Fairs of Champagne; 1204: Knights of the Fourth Crusade Capture Constantinople.

RELATED ARTICLE in *Great Lives from History: The Middle Ages, 477-1453*: Urban II.

c. 1150-1200
DEVELOPMENT OF GOTHIC ARCHITECTURE

The development of Gothic architecture introduced new structural techniques and created an aesthetic style whose soaring, light-filled spaces typify late medieval culture.

LOCALE: The Île-de-France region of France
CATEGORY: Cultural and intellectual history

KEY FIGURES

Suger (1081-1151), abbot of Saint-Denis, 1122-1151
Jean d'Orbais (fl. early thirteenth century), first architect of the Cathedral of Reims, begun in 1211
Robert de Luzarches (fl. c. 1220-1240), first architect of the Cathedral of Amiens, begun in 1220

SUMMARY OF EVENT

"Gothic," derived from "Goth," the generic name of the Teutons who invaded Europe in the fourth and fifth centuries, connotes cruelty and barbarity. It was in this opprobrious sense that "Gothic" was used by early art critics and architects such as Giorgio Vasari (1511-1574) and Sir Christopher Wren (1632-1723) to describe the dominant architecture of Europe from the twelfth century to the sixteenth. During the nineteenth century, there was a change in sentiment toward the Middle Ages, and "Gothic" ecclesiastical buildings became objects of interest, admiration, and detailed studies.

This style appears to have originated in northeastern France, especially in the Île-de-France around Paris, and from there spread throughout the Continent and across the English Channel to England. It stems out of its immediate predecessor, the Romanesque basilica, which substituted stone vaulting for wooden ceilings and consequently required heavy walls and buttresses.

The Gothic church is distinguished by a masterful combination of ribbed vaults, pointed arches, and flying buttresses. Romanesque architects regularly employed "groined" vaults to span the aisles and naves of their churches. One of the first Romanesque churches to have the groined vault in its nave was Sant' Ambrogio at Milan. These vaults were constructed by arching over the space to be covered in two different directions, the "groin" being formed by the diagonal lines where the masonry met. Though vaults of this type concentrated their vertical thrust upon columns and piers and not along a continuous wall as in the case of "barrel" vaults, they were still heavy and difficult to construct. The introduction of "ogival," or "ribbed," vaulting in Romanesque buildings of the eleventh century in northern Italy was, therefore, a significant advance in technique. In vaults of this type, the area was first outlined with diagonal, transverse, and longitudinal ribs of stone that were then filled in with webs of brick or stone. Because this type of vaulting was lighter and stronger, it became one of the distinctive features of Gothic architecture.

The Romans used only the classically proportioned round arch. Builders in Mesopotamia, however, had earlier employed the pointed arch as well. From there, the pointed arch passed to Persia, Armenia, Egypt, and Sicily. Probably the first use made of it on the European continent was in the nave arcades of the Romanesque abbey church of Cluny (1089-1131). The pointed arch proved to have a number of distinct advantages over the round: It generated less of a lateral thrust; more important, the pointed arch was more flexible in that its height was not determined by its width. Consequently, it could easily be adjusted so that the crowns of the transverse and longitudinal ribs of a vault were equal in height to the diagonal ribs, a matter of particular importance for cruciform churches. By pointing the diagonal ribs more sharply, any height commensurate with safety could be effected.

Vaulted construction required heavy buttressing by piers or relieving arches to carry the thrust to piers placed farther out. Roman and Romanesque architects concealed these piers as far as possible behind the outer walls of their buildings. Gothic architects lightened appearances by exposing the framework, the piers, and the "flying" buttresses to open view.

In comparison to earlier architecture, Gothic was revolutionary. The earlier style of building was practically turned inside out. The new style anticipated modern skyscraper construction, but in a more sophisticated way than post and lintel usage, by erecting a skeleton so that the roof was not supported directly by the walls. Instead, the roof was held aloft by an elaborate framework of piers, arches, and buttresses that at the same time absorbed and carried most of the pressures generated by the vaulting of the nave so that the walls could be filled with stained glass windows to form an airy curtain.

The interior of a Gothic church proved to be even more impressive than its exterior. While length directed attention to the sanctuary at the east end of the nave, the ribbing of piers and vaults together with the great height pulled the beholder's eyes upward. In the Cathedral of

Notre Dame Cathedral, Paris, with the flying buttresses typical of High Gothic architecture. (Hulton|Archive by Getty Images)

Amiens, the nave ceiling is 140 feet (42.5 meters) above the floor.

The new spirit dominating Gothic architecture was both philosophical and theological. From the Schoolmen (Scholastics), the medieval architects derived a feeling for order and a conviction that all temporal beauty was a reflection of divine beauty. At the same time, a deeper mystical appreciation of the humanity of Christ and his role in salvation is reflected in the many carvings and stained-glass windows that adorned the new churches.

If one individual can be singled out in this new architectural movement, it is perhaps Abbot Suger, who largely rebuilt the west facade and choir of the abbey church of Saint-Denis on the outskirts of Paris between 1130 and 1144. With its ribbed vaults, interlinking spaces, and stained glass as well as the sculptural program of the facade, this building campaign is generally conceded to be the first definitely Gothic structure. Suger fittingly commemorated the event in *Libellus alter de consecratione ecclesiae Sancti Dionysii* (1144; *Abbot Suger on the Abbey Church of St. Denis and Its Art Treasures*, 1946), in which he recounted the reasons for the rebuilding and offered the theological basis of the architectural style that transformed the material into the immaterial.

SIGNIFICANCE

Within a few years, notably at Chartres Cathedral and a number of churches located in the Île-de-France, the new aesthetic style developed with increasingly greater sophistication. By the early decades of the thirteenth century, the structural principles of ribbed vaulting and flying buttresses had been refined to the point that mature statements of the Gothic style appeared in the churches of Reims and Amiens begun by the architects Jean d'Orbais and Robert de Luzarches. These cathedrals represent the epitome of the verticality of space from floor to ribbed vault, the lightness of the stained glass, all supported by the exterior flying buttresses, and all representative of a medieval style still evident and copied today.

—*M. Joseph Costelloe, updated by Karen Gould*

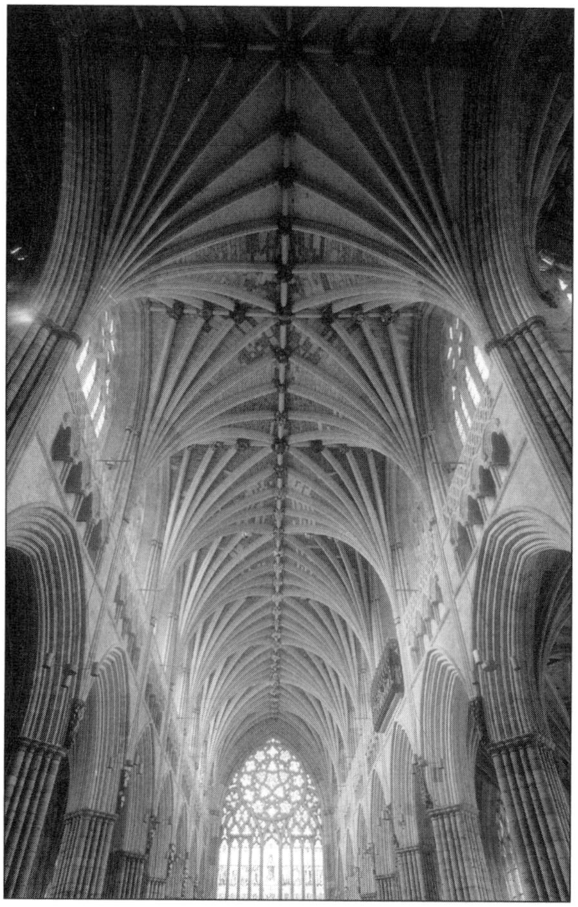

The ceiling at Exeter Cathedral, thought to be the longest Gothic vault in existence, with the ribbed, arched vaulting typical of the style. (Hulton|Archive by Getty Images)

FURTHER READING

Bony, Jean. *French Gothic Architecture of the Twelfth and Thirteenth Centuries*. Berkeley: University of California Press, 1983. A comprehensive survey of the origins and development of Gothic architecture in France.

Frankl, Paul, and Paul Crossley. *Gothic Architecture*. Rev. ed. New Haven, Conn.: Yale University Press, 2000. From Yale's Pelican History of Art series. Looks at the history of European gothic architecture. Illustrations, maps, extensive bibliography, and index.

Gerson, Paula Lieber, ed. *Abbot Suger and Saint-Denis*. New York: Metropolitan Museum of Art, 1986. A collection of essays on all aspects of Saint-Denis, Abbot Suger, and the role of this structure in the origins of Gothic architecture.

Panofsky, Erwin. *Abbot Suger on the Abbey Church of Saint-Denis and Its Art Treasures*. 2d ed. Princeton, N.J.: Princeton University Press, 1979. Includes the Latin text and English translation, together with extended notes, of two of the most important medieval documents on Gothic architecture.

_______. *Gothic Architecture and Scholasticism*. 2d ed. New York: Meridian Books, 1957. This text draws a connection between the aims of the Gothic architectural style and its contemporary philosophical system, Scholasticism.

Radding, Charles M., and William W. Clark. *Medieval Architecture, Medieval Learning: Builders and Masters in the Age of Romanesque and Gothic*. New Haven, Conn.: Yale University Press, 1992. This work juxtaposes relationships between ideas and architectural style in the transition from Romanesque to Gothic.

Simson, Otto von. *The Gothic Cathedral*. 3d ed. Princeton, N.J.: Princeton University Press, 1988. A study of the aesthetic impact of Gothic architecture as an expression of theological ideas.

Strachan, Gordon. *Chartres: Sacred Geometry, Sacred Space*. Edinburgh, Scotland: Floris, 2003. A short text presenting the architectural drawings of Oliver Perceval. Discusses the architectural history of the Gothic Chartres Cathedral, including its Islamic influences.

SEE ALSO: 11th-12th centuries: Building of Romanesque Cathedrals; c. 1025: Scholars at Chartres Revive Interest in the Classics; 1169-1172: Normans Invade Ireland; 1340: Al-ʿUmarī Writes a History of Africa.

RELATED ARTICLES in *Great Lives from History: The Middle Ages, 477-1453*: Arnolfo di Cambio; Filippo Brunelleschi; Simone Martini; Suger.

c. 1150-1200
RISE OF THE HANSA MERCHANT UNION

The Hansa, a loose union of merchants in northern Germany, evolved into an association of cities that dominated the region's maritime trade for three hundred years.

LOCALE: Baltic region of northern Germany
CATEGORIES: Economics; government and politics; organizations and institutions; trade and commerce; transportation

KEY FIGURES

Ethelred II, the Unready (968?-1016), king of England, r. 978-1013 and 1014-1016, early supporter of the rights of foreign merchants
Henry II (1133-1189), king of England, r. 1154-1189, protector of Cologne wine merchants competing with French traders in England
Henry the Lion (1129-1195), duke of Saxony, 1142-1180, and duke of Bavaria, 1156-1180, enforced peace between Germany and Gotland that encouraged trade in the Baltic

SUMMARY OF EVENT

"Hansa" is the Latin form of the German *hense*, a very old word designating a group of warriors. In thirteenth century England, this term came to mean a tribute paid by merchants from abroad. At various times the word also referred to a tax on commerce as well as to an entrance fee imposed on members of the Hanseatic League, a term that has been rejected by some scholars who prefer to refer to the confederation as the Hanseatic Community.

This confederation of merchants began roughly with the rebuilding of Lübeck in 1158-1159, which had been destroyed in 1138 and had evolved into a trade association of towns by the fourteenth century. The confederation expired in the seventeenth century. Although individual hansas were common in the Baltic region, the general use of the term hansa for a specific association of merchants and towns was not adopted until 1370.

Merchants who traveled abroad faced many hazards during the Middle Ages. Many of the early traders in the Baltic and North Seas were hardly better than pirates seizing cargoes at will. The crews of wrecked ships could be enslaved, and the flotsam and jetsam of shipwrecks were fair loot for anyone on shore, often providing considerable wealth for some of the monasteries. Besides these threats to the safety of their wares, traders were the frequent prey of noblemen greedy for exorbitant tolls. Given the hardships and the dangers they faced in foreign travel—and these early merchants were not deskbound, but quite the opposite—mutual protection on foreign shores was important right from the start in the rise of the Hansa.

As early as 978, under the reign of the young Ethelred II, the Unready, English law granted equal protection to the merchants from across the North Sea. These rights were expanded under Henry II to allow traders from Cologne to sell wine under the same provisions accorded the French. Moreover, a grant made around the year 1157 provided protection for the Cologne merchants, who by this time had their own London Guildhall. King John (r. 1199-1216) contributed to England's importance in the early history of the Hansa by enforcing his predecessors' liberal policies during his own reign, and Hansa merchants were freed from their annual tribute of two shillings in 1194. The continued strength of the feudal system in England, however, prevented the development of rich cities served by a powerful middle class of English merchants.

During the reign of Frederick I Barbarossa, German merchants fared much better. Seeking allies in his quarrels with the nobles, Frederick supported the middle class and then extracted money from it to finance his foreign interests. From one point of view, Frederick's support of this merchant middle class was shortsighted, since their independent power weakened Germany's political unity. Nevertheless, the freedom that merchants enjoyed fostered trade and encouraged the growth of the Hansa. Powerful, flourishing cities began to spring up in this period, and the Hansa emerged as a crucial factor in the decline of feudalism and the relative triumph of the middle classes over their crowns.

Once the merchant bourgeoisie received some support from sympathetic royalty, they effected many practical improvements in promoting maritime law, improving and charting the waterways, building lighthouses and digging canals, and introducing order and security into the mercantile traffic of northern Europe. For centuries, the Baltic Sea had been the main trade route between eastern and western Europe. The traders from the West did not themselves sail the Baltic but simply received goods from the Scandinavians and Slavs who came to Schleswig on the eastern shore of the narrow neck of the Danish peninsula. The overland journey from Schleswig to Hollingstedt on the Eider River leading to the North Sea was only 10 miles (15 kilometers). One prominent theory contends that the establishment of the city of Lübeck on the Trave estuary south of Schleswig in 1158-1159 opened up the first stage of the growth of the Hansa by giving Western traders direct access to the Baltic in their new "cogs," slender ships better for commerce than the northerners' vessels. Whatever Lübeck's precise role, few scholars deny its central importance in the growth of the Hansa. The spread of German commerce north and east brought German language and culture along with it into the regions of Estonia and Prussia.

The Baltic island of Gotland, a customary stopover for merchants headed east, was at first oppressed by Henry the Lion, duke of Saxony. Later, in 1161, he enforced a peace between Germany and Gotland and won German merchants the right to trade in Gotland. A community of visiting German merchants grew up in the Gottish town of Visby and were often influential in founding churches. Of the six churches that can be traced to the late eleventh century, the German merchant church of Sancta Maria Teutonicorum became the warehouse and registry of the Gotland Company. The group created its own constitution featuring rule by four aldermen elected from the merchants of Visby, Lübeck, Soest, and Dortmund.

Parallel with the growth of Gotland's importance was the German entrance into the lucrative herring fishing industry thriving off Skania on the southern tip of Sweden. For Catholic Europe, salted fish was a sought-after commodity. Fishing provided great wealth, and the herring came in great numbers to the coasts of Skania and Pomerania during the twelfth through fifteenth centuries. The city of Kolberg became famous for its salt fish, and salted herrings were a common medium of exchange and an acceptable tax offering. For the Germans trading in herring, Visby became the center of their extensive commerce. Traders enjoyed the protection of the city, for the law held that it was bound to help any merchant devastated by robbery or shipwreck.

The Russians also had a presence in the Baltic, as evidenced by churches in Gotland and other cities. Merchants in Novgorod, an old trading port in northwestern Russia, carried on business in the Church of Holy Friday, built in 1156. Germans eventually arrived in the area from Gotland and by 1184 were competing successfully against the Russians from their trading post, the Peterhof, on the Volkhov River east of Novgorod.

THE HANSEATIC LEAGUE C. 1200

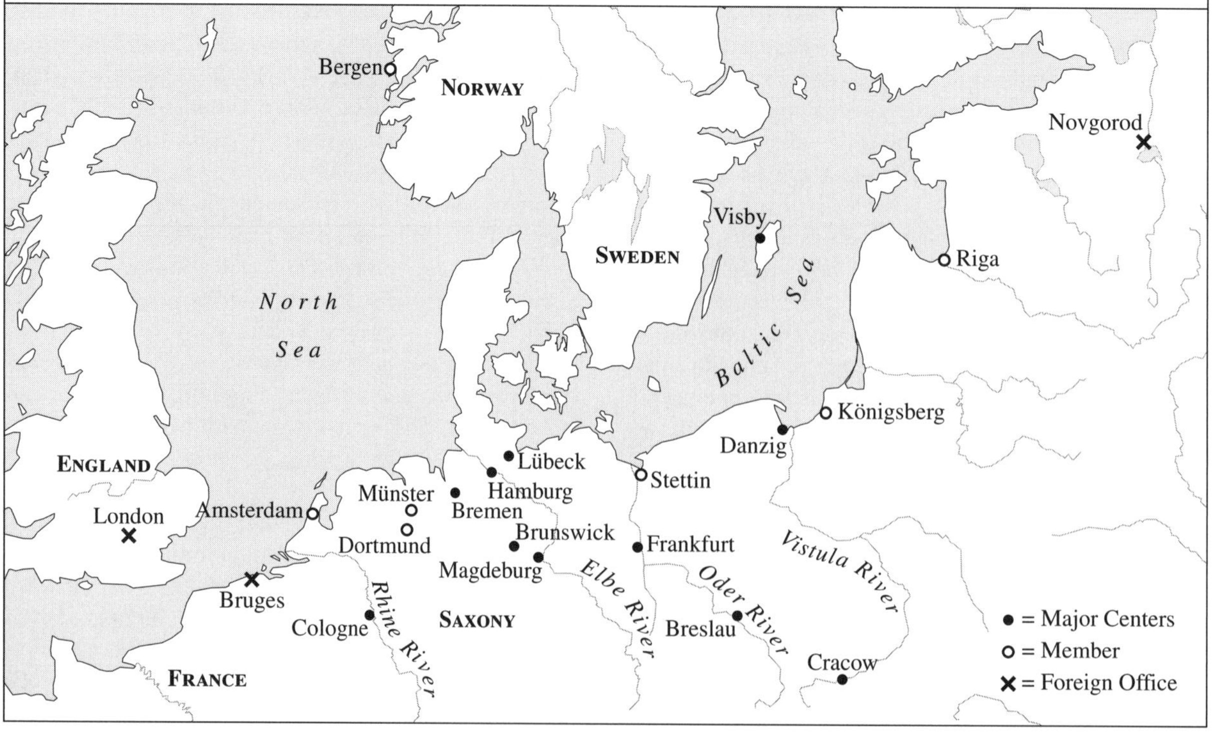

Significance

At its peak of power, the Hansa reached from Bruges (now in Belgium) in the south, over the English Channel to the eastern cities of England, north to Bergen in Norway, around the coast of Sweden and north to southern Finland and Novgorod. The heaviest concentration of Hansa cities clustered around the big centers of Bremen, Cologne, Hamburg, Lübeck, and then north up the Baltic coast to Danzig and Riga. The Hansa cities grew steadily in power until the middle of the fourteenth century, when the diverging interests of the Hansa merchants hurt their unity. From then on, the Hanseatic Community dwindled in importance, bleeding from its wars with the Dutch, the Danes, the English, and the Castilians, until the final Hanseatic diet was held at Lübeck in 1669.

—*Frank Day*

Further Reading

Corley, Brigitte. *Painting and Patronage in Cologne, 1300-1500*. Turnhout, Belgium: Harvey Miller, 2000. This study of the Cologne school of painting emphasizes the effects of trade and commerce on art and includes significant discussion of the Hanseatic League.

Dollinger, Phillipe. *The German Hansa*. Vol. 1 in *The Emergence of International Business, 1200-1800*. Reprint. New York: Routledge, 1999. The standard work on the topic, stressing the evolution of the Hansa of Merchants into the Hansa of Towns.

Durant, Will. *The Age of Faith*. Vol. 4 in *The Story of Civilization*. New York: Simon and Schuster, 1950. A brief account of the Hansa's importance is included in a chapter that places the development of the Hansa in a broad context.

Lloyd, T. H. *England and the German Hanse, 1157-1611: A Study of Their Trade and Commercial Diplomacy*. New York: Cambridge University Press, 1991. Authoritative study of England's role in the history of the Hansa.

Øye, Ingvild. "The Hansa in Europe." In *European Cultural Routes*, edited by Giovanni Mangion and Isabel Tamen. Croton-on-Hudson, N.Y.: Manhattan, 1998. An essay on the cultural history of the Hansa.

Schildhauer, Johannes. *The Hansa: History and Culture*. Translated by Kathleen Vanovitch. Leipzig, Germany: Edition Leipzig, 1985. Beautifully illustrated with detailed chapters on such topics as "The Hanseatic Townscape" and "Hanseatic Culture." Contains an excellent map, but its bibliography largely consists of German-language works.

Zimmern, Helen. *The Hansa Towns*. 1889. Reprint. New York: Kraus, 1969. A romantic narrative approach dates this study, which is nevertheless informative and extremely readable.

See also: 740: Khazars Convert to Judaism; 1150: Venetian Merchants Dominate Trade with the East; July 15, 1240: Alexander Nevsky Defends Novgorod from Swedish Invaders; June 17, 1397: Kalmar Union Is Formed.

Related articles in *Great Lives from History: The Middle Ages, 477-1453*: Ethelred II, the Unready; Frederick I Barbarossa; Henry the Lion; Henry II; King John; Margaret of Denmark, Norway, and Sweden; Valdemar II.

1152
FREDERICK BARBAROSSA IS ELECTED KING OF GERMANY

Frederick Barbarossa's reign firmly established the ideal of a united German nation as opposed to a collection of small independent political entities.

LOCALE: Holy Roman Empire
CATEGORY: Government and politics

KEY FIGURES

Frederick I Barbarossa (c. 1123-1190), duke of Swabia as Frederick III, 1147-1190, Holy Roman Emperor and king of Germany, r. 1152-1190
Conrad III (1093-1152), duke of Swabia and king of Germany, r. 1138-1152
Berthold IV of Zähringen (1152-1186), duke of Zähringen
Frederick of Rothenburg (1144-1167), duke of Swabia, 1152-1167
Henry II Jasomirgott (c. 1114-1177), duke of Bavaria, 1143-1156, and first duke of Austria, 1156-1177
Henry the Lion (1129-1195), duke of Saxony, 1142-1180, and duke of Bavaria, 1156-1180
Count Welf VI (1115-1191), margrave of Tuscany and duke of Spoleto, 1152

SUMMARY OF EVENT

By the time of Conrad III's coronation as king of Germany in 1138, the king-emperor's power and the stability of the realm had greatly eroded. The powers of a king-emperor, charged by God with the rule of Christendom and supreme lord of both the laity and clergy, had greatly diminished. The pope had taken the power of investing bishops from the emperor so the prince-bishops no longer were strictly subject to the king's control. In addition, the pope had become responsible for crowning the emperor, subordinating the emperor to the Papacy. Also, the rise of strong feudal nobles had further circumscribed the king's powers so that the emperor was dominated by the powerful ducal families. As a consequence, Conrad III's election as king was strongly contested, and he never fully gained control of the kingdom. He also never was crowned emperor.

Conrad III died February 15, 1152, and designated Frederick Barbarossa, duke of Swabia, as his successor. Frederick was elected king of Germany as Frederick I in 1152. The princes were almost unanimous in selecting Frederick, and the meeting apparently had been well planned to ensure a peaceful succession. According to one account, Conrad III designated Frederick his successor and guardian of Frederick of Rothenburg, his eight-year-old son, because Conrad realized his young son would, in all probability, be the target of inimical forces during his minority.

In any event, the election necessarily would be negotiated in the face of deep divisions among the German princes and bishops. Rivalry between the Hohenstaufen family of Conrad III and Frederick I Barbarossa, and the Welf family, led by Henry the Lion, plagued Conrad during his entire reign and easily could have disrupted the succession. Although Frederick was a Hohenstaufen, he also was the son of a Welf mother, Judith. Thus his election might be acceptable to both families. As duke of Swabia, Frederick had consistently favored his mother's family, perhaps preparing for eventual promotion to kingship. During Conrad's final illness, Frederick, in concert with Conrad's closest advisers (Abbot Wibald and Bishop Eberhard of Bamberg), offered concessions to the Welfs. Henry the Lion was promised the duchies of Saxony and Bavaria. Count Welf VI (also known as Guelph) was offered an autonomous position as margrave of Tuscany and duke of Spoleto. Henry the Lion's father-in-law, Berthold IV of Zähringen, was encouraged to carve out a sphere of influence in Burgundy. Henry II Jasomirgott, a Babenberg who feared loss of Bavaria, was prominent in a small opposition group led by Archbishop Henry of Mainz, a Hohenstaufen opponent.

After his election in Frankfurt, Frederick received oaths of loyalty from the assembled princes. On March 6, he left for Aix-la-Chapelle and his coronation. There, he was met by a large crowd assembled to see the coronation. Seated on the throne of Charlemagne, Frederick was crowned king of Germany by Arnold, the archbishop of Cologne. Immediately thereafter, Frederick began preparing an expedition to Rome to be crowned emperor of the Holy Roman Empire and to assert control over his Italian vassals. First, as was customary for newly elected kings of Germany, Frederick I Barbarossa immediately made a "grand tour" of the kingdom to receive fealty and to mediate conflicts within the kingdom. He also sent Bishop Eberhard of Bamberg to Rome to announce his election to Pope Eugene. Instead of begging papal confirmation of the election, Frederick merely informed the pope of the fact, reasserting imperial independence of papal authority.

Frederick quickly consolidated his position by confirming his Welf cousin, Henry the Lion, as duke of Saxony and granting him the dukedom of Bavaria as well. Henry, the most powerful of the German nobles, thus became Frederick's loyal ally for twenty years. In 1176, however, Henry demanded the imperial city of Goslar and its rich silver mines in return for supporting Frederick's campaign against the Lombard League. As a consequence, Frederick charged Henry with a breach of the king's peace in 1178, an event that ultimately led to Henry's eviction from his duchies in 1180. The powerful Babenberg family was compensated for its loss of Bavaria to Henry by separating the margraviate of Austria from Bavaria as a new dukedom. Frederick conferred the dukedom of Austria on Henry II Jasomirgott with rights of hereditary succession and immunity from many feudal obligations to the emperor. Thus, the Babenbergs were brought to accept Frederick's rule. Frederick also confirmed Berthold IV Zähringen's claims in Burgundy and Provence in return for Berthold's support during the coronation expedition. Through these actions, Frederick established control in Germany and converted the powerful princes to be his sworn vassals.

In setting out to gain control of his Italian lands, Frederick mounted no less than five military campaigns. Although Frederick's protracted conflict with the Lombard communes and the pope failed to establish direct royal government, he was more successful in Tuscany and central Italy. After the Peace of Venice in 1177 and the Peace of Constance in 1183, Frederick was able to extend direct imperial administration throughout Tuscany. He thus obtained enough income to expand imperial properties and ensure his maintenance in Germany.

Although his control of the Holy Roman Empire was in large part indirect, Frederick reestablished its territorial integrity and inculcated a strong sense of German nationhood. Feudal centralization of the Holy Roman Empire began with Frederick; after Hohenstaufen rule decayed, however, the centralized German state quickly reverted to an assemblage of essentially independent states uncontrolled by the emperor. The sense of nationhood developed under Frederick, however, eventually inspired reestablishment of a unified Germany in the nineteenth century.

Frederick Barbarossa receives Henry the Lion. (F. R. Niglutsch)

Frederick's reign ended when he drowned in the Saleph River of northwestern Syria while leading the Third Crusade. The actual circumstances of his death are unknown. According to one story, he was swept away while fording the river. Another report suggests that he suffered a seizure while bathing in the cold river water. Yet another tale has him thrown from his horse while crossing the river.

Artist's rendition of a statue of Frederick Barbarossa astride his horse. (F. R. Niglutsch)

SIGNIFICANCE

Although Frederick I Barbarossa's demise apparently was received calmly as a not unexpected event, he became the centerpiece of a national legend five hundred years later. According to the early nineteenth century myth, Frederick did not die, but was supposed to be living in a cave beneath Kyffhäuser Mountain in Thuringia, Germany. He was expected to return from that mountain and save the German nation in a future cataclysmic conflict. One mythic variation has Barbarossa returning when his red beard grows long enough to surround the giant round table at which he supposedly sits. These myths long antedate Barbarossa's identification as a German national hero and are steeped in contradictions. From 1250 until the sixteenth century, it was Barbarossa's grandson, Frederick II, who was believed to be in the cave. Even before Frederick II was incorporated into the legend, Kyffhäuser had been a mythic shrine from at least the time of the Celts. Many other heroes, including Julius Caesar and Wotan, had been associated with the magic mountain.

Although Frederick failed to establish lasting political order in the Holy Roman Empire, he is generally considered the most effective of medieval Holy Roman Emperors. He also has become the acknowledged German national hero who lives in the communal German mind, comparable only to El Cid in Spain, Joan of Arc in France, and King Arthur in England.

—*Ralph L. Langenheim, Jr.*

FURTHER READING

Arnold, Benjamin. *Princes and Territories in Medieval Germany.* New York: Cambridge University Press, 1991. Concentrates on fundamental institutional changes in Germany during the twelfth and thirteenth centuries.

Barraclough, Geoffrey. *Factors in German History.* 1946. Reprint. Westport, Conn.: Greenwood Press, 1979. One of the major scholars of the Middle Ages in general (and Germany in particular) provides a concise account of the major events in Barbarossa's career.

_______. *The Origins of Modern Germany.* 3d ed. Oxford, England: B. Blackwell, 1988. An excellent discussion of Frederick's effort to establish his government in the state of northern Italy. One of the best short summaries of the life and impact of Frederick.

Fuhrmann, Horst. *Germany in the High Middle Ages, c. 1050-1200.* Translated by Timothy Reuter. New York: Cambridge University Press, 1986. Provides an overview of events before, during, and after Barbarossa's reign.

Haverkamp, Alfred. *Medieval Germany, 1056-1273*. Translated by Helga Braun and Richard Mortimer. New York: Oxford University Press, 1988. A political, social, and economic history of the period, including Barbarossa's reign.

Huffman, Joseph P. *The Social Politics of Medieval Diplomacy: Anglo-German Relations, 1066-1307*. Ann Arbor: University of Michigan Press, 2000. This text uses the lens of Anglo-German relations to form a coherent picture of medieval German history from the mid-ninth to the early fourteenth century.

Kitchin, Martin. *The Cambridge Illustrated History of Germany*. New York: Cambridge University Press, 1996. Emphasizes cultural as well as political history. Recommended as an introduction for general readers.

Moore, R. I. *The First European Revolution, c. 970-1215*. Malden, Mass.: Blackwell, 2000. Frederick is discussed in the context of a study arguing that the changes in economic, political, and social structures during the eleventh and twelfth centuries were responsible for the creation of a uniquely European culture that has persisted through the centuries.

Munz, Peter. *Frederick Barbarossa: A Study in Medieval Politics*. Ithaca, N.Y.: Cornell University Press, 1969. Scholarly biography of Barbarossa, with a focus on his political accomplishments.

See also: 496: Baptism of Clovis; 735: Christianity Is Introduced into Germany; c. 1150-1200: Rise of the Hansa Merchant Union; September 17, 1156: Austria Emerges as a National Entity; 1189-1192: Third Crusade.

Related articles in *Great Lives from History: The Middle Ages, 477-1453*: Adrian IV; Alexander III; El Cid; Frederick I Barbarossa; Frederick II; Henry the Lion; Joan of Arc.

1153
Jin Move Their Capital to Beijing

The Jurchens, during the Jin Dynasty, located their capital in Beijing, bringing the city into prominence as the center of Chinese culture.

Locale: Beijing, China
Categories: Expansion and land acquisition; government and politics

Key Figure

Digunai (Ti-ku-nai; Wanyan Liang), prince of Hailing, r. 1122-1161, Jin ruler, r. 1150-1161, who effected the move to Beijing

Summary of Event

The history of China during the Song Dynasty (Sung; 960-1276) is intertwined with the Khitan Liao (907-1125), Jin (Chin; 1115-1234), and Yuan Dynasties (1279-1368), which originated from the inner Asian steppes, commonly referred to as Manchuria and Mongolia today. Since the dawn of Chinese history, these alien ethnic groups posed a significant threat to Chinese rulers who tried hard to resist militarily or, as during the Han Dynasty (206 B.C.E.-220 C.E.), to maintain peace by offering Chinese princesses to the khans as brides and sending annual tributes. These methods of pacifying China's border enemies were followed by the Song court, which made yearly tributes amounting to 200,000 taels of silver and 300,000 bolts of silk. Still, this was not enough for the ambitious Jurchens of the Jin Dynasty.

The Jurchens, led by Aguda (A-ku-ta, r. 1115-1123), became so powerful that they first allied with the Chinese to conquer the Khitans of Liao, driving them away from Chinese territory. After that, the Jurchens refused to leave, choosing to remain in China by force. The beleaguered Song government fled to the south and set up its capital in Hangzhou. The Jurchens, who had kidnapped the Song emperor Huizong (Hui-tsung; r. 1101-1125), occupied Kaifeng, the old capital of the Song administration in 1127, waiting for a chance to advance farther.

Both the Khitans and the Jurchens became sinicized. The dynastic title of Jin came from the Chinese word for "gold," which happened to be the name of a river in the Jurchens' homeland. The Jin administration encouraged translations from Confucian classics, such as Confucius's *Lunyu* (late sixth-early fifth centuries B.C.E.; *The Analects*, 1861), Mencius's *Mengzi* (early third century B.C.E.; *The Works of Mencius*, 1861; commonly known as *Mengzi*), and *Xiaojing* (fifth century B.C.E.; *The Classic of Filial Piety*, 1899). Together with Chinese historical writings such as *Chunqiu* (fifth century B.C.E.; *The Ch'un Ts'ew with the Tso Chuen*, 1872;

commonly known as *Spring and Autumn Annals*), Sima Qian's *Shiji* (first century B.C.E.; *Records of the Grand Historian*, 1960), and the *Han Shu* (also known as *Qian Han Shu*, completed first century C.E.; *The History of the Former Han Dynasty*, 1938-1955), they formed the corpus of state examinations for the Jin. Chinese language was also used as a means of communication in the Jin court. The Jin state obviously wanted its intellectuals and officials to be familiar with Chinese thought and culture.

On January 9, 1150, Digunai, whose Chinese name was Wanyan Liang, murdered his cousin, the Jin emperor Xizong (Hsi-tsung; r. 1135-1150), who was a hard drinker devoted to sensual pleasures. The new emperor, who was referred to in the *Jin shu* (thirteenth century; history of Jin) as the king of Hailing (Hailing *wang*) rather than as the emperor of Jin, revealed himself as a fierce, ruthless, and bloodthirsty man. Not only did he murder his political opponents from the imperial clan, but he also transferred the wives and concubines of his murdered cousin to his own palace. The king (or prince) of Hailing was exceptionally fond of Chinese culture and traditions and was well acquainted with the Chinese classics and history; he fought against the old tribal and feudal ways of the Jin. He brought about reforms in fiscal policy and administration in the Jin state. In his palace, he practiced the Chinese customs of chess playing and tea drinking.

The king of Hailing believed that if the Jin were to rule the Chinese, they themselves must be more Chinese. His biggest attempt at sinicizing the dynasty was his decision to move the Jin capital to Beijing. In 1152, the king took up residence in this city and constructed new palaces. The year after, he renamed the city, calling it Zhongdu, or the "central capital." There he received Song envoys and visitors who were astounded by the magnificence of his Chinese-style palaces. According to Fan Zhengda (Fan Cheng-ta), a statesman from the Southern Song court, as many as 800,000 laborers and 400,000 soldiers were employed in building the fine palaces, which were filled with precious ornaments and treasures looted from the Song during the war. In 1157, the king of Hailing, satisfied with his decision to move to Zhongdu, ordered the old Jurchen capital at Huining, Manchuria, burned and destroyed. To display his power, a new imperial residence was constructed at Kaifeng, the former Song capital, which he now referred to as his southern capital. All in all, the king of Hailing wanted to be a Chinese ruler, not a Jurchen leader. He saw himself as a legitimate overlord of China.

The king of Hailing's harshness—even to his own people—aroused anger and resentment in his court. Finally, in the winter of 1161, during one of his military campaigns against China, a group of conspirators from the conservative sect in the Jin court organized a coup, during which the king was assassinated. After the king of Hailing's demise, a more moderate ruler, Shizong (Shi-tsung; r. 1161-1190), succeeded to the throne. Compared with the king of Hailing, Shizong was not as fond of Chinese culture or as inclined toward sinicization. Nostalgic about the old capital in Manchuria, the new emperor ordered it to be partially rebuilt, and he spent almost a year there later. Although the Chinese language was still being used in court, Shizong was very pleased when a poem in the Jurchen language was presented to him as a birthday gift. Despite Shizong's efforts to revive Jurchen culture and traditions, during his reign, Beijing remained the capital of the Jin.

SIGNIFICANCE

During the Zhou Dynasty (Chou; 1066-256 B.C.E.), the area that is now known as Beijing was called Ji. Later in the Warring States Period (475-221 B.C.E.), Ji became prominent and was used as a capital city by the state of Yen, which renamed it Yenjing (Yen capital). Beijing was given the name Yuzhou during the Western Jin Dynasty (Chin; 265-316), when the city was under the control of the Hu tribes. Politically speaking, the city of Beijing occupied a strategic location on the north China plain. In the north and northeast, there was a natural mountain barrier, and toward the east was the Yellow Sea. Only two passes led to the regions over the mountains beyond the Great Wall, keeping the city rather safe. After the Grand Canal was completed in 609, Beijing became part of the main route of commerce between northern and southern China. In addition, large tax remittances in grain also traveled on the Grand Canal, adjacent to the outskirts of the city on the Beihe River, leading to the capital at Chang'an. The Sui Dynasty (581-618) named the city Zhuozhun, using it as a district administrative center.

During the Tang Dynasty (T'ang; 618-907), the city reverted to its earlier name, Yuzhou, and its political significance somewhat diminished. The government mainly used it for residences for military governors, one of whom was An Lushan, the rebel leader who almost toppled the Tang court with a rebellion that lasted from 755 to 763. The end of the Tang Dynasty heralded in another period of political division in China during which barbarians from northern China entered the Chinese plain and co-ruled China with the Song administration. The first such major alien group was the Khitans, who occupied the northern part of China down to the Huai River in the south and set up their kingdom called Liao (907-1125). The Khitans used two names in reference to Beijing and its vicinity: Nanjing (south capital) and Yenjing. After 937, the city was mostly referred to as the southern capital of Liao, differentiating it from the main capital in Manchuria in the north. The Khitans tore down the old city of Yuzhou and built in its place a city with an enclosed imperial palace, modeled on the Tang capital city of Chang'an. This marked the debut of Beijing and its vicinity as a secondary capital city in Chinese history.

The first ruler to use Beijing as his official capital was the king of Hailing, who rebuilt the city after his victory over the Song army and named it Zhongdu. However, the city of Beijing did not assume a more prominent and lasting role as a capital city until the advent of Kublai Khan (r. 1260-1294), the Mongolian leader from the Yuan Dynasty. He set up the Yuan capital at Beijing, calling it Dadu (great capital). Beijing remained the permanent home of the ruling houses during the Ming (1368-1644) and Qing (Ch'ing; 1644-1911) Dynasties and became the political center of modern-day China.

—*Fatima Wu*

FURTHER READING

Cameron, Nigel, and Brian Brake. *Peking: A Tale of Three Cities*. Tokyo: John Weatherhill, 1965. Presents Beijing in three phases: the Mongol century, the last dynasty, and in the republic. Filled with historical photographs, maps, and charts.

Franke, Herbert, and Hok-lam Chan, eds. *Studies on the Jurchens and the Chin Dynasty.* Brookfield, Vt.: Ashgate, 1997. A collection of papers on the Jurchens and the Jin Dynasty in China. Illustrations, maps, bibliography, and index.

Gernet, Jacques, *A History of Chinese Civilization.* Translated by J. R. Foster. New York: Cambridge University Press, 1982. Part 6 of chapter 6, "The Sinicized Empire," covers the Khitan Liao Dynasty; the Xixia, the empire of cattle breeders and caravaners; and the Jurchen's Jin Dynasty.

Sinor, Denis. *The Cambridge History of Early Inner Asia*. New York: Cambridge University Press, 1990. A good study of the different ethnic groups in Inner Asia, including the Scythians, Sarmatians, Xiongnu, Huns, Turks, Uighurs, Tibetans, Khitans, and Jurchens.

Tillman, Hoyt C., and Stephen H. West, eds. *China Under Jurchen Rule: Essays on Chin Intellectual and Cultural History.* Albany: State University of New York Press, 1995. Ten essays by specialists in the field and a 22-page introduction by the editors. The essays are grouped under the headings of "Politics and Institutions," "Religion and Thought," and "Literature and Art."

Twitchett, Denis, and Herbert Franke, eds. *Alien Regimes and Border States, 907-1368*. Vol. 6 in *The Cambridge History of China*. New York: Cambridge University Press, 1994. Chapter 3 on the Jin Dynasty by Franke gives a comprehensive look at the sinicized Jurchens throughout their history, in terms of their founding rulers and their relationship with the Song. The second part of the chapter deals with the Jin government structure.

SEE ALSO: 618: Founding of the Tang Dynasty; 755-763: Rebellion of An Lushan; 907-960: Period of Five Dynasties and Ten Kingdoms; 936: Khitans Settle Near Beijing; 1115: Foundation of the Jin Dynasty.

RELATED ARTICLES in *Great Lives from History: The Middle Ages, 477-1453*: An Lushan; Genghis Khan; Kublai Khan.

1154-1204
ANGEVIN EMPIRE IS ESTABLISHED

The establishment of the Angevin Empire under the three Plantagenet kings expanded English holdings to their widest extent, until Normandy was annexed in 1204 by the king of France.

LOCALE: France and England

CATEGORIES: Government and politics; expansion and land acquisition

KEY FIGURES

Matilda (1102-1167), only daughter of Henry I, married to Geoffrey IV and mother of Henry II

Henry II (1133-1189), successor to King Stephen as king of England, r. 1154-1189

Eleanor of Aquitaine (c. 1122-1204), queen of England through her marriage to Henry II

Richard I (1157-1199), third son of Henry II and king of England, r. 1189-1199

King John (1166-1216), youngest son of Henry II and king of England, r. 1199-1216

Philip II (1165-1223), son of Louis VII and king of France, r. 1179-1223

SUMMARY OF EVENT

Geographically, the Angevin Empire of the twelfth century was made up of England, Normandy, Anjou, and Aquitaine. The first two domains had been united by William the Conqueror and consolidated under his son, Henry I (1100-1135). Anjou was added by the marriage of Henry's daughter, Matilda, to Geoffrey Plantagenet, count of Anjou. Their son, Henry II, further enlarged the empire by his marriage to Eleanor of Aquitaine. The beginning of the Angevin Empire can therefore be placed at the beginning of his reign, 1154.

The empire was unified in the person of the king rather than by its subjects' loyalty to a common tradition or territory. Like his grandfather Henry and his great-grandfather William the Conqueror, Henry II enjoyed the fealty of powerful lords. These barons and earls found it to their advantage to do homage to the king because only he could prevent their destructive quarrels and give them justice. Under feudalism in its crude form, the warrior caste, while protecting those who worked their manors, had constantly challenged one another's holdings. Under Norman feudalism, the warrior lords waived their rights of ownership and instead held their lands "in fee" (*feod*, related to the word for cattle) from the king, who was recognized as the sole legal owner (especially since William owned the England he had conquered). In return for these fiefs, the king's feudal tenants-in-chief, including bishops and abbots as well as barons, promised to pay certain taxes or dues, to attend the royal councils, and to support the king with a fixed number of armed and mounted knights.

Besides superseding the manorial courts of the feudal barons, the king's justice in England absorbed the old shire courts presided over by a sheriff ("shire reeve"). Henry II revived his grandfather's practice of sending out his royal officers on circuit to sit beside the sheriffs and enforce his rights to taxes. These officers gradually expanded their jurisdiction, giving judgment in trials for murder, rape, arson, robbery, forgery, and harboring criminals. In this way, the "king's peace" was extended to the whole nation, and the king was able to fulfill his coronation oath, which bound him to see justice done and to guarantee everyone's right of appeal to his courts. For a modest fee, any freeman forcibly dispossessed of his land could get a writ, or royal command, restoring immediate possession pending a full trial. To determine property disputes, William the Conqueror had ordered juries of twelve "free and lawful men" of the neighborhood to look into the facts of the case. Henry II extended this jury inquest to cover judicial processes of every kind.

Henry claimed not to be innovating, but merely to be restoring the good old laws. He was actually depriving the feudal aristocracy of their ancient right to decide all matters either by an oath or by appealing to force (trial by combat). Henry drove the barons and their manorial courts out of business, for most of his subjects wanted to have their cases tried in the king's courts. At the same time, Henry and his sons were developing a legal system. Their writs were recorded, and they became the first body of written law since late Roman times. Royal officials had to know this written law as well as local customs; hence was born, around 1200, the profession of judge. Next came the lawyers—men trained in precedents and cases—who were hired as professional advocates by either side, recalling the professional fighters whom the parties had formerly retained for trials by combat. The fascinating evolution of English courts and law in the thirteenth century is compelling proof that the Norman/Angevin genius shaped the culture inherited by all modern English-speaking citizens.

Another innovation characteristic of the Norsemen enabled the Angevin kings to gain the upper hand over the feudal lords. This innovation was the institution of wardship, whereby the king asserted his right to take the heir of the greatest vassal into custody until the heir was of age. This right went back to the practice of Viking seafaring tribes, whose ethnic traditions were able to survive even after the ties of family had become weakened. In effect, the leader of a band of pirates held together primarily by their northern origin was transformed into the model of a feudal monarch. The model figures prominently in British history. From the works of Geoffrey Chaucer and William Shakespeare to the eighteenth century novel, it can be observed in the custom of gentry who send their children away from home at a tender age to be reared in another, aristocratic household.

The Angevin kings could develop government in such a logical and systematic way because feudal relations were considered the material out of which the state had to be formed. Especially in England, these feudal materials were molded into an original polity, in contrast to conservative Normandy, where the lords' rights were strengthened at the expense of any state, and in equal contrast to France, where the king worked with the Church to suppress feudalism in favor of an autocracy like that of Charlemagne and his Frankish forebears.

Having established the Angevin empire, Henry II was faced with the problem of bequeathing it whole to his successor. He wanted to provide for all of his sons while ensuring that the younger brothers paid homage for their provinces to the eldest. Henry's first son had died as a child, and his second son (also named Henry) died in 1183, leaving Richard I (the Lion-Hearted) next in line. When Richard I succeeded to the throne in 1189, he won great fame in Europe and the Holy Lands, and he was a reassuring presence to his Norman and Angevin vassals. Nevertheless, he spent a scant total of five months of his ten-year reign governing his inheritance in England. When Richard died unexpectedly in 1199, John, his youngest brother, took over the Crown. Although he was known to be Henry's favorite son, John was unable to command the fealty of the Norman and Angevin lords, who deserted him to pay their homage instead to the French king, Philip II.

In the empire's final phase, which saw the loss of Normandy, the Catholic Church played a major role. First, the Norman bishops, not wanting the Church to be torn apart by divided loyalty to two overlords, fell back on their original homage to the Frankish kings and their latest descendant, Philip II. For ten years after losing Normandy and Anjou, John abused his rights over his English vassals. Stephen Langton, archbishop of Canterbury, acted to preserve the monarchy painstakingly built up by Henry I and Henry II. The nobility was threatening to get rid of John as a tyrant. Rather than allow them to throw off kingly rule and plunge England back into feudal chaos, Langton announced that he had found a charter of Henry I by means of which the nobles might regain their lost liberty. He urged them not to destroy the Crown but to

THE ANGEVIN EMPIRE C. 1170

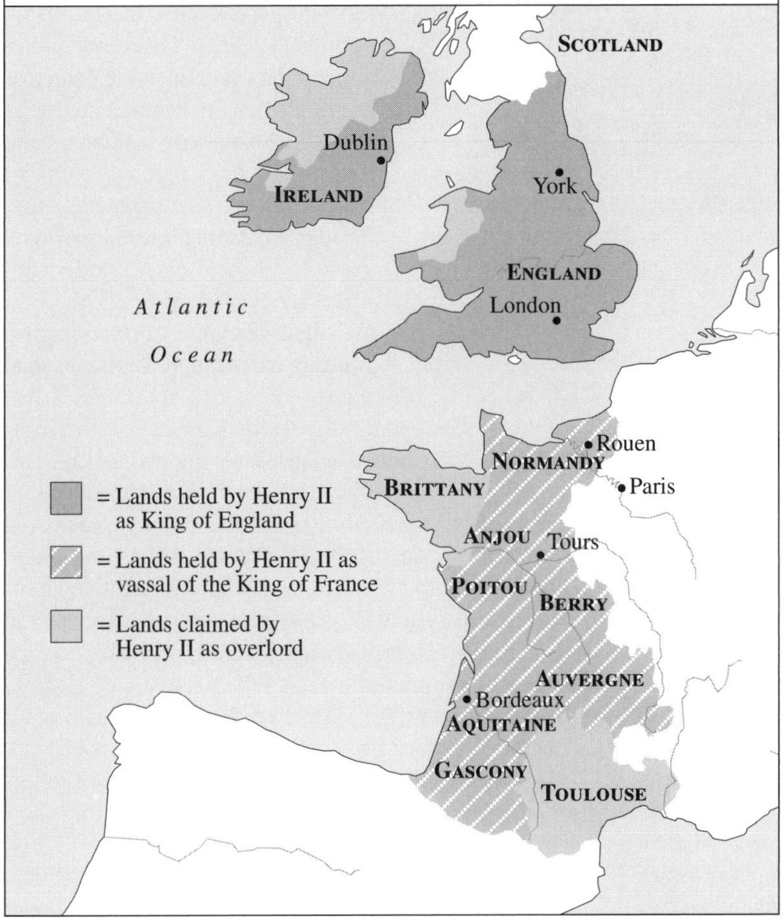

Philip II at his coronation in 1179, based on a fourteenth century manuscript in the Burgundian Library, Brussels. The Norman and Angevin lords would eventually desert Henry II's weak son, King John, to pay homage to Philip. (Frederick Ungar Publishing Co.)

demand that the king restore old customs. Although the Magna Carta that John's vassals forced on him in 1215 insists on their feudal rights as tenants- in-chief, fully thirty-two of the document's sixty-one clauses deal with the relations between the king and his *subjects*—that is, with the liberties of freemen and small-property owners that have become accepted by all those living under the common law.

SIGNIFICANCE

As summarized by historian John Gillingham, the four-part Angevin Empire became, under Henry and his sons Richard and John, "the dominant polity in western Europe." Contemporaries did not speak of an "Angevin Empire," however, nor does the term indicate a nation aware of its cultural identity. The Angevin kings did not create a political structure that might be perpetuated or conquered. Their achievement was to subordinate the feudal aristocracy, who, in spite of their diverse regions and dialects, all paid homage to their Angevin overlord.

—*David B. Haley*

FURTHER READING

Barber, Richard. *The Devil's Crown: Henry II, Richard I, John.* London: British Broadcasting Corporation, 1978. This volume is an extremely informative and popularly styled history of the Angevin period.

Bryant, Arthur. *The Medieval Foundation of England.* New York: Collier Books, 1968. A very readable account of the growth of British legal and parliamentary systems.

Church, S. D., ed. *King John: New Interpretations.* Rochester, N.Y.: Boydell Press, 1999. Discusses topics and persons such as King John and the English economy, the Church in Rome, Eleanor of Aquitaine, and Philip II.

Gillingham, John. *The Angevin Empire.* 2d ed. New York: Oxford University Press, 2001. A complete modern political account of the Angevin kings and their holdings. Includes maps, genealogical table, bibliography, and index.

_______. *Richard the Lionheart.* 2d ed. London: Weidenfeld and Nicolson, 1989. A sympathetic biography that portrays Richard as both a distinguished warrior and a capable ruler of the duchy of Aquitaine.

Mortimer, Richard. *Angevin England, 1154-1258.* Cambridge, Mass.: Blackwell, 1994. An account of the social history and customs that flourished under the Angevins. Complements Gillingham's political history of the period.

Painter, Sidney. *The Reign of King John.* Baltimore: Johns Hopkins University Press, 1949. An enduring, respected study that provides a good history of John's reign.

Powicke, F. M. *The Loss of Normandy, 1189-1204: Studies in the History of the Angevin Empire.* 2d ed. Manchester, England: Manchester University Press,

1961. Provides a fine history of the triumph and eventual supersession of Norman institutions.

Turner, Ralph V., and Richard R. Heiser. *The Reign of Richard Lionheart: Ruler of the Angevin Empire, 1189-1199*. Upper Saddle River, N.J.: Pearson Education, 2000. A survey of Richard's achievements as a military leader and administrator.

Wheeler, Bonnie, and John Carmi Parsons, eds. *Eleanor of Aquitaine: Lord and Lady*. New York: Palgrave Macmillan, 2003. A study of more than five hundred pages (with a sixty-page bibliography), discussing topics such as Eleanor's positions in the government of her reigning sons and a comparison of Eleanor with other noblewomen of the time.

SEE ALSO: June 15, 1215: Signing of the Magna Carta; 1258: Provisions of Oxford Are Established; 1337-1453: Hundred Years' War; 1366: Statute of Kilkenny; 1453: English Are Driven from France.

RELATED ARTICLES in *Great Lives from History: The Middle Ages, 477-1453*: Eleanor of Aquitaine; Henry I; Henry II; Henry III; King John; Philip II; Richard I; King Stephen; William the Conqueror.

1155
CHARTER OF LORRIS IS WRITTEN

The Charter of Lorris served as the model charter for more than eighty medieval European towns, defining the nature of the urban liberties of townspeople in France.

LOCALE: France
CATEGORIES: Laws, acts, and legal history; economics; government and politics; social reform

KEY FIGURES

Louis VI (1081-1137), king of France, r. 1108-1137
Louis VII (c. 1120-1180), king of France, r. 1137-1179

SUMMARY OF EVENT

The Charter of Lorris was an early and significant charter guaranteeing urban liberties. It served as a model of urban privileges for French towns in the twelfth and thirteenth centuries. The granting of such urban charters represented a major transformation in medieval politics, society, and economy. Roman cities in the early Middle Ages had deteriorated into stagnant markets populated mostly by the administrative or military personnel of bishoprics or lay lords. Although markets never fully disappeared and local traders still plied their wares, towns no longer were the thriving centers of long-distance trade or handicraft production. Compared with cities of imperial Rome, there were fewer governmental functions and cultural activities. The medieval population was overwhelmingly rural, and most peasants by the ninth century were serfs—they were not free and owed various forms of labor service and taxes to their lords. Serfs had to bake their bread in the lord's oven. Although legally not slaves, serfs had no access to public courts of law; they could not leave the estates and could not marry outside the estate without obtaining the lord's permission and paying a tax. Their dependency on their lords made them virtual slaves.

Beginning in the tenth century, the medieval population began to grow and rural production of grain increased. The rise in population and food production, particularly in the eleventh and twelfth centuries, made possible the reemergence of urban life. Once again towns attracted long-distance traders in luxury commodities, such as spices and silk, and in sugar, salt, metals (iron, copper, tin), precious metals (gold and silver), furs, cloth, wine, foodstuffs (grain, salted fish), and so forth. Towns became centers of important manufacturing, especially in cloth. Merchants and craftspeople organized themselves into guilds and soon demanded privileges commensurate with their growing economic power. Towns sometimes staged violent revolts against their lay or ecclesiastical lords, or peacefully obtained charters securing a high degree of autonomy and, most important, freeing townspeople from many of the exactions owed by serfs.

In Mediterranean towns, as in Italy, the concept of citizen (*civis*) was retained, encompassing all the urban dwellers, whether aristocrats or commoners. Yet northern towns beyond the Alps, as in France and Germany, drew a distinction between those living in the central fortress (bourg) and the merchants and craftspeople living outside the bourg in a trading area called a port, *vicus*, or Wik. In the north, the term "burgher" was extended to mean townspeople, socially distinct from lay lords or knights, and personally free.

The town was an association (*universitas*)—a collective legal personality, where political power belonged to the town. Towns were theoretically autonomous in administrative, judicial, and fiscal matters; they were largely freed from monarchical government. This development was more fully realized in Italy, where towns became city-states. The principle of urban autonomy and independent councils with elected officers also spread to France, Flanders, and Germany. In France, the monarchy still retained administrative prerogatives. Monarchs and other great territorial princes found it to their economic benefit to support towns and to grant charters of liberties, because towns offered vast new sources of revenue through new taxes and payments for charters.

An important element in the development of urban liberties was the growing power of the Church, which sought independence from lay control and lay investments of bishops. The Church's policy of a Pax Dei (peace of God) sought to protect the clergy and others from war. This implied exemption from the policing power of the monarchy, and the idea of Church privileges was applied to towns.

Towns, however, were not democracies. Government was generally in the hands of wealthy merchants, who formed the urban patriciate and dominated local politics through the merchant guild. Craft guilds were often represented in government but rarely exercised decisive government control, except through periodic rebellions and force. Yet the towns were also the vehicles of an economic revolution, bringing in new wealth in commerce and manufacture and offering new economic techniques and a new economic system in credit, banking and money exchange, investments, and capital.

Towns became centers of intellectual life in the cathedral schools and universities. Their economies made possible the building of the great Gothic cathedrals. Towns attracted peasants seeking to escape serfdom. Peasants who could establish that they had lived a year and a day in a town could obtained their freedom. The rural nobility encouraged peasants to trade in towns in return for new taxes. Some rural villages were given "charters" to help promote the growth of markets. The nobility required money in order to obtain the goods traded and manufactured in towns. Peasant labor services and taxes in kind were commuted to money payments. Thus the rise of towns was instrumental in slowly changing and even ending serfdom in parts of western Europe.

The Charter of Lorris was granted to a small town in north-central France, not far from Orléans. The original royal charter was given by King Louis VI, often called the Father of Communes, but was later lost. The earliest extant document is a redaction written in 1155 and granted to the town and parish of Lorris by King Louis VII. Unlike Italian towns, Lorris retained an important presence of royal power in administrative and judicial matters in the office of provost. According to article 35, all provosts and sergeants were required to uphold the liberties or customs of the charter.

CHARTER OF LORRIS: KEY PROVISIONS

- Every person with a house in Lorris pays tax to the king of sixpence for the house and each acre of land he possesses.
- No person is required to pay tax on his own provisions or on grain he has raised by his own labor.
- Burghers are exempt from road tolls on roads to Étampes, Orléans, Milly, or Melun [promoted trade].
- No burgher is required to go on any expedition that takes him farther than he can return the same day.
- With the exception of an offense against the king, no burgher is required to forfeit property he owns in the parish of Lorris in recompense for the offense.
- Those traveling to or from markets and fairs in Lorris will not be arrested unless for an offense commited the same day.
- Burghers are protected from imposition of taxes and subsidies.
- Those who have a disagreement (unless it concerns breaking into another's house), and who resolve it between themselves, are not required to pay a fine.
- Residents of Lorris are exempted from corvée [labor owed the king] except for carrying wine to Orléans twice a year.
- No one will be detained in prison if he can provide surety that he will appear in court.
- Burghers are guaranteed the right to sell their own property and go freely with their proceeds.
- Those who live in Lorris without a previous claim against him and having subjected himself to the scrutiny of the king and his provost, may reside there freely.
- As new provosts take office, they will take an oath to uphold the charter.

Source: Adapted from Milton Viorst, *The Great Documents of Western Civilization* (Philadelphia: Chilton Books, 1965), pp. 63-64.

The charter's customs clearly differentiated townspeople from the peasantry. Townspeople were exempted from taxes common to peasants, such as the tallage (or taille—a tax levied on people or land) described in article 9 and the inheritance tax (*mainmorte*). Through the provision in article 24, townspeople were freed from the peasant tax to bake bread in the lord's oven. Marriage fees were not imposed. The charter granted the right to sell one's home and to leave the town, unless one had committed a crime (article 17). Townspeople were exempt from labor service (corvée), which was typical of peasant life, except to cart the king's wine to Orléans twice a year (article 15). In article 18, the charter enshrined the concept that to live a year and a day within the town secured one's freedom.

The charter also provided important judicial privileges. These included autonomy from the abbot for those who had lands in the domain of the monastery of Saint Benedict. Townspeople had the right to be heard before the king's court within the town. They were not under the judicial authority of any provosts other than the royal provost in Lorris. These provisions effectively provided judicial freedom from neighboring powerful lay or ecclesiastical lords. The charter also preserved privileges in judicial procedures (the right to bail and the necessity of witnesses to crimes) and security over property. Judicial duels were regulated, and various fines and provost fees were reduced.

Certain limited seignorial (feudal) rights were preserved, however. A quitrent (*cens*), or fixed rent of six derniers for each house or acre of land in the parish, was levied; the king and his queen had the right to have provisions for a fortnight. Military duty could be imposed but townspeople were not required to go beyond one day's march. Taxes in rye for the provision of the sergeants were levied but restricted, and the king had the right to sell from the royal vineyards with public notice. According to article 2, however, no tax was imposed on food for one's own consumption or grain grown by one's own labor.

To encourage commerce, article 6 of the charter enacted the right of free movement of traders; commercial taxes were regulated; and no tolls were taken on the roads to Étampes, Orléans, or Milly.

SIGNIFICANCE

The Charter of Lorris became the standard custom of privileges for more than eighty towns, mostly small ones, located in the royal domain. Lorris was typical of French urban privileges in that it granted personal liberty, free movement, control over one's property, and limited autonomy. In the thirteenth century, royal power increased over many French towns, and the French bourgeoisie became politically and economically tied to the monarchy. This development would have extremely important consequences for the future political history of France.

—Lawrence N. Langer

FURTHER READING

Beatty, J., and O. Johnson. *Heritage of Western Civilization*. 8th ed. 2 vols. Englewood Cliffs, N.J.: Prentice Hall, 1995. Volume 2 contains a translation of the Charter of Lorris.

Hilton, R. H. *English and French Towns in Feudal Society*. New York: Cambridge University Press, 1992. A major comparative study of feudal urban life.

Nicholas, David. *The Growth of the Medieval City: From Late Antiquity to the Early Fourteenth Century*. New York: Longman, 1997. Discusses land ownership, commerce, industry, law, and more in the history and growth of cities and towns in early medieval Europe.

Petit-Dutailles, Charles. *The French Communes in the Middle Ages*. Translated by Joan Vickes. Amsterdam: North-Holland, 1978. This work is a classic study of French towns.

Pirenne, Henri. *Medieval Cities*. Princeton, N.J.: Princeton University Press, 1925. An important analysis of the rise of towns.

Reynolds, Susan. *Kingdoms and Communities in Western Europe, 900-1300*. Oxford, England: Clarendon Press, 1984. An examination of the nature of urban and rural communities in the Middle Ages.

Sonnenfeld, Albert, Jean-Louis Flandrin, and Massimo Montanari. *Food: A Culinary History from Antiquity to the Present*. Translated by Clarissa Botsford et al. New York: Columbia University Press, 1999. An extensive, nearly six-hundred-page collection of essays on the history and culture of the food, foodstuffs, food production, diets, eating behaviors, dining habits and formalities, and more of ancient times to the present, including an essay on the urban diet in the Middle Ages.

SEE ALSO: 11th-15th centuries: Development of the Ife Kingdom and Yoruba Culture; c. 1025: Scholars at Chartres Revive Interest in the Classics; c. 1150-1200: Rise of the Hansa Merchant Union; 1295: Model Parliament.

RELATED ARTICLES in *Great Lives from History: The Middle Ages, 477-1453*: Charles IV; Saint Fulbert of Chartres; Innocent III.

September 17, 1156
AUSTRIA EMERGES AS A NATIONAL ENTITY

Austria emerged as a national entity after the East Mark was established as the duchy of Austria. Of the German duchies in existence in 1156, it was the only one to persist as a sovereign state through the present day.

LOCALE: Regensburg, Bavaria (now in Germany)
CATEGORY: Government and politics

KEY FIGURES

Conrad III (1093-1152), duke of Swabia and king of Germany, r. 1138-1152
Frederick I Barbarossa (c. 1123-1190), duke of Swabia as Frederick III, 1147-1190, Holy Roman Emperor and king of Germany, r. 1152-1190
Henry II Jasomirgott (c. 1114-1177), duke of Bavaria, 1143-1156, and first duke of Austria, 1156-1177
Henry the Proud (c. 1108-1139), duke of Bavaria, 1126-1139, and duke of Saxony, 1137-1139
Henry the Lion (1129-1195), duke of Saxony, 1142-1180, and duke of Bavaria, 1156-1180

SUMMARY OF EVENT

Celtic and Roman civilization in Austria was crushed when Avars overran the region in the sixth century. After Charlemagne destroyed Avar power between 791 and 811, he organized the Austrian lands as the East Mark on Bavaria's eastern frontier. The East Mark then was colonized by German settlers, chiefly from Bavaria, but Magyar invaders obliterated the East Mark's German settlements between 898 and 955. Little survived, but German colonization resumed after Otto I defeated the Magyars at Lechfeld in 955, confining them to the area that became known as Hungary.

The bishops of Passau and Regensburg and the monasteries of Saint Polten, Kremsmunster, and Saint Florian were instrumental in this colonizing, joining material considerations with zeal to convert pagan Slavs and Hungarians. In 973, Margrave Leopold of Babenberg assumed secular authority in the East Mark. Shortly thereafter, in 996, the name *osterrichi* (Austria) first appeared in an imperial document. Members of the Babenberg family governed the territory until the death of Frederick the Fighter in 1246. The margraves encouraged German immigration, slowly pushed the frontier eastward, and defended the territory against the Slavs and Hungarians.

The East Mark was a no-man's-land between German civilization and peripheral ethnic groups, with boundaries determined by the balance of power. By the mid-twelfth century, German settlement was halted by Hungarians who were deeply entrenched at the Leitha River. Led by Henry II Jasomirgott, the margraves began emphasizing consolidation and internal exploitation. By this time, Vienna had reappeared, most unoccupied land was converted to agriculture, and more refined cultural aspects were in evidence. Thus, the East Mark's colonial stage of development came to an end.

For a generation, Bavaria and the East Mark were disputed by the Welfs (Guelphs) and Hohenstaufens (Ghibelins), the two most powerful German families of the period. The controversy erupted in 1137, when Emperor Lothair II died without a male heir. His daughter Gertrude had married the Welf duke of Bavaria, Henry the Proud. Through Gertrude, Henry secured Saxony, the nucleus of Lothair's possessions. Joining Saxony to Bavaria, Henry the Proud became the most powerful German prince. As duke of Spoleto, Henry's authority also reached the gates of Rome.

Henry expected to become king of Germany in early 1138, but the princes disappointed him by electing Conrad III, a member of the Hohenstaufen family who dominated the duchy of Swabia. Because the Hohenstaufens had often defied Lothair and had frequently fought with the duchy of Bavaria, Henry the Proud expressed his disappointment by preparing for war.

Conrad III deposed Henry, granting Saxony to Albert I, the margrave of Brandenburg, and presenting Bavaria to Leopold of the East Mark. Yet Conrad could not enforce his decrees. Henry recovered most of Saxony and was poised to invade Bavaria when he died in October, 1139, leaving Henry the Lion, his ten-year-old son, as his heir. The boy's grandmother and an uncle managed to compel Conrad to return Saxony to young Henry in 1142. Conrad insisted, however, that Bavaria remain in the hands of Henry II Jasomirgott of the East Mark, brother and heir of the late Leopold of Babenberg. In consequence, young Henry the Lion renounced his claim on his Bavarian inheritance.

Henry II Jasomirgott's control over Bavaria was tenuous. Opponents within the duchy warred against him, and the maturing Henry the Lion began to regret his renunciation of his claim to Bavaria. During the Second Crusade in 1147, Henry the Lion demonstrated military talent fighting against the pagan Wends. When Conrad III returned from the Crusade, Henry the Lion pressed his claim to Bavaria. Fighting had already erupted when Conrad died in February.

In 1152, Conrad III's nephew, Frederick Barbarossa, was elected king of Germany. Barbarossa (known as Frederick I Barbarossa after being crowned king) apparently recognized that Germany's constitutional structure had been forever altered by the investiture controversy and civil strife during the early twelfth century. The vast power of the princes had undermined the monarchy, and the newly crowned king needed to discover new methods of rule. Barbarossa based his plans on the inherent possibilities of feudalism, then well established in western Europe but existing only tangentially in Germany.

A strong feudal monarch required an extensive royal domain with its economic resources to create and maintain political power. Within Germany little remained of the old royal domain by 1152, so Barbarossa concentrated his initial efforts toward Italy. Here his perquisites as Holy Roman Emperor offered resources to regain his lost rights within Germany. Frederick Barbarossa therefore determined to subjugate Italy so he could eventually dominate Germany.

A second aspect of Barbarossa's policy consisted of strengthening the hierarchical structure of government within Germany with the monarch firmly entrenched at the summit, sustained by clear lines of authority and control. He needed the cooperation and support of the great dukes to construct a scheme of administration that would, with his outside resources, permit him to dominate these same dukes. He needed to grant concessions to placate powerful families, especially the Welfs, who would never rest content until they recovered their confiscated Bavarian lands. To bring this about, Barbarossa also needed to grant concessions to the Babenbergs to buy their support. The backing of the Babenbergs would counterbalance the dangerous concentration of power in the Welf family.

Frederick I Barbarossa was related to both Henry of Saxony and Henry II Jasomirgott of the East Mark. Apparently Barbarossa promised restoration of Bavaria to the Saxon duke before his election in order to ensure his support. For two years, however, Barbarossa could not persuade Henry II Jasomirgott to discuss the matter. Finally, Barbarossa and his court announced at the diet of

Frederick Barbarossa kneels to Henry the Lion. (F. R. Niglutsch)

Goslar in 1154 that Henry the Lion's claim to Bavaria overrode that of the Babenbergs. Barbarossa invested Henry the Lion with the disputed territory. Jasomirgott stubbornly refused to accept this judgment for two more years, despite negotiations in which his son Otto, bishop of Freising, took part. Jasomirgott finally yielded in 1156, on condition that he be compensated. Barbarossa delivered his compensation through a charter that converted Henry's East Mark into the newly created duchy of Austria. He granted this duchy to Henry II Jasomirgott on September 17, 1156, at Regensburg.

SIGNIFICANCE

According to this charter, known as the *privelegium minus*, the East Mark became the duchy of Austria and was legally equivalent to the other great German duchies. Furthermore, the emperor granted Duke Henry and his wife the right of inheritance in both the female and the male lines as an added guarantee of permanent succession in the Babenberg family. Moreover, no one was allowed any jurisdiction within Austria without the duke's consent, a provision that expanded the Austrian duke's sovereignty beyond that granted elsewhere.

In apparent recognition of Austria's military obligations on the Holy Roman Empire's frontier, where the Babenbergs risked continuing warfare with bordering Magyars and the Slavs, Austria was exempted from all imperial military obligations except campaigns against lands on its own borders. None of the usual ducal services to the emperor were exacted from the duke of Austria, except attendance at diets held in Bavaria. In this way, Austria became essentially independent, a status immediately sought and eventually attained by the other duchies and political subdivisions of the Holy Roman Empire.

Finally, Barbarossa's constitutional reform reinforced the internal authority of the dukes. With this authority, they could end the endemic petty warfare among the lesser nobility that was destroying Germany's internal resources. As the monarchy dominated the dukes, the dukes were expected to dominate and control the lesser potentates beneath them. The Austrian charter of 1155 illustrates Barbarossa's technique, bestowing full control of internal administration on the duke.

Of the German duchies that existed in 1156, only Austria persisted as an independent, sovereign state to modern times. Many events intervened between the twelfth and twentieth centuries, but the year 1156 witnessed Austria's decisive break with its past. Its subsequent greatness flowed, indirectly, from the charter that Frederick I Barbarossa bestowed on Henry II Jasomirgott.

—*Raymond H. Schmandt,*
updated by Ralph L. Langenheim, Jr.

FURTHER READING

Arnold, Benjamin. *Princes and Territories in Medieval Germany.* New York: Cambridge University Press, 1991. Details interrelationships between German rulers and the nature of their political status.

Barraclough, Geoffrey. *The Origins of Modern Germany.* 3d ed. Oxford, England: B. Blackwell, 1988. A thorough discussion of medieval Germany, including the establishment of Austria.

Brook-Shepherd, Gordon. *The Austrians: A Thousand-Year Odyssey.* New York: Carroll and Graf, 1997. A brief discussion of the formation of Austria is included in this survey of the nation's history.

Haverkamp, Alfred. *Medieval Germany, 1056-1273.* Translated by Helga Braun and Richard Mortimer. New York: Oxford University Press, 1988. Describes the establishment of Babenberg Austria and its subsequent history.

Huffman, Joseph P. *The Social Politics of Medieval Diplomacy: Anglo-German Relations, 1066-1307.* Ann Arbor: University of Michigan Press, 2000. This text uses the lens of Anglo-German relations to form a coherent picture of medieval German history from the mid-ninth to the early fourteenth century.

Leeper, A. W. A. *A History of Medieval Austria.* Edited by R. W. Seton-Watson and C. A. Macartney. Oxford, England: Oxford University Press, 1941. This book is unrivaled for study of Austrian history through the end of the Babenberg dynasty in 1254.

Munz, Peter. *Frederick Barbarossa: A Study in Medieval Politics.* Ithaca, N.Y.: Cornell University Press, 1969. Definitive biography of Barbarossa, including an account of his role in establishing Austria.

SEE ALSO: 496: Baptism of Clovis; 735: Christianity Is Introduced into Germany; 890's: Magyars Invade Italy, Saxony, and Bavaria; August 10, 955: Otto I Defeats the Magyars; 1147-1149: Second Crusade; c. 1150-1200: Rise of the Hansa Merchant Union; January 10, 1356, and December 25, 1356: Golden Bull.

RELATED ARTICLES in *Great Lives from History: The Middle Ages, 477-1453*: Charlemagne; Frederick I Barbarossa; Henry the Lion; Otto I; Rudolf I.

1156-1192
MINAMOTO YORITOMO BECOMES SHOGUN

In the mid-twelfth century, rival clans of provincial warriors challenged the court aristocracy for political dominance. The Taira first gained ascendancy, but Yoritomo's Minamoto clan defeated the Taira in the Gempei War and established the shogunate in Kamakura, initiating seven centuries of feudal rule.

LOCALE: Japan
CATEGORIES: Government and politics; wars, uprisings, and civil unrest

KEY FIGURES

Taira Kiyomori (1118-1181), leader of the Taira clan during its political ascendancy
Go-Shirakawa (1127-1192), retired Japanese emperor (r. 1155-1158; cloistered rule, r. 1158-1192) who sought to preserve the court's independence
Minamoto Yoritomo (1147-1199), founder of the Kamakura shogunate
Hōjō Tokimasa (1138-1215), Yoritomo's father-in-law; controlled shogunate after Yoritomo's death
Minamoto Yoshinaka (1154-1184), Yoritomo's cousin and rival, whose victories initiated the decisive phase of the war
Minamoto Yoshitsune (1159-1189), half brother of Yoritomo and brilliant general who defeated the Taira

SUMMARY OF EVENT

Through the Heian period (794-1185), Japan's monarchy weakened as Fujiwara regents and then retired emperors ruled in the emperor's stead, and state income shrank as taxed farmlands were converted to tax-free estates (*shōen*). *Shōen* were privately governed and even had their own militia. Courtiers and temples that accumulated *shōen* paved the way for feudalism by depriving the central government of revenues and local authority while fostering a provincial warrior class independent of court control—a grave situation because the national conscript army was abolished early in the period.

The warrior class was dominated by the Taira (Heike) and Minamoto (Genji) clans, both of royal descent. The Minamoto were dubbed the "tooth and claws of the Fujiwara" for helping them intimidate rivals and quell rebellions, but the court typically played the two clans off against one another. The Fujiwara's dangerous game of using warriors for political muscle proved costly when two factions called warriors to the capital in 1156. The resulting Hōgen disturbance was settled by a single battle, won by Minamoto Yoshitomo, who along with Taira Kiyomori was among those defending Go-Shirakawa, the reigning emperor, against the abdicated emperor Sutoku (r. 1123-1142) and Minamoto Tameyoshi. Tameyoshi was executed; Sutoku was exiled.

Angered when the court promoted Kiyomori while slighting him and demanded capital punishment (unused for 350 years) of fifty "rebels," including his father and brother, Yoshitomo attempted a coup (Heiji disturbance, 1159), with disaffected courtiers. He and his two eldest sons were killed. Yoritomo, the oldest surviving son at thirteen, was imprudently exiled to Izu, near many Minamoto chieftains. Hōjō Tokimasa, his second warden, later allowed Yoritomo to wed his daughter Masako and became his vassal.

Kiyomori gradually strengthened his position, insinuating his family into the court, marrying one daughter to a Fujiwara regent and another to an emperor, and securing many Taira governorships. In 1179, after a plot against his family (Shishigatani affair, 1177) and Go-Shirakawa's repossession of lands of two of Kiyomori's deceased children, Kiyomori forcibly established dictatorial rule and installed his two-year-old grandson the emperor Antoku (r. 1180-1185).

Kiyomori's arrogance provoked rebellion by a passed-over prince, Mochihito, and an aging Minamoto courtier, Yorimasa, initiating the Gempei War (1180-1185). They soon died, but in Izu, Yoritomo took up Mochihito's call to expel the Taira. Many Genji initially refused to join him. His small force was overwhelmed in his first battle (Ishibashiyama, August, 1180). However, by converting former opponents and confirming the land holdings of recruits, he expanded his force dramatically. In his next and final engagement with the Taira (Fujigawa, November, 1180), the Taira fled without a fight. He turned back to Kanto, coercing Genji holdouts to join him. At his new base, Kamakura, Kiyomori established the first of his governmental organs, the *samurai dokoro* (office of samurai), through which he curbed warrior lawlessness and organized his forces. The fact that he would have several years to develop a de facto government in the east changed Japanese history.

Widespread famine and epidemics brought a two-year hiatus in the war. Its decisive phase began when Taira attacked Yoritomo's cousin Minamoto Yoshinaka in Chubu (spring, 1183). A bold, skilled tactician who controlled five provinces and caused Yoritomo grave concern, Yoshinaka routed a larger Taira force and soon drove them from Kyoto. Urged by the court to pursue them, he dallied, fearful of Yoritomo. After unsuccessfully seeking an alliance with the Taira against him, Yoshinaka forced Go-Shirakawa to authorize an attack on Yoritomo. However, the retired emperor secretly appealed to Yoritomo, who sent an army under his half brothers Noriyori and Yoshitsune. They quickly crushed Yoshinaka and pressed west. When they attacked Ichinotani, Yoshitsune, with seventy men, struck unexpectedly from steep mountains behind the startled Taira. In disarray, they fled to Shikoku (March, 1184).

Lacking boats to pursue them, it was six months before Yoritomo sent forces west under Noriyori, who was ineffective. However, Yoritomo created two more governing entities, a secretariat (*kumonjo*, later renamed *mandokoro*), headed by Ōe Hiromoto, and a judicial board (*monchūjo*), headed by Miyaoshi Yasunobu (November, 1184). These men were experienced Kyoto scholar-administrators who contributed much to the emerging *bakufu* (tent government), whose core institutions were now in place.

The Gempei War's climax came when Yoritomo gave Yoshitsune a new army. Again audacious and strategically brilliant, Yoshitsune sailed to Shikoku in a storm with a modest force, surprising the Taira at Yashima. They fled by ship to the west. A month later, having assembled new allies and a fleet, he destroyed them at Dannoura, where Kiyomori's emperor-grandson drowned at sea (April, 1185).

Shockingly, Yoritomo quickly turned on Yoshitsune. Envious of his generalship and popularity even after Ichinotani, Yoritomo had failed to reward him, though others far less deserving received governorships. Thereafter, Yoshitsune accepted court appointments from Go-Shirakawa without Yoritomo's authorization, which Yoritomo had prohibited. Now Yoritomo ordered Yoshitsune to Kamakura, refused him entry, then sent him back to Kyoto, followed by an (inept) assassin. Forced to rebel, Yoshitsune was outlawed. A fugitive in the home

Yoritomo (seated left), jealous of Yoshitsune's generalship and popularity, turned on his brother. (F. R. Niglutsch)

provinces for many months, he found sanctuary in the north with Fujiwara Hidehira.

Before Yoshitsune's flight, the court had authorized him to attack Yoritomo, who used this to shackle the court, demanding dismissal of those supporting the authorization, creation of a court advisory council chosen by him, and appointment of his friend Fujiwara Kanezane as imperial adviser. More significant, on the pretext of the danger posed by Yoshitsune, Yoritomo gained power to appoint provincial constables (*shugo*) and estate stewards (*jitō*), and to impose a 2 percent land tax. These measures helped finance the *bakufu* and extend its local control, though placement of these officials was gradual. The final use Yoritomo made of Yoshitsune was to attack his hosts, the Ōshū Fujiwara, with a huge army after coercing them to exact his suicide. Because new western vassals were asked to demonstrate their loyalty by joining this campaign, it gave Yoritomo both control of northern Japan and a firmer grip on the west. Go-Shirakawa died in 1192. Unchallenged at court, Kanezane persuaded boy-emperor Go-Toba (r. 1183-1198) to grant Yoritomo what Go-Shirakawa had long denied: the title of *shōgun* (generalissimo; August, 1192). Thus, the *bakufu* became the shogunate, an institution that endured until 1867.

Having executed Noriyori a year later on trumped up charges, Yoritomo left no adult male relatives when he died at age fifty-two. His two immature sons were pushed aside and eventually murdered. His father-in-law, Hōjō Tokimasa, became shogunal regent, a position also held by his son and a succession of members of the Hōjō family, one of the most competent political families in Japanese history.

Eventually, court aristocrats (1219), then princes (1252) were made figurehead shogun. The last significant expansion of Kamakura's power over the court followed Go-Toba's quixotic rebellion in 1221. Once crushed, the Hōjō confiscated many *shōen* from complicit court families, extended the *jitō* system throughout Japan, and established the Hōjō-manned office of deputy shogun in Kyoto, rendering the court politically inconsequential.

SIGNIFICANCE

Yoritomo's establishment of the Kamakura shogunate (1185-1333) marked a permanent power shift to provincial warriors and their feudal lords in Kamakura. While court culture remained seductive to military chieftains, courtiers never regained political power. Though Yoritomo revolutionized Japan, politically his instincts were conservative. He was outwardly pious, lavishly supported religious institutions, and respected the court as a source of legitimacy. Moreover, the *bakufu*'s central organs were not new, being modeled on the private "house offices" though which the Fujiwara governed their *shōen* and retired emperors ruled the late Heian court.

Ruthless with potential rivals and particularly appalling in his treatment of the most brilliant general in Japanese history, his brother Yoshitsune, Yoritomo earned little love from his countrymen. However, he gave the warrior class discipline, reasonable justice, and the personal and property security that were the cornerstones of feudalism. His was the strongest national government Japan had yet achieved—one that would successfully rebuff two invasions by the mighty Mongol Empire (1274 and 1281). Warrior rule endured seven centuries, and the values of the *bushi* (warriors) remain prominent in contemporary Japan.

—*R. Craig Philips*

MAJOR EMPERORS OF THE KAMAKURA PERIOD

Reign	*Ruler*
1183-1198	Go-Toba
1198-1210	Tsuchimikado
1210-1221	Jintoku
1221	Chukyo
1221-1232	Go-Horikawa
1232-1242	Shijō
1242-1246	Go-Saga
1246-1260	Go-Fukakusa
1260-1274	Kameyama
1274-1287	Go-Uda
1287-1298	Fushimi
1298-1301	Go-Fushimi
1301-1308	Go-Nijō
1308-1318	Hanazonō
1318-1339	Go-Daigo

FURTHER READING

Mass, Jeffrey P. *Warrior Government in Early Medieval Japan: A Study of the Kamakura Bakufu, Shugo, and Jitō*. New Haven, Conn.: Yale University Press, 1974. A solid analysis of the regime Yoritomo established.

________. *Yoritomo and the Founding of the First Bakufu*. Stanford, Calif.: Stanford University Press, 1999. Revisionist work stressing Yoritomo's conservatism and the slow implementation of his system.

_______, ed. *Court and Bakufu in Japan*. New Haven, Conn.: Yale University Press, 1982. Valuable on post-Yoritomo Kamakura Japan.

Sansom, George. *A History of Japan to 1334*. Vol. 1. Stanford, Calif.: Stanford University Press, 1958. A well-written, insightful classic.

Shinoda, Minoru. *The Founding of the Kamakura Shogunate, 1180-1185, with Selected Translations from the Azuma Kagami*. New York: Columbia University Press, 1960. Fine history of the Gempei War and the *bakufu*'s genesis.

Sugawara Makoto, "Bushidō." *The East* 16-19 (1980-1983). Interesting, very detailed narrative based on Japanese historical documents.

The Tale of the Heike. Translated by Helen Craig McCullough. Stanford, Calif.: Stanford University Press, 1988. A translation of the famous war epic by a respected scholar of classical Japanese. Contains an introduction by the translator that sets the literary work within the historical context.

SEE ALSO: 792: Rise of the Samurai; 858: Rise of the Fujiwara Family; 1219-1333: Hōjō Family Dominates Shoguns, Rules Japan; 1336-1392: Yoshino Civil Wars.

RELATED ARTICLES in *Great Lives from History: The Middle Ages, 477-1453*: Minamoto Yoritomo; Taira Kiyomori.

1167
FOUNDATION OF THE NEMANJID DYNASTY

The Nemanjid Dynasty is founded in Serbia and extends its power from the eastern Sava River to the south of Thessaly by the middle of the fourteenth century.

LOCALE: Serbia
CATEGORIES: Expansion and land acquisition; government and politics

KEY FIGURES

Stephen Nemanja (d. 1200), ruler of Serbia and founder of the Nemanjid Dynasty, r. c. 1167-1196
Stephen II Nemanja (d. 1228), Stephen's son and successor as king of Serbia, r. 1196-1228

SUMMARY OF EVENT

Serbs settled in the Balkan Peninsula in the sixth and seventh centuries and were converted to Christianity in the ninth century. Their petty principalities were nominally governed by a grand zhupan (clan leader), who recognized Byzantine authority.

By the eleventh century, Serbs were beginning to form into large concentrations, opposed to both the Greeks and the Magyars. Out of the rivalry of various Serb chieftains, Stephen Nemanja triumphed, the Byzantine emperor acknowledging him as grand zhupan in 1167. A man of extraordinary energy and audacity, Nemanja united the Serbs and ruled for twenty-nine years, resigning his throne in 1196.

Not content with having forged a self-reliant nation, Nemanja conducted several successful wars against the Byzantine Empire, although he was never powerful enough to conquer it and at times had to sue for peace. Nor was he able to vanquish the Greeks, ending his career as their vassal. Nevertheless, his record among the Serbs was hallowed because he coupled his warrior's prowess with a religious sensibility. At the end of his reign, he entrusted power to his son Stephen II and retired to a monastery on Mount Athos, preparing himself through prayer and meditation for death.

The Nemanjid Dynasty, then, was founded on this legend of a ruler revered as a saint, who valued both this world and the next. Indeed, Serbs believed that oil from Stephen's grave performed miracles. One of Stephen's sons became Saint Sava, a pilgrim and statesman, revered by monks and treated by the Serbs as an embodiment of both their religion and their national aspirations.

For two hundred years, the dynasty took Serbia to the height of its power. Stephen II proved to be as effective as his father and more prudent in his military exploits, preferring to gain the advantage by diplomacy rather than war. He also enhanced the prestige and mystique of the dynasty by having himself crowned twice—by a Roman papal legate in 1217 and by the Orthodox Church in 1222. With the blessing of both the western and eastern halves of the old Roman Empire, the second Nemanja consolidated both his power and his religious standing.

All the Nemanjas adopted the name of Stephen, emphasizing their direct descent from the hallowed founder of their dynasty as well as invoking the protection of

Saint Stephen, whom the Serbs worshiped as a martyr to the Christian faith and as their patron saint. Indeed, the Nemanjid Dynasty fused the idea of Christianity and Serb unity, overriding the claims of village rulers and princelings.

By the third generation of Nemanjas, however, Serbia ceased developing at the rapid pace set by the dynasty's founders. The Nemanjas could not settle internal rivalries that led to civil war; their disputes contributed to a serious weakening of the nation, exploited by various Serb chieftains and the nobility. Nevertheless, as Schevill pointed out, the nation did slowly progress, improving both its social and economic organization. Even when the Serbs lost their independence and were defeated by the Turks in 1389, the Orthodox Church kept alive the memory of the Nemanjas, of a free and Christian state—an idea that penetrated deeply into all classes, including the peasants. The Serbs who took part in the uprising against the Turks in 1804 sang songs evoking their Nemanjid heritage of a highly developed civilization they intended to create anew. In October of 1915, when the Serbian army was faced with extinction—confronting a combined Austro-Hungarian and Bulgarian army of more than half a million men—Serbian monks and soldiers carried the coffins of their Nemanjid kings in bullock-carts, and when the roads no longer were passable by vehicles, they hoisted the coffins on their shoulders and kept going, so that their sacred rulers would not be defiled by the enemy.

After the first two Stephens, the Nemanjid kings found it difficult to protect the Serbs from the onslaught and rivalry of various Slavic peoples. Only a rare combination of shrewdness and boldness could have confirmed and extended Serbian power. On the west, Serbia had to contend with Catholic Bosnia, allied with papal Rome in efforts to attack the Orthodox Serbs. To the north, Hungary engaged in several attacks on the Serbs, and to the south the Byzantine Empire represented a perennial threat to Serb independence.

The Turkish conquest of Serbia served to embellish in the Serbian imagination a dynasty that had withstood pagan threats and remained loyal to Christianity. The religious art of the Nemanja period, found in monasteries and churches, is especially revered. The Turkish usurpation is viewed as only an interruption in Serbia's mission to defend and spread Christianity.

Significance

The Nemanjid Dynasty of old Serbia evokes images of a heroic age—not merely of great kings but of a close-knit people, fiercely independent and dynamic, creating beautiful works of art. It is an idealized image, of course, the subject of countless romantic stories. Yet the Nemanjid period also reflects a people's aspiration, a vision of the past that is simultaneously a projection of their future. At its best, the Nemanjid period also conveys the quest for religious tolerance, for the most successful representatives of the dynasty were able to live beside both Catholic and Orthodox Slavs and even encourage peaceful coexistence between different religious communities. This history of tolerance, however, was marred by other Nemanjas, who confiscated Catholic monasteries and churches and turned them over to Orthodox priests.

In the early twentieth century, the idea of the unified Yugoslavia, with the Serbs in the vanguard of a coalition of southern Slavs (Catholic and Orthodox), owed much to the example of the Nemanjas. Not until after World War II, when Yugoslavia's Communist leader Tito took control, did the idea of a Serb-led union of southern Slavs dissipate. The dissolution of Yugoslavia awakened a yearning for a union of Serbs, but the resulting wars led to more division between the south Slavs and the creation of new countries—Slovenia, Croatia, and Bosnia—establishing a fragmented region that the Nemanjid Dynasty sought to integrate.

—*Carl Rollyson*

Further Reading

Cox, John K. *The History of Serbia*. Westport, Conn.: Greenwood Press, 2002. This comprehensive history of the Serbian region includes a chapter on "The Splendor of Medieval Serbia."

Halecki, Oscar. *Borderlands of Western Civilization: A History of East Central Europe*. New York: Ronald Press, 1952. Chapter 5 provides a succinct account of the establishment and success of the Nemanjid Dynasty in the context of the Fourth Crusade and the development of Bulgarian independence.

Kaplan, Robert D. *Balkan Ghosts: A Journey Through History*. New York: St. Martin's Press, 1993. Chapter 2, "Old Serbia and Albania: Balkan 'West Bank,'" offers insights into the legacy of the Nemanjid Dynasty and describes the monasteries that perpetuate the dynasty's hold on the Serb imagination.

Laffan, R. G. D. *The Serbs: Guardians of the Gate*. 1917. Reprint. New York: Dorset Press, 1989. Chapter 1, "The Past," is still a good introduction to the geography and history of old Serbia, out of which the Nemanjid Dynasty developed.

Palmer, Alan. *The Lands Between: A History of East-Central Europe Since the Congress of Vienna.* New York: Macmillan, 1970. Chapter 1 includes a brief discussion of the Nemanjid Dynasty in terms of the eastern European tendency to glorify the past, especially episodes of valor that highlight a dedication to national mission and the quest for patriot-father figures.

Pavlowitch, Stevan K. *Serbia: The History of an Idea.* New York: New York University Press, 2002. A history focused upon Serbia as an idea that persisted even through its border changes and through its temporary "nonexistence." Includes significant discussion of medieval Serbian rulers and their relationship to the Church.

Schevill, Ferdinand. *A History of the Balkans: From the Earliest Times to the Present Day.* New York: Dorset Press, 1991. Originally published in 1933, this volume still has one of the best straightforward accounts of the founding and perpetuation of the Nemanjid Dynasty.

Stavrianos, L. S. *The Balkans Since 1453.* New York: Rinehart, 1958. Chapter 2, "Historical Background," explains the origins of the Serbs, Stephen Nemanja's role in uniting them for the first time, and his son's consolidation of Nemanja power.

West, Rebecca. *Black Lamb and Grey Falcon: A Journey Through Yugoslavia.* New York: Viking Press, 1941. Still the most evocative and dramatic account of the Nemanjid Dynasty, weaving its history and its impact on modern-day Serbia throughout this epic work of travel writing and history.

SEE ALSO: 890's: Magyars Invade Italy, Saxony, and Bavaria; 893: Beginning of Bulgaria's Golden Age; 963: Foundation of the Mount Athos Monasteries; 1204: Knights of the Fourth Crusade Capture Constantinople; June 28, 1389: Turkish Conquest of Serbia.

RELATED ARTICLES in *Great Lives from History: The Middle Ages, 477-1453*: János Hunyadi; Mehmed II; Stefan Dušan.

1169-1172
NORMANS INVADE IRELAND

Norman troops invaded Ireland in a series of small military expeditions—backed by Welsh and Flemish foot soldiers—and established a foothold in southeastern Ireland that provided the basis for England's lengthy domination of Ireland and continuing involvement in Irish affairs.

LOCALE: Ireland
CATEGORIES: Expansion and land acquisition; wars, uprisings, and civil unrest

KEY FIGURES

Henry II (1133-1189), king of England, r. 1154-1189
Adrian IV (c. 1110-1159), Roman Catholic pope, 1154-1159
Dermot MacMurrough (d. 1171), deposed king of Leinster
Eva MacMurrough (c. 1136-1177), daughter of Dermot MacMurrough and wife of Richard FitzGilbert de Clare
Rory (Roderic) O'Connor (d. 1198), king of Connacht and high-king of Ireland, r. 1166-1175
Tiernan O'Rourke (d. 1172), king of Breifne and archenemy of Dermot MacMurrough
Dervorgilla O'Rourke (fl. twelfth century), wife of Tiernan O'Rourke
Richard de Clare (d. 1176), earl of Strigoil, earl of Pembroke, and titular leader of the Norman expeditionary forces in Ireland
Laurence O'Toole (1128-1180), archbishop of Dublin, 1162-1180, who later received sainthood

SUMMARY OF EVENT

There was no well-conceived design by England's King Henry II to obtain control of Ireland. Henry, whose domains stretched from Scotland to the Pyrenees Mountains, was also duke of Normandy, count of Anjou, and ruler of Aquitaine through marriage to its duchess, Eleanor of Aquitaine. As such, Henry was lukewarm to the idea of taking on additional responsibilities. At a royal council held at Winchester in 1155, the idea of invading Ireland had been discussed but quickly put aside. It had been the English bishops, led by the archbishop of Canterbury, who had been the most enthusiastic in their support of such an invasion.

The two kingdoms were utterly different from each other. England was a centralized, medieval monarchy, with a well-developed system of bureaucracy and an effi-

Pope Adrian IV. (Library of Congress)

cient administration whose workings ultimately stemmed from the king himself. In the hands of an energetic, detail-oriented monarch such as Henry, it could be a highly effective instrument. The English Church followed the Roman model and acknowledged the pope's final authority. Ireland, however, maintained the centuries-old Celtic structure of its church. Government was decentralized, and territory was parceled into units controlled by tribal or clan groupings known as *tuath.* Tribal chieftains and clan leaders owed allegiance to different kings. Ultimately, all of the various kings theoretically pledged allegiance to an Irish high-king. The high-king, however, was considered a war leader or a "first among equals," rather than a governmental or administrative head; there was no set rule determining who would be high-king. Heredity was only one factor to consider, out of many. Order and authority were generally maintained by force of arms, and each separate kingdom often enjoyed abundant autonomy. At any given time, there might be as many as 150 Irish kingdoms. The Irish Church also operated on an independent basis, differing from the Roman Church in many of its ideas and practices. During the tenth and eleventh centuries, Danish Vikings set up independent colonies that developed into urban centers—notably Dublin, Limerick, Waterford, and Wexford—further complicating Ireland's fragmented political picture.

In 1152, Irish Church leaders had angered Theobald, the influential archbishop of Canterbury, by ignoring his claims to authority over them. In response, the archbishop pressured Henry into dispatching his emissary, John of Salisbury, on a mission to Pope Adrian IV. Born Nicholas Breakspear, Pope Adrian was the first and only Englishman elevated to the papacy. In December of 1155, Adrian issued the since-refuted papal bull Laudabiliter ("donation of Ireland"), which authorized Henry to take control of Ireland and to restore the Irish Church to Roman practices. At the time, the gesture was ineffectual; Henry did not follow up on it.

Ireland's internal politics, however, transformed the situation. Dermot MacMurrough, king of Leinster, had maintained a long-standing feud with Tiernan O'Rourke, king of Breifne. Animosity between the two kings reached such a level of intensity that MacMurrough once abducted O'Rourke's wife Dervorgilla and held her (not entirely against her will) for one year. O'Rourke never forgot this humiliation; when his powerful ally Rory O'Connor, king of Connacht, became high-king of Ireland in 1166, MacMurrough was dispossessed of his kingdom and forced into exile.

In an attempt to regain his crown, MacMurrough sought out Henry in Aquitaine and implored his assistance in its recovery. Although he expressed sympathy, Henry refused to commit himself. Nevertheless, he authorized his subjects to help in restoring MacMurrough if they so desired. MacMurrough chose to concentrate his efforts at recruitment in the border country of South Wales. There, many tough young Norman warriors had been tempering their battle skills in clashes with Welsh tribesmen.

MacMurrough found the Normans quite willing to embark on an adventure in Ireland—for a price. In return for the promise of lands, money, or both, bands of Norman knights, Flemish foot soldiers, and Welsh bowmen agreed to sail across the Irish Sea on MacMurrough's behalf. The most prominent of these mercenaries was Richard FitzGilbert de Clare, earl of Strigoil and Pembroke, who was popularly known as Strongbow. What this powerful noble asked, and received, was the hand of MacMurrough's daughter Eva in marriage and the right of succession to the kingdom of Leinster. In 1167, MacMurrough led a small force of foreigners in his first attempt to reclaim his kingdom, and it proved to be an unqualified failure. In May, 1169, however, a more formidable contingent—thirty knights, sixty men-at-arms, and three hundred archers—under the command of half brothers Robert Fitzstephen and Maurice Fitzgerald landed in County Wexford. Other landings soon followed, with Strongbow himself disembarking at Passage in County Waterford in August, 1170.

The lightly clad Irish, relying on wild, headlong charges and antiquated weaponry, proved no match for the less numerous but effective and well-disciplined Norman forces, nor could the urban Danes stand up to the Norman invaders. After a spectacular Norman success at Baginbun and the taking of Wexford and Waterford cities, Strongbow married Eva MacMurrough and marched on Dublin, which also fell into his grasp. On Dermot MacMurrough's death in May, 1171, Strongbow laid claim to his domains but had to defend his claims against various rivals. Murtough MacMurrough, Dermot's nephew, tried to wrest control of the kingdom of Leinster; Asculf, the exiled Danish ruler of Dublin, returned with Viking warriors from as far off as Norway. Cavalry charges scattered Asculf's forces, and he was beheaded after a brief trial. O'Connor and O'Rourke then besieged Dublin, but they were beaten back after two months by a Norman surprise attack on the high-king's camp.

King Henry, who became alarmed at the possibility that Strongbow might establish himself as an independent ruler, took a belated interest in the invasion and landed at Waterford in October, 1171. In the negotiations that followed, Laurence O'Toole, archbishop of Dublin, played a key role. O'Toole was largely responsible for persuading a synod of Irish bishops meeting at Cashel to submit to Henry's rule and also negotiated Strongbow's submission to the English king. Henry entered Dublin in triumph and received the submission of one Irish king after another. Although he allowed Strongbow to retain his position as ruler (not king) of Leinster, Henry appointed Hugh de Lacy, a trusted Norman, to serve as justiciar of Ireland and gave him authority over the former kingdom of Meath in order to balance Strongbow's power.

Henry's ultimate victory in Ireland occurred when he successfully negotiated the Treaty of Windsor in October, 1175. Under the terms of the treaty, High-King Rory O'Connor acknowledged Henry as his suzerain. O'Connor proved to be Ireland's last effective high-king and was increasingly unable to assert his influence over the remaining lands of his realm. He died while on a religious pilgrimage to Cong in 1198. Strongbow died at Dublin in 1176, leaving no male heir; he was buried in Christchurch Cathedral.

SIGNIFICANCE

The dominant position of the English government in Ireland had been established on an enduring foundation after the Norman invasion of Ireland and King Henry's Treaty of Windsor. The invasion and treaty not only destroyed the tradition of the high-king in Ireland but also had the effect of asserting English influence over Irish affairs even today.

—*Raymond Pierre Hylton*

FURTHER READING

Cambrensis, Giraldus. *Expugnation Hibernica: The Conquest of Ireland*. Edited and translated by A. B. Scott and F. X. Martin. Dublin: Royal Irish Academy, 1978. A primary source account of the period whose author, a Norman-Welsh cleric, expresses a distinct anti-Irish bias.

De Paor, Liam. *The Peoples of Ireland: From Prehistory to Modern Times*. Notre Dame, Ind.: University of Notre Dame Press, 1986. An overview that covers the breadth of invasions, migrations, and influences entering Ireland from prehistory to the twentieth century.

Duffy, Seán. *Ireland in the Middle Ages*. New York: St. Martin's Press, 1997. Irish historian's effort to present Irish history of the period and not English colonial history.

Flanagan, Marie Therese. *Irish Society, Anglo-Norman Settlers, Angevin Kingship: Interactions in Ireland in the Late Twelfth Century*. New York: Oxford University Press, 1989. Scholarly reevaluation of primary source material that is accessible to laypersons. Stresses the role of the English Church.

Lydon, James F. *The Lordship of Ireland in the Middle Ages*. Rev. ed. Dublin: Four Courts Press, 2003. Important study of the medieval fusion of cultures, albeit one that ultimately rendered the Irish as secondary.

Moody, T. W., and F. X. Martin. *The Course of Irish History*. Cork, Ireland: Mercier Press, 1984. One of the most complete scholarly accounts of the sequence of events culminating in the establishment of Norman political control.

SEE ALSO: October 14, 1066: Battle of Hastings; 1366: Statute of Kilkenny.

RELATED ARTICLES in *Great Lives from History: The Middle Ages, 477-1453*: Adrian V; Gwenllian verch Gruffydd; Henry II; Nest verch Rhys ap Tewdwr.

December 29, 1170

MURDER OF THOMAS BECKET

The murder of Thomas Becket and his subsequent canonization thwarted the aristocracy's effort to bring the Catholic Church, but not the English Church, under secular control and had a considerable influence on the evolution of ecclesiastical law and royal custom in England.

LOCALE: Canterbury Cathedral, England
CATEGORIES: Government and politics; religion

KEY FIGURES

Thomas Becket (1118-1170), archbishop of Canterbury, 1162-1170

Henry II (1133-1189), king of England, r. 1154-1189, and close personal friend and later opponent of Becket

Alexander III (c. 1105-1181), Roman Catholic pope, 1159-1181, torn between support of Becket and political expediency

Gilbert Foliot, bishop of London, 1163-1188, and opponent of Becket

Louis VII (1120-1180), king of France, r. 1137-1179, supporter of Becket in exile

Roger of York (d. 1181), archbishop of York and critic of Becket

SUMMARY OF EVENT

Thomas Becket was born in London in 1118 to middle-class merchant parents. He was educated first at Merton Priory in Surrey and then at Paris. About 1141, he joined the household of Theobald, archbishop of Canterbury, who sent him to Bologna and Auxerre to study law. In 1154, Becket became archdeacon of Canterbury, and in the following year Henry II chose Becket as his chancellor. Loyal courtier, able diplomat, and trusted soldier, Becket became a close personal friend of the king and vigorously pursued the interests of the Crown.

Theobald's death in 1161 was followed by a long vacancy of the see of Canterbury. Henry was aware that the archbishop of Cologne was successfully serving as chancellor of the Holy Roman Empire, and he saw in his friend an ally in his lifelong effort to gain complete control of his kingdom. Henry passed over the worthy Gilbert Foliot and asked that Becket be invested as archbishop of the see of Canterbury. If Henry expected Becket to acquiesce in his efforts to limit the independence the church had won under Stephen, he was to be disappointed; Becket resigned the chancellorship in order to devote himself completely and wholeheartedly to the service of the Catholic Church.

A crucial dispute concerning jurisdiction over felonious clerics arose between Henry and Becket in 1163. By custom, clerics accused of a felony were tried and sentenced in church courts. Because these courts were not permitted to impose any penalty involving physical punishment, criminous clerics were usually expelled from office but were spared the capital punishment often meted out to laypeople in the king's courts. In 1163, Philip de Brois, a canon accused of murder, was acquitted by a church court. Public opinion insisted that he was guilty, and the sheriff brought him before the king's justice. On Becket's protest of the action, it was dropped, but the king was determined that felonious clerics should henceforth stand trial in the secular courts. At a council held at Westminster in October, 1163, Henry insisted that all bishops swear to observe the ancient customs of the realm, without specifying what they were. Although Becket and the other bishops were aware that the unwritten customs could seriously infringe on ecclesiastical liberties, they swore to uphold them.

In January of 1164, the king held a council at Clarendon that included bishops and the lay magnates of the kingdom. In sixteen decrees, Henry proposed the regulation that should henceforth govern the relations between the Church and the Crown. The most important clause concerned criminous clerics. Henry proposed that after a cleric had been found guilty in a church court he should be stripped of his orders so that, as a layman, he could be sent to the king's judge for sentencing and for confiscation of his chattels. Henry insisted that this was the ancient custom of the realm, observed by William the Conqueror and his sons. Becket and the bishops repeated their pledge to observe the ancient customs, but when the king put them in writing, they refused to agree to them. Since medieval custom was oral and flexible, any attempt to make custom absolute by writing was considered novel and dangerous.

The *Constitutions of Clarendon* not only dealt with felonious clerics but also stated that no appeal could be made from English courts to the pope and that royal consent was required before a tenant-in-chief could be excommunicated, before a papal bull could be promulgated in the land, or before a cleric could leave England. Becket vacillated somewhat but ultimately took a position that was consistent with that of the Gregorian reformers on

The assassination of Thomas Becket in Canterbury Cathedral. (G. T. Devereux)

the Continent and of Alexander III, namely that the Church had the sole right to try and punish clerics in major orders. The question of criminous clerics and ancestral custom was actually a symptom of the deeper problem of two rival jurisdictions existing together in the same country.

When one of Becket's vassals claimed that he had been denied justice and appealed to the king, the archbishop was summoned before Henry at Northampton. Becket refused the first summons so that the assembled barons judged him guilty of contempt of court. Then the king added a demand that Becket account for the money he had handled when he was chancellor. Becket's request for time to get his accounts in order was refused. Seeing that Henry intended to ruin and imprison him or to force his resignation as archbishop, Becket fled to France, where Pope Alexander received him with honor.

During the negotiations between the pope and the French and English kings, Becket stayed at the Cistercian abbey of Pontigny in Burgundy. When Henry threatened to expel all Cistercians from England in 1166 in retaliation, Becket moved to a Benedictine abbey at Sens under the protection of King Louis VII. In 1169, Becket excommunicated two English bishops who had opposed him, and he threatened to place all England under interdict. In June of 1170, Henry had Roger, archbishop of York, crown young prince Henry, a ritual that was the prerogative of the archbishop of Canterbury. Becket, followed by the pope, excommunicated all responsible for the investiture; fearing an interdict for England, Henry was reconciled with Becket at Fréteval in Normandy in July, 1170. It was agreed that the endowments of Canterbury should be restored and the exiled followers of Becket forgiven, but nothing was said about the *Constitutions of Clarendon*, appeals to Rome, or any of the other matters in dispute.

Becket returned to England on November 30, 1170, and was received with enthusiasm. When Becket refused to lift the excommunication of Roger of York and Foliot, Henry was furious. In a fit of rage, he uttered the words, "What sluggards, what cowards have I brought up in my court, who care nothing for their allegiance to their lord. Not one will deliver me from this low-born priest!" This outburst was enough to inspire four knights to travel to Canterbury and assassinate Becket within the cathedral late in the afternoon of December 29, 1170.

The news of Becket's murder sent a shock of horror throughout Christendom. The pope refused to see any English citizens for several weeks, and Henry was afraid that his vassals would throw off their allegiance to him. The two articles of the *Constitutions of Clarendon* dealing with felonious clerics and appeals to Rome were dropped, but the remaining fourteen articles were observed, and Henry continued to control the English Church in the same manner as he had done before the struggle with Becket began.

SIGNIFICANCE

Becket was canonized by the Roman Catholic Church in 1173; he quickly became one of Europe's best-loved saints. Thousands of pilgrims visited his tomb, and churches were dedicated to him throughout Europe.

Even in death, he was a champion of the principle of clerical supremacy.

Others, however, see Henry's continued control of the English Church and his admonishing Becket as victories for secularism.

—*Carl A. Volz, updated by Hal Holladay*

Further Reading

Barlow, Frank. *Thomas Becket*. Berkeley: University of California Press, 1990. A comprehensive biography about the complex legal questions involved in the controversy.

Becket, Thomas. *The Correspondence of Thomas Becket: Archbishop of Canterbury, 1162-1170*. Edited by Anne J. Duggan. New York: Oxford University Press, 2000. A collection of Becket's letters. Includes a bibliography and an index.

Duggan, Alfred. *Thomas Becket of Canterbury*. London: Faber, 1967. A critical account of Becket's life and death based on close familiarity with the sources.

Fitz Stephen, William. *The Life and Death of Thomas Becket*. Edited by George W. Greenway. London: Folio Society, 1961. A collection of data on Becket's life and death arranged chronologically and with editor's explanatory comments.

Ide, Arthur Frederick. *Calendar of Death*. Irving, Tex.: Scholar Books, 1986. A brief study of the sociopolitical factors in Becket's attitude toward his own eminent death.

Knowles, David. *The Episcopal Colleagues of Archbishop Thomas Becket*. Cambridge, England: Cambridge University Press, 1951. Written by the author of several distinguished studies of Becket, this work contains an excellent account of the events of Northampton.

Pain, Nesta. *The King and Becket*. New York: Barnes & Noble Books, 1966. A compelling and well-documented study that takes a negative view of Becket.

Staunton, Michael, trans. *The Lives of Thomas Becket*. New York: Palgrave, 2001. A biographical look at Becket. Part of the Manchester Medieval Sources series. Includes a bibliography and an index.

Winston, Richard. *Thomas Becket*. New York: Alfred A. Knopf, 1967. A balanced, equitable, and readable study of Becket that is sensitive to the virtues as well as the flaws of both Becket and Henry.

See also: March 21, 1098: Foundation of the Cistercian Order; 1169-1172: Normans Invade Ireland; 1387-1400: Chaucer Writes *The Canterbury Tales*.

Related articles in *Great Lives from History: The Middle Ages, 477-1453*: Alexander III; Saint Anselm; Saint Thomas Becket; Geoffrey Chaucer; Eleanor of Aquitaine; Henry II.

1175
Hōnen Shōnin Founds Pure Land Buddhism

In 1175, the monk Hōnen Shōnin, discouraged by the worldly and political concerns of the Buddhist establishment, began to spread a more basic, popular philosophy in the form of the teachings of Pure Land Buddhism. This sect established the basis for what is now the most widespread form of Buddhist belief in Japan.

Locale: Kyoto, Japan

Categories: Religion; cultural and intellectual history

Key Figures

Hōnen Shōnin (1133-1212), Buddhist monk, founder of the Pure Land sect

Shinran (1173-1263), Buddhist monk, founder of the True Pure Land sect

Summary of Event

The twelfth century in Japan was a period of great strife but also of vitality in religious and cultural movements. One of the most significant developments to take place in this century was the founding of the Pure Land (Jōdo) sect of Japanese Buddhism by the priest Hōnen Shōnin in 1175. Hōnen, originally a member of the warrior aristocracy, was born into a samurai family in the province of Mimasaka (now Okayama Prefecture) in 1133. From the age of eight, he began to study Buddhist doctrine and became a monk of the Tendai sect. He studied at the headquarters of the Tendai sect, the Enryakuji temple complex located on sacred Mount Hiei to the north of Kyoto, and became a full-fledged monk of the order at the age of fifteen. This life path was not an unusual one for the younger sons of warrior families, but Hōnen's future career as both a scholar and a monk was quite unique.

The mid-twelfth century was an era of considerable political maneuvering at the Japanese court. An upstart provincial samurai family, the Taira, was able to gain influence over the imperial court and the traditional aristocracy. The Buddhist sects had their own political interests and conflicts, and Hōnen, disgusted by the increasingly political concerns of the Hiei monks, fled the monastery in favor of life as an ascetic on another part of the mountain. He continued his study of the Tendai doctrines as well as those of the other Japanese Buddhist sects but found that none of them were capable of fulfilling him spiritually. The Pure Land teachings, however, began to interest him and eventually became his exclusive subject of study and contemplation.

Pure Land Buddhist teachings centering on the Buddha Amida were brought to Japan in the sixth century and enjoyed great popularity among the aristocratic classes in the ninth and tenth centuries. The Pure Land doctrine states that the Buddha Amida pledged to deliver to the Pure Land, a paradise in the west, any believer who sincerely called his name. In Japanese, the practice of calling on Amida is referred to as *nembutsu*. The ease of salvation promised in the Pure Land teachings as well as the assurance of a better life in the next world were very attractive to a court society convinced of the fundamental transience of life.

Before Hōnen, several other famous monks had become interested in Pure Land teachings. For example, Kūya (903-972), a monk from the same Enryakuji temple complex at which Hōnen himself studied, wandered Japan teaching the value of evoking the name of Amida to the common people in the late tenth century. The peasants, frequently threatened by famine and disease, showed great interest in the transcendental philosophy associated with Amida. Despite these moments of popularity, however, the Pure Land doctrine failed to gain independence from the doctrines of other sects such as Tendai and continued to exist merely as an offshoot of other teachings.

Convinced that *nembutsu* was the path to salvation, Hōnen left the confines of Mount Hiei in 1175 and began to preach these ideas in the capital. He established a base in Kyoto at Yoshimizu, where Chionin, the main temple of the sect, now stands. This act is usually considered to be the founding of the Pure Land sect as an independent sect of Buddhism in Japan. It is recorded that Japanese of all walks of life came to listen to Hōnen's sermons. The movement that Hōnen began rapidly gained momentum, and in 1198, Hōnen wrote the *Senchaku hongan nembutsu-shū* (1198; English translation, 1997; also known as *The Selection of the Nembutsu in the Original Vow*) in which he spelled out the doctrines of the new faith and defended them against his critics. His assertion that a saintly life was no longer possible because of the corruption of the world and that the only path to salvation was through faith in the Buddha Amida found a ready audience. He also denied the idea that severe asceticism was a desirable path to religious enlightenment, a fact that made his ideas very popular.

Despite Hōnen's warm reception in Kyoto, his ideas, as well as the popularity that they were gaining, were met with hostility from the authorities. The Buddhist establishment, concerned that Hōnen's popular doctrines and denial of the superiority of monastic living would erode their own power base, began to persecute him. The fact that Hōnen not only argued the value of *nembutsu* but also asserted that the practice was far superior to all other forms of religious experience made him fall afoul of the conservative establishment. This was also the period in which the new Minamoto shogunate was attempting to assert its control over the country, and a new, mass-based religious movement was seen as a potential threat.

As a result, in 1207, Hōnen was exiled to Tosa, a remote region of the island of Shikoku, and his disciples, among them the monk Shinran, were persecuted. Hōnen, whose long religious practice had obviously brought him a broad perspective and a lack of worldly ambition, refused to renounce his religious convictions to avoid exile; instead, he said he was thankful, as it afforded him a chance to spread his teachings outside the capital. Hōnen continued to work toward the spread of the Pure Land belief during his exile. His sentence was lifted in 1211, but he died the following year. This period of persecution, however, did little to sap the vitality of the new sect, and it is clear that Hōnen laid the basis for a truly popular religious movement.

SIGNIFICANCE

After Hōnen's death his evangelical movement was continued by his disciples, who preached the practice of *nembutsu* throughout the country. The Pure Land sect of Japanese Buddhism was the first of many new Buddhist sects to be developed in the twelfth and thirteenth centuries. Its emergence marked the increasingly vital religious thought of that age and provided an impetus for the development of new ways of thinking. The Pure Land sect and its offshoot, the True Pure Land sect (Jōdo Shinshū), founded by Hōnen's disciple Shinran, became two of the most popular forms of religious worship in Japan. They developed a large following, among not only the masses but also the court nobility and warrior class. The simple teaching of the Pure Land sect meshed well with the temperament of the samurai and was easily accessible to the largely illiterate peasant class.

By the fifteenth century, methods of training monks and various rituals were systemized and received government approval, and the Pure Land sect continued to develop at a fast pace while never losing its popular base. The sect also proved to be a great creative force as it inspired depictions of Amida in art and sculpture, many of which are now hailed as national treasures, as well as changes in temple architecture.

Although the Zen sects of Japanese Buddhism are most often seen as the face of Japanese religion internationally, the Pure Land sect has enjoyed international popularity as well. Outside Japan, there are Pure Land believers in the United States, Canada, and dozens of other nations around the world. The simplicity and accessibility of the Pure Land doctrine as outlined by Hōnen as well as its tolerance and lack of a distinctly Japanese-centered perspective has resulted in Pure Land teachings becoming popular all over the globe.

—*Matthew Penney*

Further Reading

Hattori, Sho-on. *A Raft from the Other Shore: Hōnen and the Way of Pure Land Buddhism.* Tokyo: Jōdo Shū Press, 2001. A basic outline of the life of Hōnen and his teachings.

Hōnen. *Hōnen's Senchakushu: Passages on the Selection of the Nembutsu in the Original Vow.* Translated by Hirokawa Takatoshi. Honolulu: University of Hawaii Press, 1998. A translation of Hōnen's major work.

Sansom, George. *A History of Japan to 1334.* Vol. 1. Stanford, Calif.: Stanford University Press, 1958. The first volume of Sansom's three-volume study of Japanese history remains a detailed and authoritative work on the subject.

Tamura, Yoshio. *Japanese Buddhism: A Cultural History.* Translated by Jeffrey Hunter. Tokyo: Tuttle, 2001. A detailed assessment of the cultural implications and historical development of Japanese Buddhism from the introduction of the faith to modern times.

See also: 538-552: Buddhism Arrives in Japan; 607-839: Japan Sends Embassies to China.

Related articles in *Great Lives from History: The Middle Ages, 477-1453*: Kōbō Daishi; Nichiren.

c. 1175
Waldensian Excommunications Usher in Protestant Movement

The excommunication of the Waldensians from the medieval Catholic Church for preaching heretical beliefs is considered one of the marks of the beginning of the Protestant movement in Europe.

Locale: Lyons, France; Piedmont, Italy; and Europe generally

Categories: Religion; social reform

Key Figures

Peter Waldo (d. 1217), French religious leader banished from Lyons in 1184, advocate of ecclesiastical reforms

Peter II (1174-1213), king of Aragon and Catalonia, r. 1196-1213, who issued the death-by-burning edict of 1197

Summary of Event

The first Waldensians advocated a return to the simple type of Christianity reflected in the Gospels, unencumbered with ecclesiastical organization or hierarchical structure. They named themselves possibly after Peter Waldo, a rich merchant of Lyons who in 1175 or 1176 decided to distribute his wealth to the poor and also established a lay order known as the Poor Men of Lyons. Other origins of the name Waldensians suggest Vaux, or valleys of Piedmont, where the sect flourished; or Peter of Vaux, a predecessor of Waldo.

According to early accounts, Peter Waldo, after hearing of the Gospels, asked two priests to translate them into everyday language for him. He immersed himself in these translations and resolved to follow the teachings of Christ he found there in a literal fashion. He sold his property, gave the proceeds to the poor, and began begging in the streets. Soon he was joined by many of the uneducated and unlettered poor of Lyons. From this group of followers, the lay order of The Poor Men of Lyons was established. The requirements for admission to the order were "conversion," accompanied by a turning away from worldly pursuits; divesting self of personal property and vocation, along with the dissolution of any existing marriage; and unquestioned submission to the superiors in the order. Training consisted of memorization of the entire New Testament and many of the writings of the saints.

At first Peter Waldo's personal program consisted primarily of living a life of poverty, but as he became better acquainted with the Bible in the vernacular he began publicly to elucidate the Scriptures. In addition, his followers openly criticized the immorality of the clergy and their frequent indifference to Christian precepts. Although Waldo's activities, and those of his followers, were not heretical, it was contrary to the Canon Law of the Church and established practice for lay persons to preach. At the Third Lateran Council (1179), The Poor Men of Lyons sought and received authorization for their vow of poverty and were given permission to preach provided they received authorization from local Church authorities. When the Poor Men found it difficult to obtain such authorization—because they were found by the council to be unacquainted with even the most basic teachings of the Church—they ignored the council's restriction by expounding the Scriptures openly in the towns. At the Council of Verona in 1184, they were condemned along with the Albigensians and expelled from Lyons. They fled to Spain, Lombardy, the Rhineland, Bohemia, Hungary, and northern France; but as they went they came into contact with more radical heretical groups who influenced them into adopting more extreme unorthodox tenets.

As opposed to the Church, the Waldensians denied the existence of purgatory and denied the efficacy of indulgences and prayers for the dead. They held that private prayer (praying in a closet) is preferable to praying in a church. From the beginning, they especially stressed the need to make the Scriptures in the vernacular available to the laity—rather than to reserve them for the priesthood. Lying was considered an especially grievous sin, and they forbade the shedding of blood and the taking of oaths. In an age when society was bound together by a system of feudal oaths, this prohibition was considered deleterious to the social order. Furthermore, they condemned war and capital punishment. From preaching and expounding the Scriptures, it was an easy transition to hearing confessions, absolving sins, and assigning penances. At the Council of Verona (1184), they were accused of refusing obedience to the clergy, usurping the right of preaching, and opposing the validity of masses for the dead. Although the Waldensians did not espouse any significant doctoral aberration, they opposed the entire sacerdotal system, declaring that the authority to exercise priestly functions was derived not from ordination but from individual merit and piety.

In the thirteenth century, Peter Waldo led a group into upper Italy, where the sect named for him flourished in the Lombard climate of revolt and anticlericalism. (Hulton|Archive by Getty Images)

In Spain in 1194, an edict was issued allowing the confiscation of the property of all who gave food and shelter to the Waldensians. In 1197, Peter II amended this edict to include the burning of Waldensians wherever they were found. This edict was the first public document in which death by burning was prescribed as the state punishment for heresy.

By the early 1300's, the Waldensians were in such conflict with the Church that they had become a secret organization. They divided themselves into two classes, the "perfect" or *perfecti*, and the "believers" or *credentes*. Only the male descendants of the original believers—women were no longer admitted to the order—were eligible to become members. The celibate *perfecti*, having spent five or six years in study, were ordained as deacons and then required to spend as much as nine years more in theological study. They were bound by the vow of poverty, led an itinerant life of preaching, and, being exempt from manual labor, depended on the *credentes* for their support. The latter group continued to live in the world as others, even receiving the sacraments, except penance, administered by Waldensian bishops. The *perfecti* were further classified as bishops, priests, and deacons. Bishops celebrated the Eucharist and administered penance and ordination, priests preached and heard confessions, and deacons received alms and administered the temporal affairs of the church. Bishops were elected at joint meetings of priests and deacons. One bishop, the rector, seems to have enjoyed supervision over the others, but the supreme governing power was vested in a council of all the *perfecti*.

After their condemnation by Pope Lucius III at Verona, the Waldensians scattered. Waldo led a group into upper Italy, where the sect flourished in the Lombard climate of revolt and anticlericalism. As sporadic persecutions arose, however, they were gradually driven into the rugged valleys of the Piedmontese Alps. A dispute arose between the Italian and French factions in which the former, led by Waldo, rejected hierarchical organization, manual labor of the preachers, and moral requirements for one celebrating the Eucharist. The dispute reached such proportions that a majority of the sect repudiated Waldo's leadership and followed his chief opponent, Joannes de Roncho. It appears that Waldo and the French group favored a reconciliation with Rome, whereas the Italians supported the idea of a separate organization consciously opposed to Rome.

Waldo left Piedmont and, according to tradition, traveled through Italy for some time and finally went to Bohemia, where he died in 1217. The dispute was resolved at the Council of Bergamo, a city in Lombardy, in 1218, attended by delegates from several countries.

During the thirteenth and fourteenth centuries, the center of Waldensianism shifted to Milan, where the chief bishop resided and a theological school was established. Each year during Lent, a council was held attended by delegates from every nation that had an organized Waldensian church.

SIGNIFICANCE

Although harassed by numerous persecutions, the Waldensians persisted. In Bohemia, they paved the way for Jan Hus, in Switzerland for Calvin, and in France, they eventually merged with the Calvinists in the seventeenth century. The Waldensian church is considered by some to be the oldest Protestant church in existence.

—*Carl A. Volz, updated by Barbara C. Stanley*

FURTHER READING

Biller, Peter. *The Waldenses, 1170-1530: Between a Religious Order and a Church*. Burlington, Vt.: Variorum, 2001. A study of the Waldensians focusing on their beliefs and institutions.

Clot, Alberto. "Waldenses." In *The New Schaff-Herzog Encyclopedia of Religious Knowledge*. Vol. 12. Grand Rapids, Mich.: Baker Book House, 1969. Detailed history of Waldensianism, describing its place in medieval Church history and its spread to other countries in both hemispheres. Includes an extensive annotated bibliography.

Coulton, G. G. *Inquisition and Liberty*. Boston: Beacon Press, 1959. Chapters 16 and 17 detail the methodology and history of the Church's efforts to root out heresy.

Dossat, Y. "Waldenses." In *New Catholic Encyclopedia*. Vol. 4. New York: McGraw-Hill, 1967. An article maintaining that contempt for the power of the Church was the basis of the heresy.

Leff, Gordon. "Waldensians." In *The Encyclopedia of Religion*. Vol. 15. New York: Macmillan, 1987. An article setting out the historical chronology of the Waldensian movement, its belief system (biblical foundation and basic tenets), and its descent into heresy.

Shahar, Shulamith. *Women in a Medieval Heretical Sect: Agnes and Huguette the Waldensians*. Translated by Yael Lotan. Rochester, N.Y.: Boydell Press, 2001. A study that uses the story of two Waldensian women burned at the stake in 1319 to draw broader conclusions about the role of women within the sect.

Stephens, Prescot. *The Waldensian Story: A Study in Faith, Intolerance, and Survival.* Lewes, Sussex, England: Book Guild, 1998. An exploration of the trials and travails of Peter Waldo and his followers.

SEE ALSO: March 21, 1098: Foundation of the Cistercian Order; 1209-1229: Albigensian Crusade; April 16, 1209: Founding of the Franciscans; July 2, 1324: Lady Alice Kyteler Is Found Guilty of Witchcraft; 1377-1378: Condemnation of John Wyclif; 1414-1418: Council of Constance; July 6, 1415: Martyrdom of Jan Hus.

RELATED ARTICLES in *Great Lives from History: The Middle Ages, 477-1453*: Alexander III; Saint Anthony of Padua; Saint Dominic; Jan Hus; Innocent III; Alice Kyteler; Marguerite Porete; William of Saint-Amour; John Wyclif.

c. 1180
CHRÉTIEN DE TROYES WRITES *PERCEVAL*

Chrétien de Troyes wrote the Arthurian romance Perceval, *which set the stage for the creation of subsequent literary and other artistic works centered on myth, romance, fantasy, legend, and adventure.*

LOCALE: Alsace
CATEGORY: Literature

KEY FIGURE

Chrétien de Troyes (c. 1150-c. 1190), author of five Arthurian verse romances

SUMMARY OF EVENT

Not much is known about Chrétien de Troyes except for what is recorded in his works. He was evidently well-educated and must have been a cleric. Chrétien's early works were produced under the patronage of Marie de Champagne, the wife of Henry II and the daughter of Eleanor of Aquitaine and Louis VII. His last work, which remained incomplete, was *Perceval* (English translation, 1844), produced under the patronage of Philip of Flanders, count of Alsace.

The twelfth century was the era when French clerics began writing extensively in the vernacular rather than Latin, giving permanent form to the popular culture of the period. Chrétien approached this task self-consciously; the prologue to his first Arthurian romance, *Erec et Enide* (c. 1164; *Erec and Enide*, 1913), states his intention to improve on traditional storytelling by equipping his story with a better narrative structure. In doing so he laid new foundations for the newly emergent genre of romance, which was to make the leap from verse to prose in its thirteenth century heyday.

The literary sophistication of Chrétien's work increased in his later endeavors, which demonstrated a keen sense of irony and a regretfully ambivalent attitude to the chivalric code that supplied the justificatory ideology of feudalism. *Perceval*'s prologue—devoted, as convention demanded, to singing the praises of the work's patron—elects to do so by commenting on the relationship between a poet and his audience, drawing on the parable of the sower in the gospels (see Matthew 13:3-22). Chrétien likens himself to the sower casting seed on fertile ground provided by his generous patron—but in the parable, the seed is nothing less than the word of God, and much of it falls on stony ground or among weeds, so the argument is both more ambitious and more anxious than it pretends.

Perceval is a poor widow's son living in the Waste Forest (possibly in present-day Wales or Scotland), whose life is transformed following a meeting with a company of knights. They introduce him to the idea of chivalry, which his mother had concealed from him, along with his noble ancestry. Inspired by his dream, but having little understanding of the chivalric ideal, he sets off to find King Arthur and reclaim his proper place in the world. He finds Arthur's court in a dire state, and the king deeply unhappy, but he presses forward with his ambition, not realizing that every step he takes reveals his foolishness and complete ignorance of the principles of knightly behavior.

Perceval obtains the rudiments of an education in chivalry from Gornemont de Goort, which enables him to acquit himself reasonably well in taking up the cause of the beautiful Blancheflor of Beaurepaire. However, when he is offered lordship over Beaurepaire, he recalls his churlish treatment of his mother and sets out to make amends. The narrative enters its most famous and interesting phase when he seems to enter a curious parallel world, where the wounded Fisher King invites him to a magical castle. There he is gifted with a sword and witnesses a strange procession bearing a bleeding lance and a grail; he yearns to ask what it all means, but he takes Gornemont's advice far too literally and politely refuses to ask, thus creating a puzzle that has fascinated countless readers.

The remainder of the text is confusing. Although his mother is dead, Perceval begins redeeming some of his other past errors. He falls into a curious trance at the sight of three drops of blood on a field of snow but is roused by Gawain, who persuades him to return to Arthur's court, where a "hideous damsel" arrives to reproach him for having left the Grail Castle, whose people are dying and whose surrounding lands have been laid to waste in consequence. The damsel offers Arthur's knights a series of potentially redemptive quests, which are selected by various candidates, the search for the grail being left to Perceval. Instead of following Perceval, however, the text veers off to describe the markedly different and far less intriguing exploits of Gawain, a familiar figure in Arthurian legend, who had appeared as a model of chivalric virtue in Chrétien's earlier romances.

Although Gawain's exploits echo Perceval's in some respects, they are relentlessly mundane; they are, however, arbitrarily interrupted by a sequence in which Perceval, five years after his departure—during which time he has had many adventures but has not found his way back to the Grail Castle—makes a confession to a hermit, who interprets the failure of his quest as the result of a sin whose nature he has failed to comprehend. Gawain's story, like Perceval's, eventually breaks off, leaving such abundant scope for speculation as to what might have happened thereafter that the majority of surviving manuscripts include various "continuations" by an assortment of later writers, most of which are only tenuously connected to the original.

The evidence of appearances strongly suggests that Chrétien died before completing the poem constituting the first 4,815 lines of *Perceval*, which he would otherwise have brought to a conclusion befitting his commitment to good narrative structure. The adventures of Gawain—possibly by another writer—were presumably added to all the surviving manuscripts because of the interpolation featuring Perceval and the hermit, in exactly the same spirit that other "continuations" were also added to all but a few of the extant versions. The hermit episode—which clearly does not belong to the story it interrupts—is probably the first of countless attempts by later writers to figure out the significance of Perceval's visionary adventure in the Grail Castle.

Perceval differs from Chrétien's earlier works in its use of allegorical symbolism and also in affording considerable importance to prayer. This is unusual, in that one of the attractions of writing vernacular romance was that it allowed clerics some relaxation from the duties of piety and the archaic methods of religious allegory. Many later writers, including the author of the hermit episode, further increased the religious element in their interpretations of the grail episode, especially those who proposed that the grail was the cup that had collected Christ's blood during the crucifixion (the bleeding lance thus becoming the one that pierced his side). There is no evidence for this in the text, and Chrétien seems to have been far more dubious about the ideologies, pretensions, and myths supporting the crusades than many of his contemporaries and successors.

Chrétien's prologue claims that the story of *Perceval* is derived from a text supplied by his patron, but such acknowledgments were customary and no prior text survives that could have served as a model. Chrétien may well have invented the grail, although any scholar who believes that Arthurian mythology originated in Celtic folklore rather than being invented by such Norman chroniclers as Geoffrey of Monmouth have searched long and hard for evidence of a Welsh original for Perceval and a Celtic pagan grail. Versions of the story reproduced in the *White Book of Rhydderch* (c. 1300-1325) and the *Red Book of Hergest* (c. 1375-1425) are, however, more likely to be adaptations than separate versions of a common original.

Significance

Perceval's seed fell on very fertile ground, giving form to a myth that was to become astonishingly popular and pervasive, echoing through all the literary genres descended from French Medieval romance, inspiring countless scholarly fantasies and lifestyle fantasies as well as literary works and other media. Perceval's story was reproduced and elaborated in German by Wolfram von Eschenbach's *Parzival* (c. 1220), which inspired many later works, including Richard Wagner's opera *Parsifal* (1882). More significantly, it was integrated into Thomas Malory's *Le Morte d'Arthur* (1485), which became the most important sourcebook of subsequent Arthurian romance and of twentieth century Anglo-American fantastic fiction.

—Brian Stableford

Further Reading

Busby, Keith. *Chrétien de Troyes: Perceval (Le conte du Graal)*. London: Grant and Cutler, 1993. A commentary concentrating on parallels between the adventures of Perceval and Gawain.

Cazelles, Brigitte. *The Unholy Grail: A Social Reading of Chrétien de Troyes's "Conte du Graal."* Stanford, Calif.: Stanford University Press, 1996. Interprets the story of Perceval as a veiled account of a historical crisis in feudal society, in which the "revised chivalry" symbolized by the grail is part of the problem rather than the answer.

Fowler, David C. *Prowess and Charity in the Perceval of Chrétien de Troyes.* Seattle: University of Washington Press, 1959. Interprets the intended meaning of the poem as an inner "conflict of ideals."

Kelly, Douglas. *Chrétien de Troyes: An Analytic Bibliography.* Rochester, N.Y.: Tamesis, 2002. This volume is an indispensable reference tool, and it includes an index.

Loomis, Roger Sherman. *Arthurian Tradition and Chrétien de Troyes.* New York: Columbia University Press, 1949. A detailed argument supporting the case that the substance of Arthurian mythology is Welsh in origin. Book V searches for Celtic foundations for *Perceval.*

Uitti, Karl D., and Michelle A. Freeman. *Chrétien de Troyes Revisited.* New York: Twayne, 1995. An overview of Chrétien's literary work. Examines *Perceval* as a continuation of themes introduced in the earlier romances.

Weston, Jessie L. *From Ritual to Romance.* London: Cambridge University Press, 1920. A scholarly fantasy applying the theories of James Frazer's *The Golden Bough* (1890) to Chrétien's symbolism, important as the inspiration of T. S. Eliot's *The Waste Land* (1922) and other twentieth century literary works.

SEE ALSO: c. 1100: Rise of Courtly Love.

RELATED ARTICLES in *Great Lives from History: The Middle Ages, 477-1453*: Geoffrey Chaucer; Chrétien de Troyes; Edward III; Jean Froissart; Geoffrey of Monmouth; Hartmann von Aue; Henry II; Marie de France; Wolfram von Eschenbach.

c. 1181-1221
LALIBELA FOUNDS THE CHRISTIAN CAPITAL OF ETHIOPIA

Lalibela, the most illustrious of the Zagwe rulers who came to power in Ethiopia after the fall of the Aksumite kingdom, established his capital at the site that now carries his name and embarked on the construction of the famous rock-hewn churches that are wonders of the medieval world.

LOCALE: Roha, Adefa (now Lalibela in Lasta province, Ethiopia)

CATEGORIES: Architecture; government and politics

KEY FIGURES

Dil Naʿad (d. c. 1137), last in the line of Aksum rulers, r. c. twelfth century

Mara Tekle Haimanot (d. 1152), founder of the Zagwe Dynasty, r. 1137-1152

Lalibela (c. mid-twelfth century-c. 1221), Zagwe ruler, r. c. 1181-c. 1221

Yimrehane-Kristos (fl. twelfth century), third Zagwe king, revived the tradition of building rock-hewn churches, r. twelfth century

Naʿakuto Laʿab (d. 1268), Lalibela's nephew and successor, r. c. 1221-1260

Yitbarek (d. 1268), Lalibela's son and last Zagwe king, r. 1260-1268

SUMMARY OF EVENT

The last two centuries of the first millennium saw the gradual decline of the Christian kingdom of Aksum (northern Ethiopia) caused by the expansion of Muslim power in the Red Sea region. Aksumite prosperity was mainly based on its political hegemony over both sides of the Red Sea and extensive participation in the eastern and Mediterranean trade. The growth of Arab power under Umayyad and ʿAbbāsid rulers challenged Aksum's dominant position in the region. Cut off from its lucrative seaborne commercial networks, the Aksumite state entered into a period of economic stagnation and political disintegration.

In 1137, Dil Naʿad, the last Aksumite king, was overthrown by Mara Tekle Haimanot, an Agaw vassal prince from Lasta who founded a dynasty known in Ethiopian history as the Zagwe. The Zagwe rulers moved the seat of power to their home district in Bugna, in the province of Lasta. Assimilation to the Aksumite culture and the process of Christianization was so far advanced by then that the new rulers, who belonged to the Agaw ethnic group (distinct from the Semiticized Aksumites), continued the Aksumite legacy and reaffirmed the Ethiopianization of the state rather than depart from tradition. The new rulers incorporated more areas in the south to the Ethiopian state and reinvigorated Christianity by sponsoring the spread of the Ethiopian Orthodox Church among diverse groups of peoples in central and southern Ethiopia.

Among the most noteworthy achievements of the Zagwe period are the complex monolithic rock-hewn churches built by successive rulers. Although the art of carving churches out of solid mass of rock is an old Aksumite technique, it reached an extraordinary level during this period. The first major project was undertaken by the priest-king Yimrehane-Kristos, who commissioned the building of one of the most impressive and artfully decorated rock-hewn churches in the world. Some 12 miles (19 kilometers) from this church is a vast complex of eleven rock-cut churches that are described as the most incredible sights on the African continent. Most of these churches are attributed to King Lalibela.

Lalibela, the most famous of the Zagwe kings, inaugurated a period of imperial expansion and considerable literary and architectural revival. He carried out successful campaigns designed to consolidate imperial control over northern Ethiopia, including the highlands of what is now called Eritrea, and to subdue the still predominantly non-Christian regions farther south. Lalibela's reign saw the revival of foreign trade, especially through the port of Zeila in the east. Lalibela also pursued an active foreign policy, including developing good relations with Saladin in order to ensure the continuity of relations between the Ethiopian Church and the Egyptian Coptic Church and to protect Ethiopian Christians in Jerusalem. Lalibela's success in consolidating the Ethiopian state at home and his vigorous foreign policy appear to have provided the inspiration for the spread of the European myth of the legend of the Prester John.

Lalibela is most remembered as the inspired genius who built the great complex of rock-hewn churches in Roha (now Lalibela) that, according to traditional accounts, were designed to replicate Jerusalem. The eleven edifices attributed to Lalibela are all sculpted inside and out from solid volcanic rock and are interconnected by a maze of long underground tunnels and passages. Each building is architecturally unique and sumptuously decorated with a variety of paintings. Some of the buildings have immense columns. The most impressive and the largest of this complex is the Bete Medhane Alem (the Church of Our Savior), which measures 10.5 feet in length, 7 feet in width, and 3.5 feet in height (33.5 meters by 23.5 meters by 11 meters). This rectangular edifice that resembles a Greek temple is surrounded by thirty-two external colonnades. The other fascinating structure is the Bete Giyorgis (Church of Saint George), which is built in the shape of a cross from a great block of rock.

These architectural wonders have fascinated many visitors throughout the ages. Francisco Alvarez, a Jesuit priest and a member of the Portuguese mission to Ethiopia who visited the site in the sixteenth century, wrote in *The Prester John of the Indies* that the likes of such buildings "cannot, as it appears to me, be found in the world." He further wrote, "I weary of writing more about these buildings, because it seems to me that I shall not be believed if I write more."

Ethiopian legend claims that Lalibela was miraculously flown to Jerusalem, where Christ appeared to him and instructed him to build a second Jerusalem in Ethiopia.

Ethiopian Christians consider the site as the new Holy Land that was intended to replace Jerusalem, which was lost to the Muslims, as a pilgrimage center. The *Gadla Lalibela* (the hagiography of Lalibela) claims that visiting these churches is like seeing the face of Christ. Several landmarks in the area are given biblical names. The local stream that flows through the site is named the Jordan River, and the nearby mountain is called Mount Tabor. One of the eleven churches that houses the tomb of Lalibela is called Golgotha.

In spite of these accomplishments, the Zagwe hold over the Ethiopian Empire remained precarious. The Zagwe rulers were unable to remove the stigma that they were usurpers who had snatched power from the lawful rulers of the Aksumite line. Although they were the greatest patrons of the Ethiopian Church and produced three kings, including Lalibela, who were canonized as saints, the widespread perception that they were illegitimate persisted, especially in northern Ethiopia. This bias was later exploited skillfully by their rivals.

The main weakness of this dynasty, however, lay in its failure to institutionalize a smooth and effective system of succession. The Zagwe rulers seem to have regarded the state as a family property, and the death of a Zagwe king was followed by fierce scramble for power within the royal family.

The problem grew more acute after Lalibela's reign, when succession was bitterly contested between his son Yitbarek and his nephew Naʿakuto Laʿab. This internal feud aided the anti-Zagwe movement centered in the

Amhara region, a movement that was building momentum by the middle of the thirteenth century. In 1270, the last Zagwe ruler, Yitbarek, was overthrown by Yekuno Amlak, a prince from the Amhara area who claimed descent from the old Aksumite line of rulers and established what is known as the Solomonid Dynasty.

SIGNIFICANCE

King Lalibela and the other Zagwe rulers came to power at a crucial moment in Ethiopian history. By providing an alternative leadership in the south they ensured the survival of the Ethiopian state after the collapse of the old Aksumite political order. Zagwe rulers adopted the Aksumite political, literary, religious, and architectural traditions and spread them further to the south, thereby providing a common and enduring reference to the diverse communities that constituted the Ethiopian state.

Also, Lalibela's great architectural monuments and the myth that developed around them continue to be revered by the followers of the Ethiopian Church and visitors to the region.

—*Shumet Sishagne*

FURTHER READING

Alvarez, Francisco. *The Prester John of the Indies*. Translated by C. F. Beckingham and G. W. B. Huntingford. Cambridge, England: Cambridge University Press, 1961. An interesting eyewitness account of a sixteenth century Portuguese traveler in Ethiopia.

Connery, William S. "The Second Zion—The Wonder of Ethiopia's Lalibela." *World and I* 16 (August, 2001). A concise article that outlines the historical background to the construction of the Lalibela churches and provides a short description of the monolithic complex.

Gerster, Georg. *Churches in Rock: Early Christian Art in Ethiopia*. New York: Praeger, 1970. A useful account of the tradition of building rock-hewn churches in Ethiopia. The book contains some of the best pictures of the Lalibela churches ever published.

Heldman, Marilyn. "Legends of Lalibela: The Development of an Ethiopian Pilgrimage Site." *Res* 27 (Spring, 1995). A modern art historian's view of the legends associated with the building of the Lalibela monolithic churches and their place in Ethiopian national myth.

Henze, Paul B. *Layers of Time: A History of Ethiopia*. New York: Palgrave, 2000. A readable general work that is especially useful in tracing the history of the country's expansion southward during medieval times under the leadership of a series of capable Solomonid rulers. It also includes interesting information on daily life, art, architecture, religion, culture, and customs.

Munro-Hay, Stuart. *Ethiopia, the Unknown Land: A Cultural and Historical Guide*. London: I. B. Tauris, 2002. A well-researched, comprehensive, and up-to-date description of the major historical landmarks in Ethiopia.

Sergew Hable Sellassie. *Ancient and Medieval Ethiopian History to 1270*. Addis Ababa, Ethiopia: Addis Ababa University, 1972. A survey of Ethiopian history from the earliest times to the medieval period based on extensive use of primary sources.

Taddesse Tamrat. *Church and State in Ethiopia, 1270-1527*. Oxford, England: Oxford University Press, 1972. An authoritative work by one of the foremost historians of medieval Ethiopia. Contains useful information on the transition of power from the Zagwe to the new Solomonid Dynasty.

SEE ALSO: 685-691: Building of the Dome of the Rock; 12th century: Coins Are Minted on the Swahili Coast; c. 1145: Prester John Myth Sweeps Across Europe; 1270-1285: Yekuno Amlak Founds the Solomonid Dynasty.

RELATED ARTICLES in *Great Lives from History: The Middle Ages, 477-1453*: ʿAbd al-Malik; Ibn Baṭṭūṭah; Ibn Khaldūn; al-Idrīsī; Damia al-Kāhina; Mansa Mūsā; Saladin; Sundiata; Ṭāriq ibn-Ziyād.

1189-1192
THIRD CRUSADE

The Third Crusade failed to secure European control of Jerusalem but strengthened Western presence in the Middle East for generations through the acquisition of Acre and Cyprus.

LOCALE: Anatolia, Cyprus, and Palestine
CATEGORIES: Religion; wars, uprisings, and civil unrest

KEY FIGURES

Saladin (1138-1193), sultan of Egypt and Syria, founder of the Ayyūbid Dynasty
Gregory VIII (d. 1187), Roman Catholic pope, 1187, preached the Third Crusade
Frederick I Barbarossa (c. 1123-1190), Holy Roman Emperor, r. 1152-1190, and leader of the Third Crusade
Philip II (1165-1223), king of France, r. 1179-1223, leader of the Third Crusade
Richard I (1157-1199), king of England, r. 1189-1199, leader of the Third Crusade
Berengaria (1165-1230), queen of Richard I, king of England
Leopold V (1157-1194), duke of Austria, 1177-1194, adversary of Richard I

SUMMARY OF EVENT

Between 1096 and 1464, some nine or ten Crusades started from the West to attempt to regain control of the Holy Land. There was a Peasants' Crusade (1096-1097), a Barons' Crusade (1096-1204), and a Children's Crusade (1212), but one of the most colorful was the Crusade of the Three Kings (1189-1192), also known as the Third Crusade.

The Third Crusade was occasioned by the rise of the Muslim warrior Saladin. Born in Mesopotamia, Saladin became sultan in Egypt and Syria (after 1174), founding the famed Ayyūbid Dynasty (1169-1250). Determined to expel the Crusaders from the East, Saladin took Acre, Nazareth, and, finally, Jerusalem itself on October 2, 1187. Pope Gregory VIII, who was pontiff for only one year, called for a holy war to redeem Jerusalem. To his appeal, three famed kings responded.

The first of these kings was Frederick I Barbarossa, scion of the house of Hohenstaufen from Swabia, who was known for restoring peace and prosperity to his realm. As a youth, Frederick had served with the Second Crusade in 1147. Now, as a man nearing seventy, he desired once more to "take up the cross." In spite of his previous quarrels with the papacy, Frederick was reconciled to Rome and received favorably the papal legation asking him to march east. Well aware of the dangers he faced, Frederick gathered the largest crusading army yet assembled, a well-disciplined force that left Germany in May, 1189. The army peacefully crossed Hungary but encountered hostility near Bulgaria.

Frederick promptly proposed to the pope that the Crusade be redefined to target both Constantinople and Jerusalem. The Byzantine emperor quickly became more compliant. After wintering in Adrianople, Frederick avoided Constantinople, and in March, 1190, crossed the Hellespont into Anatolia. By May, the Germans had defeated the Seljuk Turks in Iconium, and the land route to Jerusalem was open. On June 10, 1190, while Frederick crossed the Calycadnus (Saleph) River in Cilicia (now Turkey), he drowned. When his troops discovered Frederick's drowned body in full armor, they lost heart for the Crusade. Many went home to Germany by sea. A much smaller force continued to Antioch under Frederick of Swabia and Duke Leopold V of Austria. Here, more discouragement occurred. Frederick's body was buried in Antioch, and not in Jerusalem, as had been planned. Without their emperor, the Germans suddenly ranked third, after the kings of England and France. A small remnant of the vast German army that had left Regensburg did prove useful in the Siege of Acre in 1191. The German contribution to the Third Crusade was virtually ended.

The second of the three kings was the youthful Richard I of England. Scion of the late Plantagenet king Henry II, Richard inherited his father's commitment to go crusading. The thirty-three-year-old "troubadour prince" was a colorful but unstable personality, dramatic but unpredictable. Often in disagreement with his family and engaged in rivalries with the king of France, Richard feared to leave his kingdom. Fortunately for the Crusaders, he did and proved to be an excellent strategist.

The third of the three kings was Philip II, commonly known as Philip Augustus, of the French House of Capet. Although he was not fond of crusading, Philip had recently waged wars with England from 1187 to 1189 in an effort to enlarge his realm. A consummate politician but an inadequate warrior, Philip agreed to meet Richard at Vezelay on July 4, 1190, to move eastward by sea.

While Philip crossed the Mediterranean and began the siege of Acre in April, 1191, Richard had landed on the island of Cyprus, where his sister, Joan, and his fiancé, Berengaria of Navarre, had been shipwrecked and were held by a local rebel prince. Richard simply conquered Cyprus. This was a fateful decision, probably the most significant outcome of the Third Crusade, since Cyprus became a permanent Western outpost in the Mediterranean. Meanwhile, Richard married Berengaria, had her crowned queen of England in the Church of Saint George at Limassol, and had his bride accompany him to Palestine.

Once in the Holy Land, Richard assisted in taking Acre, but he quarreled with Leopold in the process. After Acre fell, Philip believed that he had fulfilled his Crusader's vow and departed for France. Alone, Richard successfully took Jaffa in 1192, but he decided to negotiate peace with Saladin. On September 2, 1192, a five-year peace treaty was signed, recognizing Western control of the coast from Jaffa north, but acknowledging Muslim control of Jerusalem in exchange for guarantees of Christian access to the sacred sites. Regarding his mission as complete, Richard set out for Europe on October 9, only to be captured and held for ransom by Leopold until 1194. On his return to England, Richard went to war with his old rival, Philip. Richard died of mortal wounds near Limoges, France, in 1199.

Richard landing at Acre. (F. R. Niglutsch)

Significance

If measured by its stated goal, the rescue of Jerusalem, the Third Crusade was a failure. Since access to the Holy Sepulchre was the intent of the mission, it could be maintained that this goal was attained by diplomacy, not war. Outremer (the land beyond the sea) was militarily strengthened by the possession of Acre and the Palestinian coast. The occupation of Cyprus was the most important result of the Third Crusade. Not only did it become a powerful kingdom in its own right, but Cyprus also was a Crusader outpost in the East, a base for future campaigns, and a Western foothold in the Mediterranean for almost three hundred years.

—*C. George Fry*

Further Reading

Gibb, Christopher. *Richard the Lionhearted and the Crusades*. New York: Bookwright Press, 1986. This brief, introductory biography of the twelfth century English king discusses the origins of the Crusades and their impact on Muslim-Christian relations.

Hillenbrand, Carole. *The Crusades: Islamic Perspectives*. New York: Routledge, 2000. Chapters explore Muslim reactions to the Crusades, ethnic and religious stereotyping, daily life, the conduct of war, and more. Bibliography, index.

A depiction of the relatively insignificant siege of the Châlus castle in Limousin, 1199, where Richard died from an arrow wound after having survived the Third Crusade. From the fifteenth century Chroniques de Normandie. (Frederick Ungar Publishing Co.)

Lane-Poole, Stanley. *Saladin: All-Powerful Sultan and the Uniter of Islam*. New York: Cooper Square Press, 2002. This is the forerunner of other modern biographies of Saladin, first published under a different title in 1898, and draws extensively on original chroniclers; includes discussions of major campaigns. Illustrations, map, bibliography, index.

Lloyd, Simon. "The Crusading Movement, 1096-1274." In *The Oxford Illustrated History of the Crusades*, edited by Jonathan Riley-Smith. New York: Oxford University Press, 1999. Places the Third Crusade within the context of the medieval crusading movement, arguing its significance in the history of late medieval culture in the West.

Madden, Thomas F., ed. *The Crusades: The Essential Readings*. Malden, Mass.: Blackwell, 2002. A collection of previously published articles about the Crusades, including medieval sources, lay enthusiasm, patronage, Byzantium, and the subjection of Muslims. Bibliography, index.

Reston, James, Jr. *Warriors of God: Richard the Lionheart and Saladin in the Third Crusade*. New York: Doubleday, 2001. This history of the Third Crusade presents Saladin as a sophisticated political leader. Richard is depicted as a complex and at times brutal figure. Illustrations, maps, bibliography, index.

Riley-Smith, Jonathan. *The Feudal Nobility and the Kingdom of Jerusalem, 1174-1277*. Hamden, Conn.: Archon Books, 1973. The author examines the constitutional ideas embodied in the Crusader kingdom of Jerusalem. Notes, appendices, bibliography.

Runciman, Steven. *A History of the Crusades*. 3 vols. New York: Cambridge University Press, 1987. Prepared by a highly respected English historian, this work will long remain the definitive study of the Crusades. Volumes 2 and 3 are especially relevant to an understanding of the Third Crusade. Bibliography, index.

Smail, R. C. *The Crusaders in Syria and the Holy Land*. New York: Praeger, 1973. A fine introduction to the nature of Crusader life in the Levant. Illustrated with seventy photographs, thirty-three line drawings, three maps, and two tables. Bibliography.

See also: 976-1025: Reign of Basil II; 1009: Destruction of the Church of the Holy Sepulchre; August 26, 1071: Battle of Manzikert; 1077: Seljuk Dynasty Is Founded; November 27, 1095: Pope Urban II Calls the First Crusade; c. 1120: Order of the Knights Templar Is Founded; c. 1145: Prester John Myth Sweeps Across Europe; 1147-1149: Second Crusade; 1152: Frederick Barbarossa Is Elected King of Germany; 1204: Knights of the Fourth Crusade Capture Constantinople; 1217-1221: Fifth Crusade; 1227-1230: Frederick II Leads the Sixth Crusade; 1248-1254: Failure of the Seventh Crusade; April, 1291: Fall of Acre, Palestine; May 29, 1453: Fall of Constantinople.

Related articles in *Great Lives from History: The Middle Ages, 477-1453*: Baybars I; Bohemond I; Enrico Dandolo; Frederick I Barbarossa; Innocent III; Melisende; Philip II; Richard I; Saladin; Geoffroi de Villehardouin.

1190
MOSES MAIMONIDES WRITES *THE GUIDE OF THE PERPLEXED*

Philosopher Moses Maimonides' work The Guide of the Perplexed *attempted to reconcile Classical reason with Islamic faith and piety. It stands as the most learned Jewish presentation of rationalist philosophy in the Middle Ages.*

LOCALE: Spain and Egypt
CATEGORIES: Cultural and intellectual history; literature; philosophy; religion

KEY FIGURES

Moses Maimonides (1135-1204), Jewish philosopher
Isaac Alfasi (1013-1103), North African and Spanish Talmudist
Avicenna (980-1037), Muslim interpreter of Aristotle
Samuel ben Judah ibn Tibbon (c. 1150-c. 1230), translator of Maimonides' work
Abraham ben David of Posquieres (1120-1198), oppositional leader of the Jewish community of Provence

SUMMARY OF EVENT

Jews in the medieval world were caught between the hostile worlds of Islam and Christianity and also between the challenges and doubts that science and philosophy brought to the growing intelligentsia of traditional Judaism. This segment of society became increasingly aware of the seemingly irrational character of much Jewish teaching when Greek philosophy and science became available through numerous Arabic commentaries.

Moses Maimonides became one of the greatest Jewish philosophers of all times, not as a result of any innate drive to speculate on the riddles of existence but as a response to that very real and urgent intellectual need of his day. So effective and well recognized was the work of Maimonides that it was said of him from Yemen to France: "From Moses to Moses (ben Maimon), there was none like Moses."

As a youth Maimonides fled with his family from his native Spain before the invasion of the Islamic Almohads, a Berber dynasty. The family actually lived for about five years as Muslims until they could openly return to the practice of Judaism. Maimonides' training in Jewish law and lore was supervised by Isaac Alfasi, one of the greatest Talmudists of the time, a man whom Maimonides acknowledged as the best of his teachers. Besides being a firm student of Jewish culture, Maimonides became an outstanding physician in Egypt, writing many learned and popular medical studies. Influenced greatly by the outstanding Muslim interpreter of Aristotle, Avicenna, he became so influential as an interpreter and critic of Aristotle that even Thomas Aquinas came to owe him much.

Maimonides stands as an interesting focal point around whom three faiths concentrated their intellectual efforts. The central objective of Maimonides was to synthesize classical rationality and Hebrew piety. Judaism was presented as a rational system completely in accord with Aristotelian philosophy. *Dalālat al-Ḥā'rīn* (1190; *The Guide of the Perplexed*, 1881-1885), written in Arabic toward the end of his life, aims to resolve the problems of the "perplexed" caused by the conflict between the literal understanding of the language of the Jewish Scriptures and the demands of trained reason. Like Philo many centuries before, Maimonides believed that the application of allegory to the Bible would solve most inconsistencies. Maimonides, therefore, set out to "translate" the language of metaphor and allegory into the language of reason.

In a person's proper quest to know God, the only two available approaches are through observation and philosophy. The former seeks God in created things, tangible evidence of his providence. The alternative of studying God directly forces one into a philosophy of negation. The limitations of language and the human intellect compel humans to describe God through negative assertions that are themselves denials of negations. To say God exists, Maimonides declared, is not to affirm the existence of God but to deny that God does not exist.

Shlomo Pines, a translator of Maimonides' work, argued that Maimonides was not an eclectic or apologist but a true scholar following his own search for philosophic truth. If his goal had been to merely devise some sort of compromise between amalgams of philosophy and religion freed from obscurantism, he need only have followed the more than adequate solution devised by Avicenna. Maimonides chose, instead, to follow the ninth-tenth century Muslim philosopher al-Fārābī in interpreting prophets basically as philosophers rather than to echo Avicenna, who deemed them mystics. Similarly Maimonides preferred to abandon Avicenna, who taught the immortality of the soul, and to borrow from the views of Avempace, a forerunner of Averroës.

Maimonides found ways of working distinctly Jewish religious dispensations into his classical philosophical framework. Prophecy, for instance, he regarded as a rational aid in understanding the universe, a cooperative enterprise carried on by a rational God with the help of his creatures. The ritualistic observances commanded by the Jewish Scriptures became for Maimonides sacramentals, psychological reminders of greater verities. His other monumental work, *Mishneh Torah* (1180; *The Code of Maimonides*, 1927-1965), which reorganized and summarized the decisions of the entire Talmud, made that disorganized labyrinth accessible to more readers.

Opposition to Maimonides began to develop as soon as his work was translated in Provence, especially when a translation of *The Guide of the Perplexed* by Samuel ben Judah ibn Tibbon appeared on November 30, 1204, shortly before Maimonides' death. The criticism was so violent that after 1230, it split Provence and Spanish Jewry into two hostile camps. Led by such obscurantists as Abraham ben David of Posquieres, the reaction enlisted the assistance of the Inquisition that condemned *The Guide of the Perplexed* in 1233 as heretical and dangerous for both Jew and Christian. However, during his own lifetime and generally since, Maimonides has been recognized as one of the great minds of Judaism.

Moses Maimonides. (Library of Congress)

SIGNIFICANCE

Maimonides attracted educated, secular-minded persons of the upper classes who were eager to find in his views an excuse for abandoning both Jewish law and literal revelation. Such men seemed to some of their contemporaries to present a threat to the security and safety of the Jewish community by encouraging a schism that the militant Christian Church could exploit to degrade Judaism.

Scholar Daniel Silver denies that economic, social, or political forces were significant in marshaling opposing factions in the argument. Likewise, altercations did not stem from the scholarly world, since those who involved themselves in the intricacies of Maimonidean thought were loyal Jews. Silver, in any case, deplores the escalation of the criticism into heated controversy as a tragedy eclipsing, as it did, the merit of many able anti-Maimonists.

Another view of the controversy presents it as associated with the rise of a new cultural and social order in Western Europe that caused corresponding bitter struggles for leadership and authority within the Jewish communities of Provence and Spain.

Maimonidean thought entering a scene uncongenial to it became the ideological focus for already existing tension. The new order, based on the triumph of an irrational feudal disorder disclaiming any orderly urban integration, could no longer sustain or nurture a Maimonidean rationalism. God seemed to reveal himself to the Jews on the defensive in Spain as more arbitrary and willful than legal and national. The Maimonidean controversy therefore reflects the mortal battle that was going on between the old and the new orders.

—*Joseph R. Rosenbloom*

FURTHER READING

Arbel, Ilil. *Maimonides: A Spiritual Biography.* New York: Crossroad, 2001. A brief biographical introduction to Maimonides as a rabbi and Jewish philosopher. Bibliography, index.

Bokser, Ben Zion. *The Legacy of Maimonides.* New York: Philosophical Library, 1950. A good general introduction to the thought of Maimonides.

Inglis, John, ed. *Medieval Philosophy and the Classical Tradition in Islam, Judaism and Christianity.* Richmond, Surrey, England: Curzon, 2002. Places medieval Islamic philosophy in the context of classic philosophy. Bibliography, index.

Maimonides. *The Guide of the Perplexed*. Translated by Shlomo Pines. Chicago: University of Chicago Press, 1963. A good translation of Maimonides' work with two compelling introductory essays.

Margolies, Morris B. *Twenty Twenty: Jewish Visionaries Through Two Thousand Years*. Northvale, N.J.: Jason Aronson, 2000. Provides biographies of leading visionaries in the Jewish tradition, including Maimonides. Bibliography, index.

Martin, Richard C., Mark R. Woodward, and Dwi S. Atmaja. *Defenders of Reason in Islam: Mutazilism from Medieval School to Modern Symbol*. Boston: Oneworld, 1997. Examines Islamic Mutazilism, the belief in the primacy of reason over theological teachings, during the Middle Ages and through the twentieth century. Bibliography, index.

Neusner, Jacob, ed. *Collected Essays on Philosophy and on Judaism*. 3 vols. Lanham, Md.: University Press of America, 2003. Vol. 1 discusses Maimonides and Greek philosophy. Part of the Studies in Judaism series.

Seeskin, Kenneth. *Searching for a Distant God: The Legacy of Maimonides*. New York: Oxford University Press, 2000. Discusses the far-reaching influence of Maimonides' work in religious philosophy. Chapters cover "the urge to philosophize," monotheism, monotheism and freedom, creation, and more. Bibliography, index.

Silver, Daniel J. *Maimonidean Criticism and the Maimonidean Controversy. 1180-1240*. Leiden, the Netherlands: E. J. Brill, 1965. This interesting study tries to explain the nature and source of the criticism against *The Guide of the Perplexed*.

Yellin, David, and Israel Abrahams. *Maimonides*. Philadelphia: Jewish Publication Society, 1903. An old but particularly useful biography with excellent background material about the Muslim world.

SEE ALSO: c. 950: Court of Córdoba Flourishes in Spain; c. 1150: Moors Transmit Classical Philosophy and Medicine to Europe; c. 1265-1273: Thomas Aquinas Compiles the *Summa Theologica*; c. 1275: The *Zohar* Is Transcribed.

RELATED ARTICLES in *Great Lives from History: The Middle Ages, 477-1453*: Saint Albertus Magnus; Avicenna; al-Ghazzālī; Ibn Gabirol; Judah ha-Levi; Levi ben Gershom; Moses Maimonides; Moses de León; Naḥmanides; Thomas Aquinas.

c. 1190-1279
MA-XIA SCHOOL OF PAINTING FLOURISHES

Named after two famous artists of the Imperial Painting Academy of the Southern Song period, the Ma-Xia school was a distinctive, new style of landscape painting that suggested limitless space and otherworldliness. This style, which included innovative methods of composition, ink washes, and brush strokes, greatly influenced later generations of Chinese and Japanese artists.

LOCALE: Linan (now Hangzhou) in Zhejiang Province, China

CATEGORIES: Philosophy; cultural and intellectual history

KEY FIGURES

Ma Yuan (Ma Yüan; c. 1165-c. 1225), a Chinese court painter

Xia Gui (Hsia Kuei; c. 1180-1230), Chinese court painter and originator of the ax stroke

SUMMARY OF EVENT

During the Song Dynasty (Sung; 960-1279), the emperors were devoted patrons of the arts, and the painting profession developed as never before. When the Jurchen invaded China and captured the Northern Song capital in 1127, the Song imperial family fled to the south and established a new capital in Hangzhou. Thus, the period from 1127 to 1279 is known as the Southern Song Dynasty. During this time, the Imperial Painting Academy was the center of painting. The supreme expression of Southern Song art was the distinctive Ma-Xia style of landscape painting, named after the famous court artists Ma Yuan and Xia Gui.

Other than some basic history, there is limited biographical information on Ma Yuan. He came from a distinguished family of court artists from Hezhong, Shanxi Province. He may have first served under Emperor Xiaozong (Hsiao-tsung; r. 1163-1190). Later, under Emperor Guangzong (Kuang-tsung; r. 1190-1194), Ma Yuan attained the level of *daizhao*, or painter-in-attendance. Under Emperor Ningzong (Ning-tsung; r. 1195-1224), he achieved the Golden Girdle, the highest rank a court painter could achieve.

Xia Gui was born in Qiantang (now Hangzhou) and served in the Imperial Academy from 1200 to 1230. A contemporary of Ma Yuan, Xia attained the ranks of *daizhao* and the prestigious Golden Girdle under Emperor Ningzong. Later, he served under Emperor Lizong (Li-tsung; r. 1225-1264). Stylistically, he followed in the tradition of Li Tang (Li T'ang), whose paintings served as the transition between the earlier Northern Song monumental landscapes and the new lyrical, spontaneous, Southern Song style. Li had also developed the brushstroke technique known as the ax stroke, which resembled marks made on wood by a chisel or ax. Xia and Ma both developed Li's small ax strokes into a broader form called large ax-cut strokes.

Spontaneity, lyricism, and simplified brushstrokes are characteristic of the Ma-Xia tradition. Other qualities and techniques include mists, asymmetrical compositions, intimacy, and variegated ink tones and washes. These were all used to suggest a feeling of open space, vast atmospheric void, infinity, and otherworldliness. Ma-Xia images invited contemplation and intimacy and often suggested melancholy, perhaps reflecting the nostalgia of the exiled royal court.

Dramatic asymmetrical compositions were typical of the Ma-Xia style. Ma Yuan was often called "One-Corner Ma" because of his mastery of the one-corner composition, in which the design weight or painted elements would be focused in one corner, with the rest of the silk or paper left blank or barely tinted to suggest empty space or mist. The album leaf was the most popular form among the academy artists, and many of Ma Yuan's album and fan paintings have survived. In "On a Mountain Path in Spring" (album leaf, ink and color on silk, collection of the National Palace Museum in Taipei), the style is lyrical and intimate, as though capturing a brief moment in time. Mountains, trees, a scholar, and his servant are in the left corner. The scholar watches two birds against the vast open space. A similar compositional arrangement of painted elements appears in another album leaf, "Scholar by a Waterfall" (ink and color on silk, Metropolitan Museum of Art).

In one of Ma Yuan's major surviving paintings, "Banquet by Lantern Light" (hanging scroll, ink and color on silk, National Palace Museum in Taipei), the scene is a royal banquet, where several guests approach the royal hosts, who are hidden in a lower corner. The well-known Ma Yuan elements of a misty atmosphere, tightly constructed compositions, angular plum trees, floating distant mountains, and tall, strong pines are evident here. The painting is typical of the many nostalgic night scenes he painted.

"The Four Old Recluses in the Shang Mountains" (hand scroll, Cincinnati Art Museum) is another dramatic painting with bold diagonal movement, ax-cut textured rocks, and expressive figures. Other notable paintings include "Rain over Trees on a Rocky Shore" (hanging scroll, Seikado Foundation in Tokyo), "Early Spring" (fan-shaped, Museum of Fine Arts, Boston), "An Angler on a Wintry Lake" (hand scroll, national Museum, Tokyo), and "Two Sages and an Attendant Beneath a Plum Tree" (fan-shaped, Museum of Fine Arts, Boston).

There were many imitators of Ma Yuan's style. Xia Gui's work, on the other hand, was difficult to copy or imitate convincingly, because Xia had extraordinary technical virtuosity with the brush, ink values, and texture strokes. His "Pure and Remote Views of Streams and Mountains" (hand scroll, ink on paper, National Palace Museum, Taipei, Taiwan) is one of the most significant paintings and possibly the best example of the ink monochrome technique in the history of Chinese art. This hand or horizontal scroll is viewed like a continuous panorama, as one unrolls one end toward the other, and rolls back the parts already seen. This painting shows Xia's exacting control of ink values, ranging from soft, pale gray washes to the deepest blacks. He used swift, broken ax-cut strokes and wet and dry brush techniques to sculpt the mountains and define surface textures. Compositionally, there is a clear sense of near, middle, and far distance, and of empty space versus solid objects. Xia Gui's other classic hand scroll is "Twelve Landscape Views" (ink on paper, Nelson-Atkins Museum of Art, Kansas City), in which the scenes take the viewer through time, from morning into night.

SIGNIFICANCE

After the fall of the Southern Song Dynasty in 1279, Ma-Xia landscape painting became unpopular. Although Sun Junze, an artist in the Yuan Dynasty (1279-1368), painted in this tradition, and professional painters of the Zhe school of the Ming Dynasty (1368-1644) produced decorative variations of the style, connoisseurs considered the Ma-Xia tradition too professional—just empty technique. Some intellectuals of this period were suspicious of professionalism in the arts, which they felt should be the domain of elite literati who practiced the arts as a social pastime. For this reason, few Ma-Xia paintings survived or were collected in China.

However, the tradition was brought to Japan, where it became very popular. In Japan, the Ma-Xia paintings greatly influenced the styles of Shūbun and his student Sesshū, who are considered the two greatest masters of ink painting of the Ashikaga period (1338-1573). Sesshū (1420-1506), a Zen Buddhist monk, was often considered the greatest artist of his time. While in China from 1466 to 1469, he copied the techniques of the Southern Song painters. Xia's influence is obvious in two major hand scrolls by Sesshū, whose Chinese style of ink painting became the model for later Japanese artists.

Ma Yuan and Xia Gui are considered two of China's greatest masters of landscape painting. Their lyrical, delicate style has also become one of the most popular and recognizable styles of Chinese painting in the West.

—*Alice Myers*

FURTHER READING

Barnhart, Richard M., et al. *Three Thousand Years of Chinese Painting*. New Haven, Conn.: Yale University Press, 1997. The chapter, "The Five Dynasties and the Song Period (907-1279)," discusses the Ma-Xia painters. This oversize book includes beautiful color plates and a helpful glossary.

Cahill, James. *Chinese Paintings: XI-XIV Centuries*. New York: Crown, 1960. Includes interesting analyses of paintings by Ma Yuan and Xia Gui.

Fong, Wen C., and James Watt. *Possessing the Past: Treasures from the National Palace Museum, Taipei*. New York: Metropolitan Museum of Art, 1996. Informative discussions of the Ma-Xia school and its artists, especially in the chapter on the Imperial Painting Academy of the Song dynasty. Beautifully illustrated with examples of paintings by the Ma-Xia artists.

Lee, Sherman E. *Chinese Landscape Painting*. New York: Harry N. Abrams, 1962. Informative chapter on "The Song Dynasty," with detailed discussion of famous paintings by Ma Yuan and Xia Gui. Beautifully illustrated book with plates on almost every page.

Loehr, Max. *The Great Painters of China*. New York: Harper & Row, 1980. Includes an interesting chapter, "Painters of the Southern Song (1127-1278)," which discusses Ma Yuan, Xia Gui, and Ma Lin. Illustrated.

Sirén, Osvald. *Chinese Painting: Leading Masters and Principles*. Vol. 2. New York: Hacker Art Books, 1973. In this standard history of Chinese painting, volume 2 contains a detailed chapter on the Ma-Hsia school of painting.

Sullivan, Michael. *Symbols of Eternity: The Art of Landscape Painting in China*. Oxford, England: Clarendon Press, 1979. The chapter, "Realism Achieved and Abandoned: The Song Dynasty, 960-1279" examines the work and style of Ma Yuan and Xia Gui.

SEE ALSO: 1115: Foundation of the Jin Dynasty; 1153: Jin Move Their Capital to Beijing; 1368: Establishment of the Ming Dynasty.

RELATED ARTICLES in *Great Lives from History: The Middle Ages, 477-1453*: Ma Yuan; Xia Gui.

1193
TURKISH RAIDERS DESTROY BUDDHIST UNIVERSITY AT NALANDA

Nalanda, the greatest Buddhist monastic institution and seat of secular learning in ancient India, was destroyed by Turkish raiders, leading to the demise of Buddhism in India.

LOCALE: India
CATEGORIES: Religion; education; wars, uprisings, and civil unrest

KEY FIGURE

Ikhtar-ud-Dīn Muḥammad-ibn-Bakhtiar Khaljī (fl. twelfth century), Turkish sultan who sacked Nalanda

SUMMARY OF EVENT

Conflict between the Muslim Turkish kingdom of Ghazna (now in modern Afghanistan) and the northwest Indian states, which adhered to Buddhism, began in the ninth century. At the end of that century, the Turks conquered Jaguda, but the Indians were able to hold off the Turks until the middle of the tenth century, when a new Turkish dynasty launched a more determined effort to dominate the country. A long war ensued.

In the early eleventh century, the Turkish leader, Sultan Maḥmūd of Ghazna, amassed great riches from a series of raids on Indian states and cities. Mathura was pillaged, and the capital, Kanyakubja, was sacked. Ten thousand temples were destroyed. Although Maḥmūd's progress was eventually halted, he had established a large Turkish empire in India. Over the next 150 years, there were sporadic wars between the Turks and the Indian states, but little change in the overall position.

A new phase in the conflict began toward the end of the twelfth century. In 1173, a Turkish ruler, Sultan Ikhtar-ud-Dīn Muḥammad-ibn-Bakhtiar Khaljī, overthrew the Yamini Dynasty, which had been in power since the tenth century. Five years later, in 1178, Bakhtiar Khaljī suffered a heavy defeat after attacking the small kingdom of Gujarat in western India. However, by 1192, Bakhtiar Khaljī had recovered from this defeat and built up a new army. Some quick victories left most of northern India open to attack by the Turks. In 1193, Varanasi was looted, and a thousand temples were destroyed. They were replaced by mosques. The Turks pushed eastward and annexed Bihar and Bengal, destroying the Buddhist universities there. Uddandapura became a Turkish base, and from there, raids were launched on nearby Nalanda.

The monastery at Nalanda had been founded in the fifth century by one of the Gupta emperors. Nalanda is located in northeast India on the Ganges plain a few miles south of Patna. The Buddha visited the city of Nalanda several times on his travels through India in the sixth century B.C.E. It was then reported to be a prosperous, well-populated place. According to tradition, Nalanda was the birthplace of Sariputra, one of Buddha's chief disciples.

The monastery received royal patronage of the emperors Aśoka and Harṣa of Kanauj, and it quickly grew into the greatest center of learning in India. By the seventh century, Nalanda was more like a university than a monastery. It was no longer an institution that focused solely on spiritual enlightenment; a wide range of secular disciplines were studied. Ten thousand students were enrolled there, including many from other Asian countries, and there was a regular system of admission and registration. There were two thousand teachers, and hundreds of lectures were given every day. Courses of study included Buddhist scriptures of both Mahāyāna and Hīnayāna schools; the ancient texts known as the Vedas; and *hetu vidya* (logic), *shabda vidya* (grammar) and *chikitsa vidya* (medicine). The university was grouped with several neighboring monasteries to form a single organization. A Chinese visitor, Xuanzang (Hsüan-tsang; c. 602-664), stayed at Nalanda in the seventh century and gave high praise to the educational system there, as well as the purity of the lives of the monks. Xuangzang also admired the architecture of the university, in which rows of cells were arranged around a courtyard.

One of the great glories of Nalanda was its library. It was the biggest and the most frequently used of all the ancient Buddhist libraries. It consisted of three buildings, one of which was nine stories high. This was the Ratnodahdhi, which specialized in rare and sacred works. It was the library that enabled Nalanda University to become the embodiment of the highest ideals of education.

When the Turkish raids came in 1193, Nalanda was still a highly influential center of learning. It had been under the patronage of the Pāla emperors, who ruled northeastern India from the eighth to the twelfth centuries. However, the Turks did not spare it. Thousands of monks were killed, and the library and other buildings were burned to the ground. The majestic ruins have been excavated and can still be seen today. Other Buddhist universities, such as Vikramasila, suffered the same fate as Nalanda.

Turkish raids continued into the thirteenth century. In 1235, according to an eyewitness report from Dharmasvamin, a Tibetan pilgrim, three hundred Turkish soldiers sacked what little remained of Nalanda. Seventy scholars were forced to flee.

SIGNIFICANCE

With the loss of Nalanda, a large part of India's cultural and spiritual heritage was destroyed. The destruction of the university was followed by the demise of Buddhism in India. Buddhist monks who survived the Muslim destruction of Nalanda had to flee India and take up residence in Nepal, Tibet, China, or Burma.

Some scholars argue that the Muslim invasions were the principal cause of the end of Buddhism as an institutional religion in India. However, Hinduism and Jainism were subject to the same assaults by the Muslims, but they survived as religions in India. It has been argued that Buddhism lacked the militaristic values that can be found in Hinduism and therefore lacked the ability to organize itself against the Muslim raiders. Another reason proposed for why Buddhism disappeared from India is that it was centered around a few large monasteries and seats of learning, such as Nalanda, and did not have much organization at a local level. When such centers of knowledge, because of their riches, became the target of Muslim plunderers, there were few local centers of Buddhism to carry on the tradition. This contrasts with Hinduism, which had plenty of lay support.

There is widespread agreement among scholars that in addition to the Muslim invasions, the rise of Tantric practices within Buddhism was a contributory factor in Buddhism's decline in India. Tantra developed as a cult within the Mahāyāna school of Buddhism, a school that was strongly established at Nalanda from the sixth to the ninth century. Tantric text began to appear in the middle of the eighth century. The later form of Tantra was known as Vajrayana. It involved the use of mantras and sacred chants believed to have a magical effect and various other rituals that could, in the minds of believers, speed the path to enlightenment. The result was the erosion of the gap between Buddhist teachings and the magical practices of the Indian peasants, leading to the end of firm distinctions between Buddhism and Hinduism.

Other causes that have been advanced for the decline of Buddhism in India, in addition to the Muslim invasions, include sectarian divisions within Buddhism, the ending of royal patronage, the migration of leading Buddhist monks and scholars to other lands such as China to spread their faith, and the hostility of Hinduism toward Buddhism.

—*Bryan Aubrey*

FURTHER READING

Ahir, D. C., ed. *A Panorama of Indian Buddhism: Selections from the Maha Bodhi Journal (1892-1992)*. Delhi, India: Sri Satguru Publications, 1995. Contains fifty essays on many aspects of Indian Buddhism, including Rahul Sankrityayan's "The Rise and Decline of Buddhism in India," which argues that the decline of Buddhism in India was caused by Tantric Buddhism, which destroyed moral strength and weakened the foundation of Buddhism. Another informative essay is "Buddhist Libraries in Ancient India," by Dipak Kumar Barua.

Basham, A. L. *The Wonder That Was India*. 3d ed. 1954. Reprint. London: Sidgwick & Jackson, 2000. This is a classic study of early Indian civilization, up to the Muslim conquest. Includes information about the university at Nalanda.

De Bary, Theodore, ed. *The Buddhist Tradition in India, China, and Japan*. 1969. Reprint. New York: Vintage Books, 1972. Includes a survey of the history of Indian Buddhism from earliest times to its decline and the Muslim invasions.

Goyal, S. R. *A History of Indian Buddhism*. Meerut, India: Kusumanjali Prakashan, 1987. This is particularly informative on the many reasons for the decline and disappearance of Buddhism from India.

Warder, A. K. *Indian Buddhism*. Delhi, India: Motilal Banarsidass, 1970. A historical survey of Buddhism whose main purpose is to elucidate doctrine, but which also includes historical background. Particularly useful on the structure of the universities and the Muslim invasions.

SEE ALSO: 538-552: Buddhism Arrives in Japan; 606-647: Reign of Harṣa of Kanauj; 637-657: Islam Expands Throughout the Middle East; 791: Buddhism Becomes Tibetan State Religion; 997?-1030: Reign of Maḥmūd of Ghazna.

RELATED ARTICLES in *Great Lives from History: The Middle Ages, 477-1453*: Harṣa; Maḥmūd of Ghazna; Xuanzang.

1196-1258
CH'OE FAMILY TAKES POWER IN KOREA

During the Koryŏ Dynasty, the kingdom was under military rule from 1170 to 1270. Various generals struggled for power until General Ch'oe Ch'ung-hŏn took control, brought the country back to order, and began ruling as dictator in 1196. The Ch'oe family maintained control until 1258.

LOCALE: Korean peninsula
CATEGORY: Government and politics

KEY FIGURES

Chŏng Chung-bu (1106-1179), a Koryŏ general, leader of the military *coup d'état* in 1170

Ch'oe Ch'ung-hŏn (1149-1219), the first of the Ch'oe dictators, ruled 1196-1219

Ch'oe Ŭi (d. 1258), great-grandson of Ch'oe Ch'ung-hŏn, the fourth and the last dictator, ruled 1257-1258

SUMMARY OF EVENT

During the first two centuries of the Koryŏ Dynasty (918-1392), in spite of a few major foreign invasions and domestic uprisings, the Koryŏ kingdom enjoyed peace and prosperity. As Koryŏ entered the second half of the dynastic period, however, corruption became rampant within the court and power struggles ensued. Monarchs were weak, incompetent, and lackadaisical, and state affairs went neglected. In particular, King Ŭijong (r. 1146-1170), the effeminate eighteenth monarch of Koryŏ, led an extravagant lifestyle, building palaces, pavilions, and manmade lakes for his entertainment.

In the aristocratic Koryŏ society, civil officials ruled supreme. Military officers, on the other hand, suffered social, political, and economic discrimination. As a result, military discontent had been building for some time. On August 30, 1170 (by the lunar calendar), during one of the king's outings, a young low-ranking civil official by the name of Han Roe slapped the face of a general. This outraged the soldiers and generals who had long suppressed their building frustration and anger. That evening, General Chŏng Chung-bu and officers Yi Ŭi-bang and Yi Go led their soldiers in killing the civilian officials at the gathering, including Han Roe. Among those killed was Kim Don-jung, who earlier had burned General Chŏng Chung-bu's beard. Kim was the son of Kim Pu-sik (1075-1151), the renowned Confucian scholar, historian, and general who compiled the *Samguk sagi* (1145; history of the three kingdoms).

On returning to the palace, General Chŏng and his soldiers expelled the king and placed the king's brother Myŏngjong (r. 1170-1197) on the throne. This military coup marked the beginning of a hundred years of military rule in the Koryŏ Dynasty and was the first of many attempts by numerous generals to gain control of the kingdom. It was not until General Ch'oe Ch'ung-hŏn took power and restored order in 1196 that peace and stability were brought to the state.

Within ten years of the first revolt, all the original instigators had been killed, with the exception of Yi Ŭi-min. Born a slave, he was given the task of assassinating the banished King Ŭijong, when the movement to reinstate him was discovered and foiled in 1173. Yi eventually rose and claimed political power with his sons, but they proved to be as corrupt and lawless as their predecessors.

On April 8, 1196, General Ch'oe Ch'ung-hŏn, together with his younger brother Ch'oe Ch'ung-su and their nephew, Park Jin-jae, attacked and wiped out the Yi family. As reward, King Myŏngjong elevated the Ch'oe brothers to meritorious subjects. Nevertheless, Ch'oe Ch'ung-hŏn deposed the king the following year, replacing him with the king's brother, Sinjong (r. 1197-1204). Ch'oe held absolute power over the court and ruled the country as a military dictator. He alone made government policy decisions, rendering the king nothing more than a puppet. Ch'oe replaced kings as he saw necessary and eliminated those who opposed him. He maintained his power through his personal security force (*mun-gaek*).

The struggle to maintain power continued throughout Ch'oe Ch'ung-hŏn's life. His brother, Ch'oe Ch'ung-su, sought to marry his daughter to the crown prince in an attempt to bolster his own position. Ch'oe Ch'ung-hŏn advised against it, but when his advice went unheeded, fighting broke out in the capital city of Kaekyŏng (formerly Songak, now Kaesŏng) between the two brothers and their respective forces. Ch'oe Ch'ung-hŏn prevailed, and Ch'ung-su was killed.

There were attempts on Ch'oe Ch'ung-hŏn's life as well. King Hŭijong (r. 1204-1211) was behind one such plot in December, 1211, when Buddhist monks attacked Ch'oe in the king's palace. He was rescued barely in time by his guards. The plot was uncovered, and the king was deposed and replaced by his cousin Kangjong (r. 1211-1213). King Kangjong died after two years and was replaced by his son Kojong (r. 1214-1259). In total, General Ch'oe placed four kings on the throne and deposed two. King Kojong was the longest reigning monarch of the dynasty and witnessed Koryŏ's most turbulent time in history because of the Mongol invasions.

The Mongols launched their first invasion in 1231. Anticipating further attacks, Ch'oe U, who had succeeded his father in 1219, decided to move his court to Kanghwa Island off the Han River in 1232. The Mongols attacked that year as well, but because Kanghwa was out of reach, the Mongols ravaged the countryside instead.

While the country suffered under Mongol attacks, Ch'oe's regime built magnificent palaces on the island. The regime renewed the annual celebration *yŏndŭnghoe*, honoring the birth of Buddha, and held a more splendid event than ever before. The court seemed determined to live with abandon. Although the Mongols could clearly see the island from the opposite side of the shore, they were inexperienced and fearful of crossing water. On land, the people suffered tremendously under the marauding horde yet still had to provide for the king and nobilities on the island, as well as fight to drive the invaders from their villages.

King Kojong, meanwhile, did the only thing he could. He fervently prayed to Buddha, entertained thousands of monks on the island, and ordered the entire Buddhist scripture to be carved on wooden blocks as a supplication to Buddha to intercede. The result was the famous *Tripitaka Koreana* (thirteenth century), a collection of 81,240 blocks, each carved on both sides.

After the initial attacks in 1231 and 1232, the Mongols invaded five more times. The 1254 incursion under the leadership of Jalairtai was particularly atrocious. According to records, Jalairtai took more than 200,000 Koreans as prisoners; the dead were too numerous to count. Ch'oe U died in 1249 and was succeeded by his son Ch'oe Hang. The Ch'oe regime remained opposed to returning the court to the capital of Kaekyŏng, which was one of the conditions the Mongols demanded in exchange for their withdrawal from the peninsula. With no end to Mongol hostilities in sight, civilian officials began losing faith in the Ch'oe military regime.

Ch'oe Hang died in 1257 and was in turn succeeded by his son Ch'oe Ŭi. Neither Ch'oe Hang nor Ŭi were strong leaders. Ch'oe Ŭi was especially incompetent and was soon set on by other ambitious men. Ch'oe Ŭi was killed within a year (March 26, 1258) by one of his long-time family servants in collusion with civilian officials. The Ch'oe family's military dictatorship thus came to an end after sixty-two years and four generations. After the assassination, King Kojong and his officials sued for peace with the Mongols, resulting in the Mongols' withdrawal from the country the following year. Power transferred back to the king in 1270, when the court finally returned to Kaekyŏng.

SIGNIFICANCE

Military rule began against the backdrop of social unrest and military discontent. The numerous uprisings and rebellions were usually the result of tenuous political and social conditions, even discrimination against the military. Although most uprisings were eventually suppressed, this period saw examples of upward mobility in a society in which class distinction had been rigid. For example, Yi Ŭi-min, a man of humble beginnings, was able to climb to the highest military position. In another instance, a courageous slave from the Ch'oe house was able to incite and lead thousands of fellow slaves to revolt for their emancipation.

The Mongol invasions are regarded as playing a significant role in the demise of the Ch'oe family. However, the Ch'oe family's resistance over the years and their decision to move the capital to the island of Kanghwa prevented Koryŏ from being completely overrun. The Mongols had intended to conquer Koryŏ in their quest to dominate the Far East, as they had done to much of the known world to that point.

Although many cultural artifacts were destroyed during the Mongol invasions, the Ch'oe period saw the flourishing of cultural activities, especially related to Buddhism. This period also produced the finest specimens of Koryŏ celadon (*chŏng-ja-gi*). The aforementioned *Tripitaka Koreana* stands as a testament to the pride and tenacity of the Koreans and the spirit of defiance they exhibited against the Mongols. Indeed, such an ambitious undertaking might not have been possible in peacetime.

—*Hwa-Soon Choi Meyer*

FURTHER READING

Hulbert, Homer Bezaleel. *Hulbert's History of Korea.* London: Routledge & Kegan Paul, 1962. A history that is somewhat critical of the military era because of the sources the author consulted at the time of his writing (c. 1905), which were based on Confucian ideals.

Joe, Wanne J. *Traditional Korea: A Cultural History.* Seoul, Korea: Chung-ang University Press, 1972. A comprehensive general history of Korea from ancient times to the 1870's.

Koryŏsa. Edited by Chŏng Inji et al. Seoul, Korea: Kyŏngin Munhwasa, 1972. The Yonse edition of this classic is the most authoritative source on the history of the Koryŏ kingdom. Written from the Confucian scholars' viewpoint.

Lee, Ki-baik. *A New History of Korea*. Translated by Edward W. Wagner with Edward L. Shultz. Cambridge, Mass.: Harvard University Press, 1984. Devotes a chapter to the era.

Schultz, Edward L. *Generals and Scholars: Military Rule in Medieval Korea* Honolulu: University of Hawaii Press, 2001. The first and only book devoted to the subject in English to date. Provides a detailed account of the governmental organization and mechanism through which the Ch'oe house controlled the state.

SEE ALSO: 668-935: Silla Unification of Korea; 918-936: Foundation of the Koryŏ Dynasty; 958-1076: Koreans Adopt the Tang Civil Service Model; 1145: Kim Pu-sik Writes *Samguk Sagi*; July, 1392: Establishment of the Yi Dynasty.

RELATED ARTICLE in *Great Lives from History: The Middle Ages, 477-1453*: Wang Kŏn.

c. 1200
COMMON-LAW TRADITION EMERGES IN ENGLAND

The emergence of England's common-law tradition during the twelfth and thirteenth centuries formed the foundation of the legal systems of Britain and most of its colonies.

LOCALE: England
CATEGORIES: Government and politics; laws, acts, and legal history

KEY FIGURES

William the Conqueror (c. 1028-1087), king of England, r. 1066-1087
Henry I (1068-1135), king of England, r. 1100-1135
Henry II (1133-1189), king of England, r. 1154-1189
Edward I (1239-1307), king of England, r. 1272-1307

SUMMARY OF EVENT

William the Conqueror, in an attempt to conciliate the recently subjugated Anglo-Saxons, promised that he would "restore the laws of their last king, Edward the Confessor." In doing so, he helped to ensure that England developed a distinctive set of procedures and rules that in time came to be known as the common law. This term is used in contradistinction to Roman, or civil, law, which, except to a limited degree, was never adopted in England. Civil law was a judicial system based on written legal codes that were generally legislated by rulers. Common law, on the other hand, was never written down and was developed on a case-by-case basis. Judges rendered decisions based on earlier cases, or precedents. Although legal theorists such as Ranulf de Glanville and Henry de Bracton wrote treatises on the common law, their books were not legally binding on judges. The treatises did, however, provide summaries of cases that were used as precedents by judges making decisions.

The term "common law" refers to that law that originated in the English royal court and gradually spread until it became common to much of the realm, dealing with all persons equally as subjects of the king regardless of class. Built up gradually by the king and his judges, the common law took effect in no single year. By about 1200, however, the characteristic features of the common law were well established. William the Conqueror, in the years after the conquest of England, laid the foundations for the later emergence of the common law. A strong administrator, William introduced feudalism, grafting this system of government onto existing Anglo-Saxon legal customs. His work was mainly that of systemization and regularization. He both stated and enforced royal rights, out of which eventually grew the common law.

Although during the reign of William's son, Henry I, there was little that could accurately be called the common law, Henry I was responsible for a number of reforms and extensions of royal power. He commissioned judges to hear royal cases in the counties. Again, Henry's chief contribution to the emergence of the common law was his development of a well-run central administration that would provide the mechanism for the growth of the common law.

The most decisive period in the formation of the common law occurred during the reign of Henry II. Henry II extended the system of traveling judges. In addition, he issued the Assizes of Clarendon, which provided instructions for his justices on how to try criminal cases. Under Henry II, royal courts could prosecute criminals. He ordered that 12 men from every 104 from each township testify if anyone in their district was suspected of committing crimes. He also encouraged the use of juries, systematized the grand jury, and developed a procedure for returning land to people from whom the land had been wrongfully seized.

The common law was called "the law of the land" in part because it constituted a body of rules about pieces of land; it was a body of real property law, a law of real estate. Such a development was natural in a community such as that of twelfth century England, where the most important form of wealth was land. Naturally, one of the most important tasks of the legal system was to devise a body of rules to settle disputes concerning its ownership or possession.

Perhaps the most famous instrument of the common law was the writ. The number of writs grew from about thirty-nine in the late twelfth century to more than four hundred by the end of the thirteenth century, a clear indication of the growth of the common law. Writs were written orders in the king's name that required action by a defendant or court. Property rights were at the heart of much of the common law, and Henry II developed at least four writs to address the problem of seizure of property. Perhaps the most significant of these was the assize of *novel disseisin*, designed to quickly restore property to a property's owner. A dispossessed property owner would secure a writ, addressed to the sheriff, instructing him to assemble a jury of twelve men knowledgeable of the facts of the case. It was the task of this jury to decide before a judge whether or not the dispossession had occurred within a particular period of time. If it had, the sheriff was required to return the land to the original property owner. Since in the twelfth and thirteenth centuries the writs designed to settle the question of possession (possessory writs) were the ones most widely used, they were the ones characteristic of the common law in its formative stages. One such writ, the Assize of Mort d'Ancestor, was used to secure an inheritance of real estate, for example.

One characteristic of common law that emerged from this was its emphasis on the use of proper procedures; it did not begin with assertion of a right but designated a procedure to be used by the aggrieved party. It has been said that in the common law, "substantive law, or right, is secreted within the interstices of procedure." Moreover, it is apparent that the common law, as exemplified by the assize of *novel disseisin*, demanded considerable citizen participation. The jury of inquiry was the heart of the whole procedure, the jury here serving the same function as witnesses in later courts by providing information.

Henry's order that no one be disturbed in the possession of his land without a king's writ gave the king's law wide jurisdiction over real property and caused royal justices to formulate more and more rules about the ownership of land. In addition, his itinerant justices extended the king's law under the guise of keeping the king's peace. The application of the "grand jury," men familiar enough with events in the vills (villages) and hundreds of the shire (county) to report crimes, brought more and more cases under the competence of the royal justices. The establishment of new courts followed.

Significance

The constant extension of the number of writs until the last quarter of the thirteenth century virtually ended the application of the old feudal baronial law. By the time of Edward I, the system of royal courts, then fairly well defined, consistently applied the common law as refined by more than a century of development. By regularly calling Parliament and systematically enforcing the common law, Edward moved England toward the realization of a "community of the realm."

—Martin J. Baron,
updated by Diane Andrews Henningfeld

Further Reading

Baker, J. H. *An Introduction to English Legal History*. 3d ed. London: Butterworths, 1990. Not only provides a standard history of English law but also includes documents in Latin with accompanying English translations.

Hines, W. D. *English Legal History: A Bibliography and Guide to the Literature*. New York: Garland, 1990. A good starting place for research into English legal history, this volume provides an introduction for each facet of the law.

Hogue, Arthur R. *Origins of the Common Law*. Bloomington: Indiana University Press, 1966. Emphasizes the interrelationships among the monarchy, society, and the law, concluding with a chapter examining the legacy of medieval common law.

Pollock, Sir Frederick, and Frederic William Maitland. *The History of English Law Before the Time of Edward I*. 2d ed. 2 vols. New York: Cambridge University Press, 1968. A classic work that traces the history of English law through the maturation of the common law during the thirteenth century.

Van Caenegem, R. C. *The Birth of the English Common Law.* 2d ed. New York: Cambridge University Press, 1988. Outlines the development of the common law beginning with William the Conqueror. Discussion of royal writs and writ procedure illuminates a difficult topic.

Walker, James M. *The Theory of Common Law.* Boston: Little, Brown, 1852. Reprint. Union, N.J.: Lawbook Exchange, 1998. A classic history of common law in England, including Roman influences.

SEE ALSO: 1285: Statute of Winchester; 1295: Model Parliament.

RELATED ARTICLES in *Great Lives from History: The Middle Ages, 477-1453*: Henry de Bracton; Edward I; Henry I; Henry II; William the Conqueror.

c. 1200
FAIRS OF CHAMPAGNE

The fairs of Champagne constituted the first major organized commercial venture in Europe and provided both the place and the means for trade between Mediterranean Europe, northern Europe, the Middle East, Asia, and Africa.

LOCALE: Champagne, France
CATEGORIES: Trade and commerce; economics

SUMMARY OF EVENT

From about the middle of the eleventh century through most of the thirteenth century, the county of Champagne was the home of the fairs of Champagne, organized medieval trade fairs that encouraged and promoted interregional trade. Many factors contributed to the growth of the fairs. The location of Champagne, aristocratic patronage, technological developments, the growth of manufacturing, improved transportation, changes in business and banking practices, and the influence of the Crusades put the fairs of Champagne at the heart of the commercial revolution of the Middle Ages.

Trade fairs existed long before the Middle Ages. During the Roman period, trade fairs existed in coastal cities where people from throughout the Roman Empire met and exchanged goods. Gradually these trade fairs moved inland to locations along trade routes. In the twelfth century, virtually every trade route in Europe crossed Champagne. Champagne was well located east of Paris and between the upper Saône River and tributaries of the Rhine, Seine, and Loire. It was through these river valleys that the first traders from Flanders made their way south into Italy, and Italian traders with goods from the Mediterranean and the Arab world made their way north.

Other factors also contributed to the success of the Champagne fairs. Across Europe, improved farming techniques during the period led to growth in agriculture, which in turn led to more goods available for exchange. At the same time, Europe saw an increase in the number of manufactured goods. Textiles and metal products took the place of furs and wood as primary exports from the northern countries. In addition, the discovery of the Frieburg silver mines led to an increase in currency. Shortages of negotiable coins had traditionally hampered trade in Europe. Furthermore, returning crusaders brought with them goods from the East, spurring the demand for luxury items. The conquest of cities in the Levant by European forces led to the import of spices, gems, and other goods from the Muslim world to Europe. The Italian cities of Genoa and Pisa grew rich through this increase in trade. By 1200, European merchants were importing goods from Africa, Asia, Constantinople, Syria, and Alexandria.

Perhaps most important, however, was the patronage given to the fairs of Champagne by the counts of Champagne, who understood the potential for profit from the growing trade moving across the Champagne borders. Consequently, the counts initiated and organized the fairs of Champagne in the towns of Troyes, Provins, Bar-sur-Aube, and Lagny.

Each fair lasted for forty-nine days and was held at the same time each year. The Lagny fair started the year in January, with the Bar-sur-Aube fair usually beginning in March during Lent. The next fair, at Provins, ran from May through June and was followed by the "warm" fair of Troyes, running from July through August. In September, Provins held the fair of Saint Ayoul, and in October and November, merchants returned to Troyes for the "cold" fair.

In addition to setting the time for each fair, the counts provided many necessary amenities: a place to hold the fair, booths for individual merchants, police supervision during the fair, money changers to provide standard cur-

Hans Sebald Beham's early sixteenth century engraving depicts a country fair, or fête champêtre. (Hulton|Archive by Getty Images)

rency and maintain accounts, and judges and courts to handle disputes. The counts appointed two keepers of the fair to oversee the daily details of administration. The counts also paid nobles who lived along the major trade routes an annual income in return for fealty and a promise to protect those merchants traveling to and from the fairs of Champagne. This arrangement was called a "money fief." The counts of Champagne thus provided a regular, safe meeting place for merchants from the Mediterranean and northern Europe, making possible regular, safe transport of goods from the south to the north and from the north to the south.

Clearly, the counts of Champagne invested much money in the enterprise. They profited greatly, however, from the success of the fairs. The counts received a sales tax on all goods sold at the fairs and also realized profit from booth rental. All the fines levied against those who broke the rules of the fairs were given to the counts as well. As a result, the counts of Champagne became the richest lords in all of France.

During the first week of each fair, the merchants entered the city, registered with the keepers, set up their booths, and displayed their wares. Each day of the fair was selected for a specific commodity. For example, the first ten days of the "warm" fair at Troyes were designated for the sale of cloth. The next days were devoted to the sale of goods that could be weighed, such as spices. One surviving medieval list names more than 288 different spices available at the fairs. Over the course of each fair, an impressive number of goods were bought and sold, including wool from England and Flanders; German iron, furs, and linens; Spanish leather and steel; Mediterranean spices and dyes; Scandinavian lumber and furs; Syrian sugar; and Egyptian alum. Both raw materials and handcrafted items were traded. For example, the Champagne fairs served as a source of ivory for ivory carvers as well as a place where intricate ivory carvings were sold. Luxury goods from the Arab world such as musk, diamonds, rubies, carpets, ambergris, and ebony also found their way into the fairs of Champagne.

Until the last week of the fair, no money changed hands; only accounts were kept. During the final days of the fair, accounts were settled. The money changers provided an essential service to the Champagne fairs and made business possible in a number of ways. First, the money changers converted all the currencies from around the world into the standard currency of the fairs: the Troyes pound. Second, the money changers maintained a credit system for the merchants, and because the money changers moved from fair to fair, the credit system worked among all the fairs. For example, a merchant could have an account follow him throughout the cycle of fairs and could settle at the end of the cycle before returning home. Also, the money changers offered loans and acted as pawnbrokers. These systems, as well as an accounting system independent of the money changers called the "letter of the fair," allowed business to be transacted by proxy. Thus, a businessman could send his agent to make trades throughout the cycle. About half of the money changers were Jews, not bound by the Christian rules concerning usury. The other half of the money changers were usually Italians. During the fairs, some of the Church usury laws were relaxed. In other cases, money changers and merchants were able to hide interest in currency exchange fees.

By the fourteenth century, the fairs of Champagne were on the wane. The kings of France controlled the fairs by this time, and they were notorious for overcharging for booths and levying taxes that were too high. Furthermore, sea transportation had become more reliable and alternate trade routes had opened up.

Significance

The fairs of Champagne were some of the most significant features of the medieval commercial revolution, even with the changes begun in the fourteenth century. The fairs provided a conduit through which trade goods circulated throughout Europe and the Mediterranean. Further, because merchants from England, Scotland, Iceland, Scandinavia, Portugal, France, Germany, Switzerland, Spain, Italy, and Sicily all frequented the fairs, communication and languages spread throughout Europe. News of southern Europe reached northern Europe via the fairs. The fairs also began the process of standardization of weights, measures, and coinage necessary for trading in goods. The banking and accounting principles developed at the fairs as well as the mercantile law instituted by the counts allowed for the further expansion of commerce.

—*Diane Andrews Henningfeld*

Further Reading

Botticini, Maristella. "A Tale of 'Benevolent' Governments: Private Credit Markets, Public Finance, and the Role of Jewish Lenders in Medieval and Renaissance Italy." *Journal of Economic History* 60, no. 1 (2000). Surveys the impact of Jewish lenders on markets, finance, and credit in Italian towns of the Middle Ages and into the Renaissance.

Evergates, Theodore, ed. and trans. *Feudal Society in Medieval France: Documents from the County of Champagne*. Philadelphia: University of Pennsylvania Press, 1993. An annotated collection of more than two hundred primary source documents from twelfth and thirteenth century Champagne, including documents describing the regulation of the fairs.

Favier, Jean. *Gold and Spices: The Rise of Commerce in the Middle Ages*. Translated by Caroline Higgitt. New York: Holmes and Meier, 1998. A detailed, scholarly, accessible account of the beginnings of "modern" economies and the move from feudalism to an early form of capitalism.

Fleet, Kate. *European and Islamic Trade in the Early Ottoman State: The Merchants of Genoa and Turkey*. New York: Cambridge University Press, 1999. Chapters on a variety of traded products and commodities, including alum, grain, cloth, and metals, and discussion about the slave trade, money, and the "Latin contribution to the early Ottoman economy."

Friedman, John Block, and Kristen Mossler Figg, eds. *Trade, Travel, and Exploration in the Middle Ages: An Encyclopedia*. New York: Garland, 2000. Volume 5 of Garland's Encylopedias of the Middle Ages. A 715-page text covering the history of commerce, trade, and travel during the Middle Ages. Includes maps and illustrations.

Gies, Frances, and Joseph Gies. *Life in a Medieval City*. New York: Harper and Row, 1969. A thoroughly accessible glimpse into life in Troyes around 1250, including a full chapter on the Champagne fair. The book, aimed at the general reader, offers the details of daily life at the fair.

Lopez, Robert S. *The Commercial Revolution of the Middle Ages, 950-1350*. Cambridge, England: Cambridge University Press, 1976. This work outlines the factors that made possible the rapid economic expansion of the tenth and eleventh centuries.

Lopez, Robert S., and Irving Raymond. *Medieval Trade in the Mediterranean World*. New York: Columbia University Press, 1955. Classic book on the development of trade between the Arab world and Europe.

Postan, M. M., and Edward Miller, eds. *Trade and Industry in the Middle Ages*. Vol. 2 of *The Cambridge Economic History of Europe*. Cambridge, England: Cambridge University Press, 1987. This text has long been considered the most comprehensive study of medieval economy and is an important starting place for any study of trade.

Sarin, Amita V. "Trade as a Link to the World." *Calliope* 9, no. 8 (April, 1999). Discusses how Muslim merchants served as middlemen for trade between Europe, Asia, and Africa in the 1300's.

Weber, Max. *The History of Commercial Partnerships in the Middle Ages*. Translated by Lutz Kaelber. Lanham, Md.: Rowman and Littlefield, 2003. Part of the Legacies of Social Thought series, this work by the renowned sociologist Max Weber (1864-1920), discusses commerce and business connections during the Middle Ages. Includes a bibliography and an index.

See also: 6th-8th centuries: Sogdians Dominate Central Asian Trade; 563: Silk Worms Are Smuggled to the Byzantine Empire; 630-711: Islam Expands Throughout North Africa; 8th-14th centuries: Cahokia Becomes the First North American City; 740: Khazars Convert to Judaism; 751: Battle of Talas River; c. 1010: Songhai Kingdom Converts to Islam; c. 1100: Founding of Timbuktu; c. 1150: Refinements in Banking; 1150: Venetian Merchants Dominate Trade with the East; c. 1150-1200: Rise of the Hansa Merchant Union; c. 1200: Scientific Cattle Breeding Developed; 1230's-1255: Reign of Sundiata of Mali; c. 1250: Improvements in Shipbuilding and Navigation; 1271-1295: Travels of Marco Polo; 1290-1306: Jews Are Expelled from England, France, and Southern Italy; 1347-1352: Invasion of the Black Death in Europe.

RELATED ARTICLES in *Great Lives from History: The Middle Ages, 477-1453*: Basil the Macedonian; Benjamin of Tudela; Mansa Mūsā; Rurik.

c. 1200
SCIENTIFIC CATTLE BREEDING DEVELOPED

The scientific revolution in agricultural techniques that characterized the twelfth and thirteenth centuries was largely the result of work carried out on the monastic farms of newly founded religious orders, particularly the Cistercians, who became especially well known for their scientific approach to farming and livestock raising.

LOCALE: Europe
CATEGORIES: Agriculture; science and technology; trade and commerce

SUMMARY OF EVENT

The twelfth century origin of the Cistercian order is significant in that it forced the Cistercians into a consciousness of rural problems. Compared with the Benedictines and their already reformed Cluny, the Cistercians started late as an order. Since, by the twelfth century, the earlier monastic groups had preempted many of the more favorable agricultural sites in Europe and most of the best arable land of Western Europe had already been put to the plow, the new order was forced to retreat into less accessible areas. Also, since the Cistercians were encouraged by their rule to shun the general population, the monks tended to establish their houses in the wilder and more remote lands of England, France, and Germany. In these primitive surroundings, they were in a sense free, but this fact forced them to experiment with new techniques in agronomy.

Of significant importance in their freedom to plan was the actual management of the Cistercian lands themselves. The monasteries divided their newly acquired areas into compact groups known as granges. Each grange included arable, pasture, and timber lands, and was put under the care of one man, a cellarer, who was responsible for its effective management. Such an arrangement lifted the granges outside the normal manorial nexus and, by freeing them from the hampering restrictions, dues, rights, and obligations involved in the established agricultural structure, provided wide opportunities for innovation.

Because other orders already held the Midlands, the Cistercians in the British Isles settled mostly in the Yorkshire dales, and in the moorlands and valleys of Wales. Here they turned into exceptionally fine sheep farmers. Their close ties in the wool trade with Flanders later had its impact on the Hundred Years' War (1337-1453). In fact, the Cistercian wool trade was so highly developed that the monasteries disposed of their wool by advance contracts promising to deliver a set amount of wool for two, three, or even fifteen or twenty years. Thus wool merchants were in effect making long-term loans to the monks on the security of their future production. Because the monasteries made contracts not only for the wool of their own domains but also for that of other farmers in the area, they were actually acting as middlemen between the exporter and the small farmer. Although the Cistercians were forbidden in 1157 by their chapter general to engage in such economic speculation, they found these long-term contracts too lucrative to forgo.

Cistercian agriculture, grain production, and cattle raising were greatly stimulated on the great Flemish estates of the order when the monks began to produce for the growing towns. Intensive cultivation of the land drove out the old fallow policy, and the urban demand for meat, milk, and cheese, together with a climate favorable for pasture farming, led to a great expansion and improvement of livestock raising in the late thirteenth century.

Soon the monks became famous for their advanced concepts of animal husbandry. Cattle, sheep, and hogs were generally allowed to roam the open fields, meadows, and forests and to mate indiscriminately among their own kind, but the Cistercians began to enclose their grasslands with fencing so that undesirable strains of cattle and uncontrolled inbreeding could not contaminate their herds.

Selective breeding developed in the monks' cattle many desirable characteristics: resistance to disease, endurance of cold weather, capacity for greater milk production, and, in the case of beef cattle and hogs, greater size and weight.

In Germany and the Low Countries, the Cistercians became expert in clearing and draining vast tracts of wasteland and low-lying swamp areas. The water obtained by the drainage of swamp and fen was ingeniously stored behind specially constructed dikes and dams to reclaim additional acres by irrigation. In central and eastern Prussia, the Cistercians actually reclaimed the entire so-called Thuringian Basin. At the same time, the monastery of Waldsassen in Germany, while largely supporting itself by the export of its dressed lumber, set a standard in the conservation of its native timber.

Significance

The Cistercians, as a twelfth century reform movement in the Western Church, preferred to establish fresh religious foundations rather than to try to reform older monasteries. More from necessity than choice, they tended to locate in places uninhabited for centuries, "thick set with thorns" in mountainous and rocky areas more suited as a "lair of wild beasts than the home of human beings." Capital gained through donations and earned through the patience of hard work, together with the monks' knowledge of ancient agricultural writings, helped them turn their inhospitable abodes into fertile areas despite wars, raids, diseases, great economic hindrances inflicted on the order's trade by the state, and the sharp fall in the value of money during the twelfth and thirteenth centuries. As the monasteries prospered, thousands flocked to work as paid bands for fixed wages.

The wool industry of the Cistercians grew rapidly as well; within forty years of their foundation they were widely known as great wool raisers. By the middle of the fourteenth century the yearly export reached forty thousand sacks shipped mainly from the port of Boston not only to Flanders but also to distant parts of the world in vessels of many countries.

With such a reputation in agronomy and animal husbandry, the Cistercians were much sought after in Western Europe. They were encouraged by liberal grants to settle in Poland, for example, where they contributed not only to the economic advance of the country but to the uplift of its social and moral tone as well.

—*Carl F. Rohne*

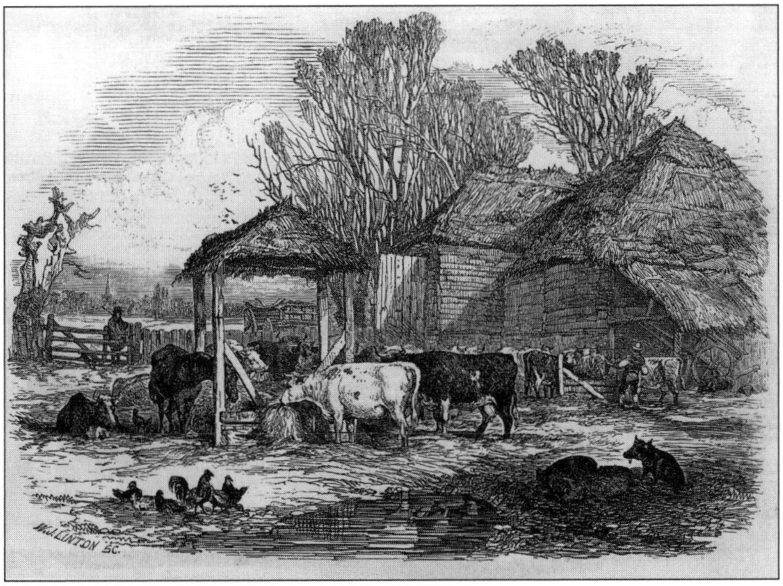

The Cistercian monks became famous for their advanced concepts of animal husbandry. Cattle, sheep, and hogs were generally allowed to roam and to mate indiscriminately among their own kind, but the Cistercians began to enclose their grasslands with fencing so that undesirable strains of cattle and uncontrolled inbreeding could not contaminate their herds. (Hulton|Archive by Getty Images)

Further Reading

Biossonade, P. *Life and Work in Medieval Europe*. 1927. Reprint. Westport, Conn.: Greenwood Press, 1982. A survey of the economic environment of the Middle Ages with special reference to agriculture.

Bokonyi, Sandor. "The Development of Stockbreeding and Herding in Medieval Europe." In *Agriculture in the Middle Ages: Technology, Practice, and Representation*, edited by Del Sweeney. Philadelphia: University of Pennsylvania Press, 1995. Examines the impact of new scientific methods of breeding livestock upon medieval European culture and society.

Duby, Georges. *Rural Economy and Country Life in the Medieval West*. Translated by Cynthia Postan. Reprint. Philadelphia: University of Pennsylvania Press, 1998. This extremely thorough analysis of all aspects of medieval agriculture includes significant discussions of animal husbandry, stockraising, and the Cistercian order.

Lekai, Louis. *The White Monks: A History of the Cistercian Order.* Okauchee, Wis.: Our Lady of Spring Bank, 1953. The author, himself a Cistercian, provides informative chapters on the agricultural pursuits of the Cistercians during the high Middle Ages: their improvement of the lands on which they settled; their extensive work in draining, clearing, and irrigating; and their significant contributions as livestock breeders.

Mullin, Francis A. *A History of the Work of the Cistercians in Yorkshire, 1131-1300.* Washington, D.C.: Catholic University of America Press, 1932. This work gives a picture of the contributions made by the Cistercians in England. Preliminary chapters deal with the founding of the Yorkshire Cistercians in 1131 and with the Cistercian ideal of charity: love of self, love of neighbor, and love of God.

Power, Eileen E. *The Wool Trade in English Medieval History.* Reprint. New York: Oxford University Press, 1955. A monograph on Cistercian work with sheep in England.

SEE ALSO: c. 700-1000: Heavy Plow Helps Increase Agricultural Yields; 1337-1453: Hundred Years' War.

RELATED ARTICLES in *Great Lives from History: The Middle Ages, 477-1453*: Beatrice of Nazareth; Saint Benedict of Nursia; Saint Bernard of Clairvaux.

c. 1200-1230
MANCO CAPAC FOUNDS THE INCA STATE

Manco Capac and his band of followers migrated northward from Pacaritambo and drove out the occupants of Acamama in the Cuzco valley. There he claimed for himself the title of Capac and divided his realm into four sections. From his male descendants, called Incas, would come successive rulers of Tahuantinsuyo.

LOCALE: Cuzco, Peru
CATEGORIES: Cultural and intellectual history; expansion and land acquisition; government and politics

KEY FIGURES

Manco Capac (fl. twelfth-thirteenth centuries), mythohistorical founder of the Incas and their state, r. c. 1200-1230

Mama Ocllo (fl. twelfth-thirteenth centuries), one of four sisters and the wife of Manco

Sinchi Roca (fl. thirteenth century), son of Manco Capac and Mama Ocllo and first successor to power, r. c. 1230-1265

Pachacuti (c. 1391-1471), ninth Incan emperor, successor to Manco Capac who reinvigorated his founding mission and created an enormous empire, r. 1438-1471

SUMMARY OF EVENT

The indigenous precontact societies of the Andes were nonliterate. The Spaniards recorded several varying accounts of the foundation of the Inca Empire told to them by surviving historians of the last Inca courts. Historians, ethnologists, and archaeologists have tried to disentangle the mythical and the historical elements of those accounts.

Archaeologists have identified a large polity they call the Huari Empire that thrived from roughly 600 to 1000 in central and southern Peru north of Lake Titicaca. After the collapse of the Huari Empire c. 1000, people in the Andean intermountain valleys returned to their traditional sociopolitical organization of kinship groups, or clans, tracing their lineage to a founding couple. These clans lived in agricultural villages called *ayllus* headed by *curacas*. Early in the thirteenth century, the *curaca* Manco Capac decided to relocate to better farmland. He grouped himself, his three brothers, four sisters, and neighboring clans of Tambos into ten *ayllus* and moved north out of Pacaritambo, in what is now Paruro Province of Peru's Cuzco Department.

Along the journey, Manco sought advice from his siblings, *ayllu* elders, priests, and his personal *huaca*, a *huaoque*, or "brother," which was a bird-shaped stone he called Inti, meaning "sun." A *huaca* was any thing, place, or person that possessed supernatural powers. Individuals, clans, and communities had *huacas* that they revered and turned to for guidance in all areas of life. This ancient custom of Andean indigenous societies persists today. Inti told Manco when to act as *sinchi*, war-chieftain, to force his way into settled areas and pause, sometimes for several years at a time, to plant and harvest crops to sustain his group while trying to locate a permanent homeland. During a prolonged stay at Tamboquiro, Mama Ocllo bore a son, Sinchi Roca. Years later, in Matagua, Manco initiated Sinchi Roca into manhood with a ceremony that included piercing his ears and placing a golden spool into each pierced hole. As Sinchi Roca grew, progressively larger spools stretched the ear lobes dramatically. These golden spools in enlarged ears became an identifying feature of all of Manco's Incas, his princes, who were male descendants and recognized as privileged elites. The Spaniards called the Incas *orejones*, big ears, because of that trait.

From Tamboquiro, Manco's band forced their way into Matagua. From Matagua they crossed the mountain ridges to the valley of Cuzco and observed a rainbow over Acamama, an *ayllu* nestled at the confluence of the Huatanay and Tullumayo Rivers. Manco declared that region to be the goal of the migration. Five groups already occupied the area. Four of the groups were Ayarmacas who were related to the newcomers and had migrated years earlier from Pacaritambo. After fierce fighting, Manco's forces drove the unrelated group out of the valley and settled Acamama. He made alliances with the other groups and cemented the alliances by exchanging brides. To the weaker groups, Manco gave daughters from the elites of his ten *ayllus*, signifying that he was the dominant partner. To the stronger groups, Manco acknowledged his subordinate status by receiving daughters of the elites whom he then married to his own elites, the Incas. The male descendants of his daughters became "Incas-by-Privilege" and shared power as semi-elites in his new kingdom.

In the center of the former Acamama, he constructed the Inticancha, a four-building complex that included his living quarters and a temple to Apu-Inti Viracocha, the sun deity. He proclaimed himself a *capac*, an exalted title that meant that his association with the solar deity made him greater than an ordinary ruler. As *capac* he was more than a *sinchi*, more than a *curaca*, more even than a *curaca* with one thousand *ayllus*, more than a person with merely temporal authority. His successors to power were also known also as Sapa Incas, or supreme rulers. The Sapa Inca's authority was absolute in all areas of society.

Radiating outward from the Inticancha, Manco Capac marked out *ceques*, "lines" dividing his realm into four sections. The *ceques* were not geometrically symmetrical but coincided with planetary alignments and allowed the Incas to calculate the arrival of planting and harvesting seasons of the various crops in the different altitudes of their vertical kingdom. Along the *ceques* he resettled

Inca kings (from top, left to right): Manco Capac, Sinchi Roca, Lloque Yupanqui, Mayta Capac, Capac Yupanqui, and Inca Roca. (Hulton|Archive by Getty Images)

his elites and semi-elites, according to their importance, and gave them administrative authority over their *ayllus*. They were to occupy and develop the fertile lands, contribute men to a common army, defend the borders, and maintain old and new shrines. Acamama he renamed Cuzco, the "navel," and called his new kingdom Tahuantinsuyo, the Four Quarters, considered the center of the world.

Tahuantinsuyo grew and prospered. The Incas expanded the acreage of irrigated lands, and llama flocks multiplied. When Manco Capac died, his *huaoque* Inti became part of the *canopa*, a collection of sacred objects kept together by his heirs.

After his death, Manco's first two heirs peacefully expanded the boundaries of Tahuantinsuyo by continuing

Manco's practice of controlling Inca marriages with neighboring elites. Before dying, the third *capac*, Lloque Yupanqui, had a vision from the solar deity Apu-Inti Viracocha. The deity told Lloque Yupanqui that his descendants would be great lords. His son, the third successor, Mayta Capac, retrieved Manco's *huaoque*, Inti, from its place of safekeeping for consultation. Inti gave the same aggressive advice it had given Manco, and Mayta Capac's army pushed the borders of the Incan state northward. He and his successors became great lords. They combined warfare with matrimonial diplomacy to expand the borders of Tahuantinsuyo.

During the reign of Viracocha Inca, the seventh successor, his son Pachacuti, who was not the designated heir, successfully repelled an attack by the powerful of the Chanca state. Pachacuti then seized power and took the name Pachacuti Inca Yupanqui. Invoking the name of Manco Capac, Pachacuti inaugurated major changes for the state. He declared that the founding eight Ayar siblings were children of Apu-Inti Viracocha. The solar deity had given Manco and the others a divine imperative and sent them to Earth through a cave on Tambotoco hill near Pacaritambo. They were to find a land chosen for them and to introduce farming, weaving, pottery making, cooking, astronomy, and all the other skills of civilization to the rest of humankind, by subjugation if necessary. One of the Ayar brothers, Ayar Cachi, was so troublesome that he had been tricked into returning to the cave. When inside, the brothers sealed the cave entrance and continued the migration without him. The other two were turned into stone and became important *huacas*. Manco recognized Acamama as the goal of the journey when his sister Mama Huaco threw a golden rod into the soil of the valley, and the rod sank all the way to its haft (handle). Pachacuti announced that all the heirs of Manco, the surviving brother who fulfilled the sacred mission entrusted to the Ayars, shared the divine essence of the solar deity. Because the divine Manco had married his sister rather than marry mere mortals, Pachacuti declared that, henceforth, Incas would marry only descendants from Manco himself. A future Inca had to be the son of the Sapa Inca and a Coya, the principal wife who was to be a sister or half sister.

SIGNIFICANCE

At his death Manco Capac left a strong state that developed into the largest of the precontact indigenous empires of the Western Hemisphere. The divine Pachacuti continued Manco's vision and rebuilt the capital of Cuzco with massive stone buildings. He replaced the Inticancha with a larger temple, called the Coricancha, the Golden Enclosure, a complex of four buildings covered with *cori*, meaning "gold." The Coricancha was a Temple of the Ancestors with sanctuaries dedicated to the sun, moon, and planets. Pachacuti renewed and accelerated the mission of spreading civilization, building stone fortresses at important junctures and connecting the major communities with an impressive road system.

When the Spaniards arrived in 1532, Manco's empire of Tahuantinsuyo had spread from Cuzco north through modern Ecuador to Colombia, south to the Maule River in central Chile, and eastward through Bolivia into northwestern Argentina.

—Paul E. Kuhl

FURTHER READING

Bauer, Brian S. *The Sacred Landscape of the Inca: The Cusco Ceque System*. Austin: University of Texas Press, 1998. An ethnologist's detailed description of the locations and functions of the *ceques* that marked the physical, social, and spiritual boundaries within the Incan empire.

Julien, Catherine. *Reading Inca History*. Iowa City: University of Iowa Press, 2000. An attempt to absorb the results of recent ethnological, archaeological, and astronomical information and provide a coherent history of the Incas. Given the complexity of the materials, a surprisingly good read.

Rostworowski de Diez Canseco, María. *History of the Inca Realm*. Translated by Harry B. Iceland. New York: Cambridge University Press, 1999. Fine reconstruction of the evolution of the Inca state, based heavily on archaeological data.

Urton, Gary. *The History of a Myth: Pacariqtambo and the Origin of the Inkas*. Austin: University of Texas Press, 1990. An anthropologist's meticulous comparisons of the Spanish chronicles and sixteenth century court records in an attempt to identify the events that could be understood in the Western sense of historicity.

SEE ALSO: After 850: Foundation of Chan Chan; c. 1000: Collapse of the Huari and Tiwanaku Civilizations.

13th century
NDIADIANE N'DIAYE FOUNDS THE WOLOF EMPIRE

The Wolof Empire emerged in the thirteenth century under the leadership of Ndiadiane N'diaye and became a powerful expansionist state, partly because of its unique location along the West African coast.

LOCALE: Senegal region expanding to the west coast of Africa
CATEGORY: Government and politics

KEY FIGURES

Ndiadiane N'diaye (fl. thirteenth century), the founder of the Wolof Empire
Alvise Cadamosto (Ca' da Mosto; 1432-1488), a Venetian explorer retained by Prince Henry the Navigator of Portugal

SUMMARY OF EVENT

The Wolof (also spelled Djolof, Jolof, or Ouolof) Empire was formed when a group of people migrated in the tenth century from the powerful Ghana Empire (situated far northwest of modern-day Ghana) and settled in the Senegal River region. The Wolof's cultural origins in Ghana are seen most clearly in the similarities of religion and culture between the Wolof and Ghana peoples.

Senegal was the site of several large kingdoms in the tenth century, as a result of its location along the borders of the Sahelian and riverine trades that converged between the Senegal and Niger Rivers in the savanna lands. In the west, the Wolof abutted the Atlantic Ocean, creating an opportunity for fish and other oceanic products to be exported in the trans-Saharan trade. However, the geographic area inhabited by the Wolof was broad and environmentally diverse. The climate varied drastically between the northern and southern ends of the Wolof territory, from arid desert in the north to tropical rain forest in the south. This environmental diversity allowed for the growth of a wide variety of crops.

Prior to the settlement of the Wolof people in the Senegal River area, there was a state north of the region known as Tekrur, which had grown to be one of West Africa's most powerful states. Tekrur had been in existence for a long time and may have expanded even before the initial growth of the Ghana Empire. Tekrur became wealthy from the trans-Saharan trade between northern and western Africa, which involved the exchange of such items as gold, slaves, and salt—three of the most highly prized possessions of that time.

The Tekrur kingdom collapsed around the time that the Wolof state was emerging under the leadership of Ndiadiane N'diaye. N'diaye claimed rule over the smaller states of Waalo, Cayor, and Baol, which had formed after the initial settlement of the Wolof people in the Senegal region toward the Atlantic coast, and N'diaye united them to form the Wolof kingdom. (Some sources note that these states, along with Djolof proper, formed in the mid-sixteenth century as the result of a fragmented Wolof Empire.)

The Wolof Empire was similar to many West African Sudanic cultures of the thirteenth century in that it was centered on a king, or *burba*. However, this *burba* did not inherit the throne through birth; he was instead chosen by a handful of nobles who made up the elite democracy. These lords chose the individual whom they saw as most fit to rule the empire from a group of qualified candidates. The lords also held the power to dethrone those they had elected if they grew to dislike the ruler's ideals or style of reign. The *burba* could retain power for decades as long as the nobles were satisfied with his leadership. These nobles obtained their status and political strength through their leadership in the military, their influence on trading systems, and their close alliance with one another through social networks under the king's rule.

The Wolof people were organized into a hierarchy of castes, a rigid structure in which the social position of the person was inherited. There were three main castes: the *jambur* or *gor* (freeborn), the *nyenyo* (artisan castes), and the *jam* (slaves). The freeborn included both the poorest commoner (*baadola*) and the royal peoples. The main economic occupation of the Wolof was farming, and the royal members were at the top of the social pyramid. The *nyenyo* caste included the *tega* (goldsmiths, silversmiths, and blacksmiths), the *rabbakat* or *maabo* (weavers), the *ude* (leatherworkers), and the *gewel* (musicians, praise singers, and historians). These occupations were inherited, and marriage outside the caste was forbidden.

Slaves were the lowest caste of people of the Wolof Empire, and there were three categories of slaves: the *jami-neg* (domestic), *jami-hareh* (traded or captured), and *jami-bur* (crown slaves). Domestic slaves were born in the household and were rarely sold. They were treated like junior members of the family, often received their own land to farm, and were allowed to marry. Trade slaves were usually captured in war and had no ties to the community. They could be bought and sold, as they had no local social network or family to support them or protect their interests. Crown slaves did manual labor for the king and for the state. They sometimes became trusted advisers of the king if they proved themselves loyal and wise. These slaves, as well as the artisans and common freeborn peoples, were required to serve the empire's nobles, working for them when necessary, and pay taxes in the form of cattle, other goods, and labor.

By the fourteenth century, the Wolof state had renounced all association with the large Mali Empire to its east and claimed a culture of its own. The Wolof became renowned for their artisans' ability to craft precious metals and prospered from their control of trade, which in turn augmented the state's political authority.

By the fifteenth century, nearly five centuries after the rise of the Wolof Empire, the Senegal River area was experiencing the influence of the Islamic religion and culture. The spread of Islam among the Wolof began with the political leaders and then expanded throughout the area among the commoner population until a majority of people of Wolof ethnicity and language had converted to Islam. Many of the Wolof practiced the Sufi form of Islam. Wolof beliefs were also characterized by "ontological absolutes," which were explanations or expectations involving ten key concepts combining Islamic and pre-Islamic ideals.

Beginning in the mid-fifteenth century, the Wolof Empire had come into contact with Europeans on the Atlantic coast south of the Senegal River. The first recorded European contact occurred with the Venetian explorer and trader Alvise Cadamosto, who in 1455 sailed along the West African coast past the mouth of the Senegal River. This contact led to trade with the Portuguese, heralding the beginning of a global commercial system based in the Atlantic. The Portuguese traded European and Asian textiles, copperware, cowrie shells, and horses in exchange for African gold, ivory, slaves, and locally made cotton cloth.

SIGNIFICANCE

The Wolof Empire serves as an example of the rise of powerful states in West Africa between the tenth and sixteenth centuries. Unlike many of the earlier western African states, however, Wolof occupied an ocean coast; virtually all other large states in West Africa emerged inland. As a result, the development of the Wolof Empire was influenced by, and benefited from, early Atlantic trade.

The Wolof Empire continued to grow until its collapse around the mid-seventeenth century, caused by conflicts within its own borders. In 1556, for example, Cayor, in the west, divided from the Wolof Empire and cut off its coastal access. The declining status of the Wolof state was exacerbated by the presence of European merchants in the eastern Atlantic through the nineteenth century. Today approximately 1.5 million Wolof still reside in Senegal and its environs.

—*Catherine Cymone Fourshey*

FURTHER READING

Boulègue, Jean. *Le Grand Jolof, XIIIe-XVIe siècle*. Paris: Façades Diffusion Karthala, 1987. Covers the history of the Wolof people in the empire between the thirteenth and sixteenth centuries.

Charles, Eunice A. *Precolonial Senegal: The Jolof Kingdom, 1800-1890*. Brookline, Mass.: African Studies Center, Boston University, 1977. Covers the history of the Wolof Empire in the nineteenth century, with some mention of earlier eras.

Diop, Samba. *The Oral History and Literature of the Wolof People of Waalo, Northern Senegal: The Master of the Word (Griot) in the Wolof Tradition*. Lewiston, N.Y.: Mellen Press, 1995. This book elaborates the epic tale of the Wolof and is concerned with the genealogy of the rulers of Waalo.

Diouf, Mamadou. *Precolonial Senegal: The Jolof Kingdom, 1800-1890*. Paris: Maisonneuve & Larose, 2001. This text covers the larger history of Senegal.

Tamari, Tal. "The Development of the Caste System." *Journal of African History* 32, no. 2 (1991): 221-250. Explains the history of the caste system in the Wolof state, focusing on griots and blacksmiths.

SEE ALSO: 992-1054: Ghana Takes Control of Awdaghust; 1062-1147: Almoravids Conquer Morocco and Establish the Almoravid Empire; 1076: Almoravids Sack Kumbi; 1230's-1255: Reign of Sundiata of Mali; 1415-1460: Prince Henry the Navigator Promotes Portuguese Exploration.

RELATED ARTICLES in *Great Lives from History: The Middle Ages, 477-1453:* Prince Henry the Navigator; Mansa Mūsā; Sundiata.

1204
GENGHIS KHAN FOUNDS MONGOL EMPIRE

The Mongols, led by Genghis Khan, defeated the Naiman, a Turkic tribe that controlled much of what is now western Mongolia, and thereby gained control of all Mongolia. Although Genghis Khan did not ascend to the throne until 1206, the victory over the Naiman gave the Mongols complete military superiority over the steppes of Mongolia and allowed them to build the Mongol Empire.

LOCALE: Mongolia
CATEGORIES: Expansion and land acquisition; government and politics

KEY FIGURES

Genghis Khan (Temüjin; between 1155 and 1162-1227), founder and ruler of the Mongol Empire, r. 1206-1227
Tayang Khan (fl. 1160-1204), ruler of the Naiman tribal confederation in western Mongolia
Toghrïl (Ong-Khan; fl. 1140-1203), ruler of Kereit tribal confederation in Central Mongolia, r. 1150-1203 (not continuously)
Jamuqa (fl. 1170-1206), leader of the Jadaran Mongols, blood brother and rival of Genghis Khan
Küchlüg (d. after 1207), militant son of Tayang Khan
Toqto'a (d. 1208), commander of the Merkit

SUMMARY OF EVENT

After a series of wars and shifting alliances, by 1204 only two tribes remained as significant powers in the steppes of Mongolia. Controlling central and eastern Mongolia were the Mongols led by Genghis Khan, and in the west were the Naiman (literally, "eight tribes"), under the leadership of Tayang Khan. In 1203, Genghis Khan had defeated his former overlord, Toghrïl (later known as Ong-Khan), khan of the Kereit tribe who ruled central Mongolia. His victory made the Naiman realize that they would have to deal with the Mongols at some point, and they decided to go to war against the Mongols. On hearing of their decision, however, Genghis Khan took the initiative and immediately marched against them. His decision was precarious, as the Mongols marched in early spring, before their horses had sufficient time to recover from the winter.

Thus, in the spring of 1204, the Mongols encountered the Naiman, who were reinforced by other tribal groups that also wished to avoid Mongol domination. One leader who joined the Naiman was Jamuqa, the leader of the Mongol Jadaran clan and *anda*, or blood brother, of Genghis Khan.

To initially confuse the Naiman, the Mongols lit numerous campfires at night, hoping to convince the Naiman that Genghis Khan's army was larger than it was. Additionally, this tactic helped stall the action so that the Mongol army and their mounts could rest. Tayang Khan, realizing the weakened state of the Mongols' horses, wanted to lure the Mongols across the Altai Mountains, where the Naiman could then ambush them. However, his more militant son Küchlüg and others insisted on attacking directly rather than relying on subterfuge. Their desires won the day, and the Naiman took the offensive. Meanwhile, Genghis Khan ordered his men to advance.

The Mongols pressed their advantage and defeated the Naiman. Tayang Khan fled but was captured at Naqu Cliff in 1204. Although Küchlüg established a fortified camp and resisted Mongol attacks for a brief time, he was forced to flee again to the Irtysh River. All the Naiman who survived the onslaught were incorporated into the Mongols. Furthermore, a number of minor tribes who had accompanied Jamuqa submitted to Genghis Khan. These included the Jadaran, Qatagin, Salji'ut, Dörben, Taychi'ut, and Onggirat.

With the victory over the Naiman, Genghis Khan now controlled the Mongolian plateau, although remnants of the Naiman and Merkit tribes continued to linger on the

MAJOR RULERS OF THE MONGOL EMPIRE

Reign	*Ruler*
1206-1227	Genghis Khan
1227-1229	Tolui (son of Genghis Khan), regent
1229-1241	Ogatai Khan
1241-1246	Toregene (wife of Ogatai), regent
1246-1248	Güyük
1248-1251	Oghul Qaimish (wife of Güyük), regent
1251-1259	Mongu
1259-1260	Arigböge (brother of Mongu and Kublai), regent
1260-1294	Kublai Khan

THE MONGOL EMPIRE IN 1260

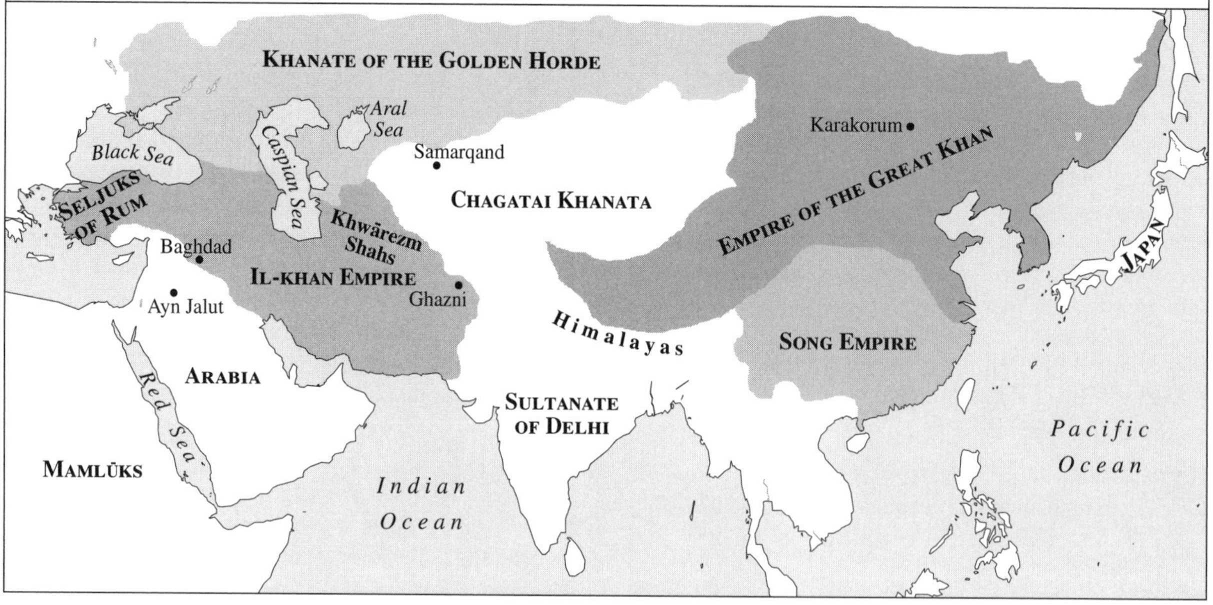

fringes of Mongolia. In addition, despite some voluntary submissions to Genghis Khan, many of the Northern Forest people remained outside Genghis Khan's control. Despite this, the Mongols still found it necessary to complete their destruction of the Naiman and their longtime foes, the Merkit, in 1206 in the Altai. In a battle near the Ulagh Tagh, the Naiman and Merkit were defeated. Factions still led by Küchlüg of the Naiman and Toqto'a of the Merkit fled farther west. Meanwhile, Jamuqa fled northwest into Tannu Tuva near the Yenesei River.

Yuan chao bishi (1240; *The Secret History of the Mongols*, 1982) does not mention any operations against the Naiman in 1206; however, historian Rashīd ad-Dīn recorded a campaign against Buyiruq Khan. It appears that Buyiruq Khan emerged as the leading figure among the Naiman after the battle in 1204. In 1206, shortly after Genghis Khan ascended the Mongol throne, he launched an attack against Buyiruq. Genghis Khan successfully defeated and killed him and thus incorporated Buyiruq's territory into his own. In a curious twist, Rashīd ad-Dīn wrote that in this battle, Küchlüg escaped and fled to the Irtysh River (now in Russia) along with Toqto'a Beki of the Merkit. It is not clear if this battle that Rashīd ad-Dīn describes was a merging of events from 1204 and those in 1208, or if it actually took place.

Not until 1207 did Genghis Khan decide to destroy any further resistance by the Naiman and Merkits. He moved westward to confront them; however, early in the winter of 1207, Genghis Khan's army halted, pausing until 1208. At this time, he also accepted the submission of the Oirad. Resuming their march, the Mongols rode through the Ulan Pass over the Altai Mountains and reached the Bukhtamra River, a branch of the Irtysh River. There the Mongols battled the Naiman and Merkits. Küchlüg, although defeated, escaped and fled first toward the Qarluqs, then toward the Uighurs of Tian Shan (now in China), and then to the ghurkhan of Karakitai (now in Kazakhstan, China, Kyrgyzstan, Turkmenistan, Uzbekistan, and Tajikistan). Toqto'a of the Merkit was slain in combat, and many of his men drowned in the river attempting to flee.

SIGNIFICANCE

The final victory over the Naiman was extremely important as it ensured that Mongolia would not face a potentially dangerous coalition of the Naiman and any other tribe dissatisfied with Genghis Khan's rule, which could include members of his own family or even supporters. Although the Mongols spent the next four years quelling rebellions or defeating the remaining tribes that had not submitted to them, the 1204 victory ended any major threat to Genghis Khan's superiority. Any remaining hostilities concerned only portions of the Mongol army.

After eliminating his rivals for dominance in the steppe, Genghis Khan could effectively become the emperor of Mongolia, assuming this position officially in

1206. He reorganized Mongolia, taking the numerous tribes that had engaged in internecine conflict and merging them into a single unit, the Yeke Mongol Ulus (great Mongol nation). This had the effect of making all tribes part of the Mongols and thus gave them a vested interest in the success of the empire. Those tribes that had served or allied with the Mongols in the past maintained their identities to some extent, whereas those that had continually resisted, such as the Naiman and the Merkits, were divided and distributed among the new units of the empire: *minggans* (thousands).

Although most of the organization of the Mongol Empire occurred in 1206, Genghis Khan had begun the organization of his empire in 1204. Shortly before the war with the Naiman, Genghis Khan had distributed spoils and divided conquered tribes among his generals and followers as a reward for their service and loyalty. The principle in this reorganization was the *minggan*. The *minggan*, or groups of a thousand households, served not only as military units but also as community units for taxation and organizational purposes. The use of the *minggan* became the standard and basis of the decimal system of organization that the Mongols used for their army as well as for organizing conquered populations for taxation and corvée labor.

In addition to removing the final obstacle to complete control over the nomads of Mongolia, the victory over the Naiman in 1204 carried additional importance. As the Naiman and the Mongols were the only significant powers remaining in Mongolia, had the Naiman been victorious, it is quite likely that the Mongol Empire would have ended before it had begun.

—*Timothy May*

FURTHER READING

Cleaves, F. W., ed. and trans. *The Secret History of the Mongols*. Cambridge, Mass.: Harvard University Press, 1982. A translation of an early Mongolian history of the life of Genghis Khan and the rise of the Mongol Empire. An excellent translation; however, Cleaves rendered it into King James English.

Grousset, René. *The Empire of the Steppes: A History of Central Asia*. Translated by Naomi Walford. New Brunswick, N.J.: Rutgers University Press, 1970. A general history of Central Asia with a considerable portion devoted to the rise and expansion of the Mongol Empire.

Hartog, Leo de. *Genghis Khan: Conqueror of the World*. New York: I. B. Tauris, 1999. While not as authoritative as Ratchnevsky's biography, Hartog's biography of Genghis Khan serves as a highly readable introduction to the rise of the Mongol Empire.

Martin, H. D. *The Rise of Chingis Khan and His Conquest of North China*. Baltimore, Md.: The Johns Hopkins Press, 1950. A study of the rise of Genghis Khan and his conquests of northern China that remains the standard more than fifty years after it was published.

Morgan, David. *The Mongols*. Oxford, England: Basil Blackwell, 1986. Morgan's volume remains the best introduction to the Mongol Empire in all of its aspects from its rise to its decline.

Onon, Urgunge, ed. and trans. *The Secret History of the Mongols: The Life and Times of Chinggis Khan*. Richmond, Surrey: Curzon Press, 2001. Another translation of *The Secret History of the Mongols* that is easier to read.

Rashiduddin Fazullah. *Jami'u't Tawarikhi: Compendium of Chronicles, a History of the Mongols*. 3 vols. Translated by W. M. Thackston. Cambridge, Mass.: Harvard University, Department of Near Eastern Languages and Civilizations, 1998. Another important source about the Mongol Empire, Rashīd ad-Dīn's (Rashiduddin's) work contains valuable information concerning the rise of the Mongols.

Ratchnevsky, Paul. *Genghis Khan: His Life and Legacy*. Translated by Thomas Nivison Haining. Cambridge, Mass.: Blackwell, 1992. The best and most scholarly biography of Genghis Khan.

SEE ALSO: 936: Khitans Settle Near Beijing; 1115: Foundation of the Jin Dynasty; 1130: Karakitai Empire Established; 1271-1295: Travels of Marco Polo.

RELATED ARTICLES in *Great Lives from History: The Middle Ages, 477-1453*: Genghis Khan; Kublai Khan; Marco Polo.

1204
KNIGHTS OF THE FOURTH CRUSADE CAPTURE CONSTANTINOPLE

The knights of the Fourth Crusade ushered in the triumph of militant Latin Catholicism and established Western political and economic power over the Byzantine Empire by capturing Constantinople.

LOCALE: Constantinople, Byzantine Empire (now Istanbul, Turkey)

CATEGORIES: Religion; wars, uprisings, and civil unrest

KEY FIGURES

Enrico Dandolo (c. 1107-1205), doge of Venice, 1192-1205

Innocent III (1160 or 1161-1216), Roman Catholic pope, 1198-1216

Isaac II Angelus (c. 1135-1204), Byzantine emperor, r. 1185-1195, 1203-1204

Alexius III Angelus (d. 1211), Byzantine emperor, r. 1195-1203

Alexius V Ducas Murtzuphlus (d. 1204), Byzantine emperor, r. 1204

Baldwin I (1172-1205), count of Flanders as Baldwin IX and count of Hainaut as Baldwin VI, 1195-1205; Byzantine emperor, r. 1204-1205

SUMMARY OF EVENT

The fall of Constantinople in 1204 was the culmination of a long historical process of Byzantine decline and the ascendancy of Western political, military, economic, and religious power in the eastern Mediterranean.

Beginning with the First Crusade in 1096, the Byzantine Empire feared that the knights were as often interested in taking Byzantine territory as they were in conquering the Holy Land. Crusading armies, particularly when they passed through the Balkans, often pillaged Byzantine provinces. From the Byzantine perspective, the Norman conquest of southern Italy made them a constant military threat to the Balkans, especially at Dyrrachium (now Durrës, Albania) on the Adriatic coast.

In the twelfth century, the Italian cities of Venice, Genoa, and Pisa obtained commercial privileges in the Byzantine Empire and established districts within Constantinople. Yet their economic power and presence within the capital were bitterly resented, and in 1182, the Latins in Constantinople were brutally massacred. Three years later, the Normans seized both Dyrrachium and the important city of Thessalonica, which was ravaged in revenge for the Latin massacre of 1182.

In the Third Crusade, the German emperor Frederick I Barbarossa raided the Balkans, seized Adrianople, and sought even to take Constantinople before crossing into Anatolia, where he died. In 1197, Barbarossa's son, Henry VI, gathered a huge fleet to attack Constantinople, but his death ended the expedition.

The Crusades were a constant threat to the Byzantine Empire, but the empire had been militarily weak ever since the destruction of the Byzantine army by the Seljuk Turks at Myriokephalon in 1176. The Italians were needed to offset the Normans and Germans. The Venetians were permitted to return to Constantinople in 1189, and the Genoese and Pisans followed in 1198.

Tensions between the Byzantine Empire and the Western knights were further strained because the Byzantines had entered into alliances with the Seljuks, as in the First Crusade, and with Egypt in the Third Crusade. The Byzantine Empire was accused of not sufficiently aiding the knights and was blamed for the failure of the Second Crusade. In addition, the Catholic and Orthodox churches were in excommunication since 1054. Doctrinal issues over the bread used in the Mass, the nature of the Holy Trinity of Jesus, and the claims of Rome as the head of the Christian world further divided east and west. In the Third Lateran Council of 1179, the pope claimed papal supremacy over the Orthodox Church. Thus, the events of 1204 were the culmination of more than a century's hostility between Byzantium and the West.

In 1198, a new pope, Innocent III, ascended the papal throne and soon called for a new Crusade. Most of the knights came from France, Flanders, England, Germany, and Sicily. They were led by Thibault of Champagne, who died just before the Crusade began, Boniface of Montferrat, Baldwin of Flanders, and Louis of Blois.

In Venice, Enrico Dandolo became doge in 1192 at the age of about eighty-five. Legend had it that he had been blinded some thirty years earlier in Constantinople as a hostage. Dandolo saw the Crusade as a means for extending Venetian influence in the eastern Mediterranean. In addition to accusing Dandolo for turning the Crusade against the Byzantine Empire, scholars have variously accused Philip of Swabia (r. 1198-1208), who succeeded his brother Henry VI as emperor of Germany and married the daughter of Byzantine emperor Isaac II Angelus, and Boniface of Montferrat, who claimed Thessalonica as king (r. 1204-1207). Such conspiracies are difficult to prove, but there was a general attitude of hostility toward the Byzantine Empire and a willingness to unify the two Christian churches.

The knights needed Venetian ships, and they agreed to pay eighty-five thousand silver marks for transport and supplies for forty-five hundred knights, nine thousand squires, and twenty thousand sergeants. Venice would also send fifty warships. A secret clause to the treaty stated that the Crusade would in fact be directed against Egypt, the center of Ayyūbid power and the base from which the Muslims had retaken Jerusalem in 1187.

As the knights gathered at Venice in April, 1202, they were able to muster only ten thousand soldiers, but the Venetians refused to lower their fees. Unable to meet the Venetian fees, the knights agreed to the doge's demand to divert the Crusaders toward Zara, a Venetian dependency on the Dalmatian coast that had been taken by the Hungarians in 1186. Zara fell to the Crusaders, but the Cistercians in the army opposed the action, and Innocent excommunicated the army. Innocent, however, did not want to lose all control of the Crusade; he later lifted the ban on the French and Germans but retained it for the Venetians. He did not forbid contact with the Venetians, however, and this allowed the army to remain together.

In Constantinople, Alexius III Angelus had taken power in 1195 by overthrowing and blinding his brother, Isaac II. Isaac's son, Alexius, escaped to the West in 1201 and sought help to restore his father to the throne. Alexius joined the Crusade; he offered two hundred thousand marks and declared his intention of unifying the churches. It was an opportunity the Venetians could not refuse. Innocent, although reluctant to change the Crusade, did not condemn the turn toward Constantinople. On July 17, 1203, the Crusaders attacked Constantinople by land and sea. Alexius III fled and the city was taken. The blind Isaac and his son were crowned as coemperors. They managed to pay one hundred thousand marks to the Venetians and knights, but a popular tide of anti-Latin feeling swept the capital, and virtually all Latins were driven from the city to Galata, where the knights were encamped. A new emperor took power as Alexius V Ducas Murtzuphlus, and both coemperors were murdered. The Crusaders then decided to destroy Byzantine independence and to subjugate the Orthodox Church to Rome. Alexius V was declared a usurper and murderer.

The taking of Constantinople in 1204, based on a sixteenth century painting by Tintoretto. (Frederick Ungar Publishing Co.)

After agreeing among themselves on dividing the Byzantine Empire, the knights launched their attack on April 12, 1204. On April 13, they breached the walls. For three days, the Crusaders ravaged the city. Alexius V was captured and executed by being thrown from a high column in the Hippodrome. Much of the plunder was dispersed to France and Venice, including the sixth century horses that adorn Saint Mark's Cathedral. One knight, Robert of Clari, remarked that "that two thirds of the wealth of this world is in Constantinople."

An electoral council of six Venetians and six Frenchmen chose Baldwin, count of Flanders, as emperor of Romania—the Latin empire of Constantinople. He was crowned in the cathedral of Hagia Sophia with the Latin rite. The Venetians had opposed the selection of Boniface of Montferrat but compensated him with Thessalonica. The Venetians and Baldwin divided Constantinople; Baldwin received five-eighths of the city and Dandolo three-eighths. Baldwin was also given southern Thrace, some area along the Bosporus, and important islands such as Lesbos and Chios. Yet the Venetians obtained major acquisitions, including Dyrrachium on the Adriatic, the Ionian islands, most of the islands of the Aegean, Crete, Gallipoli, and territory within Thrace.

Dandolo took the Byzantine title of despot and was not required to pay homage to Baldwin. Venetian clergy were given control of Hagia Sophia, and a Venetian, Morosini, was made patriarch of the Catholic Church in Constantinople. The Venetians held the most important harbors of the Byzantine Empire and secured the seas between Venice and Constantinople. The Byzantine Empire had effectively become a colony of Venice. Innocent III at first welcomed the news of Constantinople's fall and its religious union with the West, but as he learned of the details of the sack and the dominance of Venice over the church in Constantinople, he expressed concern over the direction that the Crusade had taken. In the end, however, he had to reconcile himself with the results.

Byzantine royalty and nobility formed three new kingdoms in exile: one was the empire of Nicaea just across the Sea of Marmora, a second was the despotat of Epirus in the Balkans, and the third was the empire of Trebizond on the Black Sea. The Latins occupied Constantinople but had great difficulty governing the rest of the empire. Finally, in 1261, a new Byzantine dynasty under Emperor Michael VIII Palaeologus (r. 1259-1282) was restored.

SIGNIFICANCE

Despite the restoration of the dynasty, the Byzantine Empire never fully recovered from the Fourth Crusade. It remained weak and dependent on the West until its final surrender to the Ottoman Turks in 1453. The 1204 sack of Constantinople also widened the breach between the Eastern and Western churches.

—Lawrence N. Langer

FURTHER READING

Andrea, Alfred J., ed. *Contemporary Sources for the Fourth Crusade*. Boston: Brill, 2000. Explores the varied contemporary sources that document the Fourth Crusade, including the "registers" of Innocent III. Bibliography, index.

Angold, Michael. *The Fourth Crusade: Event and Context*. New York: Longman, 2003. Examines the Fourth Crusade as a major turning point in East-West Church relations. Chapters on the Byzantine perspective, the West's assessment of Byzantium, the Venetians, the Latin empire and church of Constantinople, the Orthodox revival, and Byzantium as myth. Maps, bibliography, index.

Bartlett, W. B. *An Ungodly War: The Sack of Constantinople and the Fourth Crusade*. Stroud, Gloucestershire, England: Sutton, 2000. Surveys the Fourth Crusade, its "misguided idealism," the massive physical destruction of Constantinople, and the killing of thousands of its people. Illustrations, maps, bibliography, index.

Choniates, Nicetas. *O City of Byzantium*. Translated by Harry I. Magoulias. Detroit, Mich.: Wayne State University Press, 1984. The major Byzantine source on the Fourth Crusade. Illustrations, bibliography, index.

Clari, Robert de. *The Conquest of Constantinople*. Translated by Edgar Holmes McNeal. 1936. Reprint. Toronto: University of Toronto Press and Medieval Academy of America, 1996. A classic, brief account by an eyewitness to the 1204 sack of Constantinople. Bibliography, index.

Godfrey, John. *1204, the Unholy Crusade*. New York: Oxford University Press, 1980. A good, concise general survey of the Fourth Crusade. Illustrations, bibliography, index.

Hillenbrand, Carole. *The Crusades: Islamic Perspectives*. New York: Routledge, 2000. Chapters explore Muslim reactions to the Crusades, ethnic and religious stereotyping, daily life, the conduct of war, and more. Bibliography, index.

Madden, Thomas F., ed. *The Crusades: The Essential Readings*. Malden, Mass.: Blackwell, 2002. A collection of previously published articles about the Crusades, including medieval sources, lay enthusiasm, patronage, Byzantium, and the subjection of Muslims. Bibliography, index.

Queller, Donald E., and Thomas F. Madden. *The Fourth Crusade: The Conquest of Constantinople, 1201-1204*. 2d ed. Philadelphia: University of Pennsylvania Press, 1997. Adopts a Western European rather than Byzantine perspective on the Fourth Crusade. Maps, extensive bibliography, index.

Villehardouin, Geoffroi de, and Jean de Joinville. *Memoirs of the Crusades*. Translated by Sir Frank Marzials. Reprint. Westport, Conn.: Greenwood Press, 1983. This work contains English translations of the contemporary chronicles of the historian, military leader, and Crusader Geoffroi de Villehardouin. In the section on Villehardouin, the translator also provides a helpful summary of the earlier Crusades

SEE ALSO: 532-537: Building of Hagia Sophia; August 15-20, 636: Battle of Yarmūk; 1054: Beginning of the Rome-Constantinople Schism; August 26, 1071: Battle of Manzikert; 1077: Seljuk Dynasty Is Founded; November 27, 1095: Pope Urban II Calls the First Crusade; c. 1120: Order of the Knights Templar Is Founded; c. 1145: Prester John Myth Sweeps Across Europe; 1150: Venetian Merchants Dominate Trade with the East; 1152: Frederick Barbarossa Is Elected King of Germany; 1189-1192: Third Crusade; 1217-1221: Fifth Crusade; 1227-1230: Frederick II Leads the Sixth Crusade; 1248-1254: Failure of the Seventh Crusade; May 29, 1453: Fall of Constantinople.

RELATED ARTICLES in *Great Lives from History: The Middle Ages, 477-1453*: Enrico Dandolo; Frederick I Barbarossa; Frederick II; Innocent III; Saladin; Theoleptus of Philadelphia; Geoffroi de Villehardouin.

1206-1210
QUṬ AL-DĪN AYBAK ESTABLISHES THE DELHI SULTANATE

By establishing the Delhi sultanate, Quṭ al-Dīn Aybak laid the foundation for Muslim hegemony in northern India.

LOCALE: Northern India
CATEGORIES: Expansion and land acquisition; government and politics

KEY FIGURE

Quṭ al-Dīn Aybak (d. 1210), first sultan of Delhi, r. 1206-1210

SUMMARY OF EVENT

Muslim hegemony in northern India began with raids by Central Asian Turks, advancing through Afghanistan, which led to the establishment of the Delhi sultanate during the thirteenth century. First, the Ghaznavids (977-1186), former Turkish slave-soldiers (*mamlūk*), and then the Ghūrids (c. 1000-1215), Persians from the region of Ghūr in central Afghanistan, led repeated expeditions across the Indus into India. Although later clerical writers described these expeditions as holy wars (*jihad*) and glorified the destruction of Hindu temples and idols, the prime purpose of these raids was the acquisition of plunder, of which vast quantities were obtained.

The culmination of these activities came during the dominions of two brothers, Ghiyāṣ-ud-Dīn Muḥammad (r. 1163-1203) and Muʿizz-ud-Dīn Muḥammad (r. 1203-1206). The latter brother embarked on far-flung conquests in northern India, reaching Benares to the east and Ujjain to the south. His principal lieutenant, Quṭ al-Dīn Aybak, led many of these expeditions, and, after Muʿizz-ud-Dīn's death, became the first sultan of Delhi.

These conquests were achieved through the agency of a Muslim institution known as the *mamlūk*, or slave-soldier. Islamic religious law allowed the enslavement of non-Muslims, and at this time, the Turks of Central Asia were still shamanists, that is, unbelievers. From the time of the ʿAbbāsid caliph, al-Muʿtaṣim (r. 833-842), male Turkish slaves had been purchased and trained as professional soldiers, being much admired for their warlike qualities. Slave-armies consisted of slave-soldiers, commanded by slave-officers, and led by slave-commanders. The slave-commanders sometimes became actual rulers.

Quṭ al-Dīn Aybak was the supreme example of this curious system. A Central Asian Turk, born in the second half of the twelfth century, he was captured by slave-raiders and taken to the Persian city of Nishapur. Here, he was purchased by the city governor, who brought him up with his own sons, instructed him in the tenets of Islam, and trained him in horsemanship and archery. When his master died, he was taken to Ghazna in southeastern Afghanistan, to the court of Muʿizz-ud-Dīn Muḥammad Ghūri. The latter, impressed by Aybak's bearing and character, straightaway purchased him and placed him in his own household of *mamlūks*. When the sultan embarked on the conquest of northern India, he had Aybak by his side, promoting him within the *mamlūk* command structure.

The pace of the conquests that followed was impressive. Multan and Uch in Punjab were captured in 1175. In 1178, Muʿizz-ud-Dīn invaded Gujarat, but at Nahrwala, he suffered a massive defeat at the hands of the Cālukya ruler, Mularaja II, and was forced to withdraw. Thereafter, he proceeded to campaign in Sind, to capture Peshawar and Sialkot, and to take Lahore in 1186.

East of the Sutlej lay the sprawling realm of the Chauhan Rājput ruler, Pṛithivīrāja, which consisted of Delhi, Sambhar, and Ajmer and reached south to Mahoba. There could be no further Muslim penetration of India without first eliminating this major figure. In 1191, Muᶜizz-ud-Dīn sought to crush him in the first Battle of Tarain, near Thanesar on the upper Jumna. Pṛithivīrāja had assembled an immense army of vassals and allies. The contemporary Persian historian Minhāj Sirāj Jūzjānī has written of Hindu forces consisting of 200,000 cavalry and 3,000 war elephants. The Ghūrid army was decisively routed, and the sultan, wounded in battle, withdrew to Lahore to replenish his depleted manpower.

In 1192, Muᶜizz-ud-Dīn returned with an army said to number 120,000 to 130,000 horsemen, including 10,000 mounted archers. Again, the armies met on the plain of Tarain, but in this second battle, Pṛithivīrāja's forces were decimated, and he was captured and put to death. The sultan then advanced into Rajasthan and captured Ajmer. Further north, he appointed Aybak, who was with him on all these campaigns, *sipahsalah* (army-commander) for the upper Jumna country. By about 1193, Aybak had captured Delhi and had also taken Mirath, Baran, and Kol across the river. He made his headquarters at Delhi, where he initiated the construction of the city's first mosque, known as Quwwat al-Islam ("the might of Islam"), built out of the rubble of demolished Hindu temples, and also the foundations of Quṭb Mīnār, the immense minaret and "tower of victory" that would be completed by his successors.

The Delhi Sultanate: Muᶜizzī Slave Kings

Reign	*Ruler*
1206-1210	Quṭ al-Dīn Aybak
1210-1211	Ārām Shah
1211-1236	Iltutmish
1236	Ruknuddin Firūz Shah
1236-1240	Raziya
1240-1242	Bahram Shah
1242-1246	Masud Shah
1246-1266	Maḥmud Shah
1266-1287	Balban Ulugh Khan
1287-1290	Kay Qubādh
1290	Kayumarth

In 1194, Aybak accompanied his master on an expedition across the Ganges against the Rathor Rājput ruler of Kanauj, Jayachandra. The Muslim army penetrated as far east as Benares, and Jayachandra was defeated and killed in a bloody engagement in which Aybak is said to have shot the arrow that killed him. Afterward, Aybak sent the sultan four thousand camels laden with the spoils of Kanauj and Benares, where there had been massive destruction of temples and idols. Thereafter, Aybak put down a Rājput uprising in Ajmer in 1195-1196; in 1197, he plundered Nahrwala in Gujarat, where twenty years earlier Muᶜizz-ud-Dīn had experienced a crushing defeat; in 1199, he marched as far south as Ujjain. He captured Kalpi in 1202 and, during 1202-1203, raided into Bundelkhand. Muᶜizz-ud-Dīn played little or no part in these later campaigns. He may have already reached an advanced age or been preoccupied with affairs in Ghūr, where his elder brother, Ghiyāṣ-ud-Dīn, died in 1203.

Muᶜizz-ud-Dīn hurried back to the Ghūrid heartland to claim the succession, but within three years, he was assassinated, leaving no direct descendants. Ghiyāṣ-ud-Dīn's son, Ghiyāṣ-ud-Dīn Maḥmūd (r. 1206-1215), succeeded in Ghūr itself, but Ghazna was seized by one of the late sultan's most senior *mamlūks*, Tāj-ud-Dīn Yildiz, Aybak's father-in-law. Muᶜizz-ud-Dīn seems to have assumed that after his death, his *mamlūk* commanders would take over his conquests, although he must have known that there was bound to be bitter rivalry among them. Jūzjānī relates how, when one of his servants commiserated with him on his lack of sons, he replied that, while other rulers might have a son or two, he had his *mamlūks*, who would glorify his name by their conquests.

Of these, Aybak stood foremost, a fact recognized by Ghiyāṣ-ud-Dīn Maḥmūd in Ghūr, who sent him a canopy of state (symbol of sovereignty) and addressed him as sultan. However, Aybak did not exercise undisputed sway in India. Much of Punjab and Sind was in the possession of the *mamlūk* Nāṣir al-Dīn Qabacha, while east of Benares, Bihar and Bengal had been conquered in the 1190's by a formidable non-*mamlūk* lieutenant of Muᶜizz-ud-Dīn, Ikhtar-ud-Dīn Muḥammad-ibn-Bakhtiar Khaljī, who was virtually independent there. However, for Aybak in Delhi, the immediate bone of contention was Lahore, which was also claimed by Yildiz in Ghazna. In 1208, Aybak marched on Ghazna, expelled Yildiz, and, as Jūzjānī put it, sat on the throne of Ghazna for forty days. However, Yildiz returned with reinforcements, and Aybak was forced to relinquish the city. However, he retained Lahore, where he died in 1210, falling from his horse while playing polo. During his brief reign, his expedition to Ghazna is the only event the chroniclers mention: All his great conquests had occurred in the lifetime of his master, Muʿizz-ud-Dīn.

Although Aybak is traditionally counted as the first of the Delhi sultans, it is not certain that he used the title in the sense of exercising undisputed sovereignty: As *siparsalah*, he had minted coins in his master's name, but after the latter's death, he seems to have eschewed the exercise of that traditional prerogative of medieval Muslim rulers.

Aybak had three daughters, two of whom were married to Qabacha, and the youngest to Aybak's favourite *mamlūk*, Iltutmish. He himself was succeeded by Ārām Shah, assumed to be his son, but who survived only for a few months, struck no coins, and was apparently swept aside by the masterful Iltutmish (r. 1211-1236), the true architect of the Delhi sultanate and one of that city's greatest rulers.

SIGNIFICANCE

Aybak's biography exemplifies the ideal of the *mamlūk*. In the name of his master, his conquests made enormous inroads into northern India, establishing the first enduring Muslim polity in the subcontinent, and with it, Delhi as the future epicenter of Indo-Islamic culture.

—*Gavin R. G. Hambly*

FURTHER READING

Digby, Simon. *War-Horse and Elephant in the Dehli Sultanate*. Oxford, England: Orient Monographs, 1971. Excellent for the military dimension.

Hasan-i Nizami. *Taj al-Maathir.* Translated by B. Sarop. Delhi, India: Saud Ahmad Dehlavi, 1998. The earliest account of the period from a Muslim viewpoint.

Jackson, Peter. *The Delhi Sultanate*. Cambridge, England: Cambridge University Press, 1999. Definitive and magisterial treatment of the sultanate.

Minhāj Sirāj Jūzjānī. *Tabakāt-i Nāsirī*. Translated by H. G. Raverty. 2 vols. 1881. Reprint. Calcutta, India: The Asiatic Society, 1995. The principal contemporary account.

Wink, André. *Al-Hind: The Making of the Indo-Islamic World*. Vol. 2. Leiden: Brill, 1997. A history of the period, to be read in conjunction with the previously listed Jackson work.

SEE ALSO: 973: Foundation of the Western Cālukya Dynasty; 1193: Turkish Raiders Destroy Buddhist University at Nalanda; 1236-1240: Reign of Raziya; 1299: ʿAlāʾ-ud-Dīn Muḥammad Khaljī Conquers Gujarat.

RELATED ARTICLES in *Great Lives from History: The Middle Ages, 477-1453*: Maḥmūd of Ghazna; Raziya.

April 16, 1209
FOUNDING OF THE FRANCISCANS

The founding of the Franciscans represented the first time in Catholic Church history in which religious brothers and sisters were allowed to live in strict poverty, owning nothing, and the first time that men of a religious order were allowed to go about preaching as opposed to living in a monastery.

LOCALE: Assisi (now in Italy)
CATEGORIES: Organizations and institutions; religion

KEY FIGURES

Saint Francis of Assisi (c. 1181-1226), founder of the Franciscan Order

Saint Clare of Assisi (1194-1253), a noblewoman who became the first female follower of Francis

Innocent III (1160 or 1161-1216), Roman Catholic pope, 1198-1216, officially approved the order's founding

SUMMARY OF EVENT

Saint Francis of Assisi (then Francesco di Pietro di Bernardone), the son of a cloth merchant, was an ordinary young man, very popular with his friends, and he dreamed of knighthood and marriage. When war broke out between his hometown and the neighboring Perugia, he found himself in prison, captured by the enemy. Pietro, his father, bailed him out, but Francis had contracted some illness. When Francis recovered, he was changed. He still went out with his friends but was more reflective and thoughtful.

When the pope called for a crusade, Francis had the chance to be a knight. His father dressed him in a new coat of armor and gave him a new horse, and Francis rode off to war. Within a short time, however, he again became ill and returned home. He went to the little church of San Damiano, which was falling down, and he heard the crucifix telling him to "Rebuild my church." At first, Francis

A Beguin woman. The Beguins, composed of a variety of pious laywomen, were among the many monastic movements that, along with the Franciscans and Clares, arose in the early twelfth century; however, the Beguins were a lay order, not under vows to the Catholic Church. (Frederick Ungar Publishing Co.)

thought that he should buy or beg for stones to rebuild San Damiano. A turning point in his life occurred when he stole money from his father's store to buy stones and his father demanded the money back. Francis not only returned the money but also took off all his clothes and gave them to his father. As he handed over his clothing, Francis said that from now on his father was not Pietro but only God.

From this point forward, Francis was completely changed. With a few followers, he wandered around fixing churches and preaching poverty. At this point, Clare, a young noblewoman, heard about Francis's preaching. She was attracted to what Francis was saying about poverty and wanted to follow his style of life in a way that would be appropriate for a woman. Francis established Clare, her sister, and several other women from Clare's household at San Damiano. Other women soon joined them, and the group became known as the Damianites.

Lest he be thought heretical, Francis determined to go to Rome to get permission for his group. At first, Pope Innocent III would not listen to what looked like a pack of stragglers, but that night the pope had a dream that the church was falling down, and a man dressed like Francis was holding it up. The next day, April 16, 1209, Innocent III gave oral permission for the new order.

From this time on, Francis and his brothers spent their time preaching, rebuilding churches, and begging for whatever they needed. Francis called his group "little brothers," or friars minor. They refused money and attempted to live literally like Jesus had, having nowhere to sleep except for the ground and no clothes except rags, a rope around their waists, and no shoes. Clare and her followers also lived according to this ideal. They did not preach but prayed and fasted, eating what people brought to them or what the brothers begged for them. They spent their time doing needlework and raising some of their own food. Clare insisted that the sisters be kind and loving to one another, and Clare herself washed the feet of her sisters and cleaned their mattresses.

Before Francis died in 1226, five thousand men had been accepted into the order. As human nature would have it, controversies arose as to how the brothers should live. Francis wanted no houses or property, but there were some who could not see how the order would survive without them. In countries in which the weather was cold, the brothers needed shoes and warmer clothing. Because Francis's talent was more charismatic than administrative, he handed the running of the order to his trusted friend, Brother Elias. Yet Brother Elias felt that the order should own property. This disagreement caused dissention before and after Francis died.

About a month before he died, Francis spent the night at Mount Alverna. In the sky, there appeared a six-winged angel who marked Francis's body with the wounds of Jesus crucified. It seems that Francis's desire to live the way Jesus did reached a climax with this incident, called the stigmata. Francis died on October 4, 1226, a date on which Franciscans throughout the world celebrate his life and death. On the way to the burial, his body was taken to Clare and her sisters to view.

After Francis's death, the controversy over property and spirituality continued. A group who called themselves the Spirituals wanted to remain faithful to the primitive ideal of Francis and Clare, living a life of poverty and prayer. Before long, this movement disappeared, but in the 1300's, a group formed who called themselves Observants. They took what was best from the Spirituals and committed themselves to living a more austere life. In 1517, the Franciscans divided into two groups: the Conventuals and the Friars Minor of the Regular Observance. Some broke away from this second group to form the Capuchins, or "the strict observance." Pope Clement VII recognized them in 1527 as the third independent branch of the order. Many others also broke away and formed new convents and monasteries. In 1897, Leo X joined all families into one large order, the Order of Friars Minor.

Clare's community went through the same sort of struggle. In 1227, at eighty-two years of age, Cardinal Ugolino (1227-1241), one of the first followers of Francis, was elected the new pope, Gregory IX. Clare asked to be allowed to live according to the poverty of Francis. The pope agreed, but he determined that he would restrict this privilege to the house of Poor Ladies at San Damiano because with no property, the Poor Ladies lacked the necessities of life. Pope Gregory pleaded with Clare to accept some possessions, but Clare refused. He offered to release Clare from her vows to stop their shortages of provisions and relieve their suffering, but Clare would not yield. "Never do I wish, Holy Father, to be released in any way from following Christ."

During Clare's lifetime, many houses of Damianites sprang up throughout Italy and in most of Europe. Some 147 houses were founded before Clare's death in 1253. At least 47 houses were founded in Spain during the thirteenth century. Under the influence of Agnes of Prague, houses of Clarisses were founded in Moravia between 1242 and 1248, and a house for sixty nuns was founded in Poland in 1254 but destroyed in 1259 by the invasion of the Tartars. Meanwhile, Saint Elizabeth of Hungary in-

Saint Francis and his brotherhood. (F. R. Niglutsch)

spired many women, and a house of Poor Clares was established at Trnava in 1238. Isabelle of France, who was the only daughter of Louis VIII and Blanche of Castille, joined the Poor Ladies in 1252 and established a convent at Longchamps in 1261.

SIGNIFICANCE

By living in poverty, the Franciscans stood in opposition to the wealthy and the often corrupt church of the Middle Ages. Men and women flocked to the brotherhood and sisterhood in order to live a spiritual and holy life.

—*Winifred Whelan*

FURTHER READING

Armstrong, Regis J., J. A. Wayne Hellman, and William J. Short, eds. *Francis of Assisi: Early Documents*. 3 vols. New York: New City Press, 1999-2001. The three books of this set, *The Saint*, *The Founder*, and *The Prophet*, contain translated biographies, hagiographies, and other early writings concerning Saint Francis and the Franciscans. An excellent collection of early sources that contains explanatory notes. Maps and bibliography.

Bartoli, Marco. *Clare of Assisi*. Translated by Sister Frances Teresa. Quincy, Ill.: Franciscan Press, 1993. This scholarly biography places Clare in the larger context of later medieval Italy. In particular, her accomplishments are set against the cultural currents.

Cowan, James. *Francis: A Saint's Way*. Ligouri, Mo.: Liguori/Triumph, 2001. A devotional biography of Saint Francis of Assisi that focuses on his inner life, including questions of asceticism and poverty. Contains a bibliography.

Francis and Clare: The Complete Works. Translated by Regis J. Armstrong and Ignatius C. Brady. New York: Paulist Press, 1982. This edition of the writings of both Assisi saints contains comprehensive introductions to the life of each and clarifies the audience for and purpose of the different writings.

Frugoni, Chiara. *Francis of Assisi: A Life*. New York: Continuum, 1998. A biography of Saint Francis of Assisi. Bibliography and index.

House, Adrian. *Francis of Assisi*. New York: HiddenSpring, 2001. A treatment of the life of Francis of Assisi that attempts to deal with the miracles and other legends in a way so that non-Christians can appreciate the saint's life.

Peterson, Ingrid J. *Clare of Assisi: A Biographical Study*. Quincy, Ill.: Franciscan Press, 1993. Recent scholarship has begun to uncover the history of women of the Middle Ages. For Clare, much of this work has been done in conjunction with the 800th anniversary of her birth.

Robson, Michael. *Saint Francis of Assisi: The Legend and the Life*. London: Geoffre Chapman, 1999. A biography of Saint Francis that describes both the legends and his life. Bibliography and index.

Rotzetter, Anton, Willibrord-Christian Van Dijk, and Taddee Matura. *Gospel Living: Francis of Assisi Yesterday and Today*. Saint Bonaventure, N.Y.: Saint Bonaventure University, 1994. In three parts, this book tells the life of Saint Francis, the history of the order including the saints, writings and activities of the friars in many countries, and the present status of the order.

Sabatier, Paul. *The Road to Assisi: The Essential Biography of Saint Francis*. Brewster, Mass.: Paraclete Press, 2003. A new edition of a classic biography of Saint Francis of Assisi by a French Protestant.

Spoto, Donald. *Reluctant Saint: The Life of Francis of Assisi*. New York: Viking Compass, 2002. In this biography of the saint, Spoto tries to distinguish between legend and fact, citing reasons for his beliefs, and describes the political scene at the time.

Wolf, Kenneth Baxter. *The Poverty of Riches: Saint Francis of Assisi Reconsidered*. New York: Oxford University Press, 2003. Wolf takes a critical look at the poverty pursued by Saint Francis of Assisi and what it meant for those impoverished people in Assisi. He examines the saint's contact with the leper and his wearing of a tunic.

SEE ALSO: 963: Foundation of the Mount Athos Monasteries; March 21, 1098: Foundation of the Cistercian Order; November 11-30, 1215: Fourth Lateran Council.

RELATED ARTICLES in *Great Lives from History: The Middle Ages, 477-1453*: Saint Clare of Assisi; Saint Francis of Assisi; Innocent III.

1209-1229
ALBIGENSIAN CRUSADE

The Albigensian Crusade represented an attempt by Roman Catholic authorities to control French unification in southern Europe, which had long been the crucible of exotic influences.

LOCALE: Toulouse, southern France
CATEGORIES: Government and politics; religion; wars, uprisings, and civil unrest

KEY FIGURES

Arnaud Amalric (c. 1160-1225), abbot-general of Cîteaux and papal legate to Toulouse, preached the crusade
Innocent III (1160 or 1161-1216), Roman Catholic pope, 1198-1216, instigated the crusade
Simon de Montfort (1165?-1218), military leader of the crusade
Peter II (1174-1213), king of Aragon and Catalonia, r. 1196-1213
Raymond VI (1156-1222), count of Toulouse, 1196-1222
Raymond VII (1197-1249), count of Toulouse, 1222-1247
Philip II (1165-1223), king of France, r. 1179-1223
Louis VIII (1187-1226), king of France, r. 1223-1226

SUMMARY OF EVENT

Adherents of Manichean or dualist ways of thinking emerged in Languedoc, or southern France, in the eleventh century. This part of Europe was outside the rigid

Copy of a thirteenth century bas-relief at the Church of Saint Nazair, Carcassonne, depicting the death of Simon de Montfort at Toulouse. (Frederick Ungar Publishing Co.)

control of the French Capetian Dynasty and the Holy Roman Empire. Remnants of Jewish and Muslim cultures added to a diverse population that absorbed Middle Eastern and North African heritages easily—especially during the era of the Crusades—and wedded such influences into a capricious, often secular spirit.

The Albigensians or Cathari (purists) apparently drew their numbers from disaffected migrants from Asia Minor (Paulicians) and Bulgaria (Bogomils) who had entered the Balkans and northern Italy. Because the clergy of southern France was notoriously inefficient and disorganized, the region tolerated heterogeneous thinkers whose ideas went beyond the neo-Platonist tendencies evident in other parts of Europe. Thus, the region around Toulouse became a stronghold for Cathari beliefs.

Because all Albigensian writings were destroyed, scholars have found it difficult to ascertain any clear, systematic principles associated with the Cathari. In general, adherents were divided into two groups: ascetics and believers. The priestly class and their adepts were generally considered to be models of stoic behavior. The believers, or "auditors," however, transformed sacred principles into abhorrent practices, running the gamut from deathbed suicides, infanticide, black masses, to unbridled promiscuity and other scandalous behaviors. As a result, in 1179, the papal authorities in Rome launched a full-scale attack against Albigensians during the Third Lateran Council. Some initiates of the Cathari sect became increasingly defiant of Roman Catholic authority, and rumors spread that the Albigensians were infidels who renounced marriage, the family, Christian sacraments, crosses, icons, saints, indulgences, relics, and almost any connection to the Old Testament—presumably the work of Satan, or the Demiurge. According to popular tradition, reinforced by the songs of troubadours, the Cathari held fourteen dioceses and acknowledged their own pope. Furthermore, the Cathari notion of *consolamentum* (an initiation ceremony) openly challenged the papal decree that crusaders were granted absolution if they died in the cause of Christian perseverance. The general mind-set of southern France, rooted in cultural autonomy, drifted further away from the centrality of Philip II, who was unwilling to challenge the feudal privileges accorded to Raymond VI of Toulouse.

Pope Innocent III tried to counteract unorthodox tendencies among the Albigensians (borrowed from primitive Christian societies) by sending legates to the local bishops. While leaving the church of Saint Gilles du Gard in Toulouse, one of these legates, Peter of Castelnau, was killed by a knight in the service of Raymond VI. His death provided the pope with a pretext to call a crusade against Languedoc. Arnaud Amalric preached this Albigensian crusade in the name of Saint Dominic, who (ironically) had tried to win over the Cathari by peaceful methods. A Christian army, nominally supported by Philip II of France, gathered at Lyon and laid siege to southern France. In 1209, Béziers was assaulted, and as many as seven thousand people were indiscriminately killed. Many of the victims were unarmed citizens who had taken refuge in the church of the Madelaine. Arnaud Amalric apparently called out, "Kill them all. God will recognize his own!"

In 1226, Louis VIII crushed the Albigensian resistance, securing the capitulation of several cities in southern France. This fifteenth century miniature from the Chroniques de Hainaut *shows him entering Avignon with the pope's legate after a three-month siege of the city.* (Frederick Ungar Publishing Co.)

After this debacle, Simon de Montfort, a man known for his military acumen and fierce temperament, was appointed commander of the crusading army. Peter II, king of Aragon and Catalonia, sided with his brother-in-law, Raymond VI of Toulouse. Peter led a huge force into southern France and established headquarters at the castle of Muret. Despite being outnumbered, Simon de Montfort maneuvered around the Spanish forces and scored a resounding victory in 1213. Peter was killed and the followers of Raymond VI disbanded.

After learning about the bloodshed at Muret, Pope Innocent III suspended the crusade against the Cathari, who were renowned pacifists, and tried to find a diplomatic solution to what was essentially a political problem. Such diplomacy was conducted under the watchful eye of Philip II, who sent his son, Prince Louis, on a futile mission to force a settlement. Emboldened once again, Raymond VI fortified Toulouse. In 1218, Simon de Montfort died in an attempt to take the city.

After his father's death in 1222, Raymond VII of Toulouse continued to protect the city from invasion. Backed financially by Pope Honorius III, King Louis VIII of France crushed the Albigensian resistance in 1226 through the brutal massacre of the people of Marenaude and by securing the capitulation of Soignon and other cities in southern France. In 1229, a peace agreement was reached by which the management of Languedoc fell under the control of the French king. Caught up in this political dispute, the Albigensians went underground after Pope Gregory IV announced the Papal Inquisition of 1233 against their interest.

AN INQUISITOR DENOUNCES THE ALBIGENSIANS

[T]hey usually say of themselves that they are good Christians . . . and that they are persecuted just as Christ and his apostles were by the Pharisees. . . . [T]hey talk to the laity of the evil lives of the clerks and prelates of the Roman Church, pointing out and setting forth their pride, cupidity, avarice, and uncleanness of life. . . . They invoke, with their own interpretation and according to their abilities, the authority of the Gospels and the Epistles against the condition of the prelates. . . . Then they attack and vituperate, in turn, all the sacraments. . . . Hence they claim that confession made to the priests of the Roman Church is useless, and that, since the priests may be sinners, they cannot loose nor bind, and, being unclean themselves, cannot make others clean. . . . Moreover they read from the Gospels and the Epistles in the vulgar tongue. . . .

Source: Bernard of Gui, *Practica inquisitionis heretice pravitatis* (early fourteenth century), edited by Célestin Douais; quoted in *Readings in European History*, edited by James Harvey Robinson, abridged edition (Boston: Ginn & Company, 1906), pp. 171-172.

SIGNIFICANCE

Scholars differ as to what contributed to the significant, widespread appeal of the Cathari. Some note a strong attachment among merchants and soldiers, which partly explains the later accommodation of Calvinist ideology. Others insist on the power of a recalcitrant nobility, with secret codes derived from Middle Eastern and North African influences, all posing an obvious threat to northern European hegemony.

—*Robert J. Frail*

FURTHER READING

Burl, Aubrey. *God's Heretics: The Albigensian Crusade.* Stroud, England: Sutton, 2002. Explores the crusade against the Cathari and argues that the massacre was the first act of genocide in Europe.

Gore, Terry L. *Neglected Heroes: Leadership and War in the Early Medieval Period.* Westport, Conn.: Praeger, 1995. A lively account of military techniques in an era of siege warfare.

Madaule, Jacques. *The Albigensian Crusade: An Historical Essay.* Translated by Barbara Wall. New York: Fordham University Press, 1967. In this informative study, the author reinforces the cultural differences between northern and southern France and the role that the Albigensian Crusade played in the formation of France as a national state.

Petrus, Sarnensis. *The History of the Albigensian Crusade.* Translated by W. A. Sibly and M. D. Sibly. Rochester, N.Y.: Boydell Press, 1998. A translation of the late twelfth-early thirteenth century text *Historia Albigensium.* Includes maps, genealogical tables, bibliography, and index.

Runciman, Steven. *A History of the Crusades.* 3 vols. New York: Cambridge University Press, 1987. Places the Languedoc invasion within the context of other crusades and notes that northern extremists moved beyond the authority of the popes.

Sayers, Jane E. *Innocent III: Leader of Europe, 1198-1216.* New York: Longman, 1995. Analyzes Innocent III's attempt to impose a theocratic dominance in Eu-

rope over and against secular tendencies such as those that surfaced in Albigensian France.
Strayer, Joseph R. *The Albigensian Crusades*. Ann Arbor: University of Michigan Press, 1992. Provides a comprehensive study of the political conditions in Europe that contributed to the backlash against the Cathari.
Sumption, Jonathan. *The Albigensian Crusade*. Boston: Faber, 1999. A wide-ranging summary of the linguistic, religious, and political differences between southern and northern France that led to the clash of two cultures.

SEE ALSO: c. 1175: Waldensian Excommunications Usher in Protestant Movement; November 11-30, 1215: Fourth Lateran Council; 1233: Papal Inquisition; July 2, 1324: Lady Alice Kyteler Is Found Guilty of Witchcraft.
RELATED ARTICLES in *Great Lives from History: The Middle Ages, 477-1453*: Saint Anthony of Padua; Saint Dominic; Innocent III; Louis IX; Simon de Montfort; Philip II.

1212
CHILDREN'S CRUSADE

The Children's Crusade to the Holy Land, whether a reality or a myth, inspired and shamed adult Christians for centuries because the children who participated were seen as fervent, innocent, and pure believers and martyrs.

LOCALE: France, Germany, Italy, and the Mediterranean coast
CATEGORY: Religion

KEY FIGURES

Innocent III (1160 or 1161-1216), Roman Catholic pope, 1198-1216
Stephen of Cloyes (fl. thirteenth century), teenage leader of the young French crusaders
Philip II (1165-1223), king of France, r. 1179-1223
Hugh Ferreus (fl. twelfth century), merchant seafarer of Marseilles
William Porcus (fl. twelfth century), merchant seafarer of Marseilles
Nicholas of Cologne (fl. thirteenth century), teenage leader of the young German crusaders

SUMMARY OF EVENT

The Children's Crusade is probably one of the most familiar and least understood events of the Middle Ages. Most generally educated Western adults know the phrase "Children's Crusade" but have only vague notions about when and where it took place. The episode was not really a crusade—that is, it was neither called for nor sanctioned by the pope—and those participating in it were not granted special blessings or indulgences.

Because of its spontaneous and humble beginnings, there are no official rolls of participants or contemporary records of the crusade. It was not until twenty and more years after the year of the Children's Crusade that written accounts began to appear; these chronicles are contradictory, and many are clearly fictionalized or contain fictional elements.

The traditionally accepted version of the events, pulled together from various chronicles, is as follows. The beginning of the thirteenth century was a troubling time for Christians. The Fourth Crusade (1202-1204) had failed to drive Muslims out of what the Christians considered their Holy Land, and in 1209, Pope Innocent III's crusading armies had massacred hundreds of Albigensians, non-Christians living in southern France. In the eyes of many Christians, the Crusaders had revealed themselves to be greedy and corrupt, more interested in the spoils of war than in sacred duty and honor. The institution of the Church was found wanting, and many people looked to children as personifications of the innocence of true faith. In this climate, two boys came forward.

In France, in the small town of Cloyes near Vendôme, a shepherd boy named Stephen announced that Jesus had visited him dressed as a poor pilgrim, given Stephen a letter, and told him to present it to King Philip II of France. The letter called for a new crusade, conducted by children who were pure of heart and who would be able to accomplish what their elders could not. Stephen, then about twelve or thirteen years old, set out toward Paris to see the king, accompanied by several of his fellow shepherds, who believed that Stephen had been called to some great duty. More and more groups of children joined Stephen and his band, fervently ignoring protests by their parents. These groups included both boys and girls, poor and rich, and eventually many adults as well; they carried banners and crosses, praying and chanting Christian messages of praise. By May, 1212, when the crusaders gathered in the city of Saint Denys, just north of Paris, they numbered in the thousands.

Stephen called his followers to gather more friends and meet in Vendôme; from there they would go to the Holy Land to free the tomb of Jesus from the Muslims who then controlled the region. The children carried no weapons and had no intention of fighting. They believed that they had been called to liberate the Holy Land and that if they showed their faith by marching in, the infidels would simply fall away.

As the army grew, both the king of France and the pope studiously avoided taking any notice of it. The pope did not take the movement seriously and would not bless it. Philip II, if he ever saw Stephen's letter, apparently did not believe it; he ordered the children to return home. The faith—or the hysteria—of Stephen's followers was too well established to be set aside by the orders of an earthly king, and they continued in their quest.

The Children's Crusade, from an illustration in J. F. Michaud's Histoire des Croisades. (Hulton|Archive by Getty Images)

By late July or early August, 1212, the crusaders set off for the port city of Marseilles, more than 300 miles (483 kilometers) away on the Mediterranean. They must have been quite a sight: a procession of several thousand (some accounts say thirty thousand), banners flying, crosses held high, singing hymns and chanting "To God!" No one knows how they intended to get to the Holy Land from Marseilles—whether they expected ships to be provided for them or, as some said, expected God to part the waters of the sea.

A month later, they arrived in Marseilles. Many of the young crusaders had turned back along the way, finding their enthusiasm for the cause weakening under the harsh conditions of travel. Others had been captured and sold into slavery, or fallen ill. Some new crusaders had joined the group as it passed by. When the army reached Marseilles, they asked permission to stay a short time, expecting to be on their way soon, and permission was granted. Somehow, transportation was arranged for five thousand crusaders on the ships of two merchants, Hugh Ferreus and William Porcus. With great ceremony, they sailed out of Marseilles in August, bound, they believed, for the Holy Land.

Meanwhile, in Germany, another army of singing, banner-waving children had gathered around Nicholas, an eleven- or twelve-year-old boy from Cologne. Doubtless each of the two groups had received word of the other, and of other spontaneous uprisings by children, feeding the frenzy. In June or July, 1212, Nicholas and nearly twenty thousand followers set out for the Holy Land, via Genoa. They traveled south along the Rhine and across the Alps. Records indicate that the tired, cold, and hungry children rested at a monastery in the Alps before continuing. Like the French children, many of these German crusaders turned back, were waylaid by criminals, or died along the way. Fewer than seven thousand remained on August 25, 1212, when the group arrived at the gates of Genoa.

The army asked permission to stay only one night, expecting miraculous transportation across the sea to Palestine the next day. When it did not materialize, the group dispersed. Many returned home. Some went on to Pisa, still expecting to complete their journey. Two shiploads of children sailed from Pisa but were never heard from again. One small band eventually reached Rome and presented themselves before the pope to receive his further instructions. Innocent III coldly ordered them to return home but reminded them that they had taken vows as Crusaders and would be called to fight when they reached adulthood.

The French children who had sailed from Marseilles never reached their destination, and for eighteen years, their fate was a mystery. In 1230, an old priest came forward with a strange tale: He had sailed with the crusade out of Marseilles. Two days from port, a storm had sunk two of the ships, drowning all aboard. Those on the remaining five vessels were sold into slavery by the two merchants.

Significance

Although several contemporary chronicles tell of spontaneous gatherings of Christian children moving in procession and praying to God, it was nearly twenty years after the events that the first chronicler described them as crusaders and claimed that their destination was the Holy Land. Many scholars believe that the stories of the Children's Crusade are more legend than history. Whether factual or not, the stories of pure and innocent children setting off to do God's will, when the adults around them had failed to do so, have inspired Christians for centuries.

—*Cynthia A. Bily*

Further Reading

Armstrong, Karen. *Holy War: The Crusades and Their Impact on Today's World.* New York: Doubleday, 1988. An engaging history that delves into Christian, Jewish, and Muslim religious views. A brief section explains the theory that a spontaneous uprising by bands of wandering poor was transformed by later chroniclers into the myth of the Children's Crusade.

Dickson, Gary. "Stephen of Cloyes, Philip Augustus, and the Children's Crusade of 1212." In *Journeys Toward God: Pilgrimage and Crusade*, edited by Barbara N. Sargent-Baur. Kalamazoo: Medieval Institute, Western Michigan University, 1992. Essay examining the French participation in the Children's Crusade.

Gray, George Zabriskie. *The Children's Crusade.* New York: William Morrow, 1972. Originally published in 1870, this volume pulls together six hundred years of lore about the Children's Crusade into a romanticized, and unabashedly pro-Christian, narrative.

Hallam, Elizabeth, ed. *Chronicles of the Crusades: Eyewitness Accounts of the Wars Between Christianity and Islam.* Reprint. New York: Welcome Rain, 2000. Provides accounts of the Children's Crusade from the annals of Marbach and the monk Aubrey of Trois-Fontaines, translated into lively English prose. Lavishly illustrated and clearly annotated.

Hindley, Geoffrey. *The Crusades: A History of Armed Pilgrimage and Holy War.* New York: Carroll and Graf, 2003. Broad history of the motives, milieu, and effects of the Crusades, including a brief treatment of the Children's Crusade.

Nicolle, David. *Warriors and Their Weapons Around the Time of the Crusades: Relationships Between Byzantium, the West, and the Islamic World.* Burlington, Vt.: Ashgate/Variorum, 2002. A detailed account of the dominant technologies and strategies of warfare during the period of the Crusades.

Raedts, Peter. "The Children's Crusade of 1212." *Journal of Medieval History* 3 (1977): 279-333. Based on an extensive study of primary and secondary sources, argues that it was not religious fervor so much as peasant dissatisfaction with the wealthier classes' failures to win the Holy Land that led to the Children's Crusade.

Riley-Smith, Jonathan, ed. *The Atlas of the Crusades.* New York: Facts On File, 1990. Especially helpful for tracing the paths of the three major groups of child-crusaders through regions whose geographical names have changed several times over many centuries. Includes bibliographical references.

Zacour, Norman P. "The Children's Crusade." In *A History of the Crusades.* Vol. 2. Edited by Kenneth M. Stetton. 6 vols. Madison: University of Wisconsin Press, 1969. A detailed account, clear at every point as to which evidence from medieval chronicles can be considered reliable, and which is only speculative, at best.

SEE ALSO: c. 1175: Waldensian Excommunications Usher in Protestant Movement; 1204: Knights of the Fourth Crusade Capture Constantinople; 1209-1229: Albigensian Crusade; 1233: Papal Inquisition; August 1, 1323-August 23, 1328: Peasants' Revolt in Flanders; May-June, 1381: Peasants' Revolt in England.

RELATED ARTICLES in *Great Lives from History: The Middle Ages, 477-1453*: Enrico Dandolo; Innocent III; Philip II.

July 27, 1214
BATTLE OF BOUVINES

The Battle of Bouvines signaled the advent of a new patriotism in France when a relatively minor skirmish quickly took on mythic proportions. The battle defined France as a champion of the Catholic Church, helped make the French monarchy powerful, and heralded chivalry and knighthood.

LOCALE: Near Tournai, Flanders (now in France)
CATEGORY: Wars, uprisings, and civil unrest

KEY FIGURES

Philip II (1165-1223), son of Louis VII and king of France, r. 1179-1223
Ferrand (fl. twelfth to thirteenth centuries), count of Flanders and vassal of Philip II
Renaud (fl. twelfth to thirteenth centuries), count of Boulogne and vassal of Philip II
Otto IV (c. 1174-1218), Holy Roman Emperor, r. 1198-1215, and nephew of King John
King John (1166-1216), youngest son of Henry II and king of England, r. 1199-1216

SUMMARY OF EVENT

Drawing on four or five contemporary narratives of the brief encounter at Bouvines, poets and historians have formed the event into a legend. The essential facts reveal a much simpler story. On a hot Sunday in July of 1214, King Philip II of France was returning from Tournai, which he had devastated on the previous day to chastise Count Ferrand of Flanders, a rebellious vassal. Around midday, as the king and his knights were about to cross the bridge of Bouvines, they were unexpectedly set on by a coalition of troops led by Ferrand, Renaud of Boulogne, and Otto IV of Bavaria. A three-hour battle ensued, involving perhaps four thousand mounted knights and twelve thousand infantry. Both of the rebellious counts were taken prisoner. King Philip himself, pulled to the ground by Otto's German foot soldiers, miraculously escaped death and remounted to pursue the "false" (the excommunicated) emperor, who managed to get away. Ferrand and Renaud were led in chains to Paris, and the king's triumph was made complete by news from Poitou that his son Louis (known as "the Lion") had defeated King John of England, the remaining party to the coalition against France.

The enemy coalition was financed by King John, who simultaneously attacked Poitou in an attempt to recover the inheritance of his Angevin predecessors. John had lost these lands ten years before, when Philip had taken Normandy and Anjou from him as a disloyal vassal. The year before Bouvines, Philip had been prepared to invade England when John forestalled him by securing an intercession from the pope. (In 1216, Philip's son Louis did invade England but was defeated by the barons under the command of William Marshal.) John had been joined by two other disloyal vassals, Ferrand and Renaud; by defeating all three, Philip and his host of knights proved that vassals to the French crown were more formidable than an illegitimate coalition of mercenaries. The French monarchy was a more cohesive force than feudalism. "After Bouvines," according to French historian Georges Duby, nothing could "stand in the way of the expansion of the royal domain."

The Catholic Church had managed to harness the forces of chivalry and feudal strife by launching the First Crusade, which had freed Jerusalem in 1099. The Third and Fourth Crusades (1189-1192 and 1202-1204), however, had been failures. Philip had taken part in the Third Crusade but had fallen out with Pope Innocent III over his desire to be divorced from his second wife, Ingeborg of Denmark. Meanwhile, the pope had excommunicated and deposed Emperor Otto IV, and Philip had allied himself with the new emperor, Frederick II, in 1213. As a result, when Otto joined Philip's enemies in the surprise attack at Bouvines, Philip found himself in the heroic role of Christian champion pitted against the false emperor, or Antichrist. Coincidentally, Otto's emblem was a dragon (reminiscent of the evil dragon in the biblical Book of Revelation), which was displayed on the banner he dropped on fleeing from Bouvines. Opposing this symbol of the Antichrist, the French banner carried the Oriflamme, representing their patron, Saint Denis.

By forcing Philip to do battle on a Sunday, the enemy was violating the Lord's day. This situation invited historians to claim that God had made the king his instrument for punishing such sacrilege. The notion that the king was God's avenger powerfully supports the teaching that the Crown is the sovereign font of justice. This idea was far more potent than feudal conceptions, which held the king to be merely the strongest of mortal overlords. As the legend of Bouvines developed, Philip was given prayers like those spoken by Moses and David, as if he had foreseen the battle and directly implored God's aid. Sacred meanings could be found in all of his gestures. For example, while watching his troops cross the bridge, Philip had rested under a tree and eaten pieces of bread that he dipped in his wine. The legends also endowed Philip with a golden goblet, so that the lunchtime snack of a practical and cautious monarch resembled the taking of Communion.

If the legend made Philip to be God's champion against unruly heretics and rebels who flouted the divinely ordained social order, the miraculous victory at Bouvines also confirmed France's national role in human destiny. The underlying idea here is not truly religious, but chivalric and superstitious. Bouvines was a trial by arms—a judicial combat in which God is seen as arbitrating between the two parties by awarding victory to the just cause. In this historical event, the French entered the lists—the *champel*, or closed field, in which duels took place—as combatants on the side of honor and "romance" civilization. Their opponents were seen as evil "Teutonic" barbarians. God was believed to have rendered judgment at Bouvines by sending a definitive outcome. This divine judgment explains why Philip made no real effort to pursue and kill Otto. The flight of the Germans was the sign that judgment had been given; pressing the fight was to risk tempting God.

In what was probably the most important embellishment of the story, Bouvines was invoked, from the late thirteenth century onward, to reaffirm the belief that the king of France was "elected" by the voice of God speaking through the people. In the fullest contemporary account of the battle, Philip had completed his tour through Hainaut and Flanders and had chastised his two rebel

An artist's rendition of Philip II thanking the burghers after the Battle of Bouvines. (F. R. Niglutsch)

vassals by calculated destruction of their lands. He certainly did not plan on a pitched battle; indeed, when told of the coalition's approach, he tried to escape but could not get his army over the narrow bridge in time. Forced to make a stand, he took counsel with his knights, as was customary. He made a short speech, reminding them that although they were all sinners, they were not mercenaries like their foes and had not been excommunicated. He bade them to trust God, and, acting in his semisacred capacity, he raised his hand to bless them.

Ferrand is shown captured during the Battle of Bouvines in this miniature from Chroniques de Hainant. (Frederick Ungar Publishing Co.)

In the later legends, the king loses all trace of surprise or fear. On the contrary, Philip's self-possessed, almost theatrical speech has the effect of removing whatever perplexity and doubt the surprise attack must have raised among his followers. These legends claim that the king, obviously expecting the occasion, brought his crown with him (even though the crown was always kept in Paris). Laying that national symbol before his men—in still later legends, his forces included commoners as well as knights—Philip told them, "Without you, I cannot rule the kingdom anymore." In addition, he invited anyone who thought himself more worthy to put on the crown and lead them. Naturally, the barons cried out that they would have no king but Philip. In this way, God speaks through the "people's voice" and renews His divine choice of the king of the Franks. It is a very old ceremony that still retains its effective power, despite the advent of modern democracy.

Significance

Why, for historians, has this short and unprepared battle in the meadows of Bouvines seemed more decisive than most previous military encounters? The answer clearly lies in the importance of Philip's victory for the later development of the French monarchy. At the same time, it established the primacy of France as champion of the Catholic Church and as the model of chivalry and knighthood.

—*David B. Haley*

Further Reading

Bradbury, Jim. *Philip Augustus: King of France, 1180-1223*. New York: Longman, 1998. This biographical study explores Philip's life in the context of the Battle of Bouvines, Church history, and French history in general.

Denholm-Young, N. "The Tournament in the Thirteenth Century." In *Studies in Medieval History Presented to Frederick Maurice Powicke*, edited by R. W. Hunt, W. A. Pantin, and R. W. Southern. Reprint. Westport, Conn.: Greenwood Press, 1979. Provides insight into the court's notion of warfare.

Duby, Georges. *The Legend of Bouvines: War, Religion, and Culture in the Middle Ages*. Translated by Catherine Tihanyi. Berkeley: University of California Press, 1990. A thorough account, written by a famous medievalist. Prints a translation of the chief chronicle of Bouvines by William the Breton, together with an appendix of other thirteenth century narratives and poems on Bouvines.

_______. *The Three Orders: Feudal Society Imagined*. Translated by Arthur Goldhammer. Chicago: University of Chicago Press, 1980. An authoritative study of the three estates that, under the crown, constituted the mature feudal system of France.

France, John. *Western Warfare in the Age of the Crusades, 1000-1300*. Ithaca, N.Y.: Cornell University

Press, 1999. Historical survey of military engagements during the time of the Crusades. Includes an appendix on the Battle of Bouvines.
Hay, Denys. *The Medieval Centuries*. Rev. ed. New York: Harper and Row, 1964. Excellent source for understanding the development of the rivalry between the French and the Germans.
Painter, Sidney. *French Chivalry*. Ithaca, N.Y.: Cornell University Press, 1969. A classic account of the period.

SEE ALSO: November 27, 1095: Pope Urban II Calls the First Crusade; 1147-1149: Second Crusade; 1154-1204: Angevin Empire Is Established; 1189-1192: Third Crusade; 1204: Knights of the Fourth Crusade Capture Constantinople; 1217-1221: Fifth Crusade; 1227-1230: Frederick II Leads the Sixth Crusade; 1248-1254: Failure of the Seventh Crusade.
RELATED ARTICLES in *Great Lives from History: The Middle Ages, 477-1453*: Frederick II; Innocent III; King John; Philip II.

June 15, 1215
SIGNING OF THE MAGNA CARTA

The signing of the Magna Carta is popularly remembered as the first great confrontation between the monarchy and the lower-ranking nobility in England and the root of many important judicial practices, although many of its provisions became obsolete within a few centuries of its enactment.

LOCALE: Runnymede, England
CATEGORIES: Government and politics; laws, acts, and legal history; social reform

KEY FIGURES

King John (1166-1216), king of England, r. 1199-1216
Henry III (1207-1272), king of England, r. 1216-1272

SUMMARY OF EVENT

King John, because of his firsthand acquaintance with local government and military desertions he had suffered during campaigns in Normandy, distrusted England's barons. This distrust was met with deep discontent: English barons had paid heavily for John's wars, with eleven scutages in sixteen years (as opposed to three during the ten-year reign of John's predecessor, Richard I). As a result, in 1214 and 1215, John faced a revolt from the barons in the north and west. The barons forced his hand, and John signed the Magna Carta, or Great Charter, on June 15, 1215. In it, he agreed that even the king was subordinate to the "law of the land."

Despite its modern reputation as an early instrument of constitutional law, however, the charter was a compromise document, aiming for efficient functioning of the king's courts, not for destruction of his power. It limited the king only according to specific grievances and not in principle. The irrelevance of any compromise soon became clear: John appealed to Pope Innocent III to annul the charter, and the pope cooperated, declaring that anyone who revolted against John would be excommunicated. Two-thirds of the barons had accepted the Norman-French king Louis IX as their lord, and one-third remained loyal. John established himself in the north and continued his battles with the barons, but he soon died of dysentery.

The Magna Carta gained a reputation as a monument to constitutional freedoms through seventeenth century historians such as Edward Coke, but in fact little of the charter addresses such freedoms. Nevertheless, of the documents in which the constitutional tradition of the English-speaking peoples is enshrined, the Magna Carta is, if not the oldest, the first to have won for itself a place in the public memory. The sixty-three chapters of this "Great Charter," wrung from King John by civil war, extend a grant of liberties to all the freemen of the kingdom including barons, churchmen, and townspeople.

At first sight the fame of the Magna Carta in later centuries seems puzzling. The doctrines that were to find a prominent place in the famous libertarian documents of later centuries are absent here. The Magna Carta does not advance against the king in the name of God, or the sovereignty of the people, or the inalienable rights of humans. Yet its veneration is deserved.

The Magna Carta defined the legal relationship between king and subject in terms of the relationship that existed between a feudal lord and his vassal. The limitations that applied to the feudal lord, the Magna Carta held, were applicable in substantial measure to the king as well. In a sense a new juridical identity was created for the king; he was king no longer but feudal lord, and in this capacity his subjects could claim from him numerous rights.

An artist's rendition of King John signing the Magna Carta. (Library of Congress)

Chapter 12, for instance, states in part that no aid, or demand for payment of money, "shall be imposed in our realm except with the common council of the realm" unless it be to ransom the person of the king, to knight his eldest son, or to marry his eldest daughter. Even in these cases "only a reasonable aid shall be levied." To obtain money beyond these three designated occasions, the king must have previously obtained the consent of his subjects. This common "counsel of the realm" is to be obtained, according to chapter 14, from the Great Council convened by specific letters of summons sent by the king to his tenants-in-chief.

The three designated occasions when the king need not obtain consent are at best infrequent and, as soon as the royal government had evolved beyond the most primitive stage, the sums supplied from these sources became more and more irrelevant and inadequate so that the king was bound to obtain consent for most exactions necessary to operate government. In effect, chapter 12 of the Magna Carta secures the property right of the subject: He need yield to the Crown only those sums to which he has consented. Looked at from another viewpoint, the property right of the subject constitutes a limitation on the power of the Crown; it forms an enclave into which the king may not, so to speak, intrude without permission. Moreover, the necessity of obtaining consent led easily in time to the institution of Parliament, where eventually consent to taxation was given provisionally on the condition that the sums realized be spent for one purpose and not another.

The fact that the king needs the consent of his "tenants-in-chief" rather than of his "subjects" when he requires additional "aids" roots the Magna Carta's limitations in feudal law. The legal literature of England in the decades before the great Charter distinctly showed that the aids a feudal lord could ask of his knight or tenant-in-chief were specifically limited. For instance, the *Treatise on the Laws and Customs of the Kingdom of England* (c. 1188), a summary of English law usually attributed to Ranulf de Glanville, similarly states that the aids a lord may demand from his knights must be moderate according to the size and wealth of their fiefs and that similar moderate demands may be made by the lord only when his son is knighted or his eldest daughter married. Already, the lord is limited in what he can ask of a knight. The notion of limitation, vague in the case of Glanville but precise in the Magna Carta, is common to both documents. Since in the Magna Carta the king's subjects are his tenants-in-chief and the king is considered a feudal lord, the limitations of a feudal lord are made to do duty in limiting the king. The kings of England since William the Conqueror

THE MAGNA CARTA: KEY PROVISIONS

- The English church shall be free.
- Heirs of earls and barons shall have their inheritance.
- No scutage [tax] will be imposed without the counsel's consent.
- Offenses carry fines in proportion to the gravity of the offense.
- The king's officers will be required to adhere to rules of conduct and will not be allowed to take anyone's possessions without immediate permission and payment.
- No one may be imprisoned without the "legal judgment of his peers, or by the law of the land."
- Due process of law will not be denied or delayed.
- Merchants are protected in traveling to and from England.
- The king's promise: ". . . all these things spoken of above shall be observed in good faith and without any evil intent."

Source: Summarized from *Readings in European History*, edited by James Harvey Robinson, abridged edition (Boston: Ginn & Company, 1906), pp. 115-118.

had been feudal lords as well as kings. The Magna Carta exploited this fact.

SIGNIFICANCE

The Magna Carta contains inklings of some modern political ideas, such as the "due process" clause of the U.S. Constitution. It also guaranteed that no freeman should be imprisoned or dispossessed except by legal judgment of his peers or by the law of the land. Furthermore, justice would not be denied, sold, or delayed. Chapter 61 allowed for machinery to provide means of enforcement. Although Pope Innocent III repudiated the charter for John after the king had declared himself a papal vassal, it was confirmed seven times during the reign of Henry III and reissued again in 1297 under Edward I. The following interpretation of the Magna Carta was handed down in the statutes of Edward III (1354): "No man of what estate or condition that he be, shall be put out of land or tenement, nor taken nor imprisoned, nor disinherited, nor put to death, without being brought in answer by due process of law."

While its precedents for modern law are well known, large parts of the Magna Carta have been largely forgotten. Sir Ivor Jennings, author of *Magna Carta and Its Influence in the World Today* (1965), asserted that "if the Magna Carta were redrafted in the form of an Act of Parliament, it would contain four parts." The first part, according to Jennings, would be "a single clause from Chapter 1, protecting the rights . . . of the English church . . . so general in its terms that it has never been very important." The second part would be drawn from the fourteen provisions relating to feudal land tenure, most of which have been repealed by later law. The third part would contain the fourteen provisions relating to the administration of justice. While chapters 8, 14, and 29 have had a seminal effect on later law, the other eleven provisions "were obsolete before the end of the thirteenth century," according to Jennings. Part 4 would contain the last nine provisions of the Magna Carta, of which five are still workable under present law.

The significance of the Magna Carta therefore lies not in any one chapter or group of chapters, but rather in the fact that it established a degree of juridical equality between subjects and government, an indisputable prerequisite if the lowly subject was to claim successfully rights that the government must respect.

—*Martin J. Baron, updated by Bruce E. Johansen*

FURTHER READING

Breay, Claire. *Magna Carta: Manuscripts and Myths*. London: British Library, 2002. Argues that the Magna Carta, although symbolizing a democratic vision, was not intended as a legal document for human rights but was instead a response to political circumstances in England.

Danziger, Danny, and John Gillingham. *1215: The Year of Magna Carta*. London: Hodder & Stoughton, 2003. Investigates both the politics and social concerns of the time, including the lives of ordinary people in a time of great change.

Dickinson, J. C. *The Great Charter*. London: Historical Association, 1955. This brief work outlines the principles and historical circumstances of the Magna Carta.

Holt, J. C. *Magna Carta*. 2d ed. New York: Cambridge University Press, 1992. Examines the judicial roots of the Magna Carta, tracing the hostility toward the monarchy that developed in England after the Norman Conquest.

Jennings, Sir Ivor. *Magna Carta and Its Influence in the World Today*. New York: Her Majesty's Stationery Office, 1965. Includes the text of the Magna Carta.

Painter, Sidney. *The Reign of King John*. Baltimore: The Johns Hopkins University Press, 1966. Traces the development of the Magna Carta against the background of King John's reign.

Swindler, William F. *Magna Carta: Legend and Legacy.* Indianapolis, Ind.: Bobbs-Merrill, 1965. Discusses the use of the Magna Carta by the later generations of English and American historians.

See also: 1258: Provisions of Oxford Are Established; 1285: Statute of Winchester; 1295: Model Parliament.

Related articles in *Great Lives from History: The Middle Ages, 477-1453*: Edward III; Henry III; King John.

November 11-30, 1215
Fourth Lateran Council

The Fourth Lateran Council laid the cornerstone for medieval Christian devotion and reflected the authority of the Papacy throughout Europe.

Locale: Lateran Basilica in Rome (now in Italy)
Category: Religion

Key Figures

Innocent III (1160 or 1161-1216), Roman Catholic pope, 1198-1216
Saint Dominic (c. 1170-1221), founder of the Dominican Order of preaching friars
Saint Francis of Assisi (c. 1181-1226), founder of the Order of Friars Minor, also known as the Franciscans
King John (1166-1216), king of England, r. 1199-1216
Simon de Montfort (1165?-1218), given the Albigensian county of Toulouse in southern France by the Fourth Lateran Council

Summary of Event

Innocent III's time as pope is known as the "high noon" of the Papacy. He once likened the Papacy to the Sun and lessened the state to the satellite position of the Moon. These concepts seemed to filter through the air at the Fourth Lateran Council, in which Innocent III made his expectations known despite opposition from laity and clergy alike.

Innocent III fit the mold of many twelfth and thirteenth century popes. He was more of a jurist and an administrator than a saintly individual. Educated at Bologna, he was elected pope at the rather early age of about thirty-seven. Following in the tradition of popes Innocent II, who called the Second Lateran Council in 1139, and Alexander III, who called the Third Lateran Council in 1179, Innocent convoked a truly ecumenical council that rivaled even the earlier Eastern ecumenical councils. The number of participants (2,280) was imposing, in part because members of laity and clergy both were well represented. It was the first instance in which both estates were participants in a church council. Among the more than four hundred bishops were prelates from Bohemia, Poland, Hungary, Livonia, and Estonia, countries never before represented at a council. Innocent failed to persuade the Greeks to attend, but the Latin patriarchs of the East were present. Besides abbots, eight hundred legates of monastic chapters attended. Envoys on behalf of Frederick II of Sicily, the emperor of Constantinople, and the kings of France, Hungary, Jerusalem, Cyprus, and Aragon arrived. King John of England was not invited, since he was under the ban of excommunication, but he was represented by five proctors (three clerics and two laity).

Little is known about the council's organization. The only extant documents are Innocent's inaugural address, the record of one public session, the text of seventy approved canons, and the decree authorizing a new crusade. In addition, there are two eyewitness accounts. One describes the ceremonial splendors of the council's opening session. The council first met on November 11, following a papal mass celebrated at dawn. The ensuing papal address had such a vast audience that there were reports of several fatalities resulting from the crowded conditions, and the bishop of Amalfi was suffocated during the melee. There were two other public sessions held on November 20 and 30.

The first public session on November 11 addressed one of the major issues at hand. Innocent was eager to call a crusade, perhaps to eradicate the memory of the devastation and damage committed during the Fourth Crusade (1202-1204), when the Crusaders attacked Constantinople and succeeded in carrying off countless religious and secular treasures with reckless abandon. He ordered that all Crusaders should be ready by June to embark at Brindisi for the recovery of the Holy Land. To attract participants, the property of potential crusaders was protected. Crusaders would pay no taxes, nor would they need to address their debts during their absence. Indulgences were liberal. Despite all the careful preparation, the Crusade was doomed to failure. Frederick II was expected to participate but did not fulfill this expectation. Because of the resulting lack of leadership and the death of Innocent III in the meantime, the Fifth Crusade (1217-1221) ended in disaster in Egypt.

The Fourth Lateran Council established the number of sacraments at seven and stressed the necessity for believers to receive the sacraments in order to attain salvation. This copy of the left panel from a fifteenth century triptych by Rogier van der Weyden displays the sacraments of Baptism (administered at birth), Confirmation (youth), and Penance (maturity). (Frederick Ungar Publishing Co.)

In enacting internal Church reform, the Fourth Lateran Council was especially successful. It has been said that Innocent made more laws than fifty of his predecessors, laws that were practical and workable and entitled him to be considered virtually a cofounder of the canon law of the Church, which had been begun by Gratian in his *Decretum* (c. 1140). These laws laid the groundwork for medieval canon law through the process of assimilation of Roman law and the introduction of new church laws.

Heresy was a major concern of the council. Innocent III continued his vehement opposition to the troublesome Albigensian heresy. The council's canon 1 carefully defined the Trinity and condemned Joachim of Fiore's views against the trinity. Canon 1 also made significant use of the Aristotelian word "transubstantiation," stating that bread and wine were "transubstantiated" into the body and blood of Christ. This statement was the most significant theological definition issued by the council. It was repeated at the Council of Trent (1545-1563) and continued as a doctrine within the Roman Catholic Church. Another decree required the priest to elevate the Host with his back to the congregation. The laity subsequently became observers rather than participants in the Mass when this decree was put in place. (Following Vatican II in 1965, priests once again were able to face the congregation as they had before the Fourth Lateran Council.) Canon 21 commanded every Roman Catholic to make a yearly confession and to receive Communion at Easter.

The Fourth Lateran Council established the number of sacraments at seven and stressed the necessity for believers to receive the sacraments in order to attain salvation. Canon 50 liberally restricted marriage to the fourth degree of consanguinity. Other regulations were aimed at clerical discipline. Clergy were not to hold secular offices and were not to act in an unbecoming or exhibitionist manner. Likewise, clergy were to refrain from wearing decorous or inappropriate clothing.

Canon 2 elaborated on the pursuit of heretics. All who professed heresies contrary to the faith expressed in the first canon defining transubstantiation were condemned and left to be suitably punished by the state. To detect doctrinal deviations, bishops were ordered to visit suspected centers of heresy every year. Canon 8 marked the beginning of an episcopal Court of Inquisitions, although the Inquisition at this point in time was procedural; it was not fully developed until later in the thirteenth century. Innocent's intention at the council was to bring peace after seven years of bloody crusading against the Albigensians. The council developed these antiheresy measures into canon law, thus regularizing the legal process and making use of documentary evidence.

Canon 13 forbade the founding of new religious orders. There were new spiritual forces at work in the thirteenth century. No doubt there was fear about the radical nature of some of the new congregations compounded with a certain sense of rivalry from the older, established orders. The older orders—the Benedictines, the Augustines, the Cistercians—tried to prevail on the pope not to recognize these new orders. Innocent seems to have countermanded the council. He had already permitted the radical Francis of Assisi to preach; according to some sources, Innocent recognized the Franciscans at the council. This acceptance did not find its way into the documents but it is assumed that Innocent interceded on behalf of the Franciscans. The Franciscan rule would be recognized by Innocent III's successor, Honorius III, in 1223. Dominic Guzmán (later Saint Dominic) from Spain, lacking previous recognition, was allowed by Innocent to establish his new order after initial hesitation and against the vote of the council. After Innocent's death, the Dominican order was sanctioned by Honorius III in 1216. With good diplomatic sense, Innocent was able to reconcile dissidents within the church while simultaneously accommodating the wave of new spiritual reform orders.

The council issued decrees against Muslims and Jews. Anti-Semitism had been on the rise since the period of the First Crusade, and the nature of the crusading movement itself directed hostility toward the Muslims. With the growing self-assurance of Christians about themselves, both Jews and Muslims became "outsiders" even though they had coexisted, sometimes quite peacefully, with Christians for centuries. Canon 68 stated that Jews and Muslims should wear distinctive clothing in Christian lands so that they would not be mistaken for Christians. In the three days before Easter, particularly on Good Friday, Jews and Muslims were not to be seen in public. Innocent III did not want Jews to suffer physical persecution, and he ordered Crusaders not to harass Jews. Nevertheless, the requirement of distinctive dress paved an easier path toward the possibility of future persecution.

Other specific matters were then laid before the council for approval. These items included Innocent's choice of Frederick for German king; his suspension of Stephen Langton, the archbishop of Canterbury; his condemnation of the Magna Carta in favor of King John; and his advocacy of the claims of the Albigensian persecutor Simon de Montfort to the territory of Toulouse in southern France. Although violent opposition to the claims of de Montfort erupted among the delegates, Innocent was able to save a large part of the Toulouse inheritance for de Montfort's heir. Apart from his limited success in the Toulouse settlement, Innocent and his momentous Fourth Lateran Council failed only in launching vast crusading plans in the Holy Land.

The right-hand portion of the triptych by Rogier van der Weyden displays the sacraments of Marriage (undertaken at maturity), Orders (at old age), and Extreme Unction (at death). Not shown here is the third sacrament, the Eucharist, or communion. (Frederick Ungar Publishing Co.)

SIGNIFICANCE

The Fourth Lateran Council, by virtue of its size and inclusiveness, brought about major Church reforms in many areas and was the primary force behind the unsuccessful Fifth Crusade. It demonstrated the power of the Papacy and, through its many canons, had far-reaching effects on the clergy and laypeople alike.

—*Lowell H. Zuck, updated by Barbara M. Fahy*

FURTHER READING

Bellitto, Christopher M. *The General Councils: A History of the Twenty-one General Councils from Nicaea to Vatican II*. New York: Paulist Press, 2002. The Fourth Lateran Council is among the twenty-one councils covered in this work. Bibliography and index.

Moore, John C. *Pope Innocent III: To Root Up and to Plant*. Boston: Brill, 2003. A biography of Pope Innocent III by a noted scholar. Bibliography and index.

Moore, John C., Brenda Bolton, et al., eds. *Pope Innocent and His World*. Brookfield, Vt.: Ashgate, 1999. A collection of papers presented at a conference on Pope Innocent III at Hofstra University. Bibliography and index.

Pixton, Paul B. *The German Episcopacy and the Implementation of the Decrees of the Fourth Lateran Council, 1216-1245: Watchmen on the Tower.* New York: E. J. Brill, 1995. An examination of the Fourth Lateran Council and its effects in Germany. Bibliography and index.

Powell, James M. *Innocent III: Vicar of Christ or Lord of the World?* 2d ed. Washington, D.C.: Catholic University of America Press, 1994. A succinct collection of essays that outline the problems and interpretations of Innocent's reign.

Sayers, Jane. *Innocent III, Leader of Europe, 1198-1216*. New York: Longmans, 1994. A fresh and clear perspective of Innocent, his papacy, and the way in which his authority was viewed throughout Europe.

SEE ALSO: April 16, 1209: Founding of the Franciscans; 1209-1229: Albigensian Crusade; 1217-1221: Fifth Crusade; 1227-1230: Frederick II Leads the Sixth Crusade.

RELATED ARTICLES in *Great Lives from History: The Middle Ages, 477-1453*: Alexander III; Saint Clare of Assisi; Saint Dominic; Saint Francis of Assisi; Frederick II; Innocent III; Joachim of Fiore; King John.

1217-1221
FIFTH CRUSADE

The Fifth Crusade attempted to regain control of the Holy Land through military action against resident Muslims, but it ended as a dismal failure despite careful planning.

LOCALE: Southern Europe; Acre, Palestine; Damietta, Egypt

CATEGORIES: Religion; wars, uprisings, and civil unrest

KEY FIGURES

Innocent III (1160 or 1161-1216), Roman Catholic pope, 1198-1216, promoted the Fourth and Fifth Crusades

Honorius III (d. 1227), successor to Innocent III as Roman Catholic pope, 1216-1227, who carried out preparations for the Fifth Crusade

Andrew II (1175-1235), king of Hungary, r. 1205-1235, supporter of the Crusade

John of Brienne (c. 1148-1237), king of Jerusalem, r. 1210-1225, military leader of the Crusaders

al-Kāmil (1180-1238), sultan of Egypt, Palestine, and Syria, r. 1218-1238, commander of the forces defending Damietta

Pelagius of Albano (fl. thirteenth century), papal legate under Honorius III

SUMMARY OF EVENT

One of several Crusades that failed to drive Muslims out of what the Christians considered their Holy Land, the Fifth Crusade was nevertheless one of the most carefully planned. Pope Innocent III had been disappointed by the Fourth Crusade; although Crusaders had seized Constantinople, victory had not led to conquest of the Holy Land. Seeing the popular religious fervor that had led to the Children's Crusade in 1212, Innocent began to prepare for another Crusade in 1213. He believed that the prevailing enthusiasm for the cause would ensure a victory.

In 1213, Innocent sent a papal encyclical to Christian leaders, summoning them to a council to be held in November, 1215. The most important topic for discussion would be the formation of another Crusade, and all bishops and clergymen were instructed to begin plans to send fighting troops, arms, and supplies when the time came. Innocent also ordered all Christian churches to commence public prayers for the restoration of the Holy Land; monthly processions and daily prayers were called for in an attempt to gather spiritual support from those who would not fight. Handbooks of sermons and prayers were distributed throughout Europe. Innocent's letters and subsequent sermons by local clergymen painted dramatic pictures of devout Christians suffering under Muslim oppression and of Jesus's own sepulcher defiled by disdainful Muslims. The common folk responded enthusiastically.

Inflaming his followers was one thing, but Innocent also needed the support of kings, princes, and barons. Innocent believed that because the spirit is superior to the flesh, the pope should have authority over earthly rulers. Not surprisingly, earthly rulers disagreed. The pope dispatched carefully chosen emissaries throughout Christendom to request—or demand—support.

At the Fourth Lateran Council, which opened on November 11, 1215, the final details were arranged. Those who had taken vows as Crusaders in previous engagements would be compelled to fulfill them now. Spanish fighting against the Moors was demoted from Crusade status, and Spanish soldiers would now join this Crusade. The rules of conduct for Crusaders were spelled out, and Innocent promised indulgences and redemption for those who fulfilled their vows faithfully. The Crusaders would set off from Sicily on June 1, 1217, after the expiration of the truce between Jerusalem and the Muslims, and Innocent himself would be there to bless them.

In spite of Innocent's strong organizational skills, his carefully laid plans were not followed. He won the full support of many common people, but men of power were less willing to submit to him. No previous pope had demanded taxes to pay for a Crusade or promised redemption as repayment, and these new programs were received with great skepticism. Without the leadership of the nobles, ordinary citizens could not be drawn together into an effective force. Before he was able to press his will on secular rulers who had their own, different, agendas, Innocent III died on July 16, 1216, almost a year before the Fifth Crusade was to begin.

Pope Honorius III tried to carry out Innocent's plans, believing God's destiny for him was that he should free the Holy Land, but the difficulties were beyond him. Although Hungary and the Netherlands could be counted on, French noblemen refused to join the Fifth Crusade.

Pope Innocent III. (Library of Congress)

Sicilian king Frederick II (r. 1212; Holy Roman Emperor from 1220-1250 and leader of the Sixth Crusade) had taken up the cross, but his right to the throne was under challenge and he could not risk a long absence. The English nobility were locked in intense internal struggles, and the Spanish were unhappy at being taxed for this Crusade after they had already funded the fighting against the Moors.

King Andrew II of Hungary took the first action. In July of 1217, he set out with a large army for Spalato, where they would meet a fleet of ships. As it turned out, the number of Crusaders was larger than expected, and there were not enough ships to carry them all, resulting in a delay of several weeks. During the delay, many found their zeal weakening and returned home.

By the fall, more than one hundred thousand Crusaders from Hungary, Austria, Merano, Cyprus, and Germany gathered in Acre, Palestine. Unfortunately, Syria was experiencing a severe famine, and there was little food. Again, many Crusaders deserted the group; others starved to death or fell victim to crime and unrest. John of Brienne, the king of Jerusalem, decided to abandon his earlier plans for two massive campaigns and called instead for a series of small attacks to buy time until more Crusaders could arrive. Three times the Crusaders attacked Muslim strongholds, and three times they were defeated.

Andrew II of Hungary returned home with his army, and replacements from Germany, Italy, and Frisia arrived. The new, larger force attacked Damietta, Egypt, on May 27, 1218. Over the next eighteen months, more Crusaders gathered from Italy, France, Cyprus, and England. King John of Jerusalem was chosen as leader of the troops; he expected that with victory, Egypt would fall under his rule. The papal legate Pelagius of Albano had also arrived, however, bringing the message that the pope intended Egypt to be his own, since his authority superseded the king's. Pelagius was the stronger—and more ruthless—personality, and he gradually gained ascendancy over John.

The Crusaders camped outside Damietta. In August of 1218, they captured the Chain Tower in the middle of the Nile, and were able then to control the river. The Muslims sank several ships in the river, preventing Christian ships from passing, and the Crusaders turned to an abandoned canal. Both sides were determined, and for months neither side seemed to be winning. In February of 1219, however, internal conflict and the deposition of the new sultan led to disorder in Egypt, and the Christians were able to move in.

The Egyptians decided to negotiate. Sultan al-Malik al-Kāmil offered to surrender nearly all his territory in the kingdom of Jerusalem, and to hold to a thirty-year truce, if the Crusaders would leave Egypt. King John and others favored accepting these terms, but Pelagius did not, and he had his way. By the time the Crusaders finally conquered Damietta in November of 1219, Muslim forces outside the city were more determined than ever to resist the Christian intruders. The Crusaders themselves were disorganized and disgruntled, torn apart by the arguments of their leaders. As for Damietta, it was by this time inhabited by only a small number of starving soldiers who put up no further defense.

With Damietta taken, the conflict between John and Pelagius intensified, further dividing the Crusaders. The plan had been for Damietta to become a base from which to launch further attacks; instead, the Crusaders remained inactive and disorganized. King John departed in disgust, leaving Pelagius as an unpopular and ineffective leader. As the Muslims' strength grew, Pelagius ordered attacks, but the Crusaders were not willing to follow him. Finally, in July of 1221, ordered by the pope to rejoin the Fifth Crusade, John led the Crusaders on a march down the Nile. By then, even John had lost the popular support of the men.

Taking a route he advised against, the army was cut off and defeated by the Muslims. The Crusaders had no choice but to surrender, agreeing on August 30, 1221, to retreat from Egypt.

Significance

The Crusade that had been so carefully planned, and which had at times seemed so near to success in part because of the large numbers who joined the fight, had ended in complete failure. Once again, Crusaders failed to secure the Holy Land from Muslims.

—*Cynthia A. Bily*

Further Reading

Donovan, J. P. *Pelagius and the Fifth Crusade*. 1950. Reprint. New York: AMS Press, 1978. One of the most accessible of the book-length studies of the controversial papal legate and one of the most favorable to Pelagius. Acknowledges Pelagius's blunders but argues against those who blame those errors for the Fifth Crusade's failure. Bibliography.

Hillenbrand, Carole. *The Crusades: Islamic Perspectives*. New York: Routledge, 2000. Chapters explore ethnic and religious stereotyping, daily life, the conduct of war, and more. Bibliography, index.

Irwin, Robert. "Muslim Responses to the Crusades." *History Today* 47, no. 4 (April, 1997). Presents a rich overview of the Muslim perspective on the Crusades. Provides photographs and a short list of further readings.

Madden, Thomas F., ed. *The Crusades: The Essential Readings*. Malden, Mass.: Blackwell, 2002. A collection of previously published articles about the Crusades, including medieval sources, lay enthusiasm, patronage, Byzantium, and the subjection of Muslims. Bibliography, index.

Powell, James M. *Anatomy of a Crusade, 1213-1221*. Philadelphia: University of Pennsylvania Press, 1986. Unlike most other studies, this book praises Innocent III's extensive preparations and attributes the Fifth Crusade's failure to implementation weaknesses on the part of secular leaders. Illustrations, maps, bibliography, index.

_______, ed. *Innocent III: Vicar of Christ or Lord of the World?* 2d ed. Washington, D.C.: Catholic University of America Press, 1994. A balanced biography, with insightful discussion of Innocent's theology and his extensive theological writings. Bibliography, index.

Riley-Smith, Jonathan. *The Crusades: A Short History.* New Haven, Conn.: Yale University Press, 1987. A history for the general reader, with helpful apparatus for the nonspecialist, including nine historical maps, a unique system of transliteration, and an extensive annotated bibliography.

_______, ed. *The Oxford Illustrated History of the Crusades*. New York: Oxford University Press, 1999. Places the Fifth Crusade within the context of the medieval crusading movement, arguing its significance in the history of late medieval culture in the West. Illustrations, maps, bibliography, index.

Van Cleve, Thomas C. "The Fifth Crusade." In *The Later Crusades, 1189-1311*, edited by Robert Lee Woolf and Harry W. Hazard. Vol. 2 in *A History of the Crusades*, edited by Kenneth M. Setton. 2d ed. Madison: University of Wisconsin Press, 1969-1989. An exceptionally clear and detailed accounting of the events of the Fifth Crusade, drawn from Western and Arabic sources. Includes a map of the region. Bibliography, index.

SEE ALSO: August 15-20, 636: Battle of Yarmūk; 1009: Destruction of the Church of the Holy Sepulchre; November 27, 1095: Pope Urban II Calls the First Crusade; c. 1120: Order of the Knights Templar Is Founded; c. 1145: Prester John Myth Sweeps Across Europe; 1147-1149: Second Crusade; c. 1181-1221: Lalibela Founds the Christian Capital of Ethiopia; 1204: Knights of the Fourth Crusade Capture Constantinople; 1212: Children's Crusade; November 11-30, 1215: Fourth Lateran Council; 1227-1230: Frederick II Leads the Sixth Crusade; 1248-1254: Failure of the Seventh Crusade; April, 1291: Fall of Acre, Palestine.

RELATED ARTICLES in *Great Lives from History: The Middle Ages, 477-1453*: Enrico Dandolo; Frederick II; Innocent III.

1219-1333
HŌJŌ FAMILY DOMINATES SHOGUNS, RULES JAPAN

The Hōjō family gained control over the shoguns, reducing them to figureheads while increasing the power and prestige of the office of shogun.

LOCALE: Kamakura and Kyoto, Japan
CATEGORY: Government and politics

KEY FIGURES

Minamoto Yoritomo (1147-1199), founder of the Kamakura shogunate (1185-1333); shogun, 1192-1195; military director, 1195-1199
Hōjō Masako (1157-1225), wife of Minamoto Yoritomo, mother of Minamoto Yoriie and Minamoto Sanetomo
Hōjō Yoshitoki (1162-1224), brother of Hōjō Masako and regent to the shogun, 1205-1224
Minamoto Yoriie (1182-1204), oldest son of Minamoto Yoritomo; shogun, 1202-1203
Minamoto Sanetomo (1192-1219), second son of Minamoto Yoritomo; shogun, 1203-1219

SUMMARY OF EVENT

The position of shogun was not important politically until 1185, when Minamoto Yoritomo defeated the Taira family in the Gempei War (1180-1185). Before 1185, political power had been centered in the imperial court in Kyoto, where, since 600, the emperor had been reduced to a figurehead controlled by families at court. The position of *sei-i-tai shōgun* ("great barbarian-subduing general") had existed since the 640's as a title conferred by the emperor on a warrior who fought on the Japanese frontier (the area around present-day Tokyo), defending Japan from hostile tribes. Shogun was an honorary position, not a politically powerful one.

When new territory in the northern half of the main island of Honshū was added to the kingdom after 900, the court had less control of this newly settled region. That land and its agricultural resources were controlled by warrior families who lived there. In fact, the imperial court increasingly called on these families for services it could not provide, such as protection of property and policing. Around 900, a professional warrior class made of samurai began to evolve within these northern warrior families. However, these samurai were seen as crude and vulgar and were generally not accepted socially by the court aristocracy. The Taira family was one of these frontier samurai families, but by 1168, some of its members had managed to find a place for themselves in the sophisticated culture of court life in Kyoto and, using their wealth and military resources, had gained control of the imperial system. They lost that control when long-

MAJOR REGENTS OF THE HŌJŌ FAMILY

Regent	*Reign*
1203-1205	Hōjō Tokimasa
1205-1224	Hōjō Yoshitoki
1224-1242	Hōjō Yasutoki
1242-1246	Hōjō Tsunetoki
1246-1256	Hōjō Tokiyori
1256-1264	Hōjō Nagatoki
1264-1268	Hōjō Masamura
1268-1284	Hōjō Tokimune
1284-1301	Hōjō Sadatoki
1301-1311	Hōjō Morotoki
1311-1312	Hōjō Munenobu
1312-1315	Hōjō Hirotoki
1315	Hōjō Mototoki
1316-1326	Hōjō Takatoki
1326	Hōjō Sadaaki
1327-1333	Hōjō Moritoki

MAJOR LEADERS OF THE KAMAKURA SHOGUNATE

Shogun	*Reign*
1192-1199	Minamoto Yoritomo
1202-1203	Minamoto Yoriie
1203-1219	Minamoto Sanetomo
1226-1244	Kujo Yoritsune
1244-1252	Kujo Yoritsugu
1252-1266	Prince Munetaka
1266-1289	Prince Koreyasu
1289-1308	Prince Hisaaki
1308-1333	Prince Morikuni

standing disputes between the Minamoto, another northern samurai family, and the Taira came to a head in the Gempei War.

During the war, Minamoto Yoritomo began to work on a system for controlling Japan. Unlike the Taira, Yoritomo did not care for life at the imperial court; in fact, he saw it as perilous to the vigor of his samurai family and regime and avoided it whenever possible. When he implemented his government, he located its headquarters at a distance from the court in Kyoto, in the town of Kamakura, on the coast southeast of present-day Tokyo.

All positions in Yoritomo's government were filled by the samurai class. He developed a central administration in Kamakura with regional commanders (*shugo*) and local land stewards (*jitō*) throughout Japan. These positions coexisted with the imperial administration. Originally, the imperial administration dealt with civil matters, and the *shugo* and *jitō* dealt with military affairs, but the military bureaucracy, directed from Kamakura, gradually gained political control. Yoritomo was the first person to understand that the samurai class could rule Japan without using the imperial government structure.

Yoritomo died in 1199 after being thrown from a horse. The question arose as to which son, Yoriie or Sanetomo, would succeed him. The first successor was Yoriie, who acted as shogun but was not officially appointed until 1202. Many in the shogun system doubted that the quick-tempered, headstrong Yoriie was a good choice. Yoritomo's wife, Hōjō Masako, who came from a family of early supporters of the Minamoto, managed to have Yoriie "pushed" out of power in favor of her second son, Sanetomo, in 1203. Yoriie died from a long illness in 1204, but many historians accuse his mother and her family of having ordered his murder. Sanetomo was assassinated in 1219, leaving no heirs. Again, many historians accuse his mother and her family of arranging the murder.

Masako and her father then conspired to have Minamoto nephews and cousins appointed shogun and for the Hōjō family to serve them as regents. Masako and her brother Hōjō Yoshitoki managed to quiet the disputes within the Kamakura system and secured permanent control of the shoguns. By 1219, shoguns were mere figureheads controlled behind the scenes by Hōjō regents. In fact, the shoguns were not even direct descendants of Minamoto Yoritomo because Sanetomo had been the last direct heir. It was Masako and Yoshitoki who later engineered the Hōjō regency's victory in the Jōkyū War (1221), a last effort by Emperor Go-Toba and his supporters to reassert imperial authority. Masako is credited with changing the Hōjō strategy from a defensive posture to an offensive one, which won the war. The Hōjō continued to control shoguns until events weakened their grasp and they were driven from power in 1333.

It is ironic that under the Hōjō, the person chosen as shogun lost political power while the office of shogun increased in power and prestige. Minamoto Yoritomo had been appointed *sei-i-tai shōgun* by the emperor in 1192, but he resigned from the office in 1195 to become military director, a position he felt was more important. While Yoritomo did not see the position of shogun as particularly powerful, it was the one position the Hōjō could control. Therefore, to rule Japan from behind the scenes, they had to imbue the office with more power and prestige.

In theory, the emperor of Japan was the source of all political power. He was also the source of all moral and religious authority and was officially proclaimed a "god on earth" in the 640's. The moral and religious authority of the emperor was considered more important than his political authority and involved the emperor's conducting elaborate and almost constant rituals and pilgrimages for the good of his subjects. To perform these religious functions, the emperor delegated his political authority to administrators who oversaw the mundane tasks of ruling Japan. For the Hōjō, the appointment of shoguns by the emperor was the official delegation of political authority for the shogun to rule Japan. This ideology was used by the Ashikaga (1338-1573) and further elaborated by the Tokugawa (1603-1867) as the basis of their right to rule until it was undermined by imperial supporters in the mid-1800's.

Significance

The combination of Minamoto Yoritomo's government structure and the Hōjō's efforts to strengthen the position of shogun became the basis of Japanese government. The golden age of the shogun system came during the rule of the Tokugawa family, 1603 to 1867. The Tokugawa period saw the height of premodern Japan's prosperity and contained a span of more than two hundred years when Japan was not involved in any wars, domestic or foreign.

—*David W. Blaylock*

Further Reading

Mass, Jeffrey. *The Development of Kamakura Rule, 1180-1250.* Stanford, Calif.: Stanford University Press, 1979. Mass is an American pioneer in the study of medieval Japanese history. This volume (one of four concerning the Kamakura shogunate) deals with a major conflict, the Jōkyū War (1221), and justice in the Kamakura system.

Mulhern, Chieko Irie, ed. *Heroic with Grace: Legendary Women of Japan.* Armonk, N.Y.: M. E. Sharpe, 1991. Margaret Fukuzawa Benton's article on Hōjō Masako is the best source in English about the woman and her actions in the rise of the Hōjō family.

Perkins, George W., trans. *The Clear Mirror: A Chronicle of the Japanese Court During the Kamakura Period, 1185-1333.* Stanford, Calif.: Stanford University Press, 1998. Although this account is focused on the imperial court, it does shed light on the actions of the major players in Kamakura and Hōjō Japan.

Ruch, Barbara, ed. *Engendering Faith: Women and Buddhism in Premodern Japan.* Ann Arbor, Mich.: Center for Japanese Studies, University of Michigan, 2002. Martin Collcutt's article on Hōjō Masako covers political events and also studies her religious faith after she took tonsure as a Buddhist nun following Minamoto Yoritomo's death.

Sansom, George. *A History of Japan to 1334.* Vol. 1. Stanford, Calif.: Stanford University Press, 1958. Contains what is still the most detailed account of this period and its impact.

Souyri, Pierre Francois. *The World Turned Upside Down: Medieval Japanese Society.* Translated by Käthe Roth. New York: Columbia University Press, 2001. Discusses the Hōjō period while exploring the sweeping changes in Japan during the period from 1185 to the late 1500's.

Yamamura, Kozo, ed. *The Cambridge History of Japan.* Vol. 3. New York: Cambridge University Press, 1990. A good general introduction to Japanese history with articles written by major historians. The article by Jeffrey Mass discusses the institutions created by Minamoto Yoritomo, particularly the *shugo* and *jitō*. The article by Ishii Susumu discusses the events and actions that led to the fall of the Hōjō.

See also: 792: Rise of the Samurai; 858: Rise of the Fujiwara Family; 1156-1192: Minamoto Yoritomo Becomes Shogun; 1336-1392: Yoshino Civil Wars.

Related articles in *Great Lives from History: The Middle Ages, 477-1453*: Ashikaga Takauji; Fujiwara Michinaga; Minamoto Yoritomo; Taira Kiyomori.

1221-1259
MAI DUNAMA DIBBALEMI EXPANDS KANEM EMPIRE

Under the leadership of Mai Dunama Dibbalemi, the Kanem kingdom wielded tremendous power in the Lake Chad region and employed that authority to expand the Kanem Empire and the Islamic faith.

LOCALE: South of the Sahara Desert, northeast of Bornu, north of Lake Chad

CATEGORIES: Expansion and land acquisition; government and politics; religion

KEY FIGURES

Mai Dunama Dibbalemi (1210-1259), Kanem ruler, r. 1221-1259

Keday (fl. thirteenth century), son of Dunama, Kanem ruler, r. 1259-1277

Bir (fl. thirteenth century), son of Dunama, Kanem ruler, r. 1277-1296

SUMMARY OF EVENT

The initial empire called Kanem developed out of a federation of chiefdoms near Lake Chad. The Kanem kingdom was established around the ninth century and lasted in a reorganized and modernized form until the 1840's. It encompassed, at its height of expansion, an area covering what is now Chad, southern Libya, northeastern Nigeria, and eastern Niger. The grand scale of Kanem in the thirteenth century is attributed to the vision and campaigns of Mai Dunama Dibbalemi.

The empire included trade routes that linked sub-Saharan Africa with the Mediterranean and Red Sea trading networks. A nonsedentary population known as the Kanuri, distinctive for their culture, migrated into the Kanem area in the 1100's. By the thirteenth century, the Kanuri had developed into a sedentary population, replaced the Zaghawa rulers, and begun to conquer the surrounding areas and populations. It is postulated that the core group that came to represent Kanuri ethnicity and language emerged from the Magomi families that constituted the royal lineages of the Sefuwa Dynasty.

Dibbalemi is purported to have been the first of the Kanuri to convert to Islam. The Islamic faith was spread in the Lake Chad basin under Dibbalemi, who declared *jihad* against the surrounding populations, as a strategic element in the extensive period of conquest aimed at incorporating the neighboring territories into Kanem.

After consolidating the Kanem chiefdoms around Lake Chad, Dibbalemi and his followers set north to the Fezzan (Libya), to Kawar (between Lake Chad and the Fezzan, the region surrounding the salt mines of Bilma), and west to lands in Nigeria. This expansion was to spread Islam and to protect the Kanem state's interests in the trans-Saharan trade routes to the north. Controlling and expanding trade networks was integral to the economic and political power of the Kanem Empire. In return for its exports of fabrics, salt, minerals, and slaves, Kanem received copper, guns, and horses as imports.

At the greatest extent of Kanem, the Kanuri ruling elite controlled a large and economically strategic portion of northern Africa's trade routes. Many of the trade routes of northern Africa (Libya, Tunisia, and Egypt) had to pass through the Kanem territory at their southern terminus. As wealth increased, the Kanuri people increasingly became more sedentary in their lifestyle and became urbanized in centers such as Njimi, which is believed to have been the first capital of the Kanem Empire.

Following the death of Dibbalemi, internal rivalries and civil strife began to gravely affect the empire, although he was succeeded by two of his sons, Keday and Bir. In the early fifteenth century, the Sefuwa Dynasty moved its center from the troubles of Kanem in the northeast to Bornu a bit farther southwest, re-creating and reinventing politically the kingdom on the western shore of Lake Chad. It was not until the sixteenth century that the Kanem-Bornu Empire reemerged as a powerful force just as a power vacuum was created with the decline of the Songhai Empire further west.

The history of the Kanuri rulers from Dibbalemi onwards is recorded in the *Dīwān* (royal chronicles), which German archaeologist Heinrich Barth discovered and published in 1850. For more general historical information about Kanem-Bornu, the Arab chroniclers Ibn Saᶜīd (d. 1286), al-ᶜUmarī (1301-1349), and al-Tidjani (fl. thirteenth century) reveal a great deal.

According to the accounts of Ibn Saᶜīd, Dibbalemi expanded the Kanem Empire northward, incorporating the Kawar and Fezzan regions, and controlled Takedda, a western trade center on the road to Gao, a major seat of trade on the Niger River. Ibn Saᶜīd reported that Dibbalemi ruled Tadjuwa, Zaghawa, and Djadja in the east, and ruled over Berber populations in the south. Al-ᶜUmarī's description confirms much of Saᶜid's history. In the fourteenth century, al-ᶜUmarī wrote that it took three months to traverse the Kanem Empire from north-

A bodyguard in the entourage of the sheikh of Bornu in the early nineteenth century. At its height, the Kanem Empire extended across Chad, southern Libya, northeastern Nigeria, and eastern Niger. (Hulton|Archive by Getty Images)

Dibbalemi was also known to have developed a military force of forty-one thousand cavalry. According to Arab chroniclers, the horses used for Dibbalemi's military endeavor were imported from Tunisia. These horses were of note because they were smaller than the breeds imported from other parts of the world. Dibbalem was able to use the horses to build a powerful military for executing territorial expansions and consolidation and for spreading the Islamic faith. Dibbalemi was an Islamic reformer who organized and established madrasas (Islamic schools) for Kanem pupils to study in Cairo, Egypt. Under Dibbalemi, Islam became more profoundly established in an orthodox and all-encompassing form in Kanem-Bornu life.

east to southwest, a testament to the size of the state even after Dibbalemi's death. Al-Tidjani's records extend Kanem beyond the Fezzan, stating that in 1258 Kanem reduced the power of its rivals in the Waddan, north of the Fezzan.

While the core of the Kanem state was well defined and established, and Kanem clearly had a plan of expansion aimed at controlling trade routes and preventing the rerouting of trade to secondary uncontrolled routes, it is not as clear how strongly established was the rule of the expanded Kanem state. Was the power and authority over the Fezzan real or symbolic? Long or short-lived? While there is enough information recorded to assume some control over the north, west, and south, the evidence demonstrates that the Tubu in the east remained a defiant challenge to the conquests of Dibbalemi.

SIGNIFICANCE

According to Ibn Saʿīd, the Sefuwa Dynasty emerged in Kanem as a foreign power controlled by foreign rulers, but the dynasty became widely acknowledged as a legitimate power. It was even accepted in popular memory as indigenous within a short period of time. It seems from the available evidence that the Sefuwa were descendants of the Zaghawa Berber kings who became Islamized. In fact, a small state in the vicinity of Kanem can be dated to the sixth century, but it was the influx of Kanuri in the early twelfth century that fostered the large kingdom of renown. It was under Dibbalemi that Kanem became a large and powerful imperialist state with securely established and widely recognized territorial divisions and bureaucratic organization.

—*Catherine Cymone Fourshey*

FURTHER READING

Collins, Robert O. *Western African History.* Princeton: Markus Wiener, 1997. Primary document from western Africa. Contains a document on Kanem wars and brief discussion of Dibbalemi.

Garba, Abubakar. *Research Guidelines for the Documentation of Ancient Kanem-Borno Capitals.* Maiduguri,

Nigeria: Centre for Trans Saharan Studies, University of Maiduguri, 1988. Explains excavations of ancient cities particularly capital cities, of the Kanem-Bornu empire.

Holl, Augustin. *The Dīwān Revisited: Literacy, State Formation and the Rise of Kanuri Domination (A.D. 1200-1600)*. New York: Kegan Paul International, 2000. A history of the politics and the sultanate in the Kanem-Bornu empires. Contains an excellent bibliography of research on Kanem.

Lange, Dierk. "Ethnogenesis from Within the Chadic State: Some Thoughts on the History of Kanem-Bornu." *Paideuma* no. 39 (1993): 261-277. Examines the ethnic history of the populations in Kanem-Bornu region.

Levzion, Nehemia. "Islam in the Bilad al-Sudan to 1800." In *The History of Islam in Africa*, edited by Nehemia Levzion and Randall Pouwels. Athens: Ohio University Press, 2000. This chapter describes the history of Islamic expansion in the central Sudan. It includes a two-page section devoted to Kanem and Bornu.

Oliver, Roland, and J. D. Fage. *The Cambridge History of Africa*. Cambridge, England: Cambridge University Press, 1977. A historical account of African civilizations from c. 1050 to c. 1600.

SEE ALSO: c. 1010: Songhai Kingdom Converts to Islam; c. 1075-1086: Hummay Founds the Sefuwa Dynasty.

1225
TRAN THAI TONG ESTABLISHES TRAN DYNASTY

Tran Thai Tong, who established the long-lasting Tran Dynasty in Vietnam, firmly upheld the traditional Buddhist scholar's ideal of serving the people, protecting the country against foreign invasion, and pursuing spiritual salvation.

LOCALE: Vietnam, China
CATEGORY: Government and politics

KEY FIGURES

Tran Thai Tong (Tran Canh; 1218-1277), king of Vietnam and founder of Tran Dynasty, r. 1225-61259

Tran Thu Do (1194-1264), uncle of Tran Thai Tong and mastermind of the overthrow of the Ly Dynasty

Ly Chieu Hoang, queen of Vietnam, r. 1224-1225

Kublai Khan (1215-1294), Mongol ruler, r. 1260-1294, and Yuan Dynasty ruler, r. 1279-1294

SUMMARY OF EVENT

Though Tran Thai Tong was one of the best rulers in Vietnam's history, his ascension to power was through the manipulation of his ambitious, ruthless uncle Tran Thu Do. Ly Hue Tong's close adviser, Tran Thua, used his influence to secure for Tran Thu Do the position of commander of the imperial guards in the Ly Dynasty (1009-1225) court. With an eye on the Ly throne, in 1224, Tran Thu Do arranged a marriage between Ly Chieu Hoang, Ly Hue Tong's eight-year-old daughter, and his seven-year-old nephew Tran Canh (later known as Tran Thai Tong) and forced the ailing monarch to name his daughter as his successor and to retire and become a Buddhist monk.

In 1225, Ly Chieu Hoang turned over power to her husband, but because Tran Thai Tong was too young to assume power, Tran Thu Do was the de facto ruler of the country. When Tran Thai Tong became old enough to rule, the transition of power did not go smoothly. Because Ly Chieu Hoang did not produce a male heir, in 1238, Tran Thai Tong was forced by Tran Thu Do to wed the pregnant wife of his brother Tran Lieu in order to maintain the Tran lineage. Tran Thu Do's maneuver had two disastrous consequences: the armed rebellion of Tran Lieu and Tran Thai Tong's flight from his palace to seek refuge in a Buddhist temple. He did not return to the capital until Tran Thu Do threatened to build a new court around the temple and the abbot entreated him to listen to his uncle. A devout Buddhist who did not want to disturb the sacred environment, Tran Thai Tong eventually bowed to Tran Thu Do's demand.

After he had wrested power from Tran Thu Do, Tran Thai Tong began laying the groundwork for a promising new dynasty and proved himself a strong king. Despite Tran Thu Do's protest, he granted amnesty to Tran Lieu and made him a prince. Numerous important reforms were implemented during his thirty-three-year reign, paving the way for a government strong enough to defeat foreign invasions and to bring security and welfare to its people for several centuries.

Beginning in the early 1230's, Tran Thai Tong's government launched major reforms. In 1232, the doctoral examination was first offered as a means of recruiting candidates for top positions in the king's mandarinate. In 1242, as part of his attempt to prevent civil disobedience, reduce the central government's administrative burden, and gain firmer control of the population, Tran Thai Tong divided the country into twelve regions, each of which was headed by a governor appointed by the court. Each region was then split into numerous villages with their own governments, made up of local dignitaries. The court fully recognized each village's constitutional privileges but reserved its right to access the local registry for information about males of draft age. Using this method, by 1258, Tran Thai Tong was able to have a 200,000-man-strong army capable of resisting the first Mongol invasion.

Because Vietnam was an agricultural society, Tran Thai Tong's social programs were geared to meet the peasants' needs. Soldiers periodically returned to their own villages to participate in agriculture and other local welfare projects. In 1244, the Red River dam, the first of its kind, was built to protect the delta from annual floods. The king not only appointed qualified officials to supervise the project but also went on an inspection tour in the rainy season. In other areas of the country, if private land had to be used for public programs, appropriate compensation was paid to its owner. Sale of public land for whatever reason was strictly prohibited.

Tran Thai Tong also saw to it that commerce and industry, which primarily consisted of handicrafts, was in his reform program. Under his reign, the capital of Thang Long was a center of booming business transactions with foreign countries. Close by was Quay Van Don, where merchant ships from China and other countries in Southeast Asia came to engage in trade and commerce with Vietnam.

Tran Thai Tong planned to build national identity through cultural independence in order to prevent China from assimilating Vietnam culturally and militarily. In 1253, Quoc hoc Vien, Vietnam's first academy of letters, was founded to provide scholarship opportunities for first-rate intellectuals. In the same year, Giang vo Duong, the nation's first military academy, was inaugurated to train officers for the Vietnamese army.

The greatest test of Tran Thai Tong's leadership came in 1257, when Kublai Khan, who had unified China under the Yuan Dynasty (1279-1368), sent a powerful force southward to conquer Vietnam and the Champa. Under Tran Thai Tong's skilled command and with the Vietnamese people's support, the Mongols were defeated and withdrew from Vietnam in 1258.

Soon after his victory over the Mongols in 1258, Tran Thai Tong transferred power to his son Tran Thanh Tong and retreated to Thien Truong to practice Zen Buddhism. While studying Buddhism, he served as the new king's supreme counselor until his death in 1277.

The author of several works on poetry and Buddhism, Tran Thai Tong was best known for his famous *Khoa hu luc* (1258-1277; essays on the practice of emptiness). The book offers a fascinating interpretation of Buddhism. According to Tran Thai Tong, the purpose of practicing Buddhism is to rid oneself of suffering, not to give up one's life for the practice of Buddhism.

SIGNIFICANCE

As he matured, Tran Thai Tong, who was crowned king at the age of nine, was able to escape the influence of his powerful uncle and become a full-fledged ruler. Existing records show no significant role played by Tran Thu Do after Tran Thai Tong agreed to return to the capital, so it is likely that the king initiated and conducted all the reforms himself.

Tran Thai Tong epitomized the ideal Buddhist man in thirteenth century Vietnam. He devoted all his energy to the service of his country but did not lose sight of his self-cultivation. Although his social reforms show that he was a far-sighted and compassionate statesman in the Confucian tradition, his writings place him squarely in the Buddhist canon as they examine the root cause of human suffering and suggest ways of eliminating it. He devoted time and energy to improving his people's well-being and also pursued his spiritual salvation, maintaining a dual approach to life.

Tran Thai Tong was the first ruler to create a system of government involving a supreme counselor to the king, a practice that was followed the entire Tran Dynasty. Under this system, the crown prince served as apprentice under his ruling father, then after his coronation, retained his father as supreme counselor. This system helped eliminate the family feuds that occurred after a king's death when the crown prince was not well prepared for the job. Internally, the Tran Dynasty was perhaps one of the longest and most stable dynasties in Vietnam's history.

According to Vietnamese historians, the most important achievement of Tran Thai Tong's rule was his leaving his descendants fully prepared to resist foreign invasions. Twenty-seven years after his death, his grandson Tran Nhan Tong defeated a Chinese force of 800,000 men and 500 vessels that invaded Vietnam twice to avenge China's military debacle under Tran Thai Tong's reign.

—*Qui-Phiet Tran*

FURTHER READING

Buttinger, Joseph. *The Smaller Dragon*. New York: Frederick A. Praeger, 1958. Provides an account of Vietnam's struggle for independence from foreign rule since the tenth century. Argues that dynastic strength stemmed from political, agricultural, military, and educational reforms.

Huynh, Sanh Thong, ed. and trans. *An Anthology of Vietnamese Poems from the Eleventh to the Twentieth Centuries*. New Haven, Conn.: Yale University Press, 1966. Includes poems by Tran Thai Tong that describe his perception of life and methods for achieving spiritual salvation according to Buddhism.

Kenny, Henry J. *Shadow of the Dragon: Vietnam's Continuing Struggle with China and the Implications for U.S. Foreign Policy*. Washington, D.C.: Brassey's, 2002. Argues that United States policy toward Vietnam should be considered in light of this country's past and its recent disputes with its giant neighbor.

Whitfield, Danny J. *Historical and Cultural Dictionary of Vietnam*. Mechuen, N.J.: Scarecrow Press, 1976. Contains references to Vietnamese history and culture. The Tran Thai Tong section covers the king's victorious campaigns against the Mongol army and his major reforms after the war.

Woods, Shelton L. *Vietnam: A Global Studies Handbook*. Santa Barbara, Calif.: ABC-CLIO, 2002. Provides an overview of Vietnam's history, geography, culture, and customs.

SEE ALSO: 729: Founding of Nanzhao; 832: Nanzhao Subjugates Pyu; 863: Nanzhao Captures Hanoi; 939-944: Reign of Ngo Quyen; 982: Le Dai Hanh Invades Champa; 1323-1326: Champa Wins Independence from Dai Viet; 1428: Le Loi Establishes Later Le Dynasty.

RELATED ARTICLE in *Great Lives from History: The Middle Ages, 477-1453*: Ngo Quyen.

1225-1231
JALĀL AL-DĪN EXPANDS THE KHWĀRIZMIAN EMPIRE

During the Mongol invasions of the Khwārizmian Empire, Jalāl al-Dīn Mingburnu resisted the armies of the Mongols until Genghis Khan defeated him at the Indus River in 1231. Although much of the empire of his father, Muḥammad Khwārizmshāh II, had fallen to the Mongols, Jalāl al-Dīn still sought to carve a new empire.

LOCALE: ʿIraq-i-ʿAjam (now in Iran); Khuzistan (now in western Iran); Arran (now in Azerbaijan); and parts of Azerbaijan, Armenia, Georgia, Rum (now in Turkey)

CATEGORIES: Expansion and land acquisition; government and politics; wars, uprisings, and civil unrest

KEY FIGURES

Jalāl al-Dīn Mingburnu (d. 1231), last Khwārizm shāh, r. 1220-1231

Genghis Khan (between 1155 and 1162-1227), ruler of the Mongol Empire, r. 1206-1227

Ghiyāth al-Dīn (fl. early thirteenth century), brother of Jalāl al-Dīn Mingburnu

al-Ashrāf (d. 1237), ruler of Aleppo and Damascus, r. 1229-1237

Keykubād (d. 1236), ruler of the Seljuk sultanate of Rum, r. 1214-1236

Chormaqān (d. 1240 or 1241), Mongol general who invaded Iran in 1230-1231

Taimas (fl. 1230-1240), lieutenant of Chormaqān who led pursuit of Jalāl al-Dīn

SUMMARY OF EVENT

Following his defeat by Genghis Khan at the Indus River in 1231, Jalāl al-Dīn Mingburnu spent three years in India. After a number of failed endeavors to make an alliance with the sultanate of Delhi, Jalāl al-Dīn went west to ʿIraq-i-ʿAjam. After the death of his father, Muḥammad II, during the Mongol invasion, Jalāl al-Dīn had been named sultan. In spite of his title, Jalāl al-Dīn was a king without a kingdom. Thus, he sought to establish a new one on the ruins of his father's empire.

En route to ʿIraq-i-ʿAjam in 1224, he confirmed vassals in Kermān and Fārs (both in Iran). The rulers of these cities were former generals under his father. Rather than attempt to establish new kingdoms, they accepted his suzerainty in exchange for maintaining their governorship of their regions.

Once in ʿIraq-i-ʿAjam, Jalāl al-Dīn quickly deposed his brother Ghiyāth al-Dīn, who had established himself as ruler in the region. Jalāl al-Dīn then began to expand his new empire by invading Azerbaijan (now in Azerbaijan and Iran) in the winter of 1224-1225. By the middle of summer, he had successfully captured the capital, Tabrīz (now in Iran), on July 25, 1225. The following year, Jalāl al-Dīn invaded the Christian kingdom of Georgia and sacked Tbilisi in March, 1226.

Further conquests were placed on hold because of a rebellion in that same year. Rebellions and expansion, however, were the least of Jalāl al-Dīn's concerns in 1227, for the Mongols reappeared. After an absence of six years, the Mongols again invaded Iran. The invasion force, however, was small compared to the force that defeated Jalāl al-Dīn in 1221. Jalāl al-Dīn's army encountered the Mongols near the city of Eşfahān (now in Iran). Sources vary in the accounts of the battle, with some granting victory to the Mongols and others to Jalāl al-Dīn. In any case, because of heavy losses, the Mongols retired back to Central Asia.

With the Mongols' absence, Jalāl al-Dīn resumed his conquests and attempts to expand his new empire in Western Asia. In 1229, he again invaded Georgia and later laid siege to the city of Akhlāt (now in Turkey). The siege of Akhlāt, however, gained the attention of other Muslim powers in the Middle East, which began to view Jalāl al-Dīn as a threat to their own states. Thus, in August, 1230, Sultan al-Ashrāf of Aleppo and Damascus (now Syria) and Sultan Keykubād of Rum (now Turkey) defeated Jalāl al-Dīn at the Battle of Erzincan (now in Turkey) on August 10, 1230.

Jalāl al-Dīn's defeat had significant repercussions. First, this was his first significant defeat since returning from India, as the battle with the Mongols at Eşfahān was indecisive. Second, the defeat ended Jalāl al-Dīn's westward expansion. Although Jalāl al-Dīn had gained a reputation as a great warrior and had portrayed himself as the bulwark protecting the Islamic world from the Mongols, the defeat demonstrated that other Muslim leaders did not necessarily see a difference between his conquests and those of the Mongols. On hearing that a new and much larger Mongol army under the command of Chormaqān had entered Iran, Jalāl al-Dīn attempted to establish an alliance with al-Ashrāf and Keykubād, the very men whom he defeated earlier in the year. They declined his offer.

While Chormaqān consolidated Mongol gains in Iran, another force marched against Jalāl al-Dīn. He narrowly escaped capture and death while wintering in the Mughān plain (now in Azerbaijan). At the time, Jalāl al-Dīn thought the Mongols were still several hundred miles away, and thus he attempted to gather his forces in case of a Mongol attack in the Mughān plain, where there was plenty of pasture for his cavalry. The Mongols, however, surprised him there. He fled to the environs of Lake Urmia (now in Iran) while the Mongols shattered his army. He had eluded the Mongols.

After his forces returned without Jalāl al-Dīn, Chormaqān directed a lieutenant, Taimas, to track Jalāl al-Dīn. When Taimas returned to the Mughān, Jalāl al-Dīn again resumed his flight, first to Armenia and then to Akhlāt, again eluding the Mongols. Believing the Mongols had lost his trail, Jalāl al-Dīn then traveled to the city of Amida (now in Turkey) with the remainder of his forces. Even though his scouts found no trace of Taimas's forces, the Mongols suddenly descended upon Jalāl al-Dīn's army. Although he escaped while one of his generals, Orkhon, attempted to stave off and dispel the Mongol attack, the Mongols soon recovered and renewed their pursuit. Eventually, however, Jalāl al-Dīn again proved elusive and hid in the mountains of Kurdistan.

His success at avoiding capture, however, did not extend his career. The circumstances are unclear, but in 1231, Jalāl al-Dīn was murdered by Kurdish peasants either to avenge a past crime by Jalāl al-Dīn or simply for gain. Although the ruler of Amid recovered Jalāl al-Dīn's body and gave it a proper burial, for several years rumors abounded concerning the disappearance of Jalāl al-Dīn. Pretenders occasionally appeared, claiming to be him; this was a risky career because the Mongols often would hunt the pretenders down as well.

SIGNIFICANCE

The violent, ephemeral empire created by Jalāl al-Dīn had a significant impact on the medieval Islamic world. If not for the Mongols, Jalāl al-Dīn might have developed a stable empire consisting of northern Iraq, Transcaucasia, and western and southern Iran. However, considering that Jalāl al-Dīn's character tended to focus more on martial exploits than administrative tasks, it can only be speculated whether or not such a state would have existed.

Nonetheless, Jalāl al-Dīn's five-year expansion changed the face of the medieval world dramatically. The most immediate impact was that his presence and activities attracted the attention of the Mongols. Prior to his return from India, the Mongols had focused their attention on conquering China and made no moves into the Middle East, despite having raided extensively through Iran as well as Transcaucasia in 1220-1221. Indeed, in the years preceding Jalāl al-Dīn's return, the Mongols expressed very little interest in the area. Chormaqān's invasion was specifically meant to destroy the last remnant of Khwārizmian power, and to end any threat from Jalāl al-Dīn.

Connected with this, yet directly tied to Jalāl al-Dīn's conquest, was that the Georgian and Armenian principalities were not in position to make a determined resistance against the Mongols. Jalāl al-Dīn's efforts against them had been destructive, and the efforts were often repeated. Indeed, he often demonstrated more interest in plunder than achieving a stable empire.

Jalāl al-Dīn's ultimate defeat and the collapse of his brief empire had further ramifications in the Middle East. After the Mongols defeated him near Amid, his army dispersed across Syria and Turkey. Some entered the service of the Keykubād; others he destroyed as marauders. Still other forces drifted into Syria and served as mercenary bands. They played prominent roles in dynastic struggles among the Ayyūbids, the successors of Sultan Saladin (r. 1174-1193). In addition, one such force of Khwārizmian troops sacked Jerusalem in 1244 while in the pay of Sultan al-Ṣāliḥ Ayyūb of Egypt (r. 1239 and 1245-1249), thus taking the holy city from the rule of the Crusaders for the final time.

—*Timothy May*

FURTHER READING

Amitai-Preiss, Reuven, and David O. Morgan, eds. *The Mongol Empire and Its Legacy.* Boston: Brill, 1999. A wide-ranging examination of the Mongol Empire and its historical significance. Includes chapters on the making of the Mongol states, Mongol nomadism, and imperial ideology. Genealogical tables, maps, bibliography, index.

Barthold, W. *Turkestan down to the Mongol Invasion.* Translated by T. Minorsky and edited by C. E. Bosworth. 4th ed. Philadelphia: Porcupine Press, 1977. This classic work remains among the best accounts of the rise and fall of the Khwārizmian Empire. Bibliography, index.

Bosworth, C. E. "The Eastern Seljuq Sultanate, 1118-1157" and "The Rise and Florescence of the Khwarazm Shahs of Anushtegin's Line up to the Appearance of the Mongols, 1097-1219." In *History of Civilizations of Central Asia.* Vol. 4. *The Age of Achievement: A.D. 750 to the End of the Fifteenth Century,* edited by M. S. Asimov and C. E. Bosworth. Paris: United Nations Educational, Scientific, and Cultural Organization, 1998. Provides good background to the events just prior to Jalāl al-Dīn's rise. Bibliography.

Fitzherbert, T. "Portrait of a Lost Leader: Jalāl al-Din Khwarazmshah and Juvaini." In *The Court of the Il-Khans, 1290-1340.* Edited by Julian Raby and Teresa Fitzherbert. New York: Oxford University Press, 1996. Published proceedings of a special conference on Jalāl al-Dīn, with a solid paper on Jalāl al-Dīn by Fitzherbert. Bibliography.

Grousset, René. *The Empire of the Steppes: A History of Central Asia.* Translated by Naomi Walford. New Brunswick, N.J.: Rutgers University Press, 1970. A general history of Central Asia, with a lengthy section on the Mongols, including the activities of Jalāl al-Dīn. Maps, bibliography.

Juvayni, Ala al-Din Ata Malik. *Genghis Khan: The History of the World-Conqueror.* Translated by J. A. Boyle. 2 vols. Seattle: University of Washington Press, 1997. An annotated translation of a thirteenth century Arabic source on Genghis Khan, with a long section on not only Jalāl al-Dīn but also the Khwārizmian Empire prior to the Mongols.

Juzjani, Minhaj Siraj. *ʿAbakīt-i-Nāīrī: A General History of the Muhammadan Dynasties of Asia.* Translated by H. G. Raverty. 2 vols. New Delhi: Oriental Books, 1970. Written by a witness of the Mongol invasion of Central Asia. Contains several sections on the activities on Jalāl al-Dīn and anti-Mongol in tone.

SEE ALSO: 956: Oğhuz Turks Migrate to Transoxiana; 1040-1055: Expansion of the Seljuk Turks; 1077: Seljuk Dynasty Is Founded; 1204: Genghis Khan Founds Mongol Empire; September 3, 1260: Battle of Ain Jālūt; 1368: Tibet Gains Independence from Mongols.

RELATED ARTICLES in *Great Lives from History: The Middle Ages, 477-1453*: Baybars I; Genghis Khan; Kublai Khan; Maḥmūd of Ghazna; Saladin; Tamerlane.

1227-1230
FREDERICK II LEADS THE SIXTH CRUSADE

Frederick II led the Sixth Crusade under his imperial power, reestablished Christian rule in the Holy Land in an almost bloodless victory, and ironically earned papal condemnation and the opposition of Christian feudal interests for his efforts.

LOCALE: Southern Italy and the Holy Land
CATEGORIES: Religion; wars, uprisings, and civil unrest

KEY FIGURES

Frederick II (1194-1250), Holy Roman Emperor, r. 1220-1250, leader of the Sixth Crusade
Innocent III (1160 or 1161-1216), Roman Catholic pope, 1198-1216, Frederick's absentee guardian
Honorius III (d. 1227), Roman Catholic pope, 1216-1227, who helped plan the Sixth Crusade
Gregory IX (c. 1170-1241), Roman Catholic pope, 1227-1241
Richard Filangieri (fl. thirteenth century), Frederick's agent, who represented imperial interests in the Holy Land, 1231-1243

SUMMARY OF EVENT

In 1215, at the age of twenty-one, Frederick II took his vow as a Crusader, apparently to the surprise of Pope Innocent III, who served as his absentee guardian after Frederick was orphaned at the age of four. Frederick's father, Henry VI, was heir to the Germanic empire of Frederick I Barbarossa (r. 1152-1190), while his mother, Constance of Sicily, was heiress to southern Italy (r. 1194-1198). If he ever gained full control of his inheritance, Frederick could be the most powerful Western ruler since Charlemagne.

Frederick spent much of his early life in Sicily, at the time a half Muslim kingdom also populated by a large number of Jews and Greeks. He had a succession of tutors and appears to have absorbed much on his own from the cultural diversity of Sicily, including an attitude of toleration. Arabic and Greek texts and Muslim mathematics and science fascinated him. By the time he reached adulthood, Frederick could speak nine languages (including Arabic) and could write in seven of them. He was not a typical medieval ruler, and when he finally departed on what was the Sixth Crusade, it was a most unusual Crusade.

Also in 1215, Frederick was crowned German king at Aachen, having survived a bitter power struggle for the throne. The first five years of his reign was spent consolidating power in the north, largely by permitting considerable independent authority of the German princes. Clearly his Crusader's oath would have to await resolution of immediate political necessities. His "guardian," Pope Innocent III, dreamed of a Fifth Crusade after the Fourth Crusade (1202-1204) was diverted by the Venetians into a rapacious sacking of the Christian cities of Zara and Constantinople, and the unofficial Children's Crusade (1212) turned into an incredibly embarrassing fiasco. Innocent's plans were put into effect by his successor, Honorius III. Yet this Fifth Crusade, an attack on Damietta in Egypt led by John of Brienne, the king of Jerusalem (r. 1210-1225), in March of 1218, ended in disaster three years later.

Frederick was too preoccupied to have anything to do with the Fifth Crusade. In November of 1220, he was crowned Holy Roman Emperor in Rome with Honorius officiating. In return, he reaffirmed his vow to go on a crusade, affirmed church liberties, and promised to keep separate the crowns of southern Italy and Germany. Frederick then returned to Palermo, intent on exerting central control over what was at the time the wealthiest European kingdom because of its vast grain supplies and central position over Mediterranean trade routes.

In the wake of the failure of the Fifth Crusade, Frederick strategized with Honorius about launching a Sixth Crusade. At the suggestion of Hermann von Salza (c. 1170-1239), Frederick's friend and grand master of the Teutonic Knights (1210-1239), Frederick decided to marry Isabella, the fifteen-year-old daughter of John of Brienne and heiress to the crown of Jerusalem. Showing that this Crusade would be in imperial and not papal control, Frederick had himself crowned king of Jerusalem. This was to be a well-planned military movement using the resources of southern Italy and the Teutonic Knights. At the conference of San Germano held in 1225, Frederick pledged to the pope, under penalty of excommunication, that the Sixth Crusade would be launched by August 15, 1227.

Honorius did not live to see Frederick honor his vow as a Crusader. For his successor, Gregory IX, the eighty-six-year-old nephew of Innocent III, gaining the upper hand in the pope-emperor relationship was a more important goal than was the Crusade. Imperial control of northern and southern Italy produced serious encirclement anxieties for Gregory. Anxious to occupy the Holy

Roman Emperor in dangerous adventures far away from Italy, Gregory sent Frederick a letter containing a stern warning to go on the Sixth Crusade as scheduled, or suffer the consequences.

Unbeknown to Gregory, Frederick had already gone on the Crusade, using diplomats instead of soldiers. Taking advantage of a raging dispute between al-Malik al-Kāmil, the sultan of Egypt, Palestine, and Syria (r. 1218-1238), and his brother al-Muʿazzam, the governor of Damascus (1249-1250), Frederick was able to communicate to al-Kāmil the advantages of his kingship over Jerusalem, and to having troops at hand hostile to Syrian interests. While Gregory ordered Frederick to go east, the sultan was inviting him to come to Egypt.

Frederick and his army finally set sail from Brindisi on September 8, 1227. Disease had plagued the assembling army even before departure. Many were ill from either typhoid or cholera while on board ship. Among the sick was Frederick, who disembarked at Otranto to recover, while the rest of his fleet continued on its journey. Seizing the opportunity to catch Frederick on a technicality, Gregory excommunicated him, after denouncing the emperor in a long list of grievances. Gregory then began assembling an army to invade Sicily.

Frederick II. (Library of Congress)

While Frederick recuperated, his wife died shortly after bearing him a son, thus clouding the issue of whether Frederick would be king or regent of Jerusalem. Meanwhile his forces, led by Duke Henry of Limburg (fl. thirteenth century), recaptured Sidon, and reenforced Caesarea. Hermann of Salza established the mighty fortress of Montfort as the main base of operations of the Teutonic Knights. During his recuperation, Frederick tried, to no avail, to come to terms with Gregory. Finally, while still under excommunication, Frederick set sail for Jerusalem in June of 1228, with forty additional ships. This act, which showed the sincerity of Frederick's intentions, was a major blow to Gregory's prestige.

On his way to the Holy Land, Frederick stopped off at Cyprus, using his army's force to gain recognition of his overlordship. From Cyprus, he ventured to Tyre and then on to Acre. By this time, al-Kāmil had little reason to negotiate further with Frederick, since his brother, the governor of Syria, had suddenly died, leaving only a child to continue his claims. Yet pressure exerted by Frederick's original force (although much dwindled by the time of his arrival) and the new troops arriving with Frederick, convinced al-Kāmil to come to terms. By the treaty of February 18, 1229, the sultan surrendered Bethlehem, Nazareth, and Jerusalem. He also provided Frederick with a land corridor to the coast for supplies.

In return, Frederick promised not to fortify Jerusalem, to respect Muslim control of holy places and mosques, and to protect the sultan's interests from all adversaries (including Christians) for the length of a ten year truce.

As a final act, Frederick went to the altar of the Holy Sepulchre and placed the crown of the kingdom of Jerusalem on his own head. Instead of celebration for the return of the Holy Land to Christian rule, Jerusalem was placed under interdict and Frederick was again excommunicated for entering the church while still under excommunication and collaborating with the infidel. That the Holy Land was returned to Christianity by Frederick, without bloodshed, using only eight hundred knights and ten thousand foot soldiers, was beside the point.

To protect his kingdom of Sicily from papal invasion, Frederick had to make a speedy exit from Jerusalem. He appointed two Syrian barons as regents and headed back to Sicily. Overlordship of Cyprus was sold to five other Syrian barons. To represent imperial interests in the Holy Land, Richard Filangieri was sent in 1231, and would remain for the next twelve years. By the end of 1230, the papal invading force had been defeated and Gregory was forced to make peace. Ten years later, the hundred-year-

Pope Honorius III. (Frederick Ungar Publishing Co.)

old pope died, still battling Frederick and facing the encirclement of Rome. His successor, Innocent IV, deposed Frederick in 1245, and declared a Holy Crusade against the Holy Roman Emperor. The fact that Jerusalem had fallen the previous year, to a band of marauding Turks, allies of the Egyptians, was hardly noticed.

SIGNIFICANCE

The Sixth Crusade marked the final, successful chapter in the effort of the so-called crusading movement to capture and occupy the Holy Land, although it was not the last Crusade by Christians; that would come in 1248 with the failed Seventh and Eighth Crusades led by Louis IX. It was not until many years later, during the aftermath of World War I, that the Holy Land was again, for a time, under European (Christian) administration.

—*Irwin Halfond*

FURTHER READING

Abulafia, David. *Frederick II: A Medieval Emperor.* London: Pimlico, 1992. A demythologizing biographical study of Frederick II, containing solid and detailed analysis of his crusading venture. Illustrations, maps, bibliography, index.

Billings, Malcolm. *The Crusades.* Rev. ed. Charleston, S.C.: Tempus, 2000. Good starting point for an understanding of Frederick's role in the Crusades, and a very readable background for the Crusades as well. Bibliography, index.

Hillenbrand, Carole. *The Crusades: Islamic Perspectives.* New York: Routledge, 2000. Chapters explore ethnic and religious stereotyping, daily life, the conduct of war, and more. Bibliography, index.

Irwin, Robert. "Muslim Responses to the Crusades." *History Today* 47, no. 4 (April, 1997). Presents a rich overview of the Muslim perspective on the Crusades. Provides photographs and a short list of further readings.

Kantorowicz, Ernst. *Frederick the Second, 1194-1250.* Reprint. New York: Ungar, 1967. First published in 1931 and somewhat overdramatic in tone, this landmark biography of Frederick is still the most readable and comprehensive study of his reign. Maps, bibliography.

Madden, Thomas F. *A Concise History of the Crusades.* Lanham, Md.: Rowman and Littlefield, 1999. Presents an overview of the Sixth Crusade, with discussion of Frederick II's role in the effort. Part of the Critical Issues in History series. Bibliography, index.

_______, ed. *The Crusades: The Essential Readings.* Malden, Mass.: Blackwell, 2002. A collection of previously published articles about the Crusades, including medieval sources, lay enthusiasm, patronage, Byzantium, and the subjection of Muslims. Bibliography, index.

Marshall, Christopher. *Warfare in the Latin East, 1192-1291.* New York: Cambridge University Press, 1992. An exhaustive military history of the strategies used in the later Crusades, including detailed analysis of conflicts between fellow Christians. Bibliography, index.

Riley-Smith, Jonathan. *The Feudal Nobility and the Kingdom of Jerusalem, 1174-1277.* Hamden, Conn.: Archon, 1973. An in-depth study of the role of kings and nobles in the administration of the Latin kingdom, detailing the lack of cooperation by Frankish lords, with an excellent chapter on the Baillage created by Frederick II.

_______, ed. *The Oxford Illustrated History of the Crusades.* New York: Oxford University Press, 1999. Places the Sixth Crusade within the context of the medieval crusading movement, arguing its significance in the history of late medieval culture in the West. Illustrations, maps, bibliography, index.

SEE ALSO: August 15-20, 636: Battle of Yarmūk; 1009: Destruction of the Church of the Holy Sepulchre; November 27, 1095: Pope Urban II Calls the First Crusade; c. 1120: Order of the Knights Templar Is Founded; 1127-1130: Creation of the Kingdom of Sicily; 1147-1149: Second Crusade; 1152: Frederick Barbarossa Is Elected King of Germany; 1189-1192: Third Crusade; 1204: Knights of the Fourth Crusade Capture Constantinople; 1212: Children's Crusade; 1217-1221: Fifth Crusade; 1227-1230: Frederick II Leads the Sixth Crusade; 1228-1231: Teutonic Knights Bring Baltic Region Under Catholic Control; 1248-1254: Failure of the Seventh Crusade; May 29, 1453: Fall of Constantinople.

RELATED ARTICLES in *Great Lives from History: The Middle Ages, 477-1453*: Frederick I Barbarossa; Frederick II; Gregory IX; Innocent III.

1228-1231
TEUTONIC KNIGHTS BRING BALTIC REGION UNDER CATHOLIC CONTROL

The Teutonic knights, a military-religious order, brought the Baltic region under Catholic control and launched a series of military crusades against pagan peoples who had resisted conversion and assimilation.

LOCALE: Prussia (now Germany)

CATEGORIES: Expansion and land acquisition; government and politics; organizations and institutions; religion; wars, uprisings, and civil unrest

KEY FIGURES

Hermann Balke (d. 1239), Prussian master, 1230-1239, and Livonian master, 1237-1239

Christian (d. 1245), bishop of Prussia, 1215-1245

Conrad of Masovia (1187-1247), Polish duke

Frederick II (1194-1250), Holy Roman Emperor, r. 1220-1250

Gregory IX (c. 1170-1241), Roman Catholic pope, 1227-1241

Hermann von Salza (c. 1170-1239), grand master of the Teutonic Order, 1209-1239

SUMMARY OF EVENT

East Prussia early in the late thirteenth century lay between Poland and the Baltic Sea, bounded on the west and south by the Vistula River, on the southeast and east by the wilderness of the Masurian Lake district, on the north by the Nemunas (Memel) River. It was inhabited by eleven tribes related by language, culture, and religion to the inhabitants of Lithuania and southern Livonia (now Latvia). Pomerelia, or West Prussia, on the west bank of the Vistula, was inhabited by Slavs closely related to the Poles. Like Poland, Mecklenburg, and Pomerania, it was being settled rapidly by German immigrants who had been invited by the duke to settle in unpopulated areas. This aspect of the *Drang nach Osten* (push to the east) of the Germans was largely peaceful—in contrast to the crusading effort associated with the twelfth century Wendish Crusade and the later crusade led by the Teutonic Knights in Prussia and even later into Lithuania.

Efforts at a peaceful conversion of the Prussian pagans had failed. Earlier Slavic missionaries had become martyrs, while would-be Bishop Christian was discovering that the pagans had no desire to abandon bigamy, exposure and death of female infants, and occasional human sacrifice. Meanwhile, in Livonia, German Crusaders were exploiting their technological and organizational superiority and the ancient rivalries of the local peoples to establish themselves at Riga, and King Valdemar II (r. 1202-1241) of Denmark was crushing Estonian resistance. The example of Bishop Albert of Riga (c. 1165-1229), of the Crusader conquest of Estonia and Livonia (1198-1227), persuaded Bishop Christian and Duke Conrad of Masovia that they could organize a similar crusade, with similar success. In 1217, the pope gave his blessing to the project. From initial victories in 1219, everything went wrong—Duke Conrad could not provide an occupation force for his conquests, then could not protect his own lands from the vengeful Prussians; the Polish kingdom was entering a period of disarray, so that help from the king and other dukes was seldom available; and Prussian paganism, which was based on a military ethos, inspired its worshipers with enthusiasm for their gods' ability to give them slaves and booty from

Denmark crushed the Estonian resistance. (F. R. Niglutsch)

among the worshipers of the Christian god. The pagan offensive reached even into Pomerelia.

Unable to obtain adequate help from relatives and neighbors to repel the pagan onslaught, Duke Conrad again emulated the German model from Livonia by first attempting to found a crusading order of his own (the Dobriners), then in 1225 calling on established orders to come to his lands. Although a small number of Templars settled in Pomerelia, the only order to respond to the Masovian appeal was the Teutonic Order, and its commitment was small.

The Teutonic Order's formal name was the Knights of the Hospital of Saint Mary of the Germans at Jerusalem, which tells much about their own views of their origin and purpose. Actually founded as a hospital order at Acre (Palestine) in 1189, it was converted into a military order in 1197; as a result, in English it is often called the Teutonic Knights. *Der Deutsche Orden*, its most common German name, means only the German Order. *Der Deutschritterorden* reflects a much later period when the grandmasters served the interests of the House of Habsburg. The gifted grandmaster Hermann von Salza oversaw the order's expansion in numbers, wealth, and influence until he found it difficult to deploy the warriors in the few castles available to him in the Holy Land. In 1211, von Salza established convent-castles in Hungary to protect that kingdom from steppe warriors, but King Andrew II fearing that the newcomers were becoming too powerful, expelled them in 1225. As a result, Hermann von Salza was hesitant to give a greater response to Duke Conrad's invitation than to send a handful of knights to investigate the situation.

Frederick II issued the Golden Bull of Rimini in 1226, guaranteeing the order the protection of the Holy Roman Empire for its conquests. In 1228 and 1230, Duke Conrad signed agreements with the Teutonic Order granting the order ownership of any provinces they might conquer (apparently never anticipating that they would take more than a small area around Culm). Bishop Christian somewhat reluctantly made similar promises but came to a formal agreement only in 1231, after which he was captured by Prussians and thus vanished from the political scene for critical years. Pope Gregory IX eventually issued a crusading bull. In 1230, the first sizable contin-

TEUTONIC KNIGHTS' LANDS, 13TH CENTURY

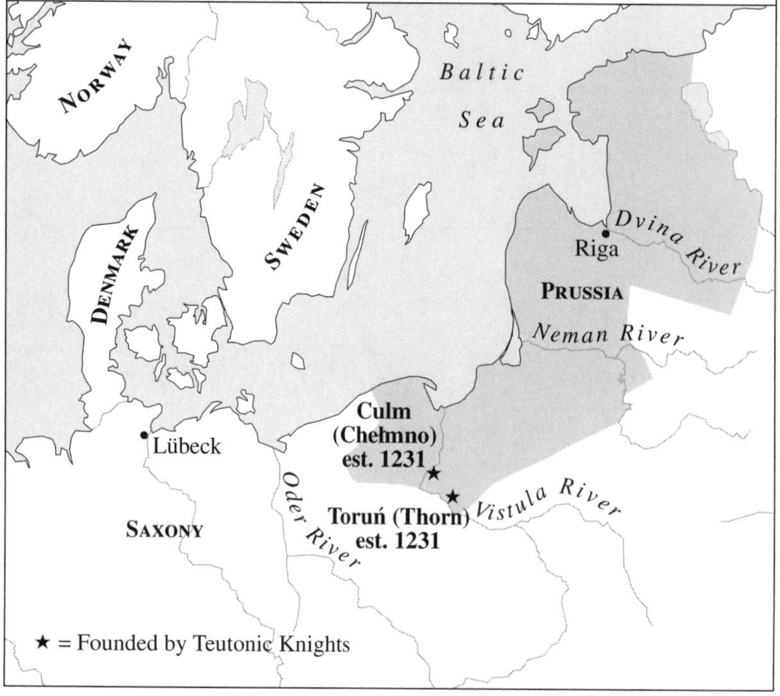

gent of Teutonic Knights arrived in Prussia under the command of Hermann Balke.

SIGNIFICANCE

The successes attained by the combined efforts of Polish, Pomerelian, and German Crusaders allowed the Teutonic Order to crush all but the most westerly tribes quickly. Also, while civil wars and the Mongol invasion of 1241 occupied the Polish dukes fully, Hermann Balke and his successors resettled the pagans in areas where they could be watched and Christianized, then attracted immigrant farmers and burghers to settle on vacant lands. Within a few decades, the Teutonic Knights had made their Prussian conquests into an independent state. By the time Duke Conrad and his heirs could protest, it was too late.

The papal legate, William of Modena, who was active during these years in Prussia and Livonia, was a practical man. Though not approving of the actions of Hermann Balke, he was not about to dismantle the state in the middle of the continuing wars in Prussia and Livonia. The Crusaders were far from attaining ultimate victory in either theater, and if the Teutonic Order were dismissed or dissolved, no competing bishop or duke had the resources to govern the areas already conquered, preach the Crusade throughout a sufficiently wide area to raise a significant number of Crusaders, and then garrison the castles after the armies of volunteers had returned home. The Teutonic Knights, with their resources in the Holy Roman Empire, could do all these things and even send replacements for fallen knights when the inevitable military disasters occurred. As a result, Masovian and Pomerelian complaints were not so much dismissed as ignored.

In 1237, Hermann von Salza sent Hermann Balke with a force of Teutonic Knights to Livonia to rescue the situation there after the local crusading order (the Swordbrothers) was largely destroyed in battle by pagan Lithuanians. In time that region came under the control of a semiautonomous branch of the Teutonic Knights called the Livonian Order. The principal distinguishing characteristic (other than the practicality of governing widely separated regions separately) was that the knights in Prussia generally spoke High German, those in Livonia Low German. To the end of the century, the grandmasters saw their order's principal duty as the defense of the Holy Land, and it was only after the loss of Acre that the order's resources in Italy, Germany, and Bohemia were used primarily to support its brethren in Prussia and Livonia.

—*William L. Urban*

FURTHER READING

Bartlett, Robert. *The Making of Europe: Conquest, Colonization, and Cultural Change, 950-1350*. Princeton, N.J.: Princeton University Press, 1993. This work offers a comprehensive overview of the expansion of Europe during the period when the Teutonic Knights conducted their conquests.

Christiansen, Eric. *The Northern Crusades: The Baltic and Catholic Frontier, 1100-1525*. Minneapolis: University of Minnesota Press, 1980. Erudite and witty study of the period that is highly informative.

Henry of Livonia. *The Chronicle*. Translated by James A. Brundage. Madison: University of Wisconsin Press, 1961. One of the very best medieval chronicles. An eyewitness account of the missionary and Crusader era, 1186-1227.

The Livonian Rhymed Chronicle. Translated by Jerry C. Smith and William L. Urban. Indiana University Publications, Uralic and Altaic Series 128. Bloomington: Indiana University Press, 1977. A useful primary source for the history of the Teutonic Knights.

Nicholson, Helen. *Love, War, and the Grail*. Boston: Brill, 2001. A study of the depictions of the Teutonic Knights, the Knights Templar, and the Knights Hospitaller in medieval literature. Details the actual history of the knights and compares it to how they have been represented.

Urban, William. *The Baltic Crusade*. Rev. ed. Chicago: Lithuanian Research and Studies Center, 1994.

_______. *The Prussian Crusade*. Lanham, Md.: University Press of America, 1980. These two works provide complete narrative accounts of the activities of the Teutonic Order during this period.

_______. *The Teutonic Knights: A Military History*. Mechanicsburg, Pa.: Stackpole Books, 2003. A complete history of the order, detailing the Knights' campaigns, individual battles, and their struggle to maintain themselves as a power to be reckoned with.

SEE ALSO: 735: Christianity Is Introduced into Germany; c. 850: Development of the Slavic Alphabet; c. 1120: Order of the Knights Templar Is Founded; c. 1150-1200: Rise of the Hansa Merchant Union; 1152: Frederick Barbarossa Is Elected King of Germany; July 27, 1214: Battle of Bouvines; April, 1291: Fall of Acre, Palestine; August 26, 1346: Battle of Crécy; July 15, 1410: Battle of Tannenberg.

RELATED ARTICLES in *Great Lives from History: The Middle Ages, 477-1453*: Saint Alexander Nevsky; Casimir the Great; Saint Elizabeth of Hungary; Frederick I Barbarossa; Frederick II; Gregory IX; Valdemar II; Władysław II Jagiełło and Jadwiga; Jan Žižka.

1230
UNIFICATION OF CASTILE AND LEÓN

The unification of Castile and León marked an early victory in the Christian Reconquest of the Iberian Peninsula and a first step toward the creation of the kingdom of Spain.

LOCALE: León and Castile (now in Spain)
CATEGORIES: Government and politics; religion

KEY FIGURES

Alfonso IX (1171-1230), king of León, r. 1188-1230
Ferdinand I (c. 1016-1065), king of Castile, r. 1035-1065, and king of Léon, 1037-1065
Ferdinand III (c. 1201-1252), king of Castile, r. 1217-1252, and king of León, r. 1230-1252

SUMMARY OF EVENT

Spain's early history is one of successive waves of invasion by German tribes. The Visigoths, the last of these invaders, obtained control of the Iberian Peninsula early in the fifth century and moved their capital from France to Toledo. The Visigoths were followers of the Arian heresy and maintained their own legal code. The Hispano-Romans were Catholic and continued to accept Roman law. Intermarriage between the two groups was forbidden. Conqueror and conquered remained separate.

Instability was characteristic of the Visigothic monarchy. The Visigothic nobles retained the elective kingship, which caused political intrigue and frequent deposition or assassination of the king. The disintegration of the Visigothic state was complete by the reign of Roderick (710-711), the last of the Visigothic kings.

Perhaps as a result of an invitation by the enemies of Roderick, Ṭārik ibn-Ziyād, the Berber governor of Tangiers, crossed the Strait of Gibraltar in 711 and defeated Roderick. A second North African army led by Ṭārik's superior, Mūsa ibn Nuṣayr, conquered the area from Mérida to Salamanca. Only the Basque and the northwestern mountains were unoccupied.

Some Visigothic nobles and their retainers retreated before the Moors into the mountains of Asturias. They elected the Visigothic prince Pelayo (c. 718-737) as king of Asturias and began the Christian Reconquest. Future kings of Spain claimed descent from Pelayo.

Alfonso I of Asturias added Galacia by conquest to his kingdom and moved the capital to Olviedo at the end of the eighth century. The discovery of the tomb of Saint James the Greater at Compostela in Galacia around 830 made the Asturian king guardian of a shrine of European significance and made Compostela a symbol of national unity. Pilgrims from Christian Spain and from Europe brought foreign ideas, customs, money, and soldiers to assist in the Reconquest. Devotion to Saint James led to legends of his appearance to Christian armies on the eve of battle signifying victory.

Succeeding kings of Asturias added additional territory, including, in the early part of the tenth century, the tablelands of León, south of the mountains. The capital was moved to the city of León, and the kingdom became known as León. Its territory included Galacia, Asturias, part of the Basque lands, Navarre, and Castile. Yet the local residents of Castile, Navarre, and the Basque lands refused to recognize the authority of the king of León. Disputes over the throne by members of the royal family weakened León and enabled the dissident areas to successfully resist the king.

Castile, located between León and Navarre, was created by the eastward expansion of León. The government of the area was given to the counts of Castile, who paid little attention to the kings. Distance, difficulty of communications, and civil strife in León contributed to making Castile independent by the middle of the tenth century. Count Fernán González united the Castilian counties, enlarged his territory, and established his family as hereditary monarchs. In 1028, Sancho García the Great of Navarre captured Castile and annexed it. On his death the territories of Navarre were divided among his sons. To his son Ferdinand, Sancho granted Castile as an independent kingdom.

Ferdinand I of Castile was obsessed with the idea of the Reconquest and was successful in battle. In 1037, he defeated King Vermundo III of León and united the two kingdoms. Taking advantage of the breakup of the caliphate of Córdoba and of the increase in population and wealth of his enlarged kingdom, Ferdinand expanded southward and westward to bring approximately a quarter of the peninsula under his control. On his death in 1065, Ferdinand divided his lands among his three sons. Within the year Alfonso VI, who had been given Castile, conquered the territories of his brothers and reunited the three crowns. The fall of Toledo to Alfonso gave him a strategic city that provided protection for the lands to the north, adversely affected the morale of the Moors, and speeded up the Reconquest.

Queen Constance, the second wife of Alfonso VI, was French. Among the Frenchmen she brought to Spain was Bernard, a monk of the Order of Cluny. The king made Bernard archbishop of Toledo, and Pope Urban III made him primate (regional or nationwide bishop) of Spain. Religious toleration had existed until this time. Christians and Moorish rulers had cooperated when it served their purposes, and both Christian and Moorish rulers became vassals of rulers of the other faith. Archbishop Bernard introduced bigotry and the spirit of the Crusades into the Reconquest. He set out to reform the church in Spain and insisted on strict adherence to orthodox Catholicism.

In 1109, Alfonso VI of Castile was succeeded by his daughter Queen Urraca, whose second husband was King Alfonso I of Aragon. The couple's marital problems caused conflict between Castile and Aragon. Alfonso seized all of Castile, Toledo, and most of León, leaving Queen Urraca Galacia and little else. Prince Alfonso, the queen's son by her first marriage to Raymond of Burgundy, was crowned king of Galacia in 1111. He recovered Castile and León from his stepfather and became Alfonso VII of Castile and León. On the death of his stepfather, Alfonso VII became pretender to the throne of Aragon. He did not attempt to conquer the kingdom, which remained separate from the crown of Castile and León.

When Alfonso VII died in 1157, he divided his lands between his two sons, Sancho III, who received Castile, and Ferdinand II, who received León. Sancho ruled only one year and was succeeded by his three-year-old son, Alfonso VIII. Alfonso assumed power at age fourteen and became one of the most successful conquerors of Moorish territory. He advertised the campaigns as Crusades, and the pope recognized them as such. Many foreigners joined the Spanish armies fighting the Moors. Alfonso also negotiated with Aragon the first of a series of treaties that determined the boundary between the two kingdoms.

In León, Ferdinand II and his son Alfonso IX greatly extended the Léonese borders southward, and Alfonso turned his attention to the conquest of Castile. The family conflict was settled in 1197 by the marriage of Alfonso IX of León to the daughter of Alfonso VIII of Castile. Their son was Ferdinand III, also known as Saint Ferdinand.

When Alfonso VIII of Castile died in 1214, he was succeeded by his son Enrique I, who died while still a minor. The crown passed to his sister, Doña Berenguela, who had been separated from her husband by the pope on grounds of consanguinity. Doña Berenguela ceded the crown to her son Ferdinand III. Alfonso IX of León opposed the cession even though he was Ferdinand's father and unsuccessfully invaded Castile to remove Ferdinand from the throne. Alfonso IX of León was so hostile to his son Ferdinand and to Castile that when he died in 1230, he bequeathed the throne of León to his two daughters by his first wife, the half sisters of Ferdinand III of Castile. Ferdinand was able to negotiate a settlement with his half sisters whereby he assumed the throne of León in return for rich dowries.

Significance

The two kingdoms that were first separated in the tenth century and temporarily joined three times in the eleventh and twelfth centuries became permanently joined in 1230. Future kings did not divide their territories as earlier kings had done. The kingdom of León and Castile included Galacia, Asturias, León, Castile, and the territories south added by conquest. The family quarrels resulting from the division of their lands by the earlier kings ended, and through unification and the desire for Reconquest, Spain was well on its way to becoming a nation of Spaniards.

—*Robert D. Talbott*

Further Reading

Altamira y Crevea, Rafael. *A History of Spain from the Beginning to the Present Day*. Translated by Muna Lee. New York: D. Van Nostrand, 1949. A classic exploration of the history of Spain from the perspectives of law, history, journalism, and art criticism.

Christys, Ann. *Christians in Al-Andalus, 711-1000*. Richmond, England: Curzon, 2002. Considers Christianity coexisting with Islam in Moorish Spain. Chapters on chronicles of the time, the city of Toledo, and more.

Descola, Jean. *A History of Spain*. Translated by Elaine P. Halperin. New York: Alfred A. Knopf, 1963. This work illustrates the author's idea of history as an art that combines a writer's imagination and a writer's knowledge.

Hillgarth, J. N. *Spain and the Mediterranean in the Later Middle Ages: Studies in Political and Intellectual History*. Burlington, Vt.: Ashgate Variorum, 2003. A survey of the political and intellectual history of Spain from 711—the time of Ṭārik's crossing—through the sixteenth century. Includes bibliography and index.

Marías, Julían. *Understanding Spain*. Translated by Frances M. Lopez-Morillas. Ann Arbor: University of Michigan Press, 1990. The major emphasis of this work is to develop an understanding of the factors that helped create Spain, factors such as geography, the Reconquest, and Moorish influences.

O'Callaghan, Joseph F. *Reconquest and Crusade in Medieval Spain*. Philadelphia: University of Pennsylvania Press, 2002. The author argues that the Papacy in the twelfth and thirteenth centuries regarded the conflict in Spain between Muslims and Christians to be a Crusade, and the popes afforded the same benefits to Crusaders in Spain as to those in the Holy Land. Includes chapters on particular battles, financing the conflicts, and Crusade warfare in general.

Reilly, Bernard F. *The Contest of Christian and Muslim Spain: 1031-1157*. Cambridge, Mass.: Blackwell, 1995. This work is a complete coverage of the rise of León-Castile and Aragon and deals extensively with the military struggle and dynastic history.

_______. *The Kingdom of León-Castilla Under Queen Urraca, 1109-1126*. Princeton, N.J.: Princeton University Press, 1982. This work covers an important period of economic and cultural advance during the Reconquest, during the final unification of León and Castile, and during Portugal's de facto achievement of independence.

See also: April or May, 711: Ṭārik Crosses into Spain; October 11, 732: Battle of Tours; c. 950: Court of Córdoba Flourishes in Spain; 1031: Caliphate of Córdoba Falls; November 1, 1092-June 15, 1094: El Cid Conquers Valencia; c. 1150: Moors Transmit Classical Philosophy and Medicine to Europe.

Related articles in *Great Lives from History: The Middle Ages, 477-1453*: Alfonso X; El Cid; Saint Isidore of Seville; James I the Conqueror; Moses de León; Ṭārik ibn-Ziyād.

1230's-1255
REIGN OF SUNDIATA OF MALI

Sundiata led the successful revolt of the Malinke people against the Susu (Soso) kingdom. In unifying the Malinke, he reasserted Mali's independence. Following this success with military expansion, he founded and established the Mali Empire, which became a major trade power in the central and western Sudanic region of West Africa.

LOCALE: West Africa (now Mali, Senegal, Guinea)
CATEGORIES: Government and politics; wars, uprisings, and civil unrest

KEY FIGURES

Sundiata (c. 1215-c. 1255), founder and king of Mali Empire, r. c. 1235-c. 1255
Sumanguru (d. c. 1235), ruler of Susu kingdom, r. thirteenth century

SUMMARY OF EVENT

Sundiata was the founder of the Mali Empire, which flourished from the thirteenth through the fifteenth centuries. At its apogee, Mali extended across the central and western Sudanic region from the Atlantic Ocean to the bend of the Niger River beyond the city of Gao. It stretched from the Sahara Desert in the north to the forest zone in the south. It covered a broad expanse of savannah-type land bound together by the upper Senegal and Niger Rivers. It was an excellent location for control of trans-Saharan trade.

The Malinke are Mande-speaking peoples. In the eleventh century, they were subjects of the Ghana Empire. With the collapse of Ghana, the region eventually fell under the control of the Susu kingdom, led by Sumanguru. In the 1220's, the various Malinke chieftaincies fell under Susu sovereignty.

Sundiata was the son of a local chief of the Keita clan. The story of his youth, as well as much of Mali's early history, is known only through the oral traditions of the Malinke. According to these narratives, the legendary Sundiata was disabled as a youth and walked with a limp. He and his mother were ridiculed by a cowife who had a healthy and handsome son, whom she feared might not become chief, or *mansa*. However, when this handsome half brother became chief, Sundiata and his mother were driven into exile.

Through a series of miraculous transformations, Sundiata regained full use of his legs and grew into a strong and wise young man. He developed into a well-known warrior and hunter. He became a member of hunters' associations and also acquired occult powers. Part of his exile was spent in the town of Mema. After the defeat of his half brother and the Susu occupation of the Malinke homeland, Sundiata, with the help of the people of Mema, returned home. He was joined by warriors and members of hunters' associations and began organizing a rebellion. The result was a series of epic battles recounted in Malinke oral traditions that have been told and retold for the past eight centuries. The battles matched the forces of Sundiata against the forces of Sumanguru. Both leaders used their occult powers against each other. Sundiata was victorious at the final battle in the town of Kirina (c. 1235) in what is now Mali. According to traditional narratives, his victory and the greatness of Mali were preordained.

Following the great victory over the Susu, Sundiata received an oath of fealty from the Malinke leaders of the various descent lineages. The title of *mansa* was reserved only for Sundiata. Previously, the Malinke had been a loose confederation of chieftaincies; now they were a centralized state.

After 1240, Sundiata took his energized forces and expanded in all directions, bringing more territory and people under Mali's rule. He succeeded in bringing the Senegal-Niger River basin under his control with non-Malinke people in a tributary status. In the process Sundiata and his successors took control of the main trade routes in the Sudanic region, especially the routes to the gold-producing areas of the south and southwest. Although agriculture was the basis of the economy, trade played a central role in the growth of the Mali Empire. Because of its key location, merchants in large trade caravans arrived in Mali's main commercial centers such as Timbuktu and Gao.

Sundiata established stability and peace, which further contributed to commercial expansion. Stability, though punctuated by periodic resistance, was based on wealth and power that derived from trade, tribute, and taxes. A standing army reinforced the authority of the *mansa*. As the empire grew, the rulers of Mali were able to develop new markets, increase trade, and draw on a larger population for taxes and soldiers. A merchant class, or *dyula*, which was dependent on the monarchy, conducted trade. Gold, salt, kola nuts, ivory, iron, and cloth were the main trade goods.

The merchant class played two key roles under Sundiata and his successors. The first involved the obvious commercial benefits they rendered, and the second was the role they played as catalysts for the expansion of Islam into Mali. Islam influenced almost all of Mali's early chiefs to one degree or another. Sundiata was considered a "nominal" Muslim, even though in times of crisis he used traditional religion to gain popular support.

The growth of Islam occurred in several ways. As Mali expanded northward it incorporated Muslim towns, and as it became a major commercial power it attracted Muslim merchants from North Africa and Egypt. These merchants developed trade relations with the Malinke merchants who were also Muslims. These merchants brought their faith with them, which spread through the commercial towns. For the rulers of Mali, Islam provided a valuable link to the north.

After Sundiata's reign Mali developed into a more Islamized state, with various kings making the pilgrimage (*hajj*) to Mecca. They established Mali's widespread reputation as a gold-trading empire. Mali reached the height of its power under Mansa Mūsā (r. 1312-1337). He is renowned for his famous *hajj* to Mecca in 1324. When passing through Cairo, he freely distributed gold and temporarily disrupted the city's economy. From this time period forward, Arab scholars such as Ibn Baṭṭūṭah, al-ʿUmarī, and Ibn Khaldūn recorded Mali's history. Mansa Mūsā gave Mali a more Islamic focus. He built mosques and schools and brought Islamic scholars and holy men to Mali. It should be noted that although the ruling families and the merchant class were Muslims, the majority of the Malinke people, who were mostly rural farmers, followed a traditional animistic religion.

After the reign of Mansa Mūsā the leadership of Mali's kings declined. The Mali Empire also outgrew itself. It became too large to be ruled effectively, as outlying areas rebelled and sought autonomy and enemies from the surrounding areas made inroads into Mali's territory and trade. Eventually Mali succumbed to the growing power of the Songhai Empire, but for two centuries it was a major power in West Africa.

SIGNIFICANCE

Sundiata was the founder of the Mali Empire. He laid the groundwork for the development of a vast multiethnic state that became a military and commercial power for more than two hundred years. The long-lasting consequences include a shift in power south from the edges of the Sahara Desert toward the forest zone of West Africa. This gave Mali greater access to gold, which opened the way for the development of a widespread commercial network. It also made possible the further penetration of Islam into the Sudanic region of West Africa. Mali's hegemony over a wide area brought peace and stability to the region.

The story of Sundiata and the rise of the Mali Empire is recited by Malinke bards or musician-entertainers, known locally as *jeliw* and as griots by the French. These traditions, recited for almost eight centuries, have become today's epic of Sundiata, Africa's most famous epic and now regarded as a classic of world epic literature. It is part of the living memory of the Malinke people. It combines history, religion, and literature and is usually recited as a narrative in a performance mode. Sundiata is a cultural hero of legendary proportions. His exploits are celebrated and his story has become a social, political, and cultural charter for the Malinke and other Mande-speaking groups.

In the last half century, a number of versions of the epic have been recorded, translated, and published. It has become part of legend and history. As a classic epic it is studied, analyzed, and taught in many parts of the world.

—*Thomas C. Maroukis*

FURTHER READING

Austin, Ralph A., ed. *In Search of Sunjata: The Mande Oral Epic as History, Literature and Performance.* Bloomington: University of Indiana Press, 1999. A series of essays that explore Sundiata's epic from a variety of disciplines and theoretical perspectives. Maps, bibliography, index.

Conrad, David C. "Searching for History in the Sunjata Epic: The Case of Fakoli." *History in Africa* 19 (1992): 147-200. This article analyzes the various versions of the Sundiata epic for historical evidence.

_______. "A Town Called Dakajalan: The Sunjata Tradition and the Question of Ancient Mali's Capital." *Journal of African History* 35 (1994): 355-377. Challenges the view of the city of Niani as Sundiata's capital.

Innes, Gordon, ed. *Sunjata: Three Mandinka Versions.* London: University of London, School of Oriental and African Studies, 1974. A translation with commentary on multiple versions of the Sundiata epic. Bibliography.

Johnson, John William. *The Epic of Son-Jara: A West African Tradition.* Bloomington: Indiana University Press, 1986. An annotated linear translation of the Fa-Digi Sisoko version of the Sundiata epic. Includes an introductory analysis of the text.

Levtzion, Nehemia. *Ancient Ghana and Mali.* New York: Africana, 1980. The classic history of two major states based on oral sources and Arabic documents. Includes discussion of the life and accomplishments of Sundiata.

McKissack, Patricia, and Frederick McKissack. *The Royal Kingdoms of Ghana, Mali, and Songhay: Life in Medieval Africa*. New York: H. Holt, 1994. A look at the history of the empires of Mali, Ghana, and Songhai, written especially for younger readers. Maps, bibliography, index.

Niane, D. T. "Mali and the Second Mandingo Expansion." In *General History of Africa: Africa from the Twelfth to the Sixteenth Century*. Vol. 4. New York: UNESCO, 1984. A well-researched history of the rise of the empire of Mali.

_______. *Sundiata: An Epic of Old Mali*. Translated by G. D. Pickett. 1965. Reprint. Harlow, England: Longman, 1994. The standard account of the rise of Sundiata based on local oral tradition.

SEE ALSO: 630-711: Islam Expands Throughout North Africa; c. 1010: Songhai Kingdom Converts to Islam; c. 1100: Founding of Timbuktu; c. 1181-1221: Lalibela Founds the Christian Capital of Ethiopia; 1324-1325: Mansa Mūsā's Pilgrimage to Mecca Sparks Interest in Mali Empire.

RELATED ARTICLES in *Great Lives from History: The Middle Ages, 477-1453*: Ibn Baṭṭūṭah; Ibn Khaldūn; Mansa Mūsā; Sundiata.

1233
PAPAL INQUISITION

The papal Inquisition developed a legal mechanism for suppressing heresy and was instituted gradually during the course of a millennium, causing the suffering and death of thousands of people during the Middle Ages.

LOCALE: Primarily Italy, southern France, Spain, and Germany

CATEGORIES: Laws, acts, and legal history; religion; social reform

KEY FIGURES

Innocent III (1160 or 1161-1216), Roman Catholic pope, 1198-1216, instigator of the crusade against the Albigensians

Frederick II (1194-1250), Holy Roman Emperor, r. 1220-1250, introduced capital punishment for heresy into secular law

Gregory IX (c. 1170-1241), Roman Catholic pope, 1227-1241, founder of the formal papal Inquisition

Innocent IV (c. 1180-1254), Roman Catholic pope, 1243-1254, organizer of the Inquisition

SUMMARY OF EVENT

When Christianity became the religion of the Roman Empire in 313, the sudden growth of Christian believers created problems of authority for both church and state. Maintenance of the social order required the prohibition of antisocial behavior such as sorcery, sacrilege, and treason. At first, coercion to ensure harmony was avoided as being contrary to Gospel precepts. Under the Christian emperors, notably Constantine's sons, physical force by the state was introduced to bring about unanimity of belief. Nonconformists were regarded as potential rebels and traitors whose activities undermined the state.

After Constantine, the unity of Christian belief was considered a guarantee of the unity of the empire. The church fathers were divided on the use of coercion, but Augustine's views became dominant in the West. He maintained that the state, like a benevolent father, was required to encourage heretics to return to orthodoxy and thus save their souls. Thus, church and state were united in a common cause.

Shortly after the year 1000, a form of neo-Manichaeism, Catharism, or Albigensianism, spread over western Europe. The popular revulsion against adherents of this sect was especially strong in France, where thirteen Cathari were burned at the stake in 1022 by order of Robert II, and the three-year-old corpse of a heretic was exhumed and taken out of Christian burial ground. Execution by fire was an innovation unheard of before that time, but in 1028, heretics were burned by popular demand at Milan. In 1051, some Cathari were hanged in the presence of Emperor Henry III. These eleventh century outbursts seem to have been prompted by the general populace rather than by the Church. Toward the end of the twelfth century, however, Catharism had spread to such an extent in southern France that the very existence of the Church seemed to be threatened.

Once attention was called to the danger, churchmen became convinced that some machinery must be set in motion to deal with it. The relatively casual approach by many bishops to heresy was changed in 1184, when the Council of Verona decreed that bishops were to make a formal inquest in each diocese to root out heretics. This was the beginning of the episcopal inquisition. The Church prescribed imprisonment, excommunication, and confiscation of property but did not condone the burning or death of heretics. In 1199, Pope Innocent III equated heresy with treason. The heretics were to be handed over to the secular powers for unspecified punishment and their lands were to be confiscated. In 1220, Frederick II decreed that relapsed heretics were to be burned and that lesser offenders were to lose their tongues.

The episcopal inquisition was not successful in stemming the tide of heretics. Pope Innocent III sent his own legatine inquisitors to southern France, and it was the murder of one emissary that touched off the crusade against the Albigensians. With the Treaty of Meaux in 1229, the crusade came to an end, but heresy was still prevalent. In 1233, Pope Gregory IX issued two papal bulls establishing the papal Inquisition, which in theory was to be implemented in cooperation with the bishops but in practice was often an instrument of papal control. Dominicans and Franciscans were generally chosen as papal inquisitors.

The inquisitor was a privileged person under the special favor of the Papacy, who could be controlled by the pope alone. He was surrounded by numerous assistants: delegates who asked preliminary questions and heard witnesses, *socii* who accompanied the inquisitor, familiars who acted as personal guards and agents, notaries, counselors, and servants. The careful preservation of records promoted the success of the Inquisition, for it rendered almost impossible the escape of any suspect. Some

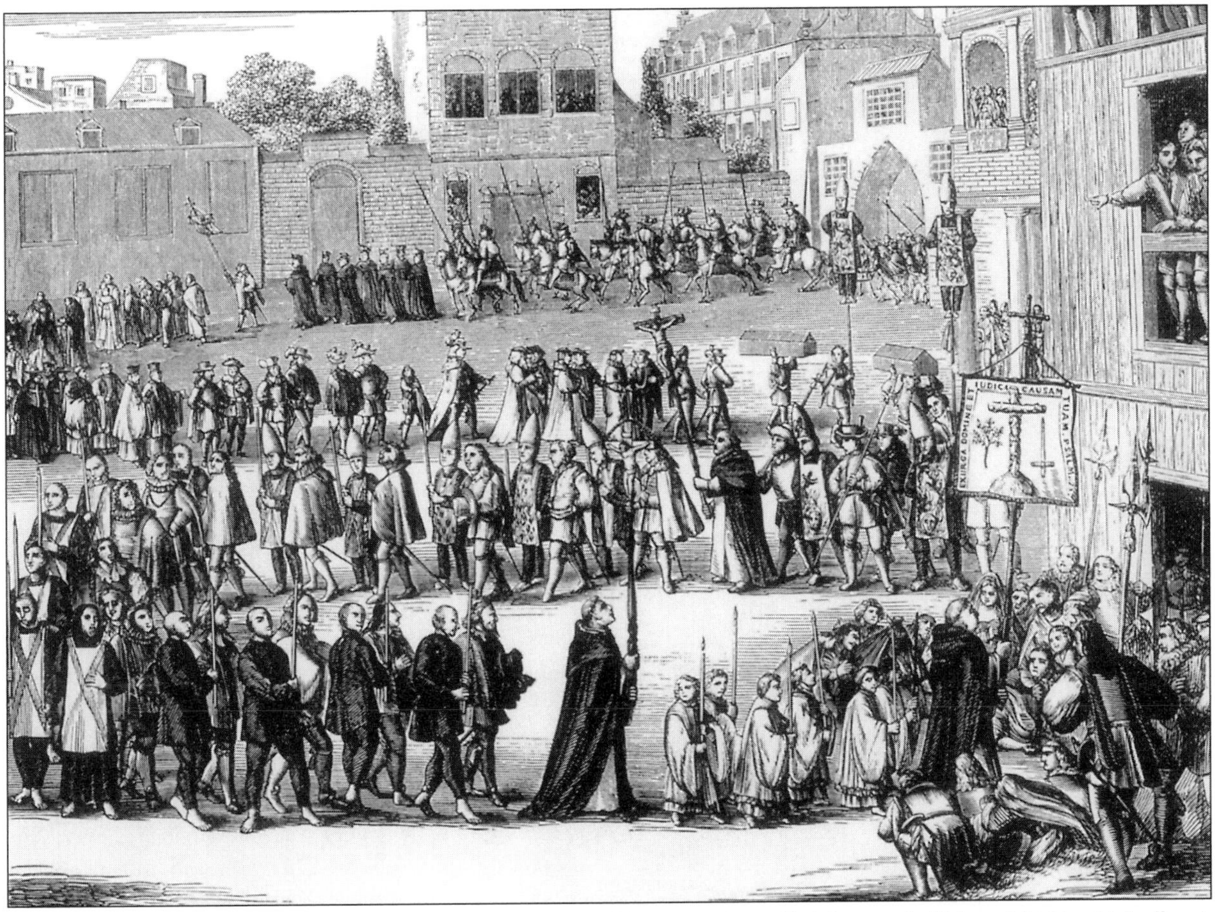

During the papal Inquisition, sentencing was pronounced at a public procession called the auto-da-fé *(act of faith), which all residents of the locality were urged to attend. This engraving appears in a 1692 edition of* Historia Inquisitionis, *by Philip of Limborch.* (Frederick Ungar Publishing Co.)

were apprehended years later, far from the scene of the original trial, on the basis of the trial records.

The inquisitor's task was formidable, as he was obliged to determine the state of a person's innermost convictions. The matter of interpretation of the nature of heresy gave abundant scope for uncovering the smallest details of a person's moral life. Inquisitors recognized a complex hierarchy of heretics, from those who were merely suspected to those who obstinately adhered to error. In the latter case, they were summarily handed over to the secular authorities to be executed, but even those who were merely suspect received some type of penance because it appeared a wrong to God that anyone whose orthodoxy was in doubt should escape penalty. The list of offenses included anticlericalism, association with heretics (including even close relatives), moral offenses, sorcery, and witchcraft. It was rare for an accused heretic to escape some form of punishment despite protestations of innocence.

After arriving at a town within his province, the inquisitor let it be known that he would receive accusations and confessions for a period of time. After that he proceeded to summon suspects who had not voluntarily presented themselves. The accused were not permitted to cross-examine their accusers, but they were permitted to draw up a list of any enemies who might gain from their conviction. Prejudiced evidence from such enemies was not to be admitted. The inquisitor was assisted by a council, and in theory, he was to reach his verdict in consultation with the council and the bishop. In practice, the verdicts were often made by the inquisitor-judge alone. Torture, which had been permitted by Pope Innocent IV in his bull *Ad extirpanda* (1252), was abrogated by Pope Boniface VIII. The sentence was pronounced at the *sermo generalis* or *auto-da-fé* (act of faith), a public exhibition that all residents of the locality were urged to attend. Sentences varied from death by fire, carried out by the state, to imprisonments of varied duration, confiscation of goods, pilgrimages, and lesser penances.

In 1233, Pope Gregory IX issued two papal bulls establishing the papal Inquisition. (Frederick Ungar Publishing Co.)

The Spanish Inquisition, which was not established until the end of the fifteenth century, bears a different character. It was established to discover heretics among converted Muslims (*Moriscos*) and Jews (*Marranos*), only later extending its activities to include Protestants. It was primarily an instrument of the state. In fact, many orthodox bishops and Jesuits were singled out for harassment and even death because of their criticism of the secular authorities.

SIGNIFICANCE

With the firmly established power, significance, and influence of the Catholic Church in medieval Europe came prescriptions for the strict adherence to Church doctrine and the swift punishment of heretics, including those accused of promulgating what were considered anti-Christian beliefs or beliefs against papal authority, and those accused of witchcraft, sorcery, and alchemy. Not only were heretics considered enemies of the Church, they were also enemies of society.

What was unique about the papal Inquisition was its practice of actively seeking out possible heretics and not simply responding to claims of heresy. The term "inquisition," from the Latin *inquiro*, means "to inquire into."

The influence of the papal Inquisition and its model reached into the mid-sixteenth century, when, in 1542, Pope Paul III established the Congregation of the Inquisition as the final court of appeals for heresy trials. The trend continued into the twentieth century. In 1908, this congregation became known as the Holy Office, and in 1965, it came to be called the Congregation for the Doctrine of the Faith.

—*Carl A. Volz, updated by Winifred Whelan*

FURTHER READING

Baigent, Michael, and Richard Leigh. *The Inquisition*. New York: Viking, 1999. A comprehensive history of the Inquisition from its medieval origins to the present.

Given, James B. *Inquisition and Medieval Society: Power, Discipline, and Resistance in Languedoc*. Ithaca, N.Y.: Cornell University Press, 1997. A detailed study of the Inquisition in one region of France. Three sections focus on the technologies employed by the inquisitors, the methods of individual and collective resistance attempted by those accused of heresy, and the social and political context in which the Inquisition in France took place.

Kieckhefer, Richard. "The Office of Inquisition and Heresy: The Transition from Personal to Institutional Jurisdiction." In *Journal of Ecclesiastical History* 46 (January, 1995): 36-61. The author indicates that there was no "Inquisition" as a systematic structured entity until 1542, a fact that is not recognized by many authors on the subject. At first, there were only individual local efforts, and only gradually did a systematic, centralized, curial inquisitional authority emerge.

Lea, Henry Charles. *The History of the Inquisition of the Middle Ages*. 3 vols. Reprint. New York: Russell and Russell, 1958. This work is considered foundational for all significant study on the topic of the Inquisition. The book outlines the gradual establishment of inquisitorial procedure and shows how after 1250 the papal legates served as an arm of central authority over the bishops as well as detectors of heresy, thus enhancing papal centralization.

Monter, E. William. *Frontiers of Heresy: The Spanish Inquisition from the Basque Lands to Sicily*. New York: Cambridge University Press, 1990. This book concentrates particularly on the Spanish Inquisition. It includes interesting tables and appendices showing the number of people who were put to death in various tribunals.

Peters, Edward. *Inquisition*. New York: Free Press, 1988. The author contends that the Inquisition began when the Church employed clergy to preserve orthodox religious beliefs from the attacks of heretics. At the time of the Protestant Reformation, these localized inquisitions were transformed into the Inquisition, mainly because it served the purpose of various political regimes. The book also includes chapters on the Inquisition in literature and art.

Shannon, Albert C. *The Medieval Inquisition*. 2d ed. Collegeville, Minn.: Liturgical Press, 1991. For its specific topic, this book singles out the period of the 1200's in Languedoc, southern France. It details how the beliefs of the Albigensians and the Waldensians resulted in the establishment of the Inquisition.

SEE ALSO: c. 1175: Waldensian Excommunications Usher in Protestant Movement; 1209-1229: Albigensian Crusade; 1212: Children's Crusade; November 11-30, 1215: Fourth Lateran Council; November 18, 1302: Boniface VIII Issues the Bull *Unam Sanctam*; July 2, 1324: Lady Alice Kyteler Is Found Guilty of Witchcraft.

RELATED ARTICLES in *Great Lives from History: The Middle Ages, 477-1453*: Arnold of Villanova; Boniface VIII; Saint Dominic; Frederick II; Gregory IX; Jan Hus; Innocent III; Innocent IV; Joan of Arc; Lady Alice Kyteler; Marguerite Porete; John Wyclif.

1236-1240
REIGN OF RAZIYA

Raziya had the distinction of being the only woman who ever occupied the throne of Delhi. Her remarkable career helps dispel the myth of the relative unimportance of women in Islamic society.

LOCALE: Northern India
CATEGORY: Government and politics

KEY FIGURES

Raziya (d. 1240), sultan of Delhi, r. 1236-1240
Iltutmish (d. 1236), her father, sultan of Delhi, r. 1211-1236
Ruknuddin Firūz Shah, her brother, sultan of Delhi, r. 1236
Jamāl al-Dīn Yakut (d. 1239), a trusted officer and Raziya's chief supporter
Ikhtiar al-Dīn Altuniya (d. 1240), Raziya's husband

SUMMARY OF EVENT

When Raziya ascended the throne of the Delhi sultanate, also known as the Turkish Slave Dynasty, she took the title sultan rather than sultana. In doing so, she was making the point that a person's gender should not be a determining factor in a ruler's ability or legitimacy.

Raziya, the first and only female sultan of Delhi, was the daughter of Sultan Iltutmish, a man who began his career in India as a slave. An able and literate man, he was purchased in Ghazna (now in Afghanistan) by the founder of the Delhi sultanate, Quṭ al-Dīn Aybak, who eventually freed Iltutmish and came to view him as his son. Iltutmish ascended the throne in 1211. As was typical of the politics of the time, the Turkish elite challenged Iltutmish's accession. After defeating the dissenters in the Battle of Tarain (1215-1216), he began expanding the territorial holdings and working toward a unified and enlightened system of government. Near the end of his distinguished reign, he named his extremely able daughter Raziya to succeed him. Although he had two sons of age and one minor son, he believed that his daughter alone had the remarkable qualities required of a good ruler. Before Iltutmish's death in 1236, he ordered his secretary general to prepare a decree naming Raziya as his successor.

Iltutmish's choice for a successor was based on objective observation and rational evaluation of his offspring. Specifically, Raziya had demonstrated her talents as a fair and able administrator when she served as regent while her father conducted a military campaign in Gwalior to the south of Delhi. Although Raziya's father trusted his daughter's abilities, a powerful group of Turkish noblemen known as the Forty Amirs objected vociferously to her accession. Taking matters into their own hands, they made Ruknuddin Firūz Shah, Iltutmish's drunkard son, sultan. The responsibility of rule unfortunately did not deter Ruknuddin from his degenerate ways, and he continued to indulge his excessive pursuit of pleasure and intoxicants. Meanwhile, Ruknuddin's mother, the notorious Shah Turkan, plotted to destroy any perceived contender for her son's rule, including Raziya, whom she viewed as a continued threat to her son's authority and her own position as high-ranking woman of the realm. In her quest for control, Shah Turkan insisted that her son, the sultan, blind and put to death Iltutmish's youngest heir, a child of ten born by a minor wife.

The shocking deed infuriated the nobility throughout the kingdom, and many became openly hostile to the throne. Rebellion broke out in the vicinity of Mansurpur and Tarain, and it had to be put down by the sultan, who led his forces on the battlefield. Meanwhile, in Delhi, Raziya, realizing that her own life was in danger, took advantage of the chaotic conditions to establish order and justice. In an open assembly at the mosque during Friday prayers, Raziya wore a red garment, the color worn by the aggrieved, and publicly accused Shah Turkan of plotting to kill her as she had her younger brother. In the name of her father, Iltutmish, she appealed to the people for help. A fiery and courageous speaker, she asked for a chance to prove her abilities, saying that if she failed, she should be decapitated. Moved by her entreaty, the people attacked the royal palace and seized Shah Turkan. When her son Ruknuddin returned to the city, he found his mother in prison and the city in revolt. The situation was so dire that the Amirs conceded, removing the sultan and placing Raziya on the throne; Ruknuddin's reign had lasted little more than six months.

Having achieved her father's goal, Raziya took the title sultan-ud-duniya-wa-ud-dīn, or king of the world and religion. For her first act as ruler, she ordered that Ruknuddin join his mother in prison. Ultimately, Ruknuddin and his mother were tried in an impartial court and were subsequently executed. Despite Raziya's popular support, her reign from the very start was troubled because of the prevailing attitude toward a woman in a position of command. Two Muslim sects, the heretical Kiramitah and Mulahidah, staged a revolt against her; more than one thousand armed heretics entered the great mosque in the city and killed many worshipers. Also, despite their initial support, some of the Amirs resented Raziya's position. Eventually, a few lay siege on Delhi, forcing Raziya and her troops into armed warfare on the banks of the Yamuna River near Delhi. The insurrection was short-lived, but dissention continued to plague the noble ranks despite Raziya's efforts to win the loyalty and support of the Amirs. In particular, she created a stir when she appointed Jamāl al-Dīn Yakut, an Ethiopian, to the high-ranking post of commander of the army. Yakut, a non-Turk who was a longtime trusted friend and supporter of Raziya and her father, had earned his new position; nonetheless, he aroused envy among the Turkish nobles and thereby provided ammunition for Raziya's detractors.

Determined to prove her worthiness and to deal with men on their own terms, Raziya began to wear men's clothing and appeared in public without the veil prescribed for women. She appeared so not only in court but also in public; she rode openly through the streets of Delhi in an attempt to connect directly to the people she ruled. Whether an act of defiance or practicality, her garb and unabashed manner added to the discord among the nobles. When a feudatory governor in Lahore rebelled, Sultan Raziya led the attack at the head of the army. Another rebellion broke out in Tabarhindah; again Raziya led the attack on the rebels. In that battle, her trusted officer Yakut was killed, and Raziya was captured and imprisoned.

DELHI SULTANATE, 1236-1398

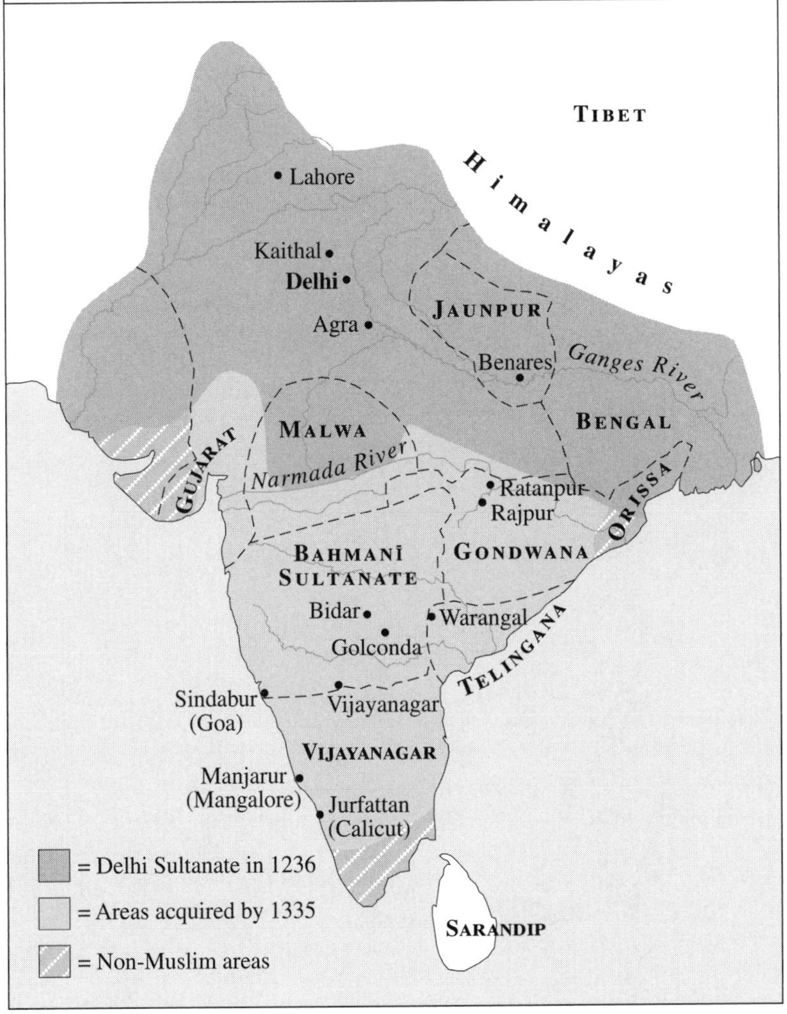

Once news of her capture reached Delhi, her brother Bahrām Shāh (r. 1240-1242) took the throne. After a short time, however, he began to lose the support of some of the nobles, including Ikhtiar al-Dīn Altuniya, a distant relative of Raziya.

An Amir of high position, Altuniya initially participated in the revolt at Tabarhindah but later switched sides and married Raziya during her imprisonment. Now aligned politically and by marriage, the two were anxious to oust the usurper, and therefore, they embarked on a plan to recapture Raziya's throne and kingdom. They assembled a large army to retake Delhi. Learning of the plan, the sultan Bāhram Shāh decided not to wait for the advancing march on the capital but led his troops as far as Kaithal, where the two armies clashed. Outflanked and outmaneuvered, both Raziya and Altuniya were killed in battle on October 13, 1240. Raziya had been sultan for three years, six months, and six days. She was not yet thirty years of age.

SIGNIFICANCE

Raziya's chief biographer, the historian Minhāj Sirāj Jūzjānī, wrote that Sultan Raziya was a great sovereign who cherished her subjects and was wise, beneficent, a patron of the learned, a dispenser of justice, and gifted with a talent in war. In fact, he claimed that she was endowed with all the attributes and qualifications necessary for a good king but that she had not attained her destiny because she was born a woman. To extol the virtues of a male king was customary, but for Jūzjānī to profusely praise a woman indicates Raziya's exceptional qualities and capacities for leadership. Her impartiality, her intolerance of racial discrimination, her quest for knowledge, and her need to establish justice were just a few of her remarkable gifts.

The historian Ferishta (c. 1560-c. 1620) wrote that Raziya possessed every good normally attributed to the ablest princes and that those who scrutinized her actions would find no fault but that she was a woman. He also noted that she read the Quʾrān with the correct pronunciation and, in her father's lifetime, employed herself frequently in the affairs of the government, a disposition that her father encouraged in her.

Sultan Raziya was the only woman to occupy the throne in her own right. She was not a proxy ruler for any male. She was not queen, but king. An able politician, she outwitted the Forty Amirs by appealing directly to her subjects, the people of Delhi. In doing so, she became the first democratically elected monarch of India. Her accession shattered the myth of the lowly position of women in Islam.

—*Katherine Anne Harper*

FURTHER READING

Brijbhushari, Jamila. *Sultan Raziya: Her Life and Times, a Reappraisal.* New Delhi, India: Manohar, 1990. A comprehensive history of the life of Raziya and the political and religious dictates of her world. Bibliography.

Madhavananda, Swami, and Ramesh Chandra Majumdar, eds. *Great Women of India.* Calcutta, India: Advaita Ashrama, 1993. An excellent general survey of the role of women in Indian culture with articles on certain important and influential Indian women throughout history. Bibliography.

Minhāj Sirāj Jūzjānī. *Tabakāt-i Nāsirī.* Translated by H. G. Raverty. 2 vols. 1881. Reprint. Calcutta, India: The Asiatic Society, 1995. The principal contemporary account.

Sharma, L. P. *The Sultanate of Delhi.* New Delhi, India: Konark, 1988. A detailed, reliable, and excellent history of this brief period in Indian history.

Zakaria, Rafiq. *Razia: Queen of India.* Bombay, India: Popular Prakashan, 1966. A fictional history based on the life of India's female sultan of Delhi. Includes epilogue and bibliography.

SEE ALSO: 1206-1210: Quṭ al-Dīn Aybak Establishes the Delhi Sultanate; 1299: ʿAlāʾ-ud-Dīn Muḥammad Khaljī Conquers Gujarat.

RELATED ARTICLE in *Great Lives from History: The Middle Ages, 477-1453*: Raziya.

July 15, 1240
ALEXANDER NEVSKY DEFENDS NOVGOROD FROM SWEDISH INVADERS

Alexander Nevsky defended the Russian land of Novgorod from Swedish invaders, checking the Swedish advance into Russian territory and allowing Novgorod's merchants to have continued access to the Gulf of Finland through the Neva River.

LOCALE: Neva River and Gulf of Finland

CATEGORIES: Expansion and land acquisition; wars, uprisings, and civil unrest; religion; government and politics

KEY FIGURES

Alexander Nevsky (c. 1220-1263), prince and then grand prince of Novgorod, r. 1252-1263

Birger Jarl (d. 1266), regent of the Swedish crown, 1248-1252

Kirill (1246-1280), metropolitan of the Russian Orthodox Church

Yaroslav Vsevolodovich (1191-1246), grand prince, r. 1238-1246

SUMMARY OF EVENT

Alexander Nevsky's leadership in the defense of Novgorod and other Russian lands from incursions of Swedes and Germans is well known. Metropolitan Kirill's *Life of Alexander* portrayed his hero as the savior of Orthodoxy. Twice Alexander was engaged in defense against Swedes, once along the Neva River on July 15, 1240, which explains the sobriquet "Nevsky." Alexander's mounted brigade surprised the encamped Swedes while infantry attacked Swedish ships in dock to prevent arrival of reinforcements. These battles (or skirmishes, as one authority avers) were part of the continuing struggle between Russians and Scandinavians for control of the Finnish and Karelian lands. Other sources, however, argue that such battles were designed by Grand Prince Yaroslav Vsevolodovich to stop the territorial and religious plans of Germans, Danes, and Swedes who hoped to absorb Novgorod at a time when it was weakened by Tatar rule. Yaroslav's action may have been designed to enhance Novgorod's military dependence on the "downstream" princes of Vladimir on whom it was already dependent for food.

Yaroslav, father of Alexander, sent him to become prince of Novgorod, a commercial city-state north of Vladimir. Unlike most Russian towns, Novgorod had a powerful assembly dominated by merchant lords and often divided in its allegiance to the grand principality of Vladimir to the south. Novgorod also maintained steady trade with the Hanseatic League of cities in northern Europe. Its furs, wax, walrus tusks, and woodwork were prized items at fairs. The so-called German quarter of Novgorod was the residence of many foreign merchants who came to the city by way of the Gulf of Finland, the Neva River, Lake Ladoga, and then south to Novgorod along the Volkhov River. When, in 1240, an army of Swedes, with Finns and Danes, arrived at the mouth of the Izhora River at the spot joining the Neva, Russians in Novgorod perceived this invasion as an effort to close their access to the sea. The merchants of Novgorod also regarded this incursion as a first step toward further acquisitions south toward the city-state itself. Meanwhile, Yaroslav was concerned about the advances of Germans and Lithuanians from the west as well as the Swedes from the north.

According to most early and modern sources, when the Swedes arrived at the Neva in "very many ships," their leader, Birger Jarl, later regent to the young king of Sweden, sent news of their presence to Novgorod, challenging the entire province to take battle. The twenty-year-old prince, Alexander, summoned an army after spending many hours praying to the Blessed Virgin in the Saint Sophia Cathedral. He was impatient to wait for reinforcements from the outlying regions of the Novgorod territories as well as others from Russian territories downstream toward Vladimir. He probably doubted the ability to raise more troops given the recent Mongol destruction of Russian mounted retainers. Thus Alexander

Alexander Nevsky, grand prince of Novgorod (1252-1263), was canonized by the Russian Orthodox Church in 1547. (Hulton|Archive by Getty Images)

began his campaign against the Swedes with a much smaller force than his opponent.

Although the encounter on July 15, 1240, is sometimes described as a skirmish by some modern writers, the description of the battle indicates that it was more than that. A certain Pelgusius, a local chieftain of a Finno-Ugric tribe at Lake Ladoga, offered to reconnoiter the Swedish encampment for Alexander. Although his tribe was pagan he was a Christian, and he told Alexander of a vision about the impending battle whereby the medieval Russian saints Boris and Gleb appeared to him with news that they intended to aid the prince against the invaders.

Despite the Swedish notification to Alexander, the fact that his armies surprised the Swedish forces in the daylight indicates that Alexander's strategy of hasty advance without additional reinforcements may have been the correct strategy. In a plan to prevent enemy reinforcements from arriving, three Swedish vessels were sunk by

Alexander's infantry, while two others escaped with fleeing soldiers. A Swedish general was killed, and one source mentions that the Birger Jarl was even wounded by Alexander and that one of the Catholic bishops was killed. Russian horsemen killed a large number of enemy as well, although the hagiography of Alexander written by Metropolitan Kirill told of an angel of death killing a multitude of Swedish soldiers who lay along the opposite banks of the Neva where Alexander's men had not crossed. At any rate the victory led to Alexander's new appellation as "Nevsky" in honor of this battle.

Among the men of Novgorod who distinguished themselves on the battlefield were six: Gavrilo Oleksich, who fought the general and son of Birger; Zbyslav Yakenovich, who fought daring encounters with his battle-ax; Jacob of Polotsk, the huntsman of Prince Alexander, who charged the enemy with his sword; Mikhail, a foot soldier who led the infantry in the attack that destroyed three Swedish vessels; Savva, who stimulated his fellow soldiers to combat when he charged the big, golden-crowned tent of the enemy, cutting its central pole; and Ratmir, who died fighting when encircled by many foes. Alexander arrived back home with losses of but twenty of his men, including those well known to contemporaries such as Konstantin Lugotinits, Giuriata Pineshchinich, Nemest, and Drochilo, son of Nezdilo the tanner.

Although he was triumphant, the new popularity of Alexander was threatening to the merchant lords of Novgorod who dismissed him as their prince. Alexander, in anger, took his courtiers and family to his former home in Pereiaslavl. A few years later, when the Germans invaded the satellite region of Pskov, Novgorod pleaded with Alexander to return. He did so, and the famous battle on the ice took place on Lake Peipus as Alexander's forces routed the German Knights of Livonia (1242). The Swedes would return again in 1247, but Alexander was then en route to the capital of the Mongols to appease their demands for conscription and taxes. The policy of appeasement was considered essential to the survival of the Russian lands, which could not have withstood simultaneously the Mongols to the south and Catholics to the west. That very year of the battle on the Neva, the Russian town of Chernigov was overwhelmed by the Mongols, as was Kiev on the Dnieper River. One year later, the Germans invaded from the west. Metropolitan Kirill thought the Catholic threat was more to be feared, since the Mongols allowed the Orthodox Church to function in Russia so long as priests prayed for the khan. Did he overstate the importance of Alexander's military defenses against the West in order to deflect criticism of the prince's appeasement of the Tatars? In any case, in 1245 the Lithuanians attacked Russian lands from the West, seizing permanently many Russian communities.

SIGNIFICANCE

A formal treaty of peace between the Russians and the Swedes was not signed until 1326. Nevertheless, because of the successful thwarting of the Swedes, Novgorod's commercial prosperity and republican political organization continued, with or without the treaty, until the late fifteenth century, when the city-state was absorbed by the Muscovite state of Grand Prince Ivan III.

—*John D. Windhausen*

FURTHER READING

Birnbaum, Henrik. *Lord Novgorod the Great: Essays in the History and Culture of a Medieval City-State*. Columbus, Ohio: Slavica, 1981. Birnbaum agrees with Soviet researchers who believe that the Swedish regent was not at the battle on the Neva, but at the later one in 1247.

Brisbane, Mark, and David Gaimster, eds. *Novgorod: The Archaeology of a Russian Medieval City and Its Hinterland*. London: British Museum, 2001. A brief, illustrated history of medieval Novgorod, exploring its archaeology. Includes maps and site plans.

The Chronicle of Novgorod. Translated by Robert Michell and Nevill Forbes. New York: AMS Press, 1970. An indispensable source for the study of Alexander's role in Novgorod, but written from the tendentious outlook of medieval churchmen.

Dukes, Paul. *A History of Russia: Medieval, Modern, Contemporary, Circa 882-1996*. 3d ed. Durham, N.C.: Duke University Press, 1998. A look at the history of Russia, including the time of formation. Extensive bibliography and an index.

Fennell, John. *The Crisis of Medieval Russia, 1200-1304*. New York: Longman, 1983. A critical account that doubts the importance of the Neva encounter.

Presniakov, A. E. *The Formation of the Great Russian State: A Study of Russian History in the Thirteenth to Fifteenth Centuries*. Translated by A. E. Moorhouse. Chicago: Quadrangle Books, 1970. First published in 1918, this work analyzes the disarray among the Russian leaders at the time of the Mongol and Western invasions. He stresses Alexander's family relationships and charismatic leadership.

Riasanovsky, Nicholas V. "Lord Novgorod the Great" and "The Mongols in Russia." In *A History of Russia*.

6th ed. New York: Oxford University Press, 2000. Two chapters, one on Alexander and the other on the Mongol influence in Russian history. Bibliography and index.

"Tale of the Life and Courage of the Pious and Great Prince Alexander." In *Medieval Russia's Epics, Chronicles, and Tales*, edited by Serge A. Zenkovsky. Rev. 2d ed. New York: Dutton, 1974. Although written forty years after the events, this book remains the basic source for the era of Alexander and depicts him as the savior of the land from the Catholic West.

Vernadsky, George. *The Mongols and Russia*. New Haven, Conn.: Yale University Press, 1953. The classic account by the late dean of American scholars of medieval Russia. It should be read in conjunction with the revisionist version of Fennell.

SEE ALSO: 850-950: Viking Era; 988: Baptism of Vladimir I; c. 1150-1200: Rise of the Hansa Merchant Union; September 8, 1380: Battle of Kulikovo.

RELATED ARTICLES in *Great Lives from History: The Middle Ages, 477-1453*: Saint Alexander Nevsky; Olaf I; Rurik; Tamerlane; Vladimir I.

1248-1254
FAILURE OF THE SEVENTH CRUSADE

The Seventh Crusade ended in failure and contributed to the growing disillusionment and anti-Crusade sentiment characteristic of mid- to late thirteenth century Europe.

LOCALE: Egypt

CATEGORIES: Religion; wars, uprisings, and civil unrest

KEY FIGURES

Louis IX (1214-1270), king of France, r. 1226-1270, leader of the Seventh Crusade

Blanche of Castile (1188-1252), mother of Louis, regent of France, r. 1223-1234 and 1248-1252

William, earl of Salisbury (c. 1212-1250), leader of the English contingent

Robert of Artois (d. 1250), younger brother of Louis, led the disastrous attack on Al Manṣūrah

Charles of Anjou (1226-1285), Crusader, brother of Louis

Alphonse of Poitiers (1220-1271), Crusader, brother of Louis

Margaret of Provence (1221-1295), wife of Louis, accompanied him on the Seventh Crusade

Jean de Joinville (c. 1224-1317), baron, joined the Seventh Crusade and described it in his memoirs

SUMMARY OF EVENT

A little more than 150 years after Pope Urban II called the First Crusade in 1095, King Louis IX of France embarked on what historians regard as the end of the crusading movement. Louis can be seen as leader of two crusades, or of one crusade in two phases. In either interpretation, it is the earlier effort that is usually called the Seventh Crusade.

It is true that there were attempts to organize crusades for several centuries after the failure of the campaigns of Louis in 1248 and 1270, but none of them succeeded in winning the kind of support that made possible the strong offensives of the twelfth and thirteenth centuries. Indeed, Louis's abortive crusade of 1270 marked the last full-scale crusade mounted by a European king.

On the diplomatic scene there were compelling reasons for a crusade in the 1240's. In the West, a succession of popes had engaged in a long vendetta with the brilliant Holy Roman Emperor and Crusader, Frederick II (r. 1215-1250). In this struggle, crusading had been a factor in several ways. First, although Frederick had promised to lead a crusade in 1215 and 1220, he did not leave until 1227. Pope Gregory IX, angered by his stalling, finally excommunicated him, a ban not lifted until Frederick's return from the Sixth Crusade.

During the Sixth Crusade, Frederick won Jerusalem in negotiations with al-Malik al-Kāmil, the sultan of Egypt, Palestine, and Syria (r. 1218-1238). The Christian victory was not long-lived, however; Jerusalem was subsequently retaken in 1244 by the Turks, who were allies of the Egyptians.

Second, Frederick once again found himself the target of papal anger in 1245, when Pope Innocent IV excommunicated him and called for a crusade against Frederick himself at the Council of Lyons.

Although his loyalty to the church was unquestioned, Louis did not support the pope in this venture. Rather, during a serious illness, Louis made a vow that he would take up the cross for the more traditional and popular purpose of reconquering the Holy Land. Louis's mother, Blanche of Castile, tried to dissuade him from his vow, saying that a vow taken in illness was not binding. Louis's response was to retake his vow on his recovery.

Conditions in the East also indicated that the time was ripe for a major thrust against the Muslims, because there was internal rivalry between the Syrian and Egyptian leaders. Another hopeful sign, though misinterpreted, was an apparent chance of allying with the Mongols against the Muslims. Several religious-diplomatic missions had been sent to the Mongol khan, Hülagü, and though they had produced no positive results, the possibilities of converting the Mongols and thus procuring a strong ally in the East was a factor in the climate that supported Louis's Crusade.

Louis prepared for the Seventh Crusade in a number of ways. First, he wanted to leave behind a stable France. He had quelled two uprisings by barons in 1241 and 1243; as he gathered his forces for the Seventh Crusade, he persuaded many of the dissident barons to accompany him. He also sent emissaries around the country to investigate any wrongdoings by his government or dissatisfaction of his subjects. As a result of this investigation, he overhauled his administration and left experienced, trustworthy officials in charge during his absence.

Second, Louis carefully planned for the material needs of his expedition. The Seventh Crusade, which was more carefully planned than any of the expeditions that had preceded it, included the construction of a port of embarkation at Aigues-Mortes, not far from Marseilles, as well as the shipping of a large number of supplies ahead to Cyprus. Further, Louis embarked on negotiations with the Genoese for transportation and the recruitment of an army of at least ten thousand men.

Apart from a small contingent from England under William, the earl of Salisbury and grandson of Henry II (r. 1154-1189), most of the force was French, and a large proportion was supported directly by the king. Among the leading barons were three of the French king's brothers: Robert of Artois, Charles of Anjou, and Alphonse of Poitiers. Louis's wife, Margaret of Provence, also accompanied the expedition, a reminder that Crusaders of knightly rank were accustomed to bringing an entire

Crusaders disembarking at Damietta, Egypt, from a woodcut in Grand Voyage de Hiérusalem *(1522).* (Frederick Ungar Publishing Co.)

The Seventh Crusade, 1248-1254

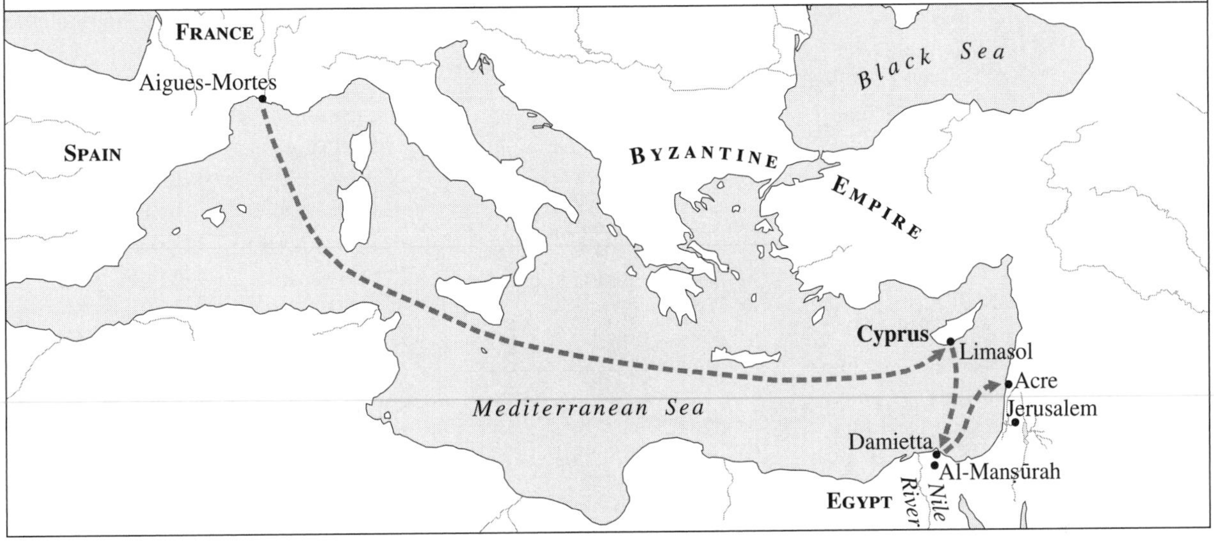

household. In this case, Margaret played a strategic role in the evacuation after Louis's defeat.

Louis received little help from the pope in organizing his Crusade. The pope's crusade against Frederick II as well as his call for a crusade in Spain diluted the crusading effort across Europe. Most of Louis's support came from within France, with the Catholic Church contributing funds that covered approximately two-thirds of his expenses. Louis also contributed a great deal of his own money to support the expedition.

After three years of preparation, the expedition sailed for Damietta after wintering at Cyprus. Louis reached the Nile River near Damietta by June of 1249. The plan called for conquering Muslims of the Ayyūbid Dynasty in Egypt, thus forcing them to make concessions in the Holy Places. Louis was following the strategy of the Fifth Crusade, when Damietta was offered in exchange for Jerusalem. In a rapid, excellently organized landing and attack, the Crusaders routed an Egyptian force that had come to the coast to meet them. Pushing on to Damietta itself by June 6, the Crusaders found the place deserted and were able to take it over with little or no loss, thus providing themselves with an ideal base of operations.

The Crusaders did not begin their march into Egypt until November 20. They did not reach Al Manṣūrah, a fortified stronghold up the Nile, until February of 1250. Al Manṣūrah was an important military objective: Whoever held Al Manṣūrah could command Cairo, and thus bargain from a position of strength.

The attack on Al Manṣūrah was a complete disaster for Louis's forces. Robert of Artois, who led the vanguard, flagrantly disobeyed orders and stormed the city with the Knights Templar before the supporting troops had time to assemble. The vanguard was trapped in the narrow streets of Al Manṣūrah, and Robert was killed. Louis, who crossed the Nile with the main body of Crusaders, fought all day and ended in possession of the battlefield outside the city when the Muslims retreated to Al Manṣūrah. Over the next days, however, the Crusaders were unable to take Al Manṣūrah and became increasingly isolated and without defense. By April, Louis and his remaining army recrossed the Nile and began their retreat to Damietta. The Muslims were able to capture the fleeing army easily. Captives worth a ransom, particularly the king, were spared.

When news of the tragedy reached Damietta, the Genoese responsible for transport planned to pull out and leave the remnant of the Crusaders to their own devices. At this juncture, Margaret bargained successfully with the Genoese and persuaded them to stay.

Louis was released on May 6, 1250, after partial payment of his ransom. He chose to remain in Acre about four years, however, as a protector of those who were waiting to be ransomed. After his mother, Blanche of Castile, who had acted as regent in his absence, died, Louis returned to France in 1254, believing that his failure had been a punishment for his sins.

Sixteen years later, Louis headed another expedition. This time, the response to the crusading call was disap-

Louis IX, captured by the Muslim forces, was held for ransom and released after its partial payment. He chose to stay in Acre for four years as protector to those waiting to be ransomed. (F. R. Niglutsch)

pointing and the army was considerably smaller than the earlier one. Some of Louis's closest associates, including Jean de Joinville, his biographer and loyal supporter on the earlier campaign, refused the second time. The army landed at Tunis, for reasons that continue to puzzle historians. It was the end for Louis, who died of a fever. It was reported that his last words were "Jerusalem, Jerusalem."

SIGNIFICANCE

The failure of Louis's crusades cannot be alleged as the sole cause for the mood of disillusionment concerning the Holy War that was so pronounced a feature after Louis's time. Nevertheless, it was undoubtedly an important factor. Louis was revered even during his lifetime as an exemplar of Christian kingship; soon after his death, he became a legend.

It was hard for the people of an age that looked to heaven for visible signs of approval to believe that a crusade could possibly be an expression of God's will, since the greatest of Christian kings that people knew had tried and failed. The old Crusaders' cry, "God wills it," could never again have a convincing ring. Whether it was Louis's failure or the political uses to which the Crusades were put during the last half of the thirteenth century that led to the end of the era is unclear. Nevertheless, although crusades continued to be mounted on a small scale for the next three hundred years, no crusade ever again achieved the scope or size of the Seventh Crusade.

—*Mary Evelyn Jegen,*
updated by Diane Andrews Henningfeld

FURTHER READING

Hallam, Elizabeth, ed. *Chronicles of the Crusades: Eye-witness Accounts of the Wars Between Christianity and Islam*. New York: Welcome Rain, 2000. A large, lavishly illustrated volume of translated primary source documents and linking essays. Bibliography, index.

Hillenbrand, Carole. *The Crusades: Islamic Perspectives*. New York: Routledge, 2000. Chapters explore ethnic and religious stereotyping, daily life, the conduct of war, and more. Bibliography, index.

Irwin, Robert. "Muslim Responses to the Crusades." *History Today* 47, no. 4 (April, 1997). Presents a rich overview of the Muslim perspective on the Crusades. Provides photographs and a short list of further readings.

Jordan, William Chester. *Louis IX and the Challenge of the Crusade: A Study in Rulership*. Princeton, N.J.: Princeton University Press, 2000. This study concentrates on the development of Louis's character and his philosophy of rulership through his preparation for and involvement in his crusades. The text unites psychological analysis with detailed economic and political data. Includes maps, illustrations, appendices, and an extensive bibliography.

Lev, Yaacov, ed. *The Medieval Mediterranean: Peoples, Economies and Cultures, 400-1453*. Vol. 9 in *War and Society in the Eastern Mediterranean, Seventh-Fifteenth Centuries*. Leiden, the Netherlands: Brill, 1997. Explores the world of the Crusades and other military encounters in the Middle East and the greater Mediterranean area, including Muslim Egypt up to the fall of Constantinople in 1453. Topics include armaments and supplies, regional administration, and the impact of the Crusaders on rural populations.

Lloyd, Simon. "The Crusades of St. Louis." *History Today* 47, no. 5 (May, 1997): 37-43. The author presents a clearly written overview of Louis's legacy and achievements, especially his devotion to the Crusades. Includes several photographs.

Madden, Thomas F., ed. *The Crusades: The Essential Readings*. Malden, Mass.: Blackwell, 2002. A collection of previously published articles about the Crusades, including medieval sources, lay enthusiasm, patronage, Byzantium, and the subjection of Muslims. Bibliography, index.

Riley-Smith, Jonathan. *The Crusades: A Short History*. New Haven, Conn.: Yale University Press, 1987. A comprehensive history of the Crusades including the crusades to the East as well as the political crusades in Europe.

Runciman, Steven. *The Kingdom of Acre and the Later Crusades*. Vol. 3 in *A History of the Crusades*. New York: Cambridge University Press, 1987. The author devotes a chapter to Louis, and he also shows the Crusades from an Eastern perspective. Maps, bibliography, index.

SEE ALSO: 630-711: Islam Expands Throughout North Africa; August 15-20, 636: Battle of Yarmūk; 1040-1055: Expansion of the Seljuk Turks; November 27, 1095: Pope Urban II Calls the First Crusade; c. 1145: Prester John Myth Sweeps Across Europe; 1147-1149: Second Crusade; 1189-1192: Third Crusade; 1204: Knights of the Fourth Crusade Capture Constantinople; 1217-1221: Fifth Crusade; 1227-1230: Frederick II Leads the Sixth Crusade; September 3, 1260: Battle of Ain Jālūt; May 29, 1453: Fall of Constantinople.

RELATED ARTICLES in *Great Lives from History: The Middle Ages, 477-1453*: Baybars I; Blanche of Castile; Frederick II; Innocent IV; Louis IX; Saladin; Urban II.

Late 13th century
MAORIS HUNT MOA TO EXTINCTION

The arrival of Polynesian people, the ancestors of the Maoris, brought about the extinction of all species of the moa, a flightless bird, in about 170 years.

LOCALE: New Zealand
CATEGORIES: Cultural and intellectual history; environment

SUMMARY OF EVENT

In the 1830's, Europeans in New Zealand found large fossilized bones that contemporary scientists concluded belonged to enormous extinct birds. Richard Owen, a noted English comparative anatomist, published a number of papers on the bones, inventing the classification *Dinornis*, "terrible bird," a term perhaps suggested to parallel the name of another recent discovery, dinosaurs. These birds are known by the Maori word *moa*, a general term for fowl. Although early studies of the fossil bones eventually named more than sixty species of moa, standard modern classifications recognize only eleven, eight smaller species in the family *Emeidae* and three large species in the family *Dinornithidae*. DNA studies suggest that there were only two large moa species, one on North Island and one on South Island.

Moa are ratite birds, flightless birds with a flat breastbone. Ratites include contemporary flightless birds such as the ostrich, kiwi, rhea, emu, and cassowary. The moa ranged in size from the upland moa, at about 55 pounds (25 kilograms), to the giant moa, which weighed around 600 pounds (272 kilograms). Early reconstructions of the giant moa oriented its neck in an upright position so that it stood about 13 feet (4 meters) tall. More recent studies have concluded that the bird carried its head and neck horizontally, stretched forward. The moa had no wings at all. The largest of the moa eggs measured 10 inches (25 centimeters) in length. The total moa population at the time of human settlement has been estimated at 158,000.

Scientists now agree that hunting by the Polynesian ancestors of the Maori caused the extinction of all moa species. The number of original settlers is not known precisely, though mitochondrial studies of living Maoris suggest that the original colonists numbered about two hundred individuals. As no other large terrestrial animals lived on New Zealand, the moa became a main source of protein for the Polynesians, with a medium-sized bird feeding fifty people for a day. The birds were easy to catch, as they did not fear human beings. Before the arrival of the Maori, the adult moa had only one predator: the Haast's eagle, whose wingspan stretched 10 feet (3 meters). Perhaps the moa instinctively guarded against danger from above but had no time to learn to fear humans. Lack of specialized tools suggests that capturing moa was readily accomplished by snaring, spearing, or clubbing. More than three hundred midden sites exist, providing much information about the extent of moa hunting. A few sites are huge, occupying up to 300 acres (120 hectares) and served as processing centers for moa kills.

Traditional scholarship places Maori settlement in the tenth or eleventh century and the extinction of the moa six hundred years later. However, carbon dating of campfire sites places the arrival of the Maoris in the late thirteenth century and indicates that no moa were killed after the middle of the fifteenth century. A model proposed by R. N. Holdaway and C. Jacomb is consistent with the carbon dates. They presented five scenarios for moa extinction based on several variables: Either one hundred or two hundred people, either low or moderate population increase, killing one adult female bird weekly for either every ten or every twenty settlers, and either with or without habitat loss. The results situated moa extinction between 1380 and 1440, requiring at most 160 years, the most rapid extinction in history. Some Europeans reported sightings of smaller moa in the 1800's, but these claims are almost certainly mistaken.

A group of Maoris dance the ceremonial Haka in 1953. (Hulton|Archive by Getty Images)

The moa life cycle aided its demise. Although Holdaway and Jacomb did not consider loss of eggs in their model, the fact is that the largest moa eggs could feed a great number of people. Moa nesting-site remains indicate that the bird laid only one or two eggs at a time. From the small clutch size and a delayed rate of maturation, scientists conclude that the moa were like the majority of New Zealand avian species: A great number of individuals survived into adulthood, and the breeding population was close to saturation most of the time. The earlier estimates that extinction took six hundred years assumed that the Maoris cropped an annual surplus of individuals. In theory, the cropping of juveniles would not have stressed the species; however, the rapidity of extinction indicates that the early Polynesians mined breeding adults.

Two other factors may have played a role. The Maori burned much of the woodland habitat of the moa, notably along the eastern coast of South Island and also areas of the rain forest on the western coast. This fact was originally not recognized, and early scholars believed that the moa inhabited grasslands. A few moa remains were discovered in upland regions, though some scientists hypothesize that the loss of woodlands drove them to the uplands. In addition, the Maori ancestors brought dogs and rats with them, and it is possible that these species contributed to the extinction of the moa by eating their eggs or attacking the young. Putting these factors together leads to the conclusion that moa hunting, made easy by the birds' habits, the nature of their life cycle, the destruction of their habitat, and the introduction of predator species, doomed the birds to extinction.

The Maori ancestors used moa bone and claws to make needles, fishhooks, and beads, and they transported water in the large eggs. A piece from an ancient cloak reveals that they used the moa skin to make clothes. However, examination of the middens also shows that they wasted parts of the moa. They threw away extant necks still attached to the heads, for example. According to one interpretation, they wasted one third of the meat, though according to another account, such waste may have resulted from a large number of kills being brought to the campsites at the same time.

SIGNIFICANCE

In the latter third of the twentieth century, a contentious debate developed concerning the assumed ecologically sustainable lives of indigenous peoples. The roots of this controversy date back to the noble savage idea of the seventeenth and eighteenth centuries. It is a common belief that primitive peoples made use of all parts of the animals that they hunted, that they hunted only for their needs, and that they lived in harmony with their environment. Despite Owen's initial judgment that human beings caused the moa's extinction, early twentieth century ethnographers promoted the view that the Maori practiced conservationism. Others promoted the idea that the moa became extinct because of climate changes, disease, or other developments. Recent studies have not supported these views. The history of the rapid extinction of the moa, coupled with the evidence of waste, leads to the conclusion that the indigenous people did not necessarily live in a sustainable manner. Moreover, many other species of birds were brought to extinction by the Maoris. The same history of the extinction of megafauna by hunting and widespread clearing and burning of woodland characterize the habits of many prehistoric peoples in the Americas, Madagascar, and Australia, while in Africa and Asia, animals had time to develop fear of human beings as they moved into new territories. It is plausible that early human beings sought to acquire food and other necessities of life in the safest and quickest manner possible, with the least expenditure of energy, and without regard for the long-term effects.

—*Kristen L. Zacharias*

FURTHER READING

Anderson, Atholl. "The Extinction of Moa in Southern New Zealand." In *Quaternary Extinctions: A Prehistoric Revolution*, edited by Paul S. Martin and Richard G. Klein. Tucson: University of Arizona Press, 1984. Examines deforestation and dates moa remains.

Belich, James. *Making Peoples: A History of the New Zealanders, from Polynesian Settlement to the End of the Nineteenth Century*. Honolulu: University of Hawaii Press, 1996. The first two chapters of this book place moa hunting in the context of Maori life.

Cassels, Richard. "The Role of Prehistoric Man in the Faunal Extinctions of New Zealand and Other Pacific Islands." In *Quaternary Extinctions: A Prehistoric Revolution*, edited by Paul S. Martin and Richard G. Klein. Tucson: University of Arizona Press, 1984. Examines the extinction of moa and other species.

Holdaway, R. N., and C. Jacomb. "Rapid Extinction of the Moas (Aves: Dinornithiformes): Model, Test, and Implications." *Science* 287 (March 24, 2000): 2250-2254.

Trotter, Michael M., and Beverly McCulloch. "Moas, Men and Middens." In *Quaternary Extinctions: A Prehistoric Revolution*, edited by Paul S. Martin and

Richard G. Klein. Tucson: University of Arizona Press, 1984. A summary of sites of moa hunting remains with radiocarbon dating.

Whelan, Robert. *Wild in Woods: The Myth of the Noble Eco-savage*. London: IEA Environment Unit, 1999. A short book that traces the origin of the idea of the environmentally-in-tune savage and argues that the habits of primitive people could be very destructive to the environment.

Worthy, Trevor H., and Richard N. Holdaway. *The Lost World of the Moa: Prehistoric Life of New Zealand*. Bloomington: Indiana University Press, 2002. A scholarly work by two leaders on the field, this book details the enormous loss of species, including the moa, in New Zealand.

SEE ALSO: c. 700-1100: Settlement of the South Pacific Islands.

c. 1250
IMPROVEMENTS IN SHIPBUILDING AND NAVIGATION

Technological advances in shipbuilding and navigation provided mariners of the Middle Ages the means for safer and swifter sea journeys and led to increased cultural, intellectual, and religious integration, as well as economic and military expansion and colonialism throughout the Eastern Hemisphere.

LOCALE: Europe and the Middle East
CATEGORIES: Engineering; science and technology; trade and commerce; transportation

KEY FIGURES

Alexander Neckam (1157-1217), author of a treatise on the mariner's compass

Raymond Lull (c. 1235-early 1316), possible inventor of the nocturnal

SUMMARY OF EVENT

It is desirable to view the achievements of medieval maritime technology under two broad headings: the actual design and construction of sailing vessels themselves and medieval methods of navigation, including their purpose and application.

The construction of vessels both for commerce and for warfare underwent significant development during the high Middle Ages, with Byzantines, Arabs, Italians, and Norsemen all contributing to the process. Greek Byzantine ship designers contributed the dromond, the classic light navy cruiser for home defense and the suppression of piracy in the eastern Mediterranean.

This relatively long ship with reasonable beam was swift and maneuverable, rugged and deadly in ship-to-ship encounters. The dromond was provided with a type of armor plating, a devastating battering ram, positions for archers, and a series of heavy catapults for throwing missiles containing the dreaded Greek fire. It is reported that some shipboard catapults could throw a half-ton weight almost half a mile, thus making the older Roman technique of boarding the opponent obsolete. These admirable ships were propelled either by banks of oars or by lateen sails, triangular sails held to a mast amidships.

Though they were seldom naval adventurers, the Arabs, too, contributed to the art of ship construction during the Middle Ages. In sheer size, the Moorish crafts were exceptional, sometimes attaining a payload of more than three hundred tons. Never venturing far from shore, these Arabic ships were supremely handy underway and could dart to shelter whenever threatened by a superior force. Muslim shipbuilders also introduced to the Western world the practice of building roomy and comfortable cabins aft for captain, officers, and supernumeraries. They depended heavily on oar propulsion.

When sails were added, they were generally carried on two masts, the forward one holding a small sail, while the midship mast carried the far larger mainsail.

The famous "long ships" of the Vikings excite both historical and aesthetic interest, for many of their actual remains were unearthed in the twentieth century. The Norse vessels are widely regarded as among the most perfect that have ever been designed and executed. Capable of withstanding the rigors of their icy home waters, these long ships with graceful lines, high freeboards, and relatively narrow beams, the ends rising high and menacing, were equally ready to meet the Atlantic swells. Skillfully constructed, the sides were built of long strakes, overlapped one above the other to provide additional rigidity. At the same time, the strakes were warped and curved, to "build in" a natural tension, thus obtaining a "royal" sheer and additional strength. Though wide amidships, the Viking hull tapered neatly to a point at each end, for exceptional maneuverability. Though gen-

The Viking "long ships" were among the best seagoing vessels, capable of withstanding the icy waters of the northern seas as well as Atlantic swells on the open ocean. (Hulton|Archive by Getty Images)

erally worked with banked oars, the Viking ships could also mount considerable canvas and were probably able to beat into the wind. Finally, the Vikings pioneered the use of the rigid long keel, around which the sides of the ship could curve and swirl, supported by the strength of the ship's stout backbone.

The inventive Venetians led the Mediterranean in the sheer numbers of vessels they produced and maintained. The famed "Serenissima" perhaps employed Europe's first assembly line, a waterborne factory that in one day could turn out a finished and equipped galley. The main subassemblies of each galley were completed in separate warehouses and then brought together in sequence along one of Venice's many canals.

In form, the Venetian galley resembled an elongated and flattened Roman trireme, with an added apostis or overhanging main deck somewhat similar to that of a modern aircraft carrier. As in most medieval vessels, oars provided the prime motive power. They were arranged on the gunwales generally in groups of three, with three rowers working from each rowing bench. When employing sails, especially for long voyages, a huge lateen rig, often square, was hung from a single mast amidships. A box at the top of the mast housed the wheels and gears necessary to raise and lower this large area of canvas. The rigging had no permanent yards or stays, sheaves, or blocks; when the ship changed direction the whole rig had to be cast off to leeward. If a radical change of weather were encountered, the whole sail, tackle and all, was exchanged for one of different configuration or size.

Medieval mariners made great advances in handling their vessels. Most medieval craft were equipped with adequate rudders, or in the case of the Vikings with outsized steering oars mounted starboard. Their bite or penetration in the water was deeper, assisting in steering a straighter course and beating farther to windward when necessary. One of the significant advances was learning how to tack, or sail a zigzag course utilizing wind pressure not directly astern. Some could sail with the wind abeam and some even with the wind quartering on the bow, no mean achievement without highly developed standing rigging.

Sailing farther from land on longer voyages, medieval mariners needed reliable instruments to assist them in plotting their courses and positions. Early Egyptians and their Phoenician inheritors probably navigated at first simply by the position of the sun, keeping it on one hand or the other in order to determine their approximate direction of travel. If the Greek historians are correct, the ancient Greeks also sailed by the sun and did not sail at night. The Romans, copiers of older cultures in this case, made few navigational improvements, preferring to leave seafaring to other peoples when possible.

During the Middle Ages, however, the compass, the astrolabe, and the nocturnal each aided the sailor in finding either his direction or his latitudinal position. The invention of the compass has been claimed by many countries. Although probably of Asian origin, it is claimed to have been invented by the Finns, the Norsemen, and the Arabs. The use of a magnetized bar or needle is first mentioned in Western medieval texts around 1200 in the works of Alexander Neckam and Guy of Provins. Probably the principle of the lodestone always pointing north had long been known and utilized for centuries in Europe, but the high Middle Ages witnessed significant refinements in the art of compass construction and utilization such as the development of the compass card, or compass "rose," which marked the cardinal directional points. Early compasses probably were nothing more than needlelike pieces of soft iron inserted into a straw and later mounted on a wooden float. Medieval mariners skillfully compensated for "needle dip" and the vexatious deviation to which magnetic compasses are prone when near ferrous metals by inscribing special lines upon compass cards.

The astrolabe, ancestor of the common sextant, was the second important navigational aid available to medieval seamen. In essence the astrolabe is a device for measuring latitude, or one's position north or south of the equator. The astrolabe was a portable tool, though it generally required three men with steady hands to operate it: one to hold it, one to take the sights, and the third to read

A Venetian galley off the Dalmatian coast. Marco Polo is supposed to have traveled in such a ship. (F. R. Niglutsch)

the attached scales. The instrument itself was a circle constructed of a heavy material to make it easier to hold. In the center of the circle was a pin with a pointer pivoting about it, a pointer with its center line carefully marked. One end of the pointer was aimed at a heavenly body, generally the sun or the North Star. The observer placed his eye at the opposite end of the pointer and aligned the two ends upon the observed object. When this was done and the astrolabe was hanging exactly plumb, the altitude could be read on the attached scale. From the observation of the altitude of a known celestial object, it was possible to calculate approximately the latitude of the observing vessel. The astrolabe was not easy to use, however, for even in a moderate sea, it was difficult to hold it steady, and when sighting the sun, troublesome shadows could confuse the observer.

A third medieval navigational instrument, less well known than the compass or the astrolabe, was the nocturnal, possibly the invention of Raymond Lull of Mallorca. The nocturnal was also used to establish latitude, using the North Star as guide. Looking like a circular slide rule, the nocturnal consisted of three discs, containing respectively hours, dates, and the figure of a man, all pinned together, with a hole in the center. The object was held at arm's length, and the observer sighted the North Star through the center hole. The disc with the figure of the man on it was then rotated until his head lined up with the "pointer" star Kochab in the Big Dipper. The observer could than read the correction to be added or subtracted from the altitude of Polaris and arrive at latitude. One could also read the time of nigh from the third disc.

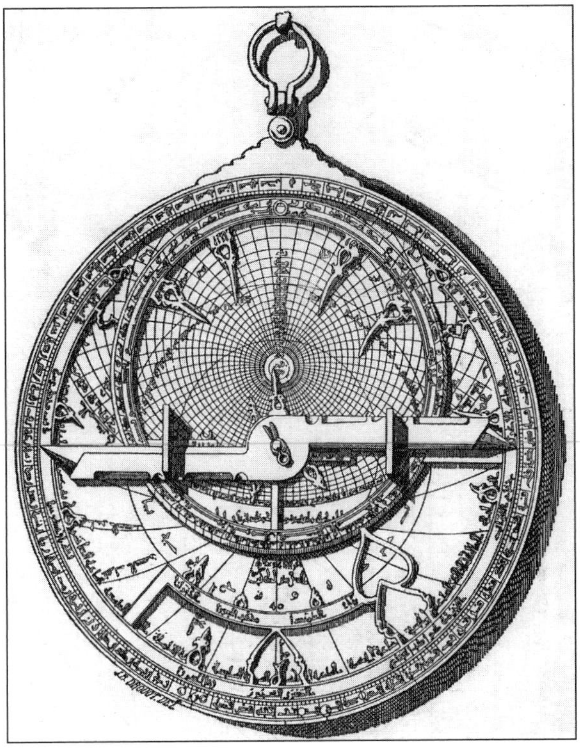

The astrolabe, ancestor of the common sextant, was an important navigational aid to medieval seamen. (Hulton|Archive by Getty Images)

SIGNIFICANCE

The advent of better ships and better navigational tools marked a new era in exploration and expansion throughout the Eastern Hemisphere, including increased interregional trade, the exchange of scientific and cultural ideas, religious conversions, military conquest, and the slave trade, especially out of Africa.

Where previously mariners navigated primarily using the sun and stars, technology such as the compass, the astrolabe, and the nocturnal, and precision ship design that took advantage of the strong and perpetual winds of the sea, increased the effects of maritime exploration on the known world.

—*Carl F. Rohne*

FURTHER READING

Aczel, Amir D. *The Riddle of the Compass: The Invention That Changed the World*. New York: Harcourt, 2001. A brief but detailed and thorough account of the invention of the compass. Also discusses the history of navigation to the fifteenth century

Calahan, Harold Augustin. *The Sky and the Sailor.* New York: Harper and Row, 1952. An account of the development of the art of navigation from the dawn of the astronomical art to the twentieth century.

Coggins, Jack. *By Star and Compass: The Story of Navigation*. New York: Dodd, Mead, 1967. A history of navigation featuring prolific maps and illustrations by the author.

Collinder, Per. *A History of Marine Navigation*. Translated by Maurice Michael. New York: St. Martin's Press, 1955. A study of the techniques and the mechanisms by which humans have navigated upon the sea since the time of the Phoenicians. It investigates the trade winds and the monsoons, the origin and development of the compass and the astrolabe, the beginnings of map making, and the problems of spherical projection.

Gardiner, Robert, and Arne Emil Cristensen, eds. *The Earliest Ships: The Evolution of Boats into Ships*. Reprint. Edison, N.J.: Chartwell Books, 2001. A comprehensive history of seafaring technology from antiquity through the Middle Ages.

Hewson, J. B. *A History of the Practice of Navigation*. 2d ed. Glasgow: Brown, Son and Ferguson, 1983. A useful and readable introduction to the instruments of navigation and their application.

Jobe, Joseph, ad. *The Great Age of Sail*. Translated by Michael Kelly. Lausanne, Switzerland: Edita Lausanne, 1967. A folio-sized volume illustrating in detail the five great centuries of the European sailing vessel.

McGrail, Sean. *Boats of the World: From the Stone Age to Medieval Times*. New York: Oxford University Press, 2002. Organized by region, covers the history of maritime travel and shipbuilding on every continent.

Taylor, Eva Germaine R. *The Haven-Finding Art: A History of Navigation from Odysseus to Captain Cook*. New ed. London: Hollis and Carter, for the Institute of Navigation, 1971. An up-to-date account of navigation "from Odysseus to Captain Cook."

Varende, Jean de la. *Cherish the Sea*. Translated by Mervyn Savill. New York: Viking Press, 1956. One of the best books available for the study of medieval ship design The author discusses technical subjects that are lightened with illustrative anecdotes. Terms and concepts are simplified and abstruse mathematical formulas are avoided when dealing with problems of practical navigation.

Whall, W. B. *Rovers of the Deep*. New York: Robert M. McBride, 1953. A work of particular interest dealing with the early Atlantic voyages of exploration after the time of Prince Henry the Navigator.

SEE ALSO: 850-950: Viking Era; 1150: Venetian Merchants Dominate Trade with the East; c. 1200: Fairs of Champagne; 1405-1433: Zheng He's Naval Expeditions; 1415-1460: Prince Henry the Navigator Promotes Portuguese Exploration.

RELATED ARTICLES in *Great Lives from History: The Middle Ages, 477-1453:* Abul Wefa; Prince Henry the Navigator; Levi ben Gershom; Raymond Lull; Alexander Neckam; Petrus Peregrinus de Maricourt; Zheng He.

c. 1250-1300

HOMOSEXUALITY CRIMINALIZED AND SUBJECT TO DEATH PENALTY

In the thirteenth century, a combination of religious and political factors led to the criminalization of homosexual behavior and the enactment of the death penalty for those engaging in practices labeled as sodomy.

LOCALE: Europe

CATEGORIES: Cultural and intellectual history; laws, acts, and legal history; religion; social reform

KEY FIGURES

Thomas Aquinas (1224 or 1225-1274), Italian theologian and philosopher

Saint Albertus Magnus (c. 1200-1280), German philosopher and theologian

Alain de Lille (c. 1128-1202), French philosopher and theologian

Peter Damian (fl. eleventh century), reformer who preached against homosexuality

SUMMARY OF EVENT

The criminalization of homosexuality developed in Europe gradually and cumulatively through the centuries, then spread to the New World. The prohibition first found expression in the Church, which led to the harsh attitudes adopted by secular institutions. Purported admonitions from the Old and New Testaments provided the basis for the prohibition of homosexuality. In addition, the writings of such figures as the church reformer Peter Damian, the canonical scholar Thomas Aquinas, and other clerics furnished justification for laws decreeing, in the thirteenth century, that homosexual acts be punishable by death.

Religious scholars through the ages cite two significant passages from Leviticus: "You shall not lie with a male as one lies with a female; it is an abomination," and "If there is a man who lies with a male as those who lie with a woman both of them have committed a detestable act; they shall surely be put to death" (18:22 and 20:13). Biblical scholars also interpreted the cautionary tale describing the destruction of Sodom as a warning against the dire consequences of homosexual behavior. When the men of Sodom expressed their desire to rape two angels who had appeared as male visitors, their city was destroyed (Genesis 19:1-25). Early in the Christian era, church and civic officials took this account literally and blamed natural disasters on homosexual conduct.

The devastated city of Sodom also provided a name for this grievous sin. In the broadest sense, sodomy is defined as any nonprocreative sexual act. While this meaning was generally accepted, a narrower definition took precedence among many moralists: that is, the anal penetration of one male by another. Both the general and the specific definition are still commonly applied in the twenty-first century.

In the eleventh century, the zealous reformer Damian denounced homosexuality as a sin comparable to blasphemy. He objected especially to sodomy among the clergy, a practice he saw as rampant. While he considered anal intercourse the most unclean act of all, he also listed solitary and mutual masturbation as sodomitical sins. He cited the death penalty that Leviticus invokes and urged that all sodomites be beaten, spat upon, chained, imprisoned, and starved. Although Pope Leo IX (1048-1054) did not sanction or institute such harsh plans for punishing homosexuals, Damian's claim that sodomy outranked all sexual sins gradually found acceptance in canon law.

In the next century, French philosopher and theologian Alain de Lille linked sodomy with murder and labeled the two acts as the most serious of all crimes. Taking up the same theme one hundred years later, Albertus Magnus (c. 1200-1280) described anal intercourse between two men as a detestable act, as a sin against nature, as an action marked by foulness and unbridled excitement, and as a contagious practice bound to infect the whole world.

Thomas Aquinas, who studied under Albert of Cologne, issued the decisive canonical declaration against sodomy and defined the word broadly. According to Thomas Aquinas, nature serves as the standard for Christian sexual ethics; therefore, carnal pleasure undermines natural harmony, which dictates that the only outcome of sex is procreation. He argued that while adultery, fornication, rape, and incest may cause harm, they are not as serious as sodomy because they can result in reproduction. Thomas Aquinas named four sexual acts that contradict nature: sex with animals, anal penetration, fellatio, and masturbation.

By the thirteenth century, the ecclesiastical obsession with homosexuality had spread to civil society as well. People outside the Church had long denounced sodomites and, given the opportunity, incorporated willingly into civil law the canonical censure of what were described as unnatural acts. During this era church and state were closely intertwined. As a result of such an alliance, the Church's campaign to cleanse the clergy of sodomites easily led to comparable tactics by civil authorities. Although acting under the guise of morality, rulers often accused political enemies, rebels, and other troublesome citizens of sodomitic acts. Whether true or not, such allegations served as convenient tools for maintaining political power. By this time, the Church had broadened its suppression of clerical homosexuality to include laypeople accused of heresy, witchcraft, and sorcery, especially after Pope Gregory IX established the Inquisition in 1233.

In the thirteenth century, the means of punishment for sodomy varied from country to country, but burning the guilty ones at the stake emerged as the favored form. Torture devices that slowly penetrated the anus also came into vogue. In one part of Italy banishment was prescribed for the first offense, followed by amputation of limbs for the second offense, then burning at the stake for habitual offenders. England, France, and Spain also took action against sodomites. In France, a man first proven to be a sodomite lost his testicles; convicted again, he lost his penis; and found guilty the third time, he met death by burning. A Spanish law decreed public castration for homosexual partners, who would then be hung by their legs until dead, their bodies left dangling in public permanently. English legal treatises recommended that sodomites be buried alive, or burned at the stake, or drawn and quartered.

SIGNIFICANCE

Although it has been some time since a person accused of homosexual acts was burned at the stake, the arguments promulgated by early religious zealots carry a familiar ring. Through the centuries the story of Sodom's destruction has been taken literally as an example of what will happen if homosexuality goes unchecked. The biblical admonitions, especially those from Leviticus, are still repeated, even though many biblical scholars point out that Leviticus contains numerous strictures that are impossible to follow or to enforce in contemporary society. Other scholars question the account of Sodom as presented in Genesis, noting that homosexual behavior is never mentioned specifically.

During the nineteenth century, the polite term "homosexuality" first came into use as a replacement for the more disparaging term "sodomy." Homosexuality continues to bedevil much of Christianity. The impact of moralistic teachings that date back centuries retain their unholy significance. The seeds that were planted early in Christian history grew to full fruition in the thirteenth century. Although the branches have been pruned through the centuries, the historical attitude toward homosexual behavior as an abomination that defies scriptural teachings still flourishes in the conservative Christian church and tradition-bound secular society.

—*Robert L. Ross*

FURTHER READING

Boswell, John. *Christianity, Social Tolerance, and Homosexuality: Gay People in Western Europe from the Beginning of the Christian Era to the Fourteenth Century.* Chicago: University of Chicago Press, 1980. An oft-cited study of Christianity and homosexuality in the period up to and including the Middle Ages in Western Europe, and a classic in the history of sexuality and in gay and lesbian studies. Bibliography, index.

Crompton, Louis. *Homosexuality and Civilization.* Cambridge, Mass.: Belknap Press, 2003. A comprehensive history of homosexuality, homophobia, and tolerance from 900 B.C.E. through 1868 C.E. Includes three sections on medieval Europe, as well as discussions of homosexuality in China and Japan during the same time period.

Dinshaw, Carolyn. *Getting Medieval: Sexualities and Communities, Pre- and Postmodern.* Durham, N.C.: Duke University Press, 1999. A concerted attempt to place the past in dialogue with the present, this text looks at issues of sexual identity and community in the late fourteenth century.

Fone, Byrne. *Homophobia: A History.* New York: Metropolitan Books, 2000. Chronicles the evolution of homophobia from the ancient world to contemporary society. Considers homophobia to be the last acceptable prejudice.

Goodich, Michael. *The Unmentionable Vice: Homosexuality in the Later Medieval Period.* New York: Dorset Press, 1979. Examines the varying attitudes toward homosexuality in the later Middle Ages, showing the gap between official Church dogma and the actual sexual behavior of the people.

Hergemöller, Bernd-Ulrich. *Sodom and Gomorrah: On the Everyday Reality and Persecution of Homosexuals in the Middle Ages.* Translated by John Phillips. 2d ed. New York: Free Association Books, 2001. An introductory text exploring the day-to-day lives of homosexual men in the Middle Ages. Includes chapters on the question of terminology, criminal law, everyday life, couplehood, religion, and more. Index.

Keiser, Elizabeth B. *Courtly Desire and Medieval Homophobia: The Legitimation of Sexual Pleasure in "Cleanness" and Its Contexts.* New Haven, Conn.: Yale University Press, 1997. Engages in an extended study of medieval homophobia to create a context for reading a fourteenth-century religious poem.

McNeill, John J. *The Church and the Homosexual.* Kansas City, Mo.: Sheed Andrews and McMeel, 1976. A Jesuit analyzes the historical and scriptural positions of the Roman Catholic Church toward homosexuality and sets out to create a revised and compassionate view of homosexuals and their relationship to spirituality.

Norton, Rictor. "The Historical Roots of Homophobia: From Ancient Israel to the End of the Middle Ages." In *Gay Roots: An Anthology of Gay History, Sex, Politics and Culture.* Vol. 2. Edited by Leyland Winston. San Francisco: Gay Sunshine Press, 1993. A comprehensive survey of the way homophobia developed and the way it continues to flourish.

Spencer, Colin. *Homosexuality in History.* New York: Harcourt Brace, 1995. An overview of homosexual behavior over the centuries that stresses its acceptance at various points in history as well as its rejection.

SEE ALSO: 1233: Papal Inquisition; c. 1265-1273: Thomas Aquinas Compiles the *Summa Theologica*; 1290-1306: Jews Are Expelled from England, France, and Southern Italy; July 2, 1324: Lady Alice Kyteler Is Found Guilty of Witchcraft.

RELATED ARTICLES in *Great Lives from History: The Middle Ages, 477-1453*: Saint Albertus Magnus; Gregory IX; Leo IX; Thomas Aquinas.

1258
PROVISIONS OF OXFORD ARE ESTABLISHED

The Provisions of Oxford transformed the centralized despotism of the Angevin Dynasty into a limited monarchy based on a written constitution.

LOCALE: Oxford, England
CATEGORY: Laws, acts, and legal history

KEY FIGURES

Henry III (1207-1272), king of England, r. 1216-1272
Innocent IV (c. 1180-1254), Roman Catholic pope, 1243-1254
Hugh Bigod (d. 1266), earl of Norfolk
Simon de Montfort (c. 1208-1265), earl of Leicester and a favorite of Henry III

SUMMARY OF EVENT

The origins of the baronial reform movement of 1258 can be traced to the early 1230's, when Henry III, a minor at his accession who came of age in 1227, began his personal rule. He was a man of multiple faces—at once aesthetical and arrogant, devout and extravagant, regnant and yet incapable of leadership—and, to quote a distinguished historian of early medieval England, "obstinate, petulant, and mercurial . . . sharp-tongued, rather ungenerous." Shrewd but not subtle, the king exhibited a disarming childlike simplicity—impervious to failures and mistakes. His reign was a period of tug-of-war between the monarch, bent on maintaining absolutism, and his barons, struggling to restrain him as well as his ministers and councillors.

The decade of Henry's minority—presided over by the regent William Marshal (earl of Pembroke, who died in 1219) and thereafter by Hubert de Burgh, the royal justiciar (1227-1232), followed by Peter des Roches and his nephew Peter des Rivaux (1232-1234) and their clerks—placed heavy strains upon the loyalty of the barons, whose traditional rights and privileges were repeatedly infringed on in the interests of peace and order. They were, however, schooled in the art of politics. In the crisis of 1234, they showed their understanding of the rule of law and of the interests of the community and supported Archbishop Edmund Rich and the clergy in forcing the king to give up his absolutist style and conform to the traditional ways of "the joint enterprise." In 1236, a baronial demonstration against foreign participation in royal governance forced him to take refuge for a time in the Tower of London, but the incident did not affect the makeup of the royal council. At a great council meeting in 1237, the barons forced the king to purge his small council and recruit "natural counselors" on pain of denying his request for aid. He submitted, albeit momentarily, appointing twelve men acceptable to the barons. Once the great council disbanded, however, the king recalled his own men.

The barons expected their monarch to assume the direction of government himself after the purge of his court and council, and they were even ready to put up with his mistakes and indiscretions in the conduct of business. Neither English nor even Norman, but French out and out, Henry unmistakably but unwittingly betrayed his misgivings about the English (though French-speaking) barons and preferred instead the Savoyard relations of his queen and his own Poitevin half brothers, the infamous Lusignans and their cronies, men who remained despised foreigners until their expulsion from England in 1258.

Ignoring the counsel of his barons, the king heedlessly pursued his dream of recovering the lost French possessions—Normandy, Anjou, Touraine, Maine, and Poitou. He paid soldiers, bribed allies, and sponsored revolts against the French king, although to little effect. He also antagonized the marcher lords in Wales by his territorial claims and his intervention in Welsh affairs. His actions provoked a rebellion at Gwynedd in 1256 by Llywelyn ap Gruffudd, grandson of Llywelyn ap Iorwerth, lord of Snowdon.

Finally, against the best advice of his barons and prelates, the king played into the politics of Pope Innocent IV and agreed to his offer of the Sicilian crown to his second son, Edmund. Until the death of Emperor Frederick II in 1250, Germany and Sicily had belonged to his Hohenstaufen family. The popes were determined to prevent the two kingdoms from being united and to destroy the influence of the Hohenstaufen dynasty. Henry's Sicilian venture in 1254 and the resulting papal ultimatum (from Pope Alexander IV, who succeeded Innocent in 1254) threatening him with excommunication unless he met the papal debts already incurred in the Sicilian war forced the king to divert the clerical contributions (tenths of the revenues of the church) for the Crusade (Henry had taken the cross in 1250) to Sicily—a venture that brought England nothing but the humiliating Treaty of Paris with France in 1259.

Yet Henry cannot be entirely faulted for all his actions and decisions. He patronized his half brothers because he wished to continue his influence in their homeland of Poitou and also because they could provide some security along the northern borders of Gascony, England's only substantial possession in France. Likewise, Henry's Sicilian scheme was not altogether misconceived. Sicily was wealthy, and an English candidature not only would block a possible French one but also was likely to provide a springboard for English expansion in the eastern Mediterranean.

The financial straits arising out of the Sicilian venture and baronial determination to obtain effective measures of reform before they could help their desperate sovereign form the background to the events of 1258. Henry summoned a parliament at Westminster on April 9, in which he conceded the baronial demand for reform. On May 2, an agreement was made in two instruments. According to the first, the king agreed to introduce reforms per baronial demands and even submitted himself to the penalty of excommunication in event of noncompliance. The second instrument contained the royal promise to reform the government by a body of twenty-four, made up of twelve of the king's council and twelve elected by the magnates, who were to convene at Oxford on June 11. The king swore to observe the majority decision of this body.

Meanwhile, the king, had called on his friends to come to the assembly at Oxford with their armed retainers. On May 25, a party of Burgundian knights and their followers were diverted from their Welsh engagement to Oxford. In self-defense, the reforming barons summoned their own armed retainers. Despite this tense atmosphere, parliament met at Oxford on June 11, and the twenty-four set to work upon a scheme of reform. This scheme is enshrined in what is known as the Provisions of Oxford. These were never formally published, but took the form of a series of memoranda.

Central to that scheme was the formation of a new council of fifteen, chosen by a complicated electoral method, including seven of the baronial twelve and three of the king's twelve, with a twelve-year tenure. It was to oversee royal ministers, appoint the great officers (especially justiciar, chancellor, and treasurer), and advise the king constantly on all matters "affecting both the king and the realm." It was to cooperate with twelve representatives of parliament, which met three times a year (October, February, and June). The justiciarship, vacant since 1234, was revived with the appointment of Hugh Bigod. Among his specific responsibilities as justiciar, Bigod was to act as chief justice with an annual tenure rather than as a leading royal minister with undefined authority, as was the case with traditional Angevin justiciars.

In these activities, the leading baron was Simon de Montfort, an aristocrat from northern France who was the king's brother-in-law and one time favorite. Montfort was absent from the Oxford parliament on June 11, negotiating the Treaty of Paris between England and France. He returned on June 14 and was present throughout the fortnight of the Oxford parliament. Together with the earls of Gloucester (Richard de Clare) and Norfolk, John FitzGeoffrey and Peter de Montfort (Simon's retainer but no relation), he was a member of the various committees concerned with reform. Although the reform movement was not solely Montfort's enterprise, his distinctive contribution lay, to quote an influential biographer, "in the moral imperatives which were part of the driving force behind the movement."

SIGNIFICANCE

Ultimately, the Provisions of Oxford limited the power of the king in England by constitutional means. The provisions passed a large measure of initiative over to each county, where four knights were to collect complaints against officials for transmission to the justiciar as he toured the counties. The justiciar was to have jurisdiction well as royal officials. The sheriffs were to be local landowners, salaried and appointed for one year only. The provisions also promised future reform of the Church and urban reforms for the city of London, the Jewry, the mint, and the royal household.

—*Narasingha P. Sil*

FURTHER READING

Brooke, Christopher. *From Alfred to Henry III, 871-1272*. London: Sphere Books, 1974. Provides a competent and compact critical history of the period.

Carpenter, D. A. "King Henry's 'Statute' Against Aliens: July 1263." *English Historical Review* 107, no. 425 (1992). Presents the text of the provisions, which includes a declaration for the exclusion from England of foreign-born persons and for the future governing of England by native-born men only.

Harding, Alan. *England in the Thirteenth Century*. New York: Cambridge University Press, 1993. A comprehensive account of the politics, government, and society of thirteenth century England.

Prestwich, Michael. *English Politics in the Thirteenth Century*. New York: Macmillan, 1990. Chapters 2 and 8 contain succinct analytical accounts of English society and government in the thirteenth century.

Sayles, George O. *The King's Parliament of England*. New York: W. W. Norton, 1974. A sound analysis of the constitutional achievements of the Provisions of Oxford.

Treharne, Reginald F. *Simon de Montfort and Baronial Reform: Thirteenth-Century Essays*. Edited by E. B. Fryde. London: Hambledon Press, 1968. A full account of Montfort's achievements as well as a competent analysis of the baronial reform movement.

Treharne, Reginald F., and I. J. Sanders, eds. *Documents of the Baronial Movement of Reform and Rebellion, 1258-1267*. Oxford, England: Clarendon Press, 1973. Superb selection and translation of primary materials.

Valente, Claire. *The Theory and Practice of Revolt in Medieval England*. Burlington, Vt.: Ashgate, 2003. Addresses the study of revolts and also discusses theories of resistance, Henry's role in the signing of the Magna Carta, and the concept of the community of the realm.

Weiler, Björn K. U., ed. *England and Europe in the Reign of Henry III, 1216-1272*. Burlington, Vt.: Ashgate, 2002. Looks at Henry's reign as it affected England and the Continent.

SEE ALSO: June 15, 1215: Signing of the Magna Carta.

RELATED ARTICLES in *Great Lives from History: The Middle Ages, 477-1453*: Hubert de Burgh; Henry III; Henry IV (of England); Innocent IV; Louis IX; Simon de Montfort.

1259
MANGRAI FOUNDS THE KINGDOM OF LAN NA

King Mangrai founded Lan Na, one of the two most important early Thai kingdoms. Through his alliance with Ramkhamhaeng of Sukhothai, the Thai people came to dominate the region now known as Thailand.

LOCALE: Northern Thailand
CATEGORIES: Expansion and land acquisition; government and politics

KEY FIGURES

Mangrai (1239-1317), king of Lan Na, r. 1259-1317
Ramkhamhaeng (c. 1239-c. 1317), king of Sukhothai, r. c. 1279-c. 1317
Ngam Muang (c. 1238-c. 1298), king of Phayao, r. 1258-c. 1298

SUMMARY OF EVENT

Through alliances and military conquests, the northern Thai (or Lao) king Mangrai established a powerful kingdom in territory that had been under Mon rule. Mangrai placed the capital of his realm in the city of Chiang Mai. He formed an alliance with King Ramkhamhaeng of Sukhothai that helped Thai people dominate the region that is now Thailand. Mangrai's kingdom of Lan Na also helped to safeguard mainland Southeast Asia from the Mongol emperors of China.

Before the Thai people established themselves as dominant in the land that is now known as Thailand, much of the region was under Khmer (Cambodian) or Mon rule. The Mon and the Khmer spoke related languages, and their descendants still live in Southeast Asia. In the northern part of Thailand, the Mon had established the kingdom of Haripunjaya in about the seventh century. Despite attacks by the neighboring Khmer, the Mon dynasty of Haripunjaya managed to remain in power until the thirteenth century.

Groups of Thai tribes had apparently migrated south from China over the course of centuries, settling in the river valleys of mainland Southeast Asia. In 1253, the Mongol conquest of the kingdom of Nanzhao, believed by many to have been a Thai state, stimulated this migration and caused an increase in the Thai population south of China. This population became the basis of the two closely related nationalities now known as Thai and Lao. Because the distinction between Thailand (earlier known as Siam) and Laos came much later in history, one can use the term "Thai" for the sake of convenience to refer to all members of this ethnic group. Scholars, however, will often use "Tai" to refer to the people speaking related languages and "Thai" to refer specifically to the people of contemporary Thailand.

The Thai tribes, in the broader sense of all members of the ethnic and linguistic group, generally lived in *muangs*, collections of settlements that acknowledged common chieftains or kings. These leaders, in turn, recognized the rule of greater regional powers, such as the Mon and Khmer dynasties. Mangrai was the son of the local Thai ruler of Ngoen Yang, located in the region of Chiang Saen. His mother was the daughter of a Thai chief from the Tai Leu group in Yunnan, China.

In 1259, Mangrai succeeded his father. The new ruler possessed considerable personal magnetism, and he rapidly brought the neighboring principalities under his leadership. Mangrai founded the city of Chiang Rai in 1262 and made it the capital of his expanding domain. He formed an alliance with Ngam Muang, the Thai king of Phayao, in 1276.

According to historical tradition, the clever Mangrai plotted to overthrow the Mon kingdom of Haripunjaya, the capital of which was in Lamphun, by enlisting the help of a merchant known as Ai Fa. Ai Fa was a trusted adviser of the Mon ruler, Yiba, and was appointed chief minister of Haripunjaya. Ai Fa adopted policies that angered the local people and estranged them from the Mon kingdom. Once popular opinion had turned against Haripunjaya, Ai Fa sent word to Mangrai that the capital was ready for easy conquest. In 1291 and 1292, Mangrai attacked the town and took it without great difficulty. Yiba fled and made some efforts at retaking his domain, without success.

The alliance with Ngam Muang helped Mangrai forge ties with Ramkhamhaeng, the powerful ruler of the growing Thai kingdom of Sukhothai. Ngam Muang and Ramkhamhaeng had studied together as children. In 1287, Mangrai and Ramkhamhaeng made their own alliance. According to legend, Mangrai helped maintain relations between Ngam Muang and Ramkhamhaeng when he convinced Ramkhamhaeng to apologize to Ngam Muang and pay reparations for seducing Ngam Muang's wife. The truth of the legend is uncertain, but the alliance with Sukhothai secured Mangrai's southern boundaries and enabled him to turn his attention to the north and successfully resist pressure from the Mongols, who ruled China.

Mangrai was continually seeking the best location for his capital. In 1268, he moved it from Chiang Rai to Fang. In 1286, he founded the city of Wiang Kum Kam, on the eastern bank of the River Ping. Still unsatisfied, in 1292, Mangrai decided to build a new capital, which he would call Chiang Mai, which means "the new city." He reportedly consulted with his two royal colleagues, and Mangrai, Ramkhamhaeng, and Ngam Muang are supposed to have planned the new city together. Present-day Chiang Mai continues to commemorate this collaboration with a statue of the three, known as the Three Kings Monument, which shows them discussing the plans on April 12, 1296, the date that is recognized as the founding of Chiang Mai.

With the building of Chiang Mai, the kingdom of Lan Na was fully established. From his seat of power there, Mangrai continued to hold off the Mongols. In 1301, the Mongols sent their greatest force against Lan Na, attacking the kingdom with 20,000 Chinese soldiers and Mongol archers. The Lan Na forces defeated the invaders, however, and afterward the Mongol emperors of China would be satisfied with payments of tribute from Lan Na.

Mangrai adhered to the Theravāda school of Buddhism and gave his support to this religion, which became the faith of almost all Thai people. He built temples and monasteries in Chiang Mai and in other parts of his kingdom. He also became known as a judge and lawgiver. The laws that he is supposed to have written have become part of the Thai legal tradition.

According to legend, Mangrai died when he was struck by lightning in the center of Chiang Mai. The place where he is thought to have died is marked today by a sacred pillar. Mangrai had three sons, and the second, Chai Songkhram, became king after his father's death. However, the passing of Mangrai resulted in a period of instability, and six kings took the throne of Lan Na from 1318 to 1328. In the latter year, though, Mangrai's great-grandson Khamfu came to power and reestablished the dynasty on a secure foundation. Descendants of Mangrai continued to rule Lan Na until the sixteenth century.

In 1558, as a result of struggles over the succession to the throne, the Burmese were able to establish their sovereignty over Lan Na. When Mangrai's dynasty finally became extinct, in 1578, the Burmese appointed their own kings to rule the northern Thai kingdom. Thailand, then known as Siam, fought with Burma over Lan Na for the next two centuries. In 1775, a Thai army took Chiang Mai. However, Lan Na continued to be ruled by its own king under guidance and control from Bangkok until 1939.

SIGNIFICANCE

Lan Na was a buffer that helped prevent the southward extension of Mongol power. The city of Chiang Mai became the most important cultural and political center of northern Thailand, and it continues to be Thailand's second major city, after Bangkok. By bringing northern Thailand together under a single rule, Mangrai and his descendants helped to establish a distinctive northern Thai identity.

—*Carl L. Bankston III*

FURTHER READING

Coedès, George. *The Indianized States of Southeast Asia*. Translated by Susan Brown Cowing. Honolulu: East-West Center Press, 1968. The classic work on Southeast Asian history. Chapter 12 gives a succinct history of the founding of Lan Na and discusses Mangrai's relations with Ramkhamhaeng.

Freeman, Michael. *Guide to Northern Thailand and the Ancient Kingdom of Lanna*. New York: Weatherhill,

2002. Illustrated guidebook and history that gives readers a good grasp of the places in the history of Lanna.

_______. *Lanna: Thailand's Northern Kingdom.* London: Thames and Hudson, 2001. Traces the settlement of northern Thailand by different ethnic groups, examines the kingdom of Lan Na, and describes the artifacts and architecture of the region.

Penth, Hans. *A Brief History of Lan Na: Civilizations of North Thailand.* Vancouver, Canada: University of British Columbia Press, 2001. Short, highly recommended history of the kingdom of Lan Na, covering its earliest times to its present-day influence, by a specialist in northern Thai history at the University of Chiang Mai.

Wyatt, David K. *Thailand: A Short History.* New Haven, Conn.: Yale University Press, 1986. Provides an introduction to Thai history, including coverage of the thirteenth century kingdoms.

Wyatt, David K., and Aroonrut Wichienkeeo, eds. and trans. *The Chiang Mai Chronicle.* 2d ed. Chiang Mai, Thailand: Silkworm Books, 1998. A translation of the major historical documents of Lan Na, from the thirteenth through the nineteenth centuries, together with helpful annotations and maps.

See also: c. 700-1253: Confederation of Thai Tribes; 729: Founding of Nanzhao; 832: Nanzhao Subjugates Pyu; 863: Nanzhao Captures Hanoi; 1204: Genghis Khan Founds Mongol Empire; 1271-1295: Travels of Marco Polo; 1295: Ramkhamhaeng Conquers the Mekong and Menam Valleys.

Related article in *Great Lives from History: The Middle Ages, 477-1453*: Kublai Khan.

September 3, 1260
Battle of Ain Jālūt

An Islamic Mamlūk Dynasty force dispatched by the sultan of Egypt defeated a Mongol army in Palestine, ending Mongolian expansion in the Middle East.

Locale: Aīn Jalūt, Palestine, near the town of Nazareth

Category: Wars, uprisings, and civil unrest

Key Figures

Baybars I (c. 1223-1277), Egyptian emir, r. 1260-1277, commander of Mamlūk forces

Quṭuz (d. 1260), Mamlūk sultan of Egypt, r. 1259-1260

Kitbuqa (d. 1260), Mongol commander in charge of Hülagü's forces in Syria and Palestine and a Nestorian Christian

Summary of Event

By 1258, the Mongols, under Hülagü (Genghis Khan's grandson and il-khan of Persia), had conquered the remnants of the old ʿAbbāsid caliphate, capturing Baghdad and slaughtering a good portion of the population in the process. Damascus, the capital of the Ayyūbid sultanate, fell in March, 1260. By the month of April, Hülagü's forces had advanced as far as Gaza in southern Palestine, thus setting the stage for an attack on Egypt, which at the time was ruled by the Mamlūks.

In response to the Mongol threat, the Mamlūk sultan of Egypt, Quṭuz, sent a force under his emir Baybars I to Palestine. It was this force that confronted and defeated a Mongol army under Kitbuqa at Ain Jālūt. The battle halted the Mongol advance on the Middle East and sealed the fate of the Crusader principalities in Palestine.

Starting in 1206, under the leadership of Genghis Khan, the Mongols (a collection of Mongolic and Turkic tribes) began to spread from their homeland in what is now Mongolia across China, Central Asia, and Eastern Europe. Genghis Khan died in 1242, and in 1251 leadership of the Mongol passed to Mangu, grandson of Genghis. Mangu's brother Hülagü was given the viceroyalty of Persia and was entrusted with the conquest of Mesopotamia and Syria.

In 1258, Hülagü's forces captured and destroyed the city of Baghdad, nominal seat of the ʿAbbāsid caliphate since 750 and one of the great cultural centers of the medieval world. After sweeping through Mesopotamia, Hülagü's armies invaded Syria, where in rapid succession they captured Aleppo and Damascus, putting an end to the Ayyūbid Dynasty, founded a century earlier by the Syrian sultan Saladin (r. 1174-1193).

In April of 1260, Mongol forces reached the southern city of Gaza. The capture of Gaza placed Hülagü in a position to attack Egypt, at the time ruled by the Mamlūk sultan Quṭuz. Hülagü sent Quṭuz an ultimatum demanding he submit to the power of the great khan. It was at this

THE MAMLŪKS C. 1300

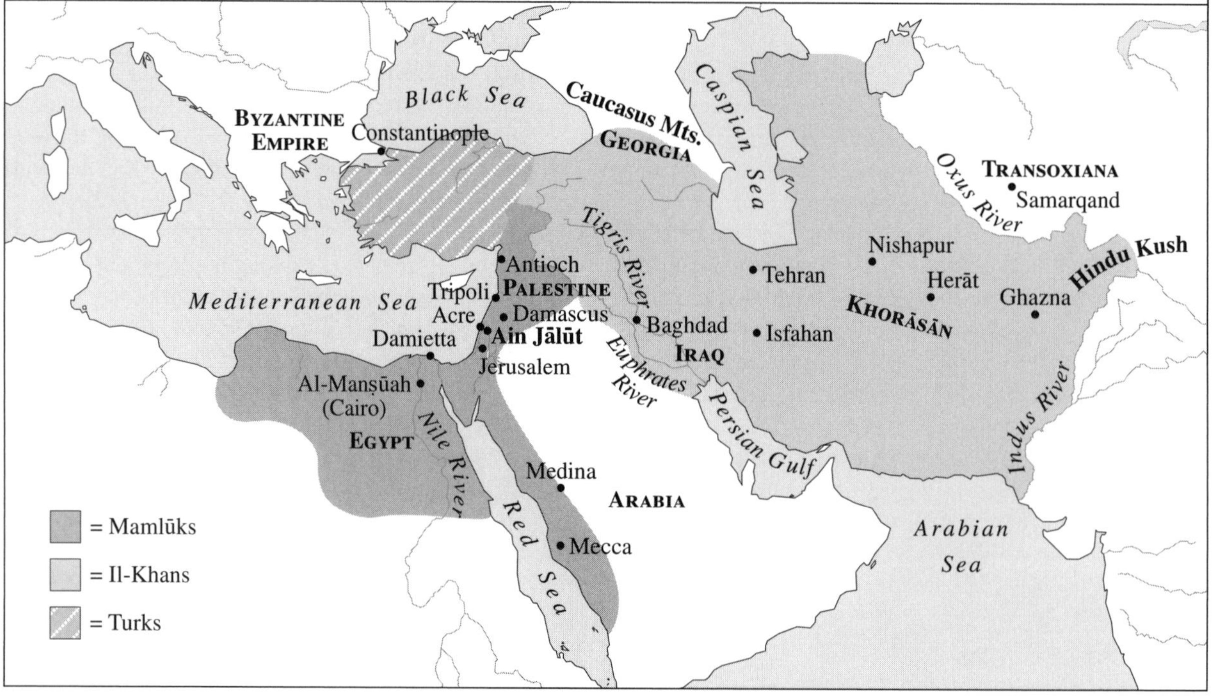

point, however, that Hülagü received news of the death of Mangu. The death of the khan brought about a confrontation between his brothers Kublai and Arigböge. Hülagü departed immediately for Persia in order to be closer to the unfolding events. The recently acquired lands of Syria and Palestine were left in charge of Hülagü's trusted general Kitbuqa, a Nestorian Christian. The forces at the disposal of Kitbuqa amounted to no more than twenty thousand warriors.

The size of the army in Kitbuqa's command was inadequate for the threat that it faced from the Mamlūk forces. However, the Mongols counted with the support of local allies. In 1244, Hayton (d. 1271), king of Little Armenia (now in Turkey), had voluntarily become a vassal of the Mongols. Hülagü had shown favorable treatment toward Christians, possibly because both his mother and his wife were members of the Nestorian sect. Consequently, Hayton saw in Hülagü a natural ally against the Muslims.

When Hülagü entered Syria in 1260, he was accompanied not only by Hayton's Armenian army but also by the Frankish troops of Bohemond VI, prince (r. 1251-1268) and count (r. 1255-1275) of Tripoli. Hayton's and Bohemond's services were generously rewarded by Hülagü. Bohemond VI tried to convince the barons of the kingdom of Jerusalem to join the alliance, but to the knights of this southern Crusader state, the Mongols seemed a greater threat than their Muslim neighbors. Shortly after the departure of Hülagü, Count Julien of Sidon (d. 1275) ambushed a Mongol patrol, killing one of Kitbuqa's nephews. Kitbuqa responded to this provocation by sacking the city of Sidon, thus ending any possibility of an alliance with the southern Franks.

Quṭuz was well aware that without the support of the Franks, who dominated the coast of Syria-Palestine, Kitbuqa would be unable to retain control of the recently conquered territories. Consequently, the sultan decided to move against the Mongols. A large Mamlūk army, under the command of Baybars, departed from Egypt on July 26, 1260. The Franks of Jerusalem declared their neutrality and allowed Baybars free passage through their territories. Baybars was allowed to camp outside the Crusader city of Acre and resupply his force; the emir, along with a number of Muslim notables, was even invited into the city as a guest of honor. After resting and reinforcing his army, Baybars advanced through Galilee, moving toward the valley of the Jordan River. Kitbuqa became aware of their advance, but he could not mobilize immediately because he had to put down an uprising of the Muslim population of Damascus.

Once the city was pacified, Kitbuqa moved south with a force that could not have numbered more than twenty thousand, including Armenian and Georgian contingents. On September 3, 1260, on the plains of Ain Jālūt, the two armies met. Since Baybar's forces were vastly superior, he deployed only part of his army in plain view of the Mongols; the rest of his troops were concealed in the surrounding hills. Kitbuqa charged valiantly with his cavalry against the Muslim forces. The initial Mongol charge failed to break the well-positioned Mamlūk lines, and as Kitbuqa's men withdrew to regroup, Baybars ordered a charge of his own. The Mongols made a stand, but at this moment the troops that Baybars had concealed in the hills came down charging on the flanks of the Mongol force. The great numbers of Mamlūk warriors overwhelmed the enemy.

Kitbuqa displayed tremendous courage during the battle, refusing to retreat as the Mamlūk warriors proceeded to surround his men. With the encirclement the battle was over. Only a small number of Mongols and their allies escaped; the great majority were killed in battle or captured. Among the captives was Kitbuqa, who was decapitated.

Following the battle, all Mongol presence in Palestine and Syria ended. Baybars and Quṭuz quickly occupied Aleppo and Damascus, taking revenge upon the Christian population who had recently collaborated with the Mongols. Hülagü sent a large Mongol force to Syria at the end of November to recover the lost territories and avenge the defeat. Although the Mongols were able to recapture Aleppo, they were halted at the Battle of Homs in December, 1281. Ain Jālūt had broken their momentum, and after Homs no further attempt was made to reconquer Syria-Palestine.

SIGNIFICANCE

The Battle of Ain Jālūt represented the end of Mongol expansion in the Middle East. The dynastic conflicts within their empire did not allow the Mongols to make an effective effort to recover Syria. By the time dynastic conflicts had been settled in the Mongol Empire, the Mamlūks had already consolidated their position in the area, making an invasion infeasible.

Beyond stopping the Mongol advance, the Battle of Ain Jālūt sealed the fate of the Crusader kingdoms of Palestine. Prior to the arrival of the Mongols, the Christian kingdoms were placed between the competing powers of Mamlūk Egypt and Ayyūbid Syria. The rivalry between these two Muslim states enabled the Franks to survive and even prosper at times. After Ain Jālūt, however, all the territories from Egypt to the Euphrates were controlled by a single Muslim power emanating from Cairo.

The aftermath of the battle left the Frankish baronies surrounded by the Mamlūks on all sides. Even though the Crusaders had provided assistance to the Mamlūks, once the Mongol threat dissipated, Baybars (by this time sultan of Egypt) felt comfortable beginning a prolonged offensive against the Christian principalities. From 1263 to 1291, the Crusader strongholds along the coast fell one by one. The city of Acre (the last Frankish principality in the Holy Land) was captured by Mamlūk forces in 1291. There would be no armed European presence in Syria and Palestine until 1917.

—Gilmar E. Visoni

FURTHER READING

Amitai-Preiss, Reuven, ed. *The Mamlūk-Ilkhanid War, 1260-1281*. New York: Cambridge University Press, 1995. A detailed account and analysis of the conflict between the Mamlūk sultanate of Egypt and the Mongol state in Persia. Also explores the Battle of Aīn Jalūt and other military battles of the time. Maps, bibliography, index.

Amitai-Preiss, Reuven, and David O. Morgan, eds. *The Mongol Empire and Its Legacy*. Boston: Brill, 1999. A wide-ranging examination of the Mongol Empire and its historical significance. Includes chapters on the making of the Mongol states during the early years of Maḥmūd Ghāzān, before his reign; Mongol nomadism; imperial ideology; and the letters of Rashīd al-Dīn. Genealogical tables, maps, bibliography, index.

Grousset, Rene. *The Empire of the Steppes: A History of Central Asia*. Translated by Naomi Walford. New Brunswick, N.J.: Rutgers University Press, 1970. An account of the historical development and influence of the nomadic peoples of Central Asia from antiquity to the eighteenth century. Maps, bibliography.

Maalouf, Amin. *The Crusades Through Arab Eyes*. Translated by Jon Rothschild. New York: Schocken Books, 1984. An account of the Crusades using contemporary Arab sources.

Morgan, David. *The Mongols*. New York: Basil Blackwell, 1987. A nonspecialist account of the Mongol Empire, this book is strongly recommended as introductory reading on the period. Maps, tables, bibliography, index.

Nicolle, David. *The Mongol Warlords: Genghis Khan, Kublai Khan, Hülegü, Tamerlane*. Poole, England: Firebird, 1990. An examination of the major Mongol rulers. Bibliographies, index.

Roux, Jean-Paul. *Genghis Khan and the Mongol Empire*. New York: Harry N. Abrams, 2003. An examination of Genghis Khan and the Mongol Empire's founding, endurance, and decline. Bibliography, index.

Runciman, Steven. *A History of the Crusades*. Vol. 3. Cambridge, England: Cambridge University Press, 1951. Part of a three-volume classic containing a comprehensive and detailed account of the Crusades. Illustrations, maps, and a genealogical table.

SEE ALSO: October 10, 680: Martyrdom of Prophet's Grandson Ḥusayn; c. 1120: Order of the Knights Templar Is Founded; 1204: Genghis Khan Founds Mongol Empire; 1225-1231: Jalāl al-Dīn Expands the Khwārizmian Empire; 1248-1254: Failure of the Seventh Crusade; April, 1291: Fall of Acre, Palestine; 1368: Tibet Gains Independence from Mongols; 1381-1405: Tamerlane's Conquests.

RELATED ARTICLES in *Great Lives from History: The Middle Ages, 477-1453*: Baybars I; Genghis Khan; Kublai Khan; Louis IX; Maḥmūd Ghāzān; Saʿdi; Saladin; Sorghaghtani Beki; Tamerlane; William of Rubrouck.

c. 1265-1273

THOMAS AQUINAS COMPILES THE *SUMMA THEOLOGICA*

Thomas Aquinas compiled the theological treatise Summa Theologica, *creating a work that attempted to combine secular and divine knowledge into one orderly rational system.*

LOCALE: Paris, France, and Naples, Italy
CATEGORIES: Cultural and intellectual history; literature; philosophy; religion

KEY FIGURES

Thomas Aquinas (1224 or 1225-1274), Italian-born Dominican theologian and philosopher
Albert the Great (c. 1200-1280), Swabian count who taught Thomas Aquinas at Cologne
William of Moerbeke (c. 1215-1286), archbishop of Corinth
Raymond of Peñafort (c. 1175-1275), Spanish canonist
Reginald of Piperno (1230-1290), confessor and companion of Thomas Aquinas
Étienne Tempier (d. 1279), bishop of Paris, 1268-1279, university chancellor

SUMMARY OF EVENT

Thomas Aquinas was born near Monte Cassino, where his parents placed him in the famous Benedictine monastery at the age of five. He was of heavy proportions with a large head, broad face, and blond hair. Although his friends called him "the great dumb ox of Sicily," history was to know him as Doctor Angelicus.

His career throughout was a distinguished one. He studied art and philosophy at the University of Naples. At the age of twenty-five, he began what could be called graduate studies at the University of Paris. He was master of theology at Paris from 1256 to 1259 and again from 1269 to 1272, adviser to Pope Urban IV and Pope Clement IV as well as to Louis IX of France, active participant in the business of his Dominican order, founder of a study house in Rome, popular preacher and debater, reorganizer of the University of Naples, and archbishop-designate of Naples, an office he declined. Death came while he was traveling to the Council of Lyons at the summons of Pope Gregory IX.

His *Summa theologiae* (c. 1265-1273; *Summa Theologica*, 1911-1921), an attempt to bring all knowledge, both secular and divine, into one orderly rational system, represents one of the most ambitious intellectual programs ever undertaken by a theologian. Aquinas deals with hundreds of theological problems, providing answers that are simultaneously consistent with Aristotelian and Platonic philosophies, medieval Christian theology, and theoretical and commonsense reasoning. The word *summa* in the thirteenth century had a technical connotation: a teaching tool for a curriculum of study in a specific scientific field. A *summa* was concise and abridged, ready to be used by the teacher and the students. Aquinas's work, of course, was facilitated by earlier scholarship, since virtually all revelationary religions that came into contact with Hellenism realized that sooner or later they must harmonize, in a monumental way, their deposit of faith with the dictates of reason. Philo and Moses Maimonides undertook the task for the Jewish tradition, Averroës for the Muslim. Within the Christian orbit, Aquinas was heir to a thousand years of scholarship that had attempted to forge a synthesis between faith and reason, revelation and observation.

Summa Theologica was created in a milieu of scholastic upheaval and in the midst of rediscovery of Aristotle. The university debate about Aristotle's inclusion in Christian theology was at a peak. Aquinas, according to his own writings, was one of the leaders of these debates in the university and theological communities in Paris.

The teaching of Saint Augustine had dominated Western thought for more than eight hundred years, and Augustinian thought insisted that in their search for truth, humans must depend on inner ideas rather than sensory experience. Aristotle had said the opposite, and it was Aristotle's insistence on empirical knowledge and the value of sense experience that caused the dichotomy between the two schools of thought. In Aquinas's time, the works of Aristotle were beginning to appear in translations accompanied by the commentaries of Arabian scholars, and French philosophers were asserting that philosophy was independent of revelation. The question was whether Aristotle could be adequately tamed to Christian theology in order to prevent weakening of the faith and even heresy.

In learning about such matters, Aquinas was greatly indebted to his famous teacher at Paris and Cologne, the eminent Albert the Great (Albertus Magnus). The contents of books of "sentences" commenting on the Scriptures and the church fathers were so influential in calling attention to the need for theological scholarship that Aquinas himself responded by first writing a *Commentary on the Sentences* of Peter Lombard. The new Latin translations of Aristotle prepared by William of Moerbeke and the early thirteenth century translation of Averroës were influential in Aquinas's conception and execution of his great work.

When Aquinas was teaching in Italy, the noted Spanish Dominican canonist Raymond of Peñafort urged him to write a new kind of *summa* as a guide for Dominican missionaries in Spain. This *Summan contra Gentiles* was directed in great measure against the radical Christian Averroists and Muslim intellectuals. According to Aquinas's fellow student Bartholomew of Lucca, the plan of the great *Summa theologiae* was conceived at Rome in 1265. Ninety-three major questions had been answered when death came to Aquinas, and the work was completed by his confessor and companion Reginald of Piperno, who extracted material from Aquinas's earlier work on Lombard's *Sententiarum libri IV* (1148-1151; *The Books of Opinions of Peter Lombard*, 1970; better known as *Sentences*), mainly from book four.

Recognizing in an enlightened way the desirability of harmonizing Aristotle and Arabic science with Christian revelation (instead of barring non-Christian scholarship as the Obscurantists insisted on doing), the *Summa Theologica* sets out to establish once and for all a compatibility between divine and human knowledge, theology and philosophy, faith and reason, and, in a sense, Plato and Aristotle. It is this kind of successful synthesis that made Aquinas indispensable to Christian theology. To cope with questions in which reason can make little progress, such as the nature of the Divine Being or Christ as the mediator of transcendency and love, Aquinas included a third epistemological category by which such knowledge was possible through a mix of reason and revelation.

Saint Thomas Aquinas. (Library of Congress)

He made his reputation where even Albert the Great had failed. Aquinas insisted that the truths of faith and those of sense experience are compatible and complementary; some truths, such as the mystery of the Incarnation, can be known only through revelation, while others, such as knowledge of the composition of earthly things, can be known only through sense experience. Moreover, Aquinas took a further step forward: Some truths require both revelation and sense experience for their perception, and among such truths he included human awareness of God. Humans become aware of God through knowledge of the material world around them, but in order to comprehend the highest truths about God one needs revelation as well. Aquinas's realism placed the universals firmly in the human mind, in contrast to the extreme realists who insisted that such universals existed independently of the human mind. The argument actually involved Platonism more than Aristotelianism. In this sense he was more like Augustine, but he used Platonic notions only when Aristotelian concepts failed; namely, he used Plato's ideas of emanation and return, and efficient and final cause.

Aquinas was concerned to show through dialectic that all revealed knowledge could be demonstrated as being not contrary to reason even if every item could not be logically proven. He relied heavily on three Aristotelian hypotheses: that since cognition starts with sense perception, then argumentation must begin with facts about the natural world; that a distinction must be made between substance and accident; and that a polarity exists between potency and action.

At first blush, *Summa Theologica* seems like a cut-and-paste project covering a collage of quasi-related topics. On closer scrutiny, however, one finds that the work is a meticulously unified and masterfully argued line of analogic reasoning, leading to a unified system of theological metaphysics. The work is in three parts, and thirty-eight sections supply answers to some 630 theological questions by quoting authorities, notably Augustine and Aristotle, and by applying impeccable logic. In the process, Aquinas answers some ten thousand objections to his own conclusions.

SIGNIFICANCE

Summa Theologica remains the greatest exposition of Christian ethics. It represents the apex of the synthesis between classical and Christian learning that had been going on since the second century. By distinguishing between philosophy and theology, it facilitated the development of Western philosophy as a distinct discipline. There was opposition to his work from Franciscans and some Dominicans; and it was condemned in 1277 by Étienne Tempier, bishop of Paris and chancellor of the university. Despite such detraction, Thomas Aquinas was canonized in 1328 and declared a doctor of the Church in 1567. Pope Leo XIII made Thomism the basis for instruction in all Roman Catholic schools, and Pius XII affirmed in an encyclical that Thomist philosophy should be regarded as the surest guide to Catholic doctrine; all departure from it should be condemned. The Roman Catholic Church, at the urging of Belgian theologians, among others, has now tended to tone down the bold rationalism of Aquinas.

The monumental work of the *Summa Theologica* shook the thirteenth century scholastic and theological worlds, as Karl Marx's writings shook political and moral sensibilities and institutions in the nineteenth and twentieth centuries. The success of Aquinas's work is attributed to his pedagogical skill rather than to his sainthood, mysticism, or complex philosophy. A closer scrutiny of his writing reveals a man of unwavering faith, with a compassionate soul and fatherly warmth, always aware of his limitations and always in search of God.

—*Lowell H. Zuck, updated by Chogollah Maroufi*

FURTHER READING

Boyle, Leonard. *The Setting of the "Summa Theologiae" of Saint Thomas*. Toronto, Canada: Pontifical Institute of Mediaeval Studies, 1982. A brief and thorough intellectual history of the *Summa*.

Eschmann, Ignatius Theodore. *The Ethics of Saint Thomas Aquinas: Two Courses*. Edited by Edward A. Synan. Toronto, Canada: Pontifical Institute of Mediaeval Studies, 1997. A treatment of the ethical system put forward by Aquinas in the *Summa*.

Gilson, Etienne. *The History of Christian Philosophy in the Middle Ages*. New York: Random House, 1955. This survey of the whole of medieval Christian philosophy puts Thomism in its historical context.

Kenny, Anthony. *Aquinas*. Oxford, England: Oxford University Press, 1980. The author, an eminent Oxford philosopher, gives a lucid, brief, and accessible account of Aquinas's theological philosophy.

Knasas, John, ed. *Thomas Papers*. Vol. 6. Houston, Tex.: Center of Thomist Studies, 1994. A challenging book, discussing the evolution of Aquinas's philosophy in various forms. Especially relevant is the section titled "Neo-Thomism, and Christian Philosophy."

Martin, C. F. J. *Thomas Aquinas: God and Explanations*. Edinburgh: Edinburgh University Press, 1997. An analysis of the relationship between science, reason, and divinity in Aquinas's thought.

Martin, Christopher, ed. *The Philosophy of Thomas*

Aquinas: Introductory Reading. London: Routledge, 1988. This work contains a representative sampling of all of Aquinas's important works, including an ample selection of his *Summa*, with excellent introductions of each selection.

Nichols, Aidan. *Discovering Aquinas: An Introduction to His Life, Work, and Influence*. Grand Rapids, Mich.: William B. Eerdmans, 2003. An introduction to Aquinas's thought and its historical impact.

SEE ALSO: 936: Khitans Settle Near Beijing; c. 950: Court of Córdoba Flourishes in Spain; 1100-1300: European Universities Emerge; c. 1150: Moors Transmit Classical Philosophy and Medicine to Europe; c. 1250-1300: Homosexuality Criminalized and Subject to Death Penalty; November 18, 1302: Boniface VIII Issues the Bull *Unam Sanctam*; c. 1310-1350: William of Ockham Attacks Thomist Ideas.

RELATED ARTICLES in *Great Lives from History: The Middle Ages, 477-1453:* Peter Abelard; Saint Albertus Magnus; Saint Anselm; Averroës; Avicenna; Boethius; Saint Bonaventure; Jean Buridan; Saint Dominic; John Duns Scotus; al-Ghazzālī; Gregory IX; Louis IX; Moses Maimonides; Alexander Neckam; Nicholas of Autrecourt; Raymond of Peñafort; Siger of Brabant; Thomas Aquinas; Vincent of Beauvais; William of Auxerre; William of Moerbeke; William of Ockham; William of Saint-Thierry.

1270-1285
YEKUNO AMLAK FOUNDS THE SOLOMONID DYNASTY

Yekuno Amlak overthrew the Zagwe Dynasty in 1270, proclaimed himself emperor of Ethiopia, and founded the Solomonid Dynasty, which produced a succession of illustrious monarchs. These monarchs built dynamic political and cultural institutions that allowed the Christian kingdom to overcome various internal struggles and to survive the incursion of Islam.

LOCALE: Northeast Africa and Ethiopia
CATEGORY: Government and politics

KEY FIGURES

Yekuno Amlak (d. 1285), founder of the Solomonid Dynasty, r. 1270-1285

Lalibela (fl. c. mid-twelfth century-c. 1221), Zagwe ruler, r. c. 1181-c. 1221, who ensured survival of Ethiopian state after the fall of the Aksumites

Yitbarek (d. 1268), last ruler of the Zagwe Dynasty, r. 1260-1268

Iyasus Moa (d. 1292), saint, important ally of Yekuno Amlak

Tekle Haymanot (d. 1312), monk and saint, who played important role in the rise of the Solomonids

Amade Tseyon (d. 1344), Ethiopian emperor, r. 1314-1344

Zera Yacob (1399-1468), Ethiopian emperor, r. 1434-1468

SUMMARY OF EVENT

After the reign of the Zagne Dynasty's last great king, Lalibela, the Zagwe hold over Ethiopia was weakened greatly by continuous succession struggles aggravated by the incursion of Islam toward the eastern border provinces. The weakening of central authority as well as the fear of Islamic resurgence galvanized the opposition to the Zagwe even in the core Christian areas. The anti-Zagwe movement was particularly strong among the Amharic-speaking Christian community of Shewa, which was on the forefront of the struggle against Muslim expansion in the east and was keen on dominating the trade routes that led to the port of Zeila on the coast. In 1268, Yekuno Amlak (also known as Tesfa Iyesus), one of the Amhara chiefs, succeeded in defeating Yitbarek, the last Zagwe king. Yekuno Amlak declared himself emperor in 1270 and founded what came to be known as the Solomonid Dynasty.

In an apparent strategy to legitimize his military victory, Yekuno Amlak presented his rebellion not as an act of insurgency against the Zagwe but as a movement to restore the old Aksumite line. He claimed ancestry from the old Aksumite rulers, who in turn were believed to have descended from the legendary king and founder of Ethiopian dynasties Menelik I, the son of King Solomon of Israel and Queen Sheba of Ethiopia. The sources for this legend appear to have been the bits and pieces of information relating to Solomon and Sheba from the Bible (1 Kings 1-13) and other Judaic, Christian, and Islamic literature.

By the thirteenth century, a fully developed narrative on the origin of the Solomonid rulers was circulating in Ethiopia in the form of a royal chronicle called the *Kebra nagast*, or the glory of the kings (fourteenth century; partial English translation, 1997). The chronicle narrates the story of how the union of King Solomon of Israel and Queen Sheba of Ethiopia resulted in the birth of Menelik I, the first Ethiopian emperor, from whom the rest of the Aksumite rulers and the later Solomonid kings were descended. By associating themselves with the House of David, the Ethiopian kings were clearly aiming at establishing a relationship with Christ himself, thereby creating an aura of divinity that arguably enhanced their legitimacy in the eyes of their Christian subjects.

Ethiopian legend maintains that on his return from a visit to his father in Jerusalem, Menelik I brought the Ark of the Covenant to Ethiopia. The Ark, which plays a central symbolic role in Ethiopian Christianity, is believed to still reside at the Church of St. Mary of Zion in Aksum. The coming of the Ark of the Covenant from Jerusalem to Ethiopia is said to symbolize the transfer of God's Covenant from Israel to Ethiopia.

Yekuno Amlak appears to have been greatly aided by the Ethiopian Orthodox Church in consolidating his rule over the Amharic- and Tigrigna-speaking areas of the northern and central highlands of Ethiopia. The church itself was eager to see the rise of a dynamic political leadership capable of challenging the Islamic threat and launching further campaigns against the pagan elements in the country to create favorable conditions for the further spread of Christianity. The highly venerated thirteenth century monk Iyasus Moa (abbot of the monastery of Debre Hayq in Wello) and his student Tekle Haymanot (founder of the famous monastery of Debre Libanos in Shewa) were said to have played key roles in the rise of the Solomonid Dynasty and in cementing the church-state alliance that characterized the Ethiopian sociopolitical order until recent times. In return for its service and loyalty to the Solomonid Dynasty, the Ethiopian Orthodox Church enjoyed generous imperial patronage including extensive land grants.

Despite a brief period of political turmoil following the death of Yekuno Amlak in 1285, Solomonid rule in Ethiopia during the medieval period was characterized by remarkable political cohesion, territorial expansion, and cultural regeneration. The most famous of the Solomonid emperors, Amade Tseyon and Zera Yacob, carried out sweeping reforms in the army and administration and conducted the greatest campaigns of territorial expansion that Ethiopian rulers had ever undertaken since the time of the Aksum king Ezana, who ruled in the fourth century.

Yekuno Amlak's successors directed their efforts first against the Muslim principalities of Ifat, Hadya, Fatagar, Dawaro, Bali, and Adal. These Muslim sultanates had taken, by the thirteenth century, virtual control of much of the area, extending from the eastern edges of the Ethiopian plateau to the coast. This Islamic resurgence in the Horn of Africa posed a serious challenge to the Christian kingdom by threatening its access to the port of Zeila (the most strategic outlet for Ethiopia by then) and by undermining its control over the trade routes that branched out to the rich resource areas in the south. Through a series of forceful campaigns, the Solomonid rulers defeated the Muslim sultanates in the east and consolidated the Christian domain. Effective control over the vital trade routes that connected the country with its Red Sea outlets led to flourishing commerce and to remarkable literary and artistic revival in medieval Ethiopia.

SIGNIFICANCE

The rise of the Solomonid Dynasty in the second half of the thirteenth century provided the Christian polity an effective political leadership and a strong ideology with which it was able to meet the challenges of Islamic resurgence in the Horn of Africa. Successive Solomonid kings, starting with Yekuno Amlak, exploited skillfully the myth of their descent from Sheba and Solomon to enhance their legitimacy. The fact that Solomonid rule in Ethiopia lasted until the overthrow of Emperor Haile Selassie (r. 1930-1974) in 1974 is a testimony to the profound influence of the legend of descent in Ethiopia.

—*Shumet Sishagne*

FURTHER READING

Crummey, Donald. *Land and Society in the Christian Kingdom of Ethiopia: From the Thirteenth to the Twentieth Century.* Urbana: University of Illinois Press, 2000. A comprehensive historical survey of Christian Ethiopia and issues of land tenure and property from the time of the Solomonids through the twentieth century. Maps, bibliography, index.

Hausman, Gerald, ed. *The Kebra Nagast: The Lost Bible of Rastafarian Wisdom and Faith from Ethiopia and Jamaica.* New York: St. Martin's Press, 1997. Presents translated selections with an introductory essay and chapters on the historical implications of the text, the ancestral tree, and more. Bibliography, index.

Henze, Paul B. *Layers of Time: A History of Ethiopia.* New York: Palgrave, 2000. A readable general work that is especially useful in tracing the history of the country's expansion southward during medieval times under the leadership of a series of capable Solomonid rulers. It also includes interesting information on daily life, art, architecture, religion, culture, and customs.

Huntingfod, G. W. B., ed. *The Glorious Victories of Amda Tseyon, King of Ethiopia*. Oxford, England: Clarendon Press, 1965. A good translation of the chronicle of the famous medieval Ethiopian emperor that details Amde Tseyon's military exploits in the east against Muslim forces in the early decades of the fourteenth century.

Marcus, Harold G. *History of Ethiopia*. New ed. Berkeley: University of California Press, 2002. A general survey of Ethiopian history from ancient times to the present. Illustrations, bibliography, index.

Munro-Hay, Stuart. *Ethiopia, the Unknown Land: A Cultural and Historical Guide*. London: I. B. Tauris, 2002. A well-researched and comprehensive description of the major historical landmarks in Ethiopia.

Pankhurst, Richard K. P., ed. *The Ethiopian Royal Chronicles*. Addis Ababa, Ethiopia: Oxford University Press, 1967. A compilation of royal chronicles, including those of the medieval Solomonid rulers. Illustrations, maps.

Tadesse Tamrat. *Church and State in Ethiopia, 1270-1527*. Oxford, England: Oxford University Press, 1972. The definitive work on the history of medieval Ethiopia by a well-known authority in the field.

_______. "The Abbots of Dabr Hayq, 1248-1535." *Journal of Ethiopian Studies* 8, no. 1 (1970). A succinct account of the prominent role in religion and in the political sphere played by the leaders of the most famous monastery in Ethiopia.

Trimingham, J. Spencer. *Islam in Ethiopia*. New York: Clarendon Press, 1952. Useful study of the history of Islam in Ethiopia, with interesting analysis of the interaction between Christianity and Islam at the local level. Maps, bibliography, index.

Ullendorff, Edward. *Ethiopia and the Bible*. London: British Academy, 1968. Written by one of the foremost authorities in Semitic studies, the book examines Ethiopia's responses to the Bible as well as the evolution of the story of the Queen of Sheba and King Solomon. Bibliography.

Yaoh, John Gay, comp. *Christianity in Ethiopia and Eritrea: An Annotated Bibliography*. Amman, Jordan: Royal Institute for Inter-Faith Studies, 1998. Provides an annotated source for the further study of Ethiopia and its history with Christianity.

SEE ALSO: c. 500-1000: Rise of Swahili Cultures; 630-711: Islam Expands Throughout North Africa; 12th century: Coins Are Minted on the Swahili Coast; c. 1181-1221: Lalibela Founds the Christian Capital of Ethiopia.

RELATED ARTICLES in *Great Lives from History: The Middle Ages, 477-1453*: Ibn Baṭṭūṭah; Lalibela.

1271-1295
TRAVELS OF MARCO POLO

The travels of Marco Polo in Asia stimulated Western interest in Eastern commerce and influenced later explorers, including Christopher Columbus.

LOCALE: Venice (now in Italy), Asia Minor, China, and Persia

CATEGORIES: Trade and commerce; cultural and intellectual history

KEY FIGURES

Marco Polo (c. 1254-1324), a Venetian traveler and merchant

Niccolò Polo (fl. 1260's), his father, also a Venetian merchant

Maffeo Polo (fl. 1260's), Niccolò's brother, also a Venetian merchant

Gregory X (1210-1276), Roman Catholic pope, 1271-1276

Kublai Khan (1215-1294), Mongol ruler, r. 1260-1294, and Yuan Dynasty ruler, r. 1279-1294

SUMMARY OF EVENT

In 1254, the year in which Marco Polo is believed to have been born, Italy was divided into warring city-states, and Genoa and Venice vied for naval dominance. Although deep in the Middle Ages, thirteenth century Europe witnessed an amazing increase in geographical knowledge as well as an increase in contact between Western Europe and the Far East. China, remote and exotic, held such a fascination for Europeans that tales of travel to that land were eagerly sought and circulated by the educated.

Before the Tatar (Mongol) conquest of Asia Minor

and the consequent arrival of Tatar embassies in the West by the late thirteenth century, contact with the Far East had already been made by such men as Giovanni da Pian del Carpini and William of Rubrouck, the latter being sent by Louis IX of France. Trade routes and opportunities that had not existed since the time of Roman rule were finally reopened. By 1260, Niccolò Polo and Maffeo Polo, the father and uncle of Marco Polo, members of an adventurous Venetian family, had left the young Marco behind and begun their epic journey eastward to the court of the khan of the Pipchak Tatars at Serai. Their hardships were compensated for by trading so successful that the brothers lingered for more than a year while amassing considerable profit. When they decided to return to Venice, however, they found that their route was cut off by local wars and mutinies, so they made a momentous decision to visit the court of the great khan of China. In Beijing, they were received graciously by that powerful medieval monarch, and after concluding business there, they were urged to return home and bring back Christian missionaries from the West for the further edification of the royal court. To expedite their journey, they were given the services of a trusted Tatar guide.

After an arduous journey overland to Venice, they learned in 1268 that Pope Clement IV had died and that no successor had yet been elected. Having decided to undertake a second journey east, they managed to secure from the new pope, Gregory X, the services of two inept Dominicans, who soon decided to desert the mission. The Polos, nevertheless, went back to Beijing, this time taking with them Marco, the teenage son of widower Niccolò Polo and a lad destined to leave a lasting record of his wanderings in the company of his father and uncle.

Marco and his two relatives began their remarkable journey in 1271, going by sea to Acre. After arriving at the mouth of the Persian Gulf, they abandoned their plan of traveling by sea and turned north, following the ancient caravan routes through Iraq and Persia, traversing Persia and Turkmenistan until they reached the Oxus River (now the Amu Dar'ya). They crossed the plain of Pamir and traveled across the incredible desolation of the Gobi Desert into the ancient mercantile cities of Samarqand, Yarkant (Shache), and Kashgar (Kashi), until they reached Tangut, in the extreme northwest of China. Finally, in the spring of 1275, the three Polos were made welcome at Shangdu, the summer capital of Kublai Khan, the Mongol emperor of China.

Marco soon became a favorite at the Chinese court of the Great Kublai Khan. He studied the native languages and in 1277 became a commissioner in the Mongol gov-

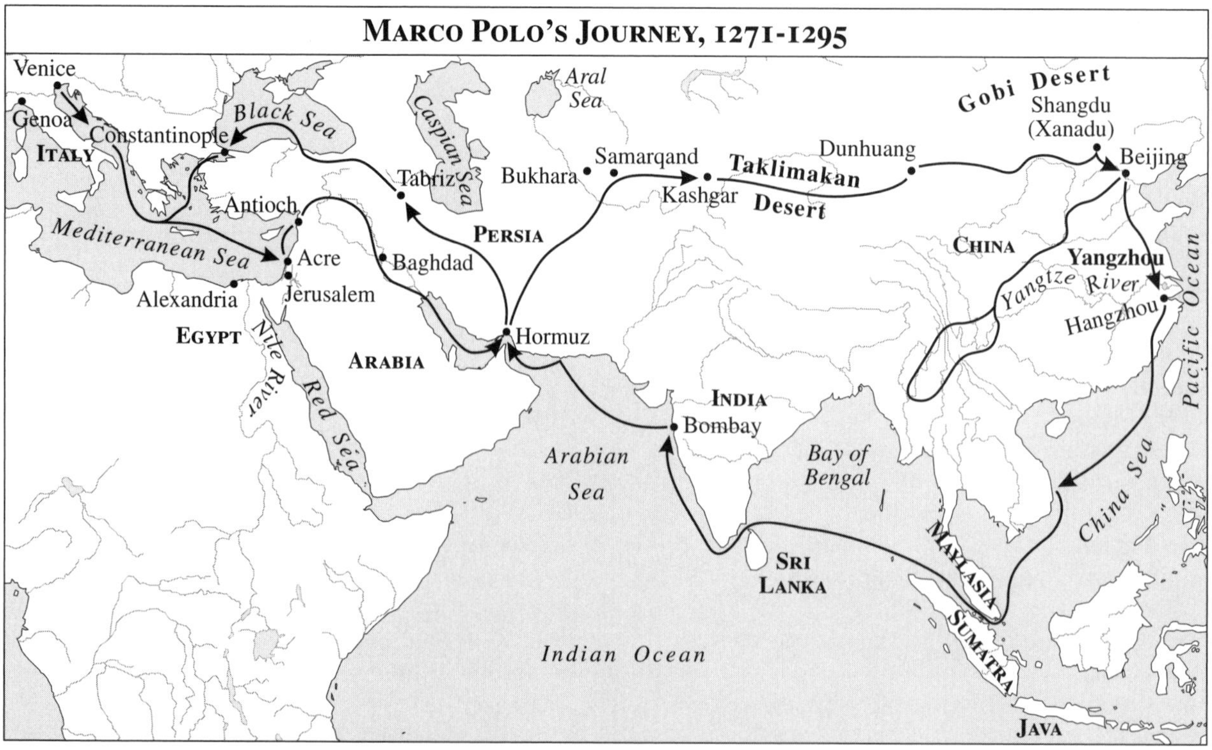

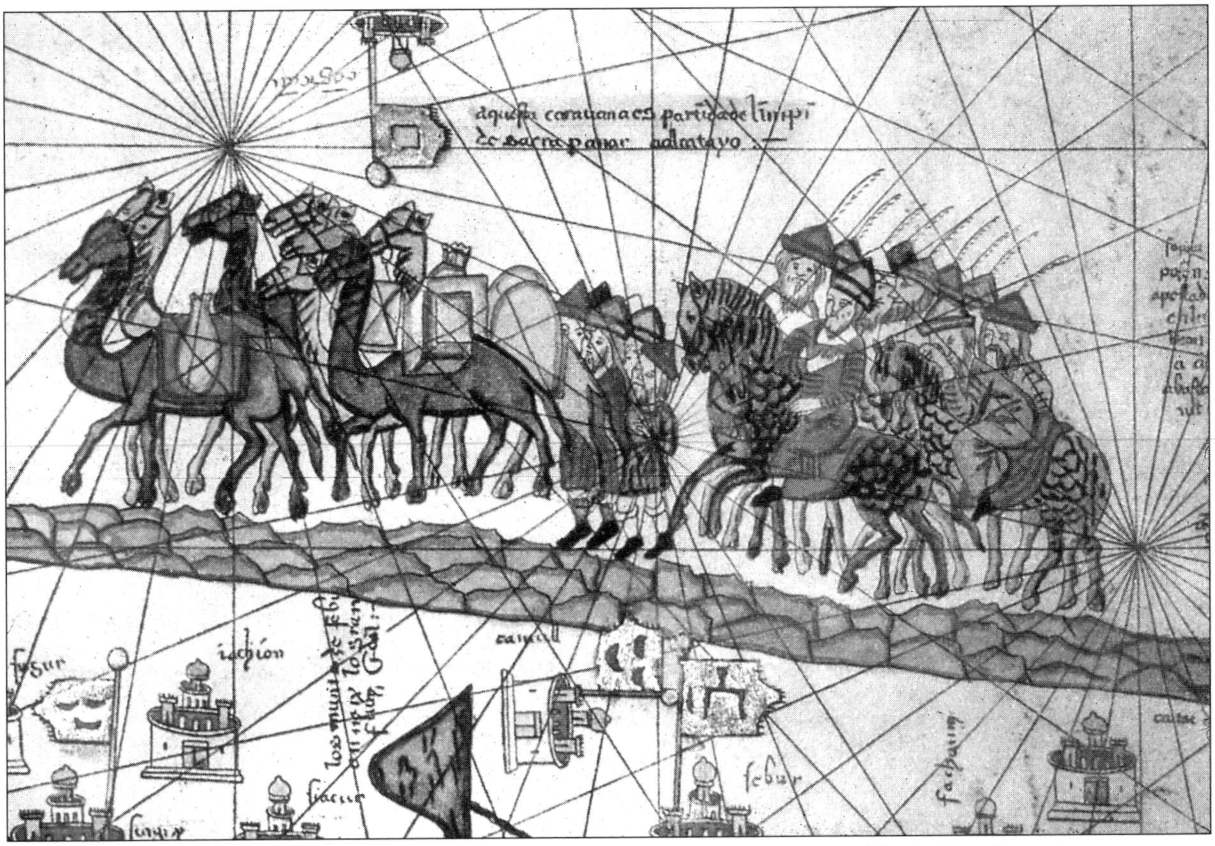

A depiction of the Polo expedition traveling along the Silk Road. (Hulton|Archive by Getty Images)

ernment. The khan came to trust the young Venetian so much that he relied on his advice in affairs of state and of commerce. Marco's descriptions of the great emperor and of his mighty palace outside the capital fired the imaginations of generations of explorers and travelers, all of whom wished to view for themselves the eight square miles (twenty-one square kilometers) of enclosed barracks, parade grounds, vast arsenals, storerooms, living quarters, library, and especially the sumptuous treasury. As a trusted agent of Kublai Khan for seventeen years, Marco Polo had the unique opportunity, seldom offered later, to observe a developed and sophisticated way of life unknown to Western society. At one point, he served Kublai Khan as governor of Yangzhou. Fortunately, he was an enlightened observer who appreciated his responsibility to record this ancient civilization for all posterity.

In his long and loyal service to the great khan, Marco Polo visited nearly every part of both northern and southern China, employing the imperial horse and packet-boat system that was kept constantly in readiness for the comfort and convenience of government officials. He cataloged and described many provinces, huge cities, and major commercial towns in lively and intriguing detail. Nothing escaped his notice; he was interested in commerce, the manufacturing arts, the character of the residents in each area, architecture, and even costumes. Marco was especially impressed with the silk industry and the staple commerce between the Levant and the West, and his account of his travels would provide Europeans with an excellent early picture of silk culture, weaving, dyeing, and finishing.

To thirteenth century Europe, the splendors of the Chinese cities must have seemed incredible. Polo's description of Hangzhou, for example, included even the fabled "twelve thousand" bridges of the city, its many huge markets and bazaars, its cavernous warehouses for its trade with India, its state-owned pavilions for wedding feasts, and even its consumption of six tons of pepper daily.

Marco Polo visited India on official business and duly recorded its commercial life. In the same way, he may also have visited the original homeland of the Mongols, the windswept steppes of Asia, where the ancestors of the great khans had grazed their herds. There is even possible reference to Siberia, though it is doubtful that the adventurous and apparently indefatigable Venetian ever traveled so far north. His account of his journey also indicates great interest in the islands to the south of China, including the Philippines.

In 1292, the Polos increasingly desired permission of the great khan to depart for their faraway home on the Adriatic. So favored were the Polos that Kublai Khan could not abide their leaving, and it was with considerable reluctance that he permitted the trio to depart, with an official commission to escort the Mongol prince's daughter to her wedding in Persia.

The voyage homeward took the Polos three years. Traveling primarily by ship, Marco recorded his impressions of Java or the "great island," Sumatra, Sri Lanka, Zanzibar, Bombay, and many other exotic and exciting islands and landfalls. The adventurers finally reached Venice, where they arrived unnoticed. An extraordinary mercantile odyssey of more than twenty years' duration at last came to a satisfying end.

SIGNIFICANCE

Shortly after returning to Venice, Marco Polo was captured by the warring Genoese in a naval battle and imprisoned. In prison, he dictated an account of his experiences to fellow prisoner and writer Rustichello of Pisa. In this famous account of his journeys, *Divisament dou monde* (fourteenth century; *The Travels of Marco Polo*, 1579), his uncle and father soon fade into the background, allowing the young and adventuresome author to become the dominant figure. The clear, colorful, and eminently readable account made a great and immediate impression on a credulous medieval Europe. It was received with awe and disbelief, and it was not until other travelers to China verified portions of the tales that they came to be sanctioned. Polo's book is responsible for stimulating Occidental interest in Eastern commerce and influencing explorers such as Christopher Columbus. Indeed, the account of Polo's travels in Asia was one of the primary sources for the European image of the Far East until the late nineteenth century.

—Carl F. Rohne, updated by M. Casey Diana

FURTHER READING

Bellonci, Maria, ed. and trans. *The Travels of Marco Polo*. Translated into English by Teresa Waugh. New York: Facts On File, 1985. This translation of Marco Polo's adventures contains many illustrations, some in color.

Larner, John. *Marco Polo and the Discovery of the World*. New Haven, Conn.: Yale University Press, 1999. A discussion of the Polo family, Marco's relationship with Rustichello, the making of the book, and the explorer's influence. Contains maps from the fifteenth century. Bibliography and index.

Polo, Marco. *The Travels of Marco Polo*. Translated by Ronald Latham. 1958. Reprint. New York: Penguin Books, 1996. One of the best translations into English of Polo's book. Contains a brief but good introduction by the translator.

Severin, Tim. *Tracking Marco Polo*. New York: Peter Bedrick Books, 1984. Entertaining account of a late twentieth century motorcycling adventurer's determination to rediscover Polo's route. Concise history of Polo's journey with photographs and maps.

Wood, Frances. *Did Marco Polo Go to China?* Boulder, Colo.: Westview Press, 1996. Wood argues that Marco Polo may not have made the fabulous journey described in his book. Wood claims that the details of that work could have been taken from the works of other travelers and that Polo's narrated tale could have been embellished by the ghostwriter who transcribed it. Wood neglects to say where Polo could have been if not in China.

SEE ALSO: 1204: Genghis Khan Founds Mongol Empire; 1368: Tibet Gains Independence from Mongols; 1381-1405: Tamerlane's Conquests; 1275: Nestorian Archbishopric Is Founded in Beijing.

RELATED ARTICLES in *Great Lives from History: The Middle Ages, 477-1453*: Giovanni da Pian del Carpini; Genghis Khan; Kublai Khan; Louis IX; Marco Polo; William of Rubrouck.

1273
SUFI ORDER OF MAWLAWĪYAH IS ESTABLISHED

Like other Sufi, or Islamic mystic, orders, the Mawlawīyah focuses on spiritual realization through renunciation of material goods, simplicity, and moving one's daily focus away from ritual and toward the seeking of spiritual truth. The Mawlawīyah also use dancing and music to achieve spiritual goals, a practice that has earned its members the name "whirling dervishes."

LOCALE: Konya, Asia Minor (now in Turkey)
CATEGORY: Religion

KEY FIGURES

Jalāl al-Dīn Rūmī (1207-1273), founder of the Mawlawīyah order
Shams al-Dīn (d. c. 1247), Rūmī's spiritual guide
Sulṭān Walad (1226-1312), Rūmī's son, leader of the order

SUMMARY OF EVENT

Sufism is the word used to describe Islamic mysticism. It derives from the Arabic term *suf*, or wool, the material from which the robes of the early mystics were made and which symbolized their avoidance of luxury. Broadly speaking, Sufism represents attempts to expand the frontiers of religion beyond ritual and to search for spiritual truth. It is a tradition based on the lives of the Prophet Muḥammad and the first generation of Muslims that emphasizes an ascetic lifestyle and embraces simplicity. The Sufi renounce the material world for the spiritual world; emphasize celibacy; and eschew material possessions, especially those beyond one's daily needs, and money not earned by one's own labor. All these emphases reflect Sufism's reactions against the dominant cultural model of the time, a model celebrating wealth, high social position, and sexuality. Thus, Sufism can be interpreted as a form of dissent and resistance to the government and orthodox religion of the period.

Jalāl al-Dīn Rūmī is considered by many to have been the most important Sufi of all time. Rūmī was born to a family of Persian origin in Balkh (Afghanistan). When Rūmī was still a young boy, he and his father left Balkh following a disagreement with local rulers. Rūmī's father was a respected religious scholar, and the Seljuk sultan of Rum invited him to bring his family and settle in Konya in modern Turkey. Konya was known as Rum (Rome) because of the area's Byzantine (Eastern Roman) past. It is because of his association with this city that Jalāl al-Dīn is known as Rūmī.

In 1244, Rūmī met the man who would be the most profound and powerful influence in his life, Shams al-Dīn, an extremely well-known religious figure. Rūmī became his disciple. Most of Rūmī's writings are dedicated to Shams, whom he called, among other things, "the absolute light of the sun and the ray of the lights of Divine Truth." Rūmī's best known work, the *Mathnawī-i ma ʿnawī* (*The Mathnawi*, 1926-1934), was one outcome of his association with his mentor, a man who appears in much of Rūmī's verse as well. Often sung as well as read, *The Mathnawi* is still considered one of the literary and religious treasures of the Persian-speaking world. Yet the inspiration Shams provided to Rūmī and the effect he had on Rūmī's spiritual development and work were not appreciated by all; Shams was eventually murdered by unidentified persons apparently unhappy with the amount of influence he had on Rūmī.

After Rūmī died in 1273, his son, Sulṭān Walad, continued his work and his leadership of the order. The order was named the Mawlawīyah (Arabic) and also called the Mevleviye (Turkish) after Maulānā (our master) Rūmī. It was under Sulṭān Walad's leadership that the order adopted the practice that would give its members their name, the whirling dervishes, though Rūmī himself began the ritual. The dancing session (*sama*) that typifies the spiritual exercise of the order is rich in symbolism, difficult to master, and an integral part of Mawlawīyah spiritual activity. The dance includes individuals turning in circles, and the overall dance proceeds in a semicircle, symbolizing movement away from God, followed by movement back to God at the end of the arc, when the dancers come near the Sufi master, or *pir*. Thus, the circular movement is symbolic of the cycle of creation.

The dance also symbolizes the soul's encounter with and awakening to reality. Each sees his own face reflected in the faces of the others, which makes individuality unreal and the other oneself. The dance is accompanied by music, including drums, flutes, and chants. The playing of the reed flute, or *ney*, is especially symbolic, as the sound of it represents the cry of the reed as it is taken from its growing point. More generally, the sound symbolizes the cry of longing to return to one's origins.

During the Ottoman Empire, the Mawlawīyah order aided conversions to Islam in urban Anatolia by pro-

A dervish c. 1910. (Hulton|Archive by Getty Images)

viding charity and aid, a focus for communal activities, and a focus for religious and devotional activities. As an order that was primarily urban and middle to upper class, and as one that did not differ with orthodox Islam in an extreme fashion, the Mawlawīyah was not seen as a particular threat to the established governmental or religious structure. In fact, the order was held in high esteem by some Ottoman sultans, including Mehmed II (r. 1451-1481), Selim III (r. 1789-1807), and Süleyman I (r. 1520-1566). The Mawlawīyah, with its inherent emphasis on dance, music, and visual art, all of which were opposed by the religious orthodoxy, also contributed greatly to the development of these art forms in Ottoman culture.

However, the popularity of the various Sufi orders was a cause for some concern on the part of the Ottoman leadership, particularly after Sufi tribal rebellions in the fourteenth to sixteenth centuries. In order to gain the support of the Sufi orders and undercut their popularity as a focus for resistance to the regime, the Ottomans attempted to co-opt the orders by giving them a symbolic role in government. Thus, the Bektashi order was incorporated into the regime as the patron order of the janissary corps; the Mawlawīyah were given a ceremonial role in the government by girding each new sultan with a holy sword, beginning in 1648. This approach worked well for the Ottomans; the Sufi orders began to be seen as protectors of the state, a state that altered their previous mass appeal as protectors of the people against the abuses of the state.

Despite its loss of political influence, the order has been spiritually, culturally, and socially influential, particularly in India, Central Asia, Afghanistan, Persia, and Turkey. Although the Mawlawīyah order was banned in Turkey in 1928 (along with all Sufi orders), it has still seen a resurgence. The Mawlawīyah today exist in many countries, including Turkey, Egypt, Syria, and other former Ottoman lands, with the most active branches in Konya and Istanbul.

SIGNIFICANCE

Jalāl al-Dīn Rūmī is arguably the most influential Sufi in history. Through his teachings, sayings, writings, and poetry, Rūmī presented a view of the human and the divine that speaks to people of all nations and all ages, helping Sufism persist through the ages. Scholar Andrew Harvey explained his impact in the following terms: "Rūmī combined the intellect of a Plato, the vision and enlightened soul-force of a Buddha or a Christ, and the extravagant literary gifts of a Shakespeare."

The broader significance of the order can be interpreted in a number of ways. In embodying an alternative view of religion, it provided potential converts with a view of Islam that stressed the spiritual, rather than the legalistic, version of the faith. Its importance in the Ottoman period can be found in its contribution to conversion, to the arts and culture, and to the ceremonial support of the state.

—*Amy J. Johnson*

FURTHER READING

Barks, Coleman. *The Essential Rūmī.* San Francisco: Harper, 1997. This popular book contains modern English translations of some of Rūmī's most captivating verses, with introductions to each section written by the translator.

Friedlander, Shems. *The Whirling Dervishes: Being an Account of the Sufi Order Known as the Mevlevis and Its Founder the Poet and Mystic Mevlana Jalāluddin*

Rūmī. Albany: State University of New York Press, 1992. This very accessible book contains basic information about the order and a wealth of photographs. Part of the SUNY series in Islam. Bibliography.

Harvey, Andrew. *Teachings of Rūmī*. Boston: Shambhala, 1999. This book contains a brief introduction to Rūmī and his works. The remainder of the book is divided into four sections, each of which contains verses and extracts from Rūmī's writings.

Kahn, Masood Ali, and S. Ram, eds. *Encyclopaedia of Sufism*. 12 vols. New Delhi: Anmol, 2003. A collection introducing Sufism and its basics in Islam, and Sufism's tenets, doctrines, literature, saints, and philosophy. Bibliography, index.

Karamustafa, Ahmet T. *God's Unruly Friends: Dervish Groups in the Islamic Later Middle Period, 1200-1550*. Salt Lake City: University of Utah Press, 1994. This academic work discusses Sufism and its role in historical context. Illustrations, bibliography, index.

Karpat, Kemal. *The Politicization of Islam: Reconstructing Identity, State, Faith, and Community in the Late Ottoman State*. New York: Oxford University Press, 2001. Discusses the role of religion in identity in the Ottoman Empire, including some discussion of the Mawlawīyah order.

Lewisohn, Leonard, and David Morgan, eds. *The Heritage of Sufism*. Boston: Oneworld, 1999. Explores Sufism from its beginnings, through the Middle Ages, and up to the mid-eighteenth century. Illustrations, bibliography, index.

Lings, Martin. *What Is Sufism?* 1975. Reprint. Cambridge, England: Islamic Texts Society, 1999. A useful general survey of the principles of mysticism and the various representatives of nonconformist religious practice and thinking in Islam. Bibliography, index.

Moyne, John A. *Rūmī and the Sufi Tradition: Essays on the Mowlavi Order and Mysticism*. Binghamton, N.Y.: Global, 1998. A very brief look at the order in the tradition of Sufism. Illustrations, bibliography.

Rūmī, Jalāl al-Dīn. *The Mathnawí of Jalālu'ddin Rūmī*. Translated and edited by Reynold A. Nicholson. 1926-1934. Reprint. London: Luzac, 1972. A complete scholarly verse translation of Rūmī's most important poetic work. Bibliography.

Vitray-Meyerovitch, Eva de. *Rūmī and Sufism*. Translated by Simone Fattal. Sausalito, Calif.: Post-Apollo Press, 1987. This book provides biographical information about Rūmī as well as discussion of Sufism, its beliefs and practices, and its role in Islamic societies.

SEE ALSO: c. 610-632: Muḥammad Receives Revelations; 637-657: Islam Expands Throughout the Middle East; Early 10th century: Qarakhanids Convert to Islam; 1077: Seljuk Dynasty Is Founded.

RELATED ARTICLES in *Great Lives from History: The Middle Ages, 477-1453*: al-Ḥallāj; al-Ḥasan al-Baṣrī; Ibn al-ʿArabī; Mehmed II; Muḥammad; Rābiʿah al-ʿAdawiyah; Jalāl al-Dīn Rūmī.

1275
FIRST MECHANICAL CLOCK

Scholars agree on the pivotal technological and social importance of the mechanical clock, but some believe that a medieval Chinese Buddhist monk invented the first water-powered mechanical clock, whereas others believe that a medieval European monk invented the first weight-driven truly mechanical clock.

LOCALE: Burgundy, in eastern France
CATEGORY: Science and technology

KEY FIGURES

I-Xing (I-Hsing; eighth century), Chinese Tantric Buddhist monk who made a hydromechanical astronomical instrument

Su Song (Su Sung; 1020-1101), astronomer and statesman at the Chinese capital Kaifeng who wrote a monograph on an astronomical clock tower

Gerbert of Aurillac (c. 945-1003), later Pope Sylvester II (999-1003), French monk to whom the invention of the first mechanical clock was long attributed

SUMMARY OF EVENT

Scholars have called the invention of the mechanical clock not only one of the most significant turning points in the history of science and technology but also one of the greatest achievements in the history of humankind. Although the term "clock" is now commonly used for a time-measuring instrument with a numbered dial and moving hands, some scholars frown on this usage, insisting that "clock" should be applied only to timekeepers that strike the hours by a bell (the Middle English *clok* directly descends from the Latin *clocca*, meaning "bell"). Devices to monitor time over both short and long periods go back to early civilizations. Ancient Babylonians, Egyptians, Greeks, and Romans developed sundials, water clocks (clepsydras), and sand clocks, and these "pre-clocks" were precursors to the mechanical clocks of the medieval Chinese, Arabs, and Europeans. The reason the medieval mechanical clock was so much more significant and influential than its predecessors was that it had the technological potential to evolve into a wide variety of timekeepers that would increasingly transform science and society.

Because many timekeepers have moving parts and because controversies exist over which country created the first mechanical clock, it is necessary to clarify the precise nature of this innovation. For many historians of technology, the mechanical clock has to be weight-driven, which means that it can work in subfreezing weather (unlike the water clock) and at night and on cloudy days (unlike the sundial). The mechanical clock also has to transmit the potential energy of a raised weight through a system of toothed wheels to a time indicator. This time-measuring mechanism—the escapement—is the crux of the mechanical clock. It consists of a rotating multinotched wheel whose cogs are periodically blocked and released by a device that rhythmically swivels back and forth and can thereby track time's flow.

Joseph Needham, an eminent Sinologist, claimed that medieval Chinese artisans, six centuries before the Europeans, had developed the escapement as part of a long evolution of astronomical devices intended to model celestial motions. To keep their observational apparatus in synchronization with the revolving heavens, Chinese astronomers used water power to regulate the revolutions of a series of wheels. Needham was able to trace the history of these devices back to the Buddhist monk I-Xing in the early eighth century. Working at the College of All Sages in the Tang Dynasty (T'ang; 618-907) capital, I-Xing and his collaborators devised what Needham calls an escapement mechanism. Water flowed into scoops at the periphery of a wheel, whose controlled rotation was transferred to the astronomical devices. In effect, time was measured by the successive weighings of scoopfuls of water. A larger and more complex hydromechanical astronomical clock was constructed by Su Song in the eleventh century. This monumental clock, more than 30 feet (9 meters) in height, was the acme of medieval Chinese horology. Unfortunately, it, like other cumbrous Chinese timekeepers, disappeared from history, the consequence of dynastic rulers who failed to understand their significance. Needham speculates that, either by emigrant or by rumor, knowledge of these hydromechanical clocks diffused westward, but other scholars doubt that they served as the stimulus for medieval European developments.

Even though Chinese hydromechanical clocks were vastly superior to clepsydras made in early medieval Europe, many scholars nevertheless believe that the first truly mechanical clock was invented in Europe during the late Middle Ages. For many years, early scholars attributed the mechanical clock's invention to Gerbert of Aurillac (later Pope Sylvester II), one of whose students wrote that this "Pope of the Millennium" had constructed a device that tracked stellar motions. Contemporary scholars wonder why, if Gerbert had invented a mechanical escapement and oscillating controller, church towers were deprived of this innovation for three hundred years. Sophisticated mechanical clocks began to appear in Europe in the late thirteenth and early fourteenth centuries, and perhaps the legend of Gerbert's invention served to bridge the gap between medieval clepsydras and fully mechanical clocks.

Some historians of technology argue that, by 1275, all the requirements for a truly mechanical clock were known. Some scholars believe that the breakthrough was made by Gerbert as early as the tenth century. He substituted a falling weight for falling water and devised a verge escapement. The descending weight caused a toothed wheel to rotate, and the verge (a spindle with pallets) engaged upper and lower teeth of the wheel alternately, causing the foliot (a rod with movable weights on each end) to oscillate. This stop-and-go mechanism, with its ticktock sound, has been called one of the most ingenious inventions in history. Other scholars point out that what was revolutionary in this mechanism was not the escapement, important though it was, but the oscillatory device, the rate of whose beats could be regulated to match nature's timekeeper, the revolution of the heavens.

These European clocks initially served a religious purpose: They regulated the monks' Mass time, prayers, meals, and work. In the late thirteenth century, clocks quickly spread from monasteries to churches, and clocks were built for St. Paul's Cathedral in London and the cathedral at Canterbury. In the early fourteenth century, clocks were built in church towers in England, France, and Italy. The earliest mechanical clock that has survived was constructed in 1386 for Salisbury Cathedral in England.

SIGNIFICANCE

Unlike the hydromechanical astronomical clocks of China, which had little influence on society, the fully mechanical European clocks had a revolutionary impact on science, technology, and culture. Lewis Mumford, an American social critic and humanist, saw the medieval mechanical clocks as the most significant contributor to the creation of the modern world. Clock time came to regulate not only work and prayer in monasteries but also all aspects of secular life. Some scholars see this time-organized society as a critical factor in the differentiation of Western from Eastern civilization. Critics of Needham's claim that the Chinese first invented the mechanical clock point out that he anachronistically misused the term "escapement" for a periodic water scoop mechanism, which was admittedly an important discovery but not the same as the European oscillating-beat escapement. The Chinese hydromechanical clock was more accurate than the early European mechanical clocks, but the Chinese clock had no future, whereas the European clock made possible the scientific, technological, and societal revolutions that helped make the modern Western world. In the sixteenth century, when the Jesuit missionaries entered China (and West finally met East), Chinese statesmen and scholars were amazed by the Jesuits' mechanical clocks, which they viewed as dazzling new inventions, unrelated to their largely forgotten horological tradition.

Initially, the European clock was an imprecise and unreliable instrument, but during the late Middle Ages and early Renaissance, it became more accurate and adaptable. When a coiled flat spring replaced the weight drive in the early fifteenth century, portable clocks became a reality. The later invention of the pendulum clock meant that fully mechanical timekeepers were increasingly more precise than any of their predecessors. These clockworks not only helped create modern science and society but also provided a philosophical model for the universe itself (the mechanistic worldview). Time measurement, once the province of obscure tinkerers and scholars, had become the catalyst in creating new ideas, new technologies, new societies, and, in the case of scientist Albert Einstein, a new vision of the universe.

—*Robert J. Paradowski*

FURTHER READING

Cipolla, Carlo M. *Clocks and Culture, 1300-1700*. 1978. Reprint. New York: Norton, 2003. This treatment of the European invention of the mechanical clock and its effect on society is highly critical of Needham's thesis that Chinese millwrights invented the first mechanical clocks.

Landes, David S. *Revolution in Time: Clocks and the Making of the Modern World*. Rev. ed. Cambridge, Mass.: Harvard University Press, 2000. This book, the first comprehensive analysis of the mechanical clock's invention and influence, has been called a "landmark." Landes, who believes that Needham's excessive Sinophilism blinded him to the true European provenance of the mechanical clock, explains in detail the origin, evolution, and impact of this great invention. This illustrated book contains an appendix on escapement mechanisms and seventy-eight pages of notes, with many references to primary and secondary sources.

Needham, Joseph. *Mechanical Engineering*. Part 2 in *Physics and Physical Technology*. Vol. 4 in *Science and Civilisation in China*. New York: Cambridge University Press, 1965. This book, with its immense bibliography, contains a condensed but updated account of the Chinese invention of mechanical clocks that was initially made public in *Heavenly Clockwork*.

Needham, Joseph, Wang Ling, and Derek de Solla Price. *Heavenly Clockwork: The Great Astronomical Clocks of Medieval China*. 2d ed. New York: Cambridge University Press, 1986. The authors argue that medieval Chinese astronomical clocks are the "missing link" between ancient water clocks and modern mechanical clocks. They survey the six centuries of mechanical clockwork in China that preceded the appearance of mechanical clocks in fourteenth century Europe.

SEE ALSO: 618: Founding of the Tang Dynasty.

1275
NESTORIAN ARCHBISHOPRIC IS FOUNDED IN BEIJING

In 1275, a Nestorian archbishopric was founded in Khanbalik, the capital of the Yuan Dynasty. Although the Nestorians reintroduced Christianity into China, they did not stay, leaving shortly after the dynasty ended.

LOCALE: Khanbalik (known to the Chinese as Dadu; now Beijing)

CATEGORIES: Religion; cultural and intellectual history

KEY FIGURE

Kublai Khan (1215-1294), great khan of the Mongols, r. 1260-1294; founder and first emperor of the Yuan Dynasty of China, r. 1279-1294

SUMMARY OF EVENT

After its disappearance at the end of the Tang Dynasty (T'ang; 618-907), Nestorian Christianity reentered the Middle Kingdom when the Nestorian tribes from Central Asia moved into northern China during the Khitan Liao (907-1125) and Jin (Chin; 1115-1234) Dynasties. In two diplomatic missions to China between 1245 and 1253, Franciscan friars reached Karakorum, the old Mongol capital, and saw a high level of religious freedom enjoyed by the Nestorians at the court and in areas under Mongol rule. When Kublai Khan proclaimed himself emperor in 1271 and called his dynasty the Yuan, or "origin," he tolerated all religions within the Mongol Empire. (The Song were defeated in 1279; thus, the dates for the Yuan Dynasty in China are generally given as 1279-1368.) In this religiously diverse environment, Nestorian Christianity claimed devotees within the ruling family and benefited from political support of the court.

The Nestorian patriarchy in Baghdad took advantage of the cosmopolitanism of the Mongol Empire and established five missionary metropolitan provinces along the ancient Silk Road—Merv (now Mary, Turkmenistan), Samarqand, Kasghar, Almalyk, and Ningxia—thereby contributing to the rapid expansion of Nestorian Christianity from the Middle East to Central Asia and China. Because of the long distance from Baghdad, the archbishops of these provinces remained independent of the control of the home church in Persia, and they did not take part in the internal administration of the home church and the selection of a new patriarch.

In 1275, a metropolitan archbishopric was founded in Khanbalik, the new capital of Yuan Dynasty China, and archdeacons were chosen from the local clergy to assist the archbishop. The only other missionary metropolitan province in China was Ningxia. After the collapse of the Southern Song Dynasty (Sung; 1127-1279), the newly conquered territory was subject to the metropolitan archbishop of Khanbalik. The Yuan officials used the Chinese word *yelikewen* to refer to Christians without making a differentiation among Nestorians, Armenian Christians, and Roman Catholics. Because the Nestorians fully recognized the authority of the Mongol rulers, they were rewarded for their loyalty with official titles in the Yuan government. As a result, the Nestorian church hierarchy was deeply integrated into the Yuan administration.

After moving his capital to Khanbalik, Kublai Khan founded the office for the Christian clergy (*chongfu si*) in 1280 to administer the Nestorian bishops, priests, monasteries, and ritual affairs in China. In 1291, he appointed an Arab Nestorian named Isa (Jesus) as the first commissioner of the office, who was succeeded by his son Elijah. With official approval, Elijah set up several Nestorian monasteries in southern China. Of all the Nestorian leaders, the most famous was Rabban Sauma, who embarked on a long journey to Europe on behalf of Kublai Khan in 1287. Another well-known leader was Bishop Mar Solomon, the supervisor of the Christians, Manichaeans, and Nestorians in southern China. In 1315, forty years after the founding of the Nestorian archbishopric in Beijing, there were seventy-two Nestorian religious offices (*yelikewen zhangjiao si*) across China.

The archbishops were usually chosen from the celibate monks, who were allowed to ordain native priests and archdeacons to assist with the church administration. Almost all the Nestorian monks, priests, and archdeacons in China were of foreign origin, except Ke Cuncheng, the only Chinese admitted into the Nestorian church hierarchy as an archdeacon. Despite their non-Chinese backgrounds, many Nestorian leaders successfully accommodated themselves to Chinese culture. Wu Anduonisi, the head of the Daming Monastery, not only adopted a Chinese surname and mastered written Chinese but also used Buddhist terminology to express his Christian faith.

Throughout the Yuan Dynasty, Nestorian Christianity was largely confined to the non-Chinese population. There were three types of Nestorian communities in Central Asia and China: the Nestorian nomads of Mongol and Turkish origins in the northern province of Lingbei (modern-day Mongolia and Siberia), the Nestorian settlements scattered across the Silk Road in Central Asia, and the Nestorian merchants who came to China through the Maritime Silk Route across the Indian Ocean and South China Sea. They lived in major coastal cities such as Quanzhou, Wenzhou, and Yangzhou, among the Buddhists, Daoists, and Muslims.

Although the support of the Mongol rulers contributed to the spread of Nestorian Christianity across Central Asia and China, the Nestorians failed to make inroads among the Chinese partly because of their confinement in foreign communities and partly because of hostility from their Buddhist and Daoist counterparts. The Nestorians were involved in several incidents of ritual and property conflicts with the Buddhists and Daoists. In 1254, a debate arose at the Mongol court about whether Christianity or Buddhism was compatible with the Mongol folk religion. The Franciscan friar William of Rubrouck supported the Nestorians in the debate and defended the Christian doctrine of monotheism against what he called Buddhist atheism. In 1304, the Mongol ruler issued an imperial edict ordering the Nestorians to stop proselytizing among the Daoist communities in Jiangnan (Lower Yangtze Valley). Because the Nestorians attempted to provide the Daoist clergy with tax exemptions in exchange for their conversion to Christianity, the Daoist leaders complained to the government that the Nestorians violated the ritual order of the Mongol Empire in which the Daoist and Buddhist monks were above the Nestorian clergy. In 1311, the Yuan government ordered the return of two Nestorian monasteries to the Buddhist communities in Zhenjiang. All these conflicts had little to do with religious differences and rather were the result of the ongoing power struggles among the Nestorian, Buddhist, and Daoist leaders at the court.

Kublai Khan proclaimed himself emperor in 1271 and called his dynasty the Yuan, or "origin" dynasty. (Hulton|Archive by Getty Images)

The end of the Yuan Dynasty in 1368 posed many obstacles to the Nestorians in China. Gone were the political protection and economic support they had received from the Mongol court, foreign merchants, and converts. Then Tamerlane's conquest of Central Asia completely cut off the overland trading routes from the Middle East to China and disrupted the communication between the home church and archbishopric in Khanbalik.

SIGNIFICANCE

The founding of the Nestorian archbishopric in Beijing in 1275 symbolized the reintroduction of Christianity into China. In the diverse ethnic and religious world of the Mongol Empire, the Nestorian faith flourished as a legal and tolerated religion across Central Asia and China. Yet the long history of cultural interaction between China and the outside world did not lead the Chinese to subscribe to Christianity. Although the Nestorian church had its devotees within the Mongol ruling family, the Chinese were rather indifferent to, if not hostile toward, the church.

The Nestorian church of the Yuan Dynasty shared the same fate of its forerunners in Tang China, which fell with their imperial patrons. In 1368, the Nestorian missionaries appeared to have left China for Central Asia with the Mongols, and in the early sixteenth century, the archbishopric of Khanbalik was incorporated into that of India. The collapse of the Mongol Empire clearly marked the beginning of the second decline of Christianity in China.

—Joseph Tse-Hei Lee

FURTHER READING

England, John C. *The Hidden History of Christianity in Asia*. Delhi: Indian Society for the Promotion of

Christian Knowledge, 1996. Provides an overview of the development of Nestorian Christianity in China.

Irvin, Dale T., and Scott W. Sunquist. *Earliest Christianity to 1453*. Vol. 1 in *History of the World Christian Movement*. Orbis, N.Y.: Maryknoll, 2001. Contains a brief section on Nestorian Christianity in Mongol China.

Moffett, Samuel Hugh. *Beginnings to 1500*. Vol. 1 in *A History of Christianity in Asia*. Orbis, N.Y.: Maryknoll, 1998. Discusses the experience of Nestorian communities in China in the wider context of the Christian expansion across continental Asia.

Rossabi, Morris. *Voyager from Xanadu: Rabban Sauma and the First Journey from China to the West*. New York: Kodansha International, 1992. A fascinating story of Rabban Sauma's journey from China to Europe in the late thirteenth century, with a brief account of the Nestorian activities in Mongol China and Central Asia.

Standaert, Nicolas, ed. *Handbook of Christianity in China: 635-1800*. Leiden, the Netherlands: E. J. Brill, 2001. Provides the most comprehensive account of the early history of Christianity in premodern China. Examines Nestorian Christianity in the Yuan Dynasty.

SEE ALSO: 845: Suppression of Buddhism; 1115: Foundation of the Jin Dynasty; c. 1145: Prester John Myth Sweeps Across Europe; 1153: Jin Move Their Capital to Beijing; 1271-1295: Travels of Marco Polo; 1368: Establishment of the Ming Dynasty; 1381-1405: Tamerlane's Conquests.

RELATED ARTICLES in *Great Lives from History: The Middle Ages, 477-1453*: Kublai Khan; William of Rubrouck; Tamerlane.

c. 1275
THE *ZOHAR* IS TRANSCRIBED

Moses de León compiled one of the most central texts of Judaism, the Zohar, *a written collection of the corpus of mystical Jewish thought known as the Kaballah. The text also has had far-reaching effects on other forms of spirituality, including paganism and religious practice based on the magical.*

LOCALE: Spain
CATEGORIES: Religion; philosophy; literature

KEY FIGURES

Moses de León (1250-1305), Spanish religious scholar, rabbi, and philosopher, probable compiler of the *Zohar*
Ibn Gabirol (c. 1020-c. 1057), medieval Jewish poet
Naḥmanides (1194-1270), Jewish mystic
Isaac ben Solomon Luria (1534-1572), disseminator of the *Zohar*

SUMMARY OF EVENT

Religions are inclined to incorporate two basic viewpoints. One, emphasizing common sense or reason, tends to observe life, attempts to explain it, and endeavors to provide mechanisms to live it in a rewarding and satisfying manner; this view plays down the mysteries of life or attempts to rationalize them. The other outlook prefers a mystical vision that concentrates on the mysteries of reality and seeks answers and guidance in difficult human situations through recourse to trust in the reliability of emotions, often leading to reliance on the occult.

Judaism is no stranger to this schism. Its corpus of mystical thought is known as the Kabbalah (also Kaballa or Cabala), meaning "tradition," and probably its greatest book is the *Zohar*. On the whole, the Kabbalah was transmitted orally, and its message was secretly guarded by those who were trusted with its esoteric mysteries. Only with the passing of time were its contents committed to writing. While the Kabbalah in its generally accepted meaning was an immediate product of medieval mystical Judaism, its roots are actually deeply embedded in the very beginnings of Jewish religious history. The Mishnah, the Talmud, and parts of the Bible, especially sections of Ezekiel and Daniel and other prophets, all in a sense may be seen as antecedents of the kind of thought that characterizes the Kabbalah. These passages and other mystic epigraphical works of the intertestamental period all profess knowledge of the means necessary to bridge the gulf between God and the world and to facilitate the passage of the human soul to the Deity. In fact, mystics assigned esoteric interpretations to passages that could support their cause. Even Philo, the great Alexandrian philosopher of the first century, came to exert a significant, if indirect, influence on the development of the

Kabbalah. Particularly attractive was his view of God as a transcendent being, outside and above the world, so far removed that intermediate forces were necessary to relate to him. These intermediate potencies, or *logoi*, identified with the "ideas" of Plato, were conceived of as personalities and identified with the angels of Scripture.

As the Kabbalah developed slowly and informally over a period of centuries, few authors were aware that they were making contributions to the growing corpus of Jewish mystical thought. One medieval pioneer was Ibn Gabirol in the mid-eleventh century, an honored Jewish poet, whose works emphasized God's glory and grandeur contrasted with humankind's weakness and insignificance. Naḥmanides, another early mystic a century later, contested the great authority of Moses Maimonides and other rationalists who held that Judaism was an open book devoid of hidden meanings. He insisted that it was replete with mysteries above the comprehension of human reason. While Naḥmanides never succeeded in developing a fully fledged system of thought, he did establish a basic intellectual framework for later mysticism. Solomon ibn-Adret (1235-1310) proved to be a moderating force in the development of the early Kabbalah; though naturally inclined toward mysticism, he sought to keep in bounds hysterical manifestations emanating from overstimulated imaginations of visionaries.

If one person can be singled out as the compiler of the Kabbalah, Moses de León is that man. Up to this time, this mysterious lore was considered suitable only for scholars and the elect initiate; moreover, it was still preserved only as an oral tradition. However, just as in the past there had been times when the Bible, the Mishnah, and the Talmud were ripe for compilation, so the time came for the oral tradition of the Kabbalah to be collated. This work of collection Moses de León carried on over a period of time, producing what later came to be called the *Zohar* or the *Book of Splendor.* While some scholars believe that de León himself composed the commentaries on the Bible that basically make up the *Zohar,* its unsystematic composition as well as its variegated content indicate that it represents the work of many different people over several generations.

The fundamental conception of the *Zohar* is that there is nothing trivial in the Bible, that the commandments as well as the narratives have higher mysterious meanings and purposes that constitute the essence of Scripture. Its conception of God identifies the Supreme Being with the emanations proceeding from him, a view leading to such a gross anthropomorphism that it permitted reference to God's eyes, his nose, his beard, and the crown of his head. It also presented vivid details of Purgatory and Hell, where the souls of the wicked were tortured by evil demons before they were purified to return to heaven.

The expulsion of Jews from Spain in 1492 triggered a new period of creativity among the Jewish mystics. Their center became Safed in Palestine, which at the time of Isaac ben Solomon Luria reached its fullest development. The Kabbalah scholar Gershom Scholem feels that the Kabbalah underwent a complete transformation following the expulsion of the Jews from Spain, and that it found its new expression best in the teachings of Luria and his school, which emphasized a mystical interpretation of exile and redemption.

The printing of the *Zohar* in 1558 allowed Luria to provide a practical, living mysticism for more than a mere elite. The concept of emanation from the Infinite, the basic principle in the Kabbalah, by this time had so far developed that God could now be conceived of as willing to contract himself into finiteness and then adjust himself to contact with humans. To receive their share of the divine indwelling, individual souls must be purified by entering more refined bodies in order to shed their imperfections. This ascent is implemented by certain practices and ceremonies in which each word and deed is directed toward the end of returning the soul to its source in God.

By its composite nature, the *Zohar* presented a confusing picture to those who tried to plumb its depths. To make the Kabbalah in general more practical and serviceable, Moses Cordovera (1522-1570) prepared his *Garden of Pomegranates*, a systematic and philosophical presentation of older Kabbalistic teachings. He also sought to find some unity among the great number of themes discussed in earlier mystical writings.

SIGNIFICANCE

The whole of the *Zohar* is permeated with stories of struggle between good and evil, holiness and profanity, a combat willed by God himself. All these ideas served the needs of the common people who hungered for supernatural visions and an opportunity to identify themselves in some way with the cosmic process itself. To such persons estranged from the goods of the world, the secrets of the Kabbalah provided new avenues of participation in a more true reality. Moses de León's compilation of the *Zohar* has resulted in centuries of intrigue—both positive and negative—for Kabbalistic thought.

—*Joseph R. Rosenbloom*

FURTHER READING

Anidjar, Gil. *"Our Place in al-Andalus": Kabbalah,*

Philosophy, Literature in Arab Jewish Letters. Stanford, Calif.: Stanford University Press, 2002. Analyzes the history of the Kabbalah, the *Zohar*, and Judaism in Andalusian Spain, also during the time of de León's compilation of the *Zohar*.

Berg, Rav Philip S. *The Essential Zohar: The Source of Kabbalistic Wisdom*. New York: Bell Tower, 2002. A practical, contemporary interpretation of the Zohar by a well-known Kabbalist, written for the general reader.

Blau, Joseph L. *The Christian Interpretation of the Cabala in the Renaissance*. Port Washington, N.Y.: Kennikat Press, 1965. The thesis of this work maintains that the Christian use of the Kabbalah was of no deep or lasting value.

Bokser, Ben Zion. *The Maharal: The Mystical Philosophy of Rabbi Judah Loew of Prague*. Northvale, N.J.: Jason Aronson, 1994. First published in 1954 as *From the World of the Cabbalah*, this book discusses the philosophy of Rabbi Judah Loew, a sixteenth century exponent of the Kabbalah's wisdom.

Scholem, Gershom G. *Major Trends in Jewish Mysticism*. New York: Schocken Books, 1995. Written by an outstanding scholar of the Kabbalah whose knowledge of basic source materials has revolutionized the study of Jewish mysticism. The author traces the development of Jewish mysticism from the time of the second Temple through the nineteenth century.

_______. *On the Kabbalah and Its Symbolism*. Translated by Ralph Manheim. New York: Schocken Books, 1996. A further elaboration of the author's earlier work on the Kabbalah.

Werblowsky, R. J. Zwi. *Joseph Karo, Lawyer and Mystic*. Philadelphia: Jewish Publication Society of America, 1977. The author presents Joseph Karo as the author of an important Kabbalistic diary describing much of the Kabbalism of the mid-seventeenth century.

SEE ALSO: c. 1150: Moors Transmit Classical Philosophy and Medicine to Europe; 1190: Moses Maimonides Writes *The Guide of the Perplexed*; 1290-1306: Jews Are Expelled from England, France, and Southern Italy.

RELATED ARTICLES in *Great Lives from History: The Middle Ages, 477-1453*: Ibn Gabirol; Moses Maimonides; Moses de León; Naḥmanides.

1285
STATUTE OF WINCHESTER

The Statute of Winchester defined the rights and obligations of British kings and subjects in military affairs and established a national police force.

LOCALE: England

CATEGORIES: Government and politics; laws, acts, and legal history; organizations and institutions; social reform

KEY FIGURE

Edward I (1239-1307), king of England, r. 1272-1307

SUMMARY OF EVENT

During his busy reign, Edward I, the so-called English Justinian, legislated a number of significant matters. The Statutes of Gloucester (1278) addressed land law. Westminster I (1275) changed a number of procedures, with the aim of receiving oppression of subjects. Westminster II (1285) and Westminster III (1290) reorganized feudalism in England, while the Statute of Mortmain (1279) attempted to limit the Church's power to acquire land and to block feudal obligations to the king and nobles. Of great significance for future English fortunes was the Statute of Winchester (1285).

Apart from providing for various contingencies, such as the supervision of strangers, clearing high roads, and guarding city gates and walls, this law called for the maintenance of a national militia, the origins of which were in the ancient Anglo-Saxon concept of the universal military obligation of freemen. Certain modifications had been made in implementing this custom even before the Norman Conquest in 1066. The land unit for providing one fighting man had been increased from one hide to five or more as the equipment of the fighting knight became more expensive than that of the old Saxon thegn (or thane). Often, too, military service came to be commuted into a money payment called "scutage."

In 1181, Henry II took a step toward reorganization of local defense with his Assize of Arms that established a graded hierarchy of military obligations based on a single recruitment system extending down to the general military duty of all freemen. By assessing military service in terms of the economic resources of the individual, the Assize of Arms interpreted feudal custom. Further, by standardizing military obligations in monetary terms Henry set a precedent that similar reforms by Henry III in 1230 and 1242 were later to incorporate into the English constitution.

By Edward I's reign, subinfeudation—the process of creating subordinate tenancies out of one landholding—had damaged the system of military tenure. Under feudalism, a lord owed the king military service. When the lord subinfeudated his land, however, the military obligation was divided among his tenants. While in theory the process of subinfeudation should not damage the ability of the king to raise an army of knights, in reality, as landowners began to create long chains of tenure, it became increasingly difficult to determine exactly what each subtenant owed in terms of military service.

At least two considerations prompted the issuance of the Statute of Winchester. One was a general rise in prices during the eleventh, twelfth, and thirteenth centuries stemming from the commercial renaissance of the period. The royal revenues were increased, but prices continued to rise ahead of income, especially the price of waging war, which rose as the use of sophisticated weapons necessitated specialized training for the infantry and limited the effectiveness of the amateur militia levies. Crossbows and the use of professional soldiers required large cash outlays, and by reaffirming the military obligation of all freemen, Edward expected to increase his revenues through scutage.

Edward's second and total victory over the Welsh in 1284 was the second and immediate cause of the Statute of Winchester. The Welsh campaigns had required large formations of expensive mercenary foot soldiers to supplement the feudal host, and because he intended to conquer rather than merely punish, Edward needed additional men as carters, woodsmen, builders, diggers, carpenters, and masons to erect castles and field fortifications in order to keep the Welsh in check. The combined pressures of needing additional revenue and additional men led Edward, in 1285, to feel the urgent need to define the rights and obligations of the king and subjects in military affairs. The Statute of Winchester was a brilliant effort at definition.

Reflecting the old Anglo-Saxon fyrd (national militia prior to the Norman Conquest) and the Assize of Arms, the statute fixed everyone's military obligation on the price of scutage in lieu of each obligation. Every freeman between the ages of fifteen and sixty was required to have armor according to his wealth. The statute defined five classes, the highest of which were those whose lands were valued at fifteen pounds and forty marks in goods.

King Edward I. (Library of Congress)

These men had to be fully equipped cavalrymen, each with chain-mail coat, iron helmet, sword, knife, and horse. At the other extreme were those freemen of little property, each of whom was obliged to have only a quilted coat, an iron helmet, a bow, and arrows. Two constables were appointed in each hundred (county subdivision) to review this host twice every year, and they could use it to repel an invader or to maintain local law and order as a police force. Constables had their own hierarchy leading up from constables of townships or villages (or "vills"), through the hundreds and counties, to king's constable of the realm.

The Statute of Winchester also represented a major change in criminal law. It placed heavy demands on local government for the maintenance of law and order. Under the Statute of Winchester, for example, in a hundred in which a robbery was committed, the whole hundred was held responsible unless the robber was found. The statute also standardized and consolidated earlier practices that required the vills to maintain night watchmen and provide necessary weapons for their constables. Furthermore, the statute specified that all people of a vill must answer the hue and cry, armed with their weapons. The vill could be punished for failure to respond to the hue and cry raised in the discovery of a crime. The vill could also be fined for failure to capture the perpetrator. There seemed to be a great concern with the number of crimes that were going unreported, and the Statute of Winchester was designed to address this concern.

Like so many medieval decrees, the Statute of Winchester was administered differently in different parts of the realm. Strict enforcement would have provided too unwieldy a force besides depriving the land of its cultivators. There was also the question of the duration and extent of service. Rather than face this problem, Edward I and his successors chose to utilize the Commissions of Array. In this case, the king appointed certain prominent men to "elect" or conscript such forces from each area as were needed for royal service at a particular time. The area, hundred, or county was responsible for supporting this force, but for strictly offensive operations the royal treasury often bore the expense, and the district provided its quota by hiring mercenaries. This arrangement paved the way for the "Bastard Feudalism" of the fourteenth and fifteenth centuries.

SIGNIFICANCE

By reestablishing that all freemen owed the king military service or scutage in lieu of military service, the Statute of Winchester was significant in the following ways. First, it raised both the money and the men needed by Edward I that the increasing cost of armament had depleted. Second, it strengthened the position of the king by creating a national force organized by counties and responsible to the monarch. Finally, the statute forced the financial burden of keeping the peace on local authorities and thus freed the king from increased outlays.

—Lynewood F. Martin,
updated by Diane Andrews Henningfeld

FURTHER READING

Baker, J. H. *An Introduction to English Legal History.* 4th ed. London: Butterworths, 2002. An accessible introduction to English law, including documents in Latin with accompanying English translations.

Lyon, Bryce. *A Constitutional and Legal History of Medieval England.* New York: Harper & Row, 1980. A study of the extent of centralization and consolidation in medieval England in comparison to France, which failed to establish a national militia as England did under the Statute of Winchester.

Maitland, F. W. *The Constitutional History of England.* New York: Cambridge University Press, 1920. Shows the connection between the old Anglo-Saxon national military force and the Statute of Winchester.

Plucknett, T. F. T. *Legislation of Edward I.* Oxford: Clarendon, 1949. An excellent study of Edward I's legislation including the significance of the Statute of Westminster.

Prestwich, Michael. *Edward I.* New Haven, Conn.: Yale University Press, 1997. A thorough biography, placing the importance of Edward I's legislation in a historical context.

SEE ALSO: 1295: Model Parliament.

RELATED ARTICLES in *Great Lives from History: The Middle Ages, 477-1453*: Edward I; Henry II; Henry III.

1290-1306
JEWS ARE EXPELLED FROM ENGLAND, FRANCE, AND SOUTHERN ITALY

The expulsion of the Jews from England, France, and southern Italy resulted in mass suffering and impeded the economic development of these European countries.

LOCALE: England, France, and southern Italy
CATEGORIES: Religion; social reform

KEY FIGURES

Frederick II (1194-1250), Holy Roman Emperor, r. 1220-1250
Charles I (1227-1285), Angevin king of Sicily, r. 1266-1285
Edward I (1239-1307), king of England, r. 1272-1307
Philip IV the Fair (1268-1314), king of France, r. 1285-1314

SUMMARY OF EVENT

Between 1290 and 1306, Jewish communities in both England and France were expelled, while in southern Italy many Jews were killed or forced to convert or to flee the region. Although the particular details vary, the dynamics are generally parallel. Unlike the larger population, most Jews lived in towns rather than on farms. Their communal numbers were small, rarely exceeding one thousand and typically under three hundred. Their occupations were limited, in large part because of legal restrictions and social discrimination. Their communities were not well integrated with the larger Christian population, many of whom were raised on a deep-seated anti-Semitism promoted by the local clergy.

In opposition to the clerical antagonism stood the king—for economic reasons. The Jews were an important source of income because they could be very heavily taxed. As the kings attempted to conquer territory, and especially during the Crusades, their economic needs - increased substantially. To ensure that the Jews could provide money, they were sometimes released from obligatory Church taxes and were granted certain economic rights.

The occasional special treatment of Jews by royalty infuriated both the Catholic clergy and those who hoped to compete economically with Jews. Over time, these Christian interests triumphed. For example, in the Third Lateran Council (1179), Church leaders forbade Jews to employ Christian servants or workers. A half century later, in 1215, the Fourth Lateran Council limited economic interaction with Jews, denied them the right to hold any public office, and compelled them to wear a distinguishing badge on their outer garments. About twenty years later, the medieval papal Inquisition began to preoccupy itself with eradicating heresy, a process that led to the Spanish Inquisition of the fifteenth century and the complete destruction of Jewish life in Spain and Portugal.

In addition to the centralized religious pressure, powerful local clergy could often impose restrictions, as could the local nobility, who were in an ongoing struggle with the monarchy. Combined with the greater royal tax burden, this increased pressure broke the back of many Jewish communities. Once their wealth was drained, they lost the special protection of the king.

The deteriorating financial conditions of the Jews led to additional restrictions. Across all three countries, Jews were stripped of their wealth, pressured and sometimes forced to convert, and in a number of cases exiled from their local communities. Several precedents were set for the more widespread expulsion later, from 1290 to 1306 and afterward, in some communities.

Jews came to England very late, starting primarily after the Norman Conquest of 1066. Unlike in the other two nations, many English Jews were financiers who loaned money at interest, a vocation closed to Christians for religious reasons.

In 1130, the Jews of London were fined a very considerable sum based on a trumped-up murder charge against a Jewish physician. In 1144, coinciding with the Second Crusade, the Jews of Norwich were accused without evidence of the ritual murder of a Christian boy. The Jewish quarter was ransacked, and Jews were forced to pay a fine. Thereafter, until 1255, about every fifteen years, another major Jewish community faced the same charges, with the same general outcome. Not incidentally, these charges and attacks took place when the Royal Treasury needed replenishing.

The most terrible incident occurred in 1190 in York, where the entire Jewish community of about six hundred was killed—including those who asked to convert; their properties were destroyed or seized; and their records of debts owed them were burned.

The Oxford Council held in 1222 prohibited Jews from owning slaves and from building new synagogues, as well as requiring that they wear a linen badge. Ten

Anti-Semitic propaganda, c. 1350: Jews are shown gathering blood from Christian children for ritualistic use. (Hulton|Archive by Getty Images)

years later, Londoners petitioned against the completion of a magnificent synagogue, which was then seized and given to the Church.

The monarch's need for money drained the Jewish communities' declining resources sufficiently to destroy many of them. A series of regulations limited the ability of Jews to collect interest on money already loaned, thus drying up their businesses. Although it was omitted in later confirmations, the original Magna Carta contained a provision restricting the claims of Jewish creditors against the estates of deceased landowners.

Throughout the thirteenth century, oppression against Jews increased, further limiting their economic opportunities. Starting in mid-century, Jews were expelled from several towns after refusing to convert. Eventually, with widespread poverty, they were of no use to the king. Finally, in order to placate the Church and lower nobility, on July 18, 1290, Edward I issued an edict of banishment for all the Jews in England—probably about six thousand. Most left for France, Germany, and Flanders.

In France, Jews had been present, in small numbers, since the first century. Unlike in England, in addition to trade and finance, some Jews were involved with wine—more in production and trade than in grape cultivation. Until the ninth century, periodic attempts were made to force conversion on the Jews. In 624, King Dagobert expelled all Jewish residents—for about fifteen years. In spite of some anti-Jewish laws, from about 800 to 1096 the Jewish communities flourished and were relatively safe. That situation changed with the advent of the First Crusade (1096-1099), after which the conditions under which the Jews lived worsened.

The first attacks on European Jews occurred in Rouen. In 1144, Louis VII issued a decree that banished converted Jewish Christians who returned to Judaism. The first of a series of blood libels occurred in 1171, when thirty-one innocent Jews were burned alive. In 1181, King Philip II imprisoned all the wealthy Jews of Paris and freed them only on receiving a large ransom. A year later, he expelled them and confiscated their real estate.

Attacks on Jewish communities continued through the thirteenth century. In 1242, both Church and king condemned and burned the Talmud, the collection of Jewish oral law. Although the order was not rigorously pursued, Jews were expelled from Poitou in 1249. In 1268, Thibaut V, count of the Champagne region, confiscated much of the Jewish wealth to pay for the Crusades. In 1283, Jews were forbidden by Philip III to live in small rural localities. In 1291, the Jews expelled from England were prohibited by Philip IV the Fair from settling in France. Finally, in July of 1306, most of the Jews of France were imprisoned and their possessions seized, and shortly thereafter they were expelled. A number of Jews were allowed to remain, mostly to collect debts they then paid to the royal coffers. In 1311, these last remnants of the Jewish population were also expelled.

Jewish life in Italy differed from that in the rest of the continent. Jews were in Rome by the first century B.C.E., and their numbers may have swelled to fifty thousand with the Jews brought as captives following the Roman conquest of Israel in 70 C.E. Conditions improved until Constantine's acceptance of Christianity as the official religion in the fourth century, after which Jews were discriminated against. For example, new synagogues were not allowed to be built, and Jews were pressured to convert to Christianity.

Conditions for Jews improved with the fall of the Holy Roman Empire, but they worsened after the conquest by the Byzantines in the sixth century, after which they improved in the south with the Arab conquest (827-1061). As a result, by the late Middle Ages, the bulk of the community was in the south. Despite the formal anti-Semitism of the Church, Jewish life developed under the rule of Emperor Frederick II, who provided protection and a monopoly in silk weaving and dyeing—in exchange for high taxes. Unlike in England and France, most Jews in Italy were craftspeople and merchants.

Frederick II's suspected liberalism brought a successful challenge by the Papacy in 1265 to replace him with the French Charles I, after which Jewish life deteriorated significantly. A series of blood libels, physical attacks, and forced conversions decimated the communities.

In 1268, the Inquisition was introduced. Following the French example, in 1270 a Jewish apostate denounced classic rabbinic literature, leading to the hunt for and burning of religious books. In about 1290, a Dominican friar accused the Jews of Apulia of ritual murder of a Christian child, leading to a series of fatal attacks.

Although there was no formal widespread expulsion, by 1294, the overwhelming majority of the approximately thirteen thousand Jews in southern Italy were forced to convert or flee, or were killed. Southern Italy never reclaimed the important presence of its Jewish population.

SIGNIFICANCE

The persecution of Jews in England, France, and southern Italy followed religious oppression by the Catholic Church and economic frustration and envy both by the nobility and by the local citizenry. Jews eventually returned to England and France, but the communities—both Jewish and non-Jewish—were forever changed in the process.

—*Alan M. Fisher*

FURTHER READING

Berger, David. *From Crusades to Blood Libels to Expulsions: Some New Approaches to Medieval Antisemitism.* New York: Touro College Graduate School of Jewish Studies, 1997. A published lecture on the xenophobic treatment of Jews in the Middle Ages.

Chazan, Robert. *Medieval Jewry of Northern France.* Baltimore: Johns Hopkins University, 1973. A detailed political history of Jewish life in medieval France.

Finestein, Israel. *A Short History of Anglo-Jewry.* London: Lincolns-Praeger, 1957. Short but informative review of Jewish life.

Foa, Anna. *The Jews of Europe After the Black Death.* Translated by Andrea Grover. Berkeley: University of California Press, 2000. A history of European Jewry from the fourteenth through the nineteenth century that emphasizes the stability and continuity of Jewish experience in the face of change and upheaval.

Hyamson, Albert M. *A History of the Jews in England.* London: Methuen, 1928. An older study, but one that provides a detailed picture of Jewish life in England.

Roth, Cecil. *The History of the Jews of Italy.* Reprint. Westmead, Farnborough, England: Gregg International, 1969. Comprehensive study of two thousand years of Jewish history in Italy.

Steiman, Lionel B. *Paths to Genocide: Antisemitism in Western History.* New York: St. Martin's Press, 1998. Examines the expulsion of the Jews as one of the events in a linear history leading up to the Holocaust.

Taitz, Emily. *The Jews of Medieval France.* Westport, Conn.: Greenwood Press, 1994. Focuses on Jewish family and domestic life.

SEE ALSO: 740: Khazars Convert to Judaism; 834: Gypsies Expelled from Persia; November 27, 1095: Pope Urban II Calls the First Crusade; 1147-1149: Second Crusade; 1189-1192: Third Crusade; c. 1200: Fairs of Champagne; November 11-30, 1215: Fourth Lateran Council; June 15, 1215: Signing of the Magna Carta; 1233: Papal Inquisition; c. 1250-1300: Homosexuality Criminalized and Subject to Death Penalty; c. 1275: The *Zohar* Is Transcribed.

RELATED ARTICLES in *Great Lives from History: The Middle Ages, 477-1453:* Benjamin of Tudela; Edward I; Frederick II; Gershom ben Judah; Moses Maimonides; Naḥmanides; Philip IV the Fair.

April, 1291
FALL OF ACRE

The fall of Acre marked the end of Christian Crusader rule and dominance in Palestine and Syria, and the resumption of Muslim control.

LOCALE: Acre (or ʿAkko), Palestine (now in Israel)
CATEGORIES: Religion; wars, uprisings, and civil unrest

KEY FIGURES

Qalāʾūn (d. 1290), Mamlūk sultan of Egypt, r. 1279-1290
Amalric de Lusignan (d. 1310), brother of Henry II; *bailie* (magistrate) of Jerusalem, 1289-1291; and regent of Cyprus, 1306-1310
William de Beaujeau (d. 1291), master of the Temple, 1273-1291
al-Ashraf Ṣalāḥ al-Dīn Khalīl (d. 1293), Mamlūk sultan of Egypt, r. 1290-1293
Henry II de Lusignan (1271-1324), ruled Cyprus, r. 1285-1324, and concurrently ruled Jerusalem, r. 1286-1291, and as titular ruler, r. 1291-1324
Otto de Grandison (d. 1320), knight errant at Acre

SUMMARY OF EVENT

A riot in late August, 1290, between Muslims and newly arrived Italian Crusaders—undisciplined, drunken, and disorderly—in the streets of Acre ended with the killing of a number of Muslims. As a consequence, Sultan Qalāʾūn of Egypt was convinced that the massacre broke the existing truce between Egypt and the already greatly contracted kingdom of Jerusalem, and he began to gather his army to finally eliminate the Franks. Outraged by the incident, the barons and knights ruling Acre suppressed the rioters and rescued many Muslims. They also immediately apologized to the sultan, who sent an embassy demanding surrender of the leaders of the riot.

The *bailie*, Amalric de Lusignan, representative of the king of Jerusalem in Acre, convened a council to frame a response. The master of the Temple, William de Beaujeau, proposed sending the criminals in the jails of Acre to Cairo as the guilty men, but the council refused. Instead of condemning Christians to die in Cairo, the council attempted to persuade the sultan's emissaries that Muslim merchants had precipitated the riot. After consulting his council, Qalāʾūn rejected this response, abandoned the truce, and began mobilizing his army.

Templar agents at Cairo reported the sultan's intentions to William de Beaujeau, who earlier had sent his own envoy to Cairo. Qalāʾūn then offered a proposal to William: He would allow the residents to leave Acre safely for a ransom of one Venetian sequin per inhabitant. When William presented this proposal to the high court in Acre, it was rejected, and the court accused William of treason.

The sultan left Cairo with his army on November 4. The invasion, however, was halted when Qalāʾūn suddenly fell ill and died on November 10. The government and citizens of Acre then relaxed, concluding that their troubles were over in the light of the usual protracted disorders accompanying the succession of sultans. The Mamlūk successional conflict, however, was settled quickly and, by March of 1291, Qalāʾūn's son, al-Ashraf Ṣalāḥ al-Dīn Khalīl, was in control. The council at Acre then sent a final embassy seeking to flatter Khalīl and to seek terms of peace. Khalīl threw them in prison, where they died. He sent his army against Acre in March, 1291. On April 6, he invested Acre and the siege began.

The inhabitants of Acre had put the double walls of the city in good repair. In anticipation of an attack after the fall of Tripoli in 1289, the authorities in Acre had broadcast appeals for help. The military orders—Templars, Hospitalers, and Teutonic knights—called in all available members from Europe. No great crusade, however, came from Europe. The only reinforcements to arrive were Tuscan and Lombard crossbow troops, who provoked the riot in August, 1290, and scattered knights errant. A few English volunteers led by Otto de Grandison came at the expense of King Edward I of England (r. 1272-1307). The Venetians and Pisans remained loyal, but the Genovese, whose business in Acre had been ruined by Venice, stood aside.

King Henry II de Lusignan, immobilized by sickness in Cyprus, sent a Cypriot group, and his brother Amalric commanded the defense. Many noncombatants were ferried to Cyprus, and supplies of food, water, and arms were in good order. In all, about 1,000 mounted men and 15,000 foot soldiers guarded the walls of Acre. The invaders reportedly brought 60,000 mounted men, 160,0000 infantry, and almost 100 catapults and mangonels. Although these figures are probably exaggerated, the besiegers most likely outnumbered defenders by ten to one.

During a month of battering, Italian catapults had knocked out some important Egyptian siege engines, and a ship fitted with a catapult did great damage behind the Mamlūk lines until it was destroyed in a storm. A moonlight sally by the Templars on April 15 began well but ended in confusion. A second sally by the Hospitalers in the dark of the moon a few days later was ambushed. Thereafter, the defenders fought from within the walls in order to conserve men and armaments. On May 4, Henry arrived from Cyprus with 100 knights and 2,000 foot soldiers. This was the last infusion of reinforcements.

Henry sent envoys to beg for peace. In reply, Khalīl demanded surrender of the city but offered to allow the defenders to leave alive. During the parley, a catapulted stone landed among the bystanders, and Khalīl had to be persuaded not to kill the ambassadors immediately. Khalīl's terms were refused and, on May 15, the Egyptians penetrated the outer wall, forcing the defenders back to the Gate of Saint Anthony and the inner wall.

On May 18, they mounted a general assault, overrunning the inner wall and the Gate of Saint Anthony. By evening, the Christians were trying to organize an evacuation by sea. Henry, Amalric, and many of the Cypriots left first. Otto de Grandison took command of the rear guard and filled the Venetian ships with wounded; he himself was the last to embark. When the elderly Nicholas of Hannape was carried to a ship by his servants, he encouraged fugitives to crowd in with him. The overloaded boat then foundered, drowning all on board.

After the ships left, the docks still were crowded with refugees. The Templars retreated to their headquarters and resisted for a few more days. Finally, the Mamlūks undermined the walls, collapsing the entire building and killing all of the defenders and many of their own men.

The Mamlūks then sacked Acre, killing or enslaving all Christians. The sultan also deliberately destroyed Acre and all of the castles along the coast. Fearing Christian sea power, Khalīl then systematically wiped out the remaining Christian outposts in the Levant.

On May 19, his army appeared before Tyre, the strongest city in the kingdom of Jerusalem. Although it might have endured a long siege, the Cypriot garrison sailed home without resisting. At Sidon, the Templars held out until July, when they left by sea. Beirut, although protected by a private truce, was taken by treachery in the same month. In August, the monasteries of Mount Carmel were sacked.

SIGNIFICANCE

By the end of 1291, no Franks remained in Outremer. The Crusader states had lasted only 192 years from the capture of Jerusalem in 1099 to their final destruction in 1291. Throughout, Outremer was plagued by persistent shortcomings. Most important, the permanent Frankish population was never large enough to defend and expand the Crusader states. Indeed, continuous reinforcement from the West was a necessity.

The many different and antagonistic European Crusader contingents seldom acknowledged any "central" authority and frequently lapsed into civil conflict. Also, the Crusaders were dependent on commercially oriented, opportunistic, and unreliable Italian city-states for transportation and commercial activity. Crusader leadership generally was unable to impose stable policy and, in any event, dependence on feudal allegiances frequently frustrated effective organization of available resources.

Acre was eventually conquered in 1516 by the Ottoman Turks, who ruled the area with minor interruptions until 1918, when the city was captured by the British. After 1922, it was governed under the British mandate of Palestine. Acre again was captured in 1948, by a Jewish terrorist group, and subsequently occupied by regular Israeli troops. In the process, most of the city's Arab population fled.

—*Ralph L. Langenheim, Jr.*

FURTHER READING

Avi-Yonah, Michael, ed. *A History of Israel and the Holy Land*. New York: Continuum, 2001. Presents a history of Palestine from the Arab conquest through the time of the Crusades, including the fall of Acre, and during the time of the Mamlūks and Ottomans. Illustrations, maps, index.

Hillenbrand, Carole. *The Crusades: Islamic Perspectives*. New York: Routledge, 2000. Chapters explore the fall of Acre, ethnic and religious stereotyping, daily life, the conduct of war, and more. Bibliography, index.

Madden, Thomas F., ed. *The Crusades: The Essential Readings*. Malden, Mass.: Blackwell, 2002. A collection of previously published articles about the Crusades, including medieval sources, lay enthusiasm, patronage, Byzantium, and the subjection of Muslims. Bibliography, index.

Payne, Robert. *The Dream and the Tomb: A History of the Crusades*. 1984. Reprint. New York: Stein and Day, 2000. Good account of the end of Outremer drawn from Arab as well as European accounts. Maps, bibliography, index.

Richard, Jean. *The Crusades, c. 1071-c. 1291*. Translated by Jean Birrell. New York: Cambridge University Press, 1999. A comprehensive history of the Crusades from its beginnings to its historical end with the fall of Acre in 1291. Genealogical tables, maps, bibliography, index.

Robinson, John. *Dungeon, Fire, and Sword: The Knights Templar in the Crusades*. New York: M. Evans, 1991.

Provides a concise historical account of the Templars' religious-military mission in battling for control of the Holy Land, and gives an account of the fall of Acre, including preceding and subsequent events. Illustrations, comprehensive bibliography.

Runciman, Steven. "The Crusader States." In *The Later Crusades, 1189-1311*, edited by Robert Lee Woolf and Harry W. Hazard. Vol. 2 in *A History of the Crusades*, edited by Kenneth M. Setton. 2d ed. Madison: University of Wisconsin Press, 1969-1989. Detailed scholarly account of the fall of Acre. Includes a map of the region. Bibliography, index.

_______. *The Kingdom of Acre and the Later Crusades*. Vol. 3 in *A History of the Crusades*. New York: Cambridge University Press, 1987. Comprehensive history of the Crusaders from the Third Crusade through final dissolution of Outremer.

SEE ALSO: 630-711: Islam Expands Throughout North Africa; August 15-20, 636: Battle of Yarmūk; 637-657: Islam Expands Throughout the Middle East; November 27, 1095: Pope Urban II Calls the First Crusade; c. 1120: Order of the Knights Templar Is Founded; c. 1145: Prester John Myth Sweeps Across Europe; 1147-1149: Second Crusade; 1189-1192: Third Crusade; 1204: Knights of the Fourth Crusade Capture Constantinople; 1217-1221: Fifth Crusade; 1227-1230: Frederick II Leads the Sixth Crusade; 1248-1254: Failure of the Seventh Crusade; September 3, 1260: Battle of Ain Jālūt; May 29, 1453: Fall of Constantinople.

RELATED ARTICLES in *Great Lives from History: The Middle Ages, 477-1453*: Baybars I; Philip II; Richard I; Saladin.

1295
MODEL PARLIAMENT

The Model Parliament established an important precedent by joining the shire knights and town burgesses with the spiritual and temporal lords, resulting in the widest political representation to that point in English parliamentary history.

LOCALE: Westminster, London, England
CATEGORIES: Government and politics; laws, acts, and legal history; social reform

KEY FIGURE

Edward I (1239-1307), king of England, r. 1272-1307

SUMMARY OF EVENT

Political historians view the evolution of the English Parliament as one of the greatest legacies of the English Middle Ages to the theory and practice of representative democracy throughout the world. Parliament had its forerunners in both Anglo-Saxon and Norman traditions and practices. It was considered normal and necessary for feudal kings to rely on their barons for advice as well as for military aid. Usually kings turned to a small council of permanent advisers, a council composed of the chief barons of the realm and important ecclesiastics. There was a prevailing tension, however, between this small council of permanent advisers, called the *curia regis*, and the larger *magnum concilium*, or Great Council of peers of the realm, who felt more and more that they, too, had a right to be consulted on matters of policy that affected their own situation.

The English kings, particularly from the time of Henry II (1154-1189), found themselves increasingly involved in costly wars with France. To gain support for these wars, particularly financial support, the kings turned to the *magnum concilium* and also to other barons and burgesses who commanded sources of wealth. Not surprisingly, therefore, some historians have tended to interpret the evolution of Parliament largely, though not solely, in economic terms.

The immediate circumstances surrounding the Parliament of 1295 can be found in Edward I's foreign policy. The king had been involved in costly wars with the Welsh. A far grander enterprise, however, was on the horizon: a war against France. Edward claimed that war was necessary to prevent France from depriving England of Gascony, a French territory (now called Gascogne, in southwestern France) rich in wine production. Both the writs summoning the members to Parliament and accounts by medieval chroniclers attest that Edward used the threat of foreign war, which was probably real, as his chief reason for calling members of the realm together to give him support. The campaign that Edward envisioned was of such a scale that the unified support of all was imperative. After negotiations between France and England failed, the king issued writs in September and October through his Chancery that required those summoned to participate in a parliament beginning the second week of November, after the feast of Saint Martin.

In composition, the Parliament of 1295 was made up of the lords spiritual, or the great churchmen; the lords temporal, or the great barons; and representatives of what was eventually to become the House of Commons. These representatives of the "commoners" came from two groups: knights of the shire, or men who held considerable land but who were not barons of the first rank or direct vassals of the king, and burgesses, or representatives of incorporated towns. Edward also summoned the two archbishops, all the bishops, the abbots of the larger monasteries, seven earls, and forty-one barons.

The composition of the 1295 Parliament thus involved the widest membership of any parliament up to that time. Edward I rarely summoned knights from the shire and burgesses from the cities and towns. In 1295, when they joined the temporal and spiritual lords in the assembly that came to be called the Model Parliament, they set an important precedent. Afterward, they began to meet in Parliament with some regularity, although representation was proportional neither to geography nor to population. The famous principle cited in the summoning writs, "that what affects all, by all should be approved," is found in Justinian's code and also in university statutes and in the Canon Law of the Roman Catholic Church. It expresses one of the most salient principles of democratic government and runs like a thread through medieval political history. The writ to the archbishop of Canterbury obligingly describes the common threat necessitating the Parliament: the king of France would "deprive us of our land of Gascony, by withholding it unjustly from us" and is conspiring "to destroy the English language altogether from the earth."

Like the lords spiritual, the great barons were also summoned by name. The summons is clearly a command, not an invitation, ordering the individual addressed to appear in person at Westminster on the Lord's day next after the feast of Saint Martin in the approaching winter.

In the cases of the bishops and great barons, the summons to Parliament was a personal one, and the work to be done by these members was in a real sense personal work, but such was not the case with the knights of the shires and burgesses, as a writ to the sheriff of Northampton makes clear. The sheriff is told "to cause two knights from the aforesaid county, two citizens from each city in the same county, and two burgesses from each borough, to be elected without delay, and to cause them to come to us at the aforesaid time and place." The writ explains that the knights and burgesses are to be "discreet," "capable of laboring," and empowered to act for their constituencies so that the business at hand could be finished then and there, evidence of the principle of representative government. Furthermore, these representatives, according to the writ, must be registered. The sheriff is enjoined to have on record the names of all knights, citizens, and burgesses elected to Parliament.

When Parliament assembled in November, each group ended by giving the king only as much as it was compelled to give. The king had to settle for a tenth of the revenue of the archbishop of Canterbury instead of the third or fourth he requested. The barons and knights gave one eleventh of their income to the king, and the boroughs gave one seventh, an indication not only of the relative wealth of the various components of the realm but also of their bargaining power. As each group assented to aid, it was dismissed and went home.

In interpreting the Parliament of 1295, a number of important features should be considered. In this Parliament, all elements of the realm were represented, but they were not yet established in the two groups which eventually became a bicameral legislature, a future development when the burgesses and the knights of the shire joined together for common discussion apart from the lords spiritual and temporal. Clearly present in 1295 was the working principle of aid for redress of grievances. The members of the Parliament of 1295 still acted within the framework of feudal grant of aid to the king. Pragmatically, this aid was now given only after collective bargaining.

SIGNIFICANCE

Parliament took an important step forward in a gradually established custom of consulting the middle class in Parliament, not outside it. The principle that "what affects all, by all should be approved" meant in effect that policies should have at least the passive support of those affected by them. This is the essential principle of broad participation in the political process and is perhaps the single most significant detail of the summons to the Model Parliament of 1295. Edward's parliaments were considered the most solemn of his councils, whose members were his representatives. The Model Parliament was not a full, functioning legislative body, nor could it challenge the authority of the king, but it did establish the consultative function of Parliament. The full implications of the Parliament of 1295 were realized only later, when lawmaking power was integrated with the consultative-judicial power of Parliament.

—Mary Evelyn Jegen, updated by Xavier Baron

FURTHER READING

Butt, Ronald. *A History of Parliament: The Middle Ages*. London: Constable, 1989. This valuable and authoritative study questions many of the assumptions about the actualities and later assessments of the Model Parliament by positioning it in the overall history of the most fundamental English political body.

Davies, R. G., and J. H. Denton, eds. *The English Parliament in the Middle Ages*. Philadelphia: University of Pennsylvania Press, 1981. The collected essays gathered here honor medieval parliamentary historian John Smith Roskell. They discuss parliament from its "prehistory" through 1509, with a good balance of constitutional and political historical analysis.

Harris, G. L. "The Formation of Parliament, 1272-1377." In *The English Parliament in the Middle Ages*, edited by R. G. Davies and J. H. Denton. Philadelphia: University of Pennsylvania Press, 1981. This chapter is the best single overview of the political and historical context of the Model Parliament, focusing on the reigns of Edward I through Edward III.

Plucknett, Theodore F. T. *English Constitutional History from the Teutonic Conquest to the Present Time*. 11th ed. Boston: Houghton Mifflin, 1960. Points to precedents of representation before the Model Parliament and so establishes a broader context for interpretation of the importance of 1295 in the history of Parliament.

Powicke, F. M. *The Thirteenth Century, 1216-1307*. 2d ed. Oxford, England: Clarendon Press, 1962. An indispensable account of the political history of the sequence of events around the Model Parliament.

Sayles, G. O. *The Functions of the Medieval Parliament of England*. Ronceverte, W.Va.: Hambledon Press, 1988. A series of documents by one of the most authoritative of British political historians, highlighting English parliamentary history.

_______. *The King's Parliament of England*. New York: Norton, 1974. This brief account is concise, accessible, and based on a lifetime of research and study. Includes an excellent bibliography.

Smith, Robert, and John S. Moore, eds. *The House of Commons: Seven Hundred Years of British Tradition*. London: Smith's Peerage, 1996. Spans the history of the House of Commons. Includes illustrations, bibliography, and index.

Wells, John. *The House of Lords: From Saxon Wargods to a Modern Senate*. London: Hodder and Stoughton, 1997. An account of the House of Lords from the time of the Anglo-Saxons to the present. Includes illustrations, bibliography, and index.

SEE ALSO: 1285: Statute of Winchester.

RELATED ARTICLES in *Great Lives from History: The Middle Ages, 477-1453*: Edward I; Philip IV the Fair.

1295
RAMKHAMHAENG CONQUERS THE MEKONG AND MENAM VALLEYS

King Ramkhamhaeng of Sukhothai spread his control over the central part of the land that would later become known as Thailand and became the first of the great Thai kings. Under his reign, the kingdom of Sukhothai established itself as a major political and cultural power in the Mekong and Chao Phraya River Valleys.

LOCALE: Central to northern Thailand

CATEGORIES: Expansion and land acquisition; government and politics

KEY FIGURES

Bang Klang Hao (c. 1200-1257), later known as Sri Indraditya, father of Ramkhamhaeng and king of Sukhothai, r. c. 1239-c. 1257

Ban Muang (c. 1230-1279), son of Sri Indraditya, elder brother of Ramkhamhaeng, and king of Sukhothai, r. 1257-1279

Ramkhamhaeng (c. 1239-c. 1317), king of Sukhothai, r. c. 1279-c. 1317

Ngam Muang (c. 1238-c. 1298), king of Phayao, r. c. 1258-c. 1298

Mangrai (1239-1317), king of Lan Na, r. 1259-1317

SUMMARY OF EVENT

In 1200, much of what is now known as Thailand was under the rule of the Khmer King Jayavarman VII, whose capital was located in Angkor, in present-day Cambodia. Other parts of the region were under the Mons, linguistic relatives of the Khmer. Groups of people speaking dialects of Thai and Lao, which scholars often refer to as Tai languages, lived in *muangs*, clusters of settlements that acknowledged the command of charismatic chieftains.

These chieftains, in turn, recognized the authority of their Khmer and Mon overlords.

After Jayavarman VII died in about 1220, the Khmer empire appears to have been weakened, opening opportunities for ambitious Thai chieftains. About 1238, two Thai chiefs, Khun Bang Klang Hao and Khun Pha Muang, formed an alliance. Together, they attacked and defeat a Khmer garrison at Sukhothai, which was at that time the capital city of the northwestern section of the Khmer empire. Khun Bang Klang Hao was acclaimed king of Sukhothai, which means "dawn of happiness," and he took the name Sri Indraditya.

Sri Indraditya had five children, three sons and two daughters. The oldest son died while still a child. The second son, Ban Muang, came to the throne on his father's death. Sukhothai's most celebrated king, though, was the youngest son. At the age of nineteen, while Sri Indraditya was still alive, this young man had won the name of Phra Ramkhamhaeng, or Lord Rama the Brave, after displaying great valor in battle. According to a stone pillar left by Ramkhamhaeng, his father's troops were about to be defeated when the youth mounted an elephant and charged the leader of the enemy to save the day by a duel on elephant back.

After the death of Ban Muang, the second Thai king of Sukhothai, Ramkhamhaeng proceeded to extend the territories he had inherited. On the stone pillar on which he detailed his accomplishments, there is a later inscription that credits him with conquering much of the Chao Phraya (Menam) River Valley. The Chao Phraya is the river that runs through the center of Thailand, and it is such an important waterway that foreigners frequently refer to it as Menam, or simply "the river" in Thai. The inscription also maintains that Ramkhamhaeng spread his rule northward to the Mekong River Valley as far as the Lao cities of Lan Chang (Luang Prabang) and Vien Chan (Vientiane). To the south, Sukhothai's empire extended down the Malay peninsula as far as Nakhon Sri Thammarat.

Although Ramkhamhaeng was absolute ruler in the territory around his capital city, his power was more questionable in his distant provinces. Much of the land was under his vassals, local lords who had sworn loyalty to him.

Ramkhamhaeng was an astute diplomat as well as a successful warrior. He forged particularly important alliances with two Thai kings to his north. As a child, he had been tutored together with Ngam Muang, the king of Phayao. Through Ngam Muang, he also established ties with Mangrai, the powerful king of Lan Na. Together, the three kings were supposed to have planned Lan Na's new capital city of Chiang Mai, which remains the second most important city in Thailand, after Bangkok.

The alliance helped all three kings. It enabled them to stand against the power of the Mons and the Khmer. The northern kingdoms served as a buffer between Sukhothai and the Mongol emperors of China. Mangrai could concentrate on defending his territory from attack by the north, with peace to the south, and Ramkhamhaeng could focus on consolidating his power in the area to the south. According to tradition, the alliance was threatened when Ramkhamhaeng seduced Ngam Muang's wife. However, Mangrai is said to have convinced Ramkhamhaeng to avoid a costly war by admitting his wrongdoing, apologizing, and paying reparations to the royal husband. The three kings are said to have renewed their alliance by drinking a brew in which they had all placed drops of their blood.

Historical tradition credits Ramkhamhaeng with establishing relations with Burma, India, Sri Lanka, and China. Sri Lanka was an important place for reasons of religion because it was a center of the Theravāda school of Buddhism, the version of Buddhism followed by Ramkhamhaeng that also became the national Thai faith. Ramkhamhaeng is said to have brought monks from Sri Lanka to instruct his subjects in proper religious practices and is reported to have sent several missions to China's Mongol rulers. According to tradition, he personally accompanied two of these missions. Following the king's embassies to China, Chinese artisans arrived in Sukhothai, where they taught the craft of making glazed ceramics. Pottery became a major manufacture in the Thai kingdom, exported to other lands, and kilns can still be seen in the ruins of Sukhothai.

In the arts of architecture and sculpture, Sukhothai found its influences close to home. Although ultimately based on Indian models, the city's great stone buildings and statues used models provided by the Mon and by the Burmese, who had themselves drawn on Mon techniques and styles.

One of the greatest accomplishments of Ramkhamhaeng's rule was the creation of Thai writing. According to the inscription on the stone pillar, the king himself was responsible for this cultural advancement, but it seems likely that he commanded and supervised it. Before the late thirteenth century, the Thais had used a writing system based on the Khmer alphabet, which was itself based on the alphabet of India. The new Thai writing brought in Mon influences. Because Thai is a tonal language, in which the meaning of words is determined by their tone or pitch, and Mon and Khmer are not tonal languages, major adaptations were required. The inscription on the king's stone pillar, believed to have been erected about 1292 as the kingdom reached its peak, may have been one of the first times the writing was used, and the pillar is the oldest existing example of written Thai.

Tradition holds that Ramkhamhaeng died when he sank beneath river rapids. After his death, his empire went into decline. It was a patchwork of feudal states, held together by his personal prowess. His son, Lo Tai, and his grandson, Lu Tai, were more dedicated to the pursuit of religion than to their kingdom. In the mid-fourteenth century, another Thai king was crowned and given the royal name of Ramadhipati. Lu Tai became a vassal of Ramadhipati, who built a new capital city, Ayutthaya. Ayutthaya is today regarded as the second Thai kingdom, after Sukhothai, and as the predecessor of the kingdom of Siam, which changed its name to Thailand in 1932.

SIGNIFICANCE

The people of modern Thailand trace their beginnings as a nation back to Sukhothai under King Ramkhamhaeng. This was the first state to establish the dominance of the Central Thai in the land that became known as Siam and, after 1932, as Thailand. Theravāda Buddhism, the religion of Ramkhamhaeng, became the majority religion of the country. The writing system that apparently came into existence in Sukhothai during Ramkhamhaeng's rule remains, with relatively minor changes, the written form of the Thai language.

—*Carl L. Bankston III*

FURTHER READING

Coedès, George. *The Indianized States of Southeast Asia.* Translated by Susan Brown Cowing. Honolulu: East-West Center Press, 1968. The classic work on Southeast Asian history. Section 8 of chapter 12 deals specifically with Sukhothai under Ramkhamhaeng.

Gosling, Betty. *Sukhothai: Its History, Culture, and Art.* Oxford, England: Oxford University Press, 1997. Describes the culture, politics, and history of the kingdom of Sukhothai from the mid-thirteenth through the mid-fifteenth centuries.

Higham, Charles, and Rachanie Thosarat. *Prehistoric Thailand: From Early Settlement to Sukhothai.* London: Thames and Hudson, 1998. The last section discusses the rise of Sukhothai.

Wyatt, David K. *Thailand: A Short History.* New Haven, Conn.: Yale University Press, 1986. Provides an introduction to Thai history, including coverage of the thirteenth century kingdoms.

SEE ALSO: c. 700-1253: Confederation of Thai Tribes; 729: Founding of Nanzhao; 832: Nanzhao Subjugates Pyu; 863: Nanzhao Captures Hanoi.

RELATED ARTICLE in *Great Lives from History: The Middle Ages, 477-1453*: Suryavarman II.

1299
ʿALĀʾ-UD-DĪN MUḤAMMAD KHALJĪ CONQUERS GUJARAT

ʿAlāʾ-ud-Dīn, sultan of Delhi, began the Muslim advance southward by invading Gujarat.

LOCALE: Gujarat, western India

CATEGORIES: Expansion and land acquisition; wars, uprisings, and civil unrest

KEY FIGURE

ʿAlāʾ-ud-Dīn Muḥammad Khaljī (d. 1316), sultan of Delhi, r. 1296-1316

SUMMARY OF EVENT

From the earliest recorded history, the Gujarat region of northwestern India, which constitutes the hinterlands of both shores of the Gulf of Cambay, saw the convergence of maritime trade-routes from southeast Asia, Sri Lanka, the Coromandel and Malabar coasts, the Persian Gulf, the Red Sea, and the east African littoral. Gujarat was therefore the scene of a continuous interchange of goods, people, and ideas.

Muslim Arab and Persian traders and seafarers, as well as Ismāʿīlī missionaries and itinerant Sufis, had long frequented the ports of Gujarat. The first Muslim military incursion into the region, however, came when Maḥmūd of Ghazna (r. 997-1030), the well-known smasher of idols and desecrator of temples, launched a devastating raid across Gujarat in 1024, his goal being the temple of Śiva at Somnath on the coast of Kathiawar. Maḥmūd returned to Ghazna with riches that made his exploit celebrated throughout the Muslim world. The temple itself had been destroyed, its devotees slaughtered, and its immense wealth shorn. Although it was rebuilt during the ensuing century and a half, it was only a matter of time before it attracted another predatory Muslim *ghazi* (holy warrior), claiming to wage *jihad* (holy war) against the Hindu idolaters.

The next person to turn his attention to Gujarat was Muʿizz-ud-Dīn Muḥammad of Ghūr (r. 1173-1206), the architect of the first Muslim state in northern India. Although his aim was to emulate Maḥmūd of Ghazna, he may also have been seeking a route to central India that would bypass the Rājput states of Rajasthan and Malwa. In 1178, he reached as far south as Anhilwara (modern Patan), where he was soundly defeated by the forces of Bhimdeva II of the Solaṅki Dynasty of Gujarat, and thereafter avoided Gujarat for the next two decades. However, in 1197, a Ghūrid army again advanced on Anhilwara, commanded by Muʿizz-ud-Dīn Muḥammad's favorite slave-commander and first sultan of Delhi, Quṭ al-Dīn Aybak (r. 1206-1210), who captured the Solaṅki capital and seized an immense treasure. Once he had withdrawn, however, Solaṅki rule was restored, and for another century, there were no further Muslim incursions.

In 1299, Gujarat was exposed to a much more intensive assault. In 1296, the throne of Delhi was seized by Sultan ʿAlāʾ-ud-Dīn Muḥammad Khaljī, who had murdered the previous sultan, his uncle, Jalāl-ud-Dīn Fīrūz Khaljī (r. 1290-1296), the first ruler of the Khaljī Dynasty (1290-1320). As a usurper and a parricide, Sultan ʿAlāʾ-ud-Dīn, facing numerous conspiracies and almost annual Mongol invasions of Punjab, needed a spectacular military triumph to consolidate his position. Thus, in 1299, he sent his younger brother, Ulugh Khan, and a trusted henchman, Nusrat Khan, jointly to invade Gujarat, which had been unmolested by Muslim raiders for more than a century and was celebrated for its fabulous wealth.

In February, 1299, the army set off, and because it chose a little-known route to avoid conflict with adjacent Rājput rulers, the local Rājput forces in Gujarat were taken by surprise, and the victorious invaders moved against Anhilwara. Rāja Karṇadeva II panicked, abandoned his capital, and fled to Devagiri (Deogir, later Daulatabad, India) in the Deccan. With comparatively little effort, the Khaljīs acquired the immense treasures accumulated by the Solaṅki Dynasty. In addition to precious metals, horses, elephants, and slaves, they captured Rāja Karṇadeva's women, including his rani (queen), Kamala Devi.

Having sacked Anhilwara, the army then (June, 1299) headed for the coast at Somnath, where, after fierce resistance, town and temple were penetrated amid a great slaughter and the acquisition of much booty, satisfying for believers in the ideological imperative of holy war (*jihad*). The objectives of the campaign, plunder and piety, were now achieved, and the army split up to lay waste the countryside in a more leisurely fashion. Ulugh Khan remained to ravage the Kathiawar peninsula, and Nusrat Khan made his way to the port of Cambay, where he levied heavy impositions on the merchant community, Hindu and Muslim alike. Here, too, he acquired his most significant prize.

He purchased from an Arab merchant a Hindu eunuch named Kāfūr for a thousand *dinars*. Of startling beauty, Kāfūr was presented to the sultan, with whom he became so great a favorite that he rose to become *malik naib* (in effect, the sultan's deputy). Appointed commander of the army, he led the advance into the Deccan in 1306-1307, reaching Madura in the far south. Toward the end of the sultan's life, however, Kāfūr plotted the downfall of ʿAlāʾ-ud-Dīn's family, and although his rivals procured his assassination (1316), by then he had undermined the foundations of Khaljī rule.

The two army commanders, Ulugh Khan and Nusrat Khan, now headed for Delhi, where they handed over an immense booty to the sultan. Strangely, they had done nothing to consolidate their conquests: They left no garrison behind, and they appointed no provincial governor. After a while, Rāja Karṇadeva quietly slipped back into Gujarat and resumed his former authority. At this point, fact and fiction merge. According to the poet-historian Amir Khusrau, Karṇadeva's former queen, Kamala Devi, now in ʿAlāʾ-ud-Dīn's harem, urged the sultan to demand that Karṇadeva send his daughter, Deval Devi, to be the wife of the sultan's heir-apparent, Khizr Khan. Karṇadeva, interpreting the dispatch of his daughter as acknowledgment of Delhi's suzerainty over Gujarat, prepared to resist. ʿAlāʾ-ud-Dīn, getting wind of this, sent an expeditionary force into Gujarat in 1304-1305, which

THE DELHI SULTANATE: KHALJĪ DYNASTY

Reign	*Ruler*
1290-1296	Jalāl-ud-Dīn Fīrūz Khaljī
1296-1316	ʿAlāʾ-ud-Dīn Muḥammad Khaljī
1316	ʿUmar Shah
1316-1320	Mubārak Shah
1320	Khusraw Khan Barwari

reached Anhilwara before Karṇadeva was aware of its presence. Karṇadeva was forced to flee precipitately, and because his former host in Devagiri was apprehensive of incurring the sultan's wrath, he sought sanctuary in Warangal, where his death passed unrecorded by the chroniclers.

This time the Khaljī troops remained in Anhilwara for a month, but they did not sack the city. Rather, their commander received orders from Delhi to appoint a temporary governor, and to return to Delhi with Karṇadeva's children, especially Deval Devi. Subsequently, in 1305-1306, ᶜAlāʾ-ud-Dīn ordered his brother-in-law and staunch supporter, Alp Arslan, to take up the governorship of Gujarat and form a permanent administration. For virtually a decade, this able official laid the foundations of Gujarat's prosperity under Muslim rule. As far as was possible, he hammered out a *modus vivendi* with the resentful Rājput elite, he assuaged the apprehensions of the Arab and other coastal trading-communities who had suffered from Nusrat Khan's depredations, and he even managed to earn the goodwill of the influential Jain community. Until it was demolished during the last decade of the eighteenth century, the fine Adina mosque in Anhilwara was the standing monument to his proconsulship. Alp Arslan left Gujarat in the autumn of 1315 for Delhi, where he was promptly assassinated by Malik Kāfūr. For the remainder of the fourteenth century, Gujarat was governed from Delhi with indifferent success, and during much of the reign of Muḥammad ibn Tughluq (r. 1325-1351), it was in revolt. Finally, a governor, Ẓafār Khan, sent to rule the province in 1391, declared himself sultan as Muẓaffar Shah in 1407.

SIGNIFICANCE

The historical sources for the Khaljī conquests of Gujarat conflict. On the Muslim side, there are the Persian histories of Amir Khusrau, Ẓiyāʾ-ud-Dī Baranī, Isami, and others, which glorify the conquest in the name of religion. On the Hindu side, there are the Rājput bardic epics, such as the *Kānhaḍade Prabandha* (fifteenth century; *Kānhaḍada prabandha: India's Greatest Patriotic Saga of Medieval Times*, 1991) by Padmanābha, which describe the heroic resistance of the Rājputs to the incursions of ᶜAlāʾ-ud-Dīn's forces. Written mainly in Old Gujarati (also termed Old Rajasthani) and sometimes in Sanskrit, these are today regarded as glowing statements of national resistance. The basic facts related in these sources differ, and so does their interpretation. Particularly problematic are the divergent traditions regarding the Rājput queens, Kamala Devi and Deval Devi.

Two broad consequences flowed from the Khaljī invasion of Gujarat. First, Gujarat in Muslim hands became a bridgehead through which central and southern India acquired a Muslim presence and eventually independent regional sultanates. Second, the establishment of Muslim rule in Gujarat during the fourteenth century paved the way for a magnificent florescence of syncretistic Indo-Islamic culture, especially in the arts, under the rule of the independent sultans of Gujarat (1391-1583).

—*Gavin R. G. Hambly*

FURTHER READING

Padmanābha. *Kānhaḍada Prabandha: India's Greatest Patriotic Saga of Medieval Times*. Translated by V. S. Bhatnagar. New Delhi: Aditya Prakashan, 1991. A translation of the Rājput epic.

Commissariat, M. S. *A History of Gujarat*. 2 vols. Bombay: Longman, Green, 1938. Authoritative account of the sultanate period.

Forbes, A. Kinloch. *Ras Mala: Or, Hindu Annals of the Province of Goozerat*. 2 vols. Oxford, England: Oxford University Press, 1924. Collection of important bardic traditions.

Jackson, Peter. *The Delhi Sultanate*. Cambridge, England: Cambridge University Press, 1999. The best general history of the period.

Misra, S. C. *The Rise of the Muslim Power in Gujarat*. Delhi, India: Munshiram Manoharlal, 1982. A thorough discussion of resources relating to Kamala Devi and Deval Devi.

SEE ALSO: 1206-1210: Quṭ al-Dīn Aybak Establishes the Delhi Sultanate; 1236-1240: Reign of Raziya; 1347: ᶜAlāʾ-ud-Dīn Bahman Shāh Founds the Bahmanī Sultanate.

RELATED ARTICLE in *Great Lives from History: The Middle Ages, 477-1453*: ᶜAlāʾ-ud-Dīn Muḥammad Khaljī.

July 27, 1302
BATTLE OF BAPHEUS

Osman I, the chief of a minor Turkish principality, defeated a Byzantine army and set his tribe on the conquest of an empire that would eventually supplant the Byzantines and encompass the Middle East and much of North Africa.

LOCALE: Yalakova Dil peninsula near Nicomedia (now İzmit, Turkey)
CATEGORY: Wars, uprisings, and civil unrest

KEY FIGURES

Osman I (c. 1258-1326), the first Ottoman leader, r. 1281 or 1288-1326
Orhan (1288-1360), Osman's son and Ottoman sultan, r. 1326-1360
Andronicus II Palaeologus (1260-1332), Byzantine emperor, r. 1282-1328

SUMMARY OF EVENT

At the beginning of the fourteenth century, Anatolia, once central to the Byzantine Empire, had fallen into disorder, part of the empire's overall decline following the Fourth Crusade (1202-1204), in which Crusaders attacked and seized Constantinople. Byzantine campaigns to reclaim sovereignty and lost lands had all but destroyed the empire's reserves of troops and money. At the same time, the rise of Genghis Khan's Mongol Empire in Central Asia had driven thousands of steppe nomads into Anatolia. One particular tribe of Turkish refugees was the Kayi tribe of the Oğhuz (also known as the Ghuzz) Turks. Initially one of a number of Turkic tribes living on the margin of the Byzantine Empire's agricultural lands, the Oğhuz began to accrue significant power in the late thirteenth century. Under the leadership of Osman and his descendants, this tribe would become the Ottoman Empire.

The Oğhuz lived the typical life of steppe nomads, moving herds of sheep and horses from pasture to pasture. For centuries, small tribes had risen to prominence by predation, by raiding the herds and wealth of their neighbors. The Byzantine crops and lands were thus attractive targets for nomadic raiders. As the Mongol conquests began to drive other nomads—including the Turks—out of Central Asia, many refugees began to convert to Islam. Under the guise of Islamic piety, the raiders became known as *ghāzīs*, or holy warriors of Islam whose raids punished their Christian neighbors. In reality, *ghāzī* raids were just a continuation of the life of predation that the nomads had always practiced. One successful leader among these *ghāzīs* was Osman (called ʿUthmān in Arabic), who became known as Osman Ghāzī. Under Osman, the Oğhuz tasted military success, and by about 1290, he became a *bey* (sometimes written as *beg*) ruling a beylik, a semi-independent Turkish principality. As a *bey*, he began a long-term campaign to seize the Byzantine province of Bithynia, located in northwestern Anatolia.

Bithynia had been a rich Roman province with major cities such as Nicomedia, Nicaea, and Bursa that were thriving centers of trade. During the Fourth Crusade, Crusaders seized the city of Constantinople and created the Latin Kingdom of Constantinople. After sixty years, the Byzantines were finally able to recover their empire, but their power had been terribly diminished and their scant resources committed to regaining lost lands in the Balkans. This diminution of Byzantine strength in the thirteenth century made Bithynian farmsteads and cities increasingly vulnerable to Turkish raids.

In 1301, Osman began to regularize the *ghāzī* raids launched by the Oğhuz with the aim of conquering the Bithynian trade. The problem was that Osman's horse archers were very mobile but lacked the siege engines and skills necessary for storming fortifications. In addition, sieges were also impractical, for cavalry armies needed huge supplies of grain or grazing land to feed their herds. Therefore, Osman began a loose blockade of Nicaea in 1301 intended to interdict supplies and force the city's surrender. Although the Byzantine emperor, Andronicus II Palaeologus, was also trying to recapture his European lands, he had to dispatch a relief force to end the blockade in order to maintain control in Anatolia.

Throughout its long existence, the Byzantine army had incorporated many different types of soldiers. In its glory days, this army had been the most professional and best-drilled force in Europe. As Byzantine lands and revenues began to decline, however, the empire had to rely more heavily on large groups of semiautonomous foreign forces that it would recruit. In 987, for example, Basil II, also known as Basil Bulgaroktonus—the Bulgar Slayer—made an alliance with Kiev, which then provided him with a corps of heavy infantrymen who became known as the Varangian Guard. In a similar fashion, Andronicus increased the size of his diminutive Byzantine army by recruiting a large number of Alan

Osman I proclaiming the Islamic faith. (F. R. Niglutsch)

horsemen in 1301. These Alans were, like the Oğhuz, horse nomads driven out of Central Asia by the relentless advance of the Mongols. Andronicus planned to use a large number of these nomads to augment a relief expedition tasked with restoring order in Bithnyia. This force of some two thousand men was under the command of George Mouzalon, a general from a distinguished military family.

As this force was prepared, Turkish spies reported its plans to Osman. On July 27, 1302 (although the traditional date ascribed to the battle is 1302, researcher Halil Inalcik provides compelling evidence that it actually occurred in 1301), as Mouzalon's men began to approach Nicomedia, they were ambushed by Osman's forces. The ambush took place near Bapheus, which the Ottomans called Koyunhisar. The Byzantine force was composed of disparate contingents that had not drilled together, and under the Ottoman fire, their formations rapidly disintegrated. In the face of the Turkish attack, the infantry, which consisted primarily of local militia, began to retreat. The Alans charged the Turks to cover the rout but were encircled by Osman's men and destroyed. As the Alans died, the rest of the Byzantine force fled, leaving Nicaea on its own.

Osman's forces of approximately five thousand men had triumphed by using the traditional tactics of nomad archers: ambush, massed archery, and encirclement. If the victory was minor in terms of the forces involved, its scope was significant. With the defeat of the only available Byzantine mobile force, Osman and his followers were free to operate in Bithynia unhindered. A number of Byzantine soldiers, frustrated by the inept leadership of their own army, joined forces with the Turks. Many *ghāzīs* from other beyliks joined Osman's retinue, for he had been proved a victorious leader. These diverse adherents soon began to refer to themselves as Osmanlis, or followers of Osman. This legitimacy was crucial, for in the nomadic Turkish culture, a leader could rise only by the acclaim and loyalty of his followers. Thus, Osman's victory at Bapheus was the key to his appeal, and by virtue of it, he was able to gain preeminence—and this was the bedrock on which the Ottoman Empire was built.

SIGNIFICANCE

Although Osman's victory effectively destroyed Byzantine power in Bithynia, the rest of Anatolia was still divided among small Turkish beyliks similar to Osman's. Each competed for prominence in the area, and diverted by their own squabbles, none combined against Osman. With their mobile force destroyed, the Byzantines could not effectively resist without weakening themselves in the Balkans, so the Ottomans could isolate and individually reduce the cities of Bithynia. As a result, Bursa fell in 1326, Nicaea in 1331, and Nicomedia in 1337. Although Osman died in 1324 during the Siege of Bursa, his son Orhan—who had operated as a general under his father—was raised to command and took the title of sultan. Orhan continued Osman's conquests.

To become more efficient in sustaining operations, Orhan and his son Murad I began to create a Byzantine-style bureaucracy and a reformed army that incorporated infantry and siege specialists. As the Ottomans began to take over an empire, they also adopted the Byzantine strategy of playing one enemy off against another. In 1346, Orhan married the daughter of the Byzantine emperor to seal an alliance that provided Ottoman support for the Byzantine emperor against his rival for the throne while giving Orhan access to Byzantine trade, which funded his campaigns against rival beyliks. This adroit diplomacy, when married to Ottoman successes on the battlefield, fostered expansion. Thus the Ottomans rose to create an empire through a combination of skill on the battlefield as exhibited by Osman and his son Orhan, administrative savvy, and their location close to Byzantine trade yet insulated by distance from the power of the Mongol Il-Khans.

—*Kevin B. Reid*

FURTHER READING

Bartusis, Mark C. *The Late Byzantine Army: Arms and Society, 1204-1453*. Philadelphia: University of Pennsylvania Press, 1992. A very good work for placing Osman's victory in the context of the competing needs of an empire struggling to regain what it had lost after the Fourth Crusade.

Inalcik, Halil. "Osman Ghazi's Siege of Nicaea and the Battle of Bapheus." In *The Ottoman Emirate (1300-1389)*, edited by Elizabeth Zachariadou. Rethymnon, Crete: Crete University Press, 1993. This chapter is the clearest and most useful study to date on the battle. It is especially useful for its discussion of the Ottoman legendary histories of the battle.

_______. *The Ottoman Empire: The Classical Age, 1300-1600*. London: Phoenix Press, 2001. A very accessible history of Ottoman society and the Ottoman conquests.

Köprülü, Mehmet Fuat. *The Origins of the Ottoman Empire*. Albany: State University of New York Press, 1992. An excellent study of the social and political milieu from which Osman sprang.

Lindner, Rudi Paul. *Nomads and Ottomans in Medieval Anatolia*. Bloomington, Ind.: Research Institute for Inner Asian Studies, 1983. Looks in great depth into the organizational structure of the *ghāzīs*, Osman's success in attracting Christian Byzantine adherents, and the structure of Osman's rule.

Nicol, Donald M. *The Last Centuries of Byzantium, 1261-1453*. New York: Cambridge University Press, 1993. Covers the intrigues over the throne that weakened the Byzantine Empire and follows the travails of the Alans recruited by Andronicus.

SEE ALSO: 956: Oğhuz Turks Migrate to Transoxiana; 1204: Knights of the Fourth Crusade Capture Constantinople.

RELATED ARTICLE in *Great Lives from History: The Middle Ages, 477-1453*: Osman I.

November 18, 1302
BONIFACE VIII ISSUES THE BULL *UNAM SANCTAM*

After much division between the church and state, Boniface VIII issued the bull Unam sanctam, *which stated that the pope held supreme power over the state.*

LOCALE: Rome (now in Italy)
CATEGORIES: Laws, acts, and legal history; religion

KEY FIGURES

Celestine V (c. 1209-1296), Roman Catholic pope, July 5-December 13, 1294
Boniface VIII (c. 1235-1303), Roman Catholic pope, 1294-1303
Philip IV the Fair (1267 or 1268-1314), king of France, r. 1285-1314
Guillaume de Nogaret (c. 1260-1313), French jurist and minister to Philip

SUMMARY OF EVENT

After the death of Pope Nicholas IV in 1292, the Papacy remained vacant for more than two years because of factionalism within the College of Cardinals. The Colonnas, a leading family in Roman politics, included two cardinals, James and Peter, who represented French interests, whereas their opponents, the Orsini, favored a Roman or Italian pontiff. The issue was resolved through the election of Peter of Murrone, an eighty-five-year-old hermit from the mountainous country of the Abruzzi. Calling himself Celestine V, the new pontiff's naïveté and inexperience made it possible for others to exploit the papal office because the pope affixed his signature to blank bulls, permitting the recipient to fill in whatever he chose. By the end of 1294, Peter, aware of his deficiencies, issued a bull declaring his right to resign, and he relinquished his office. Although the canonists affirmed the legality of Peter's decision, a papal resignation was without precedent, and it cast doubt on the legitimacy of his successor. Within less than two weeks, Benedict Gaetani was elected to succeed Celestine V, and he took the name Boniface VIII.

An aristocratic Roman who was also somewhat elderly, the new pope was reported to be of bad temper. A dispute arose between Pope Boniface and Philip IV the Fair, king of France, over the right of kings to tax the clergy in their realms. In 1296, France and England were at war, and each king taxed the Church in his lands to finance the project. The pope issued an edict or bull, *Clericis laicos*, in which he declared that any cleric who paid taxes to a secular lord, and any lord who levied or received taxes from the Church, automatically incurred excommunication. In effect, the bull denied absolute authority to a sovereign within his own kingdom. Philip retaliated by forbidding the exportation of gold and silver, jewelry, and currency from France, thereby cutting off papal revenues, and French publicists began attacking the papal position.

Early in 1297, pressured by bankers and a hostile group of cardinals who accused the pope of heresy, Boniface issued the bull *Romana mater*, which largely suspended *Clericis laicos*. The pope not only agreed to the levying of taxes on the clergy, but in certain cases, he also made it permissible without the consent of Rome. A subsequent bull left to the king the decision as to whether such assessment was necessary. One explanation that has been proposed for the pope's abrupt change of opinion was his preoccupation with a crusade against the Colonnas in Italy. At the height of this quarrel, Boniface made peace with Philip. In 1299, the Colonna stronghold, Palestrina, was razed by papal troops, plowed under, and sown with salt.

In 1300, Boniface declared a Jubilee year during which thousands of pilgrims flocked to Rome to gain the special indulgences made available. Cynics view the Jubilee merely as an attempt to line the papal coffers, but the pope was undoubtedly also prompted by religious motives. The overwhelming success of the Jubilee may have given the pope a false idea of the support he commanded among the faithful in Europe. Buoyed up with misplaced confidence, he renewed the struggle with Philip.

In 1301, Bernard Saisset, bishop of Pamiers and Boniface's legate to Paris, was arrested by Philip's agents for treason, blasphemy, and heresy. He was tried in the king's court, declared guilty, and imprisoned. A basic principle of the canon law of the Church reserved the trial of churchmen for church courts, especially when the accusation involved heresy. Boniface was compelled either to acquiesce in Philip's complete control of the French Church or to offer vigorous opposition. He ordered Saisset to be set free, and he summoned all French bishops to Rome to discuss the state of the French Church. He declared that in the case of wicked rulers, popes had the jurisdiction to take authority in temporal affairs. In a long personal letter to Philip, the pope sharply reproved him for his conduct toward the Church and went on to say, "Let no one persuade you that you have no superior or that you are not subject to the head of the ecclesiastical hierarchy, for he is a fool who so thinks."

Philip had the letter burned, and he forged another as having come from Boniface and making extreme claims for the Papacy. The forgery was calculated to stir French indignation and prompt a feeling of national hostility toward the pope. In April, 1302, Philip held an assembly of clergy, nobles, and townsmen at the Cathedral of Notre Dame in Paris, an assembly that is considered the first meeting of the Estates General. The nobility and commons, supporting the king in his antipapal position, sent a letter to the cardinals in Rome, declaring their refusal to recognize Boniface as lawful pope. The French clergy composed a less radical reply. In November, 1302, the pope's council met with about half the French bishops in attendance. One of the bulls issuing from this council was *Unam sanctam* ("one holy and catholic and apostolic church"), which was published on November 18.

In this bull, perhaps the most famous of all medieval bulls, no mention is made of the conflict with Philip. In-

FROM THE *UNAM SANCTAM*

According to the law of the universe all things are not equally and directly reduced to order, but the lowest are fitted into their order through the intermediate, and the lower through the higher. And we must necessarily admit that the spiritual power surpasses any earthly power in dignity and honor, because spiritual things surpass temporal things. . . . For the truth itself declares that the spiritual power must establish the temporal power. . . . [I]f the temporal power errs, it will be judged by the spiritual power, and if the lower spiritual power errs, it will be judged by its superior. But if the highest spiritual power errs, it cannot be judged by men, but by God alone. . . . Therefore, whosoever resisteth this power [the Papacy] thus ordained of God resisteth the ordinance of God. . . . We therefore declare, say, and affirm that submission on the part of every man to the bishop of Rome is altogether necessary for his salvation.

Source: Milton Viorst, *The Great Documents of Western Civilization* (Philadelphia: Chilton Books, 1965), p. 68.

stead, it sets forth the theoretical justification for papal primacy in Christian society regardless of time and place. It opens with statements on the unity of the Church, outside which there is no salvation or remission of sins. Numerous analogies from Scripture are used to support this unity: Noah's ark, Christ's seamless garment, the body of Christ, and the Church as a flock. In the Church, there are two swords, spiritual and temporal, "but the one is exercised for the church, the other by the church, the one by the hand of the priest, the other by the hand of kings and soldiers, though at the will and suffrance of the priest." When the earthly power errs, it can be judged by the spiritual; but when the spiritual power errs, it can be judged by God alone. The most frequently quoted assertion from the bull is its conclusion taken verbatim from a statement made by Thomas Aquinas: "Therefore we declare, state, define, and pronounce that it is altogether necessary to salvation for every human creature to be subject to the Roman pontiff."

Philip delayed a response to this challenge until the spring of 1303, when he had made plans to bring Boniface to France as a captive. In June, 1303, Philip held a council at the Louvre in which charges were brought against the pope, including simony, fornication, demon possession, illegal deposition of Celestine V, and denying the Eucharist. At the same time, Philip received word that Boniface intended to excommunicate him and had written that all subjects should deny allegiance to France. Jurist Guillaume de Nogaret, in league with Sciarra Colonna, was dispatched to Anagni, outside Rome, where Boniface was staying. With three hundred horses and a thousand footmen, they stormed the papal residence and, according to an eyewitness of the "outrage of Anagni," physically abused the aged pontiff. While the conspirators were debating their course of action, the townspeople rose up and expelled the invaders. Although Boniface was spared the ignominy of capture, he died a month later in October, 1303.

SIGNIFICANCE

Boniface's successor, Benedict XI, excommunicated Nogaret and attempted to negotiate with Philip, but he lived only a short time. Benedict was followed by Clement V, a Frenchman who succumbed to French pressure by removing the papal residence to Avignon and by lifting the excommunication from Nogaret in 1311. Clement also commended Philip for the piety and zeal he had displayed in his relations with Boniface. Both Clement and Philip died in 1314. The papal residency remained in France until 1377, during which seven popes were installed. This period became known as the Babylonian Captivity of the Church.

—*Carl A. Volz, updated by Marilyn Elizabeth Perry*

FURTHER READING

Barraclough, Geoffrey. *The Medieval Papacy.* New York: W. W. Norton, 1979. The pontificate of Boniface VIII was a disaster of the first magnitude for the Church. Not Boniface but the system was at fault, according to this author.

Boase, Thomas Sherer. *Boniface VIII.* 1933. Reprint. Wilmington, Del.: International Academic Publishers, 1979. In what is probably the best and most exhaustive work on Boniface available in English, Boase points out that the bull *Unam sanctam* contains nothing new.

Denton, Jeffrey Howard. *Philip the Fair and the Ecclesiastical Assemblies of 1294-1295.* Philadelphia: American Philosophical Society, 1991. An account of the interactions between Philip IV the Fair and Boniface VIII. Indexes.

Eno, Robert B. *The Rise of the Papacy.* Wilmington, Del.: M. Glazier, 1990. The history and doctrines of the early and medieval Roman Catholic Church.

Tierney, Brian. *The Crisis of Church and State, 1050-1300.* Medieval Academy Reprints for Teaching 21. Toronto: University of Toronto Press, 1988. A collection of documents with commentary viewing the dispute as one involving national sovereignty.

Ullmann, Walter. *A Short History of the Papacy in the Middle Ages.* 1972. Reprint. New York: Routledge, 2003. A careful survey of papal history from its development in the late Roman imperial period to the Protestant Reformation.

Wood, Charles T., ed. *Philip the Fair and Boniface VIII.* Huntington, N.Y.: R. E. Kreiger, 1976. The interpretations of fifteen historians, together with a useful annotated bibliography for further study.

SEE ALSO: November 11-30, 1215: Fourth Lateran Council; 1233: Papal Inquisition; 1248-1254: Failure of the Seventh Crusade; c. 1265-1273: Thomas Aquinas Compiles the *Summa Theologica*; 1305-1417: Avignon Papacy and the Great Schism; January 10, 1356, and December 25, 1356: Golden Bull.

RELATED ARTICLES in *Great Lives from History: The Middle Ages, 477-1453*: Boniface VIII; Philip IV the Fair; Thomas Aquinas.

1305-1417
AVIGNON PAPACY AND THE GREAT SCHISM

The Avignon Papacy (1305-1378) and Great Schism (1378-1417) inaugurated the crisis of the Catholic Church that culminated in the Protestant Reformation of the sixteenth century.

LOCALE: Medieval Europe
CATEGORY: Religion

KEY FIGURES

Clement V (c. 1260-1314), pope, 1305-1314
John XXII (c. 1244-1334), pope, 1316-1334
Benedict XII (c. 1280-1342), pope, 1334-1342
Clement VI (1291-1352), pope, 1342-1352
Innocent VI (1282-1362), pope, 1352-1362
Urban V (1310-1370), pope, 1362-1370
Gregory XI (1329-1378), pope, 1370-1378
Urban VI (c. 1318-1389), pope, 1378-1389
Clement VII (1342-1394), antipope, 1378-1394
Benedict XIII (c. 1328-1423), antipope, 1394-1423

SUMMARY OF EVENT

The power of the Church grew considerably during the central Middle Ages. The reform programs that revitalized the spiritual life of the Church in the eleventh and twelfth centuries dramatically exalted the authority of the Papacy. By the time of the mighty Innocent III (1198-1216), the pope had eclipsed the Holy Roman Emperor as the acknowledged head of western Christendom, ruling a vast administrative "state" that extended throughout the kingdoms of Europe. After 1250, however, the "papal monarchy" began to falter. The popes lost some of the reforming zeal that had won the Papacy such prestige, and they underestimated the growth of royal power in Europe's emerging "national kingdoms." When Pope Boniface VIII (1294-1303) attempted to defend ecclesiastical liberties from royal encroachment in France, Philip IV the Fair (r. 1285-1314) sent royal agents to arrest the pope; their mistreatment of the pope contributed to his death a few weeks later.

Boniface's pontificate provoked such fierce conflicts in Italy that his successors were unable to remain in Rome. After the brief pontificate of Benedict XI (1303-1304), the cardinals—themselves divided between pro- and anti-Bonifacian factions—elected the archbishop of Bordeaux, Bertrand de Got, as Clement V (1305-1314). Clement's neutrality and Gallic background made him an attractive compromise candidate, but they also left him vulnerable. He knew little of Italian affairs and had no experience with the political machinations of the Sacred College of Cardinals. Seeking refuge from the Italian storm, he turned to the familiar territory of the Midi, establishing the Papal Curia (the governmental body of the pope and Church) at Avignon in 1309. He also built up a loyal faction in the Sacred College, traditionally dominated by Italians, raising up twenty-three Gallic cardinals, most of whom came, like Clement himself, from Languedoc (in modern-day France).

Clement's death left the cardinals deeply divided. The new Gallic majority had no desire to hurry back to war-torn Rome; the Italians hoped to return as soon as possible. The factions feuded for more than two years before electing Cardinal Jacques Duèse as John XXII (1316-1334). Though elderly, John proved a forceful, capable pope. Professing his desire to return to Rome, he sent Cardinals Bertrand du Poujet (d. 1352) and Giovanni Orsini (d. 1336) as legates to Italy and took vigorous action against Emperor Louis IV (1314-1347), also called Ludwig IV, who sought to reassert imperial authority in Italy during the Papacy's absence. The legates drove Louis and his feeble antipope, Nicholas V (1328-1330; d. 1333), from Italy, but failed to pacify Italy. Yet even as he worked toward return, John undertook sweeping bureaucratic reforms that transformed Avignon into an administrative hub capable of governing the international Church indefinitely. Moreover, most of John's new cardinals were Gallic and thus unlikely to advocate prompt return to Rome. By John's death, the Papacy was no nearer to Rome than it had been at the time of his election.

In 1337, the Hundred Years' War between France and England began. Believing that they could negotiate peace more effectively in Avignon than in Rome, Benedict XII (1334-1342) and Clement VI (1342-1352) prepared to remain in Avignon indefinitely. Benedict began construction of the papal palace there and Clement bought the rights to the town from the countess of Provence in 1348. Innocent VI (1352-1362) and Urban V (1362-1370) were more energetic in pursuing return. Their remarkable legate, Cardinal Gil Albornoz, pacified Italy enough that Urban V could come to Rome, albeit briefly, in 1367. In the end, it fell to Gregory XI (1370-1378)—nephew of Clement VI—to return for good. Ignoring the pleas of the French king and his own cardinals, Gregory returned to Rome in 1377.

Gregory's premature death from malaria in 1378 engendered a more serious problem. Fearing that another

Gallic pope would return to Avignon, the Roman people forced the cardinals to elect the archbishop of Bari, Bartolomeo Prignani, as Urban VI (1378-1389). When Urban became mentally unstable, the Gallic cardinals nullified his election (though they did not have the legal power to do so) and withdrew to Avignon, where they elected Cardinal Robert of Geneva as Pope Clement VII (1378-1394). Urban refused to step down; now Christendom had two rival popes, one in Rome and one in Avignon. The Great Schism had begun.

Nor did it end with the deaths of the two principals. When Urban died, his cardinals elected first Boniface IX (1389-1404), then Innocent VII (1404-1406) and Gregory XII (1406-1415); in Avignon, Clement's cardinals elected Benedict XIII (1394-1423). Hoping to end the schism, a group of Roman and Avignonese cardinals met at Pisa in 1409. After boldly but vainly declaring Gregory XII and Benedict XIII deposed, they elected a new pope, Alexander V (1409-1410). Now, *three* popes contested the throne of Saint Peter. The division of the Church seemed more hopeless than ever.

The schism finally ended at the Council of Constance (1414-1418), summoned by the Holy Roman Emperor from Hungary, Sigismund (r. 1433-1437), and attended by representatives from all over western Christendom. Gregory XII and the Pisan pope, John XXIII (1409-1415), reluctantly agreed to abdicate; Benedict XIII was deposed in absentia, and Cardinal Oddo Colonna was elected as Pope Martin V (1417-1431). The defiance of the now marginal Benedict XIII was at worst an inconvenience. The Great Schism was over; now the work of rebuilding the Church could begin.

The Avignon Papacy and the Great Schism did great damage to the later medieval Church. Saint Brigit of Sweden (c. 1303-1373) and Saint Catherine of Siena (c. 1347-1380) spoke for many when they lamented the Papacy's abandonment of its rightful seat in Rome. The view that the Avignon popes were indifferent to Church reform is incorrect, but the largely bureaucratic nature of their reform initiatives left unaddressed the contemporary yearning for significant moral and spiritual regeneration. The continued emergence of new heresies, John

The Papal Palace at Avignon. (Hulton|Archive by Getty Images)

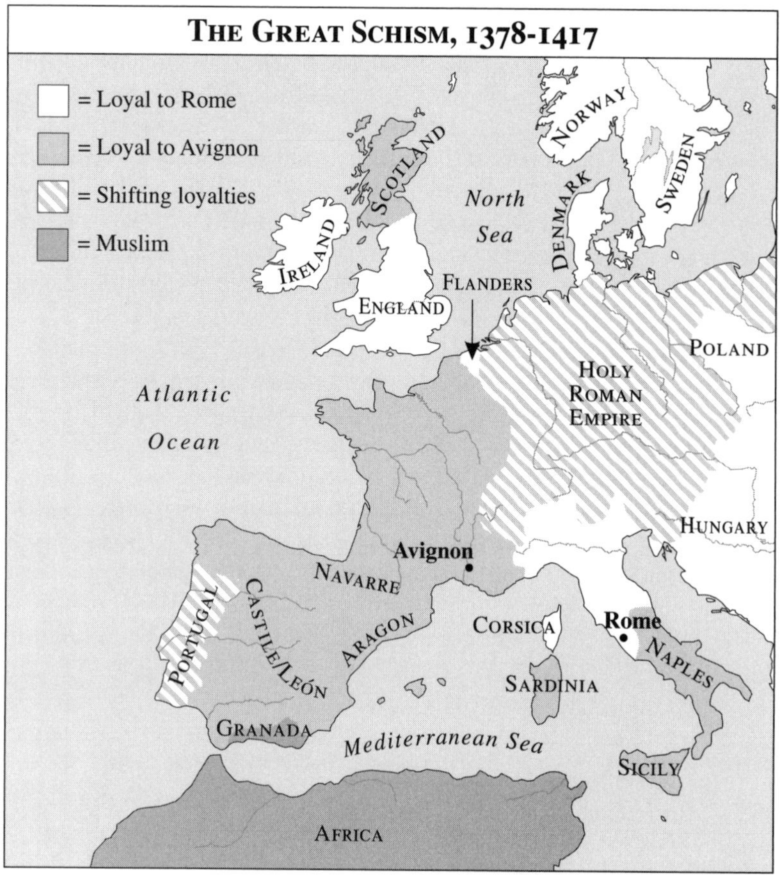

XXII's fierce battles with the Franciscans, and the growth of lay religious movements like the *devotio moderna* (a pietistic movement) all suggest that the Papacy had lost touch with new spiritual impulses at work in Christian society. Moreover, the lavishness of the Avignonese court, especially under Clement VI, was widely condemned. Not surprisingly, many contemporaries regarded the terrible Black Death (1347-1352) as divine punishment for a sinful society under the direction of a corrupted Church.

Still, the excesses attributed to the Avignon popes were exaggerated. Many of the Avignon Papacy's leading detractors—such as the Florentine poet Petrarch (1304-1374), who dubbed the Avignon Papacy the Babylonian Captivity of the Church—were Italians who resented what they saw as a Gallic appropriation of an institution that had been culturally Italian for time immemorial. Even the "Frenchness" of the Avignon Papacy was more apparent than real. Though they often favored the kings of France, the Avignon popes were by no means puppets of the French crown. Avignon itself was not part of French territory, and the popes (and most of their cardinals) were Languedocians who differed in language and culture from the French to the north.

SIGNIFICANCE

If the Avignon Papacy was chiefly a "public relations" disaster, the Great Schism was an unmitigated catastrophe. Its roots lay in the cultural tensions that the Avignon Papacy spawned, but its immediate causes and consequences evince a genuine institutional collapse. The spectacle of multiple popes hurling anathemas at one another accelerated the decline in papal prestige and prompted new challenges to the Papacy's authority. One such challenge, conciliarism, advocated the use of general councils as a means of ending the schism, arguing that the authority of a council was superior to that of the pope. Although most fifteenth century councils were dismal failures, conciliarism remained influential in intellectual circles until the 1460's.

The schism was devastating to the Church's administrative machinery, forcing Martin V and his successors to rebuild it from the ground up. Meanwhile, the power and effectiveness of secular governments grew steadily. The schism also intensified divisions within Christendom as rival powers aligned themselves with competing papal obediences to provide religious justification for ongoing conflicts. Broad-based movements such as Lollardy in England and the Hussite heresy in Bohemia, which denied the legitimacy of the Papacy, reveal the extent to which the schism eroded the notion of papal indispensability. Thus, the Catholic controversies of the fourteenth and fifteenth centuries contributed directly to the religious climate in which the Protestant Reformation was born.

—*Blake R. Beattie*

FURTHER READING

Holmes, George. *Europe, Hierarchy and Revolt, 1320-1450.* 2d ed. Malden, Mass.: Blackwell, 2000. Includes chapters on the Avignon and Roman Papacies, the Great Schism, and the Hussite movement, and several maps.

Loomis, Louise Ropes, trans. *The Council of Constance: The Unification of the Church*. Edited and annotated by John Hine Mundy and Kennerly M. Woody. New York: Columbia University Press, 1961. An excellent collection of primary sources on the Council of Constance and its inner workings.

Mollat, Guillaume. *The Popes at Avignon, 1305-1378*. Translated by Janet Love. London: T. Nelson, 1963. An essential narrative of the Avignon Papacy by one of the best scholars of the Avignon period.

Muldoon, James. *Canon Law, the Expansion of Europe, and World Order*. Aldershot, England: Ashgate, 1998. Includes the chapter, "The Avignon Papacy and the Frontiers of Christendom."

Oakley, Francis. *The Western Church in the Later Middle Ages*. Ithaca, N.Y.: Columbia University Press, 1979. Concise overview of the major developments in ecclesiastical history from the Avignon Papacy to the eve of the Reformation.

Renouard, Yves. *The Avignon Papacy, 1305-1403*. Translated by Denis Bethell. Hamden, Conn.: Archon Books, 1970. Less thorough than Mollat, but with a greater focus on the sociological and economic implications of the Avignon Papacy.

Stump, Phillip H. *The Reforms of the Council of Constance, 1414-1418*. New York: E. J. Brill, 1994. Discusses the reforms of papal provisions and members and discusses the council's "objects and agents." Includes an appendix with the reform committee's deliberations and indices of biblical texts and legal citations.

Ullmann, Walter. *The Origins of the Great Schism: A Study in Fourteenth-century Ecclesiastical History*. Hamden, Conn.: Archon Books, 1967. An excellent examination of the Schism's cultural and institutional roots.

SEE ALSO: 726-843: Iconoclastic Controversy; 1054: Beginning of the Rome-Constantinople Schism; November 18, 1302: Boniface VIII Issues the Bull *Unam Sanctam*; c. 1310-1350: William of Ockham Attacks Thomist Ideas; 1337-1453: Hundred Years' War; 1347-1352: Invasion of the Black Death in Europe; May 20, 1347-October 8, 1354: Cola di Rienzo Leads Popular Uprising in Rome; c. 1350-1400: Petrarch and Boccaccio Recover Classical Texts; January 10, 1356, and December 25, 1356: Golden Bull; 1377-1378: Condemnation of John Wyclif; 1414-1418: Council of Constance; July 6, 1415: Martyrdom of Jan Hus.

RELATED ARTICLES in *Great Lives from History: The Middle Ages, 477-1453*: Adrian IV; Giovanni Boccaccio; Saint Brigit; Saint Catherine of Siena; Charles IV; Henry V; Jan Hus; Nicholas V; William of Ockham; Petrarch; Cola di Rienzo; Thomas à Kempis; Wenceslaus; John Wyclif.

c. 1306-1320
DANTE WRITES *THE DIVINE COMEDY*

Dante's masterwork, in which he relates a journey through the three realms of the Christian otherworld—Hell, Purgatory, and Paradise—represents the summation of classical antiquity and the cultural landscape of the European Middle Ages.

LOCALE: Florence (now in Italy)
CATEGORIES: Cultural and intellectual history; literature

KEY FIGURES

Dante (1265-1321), poet and author of *The Divine Comedy*
Cacciaguida (c. 1090-1148), an ancestor of Dante
Beatrice Portinari (1266-1290), the woman who inspired much of Dante's work and a central figure in *The Divine Comedy*
Boniface VIII (c. 1235-1303), pope, 1294-1303
Henry VII of Luxembourg (1275?-1313), king of Germany, r. 1308-1313, and Holy Roman Emperor, r. 1312-1313
Vergil (70-19 B.C.E.), poet and author of the *Aeneid*, whom Dante depicts as his guide through Hell and Purgatory
Statius (between 40 and 45-c. 96 C.E.), author of the *Thebaid*, depicted as Dante's guide in the last part of *Purgatory*
Saint Bernard of Clairvaux (1090-1153), abbot of Clairvaux, depicted as Dante's last guide

SUMMARY OF EVENT

Dante Alighieri was born in the Tuscan city-state of Florence in May or June, 1265. Both his grandfather Alighiero Bellincione and his father Alighiero II were moneylenders, a fact that may have influenced the poet's reticence in speaking of his immediate family in his opus. The noble lineage of Dante's family is recorded in the poet's encounter with his ancestor Cacciaguida in *La divina commedia* (c. 1320; *The Divine Comedy*, 1802, in the first part, *Paradise*, XV-XVIII), who died in the Crusades in 1148 under Emperor Conrad III. Cacciaguida had married a noblewoman, perhaps from Ferrara, named Alighiera or Aldighiera—thus the name Alighieri.

Dante was born at a turbulent time for Florence, which was lacerated by internal and external conflicts between the Guelph and Ghibelline parties. These two factions respectively represented the merchant and "middle" classes, sympathetic to the Papacy, and the old aristocracy, sympathetic to the Holy Roman Emperor, Henry VII of Luxembourg. Dante came from a Guelph family of modest means. The Battle of Benevento (February 26, 1266), in which Charles of Anjou defeated King Manfred (*Purgatory* 3:103ff.), put an end to the Ghibelline domination of the southern Kingdom of Naples and established Guelph domination in Tuscany.

Before writing the *The Divine Comedy* (the adjective "divine" was added with the first Venetian edition of 1555), Dante was very much part of the intellectual and political life of his city. His poetic training was unmistakably linked to a group of Florentine poets, headed by his "first friend," Guido Cavalcanti (c. 1259-1300), who practiced the *dolce stil nuovo*, or sweet new style. These *stilnovisti* considered the Tuscan-Sicilian poets who preceded them to be artificial and provincial. At age eighteen, Dante, upon meeting Beatrice Portinari for the second time (he had met her nine years before, in 1274), had already written the first sonnet of *La vita nuova* (c. 1292; *Vita Nuova*, 1861; better known as *The New Life*), "A ciascun alma presa e gentil cor" (to every-loving gentle hearted friend), and had sent it to fellow troubadours and to Cavalcanti, who replied with his own sonnet.

Beatrice, a simple young maiden, became Dante's inspiration and muse, shrouded by the mystic and sublime image of the *donna gentile, donna angelicata* (the gentle, angel-like woman), a true miracle on earth and the subject of highest praise in the sonnets and *canzoni* of *Vita Nuova*. Beatrice's sublime image is enhanced by her association with the number nine, a multiple of three; it is related in chapter 30 that she died in the first hour of the ninth day of the ninth month, in the ninth decade of the century, 1290. The *Vita Nuova* is an assemblage of prose-poems, or *prosimetrum* (completed c. 1294 in imitation of Boethius), a treatise on poetry, and a *fabula* of the poet's mystical and spiritual love for Beatrice. The poet states that he will write of her things he has never said of any woman, and in the very last sonnet, he expresses the lover's desire to reach the light of Beatrice shining in the Empyrean, thus announcing the journey through the three realms of the *The Divine Comedy*.

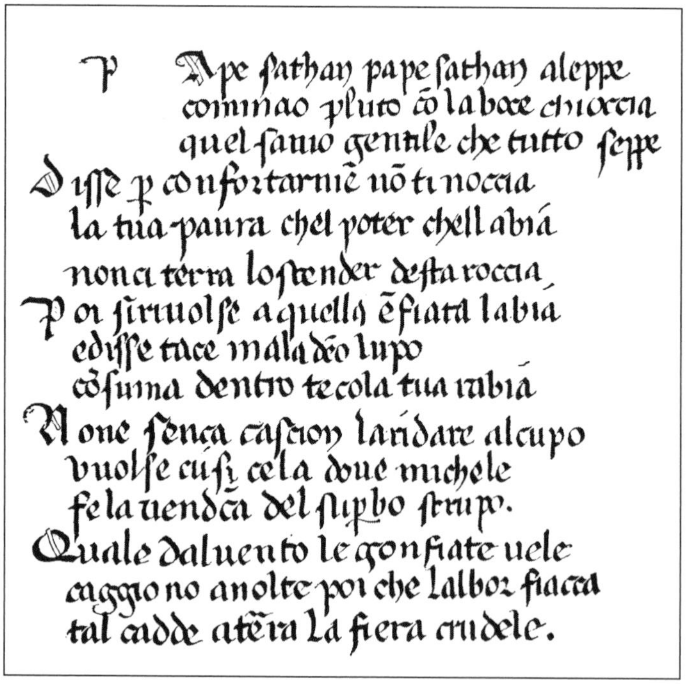
P Ape sathan pape sathan aleppe
cominciao pluto cō la boce chioccia
quel savio gentile che tutto seppe
Disse p confortarmi nō ti noccia
la tua paura chel poter chell abia
non ci terra lo scender desta roccia
Poi si rivolse a quella ēfiata labia
edisse tace maladeo lupo
cōsuma dentro te cola tua rabia
Non e sença cagion landare alcupo
vuolse cusi cela doue michele
fe la uendeta del superbo strupo.
Quale dal vento le gonfiate uele
caggiono avolte poi che lalbor fiacca
tal cadde atera la fiera crudele.

A fragment from a fourteenth century manuscript of Dante's Divine Comedy *from the Bibliothèque National de Paris.* (Frederick Ungar Publishing Co.)

In 1285, Dante married Gemma Donati, with whom he had three children, Pietro, Jacopo, and Antonia (a supposed fourth one, Giovanni, is dubious). He was a cavalryman against the Ghibelline city of Arezzo at the Battle of Campaldino (June 11, 1289) and at the Siege of Caprona (August, 1289). From 1290 (the year of Beatrice's death) to 1293, he studied philosophy and theology in religious schools such as Florence's Franciscan Convent of Santa Croce. In 1295 he joined the Guild of the Physicians and Apothecaries in order to be able to participate in the city's political life, as established by the Ordinances of Justice of 1293. In 1296 Dante became part of the Council of One Hundred, and from June 15 to August 15, 1300, he served as one of six priors.

THE NINE CIRCLES OF DANTE'S HELL

(1) Limbo: neutral souls
(2) The Carnal
(3) Gluttons
(4) Hoarders and Wasters
(5) The Wrathful and Sullen
(6) Heretics
(7) The Violent and Bestial: Murderers, Suicides, Blasphemers, Sodomites, Usurers
(8) Perpetrators of Simple Fraud: Panderers, Seducers, Flatterers, Simoniacs, Fortune-Tellers, Grafters, Hypocrites, Thieves, Evil Counsellors, Sowers of Discord, Falsifiers
(9) Perpetrators of Compound Fraud: against kin, country, guests and hosts, lords and benefactors, church and empire

In the same year, Pope Boniface VIII, Dante's fierce political enemy and supporter of the Blacks (one of two factions within the Guelphs—the other being the Whites), who believed in the supremacy of the spiritual over temporal power as he would express in his bull *Unam sanctam* (1302), proclaimed the first Jubilee. The political situation in Florence was deteriorating as a result of the civil war between Blacks and Whites, headed respectively by Corso Donati and Vieri dei Cerchi, and Dante was one of the magistrates who approved the banishment of fifteen leaders of the Blacks and Whites. Among them was his friend Guido Cavalcanti, who would contract malaria near Sarzana and die in the same year.

On June 19, 1301, in the Council of One Hundred, Dante was the sole opponent to the pope's demand for Florentine troops to aid his forces in Tuscany. In September, while Boniface was entertaining Charles of Valois in Anagni and plotting against Florence, Dante formed part of an embassy to placate the pontiff. In October, Boniface sent the ambassadors back but kept Dante in Rome. On November 1, Charles of Valois entered Florence, pretending to be a peacemaker, and Corso Donati and the Blacks took over the city.

In January of 1302, the Blacks falsely condemned Dante of barratry (breach of duty) and imposed a fine of five thousand gold florins and a two-year banishment from Tuscany. Thereafter Dante lived in exile and would never again set foot in his native city. Although he did participate in attempts to recapture the city, after the battle at Lastra in July of 1304, he spent the rest of his life in intellectual pursuits and some ambassadorial duties.

In the years following, Dante produced a body of lyric poetry or *canzoniere*, an unfinished treatise in Latin on the virtues of the Italian vernacular (*De vulgari eloquentia*, c. 1306; English translation, 1890), an unfinished philosophical work (*Il convivio*, c. 1307; *The Banquet*, 1887), a political treatise presenting logical philosophical and theological arguments on the role of the emperor and the Church (*De monarchia*, c. 1313; English translation, 1890; also known as *Monarchy*, 1954; better known as *On World Government*, 1957), thirteen epistles in Latin ("Epistola X," c. 1316; English translation, 1902), and one exegetical to Cangrande, lord of Verona, all in the lofty style essential to his ideas. In his final years, Dante composed two Latin eclogues (*Eclogae*, 1319; *Eclogues*, 1902) and the treatise *Quaestio de aqua et terra* (1320; English translation, 1902).

In the epistle dedicating the *Paradiso* to Cangrande (c. 1316), Dante explains that the work is titled *Commedia* because it ends well and is written in the humble style of the vernacular, not the lofty one of tragedy, as rhetorical rules required. The epistle, whose authenticity is disputed, proposes a fourfold exegetical method of interpretation of the *Commedia* so that the pilgrim's journey in the poem is analogous to the redemptive journey of the soul from a state of misery and confusion to one of joy and salvation—just as the nation of Israel was freed from the slavery of Egypt to the glory of Jerusalem (Psalm 113).

The actual occurrence of the journey, lasting seven days, begins on Holy Thursday, April 8 of the Jubilee year 1300. The poem consists of 14,233 verses, 100 *canti* (1 + 33 + 33 + 33) divided into three *cantiche* (each with 10 subdivisions), written entirely in terza rima, a measure that relies on the numbers 1 and 3. All this and more underscores the poem's numerological symbolism. The *Inferno*, the first and most dramatic *cantica*, begun after 1306, portrays in realistic and vivid terms a journey through a funnel-shaped Hell, after the poet is lost in a dark wood and rescued by Vergil (whose own *Aeneid*, c. 29-19 B.C.E.; English translation, 1553, appropriately, describes a journey of the Trojan hero Aeneas into the underworld). Dante, being a new Aeneas and a new Saint Paul (who was taken up to the third heaven), combines the classical and Christian traditions to explore the underworld.

The sins portrayed in the *Inferno* are structured according to an Aristotelian and Ciceronian tripartite division of incontinence, violence, and fraud corresponding to the three animals that impede the pilgrim's (Dante-Everyman's) path: Lonza-leopard, Leone-lion, and Lupa-shewolf, all with the letter *L* in Italian to represent

Lucifer, the image of the evil Trinity. The Inferno's vestibule contains the lukewarm, or neutral, souls; the first circle, or Limbo, is inhabited by those who lived before Christianity, the unbaptized virtuous pagans. The lustful, the gluttonous, the avaricious, the prodigals, the wrathful and sullen, and the heretics inhabit the second through sixth circles. The seventh circle holds three types of criminals who perpetrated violence against others: those violent against others (murderers and tyrants), those violent against themselves (suicides), and those violent against God, nature, and art (blaphemers, sodomites, and usurers). The eighth circle, devoted to simple fraud, is subdivided into ten pouches containing panderers and seducers, flatterers, simonists, diviners, barrators, hypocrites, thieves, fraudulent counselors, sowers of discord, and falsifiers. The ninth circle features compound fraud: treachery against kin (Caina), homeland or party (Antenora), guests (Ptolomea), benefactors (Judecca, holding Judas, Brutus, and Cassius), and traitors of church and empire. They are being chewed by the super traitor and rebel Lucifer, the three-headed monster, a horrible caricature of the Christian Trinity. The *Inferno* showcases memorable characters such as Francesca of Rimini, Ciacco, Farinata, Pier de le Vigne, Brunetto Latini, Ulysses, Guido of Montefeltro, Bertrand de Born, and Ugolino.

The *Purgatorio* (or *Purgatory*, completed c. 1316) is the most human and poetic canticle, a journey of love and hope from the shore of the island of Purgatory to the lofty mountain that Dante ascends in the company of Vergil and later Statius. It is divided into an Ante Purgatory of Late Repentants and a Valley of Negligent Rulers followed by seven terraces expurgating seven capital sins—pride, envy, wrath, sloth, greed, prodigality, and gluttony—and then Earthly Paradise.

The author completes the most sublime and complex *cantica*, the *Paradiso* (*Paradise*, 1316-1320), a vision and journey of heaven, guided by Beatrice and later Saint Bernard of Clairvaux, through the seven known spheres of the Ptolemaic system and the Heaven of the Fixed Stars, the Primum Mobile, and finally the Empyrean, the residence of all the blessed and God, the Beginning and the End, whose final vision is an exaltation of the human image.

Significance

Dante died on September 13 or 14, 1321, in Ravenna after having contracted malaria upon returning from an embassy to Venice on behalf of Guido Novello of Polenta. His remains, notwithstanding the efforts of the city of Florence, were never returned to his native city, perhaps ironically confirming Dante's own dictum, "Florentine by birth but not by nature" and his belief in being a citizen of the world.

His eternal legacy, *The Divine Comedy*, is a lasting masterpiece, transcending the boundaries of a Christian vision but at the same time depicting the drama of everyone's life—of human nature with all its passions, ambiguities, conflicts, and contradictions. It demonstrated immediately that the "sweet new style" of using vernacular Italian verse could communicate its lofty drama to a broad, not solely aristocratic or clerical, audience, heralding the humanism that was to characterize the Renaissance.

The journey of self-discovery that Dante outlined—from the depth and darkness of Hell to the height of reacquired freedom in the Earthly Paradise and on to the final vision of the "Love that moves the sun and the other stars" in Paradise—has left an indelible mark on all of modern literature and on the artistic and intellectual history of humanity, influencing artists, composers, and writers of all genres throughout the ages, from Michelangelo to contemporary popular culture. It has been translated into practically every known literary language and many dialects, and it consistently sees new editions and repays new readings and analysis.

—*Giuseppe C. Di Scipio*

Further Reading

Barbi, Michele. *Life of Dante*. Translated and edited by Paul Ruggiers. Berkeley: University of California Press, 1954. A concise and still reliable biography. Illustrations.

Bemrose, Stephen. *A New Life of Dante*. Exeter, England: University of Exeter, 2000. The first biography in English, for nearly eighty years, of Italy's foremost writer, from his early activity as a lyric poet and his political career in Florence to his exile and wanderings and his final years in Verona and Ravenna. Offers a chapter on the Guelphs and Ghibellines. Index, bibliographic references, list of Dante's works.

Bergin, Thomas G. *An Approach to Dante*. Boston: Houghton Mifflin, 1965. Includes a useful chapter, "Dante's Life." Bibliographic references, illustrations.

Hollander, Robert. *Dante: A Life in Works*. New Haven, Conn.: Yale University Press, 2001. Hollander, a preeminent scholar of Dante at Princeton University, examines how Dante created his masterpiece by examing the life he tells through his other works. A masterful intellectual biography. Bibliographic references, index.

Lansing, Richard, and Theodolinda Barolini, eds. *The Dante Encyclopedia*. New York: Garland, 2000. A systematic introduction to Dante's life, works, and sociopolitical milieu. Chronology, numerous illustrations, bibliographic references, index. An indispensable reference.

Wicksteed, Philip H., trans. *The Early Lives of Dante*. London: Alexander Moring, 1904. Reprint. London: Chatto and Windus, 1907. A translation of two roughly contemporaneous biographies, by Giovanni Boccaccio and Lionardo Brunis. Index.

SEE ALSO: c. 1100: Rise of Courtly Love; November 18, 1302: Boniface VIII Issues the Bull *Unam Sanctam*; c. 1350-1400: Petrarch and Boccaccio Recover Classical Texts; 1387-1400: Chaucer Writes *The Canterbury Tales*.

RELATED ARTICLES in *Great Lives from History: The Middle Ages, 477-1453*: Giovanni Boccaccio; Dante; Petrarch.

c. 1310-1350
WILLIAM OF OCKHAM ATTACKS THOMIST IDEAS

William of Ockham attacked Thomist ideas in philosophical and theological writings that questioned the teachings of the Catholic Church, preparing the way for the Protestant Reformation.

LOCALE: England and continental Europe
CATEGORIES: Cultural and intellectual history; religion

KEY FIGURES

William of Ockham (c. 1285-1347 or 1349), English theologian, philosopher, and Franciscan scholar
Thomas Aquinas (1224 or 1225-1274), Dominican friar, scholar, and Christian theologian
Louis the Bavarian (1283?-1347), Holy Roman Emperor as Louis IV, r. 1328-1347

SUMMARY OF EVENT

Although the philosophical and theological system created by Thomas Aquinas represents the highest point of medieval Scholastic thought and has long been the official philosophy of the Catholic Church, it was not without critics during its time, especially during the fourteenth century, when Thomism had not yet completely established itself. One of the sharpest and most influential of these critics was the English theologian and philosopher, William of Ockham, and his views both reflected a differing vision of truth than that of Aquinas and helped prepare the way for the Protestant Reformation.

Aquinas's greatest and definitive work, the *Summa theologiae* (c. 1265-1273; *Summa Theologica*, 1911-1921), made use of the thoughts and concepts of many of his philosophical and theological forerunners, but its greatest debt is to the Greek philosopher Aristotle. In a very real sense, Thomistic philosophy is Aristotelian philosophy Christianized, and William of Ockham's criticisms of Aquinas were inevitably linked to objections to Aristotle that stretched back to classical Greece.

The basic quarrel between Thomas Aquinas and William of Ockham involved the issue of "realism" versus "nominalism." Briefly stated, "realism" posits that universals, or the perfect form of earthly objects, exist in some real yet abstract state. Plato had taught that these universals were in fact the only reality. Thus there is, in some world beyond this one, for example, the "perfect chair" of which all earthly chairs are inferior copies. Aristotle believed that universals could exist only in specific things, but those specific things shared the essence of the universal. Aquinas, following Aristotle's lead, claimed that these universals existed in the mind of God prior to creation, but thereafter were found only in specific objects, while still retaining their universal character. A horse, for example, shares with all other horses a certain *quidditas* (roughly translated as "whatness," or even, in this case, "horseness"). This *quidditas* is the essential quality that distinguishes horses from all other creatures. Although human beings can perceive *quidditas* only as it is resident in a particular thing, it is a universal reality.

Aquinas used this relatively simple concept, linked with Christian belief, as a key part in his work to produce a broad and systematic philosophical and theological scheme. William of Ockham objected to this system because he rejected its foundation. William's cardinal principle was that universals existed not in reality but only as constructs of the human mind. Everything outside of the mind was individual. The philosophical term given to this view is "nominalism," and William's view that a universal is only a term to label a group of individuals has earned his philosophy the name "Terminism." He taught that the terms used to group individuals may be useful but they are not, in any ultimate sense, real. This led to sharp divisions with Thomistic thought.

Aquinas had sought to unite faith and reason, and so had defended the scientific character of theology. Indeed, he claimed that theology was the noblest of all the sciences, since it provides knowledge of the ultimate truths regarding God and his creation. William, on the other hand, denied that theology was a science at all, since it can rest only on the faith of the individual and the divinely granted authority of the Church. For William, science is knowledge gained from experience, principles, or conclusions drawn from the two; since the fundamental "facts" of theology are outside human experience, theology cannot be a science.

Aquinas had taught that theology is universal and unlimited, able to use all philosophical and scientific truths in order to fashion a higher and clearer vision of ultimate reality. In this way he could use what he would term universal truths to fashion various proofs for the existence of God from the natural world around him. William, who had a much more skeptical view of human reason, maintained that theology was basically a collection of mental habits, undoubtedly divinely inspired but limited by our human nature, which had the common purpose of leading human beings to salvation. He thus rejected Aquinas's belief that theology was a single characteristic of the human mind that was capable of unlimited development. Here, William anticipates a key tenet of later Protestant thought, which emphasizes the infinite gulf between God and human beings.

Thomas Aquinas and William of Ockham diverge again on the question of ethics. For Aquinas, ethics and human goodness are questions that relate to the perfection that is possible through God's sharing of his own goodness and perfection. In essence, Aquinas seems to be arguing that God wants us to be good, perhaps even perfect, and will provide the means by which to attain this. In traditional Catholic belief, this is accomplished not solely by individual action but through the assistance of the Church, which includes both the earthly version of the institution and the saints in heaven.

Again, William takes a differing view. For him, ethics and morality are based on the obligation human beings have to follow the laws laid down by God. "Goodness," a universal, does not exist as a thing in itself; it is merely a term that signifies that something is as it ought to be according to God's commandments. Here, William makes a breathtaking step and claims that God's commandments are not set according to an abstract concept of "good," but are determined purely by God's pleasure. Because God is free to do as he chooses, he can command as he pleases. People have been commanded to love God; therefore, to love him is good. Had he chosen to command people to hate him, however, "goodness" in human beings would consist of obeying that commandment, incomprehensible as that might seem. In a similar fashion, William explains, God has condemned and forbidden adultery, but God could change this and make adultery good and meritorious.

SIGNIFICANCE

The view of God's universal authority, unmediated by the presence of the Church and its traditions, has caused some to label William of Ockham "the first Protestant." Martin Luther was later to refer to William as one of his major influences, and traces of William's philosophy are clearly seen in Protestant theological thought. William's personal history adds some credence to this description. Accused, or at least suspected, of heresy by the Papacy, he was for a time confined to the Franciscan house in Avignon and later fled to the court of his protector, Louis the Bavarian, Holy Roman Emperor (known as Emperor Louis IV), where he lived until his death. As a dedicated Franciscan who rejected material goods and preached the virtues of poverty, William ran against the current of the established Church of his time.

William's ideas on the importance of the individual in the religious scheme of things and his rejection of universals in favor of directly observed particulars were later taken up and developed by empirical philosophers such as his fellow Englishman, John Locke. His major importance for both philosophy and theology is in his systematic and comprehensive marshaling of logical arguments in favor of nominalism over realism and his emphasis on the individual and the particular over the universal and general. Both views would later become central elements in the thought of the Protestant Reformation.

—*Michael Witkoski*

FURTHER READING

Adams, Marilyn McCord. *William Ockham*. 2 vols. Notre Dame, Ind.: University of Notre Dame Press, 1987. A detailed and comprehensive review of William of Ockham's thought.

Carre, Meyrick. *Realists and Nominalists*. Oxford, England: Oxford University Press, 1946. An essential study of differences between Thomas Aquinas and William of Ockham within the setting of medieval Scholastic thought.

Dancy, Jonathan, and Ernest Sousa, eds. *A Companion to Epistemology*. Cambridge, Mass.: Blackwell, 1992. Provides a brief but thorough introduction to William of Ockham's thought and helps place it within the context of general Scholastic philosophy.

Gilson, Etienne. *The History of Christian Philosophy in the Middle Ages*. New York: Random House, 1955. This survey of the whole of medieval Christian philosophy puts Thomism in its historical context.

Honderich, Ted, ed. *The Oxford Companion to Philosophy*. New York: Oxford University Press, 1995. The section on William of Ockham gives a basic introduction to his theories in an accessible fashion.

Martin, Christopher, ed. *The Philosophy of Thomas Aquinas: Introductory Reading*. London: Routledge, 1988. Contains a representative sampling of all of Aquinas's important works, including a selection of his *Summa Theologica*, with excellent introductions of each selection.

Maurer, Armand. *Medieval Philosophy*. New York: Random House, 1962. An invaluable starting point for a study of Scholastic philosophy as well as William of Ockham's individual contributions to the field.

Mole, Phil. "Ockham's Razor Cuts Both Ways: The Uses and Abuses of Simplicity in Scientific Theories." *Skeptic* 10, no. 1 (2003): 40-47. A brief, scholarly analysis of the concept "Ockham's (or Occam's) razor," which was named after William of Ockham and refers to the principle of parsimony, or simplicity, in thinking about scientific problems such as universals.

SEE ALSO: c. 1265-1273: Thomas Aquinas Compiles the *Summa Theologica*; 1305-1417: Avignon Papacy and the Great Schism; 1328-1350: Flowering of Late Medieval Physics; 1377-1378: Condemnation of John Wyclif.

RELATED ARTICLES in *Great Lives from History: The Middle Ages, 477-1453*: Peter Abelard; Jean Buridan; Francesco Landini; William of Ockham; Thomas Aquinas; William of Auvergne; William of Auxerre; John Wyclif.

June 23-24, 1314
BATTLE OF BANNOCKBURN

The Battle of Bannockburn marked the defeat of a superior English army by Scottish forces under Robert Bruce, which allowed him to secure his own reign and preserve Scotland's independence for another four centuries.

LOCALE: Stirling, Scotland
CATEGORY: Wars, uprisings, and civil unrest

KEY FIGURES

Robert Bruce (1274-1329), king of Scotland, r. 1306-1329

Edward I (1239-1307), king of England and Wales, r. 1272-1307, lost to William Wallace at the Battle of Stirling Bridge in 1297

William Wallace (c. 1270-1305), Scottish patriot who was the victor at the Battle of Stirling Bridge in 1297, executed in 1305

Edward II (1284-1327), king of England and Wales, r. 1307-1327, lost to Bruce at the Battle of Bannockburn

Gilbert, earl of Gloucester (1291-1314), nephew of Edward II and commander of English army, killed at the Battle of Bannockburn

SUMMARY OF EVENT

Margaret ("the Maid of Norway"), heir to the throne of Scotland, died in 1290 at the age of eight. Without a clear claimant to the crown, the Scottish clans permitted an eager King Edward I of England to choose between various aristocratic candidates. Edward chose John de Baliol, whom he believed he could control, over a stronger Robert de Brus, a nobleman of Anglo-Norman descent. The choice proved unfortunate when Baliol made the famous Auld Alliance with Edward's enemy France; Edward invaded Scotland, forced Baliol to abdicate, carried away the sacred Stone of Scone to England, and left Scotland without a king.

Into the vacuum of power stepped William Wallace, a landowner but not noble, who would become a hero of Scottish nationalism. Wallace rallied the disparate and often feuding clans to attack English garrisons and won a decisive victory over superior English troops at the Battle of Stirling Bridge in 1297. Wallace was defeated in a subsequent battle at Falkirk and in 1305 was betrayed, captured, and convicted of "treason" against an English king to whom he had never declared allegiance. He was hanged, drawn, and quartered, and his arms and legs were sent to four cities as a lesson to rebels.

Inspired by the support Wallace had received from the Scots, Robert the Bruce, grandson of Robert de Brus passed over for king fifteen years earlier, abandoned his earlier allegiance to England and took up Wallace's cause. He was about thirty years of age when Wallace died in 1305; and in 1306, he was crowned by the Scottish clans at Scone. He faced daunting odds. Scots rarely worked in unison. He was himself excommunicated from the Catholic Church for having murdered a rival, John (Red) Comyn, in a church. It was also certain that the English would once more invade Scotland to end the independence that a king represented.

Bruce experienced a brief breathing space when Edward I died in 1307 and his feckless son and heir Edward II showed little desire to pursue his father's ambitions in Scotland. Bruce took advantage of his reprieve to consolidate his power. He took several castles back from English control, including Edinburgh, and held a parliament of his clans at Saint Andrews. He was even recognized as king of Scots by the French, although not by the pope.

Robert Bruce. (Hulton|Archive by Getty Images)

It was not until early 1314 that Edward II came to Scotland and the struggle for independence was renewed. Edward mustered a seemingly invincible English army to end Bruce's reign and, by the middle of summer, was ready for attack. The two armies met just southeast of Stirling, only three miles from the spot where Wallace had defeated the English seventeen years earlier.

Sometime during the day of Friday, June 21, 1314, Bruce and perhaps six thousand men arrived at a small stream (a "burn" in Scots) called Bannock, which flows south of Stirling Castle and meanders through bog lands between Stirling and Falkirk to the River Forth. Stirling Castle, visible from this spot, was still held by the English, and Bruce reasoned that Edward would try to use its security as a base of operation against him in the central lowlands. He carefully chose a place north of Bannockburn on a crest atop a slope. North of the stream were only two patches of solid turf, and to cross the stream to meet him, Edward's army would have to narrow their ranks in order to avoid bogs. Strategy was particularly important because Bruce knew that he would be outnumbered almost three to one, his six thousand soldiers against between fourteen thousand and twenty thousand English. Patriotic enthusiasm alone would not be sufficient for victory.

On Saturday, June 22, scouts reported that Edward's army was proceeding along the old Roman road that connected Edinburgh to Stirling. Later reports confirmed the supposition that the English would camp for the night at Falkirk, only nine miles from Stirling.

On Sunday, June 23, the eve of Saint John's Day, Bruce and the Scottish army proclaimed a vigil and spent the day both in preparation for battle and in prayer. Late in the day, after a tiring march from Falkirk, the English army approached Bannockburn, but because of the late hour—and perhaps also because it was Sunday—the English king gave orders for his army to make camp south of the stream, at some distance from the Scots. One of his commanders, Gilbert, the earl of Gloucester, either did not hear the command or chose not to heed it and sent his three thousand soldiers against the Scots. His charge was repulsed, demonstrating the determination of Bruce's army, but the English seemed not at all dismayed by this failure. As a matter of fact, their camp reverberated late into the night with sounds of revelry, while the Scots kept vigil

Edward II at Stirling Castle. (Hulton|Archive by Getty Images)

with prayers to Saint John. Later accounts credited Bruce with one of history's greatest speeches of inspiration.

Monday, June 24, proved the fateful day. The English attacked as Bruce had anticipated and hoped, crossing the stream (almost dry at this time of the year) in the narrow spaces between the bogs, then having to climb toward the Scots on higher ground. The Scottish army formed into *schiltrons*, small, compact rings of spearmen, each man with spear leveled, as observers testified "bristling like hedgehogs." The *schiltrons* counterattacked the English and broke through their ranks, forcing them into the bogs and pursuing the English king. The earl of Gloucester was killed, and the English infantry fell into chaos. The English cavalry was crippled by the swampy turf, but the Scottish cavalry, choosing its path, disrupted the English archers. Estimates held that up to one-half of the English forces perished that day, most of their casualties coming in the bogs along Bannockburn.

His army disintegrated, Edward circled the battlefield and hurried to Stirling Castle, but its commander, knowing that he would have to surrender to Bruce, advised him to seek the safety of Dunbar. From there Edward made his way to the Lothian coast and eventually arrived back in London. He never returned to Scotland, and thirteen years later, he was deposed and murdered in a most horrible way by his queen and her lover.

Significance

The victory at Bannockburn secured Robert Bruce's (King Robert's) reign as certainly as it weakened that of Edward. Scots united behind him, and the European powers recognized him as king of Scots. In 1324, at the urging of Scots bishops, even Pope John XXII blessed his reign. In 1327, Edward III recognized his legitimacy and by implication the independence of Scotland. Robert reigned from 1306 to his death from suspicious causes in 1329.

Scotland remained a kingdom of its own for another four centuries. Yet the gravitational pull toward the stronger England continued. King Robert's son David (1329-1371) agreed to be Edward III's vassal; and the Stewart family that replaced the Bruces on the Scottish throne

SITE OF THE BATTLE OF BANNOCKBURN, 1314

continually made concessions to its powerful neighbor to the south. In the fifteenth century James IV Stewart married Margaret Tudor, sister of Henry VIII, and his great-grandson James VI inherited the English throne as James I when the "virgin" Queen Elizabeth died. The two thrones, while occupied by the same person, remained separate until the official Act of Union in 1707, which created the United Kingdom.

Even though a Scottish king became king of England, many Scots still feel that union was a mistake accomplished by deceit, when the English bribed Scottish parliamentarians to vote for the United Kingdom. Many believe that Bruce's victory at Bannockburn only delayed the inevitable. Still, when Scots talk of heroes, they remember Robert Bruce. When they desire renewal of their pride, they remember Bannockburn.

—*James T. Baker*

FURTHER READING

Barrow, G. W. S. *Robert Bruce and the Community of the Realm of Scotland.* Berkeley: University of California Press, 1965. A thorough biography of Bruce that places Bannockburn in the perspective of the king's whole career and corrects the errors of earlier scholarship.

Duffy, Seán, ed. *Robert the Bruce's Irish Wars: The Invasions of Ireland, 1306-1329.* Charleston, S.C.: Tempus, 2002. A historical overview of the military invasions of Ireland during Bruce's reign. Includes maps.

Fisher, Andrew. *William Wallace.* 1986. Reprint. Edinburgh, Scotland: John Donald, 2002. Synthesizes numerous sources into a concise factual biography that strives to be judicious in separating the legend from the man. Includes a lengthy bibliography.

Fry, Plantagenet, and Fiona Somerset Fry. *The History of Scotland.* London: Routledge & Kegan Paul, 1982. Places Bannockburn in the larger context of Scottish history and demonstrates its symbolic significance for Scots.

Linklater, Eric. *The Survival of Scotland.* Garden City, N.Y.: Doubleday, 1968. In a book that portrays the history of Scotland as a struggle to survive against great odds, Bannockburn is described as an essentially Scottish victory against a superior opposing force.

Maxwell, Herbert. *Robert the Bruce and the Struggle for Scottish Independence.* London: G. P. Putnam's Sons, 1897. This account of Bannockburn provides a balanced if romantic description of the battle, and it contains a convenient fold-out map.

Nusbacher, Aryeh. *The Battle of Bannockburn, 1314.* Charleston, S.C.: Tempus, 2000. A brief look at the battle, with color maps and other illustrations, a bibliography, and index.

Roberts, John L. *Lost Kingdoms: Celtic Scotland and the Middle Ages.* Edinburgh, Scotland: Edinburgh University Press, 1997. A history of Scotland from the eleventh to the seventeenth century, including a chapter on Bruce and Scottish independence.

Young, Alan, and Michael Stead. *In the Footsteps of William Wallace.* Stroud, England: Sutton, 2002. Wallace's story is accompanied by photographs and maps of related historic sites.

SEE ALSO: 1366: Statute of Kilkenny.

RELATED ARTICLES in *Great Lives from History: The Middle Ages, 477-1453*: Robert Bruce; David I; Edward I; Edward II; Edward III; William Wallace.

November 15, 1315
SWISS VICTORY AT MORGARTEN OVER HABSBURG FORCES

The victory at Morgarten over Habsburg forces on horseback by the allied Swiss infantry threatened the long-standing tradition that cavalries were militarily superior and laid the foundation for the modern Swiss Confederation.

LOCALE: Switzerland
CATEGORIES: Expansion and land acquisition; government and politics; wars, uprisings, and civil unrest

KEY FIGURES

Duke Leopold I of Austria (1290-1326), led attack by Habsburg forces, brother of Frederick the Fair of Habsburg
Rudolf Stauffacher (fl. fourteenth century), of Schwyz,
Werner von Attinghausen (fl. fourteenth century), of Uri, and
Walter Fürst (fl. fourteenth century), of Uri, leaders of the allied Swiss resistance against the Habsburgs
Wilhelm Tell (fl. fourteenth century), legendary leader of Swiss resistance

SUMMARY OF EVENT

The Swiss Republic includes twenty-six districts or "cantons" not united by a common ethnic stock, language, or religion, nor by natural boundaries or ancient roots. The Roman Empire never organized the Transalpine Celts into a political entity. The Germanic invaders became the majority of a population divided into four ethnic and lingual groups—Alamanni, Franks, Italians, and Romansh.

During the breakup of Charlemagne's empire, it would have been logical for these groups to be annexed by their German, French, and Italian neighbors, but this was forestalled by a thirteenth century central Alpine federative movement. Within the large and loose framework of the Holy Roman Empire of the German Nation, three small mountain valley "forest cantons"—Uri, Schwyz, and Unterwalden—bordering the shores of Lake Lucerne, formed the alliance of rebels who fought at Morgarten.

The origins of the battle and of Switzerland must be told in terms of the geography, local history, and legends of the "inner Alps." The thirteenth century brought significant changes to these forest cantons. Construction of the Devil's Bridge over the Schoellenen Gorge on the Reuss River opened a trade route through the central Alps. Travelers and pack animals could go from Milan via Lake Maggiore, the Saint Gotthard Pass and Lake Lucerne to the Basle road, the Rhine, and Flanders. The formerly poor and isolated forest cantons began to prosper. At the same time, an increasing power struggle in the Holy Roman Empire saw emperors, their rivals, and the greater princes ready to sell charters for lands, political and tax rights, or privileges to wealthy nobles, towns, and peasant communities. The forest cantons now had the money to join the bidding. As early as 1231, the freemen of Uri purchased rent freedom from their Habsburg lord, as confirmed by imperial charter. By the 1240 Faenza Charter, the Schwyzois sought to escape dues or taxes to their Habsburg lord by payments to the emperor, a privilege not recognized by a later (Habsburg) emperor.

Ultimately, the Habsburgs were the threat against which the forest cantons would join in alliance. This family from the northwestern foothills of the Alps increased its feudal estates until by 1290 it held land, tax, or political rights in nine Swiss cantons, stretching from the Rhine through the Saint Gotthard Pass, in addition to sovereignty over Austria and Styria. Habsburg rents, taxes, tariffs, trade controls, and over-zealous bailiffs all seemed to threaten the local rights of the central Alpine burghers and peasants.

In August of 1291, Schwyz, Uri, and Unterwalden signed a written alliance. This alliance largely confirmed earlier agreements for settlement of disputes and mutual defense. No particular enemy was identified and no formal declaration of sovereignty was made, but the demand for native and freeborn bailiffs and judges was clearly aimed at Habsburg lordship, and the alliance itself was inherently an act of independence. Schwyz and Uri supported an anti-Habsburg coalition that was crushed at Winterthur on April 12, 1292, and related disorders may have been the context for the legendary midnight oath of rebellion supposedly sworn at Rütli meadow in 1307. Oral tradition seems to have embellished the roles of actual leaders such as Rudolf Stauffacher (Stoupacher) of Schwyz, and Werner von Attinghausen and Walter Fürst of Uri.

A greater complication is the legend of Wilhelm Tell, supposedly an oath-taker at Rütli, resistance leader, and warrior at Morgarten. The story of the bailiff's hat, the apple shot from a son's head on the tyrant's command, the escape from the storm on Lake Lucerne, and the assassination of the bailiff sparking the war of rebellion

The Battle of Morgarten. (F. R. Niglutsch)

were recorded only in the late fifteenth century "White Book of Sarnen," polished a bit by Swiss historian Aegidius Tschudi in the sixteenth century, given historical context by Swiss historian Johannes von Müller in 1786, and popularized by Friedrich Schiller's 1804 play and Gioacchino Rossini's 1829 opera. Historians have pointed out that the apple story is a common northern tale, that the "Tell" version garbles actual history, that no fourteenth century chronicler mentions such a hero, and that "Tell" is really a Swiss equivalent to the legendary figures Robin Hood or Paul Bunyan. Some Swiss, however, point to verifiable portions of the context and argue that "Tell" is a possible composite of several heroes as well as an embodiment of the Swiss spirit.

In the Tell legend, Swiss beginnings are explained as a revolt against Habsburg injuries and insults to the self-respect of Swiss men, women, and children. In actuality, Habsburg tariffs and trade controls may have been equally important, as well as cantonal opposition in imperial politics. Certainly the immediate cause of war was the Schwyzois raid in January of 1314 on disputed properties at Einsiedeln, an abbey under Habsburg protection. The Habsburg imperial contender, Frederick the Fair, ordered an expedition to destroy the revolutionary movement.

Frederick's brother, Duke Leopold I of Austria, therefore prepared a comprehensive attack in November of 1315. One Habsburg army made a wide right-flank swing from Lucerne via the Entlebuch and Brunig Pass to attack Unterwalden, while ships from Lucerne crossed the lake to harass the western shores of Schwyz. Duke Leopold collected a main army of more than two thousand knights and perhaps seven thousand infantry at Zug, and on the moonlit night of November 14-15 set out for Schwyz. Perhaps the road through Arth was blocked, or perhaps Leopold sought a "back door" surprise, but in any case, on November 15, his army marched southward along the eastern shore of Lake Aegeri and then continued south with the Aegerisee swamp on their right and Morgarten heights on their left. Apparently the aim was to cross the watershed to the Steiner valley and use the fairly level ground between Steinen and Schwyz for the battle that would defeat the rebels.

The knights headed a column stretching over more than half a mile of mediocre track, an obviously vulnerable situation, but an attack by untrained peasants was clearly not expected. About a mile south of Lake Aegeri, the knights were brought up short, either by a roadblock or rough footing. The spare narratives written later do not fit the present terrain exactly, but the main effect is clear. The defenders—thirteen hundred Schwyzois, two hundred from Uri, and others from Unterwalden—emerged from the forests along Morgarten heights, rolled boulders and tree trunks down the rocky slope of the Figlenfluh, and attacked on foot. In addition to using arrows, spears, clubs, and axes, the Swiss defenders used the halberd—a combination of spear, axe, and hook—to pull armored knights off their mounts. Surprised, the Austrian cavalry tried to deploy their undoubtedly panicked horses into a combat formation, but the narrow way gave no room for this. The battle was simply a running rout. In less than two hours, more than half the knights were killed, some drowning in the swamp or in Lake Aegeri, and the Habsburg army completely scattered. Duke Leopold survived only by flight and, demoralized, abandoned the unsuccessful flank attack on Unterwald.

SIGNIFICANCE

For Europe, the defeat of mounted knights by infantry at Morgarten, like the similar case at Courtrai in 1302, threatened the military superiority that cavalries had claimed since the Battle of Adrianople in 378. That a small force of peasants only emerging from serfdom could outmaneuver and outfight a much larger army led by mounted knights threatened the very basis of European feudalism.

As for the forest cantons, Morgarten cemented their alliance and gained them de facto independence and credibility. Lucerne joined the alliance in 1332, Zürich in 1351, Zug and Glarus in 1352, and Bern in 1353, completing the Eight Canton Federation of the next century. In 1323, abolition of serfdom and canton government made "Switzerland" a republican exception among the feudal monarchies of Europe. The 1386 victory at Sembach followed by a treaty with Austria in 1394 effectually ended the Habsburg threat, although formal recognition by Austria came only with the 1648 Peace of Westphalia. Switzerland's expansive wars were checked, however, when a 1516 defeat by the French at Marignano and the divisive influence of the Protestant Reformation persuaded the Swiss to abandon great-power ambitions for what became a tradition of neutrality.

—*K. Fred Gillum*

FURTHER READING

Bonjour, E., H. S. Offler, and G. R. Potter. *A Short History of Switzerland.* Oxford, England: Clarendon Press, 1952. Scholarly overview of Swiss history that includes coverage of the Battle of Morgarten.

Gabriel, Richard A., and Donald W. Boose, Jr. "The Swiss Way of War: Morgarten, Laupen, Sempach." In *The Great Battles of Antiquity: A Strategic and Tactical Guide to Great Battles That Shaped the Development of War.* Westport, Conn.: Greenwood Press, 1994. Analysis of the Battle of Morgarten from the point of view of military history.

McCrackan, William D. *The Rise of the Swiss Republic.* 2d rev. ed. New York: AMS Press, 1970. Explores the legend of Wilhelm Tell.

Martin, William. *Switzerland.* New York: Praeger, 1971. Comprehensive Franco-Swiss scholarship examining Switzerland as a nation.

Wheatcroft, Andrew. *The Habsburgs: Embodying Empire.* New York: Viking Press, 1995. A history of the house of Habsburg from the early eleventh century through the late twentieth century that provides insight into the Austrian reaction to the Swiss victory at Morgarten.

SEE ALSO: September 17, 1156: Austria Emerges as a National Entity; 1414-1418: Council of Constance.

RELATED ARTICLES in *Great Lives from History: The Middle Ages, 477-1453*: Charlemagne; Rudolf I.

c. 1320
ORIGINS OF THE BUBONIC PLAGUE

In the first stage of the Black Death, much of Asia may have been ravaged by the bubonic plague.

LOCALE: Central Asia, China, the Middle East, Egypt
CATEGORY: Health and medicine

KEY FIGURE

Djanibeg (d. 1357), khan of the Golden Horde, r. 1342-1357

SUMMARY OF EVENT

Outbreaks of bubonic plague have their origins in wild rodent colonies that scientists call plague reservoirs. Fleas that feed on the blood of these rodents ingest and pass along a bacterium (bacillus) known as *Yersinia pestis*. This can be lethal to rodents under certain conditions, but in a stable reservoir, the bacilli survives in a state that is not as lethal as it can be, or the rodents develop immunity or resistance to the effects of the bacillus. In this situation, the animal disease caused by *Y. pestis* is called enzootic.

The bacillus is passed along to people when they come into contact with the reservoir, as sometimes happens with hikers in the American Southwest. It can also happen when a rodent population is disturbed and forced to migrate because of natural events such as floods or wildfires. These wild rodents may mix with household rats, creating an epizootic situation, in which the nonimmune or nonresistant animals die off in large numbers as the rodents' fleas inject the bacillus into their new hosts. Fleas seek new hosts among the human population with which the household rats—usually of the species *Rattus rattus*—share habitation.

In trying to explain the Black Death that broke out in the Near East, Europe, and North Africa in 1347, scientists and historians have long been seeking the original disturbed plague reservoir. There is no consensus on the matter, but there are three main schools of thought. One school places it in far northern India, in the foothills of the Himalayas; from there it is said to have traveled south and east to China, and westward into western Asia, Africa, and Europe. A second position places the reservoir in southeastern Russia, having moved there from northern Iraq and Kurdistan. Once located along the major trade routes from China to the Islamic world, the infected rodent and flea populations joined people and traveled with them in all directions. The third position locates the reservoir in the Gobi desert between China and Mongolia. The disease would have been carried south and then westward across Central Asia. Proponents of this explanation point to the current plague reservoirs in the Gobi and to the fact that the Mongolian Yuan Dynasty (1279-1368) ruled China and maintained regular contact with its western cousins in the Golden Horde. The image of a lone post-rider carrying a stowaway rat in his food sack and spreading the disease as he went is absurd: Large, lumbering trains of wagons accompanying traveling troops or merchants are much more likely to have harbored rats and their fleas.

China clearly was struck by some major pestilence in the early fourteenth century, though the nature of the disease or diseases involved is by no means clear. In a translated list published by William McNeill, epidemics are listed in Hopei—but only Hopei—for the years 1320, 1321, and 1323. Chinese chronicles report both civil war and a major epidemic in Hopei in 1331 in which two-thirds (or perhaps 90 percent, according to McNeill's list) of the population perished. The Chinese imperial encyclopedia *Gu jin du shu ji cheng*, compiled in 1726, provides a list of 234 nonspecific epidemics in China between 37 and 1718, including some for the years 1344, 1345, 1352, and 1356-1363. The Chinese word for epidemic is *yi* and for major epidemic *dayi*, but no researcher has yet found conclusive—or even suggestive—evidence that any of these outbreaks was bubonic plague.

In book 51 of the *Yuan shi*, the imperial chronicle of the Yuan Dynasty, the writer indicates that epidemics occurred during summer and fall, 1345, and the following year. The record is clear, however, on the string of especially severe winters in the early fourteenth century, as well as unusually frequent floods, droughts, and famines. Many people were uprooted and migrated, seeking relief. These conditions seem perfect for the induction of the bacillus into the human population and for its spread along trade and migration routes. In addition, medieval Western physicians and chroniclers, both Christian and Muslim, often placed the Black Death's origins in Cathay, an older name for China, and sometimes mention merchants coming from Asia as their sources of information. Some also reported natural calamities and "signs" in East Asia that may indeed have had an impact on plague reservoirs.

The discovery by researcher Daniel Abramowich Chwolson of three Nestorian Christian tombstones dating from 1338 to 1339 along the shore of Lake Issyk Kul, near the Kyrgyzstan-China border, added weight to the Chinese connection. Some 330 headstones mark the graves of 650 people from this community who died between 1186 and 1349. In 1338 and 1339, 106 died: On three headstones covering ten corpses from these two years, the word translated from the Syriac as "plague" appears. Both the intensive mortality and use of the word for "plague" support the idea that the Black Death passed through this region, but from which direction? Further west Sarai on the lower Volga reported great mortalities in 1345 as did Astrakhan in the Volga delta the following year. About the same time, cities in Uzbekistan reported similar high death tolls. Further and swift movement could have been facilitated by the 1346 campaigns in Kirghiz (Kyrgyzstan) of Djanibeg, khan of the Golden Horde. In 1347, he led his army back to the Black Sea to besiege the colony of Italian merchants at Kaffa (Theodosia, now Feodosyia, Ukraine). As the famous story goes, Djanibeg used catapults to hurl plague-diseased corpses among the Italians, who then took flight by sea, taking the plague with them from the Black Sea into the Mediterranean. This story had its origins with the Italian notary Gabriele de'Mussis, who was long believed to have been part of the besieged colony. Because his membership in this colony has been disproved, his story has lost its following.

SIGNIFICANCE

Assuming that the Chinese epidemics were indeed bubonic plague, their effects on China were profound. Students of China's population claim that up to 25 percent of its people died between 1330 and 1390. The dislocations among populations within China created prime conditions for the rebellions and civil wars that brought Yuan rule to an abrupt end. Although civil wars, famines, and other natural disasters befell the Chinese during this period, the record makes it clear that epidemics also played a major role in the social and political changes of the fourteenth century.

To the west, pestilence plagued the Golden Horde and eventually moved into the Middle East and North Africa. The superior records of this region clearly outline the terrible effects of the pestilence and its movement from one urban center to another. Constantinople seems to have been hit first, in the fall of 1347, with ships soon carrying the disease south to Alexandria, Egypt, and westward through the Aegean to Italy and Europe. Caravans car-

THE PLAGUE'S PROGRESS, C. 1333-1351

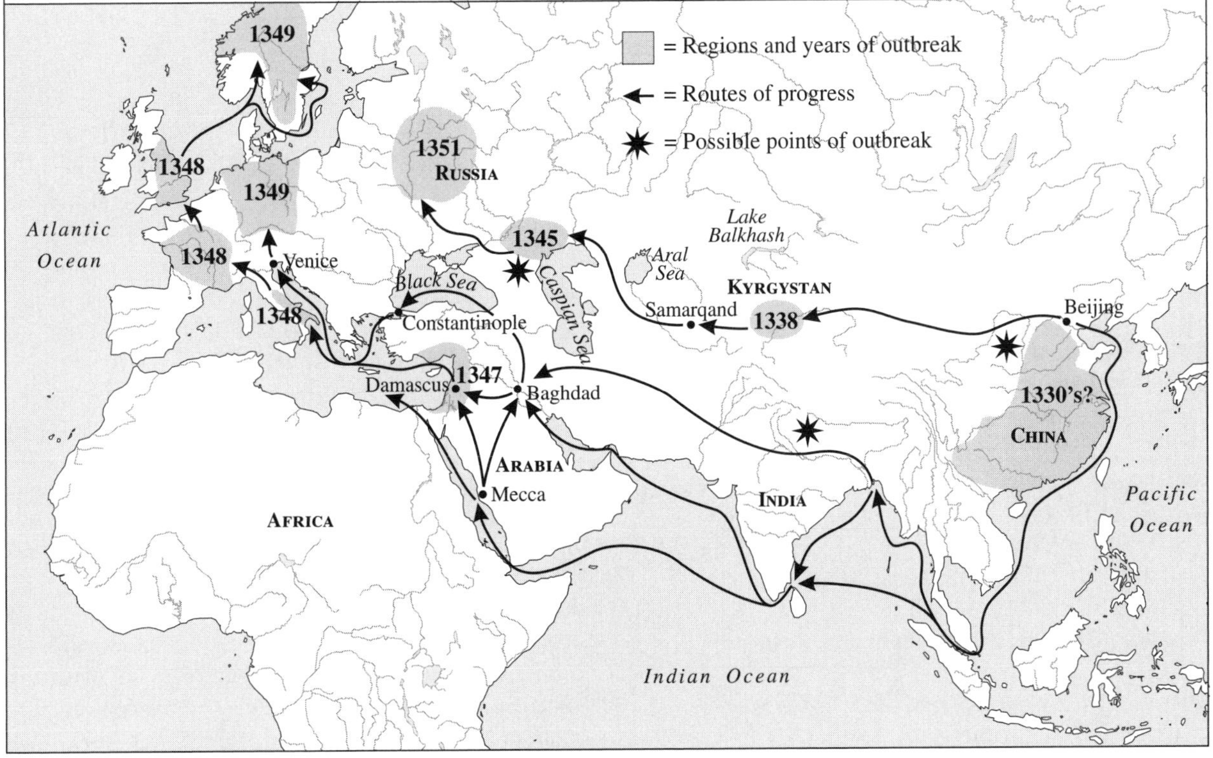

ried it to Trebizond and across Asia Minor. Throughout these regions, death tolls were staggering, with urban averages perhaps as high as 50 percent. In Egypt, the Mamlūk rulers were hit especially hard as villages in the countryside were depopulated and their aristocracy was devastated. The Black Death was in full swing.

—*Joseph P. Byrne*

FURTHER READING

Cantor, Norman. *In the Wake of the Plague: The Black Death and the World It Made.* New York: Harper, 2000. Recent overview of the plague and its effects, including possibilities of extraterrestrial origin.

Dols, Michael W. *The Black Death in the Middle East.* Princeton, N.J.: Princeton University Press, 1977. The standard work in English on the plague in the Islamic world.

Gottfried, Robert S. *The Black Death: Natural and Human Disaster in Medieval Europe.* New York: Free Press, 1983. Of particular interest is Chapter 3, "The Plague's Beginnings."

McNeill, William. *Plagues and Peoples.* Rev. ed. New York: Anchor Books, 1998. Classic work that places this epidemic in the context of world history.

Naphy, William G., and Andrew Spicer. *The Black Death and the History of Plagues, 1345-1730.* Stroud, Gloucester, England: Tempus, 2001. Well-illustrated coverage of the plague across four centuries, with an up-to-date discussion of its possible origins in the Gobi Desert.

Norris, J. "East or West? The Geographic Origin of the Black Death." *Bulletin of the History of Medicine* 51 (1977): 1-24. Challenges East or Central Asian origins of plague and locates its origin in the southern Ukraine.

Twigg, Graham. *The Black Death: A Biological Reappraisal.* New York: Schocken Books, 1985. Biologist builds case against the notion that the Black Death really was the bubonic plague.

Ziegler, Philip. *The Black Death.* New York: Harper and Row, 1969. Remains best overview of the fourteenth century outbreak. Introductory material on plague's origins is dated, but critical and useful.

SEE ALSO: 12th-14th centuries: Social and Political Impact of Leprosy; 1347-1352: Invasion of the Black Death in Europe; 1403-1407: *Yonglo Dadian* Encyclopedia Is Compiled.

1323-1326
CHAMPA WINS INDEPENDENCE FROM DAI VIET

The successful rebellion by the king of Champa and his subsequent ability to resist Vietnamese military efforts to reinstall their rule is a significant episode in the more than fifteen hundred years of strife between the Vietnamese and Cham people that would end much later with the utter defeat of the Chams.

LOCALE: Central Vietnam

CATEGORIES: Government and politics; wars, uprisings, and civil unrest

KEY FIGURES

Tran Nhan Tong (1258-1308), emperor of Vietnam, r. 1278-1293

Tran Anh Tong (1266-1320), emperor of Vietnam, r. 1293-1314

Tran Minh Tong (d. 1358), emperor of Vietnam, r. 1314-1329

Jaya Sinhavarman III (Che Man, d. 1307), king of Champa, r. 1288-1307

Huyen Tran (fl. fourteenth century), sister of Tran Anh Tong, married to King Jaya Sinhavarman III in 1306

Jaya Sinhavarman IV (Che Chi; d. 1313), king of Champa, r. 1307-1312

Che Nang (fl. fourteenth century), Vietnamese-installed vassal king of Champa, r. 1312-1318

Che Anan (d. 1342), king of Champa, r. 1318-1342

Che Bong Nga (d. 1390), king of Champa, r. 1360-1390

SUMMARY OF EVENT

From the moment the Chams entered recorded history in the first century, they were in conflict with the Vietnamese then living under Chinese rule in northern Vietnam. Most Chams are believed to have migrated from Java and Malaysia to the coast of south and central Vietnam, where they settled and intermarried with the indigenous Rhade and Jarai people of the central Vietnamese highlands. Culturally, the Chams were thoroughly Indianized, like their neighbors in Cambodia and Thailand to the west. Their Indianized culture set the Chams apart from the Chinese-influenced Vietnamese culture.

Apart from surviving inscriptions on Cham monuments, what is known of Cham history comes from Chinese and Vietnamese sources and thus has to be evaluated with caution.

The kingdom of Champa was founded by a group who rebelled against Chinese rule in 192, and it was known as Lin-yi by the Chinese and Lam Ap by the Vietnamese. After 875, the Vietnamese called the Cham the Chiem Thanh. At the height of its power in the tenth century, the kingdom of Champa stretched over a coastal area ranging south from the Gate of Annam north of modern Da Nang up to Cape Vung Tau just east of modern Ho Chi Minh City. The Chinese and Vietnamese considered the Cham fierce barbarians and pirates, but with a reputation for cleanliness.

When the Vietnamese gained independence from China in 939, their conflict with the Chams continued. In 982, the Vietnamese emperor Le Dai Hanh captured and destroyed the Cham capital of Indrapura, near the modern Vietnamese city of Quang Nam. Although the Chams would rebuild the city, intermittent warfare with the Vietnamese continued. In 1054, the Vietnamese emperor renamed his nation Dai Viet ("great land of the Vietnamese"), a name that would remain official until the nineteenth century.

In 1070, the victorious Vietnamese obtained the three northernmost provinces of Champa. They ranged south up to the modern city of Quong Tri, near where Vietnam would be partitioned into North Vietnam and South Vietnam from 1945 to 1976. This Vietnamese conquest cemented the enmity of the two people for centuries to come.

In the early 1200's, Champa was occupied by the Khmer of Cambodia. After gaining independence again in 1220, the kingdom of Champa experienced renewed warfare with the Vietnamese. However, in 1252, when Mongol invaders from the north suddenly threatened both peoples, the Chams and Vietnamese united to defeat the Mongols, and their relationship became friendly.

In 1301, the former Vietnamese emperor Tran Nhan Tong visited the king of Champa, Jaya Sinhavarman III. The former emperor promised the king of Champa his daughter, beautiful princess Huyen Tran, as the king's fifth wife. Princess Huyen was the sister of the current Vietnamese emperor, Tran Anh Tong, the son in whose favor Tran Nhan Tong had abdicated, as was the custom of Vietnam's Tran Dynasty (1225-1400). The Vietnamese debated the promise of their former emperor until 1306; their reluctance to let a Vietnamese princess marry a Cham "barbarian" was overcome only when the king of Champa agreed to cede to Vietnam two more northern Champa provinces, which included the modern cities of Hue and Da Nang.

One year after his 1306 wedding, King Jaya Sinhavarman III died. Cham aristocratic custom demanded that his young wife kill herself to be burned with her husband on his funeral pyre. The princess refused to do so, and the Vietnamese court sided with her. Her former Vietnamese lover went into Champa and rescued her. This incensed the Chams, and war broke out.

In 1312, the Vietnamese sent a punitive expedition to Champa. The new king, Jaya Sinhavarman IV, was captured and died in captivity near modern-day Hanoi. The Vietnamese formally declared the kingdom of Champa a province of Dai Viet. They replaced the king with his brother, Che Nang. Che Nang had to agree to reign as a "vassal prince of the second rank" in the service of the Vietnamese emperor, and Cham independence came to a temporary end.

In 1314, Che Nang rebelled against his Vietnamese masters but was defeated and fled to his mother in Java, Indonesia. The Vietnamese installed Che Anan as their viceroy in Champa. By 1323, Che Anan also had rebelled against the Vietnamese and refused to pay tribute. Emperor Tran Minh Tong, who had succeeded his father who had abdicated in 1314, sent troops south to subdue the Chams. However, the Chams fought off the Vietnamese. By 1326, Tran Minh Tong had abandoned the military effort against the Chams, who no longer recognized Vietnamese rule and no longer paid tribute. Thus, Champa had regained its independence from Dai Viet, which it had formally lost in 1312.

SIGNIFICANCE

King Che Anan's stubborn defeat of all Vietnamese forces sent against him from 1323 to 1326 ushered in a new era of Champa's revival. For a while, it looked as if Champa could retain its national and cultural independence from its Vietnamese enemies to the north. Although the next Vietnamese emperor claimed in an inscription carved into a huge mountain rock facing Laos that the royal heirs of Champa paid homage to him, this claim seems rather suspect to modern historians. There is evidence that Champa remained independent of Dai Viet and flourished.

Che Anan's successor failed to win back the provinces lost to the Vietnamese in 1070 and 1306, but he defeated all Vietnamese attempts to reimpose their rule in Champa. As Vietnam's Tran Dynasty declined, the Chams gained even more power.

When Che Bong Nga became king of Champa in 1360, he renewed warfare with the Vietnamese. Beginning in 1371, he plundered the Vietnamese capital of Thang Long (near modern-day Hanoi) three times. He terrorized the Vietnamese all over their country, killing their emperor in battle in 1377. A year later, Champa had recovered all five provinces once lost to Vietnam. Its power seemed unstoppable. However, Che Bong Nga died in 1390. Some accounts speak of his death in a naval battle, others relate that he was poisoned.

With Che Bong Nga's death, Champa's good fortunes came to an end. By 1401, the Vietnamese had recaptured the five northern provinces and conquered the royal Cham city of Indrapura. The Cham revival that had begun with regained independence in 1323-1326 could thrive only while Vietnam was weakened by internal dynastic decay, and Champa blossomed under its warrior king Che Bong Nga. Later, the Vietnamese would prove victorious.

In 1407, a Vietnamese fleet was poised to take the Cham capital of Vijaya, near modern-day Qui Nhon. It had to turn back only because Vietnam faced invasion by the Chinese. After a brief time of Chinese rule, from 1407 to 1428, Vietnam renewed its struggle with Champa. In 1446, Vijaya was taken, and war ended with total Vietnamese victory over Champa in 1471. The Chams lost much of their land. In the early nineteenth century, their remaining state was erased by the Vietnamese. As of the early twenty-first century, about sixty thousand descendants of the Champa lived as a minority in Vietnam. Theirs is a lost empire of Southeast Asia, with archaeological evidence speaking of its past history.

—*R. C. Lutz*

FURTHER READING

Chapuis, Oscar. *A History of Vietnam*. Westport, Conn.: Greenwood Press, 1995. Discusses the events in detail from both a Champa and a Vietnamese point of view. Very readable. Maps, bibliography, and index.

Hall, Daniel George. *A History of Southeast Asia*. 4th ed. London: Macmillan Press, 1981. Still a standard work on the period. Chapter 8 surveys the history of Champa, chapter 9 that of Vietnam, from the beginnings to the sixteenth century. Illustrations, maps, bibliography, and index.

Huard, Pierre, and Maurice Durand. *Viet Nam: Civilization and Culture*. Translated by Vu Thiên Kim. 2d ed. Hanoi: Ecole Française d'Extrême-Orient, 1994. General overview of the event from a Vietnamese perspective. Contains a general historic survey and much background on Vietnamese culture through the ages, richly illustrated.

Raj, Hans. *History of South-East Asia*. Delhi, India: Surjeet Publishers, 2002. Comprehensive account incorporating fresh historical, archaeological, and anthropological research and insights. Maps, bibliography, and index.

SEE ALSO: 939-944: Reign of Ngo Quyen; 982: Le Dai Hanh Invades Champa; 1225: Tran Thai Tong Establishes Tran Dynasty.

RELATED ARTICLE in *Great Lives from History: The Middle Ages, 477-1453*: Ngo Quyen.

August 1, 1323-August 23, 1328
PEASANTS' REVOLT IN FLANDERS

A revolt in Flanders by a coalition of peasants and city dwellers against aristocratic rule succeeded until the rebels were defeated by French authorities five years later.

LOCALE: Flanders
CATEGORIES: Social reform; wars, uprisings, and civil unrest

KEY FIGURES

Louis I (c. 1304-1346), count of Flanders, r. 1322-1346
Charles IV (1294-1328), king of France, r. 1322-1328
Philip VI (1293-1350), king of France, r. 1328-1350

SUMMARY OF EVENT

Flanders, a region of Europe bordering the North Sea and extending into areas that would later form parts of modern France, Belgium, and the Netherlands, was a separate nation during the Middle Ages. Conquered by France in a series of invasions from 1297 to 1300, Flanders won partial independence at the Battle of Courtrai on July 11, 1302. A peace treaty negotiated at Athis-sur-Orge in June of 1305 restored political power to Robert of Bethune, count of Flanders, but required that the count remain loyal to the king of France and that Flanders pay large amounts of money to France. As a result of protests by the taxpayers of Flanders, delays by the count, and the inability of France to enforce the treaty, these debts went largely unpaid.

On the death of Robert of Bethune, his grandson, Louis II of Nevers, became Louis I, count of Flanders, on September 17, 1322. Raised in France and married to the daughter of the king of France, Louis I was far more loyal to France than the previous count. He promised to pay France all money owed and appointed pro-French aristocrats to positions of power.

On July 13, 1323, Louis I gave control of the Zwin waterway, which linked the city of Bruges to the North Sea, to his granduncle, John of Namur. The city leaders feared that John of Namur was planning to direct commerce away from Bruges to the town of Sluis, located at the mouth of the Zwin. A militia from Bruges attacked John of Namur's forces at Sluis on August 1, 1323. Sluis was burned and John of Namur was held prisoner until he escaped in late September.

Louis I left Flanders for France on October 15, 1323. Peasants began to rebel against the taxes that were being collected to make payments to France in late October. Officials in charge of collecting taxes were imprisoned or forced to flee. Despite the assistance of the militias of the three large cities of Bruges, Ghent, and Ypres, the government was able to do little against this well-organized, widespread rebellion.

Louis I returned to Flanders in early 1324. He arranged a truce with the rebels and set up commissions to investigate charges of corruption made against his officials. The commissions agreed to punish corrupt officials and offered amnesty to the rebels.

The effectiveness of these commissions varied from region to region. In southwest Flanders, a commission led by Robert of Cassel, the uncle of Louis I, included representatives of city governments and listened to the testimony of the rebels. Because of this, the rebels were inclined to agree with its decisions. In Bruges, the settlement was made by Louis I and his advisers without the participation of city leaders or peasants. When Louis I later imposed heavy fines on Bruges and returned ousted officials to power, the region was ready to rebel again.

Louis I went back to France in July of 1324. Beginning in the late summer of 1324, peasants in the country-

Philip VI of France. (Hulton|Archive by Getty Images)

side north of Bruges attacked the strongholds of rural aristocrats, taking them prisoner or forcing them to flee. They also refused to pay tithes to monasteries. Local officials were driven out and replaced by representatives of the rebels.

Louis I returned to Flanders in December of 1324. Faced with a more serious rebellion than the tax protests of 1323, he gave permission for exiled aristocrats to attack the peasants with full force. He also allowed Robert of Cassel to use any means necessary to prevent the rebellion from spreading to southwest Flanders. The level of violence used on both sides quickly escalated into open warfare.

In February of 1325, peasant forces defeated the count's soldiers at the town of Gistel, southwest of Bruges. The city of Bruges joined the peasants in their rebellion at about the same time. Encouraged by their success and the support of Bruges, the rebels moved into southwest Flanders. The inhabitants of this region quickly joined the rebellion and forced Robert of Cassel to flee.

A truce was made with the rebels between March and June of 1325. A commission consisting of Robert of Cassel and representatives from the cities of Ghent and Ypres, which were still loyal to the count, was then set up. The rebels rejected the commission as too unsympathetic to their cause. Aristocrats led by John of Namur rejected it as too willing to compromise with the rebels. A meeting of the commission scheduled for June 11 failed to take place when Robert of Cassel learned that the aristocrats were conspiring to prevent him from reaching it. The other members of the commission were afraid to face the anger of the rebels waiting for them and knew that they could accomplish little without Robert of Cassel. The peace negotiations came to an end.

Louis I moved his soldiers to the town of Courtrai, between the cities of Ypres and Ghent, in an attempt to prevent the rebels from taking the town and driving a wedge between the two cities. An army of about five thousand rebels from Bruges began marching to Courtrai in mid-June of 1325. To block their approach, the count's forces set fire to the suburbs of Courtrai north of the Leie River and destroyed the bridges crossing the river. A strong wind caused the fire to spread south of the river to Courtrai. The enraged citizens of Courtrai joined the rebellion and welcomed the approaching rebels. On June 20 and 21, the rebels inflicted heavy casualties on the count's forces and took Louis I prisoner. The peasant army then moved into Ypres, which joined the rebellion.

The leaders of Bruges forced Louis I to appoint Robert of Cassel as regent on June 30, 1325. In response, John of Namur produced a document, possibly forged,

CENTERS OF THE FLANDERS PEASANTS' REVOLT, 1323-1328

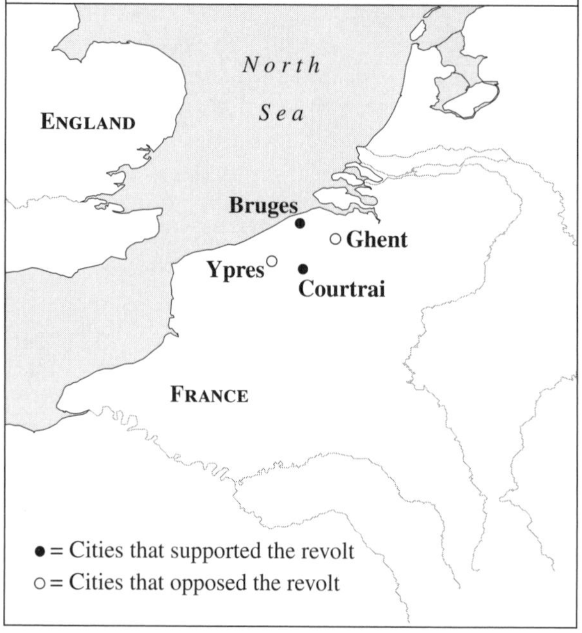

which had named him regent on June 12. The rebellion now evolved into a struggle between Robert of Cassel, allied with the rebels, and John of Namur, leading the aristocratic forces from Ghent. For several months, the two armies fought many battles, losing and gaining territory, with neither side able to break the stalemate.

In November of 1325, King Charles IV of France became involved in the struggle. He recognized the regency of John of Namur, loaned money to Ghent, and prohibited trade between France and the rebel areas of Flanders. Hoping to prevent a French invasion, the rebels released Louis I on December 1, 1325, in exchange for a promise of amnesty. Despite his promise, Louis I went to Charles IV to request military aid.

Robert of Cassel abandoned his association with the rebels and obtained a pardon from the king on March 20, 1326. Reluctant to commit troops to Flanders at a time when he expected an invasion from England, Charles IV arranged for a peace treaty to be negotiated at the town of Arques on April 19, 1326. The treaty required payment of all fees owed to France and added additional fines. Although the rebel cities generally agreed to this treaty, the peasants mostly continued as before.

After Charles IV died in 1328, his successor, Philip VI, prepared to invade Flanders. On August 23, 1328, the French and rebel armies met near the town of Cassel. The

French killed more than three thousand rebels, ending the uprising.

Significance

Philip VI's and Louis I's severe punishment of the rebels helped set up a strong centralized government that successfully resisted later attempts at social rebellion. However, the revolt marked in history a prolonged effort on the part of the peasantry and city dwellers against aristocratic rule and abuses of power and authority. Peasants in southeastern England followed with a revolt of their own in 1381.

—*Rose Secrest*

Further Reading

Fourquin, Guy. *The Anatomy of Popular Rebellion in the Middle Ages*. Translated by Anne Chesters. Amsterdam: North-Holland, 1978. An analysis of medieval uprisings that characterize the Flanders revolt as a response to an agricultural and economic crisis.

Hilton, Rodney. *Bond Men Made Free: Medieval Peasant Movements and the English Rising of 1381*. New York: Viking, 1973. Deals with the Flanders revolt and other peasant rebellions of the Middle Ages and compares them to the 1381 English peasants' revolt.

Nicholas, David. *Medieval Flanders*. New York: Longman, 1992. Provides background information on Flanders during the Middle Ages and discusses the revolt and its consequences.

_______. *Town and Countryside: Social, Economic, and Political Tensions in Fourteenth-Century Flanders*. Bruges, Belgium: De Tempel, 1971. Deals with the relationships between the cities of Bruges, Ghent, and Ypres and the rural areas of Flanders during the period of the revolt.

_______. *Trade, Urbanisation, and the Family: Studies in the History of Medieval Flanders*. Brookfield, Vt.: Variorum, 1996. Looks at the history of trade in Flanders, a critical issue during the revolt.

TeBrake, William H. *A Plague of Insurrection: Popular Politics and Peasant Revolt in Flanders, 1323-1328*. Philadelphia: University of Pennsylvania Press, 1993. A detailed account of the revolt and the complex political situation in which it took place.

See also: 1373-1410: Jean Froissart Compiles His *Chronicles*; May-June, 1381: Peasants' Revolt in England.

Related articles in *Great Lives from History: The Middle Ages, 477-1453*: John Ball; Charles IV; Jean Froissart; Wat Tyler.

July 2, 1324
Lady Alice Kyteler Is Found Guilty of Witchcraft

Kyteler's trial for witchcraft marks a transition by church and government authorities from prosecutions that pursued heresy to prosecutions and executions for witchcraft.

Locale: Kilkenny, Ireland

Categories: Cultural and intellectual history; laws, acts, and legal history; religion

Key Figures

Lady Alice Kyteler (1280-after 1324), merchant

William Outlaw (b. 1300?), merchant son of Alice Kyteler

Petronilla of Meath (d. 1324), servant of Kyteler and her first husband

Arnold le Poer (d. 1329), seneschal of Kilkenny, Wexford, and Carlow

Richard de Ledrede (d. 1360), bishop of Ossory, 1317-1360

Summary of Event

During most of the Middle Ages, witches and witchcraft were not significant concerns. Religious leaders usually maintained that witches did not really exist—people who thought they were practicing magic were thought to be simply deceiving themselves or being fooled by the devil. A superstitious belief in the efficacy of charms and the dangers of certain spirits remained among many common people, but such ideas were no threat to established faith.

Unlike imaginary witches, however, Church officials had faced a real threat in the rise of heresies. Heresy was a denial of faith in Christ and a rejection of the hierarchy of the Church and its professed dogmas and doctrines. Heretical groups began to grow during the twelfth century. Some heretics, like the Waldensians, preached a radical extremism in Christian poverty. Others, like the Catharists (or Albigensians), created an alternative religion to Christianity, believing in a dualistic conflict of good

A woodcut from a chapbook of about 1400 shows a witch, a demon, and a warlock riding broomsticks. (Hulton|Archive by Getty Images)

and evil. To eliminate these dangerous heretics, medieval authorities used the orders of Franciscans and Dominicans to preach against them, but they also attacked them with crusades and the Inquisition (mid-1100's through thirteenth century). By the fourteenth century, the Waldensians had been driven to the harmless margins of society, while the Catharists had been wiped out entirely.

In the course of these persecutions, the dominant Christian church had blamed many fantastic and impossible crimes on the heretics. Indeed, any resistance to established political or social authorities, as well as mere eccentric divergence from social norms, could be labeled as heresy and prosecuted by the evolving legal machinery. As actual heretics disappeared, however, a new scapegoat appeared: witches. The trial of Alice Kyteler illustrates this transition.

The roots of Kyteler's trial lie in a conflict over confusing jurisdictions of church and state. The king of England ruled Ireland through officials such as seneschals, but bishops there controlled certain courts and sought to protect and expand their properties and governance. In 1317, when Bishop Richard de Ledrede took possession of his diocese of Ossory in Ireland, he began to have difficulties with the locals. The Irish resented him because he was a foreigner of English birth who had spent much time in France. Instead of being appointed by the king of England, he had been provided by Pope John XXII. Furthermore, a famine and political unrest continued through the 1320's in the aftermath of a failed Scottish invasion.

In the ongoing troubles over land, revenues, and authority, Ledrede ran into trouble with the royal seneschal, Arnold le Poer. Without the support of the English king and without much local support among the powerful and wealthy, the prelate may have decided to strike at le Poer through his friend and ally, Lady Alice Kyteler.

Kyteler herself had a rather spotty past. In 1302, she had been briefly accused of murdering her first husband, William Outlaw, with the complicity of the man who became her second husband. She and her husbands were also involved in moneylending, which aroused resentment. By 1324, her fourth husband, a relative of le Poer, was deathly ill.

Kyteler's stepchildren and her sick husband chose this moment to bring complaints to Ledrede, possibly because she was arranging for her property to pass to her son, William Outlaw (named after his father, Kyteler's first husband). Ledrede had probably learned of contemporary fears of heresy and sorcery during his time at the papal court and from members of his religious order, the Franciscans. The bishop brought charges of heresy against Kyteler, her son, three other men, and seven other women.

Ledrede first accused Kyteler of a heresy. Other charges, however, were not typical of heresy but of witchcraft. Kyteler and her associates were indicted for sacrificing animals to a demon, magically excommunicating their husbands, and using the skull of a robber to mix magical ointments made from worms, hairs from buttocks, and clothing from unbaptized baby boys. These charms allegedly caused people to love or hate or even kill. Kyteler also was reputed to have slept with a demon named Robin or Son of Art. That demon reportedly appeared as a black shaggy dog or as three Ethiopians who carried iron rods; he also was said to be responsible for Kyteler's wealth.

To prevent these witchcraft charges from being heard in court, le Poer imprisoned Ledrede for seventeen days in the spring of 1324. On his release, the bishop continued to go after Kyteler, her son William, and their associates, considering them convicted and excommunicated. Kyteler's appeals were supported at a parliament in Dublin where Ledrede failed to win support from the skeptical royal government, other church officials, and representatives of nobles and townspeople. Yet on July 2, 1324, the bishop managed to get the royal justiciar to appear in his court and have Kyteler's son William (who came in full armor) confess to harboring heretics. He was heavily fined and ordered to do penance such as attending mass three times per day for a year, feeding the poor, and paying for a church roof to be covered with lead.

Helping the bishop in his case against Kyteler and William was a servant of the Kytelers, Petronilla of Meath. At some point she had been arrested and tortured to obtain incriminating information against her mistress. Technically, English law prohibited torture to extract confessions, but whipping of servants was allowed. After being whipped six times, Petronilla admitted to having witnessed Kyteler's involvement in witchcraft, much as listed in the original charges. Also, Petronilla said Kyteler would sweep the dirt on the streets toward her son's house while chanting a spell to bring all the wealth of the town to his door. Petronilla seriously implicated William Outlaw, saying he wore the devil's girdle. Petronilla also claimed that Kyteler had taught her to become a witch. She said that she and Kyteler flew through the air on a wooden beam covered with ointment.

The accused witches were punished in various ways. Believing herself to be a witch, the impenitent Petronilla was burned on November 3, 1324, the first person in Ireland to be executed by this method. Before Kyteler could be punished, she fled to England with the daughter of Petronilla. In essence, they suffered banishment, and their further fate is unknown. Imprisoned because of Petronilla's damning testimony, William gained his release by recanting heresy and sorcery and promising pilgrimages and other aids to the church. Others who were accused and captured were supposedly burnt, whipped, or forced to wear a cross. Still others remained at large.

The conflict between Arnold le Poer and Bishop Ledrede continued until the former's death in 1329 as he awaited trial for heresy. In turn, the archbishop of Dublin subsequently charged Ledrede with heresy. In the following years Ledrede lost and regained his diocese twice as he quarreled with King Edward III, the archbishop, and local magnates.

Because of source gaps, much of Kyteler's case remains a mystery. What eventually happened to her, her son, her property, and their alleged accomplices? Were proper legal procedures followed? From what source came the fantastical and obviously false charges?

SIGNIFICANCE

Kyteler's witchcraft trial itself did not spark immediate, widespread witch-hunts. Still, suspicions of conspiracies with demons, such as those against Kyteler, would be revived in years to come against other reputed witches. Within a century, as the Middle Ages ended, the hunt for witches in much of Western Europe would take on larger proportions and continue for more than two centuries afterward, surpassing the previous hunt for heretics. Subsequent witch-hunts were spurred on especially by the publication of the *Malleus maleficarum* (c. 1486; hammer against witchcraft; English translation, 1928), written by the Dominican friars Heinrich (Institoris) Krämer and Jakob Sprenger. By using torture to support incredible accusations of witchcraft, authorities would lead many innocent people, especially poor or otherwise marginalized women, to their deaths.

—Brian A. Pavlac

FURTHER READING

Cohn, Norman. *Europe's Inner Demons: An Inquiry Inspired by the Great Witch-Hunt*. New York: Basic Books, 1975. Important study of how ideas of sorcery and witchcraft from ancient times through the Middle Ages melded into the idea of witches by both intellectuals and fearful people in villages of the fifteenth century.

Davidson, L. S., and J. O. Ward, eds. *The Sorcery Trial of Alice Kyteler: A Contemporary Account (1324)*. Binghamton: Center for Medieval and Early Renaissance Studies, State University of New York at Binghamton, 1993. An account of the trial by Ledrede, comprehensively noted primary sources, supplemental texts, and an excellent introduction. Also includes a chronology, bibliography, and questions for analysis.

Heinemann, Evelyn. *Witches: A Psychoanalytic Exploration of the Killing of Women*. New York: Free Association Books, 2000. Argues for a psychoanalytic and historical approach to the study of witch-hunts.

Kieckhefer, Richard. *European Witch Trials: Their Foundations in Popular and Learned Culture, 1300-1500*. London: Routledge, 1976. Combines an examination of intellectual trends with a systematic look at legal sources. Includes a list of trials and a bibliography.

Kors, Alan Charles, and Edward Peters, eds. *Witchcraft in Europe, 400-1700: A Documentary History*. 1972. Rev. ed. Philadelphia: University of Pennsylvania Press, 2001. An extensive collection of original sources on the role of Christianity and the Papacy in prosecuting for acts of witchcraft and sorcery; the nature of evil and inquisitions, persecutions, and trials; and an introduction addressing the "problem of European witchcraft."

Levack, Brian P. *The Witch-Hunt in Early Modern Europe*. 2d ed. Harlow, England: Longman, 1995. A standard survey of the witch-hunts. Includes a bibliography, several illustrations, and a map.

Russell, Jeffrey Burton. *The Devil, Heresy, and Witchcraft in the Middle Ages*. Boston: Brill, 1998. Places the witch-hunts in the context of the history of heresy and dissent in the Middle Ages.

Thurston, Robert W. *Witch, Wicce, Mother Goose: The Rise and Fall of the Witch Hunts in Europe and North America*. New York: Longman, 2001. One of the best studies of the witch-hunts. Includes a detailed analysis of the Kyteler case and its place in the history of persecutions of witches in Europe.

SEE ALSO: c. 1175: Waldensian Excommunications Usher in Protestant Movement; 1233: Papal Inquisition; c. 1250-1300: Homosexuality Criminalized and Subject to Death Penalty; May 4-8, 1429: Joan of Arc's Relief of Orléans.

RELATED ARTICLES in *Great Lives from History: The Middle Ages, 477-1453*: Pietro d'Abano; Peter Abelard; Saint Dominic; Fredegunde; Jan Hus; Innocent III; Joan of Arc; Margery Kempe; Lady Alice Kyteler; William of Ockham; Marguerite Porete; John Wyclif.

1324-1325
MANSA MŪSĀ'S PILGRIMAGE TO MECCA SPARKS INTEREST IN MALI EMPIRE

The large entourage that accompanied Mansa Mūsā, emperor of the prosperous Mali Empire, during his famous pilgrimage to Mecca and the lavish wealth he distributed along the way left a lasting impact on North Africa and the Mediterranean. The pilgrimage prompted widespread interest in Mali's riches and placed it on the map of the medieval world.

LOCALE: Western Sudan
CATEGORIES: Government and politics; religion

KEY FIGURES

Sumanguru (d. c. 1235), founder of the Susu Empire, r. 1200-1235
Sundiata (c. 1215-c. 1255), founder of the empire of Mali, r. 1235-1255
Mansa Uli (d. 1277), son and successor of Sundiata, r. 1255-1277
Mansa Mūsā (c. 1280-1337), Mali emperor, r. 1312-1337
Mansa Maghan I (d. 1337), Mansa Mūsā's son and successor, r. 1337
Mansa Sulaymān (d. 1358), last emperor of Mali, r. 1337-1358
Ibn Baṭṭūṭah (1304-c. 1377), Arab traveler and writer

SUMMARY OF EVENT

Mansa Mūsā is best known for the famous *hajj* (pilgrimage) he made to Mecca in 1324-1325. In preparation for the pilgrimage, the emperor levied special contributions from every trading town and every province in his prosperous Mali Empire.

According to contemporary Arab writers, Mansa Mūsā traveled with an immense entourage consisting of sixty thousand porters, preceded by five hundred slaves, each carrying a staff of gold weighing about 6 pounds (3 kilograms). Each of the one hundred baggage camels carried about 300 pounds (135 kilograms) of gold.

Mansa Mūsā is said to have built a new mosque every Friday on his way to Egypt. His visit was long remembered in Cairo as one of the major events in the city's history. His gifts of gold in Cairo were so lavish that their infusion into the economy reportedly depressed the value of gold in Egypt for several years.

The splendor exhibited by Mansa Mūsā's traveling party awakened the world to the riches of Mali and the greatness of its emperor. As early as 1375, European cartographers depicted the Sudan with a portrait of Mansa Mūsā holding a gold nugget. North Africa, the Middle East, and Europe, including the Italian city-states, took an increasing interest in Mali and its gold. Trans-Saharan

Approaching Mecca. (G. T. Devereux)

trade reached a new dimension with the European and North African demand for Mali's resources. Commercial and cultural interaction between Mali and other nations was greatly stimulated by Mansa Mūsā's visit to the Middle East.

After his visit, Mansa Mūsā pursued a vigorous policy to Islamize Mali. He brought back with him many books and religious scholars and encouraged Islamic learning by opening madrasas (Islamic schools) throughout the empire. Timbuktu in particular developed into one of the foremost centers of Islamic learning, attracting scholars from all over the Muslim world. The architects Mansa Mūsā brought from the Middle East built splendid palaces and mosques and introduced a new architectural style in the Western Sudan.

It would be helpful at this point to summarize Mali's place in the history of West Africa and how it came to be the wealthy empire Mansa Mūsā ruled at the time of his pilgrimage.

The collapse of the West African kingdom of Ghana in the eleventh century led to rivalry among its former vassal states, who vied for control of the upper Niger valley and its connections with the lucrative trans-Saharan trade. By 1200, the Susu warrior Sumanguru had subdued various small chiefdoms and had welded together the Susu kingdom, which included much of the area once controlled by Ghana.

Sumanguru's hegemony was challenged by Sundiata, a chief of the Mande-speaking people who led a successful rebellion. After killing Sumanguru at the Battle of Kirina (1235), Sundiata united the Susu with other chieftaincies and forged the Mandinka state, which now is better known as the Mali Empire. Sundiata established his capital city at Niani and declared himself overall *mansa* (Malinke for king of kings or emperor). Royal authority was vested in the Keita clan, which established itself as the ruling dynasty of the burgeoning empire. Sundiata's companions and generals constituted the provincial governing elite.

Sundiata was succeeded by Mansa Uli, who continued his father's conquests and incorporated considerable areas of the Sahel region. However, the most famous of the Keita rulers was Mansa Mūsā, who carried out further campaigns of imperial expansion and consolidation. During his reign, Mali's realm extended in the north to the salt deposits of Taghaza on the fringes of the Sahara Desert and in the south to the gold country on the southern fringes of the savannah. To the west it reached as far as the Gambia and the lower Senegal valley, and to the east it controlled the copper mines and caravan center of Takedda.

The Songhai capital of Gao on the middle Niger and Timbuktu upstream were also incorporated into the empire. Mali controlled many sources of copper, salt, and gold, as well as the caravan trails between them. Complex networks of caravan routes crisscrossed the whole of the Sudan, and the numerous cities that grew along the routes flourished, becoming important centers of commerce, trade, religion, and learning.

The empire of Mali consisted of provinces and vassal kingdoms. The *mansa* controlled important provinces and major towns through directly appointed governors. At the time of Mansa Mūsā's reign, the empire had twelve provinces, each with a number of subdivisions mostly based on clan units. Mansa Mūsā's army was said to number over one hundred thousand.

With its many gold mines, Mali was the largest producer of precious metals in the medieval world. The *mansa* had an exclusive right to gold nuggets. In addition, valuable imports such as horses and metals were the monopoly of the *mansa*. The *mansa*'s commercial agents were found in all the major trading centers, including the southern termini of the Saharan trade routes. They levied duties on imports of salt, copper, and other merchandise. Command over such enormous resources enabled Mali to maintain effective security over an area the size of Western Europe.

Mansa Mūsā was succeeded by his son Mansa Maghan I, whom he had already appointed as a deputy during his pilgrimage to Mecca. However, Maghan was soon overthrown by Mansa Mūsā's brother, Mansa Sulaymān, who as the eldest male in the family contested the succession. From the accounts of Ibn Baṭṭūṭah, the Moroccan traveler who visited Mali during this time, it appears that Sulaymān maintained the empire in all its splendor. Ibn Baṭṭūṭah wrote admiringly of the prosperity, security, and justice that prevailed throughout the empire. The period after Sulaymān's reign was, however, marked by a slow decline of the empire.

SIGNIFICANCE

At the peak of its power, the empire of Mali under Mansa Mūsā extended from the Atlantic coast in the west to Hausaland in the east. An orderly system of law and government was established throughout this immensely diverse empire. Its highly developed metropolitan cities such as Timbuktu, Walata, Gao, and Jenne (Djenné) gave birth to a sophisticated urban society that actively promoted trade and crafts as well as learning and high culture.

Mansa Mūsā's impressive pilgrimage to Mecca boosted Mali's international fame and prestige and further stimulated the empire's political, cultural, and economic development. Mali's legacy continued to influence succeeding West African states such as Songhai.

—*Shumet Sishagne*

FURTHER READING

Falola, Toyin. *Key Events in African History.* Westport, Conn.: Greenwood Press, 2002. Discusses the rise of Islam beginning in the seventh century and includes the chapter, "Kingdoms of West Africa: Ghana, Mali, and Songhay, A.D. 1000-1600." Illustrations, maps, bibliography, index.

Hamdun, Said, and Noel King, trans. and eds. *Ibn Baṭṭūṭah in Black Africa.* Princeton, N.J.: Markus Wiener, 1994. A selection of the writings about Mali by Ibn Baṭṭūṭah. Illustrations, maps, bibliographical references, index.

Insoll, Timothy. "Trade and Empire: The Road to Timbuktu." *Archaeology* 53, no. 6 (2000). Valuable information on the trans-Saharan trade routes, camel caravans, and the rise of commerce in medieval Mali.

Lange, Dierk. "From Mande to Songhay: Towards a Political and Ethnic History of Medieval Gao." *Journal of African History* 35 (1994). Although its focus is on the Mande group who occupied Gao, this essay provides an excellent survey of the overall ethnic identity of the West African region and explores the common features of the medieval West African kingdoms.

Levtzion, Nehemia. *Ancient Ghana and Mali.* New York: Africana, 1980. A standard work on the evolution of the Mali Empire. Particularly useful for the early phase of the history of Mali.

Niane, D. T. "Mali and the Second Mandingo Expansion." In *General History of Africa: Africa from the Twelfth to the Sixteenth Century.* Vol. 4. New York: UNESCO, 1984. A well-researched history of Africa that includes a discussion of the rise of the Mali Empire.

_______. *Sundiata: An Epic of Old Mali.* Translated by G. D. Pickett. 1965. Reprint. Harlow, England: Longman, 1994. An account of the rise of Sundiata, the founder of the Mali Empire, based on local oral tradition.

Thobhani, Akbarali. *Mansa Mūsā: The Golden King of Ancient Mali*. Dubuque, Iowa: Kendall/Hunt, 1998. An account of the life and times of Mansa Mūsā, particularly suitable for younger readers.

Yamba, C. Bawa. *Permanent Pilgrims: The Role of Pilgrimage in the Lives of West African Muslims in Sudan*. Washington, D.C.: Smithsonian Institution Press, 1995. Although this book focuses on modern pilgrimage, it is valuable for its discussion of the history and significance of pilgrimage to African Muslims from the Sudan, Mansa Mūsā's homeland. Illustrations, maps, bibliography, index.

See also: c. 610-632: Muḥammad Receives Revelations; 629-645: Pilgrimage of Xuanzang; 630-711: Islam Expands Throughout North Africa; c. 1010: Songhai Kingdom Converts to Islam; 1062-1147: Almoravids Conquer Morocco and Establish the Almoravid Empire; c. 1100: Founding of Timbuktu; 1230's-1255: Reign of Sundiata of Mali; 1325-1355: Travels of Ibn Baṭṭūṭah; 1340: Al-ʿUmarī Writes a History of Africa; 1377: Ibn Khaldūn Completes His *Muqaddimah*.

Related articles in *Great Lives from History: The Middle Ages, 477-1453*: ʿAbd al-Malik; Ibn Baṭṭūṭah; Ibn Khaldūn; al-Idrīsī; Damia al-Kāhina; Lalibela; Mansa Mūsā; Muḥammad; Sundiata; Ṭāriq ibn-Ziyād.

1325-1355
Travels of Ibn Baṭṭūṭah

Ibn Baṭṭūṭah's extensive travels—estimated to have covered approximately 75,000 miles (120,000 kilometers)—carried him to the far corners of the Muslim world near the peak of its greatest glory.

Locale: North Africa, East Africa, Middle East, Central Asia, South Asia, Southeast Asia, China
Categories: Cultural and intellectual history; exploration and discovery; historiography

Key Figures

Ibn Baṭṭūṭah (1304-c. 1377), Arab traveler and scholar
Ibn Juzayy al-Kalbi (1321-1356 or 1357), scribe from Andalusia
Muḥammad ibn Tughluq (c. 1290-1351), sultan of Delhi, r. 1325-1351
Abū ʿInān Fāris (d. 1358), sultan of Morocco, r. 1351-1358
Khadija (d. 1379), queen of the Maldive Islands, r. 1347-1379

Summary of Event

In the early nineteenth century, German scholars published translations of manuscripts obtained in the Middle East that described the travels of a Muslim legal scholar of the fourteenth century: Ibn Baṭṭūṭah. About the same time, a British scholar produced his own translation of a similar manuscript recovered by a Swiss explorer in Egypt. During the middle of the same century, French soldiers in Algeria discovered five incomplete manuscript versions of the same work, two of them the most complete identified so far. These manuscripts were edited and assembled in both Arabic and French by two French scholars and have become the basis of what readers in the Western world know about one of the world's most indefatigable travelers.

A young member of a family of Muslim legal scholars and judges, Ibn Baṭṭūṭah set out with a party of attendants in 1325 on the *hajj*, the pilgrimage to the Arabian city of Mecca required of every able-bodied Muslim male. Ibn Baṭṭūṭah's itinerary took him from his birthplace of Tangier in what is today Morocco across North Africa to the Egyptian cities of Alexandria and Cairo, a journey of ten months. He ascended the Nile River before turning eastward across the desert to Aydhab, the port from which ships normally crossed the Red Sea to the Arabian coast.

Thwarted in this design by political unrest in the region, Ibn Baṭṭūṭah retraced his path and traveled from Cairo to Damascus in Syria, joining a caravan of fellow pilgrims headed for the holy cities of Medina and Mecca. Having finally completed the *hajj*, he turned northward to Iraq and Iran, returning to Mecca in September of 1327.

Ibn Baṭṭūṭah remained in the holy city for three years, studying Muslim law and eventually becoming a moderately successful scholar, albeit an itinerant one—for the attractions of travel had clearly taken hold. Rather than return to Morocco, he and his party set out in 1328 or 1330 on an expedition to East Africa. The group sailed down the Red Sea and into the Indian Ocean, reaching Mombasa (now in Kenya) and Kilwa (now in Tanzania), some 600 miles (970 kilometers) south of the equator. They returned to Arabia via the Persian Gulf, traveling from Oman in eastern Arabia to Mecca, which Ibn Baṭṭūṭah was visiting for the third time.

The restless scholar set out in 1330 or 1332 for India, taking a roundabout route through Egypt, the eastern Mediterranean, Turkey, the Black Sea, and what are now the nations of Ukraine, Russia, Kazakhstan, Uzbekistan, and Turkmenistan. Continuing through Persia and Afghanistan, he reached the Indian subcontinent in either 1333 or 1335. There, he spent seven eventful years as a judge, falling in and out of favor with the sultan of Delhi, Muḥammad ibn Tughluq (r. 1325-1351), and making and losing a fortune. Restored to favor and sent to China in 1341, Ibn Baṭṭūṭah fled to the Maldive Islands, far to the south in the Indian Ocean, when the ship carrying gifts to the Chinese emperor was lost in a storm. Here he found a patron in Queen Khadija, but his brief sojourn within the islands was apparently as tempestuous as his years in India, for he was forced to take refuge on the island of Sri Lanka off the southern tip of India, after only eight months.

A voyage up the eastern coast of India resulted in another disaster, when Ibn Baṭṭūṭah was shipwrecked, forcing him to return to the Maldives. In 1345, he renewed his efforts to visit China, sailing along the shores of the Bay of Bengal, rounding the southern tip of the Malay Peninsula, stopping on the island of Sumatra, and eventually reaching the city of Quanzhou on the southeast coast of China. After visiting (according to his account) Beijing, Canton, and several other Chinese cities, Ibn Baṭṭūṭah began to retrace his steps, making a final pilgrimage to Mecca in 1346-1347. He witnessed in Syria the aftermath of the plague known as the Black Death. After a visit to the Mediterranean island of Sardinia (one of the few Christian lands in which he set foot), he reached Morocco in late 1349 at the age of forty-five.

Ibn Baṭṭūṭah's travels had carried him from northwestern Africa to easternmost Asia, but they were not to be his last. In 1350, he turned northward, taking part in the defense of the peninsula of Gibraltar against Christian forces and visiting Granada, the rich region of what is now southern Spain that remained in Muslim hands. In 1353, he was sent by the sultan of Morocco on a less congenial journey deep into the Sahara Desert to investigate the empire of Mali, spending several months in the then-little-known city of Timbuktu and passing through what are today the nations of Algeria, Mali, and Mauritania.

SIGNIFICANCE

Ibn Baṭṭūṭah returned to Morocco for good in 1355. At the request of Moroccan sultan Abū ʿInān Fāris, he agreed to recount his extensive travels to a noted scribe, Ibn Juzayy al-Kalbi, who incorporated them into an elaborate work of prose and occasional poetry, completed in 1355. Its general pattern is that of the *riḥlah*, a popular form of the time that recounted a journey or journeys, usually to Mecca.

The work, *Tuḥfat al-nuẓẓār fī gharaʿib al-amsar wa-ʿajaʿib al-asfar* (1357-1358; *Travels of Ibn Battuta*, 1958-2000, best known as the *Riḥlah*), is not only an account of Ibn Baṭṭūṭah's travels but also a description of virtually the entire Muslim world. Because Ibn Juzayy also drew on earlier works, it is difficult to be sure how much of the detail of the *Riḥla*h reflects Ibn Baṭṭūṭah's own experience. Scholars even wonder whether Ibn Baṭṭūṭah actually traveled as extensively in China or East Africa as the narrative suggests.

Although copies of the *Riḥlah* reached the cities of North Africa beyond Morocco, it does not seem to have had much influence or impact. Ibn Baṭṭūṭah ended his life as a provincial judge of only modest fame. Only when his account was discovered by Europeans in the nineteenth century did its significance as the most extensive work of its kind become obvious.

—*Grove Koger*

FURTHER READING

Abercrombie, Thomas J., and James L. Stanfield. "Ibn Baṭṭūṭah, Prince of Travelers." *National Geographic* 180 (December, 1991): 2-49. Substantial article following Ibn Baṭṭūṭah's travels and showing many of the places he visited as they exist today. Map, numerous color illustrations.

Arno, Joan, and Helen Grady. *Ibn Baṭṭūṭa: A View of the Fourteenth-Century World*. Los Angeles: National Center for History in the Schools, University of California, Los Angeles, 1998. A seventy-three-page teacher's manual for teaching both Ibn Baṭṭūṭah and fourteenth century North Africa to students in grades 7-10. Illustrations, maps, bibliographical references.

Beckingham, Charles F. "In Search of Ibn Baṭṭūṭah." *Asian Affairs* 8 (1977): 263-277. Text of an informal lecture by one of Ibn Baṭṭūṭah's translators touching on his travels, their historical and geographical context, and the discovery of the manuscripts recounting them.

Dunn, Ross E. *The Adventures of Ibn Baṭṭūṭah: A Muslim Traveler of the Fourteenth Century*. Berkeley: University of California Press, 1986. The standard work in

English on the great traveler, quoting frequently from the *Riḥlah*. Includes maps, notes, an extensive bibliography, black-and-white illustrations, glossary, and elucidations of subjects such as the Muslim calendar.

Hamdun, Said, and Noël King, trans. and eds. *Ibn Baṭṭūṭa in Black Africa*. Princeton, N.J.: Markus Wiener, 1994. A selection of Ibn Baṭṭūṭah's writings during his two sub-Saharan trips—his second, to Mali, being his last recorded adventure. Illustrations, maps, bibliographical references, index.

Ibn Baṭṭūṭah. *The Travels of Ibn Baṭṭūṭah*. London: Picador, 2002. Abridged, introduced, and annotated by Tim Mackintosh-Smith, this volume is based on the Hakluyt Society translation and is the most accessible edition for the general reader.

_______. *The Travels of Ibn Baṭṭūṭah, A.D. 1325-1354*. London: Hakluyt Society, 1958-2000. Translated by Hamilton A. R. Gibb and Charles F. Beckingham. Index compiled by A. D. H. Bivar. The standard edition in English, based on the Arabic text edited by C. Défrémery and B. R. Sanguinetti and supplemented with an extensive scholarly apparatus.

Mackintosh-Smith, Tim. *Travels with a Tangerine: A Journey in the Footnotes of Ibn Baṭṭūṭah*. New York: Welcome Rain, 2001. A modern travelogue in which the author follows Ibn Baṭṭūṭah's route from Tangier to Istanbul. Includes maps, a bibliographical note, and atmospheric drawings.

Rumford, James. *Traveling Man: The Journey of Ibn Baṭṭūṭa, 1325-1354*. Boston: Houghton Mifflin, 2001. A semifictional biography designed for young readers. Color illustrations, maps.

See also: 630-711: Islam Expands Throughout North Africa; 1062-1147: Almoravids Conquer Morocco and Establish the Almoravid Empire; c. 1100: Founding of Timbuktu; 1271-1295: Travels of Marco Polo; c. 1320: Origins of the Bubonic Plague; 1324-1325: Mansa Mūsā's Pilgrimage to Mecca Sparks Interest in Mali Empire; 1340: Al-ʿUmarī Writes a History of Africa; 1377: Ibn Khaldūn Completes His *Muqaddimah*.

Related articles in *Great Lives from History: The Middle Ages, 477-1453*: Ibn Khaldūn; al-Idrīsī; Mansa Mūsā; Marco Polo; Raziya; William of Rubrouck; Yaqut; Zheng He.

1325-1519
Aztecs Build Tenochtitlán

Occupying land used by other civilizations before them, the Aztecs built one of the world's largest cities in the Valley of Mexico.

Locale: Mexico City

Categories: Architecture; cultural and intellectual history; expansion and land acquisition; religion; trade and commerce

Key Figures

Moctezuma II (c. 1480-1520), ninth emperor of the Aztec Empire, r. 1503-1520

Hernán Cortés (c. 1485-1547), Spanish conquistador

Summary of Event

The Spanish conquistadors encountered the Aztecs' remarkable civilization in its full flower, before Spanish guns, avarice, and disease laid it to waste. The center of Aztec civilization, Tenochtitlán, occupied the site of another great metropolis, what is now called Mexico City. The Aztecs called the place where they lived "Mexica," from which "Mexico" is derived. The first Spaniards to see Tenochtitlán described a city more splendid than any their well-traveled eyes ever had seen.

The Aztecs probably moved to the Valley of Mexico from the present-day Mexican state of Nayarit, about 450 miles (725 kilometers) northwest of Tenochtitlán. The marshes of the Pacific coast, not far from Mexicaltitán, fit descriptions of the Aztecs' origin place, Aztlan, "place of the herons," from which they derived "Aztec," meaning "people of the heron place."

According to the Aztecs' chroniclers, their people arrived in the Valley of Mexico in 1325. During almost two centuries between that date and the Spanish invasion led by conquistador Hernán Cortés (in 1519), the Aztecs built Tenochtitlán (meaning "place of the prickly-pear cactus"). Tenochtitlán was much larger than Paris or Rome at that same time, and it had twice the population of London. As the Aztec Empire spread to the Gulf of Mexico and present-day Guatemala, Tenochtitlán grew on land reclaimed from surrounding swamps. Two three-mile-long aqueducts were built to carry fresh water from the mainland, each with two sluices, so one could be

Artist's rendition of Tenochtitlán. (American Museum of Natural History)

closed for cleaning without interrupting the water supply.

The Aztec cosmos was filled with gods for every human activity, from fertility to death. Each community and craft had its deity. Some researchers have counted as many as sixteen hundred deities. Most Aztecs believed that the gods could not keep the Sun and Moon moving (and by implication, continue the cycle of life on earth) without a steady diet of human flesh and blood. Their cosmology propelled the Aztecs into wars to procure prisoners for sacrifice to their gods.

The Aztec Empire expanded through this warfare, which was as much a pageant as a battle. Wars were fought hand-to-hand. Aztecs disarmed their opponents and forced them to surrender, or they beat them unconscious. Soldiers wore headdresses and shirts of yellow parrot feathers set off with gold. Soldiers wore jaguar skins and hoods of gold set off by feather horns. Their shields were decorated with golden disks depicting butterflies and serpents. The armies of the Aztec Empire went to battle with two-toned drums, conch-shell trumpets, shrill clay whistles, and high-pitched screams. Priests led the soldiers into battle with trumpet-blasts calling on the gods as witnesses. The priests then waited in the rear with razor-sharp obsidian blades, ready to feed the gods with the still-warm blood of captives' beating hearts. The Aztecs transported many thousands of subject peoples to Tenochtitlán for forced labor and religious sacrifice.

Estimates of the number of people sacrificed for religious purposes range from ten thousand to eighty thousand during those three decades before the Spanish invasion. Four people at a time were sacrificed at the Great Temple in Tenochtitlán from dawn to dusk. The entire city stank of burning flesh. At times, the stench was sealed into the valley by the same atmospheric inversions that today capture some of the world's worst air pollution.

The Aztecs built a commercial network that brought to the Valley of Mexico all manner of food, rare feathers, precious metals, and other commodities, many of which were traded at a great market at Tlatelolco. Cortés reported having seen as many as sixty thousand people bartering in this grand bazaar.

While the solid temples, residences, and storehouses of the city gave Tenochtitlán an air of permanence, the city was not old by Mesoamerican standards. In less than two centuries, the site had grown from little more than a small temple surrounded by a few mud-and-thatch huts. According to Cortés's accounts, the grandeur of the Aztecs' capital outshone anything he had ever seen. In Spain, he wrote, there is nothing to compare with it. Some of Cortés's soldiers asked as if they were in a dream. The Aztec capital was a cavalcade of color—the architecture painted turquoise, yellow, red, and green.

Cortés and his roughly four hundred men forged alliances with many native peoples who were more than ready to turn against the domineering Mexicas. Through the use of informants such as the legendary Malinche (a former Mexican Indian princess who was first a slave to Cortés, then later his mistress, interpreter, and guide) and an uncanny sense of timing that Aztec leaders sometimes thought was supernatural, Cortés's small band of Spanish conquistadors reduced a state that had subjugated millions to defeat within two bloody years. The Spanish also were aided by European diseases and the Aztecs' own fear of a troublesome future.

Cortés began recruiting Indian allies against the Aztecs in Cempoalla, near the Gulf coast, home to about thirty thousand people of the Totonac nation, the first city he visited on his way to Tenochtitlán. With thousands of allies, Cortés entered the Valley of Mexico with enough human power to initiate serious combat.

Cortés and his allies found themselves received in Tenochtitlán as ambassadors of a mighty foreign country. Cortés repaid hospitality with violence: At first, he took the Aztec emperor Moctezuma prisoner, then slowly and ruthlessly undermined his power among the Mexicas. The imprisonment included physical and psychological torture. The Spaniards held Moctezuma captive for several months, while rumors regarding his health spread through the capital. After months of Spanish torment, Moctezuma was killed.

At one point, Cortés's men discovered a massive amount of gold and silver, the state treasury. The Spanish extracted 162,000 *pesos de oro* (or roughly 19,600 troy ounces) of gold from this cache. At 2003 gold prices (about $330 per troy ounce), this hoard would have been worth about $6.5 million. Much of what the Spanish purloined was part intricate artwork that they melted into bullion for convenient shipment back to Spain, except for a few pieces that Cortés preserved intact to impress his sponsors.

Following the murder of Moctezuma, Cortés and his comrades soon found the Mexica capital in full revolt. The Spanish then departed Tenochtitlán by night, along one of the causeways that connected the city with the mainland. Seven thousand Spanish and Tlascalan allies surged onto the causeway as the Aztecs attacked them from boats. The Battle of Noche Triste ("sad night"), as it was called, became an Aztec folktale, a comeuppance for many of the Spaniards who drowned because they had tied so much gold to their bodies.

Significance

The fact that Tenochtitlán was built in less than two centuries is amazing enough. When one reflects on the Aztecs' lack of construction machinery (even the wheel), this feat of Aztec construction becomes even more astounding. The island on which Tenochtitlán was built contained no construction materials, so virtually everything used to construct it had to be ferried, aboard canoes at first. Later, supplies were carried, or rolled on logs, using ropes and pulleys, along the causeways that connected the city with the mainland.

The city's size was remarkable for its time. If Tenochtitlán's population was about three-hundred thousand, which seems likely, it was the largest city in the Western Hemisphere, and the largest urban area in North or South America until after 1800. At the time the United States became independent, its largest cities (Boston, New York, and Philadelphia) housed no more than fifty thousand people each.

The Spanish invasion initiated a major demographic shift in Mexico. Henry Dobyns has estimated that the population of Mexico declined from between 30 million and 37.5 million people in 1520 to 1.5 million in 1650, a holocaust of an extent unknown in the Old World. Even if one argues that Dobyns's figures are too high, cutting them almost in half to a 1520 population of 20 million would produce a mortality rate during a 130-year period of 92.5 percent.

—*Bruce E. Johansen*

Further Reading

Brandon, William. *The American Heritage Book of Indians*. New York: Dell, 1961. Describes the Aztecs in the context of Native American life.

Carrasco, David, ed. *Aztec Ceremonial Landscapes*. Niwot: University Press of Colorado, 1999. Discusses Aztec sacred spaces, rites, ceremonies and festivals, sacrifice, shamanism, myth, and more. Includes illustrations, bibliographies, and index.

Collis, Maurice. *Cortés and Montezuma*. New York: New Directions, 1999. Provides a general overview of the history of Cortés and Moctezuma in the time of the Aztecs, from Cortés's arrival to his storming of Tenochtitlán. Includes illustrations and index.

Dobyns, Henry F. "Estimating Aboriginal American Population." *Current Anthropology* 7 (1966): 395-

449. Dobyns makes his case for large populations in Mexico and across the hemisphere.

McDowell, Bart. "The Aztecs." *National Geographic*, December, 1980, 704-752. Comprehensive history of the Aztec Empire.

Molina Montes, Augusto F. "The Building of Tenochtitlán." *National Geographic*, December, 1980, 753-766. Detailed description of the city's history.

Portilla, Miguel León. *The Aztec Image of Self and Society: An Introduction to Nahua Culture.* Salt Lake City: University of Utah Press, 1992. A detailed account of Aztec culture and society.

Stannard, David E. *American Holocaust: Columbus and the Conquest of the New World.* New York: Oxford University Press, 1992. A graphic account of the death and destruction that accompanied the Spanish conquest.

SEE ALSO: c. 600-950: El Tajín Is Built; 7th-8th centuries: Maya Build Astronomical Observatory at Palenque; c. 700-1000: Building of Chichén Itzá; c. 950-1150: Toltecs Build Tula.

RELATED ARTICLE in *Great Lives from History: The Middle Ages, 477-1453*: Itzcóatl.

1328-1350
FLOWERING OF LATE MEDIEVAL PHYSICS

Developments in kinematics and dynamics in England between 1328 and 1350 exercised a deep influence on late medieval physics and natural philosophy in Western Europe, which flourished in the fourteenth and subsequent centuries.

LOCALE: Europe
CATEGORY: Science and technology

KEY FIGURES

Thomas Bradwardine (c. 1290-1349), English mathematician and natural philosopher
William Heytesbury (before 1313-1372), English logician and philosopher
Richard Swineshead (fl. fourteenth century), English mathematician and natural philosopher
John Dumbleton (fl. fourteenth century), English mathematician and natural philosopher
Jean Buridan (1300-1358), French scholastic philosopher
Nicholas Oresme (c. 1320-1382), pupil of Buridan
Albert of Saxony (c. 1316-1390), nominalist philosopher

SUMMARY OF EVENT

Thomas Bradwardine's *Treatise on Proportions* of 1328 proposing his dynamic law of movement began a period of intense speculation in natural philosophy at Merton College, Oxford. Speculation in natural philosophy, or physics, was still associated closely in the late medieval period with classical scientists as well as their Greek and Arabic commentators whose works gradually appeared in the Latin West after the twelfth century.

Of first importance was Aristotle, whose *Physica* (335-323 B.C.E.; *Physics*, 1812), widely known and commented on in antiquity and the later medieval period, would serve as a fundamental text for students well into the seventeenth century. According to Aristotle, all things were composed of matter and form. From his postulates that the form of a substance determines its essence, that each substance has a natural inclination that dominates all the changes or movements it experiences, and that every motion presupposes a mover, Aristotle propounded a dynamic law of movement postulating that the velocity of a moving body is directly proportional to the moving force and inversely proportional to the resistance of the medium traversed. Aristotle's law implied that in a vacuum movement would take place instantaneously since the density, hence the resistance, of the medium would be zero. The impossibility of an instantaneous movement led Aristotle, in turn, to deny the existence of a vacuum.

In the sixth century, John Philoponus, in attempting to demonstrate that movement in a vacuum was possible, criticized Aristotle's dynamic law. In place of Aristotle's assertion that velocity was indirectly proportional to the resistance, he proposed that velocity was proportional to the motive force (referred to by late medieval scholars as "impetus") minus the resistance. Accordingly, movement in a vacuum was possible because the absence of a resisting medium merely reduced arithmetically the time needed to move through a given space. Philoponus's views were transmitted to the West indirectly through Averroës's commentary on Aristotle's *Physica*, which rejected criticism of Aristotle's law made by Avempace

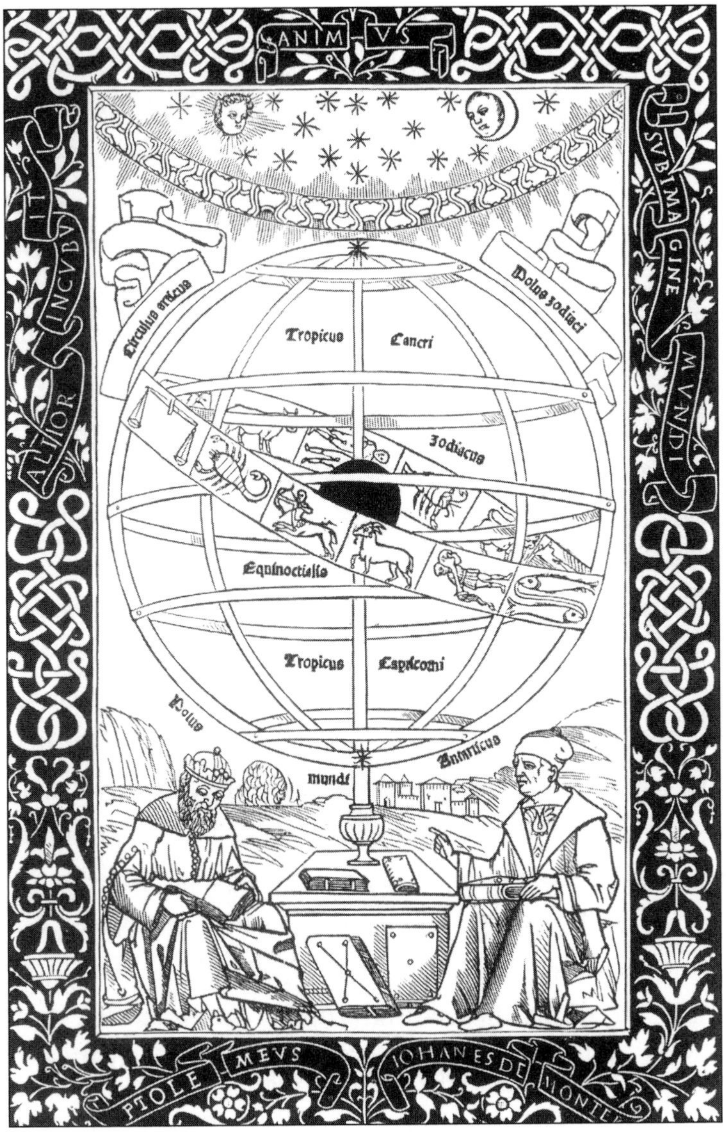

The Ptolemaic universe as explained by Johann Müller (Regiomontanus), a wood engraving in Epitome . . . Johannes de Monte Regio *(1543).* (Frederick Ungar Publishing Co.)

(a twelfth century Arabian scholar living in Spain) who repeated the views of Philoponus.

Not until Bradwardine's *Treatise on Proportions* was an attempt made to reformulate Aristotle's law in precise mathematical language. Bradwardine followed Aristotle and Averroës in characterizing the relationship between force and resistance, the parameters determining velocity, as a kind of proportion or ratio. In so doing, he rejected Avempace's and Aquinas's postulations of a law of simple arithmetical difference. Moreover, Bradwardine went beyond earlier treatments of the Aristotelian dynamic law of movement by giving it a mathematical expression that adequately reflected the observed results in cases in which the motive force is equal to or less than the resistance. In such critical cases, the simple Aristotelian proportion yielded erroneous conclusions. While Aristotle's law would predict some value greater than zero when force and resistance are equal, the velocity would in fact be zero. Even though Bradwardine used the medieval language of proportions, he expressed results more or less equivalent to the exponential function used today to define velocity.

The importance of this application of mathematical reasoning to problems of dynamics must not be underestimated. Bradwardine was followed at Merton College by such distinguished natural philosophers as William Heytesbury, Richard Swineshead, and John Dumbleton, scholars who made significant contributions to medieval kinematics. Furthermore, interest spread to Paris, where it stimulated the work of Jean Buridan, of his pupil Nicholas Oresme, and of Albert of Saxony. All these scholars helped to impart to late medieval physics a characteristic form perceptible in the key physical problems discussed, such as the laws of falling bodies, the principle of inertia, and the question of the center of gravity, as well as in the extensive use of the logical-mathematical methods of analysis and measurement. The brilliant Oresme, who was a precursor of Descartes in the development of analytical geometry, in emphasizing the daily rotation of the earth introduced a basic alteration of Ptolemaic cosmology. The scientific ferment also spread to the universities of Italy. The ardent fifteenth century German Humanist Nicholas of Cusa, in doubting the geocentric theory and in proposing that the Earth moved in rhythm with the heavens, helped to form the tradition against which the physics of Galileo developed as well as the doctrines of relativity in space and motion supported later by Bruno.

Science in the late Middle Ages had its last great exponent in Johann Müller, or Regiomontanus, and his

Averroës and his school at Córdoba in the thirteenth century played a key role in transmitting the works of Aristotle and other Greek and Arab scientists to the West. (Library of Congress)

school at Nuremberg in the latter half of the fifteenth century. His work in mathematics became the basis of trigonometry in western Europe as previously it was developed in the Arab world, and his scientific astronomical observations and charts were used by Columbus.

SIGNIFICANCE

The significance of the intellectual events described here for the study of the history of science lies in the fact that until the beginning of the twentieth century it was universally taken for granted that the history of modern mechanics began with Galileo, at the beginning of the seventeenth century. However, beginning at the turn of the twentieth century, the outstanding French historian and philosopher of science, Pierre Duhem, himself a physicist of first rank, uncovered the largely forgotten work of the Oxford and Parisian scholars here described. He then proposed the view that the scientific revolution, at least in mechanics, really began in the fourteenth century. This view ascribes to Galileo a much less dominant role than usually accepted. Duhem's thesis has been vigorously opposed by other scholars, and the dispute continues.

—*Joseph M. Victor*

FURTHER READING

Clagett, Marshall. *Giovanni Marliani and Late Medieval Physics.* Reprint. New York: AMS Press, 1967. This study deals with the problems of heat reaction and includes a discussion of Marliani's reaction to kinematic and dynamic developments at Oxford and Paris.

_______. *The Science of Mechanics in the Middle Ages.* Madison: University of Wisconsin Press, 1959. A fundamentally important work to the student of medieval mechanics that discusses the Aristotelian tradition and aspects of late medieval dynamics. The last section dealing with "The Fate and Scope of Medieval Mechanics" summarizes both the spread of the English and French physics, and the overall accomplishments of medieval mechanics, a study originally aided by concepts from scholastic philosophy.

Clagett, Marshall, and Ernest Moody. *The Medieval Science of Weights.* Madison: University of Wisconsin Press, 1952. A comprehensive survey of medieval statics, containing numerous texts and translations in addition to commentaries.

Crombie, A. C. *Augustine to Galileo: The History of Science A.D. 400-1650.* 1952. Rev. ed., *Medieval and Early Modern Science.* London: Heinemann, 1962. This work is an excellent introduction to medieval science as a whole, but it should be supplemented by more technical literature.

Dijksterhuis, E. J. *The Mechanization of the World Picture.* London: Oxford University Press, 1961. A work especially helpful in explaining the terms "intension" and "remission."

Golino, C. Q., ed. *Galileo and His Precursors.* Berkeley: University of California Press, 1966. See especially the chapter "Galileo Reappraised," by Ernest Moody.

Molland, A. G. "The Geometrical Background to the 'Merton School': An Exploration into the Application of Mathematics to Natural Philosophy in the Fourteenth Century." *British Journal for the History of Science* 4 (1968): 108-125. Outlines important features in the introduction of mathematical methods of analysis to fourteenth century natural philosophy.

Murdoch, John E. "The Medieval Science of Proportions: Elements of the Interaction with Greek Foundations and the Development of New Mathematical Techniques." In *Scientific Change*, edited by A. C.

Crombie. London: Heinemann, 1963. An important article dealing with the medieval language of proportions.

Shank, Michael H. *The Scientific Enterprise in Antiquity and the Middle Ages*. Chicago: University of Chicago Press, 2000. This anthology of essays in the history of science includes articles on Bradwardine and medieval mechanical knowledge.

Sylla, Edith D. "Thomas Bradwardine's *De Continuo* and the Structure of Fourteenth-Century Learning." In *Texts and Contexts in Ancient and Medieval Science*. New York: Brill, 1997. An examination of scientific scholarship and education using Bradwardine's work as a case study.

SEE ALSO: 595-665: Invention of Decimals and Negative Numbers; c. 950: Court of Córdoba Flourishes in Spain; c. 1100: Arabic Numerals Are Introduced into Europe; 1100-1300: European Universities Emerge; c. 1150: Moors Transmit Classical Philosophy and Medicine to Europe.

RELATED ARTICLES in *Great Lives from History: The Middle Ages, 477-1453:* Averroës; Jean Buridan; al-Khwārizmī.

November, 1330
BASARAB DEFEATS THE HUNGARIANS

Basarab, prince of Walachia, defeated the Hungarians and established the resurgence of the indigenous Walachian people. Ongoing strife between Hungary and the Danubian principalities ultimately weakened both and made them vulnerable to Turkish conquest.

LOCALE: Posada, north of Cimpulung, Walachia (now in Romania)

CATEGORIES: Expansion and land acquisition; government and politics; wars, uprisings, and civil unrest

KEY FIGURES

Basarab I (c. 1310-1352), prince of Walachia, c. 1330-1352

Charles I (1288-1342), king of the Hungarians, r. 1310-1342

SUMMARY OF EVENT

Dacia, the area of southeastern Europe that was later to become part of modern Romania, was by the first century part of the Roman Empire, although it was later overrun by the Goths and other barbarian tribes that caused the Romans to abandon the Dacian colony in 271. The original inhabitants of this area north of the Danube, thought to be Romanized Dacians, were driven out of their original homeland by these invaders. Their territory was settled by Slavic tribes, Bulgars, Avars, and, at the end of the ninth century, by the Magyars (Hungarians) and other tribes from central Asia. The Daco-Romans (later Romanians) disappeared from history for nearly a millennium, then reappeared as Vlachs, although south of their original homeland, around the eleventh century.

Although contemporary sources are scanty, it is thought that at least a sizable segment of the Daco-Roman native population retreated into the Carpathian Mountains of Transylvania, where they retained their language and culture, while the flatlands were settled by Slavs, Hungarians, Cumans, and Tatars. The extent to which this is true is still a matter of controversy between Romanians and Hungarians.

The geographical area now known as Romania formed a part of the Second Bulgarian (or Bulgaro-Vlach) Empire of the tenth and eleventh centuries, although whether Romanians made up the leadership of that empire is open to controversy. Although nominally Christianized, it was from their early contact with the Bulgarians that the Romanians were exposed to the Eastern Orthodox form of religion.

Around the end of the thirteenth century, the people now known as Romanians reappeared in Walachia, driven eastward and southward from the Carpathian Mountains of Transylvania because of religious persecution by the Catholic Hungarians and expropriation of their lands by Hungarian feudal lords. The fact that the Hungarians were still recovering from the terrible Mongol invasion of 1241, however, gave the Romanians some opportunity to rediscover their national identity. By the fourteenth century, the Walachians and Moldavians, who were excluded from the cities founded by the Hungarian kings, were increasingly dissatisfied with the political and religious climate of their Magyar suzerains. They chose the Byzantine model for church and state in preference to that of the Catholic Hungarians, a model that was Eastern Orthodox, with an absolute monarch and dynastic succession. This autocratic power eventually became subject to abuse, since there were no rival estates that could limit the power of the ruler, who often rewarded his favorites at the expense of the peasant population.

The landowners of the territory south of the Carpathians chose Basarab, a prince of the district of Arges, to serve as grand voivode (military leader) and prince. Basarab had gained recognition for his battles against the Mongol Tatars, although he was nominally a vassal of the Hungarian crown. The Basarab Dynasty, founded by Prince Basarab I, derived from the title of the prince as voivode. His status was that of sole landowner, military leader, and chief ruler and lawmaker.

Basarab unified the area between the Carpathians and the Danube, and later the area north of the Danube as well, subsequently called Bessarabia after the Basarab Dynasty. Basarab I's capital was at Cimpulung (Arges), which became his dynastic seat. His son and successor, Nicholas Alexander, continued to strengthen the dynasty and in the 1350's was the founder of the Princely Church at Curtea de Arges, which under patriarchal approval became the Eastern Orthodox metropolitan church for Walachia, thus confirming Walachia's status as a principality.

Perhaps a further factor that provided the Romanians with a national goal was the development of the Danubian trade route that extended from the Black Sea north through Walachia to Transylvania and the Adriatic Sea. This Danubian trade, and the taxes and tolls exacted from the mainly foreign merchant traders, enabled the Walachian state and its rulers to become relatively wealthy by the middle of the fourteenth century.

In Hungary, after the extinction of the native Árpád Dynasty in 1301 and a disputatious interregnum until 1310, the Angevin Dynasty was established, with the election of Charles I (later Charles IV, Holy Roman Emperor). As king, Charles succeeded in ending the anarchy that had preceded his reign and in restoring the power of the Crown against the demands of the aristocracy. Charles founded his capital at Visegrad in 1323, a year that marked his resumption of full control over Hungary. As a ruler, Charles was providential and careful, which contributed to the increasing power of Hungary during the Angevin reign.

At this time, Hungary included not only all the Danubian basin to the crests of the Carpathian Mountains, but also Walachia, northern Serbia, Bosnia, and the coast of Dalmatia.

In November, 1330, Charles invaded the domains of Basarab I in Walachia in order to reestablish Hungarian supremacy over Walachia, hoping to profit by Basarab's military reversals with his allies, the Bulgarians, who had recently been defeated by the Serbians at Velbuzhd. Although Basarab tried to buy off the Hungarian king with an indemnity of seven thousand silver marks, Charles refused. At Posada, a pass in the southern Carpathians, however, Charles was defeated by Basarab and barely escaped with his life. In spite of this victory, only a few years later Walachia again became a dependency of Hungary, only achieving full independence from Hungary in 1380.

Significance

After the Battle of Posada, both nations continued to expand under the leadership of subsequent members of their respective dynasties. The Hungarians, under Charles's son, Louis I the Great (r. 1342-1382), pursued an aggressive foreign policy against neighboring states, particularly the Venetian Republic and the Balkans, and yet the country enjoyed the benefits of domestic peace and stability. Prosperity was assured from the great mining wealth from the gold mines of Transylvania, which were mined largely by German Saxons invited by the Hungarian king. In contrast to the nobility, who held their estates as a hereditary elite, the lands newly conquered became the sole property of the king. These he used to establish a court aristocracy of his own supporters, as well as to build up a large treasury for the royal household. This social environment of wealth and privilege had a further effect of increasing the level of literacy and written documentation in Hungary at this time.

The principality of Walachia, under the Basarab Dynasty, together with the neighboring emerging principality of Moldavia, also continued to develop, although the advent of the Turks in the Balkans became an increasing threat, particularly after they defeated the Serbians and Bulgarians at the Battle of Marica in 1371. These Danubian principalities, with a large peasant population, a small boyar class under the authority of the voivode, and a disfranchised and landless class of Gypsy (Roma) and Tatar slaves, continued to be coveted by the Hungarians. Nevertheless, after the Battle of Kosovo in Serbia in 1389 and the fall of Bulgaria in 1393, Walachia also became an object of the Turkish sultan's interest. In 1394, the Turks invaded Walachia, causing the voivode Mircea the Old (r. 1386-1418) to seek refuge with the Hungarians in Transylvania, and enabling a rival boyar to gain his throne. From 1395, the Walachians began to pay a financial tribute to the Ottoman Turks. Although the Hungarians were not defeated by the Turks until 1526, the proximity of the Danubian principalities as Turkish vassals represented an enduring threat, and it influenced the desire of the subsequent Hungarian rulers to wage crusades against the Ottoman Empire.

—*Gloria Fulton*

FURTHER READING

Boia, Lucian. *Romania: Borderland of Europe*. Translated by James Christian Brown. London: Reaktion Books, 2001. A comprehensive history of Romania from the Middle Ages through the twentieth century.

Castellan, Georges. *A History of the Romanians*. Boulder, Colo.: East European Monographs, 1989. A survey of Romanian history. Chapters 2 and 3 treat the origins and early development of the Romanians.

Chirot, Daniel. *Social Change in a Peripheral Society: The Creation of a Balkan Colony*. New York: Academic Press, 1976. A monograph describing the importance of Walachia's location as a trading colony on the Danube to the area's development.

Engel, Pál. *The Realm of St. Stephen: A History of Medieval Hungary, 895-1526*. Translated by Tamás Pálosfalvi. Edited by Andrew Ayton. New York: I. B. Tauris, 2001. An extensive study of the history of medieval Hungary. Includes a chapter on Charles I. Explores the economic, social, political, cultural, and military history of the Magyars. Written especially for readers with little or no knowledge of the region and time period. Maps, tables, bibliography, index.

Georgescu, Vlad. *The Romanians: A History*. Columbus: Ohio State University Press, 1991. A survey of Romanian history by a Romanian historian. Chapter 2 covers the Middle Ages.

Papacostea, Serban. *Between the Crusade and the Mongol Empire: The Romanians in the Thirteenth Century*. Translated by Liviu Bleoca. Cluj-Napoca, Romania: Center for Transylvanian Studies/Romanian Cultural Foundation, 1998. An in-depth study of the period leading up to the Romanians' entrance into Walachia.

Seton-Watson, R. W. *A History of the Roumanians: From Roman Times to the Completion of Unity*. New York: Archon Books, 1963. Originally published in 1934, this work is a standard historical text on the formation of the Romanian nation-state.

Sugar, Peter F., ed. *A History of Hungary*. Bloomington: Indiana University Press, 1990. Chapter 5, written by Pal Angel, covers the age of the Angevins, 1301-1382.

SEE ALSO: 834: Gypsies Expelled from Persia; 1381-1405: Tamerlane's Conquests; June 28, 1389: Turkish Conquest of Serbia; 1442-1456: János Hunyadi Defends Hungary Against the Ottomans.

RELATED ARTICLES in *Great Lives from History: The Middle Ages, 477-1453*: Árpád; Mehmed II; Stefan Dušan.

1333
KILWA KISIWANI BEGINS ECONOMIC AND HISTORICAL DECLINE

Kilwa Kisiwani, once the most powerful and lucrative center of East Africa's oceanic trade, began an economic and historical decline probably caused by the Black Death in many parts of the world and a regression of gold reserves and value.

LOCALE: Kilwa Kisiwani, East African coast (now Tanzania)

CATEGORIES: Economics; trade and commerce

KEY FIGURES

ʿAlī bin al-Ḥasan (fl. twelfth century), founder of Kilwa Kisiwani

Abū al-Mawāhib al-Ḥasan bin Sulaimān (d. 1333), ruler of Kilwa Kisiwani, r. 1310-1333

Dā'ūd bin al-Ḥasan (d. c. 1351), ruler of Kilwa Kisiwani, r. 1333-c. 1351, brother of Abū al-Mawāhib al-Ḥasan bin Sulaimān

SUMMARY OF EVENT

Kilwa Kisiwani (or, simply, Kilwa) ranks among the greatest and most famous ports on the Swahili coast. According to the *Kilwa Chronicles* (c. 1550), in the ninth century a coastal east African inhabitant of the area that came to be known as Kilwa exchanged the island with ʿAlī bin al-Ḥasan for some luxury items. Al-Ḥasan was a wealthy trader who claimed to be from Persia and was the celebrated founder of the Shirazi Dynasty.

Al-Ḥasan and his descendants built a large mosque in Kilwa fostering the growth of a Muslim community.

Ḥasan and his ministers also established trade links with many nearby empires, including Great Zimbabwe in southeastern Africa and reaching as far as eastern Asia. Kilwa became exceptionally wealthy through the trade of iron, gold, and ivory in exchange for spices, jewelry, and textiles from India, China, the Arabian Peninsula, Persia, and the Mediterranean region.

By the fourteenth century under Abū al-Mawāhib al-Hasan bin Salaimān of the Mahdali Dynasty, Kilwa became the dominant trade city in the East African coastal region that stretched southward to what is now called Mozambique and northward to Somalia. Kilwa's geographical location made it a safe harbor on which to land, and its location was strategically close to several important resources such as gold mines and even elephants, all of which contributed to the city's unprecedented wealth in the early fourteenth century.

Kilwa became known to the outside world through documents recorded in several legendary visits. The first published account of a visit, in 1331, was from the celebrated Muslim explorer Ibn Baṭṭūṭah, sometimes described as the Marco Polo of Islam because of his extensive explorations. Ibn Baṭṭūṭah was amazed by the great wealth and beauty of Kilwa. He commented particularly on the stone carvings and tapestries found in the homes of the wealthy. It was during Ibn Baṭṭūṭah's visit from the western Sahara to East Africa's coast that Abū al-Mawāhib, known as the giver of gifts, was in power. Within two years of Ibn Baṭṭūṭah's visit, Dāʾūd bin al-Ḥasan, al-Mawāhib's brother, came to power.

During the reign of Dāʾūd, Kilwa's commercial economy went through a period of serious decline. Building projects such as the Husuni Kubwa palace were abandoned and maintenance of the central mosque, for Friday prayers, fell into decline, indicating that the political leadership could no longer afford opulent living.

Scholars list several reasons for Kilwa's economic decline. The gold trade from the south seems to have slipped out of Kilwa's control and, simultaneously, international markets declined with the Black Death. The Black Death affected large parts of Europe and Asia, which caused disruptions in commercial exchange at the international level. Furthermore, without total domination of gold transfer from Zimbabwe and Sofala to the outside world, Kilwa's wealth was greatly diminished during Dāʾūd's reign.

Dāʾūd lived closer to the population than did his predecessors because of Kilwa's decline in wealth. Yet despite his close connection with the people, Dāʾūd was memorialized as less than generous in comparison with his brother, likely because the economic downturn affected how the population of Kilwa viewed Dāʾūd. Under Dāʾūd, international circumstances created the decline in demand for gold, which had reached unparalleled levels in the history of the Kilwa city-state under the leadership of al-Mawāhib. The wealth of Kilwa was shared with the impoverished, the foreign, and all those in need. By the time of Dāʾūd's reign, Kilwa's commercial importance had contracted dramatically; Kilwa shifted from a leading site of trade to a remote spot on the coast.

SIGNIFICANCE

By the early fifteenth century, Kilwa experienced a resurgent period of extensive, but modest, building. In particular, homes and small mosques were fashioned from stone and coral rag (a mixture of coral and lime to create a sturdy cement). The early fifteenth century saw the construction of what is known today as "typical traditional" Swahili stone houses. The homes of the early 1400's served as ideal models among coastal east Africans in Kilwa and farther up and down the coast.

Commercial development brought great wealth to Kilwa in the thirteenth and fourteenth centuries, but by the late fifteenth century, the commercial base and networks of Kilwa brought the Portuguese navigator Pedro Álvars Cabral (1467 or 1468-1520) to Kilwa, which marked a new era of political pressure for the city. Cabral was amazed by the beautiful houses made of coral. The Portuguese navigator Vasco da Gama (c. 1460-1524) also visited the city and left with stories of beauty and riches. These men carried their reports home. Soon thereafter, the Portuguese took Kilwa by force, gaining complete control of the island by 1505. They intended to take complete control of Indian Ocean trade through this campaign.

Kilwa has been described as the "best built" settlement and "the pearl of Africa." The two most important structures of Dāʾūd's era are Husuni Kubwa and Husuni Ndogo, both of which remained unfinished as a result of the declining economy faced by Dāʾūd in the fourteenth century. Despite the fact that these structures were never completed, the vision that the building of these structures represents stands as a testament to Kilwa's earlier thriving economy and culture.

—*Evan Scott Shuey*

FURTHER READING

Bahn, Paul G. *Lost Cities*. New York: Barnes and Noble Books, 1997. A book about various great cities around the world that have declined or become extinct. Contains a section on Kilwa in its greater splendor.

Chittick, Neville. *Kilwa: An Islamic Trading City on the East African Coast*. Nairobi, Kenya: British Institute in Eastern Africa, 1974. An archaeological perspective on the material culture and history of Kilwa's trade, as well as the Islamic influence along the Swahili coast. Includes maps and floor plans of important buildings.

Freeman-Grenville, G. S. P. *The Medieval History of the Coast of Tanganyika with Special Reference to Recent Archaeological Discoveries*. Oxford, England: Oxford University Press, 1962. Recounts the medieval history of Kilwa and includes genealogical charts with names of ruling families.

Ibn Baṭṭūṭah. *Travels of Ibn Baṭṭūṭa*. Translated and edited by H. A. R. Gibb. 4 vols. Cambridge, England: Cambridge University Press, 1958-2000. This careful, amply annotated translation is by far the most important English-language source of information on the man and his milieu. Gibb's introduction and notes offer useful historical background.

Pouwels, Randall L. "The East African Coast, c. 780-1900 C.E." In *The History of Islam in Africa*, edited by Nehemia Levzion and Randall Pouwels. Athens: Ohio University Press, 2000. Details the Islamic history of coastal east Africa. Covers the history of commerce, architecture, and culture on the Swahili coast and discusses important dates, persons, and events in Swahili history. Includes maps of Kilwa and photos of Kilwa's Great Mosque.

Sutton, John. *A Thousand Years of East Africa*. Nairobi, Kenya: British Institute in Eastern Africa, 1990. Archaeology of east Africa, with a discussion of Kilwa. This book pays particular attention to the history of architecture and religion in Kilwa and its Great Mosque.

See also: c. 500-1000: Rise of Swahili Cultures; 630-711: Islam Expands Throughout North Africa; 12th century: Coins Are Minted on the Swahili Coast; 12th century: Trading Center of Kilwa Kisiwani Is Founded; 1347-1352: Invasion of the Black Death in Europe.

Related article in *Great Lives from History: The Middle Ages, 477-1453*: Ibn Baṭṭūṭah.

1336-1392
Yoshino Civil Wars

The emperor Go-Daigo, working with one of the shogunate's generals, Ashikaga Takauji, tried to seize power from the Minamoto shogunate and the Hōjō regents. However, Ashikaga turned against Go-Daigo, forcing him to flee to Yoshino, and then set up another emperor in the capital, initiating more than fifty years of civil war between the two factions.

Locale: Central Japan
Categories: Government and politics; wars, uprisings, and civil unrest

Key Figures

Go-Daigo (1288-1339), emperor of Japan, r. 1318-1339
Ashikaga Takauji (1305-1358), shogun, 1338-1358
Kusunoki Masashige (1294-1336),
Kusunoki Masatsura (d. 1348), and
Nitta Yoshisada (1301-1338), generals in Go-Daigo's army

Summary of Event

As a result of the Gempei War (1180-1185) between the powerful Minamoto and Taira families, the victorious Minamoto superseded the power of the imperial family and formed what was essentially the first military government in Japanese history. However, the power of the Minamoto shogunate was short-lived. The Hōjō, another powerful warrior family with marriage ties to the Minamoto, managed to gain power over the shogunate and began to exercise power from behind the scenes. The Hōjō were so powerful that they even able to go so far as to appoint shoguns and imperial successors.

This state of affairs continued until the fourteenth century, when, in 1326, the emperor Go-Daigo insisted on his right to appoint his own son as heir to the throne against the wishes of the Hōjō family. Go-Daigo had many allies among the warrior families, who were not satisfied with the conduct of the Hōjō and desired change. The failure to provide adequate rewards to soldiers who defended Japan during the Mongol invasions of 1274 and 1281 had damaged the prestige of the Hōjō and the shogunate in general.

In 1331, the Hōjō, desperate to preserve their power, acted by sending troops to Kyoto in an attempt to force

Go-Daigo's abdication. Go-Daigo, unprepared to mount a defense despite the support of several capable generals such as Kusunoki Masashige, fled the capital and took refuge on Mount Kasagi. He was captured, however, and exiled to the Island of Oki in 1332. The exile was short-lived, as Go-Daigo succeeded in escaping in 1333. By June of that year, he was restored to Kyoto, thanks to the efforts of Ashikaga Takauji, a general sent by the Hōjō to chastise Go-Daigo but who switched sides and began to campaign in support of the emperor. Takauji destroyed the Hōjō in the shogunate capital, Kamakura, but once again switched sides, this time turning against Go-Daigo in an attempt to seize power for himself. The period from 1333 to 1336, when Go-Daigo had reestablished imperial control is known as the Kemmu Restoration.

Takauji sought the title of shogun, which could be conferred only by imperial decree, and he concluded that the best way to arrange this was to chase Go-Daigo into exile and place a puppet emperor on the throne. In early 1336, this plan came to fruition, and Go-Daigo was again forced to flee from the capital. Takauji installed an emperor of his choosing in Kyoto, while Go-Daigo attempted to build a power base to the south of the city. This chain of events marked the beginning of the period of the Northern and Southern Courts (Nanboku-cho; 1336-1392) and a civil war that would drag on for more than fifty years.

In 1336, Takauji used his control over the imperial court at Kyoto to rally support against those loyal to Go-Daigo. He was especially successful in gaining support form several smaller warrior families on the island of Kyushu. When traveling back to Kyoto along the coast of the Inland Sea, Takauji's army was confronted by the loyalist forces at Minatogawa. Go-Daigo's armies were led by the generals Nitta Yoshisada and Kusunoki Masashige. Kusunoki, in particular, knew that this battle was a lost cause, and his death in the fighting came to be held as the pinnacle of loyalty to the throne. In line with Kusunoki's prediction, the battle was a decisive victory for the Ashikaga forces. Kusunoki Masashige was killed in the fighting but Nitta as well as Kusunoki's son Masatsura managed to escape and continued the resistance against the Ashikaga.

Go-Daigo fled to the mountains of Yoshino to the south of Kyoto, where he endeavored to continue his reign despite the military pressure of the Ashikaga. The Ashikaga continued to appoint a series of puppet emperors in Kyoto and during this period of civil war, Japan had a pair of imperial courts.

Takauji continued to increase his power and, in 1338, took the title of shogun that was previously held by the Minamoto. Also in that year, Nitta, the leader of the loyalist forces, was killed. Go-Daigo died the following year while in exile. These setbacks were tremendous but did not immediately defeat the loyalist cause. Go-Daigo was succeeded by the twelve-year-old Go-Murakami, and Kusanoki Masatsura became leader of the loyalist armies and continued to carry out guerrilla-style raids against the Ashikaga forces until he was killed in battle in 1348. This marked the end of serious loyalist resistance, although several warrior families continued to fight for the court, more out of a desire for conquered land than sincere loyalty.

The Yoshino court was able to sustain itself during this period by playing one warrior family off against an-

MAJOR EMPERORS OF THE MUROMACHI PERIOD, 1336-1573

EMPERORS: SOUTHERN COURT

Reign	*Ruler*
1318-1339	Go-Daigo
1339-1368	Go-Murakami
1368-1383	Chōkei
1383-1392	Go-Kameyama

ASHIKAGA PRETENDERS: NORTHERN COURT

Reign	*Ruler*
1336-1348	Komyō
1348-1351	Sukō
1351-1371	Go-Kogon
1371-1382	Go-En'yu

LATER EMPERORS

Reign	*Ruler*
1382-1412	Go-Komatsu
1412-1428	Shōkō
1428-1464	Go-Hanazono
1464-1500	Go-Tsuchimikado
1500-1526	Go-Kashiwabara
1526-1557	Go-Nara
1557-1586	Ogimachi

other, but it never restored the type of military power that it had during the lifetime of Go-Daigo, and its influence never extended beyond its immediate environs. The real center of power in Japan continued to be the Ashikaga stronghold at the capital of Kyoto. This state of affairs continued until the southern court surrendered without violence in 1392.

SIGNIFICANCE

The important immediate impact of the war between the northern and southern courts was the consolidation of power in the hands of the Ashikaga family. The shogunate under Takauji's grandson, Yoshimitsu (ruled 1368-1394), is considered a high point in the development of Japanese culture. Yoshimitsu was known as a patron of art, architecture, religion, and drama. He reopened trade with China, once again allowing continental influences to enter Japanese cultural circles and accelerating economic development.

Despite this short period of prosperity, this period of civil strife undermined the ordered system of government and land distribution that had been built up under the Minamoto shoguns and the Hōjō regents. The Ashikaga were able to maintain their influence over the court and the surrounding area of central Japan for more than one hundred years, but they were never able to fully control the disparate warrior clans that continued to consolidate their power at the local level at the expense of central authority. This failing of the Ashikaga power structure led to the family becoming little more than puppets by the late fifteenth century, and the emperors that they controlled became the pawns of pawns. This chaotic situation ushered in the century-long period of civil war known as the Warring States period (also known as the Sengoku period; 1476-1615).

The war between the northern and southern courts had a great impact on Japanese literature and culture. The struggles of Go-Daigo and Kusunoki Masashige were immortalized in one of the most enduringly popular Japanese historical chronicles, the *Taiheiki* (c. 1330's-1370's; *The Taiheiki*, 1959), which ironically translates as "record of the great peace." Other writings, such as those of Go-Daigo's supporter Kitabatake Chikifusa, sketched out an emperor-centered vision of Japanese history, one that would become an increasingly important part of Japanese thought in the future.

In addition, the battles of this period proved to be a model of the virtues of loyalty and sincerity in later Japanese history. Kusunoki Masashige has been an exceedingly popular historical figure. During the period of ultranationalism before and during World War II, Kusunoki was famous as a symbol of loyalty to the throne, and the tactics that he used in defending it were cited as an influence by the army and navy officers who planned the war against the Western powers.

—*Matthew Penney*

FURTHER READING

Sansom, George. *A History of Japan from 1334-1615*. Vol. 2. Stanford, Calif.: Stanford University Press, 1962. The second volume of Sansom's three-volume study of Japanese history remains a detailed and authoritative work on the subject.

Sato, Hiroaki. *Legends of the Samurai*. New York: Overlook Press, 1995. Contains a great deal of information concerning the samurai tradition, including selections from *The Taiheiki* and other original sources concerning the period of the Yoshino Civil Wars.

The Taiheiki: A Chronicle of Medieval Japan. Translated by Helen Craig McCullough. 1959. Reprint. Tokyo: Charles E. Tuttle, 1979. A translation of the most important contemporary account of the Yoshino Civil Wars.

Turnbull, Stephen. *The Samurai Sourcebook*. New York: Arms and Armour, 1999. This work provides detailed information concerning the weapons and tactics employed during the Yoshino Civil Wars.

SEE ALSO: 792: Rise of the Samurai; 858: Rise of the Fujiwara Family; 1156-1192: Minamoto Yoritomo Becomes Shogun; 1219-1333: Hōjō Family Dominates Shoguns, Rules Japan.

RELATED ARTICLES in *Great Lives from History: The Middle Ages, 477-1453*: Ashkaga Takauji; Fujiwara Michinaga; Minamoto Yoritomo; Taira Kiyomori.

1337-1453
HUNDRED YEARS' WAR

The Hundred Years' War, a series of military conflicts between France and England, resulted in France's ultimate victory at the Battle of Castillon in 1453, a rise in nationalism in a more unified France, and England's emergence—despite its withdrawal from France—as a preeminent naval power.

LOCALE: France
CATEGORIES: Wars, uprisings, and civil unrest; expansion and land acquisition

KEY FIGURES

Edward III (1312-1377), king of England, r. 1327-1377
Richard II (1367-1400), king of England, r. 1377-1399
Henry IV (1366-1413), king of England, r. 1399-1413
Henry V (1387-1422), king of England, r. 1413-1422
Henry VI (1421-1471), king of England, r. 1422-1461 and 1470-1471
Philip VI (1293-1350), king of France, r. 1328-1350
John II (1319-1364), king of France, r. 1350-1364
Charles V (1337-1380), king of France, r. 1364-1380
Charles VI (1368-1422), king of France, r. 1380-1422
Charles VII (1403-1461), king of France, r. 1422-1461
Joan of Arc (c. 1412-1431), French warrior and martyr

SUMMARY OF EVENT

The Hundred Years' War was actually waged for 116 years, from 1337 until 1453, although periods of peace occurred within that time span. The convoluted history of this drawn-out conflict, which extended through the reigns of five English and five French kings, began in 1066, when William, duke of Normandy, invaded and conquered England, thereby becoming king of England. Following the Norman Conquest, French became the language of the English court. Strong French influences were evident in the lives of the English. King Edward III was thought to speak no English, only French.

Under the feudal system prevalent in Europe after the fall of the Roman Empire in 476, the nobility granted land to people below them in rank to reward their military service in defense of the noble making the grant. This system, persisting into the fourteenth century, created a society where there was no strong central government. The populace felt greater loyalty to provinces or to sections within provinces than to the country as a whole.

In 1308, King Edward II married Isabella of France, daughter of King Philip and sister of Louis X, Philip, and Charles IV, each of whom died after brief reigns as kings of France. Isabella plotted the overthrow of her husband, anticipating that she could rule England through her young son, Edward III, who was next in the English line of succession.

At age twelve, Edward III went to France to represent his father in the court of his uncle, Charles IV, accompanied by Isabella and her lover, Roger Mortimer. A shocked Charles IV banished Isabella from court because of her adultery. Once Edward III had fulfilled his official obligations in the court of Charles IV, he, Isabella, and Mortimer went to Hainault in what is now Belgium. There Edward met and fell in love with Philippa of Hainaut, who was the same age as he. They married two years later and produced five children in the first ten years of their marriage.

The following year, 1327, after Isabella and Mortimer toppled Edward II from the throne, Edward III, in whose veins coursed royal blood from both England and France, became king of England. Edward II was subsequently murdered, and in 1330, Edward III, resisting his mother's attempts to dominate him and through him to rule England, had Mortimer hanged and his mother confined to remote castles where her influence could not compromise his reign.

Meanwhile, Charles IV died in 1328, leaving no male heir to succeed him. He was the last of the line of Hugh Capet, who ruled three hundred years earlier. It was argued that Edward III, grandson of King Philip of France, had the rightful claim to France's throne. The French, however, refused to acknowledge fifteen-year-old Edward as king, selecting instead the thirty-five-year-old Philip Valois, nephew of King Philip.

Two major factors precipitated the Hundred Years' War. In 1332, attempting to impose English rule on the Scots with whom the French were in league, Edward III led attacks on Scotland and eventually prevailed. The French supported the Scots because they were dependent on Scottish wool for a flourishing Flemish textile industry. At this time, with a population of thirteen million, three times that of England, France was clearly the strongest nation in Europe. England was viewed as a backward, impoverished place. France had a strong but limited central monarchy that did not include all of France, much of which was still ruled by feudal lords. Brittany, Burgundy, Flanders, and Guienne were beyond the control of French kings.

The English at Calais in 1347. (F. R. Niglutsch)

In 1337, Edward III, to whom Philip VI had promised to return part of Guienne to England, wrote a defiant letter to King Philip, who had not honored his pledge. This letter began the open conflict that stretched out for more than a century. In September, 1340, Edward, who had invested practically everything he and his country owned preparing for war, led an army from Flanders into France, practicing the scorched-earth policy that had worked well for Edward in Scotland a few years earlier. His troops marched to the south, laying waste to fields, ravaging dwellings, and slaughtering peasants and livestock.

The French confronted the English near Saint-Quentin, where King Philip said that he would fight the English only if they chose a place not fortified with trees and bogs. This, however, appeared to be a deception because when the two forces were about to meet in the designated location, Philip withdrew his forces, apparently unwilling to risk a humiliating defeat at the hands of the English.

After Edward III declared himself king of France, he engaged in minor land battles against the French, but his most important victory occurred in 1340 when the English overcame the French fleet in the Battle of Sluis (or Sluys). Two years later, Edward led a successful assault on Brittany, and in 1346, his forces defeated the French in the Battle of Crécy. The following year, English forces captured Calais. Following that victory, there was a considerable hiatus in the war because the Black Death (the bubonic plague) swept through Europe, killing hundreds of thousands of people and leaving the survivors too weak and dispirited to fight. In 1850, King Philip, having already lost a daughter to the plague, died himself and was succeeded by John II.

In 1356, the English defeated the French in the Battle of Poitiers, where they captured King John II, who was transported to England and held prisoner there until 1360 when the Treaty of Brétigny was negotiated, giving England Calais and nearly the whole of Aquitaine. The English also received a hefty ransom for the release of King John, who died in 1364. Charles V succeeded him.

A strained peace prevailed until 1369, when Charles V, besieged by noblemen complaining about the excessive taxation they were suffering under the English, crossed swords with Edward III over this excessive taxation and, once more, over the forfeiture of Guienne. Charles V resumed the war that had been more or less suspended for nearly a decade. By 1374, England had lost all its land in France except Calais and Guienne.

Another period of relative peace prevailed for the next quarter century, interrupted only by occasional assaults from France. In 1377, the year in which Edward III died and was succeeded by Richard II, French and Castilian ships attacked the southern coast of England, but the invasion England feared did not occur. This assault, however, emphasized to the English that they must strengthen their defenses. The English Parliament imposed head taxes on all its citizenry to pay for increased defensive measures. Everyone, regardless of financial status, paid the same tax. The poor, therefore, paid a much greater tax than the rich proportionately. This inequality led to the Peasants' Revolt of 1381.

In 1380, Charles V died and was succeeded as king of France by Charles VI, a boy of twelve quite unable to assume the responsibilities of kingship. Charles VI went insane in 1392, but in 1394, quite significantly, King Richard II of England married Isabella, daughter of Charles VI. Richard II was deposed in 1399 and replaced by King Henry IV.

All was not well in France as the king's mental and emotional deterioration progressed, but Charles VI continued to reign for thirty years after the first signs of his insanity appeared. With France in disarray, the Armagnacs of Orléans and the Burgundians vied for power. In 1407, followers of John the Fearless, a Burgundian, murdered the duke of Orléans in Paris. Four years later, King Henry IV deployed troops to France to help John the Fearless fight the Armagnacs.

With the death of King Henry IV in 1413, Henry V became king of England. In 1415, he invaded France and conquered the French at the Battle of Agincourt. The year after the murder of John the Fearless by the Armagnacs in 1419, the English occupied Paris and signed the Treaty of Troyes. Within two years, both Henry V and Charles VI were dead. Henry was succeeded by Henry VI, who was also recognized north of the Loire River as King Henry II of France.

In 1423, the English defeated the dauphins, heirs to the French throne, at Cravant and, in the following year, at Verneuil. After the English attacked and isolated Orléans in 1428, Joan of Arc emerged as both a military

The capture of King John at Poitiers in 1356. (F. R. Niglutsch)

Major Sites in the Hundred Years' War, 1337-1453

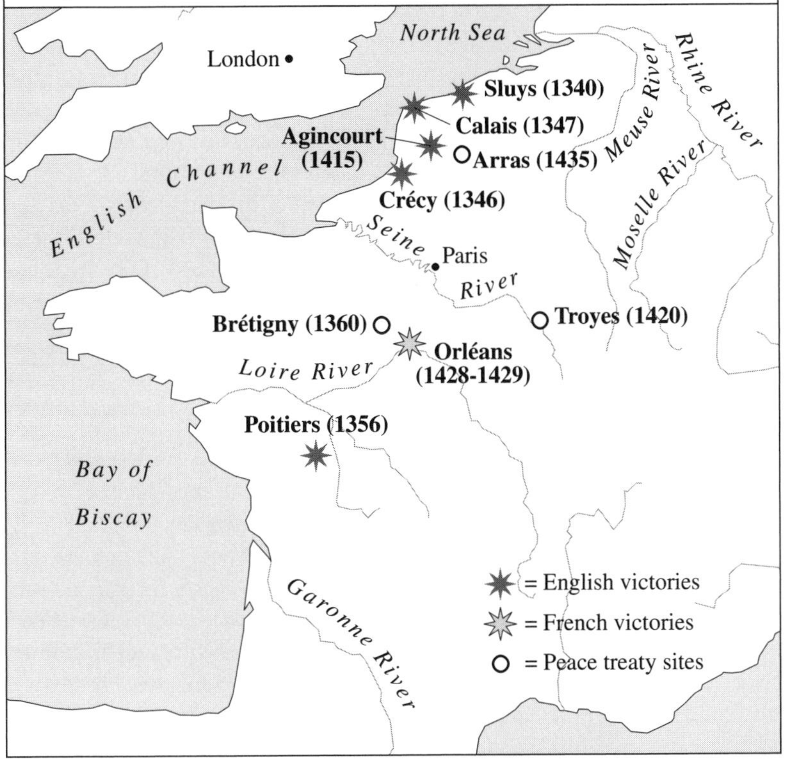

and spiritual leader as she forced the withdrawal of the English from Orléans in 1429. Charles VII became king in 1422, but was crowned in 1429. The following year, the Burgundians captured Joan and sold her to the English. She was charged as a witch and heretic and then tried. In 1431, the nineteen-year-old heroine was burned at the stake, an act that mobilized the French against the English.

In 1436, the year after Charles VII and Duke Philip of Burgundy signed the Treaty of Arras, the French regained Paris from the English. Eight years later, the Truce of Tours was enacted between France and England. King Henry VI of England married the French Margaret of Anjou in 1445. England surrendered Le Maine to France in 1448, and the next year Charles VII attacked the English at Normandy, which in 1450 became French after the English were defeated in the Battle of Formigny.

Guienne fell to the French in 1451 but was retaken by the English in an invasion led by Sir John Talbot in 1452. Talbot was overcome the following year, however, and was killed in the Battle of Castillon, whereupon the English left Guienne and the Hundred Years' War ended.

Significance

The Hundred Years' War marked the beginning of the end for the English in France. It also marked the end of the feudalism that had prevailed in Europe for nearly a millennium. It also resulted in a stronger central government in France, where an air of nationalism replaced much of the regionalism that had preceded it. England lost all of its French land holdings save for Calais, which it retained until 1558, and some of the Channel Islands, which it still holds. This conflict eliminated England as a continental power but led to its emergence as a major naval power.

William Shakespeare's major plays, such as *Henry VI, Part I* (1589-1590, pr. 1592) and *Henry V* (pr. c. 1598-1599), reflect the significant effects of the war on subsequent literature and the arts. The plays were based on historical occurrences from the war, showing Shakespeare's familiarity with the conflicts of this period. Although he took liberties in dealing with the period's history, his facts are reasonably accurate historically.

—R. Baird Shuman

Further Reading

Baker, Denise N. *Inscribing the Hundred Years' War in French and English Cultures*. Albany: State University of New York Press, 2000. This volume's eleven essays focus largely on literary accounts and the literary climate in France and England during this extended war.

Curry, Anne. *The Hundred Years' War*. 2d ed. New York: Palgrave Macmillan, 2003. A brief, reliable account of the causes and results of this conflict. Illustrations, maps, and genealogical tables.

Holmes, George. *Europe, Hierarchy and Revolt, 1320-1450*. 2d ed. Malden, Mass.: Blackwell, 2000. A fine overview of the Hundred Years' War. Captures the climate of the time and France's shift from regionalism to nationalism. Solid bibliography.

Lace, William W. *The Hundred Years' War*. San Diego, Calif.: Lucent Books, 1994. This contribution to Lucent's World History series is directed at teen readers.

The presentation is direct and accurate and is well illustrated with useful genealogical tables and maps.
Neillands, Robin. *The Hundred Years' War.* Rev. ed. New York: Routledge, 2001. A detailed account of the factors precipitating the war, of the major battles of the war, and of their outcomes. Well illustrated with genealogical tables.
Seward, Desmond. *A Brief History of the Hundred Years' War: The English in France, 1337-1453.* London: Robinson, 2003. Historical overview of the war, with illustrations, including maps.

SEE ALSO: August 26, 1346: Battle of Crécy; 1347-1352: Invasion of the Black Death in Europe; May-June, 1381: Peasants' Revolt in England; May 4-8, 1429: Joan of Arc's Relief of Orléans; 1453: English Are Driven from France.

RELATED ARTICLES in *Great Lives from History: The Middle Ages, 477-1453*: Charles d'Orléans; Charles IV; Alain Chartier; Edward III; Jean Froissart; Guy de Chauliac; Henry IV (of England); Henry V; Isabella of France; Joan of Arc; Philippa of Hainaut; Richard II.

1340
AL-ᶜUMARĪ WRITES A HISTORY OF AFRICA

Syrian Islamic chronicler al-ᶜUmarī produced a meticulous and detailed written account of medieval Africa, which serves as important primary material on Sudanic Africa in the fourteenth century.

LOCALE: Sudanic Africa and Cairo, Egypt
CATEGORIES: Cultural and intellectual history; historiography

KEY FIGURE
Al-ᶜUmarī (1301-1349), chronicler

SUMMARY OF EVENT

The writings of Ibn Faḍl Allāh al-ᶜUmarī (best known as al-ᶜUmarī) chronicled events of fourteenth century Africa. Al-ᶜUmarī's position as the sultan of Cairo's official scribe in charge of correspondence—a high post in the Mamlūk Dynasty court—gave him access to the royal archives and allowed his own work to be added to the collections in Cairo.

Al-ᶜUmarī composed a variety of works, the most important African history being *Masālik al-abṣār fī Mamālik al-amṣār* (c. 1340; partial translation, 2000), which contains at least four descriptive chapters on the various territories in Africa. In this wide-ranging, thirty-two volume work, al-ᶜUmarī gives accounts of Ethiopia, Kanem, Nubia, Mali, Aïr, Awdaghust, and Tadmekka. Al-ᶜUmarī consulted many of the inhabitants of Cairo about their encounters and meetings with the kings of the Sudan who typically passed through Cairo on their pilgrimage to Mecca. The oral and written accounts of Cairo were obtained primarily from travelers, merchants, scholars, and political ambassadors whom al-ᶜUmarī met in Cairo. On some occasions, al-ᶜUmarī references the works of previous Arab scholars who wrote on African geography, but this is rare in comparison to the primary accounts he collected.

From his fourteenth century writings, which extract information from the earlier writings of Shaykh ᶜUthmān al-Kanemi and ᶜAbd Allāh al-Salalhi, one can learn a great deal about the Sefuwa Dynasty. According to *Masālik al-abṣār fī Mamālik al-amṣār*, the Sefuwa Dynasty under Dunama bin Hummay took control of the Lake Chad city of Kanem. Al-ᶜUmarī gave an account of the rise to power of Sayf bin Dhī Yazan. According to al-ᶜUmarī's version, the Yazan were the ancestors of the Sefuwa dynastic authority who expelled the Zaghawa from power. Al-ᶜUmarī indicates that Kanem was already familiar with Islamic beliefs before Sefuwa ascendance to power. Thus, according to al-ᶜUmarī, the Sefuwa accession to power was more of a political shift than a religious change. Although the Sefuwa Dynasty under Hummay brought a more thorough conversion of the Kanem population to Islamic practice, al-ᶜUmarī writes that the Kanem king was not seen but spoke from behind a veiled covering, most likely a means of maintaining legitimacy through the Zaghawa and appeasing local Kanem beliefs in sacral Sudanic kingship. Al-ᶜUmarī reported that in terms of trade in Kanem, cowrie shells, *dende* cloth, glass beads, copper, and some coins were viable currencies.

Some of the most important writings of al-ᶜUmarī detail the history of Mali and the capital at Niani (Nyeni). The location of the old Mali Empire's capital is made clear in al-ᶜUmarī's chronicle. He places Niani in the borderlands between Mali and Guinea on the Sankani River. Furthermore, al-ᶜUmarī provides details on the role of the capital as a royal residence for the *mansas* (kings) and a seat of centralized power. Al-ʿUmarī describes Niani as a capital characterized by its conical clay residences and buildings. Al-ʿUmarī depicts even the details of how these structures were raised from foundation to ceiling. The royal residence was distinguished by the surrounding fortified walls.

Al-ʿUmarī focuses his Mali report on the reign of Mansa Sulaymān, who ruled from 1337 to 1358. Sulaymān was in fact the brother of Mansa Mūsā. According to al-ʿUmarī, Mali had fourteen provinces, which included Takrur, Ghana, Banbughu, Bambuk, and Kaukau, as well as the Mauritanean Adrar, the region inhabited by the Lamtuna Berbers. The chronicle reveals that the Mali capital was at Niani on the river that basically encircled the royal center. The palace was a site for entertaining and contained a special stage (*bembe*) for such activities. The royal regalia included an umbrella for protection of the *mansa*, a yellow flag with a red background, and drums for ceremony.

The al-ʿUmarī accounts give details about the soldiers in Mali and what types of equipment they typically used, and the author comments on the gold worn by the dignitaries. According to al-ʿUmarī, the *mansa* of Mali tolerated non-Muslims in the empire and employed them in gold mining because metalwork was viewed as requiring secret and magical rituals in which only non-Muslims could engage. Thus practitioners of African religions played a crucial role in the economy of the Malian state, which had adopted Islam as an official religion. Such accounts reveal some of the social relationships that existed among groups in medieval African societies.

Exploration and travel also figure prominently in al-ʿUmarī's accounts. There is discussion of an unsuccessful fourteenth century Malian expedition in the western Atlantic, travels along the Spanish coast, and an Egypt-Mali trade route.

Masālik al-abṣār fī Mamālik al-amṣār carefully describes seven Muslim kings from Ethiopia. In addition, al-ʿUmarī details histories of the Christian kings of Ethiopia. Beyond the scope of political history, al-ʿUmarī describes the agricultural system practiced in regions of land cultivation and the social customs of the Ethiopian populations, and he gives regional depictions. Al-ʿUmarī depicts the urban center Aksum, which he transliterates in Arabic as Akshum, and he references the provinces of Amhara and Tigre.

Al-ʿUmarī's chronicle of Ethiopia comes out of his interviews with Jamāl al-Dīn ʿAbd Allāh from Zayla, a sheikh, who received a group of Muslim representatives from Ethiopia. The Muslims petitioned the Coptic patriarch in Cairo to intervene on their behalf with the emperor of Ethiopia, Hatsi, whose name al-ʿUmarī transliterates as al-Hati. The reception of the delegation took place some time in the mid-1330's, most likely between 1332 and 1338. This is known because a Christian delegation also arrived during this period and submitted a written report to the Coptic patriarch regarding the Muslims. There were other interviewees who relayed information on Ethiopia, including merchants who had traveled there.

Other regions and topics on Africa covered by al-ʿUmarī include the Zanj (black Africans) and information about a treaty written by al-Jāḥiẓ, an eighth-ninth century theologian and writer.

SIGNIFICANCE

Al-ʿUmarī's research and writings on Africa provide a window onto the past. Al-ʿUmarī details aspects of life in different parts of Africa and, in particular, provides economic and political data that is invaluable. In addition, the chronicler provides a sense of the common people's daily life and habits. As an external source, al-ʿUmarī's work is a tremendous contribution to the field of medieval African history, particularly regarding Ethiopia in the Horn of Africa and Mali and Kanem in the Sudan.

The written sources that come from Muslim chroniclers are extremely important resources on African history, particularly for the period between the eighth and fifteenth centuries. These sources are especially valuable and useful where there are no African writing systems or translatable scripts. In regions where written sources do exist, Arabic sources serve as helpful corroborating sources for attempts to reconstruct African histories. Some of the Arabic-script chronicles were recorded by Arabs from outside the region, while others came from Muslims living in Africa. The Arabic works include a wide variety of topics ranging from geography, political commentary, religious observations, and travelers reports to news. Al-ʿUmarī's accounts in particular were highly detailed and have been of great use to modern-day historians and archaeologists.

—*Catherine Cymone Fourshey*

FURTHER READING

Abun-Nasr, Jamil M. *A History of the Maghrib in the Islamic Period.* New York: Cambridge University Press, 1990. Histories of the Maghreb under Berber, Arab, and Ottoman rulers. Includes brief references to Kanem and the Sefuwa Dynasty. Maps, bibliography, index.

Elfasi, M., and I. Hrbek, eds. "The Chad Region as a Crossroads." In *Africa from the Seventh to the Twelfth Century*. Vol. 4. Berkeley: University of California Press, 1988. Discusses selections of al-ʿUmarī's written accounts.

Hopkins, J. F. P., trans. *Corpus of Early Arabic Sources for West African History*. Edited and annotated by N. Levtzion and J. F. P. Hopkins. Princeton, N.J.: Markus Wiener, 2000. Provides a partial translation of al-ʿUmarī's history of Africa, along with translations of other chronicles about West African history. Maps, bibliography, index.

Hrbek, I., ed. *Africa from the Seventh to the Eleventh Century*. Berkeley: University of California Press, 1992. Contains a discussion of the Chad region as a crossroads. Illustrations, maps, bibliography.

Hunwick, J. O., and R. S. O'Fahey, eds. *Arabic Literature of Africa*. New York: E. J. Brill, 1994-2003. A multivolume collection of sources on writings of eastern, western, and central Sudanic Africa. Bibliography, index.

Ki-Zerbo, Joseph, and Djibril Tamsir Niane, eds. *Africa from the Twelfth to the Sixteenth Century*. Berkeley: University of California Press, 1997. Includes a chapter on the kingdoms and peoples of Chad. Illustrations, maps, bibliography.

Lewicki, Tadeusz. *Arabic External Sources for the History of Africa to the South of the Sahara*. London: Curzon Press, 1974. A description and excerpts from primary sources derived from North Africa and the Middle East regions between the eighth and the fifteenth centuries. Includes maps based on Arab sources and a bibliography.

SEE ALSO: 872-973: Publication of the *History of al-Ṭabarī*; 1010: Firdusi Composes the *Shahnamah*; c. 1075-1086 : Hummay Founds the Sefuwa Dynasty; 1230's-1255: Reign of Sundiata of Mali; 1324-1325: Mansa Mūsā's Pilgrimage to Mecca Sparks Interest in Mali Empire; 1325-1355: Travels of Ibn Baṭṭūṭah; 1373-1410: Jean Froissart Compiles His *Chronicles*; 1377: Ibn Khaldūn Completes His *Muqaddimah*.

RELATED ARTICLES in *Great Lives from History: The Middle Ages, 477-1453*: Ibn Baṭṭūṭah; Firdusi; Jean Froissart; Ibn Khaldūn; Mansa Mūsā; Sundiata; al-Ṭabarī.

August 26, 1346
BATTLE OF CRÉCY

The Battle of Crécy in France established England as an important military power because of its battlefield use of the resoundingly successful longbow, demonstrating that the mounted knights and the age of chivalry were doomed.

LOCALE: Crécy, France
CATEGORY: Wars, uprisings, and civil unrest

KEY FIGURES

Edward III (1312-1377), king of England, r. 1327-1377
Philip VI (1293-1350), king of France, r. 1328-1350

SUMMARY OF EVENT

The Anglo-Norman kings of England were so impressed with the powerful longbow they encountered in their military expeditions against Wales that they adopted it and ordered the inhabitants of every English village to practice its use on a regular basis. Thus the "Welsh" longbow had become the "English" longbow by 1346, the year of the Battle of Crécy.

Longbows varied in length from slightly more than 5.5 feet (1.5 meters) to slightly less than 6.5 feet (2 meters). The advantage of the longbow over its shorter cousins came from the increased leverage that resulted from drawing back its longer "arms." Knowledge of the principle involved was certainly no secret, but the longbow had significant disadvantages that limited its popularity. Its unwieldy length meant that the archer could carry few if any other weapons. He certainly could not put it over his back and use a sword in offensive operations. This limitation meant that it was unsuitable for any situations other than defensive battle. Perhaps more important, it was difficult to master without extensive practice, hence the royal order for regular training and practice.

Yew was the favored wood for longbow construction. Like the American aromatic cedar, the yew has an inner, red core of heartwood and an outer, white layer of sapwood. The former is strong under compression, while the latter has greater strength under tension. The bowyer took advantage of these natural properties of the yew by splitting the bow staff from the log and shaping it in such

The French charge the English at Crécy. (F. R. Niglutsch)

a way that the red layer formed the "belly," which faced the archer in use, and the white layer was on the "back" of the bow.

Arrows had to be straight to preserve their stability in flight and their accuracy. They were about 30 inches (75 centimeters) long with feathers, or "fletching," on one end to give stability in flight and a metal tip on the other. The favored tip shape was the "bodkin," which was a very elongated pyramid, square at the base and tapering to a point. On the fletched end was a notch, or "nock," made to receive the bowstring. To prevent repeated "nocking" from fraying the hemp bowstring, its central area had a thread wrapping. An archer might carry up to two dozen arrows, and an intelligent military commander would be careful to have plenty more in his baggage train.

Longbows had a "pull" of about 80 to 100 pounds (36 to 45 kilograms). They had an extreme range of more than 100 yards (90 meters) and an effective range of about 60 yards (55 meters). In other words, a good archer could expect to kill or disable an armored opponent out to 60 yards (55 meters) and could drop an arrow from a high trajectory on a general area as far as 150 yards (135 meters) away. It is difficult to be more precise because much depended on the skill of the individual archer and weather conditions such as wind. A skilled man could shoot up to twelve arrows per minute, and this speed was the greatest advantage the longbow had over its major rival—the crossbow—at the Battle of Crécy.

The crossbow was even more powerful than the longbow. Its power came from the sophisticated combination of materials in its much shorter bow. The bow was hardly more than 24 inches (60 centimeters) in length and was, essentially, a sandwich of horn on the belly, wood in the middle, and animal sinew on the back. Just as with the longbow, this combination provided materials strong under compression on the belly and strong under tension on the back but to a much greater degree. Most important, a crossbowman required little training. All of the crossbow's advantages over the longbow could not, however, compensate for one essential weakness: It was much slower to operate, and volume of fire is the most important battlefield feature of any missile weapon.

Many historians have claimed that the longbow caused a military revolution, beginning at the Battle of

Crécy, by rendering the mounted knight obsolete. This is an exaggeration. The feudal system was already in decline because of political, economic, and social developments before the Battle of Crécy. Even on the battlefield, the success of the longbow was a symptom more than a result. Although an individual on foot is almost helpless against an individual on horseback, formed infantrymen are practically impervious to attack by cavalry as long as they maintain their formation. Newly forming centralized governments were acquiring the administrative and financial skills to field and maintain capable infantry.

The Battle of Crécy was the first important battle in the Hundred Years' War between England and France that began in 1337. King Edward III of England was actually closer by strict inheritance to the throne of France than King Philip VI, and Edward was eager to assert his rights through force of arms. A more substantial and more deep-seated cause of the war was the attempt by King Philip to consolidate French territorial holdings and influence at the expense of England, which still had considerable land holdings and economic interests on the Continent. Hostile feelings and words led to open war by the late 1330's. The war proceeded in fits and starts with the French seeming to have the advantage until 1346, when Edward III mounted an invasion of Normandy. Philip came to defend his territory, and the two forces met at Crécy on August 26, 1346.

The English had about seven thousand longbowmen, some two thousand men at arms (knights), and two or three thousand auxiliaries. Philip had at least twenty thousand men at arms—the flower of French chivalry, as is often said—and many other troops. Edward deployed his men on rising ground and awaited the French attack. He could hardly do otherwise, being so badly outnumbered and so dependent on the longbowmen who were useful only in defense. Fortunately for Edward, the French obliged by attacking and in a very inept way. As the men at arms rode onto the field in piecemeal fashion, the sun was going down. Philip decided to wait until the next day to launch his attack after his men had rested and after they had all arrived, but he could not control the unwieldy mass, which continued to press forward despite his orders. He finally decided to make the best of a bad situation and ordered the attack.

Philip's Genoese crossbowmen led the assault. A brief rain shower fell on them, and this has led many historians to speculate that their wet bowstrings caused their poor performance. Whether or not this contributed, they could not withstand the more deadly shower of arrows that fell on them after the rain shower. The duke of Alençon, stationed behind the crossbowmen, decided they were acting in a cowardly fashion when they hesitated and led the mounted men at arms in a charge over them. Neither side realized exactly what a toll the longbowmen were taking because of the dark, and the French continued to press on while the longbowmen continued to shoot into the confused mass at the foot of the rise. The horsemen charged fifteen times, and the battle lasted until the "third quarter of the night." The next morning, the English discovered they had killed more than fifteen hundred French nobles and at least ten thousand others with a loss of less than one hundred on their side.

FROISSART ON THE BATTLE OF CRÉCY

. . . a heavy storm of rain came on and there were loud claps of thunder, with lightning. Before the rain, huge flocks of crows had flown over both armies, making a deafening sound in the air. Some experienced knights said that this portended a great and murderous battle. . . . The Genoese, having been marshalled into proper order and made to advance, began to utter loud whoops to frighten the English. The English waited in silence and did not stir. The Genoese hulloa'd a second time and advanced a little farther, but the English still made no move. Then they raised a third shout, very loud and clear, levelled their crossbows and began to shoot.

At this the English archers took one pace forward and poured out their arrows on the Genoese so thickly and evenly that they fell like snow. When they felt those arrows piercing their arms, their heads, their faces, the Genoese, who had never met such archers before, were thrown into confusion. . . . [T]he King of France, seeing how miserably they had performed, called out in great anger: "Quick now, kill all that rabble. They are only getting in our way!" Thereupon the mounted men began to strike out at them on all sides and many staggered and fell, never to rise again. The English continued to shoot into the thickest part of the crowd, wasting none of the arrows. They impaled or wounded horses and riders, who fell to the ground in great distress, unable to get up again without the help of several men.

So began the battle between La Broye and Crécy in Ponthieu at four o'clock on that Saturday afternoon.

Source: Jean Froissart, *Chronicles*, translated by Geoffrey Brereton (Harmondsworth, Middlesex, England: Penguin Books, 1968), quoted in *Readings in Medieval History*, edited by Patrick J. Geary (Lewiston, N.Y.: Broadview Press, 1989), p. 739.

SIGNIFICANCE

Although the Battle of Crécy raised England's international reputation and led to considerable gains by Edward III, the war dragged on. In 1356, at the Battle of Poitiers, and again in 1415 at the Battle of Agincourt, the English were to win important victories with the aid of the longbow. By the end of the war, the proud mounted knights were no longer the dominant force on European battlefields. The age of chivalry was over, and the longbow had been a significant contributor to its demise.

—*Philip Dwight Jones*

FURTHER READING

Bradbury, Jim. *The Medieval Archer.* Rochester, N.Y.: Boydell and Brewer, 1999. Discusses the role of the archer and archery during the Middle Ages.

Burne, Alfred H. *The Crécy War: A Military History of the Hundred Years' War from 1337 to the Peace of Brétigny, 1360.* New York: Oxford University Press, 1955. A classic account of the battle and its aftermath in the first part of the Hundred Years' War.

Fuller, J. F. C. *The Decisive Battles of the Western World and Their Influence upon History.* London: Eyre and Spottiswoode, 1954-1956. Contains a detailed account of the Battle of Crécy by one of the foremost military historians of the twentieth century.

Hardy, Robert. *The Longbow: A Social and Military History.* London: Bois d'Arc Press, 1998. Analyzes the use of the longbow in the history of warfare and battle.

McKisack, May. *The Fourteenth Century, 1307-1399.* Oxford, England: Clarendon Press, 1959. Part of the Oxford History of England series, this large volume contextualizes the Hundred Years' War from an English perspective. Includes maps, genealogical tables, and bibliography.

Myers, A. R. *England in the Late Middle Ages.* 8th rev. ed. Harmondsworth, Middlesex, England: Penguin Books, 1978. Concisely places the war into a broader context. Includes maps, a bibliography, and an index.

Seward, Desmond. *A Brief History of the Hundred Years' War: The English in France, 1337-1453.* Rev. ed. London: Robinson, 2003. One of the most readable accounts of the war. Includes maps and other illustrations.

Sumption, Jonathan. *The Hundred Years War.* 2 vols. Philadelphia: University of Pennsylvania Press, 1999. Volume 1, "Trial by Battle," and Volume 2, "Trial by Fire," cover the military history of the battles, including the Battle of Crécy, which make up the war period.

Verbruggen, J. F. *The Art of Warfare in Western Europe During the Middle Ages.* Woodbridge, England: Boydell Press, 1997. Covers western European warfare during the Middle Ages.

SEE ALSO: c. 700: Bow and Arrow Spread into North America; 1337-1453: Hundred Years' War; May 4-8, 1429: Joan of Arc's Relief of Orléans; 1453: English Are Driven from France.

RELATED ARTICLES in *Great Lives from History: The Middle Ages, 477-1453*: Edward III; Jean Froissart.

1347
ʿALĀʾ-UD-DĪN BAHMAN SHĀH FOUNDS THE BAHMANĪ SULTANATE

ʿAlāʾ-ud-Dīn Bahman Shāh rebelled against the sultan of Delhi and founded the independent Bahmanī sultanate of the Deccan.

LOCALE: Deccan (Central India)

CATEGORIES: Expansion and land acquisition; government and politics; wars, uprisings, and civil unrest

KEY FIGURE

ʿAlāʾ-ud-Dīn Bahman Shāh (d. 1358), Bahmanī sultan, r. 1347-1358

SUMMARY OF EVENT

The earliest Muslim state in India, the Delhi sultanate of the thirteenth century, extended from Punjab to Bengal. During the first half of the fourteenth century, the Khaljī (1290-1320) and Tughluqid (1320-1413) Dynasties expanded the sultanate into central and south India. Sultan Muḥammad ibn Tughluq (r. 1325-1351) ruled more of India than any previous sultan, but his conquests over-extended the sultanate. During the 1340's, Bengal, Gujarat, and the Deccan rebelled. In the Deccan, the revolt was largely the work of ʿAlāʾ-ud-Dīn Bahman Shāh (also known as Ẓafār Khan).

Bahman Shāh's origins are obscure and under dispute. The historian Ferishta (c. 1560-c. 1620) located him in Delhi as the servant of a Brahmin, who foretold his future greatness. A crown was also prophesied for him by the celebrated Sufi mystic, Shaykh Niẓām-ud-Dīn Awliyā (1236-1325). Another tradition linked him to Bahman, son of Iskandar, a pre-Islamic Persian hero in the *Shahnamah* (c. 1010; the book of kings) composed by the poet Firdusi. More convincing is the assumption that he was the nephew of Hizabr-ud-Dīn Yusuf Ẓafār Khan, a maternal nephew of Sultan ʿAlāʾ-ud-Dīn Muḥammad Khaljī (1296-1316) and an acclaimed military commander slain fighting the Mongols outside the walls of Delhi, c. 1300.

Nothing is known of Bahman Shāh's early life. By the 1330's, when he was in his forties, he was serving in the Deccan as a military commander (*amīr-i sada*, "emir of a hundred") under its viceroy, Qiwan-ud-Dīn Qutlugh Khan, a trusted lieutenant of Sultan Muḥammad ibn Tughluq and an experienced soldier-administrator from whom he would have learned much. Qutlugh Khan ruled the Deccan for a decade from its capital of Devagiri (Deogir, later Daulatabad, India), but in 1344-1345, the sultan recalled him, contributing to the loss of the province three years later.

Muḥammad ibn Tughluq sent new men from Delhi to the Deccan to enforce order and enhance revenue collection. The historian Ẓiyāʾ-ud-Dī Baranī describes them as men eager to shed blood, and the province awaited their arrival with apprehension. One of these newcomers, on reaching Dhar north of the Narbada River, summarily executed eighty military officers. When this news reached the Deccan, the military commanders (*amīran-i sada*) rose in revolt and killed the sultan's commissioners sent to chastise them. The rebels then converged on Daulatabad, where the garrison went over to them. From that time (September, 1346), the Deccan was virtually independent of Delhi.

Hurriedly, the rebels chose a leader, the elderly Ismāʿīl Mukh Afghan, whose appeal lay in the fact that his brother commanded the sultan's army in Malwa and might defect to support his brother. Ismāʿīl Mukh was acclaimed the first sultan of the Deccan under the title of Nāṣir-ud-Dīn Ismāʿīl Shāh. Among his fellow conspirators who received honors was Bahman Shāh, who was granted the title of Ẓafār Khan, a title made famous by his heroic uncle.

Muḥammad ibn Tughluq reacted to the news of the rebellion by setting out for Daulatabad with an avenging army, but after learning of a fresh revolt in Gujarat, he diverted his forces to that valuable province. Meanwhile, his local representative in the Deccan, ʿImād-ul-Mulk, set off to restore Tughluqid authority in the province, eventually capturing Bidar. Ẓafār Khan set off for Bidar to confront him, but with only twenty thousand horses, he hesitated to force an engagement. Reinforced by a further five thousand horses sent by Nāṣir-ud-Dīn Ismāʿīl Shāh and fifteen thousand infantry provided by the raja of Tilangana, he defeated and killed ʿImād-ul-Mulk, whose fugitive forces either streamed into Bidar fort or made their way into Malwa.

Leaving his companion-in-arms, Malik Saif-ud-Dīn Ghūri, to besiege Bidar, Ẓafār Khan made a triumphant progress back to Daulatabad, where Nāṣir-ud-Dīn Ismāʿīl Shāh, seeing Ẓafār Khan's popularity with the army, prudently declared that he himself was unfit to retain the sultanate and recommended that the army choose Ẓafār Khan in his stead.

In 1347, Ẓafār Khan was crowned sultan by the Sufi saint, Shaykh Siraj-ud-Dīn Junaydi, assuming the titulature of ʿAlāʾ-ud-Dīn Ḥasan Bahman Shāh. He then distributed the honors, titles, and largess expected from a new ruler. Four hundred pounds weight of gold and a thousand pounds weight of silver were distributed to charities in the name of Shaykh Niẓām-ud-Dīn Awliyā, who had foretold that Bahman Shāh would one day gain a throne. His eldest son, Muḥammad (the future sultan Muḥammad I, 1358-1375), was designated heir-apparent with the title of Ẓafār Khan, and married the daughter of Saif-ud-Dīn Ghūri, who, returning triumphantly from Bidar, was appointed *vakil-i mutlaq* (chief minister).

Bahman Shāh's position at his accession was not an easy one. Despite the diverse terrain of the Deccan, the central core consisted of stony wolds, broken by deep escarpments and crowned by rocky crags on which were perched innumerable forts. It was a land easy for a possessor to retain but difficult for an outsider to conquer. Some officers willingly supported him, others grudgingly, nursing their own ambitions, while others were loyal to the Tughluqs. Among the Hindu rajas and chieftains, some held back, hedging their bets. Also, the new regime had dangerous neighbors: To the north, Malwa was loyal to Delhi; to the east, the Hindu kingdom of Tilangana, with its capital at Warangal, was formidable; most dangerous was the newly founded Hindu kingdom of Vijayanagar, south of the Tungabhadra.

At his accession, Bahman Shāh was said to have dreamed of conquering the far south, but his prudent henchman, Saif-ud-Dīn Ghūri, advised against it, reminding him that the campaigns of ʿAlāʾ-ud-Dīn Muḥammad Khaljī and Muḥammad ibn Tughluq had contributed to the misfortunes of their last days; rather, he urged consolidation in the Deccan and aggression against Malwa and Gujarat. Consequently, for the next four years, Bahman Shāh concentrated on suppressing refractory chieftains and disloyal subordinates. Reportedly, fearful of leaving the impregnable defences of Daulatabad, he was visited in a dream by Uwais Qarani (a legendary contemporary of the Prophet Muḥammad), who assured him of victory if he would take the field in person. Fortified by the saint's assurances, he set out for Gulbarga, only to learn of the death of Muḥammad ibn Tughluq (March, 1351), which made the future independence of the Deccan virtually certain. Bahman Shāh then made Gulbarga, in place of Daulatabad, the capital of the new sultanate.

Bahman Shāh strengthened Gulbarga's fortifications, and within the citadel, he probably initiated the building of the Jami Masjid (congregational mosque), completed in 1367 by a Persian architect from Qazvin, and also the solid donjon known as the Bala Hisar. A surviving inscription, dated 1353-1354 (the earliest Muslim inscription known in south India), records another mosque in Gulbarga, no longer extant, founded by Bahman Shāh's *vakil-i mutlaq*, Saif-ud-Dīn Ghūri.

Bahman Shāh remained active throughout the remainder of his reign. In the west, he conquered Kolhapur, Goa, and Dabhol (south of modern Bombay), which became the main port of the sultanate, while his forces pressed north into Malwa and occupied Warangal in the east. By the time of his death, the new state stretched from the Narbada southward to the Tungabhadra and from the Arabian Sea almost to the Bay of Bengal.

He was a plain soldier, and ceaseless campaigning left him little time to cultivate the arts of peace, although he is identified with one major work of literature, the *Futūḥ al-Salātīn* (fourteenth century; *Futuhus-salatin by Isami*, 1948) of ʿAbd al-Malik ʿIṣāmī, an epic account of India's Muslim rulers inspired by Firdusi's *Shahnamah*. As a successful rebel who had usurped a kingdom by force, Bahman Shāh sought the legitimizing approval of the charismatic Sufi shaykhs who dominated the religious life of the period. Therefore, he honored Shaykh Niẓām-ud-Dīn Awliyā in distant Delhi and regarded Shaykh Siraj-ud-Dīn Junaydi as his spiritual mentor. Although the latter did not finally settle in Gulbarga until after Bahman Shāh's death, the sultan's tomb is located adjacent to the saint's.

Significance

Bahman Shāh's founding of an independent sultanate in the Deccan marked the end of a single, Delhi-based Muslim state in India and heralded the emergence of regional sultanates that would develop their own distinctive cultural traditions and artistic styles. The Bahmanī sultanate served a dual function: of extending the Islamic presence southward while barring the northern expansion of the Hindu Vijayanagar kingdom.

—*Gavin R. G. Hambly*

Further Reading

Briggs, John. *History of the Rise of the Mahomedan Power in India*. 4 vols. 1829. Reprint. Calcutta, India: Editions Indian, 1966. Translation of some of the work of the Deccani chronicler, Ferishta.

Husaini, S. A. Q. *Bahman Shāh*. Calcutta, India: Firma K. L. Mukhopadhyay, 1960. The only biography of the sultan.

Jackson, Peter. *The Delhi Sultanate*. Cambridge, England: Cambridge University Press, 1999. The best general account of the period.

Michell, George, and Mark Zebrowski. *Architecture and Art of the Deccani Sultanates*. Cambridge, England: Cambridge University Press, 1999. Outstanding for the arts.

Sherwani, H. K. *The Bahmanis of the Deccan*. Delhi, India: Munshiram Manocharlal, 1985. Excellent account of the dynasty.

See also: 1206-1210: Quṭ al-Dīn Aybak Establishes the Delhi Sultanate; 1236-1240: Reign of Raziya; 1299: ʿAlāʾ-ud-Dīn Muḥammad Khaljī Conquers Gujarat.

Related article in *Great Lives from History: The Middle Ages, 477-1453*: Firdusi.

1347-1352
INVASION OF THE BLACK DEATH IN EUROPE

The invasion of the Black Death, or plague, created physical and psychological devastation, but also brought an end to Church domination in the Middle Ages and ushered in numerous social and economic reforms.

LOCALE: Western and central Europe
CATEGORIES: Environment; health and medicine; social reform

KEY FIGURES

Giovanni Boccaccio (1313-1375), Italian author
Geoffrey Chaucer (c. 1343-1400), British author
Guy de Chauliac (c. 1290-1368), French physician and author
Jean de Venette (1307/1308-1368/1369), Carmelite friar and writer

SUMMARY OF EVENT

Apparently originating near Delhi in the 1330's, the plague spread to southern Asia by 1346 and to the cities of Kaffa and probably Constantinople by the end of the following year. Merchants traveling from Kaffa and probably from Constantinople effectively transmitted the plague to the ports of Genoa and Venice in northern Italy, to Messina in Sicily, and to Marseilles in southern France. The pandemic spread through Spain and France in 1348, arriving in England in the autumn of that year and eventually reaching Scandinavia and northern central Europe in 1349. Northern Russia first suffered its effects in 1352, after the plague had declined in Western Europe. China experienced the disease between 1352 and 1369; Iceland and Cyprus were totally depopulated.

An increase in both maritime and overland trade facilitated the movement of the plague bacillus, and the southern European seaports were devastated first. Boats were loaded with two commodities: spices and disease-ridden rats. The "king of terrors" ravaged populated areas so severely that at least one-fourth of Europe's inhabitants had died by 1350. Sometimes entire villages were depopulated by death, since 60 percent to 80 percent of those infected failed to survive. Half of Florence's ninety thousand people vanished; some two-thirds of the population of Siena and Hamburg died.

French physician Guy de Chauliac encouraged rational and professional courtesy in the face of the disease and also understood some of the demographics and social conditions that encouraged its persistence. The biological spread of the plague bacillus (*Yersinia pestis*) was facilitated when engorged, bacilli-infested fleas would leave their original animal hosts in search of new hosts, usually humans. The bite of the flea produced oval swellings called buboes. These chestnut-sized lumps appeared commonly near an area of lymph nodes, usually in the groin, the armpit, or the neck. The blackened color of these buboes gave the disease its common name—the Black Death. It appears that three types of plague existed. The first was the simple bubonic plague. The second and the most common type was pneumonic plague, which occurred when the bacillus invaded the lungs or was transmitted through exposure to a coughing plague victim. The third type was the always fatal septicemic plague, which occurred when the bacillus fully invaded the bloodstream and overwhelmed the nervous system before producing pustules.

Europe experienced great physical and mental anguish as whole families vanished. The plague created an even greater sense of demoralization, anomie, and relative deprivation, exacerbated by numerous viral epidemics, including measles, smallpox, influenza, dysentery, typhus, tuberculosis, and whooping cough. Medical treatment was invariably irrational, even dangerous to the patient, as were numerous preventive procedures.

The practice of "sewage pharmacology" became widespread as people turned to unusual treatments in the hope of preventing the disease. Believing that strong odors could prevent transmission of the disease, some people would bathe daily in urine and even drank urine; others smeared human excrement on their clothing. Attempts were made to bottle flatulation; others allowed male goats to live in their houses, filling rooms with the malodorous smell of their urine. It was also the practice for people to hover over open latrines and inhale the stench. One witness reported "many were so courageous that they swallowed the pus from the mature boils in spoonfuls." Boils were incised, dried, and powdered for inhalation or administered orally in a drink. Geoffrey Chaucer's *The Canterbury Tales* (1387-1400) describes such psychological and behavioral responses to the plague.

Attempts at prevention assumed other procedures as when walls, furniture, and even a person's face and hands were washed in rose-water or vinegar. It was not an un-

This wood engraving, from a fifteenth century German book in the Rosenwald collection (Library of Congress) depicts a plague victim pointing out his boils to three physicians. (Library of Congress)

common sight to see people with garlands, wearing nosegays, and even cloth masks with large noses stuffed with flowers, which were believed to act as a filter against miasma. Further evidence of this belief is revealed in the nursery rhyme "Ring Around the Rosey, Pocket Full of Posies," which signified the rose-colored swelling "ring" on the skin as an early stage of plague. Even the wearing of pointed shoes was avoided because such shoes were thought to resemble Satan's cloven hoof.

In keeping with Galenic medicine and the concept of humors, people were advised to avoid any excesses in eating, drinking, exercise, and even sexual relations. At the same time, many people felt doomed and frequently indulged in extreme forms of debauchery and antisocial behavior. Individuals and groups roamed streets robbing people or entering houses to rape and plunder. In Spain, the Tarrantella dance (bite of the tarantula spider) was forbidden.

Mass hysteria became endemic to much of Europe. Various social movements became the focus of the people's frustration. Italian writer Giovanni Boccaccio, in his work *Decameron: O, Prencipe Galeotto* (1349-1351; *The Decameron*, 1620), presented a series of graphic biographies explaining social dysfunction and class structure during the plague. In one such display of social dysfunction, pilgrimages of the Brethren of the Cross or the Brotherhood of the Flagellants would go from village to village whipping themselves and others with metal-tipped leather thongs as penitence for presumed wrongs. This form of mortification of the flesh was actually based on an earlier concept of exorcism, one that the Church later came to despise. The Flagellants roamed throughout much of Europe, releasing criminals and patients from insane asylums. Carmelite friar Jean de Venette made a number of astute observations and descriptions of flagellantism.

A similar social movement was the so-called *charisant mania*, whereby hundreds, sometimes thousands, would dance and sing uncontrollably in village or city streets. The sinister aspect of this mania was that some would dance themselves to death through exhaustion or trample others to death while performing awkward and erratic dances. Yet for some, the dance of death was not a psychological disorder but rather represented a later stage of plague, when the subcutaneous hemorrhaging created black blotches on the victim's skin. Eventually, the victim's central nervous system deteriorated, creating bizarre and painful neurological dysfunction and disorientation.

Unfortunately, another antisocial movement, also documented by Jean de Venette, was the rise of anti-Semitism, particularly later in Germany and central Europe, although the first instances of widespread persecution were in Marseilles in 1348 when thousands of Jews were burned to death. The notion of anti-Semitism probably developed as early as the First Crusade (1095-1099), when the Catholic Church contended that Jews represented demons of Satan, poisoning the wells of plagued communities. By 1349, the number of persecutions had begun to decline, perhaps because the populace realized that Jews were also victims of the plague. With the decline of the Black Death in 1351, the persecution of the Jews waned.

SEARCHING FOR SCAPEGOATS: JEAN DE VENETTE ON THE PLAGUE AND ANTI-SEMITISM

Some said that this pestilence was caused by infection of the air and waters, since there was at this time no famine nor lack of food supplies, but on the contrary great abundance. As a result of this theory of infected water and air as the source of the plague, the Jews were suddenly and violently charged with infecting wells and water and corrupting the air. The whole world rose up against them cruelly on this account. In Germany and other parts of the world where Jews lived, they were massacred and slaughtered by Christians, and many thousands were burned everywhere, indiscriminately. The unshaken . . . constancy of the [Jewish] men and their wives was remarkable. For mothers hurled their children first into the fire that they might not be baptized and then leaped in after them to burn with their husbands and children. It is said that many bad Christians were found who in a like manner put poison into wells. But in truth, such poisonings, granted that they actually were perpetrated, could not have caused so great a plague nor have infected so many people. There were other causes; for example, the will of God and the corrupt humors and evil inherent in air and earth.

Source: Jean de Venette, *A Chronicle of Jean de Venette*, translated by Jean Birdsall and edited by Richard A. Newhall (New York: Columbia University Press, 1953), pp. 48-51.

SIGNIFICANCE

The Black Death resulted in many lasting changes: better medical literature, programs of public sanitation, decline of feudalism and the manorial systems, the beginning of the end of the medieval period, and almost complete control of all ecclesiastical matters by the Catholic Church. For example, certain city governments imposed programs to prevent contagion and improved sanitation. Florence and Venice established commissions for public health in 1348; in the same year, the Italian city of Pistoia issued regulations on burial, clothing, and food to counter the spread of plague.

—*John F. McGovern, updated by John Alan Ross*

FURTHER READING

Aberth, John. *From the Brink of the Apocalypse: Confronting Famine, War, Plague, and Death in the Later Middle Ages*. New York: Routledge, 2001. A study of social upheaval and strife in the late medieval period, thematically organized around the Four Horsemen of the Apocalypse.

Campbell, Anna M. *The Black Death and Men of Learning*. Reprint. New York: AMS Press, 1966. The author argues that education suffered a decline after the Black Death since the number as well as training of professors had deteriorated.

Cantor, Norman F. *In the Wake of the Plague: The Black Death and the World It Made*. New York: Perennial, 2002. A broad-ranging, multifaceted text, this study covers the effects of the plague on individuals and society at large, as well as surveying all major theories of the cause of the Black Death, from contemporary superstition to modern science.

Coulton, George. *The Black Death*. New York: Robert M. McBride, n.d. In this work, published c. 1930, the author is convinced that the plague gave rise to the Protestant Reformation and was instrumental in major changes in land rights and in the sense of individualism.

Gasuet, Francis. *The Black Death of 1348 and 1349*. 2d ed. London: George Bell and Sons, 1908. A lucid treatment of the subject anticipating Coulton's thesis that the plague brought about a revolution in Church development.

Gottfried, Robert. *The Black Death: Natural and Human Disaster in Medieval Europe*. New York: Free Press, 1988. A thorough study of how the plague brought dramatic transformation to medieval Europe, particularly within the Church.

Shrewsbury, J. *A History of Bubonic Plague in the British Isles*. Cambridge, England: Cambridge University Press, 1970. Detailed descriptions of socioeconomic and demographic effects of the plague.

Twigg, Graham. *The Black Death: A Biological Reappraisal*. New York: Schocken Books, 1985. The author presents significant data to demonstrate that plague diseases produced clinical signs akin to anthrax, which was a major killer in medieval Europe.

Ziegler, Philip. *The Black Death*. London: Collins, 1969. A critical review of the major historians who describe the social and economic consequences of the plague.

SEE ALSO: November 27, 1095: Pope Urban II Calls the First Crusade; 12th-14th centuries: Social and Political Impact of Leprosy; c. 1320: Origins of the Bubonic Plague.

RELATED ARTICLES in *Great Lives from History: The Middle Ages, 477-1453:* Giovanni Boccaccio; Geoffrey Chaucer; Guy de Chauliac.

May 20, 1347-October 8, 1354
COLA DI RIENZO LEADS POPULAR UPRISING IN ROME

Cola di Rienzo led a popular uprising against the aristocratic families of Rome, ruling the city as a dictator until he was murdered by the commoners who had supported him.

LOCALE: Rome (now in Italy)
CATEGORIES: Social reform; wars, uprisings, and civil unrest

KEY FIGURES

Cola di Rienzo (1313-1354), ruler of Rome, 1347 and 1354
Clement VI (c. 1291-1352), Roman Catholic pope, 1342-1352
Charles IV (1316-1378), king of Bohemia as Charles I, r. 1346-1378, and Holy Roman Emperor, r. 1355-1378
Innocent VI (1282-1362), Roman Catholic pope, 1352-1362

SUMMARY OF EVENT

In 1309, Pope Clement V moved the headquarters of the Papacy from Rome to Avignon (now in France), where it would remain until 1377. Although Rome was in the region of central Italy known as the Papal States and was therefore theoretically under the direct rule of the pope, the long absence of the Papacy led to a struggle for power among Rome's aristocratic families.

Cola di Rienzo (a shortened version of his original name, Nicola di Lorenzo) was an outspoken critic of the aristocrats. In 1343, he was a member of a delegation sent from Rome to Avignon to ask Pope Clement VI to return the Papacy to Rome. Although Clement VI remained in Avignon, he appointed Rienzo to the post of notary of the civic treasury of Rome. He also declared 1350 to be a Holy Year, which would bring numerous pilgrims to Rome and help relieve the poverty of the Roman people.

On his return to Rome in 1344, Rienzo continued his public speeches denouncing the aristocrats. Although the common people were influenced by his oratory, the aristocrats failed to take him seriously. Some even amused themselves by inviting him to dinners, where they laughed at his verbal attacks. Secretly, Rienzo began planning a revolution with the commoners, financed by merchants who were eager to end the crime and bloodshed that filled Rome under the rule of the aristocrats.

On May 20, 1347, after attending a midnight mass at the church of Sant'Angelo in Peschiera, Rienzo led a group of his followers to the Capitoline Hill. Dressed in full armor with only his head bare, he made an impassioned speech against the aristocrats. A new constitution for Rome was read to the crowd, who accepted Rienzo as their leader. A few days later, he took the title of "tribune," from the title of an official of ancient Rome who served as a representative of the common people.

The aristocrats, intimidated by the number of Rienzo's supporters, some of whom bore weapons paid for by the merchants, were forced to swear loyalty to the new ruler of Rome. Rienzo proclaimed reforms of the financial, judicial, and political systems of Rome and enacted severe punishments for lawbreakers.

After these initial declarations, Rienzo announced his plan to unite Italy into a single nation. He sent representatives into all parts of Italy, inviting the rulers of its various regions to an assembly that would enact this goal. Many of these regional governments accepted the invitation, and the assembly began on August 1, 1347.

Following an elaborate ceremony in which he awarded himself a knighthood, Rienzo announced to the assembly that all the inhabitants of Italy were now Roman citizens and that Rome held jurisdiction over all other nations. He also declared that he and the pope held power over all other rulers. It seemed that Rienzo was attempting to transform Italy into a new Roman empire, with himself as emperor.

Many of Rienzo's followers withdrew their support because of his increasingly grandiose pronouncements. Meanwhile, the ousted aristocrats began gathering troops outside the city. On November 20, 1347, Rienzo's forces defeated the aristocrats' army, leaving eighty aristocrats dead.

Despite this victory, Rienzo continued to lose popular support. Although Pope Clement VI had at first accepted Rienzo as the ruler of Rome, he issued a decree declaring him a criminal and a heretic whom the people of Rome should remove from power. Faced with his declining popularity as well as another uprising by the aristocrats, Rienzo resigned on December 15, 1347.

For two years, Rienzo lived as a hermit among monks in the mountains east of Rome. Meanwhile, the struggle between the aristocrats and the commoners continued. After the Holy Year, the aristocratic families seized all power in Rome, forcing the papal representative to flee. Encouraged by the pope, a group of Roman citizens appointed an elderly, respected Roman named Giovanni Gerroni as the ruler of Rome with the title of "rector" on December 26, 1351. He had not been in office long when he discovered a conspiracy plotting his downfall. Declaring himself unequal to the task of ruling Rome, he left the city.

The aristocrats took power again. Once again the commoners rose in rebellion, this time selecting Francesco Baroncelli as their leader. He proved to be no more effective against the aristocrats than the previous leader. Many Romans wished for the return of Rienzo. Despite his vanity and extravagant ambitions, he seemed to be the only popular leader capable of defeating the aristocrats.

In 1350, Rienzo traveled to the court of Charles IV, king of Bohemia (later to be the ruler of the Holy Roman Empire), in an attempt to win his aid in regaining power in Rome. Charles IV reported his visit to Pope Clement VI, who ordered him to be placed under the custody of the archbishop of Prague. Rienzo was again declared a heretic, given a death sentence, and held prisoner in Avignon beginning in August of 1352.

Clement VI died on December 6, 1352. The new pope, Innocent VI, was more sympathetic to Rienzo's cause and thought he might be useful in returning papal authority to Rome. Innocent VI lifted the charge of heresy and freed him from imprisonment. On August 1, 1354, Rienzo returned to Rome with the new title of "senator."

Rienzo's behavior during his second period as the ruler of Rome was even more dictatorial than before. Desperate for money to pay the soldiers who protected him from the aristocrats, he raised taxes to extremely high levels. He arrested wealthy merchants and forced their families to pay large ransoms for their release.

One of Rienzo's most notorious actions occurred when he arrested one of his supporters, Pandolfuccio di Guido dei Franchi, on suspicion of attempting to overthrow him. Without a trial, Rienzo had him beheaded. Many of the people of Rome had respected this man and were outraged by his execution. This act, along with heavy taxes and Rienzo's erratic behavior, turned many against him.

Cola di Rienzo vows to avenge his brother's death. (Hulton|Archive by Getty Images)

On October 8, 1354, a mob surrounded the palace in which Rienzo lived. He attempted to address the crowd from the balcony of the palace but could not be heard over their shouts. The mob began throwing stones at him and set fire to the wooden fortifications surrounding the palace. Rienzo attempted to escape by disguising himself to blend in with the crowd, but he was soon recognized and taken prisoner.

After confronting the crowd in silence for a time, Rienzo was stabbed with a sword by one of his former officials. The mob began to beat and tear at his body and his head was cut off. His corpse was left hanging by its feet for two days, then taken down and burned.

SIGNIFICANCE

Rienzo has been viewed as both a patriot and popular hero and as a dictator whose desire for glory brought him down. He saw himself as a visionary and vigorously pursued his dreams. However, the political and social turbulence that marked Rome in the late Middle Ages brought an end to his dreams of leading Rome to rediscover its strength and importance in the Mediterranean world.

—*Rose Secrest*

FURTHER READING

Cheetham, Nicolas. "Avignon and the Great Schism (1305-1389)." In *Keepers of the Keys: A History of the Popes from Saint Peter to John Paul II*. New York: Charles Scribner's Sons, 1983. Describes the move of the papacy to Avignon and the career of Cola di Rienzo as seen by Clement VI.

Collins, Amanda. *Greater than Emperor: Cola di Rienzo and the World of Fourteenth Century Rome*. Ann Arbor: University of Michigan Press, 2002. This biography of Rienzo focuses on his power and the environment in which he governed. Bibliography and index.

The Life of Cola di Rienzo. Translated by John Wright. Toronto: Pontifical Institute of Mediaeval Studies, 1975. The anonymous fourteenth century biography that is the primary source of information on Rienzo. Contains an excellent introduction by the translator, who provides a concise historical background of the period and the various critical views of Rienzo's character.

Musto, Ronald G. *Apocalypse in Rome: Cola di Rienzo and the Politics of the New Age*. Berkeley: University of California Press, 2003. A biography of Cola di Rienzo that describes his role as tribune. Bibliography and index.

Petrarca, Francesco. *The Revolution of Cola di Rienzo*. 3d ed. New York: Italica Press, 1996. A translation of Petrarch's letters and the letters of Cola di Rienzo as well as from the Church's archives. The introduction by Ronald G. Musto provides valuable information on the letters and Rienzo. Bibliography and index.

Wood, Diana. "Propriissima Sedes Beati Petri: The Problem of Old Rome." In *Clement VI: The Pontificate and Ideas of an Avignon Pope*. New York: Cambridge University Press, 1989. An account of the struggle between Clement VI and Cola di Rienzo.

SEE ALSO: November 18, 1302: Boniface VIII Issues the Bull *Unam Sanctam*; 1305-1417: Avignon Papacy and the Great Schism.

RELATED ARTICLES in *Great Lives from History: The Middle Ages, 477-1453*: Charles IV; Cola di Rienzo.

1350
RAMATHIBODI I CREATES FIRST THAI LEGAL SYSTEM

The kingdom of Ayutthaya, later known as Siam and today as Thailand, was one of the most stable political systems in Southeast Asia. Its founder, Ramathibodi, was responsible for building a government composed of four ministries and a law code. Both of these innovations survived well into the twentieth century in the modern state of Thailand.

LOCALE: Kingdom of Siam (now Thailand)
CATEGORIES: Government and politics; laws, acts, and legal history

KEY FIGURE

Ramathibodi I (1315-1369), founder and ruler of the Kingdom of Siam, r. c. 1351-1369

SUMMARY OF EVENT

The beginnings of the Kingdom of Siam (now Thailand)—nestled between several neighboring empires, the Khmer to the east, India to the west, and China to the north—can be traced to the Ayutthaya (also Ayudhya, Ayuthia, or Ayuthaya) period. The founder of this state was Ramathibodi I, who not only conquered and combined several neighboring states but also developed a political system for the region that continued into the twentieth century.

Ramathibodi was a member of a tribe originating in southwestern Siam. During his reign, it was rumored that he was a brother of the great leader Ramkhamhaeng, who had ruled most of Siam until his death in 1317. It was said that Ramathibodi descended from the same bloodline as the former monarch, and the story allowed him to claim his rule as a continuation of the original dynasty.

On Ramkhamhaeng's death, his empire splintered into many small states with their own rulers. These states were too small to protect themselves from outside invaders, including the Khmer. Ramathibodi's first great achievement was to move his army into central Siam, conquering a broad swath of territory and founding Ayutthaya as the first city of his empire. Calling the new state the Kingdom of Ayutthaya, he made the city into a commercial and political center for Siam. By 1352, the kingdom had expanded to the Bay of Bengal in what is now modern Myanmar (Burma). Ramathibodi's armies also invaded and conquered most of the Malay Peninsula and defeated the Khmers in the east.

With the borders of the empire set, Ramathibodi focused on creating a permanent system of government. He began with the selection of four great offices or ministries of the state and then developed a law code that would be enforced by them. The four ministries addressed the interior, providing the internal security for the state and the people; the treasury; the king's household and the ritual of the monarchy; and agriculture. This final ministry, called the Ministry of Na, was probably the most important of the four, because it handled the rice fields so necessary for the people to survive (Ramathibodi had set up his city and empire along the Siam River system to ensure the plentiful rice harvests that would be overseen by this ministry). The four ministries became the focus of power in the government and enforced the new laws drawn up by Ramathibodi.

Prior to the Kingdom of Ayutthaya, much of the law for the region was based on tradition, with local customs and the dictates of local monarchs setting the rules. Ramathibodi sought to consolidate these laws, making them more systematic and understandable for ordinary people. His code, known as the Thamanasat, was partly based on the Indian form of law known as the Manu. Elements of Manu were combined with ancient customs and modern rulings to form the code. The process took years as Ramathibodi eliminated outdated or contradictory laws and built the code from the remainder.

Ramathibodi's code focused primarily on public law rather than private affairs. He set the guidelines for the relationship between the people and the state while leaving many individual decisions to the people. One area where he legislated heavily was in public works. Under his law each male citizen of the kingdom participated in the corvée system whereby they "donated" six months of their time working on public projects, including farming and road construction. Ramathibodi's 1356 Law of Abduction criminalized the act of helping slaves escape mandated service in the corvée system. The punishment was severe, sometimes death.

The code also established a hierarchy among men in the society, including defining freemen and slaves. This hierarchy was apparent in Ramathibodi's 1350 Law of Evidence. The law created the rules for who could testify in court and against whom they could testify. Freemen were allowed to testify against slaves, but slaves had no such rights.

In 1351, the Law of Offenses Against Government set the punishments for government officials who cheated or stole from the government. Those officials could be suspended, fined, lashed, or executed based on the severity of the crime.

The laws also created the system of Sadki Na, or Degrees of Dignity, for government officials. The Sadki Na determined classes of officials based on the amount of land they received from the king. The more land they received, the higher was their level of dignity and authority. The Sakdi Na also forced officials to treat one another with respect and to work with one another for the advancement of the state.

Ramathibodi's code also set the commercial regulations for the state. Under the code, the king owned all the land in the kingdom. He would grant land to important officials, but they did not own that land. Instead, they held the land until death or the time when they no longer served the king. Ownership of all land gave Ramathibodi total control over his population and his government officials.

One major change in private law instituted by Ramathibodi was the 1359 law governing husbands and wives. This law, which was greatly influenced by Khmer and Indian law, legalized polygamy and made it easier for men and women to get a divorce.

Like all law codes, there was a procedure for changing the codes and modernizing them. Under Ramathibodi's law, the kings retained the absolute power to issue laws to handle current situations. These royal decisions were known as Rajasattham. The decisions were collected and became part of two sets of law. The original code became known as the Mula Attha. The Sakha Attha was a digest of all the monarch's decisions that supplemented the law code. Kings could discard the decisions of their predecessors, particularly if they found them to contradict Manu.

SIGNIFICANCE

Ramathibodi's code was the basis for Siamese and then Thai law into the middle of the twentieth century. While Ramathibodi's dynasty lasted only a few years after his death, his system of government created a stable society with the rule of law for most people. Ramathibodi's reign witnessed the creation of government ministries and a law code that would last several centuries, to be replaced by a more democratic system only in the twentieth century.

—Douglas Clouatre

FURTHER READING

Baker, Christopher. *A History of Thailand.* New York: Cambridge University Press, 2003. A wide-ranging book describing the culture, government, and people of Thailand from ancient to modern times.

Chakrabongse, Prince Chiela. *Lords of Life: A History of the Kings of Thailand.* London: Redman, 1982. A series of portraits of the leading rulers of Thailand throughout its history

Englehart, Neil. *Culture and Power in Traditional Siamese Government.* Ithaca, N.Y.: Southeast Asia Program Publications, Southeast Asia Program, Cornell University, 2001. Details the duties and authority of Thai monarchs and their use of absolute power in the twentieth century.

Gervais, Nicolas. *The Natural and Political History of the Kingdom of Siam.* Bangkok: White Lotus Press, 1989. An overview of the government system of Thailand and its economic development.

Peleggi, Maurizio. *Lords of Things: The Fashioning of the Siamese Monarchy.* Honolulu: University of Hawaii Press, 2002. Describes the development of the Thai monarchy, with its rituals, ministries, and powers.

Rajchagool, Chaigan. *The Rise and Fall of the Thai Absolute Monarchy.* Bangkok: White Lotus Press, 1994. Details the medieval Thai monarchy and how it advanced into modern times and lost its absolute authority.

Smith, Ronald Bishop. *Siam or the History of the Thais.* Bethesda, Md.: Decatur Press, 1986. Examines Siam, its government, and the development of Siamese society.

Wood, William R. *A History of Siam, from the Earliest Times to the Year A.D. 1781.* 1933. Reprint. San Diego, Calif.: Simon, 2001. The first Western book on the history of early Thailand book, by a British consul and based on ancient Thai documentation.

Wyatt, David. *Thailand: A Short History.* New Haven, Conn.: Yale University Press, 2003. A brief work touching on the major events—political, military, and cultural—in Thai history.

SEE ALSO: 682-1377: Expansion of Śrivijaya; c. 700-1253: Confederation of Thai Tribes; 729: Founding of Nanzhao; 802: Founding of the Khmer Empire; 877-889: Indravarman I Conquers the Thai and the Mons; 1295: Ramkhamhaeng Conquers the Mekong and Menam Valleys.

RELATED ARTICLE in *Great Lives from History: The Middle Ages, 477-1453*: Suryavarman II.

c. 1350-1400
PETRARCH AND BOCCACCIO RECOVER CLASSICAL TEXTS

Petrarch and Boccaccio brought humanist ideals to the forefront of European education through the preservation and circulation of neglected manuscripts from the classical age.

LOCALE: Florence and Naples (now in Italy) and Avignon (now in France)
CATEGORY: Cultural and intellectual history

KEY FIGURES

Petrarch (1304-1374), Italian literary scholar, classicist, and author
Giovanni Boccaccio (1313-1375), Italian diplomat, poet, and storyteller, author of the *Decameron*
Dante (1265-1321), Italian poet and author of *The Divine Comedy*

SUMMARY OF EVENT

In 1350, Petrarch stopped over in Florence on his way to Rome for the mid-century papal Jubilee. There, he met Giovanni Boccaccio who, like Petrarch, had already established himself as an innovative literary figure in Europe. Petrarch's reputation was reinforced by *Rerum vulgarium fragmenta* (1470, also known as *Canzoniere*; *Rhymes*, 1976), which had been largely completed by 1335. This collection of 366 poems (317 sonnets, 29 canzoni, 9 sestine, 7 ballates, and 4 madrigals) represents a fusion of classical and Christian values. More important, it continued the enterprise, begun by Dante, of writing in the vernacular—in this case, the refined Tuscan dialect of northern Italy.

Petrarch drew from numerous sources, chiefly the influential poets of Roman antiquity—Vergil, Horace, Catullus, Propertius, and especially Ovid. Saint Augustine's moral precepts added a formidable coloring, as did Dante's *La vita nuova* (c. 1292; *Vita nuova*, 1861; better known as *The New Life*). The sprightly lyrical quality derives some of its vigor from the Provençal troubadours—notably Arnaut Daniel and Bernart de Ventadorn. In addition, courtly love resonances from Guido Cavalcanti's late thirteenth century poems are discernible. This extraordinary synthesis of biblical and classical themes inspired the humanist movement and contributed to Petrarch's moment of recognition on April 8, 1341, when he was crowned Poet Laureate of the Holy Roman Empire. This event was orchestrated by King Robert of Naples, perhaps the most dynamic patron of the arts during the formative years of Petrarch and Boccaccio.

Boccaccio's *Decameron: O, Prencipe Galeotto* (1349-1351; *The Decameron*, 1620) also relied on classical sources and fourteenth century prose works. Among the latter, the *Gesta Romanorum*—a popular collection of tales and fables from antiquity that reached its final form during Boccaccio's lifetime—and the French *fabliaux* tradition represent noticeable influences. Boccaccio's Italian writings leading up to the *Decameron* reveal tendencies that clearly suggest the revival of classical literary modes. Early prose works from his Naples period of the 1330's, *Il filocolo* (c. 1336; *Labor of Love*, 1566) and *Il filostrato* (c. 1335; *The Filostrato*, 1873), derive their energy from historical parallels. *Il ninfale d'Ameto*, also known as *Commedia delle ninfe* (1341-1342; comedy of the nymphs), the *Elegia di Madonna Fiammetta* (1343-1344; *Amorous Fiammetta*, 1587, better known as *The Elegy of Lady Fiammetta*), and *Il ninfale fiesolano* (1344-1346; *The Nymph of Fiesole*, 1597) from his Florentine period of the 1340's continue this pattern as Boccaccio

Francesco Petrarch. (Hulton|Archive by Getty Images)

added psychological and mythological elements to pastoral idylls.

The sensuality of these works can be traced to the Angevin court at Naples, where the chivalric codes of northern France were deeply embedded. Boccaccio's prose style, a mixture of classical decorum and robust local Italian color, became the model for Renaissance realists who admired the broad spectrum of his imagination, by which characters and social setting are vividly conveyed and at times viciously satirized.

Petrarch had a profound effect on Boccaccio's appreciation for classical writers. As Petrarch used his papal connections in Avignon to move around Europe visiting cathedrals and monasteries in search of ancient manuscripts, he developed a lively correspondence with Boccaccio. The two met regularly—in Milan (1359), Venice (1363 and 1367), and Padua (1368)—planning projects and trading books. Boccaccio translated into Italian the works of the Roman historian Livy, studied the *Thebais* (c. 90; *Thebaid*, 1767) of Statius, restored the reputation of Ovid, and wrote "eclogues" in imitation of Vergil. To Petrarch, he sent Dante's *La divina commedia* (c. 1320; *The Divine Comedy*, 1802), Augustine's "Commentary on the Psalms of David," and excerpts from Cicero and Marcus Terentius Varro. Furthermore, Boccaccio popularized one of his favorite works, *Metamorphoses* (second century; *The Golden Ass*, 1566) by Lucius Apuleius, and galvanized European interest in classical mythology in a series of Latin books written between 1350 and 1360.

Petrarch elevated Seneca, Sappho, Cicero, Horace, and Quintilian to celebrated positions of esteem and contributed to new considerations of historical documentation by praising the accomplishments of Julius Caesar, Sallust, and Livy. Petrarch wrote a philological commentary on portions of Livy's *Decades* from a manuscript retrieved by Landolfo Coronna, one of his patrons. Many of the ideals of the Humanist tradition concerning civic duty, eloquence, and moderation derive from Petrarch's study of lost manuscripts of Cicero's works—the *Pro archia* and fragments of his letters—uncovered by Petrarch at Liège (1333) and at Verona (1345), respectively.

Giovanni Boccaccio. (Library of Congress)

Significance

Petrarch and Boccaccio owned copies of Vitruvius's *De architectura*, which they circulated. Developments in Renaissance architecture can be attributed to this effort. They supervised the translations of Homer and Plato into Latin, along with annotations to the ecclesiastical chronicles of Eusebius of Caesarea. Petrarch continued to explore classical literature and history in several Latin books, notably *De viris illustribus* (1351-1353; reorganized as *Quorundam virorum illustrium epithoma*)—an unfinished biography of famous Romans. Boccaccio concentrated on *Trattatello in laude di Dante* (1351, 1360, 1373; *Life of Dante*, 1898), which led to his appointment as a lecturer on Dante in Florence (1373). The scope and depth of the Latin writings of Petrarch and Boccaccio perhaps outweigh their contributions to the European vernacular traditions because they provided the essential materials for the blossoming of Humanism in the fifteenth century.

As Latinists and Italian lyric poets, Petrarch and Boccaccio paved the way for the secular spirit that imbues the work of Geoffrey Chaucer and a host of Renaissance vernacular writers. These authors attempted to capture, for the first time since classical antiquity, the complex world of human emotions seen freely from all sides, without class bias or religious restriction. They added a wealth of nuances and perspectives to the predetermined framework of Christian culture that houses their ideas. Chaucer's *The Canterbury Tales* (c. 1387-

1400), Boccaccio's *Decameron*, and, to a lesser extent, Petrarch's *Canzoniere* present a series of vignettes rooted in middle-class competitive practicality. Eroticism is equally as powerful as Christian morality, and the metaphysical dimensions of life are mirrors of worldliness.

The Humanism articulated by Petrarch and Boccaccio introduced impulses at odds with Scholastic thought, and thus it may be viewed as the mentality of a transitional phase, between the medieval and the modern. While discovering, editing, and restoring classical texts, Petrarch and Boccaccio also contributed to an imaginative understanding of ages past; this understanding gave classical literature a pedigree that it had not yet attained. Moreover, Petrarch and Boccaccio offered their contemporaries a new appreciation for the literary qualities of Greek, Roman, and early Christian authors, with a deeper sense of how they achieved their effects. As a result, humanist scholars were endowed with a finer vision of their own turbulent era.

—*Robert J. Frail*

FURTHER READING

Fubini, Riccardo. *Humanism and Secularization: From Petrarch to Valla*. Durham, N.C.: Duke University Press, 2003. An examination of Humanism and its relationship with Petrarch, Bracciolini, and Poggio. Bibliography and index.

Jones, Frederic J. *The Structure of Petrarch's "Canzionere": A Chronological, Psychological, and Stylistic Analysis*. Rochester, N.Y.: Boydell and Brewer, 1995. An analysis of Petrarch's poetry, particularly his *Canzionere*. Bibliography and indexes.

Koff, Leonard Michael, and Brenda Deen Schildgen, eds. *"The Decameron" and the "Canterbury Tales": New Essays on an Old Question*. Cranbury, N.J.: Associated University Presses, 2000. A collection of essays on the relationship between the two works. Bibliography and index.

Mazzotta, Giuseppe. *The World at Play in Boccaccio's "Decameron."* Princeton, N.J.: Princeton University Press, 1986. Connects the stories of the *Decameron* to commercial, legal, and political events in early fourteenth century culture.

Quillen, Carol E. *Rereading the Renaissance: Petrarch, Augustine, and the Language of Humanism*. Ann Arbor: University of Michigan Press, 1998. Examines Petrarch as a reader and writer as well as his correspondence in relation to Humanism. Also looks at Saint Augustine. Bibliography and index.

Serafini-Sauli, Judith Powers. *Giovanni Boccaccio*. Boston: Twayne, 1982. A very useful introduction to Boccaccio's works. Introductory chapters deal with the writer's background and the early years in Naples. Each section is preceded by biographical information as a preface to the commentary. Contains a good bibliography, with details of the works in Italian, Latin, and English translations.

Staples, Max. *The Ideology of the "Decameron."* Lewiston, N.Y.: Edwin Mellen Press, 1993. This wide-ranging study offers a fairly comprehensive account of Boccaccio's sources and demonstrates the classical depth established early in his writings.

SEE ALSO: c. 1100: Rise of Courtly Love; 1305-1417: Avignon Papacy and the Great Schism; c. 1306-1320: Dante Writes *The Divine Comedy*; 1387-1400: Chaucer Writes *The Canterbury Tales*.

RELATED ARTICLES in *Great Lives from History: The Middle Ages, 477-1453*: Giovanni Boccacio; Guido Cavalcanti; Geoffrey Chaucer; Dante; Petrarch.

January 10, 1356, and December 25, 1356
GOLDEN BULL

The Golden Bull, a constitutional settlement presented by Emperor Charles IV, reiterated the power of the electors of the Holy Roman Empire.

LOCALE: Nuremberg, Holy Roman Empire (now in Germany) and Mete, France, Holy Roman Empire (now in France)

CATEGORIES: Expansion and land acquisition; government and politics; laws, acts, and legal history; religion

KEY FIGURE

Charles IV (1316-1378), king of Bohemia as Charles I, r. 1346-1378, and Holy Roman Emperor, r. 1355-1378

SUMMARY OF EVENT

Policies decreed in the Golden Bull of 1356 were intended to resolve constitutional problems remaining from the reign of Charles II's predecessor as Holy Roman Emperor, Louis the Bavarian (r. 1328-1347), also known as King Louis IV of Germany (r. 1314-1347). These problems concerned disputed claims to certain electorates of the Holy Roman Empire, the powers and functions of the electors, and papal prerogatives to decide the validity of elections and confer imperial authority on the elected candidate.

Traditionally, the seven electors of the empire chose one of the German princes as king, who then usually went before the pope to be crowned emperor. After an Avignon pope refused to confirm claim to the *emperium*, the electors issued, in 1338, the Declaration of Rense and the ordinance *Licet juris* proclaiming a prince's election as German king as tantamount to his election as emperor. Although the electors conceded the pope's right to crown the emperor, they rejected the assumption that the election required papal confirmation or that the emperor's authority stemmed from the pope.

During the medieval period, the Holy Roman Empire was beset by the intervention of France and the Avignon Papacy. Behind a Papacy seeking to meddle in imperial elections lurked a French monarch who hoped to secure territorial gains at the expense of the Holy Roman Empire in both the Rhoneland and the Rhineland. Thus Emperor Charles IV's German pacification problem was greatly facilitated by serious French losses at the hands of the English in the opening phases of the Hundred Years' War which broke out in 1337. The mutual desires of both the Avignon popes and the kings of France to benefit at the expense of imperial Germany thus were less threatening because the Avignon popes were henceforward supported by a weakened France.

Deterioration of Louis's popularity and support after 1338 finally enabled the Papacy to depose him in favor of the Luxembourger, Charles of Bohemia, in 1346. Charles was elected emperor in July, 1346, but was not formally crowned in Rome by a papal legate until 1355, and only upon renouncing interference in Italian affairs.

One of Charles's basic intentions was to secure internal peace in Germany. He had already quelled one great disturbing element, the disgruntled Wittelsbach Dynasty, by consolidating his own authority in Germany between 1346 and 1354. By strengthening the electoral process, perhaps future schisms might be contained.

Immediately after returning from Italy, Charles summoned a Reichstag, or diet, at Nuremberg. There, he presented proposals for a constitutional settlement clarifying membership in the electoral college and defining the territorial powers of princes governing territories officially designated as imperial electorates. Accepted by the Reichstag, these proposals were promulgated by Emperor Charles on January 10, 1356; together with a supplement approved by the Reichstag of Metz on December 25 of the same year. These acts comprise the Golden Bull, so called after the golden seal affixed to important imperial documents.

To avoid long disrupting vacancies of the throne, the edict provided that the archbishop of Mainz was to communicate with his fellow electors within one month after the emperor's death and summon them to appear within three months at Frankfurt to choose a successor. Furthermore, subjects of the Holy Roman Empire were required to facilitate safe passage of the electors. To avoid misunderstandings and bickering, electors who failed to appear or send proxies forfeited their votes. To assure results, electors were required to remain in Frankfurt until they named a successor. If they failed to reach a decision within thirty days, they were to be fed thereafter on bread and water. A majority vote constituted a valid election, which would be declared unanimous so as to preclude double elections.

The Golden Bull reaffirmed the right of the seven traditional electoral princes to choose the German king. The decree designated the seven electors by name and bestowed semiregal autonomy, immune from imperial ju-

Charles IV. (Library of Congress)

abandoned its universalism so that by the second half of the fifteenth century it became popular in the Germanies to speak of the Holy Roman Empire of the German Nation. Charles IV designed the Golden Bull to strengthen his external position with respect to the pope. Also, recognition of the electors' sovereignty created a conservative force contributing to maintaining peace among the German states.

The edict did much to undermine the emperor's internal position, however, because it made the electoral princes the first estate of the empire. Almost immediately, the nonelectoral princes claimed the same sovereign rights, including the principles of indivisibility and primogeniture, enjoyed by the electors. Thus in 1359, Duke Rudolf IV of Habsburg arbitrarily bestowed upon his house the so-called major privileges. Among other things, these privileges made the duchy of Austria an archduchy independent of the empire with the Habsburg lands indivisible. Other states, such Wurtemberg, Lippe, and Baden, soon did the same, adopting the principles of primogeniture and the indivisibility of principalities as well as privileges preventing recourse from electoral courts to the imperial *Hoffgerticht*. By 1500, most princes managed to consolidate their territorial authority at the expense of the emperor and the local aristocracy. Thus Charles, in his quest for peace, acknowledged the division within Germany and the futility of attempting to maintain a centralized monarchy. The electors of the Holy Roman Empire became upholders of the status quo, working with the emperor to preserve peace within the empire.

risdiction, upon their principalities. All electoral territories were indivisible and retained their vote permanently. In the case of lay electorates, the law of primogeniture was invoked to exclude rival claimants for the same title and its attendant vote. The electors were granted full right to all metal and salt mines on their lands and to the taxes payable by Jews for protection. The electors also could coin their own money. No appeal would be recognized from an electoral court to any higher court of the empire. Finally, the bull forbade the formation of leagues of cities except under the emperor's patronage.

The Golden Bull, seeking to eliminate papal interference in imperial elections and politics, stipulated that a simple majority of the seven votes conferred unqualified authority as emperor from the moment of an emperor's election. Designation of the count palatine of the Rhine and the duke of Saxony as regents during any interregnum automatically excluded the pope's claim to act as vicar in such a period. These constitutional procedures of the Golden Bull thus ended the pope's authority in German affairs. They were Charles's response to his earlier exclusion by the Papacy from Italy.

The Golden Bull of 1356 had several far-reaching effects on subsequent German history. In the first place, the Holy Roman Empire, by its prior withdrawal from Italy,

SIGNIFICANCE

The Golden Bull, while containing some innovations, actually legally confirmed historical developments dating from the late eleventh century. Its effect was to accelerate further development of German particularism, thus blocking all attempts to unify Germany until well into the nineteenth century. It can be asserted that historical experiences following the Golden Bull were so firmly rooted in the German memory that they "constituted an iron framework, a mold" so firm that it shaped subsequent German efforts to deal with contemporary problems as late as 1939. The Germany of the First Reich, the Holy Roman Empire, had a direct impact on the attitudes of the late Second and Third Reichs.

Not only did the Golden Bull contain provisions that related to international conditions impinging on Germany but also its ultimate impact was international as it encouraged a shift in the medieval theory of world government. Since 962, the emperor and pope had been, in theory, twin depositories of God's authority exercised through states. In breaking the imperial and papal interdependence, the ideal of Charlemagne and Otto was relinquished in favor of a secular justification for sovereignty, a move facilitating rationalization of the later system of the authority of states that emerged fully in the seventeenth century.

—*Edward P. Keleher, updated by Ralph L. Langenheim, Jr.*

Further Reading

Barraclough, Geoffrey. *The Origins of Modern Germany.* 3d ed. Oxford, England: B. Blackwell, 1988. Probably the most useful account of German history in the English language.

De Booulay, F. R. H. *Germany in the Later Middle Ages.* London: Athlone Press, 1983. Includes a brief description of the Golden Bull, its purpose, and its result.

Detwiler, Donald S. *Germany: A Short History.* 3d ed. Carbondale: Southern Illinois University Press, 1999. A broad survey of German history from antiquity through the twentieth century.

Ferguson, Wallace K. *Europe in Transition, 1300-1520.* Boston: Houghton Mifflin, 1962. This study of the Renaissance contains discussions of the background to the Golden Bull.

Kitchin, Martin. *The Cambridge Illustrated History of Germany.* New York: Cambridge University Press, 1996. Emphasizes cultural as well as political history; easy reading.

Schulze, Hagen. *Germany: A New History.* Translated by Deborah Lucas Schneider. Cambridge, Mass.: Harvard University Press, 1998. Comprehensive history of Germany that begins with a chapter on the Roman Empire and German lands.

Scott, Tom. *Society and Economy in Germany, 1300-1600.* New York: Palgrave, 2002. Organized thematically rather than chronologically, this book surveys the political, social, and economic history of late medieval and early modern Germany.

Waugh, W. T. "Germany: Charles IV." In *The Cambridge Medieval History*, Vol. 7, edited by J. R. Tanner et al. Cambridge, England: Cambridge University Press, 1932. Discusses the constitutional problems that Charles IV attempted to resolve in the Golden Bull.

See also: September 17, 1156: Austria Emerges as a National Entity; November 18, 1302: Boniface VIII Issues the Bull *Unam Sanctam*; 1305-1417: Avignon Papacy and the Great Schism; 1337-1453: Hundred Years' War.

Related articles in *Great Lives from History: The Middle Ages, 477-1453*: Charlemagne; Charles IV; Otto I.

c. 1360-1440
Kan'ami and Zeami Perfect Nō Drama

Kan'ami and his son Zeami transformed the nature of Japanese theater by merging the existing popular form of sarugaku *with samurai culture and Zen Buddhism, creating the vastly more refined and elegant form of Nō, which has survived for more than six hundred years.*

Locale: Japan
Categories: Cultural and intellectual history; literature

Key Figures

Kan'ami Kiyotsugu (1333-1384), actor and playwright, principal reformer of Nō theater
Ashikaga Yoshimitsu (1358-1408), shogun, 1368-1394
Zeami Motokiyo (1363-1443), actor, playwright, principal theorist of Nō theater

Summary of Event

In the mid-fourteenth century, Japanese theater was largely if not exclusively a popular entertainment, and actors were outcasts. However, Kan'ami Kiyotsugu initiated a series of developments and refinements to the existing forms of *dengaku* ("rice-field entertainment") and *sarugaku* (literally "monkey music," an amalgam of entertainment forms emphasizing comical-pantomimic elements). By 1374, Kan'ami and his company were sufficiently established that they were invited to perform for

ZEAMI ON THE ART OF NŌ

On the text:

The writing of Nō consists of three stages: choice of "seed," construction, and composition. The "seed" is the story on which the play is based. This story must be well considered and divided into Introduction, Development, and Climax. . . . If the writer wishes to make a new play—one that does not use an existing story—he should bring in some famous place or ancient monument and may thus produce a spectacle which will move his audience. . . . Moreover, he must bear always in mind whether his play be one of prayer, mystery, love, recollection, or longing.

On the stage:

The stage should not stand back or forward, to right or left, but right in the middle of the auditorium, for the voice always travels best in a straight line. Before a performance the stage and "bridge" should be carefully examined and any nails or other dangerous places put to rights.

On music:

Before [the play] begins, the flute should play for a while in order to quiet the audience and put them in the right mood. When the dancing and singing has begun, the flute-player must listen to the actor's voice, follow its rhythm and, as it were, "shadow" it. . . . [The drummers] must not go their own way. Their business is to understand the actors' intentions and follow the rhythms of the singing and dancing.

On acting:

Not more than four or five actors ought to take part in a play. In old times, even if more actors were at their disposal, in a play which only needed one or two they did not use more than one or two. Nowadays, excusing themselves on the plea that there are some actors "over," they set in rows a number of persons . . . and let them sing in unison. This is contrary to the principles of our art.

An old actor cannot take the part of a girl or of young warriors. . . . The writer of a play must bear in mind his [actor's] style and write a part for him which will not be inappropriate to his appearance.

Source: Quoted by Arthur Waley in *The Nō Plays of Japan* (1922; reprint, New York: Dover Publications, 1998), pp. 26-36.

the shogun Ashikaga Yoshimitsu in Kyoto. The shogun was only a teenager at the time, but he had already developed the sophisticated aesthetic sensibilities that would mark his rule.

The performance was an enormous success. Not only did the shogun appreciate the grace and elegance of the actors, but also he was impressed by the skill—and the physical beauty—of Kan'ami's eleven-year-old son, Zeami, who performed the *kokata* (child actor) role. Thus began a personal as well as professional relationship between the most powerful political figure in the country and the family that was to transform the nature of traditional Japanese theater. The relationship between Yoshimitsu and Zeami gave the actor and his father political cover for the kinds of reforms they were attempting. Also, the tastes and predilections of the shogun were at the center of Kan'ami's and Zeami's transformations of the form. Zeami, in particular, took advantage of the opportunity not only to meet and converse with the most influential courtiers but also to observe outstanding performances in music, dance, and other means of artistic expression.

Not surprisingly, however, the apparent homosexual affair between the shogun and a mere actor led to rivalries and jealousies. After Yoshimitsu abdicated the shogunate, Zeami's political stature waned—largely because the new shogun, Yoshimochi (ruled 1395-1423), preferred a rival actor named Zōami, whom Zeami himself also admired—and the process of decline accelerated after the death of Yoshimochi in 1428. Ultimately, Zeami was exiled to the island of Sado in 1434 and is said to have ended his life as a Buddhist monk. The drop in Zeami's personal fortunes seems to have been idiosyncratic, however: His nephew Motoshige (better known as On'ami) and son-in-law Komparu Zenchiku (Zeami's chosen successor) became popular with later shoguns, and Nō retained its status as elegant court entertainment for centuries.

Today, Kan'ami and Zeami are both regarded as among the foremost actors, theorists, and playwrights of Nō. Nō plays were constantly being adapted and revised throughout the late fourteenth and fifteenth centuries, so it is often difficult if not impossible to attribute a particular Nō play to a specific dramatist. Still, it is certain that many of the best-known and most compelling Nō plays were written by either Kan'ami or Zeami—or, in many cases, adapted by Zeami from an original work by his father. The two men were unquestionably at the forefront of a movement to raise the literary value of Nō; indeed, many of their plays rank among the most evocative works of poetry in any language. Kan'ami was also responsible for changes in the dramatic structure of existing texts and for integrating new forms of both music and dance into the Nō. Thus, he is generally credited with being the first playwright of what is now called Nō.

A Nō play, however, is only partially about the dramatic text. To attempt to comprehend a Nō play based only on its words is at least as risky a proposition as trying to understand the true nature of a Western opera solely on the basis of the libretto. Nō (the word simply means "skill" or "ability") is the synthesis of a host of source elements, including folk dance, poetry, court music, Buddhist (especially Zen) thematic material, popular entertainment, and Chinese drama. There are often allusions to works of literature or historical and legendary figures: The seemingly casual assurance that spectators will understand such references simultaneously flattered and affirmed the cultured samurai audience. Similarly, the religious and philosophical elements of the Nō style not only supported the court but also were intended, in Zeami's words, as a "means to pacify people's hearts, to bring about a sense of contentment and to promote a long life."

Probably the most important advance in Nō attributable to Kan'ami and Zeami is the fusion of the aesthetic principles of *monomane* (roughly akin to the Greek "mimesis," but perhaps better translated simply as "role playing") and *yūgen*. This latter term is difficult to translate, but refers to a transcendent, mysterious, depth of feeling, a sense of grace and harmony. At the most fundamental level, the concept of *yūgen* links the Nō theater to other, preexisting elements of Japanese aesthetics, most notably the notion that what is implied is of greater import than what is presented more overtly. This subtle quality of evocation is apparent in both the written texts and in the performance style, which is stately, elegant, and—by Western standards, at least—extremely slow.

The fullest articulation of the aesthetics of Nō comes in Zeami's theoretical writings, begun in approximately 1400 and continued throughout the rest of his life. Originally intended as secret treatises to be read only by the successive leader of the Kanze school of Nō, these essays are collectively referred to as the *Fūshikaden* (teachings on style and the flower) or the *Kadensho* (English translation, 1968; literally, the book of the transmission of the flower). The central image here is of the flower, which represents the pinnacle of aesthetic expressiveness: a synthesis of the physical, the vocal, and the spiritual. The actor's job, then, is to nurture and develop his delicate flower from his first training at the age of seven through youth, maturity, and ultimately old age. Of significance are both the emphasis on the spiritual nature of performance and the link to the natural world. For example, Zeami, one of the first to articulate the aesthetic principle of *jo-ha-kyu* ("slow, medium, and fast," with the sense of "exposition, development, and climax"), regards the concept as a natural extension of the physical world.

SIGNIFICANCE

Nō theater is one of the oldest continuously performed art forms in the world, considered so important to world culture that the Allied occupation force actively supported its reintroduction after World War II. Apart from its intrinsic value, Nō has also influenced such modern musical and theatrical artists as Benjamin Britten, Ezra Pound, W. B. Yeats, and Robert Wilson. Nō is both a means of entry into the court life of the Muromachi period (1336-1573) and the distillation of Japanese aesthetics. The refinements wrought by Kan'ami and Zeami in the late fourteenth and early fifteenth centuries form the basis for everything Nō was to become: They were the foremost playwrights, actors, and theorists not only of their day but also in the entire history of the form.

—Richard Jones

FURTHER READING

Brandon, James, ed. *The Cambridge Guide to Asian Theater*. Cambridge, England: Cambridge University

A modern Nō actor. (Hulton|Archive by Getty Images)

Press, 1993. Comprehensive overview of traditional Asian theater forms.

Keene, Donald, ed. *Twenty Plays of the Nō Theater.* New York: Columbia University Press, 1970. Translations of some of the best-known Nō plays, with an introduction by Keene.

LaFleur, William R. *The Karma of Words: Buddhism and the Literary Arts of Medieval Japan.* Berkeley: University of California Press, 1983. Includes two chapters devoted largely to the parallels between Nō and Buddhist thought.

Ortolani, Benito. *The Japanese Theater: From Shamanistic Ritual to Contemporary Pluralism.* Rev. ed. Princeton, N.J.: Princeton University Press, 1995. Standard text for traditional and contemporary Japanese theater forms.

Terasaki, Etsuko. *Figures of Desire: Wordplay, Spirit Possession, Fantasy, Madness, and Mourning in Japanese Noh Plays.* Ann Arbor: Center for Japanese Studies, University of Michigan, 2002. An analysis of six plays attributed to Kan'ami and Zeami. Bibliography and index.

Thorndike, Arthur H., III. *Six Circles, One Dewdrop: the Religio-Aesthetic World of Komparu Zenchiku.* Princeton, N.J.: Princeton University Press, 1993. Includes translations of Zenchiku's theoretical work and an extensive commentary.

Tsubaki, Andrew T. "Zeami and the Transition of the Concept of Yūgen: A Note on Japanese Aesthetics." *Journal of Aesthetics and Art Criticism* 30, no. 1 (Fall, 1971): 55-67. Explication of *yūgen*, one of the most problematic terms of Japanese aesthetics.

Waley, Arthur. *The Nō Plays of Japan.* New York: Knopf, 1922. Important early work includes translations of nineteen plays and an introduction.

Zeami Motokiyo. *Kadensho.* Translated by Sakurai Chuichi, Hayashi Shuseki, Satoi Rokuro, and Miyai Bin. Kyoto: Sumiya Shinobe Publishing Institute, 1968. One of Zeami's most influential treatises.

_______. *On the Art of the Nō Drama: The Major Treatises of Zeami.* Translated by J. Thomas Rimer and Yamazaki Masakazu. Princeton, N.J.: Princeton University Press, 1984. Translations of Zeami's most important theoretical work; includes a 30-page introduction.

SEE ALSO: 538-552: Buddhism Arrives in Japan; March 9, 712, and July 1, 720: Writing of *Kojiki* and *Nihon Shoki*; 792: Rise of the Samurai; c. 800: *Kana* Syllabary Is Developed; c. 1001: Sei Shōnagon Completes *The Pillow Book*; c. 1004: Murasaki Shikibu Writes *The Tale of Genji*; 1336-1392: Yoshino Civil Wars.

RELATED ARTICLES in *Great Lives from History: The Middle Ages, 477-1453*: Ashikaga Takauji; Zeami Motokiyo.

1366
STATUTE OF KILKENNY

The Statute of Kilkenny was one of several unsuccessful efforts by medieval English kings to control Irish nobles. The statute outlawed virtually all significant interaction between English and Irish persons, forbade the practice of Irish customs by the English, defined the king's legal authority, and prohibited Irish military activities.

LOCALE: Kilkenny, Ireland

CATEGORIES: Government and politics; laws, acts, and legal history; social reform

KEY FIGURES

Edward III (1312-1377), king of England, r. 1327-1377

Lionel of Antwerp, duke of Clarence (1338-1368), third son of Edward III and lord lieutenant of Ireland, 1361-1366

SUMMARY OF EVENT

Throughout the medieval period, English monarchs endeavored to extend royal authority throughout their kingdom, a task made virtually impossible by the extent of their claims. Based in Normandy, the Anglo-Norman (or Angevin) Empire stretched from Scotland to the south of France.

Although unable to maintain their continental empire into the modern era, a basis for effective political influence by the monarchy over the British Isles was acquired. This was achieved over a period of five hundred years through successful wars and diplomacy against Scottish, Welsh, and Irish kings and nobles. By 1500, an Anglo-Norman/English aristocracy was in place throughout the British Isles. This resulted ultimately in an English ascendancy throughout Britain, but success was never continuous or even assured. Strong English kings advanced monarchical power, but weak kings witnessed the reverse. Ireland provides a clear example of this process.

In 1169, Richard de Clare, an Anglo-Norman noble known as Strongbow, pressured Irish warlords into paying homage to Henry II (r. 1154-1189), then king of England. Henry was most interested in protecting his continental possessions and in limiting papal authority in England, but he readily accepted the offer of allegiance. He then created Anglo-Norman aristocrats to rule Ireland in his name. Despite the claim of suzerainty (overlordship), however, Anglo-Normans were not a significant presence because the Irish greatly outnumbered their nominal overlords.

Over the next two centuries, with few settlers arriving from England, the descendants of those Anglo-Norman lords, while not absorbed by the Irish, fused with the locals to the point where they were hardly distinguishable from the natives. Marriages between Anglo-Norman aristocrats and daughters of Irish chieftains meant reduced loyalty to London. Irish language and customs replaced Anglo-Norman; Irish names replaced Norman (for example, De Burgh became Burke); Irish law was used in place of English law; and most significantly, Irish military prowess improved to the point that the Irish were a match for English forces. Direct English rule was thus sporadic and intermittent at best; efforts to give substance to a real alien presence met only resistance.

Edward I (r. 1272-1307) was a strong English king determined to assert himself in his kingdom. In Ireland, he effected stronger bonds with a few, powerful Anglo-Irish nobles and encouraged them to be more proactive for him. In return for his blessing and aid, they were to renounce native ways. Several Irish parliaments at Kilkenny issued edicts and proclamations or enacted laws ordering Englishmen in Ireland to abandon their Irish ways. That such proclamations and laws were issued repeatedly is an indication that they were ignored and that they were not enforceable. Edward's initiative was lost by his timorous son, Edward II (r. 1307-1327), but Edward III attempted to regain the initiative. Yet the king's plan for Ireland, as had so often been the case, was undermined by more important problems elsewhere. War with Scotland (1333) and the outbreak of the Hundred Years' War (1337-1453) once again focused the English monarchy's attention on the Continent.

Despite this, there were those in Ireland who viewed a rigid defining of the Anglo-Norman as an aid to their own power. Edward was quite willing to assist them as long as a military expedition was not required. A request in 1347

King Edward III. (Library of Congress)

for the prohibition of marriages between Irish and English was validated by proclamation. A Kilkenny assembly of 1351 prohibited nineteen specific relations between the Irish and the English. A political marriage between Lionel of Antwerp, Edward's third son, to Elizabeth de Burgh provided the title of earl of Ulster and a real claim of power. The king appointed Lionel lord lieutenant of Ireland in 1361, and it was he who summoned the Parliament of Kilkenny in 1366. The assembly was in no way representative of Ireland, for its members were primarily Anglo-Norman nobles and their church allies. The Statute of Kilkenny was their statement of acceptable behavior for both the English and the Irish.

Written in Norman-French, which connoted linguistic superiority, a preamble to the statute described the lawlessness that existed in Ireland. The church was declared free (albeit under the protection of the king), and things Irish were condemned. Sexual interactions of any kind—legal or otherwise—between the English and Irish were deemed acts of treason, as were any acts of war against the king. Englishmen were to speak English, and Irish customs (such as hurling and riding Irish style) were not to be practiced by the English. English law was the only acceptable legal code, and enforcement of the law was to be by English judicial representatives only. Additionally, Irishmen were prohibited from taking orders in religious houses (they could not become church leaders or clerics), and excommunication was prescribed for those who refused to accept the rules set forth. The overall purpose was twofold: Those who would rule had to be English, and those who retained Irish ways were considered inferior before the king's law.

Had the Statute of Kilkenny been enforced, or even if it were enforceable, English monarchs would have acquired a decisive ally in their desire to control Irish nobles. Anglo-Irish/English nobles could rely only on the king for their continued position and power, which meant that loyalty to the king was essential. Irish nobles, on the other hand, would have had their political power severely curtailed and their ability to wage war eliminated.

The short-term impact of the Statute of Kilkenny on Ireland was like most edicts, decrees, and laws put forward by English rulers of earlier or later times, that is, it had little effect. Throughout the medieval era actual royal authority was usually a reflection of the ability and longevity of the monarch on the throne. Many English monarchs were either incapable of asserting authority in Ireland or were challenged in venues far more critical to their power. Hence English stipulations regarding proper Irish noble behavior were neither acceptable to Irish nobles nor enforceable by their English sovereign. By 1500, English monarchs controlled only the Pale, a thin strip of land centered on Dublin along the eastern coast of Ireland. By 1600, however, when the security of England vis-à-vis continental powers made control of Ireland (and other parts of the British Isles) imperative, Irish nobles were truly brought to heel. Moreover, the religious struggles of the seventeenth century relegated Roman Catholics to subservient status (most of the Irish were Catholic). In sum, by 1700, many of the concepts propounded within the Statute of Kilkenny were enforced strictly and effectively, although for different reasons and by different groups.

SIGNIFICANCE

The long-term relevance of the Statute of Kilkenny is perhaps more important than its short-term impact. If the document is interpreted from the perspective of 1366, it is clearly a feudal statement of lord/vassal expectations. It dealt with specific issues that pertained to a particular time. However, if that context is ignored or overlooked, inchoate ideas of imperialism and nationalism are most certainly discernible. The statute has been described as a document put forward to protect the "racial purity of [the] English" or to denigrate the Irish nation. Such concepts are more closely associated with later ages, and to interpret the document as an imperial or racist statement is a clear misrepresentation of both the facts and the definition of the terms.

—*William S. Brockington, Jr.*

FURTHER READING

Cosgrove, Art, ed. *A New History of Ireland*. Vol. 2 in *Medieval Ireland, 1169-1534*. New York: Clarendon Press, 1987. Irish history by Irish historians. Extensive bibliography.

Duffy, Seán. *Ireland in the Middle Ages*. New York: St. Martin's Press, 1997. Irish historian's effort to present Irish, not English colonial, history of the period.

Frame, Robin. *Colonial Ireland: 1169-1369*. Dublin: Helicon, 1981. Told from the Irish perspective, focus is on English efforts to destroy the existing Irish power structure and to implement English institutions.

_______. *English Lordship in Ireland, 1318-1361*. New York: Clarendon Press, 1982. Significant study of the decades leading to the statute, especially the earlier attempts by English kings to control their Irish lords.

Lydon, James F. *The Lordship of Ireland in the Middle Ages*. Rev. ed. Dublin: Four Courts Press, 2003. Important study of the medieval fusion of cultures, albeit one that ultimately rendered the Irish as secondary.

_______, ed. *The English in Medieval Ireland: Proceedings of the First Joint Meeting of the Royal Irish Academy and the British Academy*. Dublin: Royal Irish Academy, 1984. Contains a collection of articles on English-Irish relations.

Otway-Ruthven, A. J. *A History of Medieval Ireland*. 2d ed. New York: St. Martin's Press, 1980. Overview of Irish history, culture, and political changes in a British context.

"A Statute of the Fortieth Year of King Edward III, Enacted in a Parliament Held in Kilkenny, A.D. 1367, Before Lionel Duke of Clarence, Lord Lieutenant of Ireland." In *Statutes and Ordinances, and Acts of the Parliament of Ireland: King John to Henry V*, edited by Henry F. Berry. Vol. 1 in *Statute Rolls of the Parliament of Ireland*. Dublin: H. M. Stationery Office, 1907. Translated text of the statute, also in Norman-French.

SEE ALSO: 1169-1172: Normans Invade Ireland.

RELATED ARTICLES in *Great Lives from History: The Middle Ages, 477-1453*: Edward I; Edward II; Edward III; Henry II.

1368
ESTABLISHMENT OF THE MING DYNASTY

The establishment of the Ming Dynasty by Zhu Yuanzhang marked the restoration of Han Chinese rule in China and the beginning of a new era, in which Chinese civilization experienced further developments.

LOCALE: China
CATEGORY: Government and politics

KEY FIGURE

Zhu Yuanzhang (Chu Yüan-chang; 1328-1399), founder and first emperor of the Ming Dynasty, r. 1368-1398

SUMMARY OF EVENT

The Ming Dynasty (1368-1644) was founded by Zhu Yuanzhang amid intensive military conflicts: Han Chinese uprisings against the Mongol rulers of the Yuan Dynasty (1279-1368) and warfare among Chinese power contenders.

Zhu Yuanzhang was born into a family of poor tenant farmers in the district of Haozhou (modern Fengyang county) in the Huai River plain of modern-day Anhui Province. His earliest years were ones of great hardship. In his childhood, he tended sheep for others, often suffering from hunger. Orphaned at the age of sixteen, Zhu became a Buddhist monk and wandered through the Huai region, begging for his existence. These experiences proved useful for Zhu's later rise to power—they acquainted Zhu with local socioeconomic and geographical conditions. They also were to shape many of Zhu's policies after he became emperor.

A fortuitous turning point in Zhu's life came in 1352, when he joined the insurgent forces under Guo Zixing (Kuo Tzu-hsing), then stationed in the Haozhou area. Guo's forces belonged to the Red Turban Rebellion (1351-1356), an anti-Mongol movement that consisted of various independent armed rebellious forces. Participants in this movement believed that the Maitreya Buddha would be coming to save the unfortunate and destroy evil forces, especially the Mongols. The movement started in Jiangsi and Hunan Provinces in the 1330's and quickly spread throughout half of China within a dozen years. Guo Zixing was one of the many independent Red Turban leaders.

Under Guo Zixing's command, Zhu Yuanzhang fought bravely and demonstrated remarkable ability to use military tactics. Because of this, he quickly gained the admiration of his fellow soldiers and became Guo's favored follower and trusted aide as well as a member of Guo's household (by marrying Guo's adopted daughter). While remaining loyal to Guo, Zhu managed to build his own military contingent, whose leaders were mostly Zhu's former friends and childhood companions and included his future chief of staff, Xu Da (Hsü Ta). This group of military leaders formed the core of his personal following for the next twenty years.

Shortly after Guo Zixing died in 1355, Zhu Yuanzhang took command of Guo's forces. In 1356, Zhu's army crossed the Yangtze River and captured the city of Nanjing. Zhu began building a regional state with Nanjing as its capital. His reputation drew many important military leaders to him, and his force grew rapidly. Zhu became one of several regional leaders competing for mastery of the whole realm. From 1356 to 1367, Zhu defeated his rivals one by one in the middle and lower Yangtze region and firmly established his control there. In January, 1368, Zhu proclaimed the founding of a new dynasty, the Ming ("bright"), and took the title of emperor, ruling as Hongwu (Hung-wu; literally, the "great martial emperor"). Meanwhile, Zhu launched military expeditions against his remaining enemies to the south, west, and especially the Mongols to the north. The Mongol rulers and their forces were driven out of Dadu (Beijing) and fled further to the north, the Gebi Desert. By the end of the 1380's, the whole country was brought under the control of Zhu's Ming Dynasty.

Zhu Yuanzhang was the only founder of an imperial Chinese dynasty who came from a household of destitute farmers—the bottom layer of Chinese society. Zhu's success in gaining the throne is generally attributed to his military leadership, his efforts to help ordinary people, and his search for talented people to run his government.

Zhu built and maintained an effective and loyal military leadership. He attempted to impose discipline on his troops and took care to minimize harm to the civilian population, particularly forbidding his soldiers to bully women and to engage in looting. This ensured that his troops behaved better than other insurgent forces and helped win the goodwill of conquered populations. Zhu paid considerable attention to rehabilitating the lives of ordinary people in the farming villages, granting tax remissions to war-ravaged regions and helping resettle displaced people. In so doing, he strove to create the image of a compassionate future ruler. Zhu also proved open-minded and eager in searching for and recruiting talented

MAJOR RULERS OF THE MING DYNASTY

Reign	*Ruler*
1368-1398	Hongwu (Zhu Yuanzhang)
1399-1402	Jianwen (Zhu Yunwen)
1402-1424	Yonglo (Zhu Di)
1424-1425	Hongxi
1426-1435	Xuande
1436-1449	Zhengtong
1450-1457	Jingtai
1457-1464	Tianshun
1465-1487	Chenghua
1488-1505	Hongzhi
1506-1521	Zhengde
1522-1567	Jianjing
1567-1572	Longqing
1573-1620	Wanli
1620	Taichang
1621-1627	Tianqi
1628-1644	Chongzhen

personnel, including eminent scholars. At the capture of each administrative town, local literati, either officials in the service of the enemy or in private life, were interviewed and often appointed to office. Because of this policy, many scholars presented themselves to Zhu, serving as Zhu's advisers, literary tutors, officials, and strategists and playing a critical role in formulating many of Zhu's wartime policies and in transforming Zhu from an insurgent peasant leader to the ruler of an empire.

As emperor, Zhu Yuanzhang is traditionally believed to have been both a ruthless autocrat and a compassionate sovereign. Both reputations have fact behind them. Zhu was autocratic, more so than any of the previous Chinese rulers, as evidenced by Zhu's abolishment of the post of prime minister and his recourse to a reign of terror. Zhu was extremely concerned with the consolidation and perpetuation of the rule of his dynasty. This concern led him to suspect all his veteran and high-ranking officials and regard them as potential usurpers of imperial power. He particularly distrusted the prime minister, the head of civil administration with strong executive power. Therefore, Zhu abolished the office of prime minister in 1380 and warned that it should never be restored by his successors. Zhu acted as his own prime minister, making the six ministries directly responsible to him and thus gathering all important executive powers in his own hands. (In previous dynasties, the sovereign and the prime minister shared power.) The emperor became a true autocrat, omnipotent and unchecked. However, the emperor alone was unable to handle all state affairs. Increasingly, he turned to the inner court for help. The inner court, distinct from the outer court (the civil administration), was composed of the emperor's personal secretaries (mostly scholars). During the reigns of Zhu's descendants, the inner court expanded to include eunuchs, who became omnipresent and powerful and four of whom actually became dictators and controlled the court politics.

Zhu's reign was also marked by the systematic use of terror, primarily targeting bureaucrats, especially those in high posts. Zhu's terrorist techniques included tight surveillance and various brutal punishments—such as beating, torture, amputation, and execution—that were often random and massive. Some officials were subjected to severe punishments for their misconduct, especially for corruption. Many others, however, were punished only for alleged or suspected offenses and even for no legitimate reasons. As Zhu got older, he became ever more obsessed with the execution of senior officials, particularly meritorious and prestigious military generals and their family members. One case of execution could lead to the decimation of one or several whole clans and the deaths of hundreds and even thousands of innocent people. Zhu's reign of terror was a well-conceived political strategy designed to intimidate his officials into total submission and to remove potential challengers not only to himself but also to his young and weak successor.

This image of Zhu Yuanzhang as a cruel autocrat contrasts sharply with his other image, that of a compassionate ruler who cared about the common people, farmers in particular. Partly because of his poor peasant background and his childhood experiences, Zhu seems to have had genuine sympathy for the plight of the peasants. In his numerous pronouncements, he often mentioned how difficult a peasant's life could be and urged local officials not to bully the people but to make efforts to improve the people's livelihood. He even allowed local people to punish corrupt local officials by taking them to the capital. The emperor was concerned with the building and repairing of irrigation systems. When natural disasters occurred, he ordered the opening of public granaries to the people in disaster-stricken areas and the reduction or remission of their taxes.

Scholar Edward L. Farmer has presented yet another image of Zhu Yuanzhang, viewing him as a "shrewd and far-sighted legislator." Zhu legislated for all sectors of the society—the imperial family, the eunuchs, officials, nobles, and commoners. In so doing, Zhu proved careful, energetic, persistent, and creative.

SIGNIFICANCE

The rise of the Ming Dynasty ended nearly a century of alien (Mongol) control over China and resorted Han Chinese rule. For this reason, Zhu Yuanzhang, the founder of the Ming Dynasty, has been hailed as a national hero by many Chinese, including Sun Yat-sen, the father of the 1911 Revolution. Zhu's anti-Mongol activities inspired nationalist movements in later generations. The fact that Zhu rose to imperial power from a poor farmer's household encouraged later peasant revolutionaries such as Mao Zedong (Mao Tse-tung), the history-conscious leader of the Communist revolution

As an effective and diligent monarch, Zhu gave a new shape to the structure of Chinese central government that would last through all of Ming and Qing times until the revolution of 1911. The legacy of his autocratic rule could even be seen in modern times, in the authoritarian style of rule of rulers such as Chiang Kai-shek (Jiang Jieshi) and Mao.

—*Yunqiu Zhang*

FURTHER READING

Brook, Timothy. *The Confusion of Pleasure: Commerce and Culture in Ming China*. Berkeley: University of California, 1998. An account of the impact of commercialization on social and cultural life during the Ming dynasty.

Cass, Victoria Baldwin. *Dangerous Women: Warriors, Grannies, and Geishas of the Ming*. Lanham, Md.: Rowan & Littlefield, 1999. Contains valuable information about official attitudes toward women and women's issues in Ming times.

Chan, Hok-Lam. *China and the Mongols: History and Legend under the Yuan and Ming*. Brookfield, Vt.: Ashgate, 1999. Contains a chapter examining the official records on the rise of Zhu Yuanzhang.

Farmer, Edward L. *Zhu Yuanzhang and Early Ming Legislation*. Leiden, the Netherlands: E. J. Brill, 1995. An analysis of Zhu Yuanzhang's legislative activities.

Hucker, Charles O. *The Traditional Chinese State in Ming Times*. Tucson: University of Arizona Press, 1961. An examination of the Ming political system.

Mote, Frederick W., and Denis Twitchett, eds. *The Ming Dynasty, 1368-1644*. Vol. 7 in *The Cambridge History of China*. Cambridge, England: Cambridge University Press, 1988. An account of the political history of the Ming Dynasty, including chapters on Zhu's founding of the dynasty.

Taylor, Romeyn. *Basic Annals of Ming T'ai Tsu*. San Fransico, 1975. English translations of some primary materials about the founding of the Ming Dynasty.

Wu, Han. *Biography of Zhu Yuanzhang*. Beijing: Chinese Press, 1949. Still the most authoritative account of Zhu Yunzhang's life and career.

SEE ALSO: 1115: Foundation of the Jin Dynasty; c. 1387: Chinese Create the Eight-Legged Essay; 1397: Publication of the Laws of Great Ming.

RELATED ARTICLES in *Great Lives from History: The Middle Ages, 477-1453*: Kublai Khan; Zheng He.

1368
TIBET GAINS INDEPENDENCE FROM MONGOLS

The collapse of Mongol overlordship of Tibet led to the rebirth of Tibetan culture and political independence. The resulting secular dynasty ruled most of the Tibetan plateau for the next hundred years, when conflicts between monastic and lay leaders led to its downfall.

LOCALE: Central Tibetan plateau (now the Tibet Autonomous Region, People's Republic of China).

CATEGORY: Government and politics

KEY FIGURES

Changchub Gyaltsen (Byang-chub rgyal-mtshan; 1302-1364), Tibetan administrator who became the ruler of Tibet after the collapse of Mongol power on the plateau, r. 1350-1364

Zhu Yuanzhang (Chu Yüan-chang; 1328-1398), first emperor of the Chinese Ming Dynasty, r. 1368-1398

Sakya Pandita (1182-1251), a Tibetan monk and scholar.

SUMMARY OF EVENT

At the beginning of the fourteenth century, the Mongols ruled both China and Tibet. In the former, they exercised rule through a succession of emperors of the Yuan Dynasty (1279-1368), while in Tibet, they maintained a loose overlordship through the abbots of the Sakya order of Tibetan Buddhism. The head abbots of the primary monastery, Sakya, which is located in central Tibet to the west of the modern town of Shigatse, were given the title of imperial preceptor, and ruled for the Mongols through a series of lower level administrators, both clerical and secular. The nature of the Tibetan-Mongol relationship at the time is best described as one of lama-patron, which stems from the conversion to Buddhism of Godan Khan, a grandson of Genghis Khan and overlord of northeastern Tibet, by Sakya Pandit in 1247. In effect, he offered Tibetan loyalty for Mongol protection and control. This arrangement effectively centralized political leadership of the plateau in the hands of the Sakya order, and because the Mongols allowed the Sakya abbots great latitude, they became the de facto rulers of Tibet.

Although Sakya rule was resented by the other monastic orders and some local secular rulers, none could offer a serious challenge to them because of the strength of the lama-patron relationship during the rule of Kublai Khan (r. 1279-1294) and his successor, Temür Oljeitu (Chenzong; r. 1294-1307), the first two emperors of the Yuan Dynasty. Both had a strong interest in Tibetan Buddhism and lavished wealth on Sakya monasteries. One of the principal opponents of the Sakya was the Kagyu order, especially those monks from Drigung monastery. These two groups battled for prestige, economic resources, and territory, and the conflict reached its peak when, with Mongol assistance, the Sakya looted and burned Drigung in 1290. Although it was subsequently rebuilt at the behest of the victorious Sakya, the conflict only served to harden the attitudes of their rivals and led to widespread hatred of the Mongol presence in Tibet.

The death of Temür in 1307, however, marked a radical change in this relationship. Subsequent Yuan emperors were corrupt, ineffective, or uninterested in Tibet, and consequently, the Sakya lost their protection and patronage. New rivalries sprang up between the Sakya and other orders, which had sought their own Mongol patrons as the Yuan Dynasty began its decline. Corruption within the Sakya order itself, where abbots of different monasteries sought political advantage through secret alliances, bribery, and poisoning of rivals, worsened this situation.

A key figure in the eventual overthrow of Sakya dominance was Changchub Gyaltsen, a former Sakya monk who began his career as a minor administrator at Sakya but who rose to prominence in 1332 as a myriarch, or governor, of one of thirteen large administrative districts under Mongol rule. He was a member of the large and influential Lang family that hailed from the Yarlung region. Despite his importance, he was persecuted, arrested, jailed, and tortured during the intrigues surrounding the Mongol decline. These experiences led him to take an active role in countering Sakya power. Through alliances with monastic rivals and secular Tibetan patrons, he eventually broke Sakya power and, in 1354, occupied Sakya itself, effectively ending its dominance. Although the Mongols remained nominal rulers of the plateau for another fourteen years, they appeared to be uninterested in supporting their Sakya allies, and in any case, Changchub Gyaltsen apparently made a strong effort to avoid provoking the Mongols to do so.

The Yuan Dynasty was finally broken in 1368 by Zhu Yuanzhang, a former Buddhist monk of peasant origin who led the final revolt against the Mongols and who, as Hongwu (Hung-wu), became the first emperor of the Ming Dynasty (1368-1644). His primary concerns were the consolidation of his power and the removal of remaining Mongol influence in China, and therefore, he took little interest in Tibet. Although Changchub Gyaltsen died in 1364, his successors were able to continue his efforts, and they formed a dynasty that ruled Tibet for a century.

Many later authors describe the reign of Changchub Gyaltsen and his initial successors as a kind of golden age in Tibet. His goal was simple: to establish an authentic Tibetan state and to rid the plateau of all foreign influence. He demanded that foreign dress and manners be abandoned at his court and took a series of Tibetan royal titles that emphasized his right to rule and his rejection of ties to foreign powers. He deliberately invoked the image of the most famous of the ancient religious (Dharma) kings of Tibet—Songtsen Gampo, Trisong Detsen, and Ralpachen—and directed his own court to mimic those of the past. He relocated the capital from Sakya to Neugong, the former seat of power of the Yarlung kings, and transformed the taxation and tribute system of the Mongols, replacing it with a series of local administrators who were responsible for the collection of local taxes, of which a one-sixth were to be delivered to the state. He also sought to better protect his frontiers and established a series of guard posts along it. Perhaps most important, he and his successors saw themselves as equals to the Ming rulers and made little or no move to establish political or diplomatic relationships with them. This did not prevent the Chinese from attempting to influence the course of political development on the plateau, however. The Ming rulers became patrons of a number of monasteries, especially those of the Karmapa order, and bestowed wealth and Chinese titles on their abbots. However, this led to no significant influence on local politics.

Aside from promoting Tibetan nationalism and urging a return to the laws and legal codes of the Dharma kings, the dynasty did not seek to transform religious belief in Tibet. The Sakya were able to continue their teachings, as were all other orders. However, one interesting development during this period was the emergence of the so-called *terma*, or "treasure" texts. These "re-discovered" texts were said to have been written in deep antiquity and could only emerge in a new age ready to receive them. The most famous of these texts, the "Fivefold Set of Scrolls," documented, among other things, the glories of the ancient kings, the establishment of Buddhism in Tibet, and other clearly nationalistic themes. Lamas who discovered them were known as *tertons*, or "revealers of treasure." It is obvious how these *terma* served the developing Tibetan state, but other texts were rediscovered by monastic orders such as the Nyingma, and these served as means by which they could reestablish themselves in this new age.

Into this period of broad religious tolerance was born one of the most important figures of Tibetan history, Tsongkhapa, the founder of the Gelugpa monastic order, which came to dominate both political and religious life on the plateau from the mid-seventeenth century until the modern era.

Significance

The decline of the Mongol Yuan Dynasty led to a stunning rebirth of Tibetan nationalism from the mid-thirteenth century to the mid-fourteenth century. Tibet shook off foreign influence at this time, and laid a solid foundation for an indigenous centralized government. Buddhism witnessed a resurgence as well during this period, and religious tolerance was promoted. Despite the broad appeal of this new Tibetan ruling dynasty, continued factional politics eventually undermined its authority, and Tibet was soon returned to conflict and hostilities between rival groups of monasteries and secular rulers.

—*Mark Aldenderfer*

Further Reading

Amitai-Preiss, R., D. Morgan, and C. Griggs, eds. *The Mongol Empire and Its Legacy.* Boston: Brill Academic Publishers, 2000. A compilation of papers on the social, economic, military, and political impact of the Mongol conquests of Eurasia, with a thorough review of major controversies in Mongol studies.

Department of Information and International Relations. *The Mongols and Tibet: A Historical Assessment of Relations Between the Mongol Empire and Tibet.* Dharamsala, India: Central Tibetan Administration, 1996. An analysis of the historical ties between the two cultures from a strongly Tibetan perspective.

Petech, Luciano *Central Tibet and the Mongols: The Yüan-Sa-skya Period of Tibetan History.* Series Orientale Roma 65. Rome: Istituto Italiano per il Medio ed Estremo Oriente, 1990. A complete and thorough review and analysis of the relationship between the Mongols and the Sakya order of Tibetan Buddhism.

Richardson, Hugh. "The Political Role of the Four Sects in Tibetan History." *Tibetan Review* 11 (1976): 18-23. An overview of how the four major sects of Tibetan Buddhism influenced political processes on the plateau with a clear description of the Mongol period.

_______. *Tibet and Its History.* 2d ed. Boston: Shambhala, 1984. One of the most authoritative histories of Tibet in English, revised and expanded since its first edition in 1962. Illustrations, bibliography, index.

Saunders, J. J. *The History of the Mongol Conquests.* London: Routledge and K. Paul, 1971. A comprehensive history of the Mongol empire.

Stein, R. A. *Tibetan Civilization.* Stanford, Calif.: Stanford University Press, 1972. Useful and accessible historical overview of Tibet's history and culture.

See also: 627-650: Reign of Songtsen Gampo; 763: Tibetans Capture Chang'an; 838-842: Tibetan Empire Dissolves; 1271-1295: Travels of Marco Polo; 1368: Establishment of the Ming Dynasty.

Related articles in *Great Lives from History: The Middle Ages, 477-1453*: Genghis Khan; Kublai Khan.

1373-1410
JEAN FROISSART COMPILES HIS *CHRONICLES*

Jean Froissart compiled his Chronicles, *offering a vivid panorama of an age in transition that relied for its inspiration on waning codes of chivalry and a growing spirit of secular humanism.*

LOCALE: England, France, Flanders, and Burgundy
CATEGORIES: Historiography; literature; cultural and intellectual history; government and politics; wars, uprisings, and civil unrest

KEY FIGURES

Jean Froissart (1337?-c. 1404), Flemish court historian, poet, and secretary to Philippa of Hainaut, 1361-1366
Philippa of Hainaut (c. 1312-1369), queen of England, r. 1327-1369
Edward III (1312-1377), king of England, r. 1327-1377

SUMMARY OF EVENT

Jean Froissart entered the service of Margaret of Hainaut sometime between 1350 and her death in 1356. This was the first of many court appointments that enabled Froissart to establish a network of contacts in aristocratic circles. In 1362, he went to England to serve as secretary to Philippa of Hainaut, wife of Edward III. Froissart remained in Phillipa's entourage until her death in 1369. During these years of service, Froissart traveled to Scotland, France, Spain, and Italy. While in England, he presented to the court a verse chronicle of the Battle of Poitiers (1356) and continued to write traditional poetry. Under the patronage of Wenceslas I of Luxembourg, duke of Brabant, Froissart received a position as rector of a small parish from 1373 to 1384. There, he began to formulate his principal literary and historical accomplishment: the four books entitled *Chroniques de France, d'Engleterre, d'Éscose, de Bretaigne, d'Espaigne, d'Italie, de Flandres et d'Alemaigne* (1373-1410; *The Chronycles of Englande, Fraunce, Spayne . . .*, 1523-1525, better known as *Chronicles*).

Froissart contributed to the formation of French historiography that began with the Crusades. In this tradition, the difference between a chronicle and a history depended on the amount of information supplied. Chronicles in general, particularly those following the thirteenth century annalist method developed at the monastery of Saint-Denis, present a simplified narrative, whereas a historical approach demands greater depth and detailed descriptions. (Chroniclers are also called annalists.) Thus, Froissart relied not only on original documents but also on eyewitness accounts and interviews. Once Froissart's reputation was established, members of the aristocracy sought to provide him with the financial resources and protection necessary to gather data. Even though he was a priest, Froissart was at ease in sophisticated society, and *Chronicles* reflects the mannerisms, speech, dress, and value systems that characterize the period.

Chronicles covers significant events in European history from 1326 until 1400. Book 1, completed before 1371, begins with the coronation of Edward III in England and the accession of Philip VI of Valois to the crown of France in 1328, thus setting the stage for the Hundred Years' War (1337-1453). This first volume was later revised to include events up to 1379 and serves as a valuable indicator of Froissart's methodic development as a historian. Book 2, written between 1385 and 1388, recapitulates the events of the last years of the preceding volume, with new information added, and concludes with the peace treaty of Tournai (December, 1385) between Ghent and Philip the Bold, duke of Burgundy.

Book 3, finished in 1392, recites events that had occurred since 1382, but gives a fuller account of them. This volume ends in 1389 with a three-year truce concluded between France and England. In his study of the political events in Portugal between 1383 and 1385 that led to the invasion launched by John of Gaunt, duke of Lancaster, Froissart made considerable use of Portuguese narrative and anecdotal information provided by the Gascon knights who served under Edmund Cambridge, duke of York.

The first fifty chapters of book 4 follow closely on the material of book 3 as Froissart reexamined the political machinery of France under Charles VI. In 1392, a series of truces between England and France was announced, and Froissart took advantage of this opportunity to visit England for three months under the patronage of William, count of Ostrevant, cousin to Richard II. Froissart was well received by Richard, but felt uncomfortable in what he sensed was a highly unstable environment. Thus, book 4 recounts the confusion in England leading to the deposition of Richard in 1399 and his death the following year.

Chronicles does not constitute a formal history of the aristocracy, yet Froissart used a process of selection in order to demonstrate significant acts of gallantry, diplomacy, and heroism. Hence, he overlooked issues that attracted the attention of other chroniclers—administration of estates, enactment of laws, and collection of taxes. Nevertheless, Froissart commented openly on French policy during the reign of Charles V, on the relationship between the French monarchy and the vassals of Brittany and Flanders, and on the Papal schism. These brief personal judgments reveal the techniques of composition and variations found in the different manuscripts of *Chronicles*. The mobility evident in these texts is most likely the result of collaboration with other compilers who may have played a considerable role in the elaboration of certain episodes. Thus, the *Chronicles*' form is derivative of the Arthurian romances, which usually included a fair number of overlapping accounts.

Froissart was an insightful observer of strategic warfare. One of his intentions was to give a faithful account of siege warfare and pitched battles. He commanded a wide military vocabulary, which he used to document changes in fourteenth century combat. He observed that warriors were motivated less by nationalism than by personal honor or monetary gain. One-to-one encounters on horseback no longer had the advantage over the use of well-disciplined archers. Froissart's saga of military exploits stresses individual action, yet his accounts make it clear that in large engagements, the victor was usually the side that managed some degree of coordinated tactics. Froissart's astute analysis of tactical warfare and individual heroics lends extraordinary depth to the narrations of the most famous battles of the fourteenth century.

A portrait of Jean Froissart based on a chalk drawing in the Arras Town Library. (Frederick Ungar Publishing Co.)

Froissart observed the decline of chivalry as the concept of courtesy often degenerated into greed and meaningless pageantry. His description of the tournament held at Smithfield in 1390 under the aegis of Richard II implies that courtesy had become a code of etiquette observed by members of the upper class in dealing with one another; it was rarely associated with the protection of the weak by the strong. Froissart did not openly take sides in the conflicts of knights, although in the evolution of *Chronicles* there are shifts in partisanship from the English to the French, and, in book 4, to the Burgundian side. He consistently chose to accentuate moderation as an ideal, exemplified by the conduct of Philip the Bold. Although Edward the Black Prince was the hero of the Battle of Poitiers, Froissart criticized the massacre of civilians at Limoges (1370), just as he condemned the brutality of Edward III's treatment of the burghers of Calais in 1347. In general, Froissart was concerned with deeds and actions, not with biography. Because of his accomplished literary talent, the portraits of the protagonists of *Chronicles* are imbued with a legendary quality.

Froissart often invoked divine Providence to justify the outcome of events. His philosophical observations reveal a trust in social order controlled by a just prince who watches over the commonweal. His accounts of the Jacquerie movement (a peasants' revolt) in France (1358) and the English Peasants' Revolt of 1381 clearly indicate that urban disintegration was a threat to national stability. Nevertheless, his portrayal of John Ball, the vagrant priest who incited the English revolt, conveys a well-intentioned sympathy for lower-class misery. Froissart's ability to synthesize epic conflicts, like the struggle for dominance in Europe between the Plantagenet and Valois dynasties, gives *Chronicles* its distinctive pedigree. The comparison of the last Crusade, which ended in the defeat of the French at Nicopolis, to the French epic *La Chanson de Roland* (twelfth century; *Song of Roland*, 1880) implies that the history of Europe was irrevocably determined.

SIGNIFICANCE

Froissart often repeated his contention that the purpose of *Chronicles* was to illustrate "les grans merveilles et les beaux faits d'armes" (heroic exploits and military prowess). He accomplished this aim with astonishing regularity despite errors in topology (regional history) and inconsistencies in dating. There was no attempt to outline historical patterns; instead, a strong emphasis on human factors, along with Froissart's objectivity, political acumen, variety, and poetic effects, gives *Chronicles* a dramatic flair that is not always evident in historical works produced by his contemporaries. The scope and dynamism of Froissart's observations and his effort to create a social tableau of fourteenth century culture have contributed to his reputation as a narrative historian who compares favorably with Herodotus.

Chronicles benefited greatly from the advent of the printing press, and in the hundred years after Froissart's death, at least ten editions appeared, including a Latin abridgment in 1537—which was, in turn, translated into English, French, and Dutch. This transmission made the work available to Humanist scholars and aristocratic readers across Europe, who considered it prestigious to own a copy. By the mid-sixteenth century, *Chronicles* emerged as the most widely read account of the first half of the Hundred Years' War.

—*Robert J. Frail*

FURTHER READING

Ainsworth, Peter F. *Jean Froissart and the Fabric of History: Truth, Myth, and Fiction in the "Chroniques."* New York: Oxford University Press, 1991. An impressive, comprehensive account of Froissart's ability to weave an intricate narrative out of such diverse strands of information.

Archambault, Paul. *Seven French Chroniclers: Witnesses to History.* Syracuse, N.Y.: Syracuse University Press, 1974. This work contains an instructive essay on Froissart that places him within the context of the French annalist tradition and delineates the trajectory of French chronicle writing from 1200 to 1500.

Dahmus, Joseph. *Seven Medieval Historians.* Chicago: Nelson-Hall, 1982. A well-researched, fairly comprehensive study of the way in which Froissart conceived of history as a conflict of interests among individuals of prominent rank and prestige. The chapter on Froissart includes generous quotations from *Chronicles.*

De Looze, Laurence. *Pseudo-autobiography in the Fourteenth Century: Juan Ruiz, Guillaume de Machaut, Jean Froissart, and Geoffrey Chaucer.* Gainesville: University Press of Florida, 1997. Looks at Froissart's work in the context of other autobiographical writings of the Middle Ages.

Figg, Kristen M., ed. and trans. *Jean Froissart: An Anthology of Narrative and Lyric Poetry.* New York: Routledge, 2001. Translated selections of Froissart's poetry and prose writings.

Palmer, J. J. N., ed. *Froissart: Historian.* Totowa, N.J.: Boydell Press, 1981. An appraisal of Froissart's technique in light of modern historical scholarship.

Tuchman, Barbara. *A Distant Mirror: The Calamitous Fourteenth Century.* New York: Alfred A. Knopf, 1978. A spirited and kaleidoscopic re-creation of European culture during the Hundred Years' War.

SEE ALSO: c. 700: Bow and Arrow Spread into North America; c. 1100: Rise of Courtly Love; 1305-1417: Avignon Papacy and the Great Schism; 1337-1453: Hundred Years' War.

RELATED ARTICLES in *Great Lives from History: The Middle Ages, 477-1453*: John Ball; Edward III; Jean Froissart; Guillaume de Machaut; Philippa of Hainaut; Richard II; Jean de Venette.

1377
IBN KHALDŪN COMPLETES HIS *MUQADDIMAH*

Ibn Khaldūn's Muqaddimah *is a foundational and stimulating sociological work, a philosophy of history, and a comprehensive description of the societies, cultures, and politics of Muslim North and Northwest Africa.*

LOCALE: North Africa and Northwest Africa
CATEGORIES: Cultural and intellectual history; historiography

KEY FIGURE
Ibn Khaldūn (1332-1406), Arab historian known for his theories on the rise and fall of empires

SUMMARY OF EVENT
Ibn Khaldūn's writings were closely intertwined with his personal experiences and stormy political career. Born the son of a scholarly nobleman in Tunisia, he had the advantage of receiving personal instruction by some of the most eminent teachers of the day.

In addition to memorizing the Qurʾān, he studied rhetoric, mathematics, logic, astronomy, and philosophy. In about 1347, both of his parents died from the Black Death, which devastated much of the Mediterranean region. A few years later, the sultan of Tunis, Ibn Tāfrākīn, appointed the young man as master of the signature, which meant that he helped copy official documents. This position gave him early insight into the inner workings of the government, including the intrigue of court politics.

During Ibn Khaldūn's time, the Maghreb was a prosperous trading region. Politically, however, the region was quite disorderly, with many competing groups—dynastic states, semi-independent towns, and powerful Arab and Berber tribes—fighting constantly for territory and the right to collect taxes. In 1352, when Abū Ziad, the emir of Constantine, went to war with Tunis, Ibn Khaldūn escaped the turmoil by moving westward. Using his family's connections, he settled in Fès, Morocco, where the new sultan, Abū ʿInān Fāris, had been establishing a major center of Muslim scholarship.

In Fès, Ibn Khaldūn continued his education and became personal friends with some of the most outstanding historians and philosophers of the day. In this early period, he wrote a textbook about logic and an abridgment of the rationalist writings of Averroës.

For a short time, Ibn Khaldūn served as the sultan's secretary. In 1357, the sultan, suspecting that Ibn Khaldūn remained loyal to Tunis, had him imprisoned, where he remained until the sultan's death in 1359. While in prison, he was apparently able to spend his time reading and meditating. After he was released, Fès had a series of weak sultans, with military commanders and civilian leaders competing for power and prestige. Ibn Khaldūn participated skillfully in this dangerous game. The new sultan of Morocco, Abū Sālim (r. 1359-1361), recognized his abilities and appointed him secretary of state in charge of law enforcement. However, in less than two years, Abū Sālim was murdered, and Ibn Khaldūn decided to flee the increasingly unstable country.

In 1362, Ibn Khaldūn moved to Granada, which was the only remaining Muslim state in Andalusia (now Spain). Already on good terms with Granada's rulers, he soon acquired a prominent position in the court and even led a diplomatic mission to negotiate a peace settlement with the Christian kingdom of Castile. Ambitious for greater power, he soon accepted an offer to be the governor of Bejaïa (now in northeast Algeria). Within two years, however, the unpopular sultan of Bejaïa was assassinated, and the sultan of Constantine conquered the city. Ibn Khaldūn fled Bejaïa and found refuge with the Dawawida, a powerful Arab tribe.

The following nine years were the most turbulent ones of his career. Entering into a series of temporary alliances with the warring sultans of Tlemcen, Tunis, Constantine, and Fès, his place of residence changed almost every year, and he barely escaped death on several occasions. By establishing very close relations with the Arab tribes of the region, he mediated numerous conflicts and thereby exercised considerable influence as a power broker.

By 1375, having become thoroughly disgusted with the dangers of wars and conflict, Ibn Khaldūn decided to leave politics and devote his energies to historical research and writing. As a result of his active public life, he had acquired a great deal of concrete knowledge about the cultures and political realities of North Africa. Always a contemplative man, he had long been thinking about the reasons for the events that he observed. Thus, he happily accepted an offer to live in a small village with an Arab tribe near what is now Frenda, Algeria. It was here that he completed the first edition of his most celebrated work, *Muqaddimah* (1375-1379; *The Muqaddimah*, 1958). Although conceived originally as the first volume of a larger "universal history" (*Kitāb al-ʿibar*), it became known as an independent book in his own lifetime. He would later modify and make additions to *The Muqaddimah*, but its basic structure and most important ideas appeared in the 1377 edition.

The Muqaddimah begins with a discussion of the purposes and methods of history, which Ibn Khaldūn conceived to be a systematic science dealing with the social organization of humanity's past and present. Although he attempted to analyze social and political institutions as universal phenomena, most of his work was actually about the Maghreb. Some of his views were naturally ethnocentric, for his opportunities to learn about Europe and non-Islamic religions were very limited. He wrote about all components of Maghreb culture, including the sciences, the arts, technology, philosophy, commerce, forms of government, and the different ways that people earned their livelihood.

His sociological analysis emphasized the differences between traditional nomadic societies (which he admired) and the developed urban societies (which he criticized as soft and corrupt). He argued that all societies must be held together by a shared sense of social cohesiveness or group spirit (*ʿaṣabīyah*), which is promoted by the unifying forces of religion, kinship, fear, and perceptions of self-interest.

The Muqaddimah outlined a coherent philosophy of historical change, asserting that the rise and fall of political regimes tends to follow cyclical patterns that can be discovered empirically. Ibn Khaldūn believed that historical outcomes were determined by combinations of variables, including economic conditions, internal rivalries, institutional corruption, the effectiveness of leadership, and the extent of the relevant societies' cohesiveness. Because many of these variables were intangible and impossible to measure, Ibn Khaldūn did not claim that historical analysis would allow dependable predictions of outcomes in specific instances. Contrary to many religious philosophers, moreover, he never affirmed that the course of human history followed a divine plan or moved toward a definite end.

Probably more than any other medieval historian, Ibn Khaldūn searched for natural causes, attempted to be impartial, and applied rigid criticism of his sources. In discussing what caused events, he usually expressed a skeptical and secular point of view, leading some commentators to conclude that he was influenced by rationalist philosophers. Yet, when he wrote about the Qurʾān and Islam, he consistently defended religious orthodoxy and refuted the arguments of the skeptics and rationalists.

Apparently, Ibn Khaldūn did not see any contradiction in the two approaches. He frequently encouraged readers to find refuge in religion and to trust the divine revelation given to Muḥammad. His contemporaries reported that he was a devout Muslim and was firmly committed to austere Sufi doctrines.

The Muqaddimah enhanced his reputation as a scholar. In 1382, he was appointed lecturer at the famous Al-Azhar University in Cairo. While there, he revised *The Muqaddimah* and completed his *Kitāb al-ʿibar*, of which the last two volumes are especially noteworthy; they are considered the most important primary sources for the history of Arabs and Berbers in North Africa.

Ibn Khaldūn also served several terms as the chief Maliki judge of Cairo. In 1400, he accompanied the Egyptian army in an expedition to Syria in order to resist the invasion of the Mongol conqueror, Tamerlane (1336-1405). He had numerous conversations with Tamerlane, including the negotiation of freedom for civilians caught and held in the siege, before returning to Cairo. He completed his autobiography there a few months before dying in 1406.

SIGNIFICANCE

Ibn Khaldūn's enduring fame is primarily due to *The Muqaddimah*. Prior to this innovative work, most historians and chroniclers had been content to describe the facts of political events, dynastic rulers, and military conquests. Ibn Khaldūn emphasized causation, and he was perhaps the first historian to have looked seriously for underlying causes of events in economic forces and the dynamics of social institutions. In addition, he was the first Muslim historian to give a comprehensive description of the various accomplishments of the Islamic world.

He was almost forgotten after his death, but beginning in the sixteenth century, his writings became very popular among Turkish scholars of the Ottoman Empire. In the nineteenth century, his stature increased as European historians and sociologists discovered that he had anticipated many of their theoretical views.

—*Thomas Tandy Lewis*

FURTHER READING

Ahmad, Zaid. *The Epistemology of Ibn Khaldūn*. New York: Routledge, 2003. Analytical approach to Khaldūn's epistemology, with a close examination of chapter 6 of the Muqaddimah, in which Khaldūn sketches his thoughts on the relationship and usefulness of science to human civilization.

Azmeh, Aziz al-. *Ibn Khaldūn: An Essay in Reinterpretation.* 1981. Reprint. New York: Central European University Press, 2003. One of the foremost authorities on Ibn Khaldūn reexamines *The Muqaddimah.* Emphasizes the extent to which his work is a culmination of medieval Muslim literature. Includes a detailed bibliography of works on Ibn Khaldūn in various languages.

Baali, Fuad. *Social Institutions: Ibn Khaldūn's Social Thought.* Lanham, Md.: University Press of America, 1992. A scholarly study of his theories about social institutions, focusing on the similarities between these theories and those of modern sociologists.

Dahmus, Joseph. *Seven Medieval Historians.* Chicago: Nelson-Hall, 1982. Includes an interesting and succinct chapter devoted to Ibn Khaldūn.

Fischel, Walter. *Ibn Khaldūn in Egypt: A Study in Islamic Historiography.* Berkeley: University of California Press, 1967. Concentrates on Ibn Khaldūn's career after 1382 and provides a scholarly and readable analysis of all his historical works.

Ibn Khaldūn. *Ibn Khaldūn and Tamerlane: Their Historic Meeting in Damascus, 1401 A.D.* Translated by Walter J. Fischel. Berkeley: University of California Press, 1952. A short work supplemented with many explanatory remarks and notes. Gives Ibn Khaldūn's account of his meeting with Tamerlane during the siege of Syria.

_______. *The Muqaddimah: An Introduction to History.* Translated by Franz Rosenthal. 3 vols. Princeton, N.J.: Princeton University Press, 1986. The first volume includes the translator's helpful introduction to Ibn Khaldūn's life and works.

Lacoste, Yves. *Ibn Khaldūn: The Birth of History and the Past of the Third World.* Translated by David Macey. London: Verso, 1984. An excellent analysis of Ibn Khaldūn's thought, arguing that his skeptical approach to history did not affect his religious orthodoxy.

Rosenthal, Franz. *Introduction to "The Muqaddimah": An Introduction to History, by Ibn Khaldūn.* Rev. ed. 3 vols. Princeton, N.J.: Princeton University Press, 1967. A complete English translation. Rosenthal introduces the first volume with a long and informative section on the life and work of Ibn Khaldūn and the many factors that might have influenced his views.

Schmidt, Nathaniel. *Ibn Khaldūn: Historian, Sociologist, and Philosopher.* New York: AMS Press, 1967. A fifty-page essay that contains a good summary and many perceptive insights.

SEE ALSO: April or May, 711: Ṭārik Crosses into Spain; 872-973: Publication of the *History of al-Ṭabarī*; c. 950: Court of Córdoba Flourishes in Spain; 972: Building of al-Azhar Mosque; 1031: Caliphate of Córdoba Falls; 1230: Unification of Castile and León; 1271-1295: Travels of Marco Polo; 1324-1325: Mansa Mūsā's Pilgrimage to Mecca Sparks Interest in Mali Empire; 1325-1355: Travels of Ibn Baṭṭūṭah; 1340: Al-ʿUmarī Writes a History of Africa; 1347-1352: Invasion of the Black Death in Europe; 1373-1410: Jean Froissart Compiles His *Chronicles.*

RELATED ARTICLES in *Great Lives from History: The Middle Ages, 477-1453*: Averroës; Jean Froissart; Ibn Baṭṭūṭah; Ibn Khaldūn; al-Idrīsī; Damia al-Kāhina; al-Masʿūdī; Mansa Mūsā; Marco Polo; al-Ṭabarī; Tamerlane; Ṭāriq ibn-Ziyād; Yaqut.

1377-1378
CONDEMNATION OF JOHN WYCLIF

Reformer John Wyclif was condemned for attacking English Church authority and advocating a separation of church and state. A number of theological reforms that he propounded were later adopted by the Protestant reformers of the sixteenth century.

LOCALE: Oxford and London, England
CATEGORIES: Government and politics; religion; literature

KEY FIGURES

John Wyclif (c. 1328-1384), Oxford professor and English ecclesiastical reformer
John of Gaunt (1340-1399), the fourth son of King Edward III and an early and staunch supporter of Wyclif
Simon of Sudbury (d. 1381), archbishop of Canterbury who summoned Wyclif to answer charges at Lambeth Palace in 1378
William of Ockham (c. 1285-1347 or 1349), Oxford philosopher and political thinker whose work strongly influenced Wyclif
Marsilius of Padua (c. 1280-c. 1342), political theoretician who influenced markedly the young Wyclif's conceptions of state and sovereignty

SUMMARY OF EVENT

John Wyclif (sometimes spelled Wycliffe) was an English ecclesiastic and statesman of the first order. His early life, partly spent preparing himself at Oxford for an ecclesiastical career, saw England in the throes of great changes. Everywhere an air of restlessness prevailed as a result of the long and costly Hundred Years' War (1337-1453) with France, to which the Black Death (bubonic plague) added social, physical, and psychological horrors. A rising middle class caused dislocations of society, and the increasingly heavy taxation levied on England by an unsympathetic papal court at Avignon aroused national resentments.

Wyclif, quick in mind, tenacious of memory, and profound in religious sympathies, hungered for security in a cleansed Church. He carried out his campaign for a reformed Church both as an academic and as a popular preacher. He was ordained a priest in 1355 and established himself as a popular preacher. In 1374, the Crown presented him with the rectory of Lutterworth in Leicestershire that would serve as the base of his reform movement until his death. Additionally, however, he continued his academic training and accepted a position a Oxford where he lectured with few interruptions from 1360 to 1381. He served as a member of the famous Good Parliament and early advocated English national resistance to unjust financial claims made by the Papacy. His work, *De civili dominio* (on civil dominion or lordship; 1895-1904), presented the arguments that were used by the Good Parliament to resist papal claims.

While it is extremely difficult to trace the precise course of Wyclif's intellectual maturation and the development of his controversial views, his impact on his contemporaries was so great that he became an intellectual institution among European liberals and reformers by the time of his death in 1384. His initial attacks on the Church focused on the abuse of Church power. Skeptical of the famous Donation of Constantine (exposed as a fraudulent document in 1440), Wyclif was firmly against the Roman clergy possessing either secular property or office. As a close corollary, Wyclif later held that the Church ought not to interfere in the secular affairs of Christians, least of all in the affairs of Christian princes who were themselves ordained by God to their high offices. Finally, Wyclif argued that secular rulers had a moral obligation to restrain the excesses of clergymen who trafficked in secular matters, and supported the right of civil authorities to confiscate the properties of clerics that were improperly attained or legally misused. He was supported in these attacks and received political protection from John of Gaunt who shared his anticlerical views.

Wyclif's criticisms escalated following the Great Schism (1378-1417). The French, angered by the appointment of Urban VI as pope, appointed their own pope, Clement VII, leading to a conflict in Church authority. Angered by the obvious political intrigue in Church politics, Wyclif gradually evolved a series of doctrines that served effectively to undermine the whole structure of the organized Church. In pamphlets and lectures, he began to attack historical papal claims and prerogatives in both the religious and the secular spheres. He questioned the time-honored concept of Petrine supremacy and the power of the pope to excommunicate, and went so far as to call the pope the Antichrist, a claim later to be reiterated by Martin Luther. The sale of indulgences he viewed as fraudulent, and he declared that there could be no justification for the hierarchy within the Church it-

John Wyclif, from a portrait in a 1581 edition of Jean de Laon's Vrais Pourtraits des hommes illustres. (Frederick Ungar Publishing Co.)

self, much less for a differentiation between priest and layman. He also attacked such standard medieval practices as the veneration of relics, communion in one kind for the laity, pilgrimages, confession, penance, and absolution, asserting that each Christian had ultimately to be responsible for his own conduct.

Wyclif sharpened his attack on Church authority by offering sweeping doctrinal claims that stood in opposition to orthodox beliefs. He proclaimed that Scripture alone is the final authority in matters of faith. He likewise declared that each individual stands alone before God and has no need for a priest or Church to act as mediator. One of the most radical views was his denial of transubstantiation, the belief that the bread and wine are transformed into the body and blood of Christ during the celebration of the Eucharist. To popularize his views, he made his most outstanding contribution to popular religion by supporting the translation of the Bible into the developing English vernacular. In 1378, he also supported the commissioning of lay preachers, the Lollards, to preach his doctrines in a simple style to the masses.

That Wyclif was allowed to preach such doctrines at Oxford is a revealing commentary on the dissatisfaction then current in England. Only twice was Wyclif required to testify about his views; and on neither occasion was he permanently silenced. It was obvious that the authorities of Oxford were not willing to interfere with his brilliant lecturing, and the Church was also apparently hesitant to make a formal issue of his views. In 1377, however, Archbishop Simon of Sudbury commanded Wyclif to appear before a special convocation at Saint Paul's, London. Wyclif's supporters of all classes came out in force, and a large crowd of Londoners invaded the hall of convocation to defend him. A near riot resulted, and the proceedings were canceled.

Eventually, the pope took note of his heretical views and formally requested an inquiry into his work. In 1377, Gregory XI addressed letters to the archbishop of Canterbury and other dignitaries, declaring a number of points in Wyclif's writings heretical and demanding that he be silenced. Wyclif was to be arrested and taken before the archbishop of Canterbury and the bishop of London, who were to conduct the inquiry into his revolutionary views. Part of the basis for the attack on Wyclif was his heavy reliance on the work of both William of Ockham, a realist whose views challenged some Church doctrines, and Marsilius of Padua who had seriously attacked the right of the Church to be involved in the affairs of the secular state. For several reasons, the two prelates did not take action against the heretical Oxford don for many months. Perhaps they resented orders from a "schismatic" pope, who was suspected of being a tool of French foreign policy. Perhaps the nation was too preoccupied with the death of Edward III and preparations for the coronation of the new king. It is also possible the Wyclif's support among many of the British intelligentsia of the period made circumspection necessary. In 1378, Wyclif was again summoned by the archbishop to London, but this time to the relative privacy of Lambeth Palace. Word again reached Wyclif's supporters, however, and a noisy crowd quickly gathered outside the gates. The clergy present, wishing to avoid a debacle like the one they had witnessed the year before, merely recommended that Wyclif cease discussing such controversial matters in public.

The year 1381, however, marked the outbreak of the short-lived Peasants' Revolt and a change in Wyclif's fortunes. While Wyclif had no direct role in the revolt, many of those involved had been influenced by Wyclif's

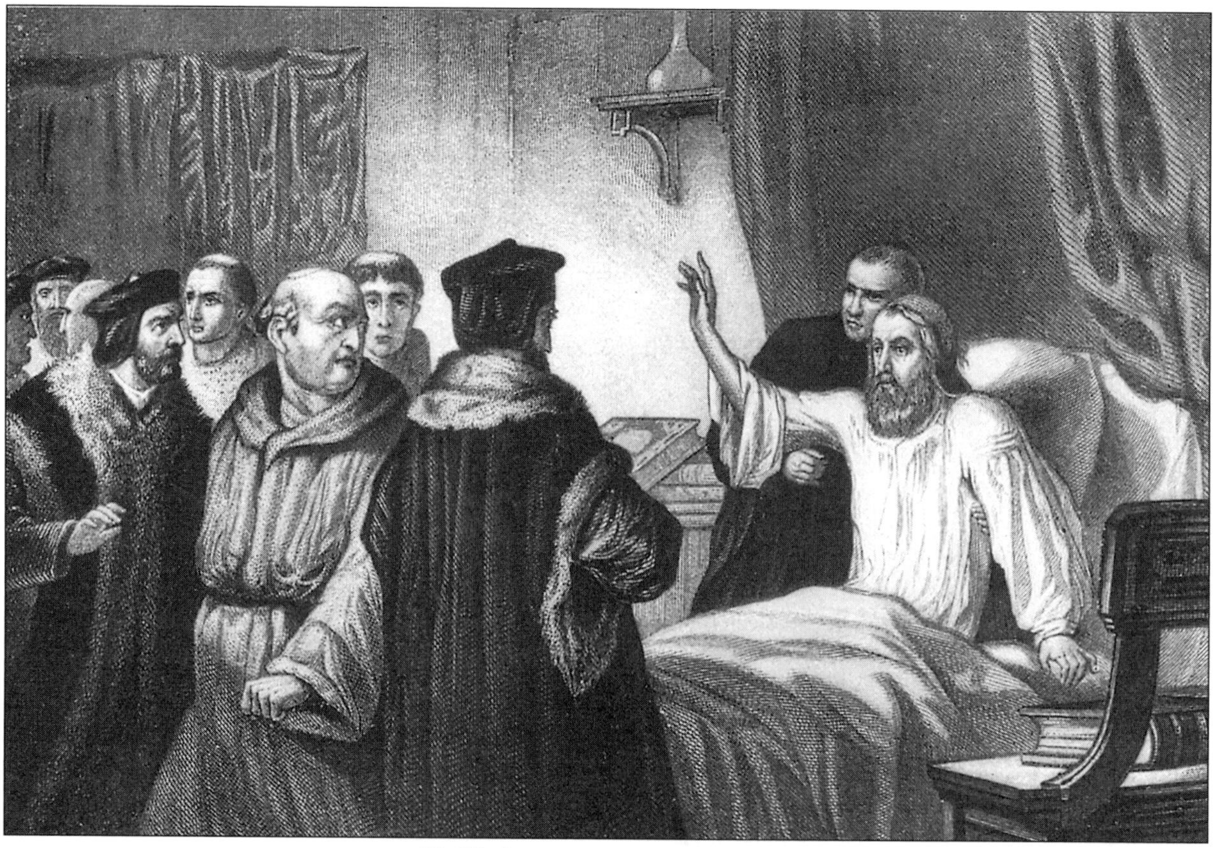

Wyclif's last moments. (F. R. Niglutsch)

attack on Church authority. In response to the revolt, political and religious conservatives banded together, and Wyclif lost much of his royal political support. Wyclif was again summoned by the archbishop to London to the Blackfriar's convent for a hearing. The new archbishop was William of Courtenay, a longtime opponent of Wyclif. Despite continued support from the Oxford faculty for Wyclif as a person, the faculty found it necessary to bow to Church pressure. Although Wyclif was not arrested, he was required to withdraw from Oxford and from public preaching. He retired to Lutterworth, where he engaged in an intense period of pamphlet and treatise writing and from which he continued to direct the Lollard movement. After the Council of Constance (1414-1418) condemned 251 articles of his writings in 1415, Wyclif's body was disinterred, burned, and scattered on unconsecrated ground.

SIGNIFICANCE

Wyclif's movement was nothing short of a revolution in the medieval Church. He greatly influenced Jan Hus in Bohemia, who also spoke out for radical Church reform, and his views merely went underground for a time to reappear later in the Reformation.

—*Carl F. Rohne, updated by Charles L. Kammer III*

FURTHER READING

Hall, Louis Brewer. *The Perilous Vision of John Wyclif.* Chicago: Nelson-Hall, 1983. A comprehensive biography of Wyclif that is grounded solidly in the political and social unrest of the time.

Hudson, Anne. *The Premature Reformation: Wycliffe Texts and Lollard History.* Oxford, England: Clarendon Press, 1988. A comprehensive account of the political and theological views of Wyclif and the Lollards, with a discussion of their influence on the later Reformation.

Hudson, Anne, and Michael Wilks, eds. *From Ockham to Wyclif.* Oxford, England: Blackwell, 1987. Includes essays on Wyclif and locates his work in the context of early Church reformers.

Lahey, Stephen E. *Philosophy and Politics in the Thought*

of John Wyclif. New York: Cambridge University Press, 2003. Part of the Cambridge Studies in Medieval Life and Thought series. Includes a bibliography and index.

Lechler, Gotthard. *John Wycliffe and His English Precursors*. London: Religious Tract Society, 1878. This work remains a standard for all Wyclif research.

Stacey, John. *John Wyclif and Reform*. Philadelphia: Westminster Press, 1964. A good study of Wyclif's influence on Church reform in England and on the later Reformation.

See also: 1305-1417: Avignon Papacy and the Great Schism; c. 1310-1350: William of Ockham Attacks Thomist Ideas; 1347-1352: Invasion of the Black Death in Europe; May-June, 1381: Peasants' Revolt in England; 1414-1418: Council of Constance; July 6, 1415: Martyrdom of Jan Hus; 1440: Donation of Constantine Is Exposed.

Related articles in *Great Lives from History: The Middle Ages, 477-1453*: Edward III; Jan Hus; Margery Kempe; William of Ockham; Thomas à Kempis; Wat Tyler; Lorenzo Valla; John Wyclif; Jan Žižka.

c. 1380
Compilation of the Wise Sayings of Lal Ded

The great female spiritual leader, Lal Ded, preached harmony and love between all people and religions. Her wise sayings laid the foundation for the modern Kashmiri language and remain popular proverbs today.

Locale: Kashmir (now in India)
Categories: Literature; philosophy; religion

Key Figure

Lal Ded (c. 1320-1390), Kashmiri saint, philosopher, mystic, and poet

Summary of Event

Lal Ded (also known as Lalleshwari by Hindus and Lalla Arifa by Muslims) was born into a Brahman family in Puranadhisthana (now Pandrenthan) near the capital city of Srinagar, in Kashmir (now the northernmost province of India), when the region was experiencing a great deal of political and religious upheaval. At an early age, she was tutored in the Sanskrit classics such as the *Bhagavadgītā* (c. 200 B.C.E.-200 C.E.; *The Bhagavad Gita*, 1785) and the Upaniṣads (c. 1000-c. 200 B.C.E.). Early in her second decade of life, she was married to a boy in the village of Padmanpora (now Pampore). She was renamed "Padmavati" by her in-laws. Her mother-in-law mistreated her and tried to starve her by giving her meals consisting of big, round stones covered with a veneer of rice. This story is reflected in the popular Kashmiri proverb: "Whether they killed a large sheep or a small one, Lalla had her round stone."

After about a decade of marriage, Lal left and began her lifelong spiritual quest. Her teacher was Siddha Srikantha, who was known as a scholar of Sanskrit literature as well as a master of yoga. Lal used the vernacular Kashmiri language of her time to engage in dialogues with Muslim mystics, some of whom had come to Kashmir to escape the ravages of Timur, who was plundering large parts of Central Asia and the Middle East. She excelled in her studies of yoga and became a wandering preacher, with little regard for clothing and possessions, as a way of renouncing the world. Although many of her male counterparts in India had become wandering ascetics, it was (and remains) highly unusual for a woman to follow this practice.

Kashmir had for centuries been known as a center of devotion to the Hindu god Śiva. Three centuries before Lal, the famous Shaivite scholar-saint Abhinavagupta had outlined a Tantric devotional practice through which the individual rises to a state of universality through realization of internal energy. However, in the Kashmir of Lal's time, passionate religious practice had become buried in ritual. Lal was able to use the Kashmiri vernacular language, Shaivite symbolism, and the example of her own life to revive general interest in spirituality, which she expanded to embrace the monotheism of the Muslim mystics as well as other Hindu practices.

The revered teacher began to compose *vakhs* (small devotional poems) in the vernacular to convey her teachings, experiences, and feelings. These entered the oral tradition and are still recited and sung today. She used concrete imagery from everyday life to aid in the understanding of how people should proceed in the path to self-realization. This body of literature, which contributed to the development of the Kashmiri language before the extensive Persian influence of subsequent years, is referred to as the Lalla Vakyani. The poems are written as quatrains in which the second and fourth lines (and also usu-

A yogi feeding a peacock. (Hulton|Archive by Getty Images)

ally the first and third lines) rhyme. Their rhythmic quality is very free flowing, with emphasis on the content. As part of Kashmiri repertoire, they are often sung and accompanied in a musical style inspired by Persian tradition.

The *vakhs* of Lal Ded focus on the path to self-realization. In some, she emphasized self-recognition as a path to the divine, identifying the ego as an obstacle to that awareness. She also criticized extreme self-mortification, which she felt was not productive. In spite of her own dramatic forms of renunciation, she advocated that devotees take care of themselves physically so that they would have more time to develop their spirits. She disapproved of idol worship and animal sacrifice, and derided them in her poetry.

There are many anecdotes and stories associated with Lal Ded. Some of them are accounts of miracles, but others illustrate her religious philosophy and her interactions with contemporary religious figures. According to one of these stories, the person who eventually became the Sufi saint Nuru'ddin Shah, known to the Hindus as Nand Rishi, was once ordered to break into a house by his stepbrothers, who were professional thieves. Lal happened to be in the neighborhood and admonished him to seek something of better value, suggesting that he break into the house of God to find something truly great. This statement, consistent with Lal's boldness and disregard for social conventions, captured his imagination and inspired him to meditate in seclusion.

Another story describes a conversation by the river with her guru, Siddha Srikantha. He was curious as to why Lal Ded was scrubbing the outside of an earthen pot instead of the inside. She replied with a question of her own, asking him what good would it do to cleanse the body while the inner self was not pure. The very impracticality of her act was used to reenforce a kind of spiritual symbolism.

Significance

Lal Ded is highly significant in several ways. She is one of South Asia's major women poets and religious figures. She was able to express the esoteric subtleties of yoga and Hindu philosophy in terms of her personal experience, and she delivered them in a vernacular language that made them accessible to the illiterate masses. She was one of the very first in a series of great syncretist mystics—including Kabir and Guru Nanak—who transcended sectarian beliefs, asserting what they saw as the common truths in Islam and Hinduism. She contributed to the development of the Kashmiri language, and she is still revered in Kashmir, where in 1981-1982, a women's hospital in Srinagar was named in her honor.

—*Alice Myers*

FURTHER READING

Kaul, Jayalal. *Lal Ded.* New Delhi, India: Sahitya Akademi, 1973. Scholarly study that covers the life and legend of Lal Ded, the text and content of Lalla Vakyani and translations. There is an extensive bibliography that includes Persian chronicles, manuscripts, and published books.

Kaul, R. N. *Kashmir's Mystic: Poetess Lalla Ded Alias Lalla Arifa.* New Delhi, India: S. Chand, 1999. Discusses her life and legend but focuses on her use of the theory and practice of Kashmir Shaivism and her mystical experience.

Kotru, Nil Kanth. *Lal Ded: Her Life and Sayings.* Kashmir, India: Utpa, 1989. A long introduction discusses her life, but most of the book consists of her translated sayings and extensive notes on the verses.

Odin, Jaishree Kak. *To the Other Shore: Lalla's Life and Poetry.* New Delhi, India: Vitasta, 1999. A scholarly and feminist reappraisal of Lalla. Includes a wide range of Lalla's verses, transcribed and translated from the Kashmiri, a concordance of various Lalla collections, and a bibliography.

Parimoo, B. N. *The Ascent of Self: A Reinterpretation of the Mystical Poetry of Lalla-Ded.* Delhi, India: Motilal Banarsidass, 1978. Based on analyses of her verses, the thesis of the book is that Lal Ded attained yogic perfection.

_______. *Lalleshwari.* New Delhi, India: National Book Trust, 1987. Includes interesting biographical information on her early life, marriage, and miracles, as well as chapters on her verses.

Temple, Sir Richard Carnac. *The Word of Lalla the Prophetess.* Cambridge, England: Cambridge University Press, 1924. This study covers the sources of Lalla's religion, its theory, and doctrine as well as her teaching. Includes a useful glossary and index.

Toshkhani, S. S. *Lal Ded: The Great Kashmiri Saint-Poetess.* New Delhi, India: A. P. H. Publishing, 2002. The papers and proceedings of the national seminar on Lal Ded held on November 12, 2000, in New Delhi. Scholars discuss her spiritual vision and the facts, myths, and legends about her. There is also a section of selected verses.

SEE ALSO: 788-850: Śaṇkara Expounds Advaita Vedānta.

RELATED ARTICLES in *Great Lives from History: The Middle Ages, 477-1453*: Rāmānuja; Śaṅkara.

September 8, 1380
BATTLE OF KULIKOVO

The Battle of Kulikovo marked the decisive defeat of the Mongols by Grand Duke Dmitry Donskoy of Moscow, which dispelled the myth of Mongol invincibility and elevated Dmitry as a legendary hero in Russia.

LOCALE: Tula region of Russia, south of Muscovy (now Moscow)
CATEGORY: Wars, uprisings, and civil unrest

KEY FIGURES

Dmitry Donskoy (1350-1389), grand duke of Moscow, r. 1359-1389

Jogaila (c. 1351-1434), grand prince of Lithuania, later king of Poland as Władysław II Jagiełło, r. 1386-1434

Mamai (d. 1380), Mongol general and leader of western part of the Golden Horde

Oleg (1350-1402), grand prince of Riazan principality

SUMMARY OF EVENT

For much of the thirteenth and fourteenth centuries, Russia was under domination by the Mongols, or Tatars as they were known in Russian. The Mongols had invaded southern Russia in 1237, and by 1241 had succeeded in conquering Kiev. Thus began a long period known as the Tatar yoke, whereby the Mongols maintained exploitive control over the Russian lands. Although the Mongol conquest was savage, the Golden Horde allowed Russian princes to rule the day-to-day affairs of their regions. The Mongol yoke largely took the form of periodic demands for tribute and, less frequently, plunderous raids.

During this time, Muscovy (Moscow) was surpassing Kiev and Novgorod as the preeminent Russian principality. First emerging as a significant principality in the late thirteenth century, Muscovy grew partly as a result of the sycophancy of its princes toward the Golden Horde. In 1327, Muscovy became the residence of the metropolitan (chief religious leader) of the Russian Orthodox

Dmitry Donskoy refuses to pay tribute to the Tatars. (F. R. Niglutsch)

Church, which not only elevated the city's status as a religious capital but also laid the groundwork for the claim of Moscow to be the "Third Rome." During the middle of this important period in Muscovy's (and Russia's) development came the reign of Grand Duke Dmitry Donskoy in the late fourteenth century, setting the stage for an eventual escape from Mongol domination and the consolidation of a Muscovite state.

The Golden Horde was experiencing internecine struggles among its rival khans when Dmitry came to power in Muscovy. One especially powerful khan named Mamai sought to recentralize Mongol authority. At the same time, Mamai was concerned about the growing independence of the Russian princes and particularly about the growing strength of Muscovy. In 1378, Mamai sent a Mongol force under the command of one of his generals, Begich, to Riazan, a principality at the southeastern border of Muscovy. Dmitry interpreted this as a threat to his own domain, and responded by personally leading his troops to head off Begich's advance. A battle ensued between the two forces at the Vozha River on August 11, with Dmitry's troops emerging victorious.

The Mongol defeat in that small battle only served to enrage Mamai, who already had resolved to reimpose on the Russians stricter discipline and extract from them greater tribute. In the months following Begich's defeat, Mamai prepared for a major assault on Muscovy. His decision to personally lead his army into battle ensured that the resulting clash would have epic-heroic aspects. Mamai also secured promises of assistance from the princes of Riazan and Lithuania. Oleg of Riazan felt compelled to acquiesce to Mamai's demand for assistance in order to save his region from yet another assault. Oleg did, however, alert Dmitry to Mamai's planned attack and delayed the deployment of his troops for so long that they failed to meet up with Mamai's army.

Having been alerted to Mamai's plan by Oleg in the summer of 1380, Dmitry prepared for the Mongol attack. Legend has it that Dmitry was blessed by Abbot (later Saint) Sergius of Zagorsk, who also foretold the Mongols' defeat at Dmitry's hand. Dmitry assembled a large force of men from Muscovy, but received little assistance from the other major Russian cities and principalities. He did secure men from other lands, including Lithuanians,

Belorussians, and Ukrainians. As these forces were being assembled, Mamai's emissaries approached Dmitry with a demand for tribute backed by a threat of attack. Dmitry stalled for a time in diplomatic negotiations through his own envoy, but shortly began moving his troops toward the Don River without the knowledge of Mamai. On September 7, they crossed the Don near the point where it was met by the Nepriadva River and set up positions in Kulikovo Pole (Snipes's Field).

Mamai had planned for his army to be joined by Jogaila's Lithuanian forces on September 1. Jogaila's forces were late, however, and Mamai went on toward Moscow without those reinforcements. In the early morning of September 8, Mamai's army entered the Kulikovo Pole from the end opposite Dmitry's forces, as Dmitry had anticipated. As a thick fog obscured the vision of the two armies, however, both sides waited in relative silence for several hours. When the fog lifted, both armies immediately sprang into preparations for battle. True to his somewhat self-styled heroic character, Dmitry chose to ride with his central mounted units as a soldier under the grand prince's banner. Mamai directed his troops' attack from behind the front lines.

The first hours of the battle were favorable for the Mongols, who began compressing the Russian troops against the Don. Yet Dmitry had earlier hidden an elite group of cavalrymen behind his left flank. This ambush force now came into play, taking the Mongols entirely by surprise. The Mongol cavalry panicked and fled the battlefield, driving off and trampling their own infantry. As they had at Vozha two years earlier, Dmitry's forces pursued the fleeing Mongols to seize spoils. Mamai himself managed to escape even before the battle had subsided. Dmitry had fallen unconscious on the battlefield, but survived.

The Russian victory did not owe entirely to Dmitry's tactics and his forces' fighting ability. Certainly the absence of Jogaila's forces contributed to Mamai's defeat. Still a day's ride away when Mamai fled the battlefield, Jogaila chose to turn back rather than face Dmitry's army alone. Dmitry's victory was further diminished by the heavy losses sustained by Russian troops.

SIGNIFICANCE

Dmitry was credited with standing up to the Mongols, halting Mamai's raid, and weakening the Golden Horde. Out of respect for these accomplishments Dmitry became known as Dmitry Donskoy, or Dmitry of the Don. Russians in Muscovy and far beyond looked to Dmitry as a leader of the Russian people against the Tatars, thus marking a step toward an eventual consolidation of the Russian principalities into a national Russian state.

Despite the symbolic power of Dmitry's success at Kulikovo in destroying the myth of Mongol invincibility, Russia would suffer under the Mongol yoke for another century. It was not until 1480 that Ivan III (the Great) of Moscow successfully renounced Russian subordination to the khan. During that century, Kulikovo would remain a source of pride and hope for the Russians, and Dmitry Donskoy became a symbol of Russian strength and resistance to invaders throughout Russian and later Soviet history.

—*Steve D. Boilard*

FURTHER READING

Bogatyrev, Sergei. *The Sovereign and His Counsellors: Ritualised Consultations in Muscovite Political Culture, 1350's-1570's.* Helsinki: Academia Scientiarum Fennica, 2000. An in-depth study of medieval Muscovy's political structure, beginning in the 1350's.

Crummey, Robert O. "Moscow and Its Rivals, 1304-1380." In *The Formation of Muscovy, 1304-1613.* London: Longman, 1987. A discussion of Moscow's conflicts and rivalries in the fourteenth century, culminating in the Battle of Kulikovo.

Halperin, Charles J. *Russia and the Golden Horde.* Bloomington: Indiana University Press, 1985. An analysis of Russia under the Tatar yoke. The Battle of Kulikovo is noted in various parts of the narrative.

Hartog, Leo de. *Russia and the Mongol Yoke: The History of the Russian Principalities and the Golden Horde, 1221-1502.* New York: British Academic Press, 1996. Explores the Mongolian beginnings of the Russian Empire and the Golden Horde. Covers the Mongolian invasion and subsequent dominance of Russia, the rise of Moscow and Lithuania, and more. Genealogy of principal persons, maps, a bibliography, index.

"Moscow's First Successful Challenge of the Mongols, 1380." In *Medieval Russia: A Source Book, 850-1700,* edited by Basil Dmytryshyn. 3d ed. Fort Worth, Tex.: Holt, Rinehart and Winston, 1991. A translated excerpt from a nineteenth century Russian source. This account is heavily biased, with reference, for example, to the "godless Tatars."

Neville, Peter. "The Rise of Muscovy." In *A Traveler's History of Russia and the USSR.* Brooklyn, N.Y.: Interlink, 1990. A brief description of Muscovy's rise to prominence in the thirteenth and fourteenth centuries, focusing on the Russians' efforts to escape the Mongol yoke.

"Orison on the Life and Death of Grand Prince Dmitry Ivanovich." In *Medieval Russia's Epics, Chronicles, and Tales*, edited by Serge A. Zenkovsky. New York: E. P. Dutton, 1974. A highly symbolic and reverent tribute to Dmitry written shortly after his death, with particular focus on his defeat of Mamai. This work conveys the idolization felt by Russians toward Dmitry, and their epic-heroic interpretation of Kulikovo.

Ostrowski, Donald. *Muscovy and the Mongols: Cross-Cultural Influences on the Steppe Frontier, 1304-1589*. New York: Cambridge University Press, 1998. A study of the cultural effects on the Tatars and Muscovites upon one another. Covers both cross-cultural exchanges in which one culture absorbed part of the other and xenophobic reactions in which one culture was shaped by its resistance to the other.

Riasanovsky, Nicholas V. "The Mongols in Russia." In *A History of Russia*. 6th ed. New York: Oxford University Press, 2000. A chapter on the Mongol influence in Russian history. Bibliography, index.

SEE ALSO: 988: Baptism of Vladimir I; 1204: Genghis Khan Founds Mongol Empire; July 15, 1240: Alexander Nevsky Defends Novgorod from Swedish Invaders; 1368: Tibet Gains Independence from Mongols; 1381-1405: Tamerlane's Conquests; July 15, 1410: Battle of Tannenberg.

RELATED ARTICLES in *Great Lives from History: The Middle Ages, 477-1453*: Saint Alexander Nevsky; Genghis Khan; Kublai Khan; Tamerlane; Vladimir I.

May-June, 1381
PEASANTS' REVOLT IN ENGLAND

This popular protest against an oppressive tax consolidated agrarian discontent and eventually brought about the demise of villeinage in England.

LOCALE: Southeastern England
CATEGORIES: Social reform; wars, uprisings, and civil unrest; government and politics

KEY FIGURES

Wat Tyler (d. 1381), chief rebel leader from Maidstone, Kent
Richard II (1367-1400), king of England, r. 1377-1399
Abel Ker (fl. fourteenth century), rebel leader from Erith, Essex
Robert Cave (fl. fourteenth century), rebel leader from Dartford, Kent
John Ball (d. 1381), priest from Blackheath, Kent
Simon of Sudbury (d. 1381), archbishop and chancellor of England
Robert Hales (fl. fourteenth century), treasurer of England

SUMMARY OF EVENT

Wat Tyler (also known as Walter) was the leader of the Peasants' Revolt, which lasted from late May to the end of June, 1381. It was an outcome of the growing conflict between landlords and tenants since the Black Death (bubonic plague) of the midcentury, declining population, and the consequent shortage of laborers. Landowners before the epidemic used to charge high rents for leasing their lands and pay low wages to men eager for a livelihood. After the plague, the scarcity of labor threatening a rise in wages led to the Ordinance of Laborers of 1349 and the Statute of 1351, which limited mobility of labor and pegged wage rates at the 1346 level. These measures provoked agricultural unrest. From 1372, basic food prices fell as a result of improved harvests as well as a declining population in the wake of later outbreaks of plague, but wages did not drop, thus threatening the profit margins of the manorial landlords. Consequently, there were attempts to control wages by law, and these efforts contributed to the outbreak of the Peasants' Revolt in 1381.

Another contributing factor to the revolt was a crisis of confidence in government, generated partly by England's failures in the Hundred Years' War (1337-1453). From the later part of the 1360's through the 1370's, the French commanded greater advantage over the English. English leadership suffered as Edward III was aging with no adult male to succeed him, his two eligible sons having predeceased him. The surviving third son, John of Gaunt, was inexperienced and unpopular. When Edward III died, no regent was appointed for Richard II, the Black Prince's son, who succeeded to the throne in 1377 at the age of ten.

Since 1371, parliament had been disenchanted with clerical incompetence. The clergy was also accused of avoiding taxes. In the Good Parliament of 1376, the Commons meeting at Westminster indicted a number of royal servants for corruption and the accused were tried before the Lords. Although the leader of the Commons, Sir Peter de la Mare, was arrested in the spring parliament of 1377, he was back again as the speaker in autumn, demanding a list of the members of the king's council.

In spite of these signs of uneasiness, throughout 1377 to 1381, Parliament was generous with money grants, though demanding accountability from the government. It granted a poll tax of four shillings per head on all males between the ages of twelve and sixty in the spring of 1377, a double subsidy in autumn, and another poll tax in the spring of 1379. In 1380, a subsidy was granted on condition that the king's continual council be dismissed. The parliament meeting at Northampton in autumn approved a poll tax at the rate of a shilling a head for all males above the age of fifteen. This tax was to be collected in two installments in January and June of 1381. The attempt to collect it led to the Peasants' Revolt of 1381.

WAT TYLER MEETS KING RICHARD

At the time of the Peasants' Revolt, King Richard II was only fourteen years old. As told in the Anonimalle Chronicle, *he nevertheless showed great diplomatic skill in dealing with Tyler, promising to free his men from villeinage. The chronicler contrasts the young king's presence of mind with Tyler's ingratitude:*

[Tyler], in the presence of the king, sent for a flagon of water to rinse his mouth, because of the great heat that he was in, and when it was brought he rinsed his mouth in a very rude and disgusting fashion before the king's face. And then he made them bring him a jug of beer, and drank a great draught, and then, in the presence of the king, climbed on his horse again. At this time a certain valet from Kent . . . said aloud that he knew him for the greatest thief and robber in all Kent. Watt heard these words, and bade him come to him . . . and would have slain him in the king's presence, but because he strove to do so, the mayor of London, William Walworth, reasoned with the said Watt for his violent behavior and despite [malice], done in the king's presence, and arrested him. And because he arrested him, the said Watt stabbed the mayor with his dagger in the stomach. . . . But, as it pleased God, the mayor was wearing armour and took no harm, but like a hardy and vigorous man drew his cutlass, and struck back at the said Watt, and gave him a deep cut . . . mortally wounding him.

Source: From *Anonimalle Chronicle*, translated by C. Oman in *The Great Revolt of 1381* (Oxford, England: Clarendon Press, 1906), quoted in *The Portable Medieval Reader* (New York: Penguin Books, 1977), edited by James Bruce Ross and Mary Martin McLaughlin, pp. 188-191.

The earliest decisive event occurred in Essex on May 30, when about one hundred peasants and fishermen of Fobbing, Corringham, and Stanford refused to pay and stoned the party of collectors headed by the commissioner John Bampton out of Brentwood. On June 2, the chief justice of the common pleas, Robert Belknap, who came with a commission of trailbaston (special judicial power to put down hoodlums), was manhandled and forced to swear never to hold such a session. Although Belknap's life was spared, six of his local aides were killed. The Brentwood murders were followed by a general outbreak of violence throughout the county during the first week of June.

In Kent, rebel gangs under the leadership of Abel Ker of Erith invaded the monastery of Lesnes and incited the men of Dartford, where a baker named Robert Cave led men from the neighboring villages to Rochester. On June 7, at Maidstone, Wat Tyler (also spelled Tegheler and Heller) emerged as the leader of the rebels. An artisan from Dartford, Tyler reportedly was a discharged soldier from the French wars who had become a felon. His military background perhaps helped him command the insurgents, many of whom were probably war veterans. His success in rallying the rebels was no doubt owed also to the fiery sermons of John Ball, a vagrant priest from Blackheath, held at the archbishop's prison, whom he freed.

On June 8-9, the rebellion spread in all directions and fresh recruits from every village between Weald and the Thames estuary joined the horde targeting royal officials, lawyers, and unpopular landlords. They seized as hostages four prominent country gentlemen and made them swear an oath of fealty to "King Richard and the Commons of England." They also broke open all the gaols, releasing the inmates. On June 10, Tyler turned toward Canterbury, sacked the palace of the archbishop and chancellor Simon of Sudbury, and forcibly entered the cathedral to terrorize the monks. Thereafter, the rebels made the Kentish sheriff William Septvans surrender all judicial records and financial rolls that were destroyed.

On the same day a band of rebels from southwest Essex destroyed the properties connected with the treasurer, Sir Robert Hales, and with the sheriff, John Sewell.

On June 13, the rebels from Essex and Kent entered London and destroyed numerous properties, including John of Gaunt's manor of the Savoy. The royal court, besieged in the Tower of London, was forced to negotiate with the rebels. On June 14, at the meeting at Mile End in east London, Richard agreed to abolish villeinage and declared that the rebels could seize those they regarded as traitors and bring them to the king's justice. Consequently, Tyler and his men entered the Tower and beheaded chancellor Sudbury and treasurer Hales. These murders were followed by a massacre of alien workers of the city.

These acts of violence resulted in a decline of the rebel force as many of the insurgents joined in a drinking spree to celebrate their success. Meanwhile mayor William Walworth had organized the city's defense and advised Richard to meet the rebels at Smithfield. Here, on June 15, came mostly Kentish men, their Essex cohorts having departed after the Mile End meeting. Desperate and defensive, Tyler behaved rudely, addressing the king as "brother" and shaking the boy's hands "forcefully and roughly." He demanded that there be only one bishop and one prelate for the whole of England; that the properties of the rest of the clergy be distributed among the people; and that "there should be no . . . serfdom nor villeinage . . . but that all men should be free." He further demanded that "there should be no law except for the Law of Winchester [probably the Statute of Winchester of 1285, which provided for mutilation instead of death of felons] . . . and that no lord should have lordship in future . . . except for the king's own lordship."

Showing remarkable tact and courage, the king promised everything and urged Tyler to go home. The latter, feeling thirsty as a result of the heat, called for beer, drank a great draught in the king's presence, and mounted his horse. At that point, he was recognized by one of the royal valets, Sir John Newentone, to be "the greatest thief and robber in all Kent." As Tyler proceeded to kill his accuser, he was intercepted and wounded by Walworth. Thereupon another king's man, Ralph Standish, delivered the coup de grâce. Yet Tyler did not succumb. He spurred his horse, though only to ride some thirty yards before collapsing from his charge half dead. His followers carried him into the adjoining hospital of Saint Bartholomew from where he was dragged out later by Walworth and beheaded.

SIGNIFICANCE

Tyler's death brought the peasant's rebellion, born as a result of an oppressive series of poll taxes and widespread discontent among the peasantry, to its end, but its memories lingered on to wipe out villeinage from English society in the course of a century.

—*Narasingha P. Sil*

Wat Tyler did not die immediately after receiving the blows from Walworth and Standish; he managed to ride on his horse some thirty yards before collapsing and being carried to Saint Bartholomew's Hospital. (H. Bricher)

FURTHER READING

Dobson, R. B. *The Peasants' Revolt of 1381.* London: Macmillan, 1970. A useful collection and translation of important contemporary chronicles of the revolt together with a masterful introduction.

Dunn, Alastair. *The Great Rising of 1381: The Peasants' Revolt and England's Failed Revolution.* Stroud, Gloucestershire, England: Tempus, 2002. Novelistic rendition of the uprising by a lecturer in medieval history at the University of St. Andrews. Color illustrations, bibliographic references, index.

Fryde, E. B. *Peasants and Landlords in Later Medieval England: c. 1380-c. 1525.* New York: St. Martin's Press, 1996. A social history

of rural England during the century the led up to the Tyler uprising and beyond. Illustrations, bibliographic references, indexes.
Galbraith, V. H. "Thoughts About the Peasants' Revolt." In *The Reign of Richard II*, edited by F. R. H. Du Boulay and Caroline M. Barron. London: Athlone Press, 1971. A valuable study claiming William Parkington, keeper of the king's wardrobe, as the author of the *Anonimalle Chronicle, 1333-1381*, a major eyewitness account of the revolt in London.
Hill, Douglas, comp. *The Peasants' Revolt: A Collection of Contemporary Documents*. 1968. Reprint. Amawalk, N.Y.: Jackdaw, 1998. A study guide accompanies facsimile reproductions of a map, a pamphlet, and transcripts.
Hilton, R. H. *Bond Men Made Free: Medieval Peasant Movements and the English Rising of 1381*. New York: Viking Press, 1973. A persuasive analysis of the nature and origins of this uprising.
Hilton, R. H., and T. H. Aston, eds. *The English Rising of 1381*. New York: Cambridge University Press, 1984. A collection of eight specialized articles on the revolt.
Justice, Steven. *Writing and Rebellion: England in 1381*. Berkeley: University of California Press, 1994. Examines six texts by rebels in the uprising that, the author argues, demonstrate a cohesive insurgent ideology.
Oman, Charles. *The Great Revolt of 1381*. Oxford, England: Clarendon Press, 1906. Reprint. London: Greenhill, 1989. A pioneering study of the revolt.
Valente, Claire. *The Theory and Practice of Revolt in Medieval England*. Burlington, Vt.: Ashgate, 2003. Addresses in its opening chapter the study of revolts and also discusses theories of resistance.

SEE ALSO: 1285: Statute of Winchester; August 1, 1323-August 23, 1328: Peasants' Revolt in Flanders; 1337-1453: Hundred Years' War; 1347-1352: Invasion of the Black Death in Europe; 1373-1410: Jean Froissart Compiles His *Chronicles*; 1453: English Are Driven from France.
RELATED ARTICLES in *Great Lives from History: The Middle Ages, 477-1453*: John Ball; Edward III; Jean Froissart; Richard II; Wat Tyler; John Wyclif.

1381-1405
TAMERLANE'S CONQUESTS

Tamerlane reunited much of the Mongols and became the greatest conqueror since Genghis Khan.

LOCALE: Moghulistan (now part of Kazakhstan and China), Transoxiana (now part of Uzbekistan, Turkmenstan, Afghanistan, and Iran), Armenia and Anatolia (now Turkey), Syria, Iraq, and Georgia
CATEGORIES: Expansion and land acquisition; wars, uprisings, and civil unrest

KEY FIGURE
Tamerlane (Timur; 1336-1405), *seheb caran* and emperor of the Mongols and Turks, r. 1370-1405

SUMMARY OF EVENT
By 1380, Tamerlane had risen from obscurity in the Turko-Mongol world to command first a tribe and then the key to Central Asia—the Ulus Chagatai. The *ulus*, or kingdom, of Chagatai, had as its western nucleus Transoxiana, a principality framed on the north by the Aral Sea and on the south by the Hindu Kush Mountains. On its west and east were the Oxus and the Jaxartes Rivers, and this rectangular dominion linked the trade of China and India with that of the eastern Mediterranean. Transoxiana provided agricultural and pastoral lands for its inhabitants, including some of the best cotton and silk produced anywhere in the world. These lands, with Moghulistan to the east, were the heart of the inheritance of Chagatai, the third son of Genghis Khan.

Tamerlane, unrelated to the great khan or to Chagatai, gained sway over the western *ulus* in the 1360's and established his capital at Samarqand, the greatest city of Central Asia. Although a nomad, he understood the importance of settled allies, and he spent the next four decades courting the agriculturalists, merchants, and village and city peoples. He enlarged, strengthened, and fortified Samarqand, Bukhara, and other cities in the region. He preserved the peace, constructed new markets, and protected the caravans and trade routes. He never claimed to be khan because he knew that he was not a descendent of the family of Genghis Khan. Yet, he did not hesitate to use the tribal assembly, or *kuraltai*, to claim the title of *saheb caran*, "emperor of the age and conqueror of the world."

TAMERLANE'S EMPIRE C. 1400

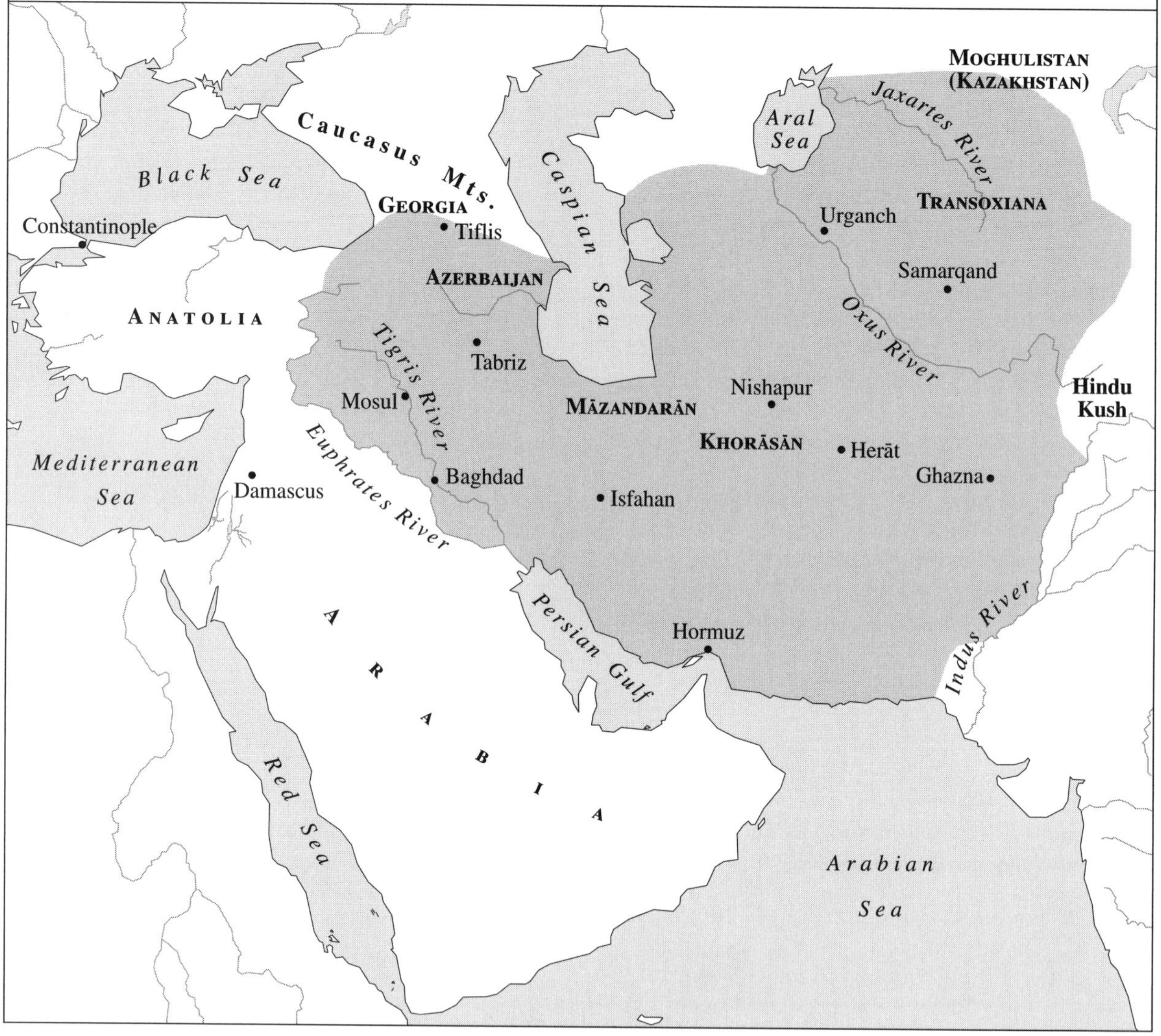

At the same time, he slowly undercut the tribal system by depriving the tribe and its leadership of traditional lands, powers, and warriors. In doing this, he limited the ability of each tribe to act independently, and he established new military units, commanded by family or companions, that he could control in their place. His administrators, unlike his soldiers, were either taken from the settled peoples of Transoxiana or from among those that he conquered. All were, of course, chosen for their loyalty and their dependency on him. Using these vehicles, the lord of Samarqand extracted land and trade taxes to support his campaigns and requisitioned food, fodder, and animals for his armies. He also subdivided the Chagatai into *tumens*, or regions capable of supporting ten thousand soldiers. As in mongol times, the *tumen* was required to furnish soldiers for war, and beginning in 1380, war it would be.

Secure in the Chagatai and with a large and dependable army at his back, the *saheb caran* moved westward against Khorāsān and Māzandarān. Both had originally been part of the *ulus*, and Herāt, the chief city of Khorāsān, had previously sworn loyalty to him. When the city refused to resubmit to his control in 1381, Tamerlane besieged Herāt, demanding the submission of its leaders as well as tribute for his army. These were forthcoming, and he retired, only to return in 1384 when all Khorāsān rose against him. As would become his custom, when a city fell a second time into his hands, he replaced its rulers by those more favorable to his cause. In the case of Herāt, which had broken faith with him, he made it a conspicuous example. The emperor cemented two thousand of its residents while still alive into twin towers in front of the municipality. Then, he devastated the cities of southern Khorāsān, stripping them of their fortifications, before moving north to the Caspian Sea, and secured Māzandarān and part of Azerbaijan, including the critical fortress of Tabrīz.

The capture of Tabrīz, however, created an unforeseen problem and Tamerlane's greatest challenge. The city was formerly a vassal of the khan of the Golden Horde, and the Horde, another of the fourfold divisions of Genghis Khan's inheritance, spanned the Caucasus. The leader of the Horde, Toktamish, was one of Tamerlane's oldest allies and owed his crown to the emperor. Yet, in 1386, the khan broke their treaty, captured Tabrīz, and killed Tamerlane's garrison. Unexpectedly betrayed, Tamerlane seized Tiflis on Toktamish's border. This city, an important preliminary to any attack on the Caucasus, brought the submission of the king of Georgia and other regional leaders, who had previously been allies of the Horde. With Tiflis in hand and the khan seemingly on the defensive, Tamerlane turned his army on southern Iran. Isfahan, which had once been the greatest city of ancient Persia, surrendered but then slaughtered a party of the conqueror's soldiers. The earlier treachery of the khan; the discovery while at Isfahan that Toktamish, the Mongols of Moghulistan, and some of Tamerlane's allies were looting Transoxiana; and the attack on his men were too much to be ignored. Isfahan, even more than Herāt earlier, paid the price. With the exception of only those citizens who had sheltered soldiers, 70,000-100,000 were butchered and their heads stacked into towers as an example. Still, this scarcely disguised the fact that the ruler of Samarqand had been caught off guard again. Unprepared to meet the challenge, Tamerlane hurried north to meet Toktamish.

The emperor first secured the land between the rivers, his homeland. One city, Urganch, which had risen against him, was now completely destroyed and the ground sowed with grain. Others cities were sacked, and Toktamish and the Mongols retreated. While one force checked Toktamish, a second drove deep into Moghulistan in both 1388 and 1389, dispersing enemy concentrations. With this accomplished, Tamerlane assembled a

Tamerlane (Timur) places the Ottoman sultan Bayezid I on public display in 1402. (F. R. Niglutsch)

great force, said to be nearly 200,000 men, at Samarqand and set out to break up the Golden Horde. By the summer of 1391, he had captured the khan's capital, defeated its leader, and killed most of the khan's army. It was Tamerlane's greatest triumph. Now, as many times before, the conqueror's army returned to Samarqand laden with the spoils of war.

The triumph was short-lived. By 1393, the army was back in Azerbaijan and Māzandarān in order to complete the subjugation of the provinces. Those who opposed the emperor fled, enabling him to secure both Baghdad and Mosul. He defeated the Turks of eastern Anatolia, and when Toktamish again challenged him in 1394, he drove the khan much of the way to Moscow, destroying in the process the khan's alliance with that state. The Horde was now effectively broken up, and the khan and his allies ruined.

However, Tamerlane, by now in his sixties, was so weak that he could no longer walk. Unlike in the past, he began to spend more and more time in Samarqand. He rested from 1396 to 1398 before invading India, probably with the intention of securing his southern flank. He conquered northern India and besieged and captured Delhi. Possibly because of his advancing age, the army's morale, or local conditions, the soldiers turned on the prisoners and slaughtered nearly 100,000 people. Whatever the reason, the campaign was quietly abandoned in 1399.

Tamerlane again returned to his conquests. His lieutenants, aware of their leader's failing health and the unreliability of the army, suggested a delay of a year. The emperor would not hear of it. To prove them wrong, he returned to the west and, in a brief campaign, gained Aleppo, Damascus, Armenia, and Anatolia, excluding Constantinople. He defeated the sultan of the Turks and retained him as a captive in his entourage for all to see. With the west, the north, and the south now secure, the army made its way back to Samarqand in 1404.

There, in a leisurely fashion, he summoned his *tumens*, as he had done against Toktamish more than a decade before. After celebrations, drinking, and dancing, preparations were at last begun to conquer the Moghulistan, the heartland of Genghis Khan. First, Tamerlane reviewed the troops, a difficult task considering that he could hardly see and could no longer walk. The soldiers had to pass before him. Then, he issued final instructions to those whom he left behind. In October, 1404, as winter approached, he set out. Three months later, Tamerlane, often called the World Conqueror or the Earth Shaker, died of an intestinal ailment at Otrar on the Jaxartes River. Like Genghis Khan and others before him, he died as he wished, preparing to assume the offensive.

SIGNIFICANCE

Tamerlane, in spite of his lowly beginning and infirmity, became one of the great conquerors of history, ranking with Nebuchadnezzar, Cyrus the Great, Alexander the Great, Attila, Genghis Khan, and Napoleon. As a soldier, he first brought war and then peace and continuity to the region. He was, at times, brutal, particularly to those outside his core territories, and required heavy taxes of his subjects. Still, he brought prosperity and stability during his lifetime.

However, unlike Nebuchadnezzar and Genghis Khan, his reputed mentor, he failed to establish a permanent state. His army and those who performed his administrative duties did so out of personal loyalty and not because they were committed to a Tamerlaneian state. His empire quickly followed him to its grave.

—*Louis P. Towles*

FURTHER READING

Clavijo. *Embassy to Tamerlane, 1403-1404*. New York: Harper, 1928. Possibly the best contemporary source on Tamerlane and his court.

Hookham, Hilda. *Tamburlaine the Conqueror*. London: Hodder, 1962. A readable and most thorough account of his campaigns.

Lamb, Harold. *Tamerlane: The Earth Shaker*. New York: Robert M. McBride, 1928. One of the most popular of the accounts.

Manz, Beatrice. *The Rise and Rule of Tamerlane*. New York: Cambridge, 1999. A thoughtful analysis of the conqueror's work.

Nicolle, David. *The Mongol Warlords*. New York: Firebird, 1990. More informative on the subject of Genghis Khan than on Tamerlane.

Sokol, Edward. *Tamerlane*. Lawrence: Coronado, 1977. The author provides valuable insights into the conquerer's campaigns.

SEE ALSO: 956: Oğhuz Turks Migrate to Transoxiana; 1040-1055: Expansion of the Seljuk Turks; 1204: Genghis Khan Founds Mongol Empire; 1399-1404: Tamerlane Builds the Bibi Khanum Mosque.

RELATED ARTICLES in *Great Lives from History: The Middle Ages, 477-1453*: Alp Arslan; Genghis Khan; Kublai Khan; Osman I; Tamerlane.

1382-1395
REIGN OF STHITIMALLA

Sthitimalla was the greatest ruler of the Malla Dynasty of medieval Nepal. Although his ancestral origins are obscure, he ascended to the Malla throne and secured the kingdom after a long and extremely turbulent period lasting nearly eight decades.

LOCALE: Kathmandu Valley, Nepal
CATEGORY: Government and politics

KEY FIGURES

Ari Malla (d. 1216), founder of the Malla line, r. 1200-1216
Sthitimalla (1354-1395), king of Malla, r. 1382-1395
Rajalladevi (1347-1385), his wife, queen of Malla

SUMMARY OF EVENT

Malla rule began in the Kathmandu Valley at the beginning of the twelfth century when a king named Ari Malla came to the throne after a long transitional period of chaos and strife. The ancestry of the Mallas in Nepal has not been clearly established, but they may have originated in north India. The word *malla* means wrestler and, by extension, one who is able to grapple with adversaries; it has been postulated that its use as a name suggested the strength of the ruler and eventually was employed as the family name for the powerful clan. It is not known if the first Malla ruler acquired the throne through conquest or by some other means, but the beginning of Ari Malla's reign can be dated to October, 1200. By taking various titles as noted in inscriptions, he consolidated a somewhat tentative authority in the region with the Malla seat of power at Bhadgaon (modern Bhaktapur) in the Tripura Palace.

He was followed by his son Abhaya Malla (r. 1216-1255), whose turbulent reign was challenged and subjected to raids from Doyas, a neighboring people, and weakened by natural disasters. In 1255, the country was so devastated by plague and earthquakes that one-third of the population perished. Abhaya's son Jayadeva Malla (r. 1255-1258) also ruled a kingdom made insecure by various disasters and severe internal dissension. Both of Jayadeva's sons died in childhood. Although a number of kings followed throughout the remainder of the thirteenth and much of the fourteenth centuries, Malla rule was insecure and often threatened by external forces. One disaster of great importance was the devastating raid of Sultan Shams-ud-din Ilyas of Bengal in 1345-1346 in which all of the major shrines of the Kathmandu Valley were looted and burned. The years following the raid were a time of terrible upheaval in Nepal. The prestige and power of the monarchy was seriously curtailed, and the population suffered terribly. It was not until an unknown noble named Jayasthiti married a Malla princess and began to assert authority in the Kathmandu Valley that peace and stability gradually were restored to the region.

The lineage of Jayasthiti, later called Sthitimalla, is not clearly known and is debated among scholars. Some have connected him to the line of Harisimha of Tirhut (Mithila, northern Bihar), an Indian kingdom bordering Nepal. Others argue that he was Malla royalty but was connected to a lateral branch of the family. There can be no doubt, however, that his authority on the throne resulted from his marriage in 1355 to an eight-year-old Malla princess named Rajalladevi, the granddaughter of Rudramalla of Bhadgaon (1295-1326), the previous Malla king. Rajalladevi was under the guardianship of her grandmother, the regent Devaladevi (d. 1366). An obscure king named Rajadeva and subsequently his son Arjunadeva (r. 1361-1370) nominally occupied the throne, but the real power seems to have been in the hands of the regent Devaladevi. It is recorded that the regent queen selected the husband of her ward and summoned Sthitimalla from somewhere south of Kathmandu Valley. Little more is certain other than Jayasthiti must have been of noble lineage to warrant the hand of the royal princess.

At first Jayasthiti played a nominal role in the politics of the day. His activities for many years after his marriage are undocumented. By 1372, Sthitimalla had become co-ruler with Arjunadeva. Shortly thereafter, he had Arjunadeva imprisoned and eventually killed. Immediately after the demise of the co-ruler, on September 15, 1382, Sthitimalla officially was crowned king. There were some nobles who opposed his rule, but even those critics in due course succumbed to his intelligent leadership and administration.

Although some may have questioned his tactics in gaining the throne, he nonetheless brought much needed stability to the land after nearly a century of anarchy. Until Sthitimalla's accession to the throne, Nepal had been divided into small independent and often warring kingdoms centering on important towns. The nobles of the autonomous states attempted to influence the politics of the Kathmandu Valley and sought to undermine the country's stability. Certainly the biggest threat was the destabilization of the throne. Sthitimala, however, proved an able politician. Even as co-ruler he had brought under his control the aggressive nobles of the nearby city of Patan, and in 1374, his forces defeated the neighboring kingdoms of Banepa and Pharping, his two most belligerent opponents. He had full control of the country from 1382 until his death in 1395. Not only did Sthitimalla ensure internal peace, but also stability meant that the borders of Nepal were secure from the outside danger of invasion.

Jayasthiti Malla was a visionary ruler who sought to consolidate Nepali society through conquest and legislation. He introduced a program of social reforms, some of which were ceremonial in nature; for example, he determined the requirements of the cremation ceremony for a deceased king, which was to be attended by all subjects. With his advisers, he undertook the first comprehensive codification of law in Nepal that was based largely on the ancient Hindu laws set down by Manu. Traditionally, he is credited with obtaining the help of Brahmans from both north and south India in formulating a code of religious and social conduct. Although the caste system was known in Nepal from as early as the Licchavi Dynasty (fourth-ninth century), the king reformed the caste system in a way that did not stress the traditional four *varnas* (castes), but classified people into sixty-four subcastes. In addition, he laid down detailed guidelines for marriage, dining, maintaining drinking water, and, in fact, all actions and interactions between the various groups. Jayasthiti also standardized weights and measures and introduced laws for the use of pasturelands and water for irrigation as well as for property rights and inheritance. He also introduced a penal code prescribing criminal offences to be punished by fines rather than inhumane treatment and abuse. Many of the laws introduced by Jayasthiti continue to be used today with little modification.

An ardent Hindu, Sthitimalla was a devotee of Viṣṇu (Vishnu), particularly in his avatar as Rama. He is renowned for staging several dramas based on the great Hindu epic, the *Rāmāyaṇa* (c. 550 B.C.E., some material added later; English translation, 1870-1889). He was equally devoted to the god Śiva and was a patron of Śiva's famous temple at Pasupatinath, and he undertook restoration of the sacred site after the Muslim destruction. He also restored the Great Stupa and Svayambunatha, a much-revered Buddhist holy site, after it too suffered ruin at the hands of the Muslims. An even-handed ruler, he maintained peaceful relations with the Buddhists, although he was directly or indirectly responsible for the increasing authority of Hinduism in Nepal.

Jayasthiti was particularly important in the evolution of the cult of the goddess in Nepal. A goddess known as Manesvari had been the patron deity of the earlier Licchavi kings and their successors. By the fourteenth century, a form of the goddess Durga called Taleju, or Taleju Bhavani, had been introduced into the Kathmandu Valley from northern India. The two goddesses, Manesvari and Taleju, fused to form what was to become the focus of a major cult in Nepal. Jayasthiti adopted Taleju as his tutelary goddess, and he inaugurated the use of Taleju's name in the royal edicts and inscriptions. Taleju was the royal divinity, and as such, she has been worshiped by all the kings of Nepal until modern times.

Sthitimalla had three sons: Dharmamalla, Jyotimalla, and Kirtimalla. Many of the plays staged by Sthitimalla were performed as part of the celebration of the births or marriages of his sons. Sthitimalla died in 1395, and his sons ruled jointly and collegially thereafter for many years. Two of the sons died, and leaving Jyotimalla (d. 1428) as the sole ruler of Nepal. Sthitmalla's sons maintained the strong and peaceful kingdom that he had established.

SIGNIFICANCE

King Sthitimalla of Bhadgoan was unquestionably one of the major figures in Nepal's history. He also was the most important king of the Malla line. He began by asserting his rule from the small principality of Bhadgaon but eventually was able to bring under his control the kingdom of Patan and other parts of the Kathmandu Valley. In addition, he exerted considerable control over the rebellious neighboring states of Banepa and Pharping. By curbing the power of the antagonistic and manipulative nobles throughout the region, he was able to bring great stability and prosperity to Nepal. Whatever Sthitimalla's obscure origins, most of the old Nepali aristocracy eventually rallied to his support. His profound and enduring influence is particularly evident in his reformation of the social and legal codes as well as the increased prominence of Hinduism in Nepal. Particularly important were his strong hand in reunification of central Nepal after nearly a century of chaos. In addition, his social reforms have had a lasting impact on Nepal's society and culture.

—*Katherine Anne Harper*

FURTHER READING

Petech, Luciano. *Mediaeval History of Nepal (c. 750-1482).* Rome: Istituto Italiano Per Il Medio Ed Estremo Oriente, 1984. Provides known inscriptions of the period and a reconstruction the very fragmentary medieval period in Nepal. Bibliography.

Regmi, D. R. *Medieval Nepal*. Calcutta, India: Firma K. L. Mukhopadhyay, 1965. A carefully considered reconstruction of the period. The author offers several important interpretations of the remaining fragmentary evidence. Some inscriptions and a bibliography.

Shaha, Rishikesh. *Ancient and Medieval Nepal*. New Delhi, India: Manohar, 1997. An excellent short history that succeeds in clarifying its complex subject matter. Bibliography.

Slusser, Mary Shepherd. *Nepal Mandala: A Cultural Study of the Kathmandu Valley*. Kathmandu, Nepal: Mandala Book Store, 1998r. A superior and interesting work that recounts the fragmentary history of medieval Nepal in minute detail. Bibliography.

SEE ALSO: 1368: Tibet Gains Independence from Mongols; 1381-1405: Tamerlane's Conquests.

c. 1387
CHINESE CREATE THE EIGHT-LEGGED ESSAY

This poetic essay form with its rigid structure of parallelism and character count became the mainstay of the Chinese examination system and was ultimately blamed for stultifying Chinese thought.

LOCALE: China
CATEGORY: Education

KEY FIGURE

Confucius (551-479 B.C.E.), Chinese philosopher whose teachings became the primary subject matter of the imperial civil service examinations

SUMMARY OF EVENT

China has a long history of emphasizing scholarship and excellence in literary achievement, dating back to the earliest roots of Confucian thought. The Confucian principle that the people would be ruled best by the erudite and wise inspired the creation of the Chinese civil service system, which was first developed in the Qin Dynasty (Ch'in; 221-206 B.C.E.). This system involved a series of examinations that selected individuals worthy of government employment. The examinations were intended to be a forum in which the candidates could demonstrate their knowledge of the Confucian classics (works written or compiled by Confucius and his followers) and of history as well as their ability to apply that body of knowledge to general philosophical principles and to specific political issues.

These examinations were exceedingly rigorous and required lengthy periods of preparation, which effectively restricted them to those persons who could afford a lengthy period of nonproductive study, although, in theory, the examinations were open to all. A candidate had to pass through a series of examinations, starting at the local level and progressing to district, provincial, and palace examinations. Examinations were held every three years, and successfully passing them entitled the applicant to several privileges, including exemption from corporal punishment and from certain feudal labor taxes, effectively making the scholars members of the lower gentry. Obtaining a civil service position generally required passing the provincial level exam, which required enough study that it was unlikely for a candidate to pass it before the age of thirty, and the higher levels of examinations that qualified a person for higher-level positions often could not be passed except by elderly and particularly accomplished scholars. The emperor himself might well read and grade the examination essays of candidates for the highest ministerial posts.

As the centuries passed, the prescribed forms in which candidates were expected to phrase their responses to the examinations grew increasingly rigid. This rigidity reached its height after the end of the Mongol occupation around 1387, with the development of the *bagu wen*, or eight-legged essay, which would form the principal mode of composition throughout the Ming (1368-1644) and Qing (Ch'ing; 1644-1911) Dynasties. The term "eight-legged essay" is derived from the eight major parts of the essay: the presentation, amplification, preliminary exposition, initial argument, inceptive paragraphs, middle paragraphs, rear paragraphs, and concluding paragraphs. The fifth through eighth parts were expected to be constructed of two "legs," that is, two antithetical paragraphs in perfect balance. (By contrast, most Western essay formats are tripartite—introduction, body, and conclusion.)

The eight-legged essay was constructed on principles of strict parallelism, to the point that each portion of it was to contain a precise number of characters, and the entirety was expected to follow certain schemes of contrasting tonal patterns when read aloud. A properly written eight-legged essay thus consisted of pairs of columns of characters (Chinese was traditionally written from top to bottom, rather than across the page), in which each paragraph responded to the other, word for word, phrase for phrase, sentence for sentence, all perfectly balanced in both concept and tonal quality. In many ways, the eight-legged essay was more like some of the stricter forms of verse than the prose forms that most Westerners would connect with the term "essay."

Because of this rigid structural requirement, it soon became easier for candidates to concentrate on the outward form of the essay to the exclusion of all content. Writing a proper eight-legged essay was reduced to a game of juggling words, and all pretense of genuinely analyzing the Confucian Classics or relating them to contemporary political issues was lost. The effect of this stylized form of writing examination responses was ultimately the repression of creative thought, and as a result, the officials produced by these examinations lost the ability to respond flexibly to new problems in a changing Chinese society. However intelligent or well-trained the resultant scholars might have been, all their intellectual energies had been so completely trained in the Classics that they became backward-looking, unable to move beyond traditional answers to find solutions to the new problems facing China.

It is possible to express original thought within the rigid form of the eight-legged essay, just as it is within the strict verse form of a sonnet. A true master of the form could use the eight-legged essay to develop creative ideas just as the English bard William Shakespeare wrote sonnets whose literary power has awed readers for centuries. The problem arose because candidates for civil service were more reliably rewarded for strict adherence to outward form over the production of any real content, so much so that the eight-legged essay became an exercise in producing empty verbage. Translations of award-winning examination essays into English often reveal a

Early Ming civil servants (left) addressing their superiors c. 1400. (Hulton|Archive by Getty Images)

shocking lack of content, with words just going around in circles without forming any logical argument. As a result of this misplaced emphasis on form over content, the eight-legged essay became the frequent target of satirists such as Wu Jingzi (Wu Ching-tzu; 1701-1754), whose novel *Ru lin wai shi* (eighteenth century; *The Scholars*, 1957) mocked the endless efforts to write the perfect eight-legged essay.

Significance

The eight-legged essay form became so firmly entrenched in Chinese composition that the term appears even in Communist discourse, although often as a term of opprobrium for a person who mindlessly spouts official catchphrases. Although the eight-legged essay was originally intended to show that scholars had mastered formal organization, it decayed into a test of would-be scholars' ability to plug the appropriate clichés into the proper places. By the nineteenth century, the problem had become so severe that there were strong calls for the abolition of the eight-legged essay as a practice that hindered China's ability to adapt to change and thus reinforced its backwardness. During the Hundred Days Reform of 1898, the eight-legged essay was supposed to be abolished, but its use was not fully set aside until 1901. It can be argued that the modern Chinese university entrance examination is a descendent of the old imperial Chinese civil service examination system.

—*Leigh Husband Kimmel*

Further Reading

Ebrey, Patricia Buckley, ed. *Chinese Civilization and Society: A Sourcebook*. New York: Free Press, 1981. A useful overview on Chinese history from ancient times to the present, including excellent bibliographies to help find more in-depth information.

Elman, Benjamin A. *A Cultural History of Civil Examinations in Late Imperial China*. Berkeley: University of California Press, 2000. An extensive study of the civil examination system as a cultural fixture of imperial China and the social consequences it created.

Lee, Thomas H. C. *Education in Traditional China: A History*. Boston: Brill, 2000. A history of the development of education in ancient China, and of the importance of the imperial civil service examination system in shaping the curriculum and teaching methods.

Mao Zedong. *Oppose the Party "Eight-Legged Essay."* Beijing: Foreign Languages Press, 1960. This speech by the leader of the Chinese Revolution, in which he attacks what he perceives as persistent backwardness, shows how deeply the concept of the eight-legged essay as a fixed form of expression had penetrated into Chinese culture.

Miyazaki, Ichisada. *China's Examination Hell: The Civil Service Examinations of Imperial China*. Translated by Conrad Schirokauer. New Haven, Conn.: Yale University Press, 1982. A study of the form and problems of the civil service examinations as they reached their peak of complexity in the Qing Dynasty but with references to their historical development. The system is specifically compared and contrasted with the modern Japanese experience of "examination hell," the intensive examinations at the end of secondary schooling that can make or break a person's career.

Roberts, J. A. G. *A Concise History of China*. Cambridge, Mass.: Harvard University Press, 1999. A basic overview of Chinese history. Outlines the cultural matrix in which the imperial civil examination and the eight-legged essay developed and how they in turn affected the culture and society.

See also: 606: National University Awards First Doctorate; 868: First Book Printed; 960-1279: Scholar-Official Class Flourishes Under Song Dynasty; 1130: Birth of Zhu Xi; 1368: Establishment of the Ming Dynasty.

Related article in *Great Lives from History: The Middle Ages, 477-1453*: Zhu Xi.

1387-1400
CHAUCER WRITES *THE CANTERBURY TALES*

Chaucer developed English vernacular narrative in The Canterbury Tales, *creating a unique English literary language and bringing to life the experiences of a broad variety of fourteenth century English types.*

LOCALE: England
CATEGORIES: Literature; cultural and intellectual history

KEY FIGURE

Geoffrey Chaucer (c. 1343-1400), English poet and diplomat

SUMMARY OF EVENT

Geoffrey Chaucer's father was a well-to-do wine merchant, whose connections to the court of King Edward III undoubtedly enabled him to place his son in a royal household as a page. In such a position, Chaucer would have imbibed the values of the aristocracy and would have made valuable connections with powerful people. Those connections, along with his native intelligence and talents, led to a long career as a public servant, which included stints as a soldier, diplomat, controller of wool customs for the port of London, justice of the peace, member of Parliament, and clerk of the king's works. It was while on diplomatic missions to Italy that Chaucer came in contact with and was deeply influenced by the literary works of Dante, Petrarch, and Giovanni Boccaccio. In 1399, Chaucer leased a house near Westminster Abbey; when he died the following year, he was buried in the Abbey in a location that would later become known as Poets' Corner.

Although Chaucer's life as an active public servant is relatively well documented, the official records never mention his poetry. Clearly, however, he seems to have written a variety of literary works throughout his adult life. The once-traditional division of his literary career into three successive periods is considered simplistic by modern scholars. If these divisions are not rigidly imposed, however, they do help readers grasp a general movement in the poet's reading interests, which are reflected in his own writing: the French period, when he was influenced by French courtly poetry; the Italian period, when he later discovered and was influenced by Italian literature; and, finally, the English period, in which he synthesized the earlier influences and produced his own unique poetry, specifically representing the English scene in *The Canterbury Tales* (1387-1400).

Chaucer's decision to write poetry in English (later known as Middle English) was by no means inevitable in fourteenth century England. From the time of the Norman Conquest in 1066 right up to Chaucer's lifetime, the prestige language in England was French, the spoken language of royalty and the aristocratic ruling class. Meanwhile, the written language of learning (in the universities), of the church, and of government was Latin. By contrast, English was the unassuming language of the common people. By Chaucer's time, however, the common spoken language, or vernacular, had reasserted itself to the point that, in 1362, Parliament decreed that legal proceedings should be conducted in English instead of French. Thus, Chaucer lived in a period of linguistic transition. He probably would have heard English spoken in his home but would have studied Latin and French at school.

Chaucer's decision to write in English should also be seen in the context of the emerging vernacular literatures in Western Europe. Well before Chaucer's time, sophisticated literature began to be written in the vernacular in France, Italy, and Spain. As noted earlier, Chaucer was especially influenced by artful and complex literary works written in French (for example, *Le Roman de la rose*, thirteenth century; *The Romance of the Rose*, partial translation c. 1370, complete translation 1900) and Italian. Although there were certainly literary works written in English before Chaucer's time, including lyrics and romances, these did not provide him with major literary models, as did continental and Latin writing. One of Chaucer's main contributions was to fashion a literature in English that was capable of the complexities and sophistication of some of his continental and Latin models.

Given the prestige of French language and literature during Chaucer's formative years, it is not unlikely that some of his earliest writing would have been poetry in French imitating French literary styles. In any event, it is clear that Chaucer from early in his writing career successfully adapted into English the styles and subject matters of the French courtly tradition. For Chaucer, it is important to note, such adaptations were not servile renderings of the originals. For example, the French courtly or chivalric love (the idealistic code of romantic love in which the man is a humble supplicant and the lady an impossibly high ideal) is treated by Chaucer in a lighter, often ironic way, which undercuts the courtly sentiment.

In his adaptations from the French, and from Italian

Chaucer's English

One of the enduring attractions of Chaucer's tales is that he wrote them in the English commonly spoken in his day rather than in Latin, the language of scholars and bureaucrats. He showcased his love of English in all its variety through the diverse voices of his pilgrims, from the worthy Knight to the bawdy but worldly-wise Wife of Bath. The beauty of what we now call Middle English is evident in the famous lines that open The Canterbury Tales:

Whan that Aprill with his shoures soote	When April with its sweet showers
The drought of March hath perced to the roote,	Has pierced the drought of March to the root
And bathed every veyne in swich licour	And bathed every vein in the liquor
Of which vertu engendred is the flour;	That engenders flowers
Whan Zephirus eek with his sweete breeth	And when Zephyr with his sweet breath
Inspired hath in every holt and heeth	Has inspired in every grove and heath
The tendre croppes, and the yonge sonne	The young shoots, and the young sun
Hath in the Ram his halve cours yroone,	Has coursed halfway through Aries
And smale foweles maken melodye,	And small birds are making melody
That slepen al the nyght with open ye	That sleep through the night with open eye—
(So priketh hem nature in hir corages);	(So Nature prompts them in their hearts—)
Thanne longen folk to goon on pilgrimages. . . .	That's when folks long to go on pilgrimages. . . .

Source: Middle English from *The Works of Geoffrey Chaucer*, edited by F. N. Robinson (Boston: Houghton Mifflin, 1957), p. 17; translation by Christina J. Moose.

and Latin as well, Chaucer also enriched English literature by integrating into his writing a range of classical allusions, references to philosophical and theological topics, and a host of other subjects—dream-lore, astrology, literary genres. In this way, Chaucer pioneered (created, really) English literature capable of sophistication and intellectual complexity equal to that of his continental models. Again, however, Chaucer did not in this enterprise simply translate literally from one culture to another. He had to create an English idiom that expressed these complexities, and in so doing he succeeded in creating a unique English literary language.

Chaucer also adapted, primarily from the French literary tradition, metrical patterns that have been hugely influential in English literature since his day. In place of the native alliterative verse form (for example, in William Langland's *The Vision of William, Concerning Piers the Plowman*, c. 1362, c. 1377, and c. 1393), Chaucer characteristically looked to and adapted the metrical verse form employed by French poets. Metrical verse provided a set number of syllables and a regular pattern of alternating stressed and unstressed syllables. Some Middle English poetry had been written in metrical verse before Chaucer's time, but it had followed the French octosyllabic model of employing eight syllables per line. Chaucer adapted the greater flexibility of the ten-syllable (decasyllabic) line for English poetry. This resulted in Chaucer's characteristic iambic pentameter line, in which there is an unstressed syllable followed by a stressed syllable (an iambic foot) in a regular pattern in a ten-syllable line: "A Knyght ther was, and that a worthy man."

Chaucer's additional important innovation was to employ these iambic pentameter lines in rhyming couplets, the form seen in the general prologue to *The Canterbury Tales* and the well-known tales from that work. In Chaucer's hands, the pentameter couplets became a remarkably supple form, capable of narrative momentum as well as conversational tone and exchange. The pentameter line became a staple verse form in the English literary tradition, making possible the blank verse later used by William Shakespeare and John Milton, among others.

Another important contribution of Chaucer to English literature is the reflection in his writing of lifelike experience, of credible characters in ordinary circumstances, if not credible actions. Again, Chaucer in this development of verisimilitude is heir to many continental influences, notably the comic realism of the bawdy French fabliaux, which he exploited fully in "The Miller's Tale." Yet when, in the general prologue to *The Canterbury Tales*, he gathered an assorted company of "nine and twenty" pilgrims, representing a wide cross section of fourteenth century English society, in Southwark at the Tabard Inn (which actually existed on the south bank of the Thames in London and would have been a natural starting point

Detail from the illuminated Ellesmere manuscript (c. 1400-1410) of Chaucer's Canterbury Tales *showing the knight and his squire.* (Hulton|Archive by Getty Images)

for pilgrimages to Canterbury), he succeeded in bringing this distinctly English scene to life using the subtle illusions of his art.

Furthermore, in describing the pilgrims, Chaucer made them both representatives of their vocation or "estate" and individuals, who are possessed of unique characteristics and intentions. Through an apparently haphazard description of details about each pilgrim, Chaucer's narrator allowed readers to glimpse the character's internal world of values, although the Chaucerian narrator himself is remarkably free from value judgments about the pilgrims, except for comments of general approval about everyone, including the obvious scoundrels. The result is a complexity of "characterization" and motivation that is central to the English literary tradition.

SIGNIFICANCE

Chaucer's decision to write poetry in English was a watershed event in the English linguistic and literary traditions. His use of English helped to bring prestige to that language, and it demonstrated the fluency and stylistic variety of which the language was capable. In *The Canterbury Tales* in particular, Chaucer contributes important stylistic innovations as well as humanistic values to the development of English literature.

Arguably, Chaucer's most important contribution to the development of vernacular narrative is the way he matched the unique personalities of his pilgrims to the tales they tell on the way to Canterbury. Thus, the knight tells a courtly romance, the miller a bawdy fabliau, the prioress a miracle of the virgin, and so forth. This stylistic enhancement has long been recognized as one of Chaucer's greatest innovations in the vastly influential *Canterbury Tales*.

—*James Flynn*

FURTHER READING

Cooper, Helen. *Oxford Guides to Chaucer: The Canterbury Tales*. New York: Oxford University Press, 1989. Provides detailed introductions to each of the tales. Comprehensive, reliable, and extremely useful as a reference tool.

Donaldson, E. Talbot. *Speaking of Chaucer*. New York: W. W. Norton, 1970. A collection of essays notable for their learning and wit. Many are classics concerning *The Canterbury Tales*.

Finley, William K., and Joseph Rosenblum, eds. *Chaucer Illustrated: Five Hundred Years of the Canterbury Tales in Pictures*. New Castle, Del.: Oak Knoll Press, 2003. An illustrated survey of *The Canterbury Tales* and its reception in the world of art.

Fisher, John H. *The Importance of Chaucer*. Carbondale: Southern Illinois University Press, 1992. A judicious overview of Chaucer's accomplishments and innovations, especially with respect to linguistic matters.

Hirsh, John C. *Chaucer and the Canterbury Tales: A Short Introduction*. Malden, Mass.: Blackwell, 2003. An introduction to Chaucer's tales for the general reader.

Horobin, Simon. *The Language of the Chaucer Tradition*. Rochester, N.Y.: D. S. Brewer, 2003. A discussion of the development of Middle English during Chaucer's time.

Muscatine, Charles. *Chaucer and the French Tradition*. Berkeley: University of California Press, 1957. A landmark critical work that remains useful for its scholarly insights.

Pearsall, Derek. *The Canterbury Tales*. London: Allen &

Unwin, 1985. Insightful critical account of the work, along with some helpful reviews of scholarship.

SEE ALSO: December 29, 1170: Murder of Thomas Becket; c. 1180: Chrétien de Troyes Writes *Perceval*.

RELATED ARTICLES in *Great Lives from History: The Middle Ages, 477-1453*: Saint Thomas Becket; Geoffrey Chaucer; Chrétien de Troyes; Eleanor of Aquitaine; Jean Froissart; Guillaume de Machaut; Vincent of Beauvais.

June 28, 1389
TURKISH CONQUEST OF SERBIA

The Turkish conquest of Serbia heralded the end of Serbia's golden age as a major power in the Balkan Peninsula and the beginning of more than four hundred years of Ottoman occupation and domination of southeast Europe.

LOCALE: Kosovo Plain, Serbia
CATEGORIES: Expansion and land acquisition; wars, uprisings, and civil unrest

KEY FIGURES

Lazar I Hrebeljanovič (c. 1329-1389), prince of Serbia, r. 1371-1389
Stefan Dušan (1308-1355), king of Serbia, r. 1331-1346, emperor of the Serbs and Greeks, r. 1346-1355
Murad I (c. 1326-1389), Ottoman sultan, r. 1360-1389
Stefan Lazarevich (d. 1427), prince of Serbia, r. 1389-1427
Bayezid I (c. 1360-1403), Ottoman sultan, r. 1389-1402
George Brankovich (c. 1374-1456), Serbian despot, 1426-1456
Mehmed II (1432-1481), Ottoman sultan, 1444-1446 and 1451-1481, conqueror of Constantinople
Milica (c. 1335-1405), princess of Serbia, r. 1389
Tvrtko I (c. 1338-1391), king of Bosnia, r. 1353-1391, ally of Lazar I

SUMMARY OF EVENT

The Ottoman Turks conquered Serbia between 1389 and 1459. The conquest began less than a century after the Ottoman Turks first appeared in Europe from their homeland in Asia Minor where they had emerged around 1290 under the leadership of Osman I. In 1345, John Cantacuzenus, one of the claimants to the throne of the shrinking Byzantine Empire, had called on the Turks for military support as mercenaries, but they had seized on the opportunity to extend their domains into southeastern Europe. They captured the city of Gallipoli and under Murad I occupied Byzantine Thrace, clashing for the first time with Slavic kingdoms in the central Balkans.

The condition of these kingdoms made them ripe for conquest by Murad. Serbia, Bosnia, and Bulgaria were racked by the internal strife of rival pretenders, rival religions, rebellious nobles, and oppressed peasants. Under the strong Serbian Nemanjid Dynasty, particularly the Serbian czar of the Serbs and Greeks, Stefan Dušan, the Serbs had extended their state to include Albania, Epirus, Thessaly, Macedonia, and most of the Adriatic and Ionian coasts. The Serbian Orthodox Church, under its patriarchate at Pech, was autocephalous and a center of cultural life. Serbia had a strong economy, with considerable activity in mining, trade, and agriculture. Ostensibly the strongest state in the Balkans at the time of the Turkish arrival in Europe, Serbia had in reality overextended itself; to some of the peoples languishing under Serbian oppression, the Turks appeared as liberators.

In 1365, Murad captured Adrianople and made it the Ottoman capital, a status it retained until the Turkish conquest of Constantinople in the fifteenth century. Having smashed a Christian crusading army of Hungarians, Serbs, Bosnians, and Walachians that had set out to recapture the city, Murad overran western Bulgaria in 1366, forcing its leaders to become his vassals. After disastrously defeating the Serbs in 1371 at the Battle of Marica near Adrianople, the strong Nemanjid Dynasty of the Serbs was at an end, and the throne of Serbia passed to weaker incumbents.

The Ottomans turned their attentions to Anatolia and the dynastic troubles of the Byzantine Empire after 1371. Then they again entered the Balkans, conquering Sofija in Bulgaria and the Byzantine city Salonika (Thessaloniki). Finally, the sultan invaded Serbian Macedonia and the Serbian homeland itself. Murad had left most of Serbia under the rule of its prince, Lazar I Hrebeljanovič, as a vassal. Unwilling to accept Turkish suzerainty, Lazar

Battle on the Kosovo Plain. (F. R. Niglutsch)

I formed an alliance with the king of Bosnia, Tvrtko I, and John Stratsimir of Vidin Bulgaria. While Murad was quieting disorders in Asia Minor, the two Slavic rulers organized a military coalition of Bosnians, Serbs, Croats, Bulgarians, Walachians, and Albanians. In 1388, the coalition won three successive victories over the Turks. Murad, in response to this challenge, hurried back to Europe and on June 28, 1389, inflicted an overwhelming defeat upon the South Slavic and other Balkan forces at Kosovo, although he was assassinated in the course of the battle.

The Battle of Kosovo, because of its dramatic consequences for the entire Balkan Peninsula, and especially for the Serbs, has been the subject of myth and legend since shortly after its occurrence. It is the subject of an oral epic cycle, Prince Lazar I and other combatants have been given semilegendary status, and the region of Kosovo, the site of the battle as well as the location of a number of ancient Serbian monasteries and other monuments, has achieved an importance to the Serbs that goes beyond the merely geographical.

After the decisive Battle of Kosovo, or the Field of Blackbirds, Bayezid I, the new sultan, avenged his father Murad's death by ordering the execution of the captive Lazar I. Princess Milica, Lazar's wife, ruled Serbia until her infant son, Stefan Lazarevich, was of age. She founded several monasteries, became a nun, and assembled around her the widows of men who died at Kosovo.

When Lazar's son and successor, Stefan Lazarevich, was made a tributary vassal of the Ottoman Turks, Serbia's real independence ended, though the ruling dynasty and some measure of limited autonomy were retained. Stefan Lazarevich even took part in later battles on the side of the Turks, although he visited the Byzantine emperor on his return from Bayezid's battle at Ankara in 1402.

In the wake of the Battle of Kosovo, Bayezid managed by 1395 to incorporate eastern Bulgaria, to extend his influence over Walachia, and to begin the first Turkish siege of Constantinople.

The Ottoman Turks continued to strengthen their hold over the Balkans during the fifteenth century. In

1402, Bayezid's devastating defeat at Ankara at the hands of the great Mongol conqueror Tamerlane marked a temporary setback for Ottoman fortunes in Asia Minor, but in Europe, the Turks remained strong, waging war intermittently with the Venetian Republic, Hungary, Serbia, and the Byzantine Empire. When Stefan Lazarevich died without heirs, his nephew George Brankovich became ruler of Serbia, which by this time had the status of a despotate, a title conferred on Stefan Lazarevich by the Byzantine emperor. Brankovich built a new fortified city at Smederovo, on the Danube, in 1430.

With the help of his Hungarian ally János Hunyadi, Brankovich was able to throw off the Turkish yoke in 1444. Yet the Turks more than recovered their losses within a few years, and at a second battle at Kosovo, in 1448, defeated the forces of the Hungarian leader Hunyadi. In the meantime, Murad II had died, and the new sultan, Mehmed II, set about capturing the silver mining town of Novo Brdo, the source of Brankovich's wealth. In 1456, the Serbian despot Brankovich died at Smederovo. Three years later, Mehmed led his troops to the fortress and captured it. This signaled the final defeat of Serbia, which was not to revive as a nation until the nineteenth century. In Europe, the fall of the fortress at Smederovo was considered a disaster equal to the fall of Constantinople, because it signaled the fact that what was called the Turkish menace had the potential of overrunning the entire continent. Under Sultan Mehmed II, the Ottoman Turks finally captured Constantinople in May, 1453, thus terminating the thousand-year-old Byzantine state.

Significance

The definitive Turkish conquest of Serbia in 1459 had several important consequences. It gave the Ottoman Empire control over the entire southern bank of the lower Danube River. Fearing Hungarian attacks, the Turks extended their complete sway over Walachia in 1462, to gain control over most of the northern bank of the lower Danube. The Turkish occupation of Serbia facilitated Mehmed's conquest of Bosnia in 1463 and neighboring Herzegovina by his successor some twenty years later. These Turkish acquisitions had the net effect of transforming Hungary, as Byzantium of old, into an outpost of Christian civilization against the infidels. In its subsequent defeat by the Turks in 1526, Hungary abdicated this mission to neighboring Habsburg Austria. Against the impenetrable walls of Vienna, the Turkish advance was finally shattered toward the end of the seventeenth century, and Turkish power thereafter declined at the hands of Austria, Russia, and the reemerging Balkan states.

—Edward P. Keleher, updated by Gloria Fulton

Further Reading

Cox, John K. *The History of Serbia*. Westport, Conn.: Greenwood Press, 2002. This comprehensive history of the region includes chapters on Serbia's golden age and the Ottoman rule of the Balkans.

Edwards, Lovett. *Yugoslavia*. New York: Hastings House, 1971. Chapters 3 and 4 contain an account of the aftermath of the Kosovo battle as well as cultural history of the region.

Emmert, Thomas A. *Serbian Golgotha: Kosovo, 1389*. New York: Columbia University Press, 1990. A book-length study of the Battle of Kosovo, including the decline of Serbia in the years leading up to the battle, the event itself, the legends to which it gave rise, and the effects of those legends on nineteenth and twentieth century Balkan history.

Fine, John V. A. *The Late Medieval Balkans: A Critical Survey from the Late Twelfth Century to the Ottoman Conquest*. Ann Arbor: University of Michigan Press, 1987. Scholarly work covering the rise of the Serbian state and the Ottoman invasion.

Gerolymatos, André. *The Balkan Wars: Conquest, Revolution, and Retribution from the Ottoman Era to the Twentieth Century and Beyond*. New York: Basic Books, 2002. A history of the region that includes discussion of the Battle of Kosovo and the Ottoman era. Asserts that Balkan wars throughout history have been motivated by the same forces: religion and nationalism.

Singleton, Fred. *A Short History of the Yugoslav Peoples*. New York: Cambridge University Press, 1985. Chapters 3 and 4 cover the Ottoman invasion and occupation of the Yugoslav lands.

Sugar, Peter F. *Southeastern Europe Under Ottoman Rule, 1354-1804*. Seattle: University of Washington Press, 1977. A detailed scholarly treatment of the changes wrought in the Balkans by the introduction of Ottoman rule.

Temperley, Harold W. V. *History of Serbia*. Reprint. New York: AMS Press, 1970. First published in 1917, this historical survey includes in Chapter 6 a detailed discussion of the battle at Kosovo and its importance for the Serbs.

West, Rebecca. *Black Lamb and Grey Falcon: A Journey Through Yugoslavia*. New York: Viking Press, 1943.

A discussion of the Kosovo myth and its importance for the Serbs.

SEE ALSO: 893: Beginning of Bulgaria's Golden Age; 1040-1055: Expansion of the Seljuk Turks; 1077: Seljuk Dynasty Is Founded; 1167: Foundation of the Nemanjid Dynasty; November, 1330: Basarab Defeats the Hungarians; 1442-1456: János Hunyadi Defends Hungary Against the Ottomans; 1444-1446: Albanian Chieftains Unite Under Prince Skanderbeg; May 29, 1453: Fall of Constantinople.

RELATED ARTICLES in *Great Lives from History: The Middle Ages, 477-1453*: János Hunyadi; Mehmed II; Stefan Dušan; Tamerlane.

c. 1392
FOUNDATION OF THE GELUGPA ORDER

The founding of the Gelugpa (Yellow Hat, Geluk-pa, or Dge-lugs-pa) order of Tibetan Buddhism created the basis for the development of lamaist rule across the central Tibetan plateau.

LOCALE: Central Tibetan plateau (now the Tibet Autonomous Region, People's Republic of China)
CATEGORIES: Government and politics; religion

KEY FIGURES

Tsongkhapa (1357-1419), a Tibetan Buddhist scholar, yogi, and monk who founded the Gelugpa order of Tibetan Buddhism

Padmasambhava (Guru Rinpoche; fl. c. eighth century), founder of the Nyingma order of Tibetan Buddhism

Sakya Pandita (1182-1251), a Tibetan monk and scholar

Sonam Gyatso (Bsod-nams-rgya-mtsho;1543-1588), abbot of Drepung monastery, later known as the Third Dalai Lama

SUMMARY OF EVENT

At the start of the fourteenth century, the four major orders (or sects) of Tibetan Buddhism were the Nyingma, Kadam, Kagyu, and Sakya. Each of these had its origins in the florescence and reestablishment of Buddhism on the plateau at the end of the tenth century through the eleventh century. A fifth sect of Buddhism, Bon, often thought to be an amalgam of pre-Buddhist Tibetan religious belief and Buddhism, was also important. Although broadly similar in their content, each order followed its own interpretations of Indian Buddhist thought and, consequently, emphasized different pathways to the achievement of enlightenment, or nirvana.

Each order owed its origins to a charismatic founder. The Nyingma, the earliest order, was founded by a mendicant yogi from India, Padmasambhava, who emphasized the Tantric tradition of Indian Buddhist thought. Although followers of the Nyingma tradition founded the first Tibetan monastery at Samye, most practitioners of this order were often laypeople or adepts, who practiced magic and incorporated shamanic elements into their religious practice. In contrast, the Kadam was founded on the ancient Indian Buddhist cornerstone of the monastic community. This order emphasized rigorous study within the confines of the monastery as the true means by which to achieve enlightenment, and its followers rejected Tantric practice. Because of its lack of appeal and demanding lifestyle, the Kadam order never rose to prominence on the plateau.

The Kagyu and Sakya orders dominated religious life on the plateau from the twelfth to mid-fourteenth centuries, achieving this through spiritual innovation and the formation of alliances with powerful secular patrons. The Kagyu combined asceticism with monastic organization. Hermit monks would travel to sacred caves and meditate, and in time, some of these locales became the seats of major monastic institutions. Five major suborders of Kagyu were founded, each with its primary monastery, and of these, Drigung, Shangpa, and Karma were the most prominent. Each was supported by a local clan or family. Drigung and Shangpa were located in Ü (central Tibet near Lhasa and the Kyichu River), and the Karma became particularly powerful in Kham (now eastern Tibet and western Sichuan) and southeastern Tibet through its alliances with the Chinese court, especially during the thirteenth century.

Sakya was the most powerful of the four orders. Its major center at Sakya was founded in 1073, and the order emphasized the teaching of the so-called New Tantras, to be distinguished from the Old Tantras taught by the Nyingma and Bon. The Sakya emphasized a clerical and monastic form of Buddhism focused on lineages of celibate monks. An influential clan, the K'ön (or Khön) from

Tsang (the area west of the modern Tibetan town of Shigatse) were instrumental in the rise of the Sakya and provided them with land, serfs, and protection.

The appearance of the Mongols on the Tibetan plateau was the primary catalyst for the rise of Sakya power. Genghis Khan made forays into the plateau by 1206 and, at the time, received submission from the leaders of both Shangpa and Sakya. The abbot of Sakya monastery was invited to Mongolia to teach Buddhism, and this provided a considerable boost to Sakya fortunes in Tibet. However, with the death of Genghis Khan in 1227 and the division of his domain between his sons and grandsons, other orders and suborders began to compete for political advantage. A period of uncertainty and conflict followed as orders and their patrons schemed for power.

In 1247, Sakya Pandit, a monk of Kön lineage and recognized as a brilliant scholar and synthesizer of Buddhist doctrine, was sent to the Mongol prince Godan Khan, a grandson of Genghis Khan and overlord of northeastern Tibet, to intercede on the behalf of a group of Tibetan nobles. Sakya Pandit offered Tibetan loyalty in exchange for Mongol protection and control, and although he died in 1251, one of his nephews, P'agpa, became the ruler of Tibet under the sponsorship of Kublai Khan in 1276. This event was of great importance to Tibetan political developments because it formalized the principle of the lama as a head of state. The head abbots of Sakya monastery were given the title of imperial preceptor and ruled for the Mongols through a series of lower level administrators, both clerical and secular. Despite Mongol support, Sakya was unable to maintain its dominance because of a long series of corrupt administrators. By 1354, political and clerical power had shifted eastward toward the Yarlung valley (in eastern Ü), which at the time was controlled by a suborder of Kagyu. This pattern of shifting power between Ü and Tsang was to last for the next three hundred years.

A stupa at the Thame Monestary in Nepal, center for the Gelugpa, or Yellow Hat, Order of Tibetan Buddhism. (Hulton|Archive by Getty Images)

The Gelugpa (translated as "those who follow virtuous works") order was created during this political chaos, about 1392, by the great Tibetan scholar Tsongkhapa. Although often seen as a reforming figure, his great contribution to Tibetan Buddhism was in fact a masterful synthesis of scholarly insight and Tantric thinking. In the *Lamrim Ch'enmo* (fifteenth century; *The Great Treatise on the Stages of the Path of Enlightenment*, 2001) and other works, he argued that reliance on reason and philosophical education in Buddhism was the only real path to enlightenment and that Tantric practice toward that end could be employed only by true masters after long years of study and reflection. This was to be performed not in the hermitage or isolated retreat but instead within the confines of the monastery, where strict discipline and withdrawal from life could be achieved. In this sense, the Gelugpa order was first known as the New Kadam, and over time, many Kadam monasteries were absorbed into the Gelugpa tradition. Very few monks ever reached the highest levels of this rigorous study, although large numbers of monks received basic academic training in this philosophy. In practice, this system led to the creation of rigid hierarchy of power, with a small number of lamas and scholars at the top supported by very large numbers of academic and nonacademic monks. This stood in stark contrast to the much smaller monasteries of the other established orders.

Tsongkhapa founded Ganden monastery near Lhasa in 1409, and his disciples founded Sera (1419), Drepung (1416), and Tashilunpo (1447). These monasteries became the largest in all Tibet, attracting students from the entire plateau and from all orders. The leaders of the Gelugpa understood the potential political power of these large institutions, and began the systematic establishment of other monasteries across the plateau. Given their staffing requirements, they soon began to demand the compulsory recruitment of monks from the local area, a process generally supported by the local secular elites, who saw political advantage in alliance with the Gelugpa. However, resistance from the leaders of Tsang and the Karma suborder, among others, prevented the Gelugpa from exercising control over the entire plateau until the Gelugpa sought foreign patrons. In the mid-sixteenth century, the abbot of Drepung monastery and nominal head of the Gelugpa order, Sonam Gyatso (later known as the Third Dalai Lama, a title bestowed on him by the Mongols), converted the Mongol overlord Altan Khan to Buddhism. This gave the Gelugpa a powerful foreign patron who eventually helped them gain political control of all of Tibet by 1642.

Two Gelugpa (Yellow Hat) Buddhist monks blowing conch shells atop the Dalai Lama's temple in Dharmsala, India. (Hulton|Archive by Getty Images)

SIGNIFICANCE

Although the roots of lamaist control over both religious and secular life on the Tibetan plateau can be traced to the mid-thirteenth century Sakya offer of political submission to the Mongols, it was not until the founding of the Gelugpa order that true political centralization in the hands of a religious elite occurred. Tsongkhapa's reforms led to the creation of a powerful monastic system, and with Mongol support, the Gelugpa were able to crush resistance to their rule and establish what has become known as the lamaist state with its seat in Lhasa. The Mongols created the title Dalai Lama (ocean of wisdom) to refer to the head of the Gelugpa order, and thus the Dalai Lama became the nominal head of the lamaist state. A succession of Dalai Lamas ruled over Tibet until the overthrow of the state following the invasion of Tibet by the People's Republic of China in 1950.

—*Mark Aldenderfer*

FURTHER READING

Mills, Martin A. *Identity, Ritual and State in Tibetan Buddhism: The Foundations of Authority in Gelukpa Monasticism*. Richmond, Va.: Curzon, 2001. A review and analysis of how authority is maintained within the Gelugpa order, with a useful historical overview.

Stein, R. A. *Tibetan Civilization*. Stanford, Calif.: Stanford University Press, 1972. Useful and accessible historical overview of Tibet's history and culture.

Thurman, Robert. *Tsongkhapa's "Speech of Gold in the Essence of True Eloquence": Reason and Enlightenment in the Central Philosophy of Tibet*. Translated with an introduction by Robert Thurman. Princeton, N.J.: Princeton University Press, 1984. A discussion and analysis of Tsongkhapa's thinking and synthesis of philosophy by one of the West's leading scholars of Tibetan Buddhism.

Tucci, Giuseppe. *The Religions of Tibet*. Berkeley: University of California Press, 1988. First published in 1970, this volume provides a masterful and very detailed overview of Tibetan religious thought from its origins to the modern era. It also describes important aspects of ritual practice and its interpretation.

SEE ALSO: 627-650: Reign of Songtsen Gampo; 763: Tibetans Capture Chang'an; 791: Buddhism Becomes Tibetan State Religion; 838-842: Tibetan Empire Dissolves; 1368: Tibet Gains Independence from Mongols.

RELATED ARTICLES in *Great Lives from History: The Middle Ages, 477-1453*: Genghis Khan; Kublai Khan.

July, 1392
ESTABLISHMENT OF THE YI DYNASTY

The Yi Dynasty was founded by the Koryŏ general Yi Sŏng-gye, who first staged a nearly bloodless coup against King U, then forced the abdication of Kongyang, the last king of Koryŏ.

LOCALE: Korean peninsula
CATEGORY: Government and politics

KEY FIGURES

Kublai Khan (1215-1294), Mongol ruler, r. 1260-1294; Yuan Dynasty founder and ruler, r. 1279-1294
King U (d. 1388), king of Koryŏ, r. 1374-1388
Yi Sŏng-gye (T'aejo; 1335-1408), Koryŏ general, later founder and ruler of Yi Dynasty, r. 1392-1398
Chŏng To-chŏn (fl. fourteenth century), neo-Confucian scholar, most influential government official under Yi Sŏng-gye

SUMMARY OF EVENT

The end of the Koryŏ Dynasty (918-1392) was plagued by social disorder and foreign invasions. In the thirteenth century, the increasingly powerful Mongols, nomads from the north central Asian steppe, were destined to make a significant mark on Koryŏ's history. The Mongols swooped down on China and defeated the Jurchen Jin (Chin; 1115-1234) and Southern Sung Dynasties (Song; 1127-1279).

Koryŏ suffered more than a half dozen invasions by the Mongols from 1231 until it finally surrendered in 1259. Koryŏ was able to resist for as long as it did because the court moved to the island of Kanghwa, at the entrance of the Han River. Though but a short distance from the mainland shore, the court's location was nevertheless a major factor, for the Mongols were not familiar with sea warfare. Rather than waging war on the island, the Mongols ravaged the peninsula instead. After Koryŏ's surrender, Kublai Khan invaded Japan twice (1274 and 1281) by way of Korea, forcing Koryŏ to contribute material and troops.

Although thirty years of war with the Mongols brought about the physical destruction of Koryŏ, after Koryŏ's surrender, its court developed a unique relationship with that of the Mongols. In an attempt to bolster his power in court, Koryŏ king Wŏnjong (r. 1260-1274) received Kublai Khan's daughter as consort for his crown prince. Henceforth, several succeeding kings took Mongol princesses as their wives.

After marriage, the crown princes of Koryŏ would stay in the Mongols' Yuan court under hostagelike conditions until it was time to ascend the throne. Although the Koryŏ kings received some protection from the Mongols, the authority of the kingship was severely weakened, and Koryŏ all but lost its independence. The Mongols involved themselves with Koryŏ's internal affairs and made what the Koreans viewed as excessive demands for materials as well as for eunuchs and maids. Also, under the protection of the Yuan court, abuses of power and other official misconduct were rampant. This relationship lasted for more than a hundred years until the end of the Yuan Dynasty (1279-1368).

In the 1350's, Yuan's power waned, and the Mongols were driven back north by the rising Ming Dynasty (1368-1644). During this transitional period, a power vacuum emerged in the northeastern part of Korea and in Manchuria, which presented a window of opportunity for Koryŏ. King Kongmin (r. 1351-1374) seized the opportunity by retaking the northeastern territory of Hamkyŏng Province (1356). Yi Chach'un, the father of Yi Sŏng-gye who would later found the Yi Dynasty, led the expedition. For his valor, the king rewarded Yi Chach'un and appointed him general for the region. Following in his father's footsteps, Yi Sŏng-gye distinguished himself in many military campaigns.

Koryŏ's border troubles not only involved China but Japan as well. Attacks by Japanese pirates were not new, but during the late Koryŏ period, especially beginning in 1350, their depredation amounted to a national crisis. Half-naked and armed with long swords, these marauders would land at any time and any place along the coastline of the peninsula, pillaging and burning coastal villages and carrying away their booty. According to historian Wanne J. Joe, during King U's reign alone, 378 incursions took place. Here, too, Yi Chach'un, and later, Yi Sŏng-gye, played important roles in repelling the Japanese.

MAJOR RULERS OF THE YI DYNASTY, 1392-1608

Ruler	*Reign*
1392-1398	Yi T'aejo
1398-1400	Chŏngjong
1400-1418	T'aejong
1418-1450	Sejong
1450-1452	Munjong
1452-1455	Tanjong
1455-1468	Sejo
1468-1469	Yejong
1469-1494	Sŏngjong
1494-1506	Yŏnsan Gun
1506-1544	Chungjong
1544-1545	Injong
1546-1567	Myŏngjong
1567-1608	Sŏnjo

Note: This table ends with the Japanese invasions of Korea (1592-1598), although the Yi Dynasty lasted until 1910.

Yi Sŏng-gye distinguished himself in battles repulsing the Red Head Robbers, one of the Chinese groups from the north who were then ravaging the country, even occupying the capital, Songdo (Songak), in 1360. In 1370, Yi captured the Liaotung region of south Manchuria from the retreating Mongols, albeit for a short time, fulfilling Koryŏ's long cherished desire to retake what had once been part of Koguryŏ, as Koryŏ claimed to be the legitimate heir to that kingdom. Only a few generations earlier, this upstart Yi family from Chŏlla Province had moved to the Hamkyŏng Province in search of better opportunities. Eventually, Yi Sŏng-gye became one of the most renowned generals of the era.

In February, 1388, the Ming Chinese threatened to retake the Hamkyŏng Province area by establishing a Ch'ollyŏng commandery and arguing that the area had earlier belonged to the Mongols and therefore must be a part of the Liaotung region, which was then under Ming control. Koryŏ's supreme commander, general Ch'oe Yŏng, responded by mobilizing an army to attack the Liaotung peninsula once again. However, there was dissension within the ranks. General Yi Sŏng-gye, one of the two deputy commanders who were to direct the campaign under Ch'oe Yŏng, objected to the campaign, despite having successfully attacked the same region in the past. One of the main points of his objections was characteristically Confucian. He said, "It is wrong for a small country to attack a large one."

General Yi set out reluctantly. However, in the middle of the campaign, defying King U's order to march on to Liaotung, he turned his army around at Wihwa Island on May 22, 1388, crossed the Yalu River again, and marched back to the capital. He overthrew King U and exiled his superior, General Ch'oe Yŏng, both of whom he later killed. The withdrawal from Wihwa signaled the beginning of the end of Koryŏ as Yi Sŏng-gye now controlled the military. Referring to the botched campaign of Manchuria, the historian Joe wrote, "The evil that defeated this heroic venture was the enemy within, as represented by Yi Sŏng-gye." Yi Sŏng-gye adopted the old name of Chosŏn for his state, known as the Yi Chosŏn Dynasty. Two years later, he moved the capital from Kaesŏng (former Songdo) to Hanyang (present-day Seoul).

Although Koryŏ had been firmly Buddhist, Yi T'aejo (posthumous title) filled his government with followers of the Chinese philosopher Confucius, most notably Chŏng To-chŏn, Yi's deputy commander and a neo-Confucian scholar who later formulated many policies in the fields of government, law, and religion. Many decrees were issued that, over time, effectively made Confucianism the dominant philosophy in the kingdom. One of the central tenets of Confucianism is the importance of the five cardinal relationships: ruler and subject, father and son, husband and wife, brother and brother, and friend and friend. The unconditional loyalty and respect that Confucianism prescribes within these relationships have long been characteristic of the Korean people.

Significance

Yi Sŏng-gye succeeded in ridding Koryŏ of many foreign invaders and was the forefather of a new line of monarchs that lasted more than five hundred years and had a lasting impact on Korean society. He established Seoul as the capital of the state. The rise of Confucianism greatly affected the way the Korean people view their relationship to their government and to each other. During the reign of Yi Sŏng-gye's grandson King Sejong (r. 1418-1450), Korea enjoyed some of its most peaceful and prosperous years, including the invention of the Korean alphabet, *hasngŭl*, which because of its scientific logic and simplicity is so easy to learn that illiteracy in Korea is nearly nonexistent.

—*Hwa-Soon Choi Meyer*

Further Reading

Duncan, John B. *The Origins of the Chosŏn Dynasty.* Seattle: University of Washington Press, 2000. Deals with the question of the main cause of the dynastic change from Koryŏ to Yi.

Hulbert, Homer B. *Hulbert's History of Korea.* 2 vols. London: Routledge & Kegan Paul, 1962. Presents the most detailed account of Korean history from antiquity to 1904 in the style of annals. However, some of Hulbert's accounts disagree with from more recent works.

Joe, Wanne J. *Traditional Korea: A Cultural History.* Vol. 1 in *A History of Korean Civilization.* Seoul: Chung-ang University Press, 1972. Gives a comprehensive and well-balanced view of Korean history.

Lee, Ki-baik. *A New History of Korea.* Translated by Edward W. Wagner. Cambridge, Mass.: Harvard University Press, 1984. A concise overview of Korean history. The "Dynastic Lineages" section is especially helpful.

Rutt, Richard. *James Scarth Gale and His History of the Korean People.* 2d ed. Seoul: The Royal Asiatic Society, Korea Branch, 1983. Based on the history written by James Gale, a contemporary of historian Homer B. Hulbert. Gale and Hulbert were born a month apart and served together at the court of the emperor Kojong (r. 1864-1907) at the end of the Yi Dynasty.

See also: 668-935: Silla Unification of Korea; 918-936: Foundation of the Koryŏ Dynasty; 958-1076: Koreans Adopt the Tang Civil Service Model; 1145: Kim Pu-sik Writes *Samguk Sagi*; 1196-1258: Ch'oe Family Takes Power in Korea.

Related article in *Great Lives from History: The Middle Ages, 477-1453*: Wang Kŏn.

1397
PUBLICATION OF THE LAWS OF GREAT MING

Hongwu, the first emperor of the Ming Dynasty, published the Great Ming Code, a set of laws designed to help the emperor centralize power within the dynasty and create an authoritarian government that would control people's everyday lives.

LOCALE: China
CATEGORY: Laws, acts, and legal history

KEY FIGURE
Hongwu (Hung-wu or Zhu Yuanzhang; 1328-1398), first emperor of Ming Dynasty, r. 1368-1398

SUMMARY OF EVENT

The publication of the Great Ming Code in 1397 was the culmination of the work of the first Ming emperor, Hongwu (born Zhu Yuanzhang, or Chu Yüan-chang), and a variety of legal advisers who were ordered to transform the Chinese code into a more modern one fit for a new dynasty and empire. The story of the Great Ming Code can be found in the history of its development.

The latter half of the fourteenth century saw a dramatic change in Chinese politics. Since 1260, when Kublai Khan defeated the Chinese, the Mongols had ruled China. The Yuan Dynasty (1279-1368) was a Mongol dynasty, although it ostensibly was a continuation of the Chinese dynasty system. By 1360, however, the Mongol hold over the country had begun to weaken, and regional leaders in China began to challenge the Mongols' power. One of the those challenges came from a Buddhist monk, Zhu Yuanzhang (Chu Yüan-chang), who was able to rally Chinese support around a military insurgency against the Yuan Dynasty. By 1368, Zhu had led the Chinese people to sweep the Mongols from much of China.

Zhu, who would reign as Hongwu, began to create a governmental system that would become the Ming Dynasty. He reworked the Chinese legal and political systems while acquiring a reputation as a brutal leader who would allow no one to slow his reforms. His Great Ming Code became the basis for the Chinese imperial legal system and was used for the next five centuries.

The century-long Mongol conquest and occupation had caused Chinese law to dwindle in importance as the Mongol political leadership placed priority on fulfilling its own needs. The basis of Chinese law before the thirteenth century had been the code drawn up during the Tang Dynasty (T'ang; 618-907). After gaining power, Hongwu immediately sought to revive the Tang code. He commissioned between twenty and one hundred legal scholars to search through the Tang code and rewrite it by removing out-of-date portions and composing new ones. The first revision of the Tang code was presented to Hongwu in 1373. The code had been reduced to 285 articles and 145 statutes and was presented for the emperor's approval. The final publication of the Great Ming Code was made in 1397, at which time, the emperor approved it.

Known as the Daming (Ta-ming), the code was divided into seven sections, some adapted from the Tang code, and others added to it. The first section was general, outlining the principles to be used throughout the code. These principles included the method of interpretation of the code and the process by which it would be used in court cases. The second section was civil and applied to the different parts of the government. It included the powers of each ministry and the authority and restrictions placed on government officials. Judicial power was also covered under the civil section, and restrictions were placed on judges when using the code.

The third section, the fiscal codes, focused on land taxes, the main source of revenue for the Chinese government. The fiscal section also established the government's authority to take a census. The fourth section, involving rituals, set out the social and religious requirements that people would have to perform to satisfy their ritual duties and outlined the requirements for marriage. The fifth part of the code dealt with the military. This section was specific in that it outlined how the palace stables were to be kept, the duties of imperial couriers, and the security that was to be provided for the palace. The sixth portion of the code involved public works. One of the areas regulated was the construction of dikes along the many rivers of China, a critical action because much of the population lived along the rivers and uncontrolled seasonal flooding could wipe out much of Chinese civilization. This portion also listed the method of constructing and inspecting public buildings. The seventh portion, the criminal code, identified crimes and the punishments associated with them.

For a country populated by tens of millions, the Daming was surprisingly short, leaving broad interpretive powers to judges and the emperor. Courts and their judges had the power of interpretation, known as the

Dagao. Cases decided by judges were used as guides for future disputes, not unlike the procedure in a common law system. The emperor also retained the power to issue edicts that would amend the Daming: He could replace the old law, *lu*, found in the code, with new law, *li*. This became an important tool as Hongwu found his attempts to centralize power were restricted by portions of the code. Under the Daming, all government officials were prohibited from abusing their official positions or from administering the horrific punishments that had been part of previous dynasties and the Mongol occupation. However, as Hongwu began to consolidate power, he was forced to issue new *li* so that he could remove high officials who displeased him.

The code also included a reworking of the political system begun by Hongwu with a series of purges. The emperor emptied his ministries of many officials and combined them into three major centers of power. The three ministries—military, finance, and public works—controlled the lives of most Chinese and held them within a rigidly defined status in society. The military ministry forced its members and families to live along the frontiers where the greatest military threat existed. All members of the military had fathers in the military, and their children would be required to serve. The finance ministry workers were all located within the large cities so that they could carry out most government duties. The children of the men who worked for the ministry would be expected to work for the ministry as well. The public works committee controlled the countryside and the largest portion of the Chinese community, the peasants who worked the farms.

The final publication of the Great Ming Code also included various edicts handed down by Hongwu during his reign. These included regulations regarding mourning and funerals. The emperor regulated the rituals, both political and religious, to be performed by the citizens. There were regulations concerning the nobility, education, and university training. The code exhorted the Chinese to follow the Confucian ideals of education and of staying within one's proper social grouping.

Hongwu's death in 1398 is seen as the beginning the Ming Dynasty succession. With the Great Ming Code, he had provided his successors with the tools for maintaining the dynasty and protecting Chinese civilization for centuries to come.

SIGNIFICANCE

The development of the Great Ming Code created the conditions for the establishment of an authoritarian system of government in China. The code became the method by which Hongwu and his successors were able to control the Chinese people and form an empire in which the everyday lives of the people were dictated by the central government. The code, with its additions and edicts provided by the emperor, detailed everything from proper mourning at funerals to marriage rituals and the careers that people would choose. The code further strengthened the rule of the emperor, as Hongwu used it to mandate where his citizens would live and how they would work. The Great Ming Code became the legal basis for the Chinese empire into the twentieth century.

—*Douglas Clouatre*

FURTHER READING

Brook, Timothy. *The Confusions of Pleasure: Commerce and Culture in Ming China*. Berkeley: University of California Press, 1998. This works examines how Ming law was used to restrict both the commercial and cultural activities of the Chinese people throughout the entire dynasty.

Chan, Albert. *The Glory and Fall of the Ming Dynasty*. Norman: University of Oklahoma Press, 1992. Focuses specifically on the political side of the Ming Dynasty, its emperors and governing system and how that eventually led to its disintegration.

Johnson, Wallace. *The Tang Code*. Princeton, N.J.: Princeton University Press, 1989. A detailed analysis of the early law code of the Chinese empire and how the legal process in this code was used by later dynasties, including the Ming.

Mote, F. W. *Imperial China 900-1800*. Cambridge, Mass.: Harvard University Press, 1999. A wide-ranging book that deals with the several dynasties that ruled China from the medieval period into the modern era.

SEE ALSO: 1115: Foundation of the Jin Dynasty; 1153: Jin Move Their Capital to Beijing; 1368: Establishment of the Ming Dynasty; c. 1387: Chinese Create the Eight-Legged Essay; 1403-1407: *Yonglo Dadian* Encyclopedia Is Compiled.

RELATED ARTICLE in *Great Lives from History: The Middle Ages, 477-1453*: Yonglo.

June 17, 1397
KALMAR UNION IS FORMED

The Kalmar Union was formed through the diplomatic skills of Margaret I, bringing Sweden, Norway, and Denmark under the rule of a single sovereign in a union that lasted more than a century.

LOCALE: Sweden, Norway, and Denmark
CATEGORIES: Government and politics; trade and commerce; diplomacy and international relations; laws, acts, and legal history

KEY FIGURES

Albert (1340-1412), king of Sweden, r. 1364-1389
Margaret of Denmark, Norway, and Sweden (1353-1412), regent of Denmark, 1376-1412, regent of Norway, 1380-1410, and regent of Sweden, 1389-1412
Erik of Pomerania (c. 1381-1459), king of Denmark, Norway, and Sweden, r. 1397-1439
Christian II (1481-1559), king of Denmark and Norway, r. 1513-1523, and king of Sweden, r. 1520-1523
Gustav I Vasa (c. 1496-1560), king of Sweden, r. 1523-1560

SUMMARY OF EVENT

During the fourteenth century, the three Scandinavian nations of Denmark, Norway, and Sweden were involved in numerous complex struggles for political power. In addition to wars among the three nations and conflicts between the nations of Scandinavia and the Hanseatic League (a powerful federation of German trading towns), there were internal struggles as well.

During one of these struggles, the nobles of Sweden, in alliance with the Hanseatic League, invited Albert of Mecklenburg, a German prince, to drive out the current king of Sweden, Magnus II, who was his uncle. Albert invaded in 1363, taking the title of king. He defeated the forces of Magnus II in 1365 and took him prisoner. Magnus II was released in 1371 in exchange for recognizing Albert as king.

The reign of Albert was a constant struggle with the Swedish nobles, who held most of the real power. The most powerful of these nobles was Bo Jonsson Grip, who owned large amounts of land in Sweden, including all of Finland (which was at the time a part of Sweden). When Grip died in 1386, Albert attempted to seize his estates, and this act caused the nobles to unite against him.

Meanwhile, the future ruler of all three nations was consolidating her own power. The daughter of King Valdemar IV of Denmark, Margaret I married King Håkon VI of Norway, the son of Magnus II, in 1363, when she was ten years old. During the reign of Albert, Håkon VI lost his claim to the throne of Sweden but retained Norway.

In 1370, Margaret gave birth to a son, Olaf. When Valdemar IV died in 1375, she was able to convince the nobles of Denmark to elect Olaf king. Because he was still a child, Margaret ruled Denmark as regent in his place.

In 1380, Håkon VI died and Olaf inherited the throne of Norway. Margaret was now the regent of both Denmark and Norway. When the Swedish nobles turned against Albert in 1386, Margaret was ready to offer military aid to them in exchange for making Olaf king of Sweden as well. Her plans were destroyed when Olaf died suddenly on August 3, 1387, possibly from poison.

During this crisis, Margaret proved to have great skill at diplomacy. She had no claim to the throne of any of the three nations, and Scandinavian law and tradition prevented a woman from reigning as a monarch. Despite this restriction, she managed to persuade the nobles of both Denmark and Norway to allow her to continue to rule as regent, with the right to name her heir. The heir she chose was her grandnephew, Erik of Pomerania, who was a young child at the time.

In March of 1388, the Swedish nobles accepted Margaret as regent of Sweden also, beginning a war for control of Sweden between Margaret and Albert. On February 24, 1389, a decisive battle was fought near the Swedish town of Falköping. The forces of Margaret defeated the forces of Albert, and he was taken prisoner. Margaret was now the ruler of all three Scandinavian nations.

The Swedish city of Stockholm continued to be controlled by the supporters of Albert. These supporters allied themselves with pirates who were disrupting trade on the Baltic Sea. The Hanseatic League, which depended on the Baltic trade routes, formed an alliance with Margaret against the pirates. In 1395, Margaret made an agreement with the supporters of Albert to release him from imprisonment in exchange for a large ransom. If the ransom was not paid, Stockholm would be turned over to the Hanseatic League for three years, after which it would be given to Margaret. Albert was unable to raise enough money for the ransom, so the Hanseatic League took over the city and spent the next three years destroying the pirates.

Erik of Pomerania was accepted as king of Norway in 1389, and was elected king of Denmark and Sweden in 1396. On June 17, 1397, representatives of all three nations, nobles and clergymen, gathered at Kalmar, Sweden, to witness the coronation of Erik of Pomerania as the king. This ceremony was the birth of what would later be known as the Kalmar Union.

Little is known of the negotiations that took place between Margaret and the nobles at Kalmar at this time, but they seem to have taken about a month to complete. The two documents produced by these negotiations were both dated July 13, 1397. The first document, known as the Coronation Letter, was written on parchment and announced the coronation of Erik of Pomerania in a way that implied a centralized, hereditary monarchy.

The second document, known as the Union Letter, has been closely studied by historians because it poses several questions. Although the text of this document states that it is written on parchment and that it is hung with seventeen seals, it is actually written on vellum and contains only ten seals, which are stamped into it rather than hanging from it. These discrepancies, along with the fact that the Union Letter contains written corrections, leads scholars to believe that it is an unapproved draft of an agreement that was never completed.

Apparently Margaret wanted a closer union of the three nations than the nobles, who wanted to ensure that each nation would retain its own laws and customs. Unable to come to a formal agreement with the nobles about the exact details of the union, Margaret continued to rule as before, relying on her diplomatic skills to avoid conflicts.

Although Erik of Pomerania reached the age at which he no longer needed a regent in 1401, Margaret remained the unofficial power behind the throne until her death on October 28, 1412. She spent the last years of her life strengthening the union and increasing the power of the sovereign by appointing loyal and efficient officials to administer her government.

Erik of Pomerania proved to be a less effective ruler than Margaret. His attempt to build an empire on the Baltic coast led to an expensive war with the Hanseatic League. A blockade of Swedish exports of iron and copper by the Hanseatic League in 1434 led to a rebellion by Swedish miners. Eventually Erik of Pomerania was deposed from the thrones of Denmark and Sweden in 1439 and Norway in 1442.

Erik of Pomerania was replaced by Christopher III, who died in 1448 with no heir. Danish nobles selected Christian I as his successor while Swedish nobles selected Karl Knutsson. The conflict between Denmark and Sweden continued for the next several decades, as one side or the other gained control over the throne of Sweden.

On January 19, 1520, Christian II, the king of Denmark and Norway, defeated the forces of Sten Sture the Younger, the regent of Sweden. After months of attempting to take the city of Stockholm by force, Christian II convinced it to surrender by promising amnesty to his opponents. He was crowned king of Sweden on November 4, 1520. Four days later, despite his promise of amnesty, he executed eighty-two supporters of Sten Sture the Younger in an event later known as the Stockholm Bloodbath. The bloodbath alienated most Swedish factions, and the union was in great disfavor.

The Swedish nobleman Gustav I Vasa led a war of independence against Christian II, defeating him with the financial help of the rich German trading city of Lübeck. He was crowned king of Sweden on June 6, 1523, ending the Kalmar Union.

SIGNIFICANCE

Despite Margaret's diplomacy and tact, the Kalmar Union never formally materialized. What was significant about Margaret's attempts to bring the three nations together is their turning back a German (Hanseatic League) economic and cultural advance into Scandinavia and the Baltic region. Also, Scandinavia remained a great union under one sovereign, one of Margaret's goals, for more than one hundred years.

—Rose Secrest

FURTHER READING

Butler, Ewan. "Royal Union, Peasant Separatism." In *The Horizon Concise History of Scandinavia*. New York: American Heritage, 1973. Focuses on the wars and rebellions that threatened the Kalmar Union throughout its history.

Derry, T. K. "The Union of Three Crowns." In *A History of Scandinavia*. Minneapolis: University of Minnesota Press, 1979. A detailed account of the rise and fall of the Kalmar Union. Gives a contextual discussion on life in the Middle Ages. Includes maps, family trees, and a helpful time line of parallel events in all the Scandinavian countries. Excellent bibliography.

Larsen, Karen. "Scandinavian Union." In *A History of Norway*. 1948. Reprint. Princeton, N.J.: Princeton

University Press, 1974. An account of the Kalmar Union from the viewpoint of Norway.
Sawyer, Birgit, and Peter Sawyer. *Medieval Scandinavia: From Conversion to Reformation, Circa 800-1500.* Minneapolis: University of Minnesota Press, 1993. Provides a history of Scandinavia in the Middle Ages, from its lands and people, to its politics, trade, towns, religions, ancestry, and more. Maps, bibliography, index.
Scott, Franklin D. "Margareta and the Union of Kalmar." In *Sweden: The Nation's History.* Carbondale: Southern Illinois University Press, 1988. Discusses Margaret I and the Kalmar Union as seen by Sweden. Includes maps, bibliography, and index.
Singleton, Fred. "Finland and Sweden." In *A Short History of Finland.* 2d ed. Cambridge, England: Cambridge University Press, 1998. Describes the effect of the Kalmar Union on Finland.

SEE ALSO: c. 1150-1200: Rise of the Hansa Merchant Union.
RELATED ARTICLES in *Great Lives from History: The Middle Ages, 477-1453*: Margaret of Denmark, Norway, and Sweden; Valdemar II.

1399-1404
TAMERLANE BUILDS THE BIBI KHANUM MOSQUE

After winning many victories and expanding his empire, the Turkish leader Tamerlane hoped to make his capital Samarqand the most glorious city in the Islamic world. The crowning edifice was to be the Bibi Khanum Mosque.

LOCALE: Samarqand, Central Asia (now in Uzbekistan)
CATEGORY: Architecture

KEY FIGURE

Tamerlane (Timur; 1336-1405), warrior and ruler of the Barlas tribe, r. 1370-1405, who expanded his small state into an empire

SUMMARY OF EVENT

Tamerlane, also known as Timur, burst on the Central Asian scene as leader of the Barlas tribe in the late thirteenth and early fourteenth century. *Timur* is Turkish for "iron," suitable for this conqueror, but he is popularly called Tamerlane from the Persian Timur-i-lenk (Timur the Lame), a name that reflected his limp, the result of a wound he received as a young man. The leader of a small Mongolian-Turkic tribe, he created an empire stretching from India to Asia Minor.

Born in 1336 in Kesh, south of Samarqand (now in Uzbekistan), Tamerlane was the son of the chief of the Barlas tribe, one of numerous small Turkish clans in the empire of Genghis Khan (r. 1206-1227), which was divided after his death among his descendants. The Barlas were in the western group in Transoxiana. By the mid-fourteenth century, Mongol control over the area was in name only, and Tamerlane was able to build a following among the other Turks and create his empire.

Tamerlane was a conscientious builder. He would destroy a city and then bring in architects and artisans to rebuild it. Sculptors, stone masons, stucco and mosaic workers, weavers, glassblowers, and potters came from all over his empire. On one of his buildings, he inscribed the Arab proverb "If you want to know us, examine our buildings."

He built magnificent buildings in several cities, including the White Palace of Shahr-i-Sabz and Hojo Ahmed Yesevi Mosque of Turkistan, built in honor of the great poet and sheik. However, his capital, Samarqand, was the location of most of his structures: secular and religious edifices containing walled gardens decorated in gold and silk and furnished with magnificent carpets. Most of the buildings have not survived, but some remain. Outstanding features of these buildings include the entrance ways, with the characteristic arched *ivans* (barrel-vaulted openings) copied from the Persian buildings to which Tamerlane looked for inspiration. Timurid structures are also noted for their glazed tile work, an advancement over the earlier Mongolian lead glazes, which oxidized too quickly. Reflecting the advanced techniques of the Timurid period, more durable colored glazes were used. Instead of single-colored tiles, which limited the designs to the shape of the tiles used, the Timurid artisans used inlaid mosaics employing smaller bits of tile.

The Bibi Khanum Mosque was built as a memorial for Saray Mulk Khanum, Tamerlane's wife and the daughter of Chagatai Khan, the dependent ruler Tamerlane put on the throne after his conquest of Transoxiana. Its formal name is Masjid-i Jami or the congregational mosque.

The mosque continued the Persian architectural traditions and served as a testament to his achievements as a conqueror. He began the work in 1398-1399 and had part of it reconstructed in 1404. Saray Mulk Khanum had ordered the construction of the attached *madrasa* (school) and mausoleum. Ruy Gonzales de Clavijo, Spain's ambassador to Tamerlane who observed the final stages of the construction, recorded in his memoirs that the ailing Tamerlane was brought on a litter every day to oversee the work. He would supervise construction, having his meals brought to him and tossing the leftovers down into the pits for the workmen. He would also throw coins to the workers urging them on. Construction went on day and night. Clavijo also wrote about disagreements between Tamerlane and his architects, particularly concerning the facade of the mosque, which he wanted to possess a grandeur worthy of his beloved wife.

Tamerlane modeled the Bibi Khanum on the mosque of the Mongol ruler Uljaytu at Sultaniyya. He imported architects from Persia and India whom he had defeated the year before construction began. Ninety-five elephants hauled the building materials to Samarqand. Two hundred architects, artists, masons, and craftspeople from around the empire and six hundred slaves worked on the building. One observer said, "Its dome would have been unique if not for the heavens and its entrance unique if not for the Milky Way."

The mosque was exceptionally large: a 182-by-119-yard (167-by-109-meter) rectangle. It had typical Timurid features such as creative use of domes and columns and various styles of tiles and inscriptions. The mosque was built for public use. Saray Mulk Khanum was not buried near the mosque but in a madrasa (school) complex located on the road between the old capital of Afrasiab, north of Samarqand, to the Registan, and the center of Samarqand. Two smaller side mosques were also located in the Bibi Khanum complex. One of the mosque's notable features was the large Qurʾān stand—90 inches, or 230 centimeters, long—originally located inside one of the mosque's alcoves but later moved to the courtyard. At the entrance as well as over the gate to the sanctuary inside, an inscription assigns the building to "the great sultan, pillar of the state and the religion, Amir Timur Gurgan." At the time, it was the largest and one of the grandest buildings in the Muslim world, designed to boast the ruler's prowess; however, its very size and grandeur contributed to its ruin as it stretched medieval architectural technology to the limits, which led to its crumbling over time. Eventually, it was destroyed almost completely in a nineteenth century earthquake.

Among the legends that have grown up about the Bibi Khanum is the story of the architect who was so in love with Saray Mulk Khanum that while Tamerlane was on campaign, he refused to work until she allowed him to kiss her. She finally gave in but put her fingers between his lips and her cheek. However, his passion was so great that the imprint of his lips penetrated and remained on her cheek. On his return, Tamerlane went into a rage, but the architect escaped by climbing to the height of the mosque, grew wings, and flew away. Tamerlane had his Indian elephants trample the mosque to the ground and ordered all women afterward to wear veils to hide their beauty. Later generations told this tale to explain the custom of Muslim women wearing veils and the sad state of disarray to which the mosque had fallen.

SIGNIFICANCE

The Bibi Khanum Mosque successfully fulfilled the goals that Tamerlane set for it. It was the crowning glory of his building projects for Samarqand. It marked him as a great warrior, builder, and champion of Islam for posterity. It continued the architectural traditions of Persia while adding innovations that would influence Islamic architecture. Among the innovations his architects introduced were new designs for domes and gateways and technically advanced glazed tiles. The mosque also made Samarqand one of the major cities of Central Asia, a political and cultural center, for all the generations to follow. The mosque served to unify Tamerlane with people he conquered and ruled. It demonstrated his power and influence as a leader and administrator beyond his role of conqueror, as history mainly regards him. Among the mosques that have used Bibi Khanum as a model are Masjid-i Shan in Isfahan, Iran, and some of the mosques of India built by the Mughals. Although Tamerlane hoped the mosque would be a memorial for him and his beloved wife for the ages, the building did not stand the ravages of time.

—Frederick B. Chary

FURTHER READING

Blair, Sheila S., and Jonathan M. Bloom. *The Art and Architecture of Islam, 1250-1800*. New Haven, Conn.: Yale University Press, 1994. An important scholarly study. Chapter 4 covers the mosque.

Golombek, Lisa, and Donald Wilber. *Timurid Architecture of Iran and Turan*. Princeton, N.J.: Princeton University Press, 1988. Specifically deals with Tamerlane's and his successors' buildings.

Gonzalez de Clavijo, Ruy. *Embassy to Tamerlane, 1403-1406*, New York: Harper, 1928. An important primary document by Spain's ambassador to Tamerlane.
Knobloch, Edgar. *Beyond the Oxus: Archaeology, Art, and Architecture of Central Asia*. London: Ernest Benn, 1972. A major contribution to study of Timurid and other buildings in Central Asia.
Voronina, V. *Architectural Monuments of Middle Asia: Bokhara, Samarqand*. Leningrad: Aurora, 1969. A popular book of Central Asia buildings including the Bibi Khanum Mosque.

SEE ALSO: 637-657: Islam Expands Throughout the Middle East; 685-691: Building of the Dome of the Rock; 972: Building of al-Azhar Mosque; 1381-1405: Tamerlane's Conquests.
RELATED ARTICLE in *Great Lives from History: The Middle Ages, 477-1453*: Tamerlane.

1400-1500
FOUNDATION OF THE WEST AFRICAN STATES OF BENIN

Commerce helped Benin become the earliest great West African empire and the largest polity in West Africa's forest area. The divine monarch, or oba, *exercised a system of political checks and balances that controlled all key appointments and political rewards.*

LOCALE: Southern Nigeria
CATEGORY: Government and politics

KEY FIGURES

Oduduwa, legendary first king of Ife
Oranmiyan (fl. possibly the thirteenth century), semihistorical founder of the Benin monarchy
Eweka (fl. late thirteenth or early fourteenth century), first *oba* of Benin
Ewedo (fl. late fourteenth century), fourth *oba* of Benin
Ewuare the Great (fl. fifteenth century), twelfth *oba* of Benin, r. c. 1440-1480

SUMMARY OF EVENT

The highly centralized state of Benin became one of the major kingdoms of West Africa. It was located west of the Niger River in the forested area of what is now southern Nigeria. It was a powerful monarchy between the thirteenth and the nineteenth centuries, although evidence suggests earlier political organization.

The Portuguese who came into contact with the kingdom in 1485 described its wealth and orderly administration, but its history before European contact is speculative. Attempts to reconstruct this area's early past have relied on multidisciplinary approaches using oral traditions, archaeological and linguistic evidence, and material culture.

Evidence shows that the area has been inhabited for several millennia. Linguistic studies indicate that the basic language, Edo, developed in relative isolation over the past four thousand years. Although the original inhabitants may have been affected by external influences, immigrant groups and outside innovations seem to have been absorbed by the developing Edo-speaking culture.

It is impossible to determine the date of the first monarchy or its origins. The autonomous village was the basic political unit of early Edo (also called Bini) agricultural settlements. Traditions state that rulers known as the *ogiso* emerged around 950 and ruled for several centuries. Such narratives claim that the *ogiso* period ended with the dethroning of the ruler and the appointment of a group of chiefs, who were commissioned to develop new leadership.

Both Edo and Yoruba narratives tell the story of how these Edo chiefs asked Oduduwa, the king of Ife, to send one of his children to rule them. When his son Oranmiyan arrived in Benin, he realized that as a foreigner to Edo culture and language, he would be unable to rule effectively. Oranmiyan fathered a child with the daughter of a local Edo chief and returned to Ife. Their son, Eweka, became the first king, or *oba*, of Benin.

The story of Oranmiyan may be semilegendary, but the derivation of the new dynasty from Ife is possibly true. However, it has been suggested that these narratives reflect a conquest rather than an orderly establishment of monarchy. It is important to note that although the kingship derived from Ife, the first *oba* was Edo, suggesting that the new and alien kingship adapted to the indigenous culture. Whatever the circumstances, the establishment of a central monarchy, probably in the late thirteenth or early fourteenth century, marked a new period in the development of the Benin state.

Benin City, located inland from the coast and about 80 miles (129 kilometers) west of the Niger River, was the capital of the kingdom. Archaeological evidence shows that the site was developed by the beginning of the common era. Its origins are unclear, but there are indications that it grew from a cluster of independent settlements. Studies of the city's walls indicate such a fusion of communities before the emergence of a centralized kingdom. The merging was unusual for the Edo who generally organized into small autonomous villages.

Benin City established control of the surrounding countryside for a radius of 10 to 15 miles (16 to 24 kilometers). The town's development most likely resulted from a combination of factors, including improved methods of food production and evolution of metal technology for better tools and farming implements. Whatever the initial impetus for the city's origin, its growth was built on commerce. Situated near the Benin River northwest of the Niger Delta, it controlled trade routes in all directions. Its interior location and highly organized political system enabled its inhabitants to control early European trade in the area.

The emergence of the new dynasty was a key point in Benin's evolution from a small state to a powerful kingdom. However, the transformation was not a sudden one. According to traditions, the first *obas* lived under the influence of a hereditary council of local chiefs known as the Uzama. Late in the fourteenth century Ewedo, the fourth *oba*, is believed to have reduced the power of the Uzama and set up the first hierarchy of chiefs to serve in his new palace. Under Ewedo, the state became highly centralized as the *oba* developed more autocratic control. Along with the new form of government came innovations such as new weapons and war tactics that enabled Benin to pursue a course of military expansion.

Traditions indicate that advances in metallurgy, such as the lost-wax casting process, were introduced to Benin City from Ife about this time. Copper was imported to make the alloys for casting. The city came to be known for its brass sculptures as well as its ivory and wood carvings. Portrait heads, figural works, and bas-reliefs glorified the monarchy through depictions of *obas* and others connected with palace life. There are stylistic affinities that link this early court art with the terra-cotta sculptures of the Nok culture (c. 500 B.C.E.-200 C.E.) in central Nigeria. Although Edo works portrayed the same royal themes that were found in Ife sculpture, they lacked the naturalism that was so characteristic of their Yoruba neighbors.

Ewuare the Great was among the most powerful *obas*. It is believed that he seized the throne in what may have been a domestically disputed succession or part of a more widespread conflict. His reign was noted for political reform, consolidation of power, and military expansion. He further reduced the power of the Uzama and created new categories of leadership. In addition to "palace chiefs" dedicated to serving the *oba* and his family, he appointed "town chiefs" from the rural areas that had sometimes organized resistance to central power. Nonhereditary hierarchies of authority were established. Even male commoners had opportunities for advancement. Controlling all appointments, the *oba* rewarded service and loyalty, satisfied ambitions, and resolved conflicts. He developed a system of checks and balances. Palace and town chiefs

A Bronze "choker head" from Benin, displaying the court dress. (Leon Underwood, *Bronzes in West Africa*; London: Alec Tiranti, 1968.)

competed with each other and with the Uzama for influence.

Ewuare rebuilt Benin City and fortified it with great walls and moats. He organized a powerful war machine and greatly extended the boundaries of the kingdom. Although the state never incorporated all of the Edo, under Ewuare's military command additional Edo as well as non-Edo territories were incorporated into the kingdom. The *oba* became the supreme political, military, and judicial leader. He was elevated to divine status and was believed to possess supernatural powers. From this time, Benin had a central ruler and a central government with the means of ruling an empire.

SIGNIFICANCE

The emergence of Benin marked a new development for the Edo, who had traditionally organized into small village-based communities. Although it emerged later than the great kingdoms in the grasslands to the north, Benin became the earliest great empire and the largest political system to rise in West Africa's forest region. At its zenith, it extended from the Niger River westward to what is now Lagos. Through its highly centralized political structure and its complex nonhereditary reward system, the *oba* was able to manipulate competing interests and control the diverse constituencies of the kingdom.

When the first Europeans arrived in this area, Benin was a thriving empire. Portuguese merchants wrote of the kingdom's size, wealth, and power. Early European contacts with the Edo involved relationships of equal partners. The *oba* received ambassadors from Portugal and sent Edo ambassadors to Europe. Benin regulated trade between inhabitants of the West African interior and Europeans seeking ivory, palm oil, pepper, and, eventually, slaves.

—*Cassandra Lee Tellier*

FURTHER READING

Bradbury, R. E. *Benin Studies*. London: Oxford University Press, 1973. A collection of essays reflecting Benin's complex cultural and political history.

Davidson, Basil. *West Africa Before the Colonial Era: A History to 1850*. New York: Longman, 1998. An overview of early West African social, political, and economic history.

Egharevba, Jacob. *A Short History of Benin*. 1934. Reprint. Ibadan, Nigeria: Ibadan University Press, 1991. A pioneering work in Benin history with materials from informants who remembered the British conquest of 1897.

Eisenhofer, Stephan. "The Origins of the Benin Kingship in the Works of Jacob Egharevba." *History in Africa: A Journal of Method* 22 (1995): 141-163. Reconstruction of the history of Benin has been based on Egharevba's data, some of which have proven to be questionable.

Girshick, Paula Ben-Amos, and John Thorton. "Civil War in the Kingdom of Benin, 1689-1721: Continuity or Political Change?" *Journal of African History* 42 (2001): 353-376. Benin's civil war marked a modification of earlier centralized political structure.

Ryder, A. F. C. *Benin and the Europeans: 1485-1897*. New York: Humanities Press, 1969. An interdisciplinary approach to reconstructing the history of the kingdom of Benin.

SEE ALSO: 11th-15th centuries: Development of the Ife Kingdom and Yoruba Culture.

1403-1407
YONGLO DADIAN ENCYCLOPEDIA IS COMPILED

In 1403, Emperor Yonglo commissioned the compilation of a work, the Yonglo Dadian, *which would record all existing knowledge and include every monograph in the Chinese empire. Completed in 1407, the encyclopedia consisted of 917,480 handwritten pages within 22,937 sections, filling 11,095 manuscript volumes.*

LOCALE: China
CATEGORIES: Cultural and intellectual history; literature

KEY FIGURES

Yonglo (Yung-lo; 1363-1424), third emperor of the Ming Dynasty, r. 1402-1424
Xie Jin (Hsieh Chin; 1369-1415), scholar official and trusted adviser of Yonglo
Dao Yan (Tao-yen; 1335-1419), Buddhist monk, poet, and official who helped the Yonglo usurp the throne

SUMMARY OF EVENT

Zhu Di (Chu Ti; the future emperor Yonglo) was the fourth son of Zhu Yuanzhang (Chu Yüan-chang; the emperor Hongwu), the founder of the Ming Dynasty (1368-1644). His eldest brother, Zhu Biao (Chu Piao) had died in 1392, and Zhu Biao's son and heir apparent, Zhu Yunwen (Chu Yun-wen), was named the successor to the throne. When Emperor Hongwu died in 1398, Zhu Yunwen ascended the throne as Emperor Jianwen (r. 1399-1402). After years of civil war beginning in 1399, Zhu Di, also known as the prince of Yan (Yen), usurped the throne from his nephew and became the new emperor on July 17, 1402. His reign was known as the era of Yonglo ("perpetual happiness"), and one of the great achievements of his reign was the compilation of the *Yonglo Dadian* (the grand encyclopedia of Yongle), the earliest and largest of its kind in the world.

In the first year of his reign, Yonglo saw the need to collect, copy, and preserve all existing Chinese literature in every area of knowledge. In September, 1403, he appointed Xie Jin, the grand secretary and a Hanlin academician, to serve as general director of the project. With a staff of 147 assistants, Xie Jin completed the work by December, 1404. However, Yonglo thought the manuscript was inadequate, so he commissioned his longtime adviser Dao Yan (also known as Yao Guangxiao, or Yao Kuang-hsiao) to serve as a codirector of a major revision. The Chinese government hired 2,180 scholars from the Hanlin Academy, the National University, and government agencies to search the country for texts not found in the imperial library or to work on the copying and editing at the Literary Erudition Pavilion. The final compilation, finished in December, 1407, encompassed approximately 8,000 books from various areas, including art, animals, astronomy, Buddhism, agriculture, Buddhism, classical texts, codes of law, Confucian canon, drama, fiction, geography, geology, history, institutions, literature, mathematics, medicine, military affairs, natural sciences, novels, philosophy, plants, religion, ritual, technology, and Daoism.

The final vast compilation consisted of more than 370 million words, 917,480 pages, and 22,937 sections or chapters (sixty of which were tables of contents) in 11,095 handwritten folio volumes. Subject headings appeared in the outer edges of the pages. The emperor named this work *Yonglo Dadian*, incorporating the name of his reign. He also wrote a long preface, which included this explanation of why he undertook such an ambitious project:

> Ever since I succeeded to my father's throne, I have thought about writing and publication as a means of unifying confusing systems and standardizing government regulations and social customs. . . . Nevertheless, I ordered my literati-officials to compile *The Four Treasuries*, to purchase lost books form the four corners of the country, to search and to collect whatever they could find, to assemble and classify them according to both topical and phonetic order, and to make them into enduring classics. The fruit of their labor is this encyclopedia, which includes the breadth of the universe and all the texts from antiquity to the present time, whether they are big or small, polished or crude. . . . I've been assiduously studying the Dao taught by the sages and often discuss its aims with learned people

Although obviously proud of this encyclopedia, Yonglo never sent the manuscript for printing. In 1421, when Yonglo transferred the capital from Nanjing (Nanking) to Beijing (Peking), the encyclopedia was also moved to the Forbidden City.

There is controversy regarding Yonglo's real motives for compiling but not publishing the encyclopedia. According to what he said in the preface, Yonglo's purpose was to preserve all extant Chinese literary treasures and heritage, and he had a genuine scholarly interest in the project. Also, it appears likely that the additional expense of woodblock cutting for such a huge work would have been too much of a burden on the imperial treasury by the time the encyclopedia was completed.

The preface also suggests some political motivation. Yonglo was a warrior king, but he sought the reputation and legacy of being a sage ruler and patron of learning in the traditional sense, as evidenced in his references to the Dao, sages, and learned people. He also sponsored numerous other literary projects and thus helped legitimize his rule. Posthumously, he was given the name, Wen Huangdi (Wen-huang-ti), or "emperor of culture," a high distinction for a Chinese emperor. However, the Qing scholar, Sun Chengze (1593-1675), held another opinion; he concluded that Yonglo used the encyclopedia project to employ and placate the restless literati, who were resentful of Yonglo's bloody usurpation of the throne.

Whatever the reason for not printing the encyclopedia, it was unfortunate that it never went to the printing shop or into multiple production. After the encyclopedia narrowly escaped destruction in a fire in 1556, Emperor Jiajing (Chia-ching; r. 1522-1567) ordered that two manuscript copies be made. After five years, the project was completed, and the copies were placed in the Literary Erudition Pavilion and the Imperial Library. The original was returned to Nanjing. Unfortunately, the original and one of the copies were destroyed with the collapse of the Ming Dynasty in 1644. During the reign of Emperor Yongzheng (Yung-cheng; r. 1723-1735), the remaining copy was transferred to the Hanlin Academy Library. Unfortunately, due to theft, rodents, and poor environmental conditions, much of the encyclopedia was lost. By 1900, it was estimated that of the original 11,095 volumes, only about 800 had survived. Then in 1900, during the Boxer Rebellion, the Hanlin Academy was set on fire and the *Yonglo Dadian* was almost completely destroyed or stolen.

SIGNIFICANCE

The *Yonglo Dadian* was one of the greatest achievements of the Ming Dynasty and helped establish Emperor Yonglo as a patron of Chinese literature and culture. Involving more than two thousand scholars, it was the largest compilation project in Chinese history. The scope of the encyclopedia included all existing literature that could be found in the country. One of the largest encyclopedias ever produced, the *Yonglo Dadian* helped preserve rare and fragile works that otherwise would have disappeared.

It is estimated that only about four hundred books remain, but they are the only copies of numerous ancient works that were lost or destroyed. In April, 2002, acknowledging its significance in Chinese cultural history and scholarship, the Xinhua news agency announced that the Beijing Library Press would begin publishing photocopies of the entire encyclopedia in its original size, color, and style.

—*Alice Myers*

FURTHER READING

Chan, Albert. *The Glory and Fall of the Ming Dynasty*. Norman: University of Oklahoma Press, 1982. Contains a section on the *Yonglo Dadian* and a well-researched history of the loss and survival of parts of the encyclopedia.

Chan, David B. *The Usurpation of the Prince of Yen, 1398-1402*. San Francisco: Chinese Materials Center, 1976. Provides a detailed study of how the Yonglo emperor, also known as the prince of Yan, usurped the throne. Especially interesting is the active role in the usurpation by the monk Dao Yan, who later was assigned a major role in the *Yonglo Dadian* project.

Davis, Donald G., and Cheng Huanwen. "The Destruction of a Great Library: China's Loss Belongs to the World." *American Libraries* 28 (October, 1997): 60-62. This article focuses on the destruction during the Boxer Rebellion of the Hanlin Academy library housing the encyclopedia.

Mote, Frederick, and Denis Twitchett, eds. *The Ming Dynasty, 1368-1644*. Vols. 7-8 in *The Cambridge History of China*. Cambridge, England: Cambridge University Press, 1988. Scholarly work on the Ming Dynasty, including sections on the *Yonglo Dadian*.

Tsai, Shih-shan Henry. *Perpetual Happiness: The Ming Emperor Yongle*. Seattle: University of Washington Press, 2001. A biography about the emperor who had the encyclopedia created. Includes a detailed description of the compilation and the later history of the work. Extensive bibliography, notes, and a glossary of Chinese characters.

SEE ALSO: 1368: Establishment of the Ming Dynasty; c. 1387: Chinese Create the Eight-Legged Essay; 1397: Publication of the Laws of Great Ming.

RELATED ARTICLE in *Great Lives from History: The Middle Ages, 477-1453*: Yonglo.

1405-1433
ZHENG HE'S NAVAL EXPEDITIONS

The seven Ming Dynasty diplomatic expeditions led by Admiral Zheng He mark the high point of Chinese naval power, involving the greatest naval armadas in history up to that time.

LOCALE: Pacific Ocean off the coast of East and Southeast Asia, the Indian Ocean, and the waters along the Arabian Peninsula and East Africa
CATEGORIES: Diplomacy and international relations; trade and commerce

KEY FIGURES

Zheng He (Cheng Ho; c. 1371-between 1433 and 1436), grand admiral who led the expeditions
Hongwu (Hung-wu or Zhu Yuanzhang; 1328-1398); founder and first emperor of the Ming Dynasty, r. 1368-1398
Yonglo (Yung-lo or Zhu Di; 1363-1424), third emperor of the Ming Dynasty, r. 1402-1424, who supported Zheng He's expeditions
Hongxi (Hung-hsi; 1378-1425), fourth emperor of the Ming Dynasty, r. 1424-1425, who halted Zheng He's expeditions
Xuande (Hsüan-te; 1399-1435), fifth emperor of the Ming Dynasty, r. 1426-1435, who permitted a final expedition in 1431-1433
Xia Yuanji (Hsia Yüan-chi; 1366-1430), finance minister opposed to Zheng He's expensive expeditions

SUMMARY OF EVENT

In his twenty-two-year reign as the Yonglo emperor, Zhu Di (Chu Ti) reversed many of his father's policies. He relocated the national capital from Nanjing to Beijing in the north, rebuilt both the Great Wall and the Grand Canal, began diplomacy and trade with China's nearer neighbors such as Japan and Korea, and sent armies to control both Vietnam in the south and his northern neighbors, the Mongols and Jurchens. His reign both at home and abroad was one of the most dynamic and expansive in all Chinese history.

Yonglo's principal aim behind the expeditions of Zheng He was to establish the greatness and power of the Ming Dynasty (1368-1644) by having foreign rulers recognize Chinese suzerainty. Most of the places visited by Zheng He's ships were known in China through earlier reports from Chinese and Arab merchants and travelers. The fleets featured hundreds of ships, dominated by nine masted treasure ships of three thousand tons burden, as well as specialized troop and supply ships, all accompanied by well-armed warships. These armadas awed everyone they encountered.

Zheng He's ships returned to China with exotic treasures and foreign envoys that added luster to the Yonglo emperor's rule. African giraffes drew great wonder at the Chinese court while two well-known food delicacies—shark's fin and bird's nests—were said to have been introduced through Zheng He's missions. Commercial transactions were a secondary purpose at best. The first three voyages visited areas known to Chinese seamen, but not previously visited by official Ming envoys. Later voyages ventured into lesser-known waters in the India Ocean, along the Arabian Peninsula and the East African coast. The intent, however, was not exploration in the sense of opening areas to Chinese commerce, religion, or residence, but rather to have the rulers they encountered recognize the great power of the Ming Dynasty.

Yonglo placed a trusted member of his own household, the eunuch Zheng He, in charge of the first expedition in 1405. Based on the considerable achievements of Song (Sung; 960-1279) and Yuan (1279-1368) Dynasty seamanship, Zheng He built special treasure ships in Chinese shipyards. These vessels carried large sails and boasted rudders of advanced design, superior navigational equipment, and stabilization gear for rough seas. Zheng He's largest ships were 400 feet (120 meters) long while Columbus's caravel, the *Santa Maria*, for example, was only 85 feet (26 meters) long. Each expedition required at least a year's preparation and most lasted for about two years.

Zheng He led the first expedition with more than thirty great treasure ships and hundreds of other vessels. He established diplomatic relations especially at Malacca on the Malay Peninsula and Calicut, a famous pepper trading port, on the southwest coast of India before returning to China with cargos of exotic goods as well as envoys to the Ming court. Zheng He and many of his subordinate eunuch commanders, as well as unknown numbers of his crews, were Muslims. In their journeys through the waters of Southeast Asia and the Indian Ocean, they dealt with many Muslim rulers, merchants, and seafarers. The five remaining naval expeditions Zheng He undertook during Yonglo's reign followed the pattern of the first, but each sought new treasures and new evidence of China's dominance.

Zheng He's fleets sailed as far west as the west coast of India in early voyages. The fourth expedition of 1411 reached the Persian Gulf and the fifth the coast of East Africa. Zheng He often dispatched smaller squadrons of ships commanded by eunuch subordinates to undertake special exploratory cruises. The sixth and final effort of Yonglo's reign came in 1421. These missions testify to the skill of the Ming Chinese in shipbuilding, navigation, and naval command, which far exceeded the abilities of the Arabs, their only real rivals at the time.

Several factors mark major differences between Zheng He's voyages and those of Europeans in the late fifteenth and early sixteenth centuries. Most important was that Zheng He's goal was not exploration or discovery but to establish diplomatic relations. Also, at the time of Zheng He's voyages in the early fifteenth century, Spanish and Portuguese explorers had just begun their first assays into the Atlantic and along the coast of Africa. In the early fifteenth century, Europeans lacked the skills to undertake voyages comparable to Zheng He's in terms of duration and distance. Further, the scale of Zheng He's expeditions, the size of the ships, and the numbers of people were far greater than those of fifteenth and sixteenth century Europeans. For example, with only three small ships and about one hundred men, Vasco de Gama reached Calicut on India's coast about a century later than Zheng He's ships. Zheng He had led dozens of huge ships, along with a supporting fleet of hundreds and a crew of twenty-five thousand.

The emperor Hongxi, also known as Zhu Gaozhi (Chu Kao-chih), halted the expeditions in 1426. In 1431, his successor, the emperor Xuande, also known as Zhu Zhanji (Chu Chan-chi), authorized a seventh expedition in order to reestablish diplomatic linkages. Zheng He again led the fleet but died on the return to China and was buried at sea. His death marked the end of great Chinese naval projects.

SIGNIFICANCE

Zheng He's voyages reflect the boundless ambition of the emperor Yonglo but were only one of that great ruler's many bold undertakings. After Zheng He's death, Ming rulers ended naval diplomatic missions. It is only in retrospect that Zheng He's expeditions have attracted historians' attention. The Chinese superiority in shipbuilding, navigation, and seamanship withered quickly. The Ming Dynasty's abandonment in 1433 of efforts to project its power via the ocean contrasts with increasing European interest and success in seaborne exploration, commerce, and colonization beginning about fifty years later at the end of the fifteenth century. Thus, the termination of Zheng He's expeditions are considered a precursor of the great shift in power from China to Europe that was finalized only in the nineteenth century.

—David D. Buck

FURTHER READING

Fairbank, John King, and Denis Twichett, eds. *The Ming Dynasty, 1368-1644*. Vols. 7-8 in *The Cambridge History of China*. New York: Cambridge University Press, 1988. Contains discussions of Zheng He's voyages.

Goodrich, L. Carrington, and Chaoying Fang, eds. *Dictionary of Ming Biography, 1368-1644*. 2 vols. New York: Columbia University Press, 1976. Contains biographies of Zheng He and other important people.

Levathes, Louise. *When China Ruled the Seas: The Treasure Fleet of the Dragon Throne, 1405-1433*. New York: Oxford University Press, 1994. An engagingly written popular account of Zheng He and his voyages.

Menzies, Gavin. *1421: The Year China Discovered America*. New York: HarperCollins, 2003. Menzies claims ships from Zheng He's fleets explored the Atlantic and most of the Pacific. The record, however, does not support his speculations. His book is a fanciful tale that masks the true accomplishments of Zheng He and his fleets, which were the greatest and most accomplished navies the world had yet seen. Menzies' fertile nautical imagination, along with his misuse of historical maps and archeological evidence, have led him far astray. There is no reason to believe that Zheng He's missions ever sailed beyond East African or Southeast Asian waters.

Mote, F. W. *Imperial China, 800-1800*. Cambridge, Mass.: Harvard University Press, 1999. Chapter 24 is a brilliant account of the Yongle period and Zheng He's place in it.

SEE ALSO: 1368: Establishment of the Ming Dynasty; 1397: Publication of the Laws of Great Ming; 1403-1407: *Yonglo Dadian* Encyclopedia Is Compiled.

RELATED ARTICLES in *Great Lives from History: The Middle Ages, 477-1453*: Yonglo; Zheng He.

July 15, 1410
BATTLE OF TANNENBERG

The Battle of Tannenberg marked the declining dominance of the knights of the Teutonic Order along the Baltic coast, the consequent rise of Poland as the most powerful state in east central Europe, and the preeminence of Lithuania in eastern Europe.

LOCALE: Between the village of Tannenberg and the forest of Grunwald in southern East Prussia (now near Stębark, Poland)

CATEGORY: Wars, uprisings, and civil unrest

KEY FIGURES

Władysław II Jagiełło (c. 1351-1434), king of Poland, r. 1386-1434, converted to Christianity in 1386

Vytautas (1350-1430), grand prince of Lithuania, r. 1392-1430, cousin of Jagiełło

Ulrich von Jungingen (d. 1410), grandmaster of the Teutonic Knights, ruler of Prussia, r. 1407-1410

SUMMARY OF EVENT

Since the thirteenth century, the knights of the Teutonic Order had led crusades against the pagans in Lithuania and against schismatics (Orthodox Christians) in Russia. During much of this time, the Germans of the Teutonic Order had been allied with the Polish kings, who were advancing eastward to the south against the same combination of enemies. It had seemed that the Peace of Kalish (1343) had brought an end to the conflicts over possession of Pomerellia (West Prussia). The conversion of the Lithuanian grand duke, Władysław II Jagiełło, and his 1386 marriage to the Polish heiress, Jadwiga, ended the Polish need for an alliance with the Germans. Jadwiga's death in 1399 removed the last voice for peace.

Nevertheless, war was not inevitable. The Teutonic Knights had once been allied with Jagiełło against Vytautas's father, and Vytautas had held him partly culpable for his murder. Twice Vytautas had been allied with the Teutonic Knights against Jagiełło. Each time Vytautas had rebelled, cleverly disguising his intent until he could do maximum damage to the Teutonic Order's position in Samogitia. Afterward, when Vytautas realized that he could seize Russia from the weakening hands of the Tatars, he made peace with the Teutonic Order, surrendering Samogitia at the Treaty of Sallinwerder (1398) in return for military aid. Having similarly reconciled himself with Jagiełło, he could count on having Polish knights support his campaigns against Tatars, the grand duke of Moscow, and Novgorod the Great.

Samogitia was important to the Teutonic Knights as the land bridge to their possessions in Livonia. It was also home to the last pagans in Europe, doughty warriors who had refused to convert when the rest of the Lithuanians obeyed Jagiełło's instructions to consider themselves henceforth Roman Catholics. Samogitia was also the homeland of Vytautas's mother, and most of Vytautas's boyars were unhappy that it was in foreign hands. In 1409, after an unusually cold winter and a very dry summer, the crops failed. Several thousand Samogitians fled to Vytautas. Grandmaster Ulrich von Jungingen asked Vytautas to return the "serfs" according to treaty promises. Vytautas responded that they were not serfs and, therefore, he was allowing them to stay. Ulrich then ordered vessels carrying Polish grain to Lithuania be searched, and when weapons were allegedly found, supposedly destined for Samogitian rebels, he confiscated the cargos. Vytautas was furious. Soon thereafter a rebellion began in Samogitia, and Vytautas appeared with an army, supposedly in support of the Crusader order, but in actuality aiding the rebels. Grandmaster Ulrich then attacked Jagiełło, hoping to intimidate him into abandoning his support of Vytautas.

The grandmaster had good reason for confidence in his ability to challenge two great powers at once: Most of the border wilderness between Prussia and Poland's northeast province, Masovia, was impassible for large armies. In addition, the Masovian dukes were not eager to become involved in the war. The Polish forces were on the west bank of the Vistula River and could not easily cross to join the Lithuanians. At the time, the armies of the Teutonic Order were considered invincible, and their border fortifications were the best in east central Europe. Finally, Sigismund of Hungary and Holy Roman Emperor Wenceslas of Bohemia were expected to attack Poland's southern and western frontiers, while the Livonian forces would ravage Lithuania.

Sigismund and Wenceslas had other problems to deal with, however, and the Livonians had signed a truce with Vytautas. The grandmaster prepared for war, anticipating an invasion of West Prussia. To Ulrich's surprise, Vytautas marched into Masovia in June with eleven thousand men, while Jagiełło's engineers built a pontoon bridge and transported his eighteen thousand to twenty-one thousand men across the Vistula. The grandmaster had to hurry to take his own twenty thousand men into East Prussia and cut off the invaders at the Dzewa (Drwęça)

Władysław (or Ladislaus) II Jagiełło, king of Poland 1386-1434. (Hulton|Archive by Getty Images)

River. Jagiełło then feigned a retreat and marched around the eastern flank of the Crusader forces through the Grunwald forest. Grandmaster Ulrich again cut off the invaders' line of march, passing through Tannenberg before dawn on July 15 to confront the Poles and Lithuanians on a broad field at the edge of the forest.

Ulrich did not exploit the advantage of surprise. He apparently wanted to fight a defensive battle, holding his heavy cavalry in reserve for the moment that his light cavalry and infantry drove their opponents back, then charging into the rear of the retreating forces. Yet Jagiełło delayed deploying his forces. He remained in his tent, hearing Mass after Mass. After a while, the grandmaster pulled his forces back somewhat so that his enemies would have space to line up their forces. This strategy had the disadvantage of placing the order's excellent artillery in a poor location and abandoning the obstacles the infantry had erected to protect their position. Meanwhile, his troops had nothing to eat or drink. As the morning wore on, the grandmaster sent two swords to the king, challenging him to come out and fight. At that Jagiełło ordered the attack.

Vytautas's Lithuanians, Russians, and Tatars swept down on the Crusader lines; the Poles advanced singing their anthem. After a desperate struggle, most of Vytautas's cavalry fled the field, pursued by elated, undisciplined Crusaders from Germany. Vytautas, however, remained on the field, exhausting horse after horse in directing the fighting. Polish units, meanwhile, noticed the gap the Crusaders had left in their lines. Charging into that gap, the Poles began to roll up the German position. Grandmaster Ulrich, instead of ordering a retreat (perhaps because he did not think he could extract his forces successfully), collected every knight he could into a column and charged directly toward Jagiełło's great banner. The attack had a good chance of success, and one knight almost struck down the king before he himself was unhorsed. When Ulrich's banner went down, however, the advance stalled. The order to retreat could not be obeyed. Ulrich, most of his officers, and most of his knights were surrounded and killed; a few were taken prisoner.

Panic set in among the German forces, a panic that became worse when they realized that even abandoning weapons and armor could not speed their flight through the forest significantly. The pursuers cut down the slowest, stopping only to loot the dead, steal the belongings of the prisoners before murdering them, and protect those they considered sufficiently wealthy to ransom.

About eight thousand soldiers had fallen in each army. Jagiełło ordered a search for the grandmaster's body, the collection of weapons, the burial of the dead in mass graves, and care for the wounded. His army, though victorious, was too exhausted to move for three days. Vytautas, more active and a better leader, sent his Tatars to burn and loot throughout East Prussia.

When Jagiełło did move north, he was met by delegations of clerics, towns, and secular knights, all eager to obtain favorable terms of surrender. He expected that the entire country would come under his sway. He did not reckon on the unusual initiative of a minor officer of the Teutonic Order, Heinrich von Plauen, who took his small force directly to Marienburg, the greatest fortress in Prussia, where grandmasters had entertained the thousands of Crusaders who used to come annually to earn knighthood, to witness the elaborate chivalric spectacles and, if sufficiently prominent, to sit at the Table Round. In three days, he made Marienburg defensible, so that all Jagiełło could do was sit outside the walls, without siege guns or a sufficient supply of food. When disease began to break out among Vytautas's troops, Jagiełło ordered a

Jadwiga (or Hedwig), queen of Poland 1384-1399. (Hulton| Archive by Getty Images)

retreat. Heinrich von Plauen followed, recapturing the towns and castles one by one easily because the king could not leave behind a large occupation force. Such was the disadvantage of the king having to rely on a feudal levy and foreign allies.

Significance

Although Jagiełło did not occupy Prussia, he had struck a deadly blow at the order, destroying the flower of its fighting machine, its most experienced leaders, and its reputation for invincibility. The Treaty of Thorn (1411) imposed a crushing indemnity on the Teutonic Order that ultimately drained its resources beyond recovery. Poland was henceforth the dominant power in the region.

—*William L. Urban*

Further Reading

Christiansen, Eric. *The Northern Crusades*. New ed. New York: Penguin, 1997. The best of the general surveys that set the Battle of Tannenberg in context.

Davies, Norman. *God's Playground: A History of Poland in Two Volumes*. Vol. 1. New York: Columbia University Press, 1982. A lively account with no controversial opinions repressed.

Evans, Geoffrey Charles. *Tannenberg: 1410-1914*. London: Hamilton, 1970. Succinct standard interpretation of two major battles at this site by a military historian.

Jasienica, Pawel. *Jagiellonian Poland*. Miami, Fla.: American Institute of Polish Culture, 1978. Polish interpretation of the battle that gives credit for victory to Jagiełło.

Koncius, Joseph. *Vytautas the Great, Grand Duke of Lithuania*. Miami, Fla.: Franklin Press, 1964. Lithuanian interpretation of the battle that gives credit to Vytautas.

Longworth, Philip. *The Making of Eastern Europe: From Prehistory to Postcommunism*. 2d ed. New York: St. Martin's Press, 1997. This comprehensive history begins with the twentieth century and moves backward in time in each successive chapter. The Jagiellons are discussed in the chapter on the cultural and religious tensions of 1352-1526.

Lukowski, Jerzy, and Hubert Zawadski. *A Concise History of Poland*. New York: Cambridge University Press, 2001. A general introduction to Polish history. Includes a chapter on Jagiellonian Poland.

Urban, William. *The Teutonic Knights: A Military History*. Mechanicsburg, Pa.: Stackpole Books, 2003. A complete history of the order, detailing the knights' campaigns, individual battles, and their struggle to maintain themselves as a power to be reckoned with. Includes a dramatic account of the Battle of Tannenberg.

See also: 735: Christianity Is Introduced into Germany; c. 1120: Order of the Knights Templar Is Founded; c. 1150-1200: Rise of the Hansa Merchant Union; July 27, 1214: Battle of Bouvines; 1228-1231: Teutonic Knights Bring Baltic Region Under Catholic Control; August 26, 1346: Battle of Crécy.

Related articles in *Great Lives from History: The Middle Ages, 477-1453*: Saint Alexander Nevsky; Casimir the Great; Władysław II Jagiełło and Jadwiga; Jan Žižka.

c. 1410-1440
FLORENTINE SCHOOL OF ART EMERGES

The emergence of the Florentine School of Art established the principal characteristics of Italian Renaissance art through the works of Donatello, Masaccio, and Filippo Brunelleschi.

LOCALE: Florence (now in Italy)
CATEGORY: Cultural and intellectual history

KEY FIGURES

Filippo Brunelleschi (1377-1446), a Florentine artist, goldsmith, and first architect of the new Renaissance style

Donatello (c. 1386-1446), a Florentine artist who trained as a goldsmith, engraver, and carver before becoming a sculptor

Lorenzo Ghiberti (c. 1378-1455), a Florentine artisan and master of perspective under whom Donatello worked

Masaccio (1401-1428), a Florentine painter whose altarpieces and frescoes were influenced by Giotto, Brunelleschi, and Donatello

SUMMARY OF EVENT

Although they built on foundations and developments in early Italian Renaissance art during the early fourteenth century, the work of three artists, Filippo Brunelleschi, Donatello, and Masaccio, converged in the early fifteenth century to define the character of Italian Renaissance art and establish Florence as a leading artistic center. Because their work represented the major art forms—architecture for Brunelleschi, sculpture for Donatello, and painting for Masaccio—collectively, they articulated the principal ideals of Italian Renaissance art.

A famous competition of 1401 for the design of a pair of bronze doors for the baptistery of Florence was important for the emergence of Florentine art. The winner, Lorenzo Ghiberti, narrowly defeated Filippo Brunelleschi, who then turned to architecture. Ghiberti's assistant while working on the doors was Donatello. Thus, while Ghiberti's doors were significant artistic achievements in their own right, they can also be said to have influenced the careers of Brunelleschi and Donatello.

When Brunelleschi lost the competition, he went to Rome to study the ancient architectural monuments. The subsequent architectural projects that Brunelleschi designed in Florence are marked by a consistent application of harmonious geometrical proportions and the use of classically inspired architectural members and ornament.

The most famous of Brunelleschi's architectural works is the dome of Florence cathedral, which was begun in 1420 and completed around 1436. As the largest dome since Roman times, its octagonal structure was composed of an inner and outer shell. The structural ingenuity combined with the simple, basic shapes point to the ideals that Brunelleschi's architecture conveyed.

Because it was added to an earlier essentially Gothic structure, Brunelleschi's dome did not reveal the full extent of his architectural innovations. Several buildings that he designed between 1420 and his death in 1446, however, demonstrate the classicism of his approach to architecture. In the Ospedale degli Innocenti (foundling hospital), an orphanage begun in 1419, the plan and elevation rely on modular proportions based on the geometrical system of the ancient Greek mathematician, Pythagoras, as revealed in the exterior arcade with its rhythmical row of arches supported on slender Corinthian columns. A similar use of proportion as well as nave arcades with rounded arches and Corinthian columns characterize two Florentine churches: San Lorenzo, which was begun sometime around 1425 and completed 1470, and Santo Spirito, which was designed in 1434-1436. In many ways, the most perfect structure that Brunelleschi designed was the Pazzi Chapel, the chapter house of the church of Santa Croce in Florence, begun in 1433. The plan focuses on a central square with the space of half a square to either side covered by a dome. The consistency of the proportional module and the centralized space give this structure a feeling of perfect balance and harmony that became a hallmark of Renaissance culture.

Donatello assisted Ghiberti but soon established himself as a sculptor. Whereas Ghiberti's reliefs were still marked by active diagonals in the compositional lines and sharp drapery folds that had a decorative quality reminiscent of the late Gothic style, Donatello's early works such as the Saint George for one of the exterior niches of the Florentine guildhall of Orsanmichele portrayed a fully three-dimensional body whose taut form protrudes into the viewer's space. A low relief of Saint George slaying the dragon just beneath this statue uses architectural forms with the kind of perspective that Brunelleschi constructed with his architecture.

Throughout a long career, Donatello combined several important features that characterized Renaissance art. First, he brought a three-dimensional corporeality to depictions of the human body. Second, his sculptures emanated a powerful psychological persona appropriate to the subject. Third, he revived several classical sculptural types such as the nude body and the equestrian statue. Finally, his technique of low relief utilized perspective to create a believable spatial context.

The three-dimensional reality of the human body combined with the idealistic beauty of the nude figure to produce a bronze sculpture of *David* (c. 1450) for Cosimo de' Medici. The unusual depiction of a nude David posed in classical *contrapposto* is the first freestanding nude sculpture since antiquity. In Padua, Donatello executed an equestrian statue of a *condottiere*, or soldier, nicknamed *Gattamelata* (c. 1445), which revives the Roman equestrian monument. Done in bronze, both horse and rider have a powerful physical presence. The individual personality that emerges from the portrait-quality of the soldier's face also draws inspiration from Roman portrait sculpture.

Part of Donatello's genius was the ability to infuse many of his subjects with psychological insight. His prophets for Florence Cathedral emanate a striking sense of their calling. The large bald head and penetrating eyes of *Habbakuk* (c. 1430), give this prophet an intense inner character. Most startling is his wooden statue of Mary Magdalene carved in the last decade of his life; her gaunt face and body graphically portray spiritual strength through physical mortification.

Donatello continued to perfect the depiction of space using low relief that he pioneered in the early *Saint George and the Dragon*. He created the effects of aerial perspective with landscape elements as in a relief of the *Ascension of Christ and the Giving of the Keys to Saint Peter* (c. 1425-1430). He used architectural perspective not only to convey three-dimensional space but also to unify several narrative scenes, for example in the gilt bronze relief of the *Feast of Herod* done around 1425 for the font in the baptistery of Siena. Thus, in many forms, Donatello's work epitomized the new directions in Renaissance art that focused on human qualities within a believable spatial setting.

Of the three artists whose work revolutionized not only Florentine but also Italian Renaissance art in general, Masaccio, the painter, was the youngest. He was born in a small town near Florence in 1401, the year that

Brunelleschi's Dome in Florence, Italy. (Digital Stock)

the competition for the bronze doors of the Florentine baptistery took place. Thus, Masaccio benefited from some of the visual ideas about architectural perspective and the monumentality of the human figure articulated by Brunelleschi and Donatello.

Masaccio's life was quite brief; he died before he was thirty years old. In this short time, however, he painted several works that summarized the innovations in form and space with his own artistic creativity and vision. His most famous works are the frescoes of the *Lives of Saints Peter and Paul* in the Brancacci Chapel of Santa Maria del Carmine in Florence (c. 1425-1428) and a fresco of the Trinity in the Florentine church of Santa Maria Novella (c. 1427-1428). These paintings share several characteristics. The figures have a sculptural monumentality achieved by modeling with a consistent light source. They also display an inner awareness of the psychological import and drama of a scene. The *Expulsion of Adam and Eve* in the Brancacci Chapel illustrates these characteristics. The weightiness and corporeal quality of the nude bodies of Adam and Eve accentuate their expression of shame at the realization of their human fallibility.

The three-dimensional reality of the human body combined with the idealistic beauty of the nude figure to produce Donatello's bronze sculpture of David. (Hulton|Archive by Getty Images)

To create a spatial context, Masaccio combined the unifying force of a single light source with the device of one-point perspective. The spatial recession in *The Tribute Money*, a fresco from the Brancacci Chapel, gives a convincing pictorial illusion of the depth of the landscape setting while simultaneously unifying several different scenes into a continuous narrative. In the fresco of the Trinity in Santa Maria Novella, a single-point perspective is used to create spatial unity that connects the spectator's viewpoint with the illusion of architectural space in the painting.

SIGNIFICANCE

The work of Brunelleschi, Donatello, and Masaccio shared common aesthetic ideas. Although they did not work as a group, they knew each other. Brunelleschi and Donatello studied ancient monuments in Rome together. Masaccio included a portrait of Donatello in one his frescoes that is now lost. Beyond these personal ties are the visual interrelationships that their work displays. Revival of the aesthetic principles of classical architecture and sculpture led to the use of proportion and perspective to articulate space in all media. It also helped to develop portrayal of human figures as substantial, three-dimensional bodies. For Donatello and Masaccio, the expression of inner emotion and character was an integral part of the human condition that they depicted in the sculpture and painting. The convergence of these three great artists in Florence during the first half of the fifteenth century set the direction of Renaissance art that accorded with the new spirit of the age.

—*Karen Gould*

FURTHER READING

Ahl, Diane Cole, ed. *The Cambridge Companion to Masaccio*. New York: Cambridge University Press, 2002. A comprehensive look at Masaccio and his works as well as fifteenth century art in Florence. Bibliography and index.

Avery, Charles. *Donatello: An Introduction*. New York: Icon Editions, 1994. A concise, illustrated survey of the life and work of Donatello, this book provides balanced coverage of Donatello's sculpture in different media and in different cities of Italy, and discusses his importance and indifference. An ideal introduction, Avery's book shows how Donatello's influence helped to create a new humanism that was a hallmark of the Renaissance.

Battisti, Eugenio. *Filippo Brunelleschi*. London: Phaidon, 2002. A translation and revision from an earlier Italian version, this scholarly study thoroughly examines Brunelleschi's life and career, including such aspects as his military engineering, theatrical machinery, and verse. Illustrated. Contains index.

Donatello. *Donatello*. Florence: Giunti, 1999. A catalog of Donatello's sculpture. Contains forty-four leaves of plates, mostly color.

Fremantle, Richard. *Masaccio*. New York: Smithmark, 1998. A catalog of the artist's works along with criticism and interpretation. Illustrations and bibliography.

Hartt, Frederick, and David G. Wilkins. *History of Italian Renaissance Art*. 5th ed. New York: Harry N. Abrams, 2003. A comprehensive history of Italian Renaissance art with discussions of Brunelleschi, Donatello, and Masaccio and their influence on the development of Renaissance art.

King, Ross. *Brunelleschi's Dome: How a Renaissance Genius Reinvented Architecture*. New York: Walker, 2000. King focuses on Brunelleschi's construction of the dome of the cathedral of Santa Maria del Fiore. Illustrations and index.

Walker, Paul Robert. *The Feud that Sparked the Renaissance: How Brunelleschi and Ghiberti Changed the Art World*. New York: William Morrow, 2002. Walker examines the interactions of Brunelleschi and Ghiberti, including their competitions. Illustrated with eight pages of plates. Bibliography and index.

See also: c. 1350-1400: Petrarch and Boccaccio Recover Classical Texts.

Related articles in *Great Lives from History: The Middle Ages, 477-1453*: Filippo Brunelleschi; Donatello; Lorenzo Ghiberti; Masaccio.

1414-1418
Council of Constance

The Council of Constance ended the Great Schism within the Catholic Church, but it failed to institute basic reforms, especially the sharing of papal powers with regular assemblies of churchmen, and it sparked Hussite revolt in Bohemia.

Locale: Constance (now in Switzerland)
Categories: Government and politics; religion

Key Figures

Jan Hus (1372 or 1373-1415), Bohemian reformer accused of heresy
John XXIII (d. 1419), former mercenary general, antipope, 1410-1415
Sigismund (1368-1437), king of Hungary, r. 1387-1437, and Holy Roman Emperor, r. 1433-1437

Summary of Event

In the early fourteenth century, European public life seemed to be unraveling. There had been divisions in the Roman Church before, but the Great Schism that began in 1378 was worse than any previous contest of pope and antipope. After the Council of Pisa met in 1408 in an effort to remove both the Roman and Avignon popes, they achieved little more than declaring a third pope, who was soon succeeded by a former mercenary soldier, John XXIII, whose personal life and politics were more distasteful than those of either of his rivals.

Similarly, the Holy Roman Empire was being contested by three claimants: Wenceslas of Bohemia, who had refused to accept his deposition by the electors on the grounds of incompetence and alcoholism; Ruprecht of the Rhine, a minor prince; and Wenceslas's half brother, Sigismund of Hungary, whose qualifications were geniality, a gift for foreign languages, and the expectation that he would be Wenceslas's heir. France was ruled by an insane king, with the regency contested between Burgundian and Orléanist factions. England, having finally resolved its internal problems, saw an opportunity to resume the Hundred Years' War. Bulgaria and Serbia had fallen to the Ottoman Turks, Constantinople was surrounded, and the French and Hungarian Crusaders of 1396 had suffered a humiliating defeat at Nicopolis on the Danube.

In the end, everyone turned to Sigismund for leadership. Ruprecht had died, Wenceslas was unable even to maintain peace in his own kingdom, and John XXIII had been driven out of Rome by King Ladislas of Naples. In 1413, the electors of the Holy Roman Empire proclaimed

Sigismund as the German king and saw to his coronation in Aachen; then they contributed a small number of knights to accompany him to Italy. There, Sigismund won general agreement to participate in general council, which would attempt to resolve some of Christendom's most pressing crises.

The site was to be Constance, a beautiful city on a lake that everyone could reach easily via the Rhine and the Alpine passes, which had sufficient lodgings and food, enjoyed a mild climate, and was relatively neutral in politics. For convenience, the delegates would be divided into four "nations" according to the practice common in universities: the German, the Italian, the French, and the Spanish. Because the Spanish refused to attend, however, their place was awarded to the English.

Because it was not easy to get all the representatives to Constance on time, the council took up important business slowly even after John XXIII formally opened its sessions in late 1414. Sigismund did not appear until Christmas Eve. This time, however, was not wasted. The adherents of the three popes conducted informal discussions that led them to the conclusion that the present claimants had to go. As it dawned on John XXIII that he would not have an honorable retirement, he slipped out of Constance on March 20, a day when the entire populace and most of the council members were watching a tournament, leaving behind a proclamation that the council was dissolved.

Sigismund responded promptly by ordering the councilmen to stay in session, setting pursuers on the fugitive's trail, and raising an army to attack John's protector, Friedrich of Austria. In late April, John XXIII was captured and brought to Constance. In early May, he was put on trial for heresy, simony, and a long catalog of crimes mortal and venal. By the end of the month, John XXIII had been convicted and deposed.

Meanwhile, another trial was in process, that of Jan Hus of Bohemia. Hus was the leader of the Czech reformers, a brilliant orator, a man of highest personal integrity, but hated by the German churchmen in Prague who were the target of his unrelenting attacks. Because Hus's philosophy was strikingly similar to that of John Wyclif, he was repeatedly accused of heretical beliefs and practices. The council was an opportunity for Hus to defend himself against his enemies' charges and to persuade others to make the kind of basic reforms that would transform the Church into a servant of the people rather than the great landed families.

Sigismund had given Hus safe conduct to Constance, then rather shamefacedly arrested him when churchmen threatened to break up the council and go home unless the excommunicated scholar was put on trial for heresy. The trial was a travesty. Hus was condemned and burned at the stake in July. His follower, Jerome of Prague, came to Constance to defend Hus's teachings. He was burned in May of 1416, shouting his defiance to his last breath.

Immediately, the smoldering unrest in Bohemia burst into flame. Czech nationalism joined religious and class motives to create several Hussite parties. Soon, moderate Hussites were celebrating communion "in both kinds," with the communicants drinking from the chalice as well as the priest; radicals were advocating social revolution.

THE *SACROSANCTA*, 1415

One of the most important canons produced by the Council of Constance, the Sacroscanta *declared the council's supremacy over the Papacy, claiming that its authority derived directly from Christ:*

This holy synod of Constance, forming a general council for the extirpation of the present schism and the union and reformation, in head and members, of the Church of God, legitimately assembled in the Holy Ghost, to the praise of Omnipotent God, in order that it may the more easily, safely, effectively and freely bring about the union and reformation of the church of God, hereby determines, decrees, ordains and declares what follows:

- It first declares that this same council . . . has its power immediately from Christ, and every one, whatever his state or position, even if it be the Papal dignity itself, is bound to obey it in all those things which pertain to the faith and the healing of the said schism, and to the general reformation of the Church of God, in head and members.
- It further declares that any one, whatever his condition, station or rank, even if it be the Papal, who shall contumaciously refuse to obey the mandates, decrees, ordinances or instructions which have been, or shall be issued by this holy council, or by any other general council, legitimately summoned . . . shall, unless he repudiate his conduct, be subject to condign penance and be suitably punished, having recourse, if necessary, to the other resources of the law.

Source: Translated by J. H. Robinson in *Translations and Reprints from the Original Sources of European History,* series 1, vol. 1 (University of Pennsylvania Press, 1912), pp. 31-32.

Sigismund's personal diplomacy persuaded the remaining popes to resign, which required the creation of a fifth nation in order to seat the Spanish delegates. Sigismund visited France and England, hoping to bring an end to the Hundred Years' War (Henry V had landed in Normandy in August and fought the Battle of Agincourt). The repercussions of this conflict were felt in Constance, where it was widely believed that the French nation wanted to break up the council.

There were two trials that touched on the question of tyrannicide. The first was that of John Petit, who had defended the assassination of Louis of Orléans. The second concerned the Dominican Johannes Falkenberg, who had called for the murder of King Władysław II Jagiełło of Poland, whom he accused of being an idolater and a secret pagan. In the end, it was decreed that Catholics cannot commit murder, even for a good cause.

With the French not cooperating, with the cardinals angry at having lost influence, with national issues intruding on the deliberations at every level, and with Sigismund absent on diplomatic missions, management of the council fell to the archbishops of Milan, Antioch, Riga, and Salisbury. Only in October of 1417 were they able to bring the nations together to pass several important decrees: *Frequens* established the principle of holding regular general council, the next in five years, the following in seven years, and thereafter every ten years; another established a procedure for dealing with future schisms; and a commission was established to determine a method of electing a pope.

In November, the electoral conclave met. Consisting of all the cardinals and delegates from each of the nations, this conclave came to agreement within three days on Cardinal Odo Colonna, who took the name Martin V. The enthusiasm of the moment hardly lasted past the naming of a reform commission; in January of 1418, the pope listed matters the commission should study, but he insisted on an impossible unanimity before any changes could be adopted. Papal authority was safe.

SIGNIFICANCE

Martin V was not eager to call another council, nor was his successor, Eugenius IV. They, the cardinals, and the papal bureaucrats recognized the danger presented by an effort to create a representative government for the Church. Who could resolve matters quickly and effec-

John Hus before the Council of Constance. (Frederick Ungar Publishing Co.)

tively, who could call for a crusade, who could decide whether a Holy Roman Emperor had been properly elected, if not the pope? Reforms would win public respect at the cost of bankrupting the Papacy and tying the pope's hands.

The Council of Constance had been a magnificent effort. The councilmen had restored the unity of the Roman Catholic Church, but they left some important disputes to be resolved by Martin Luther, others by the Council of Trent, and the rest by time.

—*Roger Smith*

FURTHER READING

Bellitto, Christopher M. *The General Councils: A History of the Twenty-one General Councils from Nicaea to Vatican II*. New York: Paulist Press, 2002. Detailed historical discussion of each of the general councils, including that of Constance.

Fudge, Thomas A. *The Crusade Against Heretics in Bohemia, 1418 to 1437: Sources and Documents for the Hussite Crusades*. Aldershot, Hampshire, England: Ashgate, 2002. A collection of primary sources drawn together to illustrate the Bohemian aftermath of the Council of Constance and the crusades that followed.

Holmes, George. *Europe, Hierarchy and Revolt, 1320-1450*. 2d ed. Malden, Mass.: Blackwell, 2000. Includes chapters on the Avignon and Roman papacies, the Great Schism, and the Hussite movement, and several maps.

Hughes, Philip. *The Church in Crisis: A History of the General Councils, 325-1870*. Garden City, N.Y.: Doubleday, 1964. Narrative account of the crises for a general audience by a prominent Roman Catholic scholar.

Lewin, Alison Williams. *Negotiating Survival: Florence and the Great Schism, 1378-1417*. Madison, N.J.: Farleigh Dickinson University Press, 2003. Provides the Florentine point of view on the Great Schism and the Council of Constance, as well as detailing the effects of these events upon the lives of the state's inhabitants.

Oberman, Heiko. *Forerunners of the Reformation: The Shape of Late Medieval Thought Illustrated by Key Documents*. New York: Holt, Rinehart and Winston, 1966. Provides a chapter on the intellectual nature of the Church, with emphasis on Hus's views, by a prominent theologian.

Pelikan, Jaroslav. *Reformation of Church and Dogma, 1300-1700*. Vol. 4 in *The Christian Tradition: A History of Development of Doctrine*. Chicago: University of Chicago Press, 1984. Citation-filled scholarly work, especially for theological students and scholars.

Spinka, Matthew. *John Hus at the Council of Constance*. New York: Columbia University Press, 1965. Contains a lengthy account of Hus's trial and execution.

Stump, Phillip H. *The Reforms of the Council of Constance, 1414-1418*. New York: E. J. Brill, 1994. Rehabilitative history of the council that claims it was more successful than generally thought, and explains the failures that existed.

Waugh, W. T. "The Councils of Constance and Basle." In *The Cambridge Medieval History*. Cambridge, England: Cambridge University Press, 1964. Straightforward, scholarly account of the council.

SEE ALSO: 735: Christianity Is Introduced into Germany; c. 1175: Waldensian Excommunications Usher in Protestant Movement; 1209-1229: Albigensian Crusade; 1305-1417: Avignon Papacy and the Great Schism; November 15, 1315: Swiss Victory at Morgarten over Habsburg Forces; 1337-1453: Hundred Years' War; 1377-1378: Condemnation of John Wyclif; June 28, 1389: Turkish Conquest of Serbia; July 6, 1415: Martyrdom of Jan Hus.

RELATED ARTICLES in *Great Lives from History: The Middle Ages, 477-1453*: Henry V; Jan Hus; Wenceslaus; Władysław II Jagiełło and Jadwiga; John Wyclif.

July 6, 1415
MARTYRDOM OF JAN HUS

The martyrdom of Jan Hus at the Council of Constance made him a Bohemian national hero and led to a Hussite revolt against the Holy Roman Emperor and a new schism within the Catholic Church.

LOCALE: Constance, South Germany, and Bohemia
CATEGORIES: Government and politics; religion

KEY FIGURES

Jan Hus (1372 or 1373-1415), Bohemian theologian and martyr
Jerome of Prague (c. 1365-1416), fellow martyr, brought John Wyclif's writings to Bohemia
Zajic Zbynêk (d. 1411), archbishop of Prague, 1403-1411, condemned Wyclif's teachings and tried to thwart Hus
John XXIII (d. 1419), antipope, 1410-1415
Sigismund (1368-1437), king of Hungary, r. 1387-1437, king of Bohemia, r. 1419-1437, and Holy Roman Emperor, r. 1433-1437
Wenceslas (1361-1419), king of Bohemia, r. 1378-1419, supporter of Hus

SUMMARY OF EVENT

In 1382, Ann of Bohemia married Richard II and became queen of England. Through that connection, Czech students began to attend Oxford University and came under the influence of John Wyclif's teaching. Although the Catholic Church had condemned Wyclif for holding heretical beliefs, the legacy of his teaching at Oxford remained after he had to leave the faculty. Jerome of Prague became acquainted with the writings of the English theologian and took them to Bohemia, where he presented them to Jan Hus, who already had been assailing abuses and corruptions in the late medieval church.

Hus, a master of arts at the University of Prague, joined its faculty in 1398 and was dean in 1401-1402. He was a popular preacher at Bethlehem Chapel, where he expounded Scripture in the Czech language and called for reforms in the Church in a manner similar to that of Wyclif.

As in Wyclif's England, the religious issues in Bohemia were connected with national resentment against foreign interference. Until the fourteenth century, Bohemia inclined more toward Constantinople than toward Rome for leadership in religion, because the country had received Christianity originally from the Eastern Church. The University of Prague had Czech and German faculties that opposed each other over various teachings of Wyclif. The Czechs distrusted the Germans and Rome, and antipapal sects such as the Waldensians had gained a following in Bohemia.

At first Archbishop Zajic Zbynêk supported Hus's efforts to cleanse the Church, but his vehement attacks upon clergymen involved in corruptions led Zybnêk to oppose Hus and other reformers. The Papacy at that time was divided between rivals at Rome and Avignon, and both would-be pontiffs urged the archbishop to suppress the dissidents on the grounds that they promoted Wyclif's heresies.

Hus, like Wyclif, espoused the Augustinian understanding of the true church as the body of people God predestined for salvation. Although the Bohemian reformer acknowledged the authority of the visible Catholic Church, he refused to equate it with the true church because so many of its members led evil lives and some of its practices were corrupt. In a book entitled *De ecclesia* (*The Church*, 1915), Hus published his doctrine, which ecclesiastical leaders deemed subversive. When the antipope Alexander V ordered the burning of Wyclif's books, Hus defended some, but not all, of the English reformer's doctrines. King Wenceslas of Bohemia protected Hus, so Archbishop Zbynêk and Alexander V denounced him. Zybnêk ordered the execution of several Hussite students. The Catholic Church at that time was seething with dissension over the divided Papacy, as rival claimants sat in Rome, Avignon, and Pisa, and a general council of bishops convened at Constance in an effort to heal the schism. Any unconventional teaching about the character of the true church was therefore unwelcome.

The archbishop of Prague tried to silence Hus, but he preached anyway. Zybnêk accused him of heresy. When the pope at Pisa, John XXIII, announced a sale of indulgences, Hus cited that as evidence of financial abuses in the highest Church office. King Wenceslas broke with Hus over this issue, so the reformer lost his protector. In 1414, Sigismund, king of Hungary and of Bohemia, who was to become Holy Roman Emperor, requested that Hus and Jerome appear before the Council of Constance to answer charges of heresy. He promised them safe conduct to and from the council, but a trial led on July 6, 1415, to condemnation and death by burning for both of the accused.

Perhaps Sigismund thought the executions at Constance would intimidate Bohemian dissidents, but they provoked a violent revolt instead. It began in Prague in 1419, under the leadership of Hussite noblemen, and so several Bohemian cites adhered to the defense against the Catholic forces. Sigismund's efforts to suppress the Hussites by force failed, but the rebels weakened their own cause by dividing among themselves. The conservative faction sought Church reforms in accord with Hus's teachings, but the radicals wanted sweeping social and political changes as well. The Taborites, as the radicals were known, decried the traditional feudal society and enlisted common people and lowly knights and clergymen, as they fought tenaciously until 1434, when imperial forces defeated them with aid from conservative Hussites.

Defeat in battle did not destroy the Hussites. Emperor Sigismund and the Catholic hierarchy agreed to a compromise in 1436 that allowed the Hussites to practice their religion and to enjoy the same political rights as Catholics. Many Hussite nobles kept Catholic properties they had seized during the revolt. The Papacy, reunited at the Council of Constance, did not accept the compromise, but it lacked the means to thwart it.

The Hussites had won politically as well as religiously, perhaps because of the defeat of the Taborite radicals. Large numbers of Bohemians and some Moravians aligned with the Hussite movement in opposition to the Roman Catholic Church. Bohemian nobles continued to elect their kings and to exert decisive influence in the national diet and thereby to maintain protection of the Hussites until the forces of the Habsburg Empire conquered Bohemia in the Thirty Years' War (1618-1648). The remaining Taborites who resisted absorption into the major Hussite church became known as United Brethren, which maintained a separate existence and refused all agreements with the Catholics and did not enjoy legal recognition. The Brethren were very receptive toward Lutheranism and Calvinism, when those beliefs entered Bohemia in the sixteenth century. Hussites of both connections suffered horribly during recurrent persecutions by Catholic authorities well into the eighteenth century.

John Hus. (Frederick Ungar Publishing Co.)

SIGNIFICANCE

Although the Hussites eventually became Protestants, Hus himself was almost completely orthodox when judged by the standards of medieval Catholicism. The account of his trial at the Council of Constance shows clearly that he accepted all seven sacraments and that he believed in transubstantiation, the teaching that the bread and wine of the Eucharist become the actual body and blood of Christ when a priest consecrates them. Hus believed in Purgatory and in prayers for the dead who were confined there, and he thought that living believers could perform good works to benefit the deceased in Purgatory. He believed the Virgin Mary had been raised from the dead and exalted to Heaven above the angels, where she intercedes for Christians on earth and in Purgatory. While he awaited execution, Hus confessed his sins to another priest, and he implored Saint John the Baptist to intercede for him with God.

It appears that his rejection of papal supremacy was Hus's only actual heresy. He upheld the authority of the Bible but as interpreted by the early ecumenical councils and the church fathers. He would not affirm the right of the pope to issue the infallible interpretations of either the Scriptures or the fathers. Hus preached and wrote in an era when the matter of supreme ecclesiastical authority was hotly contested, so his views appeared dangerous both to the Papacy and to advocates of the conciliar theory of church government.

—*James Edward McGoldrick*

FURTHER READING

Budgen, Victor. *On Fire for God*. Welwyn, England: Evangelical Press, 1983. A readable biography that extols Hus as an example of heroic faith.

Fudge, Thomas A. *The Crusade Against Heretics in Bohemia, 1418 to 1437: Sources and Documents for the Hussite Crusades*. Aldershot, Hampshire, England: Ashgate, 2002. A collection of primary sources drawn together to illustrate the Bohemian aftermath of the Council of Constance and the crusades that followed.

_______. *The Magnifcent Ride: The First Reformation in Hussite Bohemia*. Brookfield, Vt.: Ashgate, 1998. A detailed account of Hus's theology, his politics, and his historical legacy. Places the Hussites in the context of the political and cultural situation in fourteenth and early fifteenth century Bohemia.

Hus, John. *The Church*. Translated by David Schaff. Westport, Conn.: Greenwood Press, 1974. A reprint of an edition of Hus's most controversial writing, *De ecclesia*, first published in translation in 1915. Essential reading for an understanding of his beliefs.

_______. "Hus on Simony." In *Advocates of Reform*, edited by Matthew Spinka. Vol. 14 of Library of Christian Classics. Philadelphia: Westminster Press, 1953. An important tract that shows Hus's exposé of ecclesiastical corruption.

Kaminsky, Howard. *A History of the Hussite Revolution*. Berkeley: University of California Press, 1967. A thorough study of Hussite ideas and their revolutionary consequences.

Klassen, John M. *Warring Maidens, Captive Wives, and Hussite Queens: Women and Men at War and at Peace in Fifteenth Century Bohemia*. New York: Columbia University Press, 1999. A useful text for broadening one's understanding of the cultural effects of the Hussite revolution. Examines the changing roles of women in fifteenth century Bohemia. The author argues that women gained more freedom from traditional roles as men came to respect those dissident women working to resist women's oppression and subordination.

Roubiczek, Paul, and Joseph Kalmer. *Warrior of God*. London: Nicholson and Watson, 1947. A valuable biography by enthusiasts who portray Hus as a saint.

Spinka, Matthew. *John Hus*. Princeton, N.J.: Princeton University Press, 1968. The best biography of Hus published in English. Scholarly, readable, and fair.

_______. *John Hus and the Czech Reform*. Chicago: University of Chicago Press, 1941. An important study of Hus's concept of reform and the extent of his debt to Wyclif.

_______, ed. and trans. *John Hus at the Council of Constance*. New York: Columbia University Press, 1965. The records of Hus's trial and execution. Shows clearly that he was not a proto-Protestant.

SEE ALSO: 735: Christianity Is Introduced into Germany; 1054: Beginning of the Rome-Constantinople Schism; c. 1175: Waldensian Excommunications Usher in Protestant Movement; 1209-1229: Albigensian Crusade; November 11-30, 1215: Fourth Lateran Council; 1305-1417: Avignon Papacy and the Great Schism; 1337-1453: Hundred Years' War; 1377-1378: Condemnation of John Wyclif.

RELATED ARTICLES in *Great Lives from History: The Middle Ages, 477-1453*: Henry V; Jan Hus; Wenceslaus; William of Saint-Amour; Władysław II Jagiełło and Jadwiga; John Wyclif; Jan Žižka.

1415-1460
PRINCE HENRY THE NAVIGATOR PROMOTES PORTUGUESE EXPLORATION

Prince Henry dispatched exploratory expeditions that removed the imagined terrors of the deep sea, established the first commercial trade ventures of modern times, and marked the start of the African slave trade.

LOCALE: Sagres, Largos, and Lisbon, Portugal
CATEGORIES: Exploration and discovery; trade and commerce

KEY FIGURES

Prince Henry the Navigator (1394-1460), third son of King John of Portugal
John Gonçalves (c. 1400-c. 1465), explorer who rediscovered the Canary Islands and Madeira in 1418
Antão Gonçalves (fl. fifteenth century) and
Nuno Tristão (fl. fifteenth century), originators of Portuguese slave interests in 1441
Diogo Gomes (fl. 1440-1484), explorer of Cape Verde Islands between 1458 and 1460

SUMMARY OF EVENT

The court of Prince Henry the Navigator at Sagres became famous as a place that attracted mathematicians, geographers, and, in general, any scientific-minded person from East or West interested in exploration, discovery, and the expansion of maritime knowledge. The center of Henry's maritime activity was not his court at Sagres, but at Lagos, where nearly all the early expeditions were equipped. Although Henry financed and directed many expeditions along the coast of Africa, he did not accompany them. His aim was not personal adventure, but rather the expansion of scientific knowledge and the extension of Portugal's wealth.

Inspired by the crusading zeal of his mother, he claimed that his primary goal was the propagation of Christianity even beyond Moorish lands. While he also sought to draw commercial profit from the new-found lands to underwrite the vast expense of the voyages, the sincerity of his religious and scientific motives is not easily discredited. Determined to wipe out medieval fears of the sea and unknown lands, he was passionately involved in supervising the compilation and dissemination of the knowledge gained from new voyages. The influence of the ancient Greek astronomer Ptolemy was still great: His view that the world was flat attracted supporters, and many believed that while the known portion of the earth was neatly divided into ordered segments, the unknown area was full of sea monsters and boiling waters. Henry not only studied the ancient geographers and medieval maps, but engaged an expert map and instrument maker, James of Majorca, so that his explorers might have the best nautical information.

Henry's enthusiasm was fed not only by the experiences of the traders of his own day, but also by his knowledge of past expeditions of Crusaders and explorers such as Marco Polo and John de Plano Caprini. Little was known of the Viking adventures in crossing the Atlantic to Greenland and America or their penetration of Russia, but Henry became interested in studying their sea ventures and was strongly influenced by them. Between 1250 and 1410, many new geographical vistas had opened up. In 1270, the Italian Lancelot Malocello found the Canary Islands, and in 1281 and 1291, the Italians Tedisio Doria and Vivaldi discovered Cape Horn while trying to reach India by sea. Around 1350, the Catalonians found Guinea. The Englishman Robert Machin reached Madeira, only to die there; however, his servant managed to escape from the island and eventually reported the discovery to Henry.

Henry's captains used all the reliable knowledge of the sea available to them from such explorations, and used the compass and other instruments to navigate in the open sea. Henry's first venture in expansion, however, was the Portuguese conquest in 1415 of Ceuta, the Moorish port opposite Gibraltar. Fulfilling the mission of the Military Order of Christ, of which he was grandmaster, his ships carried on a constant war against the Muslims. He envisioned the conquest of Ceuta as part of the Crusade against Islam. The permanent occupation of Ceuta marks the beginning of imperialism by nation-states three generations in advance of the general movement. Again in 1418, when John Gonçalves rediscovered the Canaries and Madeira, colonization followed.

It was after the fall of Ceuta that Henry entered his career of discovery, and his immediate objects were to know the country beyond Cape Bojador, the farthest limit of the known world on the west side of Africa, to open up trade relations and to spread the Christian faith. After twelve years of voyages down the African coast, one of his seamen, Gil Eanes, finally rounded Cape Bojador off the coast of modern Rio de Oro in 1434 or 1435. He found habitable land and not sea monsters. From that date events moved quickly.

An unsuccessful attempt to take Tangier occupied Henry's attention between 1437 and 1445. Nevertheless, Antão Gonçalves landed on the coast of Africa in 1441 and brought back the first captives. Nuno Tristão penetrated as far as Cape Blanco, and a few years later to Arguim Bay, and also returned with captured indigenous people, thus inaugurating the slave trade of Guinea. Although Henry's school has been reproached with encouraging slavery, it was an age that saw no harm in the traffic, and he would claim that the Africans brought to Portugal were employed in domestic offices and fairly treated, and that nearly all of them became Christians. There is little doubt, however, about his interest in the discovery of gold around Guinea. In 1445, a number of caravels sailed to Cape Verde. Ten years later, Alvise Cadamosto (whose narrative proved a most significant contribution to the knowledge of Africa and its adjoining waters) sailed 500 miles (800 kilometers) farther to Cape Palmar. The discovery of the Azores to the west of Spain by Gonzalo Cibial in 1436, and the further discovery of two more groups of islands before 1450, led to the colonization of the whole archipelago before Henry's death in 1460.

Prince Henry of Portugal, in armor after the conquest of Ceuta (1415), the Moorish port on the African side of the Strait of Gibraltar. (Hulton|Archive by Getty Images)

From 1458 to 1460, Diogo Gomes explored the Senegal and the Gambia, and sailed down the coast as far as Sierra Leone, marking the final exploring effort during Henry's lifetime. Henry's last labor was the commissioning and supervision of the beautiful Camaldalese Chart of Fra Mauro, which carefully illustrated the systematic and scientific discoveries of Henry's "school." He died in November, 1460, deeply in debt as the price of his lifelong service to the cause of Christianity and science and to the pursuance of his motto, *Talent de bien faire* ("The desire to do well").

Significance

The more remote achievements resulting from the pioneering efforts of Henry and his court include the voyage of Bartholomeu Dias around Cape Horn in 1486, the voyage to India round Africa by Vasco da Gama from 1497 to 1499, and the establishment of the first outpost of empire by Albuquerque between 1506 and 1515. All of these men were trained in the techniques of Prince Henry's techniques, and their voyages were inspired or encouraged by his school. Ultimately, the discovery of America by Columbus—and by the Italian Amerigo Vespucci—and the circumnavigation of the globe by Magellan's crew were inspired by the achievements of Henry's captains and their successors. Thus, Henry's thirst for inquiry, empire, and crusading led to the opening of a new age and a new world.

—*Carl F. Rohne, updated by Marian T. Horvat*

Further Reading

Aczel, Amir D. *The Riddle of the Compass: The Invention that Changed the World.* New York: Har-

AFRICAN EXPEDITIONS SPONSORED BY PRINCE HENRY

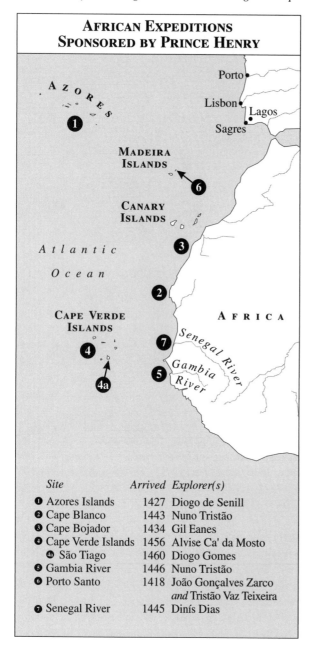

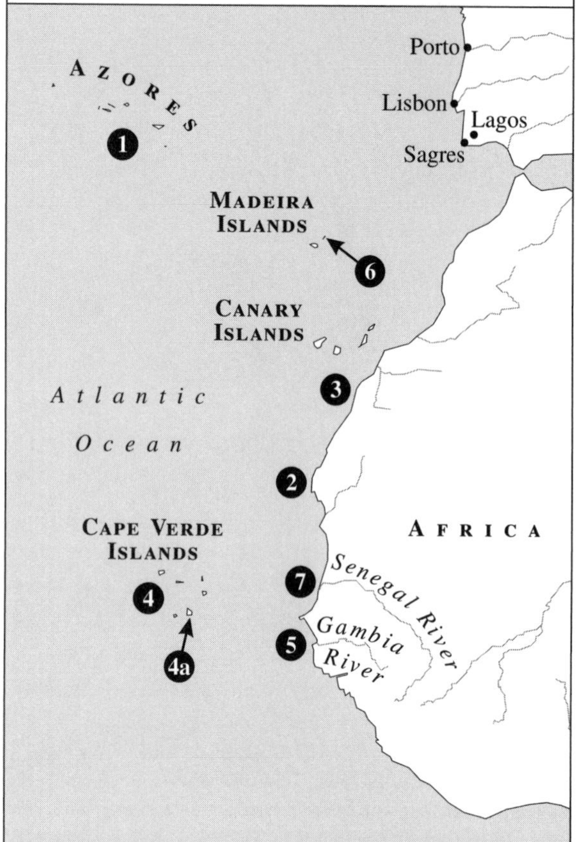

Site	*Arrived*	*Explorer(s)*
1 Azores Islands	1427	Diogo de Senill
2 Cape Blanco	1443	Nuno Tristão
3 Cape Bojador	1434	Gil Eanes
4 Cape Verde Islands	1456	Alvise Ca' da Mosto
4a São Tiago	1460	Diogo Gomes
5 Gambia River	1446	Nuno Tristão
6 Porto Santo	1418	João Gonçalves Zarco *and* Tristão Vaz Teixeira
7 Senegal River	1445	Dinís Dias

court, 2001. A brief but detailed and thorough account of the invention of the compass. Also discusses the history of navigation to the fifteenth century.

Beazley, Charles Raymond. *Prince Henry, the Navigator: The Hero of Portugal and of Modern Discovery, 1394-1460 A.D.* New York: G. P. Putnam's Sons, 1894. Reprint. New York: Burt Franklin, 1968. Considered a standard biography of Prince Henry that closely follows primary sources and presents a sympathetic picture.

Bradford, Ernle D. S. *A Wind from the North: The Life of Henry the Navigator.* New York: Harcourt, Brace, 1960. A favorable assessment of the character and outlook of Prince Henry based on source documents.

Goodman, Jennifer R. *Chivalry and Exploration, 1298-1630.* Rochester, N.Y.: Boydell Press, 1998. A survey of medieval exploration, with chapters on Prince Henry's chivalry, chivalric literature in the age of exploration, and the romance as a literature of travel. Includes a bibliography and index.

Hanson, Carl. *Atlantic Emporium: Portugal and the Wider World, 1147-1497.* New Orleans, La.: University Press of the South, 2001. A brief survey of Portugal's period of discovery, including Henry's expeditions. Includes illustrations, a bibliography, and index.

Oliveira Martins, J. P. *The Golden Age of Prince Henry, the Navigator.* Translated by James Johnston Abraham and W. Edward Reynolds. London: Chapman and Hall, 1914. Classic Portuguese work by a noted scholar in the field with a primary emphasis on politics and the personalities of the court. Makes a critical portrayal of Prince Henry.

Russell, Peter. *Portugal, Spain, and the African Atlantic, 1343-1490: Chivalry and Crusade from John of Gaunt to Henry the Navigator and Beyond.* Brookfield, Vt.: Variorum, 1995. A history of Portuguese—and Spanish—exploration along the African coast during Prince Henry's time.

_______. *Prince Henry "the Navigator": A Life.* New Haven, Conn.: Yale University Press, 2000. A history of Prince Henry and his expeditions. Provides many illustrations, a map of discoveries, and a translated letter of Henry's, written to his father. Includes an extensive bibliography and index.

Sanceau, Elaine. *Henry the Navigator: The Story of a Great Prince and His Times.* New Haven. Conn.: Archon Books, 1969. A factual and easy-reading narrative by a noted English scholar of Portuguese history.

Ure, John. *Prince Henry the Navigator.* London: Constable, 1977. Portrays Prince Henry as a more complex figure, a man torn between the conflicting influences of his medieval background and a pragmatic, forward-looking personality.

Winius, George D., ed. *Portugal, the Pathfinder: Journeys from the Medieval Toward the Modern World,*

1300-circa 1600. Madison, Wis.: Hispanic Seminary of Medieval Studies, 1995. Chapters look at figures such as Prince Henry, Vasco de Gama, and their successors; the "discovery" of the Atlantic as a space; the evidence of medieval maps; and Portuguese expansion in West Africa. Includes a bibliography and index.

SEE ALSO: 850-950: Viking Era; c. 1145: Prester John Myth Sweeps Across Europe; c. 1250: Improvements in Shipbuilding and Navigation; May 29, 1453: Fall of Constantinople.

RELATED ARTICLES in *Great Lives from History: The Middle Ages, 477-1453*: Prince Henry the Navigator; Petrus Peregrinus de Maricourt.

1428
LE LOI ESTABLISHES LATER LE DYNASTY

Le Loi's victory over Chinese occupiers demonstrated both the superiority of guerrilla and psychological warfare and the Vietnamese people's determination to resist foreign rule.

LOCALE: Vietnam, China
CATEGORIES: Government and politics; wars, uprisings, and civil unrest

KEY FIGURES

Le Loi (1385-1443), king of Vietnam, r. 1428-1443
Nguyen Trai (1380-1442), principal strategist and close adviser to Le Loi
Yonglo (Yung-lo; 1363-1424), emperor of China, r. 1402-1424

SUMMARY OF EVENT

Taking advantage of Ho Qui Ly's usurpation of the Tran throne in 1400, which caused popular resentment among the Vietnamese people, Yonglo sent his armies southward to conquer Vietnam. After removing the last king of the Ho Dynasty (1400-1407) from power and destroying all the pocket resistance by Tran Dynasty (1225-1400) loyalists, he set up Chinese rule over Vietnam in 1414. Though Vietnam in the past had been made a Chinese province, this occupation was particularly cruel. Chinese rulers pursued a systematic policy meant to destroy Vietnam's identity: Its people were forced to adopt Chinese customs and to scour the jungle and the sea for treasures. Books and all valuable items were confiscated and taken to China, along with the colony's skilled artisans and topnotch professionals.

A landlord and farmer, Le Loi used his wealth and popularity to organize an armed resistance to the Chinese occupation, officially declared in 1417. Though he was able to rally many Vietnamese to his cause, his early military campaigns were not always successful. In one desperate battle, Le Loi's life was saved by one of his generals, who disguised himself as his commander in chief. The Chinese captured the general, whom they mistook for Le Loi, and unknowingly let their enemy escape.

By as early as 1425, using alternately guerrilla and large-scale operations, Le Loi had scored victory after victory over the Chinese. To bring the war to a quick end, he successfully employed psychological warfare, a sophisticated strategy developed by his close adviser and principal strategist Nguyen Trai. For example, to create in the minds of the people and the troops a superstitious belief in Le Loi as Heaven's choice to lead the resistance, Nguyen Trai had the saying "Le Loi Shall Be King" engraved on rocks and old trees. The powerful occupying force was reduced to a few, isolated garrisons and lost the will to fight when Le Loi's troops ambushed and destroyed periodic reinforcements. The most decisive battle took place in 1427 at Chi Lang Pass near the Chinese border, where elite units of the newest reinforcement suffered heavy losses, and their commander Liou Cheng was killed. Vietnam was totally liberated, and Le Loi proclaimed himself emperor in 1428.

The first thing Le Loi did after the country became independent was seek reconciliation with China. It had become a rule that for Vietnam to live in peace, its king must have China's recognition. Le Loi scored another diplomatic victory, except he was required to submit triannually two effigies in pure gold—probably a compensation for the killing of China's two generals during the war—as part of a vassal's tribute to his Chinese sovereign.

After a long period of Chinese rule and protracted war, Vietnam was literally asunder. Le Loi began to launch reforms as soon as he assumed power. Most of his reforms were important and necessary, but they were by and large extreme and severe.

Reforms were from the top down to the grassroots level.To train qualified administrators, Le Loi founded

Quoc tu Giam (institute for the education of the children of the nation), which enrolled high officials' children as well as gifted students from the populace. An annual special exam was required for all government officials of lower ranks, forcing them to keep their administrative skills updated. At the local level, schools were open to all students, regardless of their family status and origin. Even Buddhist and Daoist monks were required to pass a qualifying exam to be licensed to practice their faith.

To protect social order and morality, which had eroded because of the wars, severe penalties ranging from caning to severing fingers and toes were meted out for minor violations such as creating a public disturbance, gambling, petty theft, and vagrancy.

Military reforms were implemented with the agricultural nature of the country in mind. Because Vietnam was in peacetime, Le Loi reduced his 250,000-man-strong army to 100,000 troops. Only one-third of the number remained as the standing army, the rest returned to their villages to do agricultural work.

Le Loi's most important reforms were in matters of land redistribution and private property. Because public land was occupied by profiteers during the war, veterans had no means of living when they returned to their villages. To remedy the situation, Le Loi confiscated the illegally owned land and redistributed it to those who had participated in the resistance, including retired high officials, able-bodied war veterans, orphans, widows, the invalids, and the elderly.

SIGNIFICANCE

According to Sunzi in *Sunzi Bingfa* (c. 5th-3d century B.C.E.; *The Art of War,* 1910), to be successful in a conquest, a king must see to it that he meets these three requirements: First, he must have Heaven's consent; second, he must engage the enemy at a propitious location; and third, he must have the local people's support. Le Loi's conduct of the resistance to Chinese rule shows that he exceeded these three demands.

By "Heaven's consent," Sunzi meant the right time for action. According to the Daoist concept of timeliness, a response not thought through to a premeditated provocation brings harm only to the self as one does not know what the enemy will do next. Daoism therefore calls for vigilance and careful planning in order to guarantee sure success for the eventual retaliation. Le Loi brilliantly applied Sunzi's teaching in all phases of his struggle against the Chinese. First, in the early stages of war, he used guerrilla tactics to harass rather than confront the enemy. Large-scale attacks were launched only when his force was strong enough and when the enemy was exhausted. Second, Le Loi engaged the enemy where he wanted by having a small contingent harass them and flee, thus luring them into ambushes that destroyed them. Finally, Le Loi's greatest asset was his people's unconditional support for his cause. The period of Chinese rule was too long and too brutal for the Vietnamese to bear. They now turned to Le Loi as their savior who they believed could take them out of what they perceived as slavery.

Another human factor contributed not only to Le Loi's smashing military victory but also to the king's prestige and Vietnam's dignity vis-à-vis China after the war. In all phases of the resistance, it was Nguyen Trai who developed proper strategies to win the war. One of his favorite tactics to avoid unnecessary bloodshed was to persuade the embattled enemy to surrender. Nguyen Trai's arguments were so convincing that numerous commanders of the Chinese army turned over their bastions to Le Loi's troops. Nguyen Trai's literary genius was shown in his masterpiece *Binh ngo dai cao* (1428; proclamation on the pacification of the Wu), in which he justified the victorious uprising against the Chinese by Le Loi as well as the legitimacy of his kingship and the dignity of being the free citizens of Vietnam. On the diplomatic front, Nguyen Trai also helped Le Loi win an important victory when the Chinese emperor, convinced by Nguyen Trai's rhetorical skills, agreed to appoint Le Loi king of Vietnam.

Le Loi's social reforms were far more radical and progressive than those carried out by kings of previous and later dynasties. Vietnam's modern private property system, for example, was derived from Le Loi's so-called *quan dien* (public land) system described above. The Later Le Dynasty (1428-1789) marked the first long period of national independence from imperial China.

—*Qui-Phiet Tran*

FURTHER READING

Buttinger, Joseph. *The Smaller Dragon.* New York: Frederick A. Praeger, 1958. Provides an account of Vietnam's struggle for independence from foreign rule since the tenth century. Argues that dynastic strength stemmed from political, agricultural, military, and educational reforms.

Huynh, Sanh Thong, ed. and trans. *An Anthology of Vietnamese Poems From the Eleventh to Twentieth Centuries.* New Haven, Conn.: Yale University Press, 1966. Includes selected poems by Nguyen Trai that describe his concept of living after his retirement from Le Loi's imperial court.

Kenny, Henry J. *Shadow of the Dragon: Vietnam's Continuing Struggle with China and the Implications for U.S. Foreign Policy.* Washington, D.C.: Brassey's, 2002. Argues that American policy to Vietnam should be considered in light of the country's past and modern-day disputes with its giant neighbor.
Whitfield, Danny J. *Historical and Cultural Dictionary of Vietnam.* Metuchen, N.J.: Scarecrow Press, 1976. Contains references to Vietnam's history and culture. The Le Loi section discusses the king's victory campaigns against the Ming army and his major reforms after the war.
Woods, Shelton L. *Vietnam: A Global Studies Handbook.* Santa Barbara, Calif.: ABC-CLIO, 2002. Provides an overview of Vietnam's history, geography, culture, and customs.

SEE ALSO: 729: Founding of Nanzhao; 832: Nanzhao Subjugates Pyu; 939-944: Reign of Ngo Quyen; 1225: Tran Thai Tong Establishes Tran Dynasty; 1323-1326: Champa Wins Independence from Dai Viet.
RELATED ARTICLES in *Great Lives from History: The Middle Ages, 477-1453*: Ngo Quyen; Yonglo.

May 4-8, 1429
JOAN OF ARC'S RELIEF OF ORLÉANS

Joan of Arc's military leadership in the relief of Orléans began a series of French victories that shattered the myth of English invincibility and turned the tide in the Hundred Years' War. Her legacy as a national savior, warrior, and martyr remains to this day.

LOCALE: France
CATEGORIES: Wars, uprisings, and civil unrest; government and politics; religion

KEY FIGURES

Joan of Arc (c. 1412-1431), French heroine also known as the Maid of Orléans
Charles VII (1403-1461), Valois claimant to the French throne
Jean Dunois (1403-1468), bastard child of the duke of Orléans, later comte de Dunois, French commander at Orléans
John of Lancaster (1389-1435), duke of Bedford and regent in France for Henry VI
John Talbot (c. 1384-1453), earl of Shrewsbury and English troop commander at Orléans

SUMMARY OF EVENT

During the Anglo-French Hundred Years' War (1337-1453), the English invaders repeatedly defeated France's feudal armies in battles such as Crécy (1337) and Poitiers (1356). With Henry V's victory at Agincourt in 1415, English mastery of all France seemed possible. Defeated and demented, King Charles VI of France, by the 1420 Treaty of Trois, gave Henry his daughter Catherine in marriage and regency powers and inheritance rights, in effect disinheriting his own son, the dauphin Charles. Henry V and Charles VI died in 1422, leaving an infant Henry VI as sovereign of both kingdoms. Henry's regent for France, John of Lancaster, duke of Bedford, held Paris and northern France with the alliance of Burgundy and the acquiescence of Brittany. The former dauphin, claiming the throne as Charles VII, was an uncrowned and generally unsuccessful challenger. His "capital" at Bourges and a residence at Chinon were threatened as Bedford's commanders advanced. On October 12, 1428, the English attacked the key city of Orléans on the north bank of the Loire.

The invaders had scattered so many troops in Loire valley garrisons that less than five thousand were at hand to take the walled city, and even these forces were dispersed—some in connected forts northwest of Orléans, others in isolated forts upstream or downstream or at the south end of the nine-span Loire bridge. Despite this, river traffic continued, there was an upstream ford, and the city's eastern gate admitted supplies. Orléans' seventy-one heavy cannon and numerous field pieces outgunned the besiegers. John Talbot, the effective English siege commander, was essentially waiting for the city of perhaps forty thousand, including refugees, to starve. On the other hand, the capable French commander, Jean Dunois, felt that with only two thousand troops and two thousand militia, he could not attack, and so waited for reinforcements. The bishop and several leading citizens left, and, by early 1429, the people of Orléans began to feel abandoned. At Chinon in March, while King Charles was trying to organize a relief force, a seventeen-year-old peasant girl arrived and volunteered to lead the expedition.

Joan of Arc entering Orléans. (F. R. Niglutsch)

Joan the Maid, or Jehanne la Pucelle, as she described herself, was one of five children born to Isabelle Romée and peasant farmer Jacques in the Lorraine village of Domrémy. Her childhood was "like the others" until about 1425, when she began to sense voices and visions of saints telling her that God wished Joan to drive the English from France. By 1428, she was petitioning local officials for support, and in February of 1429, Joan was given an escort for the 240-mile (386-kilometer) journey to Chinon. There the court awaited her with a mixture of curiosity, skepticism, and faint hope.

Joan presented to Charles a still secret "personal message" as well as her service toward raising the siege of Orléans and leading the troops to Reims, where Charles could be anointed with the sacred oil kept there for traditional French coronations. Charles was impressed by Joan's confidence, but he cautiously had her examined by clerics and matrons to make sure the virgin claiming divine inspiration was not a witch deceived and seduced by the devil. Once cleared of Satanic associations, Joan was equipped with white armor, a sword, a small battle-ax, a white religious standard of her own design, a large black charger that she rode with admirable skill, and a vague status as a commander (but not a knight or chevalier) in the four-thousand-man relief force that set out from Blois for Orléans on April 27. The march seemed an uncertain combination of supplies, military force, religious devotion, and showmanship.

The French relief army, keeping south of the Loire, arrived upstream from Orléans on the afternoon of April 28 or 29, and were met by commander Dunois. He was impressed by Joan's forcefulness and anxious to show this much-expected arrival to the people of Orléans. Accordingly, in the early evening Joan rode through the eastern gate, escorted by Dunois and other captains. Torches dramatized the procession and crowds pressed forward to touch the garments or at least the horse of this girl they hoped would save them. For several days, while the French commanders debated plans of attack, Joan mingled with the garrison and citizens of Orléans, while also sending surrender demands to the English commanders. The English troops hailed her with earthy insults, but the French soldiers increasingly accepted her as a leader.

On May 4, French troops attacked Saint Loup, an English fort east of Orléans. Joan hastened to the fight, which Dunois was ready to discontinue, and rallied the French to capture the position. Thereafter, Joan was one of the military council, and she also played a leading part in taking Les Augustins near the south end of the bridge. On May 7, while fighting at the Tourelles fortification (towers) and guarding the bridge itself, Joan was seriously wounded by an arrow, but still took charge of the attack that captured the towers. By nightfall of May 7, the Loire bridge was in French hands, and Orléans was no longer isolated. The following day, after challenging the French to battle (which they declined) the English army marched north. On the evening of May 8, the long-besieged citizens celebrated their rescue by the Maid of Orléans.

The relief of Orléans was accomplished without a major battle of main forces—only a few hundred lives were lost on each side, and the odds clearly favored the French after April 29. Nevertheless, the prolonged September to May "siege" was lifted unexpectedly only nine days after Joan's arrival, enough of a "miracle" to encourage the French and disquiet the English, as Bedford reported to London. Joan, Dunois, and other French commanders captured English garrisons along the Loire at Jargeau, Meung, and Beaugency. On June 17, the English and French main armies, each numbering about five thousand, encountered each other near Patay. While Talbot and Sir John Fastolf began to deploy in the usual English "hedgehog" defense line of stakes and archers, Joan's insistence on immediate attack took them by surprise. In a paralyzing defeat, the English lost thousands, Talbot was captured, Fastolf fled, and the English, decisively beaten in the field, fell back on Paris. Patay ranked with Orléans as a decisive French victory and a blow to English morale.

French debates over strategic direction continued until Charles reluctantly tried Joan's plan to advance through Champagne for a coronation at Reims. The march became a triumph—popular enthusiasm (and a few bribes) disarmed opposition and avoided any divisive battle between the French. The idolized girl on horseback achieved her greatest political success with the Reims coronation, which dramatized Charles as the crowned, anointed, and rightful king of France.

In 1430, however, Joan failed to take Paris, was captured near Compiègne in May by Burgundian forces, sold to the English-controlled Paris authorities, and tried by a Church court at Rouen from January through May, 1431. The judges and Joan disagreed somewhat dogmatically concerning God's will, and the court predictably insisted that Joan's anti-English voices must be either imaginary or proof of Satanic possession. After a brief "recantation" of the voices, Joan "relapsed" and as a convicted heretic and tool of the devil, was turned over to the civil authorities and burned at the stake in Rouen on May 30, 1431.

The popular nationalism that Joan had harnessed so dramatically in 1429 did not by itself drive the English from France. Those who could pay for such a war wanted to be able to profit from the outcome. King Charles (who made no attempt to ransom Joan in 1430) methodically pursued governmental, fiscal, and military reforms and in 1435 also won the support of Burgundy for expelling the English. Only in 1450, with success assured, did Charles order the inquiry that cleared Joan (and the king) of any taint of witchcraft or heresy. Papal authorities declared Joan rehabilitated in 1456, and in a later and different context, the Church declared her "venerable" in 1904, "blessed" in 1909, and canonized on May 16, 1920, as "Saint Joan."

SIGNIFICANCE

Joan of Arc added the spark of moral and combat leadership needed to give the French a season of military and political success and the confidence and credibility for ultimate victory at Orléans. Yet in the long run, Joan's life was seen as a human drama even more compelling than the war itself. She was a "guided" heroic savior by the age of nineteen—a sort of fairy tale, but with a brutal ending.

—*K. Fred Gillum*

FURTHER READING

Burne, Alfred H. *The Agincourt War: A Military History of the Latter Part of the Hundred Years' War from 1369 to 1453*. Ware, Hertfordshire, England: Wordsworth Editions, 1999. An English military analysis of the Battle of Agincourt, originally published in 1956.

DeVries, Kelly. *Joan of Arc: A Military Leader.* Phoenix Mill, Mich.: Sutton, 1999. A biography exploring Joan as a saint and a military leader. Includes illustrations, a bibliography, and an index.

Elliott, Dyan. "Seeing Double: John Gerson, the Discernment of Spirits, and Joan of Arc." *American Historical Review* 107, no. 1 (February, 2002). Argues that the work of the French theologian Jean de Gerson (1363-1429) attempted to use clerical control to "contain" female spirituality, including Joan's.

Gies, Frances. *Joan of Arc: The Legend and the Reality.* New York: Harper and Row, 1981. A scholarly account, but omits some "legends." Includes a bibliography and an index.

Pernoud, Régine. *Joan of Arc by Herself and Her Witnesses*. Translated by Edward Hyams. 1966. Reprint. Lanham, Md.: Scarborough House, 1994. A work of great integrity and judgment by the former director of the Centre Jeanne d'Arc in Orléans, who culled documents of Joan's own times for this extremely useful book.

Sackville-West, Vita. *Saint Joan of Arc*. New York: Grove Press, 2001. A comprehensive and well-balanced biographical account of Joan, first published in 1936 and written by the noted twentieth century British author. Includes discussion of the history of France during the reign of Charles VII.

Warner, Marina. *Joan of Arc: The Image of Female Heroism*. Berkeley: University of California Press, 2000. The author ranges through the centuries and provides, for example, a hard look at how little is known about Joan's appearance and image as a hero.

Wheeler, Bonnie, and Charles T. Wood, eds. *Fresh Verdicts on Joan of Arc*. New York: Garland, 1999. A wealth of essays ranging from topics such as Joan's military leadership of men, her gender expression, her interrogation at trial, errors in histories of Joan, comparisons with Christine de Pizan, and more.

SEE ALSO: 1233: Papal Inquisition; c. 1250-1300: Homosexuality Criminalized and Subject to Death Penalty; July 2, 1324: Lady Alice Kyteler Is Found Guilty of Witchcraft; 1337-1453: Hundred Years' War; 1453: English Are Driven from France.

RELATED ARTICLES in *Great Lives from History: The Middle Ages, 477-1453*: Charles d'Orléans; Alain Chartier; Christina of Markyate; Christine de Pizan; Fredegunde; Henry V; Joan of Arc; Damia al-Kāhina; Margery Kempe; Lady Alice Kyteler; Philip the Good.

1440
DONATION OF CONSTANTINE IS EXPOSED

The Donation of Constantine was exposed as fraudulent, casting doubts on the legitimacy of papal authority.

LOCALE: Kingdom of Naples (now in Italy)
CATEGORIES: Cultural and intellectual history; religion

KEY FIGURES

Nicholas of Cusa (1401-1464), philosopher and theologian
Lorenzo Valla (1407-1457), philosopher
Alfonso V (1396-1458), king of Aragon, r. 1416-1458, and king of Naples, r. 1442-1458
Eugenius IV (1383-1447), Roman Catholic pope, 1431-1447

SUMMARY OF EVENT

The Donation of Constantine (known in Latin as the *Constitutum Constantini*) is a document supposedly written by Constantine the Great, the first Christian emperor of Rome, to Pope Sylvester I in the early fourth century. The document consists of about three hundred lines of Latin text and is divided into two parts. The first half is known as the *Confessio* and the second half is known as the *Donatio*.

The *Confessio* describes how Constantine the Great rejected the advice of pagan priests to bathe in the blood of children to cure his leprosy. He then had a dream in which Saint Peter and Saint Paul appeared to him and told him he would be cured if he visited Pope Sylvester I and became baptized as a Christian by him. Constantine followed this advice and was miraculously cured.

The *Donatio* relates how Constantine, in gratitude for his cure, declared that Pope Sylvester I and his successors would have rule over all Christian churches in the world. Constantine also granted them the use of his Lateran Palace and the use of numerous imperial insignias. Most important, he gave them political power over all the western part of the Roman Empire and stated that he would move his own court to a new capital (Constantinople) in the eastern part.

Throughout the Middle Ages, the Donation of Constantine was used to defend the authority of the pope over all other Christian clergy and over the secular rulers of western Europe. Although some questioned the validity of the Donation of Constantine on the grounds that the emperor could not legally donate his authority over the empire, the authenticity of the document itself was rarely challenged. The only known accusation of forgery before the fifteenth century came from Otto III, ruler of the Western Roman Empire, in 1001.

The first important attempt to prove that the Donation of Constantine was a forgery came from the German priest, philosopher, theologian, and mathematician Nicholas of Cusa. In his book *De concordantia catholica* (1433, on unity), he noted that the Donation of Constantine was not mentioned in any of the numerous church histories of its time. He also used historical records to show that the pope acknowledged the authority of the emperor in Western Europe until the eighth century.

The most critical attack on the authenticity of the Donation of Constantine came seven years later when the Italian philosopher Lorenzo Valla wrote *De falso credita et ementita Constantini donatione declamatio* (1440; *The Treatise of Lorenzo Valla on the Donation of Constantine*, 1922). In this work, Valla used both historical evidence and linguistic analysis to demonstrate that the Donation of Constantine could not have been written during the time of Constantine I.

Like Nicholas of Cusa, Valla noted the lack of historical records mentioning the document. He also noted that the Donation of Constantine made reference to the controversy over the use of images in worship services, an issue that did not come up until the eighth century. The document also mentioned satraps, a type of official that did not exist in the government of Constantine I.

Valla also studied the style of Latin used in the Donation of Constantine to prove that it could not have been written in the fourth century. By carefully examining the grammar and vocabulary used in the document, he was able to demonstrate that the Latin of the Donation of Constantine was not the Latin used during the time of Constantine I but the Latin used hundreds of years later.

Valla had many political, theological, and philosophical reasons for his attack on the authenticity of the Donation of Constantine. Besides a concern for exposing the truth, he also hoped to demonstrate that it would be evil for the pope to accept secular power from Constantine the Great because his Roman Empire was tyrannic. In a similar way, he advocated the spiritual freedom of the individual over the absolute spiritual authority of the pope. Philosophically, he defended the use of objective evidence over reliance on accepted authority.

Valla also had a more practical reason for denying the authenticity of the Donation of Constantine. He was employed as a secretary and historian to Alfonso V, king of Aragon, who was at war with Pope Eugenius IV over control of the kingdom of Naples. By exposing the Donation of Constantine as a forgery, Valla denied the authority of the pope to determine who would rule the kingdoms of Western Europe.

At the beginning of the Reformation, the leaders of the Protestant movement used Valla's book to demonstrate that the power of the pope was based on falsehoods. In defense of the Catholic Church, the Italian philosopher Agostino Steuco pointed out that Valla's work was seriously flawed by being based on an abridged and distorted version of the Donation of Constantine rather than on the best text available.

Despite this attack on Valla's methods, modern scholars agree that the Donation of Constantine is a forgery. The evidence suggests that it was composed shortly after the year 750, probably by a cleric at the Church of the Savior, which was built within the Lateran Palace mentioned in the document.

Significance

Several theories have been advanced to explain the motive behind the forgery of the Donation of Constantine. In the 1960's, it was suggested that it was used to defend the authority of the pope during diplomatic negotiations with the Franks in the eighth and ninth centuries. Later in the twentieth century, it was suggested that the Donation of Constantine was composed to associate the Church of the Savior with the glory of the first Christian emperor and that it was more an embellished version of what was believed to be the truth rather than a deliberate fraud.

The author of the Donation of Constantine apparently based the *Confessio* section of the document on well-known fifth century legends about Pope Sylvester I. The *Donatio* section is more original, although such a donation was vaguely mentioned in the same legends. The final part of this section, in which the pope was given power over all other rulers in Western Europe, was of great political and theological importance from the eleventh to the fifteenth centuries.

Despite its later significance, this section may have been an afterthought added by the author after the importance of the Church of the Savior had been established earlier in the document. The claims of papal power made at the end of the Donation of Constantine were either well-established by the middle of the eighth century or were so broadly expressed as to be virtually without any specific meaning.

The critiques of the authenticity of the Donation of Constantine by Nicholas of Cusa and Lorenzo Valla in the middle of the fifteenth century were important precedents in the development of textual criticism in the early Renaissance. Later philosophers would use their methods to question the validity of other old documents. This movement away from accepting the writings of ancient authorities to making use of scientific evidence was one of the important factors in the philosophical transition from medieval Scholasticism to Renaissance Humanism.

—*Rose Secrest*

FURTHER READING

Camporeale, Salvatore I. "Lorenzo Valla's Oratio on the Pseudo-Donation of Constantine: Dissent and Innovation in Early Renaissance Humanism." *Journal of the History of Ideas* 57 (January, 1996): 9-26. Discusses the political and theological implications of Lorenzo Valla's attack on the authenticity of the Donation of Constantine.

Delph, Ronald K. "Valla Grammaticus, Agostino Steuco, and the Donation of Constantine." *Journal of the History of Ideas* 57 (January, 1996): 55-77. Describes Agostino Steuco's criticism of the methods used by Lorenzo Valla to expose the Donation of Constantine as a forgery.

Fubini, Riccardo. "Humanism and Truth: Valla Writes Against the Donation of Constantine." *Journal of the History of Ideas* 57 (January, 1996): 79-86. An analysis of the philosophical motivations behind Lorenzo Valla's critique of the Donation of Constantine.

Ginzburg, Carlo. *History, Rhetoric, and Proof.* Hanover, N.H.: University Press of New England for Brandeis University Press/Historical Society of Israel, 1999. Contains a chapter on Lorenzo Valla and the Donation of Constantine. Bibliography and index.

Valla, Lorenzo. *The Treatise of Lorenzo Valla on the Donation of Constantine.* Translated by Christopher B. Coleman. Toronto: University of Toronto Press in association with the Renaissance Society of America, 1993. A translation of *De falso credita et ementita Constantini donatione declamatio.* Includes analysis and biographical material on Valla.

SEE ALSO: 1127-1130: Creation of the Kingdom of Sicily; 1377-1378: Condemnation of John Wyclif.

RELATED ARTICLE in *Great Lives from History: The Middle Ages, 477-1453*: Lorenzo Valla.

1442-1456
JÁNOS HUNYADI DEFENDS HUNGARY AGAINST THE OTTOMANS

János Hunyadi defended Hungary against Ottoman invaders, which delayed the Ottoman conquest of Europe and contributed to the development of a Hungarian national identity.

LOCALE: Hungary and the Balkan Peninsula
CATEGORY: Wars, uprisings, and civil unrest

KEY FIGURES

János Hunyadi (c. 1407-1456), Hungarian national hero who preserved Hungary from Ottoman conquest

Władysław III (1424-1444), king of Poland, r. 1434-1444, king of Hungary as Ulászló I, r. 1440-1444

Ladislas V Posthumous (1440-1457), king of Hungary, r. 1444-1457, king of Bohemia, r. 1440-1457, ward of Frederick III of Austria until 1453

Giovanni da Capestrano (1386-1456), coleader with Hunyadi in defending Belgrade in 1456, later canonized by the Catholic Church as John of Capistrano

Murad II (1404-1451), Ottoman sultan, r. 1421-1444, 1446-1451

Mehmed II (1432-1481), Ottoman sultan, r. 1444-1446, 1451-1481

SUMMARY OF EVENT

In 1437, Hungary fell into chaos when King Sigismund died without leaving a male heir. Sigismund's daughter, Elizabeth, however, was married to Albrecht, king of Austria, whom Sigismund had designated his successor. Albrecht, however, died after two years without an heir but leaving Elizabeth pregnant. Some Hungarians then supported Elizabeth as regent but others, demanding a male king, elected Władysław III, then king of Poland, as King Ulászló I of Hungary. This action precipitated a civil war.

Sultan Murad II, taking advantage of the confusion, expanded into Walachia (part of what is now Romania) and resumed raids into Hungary across the Danube River. In response, Władysław III appointed János Hunyadi (nicknamed Yanko by the Turks) as captain general of Belgrade and *voivade* (military leader) of Transylvania and charged him with defending Hungary's southern border. Hunyadi, son of a minor Vlalch (Romanian) nobleman, Vajk Oláh, and reputed to be an illegitimate son of King Sigismund, was an effective leader. Previously, Hunyadi had been appointed to high command by Sigismund and had been made *ban* (commander) of Szörény by Albrecht. As the "white knight" of the Serbs and Hungarians, Hunyadi led cavalry charges wearing shining silver armor, quickly winning victories over Władysław's domestic opponents and over the Ottomans along the 200 miles (320 kilometers) that makes up the southern Hungarian border.

His decisive victory at Bataszek in 1441 against Elizabeth's supporters was his first victory of national significance. He defeated a Turkish army under Mezit Beg at Nagyszeben in Transylvania and routed another Turkish army of an estimated eighty thousand men near the Iron Gates on the Danube in 1442. Soon after, Sultan Murad II offered to sign a treaty of peace, but Hunyadi persuaded Władysław to take the offensive against the Turks in 1443. Following Sigismund's prior effort, Hunyadi attempted to generate enthusiasm for a new Crusade to drive the Turks out of Europe. Support from western Europe was minimal; only Pope Julian accompanied the Crusade. Thus, the Crusaders were primarily Poles and Hungarians and, later, Walachians, along with a few Serbs, Bulgarians, Bosnians, and Albanians.

The Crusade crossed the Danube in July of 1443 and captured Nish in what is now western Serbia with great losses to the Ottomans. Next, they occupied Sofia (now in Bulgaria), and attempted crossing the Balkan Range in midwinter. After winning a victory on Christmas Eve near Phillipolis, they found the weather, supply problems, and increased Turkish pressure insurmountable, so Hunyadi ordered a return to Buda. Arriving in February, 1444, his chilled and gaunt army, led by King Władysław on foot, triumphantly entered the city singing hymns and flaunting Ottoman banners. Murad II, essentially a man of peace, did not pursue the Crusaders across the Danube but negotiated a ten-year truce on July, 1444, at Szeged, in which Serbia and Walachia were freed from Ottoman rule and the Hungarians agreed to not cross the Danube or press claims on Bulgaria.

Julian Cesarini, the papal cardinal legate, however, persuaded Władysław that word given to an "infidel" need not be honored, so Hunyadi and Władysław again invaded the Balkans in 1444, leading an army of about 20,000 Hungarians and Walachians. Murad, however, succeeded in returning from a campaign in Asia Minor and confronted the Hungarians with 100,000 men at Varna on November 10, 1444. Hunyadi and Władysław were decisively defeated. Władysław was unhorsed and decapitated and his head was mounted on a lance, as was a copy of the broken treaty. These symbols were returned to Bursa, then the Ottoman capital, for public display as a warning to the perfidious. Cardinal Julian fled and was never seen again, dead or alive, reportedly having been executed by his own defeated troops. Most of the army was killed in battle or beheaded on the field.

Hunyadi, however, escaped and returned to Hungary, where he successfully mediated the dynastic conflict.

Giovanni da Capestrano, defender of Belgrade in 1456 and later canonized as Saint John of Capistrano, from a painting by Bartolommeo Vivarini at the Louvre, Paris. (Frederick Ungar Publishing Co.)

Elizabeth had died, leaving her very young son, King Ladislas V Posthumous, under the protection of his uncle, Emperor Frederick. The Hungarian diet of 1445, an assemblage of nobles, sent negotiators to Frederick requesting return of Ladislas as king, but in the interim, the diet appointed a council of regency to restore internal peace. Failing to retrieve Ladislas, the 1447 diet elected Hunyadi governor with limited sovereign rights. Hunyadi succeeded in restoring peace in most of the country, although he was defeated by a Czech leader Giskra, who retained control of Northwestern Hungary.

In 1448, allied with Albania's leader, Skanderbeg, Hunyadi again invaded the Balkans. They were again defeated by Murad II in the Second Battle of Kosovo (Rígomezö in Hungarian). As a result, Serbia lost its independence, Bosnia became an Ottoman vassal state, and Hungarian military power was crippled. Skanderbeg retreated to Croia in Albania, where he remained independent for two decades. Hunyadi, however, still succeeded in holding back Ottoman advance into Hungary.

In 1450, Hunyadi abandoned his supporters in the diet and allied himself with the Habsburg party. In this way, he acquired new Moravian territories and became the legitimate regent for the child king. In 1452, the Austrian and Bohemian Estates forced Emperor Frederick to release Ladislas from tutelage. Ladislas was then instated as king of Hungary, but allowed Hunyadi to remain de facto regent.

János Hunyadi and Giovanni da Capestrano leading the charge at Belgrade. (F. R. Niglutsch)

After capturing Constantinople in 1453, Mehmed II, the son of Murad II, conquered most of Serbia during 1454 and 1455. In 1456, he besieged about 7,000 men in the fortress of Nándofehérvár (Belgrade) with an army of about 100,000. Hunyadi and the monk, Giovanni da Capestrano, broke through the Ottoman fleet blockading the Danube and entered the citadel of Nándofehérvár. After severe bombardment breached the fortress walls, the Turks penetrated the citadel. Here, Hunyadi ordered his men to hide, while the Janissaries scattered to plunder the town. At a prearranged signal, the Hungarians fell on the disorganized Turks, killed many, and drove the remainder out of the city, where many more were trapped in the moats and burned to death. The Hungarians and Capestrano's Crusaders then charged the remaining Turks, wounded the sultan, and broke the Ottoman army on July 22. The Ottomans thereafter retreated, leaving their siege guns behind and did not again invade Hungary for seventy years. Hunyadi died of the plague two weeks after the battle, and Capestrano also died a few months afterward. Hungarian affairs again lapsed into internal conflict.

SIGNIFICANCE

Hunyadi was immediately and uncritically hailed as the person who saved Hungary and Europe from the Ottomans. He thus became the national hero around whom Hungarian national identity has centered. Critical analysis, however, shows that Hunyadi was far from an invincible military leader, having commanded at two major military disasters. He also failed to end the Ottoman threat as his actions only delayed the advent of Ottoman control. His effect on Hungarian political evolution lies mostly in having prepared the way for Hungary's first centralized royal government. This government, however, did not survive Ottoman conquest seventy years after Hunyadi's death.

—*Ralph L. Langenheim, Jr.*

FURTHER READING

Bak, János M., and Béla K. Király, eds. *From Hunyadi to Rákóczi: War and Society in Medieval and Early Modern Hungary.* New York: Columbia University Press, 1982. Includes a critical essay, "János Hunyadi, the Decisive Years of His Career, 1440-1444," written by Pál Engel. Also contains useful background material on fifteenth century Hungary.

Bideleux, Robert, and Ian Jeffries. *A History of Eastern Europe: Crisis and Change.* New York: Routledge, 1998. This comprehensive work explores, among other topics, the history between the Ottomans and the Hungarians before, during, and after Hunyadi's time. Maps, bibliography, index.

Held, Joseph. *Hunyadi: Legend and Reality.* Boulder, Colo.: Westview Press, 1985. Critical evaluation of Hunyadi's career and an extensive description of the social and political environment of the times.

Kinross, Lord. *The Ottoman Centuries: The Rise and Fall of the Turkish Empire.* New York: William Morrow, 1977. Analyzes Hunyadi's battles with the Turks from the Turkish point of view.

Muresanu, Camil. *John Hunyadi: Defender of Christendom.* Translated by Laura Treptow. Iaşi, Romania: Center for Romanian Studies, 2001. Considers Hunyadi as soldier and statesman. Although this work might be difficult to locate and obtain, it is one of only a few sources in English on Hunyadi. Bibliography, index.

Pamlényi, Erving, ed. *A History of Hungary.* London: Collets, 1975. A detailed history with good introductory material.

Sugar, P. F., ed. *A History of Hungary.* Bloomington: Indiana University Press, 1990. Includes an essay by János M. Bak entitled "The Late Medieval Period," which outlines the political and cultural history of Hunyadi's regime.

SEE ALSO: August 10, 955: Otto I Defeats the Magyars; 1040-1055: Expansion of the Seljuk Turks; 1077: Seljuk Dynasty Is Founded; November, 1330: Basarab Defeats the Hungarians; 1381-1405: Tamerlane's Conquests; June 28, 1389: Turkish Conquest of Serbia; 1444-1446: Albanian Chieftains Unite Under Prince Skanderbeg; May 29, 1453: Fall of Constantinople.

RELATED ARTICLES in *Great Lives from History: The Middle Ages, 477-1453*: Árpád; János Hunyadi; Saint László I; Mehmed II; Stefan Dušan; Stephen I.

1444-1446
ALBANIAN CHIEFTAINS UNITE UNDER PRINCE SKANDERBEG

Albanian chieftains united under Skanderbeg as part of the League of Lezha, which preserved Albanian freedom for nearly forty years and established Albanian national identity.

LOCALE: Albania
CATEGORIES: Government and politics; wars, uprisings, and civil unrest

KEY FIGURES

John Kastrioti (fl. 1410), prince of Emathia and father of Skanderbeg
Skanderbeg (1405-1468), prince of Emathia
Moïse Golem (fl. 1443-1456), a principal commander under Skanderbeg
Murad II (1404-1451), Ottoman sultan, r. 1421-1444 and 1446-1451
Mehmed II (1432-1481), Ottoman sultan, r. 1444-1446 and 1451-1481

SUMMARY OF EVENT

Born George Kastrioti, Skanderbeg was the youngest son of John Kastrioti, prince of Emathia. Although John Kastrioti was a vassal of the Ottoman Turks, he participated in a series of unsuccessful revolts against them during the 1430's. His youngest son, George, was sent to the sultan as a hostage in 1414, and probably was sent again in 1423. Here, George was given the name Skander (Alexander) and was enrolled as a Janissary, a corps of troops recruited by taking non-Muslim children as slaves of the sultan. Skander attended the military school for pages.

In 1426 or 1427, Skander became a *siphai*, a landed vassal required to supply mounted troops to the sultan. In 1438, Skander was made a *beg* (or *bey*, a title of nobility) and was appointed governor (*vali*) of three small communities in the *vilayet*, or province, of Kruja. Later, in 1440, he apparently moved to the large province of Dibra.

In 1443, the Hungarian leader János Hunyadi organized a campaign against the Ottomans and called the Balkan princes to join him as his Hungarians marched south. The sultan rallied his vassals, and Skanderbeg marched to join him. On November 3, the Hungarians attacked at Niš and forced an Ottoman retreat. At this point, Skanderbeg deserted the Ottomans and returned to Dibra with three hundred Albanian horsemen. Finding Dibra ready for revolt, Skanderbeg proceeded to Kruja, where he presented a false *firman* (order from the sultan) giving him command of the town and citadel. That night, Skanderbeg attacked and annihilated the Ottoman garrison. He then spread the rebellion, evicting Ottoman landed vassals from the region. After triumphantly returning to Kruja, he proclaimed Albanian freedom on November 28, 1443, and raised the Kastrioti banner over the citadel. Skanderbeg then organized volunteers to capture several citadels in central Albania during December. He also called a conclave of Albanian lords in Venetian territory at Lezha.

At this conclave, he organized an alliance or confederation known as the League of Lezha. This league was an important innovation, since it marked the first embryonic centralized state in the region. A league army supported by a common fund was organized to counter the much larger Ottoman forces. Skanderbeg was appointed commander in chief and head of the league. Loyal garrisons were installed in fortresses, some lords were deposed, and outstanding soldiers were rewarded with domains of their own. The league, however, was a confederation in which individual nobles retained local authority and the right to withdraw. Encroachments on feudal authority and opportunism made defections a recurring problem and ultimately destroyed the league.

During the spring of 1444, Skanderbeg enrolled an army of some 8,000 to 10,000 regular troops with approximately 10,000 reserves. He also reinforced fortresses and organized a look-out system to warn of attack. About 3,000 troops, mostly mounted cavalry, were under his direct command with another 3,000 under Moïse Golem guarding the eastern frontier. The remaining troops were under the command of individual nobles.

In June, 1444, 25,000 Ottomans under the command of Ali Pasha invaded Albania through Ochrid. After they were routed by Skanderbeg, the Ottomans withdrew to combat a Hungarian-Polish invasion. After annihilating the Hungarians and Poles at Varna in November of 1444, the Ottomans again invaded Albania. Skanderbeg and his troops defeated the Ottomans at Modr in October, 1445, and at Dibra in September, 1446. The Ottomans did not attempt another invasion in 1447, but war did break out between the league and the Venetian Republic over Danja and Lezha. Lacking artillery, the Albanians were unable to take these citadels.

In 1448, Murad II laid siege to Sfetigrad (Kodjadjik)

Skanderbeg demands that the Ottomans surrender. (F. R. Niglutsch)

on Albania's eastern border. Failing to arrange a peace, Skanderbeg quickly defeated the Venetians near Drin in July, 1448, and immediately set off to relieve Sfetigrad. The city capitulated in August, however, so Skanderbeg compromised with the Venetians, giving up Danja for a payment of fourteen thousand ducats per year. The Venetians also agreed to subsidize a Hungarian-Albanian alliance under which Skanderbeg joined János Hunyadi's new offensive against the Turks. The Hungarians, however, were defeated in the Second Battle of Kosovo on October 12, 1448, and the alliance ended.

In early May of 1450, Murad again invaded Albania with a force of about 100,000. Skanderbeg's call to arms raised nearly 18,000 men. Besieged by Murad's army, Kruja was garrisoned with 1,500 men, but Skanderbeg held 8,000 troops on nearby Mount Tumenisht, from which he repeatedly attacked Murad's troops. The remaining Albanian units ambushed Ottoman reinforcements and supply caravans. After a siege of four and a half months, Murad purportedly lost 20,000 men and was forced to retreat to Adrianople (now Edirne).

The Treaty of Gaeta between Skanderbeg and Alfonso V of Aragon on March 26, 1451, brought minor support against Ottoman offensives in 1452-1453. In 1453, Skanderbeg traveled to Naples and persuaded Alfonso to send troops and artillery to Albania. He also persuaded Ragusa to organize a coalition of troops from Albania, Hungary, and Serbia to fight against the Ottomans. With this support, Skanderbeg laid siege to Berat. Just as the citadel was at the point of surrendering, however, he was assaulted from the rear by 40,000 Ottoman troops who had crossed the frontier through the connivance of Moïse Golem, who had defected. Skanderbeg's defeat renewed Venetian opposition, and Alfonso withdrew his support. In 1456, Golem led 15,000 Ottoman cavalry into Albania, but was defeated by Skanderbeg at Oranik. Skanderbeg's nephew, George Stres Balsa, became the next to defect and gave up the frontier citadel of Modrica to the Ottomans. Skanderbeg's other nephew, Hamza Kastrioti, also joined the Ottomans.

In 1457, some 80,000 Ottomans under the command of Isaac Bey Evernos entered Albania accompanied by

Hamza Kastrioti, who had been named governor of Kruja by the sultan. Skanderbeg avoided direct combat with the invaders until September 7, when he surprised the Ottomans near Kruja and captured thousands of prisoners, including Hamza Kastrioti. Skanderbeg then signed a three-year truce; during this period, he took his army to Italy to support Ferdinand of Naples in 1461. In Italy, Skanderbeg won battles at Barletta and Trani. Returning to Albania in 1462, he defeated three separate invasions at Mokra, Pollog, and Livad. After these victories, Skanderbeg persuaded Mehmed II to sign a ten-year peace treaty in April, 1463. Shortly thereafter, Venice declared war on the Ottomans and promised aid to the Albanians. Pope Pius II announced a crusade, and Skanderbeg renewed hostilities. Unfortunately, the crusade collapsed after Pius II's death in 1464, leaving the Albanians unsupported.

Mehmed sent an army of 14,000 into Albania from Ochrid, but was promptly crushed in August, 1464. In June, 1466, he proclaimed a holy war of extermination and besieged Kruja with the entire Ottoman army of 150,000 men. In July, Mehmed left with part of the army, leaving Ballaban Pasha to continue the siege. During the winter of 1466-1467, Skanderbeg went to Rome and Naples seeking aid, but accomplished little. In April, 1467, the Albanians defeated reinforcements who were advancing to strengthen Ballaban Pasha; a few days later, they broke the siege and killed Ballaban. Mehmed countered by again invading Albania with his entire imperial army. Winning a bloody battle at Buzurshek (near what is now Elbasan), he again laid siege to Kruja. After three weeks, however, Mehmed left the field of battle, and Skanderbeg again freed his capital.

In the face of continuing hostilities, depleted forces, and low finances, Skanderbeg planned an assembly of nobles at Lezha to be held in 1468. In midwinter, however, Skanderbeg contracted fever, and he died on January 17, 1468. His son, John, fled with his mother to Naples. Resistance continued but depended heavily on Venetian support. Venice quit the war in 1479, and the Ottomans quickly captured the Albanian citadels. At this point, Skanderbeg's son returned but was unable to stem the tide. After he fled the country in 1482, Albanian independence was lost.

SIGNIFICANCE

Skanderbeg's League of Lezha began the process of creating a nation-state in Albania. It successfully maintained an independent Albania for some twenty-five years, thus delaying and partially checking the Ottoman advance into Europe. Skanderbeg's successors, however, were unable to keep the league together, and most of Skanderbeg's accomplishments were undone. As a result of his efforts to establish Albanian independence, Skanderbeg has been honored as the national hero of modern Albania.

—*Ralph L. Langenheim, Jr.*

FURTHER READING

Chekrezi, Constantine A. *Albania Past and Present.* 1919. Reprint. New York: Arno Press, 1971. This work on Albanian history includes a section on Skanderbeg and covers the highlights of his career.

Giaffo, Lou. *Albania: Eye of the Balkan Vortex*. Princeton, N.J.: Xlibris, 1999. Comprehensive survey of Albanian history from 1500 B.C.E. through the fall of Communism. Includes discussion of Skanderbeg.

Jacques, Edwin C. *The Albanians: An Ethnic History from Prehistoric Times to the Present.* Jefferson, N.C.: McFarland, 1995. Written by an American who was a former Protestant missionary teacher, this work presents a history of Albania through the early 1990's.

Marmullaku, Ramadan. *Albania and the Albanians.* Translated by Margot Milosavljevic and Boško Milosavljevic. Hamden, Conn.: Archon Books, 1975. Includes a brief account of Skanderbeg's career, placing him within the context of his times.

Pollo, Stefanaq, and Arben Puto. *The History of Albania from Its Origins to the Present Day.* London: Routledge and Kegan Paul, 1981. Contains a fairly detailed discussion of Skanderbeg from the perspective of communist historians.

Swire, J. *Albania: The Rise of a Kingdom.* 1929. Reprint. New York: Arno Press, 1971. This work includes a readable short account of the military and political accomplishments of Skanderbeg.

Vickers, Miranda. *The Albanians: A Modern History.* Rev. ed. London: I. B. Tauris, 1999. Includes extensive discussion of Ottoman rule and the rise of Albanian nationalism.

SEE ALSO: 1040-1055: Expansion of the Seljuk Turks; 1077: Seljuk Dynasty Is Founded; 1381-1405: Tamerlane's Conquests; June 28, 1389: Turkish Conquest of Serbia; 1442-1456: János Hunyadi Defends Hungary Against the Ottomans; May 29, 1453: Fall of Constantinople.

RELATED ARTICLES in *Great Lives from History: The Middle Ages, 477-1453*: János Hunyadi; Mehmed II.

c. 1450
GUTENBERG PIONEERS THE PRINTING PRESS

Johann Gutenberg invented the printing press by developing the technology of printing with movable metal type. The printing press ushered in a cultural revolution and made written materials more widely available at a lower cost.

LOCALE: Germany
CATEGORIES: Communications; cultural and intellectual history; literature; science and technology

KEY FIGURES

Johann Gutenberg (1394/1399-1468), probable inventor of movable type
Laurens Janszoon Coster (c. 1370?-1440), Dutch sexton of Harlem, claimed by some to be inventor of movable type
Johann Fust (c. 1400-1466), Mainz businessman, backed Gutenberg before establishing a printing firm with Peter Schöffer
Peter Schöffer (c. 1425-1502), an early Mainz printer

SUMMARY OF EVENT

A concise, factual account of the invention of printing with movable type is not possible because surmises far outnumber facts. The few early printed works bearing dates and names are of little help in identifying early experimenters.

Wang Jie (Wang Chieh) used the first block print in China in 868 to produce the *Diamond Sutra*; in the eleventh century, his fellow countryman Bi Sheng (Pi Sheng) arranged molded and baked clay characters on a frame for printing. Except in Arabic Spain, the West did not make paper until 1270, in Fabriano, Italy; Ger-

Gutenberg examines his first proof. (F. R. Niglutsch)

many did not begin the process until the fourteenth century.

Between the painstaking copying of manuscripts by hand and the earliest printing with movable type that imitated their calligraphy, an intermediate process of "block books" or xylographica appeared. As early as 1418, pictures were carved in wood and printed in thin brownish ink on one side of a leaf. Later, descriptive text accompanied the picture, and printing was done on both sides of the paper in improved ink made of pine shavings and soot. Examples of block books are the *Biblia pauperum* (poor man's Bible), the *Apocalypse*, and the *Ars moriendi* (the art of dying). Between the middle and end of the fifteenth century, about thirty thousand editions of "cradle books," or incunabula (so called because they were Europe's earliest printed books), appeared in Europe.

Unlikely credit has been given to Laurens Janszoon Coster for the invention of movable type in 1423; however, contemporary documents fail to mention him. A 1570 book by Adrian Young, *Batavia*, gave Coster credit, but most modern scholars ignore this shadowy claim. Although no extant book bears his name, a more plausible inventor of printing with movable type is Johann Gutenberg, from Mainz, Germany. During a time when he was working in Strasbourg between 1430 and 1440, he seems to have been adapting the *prelum*, or winepress, for printing. Although he produced fewer than thirty works, he devoted years to mechanical perfection of the new process of printing. Among his alleged works are a thirty-six-line Bible; a forty-two-line Bible (the Mainz, Mazarin, or Gutenberg Bible); *Catholicon*, a theological grammar of Johannes Balbus; two indulgences (for 1454 and 1455); and some calendars, including one for the year 1448.

Supporting Gutenberg as the inventor of printing are court records and documents of Mainz, which show his need for funds and detail his lawsuits regarding the press. In 1448, a loan made by Johann Fust facilitated the printing with movable type of the forty-two-line or Gutenberg Bible between 1452 and 1455, antedating the thirty-six-line Bible of 1459-1460. That Gutenberg's press produced the early calendars of 1447 or 1448, and the 1454 and 1455 indulgence slips (used to issue indulgences) seems plausible because of the similarity of type. The appearance of printed indulgence slips has tempted some to suggest that the Papacy was planning a great retaliatory campaign against the Turks after the fall of Con-

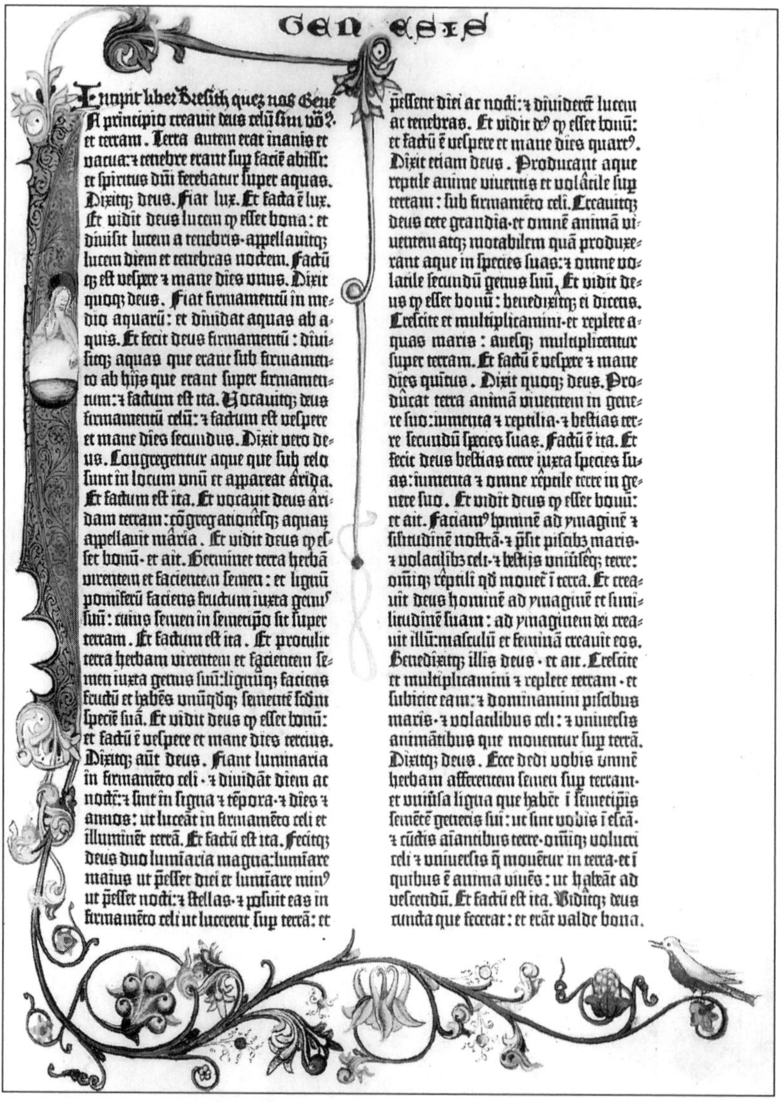

A page from the Mazarin Bible, the first major work Gutenberg published, named later for the Mazarin Library, Paris, where it was housed. Also known as the forty-two-line Bible for the number of lines per page. (Hulton|Archive by Getty Images)

stantinople in 1453. The papal legate in Mainz supposedly ordered both Gutenberg and Johann Fust to print indulgences to help defray the expenses of the campaign.

A lawsuit of 1455 indicates that Johann Fust sued to recover his expenses incurred in the loans he made to Gutenberg. Around this time, Fust and Gutenberg's former chief workman, Peter Schöffer, formed a new printing firm. Before this setback, however, Gutenberg's press yielded 210 copies of the Bible using 290 different typefaces. From 1455 to 1460, Gutenberg used equipment supplied by his new patron, Dr. Humery of Mainz. The 1460 *Catholicon* marks the end of Gutenberg's supposed work. In that year, he accepted a court position offered by the archbishop of Mainz, leaving Fust and Schöffer dominant in the new art in that city.

The chief credit given to Fust and Schöffer derives from their 1457 *Psalter*, the first book whose colophon dates and names its printer. Some scholars claim its *U* and *V* capitals link it to the 1454 and 1455 indulgence slips. The *Psalter* contains black and red print and blue initials, an innovation since earlier rubrication had been done by hand. In addition, the woodcuts in the *Psalter* are delicate and profuse. Fust and Schöffer followed this work in 1462 by a forty-eight-line Bible. From 1466 until his death, Schöffer worked alone. He was known for his use of marginal notes, Greek printed characters, and spacing between lines. A poster of his—the first of its kind—that advertised printed books shows that he had become a large-scale businessman.

In Cologne in 1466, Ulrich Zell produced perhaps the first printed Latin classic, Cicero's *De officiis*. Elsewhere in Germany, Anthony Koberger published the *Nuremberg Chronicle* in 1493, using much illustration and both Gothic and Roman typefaces. In Augsburg, Erhard Ratdolt printed missals and ecclesiastical books with border designs and engraved initials, such as his *Obsequiale Augustense* (1487).

In Italy, two German clerics, Konrad Sweinheim and Arnold Pannartz, established presses in a Subiaco monastery (1461) and in Rome (1467). These originators foreshadowed the Humanist Aldus Manutius, the Elder, most famous of all Italian printers. In Venice from 1485 until about 1505, he printed Greek and Latin editions of works by Aristotle, Aristophanes, Bion, Moschus, and others. His small pocket-size books of cheap quality and legible italic typeface helped to disseminate learning to the less wealthy classes.

A Frenchman, Nicolaus Jenson, studied in Mainz and worked in Venice in the 1460's. Printing in France itself produced the early names of Jean Heynlin and Guillaume Fichet of the Sorbonne, and of others such as Ulrich Gering, Martin Krantz, and Michael Freiburger. In 1470, a volume of the letters of Gasparino Barzizi of Bergamo appeared followed by the first Bible printed in France, in 1476.

Printing in Spain started in 1468, when a Barcelona press produced a grammar book. Later, Lambert Palmart of Valencia published its city laws during 1477-1490 in fifteen volumes. Spain produced mostly ecclesiastical works, with some poetry and romances.

In the Low Countries, the Brothers of the Common Life set up a press at Marienthal in 1468; by 1490, more than sixty establishments acknowledged their supervision. In Bruges, Colard Mansion taught William Caxton, an Englishman who translated and printed Raoul Le Fever's *Recuyell of the Historyes of Troye* in 1475. By 1477, Caxton returned to England to print the country's first book, significantly in the vernacular.

SIGNIFICANCE

Within fifty years of its invention, printing by movable type spread over Europe to become—as a vehicle for the mass dissemination of information—one of the most significant events in the history of Western culture.

—John J. Healy, updated by Karen Gould

FURTHER READING

Chappell, Warren. *A Short History of the Printed Word*. Reprint. Boston: Nonpareil Books, 1980. Contains a good introduction to the basics of printing technology along with a survey of printing's history, placing the invention of printing and the incunable era in context.

Davies, Martin. *Aldus Manutius: Printer and Publisher of Renaissance Venice*. London: British Library, 1995. A concise introduction to the works of Aldus and his contributions to the development of printing.

Febvre, Lucien, and Henri-Jean Martin. *The Coming of the Book: The Impact of Printing, 1450-1800*. Translated by David Gerard. 1976. Reprint. London: Verso, 1997. A study of the transformations that printing brought to book production and the book trade.

Ing, Janet. *Johann Gutenberg and His Bible*. 2d ed. New York: Typophiles, 1990. A concise, readable account of the evidence concerning Gutenberg and his role in the invention of printing and the production of the Gutenberg Bible.

Jensen, Kristian, ed. *Incunabula and Their Readers: Printing, Selling, and Using Books in the Fifteenth Century*. London: British Library, 2003. An anthology of essays exploring why books became the first mass-produced and mass-marketed commodities in history. Examines the European cultural and economic situation to account for both the possibility and the appeal of print in the fifteenth century.

Kapr, Albert. *Johann Gutenberg: The Man and His Invention*. Translated by Douglas Martin. Brookfield, Vt.: Scolar Press, 1996. Covers Gutenberg's origins, early life, apprenticeship, and travel; the technical problems of inventing the printing press; his business; and more.

Lehmann-Haupt, Hellmut. *Peter Schoeffer of Gernsheim and Mainz*. Rochester, N.Y.: L. Hart, 1950. A short biography of Peter Schöffer and his pioneering role in the development of printing.

Man, John. *Gutenberg: How One Man Remade the World with Words*. New York: John Wiley and Sons, 2002. At once a macro and a micro study, the author describes the international sociopolitical background for the invention of the printing press, the background of key fifteenth century cities, and the individual biographical background of Gutenberg himself. Practical technical details of the construction and use of the printing press are provided alongside broadly focused arguments about its global effects.

Painter, George D. *William Caxton: A Quincentenary Biography*. New York: G. P. Putnam's Sons, 1977. A complete biography of England's first printer from his first career as a merchant-trader to his later years when he set up a printing establishment in England.

Scholderer, Victor. *Johann Gutenberg: The Inventor of Printing*. 2d ed. London: British Museum, 1970. An overview of Gutenberg's life and accomplishments.

SEE ALSO: 7th-8th centuries: Papermaking Spreads to Korea, Japan, and Central Asia; 713-741: First Newspapers in China; 868: First Book Printed; c. 1045: Bi Sheng Develops Movable Earthenware Type.

RELATED ARTICLES in *Great Lives from History: The Middle Ages, 477-1453*: Jean Froissart; Johann Gutenberg; Poggio.

1453
ENGLISH ARE DRIVEN FROM FRANCE

The English were driven from France through French numerical superiority, nationalism, Burgundian support, and the creation of a national army that later gave France the leadership of early modern Europe.

LOCALE: France
CATEGORIES: Government and politics; wars, uprisings, and civil unrest

KEY FIGURES

Joan of Arc (c. 1412-1431), patriotic heroine of France, canonized 1920
Philip the Good (1396-1467), duke of Burgundy, 1419-1467
Charles VII (1403-1461), king of France, r. 1422-1461
John of Lancaster (1389-1435), duke of Bedford, English regent in France, 1422-1435
John Talbot (c. 1384-1453), earl of Shrewsbury, English commander in defeat

SUMMARY OF EVENT

After 1066, when Duke William of Normandy (William the Conqueror) conquered England at the Battle of Hastings (part of the Norman Conquest) and became its king, English monarchs also ruled provinces in France. These holdings, extensive under Henry II (r. 1154-1189), were lost by his son John (r. 1199-1216) to the French king Philip II (r. 1179-1223) except for the wine-producing Guienne of southwestern France. From 1337 to 1453, English monarchs repeatedly invaded France—in a series of battles known now as the Hundred Years' War—hoping to regain lost provinces and claiming that their descent from Philip IV the Fair (r. 1285-1314) through his daughter Isabella of France gave them title to the French throne itself. English victories at Crécy (1346) and Poitiers (1356), thanks to their longbows, brought territorial gains under the 1360 Treaty of Brétigny, although French guerrilla tactics regained most of these by 1396.

The war was renewed in 1415, however, when Henry V soundly defeated the French army at Agincourt and then launched a major English effort to gain control of all France. This was an ambitious project. There were about six Frenchmen for every Englishman, and the recruitment, equipment, transport, conquest, and occupation costs would require special taxes voted by Parliament.

Meanwhile, the French people were becoming increasingly hostile to the English invaders, and the French feudal levies (conscripts) were learning to avoid futile frontal assaults. Henry's second invasion of Normandy in 1417, however, met little opposition from France's Valois king, the intermittently insane Charles VI. His teenage son, the dauphin Charles, trying to organize a patriotic front, blundered with a treacherous assassination of Duke John the Fearless of Burgundy in 1419. This threw John's son, Philip the Good, into the English camp, and King Charles capitulated. By the Treaty of Troyes, signed on June 14, 1420, Charles VI accepted Henry as his regent and heir, disinherited the dauphin as a dishonorable murderer, and gave his daughter Catherine in marriage to Henry. Their anticipated son (the future Henry VI, born in 1421), was to rule France as well as England. Paris opened its gates, and Henry's conquest of France seemed well under way.

King Edward III crossing the Somme River during the French campaign. (F. R. Niglutsch)

Unfortunately, both Henry V and Charles VI died in 1422, leaving Henry VI as an infant sovereign for France and England. While his regent in France, John of Lancaster, duke of Bedford, was capable, the regent in England, Humphrey, duke of Gloucester, failed to provide money or control policy.

One result was London's insistence on an advance to Orléans on the Loire without providing enough men, supplies, and artillery to take this fortified city. Consequently, the scene was set for an English reverse when Charles reinforced the capable leaders at Orléans with five thousand troops plus Joan of Arc, a teenage country girl claiming a divine mission. She took center stage with remarkable effect. Her infectious confidence was a factor in breaking the siege of Orléans, and her participation and influence increased with the victories at Jargeau and Patay, culminating in the march through Champagne to a ceremonious coronation of Charles at Reims on July 17, 1429.

These spectacular victories, however, did not dislodge the English from northwestern France and the Guienne. After Joan's capture in 1430 and execution in 1431, the war languished. While English war policy in the 1430's was hampered by financial shortages and the death in 1435 of Bedford, Charles prepared methodically. An essential reconciliation with Burgundy by the 1435 Treaty of Arras meant the recovery of Paris on April 13, 1436. Expelling the capable English army commanders from northwestern France required war,

ENGLAND BEFORE AND AFTER THE HUNDRED YEARS' WAR

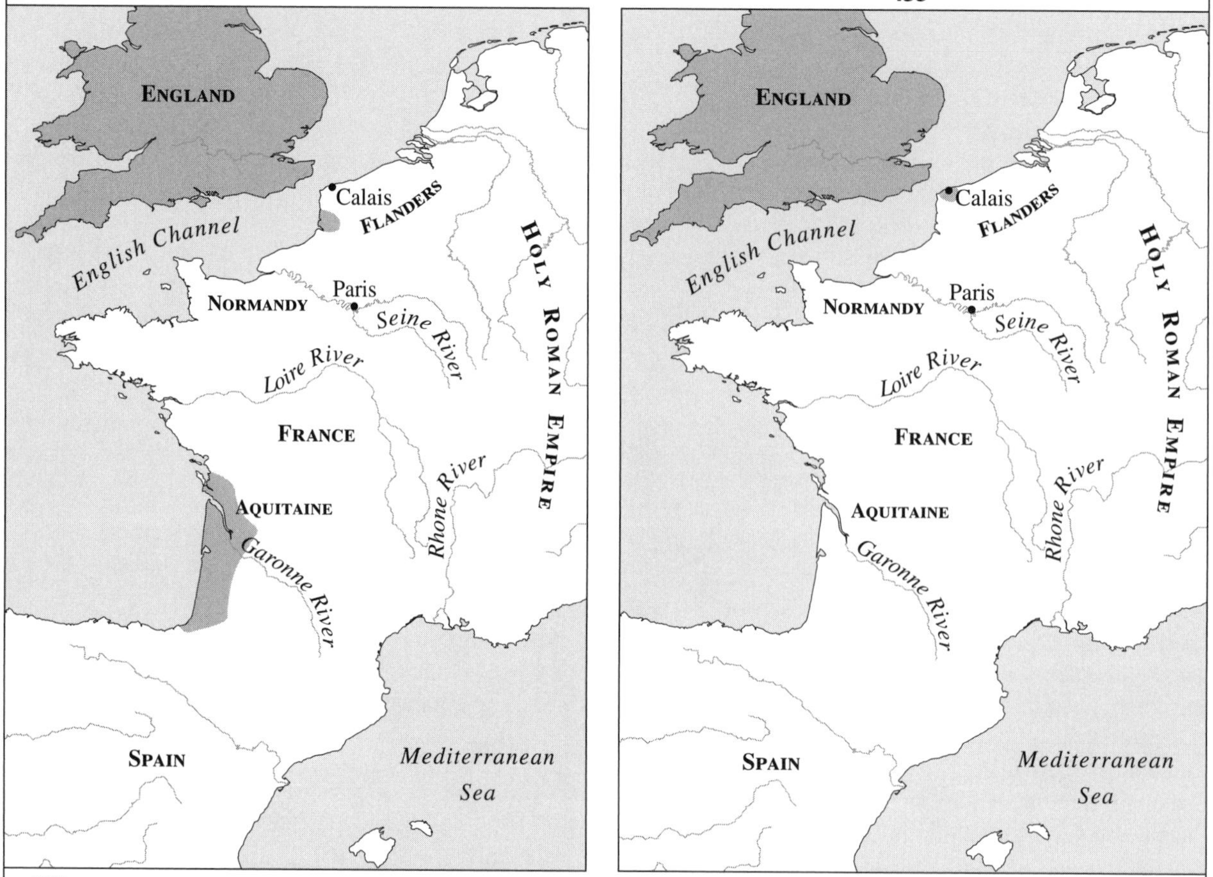

English territory: Note the reduction in holdings on the Continent to Calais by war's end.

which in turn required money and an improved army. Indirect taxes and a hearth tax became permanent (if unpopular) annual revenues for the central government. The feudal levies of local lords were replaced by a national army under royal control while on the technical side, Jean and Gaspard Bureau developed more effective artillery. With "corned" gunpowder firing cast iron or lead shot, the new French army gained missile superiority over the English.

Finally, in 1441, Charles launched a well-prepared attack. Pontoise fell to French artillery, weakening the English position in the lower Seine valley, and in 1442 sieges reduced the English outer fortresses in Guienne. A 1443 English expedition proved fruitless; in 1444, Henry VI and the English "peace party" tried the path of negotiation. The Truce of Tours provided for the 1445 marriage of Henry with Margaret of Anjou, a niece to Charles VII, with a secret clause calling for the cession of Maine, including its line of strong fortresses, to France. These surrenders dragged on through 1448, but when English aggression against Brittany broke the truce, Charles invaded Normandy in 1449. The new French armies swiftly took many fortified towns and held the countryside, gaining a major success for "Charles the Well-Served."

Early in 1450, the English made a belated effort to save Normandy. An army under Sir Thomas Kyriell landed at Cherbourg, recovered Valognes, and moved east through Carentan to reinforce the Bayeux garrison. Kyriell's force of perhaps five thousand to six thousand spent the night of April 14 at the village of Formigny and early on April 15 found the road back to Carentan blocked by a French army of three thousand under the count of Clermont. The English deployed west of Formigny, and for some hours, the opposing forces sought to provoke the other to attack, each hoping for a defensive victory. A melee eventually developed over two French culverins (light cannon) but the decisive factor was the arrival from Saint Lo of about twelve hundred French troops under the constable of Richemont, on the English left flank. Simultaneous French attacks broke the disjointed English defenses. The French claimed 3,774 English dead on the field, plus "more than a thousand whom shameful flight . . . did not save," as well as fifteen hundred prisoners, including Kyriell. The reported French loss of only six, eight, or twelve is not credible, but the significant result of this decisive battle was that Kyriell's army no longer existed. English garrisons at Bayeux, Avranches, Caen, Falaise, and elsewhere fell quickly. Cherbourg surrendered on August 12, 1450, after "such a heavy battering from cannons and bombards that the like had never been seen before," and no part of France remained under English rule except Guienne, Calais, and the Channel Islands.

Following the defeat at Formigny, the English government was shaken by disorders at home leading to Cade's Rebellion of 1450, and Charles VI seized the opportunity to attack in the Guienne. Again the French employed a broad-front invasion, brief sieges, threats, and bribery to converge on the English positions. The Bordeaux garrison surrendered on June 30, and Bayonne on August 20, 1451. The expulsion of the English from southwestern France was complete, although only for a year's space. King Charles's administrators and tax collectors became so immediately unpopular that influential Guiennese leaders promised in 1452 to support whatever expedition London could send to restore English rule. Accordingly, in October of 1452, the English sent an army of three thousand commanded by John Talbot, earl of Shrewsbury, a veteran of close to fifty years of campaigning, to liberate Guienne. Bordeaux indeed rose against its French garrison, and all western Guienne rallied to Talbot, soon strengthened by a reinforcement of three thousand more troops from England. In July of 1453, however, French armies advanced into Guienne, and a force of seven thousand under the direction of artillery master Jean Bureau besieged Castillon in the Dordogne valley. Talbot marched from Bordeaux to relieve Castillon with an Anglo-Guiennese army of about the same number, but these forces were evidently scattered by the time he arrived before Castillon on July 17.

Exactly why Talbot chose to make a dismounted frontal assault on the French lines with his straggling force is unclear. The attack was riddled by enfiladed artillery fire and the right flank crumpled by Franco-Breton reinforcements. In the rout, Talbot was killed and the Anglo-Guiennese army destroyed. Bordeaux surrendered to France on October 19. Only Calais remained, until 1558, as part of continental France under the English flag. The war was over, and the French king

Charles VII enters Rouen in 1450, after the French had secured Normandy. From a miniature in a fifteenth century account of the Hundred Years' War. (Frederick Ungar Publishing Co.)

emerged as "Charles the Very Victorious" while English frustration in defeat helped cause their own divisive "War of the Roses."

SIGNIFICANCE

Throughout the Hundred Years' War, England's apparent initiative depended on battles won by superior archery. Their repeated invasions, however, antagonized the French population, gradually creating the nationalism dramatically embodied by Joan of Arc. Equally important were the systematic administrative reforms of Charles VII in giving France an army decisively superior in equipment and method to the English forces.

Three hundred years of antagonism between England and France, beginning with the Norman Conquest of England in 1066 and culminating with the Hundred Year's War, came to fruition in 1453. This year marked the end of a divisive period in the history of the Middle Ages in Europe and a new period of nationalism and military superiority for France.

—*K. Fred Gillum*

FURTHER READING

Allmand, C. T., ed. *War, Literature and Politics in the Late Middle Ages*. New York: Barnes and Noble Books, 1976. Several informative articles covering topics such as espionage, artillery, chivalry, and the Hundred Years' War.

Burne, Alfred H. *The Agincourt War: A Military History of the Latter Part of the Hundred Years' War from 1369 to 1453*. Ware, Hertfordshire, England: Wordsworth Editions, 1999. A military analysis of the Agincourt war. Includes bibliography and index.

Contamine, Philippe. *War in the Middle Ages*. Translated by Michael Jones. New York: Basil Blackwell, 1984. Rich in details, this book offers a history of the art and science of militarism in medieval Europe. Includes an extensive bibliography and an index.

Holmes, George. *Europe, Hierarchy and Revolt, 1320-1450*. 2d ed. Malden, Mass.: Blackwell, 2000. A good overview of the Hundred Years' War. Explores France's shift from regionalism to nationalism. Includes a good bibliography.

Sackville-West, Vita. *Saint Joan of Arc*. New York: Grove Press, 2001. A biographical account of Joan, first published in 1936, including discussion of the history of France during the reign of Charles VII.

Seward, Desmond. *A Brief History of the Hundred Years' War: The English in France, 1337-1453*. London: Robinson, 2003. Historical overview of the war, with illustrations, including maps.

Vale, M. G. A. *Charles VII*. Berkeley: University of California Press, 1974. Scholarly analysis of war policies.

Walker, David. *The Normans in Britain*. Cambridge, Mass.: Blackwell, 1995. An overview of the Anglo-Norman period in England, beginning with the Battle of Hastings in 1066.

SEE ALSO: October 14, 1066: Battle of Hastings; 1337-1453: Hundred Years' War; August 26, 1346: Battle of Crécy; May 4-8, 1429: Joan of Arc's Relief of Orléans; 1453: English Are Driven from France; May 29, 1453: Fall of Constantinople.

RELATED ARTICLES in *Great Lives from History: The Middle Ages, 477-1453*: Henry II; Henry V; Isabella of France; Joan of Arc; King John; Philip the Good; Philip II; Philip IV the Fair; William the Conqueror.

May 29, 1453
Fall of Constantinople

The end of the Byzantine Empire came with the fall of Constantinople and the rise of the Turkish and Muslim Ottoman Empire, considered to mark the end of the Middle Ages.

Locale: Constantinople, Byzantine Empire (now Istanbul, Turkey)
Categories: Government and politics; religion; wars, uprisings, and civil unrest

Key Figures

Mehmed II (1432-1481), Ottoman sultan, r. 1444-1446, 1451-1481
Constantine XI Palaeologus (1404-1453), Byzantine emperor, r. 1449-1453
Giovanni Giustiniani (d. 1453), Genoese soldier, assisted Greeks during the siege
Zagan Pasha (fl. fifteenth century), Turkish commander and zealot

Summary of Event

By 1453, relations between Christians of the Greek East and Christians of the Latin West were near the breaking point. The Greeks remembered with bitterness the capture of Constantinople in 1204 at the hands of Western Crusaders. This led to a struggle between the Greeks and Latins to control Constantinople after 1261, with control eventually going to the Greeks.

By the fifteenth century, the failure of the Orthodox Church and the Catholic Church to reconcile their differences and present a united front against the encroaching Turks left Constantinople and the Byzantine Empire vulnerable to invasion. The young sultan of the Turks, Mehmed II, saw in this division within Christendom the chance to crush the might of the Byzantine Empire. He had decided early in his reign that one of his principal objectives would be the seizure of the "God-protected city," and by the spring of 1453 he had determined his plan of attack.

When the Greeks awoke on the morning of April 5, 1453, they were amazed at the sight of more than one hundred thousand Turkish troops outside the high walls of Constantinople, stretching in a formidable line from the Sea of Marmora to the Golden Horn. The city had withstood sieges from all the migratory barbarians of the East, yet never had it faced such peril as it did on that April morning.

The hosts of the Turkish sultan seemed numberless. Cattle, supply wagons, tents, heavily armed soldiers, and cursing officers intermingled in a terrifying scene of purposeful confusion. By the middle of the morning, the defenders on top of the stout walls could see the huge Turkish cannon being maneuvered into place by thousands of sweating laborers.

While the Turkish land army had been making its preparations, the sultan's navy had not been idle; soon the harried defenders saw 493 Turkish ships sail quickly into the Bosporus, fully armed and ready to match the Greek fleet.

The opposing forces were unevenly matched. The sultan, having mustered more than one hundred thousand men, including the elite Janissaries, and five hundred ships, could surely overwhelm the legions of beleaguered Byzantium, which numbered some seven to eight thousand supported by fifteen ships. Mehmed II had built forts to control the naval approaches to Constantinople, forestalling any naval reinforcements coming to the aid of the emperor. It was impossible to doubt the outcome of such odds; yet the defense of Constantinople was maintained brilliantly and bravely for nearly two months.

The Byzantines, it is to be noted, had more than high walls on their side. The leader of their forces, the Genoese Giovanni Giustiniani, was a man of outstanding military ability, as he proved time and time again in repelling successive attacks of the Turks. Giustiniani was part of the force sent from Venice and Genoa, whose traders and merchants had realized that Constantinople was the central crossroads to trade with the East. The Greeks also had their famous chain boom with which they could block off their harbor, and they had courage and belief in the protection of the Christian God.

On April 12, the siege began in earnest. The Royal One, the biggest siege gun the Turks possessed, was moved ponderously into position. The barrel of this gargantuan weapon was three feet in diameter and fired stone projectiles weighing nearly a ton. From its first shot the huge gun posed a dramatic threat to the garrison on the walls. Week after week, it hammered slowly and inexorably at the crumbling defenses. Citizens were roused at any hour of the day to repair the holes in the battlements. The strain told. Nerves stretched tighter, and fatigue began to take its enervating toll.

In actual fighting, however, the vastly outnumbered Greeks decisively won the first two major engagements of the siege. On April 18, Giustiniani and his armored

Genoese followers beat back wave after wave of Turks who attempted to scale the walls, while the very next day the Greek naval forces successfully repelled a frenzied attack by almost three hundred of the smaller Turkish men-of-war. In a crescendo of death, even more attacks by the Turks took place throughout the following weeks. Slowly and grimly, they set out to wear down the defenders. Day after hot day, the siege continued. The Greeks stayed at the walls, their numbers so low that they had their food and ammunition brought to them on the parapets.

Even the redoubtable Mehmed II began to doubt the wisdom of the siege when it had become obvious that the Greeks would fight to the bitter end. His own troops were becoming restive, and he suspected that help for the Greeks might soon arrive. By the evening of May 27, 1453, Mehmed II was in favor of negotiating with the stubborn defenders. At a council meeting that evening, however, the zealous warrior Zagan Pasha rose to his feet and passionately exhorted his colleagues to finish the task they had begun nearly two months before. The Turks broke up their conference determined once more to take the city.

Mehmed II, called the Conqueror, victor at Constantinople and founder of the Ottoman Empire. (Hulton|Archive by Getty Images)

On the morning of May 28, the final attack on the city of Constantinople began. Assault after assault was beaten back by the exhausted Greeks. On the night of the last day of the empire, the citizens of Constantinople, Greek and Latin, gathered together for Mass at the hallowed shrine of Byzantine Christendom, Santa Sophia, known as Hagia Sophia. Old differences between Latins and Greeks were forgotten in these final moments as haggard soldiers of the East and the West worshiped together in the sacred basilica. The ancient lights, the gold decorations, the priceless icons, must have moved the tired warriors.

On May 29, 1453, the Turkish forces at last forced their way into the city. Finally, even Emperor Constantine XI Palaeologus, the last of the caesars, descended from his horse. With an air of fatality, he removed his imperial vestments and, clad only in his simple tunic and the red leather imperial boots, took up his sword to fight to the death at the side of his last troops. The last link with ancient Rome was broken. The empire of a thousand years had ended.

SIGNIFICANCE

The consequences of the fall of Constantinople are vast. Besides the cultural impact on the West from refugee Greeks, the East slowly sank into poverty and an intellectual decline. The foothold of the Turks into southern Europe consolidated their base for further invasion of central and southern Europe, eventually resulting in the complete conquest of the Balkans.

The Ottoman Empire, whose attachment to Constantinople was as strong as the Greeks and Latins, made Constantinople its capital and principal city. Mehmed II himself destroyed the altar at Hagia Sophia and turned the church into a Muslim mosque. It later became a museum.

Constantinople is still the seat of the patriarch of the Orthodox Church, and one of the most important cities for the Turkish Muslims. Constantinople, whose name was changed to Istanbul in the early 1900's, is truly a cosmopolitan city.

—*Carl F. Rohne, updated by Elizabeth L. Scully*

FURTHER READING

Diehl, Charles. *Byzantium: Greatness and Decline.* Translated by Naomi Alford. New Brunswick, N.J.: Rutgers University Press, 1957. An interpretive ac-

The Siege of Constantinople in 1453. (Library of Congress)

count of the factors in Byzantine life that contributed both to the maintenance of the empire and its gradual decline.

Freely, John. *Istanbul: The Imperial City.* New York: Viking, 1996. Explores the history of the city now known as Istanbul, from the seventh century B.C.E. through the fall of the Ottoman Empire in the early twentieth century. Includes chapters on the city when it was known as Constantinople and its fall during Mehmed's time. Illustrations, spelling and pronunciation guide, bibliography, index.

Goodwin, Jason. *Lords of the Horizons: A History of the Ottoman Empire.* New York: Picador, 2003. A history of the Ottoman Turks beginning in 1288. Looks at the empire's artistic achievements, the first use of the cannon in the seizure of Constantinople, religious tolerance and the empire's longevity, harems, and more. Illustrations, maps, bibliography, index.

Imber, Colin. *The Ottoman Empire, 1300-1650: The Structure of Power.* New York: Palgrave Macmillan, 2002. A comprehensive survey for the general reader of the Ottoman Empire from its origins to the seventeenth century. Using original, contemporary sources as well as modern scholarship, the author analyzes the tradition of sultans and male succession, law and legal education, the military, political power, palace life, harems, religion, and more. Maps, glossary, bibliography, index.

Nicol, Donald M. *The Last Centuries of Byzantium, 1261-1453.* 2d ed. New York: Cambridge University Press, 1993. A political and social history of the Byzantine Empire from the Greek restoration in 1261 until the fall of Constantinople.

Palmer, Alan. *The Decline and Fall of the Ottoman Empire.* New York: Barnes and Noble, 1994. Although only the introduction deals with the actual fall of Constantinople, the book explores the consequences of the fall until World War I.

Pears, Edwin. *The Destruction of the Greek Empire and the Story of the Capture of Constantinople by the Turks.* London: Longmans, Green, 1903. Still one of the best balanced accounts regarding the political, social, and religious aspects of the fall.

Runciman, Steven. *The Fall of Constantinople, 1453.* New York: Cambridge University Press, 1990. This study by a distinguished Byzantinist, originally published in 1965, is probably the standard work in English on the famous siege. Attention to scholarly detail does not impede the retelling of enthralling and tragic episodes from the last days of the city's resistance to the Ottomans. Illustrations, maps, bibliography, index.

Sicker, Michael. *The Islamic World in Ascendancy: From the Arab Conquests to the Siege of Vienna*. Westport, Conn.: Praeger, 2000. Presents a history of the rise and expansion of the Islamic empire, including the conquests of Mehmed. Concludes with a chapter on the end of the ascendancy. Bibliography, index.

SEE ALSO: 532-537: Building of Hagia Sophia; August 15-20, 636: Battle of Yarmūk; 976-1025: Reign of Basil II; 1040-1055: Expansion of the Seljuk Turks; 1054: Beginning of the Rome-Constantinople Schism; 1077: Seljuk Dynasty Is Founded; November 27, 1095: Pope Urban II Calls the First Crusade; c. 1145: Prester John Myth Sweeps Across Europe; 1147-1149: Second Crusade; 1150: Venetian Merchants Dominate Trade with the East; 1189-1192: Third Crusade; 1204: Knights of the Fourth Crusade Capture Constantinople; 1217-1221: Fifth Crusade; 1227-1230: Frederick II Leads the Sixth Crusade; 1248-1254: Failure of the Seventh Crusade; April, 1291: Fall of Acre, Palestine; July 27, 1302: Battle of Bapheus; June 28, 1389: Turkish Conquest of Serbia; 1442-1456: János Hunyadi Defends Hungary Against the Ottomans.

RELATED ARTICLES in *Great Lives from History: The Middle Ages, 477-1453*: Basil the Macedonian; Hārūn al-Rashīd; Justinian I; Mehmed II; Nicholas V; Osman I; Tamerlane.

Time Line

The time line below includes the events and developments covered in the essays in this publication (appearing in small capital letters) as well as more than five hundred other important events and developments. Each event is tagged by general region or regions, rather than by smaller nations or principalities, which changed significantly over the millennium covered in this publication; by this means, the time line can be used to consider general trends in the same region over time. However, because many events, although occurring in one or two regions nevertheless had a global or cross-regional impact, they have been left in strict chronological order to facilitate a better understanding of simultaneous events and their occasional interaction. The abbreviation "c." is used below to stand for both "circa" (when it precedes the date) and "century" or "centuries" (when it follows the date).

Date	Region	Event
5th-6th c.	East Asia	CONFUCIANISM ARRIVES IN JAPAN
455	Europe	Vandals sack Rome
c. 456	Europe	Saint Patrick begins his missionary work in Ireland
476-493	Europe	Reign of Odoacer, first barbarian king of Italy
481-511	Europe	Reign of Clovis, king of the Franks
484	Central and South Asia	WHITE HUNS RAID INDIA
493-511	Europe	Reign of Saint Clotilda, queen consort of France
493-1364	Europe and Middle East	Bulgarian-Byzantine wars for control of the area south of the Danube River and the border between the Byzantine Empire and the Bulgarian kingdom
495-516	Europe	Battle of Mount Badon puts a stop to Anglo-Saxon expansion
496	Europe	BAPTISM OF CLOVIS
499	South Asia	Āryabhaṭa the Elder writes his magnum opus on mathematics and astronomy, *The Aryabhatiya*
500-534	Europe	Burgundian-Frankish wars for control of Burgundy
c. 500-1000	Africa	RISE OF SWAHILI CULTURES
c. 500-1000	Americas	TIWANAKU CIVILIZATION FLOURISHES IN ANDEAN HIGHLANDS
6th-8th c.	Central Asia	SOGDIANS DOMINATE CENTRAL ASIAN TRADE
Aug. 502-591	Europe and Middle East	Byzantine-Persian wars for control of Asia between the Bosporus and beyond the Euphrates River
Feb. 2, 506	Europe	ALARIC II DRAFTS THE *BREVIARUM ALARICI*
507	Europe	Clovis defeats the Visigoths at Vouillé and unifies Gaul
524	Europe	IMPRISONMENT AND DEATH OF BOETHIUS
526	Europe	Priscian writes *Institutiones grammaticae*
Before 527	Central Asia	Translator and church historian Dionysius Exiguus devises the Christian-based calendar
527-548	Europe	Reign of Theodora, Byzantine empress
529	Europe	Saint Benedict of Nursia founds the Benedictine monastic order at Monte Cassino in southern Italy
529-534	Middle East	JUSTINIAN'S CODE IS COMPILED: Justinian definitively codifies Roman law, wages war against the Germans and Persians, and changes the nature of the Eastern Roman (Byzantine) Empire to an absolute monarchy
531-579	Middle East	Reign of Khosrow I, king of Persia
532-537	Middle East	BUILDING OF HAGIA SOPHIA

DATE	REGION	EVENT
534-535	Europe	Reign of Amalasuntha, queen of the Ostrogoths
534-554	Europe	Gothic wars for control of the Italian peninsula
538-552	East Asia	BUDDHISM ARRIVES IN JAPAN
543-1189	South Asia	Cālukyan wars for control of southern India
c. 550	East Asia	The Tuque (T'u-chüeh), a Turkish steppe people, create a loose dominion north of China, stretching from Korea to Karashar
July 552	Europe	Battle of Taginae: Justinian's general Narses defeats the Ostrogoths in Italy
563	Europe, Middle East, East Asia	SILK WORMS ARE SMUGGLED TO THE BYZANTINE EMPIRE
567-568	Central and South Asia	SĀSĀNIANS AND TURKS DEFEAT THE WHITE HUNS
567-597	Europe	Reign of Fredegunde, queen of Neustria
568-571	Europe	LOMBARD CONQUEST OF ITALY and reign of Alboin
Late sixth c.	Europe	Irish abbess Saint Brigit makes Kildare a center of scholarship and a school of art
Late sixth c.	Europe	Gregory of Tours writes his history of the Franks, *Historia Francorum*
581	East Asia	SUI DYNASTY REUNIFIES CHINA
590-604	Europe	REFORMS OF POPE GREGORY THE GREAT
593-604	East Asia	REGENCY OF SHŌTOKU TAISHI
593-628	East Asia	Reign of Suiko, Japanese empress
c. 595/598	Europe	Battle of Catraeth, ground battle in defense of Britain
595-665	East and South Asia	INVENTION OF DECIMALS AND NEGATIVE NUMBERS, including the zero value
596-597	Europe	SEE OF CANTERBURY IS ESTABLISHED
598-668	East Asia	Sino-Korean wars: Chinese conquest of north Korea
c. 600-950	Americas	EL TAJÍN IS BUILT
7th c.	Africa	Aksumite kingdom is weakened by the spread of Islam throughout Arabia and North Africa
7th-early 8th c.	Americas	MAYA BUILD ASTRONOMICAL OBSERVATORY AT PALENQUE
7th-8th c.	East Asia	PAPERMAKING SPREADS TO KOREA, JAPAN, AND CENTRAL ASIA
7th-13th c.	Americas	MOGOLLONS ESTABLISH AGRICULTURAL SETTLEMENTS
605-610	East Asia	BUILDING OF THE GRAND CANAL
606	East Asia	NATIONAL UNIVERSITY AWARDS FIRST DOCTORATE
606-647	South Asia	REIGN OF HARṢA OF KANAUJ
607-839	East Asia	JAPAN SENDS EMBASSIES TO CHINA
c. 610-632	Middle East	MUḤAMMAD RECEIVES REVELATIONS
610-638	Europe	Constantinople's Sergius I is patriarch of the Orthodox Church
610-641	Europe	Heraclius reigns over the Byzantine Empire, Hellenizing the culture and introducing a system of provinces ruled by military governors
c. 611-642	South Asia	REIGN OF PULAKEŚIN II
618	East Asia	FOUNDING OF THE TANG DYNASTY
619	Middle East	Death of Khadīja, wife of the Prophet Muḥammad and first convert to Islam

DATE	REGION	EVENT
622	Middle East	The Prophet Muḥammad flees from Mecca to Medina to avoid persecution
627-649	East Asia	Reign of Taizong, Chinese emperor
627-650	Central and South Asia	REIGN OF SONGTSEN GAMPO
c. 628	South Asia	Indian mathematician Brahmagupta completes his masterwork on astronomy, the *Brahmasphuṭasiddhānta*
629-645	East, Central, and South Asia	PILGRIMAGE OF XUANZANG
630-668	South Asia	REIGN OF NARASIṂHAVARMAN I MAHĀMALLA
630-711	Africa	ISLAM EXPANDS THROUGHOUT NORTH AFRICA
June 8, 632	Middle East	Death of the Prophet Muḥammad, followed by creation of the Islamic caliphate
633	Europe	At the Fourth Council of Toledo, Isidore of Seville orders the establishment of liberal arts schools in all dioceses of Hispania
634-644	Middle East	Reign of ʿUmar I, first caliph
635-800	Europe	FOUNDING OF LINDISFARNE AND CREATION OF THE *BOOK OF KELLS*
Aug. 15-20, 636	Middle East	BATTLE OF YARMŪK: Muslim forces capture the holy regions of Syria and Palestine from the Byzantine Empire
637	Middle East	Battle of Qadisiyah: Arab forces destroy the Sāsānian Persians, heralding the decline of their empire
637-657	Middle East	ISLAM EXPANDS THROUGHOUT THE MIDDLE EAST
641-642	Middle East	Siege of Nahavand: Muslims invade the Persian highlands
645-646	East Asia	ADOPTION OF *NENGO* SYSTEM AND TAIKA REFORMS
c. 650	East Asia	Portraitist Yan Liben paints his *Scroll of the Emperors*, depicting thirteen of China's emperors
652-c. 1171	Africa	CHRISTIAN NUBIA AND MUSLIM EGYPT SIGN TREATY
657-661	Middle East	Muslim Civil War for control of the Islamic world: ʿAlī's claim to the caliphate creates a rift in Islamic unity between Syrian and Iraqi Muslims, leading to the formation of the Shīʿite and Sunni sects
c. 667-c. 702	Africa	Reign of the Berber queen Damia al-Kāhina
668-935	East Asia	SILLA UNIFICATION OF KOREA
674-678	Europe	The flammable liquid Greek fire is used by the Byzantines against Arab ships during the Siege of Constantinople
c. 675-719	Europe	Frankish civil wars for control of the Frankish kingdom
c. 680	Europe	Cædmon composes the earliest known English poetry
Oct. 10, 680	Middle East	MARTYRDOM OF PROPHET'S GRANDSON ḤUSAYN at the Battle of Karbalāʾ
682-1377	Southeast Asia	EXPANSION OF ŚRIVIJAYA
685-691	Middle East	BUILDING OF THE DOME OF THE ROCK
685-705	Middle East	Reign of Caliph ʿAbd al-Malik
687	Europe	Pépin of Herstal wins the Battle of Tertry, solidifies rule over all Franks, and unifies the office of Mayor of the Palace
687-701	Europe	Saint Sergius I is pope
Nov. 17, 689	Europe	Death of Saint Hilda of Whitby, English abbess

DATE	REGION	EVENT
c. 690	Europe	Death of Paul of Aegina, Byzantine physician and writer
690-705	East Asia	REIGN OF EMPRESS WU
c. 700	Americas	BOW AND ARROW SPREAD INTO NORTH AMERICA
c. 700	East Asia	Porcelain is invented in China
c. 700	Middle East	Windmills are invented in Persia
c. 700-1000	Americas	BUILDING OF CHICHÉN ITZÁ
c. 700-1000	Europe	HEAVY PLOW HELPS INCREASE AGRICULTURAL YIELDS
c. 700-1100	Australia/Pacific	SETTLEMENT OF THE SOUTH PACIFIC ISLANDS
c. 700-1253	Southeast Asia	CONFEDERATION OF THAI TRIBES
8th c.	Europe	Composition of *Beowulf*, England's national epic
8th-14th c.	Americas	CAHOKIA BECOMES THE FIRST NORTH AMERICAN CITY
8th-15th c.	Americas	HOHOKAM ADAPT TO THE DESERT SOUTHWEST
701	East Asia	TAIHŌ LAWS REFORM JAPANESE GOVERNMENT
c. 710	South Asia	CONSTRUCTION OF THE KĀILAŚANĀTHA TEMPLE
Apr./May 711	Europe	ṬĀRIK CROSSES INTO SPAIN, overcoming the Visigoths in the seven-day Battle of La Janda
711-1492	Europe	Reconquista (Reconquest) of Spain: Christian principalities launch a four-hundred-year campaign to retake the southern Iberian Peninsula from Muslim rule
712-720	East Asia	WRITING OF *KOJIKI* AND *NIHON SHOKI*
713-741	East Asia	FIRST NEWSPAPERS IN CHINA
714	Europe	Pépin's illegitimate son, Charles Martel, seizes control of the Frankish kingdom
717-718	Europe	Siege of Constantinople: The Islamic Empire expands into Europe
718-759	Europe, Middle East	Frankish-Moorish wars for control of Gaul
719-741	Europe	Charles Martel is Frankish mayor of the palace
721	Europe	Battle of Toulouse: Eudo, duke of Aquitaine, defeats the Muslims
726-843	Europe	ICONOCLASTIC CONTROVERSY
728	Middle East	Death of the Islamic sage al-Ḥasan al-Baṣrī
729	Southeast Asia	FOUNDING OF NANZHAO
730	South Asia	RISE OF THE PRATIHĀRAS
730's	East Asia	Li Bo is traveling through China and writing lyric poetry
731	Europe	BEDE WRITES *ECCLESIASTICAL HISTORY OF THE ENGLISH PEOPLE*
Oct. 11, 732	Europe	BATTLE OF TOURS: Christian victory discourages Muslim incursions beyond the Pyrenees
733-750	Europe	Æthelbald's wars for control of the Anglo-Saxon kingdoms: Mercia becomes the most important power in England
734-755	East Asia	Wang Wei is writing poetry in China
735	Europe	CHRISTIANITY IS INTRODUCED INTO GERMANY by Saint Boniface, archbishop of Mainz
740	Europe	KHAZARS CONVERT TO JUDAISM
c. 740	Middle East	Abū Ḥanīfah founds the Hanifite school of Islamic law

DATE	REGION	EVENT
744-840	Central Asia	UIGHUR TURKS RULE CENTRAL ASIA: Uighurs destroy the Tuque (T'u-chüeh) Empire and dominate Mongolia and Central Asia
747-750	Middle East	ʿAbbāsid Revolution: Establishment of a legitimate Islamic government and control of tax revenues
Dec. 4, 749	Europe	Death of John of Damascus, writer, monk, and religious scholar
c. 750	East Asia	Carbon-steel swords first appear in Japan
c. 750	South Asia	Śaṅkara founds the Advaita school of Hindu philosophy and makes a pilgrimage throughout the Indian subcontinent
750-1035	Europe, Middle East	Byzantine-Muslim wars to determine Christian vs. Muslim influence in the Middle East
c. 750-1240	Africa	RISE AND FALL OF GHANA
751	Central Asia	BATTLE OF TALAS RIVER: Arabs defeat the Chinese near Samarqand in Central Asia
754	Europe	CORONATION OF PÉPIN THE SHORT
755-763	East Asia	REBELLION OF AN LUSHAN
759-770	East Asia	Chinese poet Du Fu writes his most mature lyrics
763	Central Asia	TIBETANS CAPTURE CHANG'AN
764-770	East Asia	Reign of Kōken, Japanese empress
c. 770	Worldwide	Iron horseshoes come into common use
770-810	South Asia	REIGN OF DHARMAPĀLA
771-786	Europe	Offa's wars for Mercian hegemony in England
771-814	Europe	Wars of Charlemagne: expansion and protection of the Frankish empire
775-802	Europe	Reign of Saint Irene, Byzantine empress
775-840	Southeast Asia	BUILDING OF BOROBUḌUR
780	Middle East	BEGINNING OF THE HAREM SYSTEM
780	Southeast Asia	RISE OF THE SAILENDRA FAMILY
781	Europe	ALCUIN BECOMES ADVISER TO CHARLEMAGNE
782	Europe	Saxon chieftain Widukind leads a revolt against the Franks near the Weser River
786-809	Middle East	REIGN OF HĀRŪN AL-RASHĪD
788-850	South Asia	ŚAṄKARA EXPOUNDS ADVAITA VEDĀNTA
791	Central Asia	BUDDHISM BECOMES TIBETAN STATE RELIGION
792	East Asia	RISE OF THE SAMURAI
June 7, 793	Europe	NORSE RAID LINDISFARNE MONASTERY
794-1185	East Asia	HEIAN PERIOD
c. 796	Europe	Completion of Offa's Dyke, built on the Welsh border to defend the Mercian kingdom
800	Europe	Pope Leo III crowns Charlemagne Holy Roman Emperor
c. 800	East Asia	*KANA* SYLLABARY IS DEVELOPED
9th-11th c.	Africa	Kanem-Bornu Sultanate expands throughout western Sudan
c. 800-1100	Australia/Pacific	Polynesians make unique stone images on Necker Island in Hawaii
c. 800-1350	Americas	MISSISSIPPIAN MOUND-BUILDING CULTURE FLOURISHES
9th-14th c.	Africa	RISE OF THE TOUTSWE KINGDOM

DATE	REGION	EVENT
9th-15th c.	Americas	PLAINS VILLAGE CULTURE FLOURISHES
9th-15th c.	Middle East, Africa	Throughout the Islamic world, *mamlūks* (military slaves) are recruited into elite regiments, providing military support to many Islamic emirates and caliphates
801	Middle East	Death of Sufi mystic Rābiʿah al-ʿAdawiyah
802	Southeast Asia	FOUNDING OF THE KHMER EMPIRE
802-839	Europe	Reign of Egbert, king of England
809	Middle East	FIRST ISLAMIC PUBLIC HOSPITAL
c. 810	Europe	Rabanus Maurus's "figural poems" revive the classical practice of joining text to pictures
c. 810-815	Europe	Theophanes the Confessor writes *Chronographia*, the main source for the history of the Byzantine Empire from about 600 to 813
812	East Asia	PAPER MONEY FIRST USED IN CHINA
815	Middle East	Death of Abū Mūsā Jābir ibn Ḥayyān, Arabian chemist and alchemist
832	Southeast Asia	NANZHAO SUBJUGATES PYU
834	Middle East	GYPSIES EXPELLED FROM PERSIA
Apr. 22, 835	East Asia	Death of Japanese monk Kōbō Daishi
838-842	Central Asia	TIBETAN EMPIRE DISSOLVES
840-846	Central Asia	UIGHUR MIGRATIONS
840-920	Central Asia	Nomadic Kirghiz horsemen invade Mongolia and drive out the Uighurs
c. 841	Europe	Dhuoda writes *Liber Manualis*, the only extant book by a woman from the Carolingian period
June 25, 841	Europe	Battle of Fontenay, ground battle in the Carolingian civil wars
843	Europe	TREATY OF VERDUN divides the Carolingian Empire among Charlemagne's sons
843-876	Europe	Reign of Louis the German, king of Germany
845	East Asia	SUPPRESSION OF BUDDHISM
Mid-9th c.	East Asia	INVENTION OF GUNPOWDER AND GUNS
c. 850	Europe	DEVELOPMENT OF SLAVIC ALPHABET
c. 850	Middle East	Death of Arabic mathematician and astronomer al-Khwārizmī
c. 850	Middle East	The coffee beverage is invented in Arabia
c. 850-950	Europe	VIKING ERA: Vikings raid the British Isles, Iceland, continental Europe, and Russia
850-1257	South Asia	Cōla Kingdom rules much of southern India
After 850	Americas	FOUNDATION OF CHAN CHAN
852-889	Europe	Reign of Boris I of Bulgaria, czar of Bulgaria
July 855	Middle East	Death of Aḥmad ibn Ḥanbal, Muslim theologian and jurist
858	East Asia	RISE OF THE FUJIWARA FAMILY
858	Middle East	Birth of Arab astronomer and mathematician al-Battānī
858-867	Europe	Nicholas the Great is pope
859-862	Europe	Varangian incursion: Vikings invade northwestern Russia
c. 860-879	Europe	Rurik becomes the first prince of Kievan Rus
861-870	Middle East	Muslim civil war for control of the caliphate in Baghdad

DATE	REGION	EVENT
863	East and Southeast Asia	NANZHAO CAPTURES HANOI
863-885	Europe	In Moravia, Saints Cyril and Methodius are developing the Slavonic liturgy and alphabet
864	Europe	BORIS CONVERTS TO CHRISTIANITY
867-886	Europe	Reign of Byzantine emperor Basil the Macedonian
868	Middle East	Death of Arabic zoologist and scholar al-Jāḥiẓ
868	East Asia	FIRST BOOK PRINTED: The *Diamond Sutra* is the earliest extant printed book
869-883	Middle East	ZANJ REVOLT OF AFRICAN SLAVES
871-899	Europe	Reign of Alfred the Great, king of England
872	Middle East	Arab historian al-Ṭabarī writes his history of the world
872-973	Middle East	PUBLICATION OF *THE HISTORY OF AL-ṬABARĪ*
875-877	Europe	Reign of Charles the Bald, king of France and Holy Roman Emperor
877-889	Southeast Asia	INDRAVARMAN I CONQUERS THE THAI AND THE MONS
878	Europe	ALFRED DEFEATS THE DANES at the Battle of Edington
886	Europe	Last Viking siege of Paris
890's	Europe	MAGYARS INVADE ITALY, SAXONY, AND BAVARIA
893	Europe	BEGINNING OF BULGARIA'S GOLDEN AGE
c. 896-907	Europe	Reign of Árpád, founder of the first Hungarian state
899-918	Europe	Reign of Æthelflæd, queen of Mercia
899-924	Europe	Reign of Edward the Elder, king of England
Early 10th c.	Central Asia	QARAKHANIDS CONVERT TO ISLAM
10th c.	Americas	CULT OF QUETZALCÓATL SPREADS THROUGH MESOAMERICA
10th c.	Central and South Asia	Ghaznavid Turks invade India from Afghanistan, introducing an Islamic influence that will continue until the early sixteenth century
10th-11th c.	Africa	FIRST HAUSA STATE ESTABLISHED
10th-11th c.	Europe	The crossbow makes its first European appearance, in Italy
10th-11th c.	Europe	Under the Umayyad caliphate, the Iberian Peninsula experiences a golden age of philosophy, literature, science, and relative religious tolerance
c. 900-1150	Middle East	Philosophy, science, and scholarship flourish in Iran under such figures as al-Bīrūnī, physician-philosopher Avicenna, the Islamic theologian al-Ghazzālī, and the physician al-Rāzī
907-960	East Asia	PERIOD OF FIVE DYNASTIES AND TEN KINGDOMS
907-1125	East Asia	The Liao Dynasty rules northwestern China
911	Europe	Rollo receives the county of Normandy from the French king
911-c. 932	Europe	Rollo's reign establishes the Norman Dynasty
912-961	Europe	ʿAbd al-Raḥmān III al-Nāṣir, Umayyad emir and caliph, rules Córdoba
c. 915	Africa	Arab historian and geographer al-Masʿūdī begins his extensive travels through the Middle East and Asia

DATE	REGION	EVENT
915	South Asia	PARĀNTAKA I CONQUERS PĀṆḌYA: Parāntaka expands Cōla territory into southern India with his victory against the Pāṇḍyas at the Battle of Vellur
918-936	East Asia	FOUNDATION OF THE KORYŎ DYNASTY
920	East Asia	Khitans drive out Kirghiz and establish an empire in Mongolia and China
Sept. 15, 921	Europe	Death of Saint Ludmilla, duchess of Bohemia
c. 922	Middle East	Persian physician al-Rāzī writes his treatise on smallpox
927	East Asia	COMPILATION OF THE *ENGI SHIKI*
c. 930	Europe	Vikings settle Iceland
c. 930	Middle East	Islamic theologian al-Ashʿarī founds Ashʿarism, a movement to achieve a true synthesis of purely logical argument and the transcendental elements of revealed Islam
936	East Asia	KHITANS SETTLE NEAR BEIJING
937	Europe	Battle of Brunanburgh: Æthelstan defeats Scots and Vikings
939-944	Southeast Asia	REIGN OF NGO QUYEN
945-964	Europe	Reign of Saint Olga, princess of Rus
945-1055	Middle East	The Buyid Dynasty dominates the ʿAbbāsid caliphate in Iraq
c. 950	Europe	COURT OF CÓRDOBA FLOURISHES IN SPAIN
c. 950-1100	Middle East	RISE OF MADRASAS
c. 950-1150	Americas	TOLTECS BUILD TULA, the largest city in central Mexico, with a population of about 60,000 and covering some 5 square miles
Aug. 10, 955	Europe	OTTO I DEFEATS THE MAGYARS at the Battle of Lechfeld
956	Central Asia	OĞHUZ TURKS MIGRATE TO TRANSOXIANA
958-1076	East Asia	KOREANS ADOPT THE TANG CIVIL SERVICE MODEL
960	East Asia	FOUNDING OF THE SONG DYNASTY
c. 960	Europe	JEWS SETTLE IN BOHEMIA
960-1279	East Asia	SCHOLAR-OFFICIAL CLASS FLOURISHES UNDER SONG DYNASTY
962	Europe	FOUNDATION OF THE MOUNT ATHOS MONASTERIES
962-973	Europe	Coronation of Otto I as Holy Roman Emperor
c. 963	Europe	German-Saxon poet, playwright, and historian Hrosvitha is writing plays in Gandersheim
969-1171	Africa	REIGN OF THE FĀṬIMIDS: Shīʿite Muslims based in Cairo, the Fāṭimids challenge Baghdad's Sunni ʿAbbāsid caliphate for control of the holy cities of Mecca and Medina
972	Africa	BUILDING OF AL-AZHAR MOSQUE
972-1152	Africa	The Zirid and Hammadid Berbers, under the Fāṭimid caliphate, dominate Tunisia and eastern Algeria
973	South Asia	FOUNDATION OF THE WESTERN CĀLUKYA DYNASTY
976-1025	Europe	REIGN OF BASIL II

DATE	REGION	EVENT
977-1186	Central and South Asia	The Ghaznavid Empire, based in modern-day Afghanistan, is the first Islamic state dominated by a Turkic military class, spreading Islam into India
978-980	Europe	Franco-German war for control of the province of Lorraine
978-1016	Europe	Reign of Ethelred II, the Unready, king of England
980-1015	Europe	Reign of Vladimir I, grand prince of Kiev
982	Southeast Asia	LE DAI HANH INVADES CHAMPA
c. 983-998	Middle East	Persian mathematician and astronomer Abul Wefa develops his theory of sines and cosines
c. 985-1014	South Asia	REIGN OF RĀJARĀJA I
987	Europe	HUGH CAPET IS ELECTED TO THE FRENCH THRONE
988	Europe	*BAPTISM OF VLADIMIR I*
989	Europe	Byzantine princess Anna marries Vladimir I and lays the foundation for the Christian conversion of Russia
990's	Europe	The first stone keeps appear in northwestern Europe
991	Europe	Battle of Maldon: Danish Vikings defeat the English and force them to pay Danegeld
992-1054	Africa	GHANA TAKES CONTROL OF AWDAGHUST
995-1000	Europe	Reign of Olaf I, king of Norway
997-1038	Europe	Reign of Stephen I, king of Hungary
998-1030	Central and South Asia	REIGN OF MAḤMŪD OF GHAZNA
999-1003	Europe	Sylvester II is pope
c. 1000	Americas	COLLAPSE OF THE HUARI AND TIWANAKU CIVILIZATIONS
c. 1000	Americas	Pueblo villages are built and black-on-white ceramics are manufactured in New Mexico's Mimbres Valley
c. 1000	East Asia	FOOTBINDING DEVELOPS IN CHINESE SOCIETY
c. 1000	South Asia	HINDI BECOMES INDIA'S DOMINANT LANGUAGE
c. 1000	South Asia	Construction of the Lingaraja and Rajarani temples in Orissa on India's east coast
c. 1000	Americas	Metalworkers in southern Costa Rica and western Panama produce gold pendants depicting figures with the heads of frogs, turtles, bats, and crocodiles
c. 1000	Europe	Death of Leif Eriksson, Norwegian explorer
Sept. 9, 1000	Europe	Battle of Svalde, a naval conflict during the Viking raids
1000-1471	Southeast Asia	Vietnamese-Cham wars for control of the kingdom of Champa (southern Vietnam)
11th c.	Africa	EXPANSION OF SUNNI ISLAM IN NORTH AFRICA AND IBERIA
11th c.	Central Asia	Tibet undergoes a Buddhist renaissance, with growth of monasteries, schools, and art
11th-12th c.	Europe	BUILDING OF ROMANESQUE CATHEDRALS
11th-12th c.	Americas	FIRST EUROPEAN-NATIVE AMERICAN CONTACT: Norse expeditions reach Baffin Island, Labrador, and Newfoundland, 986-1008

DATE	REGION	EVENT
11th-15th c.	Africa	DEVELOPMENT OF THE IFE KINGDOM AND YORUBA CULTURE: Ife becomes a major urban center during the Pavement period, named after mosaics constructed to form a distinctive herringbone pattern. Ife's famous terracotta and metal heads are sculpted to represent identifiable individuals
11th-15th c.	Africa	GREAT ZIMBABWE URBANISM AND ARCHITECTURE: develops after the city is founded by Bantu-speaking ancestors of the Shona people
11th-15th/16th c.	Africa	Tellem people, seeking to avoid conversion to Islam, migrate from the inland Niger River Delta and Jenne-Jeno to the Bandiagara escarpment
After 1000	Europe	DEVELOPMENT OF MIRACLE AND MYSTERY PLAYS
1001	Southeast Asia	Thailand's Lopburi Kingdom requests China's assistance in securing independence from the Khmers
c. 1001	East Asia	SEI SHŌNAGON COMPLETES *THE PILLOW BOOK*
c. 1004	East Asia	MURASAKI SHIKIBU WRITES *THE TALE OF GENJI*
1009	Middle East	DESTRUCTION OF THE CHURCH OF THE HOLY SEPULCHRE
1010	Middle East	FIRDUSI COMPOSES THE *SHAHNAMAH*, Iran's national epic
c. 1010	Africa	SONGHAI KINGDOM CONVERTS TO ISLAM
c. 1010-1015	Middle East	AVICENNA WRITES HIS *CANON OF MEDICINE*
1012	East Asia	RICE IS INTRODUCED INTO CHINA
1013	Europe	Danish king Sveyn I Forkbeard defeats English king Ethelred I and forces him into exile
Apr. 23, 1014	Europe	BATTLE OF CLONTARF: Brian Boru and his son Murchad defeat the Norse-Leinster alliance, but Brian is killed
1014-1024	Europe	Henry II the Saint reigns as Holy Roman Emperor
c. 1015	Europe	The two republics of Genoa and Pisa send ships to Sardinia and Corsica to oust the Arabs from those islands, then vie for their control for the next three hundred years
1016-1017	East Asia	Regency of Fujiwara Michinaga
1016-1028	Europe	Reign of Saint Olaf, king of Norway
1016-1035	Europe	CANUTE CONQUERS ENGLAND and reigns as king of England, Denmark, and Norway
1016-1070	Europe	Normans migrate into southern Italy, eventually subverting Byzantine dominance
c. 1017	South Asia	Cōlas conquer Sri Lanka
c. 1018	Middle East	Arab scholar and scientist al-Bīrūnī becomes official astronomer/astrologer to the court of Maḥmūd of Ghazna
1018	Europe	Emperor Basil II conquers Bulgaria, expanding the Byzantine Empire to its largest extent until the second Bulgarian kingdom is established under the Asen line in 1186
1019	Central and South Asia	Maḥmūd of Ghazna raids northern India and destroys Kanauj, the capital of the Gurjara-Pratihāra Empire
1019	Southeast Asia	Airlangga founds the Kahuripan kingdom in Java; during his reign Hindu and Buddhist arts flourish

DATE	REGION	EVENT
1020-1057	East Asia	Japanese sculptor Jōchō is developing his joined-wood technique
1020's	Middle East	Arab physicist Alhazen, the most important figure in optics between antiquity and the seventeenth century, writes his treatise *Optics*
c. 1025	Europe	SCHOLARS AT CHARTRES REVIVE INTEREST IN THE CLASSICS
1025	South and Southeast Asia	South India's Cōla kingdom invades Śrivijaya
After 1026	Europe	Italian music theorist Guido d'Arezzo publishes the *Micrologus*, a manual on musical notation and one of the most influential books of its time
Apr. 10, 1028	Europe	Death of Saint Fulbert, founder of the cathedral school at Chartres
c. 1028	Europe	Death of Gershom ben Judah, French-German rabbi who played a major role in establishing the scholarly autonomy of Franco-German Jewry
1030	South Asia	Al-Bīrūnī completes his history of India, *Tārʾīkh al-Hind*
1031	Europe	CALIPHATE OF CÓRDOBA FALLS
1031-1086	Europe	Ta'ifa rulers assume power in Islamic Spain after the fall of Córdoba, becoming patrons of the arts and architecture and building huge palaces
1032-1227	East Asia	Rise of the Xixia Empire in northwestern China
1037	Middle East	Death of Avicenna, Persian philosopher and scholar
1038	Central Asia	Battle of Nishapur: Seljuks defeat the Ghaznavids and move into the Khorāsān grazing grounds of northeastern Persia
May 24, 1040	Middle East	Battle of Dandāngān Castle: Seljuks overcome the Ghaznavid Masʿūd I
1040's	Europe	Ibn Gabirol is writing poetry in biblical Hebrew
1040-1055	Middle East	EXPANSION OF THE SELJUK TURKS
c. 1042	Central Asia	The "second transmission," a renaissance in Tibetan Buddhism, is born when Atisha, an Indian mystic, settles in Tibet
1043-1066	Europe	Reign of Edward the Confessor, king of England
c. 1044	East Asia	The first book containing a formula for gunpowder appears, listing coal, saltpeter, and sulfur as the primary ingredients
1044	Southeast Asia	Anawrahta founds the first Burmese kingdom, the Pagan Empire
c. 1045	East Asia	BI SHENG DEVELOPS MOVABLE EARTHENWARE TYPE
1048	Africa	ZĪRIDS BREAK FROM FĀṬIMID DYNASTY AND REVIVE SUNNI ISLAM
1049-1054	Europe	Leo IX is pope
c. 1050	East Asia	Worldwide proliferation of block-printed books and paper
1050-1203	Southeast Asia	Khmer-Cham wars: Khmer territorial expansion and political control over Champa
1054	East and South Asia	Chinese and American Indian astronomers observe the Crab supernova explosion

DATE	REGION	EVENT
1054	Europe	BEGINNING OF THE ROME-CONSTANTINOPLE SCHISM
1055	Europe	Llewelyn ap Gruffydd, prince of Powys, briefly unifies Wales, but the country dissolves after his death
1055	Middle East	The Seljuk Turks take Baghdad, ending Buyid rule
1059	East Asia	Chinese writer and philosopher Ouyang Xiu revivifies the *fu*, a Chinese poetic form, with "The Sounds of Autumn"
1062-1147	Africa	ALMORAVIDS CONQUER MOROCCO AND ESTABLISH THE ALMORAVID EMPIRE
1063-1072/73	Middle East	Reign of Alp Arslan, second Seljuk sultan; Seljuk vizier Niẓām al-Mulk is in power
Sept. 25, 1066	Europe	Battle of Stamford Bridge: English king Harold II defeats Norwegian and Norman invaders
Oct. 14, 1066	Europe	BATTLE OF HASTINGS: William of Normandy defeats Harold II in this decisive battle in the Norman Conquest
1066-1086	Europe	The abbot Desiderius restores the abbey at Monte Cassino
1066-1087	Europe	Reign of William the Conqueror, king of France
1067	East Asia	Chinese statesman Sima Guang presents his *Zizhi tongjian* to Emperor Yingzong
1069-1072	East Asia	WANG ANSHI INTRODUCES BUREAUCRATIC REFORMS
1070's	Middle East	Mathematician and poet Omar Khayyám writes his *Rubáiyát*
Aug. 26, 1071	Middle East	BATTLE OF MANZIKERT: marks the beginning of Byzantine decline as Seljuk Turks conquer Anatolia and Hellenistic Asia Minor; prompts the First Crusade two decades later
After 1071	Europe	Byzantine philosopher and historian Michael Psellus writes *Chronographia*
1073-1085	Europe	Gregory VII is pope
c. 1075-1086	Africa	HUMMAY FOUNDS SEFUWA DYNASTY
1075	Europe	In Spain, work begins on the cathedral of Santiago de Compostela, the most important destination for Christian pilgrims after Rome and Jerusalem
1075-c. 1220	Africa	EMERGENCE OF MAPUNGUBWE
1076	Africa	ALMORAVIDS SACK KUMBI
1076	Europe	Investiture Controversy begins: Pope Gregory VII excommunicates Emperor Henry IV for insisting on his right to name bishops and other clerics within his realm
c. 1077	Europe	Bayeux Tapestry is created: More than 200 feet long, it tells the story of the Battle of Hastings in 1066
1077	Middle East	SELJUK DYNASTY IS FOUNDED: Süleyman founds Seljuk Rum, beginning the golden age of the Seljuk Empire
1077-1095	Europe	Reign of Saint László I, Polish-born king of Hungary
1077-1214	Europe	German civil war over control of the Holy Roman Empire
1081-1085	Europe	Norman-Byzantine wars result in Norman defeat and preservation of Byzantine autonomy
1084-1106	Europe	Henry IV of Germany reigns as Holy Roman Emperor

DATE	REGION	EVENT
1086	Africa	Battle of Al-Zallāqah: Major battle during the Reconquista; after Castilian king Alfonso VI conquers Toledo in 1085, the Almoravid Tāshufīn enters Iberia to support the Islamic principalities and establish control in the south
1086	Europe	DOMESDAY SURVEY: Ordered by William the Conqueror, first Norman king of England, the Domesday Book records a systematic survey of England's lands
1086-1091	Europe	Bogomil (Bulgarian) revolt and Pecheneg-Byzantine war
1088-1099	Europe	Urban II is pope
1092-1093	Europe	Saint Anselm intercedes with King William Rufus on behalf of oppressed clerics in England, is named archbishop of Canterbury
1092-1094	Europe	EL CID CONQUERS VALENCIA: After cavalry and infantry battles and sieges, El Cid holds Valencia during his lifetime, although Muslims reconquer it at his death
Nov. 27, 1095	Europe, Middle East	POPE URBAN II CALLS THE FIRST CRUSADE
1095-1105	Middle East	Muslim mystic al-Ghazzālī abandons Baghdad for a life of poverty, producing *The Revival of the Religious Sciences*
Aug. 1096	Europe	Battle of Cibotus: Crossing the Bosporus into Asia, participants in the Peasants' Crusade are annihilated by the Turks
Before 1097	Europe	Italian physician Trotula is writing her manuals of the treatments of women's diseases and conditions
July 1, 1097	Europe, Middle East	Battle of Dorylaeum: Bohemond I defeats the Turks
Mar. 21, 1098	Europe	FOUNDATION OF THE CISTERCIAN ORDER
June 3, 1098	Europe, Middle East	Fall of Antioch to Bohemond I and Crusaders after an eight-month siege
July 15, 1099	Middle East	Crusaders retake Jerusalem
c. 1100	Europe	ARABIC NUMERALS ARE INTRODUCED INTO EUROPE
c. 1100	Africa	FOUNDING OF TIMBUKTU
c. 1100	Africa	ORIGINS OF SWAHILI IN ITS WRITTEN FORM
c. 1100	Europe	RISE OF COURTLY LOVE
1100	Americas	Building of the Pueblo Bonito, the largest of the Chaco Canyon multistory houses
1100	Europe	European knights adopt the use of the couched lance, which provides more force than previous hand-thrust weapons
1100-1125	East Asia	Reign of Huizong, famous for his paintings and as a patron of the arts
1100-1135	Europe	Reign of Henry I, king of England
1100-1300	Europe	EUROPEAN UNIVERSITIES EMERGE
12th c.	Africa	Gao, near the Niger River on the border between the Sudan and the Sahel, becomes a key trading center of the Songhai Empire
12th c.	Africa	COINS ARE MINTED ON THE SWAHILI COAST
12th c.	Africa	TRADING CENTER OF KILWA KISIWANI IS FOUNDED
12th c.	East Asia	WANG CHONGYANG FOUNDS QUANZHEN DAOISM
12th-14th c.	Europe	SOCIAL AND POLITICAL IMPACT OF LEPROSY

DATE	REGION	EVENT
12th-15th c.	Africa	Creation of the Esie sculptures, soapstone images of humans and animals found near this Yoruba town in Nigeria
c. 1100-1500	Australia/Pacific	On Easter Island, the earliest of the giant stone figures called *moai* are being carved
1101	East Asia	Li Qingzhao is writing her poetry
1101	Europe	Tancred becomes regent of Antioch
July 28, 1101	East Asia	Death of Chinese poet and scholar Su Dongpo
Sept. 6, 1101	Middle East	Battle of Ramleh, a ground battle in the Crusades
1107	East Asia	Death of Chinese calligrapher Mi Fei
1112	East Asia	The Miyazedi stone inscriptions, recording the earliest known written form of the Burmese language, are created
1113-1150	Southeast Asia	Reign of Khmer king Suryavarman II, who captures parts of Vietnam, Laos, and Thailand, and builds Angkor Wat
1115	East Asia	FOUNDATION OF THE JIN DYNASTY: Jurchens conquer northern China, Mongolia descends into tribal warfare between Jurchens and Khitan-Liao, and Chinese are driven south
1115	Europe	Saint Bernard founds the abbey of Clairvaux and revives the Cistercian monastic order
July 24, 1115	Europe	Death of Matilda of Canossa, defender of the Papacy during the Investiture Controversy
1117	Europe	French Scholastic philosopher and university teacher Peter Abelard is tutoring his pupil Héloïse in Paris
c. 1119	East Asia	Earliest known record of a compass, although the instrument was invented centuries before
c. 1119-1120	Europe	William of Saint-Thierry becomes abbot of the monastery at Saint-Thierry near Reims
c. 1120	Middle East	ORDER OF THE KNIGHTS TEMPLAR IS FOUNDED
1122	Europe	Concordat of Worms settles the Investiture Controversy, which began in 1076
1123	Europe	Battle of Ascalon: Venetian fleet defeats a Muslim fleet, ensuring Christian control of the Kingdom of Jerusalem for another generation
1124-1153	Europe	Reign of David I, king of Scotland
1127-1130	Europe	CREATION OF THE KINGDOM OF SICILY: Roger II unifies Norman territories in southern Italy, Sicily, Malta, and North Africa
1127-1279	East Asia	Southern Song Dynasty
1130	East Asia	BIRTH OF ZHU XI, who later consolidates Confucian thought into four books
1130	Central Asia	KARAKITAI EMPIRE ESTABLISHED
1130-1163	Africa	Reign of ʿAbd al-Muʾmin, Berber founder of the Almohad Dynasty
1130-1170	Europe	Owain Gwynedd rules in Wales, overseeing a revival of Latin scholarship and literature
1131-1153	Middle East	Reign of Melisende, queen of Jerusalem

Date	Region	Event
1134-1141	East Asia	In China, Yo Fei, a military commander in the displaced Song Dynasty, conducts campaigns against the Jin and Qi invaders under the slogan "Give us back our rivers and mountains!" He is murdered
1135-1154	Europe	Reign of King Stephen, king of England
c. 1136	Europe	Geoffrey of Monmouth's *History of the Kings of Britain* appears
1136	Europe	In Kidwelly, Carmarthenshire, Wales, Gwenllian verch Gruffydd is killed fighting against Norman invaders
1136	Europe	Hildegard von Bingen Becomes Abbess
1137	South Asia	Death of Rāmānuja, Indian philosopher
July 1137	Europe	Eleanor of Aquitaine marries Louis VII, king of France, significantly increasing the size of France by adding her land holdings to the kingdom
1139	Europe	Pope Innocent II prohibits the use of the crossbow in Christian Europe
1139	Europe	Hebrew poet, physician, and philosopher Judah ha-Levi writes his *Book of the Kuzari*
1139-1185	Europe	Reign of Afonso I, king of Portugal
1140's	Africa	Arab geographer and cartographer al-Idrīsī produces a globe and maps of the world at the court of Roger II, king of Sicily
1140-1150	Europe	Abbot Suger reforms the architecture of Saint-Denis outside Paris and furnishes it with newly commissioned artworks
1141	Central Asia	Battle of Qatwan: Seljuks are defeated in a clash with the nascent Karakitai Empire near Samarqand
1142-1180	Europe	Henry the Lion is duke of Saxony and Bavaria
1143	Europe	Portugal becomes an independent state under the leadership of Afonso I
1143-1180	Middle East	Reign of Byzantine emperor Manuel I Comnenus
1145	East Asia	Kim Pu-sik Writes *Samguk Sagi*, Korea's first written histories
c. 1145	Europe	Prester John Myth Sweeps Across Europe
1145-1232	Europe	Almohad Berbers from the south overcome the Almoravids in northern Africa and Islamic Spain
1147-1149	Europe	Second Crusade is prompted by Muslim conquest of the principality of Edessa in 1144, unsuccessfully led by the kings of France and Germany
1147-1186	Europe	Sicilian-Byzantine wars: Byzantines fail to reconquer southern Italy and Sicily
After 1148	Europe	Death of Anna Comnena, Byzantine princess and historian
c. 1150	Europe	Moors Transmit Classical Philosophy and Medicine to Europe
c. 1150	Europe	Refinements in Banking
1150	Europe	Venetian Merchants Dominate Trade with the East
1150	Americas	Inhabitants of Chaco Canyon abandon their settlements during a long drought

DATE	**REGION**	**EVENT**
1150-1160	Europe	German mystic and Benedictine abbess Hildegard von Bingen is writing hymns, canticles, and morality plays
c. 1150-1200	Europe	DEVELOPMENT OF GOTHIC ARCHITECTURE allows higher cathedral ceilings and more numerous windows filled with stained glass, leading to some of the most breathtaking architecture in Europe
c. 1150-1200	Europe	RISE OF THE HANSA MERCHANT UNION: The Hanseatic League dominates trade in the Baltic and becomes the northern European hub for world trade
1152	Europe	FREDERICK BARBAROSSA IS ELECTED KING OF GERMANY, reigns as Holy Roman Emperor until 1190
1153	East Asia	JIN MOVE THEIR CAPITAL TO BEIJING
1153-1186	South Asia	Construction in Sri Lanka of the Parakrama Samudra, a huge artificial lake for irrigation and one of the greatest feats of engineering in the world
1154-1159	Europe	Adrian IV is pope
1154-1204	Europe	ANGEVIN EMPIRE IS ESTABLISHED: Henry II, the first Plantagenet, reigns in England (1154-1189) and reforms English law and its enforcement; Eleanor of Aquitaine reigns as queen, adding her domains in France to England's holdings; the empire dissolves on her death in 1204 when their weak son King John cannot hold the empire together
1155	Europe	CHARTER OF LORRIS IS WRITTEN
1156	East Asia	The Hōgen disturbance in Japan, between the Minamoto (Genji) and Taira (Heike) clans, inaugurates the decline of Fujiwaras
Sept. 17, 1156	Europe	AUSTRIA EMERGES AS A NATIONAL ENTITY
1156-1192	East Asia	MINAMOTO YORITOMO BECOMES SHOGUN: establishes *bakufu*, government by warrior chieftains (shoguns) or their regents, which will endure for seven centuries
1157-1182	Europe	Valdemar I the Great reigns during Denmark's golden age
c. 1159	Europe	Geographer Benjamin of Tudela embarks on his journey to Baghdad
1159-1181	Europe	Alexander III is pope
1160	Europe	Death of the religious mystic Christina of Markyate
1160's	Europe	Marie de France is composing her *Lais*
1167	Europe	FOUNDATION OF THE NEMANJID DYNASTY: emergence of an independent Serbia under Stefan Nemanja
1167-1183	Europe	Wars of the Lombard League result in free government of Lombard cities and their retention of the royal revenue
1169-1172	Europe	NORMANS INVADE IRELAND: English incursions into Ireland will last for more than four centuries
1170	Europe	While acting as Venetian ambassador in Constantinople, Enrico Dandolo is blinded on order of the Byzantine emperor
Dec. 29, 1170	Europe	MURDER OF THOMAS BECKET, English statesman and archbishop of Canterbury, in Canterbury Cathedral

Date	Region	Event
1171	Africa	Saladin establishes the Ayyūbid Dynasty in Syria and Egypt
1171	Europe	Averroës (Ibn Rushd) becomes physician to Alomoravid caliph Abū Yaʿqūb Yūsuf in Marrakech
1174-1178	Europe	After it was destroyed by fire, Canterbury Cathedral is rebuilt in a distinctly English architectural style
c. 1175	Americas	The major city Tula, in central Mexico, is destroyed by peoples from northern Mexico
c. 1175	Central and South Asia	In Punjab, Ghūrid Turks defeat the Ghaznavids
1175	East Asia	Hōnen Shōnin Founds Pure Land Buddhism
c. 1175	Europe	Waldensian Excommunications Usher in Protestant Movement
1175-1206	South Asia	Conquests of Muḥammad of Ghor, laying the groundwork for Islamic rule in India
May 29, 1176	Europe	Battle of Legnano: Lombard League defeats Frederick I Barbarossa
1179-1223	Europe	Reign of Philip II Augustus, the first French monarch referred to as King of France (rather than "of the Franks")
c. 1180	Europe	Chrétien de Troyes Writes *Perceval*
1180's	East Asia	Saigyo, a Buddhist monk, composes three volumes of poetry known as the *Sankashu* (mountain hermitage)
1180-1185	East Asia	In the Gempei War, the Minamoto clan defeats the Taira clan and establishes the *bakufu* (shogunate) government in Kamakura
c. 1180-1230	Africa	Expansion of the Soso Kingdom under the Kante Dynasty, which absorbs much of ancient Ghana
c. 1181-1221	Africa	Lalibela Founds the Christian Capital of Ethiopia
c. 1181-1243	Southeast Asia	In Khmer, Jayavarman VII builds the city of Angkor Thom, supporting Mahayana Buddhism with the Bayon temple
1183	Europe	Peace of Constance allows Frederick I Barbarossa to extend direct imperial administration throughout Tuscany
1184-1212	Europe	Reign of Queen Tamara, Georgian queen
1185-1208	Europe	Saxo Grammaticus composes his history of the Danes, *Gesta Danorum*
July 4, 1187	Middle East	Battle of Hattin: Saladin's forces capture this walled city, prompting the Third Crusade
1189-1192	Europe	Third Crusade: The participation of Richard I helps to restore some Christian possessions, including Acre and Cyprus but not Jersalem
1189-1199	Europe	Reign of Richard I, king of England
c. 1190	Europe	Hartmann von Aue composes the first German Arthurian romance, *Erec*
1190	Europe	Moses Maimonides Writes *The Guide of the Perplexed*
1190's	Europe	Alexander Neckam becomes the first Scholastic theologian to teach at Oxford University
c. 1190-1279	East Asia	Ma-Xia School of Painting Flourishes

DATE	REGION	EVENT
1191	East Asia	Eisai, a Buddhist monk, is teaching Zen Buddhism in Japan, marking the growth and influence of this form of Buddhism
1192-1203	Central and South Asia	The Ghūrid Empire, headed by Muḥammad Ghūri, invades India, defeats the Rājputs, and sacks Buddhist monasteries
1193	Central and South Asia	TURKISH RAIDERS DESTROY BUDDHIST UNIVERSITY AT NALANDA
1194	Europe	Pope Celestine III issues Joachim of Fiore a charter to establish new monastery at San Giovanni in Fiore
1196-1258	East Asia	CH'OE FAMILY TAKES POWER IN KOREA
1198	Europe	Pope Innocent III calls for the Fourth Crusade
c. 1198-1200	Europe	French musician Pérotin, a pioneer of Western music, is developing polyphonic forms
1198-1216	Europe	Innocent III is pope
Feb. 9, 1199	East Asia	Death of Japanese shogun Minamoto Yoritomo
1199	Europe	Burgundian historian and military leader Geoffroi de Villehardouin joins the Fourth Crusade
1199-1216	Europe	Reign of John, king of England
c. 1200	Europe	As forged steel processes are refined, several European cities, including Sheffield, Brussels, and Toledo, emerge as swordmaking centers
c. 1200	Americas	In North America, the southwestern Anasazi culture is destroyed, possibly by raiding Ute, Apache, Navajo, and Comanche tribes
c. 1200	Europe	COMMON-LAW TRADITION EMERGES IN ENGLAND
c. 1200	Europe	FAIRS OF CHAMPAGNE: Such international markets introduce Asian and other world goods into Europe
c. 1200	Europe	SCIENTIFIC CATTLE BREEDING DEVELOPED
c. 1200	Europe	Nicholas of Verdun produces the Klosterneuburg Altarpiece, an elaborate metalwork shrine in Cologne Cathedral considered the most important metal artwork of the Middle Ages
c. 1200	Australia/Pacific	Polynesians reach the Chatham Islands east of New Zealand
c. 1200	Australia/Pacific	Construction begins on Nan Madol, a city on Pohnpei Island in Micronesia
1200	Americas	Moundville, on the Black Warrior River in Alabama, is one of the largest cities in North America at this time, producing ceramic, stone, and copper tools and implements
1200	Americas	In New Mexico, people are living in cliff dwellings such as those at Mesa Verde; in Arizona, Snaketown is abandoned
Apr. 23, 1200	East Asia	Death of Confucian scholar Zhu Xi

DATE	REGION	EVENT
Early 13th c.	East Asia	Composition of the Japanese war epic *Heike monogatari* (*The Tale of the Heike*), the tale of the Taira and Minamoto clans from the Hōgen disturbance in 1156 to the end of the Gempei War in 1185
c. 1200-1210	Europe	German poet Wolfram von Eschenbach writes his epic *Parzifal*
c. 1200-1230	Americas	MANCO CAPAC FOUNDS THE INCA STATE
1200-1300	Central Asia	Tibetan monks translate 4,569 works in the Buddhist canon, which along with Chinese translations preserves India's Buddhist doctrines
1200-1482	South Asia	King Ari Malla founds the Malla Dynasty in the Kathmandu Valley; it will dominate the region until 1482
c. 1200-1500	Central and South Asia	Development of the Urdu language, a combination of Persian, Arabic, and regional dialects
13th c.	Africa	The Great Mosque of Kilwa begins construction in Tanzania and marks the flowering of Swahili architecture and powerful trade cities along the East African coast
13th c.	Africa	The centralized city-state of Benin is founded by Edo-speaking people; kingship at Benin state is formalized in the thirteenth century, and by the mid-fifteenth century, under Oba (King) Ewuare the Great, Benin develops into an empire
13th c.	Africa	Muslim Soninke people found the major trade city of Jenne on the Niger Delta in West Africa, although Jenne's founding has been dated as early as the eighth century, according to oral tradition
13th c.	Africa	NDIADIANE N'DIAYE FOUNDS THE WOLOF EMPIRE in the region of modern Senegal
13th c.	East Asia	Korean printers complete the Buddhist *Tripitaka Koreana*
13th c.	Europe	Rise of the guild system, in which groups formed by professional craftsmen begin to assume political as well as economic power, in turn leading to powerful city-states such as Venice and Florence
13th c.	Europe	The cog, a large merchant vessel associated with the Hanseatic League, is developed in northern Europe
13th-16th c.	Africa	Mali Empire: Through a series of successful military campaigns, the emperors of Mali created a massive kingdom stretching across a vast section of West Africa
1202	Europe	The first great medieval European mathematician, Leonardo Fibonacci (Leonardo of Pisa), publishes *Liber abaci* (book of calculations), which popularizes the decimal system first devised in India
1202-1241	Europe	Reign of Valdemar II, king of Denmark
1204	East and Central Asia	GENGHIS KHAN FOUNDS MONGOL EMPIRE
1204	Europe	KNIGHTS OF THE FOURTH CRUSADE CAPTURE CONSTANTINOPLE

DATE	REGION	EVENT
1206-1210	South Asia	QUṬ AL-DĪN AYBAK ESTABLISHES THE DELHI SULTANATE
1206-1526	South Asia	Wars of the Delhi Sultanate: struggles for hegemony in India result in Muslim domination
Apr. 16, 1209	Europe	FOUNDING OF THE FRANCISCANS
1209-1229	Europe	ALBIGENSIAN CRUSADE is led by Simon de Montfort
1210	Middle East	Death of Fakhr al-Dīn al-Rāzī, Muslim theologian and scholar
1212	Europe	CHILDREN'S CRUSADE
1212	Europe	Saint Clare of Assisi receives the tonsure from Saint Francis of Assisi and settles at the nearby monastery of San Damiano, where she will establish the Poor Ladies of Assisi
July 16, 1212	Europe	Battle of Las Navas de Tolosa; the armies of Aragon and Castile defeat the Almohads, a turning point in the Reconquista, the campaign of Christian kingdoms to defeat Islamic rule
c. 1213	Middle East and Central Asia	Muslim historian and geographer Yaqut begins his travels through the Middle East and Central Asia
July 27, 1214	Europe	BATTLE OF BOUVINES, during the German civil war of 1077-1214, establishes France as champion of the Catholic Church and sets a precedent for popular support of the monarchy
1215	East Asia	Genghis Khan captures Beijing during the Mongol invasion of China
1215	Europe	Saint Dominic establishes the Dominican monastic order
June 15, 1215	Europe	SIGNING OF THE MAGNA CARTA
Nov. 11-30, 1215	Europe	FOURTH LATERAN COUNCIL reinforces the power of the Papacy and initiates the unsuccessful Fifth Crusade
1215-1217	Europe	English civil war over absolute monarchy vs. baronial rule and English land in France results in King John's victory and negotiation of the Magna Carta
1216-1272	Europe	Reign of Henry III, king of England
1217-1221	Africa, Middle East	FIFTH CRUSADE: organized to attack the Islamic power base in Egypt, succeeds in capturing the port city of Damietta but ends in defeat
1217-1276	Europe	Reign of James I the Conqueror, king of Spain
1219	Europe	While a student in Paris, Johannes de Muris begins writing his controversial treatise on musical notation, *Ars novae musicae*
1219-1333	East Asia	HŌJŌ FAMILY DOMINATES SHOGUNS, RULES JAPAN
c. 1220	Europe	Saint Elizabeth of Hungary establishes the first orphanage for homeless children in Central Europe
1220's	Europe	Walther von der Vogelweide is writing poetry in Germany
1220's	Europe	Franciscan theologian Saint Anthony of Padua is preaching to large crowds throughout Italy
1220's	Middle East	Ibn al-ʿArabī formulates the doctrines of Sufism
1220-1250	Europe	Reign of Frederick II, king of Sicily and Holy Roman Emperor

DATE	REGION	EVENT
1221	Middle East	Battle of Eşfahān: Mongols retreat from Iran to Central Asia
1221-1256	Middle East	Mongols invade and dominate Iran
1221-1259	Africa	MAI DUNAMA DIBBALEMI EXPANDS KANEM EMPIRE
1223	East Asia	Death of Japanese sculptor Unkei
1223-1252	Europe	Reign of Blanche of Castile, queen of France
c. 1225	East Asia	Death of Chinese painter Ma Yuan
1225	Europe	Mathematician Leonardo Fibonacci (Leonardo of Pisa) publishes his numbers theory in *Liber quadratorum* (the book of square numbers), dedicated to his patron, Holy Roman Emperor Frederick II
1225	Southeast Asia	TRAN THAI TONG ESTABLISHES TRAN DYNASTY
1225-1231	Middle East	JALĀL AL-DĪN EXPANDS THE KHWĀRIZMIAN EMPIRE
1226	East Asia	Battle of Yellow River destroys the Western Xia kingdom and leaves the Song Dynasty vulnerable to Mongol attack
Oct. 3, 1226	Europe	Death of Saint Francis of Assisi
1226-1270	Europe	Reign of Louis IX, king of France
1227-1230	Middle East	FREDERICK II LEADS THE SIXTH CRUSADE
1227-1241	Europe	Gregory IX is pope
1227-1502	Middle East	The Golden Horde khanate rules the western Mongol Empire, stretching from the Caucasus Mountains and the Volga River Basin to the Irtysh River in Siberia
1228	Europe	William of Auvergne becomes bishop of Paris
1228-1229	Middle East	In what is sometimes referred to as the Sixth Crusade, the excommunicated Holy Roman Emperor Frederick II sails to the Holy Land and negotiates a reoccupation of Jerusalem
1228-1231	Europe	TEUTONIC KNIGHTS BRING BALTIC REGION UNDER CATHOLIC CONTROL: in particular East Prussia, which, together with Brandenburg, forms the nucleus of the Prussian state
1228-1454	Middle East	The Rasulid sultanate rules in Yemen
1229-1574	Africa	The Hafsid Berbers replace the Almohads as the dominant force in northwestern Africa's Maghrib
c. 1230	Europe	German mystic Mechthild von Magdeburg leaves home to join the Beguines in Magdeburg
1230	Europe	UNIFICATION OF CASTILE AND LEÓN
1230	East Asia	Death of Chinese painter Xia Gui
Aug. 10, 1230	Middle East	Battle of Erzincan: Defeat of Jalāl al-Dīn ends his westward expansion
c. 1230-1235	Europe	Snorri Sturluson writes the *Heimskringla*, his chronicle of the kings of Norway
1230's-1255	Africa	REIGN OF SUNDIATA OF MALI
1231	East Asia	The Koryō Dynasty is forced into exile when the Mongols begin a series of invasions into the Korean peninsula

DATE	REGION	EVENT
1232-1492	Europe	The Nasrid Dynasty rules Granada but becomes a vassal to northern Christian states by 1243; the Nasrids build the Alhambra, the last major monument to Islam on the Iberian Peninsula
1233	East Asia	The Jin capital at Kaifeng surrenders to the Mongols
1233	Europe	PAPAL INQUISITION
c. 1235	Europe	Henry de Bracton writes his treatise on English common law, *De legibus et consuetudinibus Angliae*
1235	Africa	Battle of Kirina: Sundiata of Mali defeats Sumanguru of Ghana
1236-1240	South Asia	REIGN OF RAZIYA, fifth sultan of Delhi
1236-1242	Europe, Middle East, Asia	The Mongols make conquests in Russia, Eastern Europe, Iran, and Transcaucasia
July 15, 1240	Europe	ALEXANDER NEVSKY DEFENDS NOVGOROD FROM SWEDISH INVADERS
Apr. 11, 1241	Europe	Battle of Sajó River, during the third Mongol invasion of Eastern Europe
1243	Middle East	Battle of Köse Dagh: fall of the Seljuks to the Il-Khanids
1243-1254	Europe	Innocent IV is pope
1243-1295	Southeast Asia	Reign of Jayavarman VIII and restoration of Hinduism in the Khmer nation
1244	Middle East	Muslim Turks retake Jerusalem from Christian Crusaders
Apr. 16, 1245	Europe	Franciscan missionary Giovanni da Pian del Carpini leaves Lyon to lead a mission to the Mongols in Kiev, three thousand miles away
1248-1254	Middle East	FAILURE OF THE SEVENTH CRUSADE
1248-1257	Europe	Saint Bonaventure is writing his theological works
1249-1250	Middle East	Battle of Mansura (Al Manṣūrah), ground battle in the Seventh Crusade: King Louis IX's forces are routed, and Louis is taken for ransom
1249-1286	Europe	Alexander III of Scotland unifies mainland Scotland
Late 13th c.	Australia/Pacific	MAORIS HUNT MOA TO EXTINCTION in New Zealand
c. 1250	Europe	IMPROVEMENTS IN SHIPBUILDING AND NAVIGATION
c. 1250	Americas	Chichén Itzá is abandoned as a population center but remains a destination for Mayan pilgrims
c. 1250	Americas	The Toltecs conquer the major religious and cultural center at Cholula, east of the Mexican Basin
1250	Americas	The Hohokam settlement of Casas Grandes, in northern Chihuahua, undergoes major construction, including ballcourts, wells, and a sewer system
1250's	Middle East	Muslim poet Jalāl al-Dīn Rūmī composes Sufi lyrics of *Dīwan-i Shams-i Tabrīz*
c. 1250-1300	Europe	HOMOSEXUALITY CRIMINALIZED AND SUBJECT TO DEATH PENALTY
c. 1250-1532	Americas	The Inca Empire conquers Chanca, Chincha, Chinchasuyu, Chimor, and other Andean states, creating the largest indigenous state in the Western Hemisphere, with an estimated thirteen million inhabitants

DATE	REGION	EVENT
Feb./Mar. 1252	East Asia	Death of Mongolian princess and kingmaker Sorghaghtani Beki
1252-1284	Europe	Reign of Alfonso X, king of Castile and León
1252-1517	Middle East	The Mamlūk sultans, former slaves to the declining Ayyūbids, assume rule in Egypt, Palestine, Syria, and the holy cities of Mecca and Medina on the Arabian Peninsula, defeating the Crusaders at the end of the thirteenth century and becoming the most important Islamic power of the Middle Ages
1253-1254	Europe	Dutch geographer William of Rubrouck is traveling through Central Asia
1254-1273	Europe	Great Interregnum: The Holy Roman Empire loses its authority over Italy as the Papacy invites Charles of Anjou to establish Angevin power in southern Italy and Sicily
1255	Europe	Birger Jarl, regent of the Swedish crown, founds the city of Stockholm
1256	Middle East	Medina's mosque is destroyed by fire
1256	Europe	French theologian William of Saint-Amour writes *De periculis novissimorum temporum*
1257-1258	Middle East	The Persian writer Shaykh Saʿdi writes *The Orchard* and *The Rose*
1257-1266	Europe	Roger Bacon is in Paris teaching mathematics, perspective, and philosophy and conducting scientific investigations
1257-1299	Europe	The republics of Venice and Genoa battle for control of trade routes and ports in the eastern Mediterranean and Black Sea; although neither side clearly defeats the other, Venice proves more resilient and Genoa never recovers
1258	Middle East	Il-Khanid Mongols sack the Islamic capital, Baghdad, and murder the caliph al-Mustaʿṣim, ending the ʿAbbāsid caliphate—a major blow to Islamic civilization
1258	Europe	PROVISIONS OF OXFORD ARE ESTABLISHED
1259	Southeast Asia	MANGRAI FOUNDS THE KINGDOM OF LAN NA
Sept. 3, 1260	Middle East	BATTLE OF AIN JĀLŪT: Mongols invade Syria and capture Damascus but are defeated by Mamlūk slave cavalry
1260-1277	Middle East	Reign of Baybars I, sultan of Egypt and Syria
1260-1278	Europe	William of Moerbeke translates Aristotle's works
1260-1294	East Asia	Reign of the Mongol Kublai Khan, who moves his capital to Beijing and establishes the Yuan Dynasty
1260-1315	Europe	Nicola and Giovanni Pisano are creating cathedral sculptures in northern and central Italy
1261	Middle East	Byzantine emperor Michael VIII Palaeologus retakes Constantinople from the Venetians, who had captured the city in 1204, but the Byzantine Empire will never regain its former power
1261	Europe, Asia	Civil war between Il-Khanate of Persia and the Golden Horde of Russia begins

DATE	REGION	EVENT
1262-1288	Europe	Salimbene writes his *Chronicle*
1263	Europe	Jewish scholar and physician Naḥmanides is forced to debate a Dominican friar as a stratagem to convert him to Christianity; despite the rigged and unfair restrictions of the debate, Naḥmanides rebuts the Dominican's claims and defeats him
1263-1265	Europe	Barons' War over baronial participation in English government; royalist victory results in restoration of King Henry III
1264	Europe	Death of Vincent of Beauvais, French scholar and historian
c. 1265-1273	Europe	THOMAS AQUINAS COMPILES THE *SUMMA THEOLOGICA*
Feb. 26, 1266	Europe	Battle of Benevento: Charles of Anjou conquers Sicily, establishing Angevin rule
1268	Europe	Death of Flemish mystic Beatrice of Nazareth
1269	Europe	Petrus Peregrinus de Maricourt publishes his treatise on the properties and uses of magnetism
1269-1270	Africa	Eighth Crusade is organized by a now elderly Louis IX, who dies upon landing in Tunisia
1269-1465	Africa	The Marinid Dynasty conquers the Maghrid and ends Almohad rule in northwestern Africa
1270-1272	Middle East	Edward I, the son of Henry III of England, decides to press on alone to Palestine after the French abandon the Eighth Crusade and achieves some modest success with a truce before the ultimate fall of Acre, the last bastion of the Crusader states, in 1291
1270-1277	Europe	Siger of Brabant is condemned by the Church for his heretical teaching of Averroistic doctrines and finally flees Paris for Rome
1270-1285	Africa	YEKUNO AMLAK FOUNDS THE SOLOMONID DYNASTY: The Solomonic period is a golden age of trade and cultural exchange for Ethiopia and the surrounding region
1271-1276	Europe	Gregory X is pope
1271-1295	Europe, Mideast, and Asia	TRAVELS OF MARCO POLO
1272-1307	Europe	Reign of Edward I, king of England
1273	Europe	Catalan mystic Raymond Lull writes his *Book of Contemplation*
1273	Middle East	SUFI ORDER OF MAWLAWĪYAH IS ESTABLISHED
1273-1291	Europe	Reign of Rudolf I, Holy Roman Emperor
1274-1278	Europe	Habsburg-Bohemian War: Rudolf's victory results in establishment of the Habsburg Dynasty in Austria
1274, 1281	East Asia	The Mongols attempt naval invasions of Japan but are forced to retreat by devastating typhoons
1275	Europe	FIRST MECHANICAL CLOCK
1275	East Asia	NESTORIAN ARCHBISHOPRIC IS FOUNDED IN BEIJING
c. 1275	Europe	THE *ZOHAR* IS TRANSCRIBED
1275	Europe	Theoleptus of Philadelphia retires as a monk to Mount Athos in northeastern Greece, where he practices a form of prayer and spirituality known as Hesychasm

DATE	REGION	EVENT
Jan. 6, 1275	Europe	Death of Spanish religious scholar Raymond of Peñafort
c. 1276-1277	Europe	Adam de la Halle writes his play *Jeu d'Adam*
Nov. 15, 1280	Europe	Death of Saint Albertus Magnus, German philosopher, theologian, and scientist
c. 1280-1300	Europe	Guido Cavalcanti is writing love poetry in the "sweet new style"
c. 1281/88-1326	Middle East	Reign of Osman I, founder of the Ottoman Empire
Nov. 14, 1282	East Asia	Death of Japanese monk Nichiren
c. 1284	Europe	Arnolfo di Cambio becomes Florence's *capomaestro*, or chief architect
1284	Europe	The 64-meter-high vault of the Cathedral of Saint-Pierre Beauvais collapses, revealing limits to the height of Gothic cathedrals
1285	Europe	STATUTE OF WINCHESTER
1285-1314	Europe	Reign of Philip IV the Fair, king of France
1290-1306	Europe	JEWS ARE EXPELLED FROM ENGLAND, FRANCE, AND SOUTHERN ITALY
c. 1290-1326	Middle East	Reign of Osman I, founder of the Ottoman Empire in northwestern Anatolia
1290-1388	Europe	Anglo-Scottish wars produce Scottish independence until the seventeenth century
Apr. 1291	Middle East	FALL OF ACRE, PALESTINE marks the end of the Crusader kingdom in Palestine
Aug. 1291	Europe	The principalities of Schwyz, Uri, and Unterwalden sign a written alliance for mutual defense; it will form the basis for the state of Switzerland
Dec. 8, 1292	Europe	Death of John Pecham, archbishop of Canterbury
1293-1310	Southeast Asia	Rise of kingdom of Majapahit in Java, which emerges in the fight against the Mongols
1294	Europe	Edward I of England attacks La Rochelle; in response, Philip IV seizes the English duchy of Aquitaine
1295	Europe	MODEL PARLIAMENT establishes broad political representation in England
1295	Southeast Asia	RAMKHAMHAENG CONQUERS THE MEKONG AND MENAM VALLEYS
1295-1304	Middle East	Reign of Maḥmūd Ghāzān, Mongol il-khan of Iran
1296	Europe	Franciscans found the church of Santa Croce in Florence
1296-1316	South Asia	Reign of ʿAlāʾ-ud-Dīn Muḥammad Khaljī, Khaljī sultan of Delhi
Sept. 11, 1297	Europe	Battle of Stirling Bridge: William Wallace defeats the English in this battle in the Anglo-Scottish wars
July 22, 1298	Europe	Battle of Falkirk: English defeat William Wallace
1299	South Asia	ʿALĀʾ-UD-DĪN MUḤAMMAD KHALJĪ CONQUERS GUJARAT
Dec. 22, 1299	Middle East	Battle of Homs: Ghāzān defeats the Mamlūks
1290's-c. 1310	Europe	Arnold of Villanova develops alcohol distillation and writes numerous medical treatises
1300	Americas	The mound-builder city of Etowah, in northeastern Georgia, dominates the region

DATE	REGION	EVENT
1300	East Asia	Japanese sword makers create the *katana*, a curved sword used by samurai warriors
c. 1300	Americas	Distinct tribal identities among North American indigenous peoples develop in response to the increasing importance of agriculture and sedentary cultures
c. 1300	Europe	Early oil painting on a Norwegian church altar heralds the refinement and proliferation of the technique a century later
c. 1300-1350	Europe	Albanians migrate southward from the Balkans into central Greece
1300's	Europe	The population of France is estimated to be about 20 million, far greater than that of Germany (14 million) or England (only 4 million)
c. 1300-1400	Central and South Asia	Nepalese artists begin to influence Tibetan art
14th c.	Africa	The semilegendary founder of Benin and Oyo, Prince Oranmiyan, flourishes in West Africa
14th c.	Europe	The carrack, an efficient sailing ship with multiple masts, becomes popular in Atlantic and Mediterranean waters
14th-15th c.	Europe	The increasing predominance of firearms in Europe results in the diminishing use of archers in warfare
July 11, 1302	Europe	Battle of Courtrai: The eight-year battle between England's Edward I and France's Philip IV ends when the count of Flanders, an English ally, defeats Philip
July 27, 1302	Middle East	BATTLE OF BAPHEUS: first battle of the Byzantine-Ottoman wars; the Byzantines attempt to meet the challenge of Ottoman power but are defeated
Nov. 18, 1302	Europe	BONIFACE VIII ISSUES THE BULL *UNAM SANCTAM*
1302-1461	Europe, Middle East	Byzantine-Ottoman wars test whether the reduced Byzantine Empire can defend itself against the growing Ottoman Empire, marking the rise of Ottoman domination of Balkans and Middle East
1304	Europe	Giotto begins painting his frescoes in Padua
1305	Europe	Dietrich von Freiberg investigates rainbows to understand reflection and refraction
1305-1307	Europe	Scholastic theologian John Duns Scotus is teaching in Paris
1305-1417	Europe	AVIGNON PAPACY AND THE GREAT SCHISM
Before 1306	Europe	Marguerite Porete writes *The Mirror of Simple Souls*
c. 1306	East Asia	Japanese poet Nijō writes *Towazugatari*, or *The Confessions of Lady Nijō*, concerning her life at court
c. 1306-1320	Europe	DANTE WRITES *THE DIVINE COMEDY*
1306-1329	Europe	Reign of Robert Bruce, king of Scotland
1307-1327	Europe	Reign of Edward II, king of England
1308-1330	Europe	Reign of Isabella of France, queen of England
1309-1466	Europe	Teutonic Knights' wars with Poland: The Teutonic Order becomes the dominant power on the Baltic coastline
1310-c. 1350	Europe	WILLIAM OF OCKHAM ATTACKS THOMIST IDEAS
1312-1337	Africa	Reign of Mansa Mūsā, king of Mali
1313-1357	Europe	Ghibelline-Guelph struggle for domination of Tuscany

DATE	REGION	EVENT
1314	Africa	Emperor Amda Tseyon comes to power in Ethiopia, expanding the Solomonid Dynasty
June 23-24, 1314	Europe	BATTLE OF BANNOCKBURN: Robert I's victory ensures Scottish independence
1314-1325	Europe	German civil war for control of the Holy Roman Empire: Wittelsbach victory confines the Habsburgs to their Austrian possessions
1315	Europe	Simone Martini produces his masterpiece, the Siena *Maestà*
Nov. 15, 1315	Europe	SWISS VICTORY AT MORGARTEN OVER HABSBURG FORCES
1316-1334	Europe	John XXII is pope
1317-1329	Europe	Jewish rabbi and philosopher Levi ben Gershom writes *The Wars of the Lord*
c. 1320	Middle East	ORIGINS OF THE BUBONIC PLAGUE: The point of origin is contested but may be in Crimea, carried back to China by Mongol soldiers; epidemics begin to emerge in the 1330's in China and spread west
1320	Europe	Philippe de Vitry produces his treatise on music, *Ars nova*
1320-1328	Europe	Luccan-Florentine war: In the Ghibelline-Guelph struggle for domination of Tuscany, a major setback for the Ghibellines
1320-1334	Europe	French painter Jean Pucelle is illuminating manuscripts in Paris
1323-1326	Southeast Asia	CHAMPA WINS INDEPENDENCE FROM DAI VIET
1323-1328	Europe	PEASANTS' REVOLT IN FLANDERS
1324	Europe	Aragon conquers Sardinia
July 2, 1324	Europe	LADY ALICE KYTELER IS FOUND GUILTY OF WITCHCRAFT
1324-1325	Africa	MANSA MŪSĀ'S PILGRIMAGE TO MECCA SPARKS INTEREST IN MALI EMPIRE
1325-1355	Africa	TRAVELS OF IBN BAṬṬŪṬAH
1325-c. 1400	Americas	Rise of the Kachina cult in the American Southwest
1325-1519	Americas	AZTECS BUILD TENOCHTITLÁN: Mexican people settle on a marshy island in the Basin of Mexico's Lake Texcoco, building monuments to gods such as Huitzilopochtli and Tlaloc
1327-1369	Europe	Reign of Philippa of Hainaut, queen of England
1327-1377	Europe	Reign of Edward III, king of England
1328	Europe	Philip VI, the first French king from the Valois branch of the Capetian dynasty, ascends the French throne
1328	Europe	King Edward III of England signs the Treaty of Northampton, formally recognizing Scottish sovereignty
1328	Europe	William of Ockham challenges Church authority and upholds the rights of lay rulers
1328-1350	Europe	FLOWERING OF LATE MEDIEVAL PHYSICS
1329-1371	Europe	Reign of David II, king of Scotland
Nov. 1330	Europe	BASARAB DEFEATS THE HUNGARIANS at the Battle of Posada
1331	Europe	Siege of Friuli in Italy is marked by early use of gunpowder weaponry on the battlefield

DATE	REGION	EVENT
1331-1355	Europe	Reign of Stefan Dušan, king of Serbia
1333	Africa	KILWA KISIWANI BEGINS ECONOMIC AND HISTORICAL DECLINE
1333-1370	Europe	Reign of Casimir the Great, king of Poland
1333-1466	Europe	Polish wars of expansion: Poland comes into power, achieving access to trade ports and political dominance of eastern central Europe
1334-1360	Europe	The bell tower at the Cathedral of Florence is built
1335	Middle East	Il-Khanate of Persia ends
1336-1392	East Asia	YOSHINO CIVIL WARS: Ashikaga Takauji ousts Emperor Go-Daigo from Kyoto, establishing the Northern Court in Japan as Go-Daigo takes refuge in the south at Yoshino and founds the Southern Court; thus begins the Muromachi period, a time of intense rivalry and warfare between competing warlords known as *daimyo*
1337-1453	Europe	HUNDRED YEARS' WAR: a series of military conflicts between France and England that resulted in France's ultimate victory at the Battle of Castillon in 1453, a rise in nationalism in a more unified France, England's withdrawal from its French holdings, and England's emergence as a preeminent naval power
1340	Africa	AL-ʿUMARĪ WRITES A HISTORY OF AFRICA
June 24, 1340	Europe	Battle of Sluis: English fleet overcomes the French in this naval battle in the Hundred Years' War
1340's	Europe	Jean Buridan is writing his commentaries on the works of Aristotle
c. 1343	South Asia	Completion of Vijayanagar in southern India, one of the most lavishly appointed cities in the world, with palaces, temples, and huge gateways
1346	South Asia	Muslim armies raid the Kathmandu valley in Nepal, destroying images and temples
Aug. 26, 1346	Europe	BATTLE OF CRÉCY: Key battle in the Hundred Years' War, notable for the use of longbows by the English to defeat French knights; also marked the role of gunpowder artillery. English victory at Crécy foreshadowed the decline of the mounted knight and a greater emphasis on missile warfare
Oct. 17, 1346	Europe	Battle of Neville's Cross: English defeat David II and the Scots
1346-1381	Europe	Hungarian-Venetian wars: Hungary gains Dalmatia
1347	Europe	Siege of Calais ends when the English capture this city on the French coast of the English Channel, after a yearlong siege
1347	South Asia	ʿALĀʾ-UD-DĪN BAHMAN SHĀH FOUNDS THE BAHMANĪ SULTANATE

Date	**Region**	**Event**
1347-1352	Europe	Invasion of the Black Death in Europe: Traveling on flea-infested rats from the east, the plague erupts first in Constantinople and then travels west to Italy and north throughout Europe for the next three years, killing a third of the population; more than any other natural event, this epidemic shaped Europe for centuries, not only economically, as labor shortages gave rise to a new middle class, but also religiously and politically, as social reforms were instituted to cope with the epidemic's aftermath
1347-1354	Europe	Cola di Rienzo Leads Popular Uprising in Rome
c. 1350	Americas	Mixtecs and Zapotecs intermarry to extend their territories in Mexico's Oaxaca Valley
c. 1350	Australia/Pacific	On the islands of central Vanuatu (New Hebrides) in the southwestern Pacific, the legendary king Roy Mata is in power, as evidenced by a burial site containing his body and shell artifacts
1350	Americas	Eastern Woodland culture, characterized by religious practices and artifacts displaying warrior, bird-man, and serpent imagery, flourishes in eastern North America
1350	Southeast Asia	Ramathibodi I Creates First Thai Legal System
1350-55, 1378-80	Europe	More Venetian-Genoese battles for control of trade routes and ports in the eastern Mediterranean and Black Sea; Venice thrives while Genoa declines
c. 1350-1400	Europe	Petrarch and Boccaccio Recover Classical Texts, leading to the emergence of Humanism and laying a foundation for the Renaissance
1352-1434	Southeast Asia	Khmer-Thai wars: Siamese attempts to exert political dominance over Cambodia cause the decline of the Khmer Empire
1353-1373	Southeast Asia	Fa Ngum founds the Lan Xang, a kingdom that controls Laos and parts of Thailand
1354	Europe	Ottoman Turks capture the Byzantine fortress of Gallipoli and begin expansion into the Balkans
1354	Europe	Andrea Orcagna is commissioned by Strozzi family to paint an altarpiece in the church of Santa Maria Novella in Florence, *Christ Conferring Authority on Saints Peter and Thomas Aquinas*
1355-1378	Europe	Reign of Charles IV, Holy Roman Emperor
1356	Europe	Golden Bull: Charles IV reiterates the power of the electors of the Holy Roman Empire, thus limiting German unity
Sept. 19, 1356	Europe	Battle of Poitiers: English defeat the French and capture the French king John II, who is held prisoner in England until 1360
1358-1384	Middle East	Persian poet Hafiz is composing his *ghazal*
1360	Europe	Treaty of Brétigny: England gains Calais and nearly the whole of Aquitaine

DATE	REGION	EVENT
1360	Europe	Jean de Venette records the trauma of plague and war during his times in his *Chronicon*
c. 1360-1406	Middle East	Jalayirid Dynasty rules Iraq and northwestern Iran after the collapse of the Il-Khans
c. 1360-1440	East Asia	KAN'AMI AND ZEAMI PERFECT NŌ DRAMA
1361-1370	Europe	Danish wars with the Hanseatic League: The League maintains its supremacy in the Baltic region
1363	Europe	Guy de Chauliac completes his treatise on surgery, *Chirurgia magna*
1366	Europe	STATUTE OF KILKENNY
1368	Southeast Asia	Burmese civil wars for provincial supremacy of Burma begin; Burma is united by 1555
1368	East Asia	ESTABLISHMENT OF THE MING DYNASTY: The native Chinese population reasserts itself, burning the Mongol palaces of the Yuan Dynasty in Beijing
1368	Central Asia	TIBET GAINS INDEPENDENCE FROM MONGOLS
1369	Europe	A sense of national identity begins to form in the Low Countries (Netherlands) with the marriage of Margaret of Flanders to Philip the Bold of Burgundy, inaugurating more than a century of Burgundian rule of the region
1369-1388	Europe	Portuguese-Castilian war over reciprocal claims by Portugal and Castile to each other's thrones; mutual independence is assured for Portugal and Castile, and Portugal and England begin a long alliance
c. 1371	Americas	In Mexico, Tezozomoc becomes king at Azcapotzalco and takes control of Tenochtitlán, naming Acamapichtli as its king
1371	Europe	Battle of Marica: Turks defeat the Serbians and Bulgarians
1371-1529	Southeast Asia	Thai kingdom and the provinces of Ayutthaya and Chiengmai struggle for dominance
1373-1410	Europe	JEAN FROISSART COMPILES HIS *CHRONICLES*
1375	Middle East	The Armenian kingdom of Cilicia, in southern Anatolia, falls to the Mamlūks
1376	Africa	Ibn Khaldūn abandons his political career to live among North Africa's nomadic tribes and write
1376	Europe	Catherine of Siena travels to Avignon to urge the pope to return to Rome
1377	Southeast Asia	The Majapahit kingdom conquers Palembang in Sumatra, ending Śrivijayan dominance
1377	Africa	IBN KHALDŪN COMPLETES HIS *MUQADDIMAH*
Apr.?, 1377	Europe	Death of Guillaume de Machaut, French poet and composer of polyphonic music
1377-1378	Europe	CONDEMNATION OF JOHN WYCLIF
1377-1399	Europe	Reign of Richard II, king of England
1378-1419	Europe	Reign of Wenceslaus, king of Bohemia
c. 1380	South Asia	COMPILATION OF THE WISE SAYINGS OF LAL DED
Sept. 8, 1380	Europe	BATTLE OF KULIKOVO: defeat of the Mongols by Grand Duke Dmitry Donskoy of Moscow

Date	Region	Event
May-June 1381	Europe	Peasants' Revolt in England, led by Wat Tyler
July 15, 1381	Europe	John Ball is executed near St. Albans Abbey for his part in Wat Tyler's Peasants' Revolt
1381-1405	Middle East	Tamerlane's Conquests: After establishing Timurid rule in Central Asia, Tamerlane gains control over most of Iran, Iraq, Syria, and Anatolia, as well as southern Russia and India
1382-1395	South Asia	Reign of Sthitimalla
1382-1516	Middle East	In the Mamlūk sultanate, the Burjī sultans, Circassian military elites, replace the Baḥrī line
1384-1399	Europe	Reign of Władysław II Jagiełło and Jadwiga, king and queen of Poland
1385-1499	Europe	Austro-Swiss wars: Swiss victory secures the de facto independence of Switzerland
c. 1387	East Asia	Chinese Create the Eight-Legged Essay
1387-1400	Europe	Chaucer Writes *The Canterbury Tales*
1387-1412	Europe	Reign of Margaret, queen of Denmark, Norway, and Sweden
1389	Europe	Battle of Falköping: Margaret's forces were victorious in this battle of the Swedish civil war
June 28, 1389	Europe	Turkish Conquest of Serbia: Battle of Kosovo
1389-1402	Middle East	Reign of the Ottoman sultan Bayezid I, who will defeat Tamerlane and the Timurids
1391	Europe	Jews on the Iberian Peninsula are persecuted and massacred
c. 1392	Central Asia	Foundation of the Gelugpa Order of Buddhist monks
July 1392	East Asia	Establishment of the Yi Dynasty
Sept. 25, 1396	Middle East	Battle of Nicopolis: European Christians fail to drive back the Muslim Turks, leaving them in control of the Balkans
1397	East Asia	Publication of the Laws of Great Ming
June 17, 1397	Europe	Kalmar Union Is Formed: Sweden, Norway, and Denmark are united
Dec. 17, 1399	South Asia	Battle of Pānīpat, major battle during Tamerlane's invasion of India
1399-1404	Central Asia	Tamerlane Builds the Bibi Khanum Mosque in Samarqand
1399-1413	Europe	Reign of Henry IV, king of England
c. 1400	Americas	The Mayan codexes are being created
c. 1400	Americas	In Mexico, the population of the Tarascan state grows to about 35,000, centered on its capital at Tzintzuntzan
1400	Africa	The Kongo kingdom becomes central Africa's largest state, with its capital at Mbanza
1400	Americas	In southeastern North America, Moundville, Etowah, and Spiro are in decline
1400	Europe	Iceland enters a five-century period of decline following natural disasters, climate change, disease, and depleted resources
Oct. 25?, 1400	Europe	Death of Geoffrey Chaucer

DATE	REGION	EVENT
c. 1400-1401	Middle East	Tamerlane's armies burn and loot Aleppo and Damascus in Syria and Baghdad in Iraq
1400-1402	East Asia	Zeami Motokiyo writes his first treatise on the aesthetics of Nō drama, *Fūshikaden*
1400-1403	Europe	Christine de Pizan composes *Le Livre de la mutacion de fortune* and *Le Livre du chemin de long éstude*
1400-1409	Europe	Glendower's Revolt: This struggle for Welsh independence from England results in English victory and Welsh submission, impoverishment, and social restructuring
Aug. 20, 1400-11	Europe	German civil war: Wenceslaus of Bohemia wins this struggle for the Holy Roman Empire and the Rhine-Main area of Germany, but his power continues to decline, enabling his brother Sigismund to replace him as king
1400-1500	Africa	FOUNDATION OF THE WEST AFRICAN STATES OF BENIN
15th c.	Europe	The Medici merchant-banker family rules Florence, exerting not only economic and political but also cultural influence stemming from their patronage of the arts
July 28, 1402	Central Asia	Battle of Ankara: Tamerlane defeats Bayezid I
1402-1421	Middle East	Mehmed I reestablishes a unified Ottoman state after the death of his father Bayezid I
1402-1424	East Asia	Reign of Chinese Ming emperor Yonglo is marked by five military campaigns, the development of porcelains and textiles, and the proliferation of Buddhist influence
1403-1407	East Asia	*YONGLO DADIAN* ENCYCLOPEDIA IS COMPILED
1404-1406	Southeast Asia	Malacca emerges as the most important trading center on the Malay Peninsula
1405	Central Asia	Death of Tamerlane
1405-1433	East Asia	ZHENG HE'S NAVAL EXPEDITIONS
1406	Europe	Pisa falls to Florence
c. 1406-1408	East Asia	In Beijing, work begins on the Forbidden City
1406-1428	East Asia	The Chinese take control of Vietnam
1408	Europe	Donatello sculpts his bronze *David*
1409-1419	Central Asia	Gelugpa Buddhists build three major monasteries in Lhasa: Ganden in 1409, Drepung in 1416, and Sera in 1419
1409-1613	Europe	Kalmar wars: Sweden achieves independence
July 15, 1410	Europe	BATTLE OF TANNENBERG: marks the decline of the Teutonic Knights and the rise of Polish influence in the Baltic
c. 1410-1440	Europe	FLORENTINE SCHOOL OF ART EMERGES
1413-1422	Europe	Reign of Henry V, king of England
1414-1418	Europe	COUNCIL OF CONSTANCE ends the Great Schism
July 6, 1415	Europe	MARTYRDOM OF JAN HUS
Oct. 25, 1415	Europe	Battle of Agincourt: English rout the French in the first of a string of English victories in the Hundred Years' War
1415-1460	Europe	PRINCE HENRY THE NAVIGATOR PROMOTES PORTUGUESE EXPLORATION: Portuguese establish contact along West African coast

Date	Region	Event
1417	East Asia	The Confucian texts known as the *Great Compendium of the Philosophy of Human Nature* appear; with the Five Classics and the Four Books, they set the standard for Chinese scholarship
1418-1450	East Asia	The reign of the Yi Dynasty emperor Sejong is marked by the creation of a written Korean language
1419-1436	Europe	Hussite wars: Prompted by the martyrdom of Jan Hus, a Bohemian civil war in which Czech Hussites, nationalist followers of Hus, attack clerics and churches
c. 1420	Americas	Cozumel, an island off the coast of Yucatan, becomes a destination for women seeking to worship the Mayan fertility goddess Ixchel
1420's	Europe	The works of Masaccio, the foremost painter of the early fifteenth century, mark the transition from medieval to Renaissance art
1423	Europe	Battle of Cravant: English defeat French
1423	Europe	Appearance of the earliest dated woodcut, depicting Saint Christopher
1423-1454	Europe	Venetian-Milanese wars result in a strong Venetian mainland with protected routes to European markets and long-term peace between Venice and Milan
1424	Europe	Battle of Verneuil: English defeat French
c. 1425	Europe	The corning, or granulating, process is developed to grind gunpowder into smaller grains
1425	Americas	Growth of the Zuni villages of New Mexico
1425-1462	Europe	Russian civil war determines principle of succession from father to son
1426-1435	East Asia	Reign of the Ming emperor Xuande, known for his patronage of the arts
c. 1427	Europe	Thomas à Kempis writes *The Imitation of Christ*
1427	Southeast Asia	Battle of Chi Lang Pass: Vietnam is liberated
1427?-1440	Americas	Reign of Itzcóatl, king of the Aztecs: The Aztec Empire begins when the Mexica of Tenochtitlán form the Triple Alliance with Tlacopan and Texcoco and defeat Azcapotzalco
1428	East and Southeast Asia	LE LOI ESTABLISHES LATER LE DYNASTY
May 4-8, 1429	Europe	JOAN OF ARC'S RELIEF OF ORLÉANS
1429	Europe	Alain Chartier writes about Joan of Arc in *Epistola de Puella*
1430	Europe	Philip the Good creates the Order of the Golden Fleece, which he awards to nobles in the Low Countries as a means of uniting them politically under his Burgundian control
1430's	Europe	Florentine painter Fra Angelico is painting his *Annunciation*
1430's	Europe	The Van Eyck brothers are painting their masterpiece, a polyptych known as *The Ghent Altarpiece*

DATE	REGION	EVENT
c. 1430's-1450	Europe	Leonello d'Este establishes Ferrara as a major center for Humanism and the arts
1431	Southeast Asia	The Khmer Empire falls to Thais after they sack Angkor
May 30, 1431	Europe	Joan of Arc is burned for heresy
1431-1447	Europe	Eugene IV is pope
1431-1449	Europe	The Council of Basel rejects and weakens papal authority in the wake of scandals over church corruption; the Church is in a state of crisis, which paves the way for the Reformation
c. 1435-1464	Europe	Architect Leon Battista Alberti writes his influential treatises on painting, architecture, and sculpture
c. 1436	Europe	English mystic Margery Kempe dictates her memoirs, *The Book of Margery Kempe*
1436	Europe	Filippo Brunelleschi completes his revolutionary dome for the cathedral of Santa Maria del Fiore in Florence
1438-1769	East and Southeast Asia	Burmese-Chinese wars: Border ambiguity gives rise to this conflict, but both sides tire of war, sign a treaty, and resume peaceful trade
1439-1459	Europe	Frederick III of Habsburg is elected Holy Roman Emperor; during his reign, the German principalities will become increasingly independent
1440	Europe	DONATION OF CONSTANTINE IS EXPOSED
c. 1440-1480	Africa	Oba Ewedo rules Benin, establishing a highly centralized, autocratic form of government and devising new military weapons and tactics
1442-1456	Europe	JÁNOS HUNYADI DEFENDS HUNGARY AGAINST THE OTTOMANS
1443-1468	Africa	The Tuareg, a group of nomadic, semisedentary tribes and slave traders, take control of Timbuktu and Gao
1443-1478	Middle East, Europe	Albanian-Turkish wars: Albania becomes part of the Ottoman Empire
Nov. 10, 1444	Hungary	Battle of Varna: Murad defeats János Hunyadi and Władysław
1444-1446	Europe	ALBANIAN CHIEFTAINS UNITE UNDER PRINCE SKANDERBEG
1447	Europe	Visconti rule of Milan ends with the death of Filippo Maria Visconti and the ascension of the Sforza family
1447-1450	Europe	Pope Nicholas V's Roman Jubilee year (1450) is preceded by massive building and renovation projects, including the Senators' Palace on Capitoline Hill, the Vatican Palace, and an expansion of Saint Peter's
1448-1471	Europe	Bohemian civil war over control of the Bohemian crown
1448-1471	Europe	Sweden breaks from Denmark and Norway and becomes independent

DATE	REGION	EVENT
c. 1450	Europe	GUTENBERG PIONEERS THE PRINTING PRESS: The ability to print and publish a broad variety of documents, combined with the rise in use of vernacular languages, has a revolutionary impact on European civilization and helps lay a foundation for the Reformation and the proliferation of Humanist thought
1450	Africa	Songhai incorporates the former kingdom of Mali and becomes one of the largest empires in Africa
1450	Europe	Battle of Formigny: French defeat English and Normandy becomes French territory
1450-1550	East Asia	Japanese civil wars for control of Japanese provinces eventually lead to consolidation of power on a national scale
1451-1481	Middle East	Reign of the great Ottoman sultan Mehmed II
1452	Europe	Florentine sculptor Lorenzo Ghiberti completes work on the bronze doors of the Baptistery of San Giovanni, Florence
1452	Europe	The great Renaissance artist and engineer Leonardo da Vinci is born in Tuscany
1453	Europe	ENGLISH ARE DRIVEN FROM FRANCE after the Battle of Castillon, marking the virtual end of English possessions on the Continent and the end of the Hundred Years' War
May 29, 1453	Europe	FALL OF CONSTANTINOPLE marks the end of the Byzantine Empire and the ascendancy of the Muslim-Turkish Ottoman Empire

Glossary

Abbey: A self-sufficient religious community of either monks or nuns (sometimes both housed separately), run by an abbot or abbess and sometimes subject to a higher secular authority through feudal obligation. Abbots and abbesses occupied posts that were socially and politically as well as spiritually important and powerful. *See also* Monastery.

ʿAbd: Arabic for "slave," often seen in proper names combined with other words referring to Allah ("slave of God"), one of his attributes ("servant of the Merciful"), or royalty ("servant of the king").

Acre: In the Middle Ages, roughly the area that could be plowed in one day.

Adamites: A religious sect, considered heretical, which sought to render humankind able to return to Adam's state in paradise prior to Original Sin.

Aketon: A shirt stuffed with cotton and worn under a hauberk as padding. *See also* Hauberk.

Albigensians: Members of the heretical Catharistic sect who lived in and around Albi, France. The Cathars in general held a dualistic belief that matter was evil and thus Christ never took human form. The Albigensians became the target of the anti-Catharistic Albigensian Crusade during the years 1209-1229.

Alderman: From Old English *ealdorman* ("old" or "parent" man), an Anglo-Saxon office under the king constituting the head of a shire. The office evolved into that of the earl, which eventually became a title of nobility; also, in the towns, heads of merchant guilds or community office were known as aldermen.

Allegory: A story, literary work, or play in which characters in the narrative personify abstract ideas or qualities and so give a second level of meaning to the work, in addition to the surface narrative.

Almoner: An officer who distributed alms to the sick and poor.

Amercement: A fine imposed for a minor offense; imposed in place of harsher punishment and therefore said to be "at the mercy" of the king.

Amir: *See* Emir.

Anchorite, anchoress: Respectively, a man or woman living a solitary and ascetic religious life, sometimes a cleric attached to a monastery and sometimes an individual living in the wilderness.

Angles: A Germanic people who infiltrated and settled in England during the fifth century and assimilated with local tribes to form the Anglo-Saxons. *See also* Jutes, Saxons.

Apostate: One who renounces religious orders or other duty, considered a serious breach of faith.

Apostolic succession: The belief that the authority of Jesus Christ passes down from his apostles through the bishops (popes).

Appanage: A large grant of land donated by a ruler to a member of his family, such as a son, along with a title (duke or count) conferring rights to collect taxes.

Apprentice: *See* Craft.

Archdeacon: Subordinate of a bishop with responsibility for supervising the diocesan clergy and holding ecclesiastical courts within his archdeaconry.

Arianism: The belief of the fourth century Alexandrian priest Arius and his followers, who in the next three hundred years included many Germanic Visigoths and Lombards, that Jesus was the greatest *created* being but, because he was a creature and not Creator, was therefore not the same as God.

Armet: A closed helmet consisting of the rounded cap of the bascinet with two cheek pieces overlapping at the front when closed. *See also* Bascinet.

Armor: Protective clothing and gear used during combat and made of a variety of materials such as leather and mail, and including a wide range of pieces. *See also* Aketon, Armet, Aventail, Bavier, Besagues, Bevor, Bracers, Burgonet, Byrnie, Cabacete, Cerevelliere, Close helmet, Coif, Couter, Cuisses, Gambeson, Gorget, Greaves, Haketon, Haubergeon, Hauberk, Jack, Kettle, Pauldron, Poleyn, Rerebrace, Sabaton, Sallet, Sollerets, Spaudler, Surcoat, Tabard, Vambrace.

Arthurian romance: Literature that includes the legendary King Arthur or his Knights of the Round Table, often referred to as the Matter of Britain. At the core of this literature are the medieval romances that are closely allied with the founding of Britain, including stories about the birth of Arthur, his assumption of the throne (pulling the sword Ex Calibre from the stone in which it was embedded), his love affair with Guinevere and her betrayal with the knight Lancelot, the exploits of the Knights of the Round Table, and stories of Arthur's downfall at the hands of his illegitimate son Mordred. Arthurian romance is found in the twelfth century chronicler Geoffrey of Monmouth's *History of the Kings of Britain* (c. 1136), the twelfth century French romances of Chrétien de Troyes, Layamon's *Brut* (c. 1205), the anonymous *Sir Gawain and the Green Knight* (fourteenth century), and Sir Thomas Malory's *Le Morte d'Arthur* (1485), among others.

Assart: As a noun, a piece of wasteland or previously unfarmed forest land that has been cleared or drained and prepared for farming. As a verb, to clear and prepare a piece of land for farming, which was generally illegal without acquiring the appropriate license.

Assize: A broadly applied term referring to any legal procedure, the court, judge, or jury applying that procedure, or a court enactment; generally these were civil and not criminal and related to real estate or market regulations, such as standard weights and measures, or quantities of commodities, such as wine, bread, or ale.

Atheling: The eldest son or heir apparent of an Anglo-Saxon king.

Aventail: A mail garment that hung down from the helmut like a curtain, designed to protect the neck.

Bailey: An outer wall of a castle or the courtyard or a wall surrounding the keep; also, the space between such walls. *See also* Keep.

Bailiff or bailli: The officer appointed by the landlord of a manor or town who was responsible for collecting rents owed to the landlord and distributing services owed to the tenants. A town might have more than one bailiff with different duties, who together acted as the town's executive officer reporting to the landlord.

Ballista: A war machine used to hurl large arrows or other missiles. *See also* Catapult, Trebuchet.

Bard: A minstrel or poet who played an important role in relating the exploits of his lords and people through verse that could be remembered and, later, written down for posterity.

Barony: An administrative division of certain counties or a land grant from the king, overseen by a baron.

Barrow: An earthen burial mound.

Bascinet: An open-faced helmet, either round or pointed and reaching down to the cheeks and neck, used in the fourteenth century.

Bastard: An illegitimate son of a noble or king.

Bastion: A tower projecting from the walls of a castle.

Battlement: A small wall or indented parapet used as a shield for defense.

Bavier: A chin piece used in armor.

Beg or bey: The title of an Ottoman governor.

Beguines or Beghards: In twelfth century and later, particularly in the Low Countries, small groups of devout women (Beguines) or men (Beghards) who lived together for religious purposes but did not take religious vows. They could own property and marry.

Benedictines: A monastic order founded by Saint Benedict. The monks, known as Black Friars for their black habits, took vows of poverty, chastity, and obedience to Benedictine Rule and their monastery's abbot. *See also* Carmelites, Carthusians, Cistercians, Dominicans, Franciscans, Mendicants.

Benefice or benefit: From the Latin *beneficium*, land in reward for service. In secular terms, a land awarded to a member of the aristocracy, a bishop, or a monastery in exchange for services. In ecclesiastic terms, an endowed church office that returns revenue.

Benefit of clergy: The exclusion of clerics from the jurisdiction of secular courts. Even minor clerics who committed offenses could be remanded to the authority of the bishop. Clerics accused of offenses proved their status by exhibiting their literacy (reading Scripture, for example); as the ability to read spread during the later Middle Ages, the benefit was abused.

Besagues: Circular plates of armor at the elbow joint and front of the shoulder.

Bestiary: A form of literature, popular from classical times to the Middle Ages, in which animals were used to teach moral lessons or impart knowledge, often Christian doctrine. Examples include Isidore of Seville's *Etymologiae* (sixth century C.E.) and to some degree Geoffrey Chaucer's *Parlement of Foules* (1380). *See also* Allegory.

Bevor: A collar plate covering the lower face.

Bishop: An important and powerful office, held by an ordained priest who was also often a nobleman and an accomplished military leader, with religious authority over an administrative territory called a diocese, as well as legal authority over its clergy, friars, monks, and nuns.

Black Death: The name for the bubonic plague that decimated the population of western Asia and Europe in the mid-fourteenth century.

Black Friars or Monks: *See* Benedictines, Dominicans.

Bloodfeud: A conflict between families that often extended for generations and usually was instigated by an act of revenge.

Bogomils: A heretical sect that began in the mid-tenth century in Bulgaria, spreading into the Byzantine Empire and west into Europe. Bogomils held the dualistic belief that God had two sons, the good Jesus and the evil Satan.

Bondman: A serf or slave. Bondmen and their families routinely formed part of the package in a grant or transfer of land from one property owner to another—often by name.

Book of hours: A medieval prayer book for the layperson, often small in size to be portable and sometimes beautifully illuminated.

Bordar or bordarii: A type of peasant who occupied a cottage but often one with no farmland; this class was lower than that of villein but higher than that of a cottager. *See also* Cottager, Serf, Villein.

Borough, burg, burgh, or burh: In Anglo-Saxon England, a planned town designed for military defense or as a political center; the term came to mean any town granted the right of self-government.

Bot: Compensation for damages, penalty fee, amends, reparation. Used in compounds for more precise legal terms, such as cynebot (compensation for killing a king) or manbot (compensation for a crime).

Boyar or bojar: A Bulgarian or Russian member of the landed military aristocracy.

Bracers: Plate armor worn to protect the arms.

Breviary: A book containing the Divine Office (lessons, psalms, and hymns) day by day. *See also* Divine Office.

Brigandine or brigantine: A material used for light body armor, consisting of metal plates, strips, or scales sewn on or into a thick material such as canvas or leather. *See also* Jack.

Buckler: A small, round shield used by foot solders to defend themselves against blows in hand-to-hand combat. *See also* Pavise, Targe.

Buckram: A stiff, heavy linen or cotton fabric.

Buffet: A ceremonial blow administered when a new knight was dubbed.

Bull: An papal letter or document that issued an authoritative statement or policy. Named for the pope's lead seal, or *bulla*.

Burgage: In England and Scotland, a property held in "burgage tenure," that is, a property, usually located in a borough as opposed to a rural area, that normally consisted of a house or living quarters either with or without additional land and was rented to an occupant for money as opposed to service. A burgage could be subdivided to accrue additional rents.

Burgess: In England, a member of a borough community, generally but not always a freeman; later generalized to refer to the more prosperous residents of a town.

Burgher: In German countries, a townsman.

Burgonet: A steel cap with a chin piece common in the sixteenth century.

Burgundians: A Germanic tribe of the eighth through tenth centuries eventually incorporated into the Frankish kingdoms.

Buttress: A projection from a wall for additional support.

Byrnie: A mail shirt that eventually developed into the hauberk. *See also* Hauberk.

Byzantine Empire: The Eastern Roman Empire, the successor to the Roman Empire after its fall in 476, with the capital at Constantinople; it ended in 1453 with the fall of Constantinople to the Ottoman Turks.

Cabacete: A tall, narrow helmet of the Spanish infantry in the late fifteenth century; it had a brim that was drawn up to a point at front and rear.

Caliph: From the Arabic *kalifah*, "successor," the title of the successors of the Prophet Muḥammad in the Orthodox, Umayyad, ʿAbbāsid, and Fāṭimid caliphates. Their status waned with the increasing military powers of regional emirs and sultans.

Canon law: The system of governing the Roman Catholic Church, its bishops, clerics, and laypersons. In the Middle Ages, this influence was pervasive in Europe, not only among the clerics but also, for the laity, in areas that today are generally governed by secular laws regarding marriage, divorce, slander, defamation, inheritance, and other social matters.

Canonical hours: The times of day and night during which specific services were sung or recited: matins, lauds, prime, tierce, sext, nones, vespers, and compline.

Cardinal virtues: Prudence, temperance, fortitude, and justice, the four classic virtues. *See also* Seven Deadly Sins, Seven Moral Virtues.

Carmelites: Also known as the White Friars or Monks from the color of their habits, a mendicant order of monks known for study and meditation. *See also* Benedictines, Carthusians, Cistercians, Franciscans, Mendicants.

Carrack: Large square rigged sailing vessel of Genoese origin, clinker built.

Carthusians: An order of clergy in the late Middle Ages known for their learning and asceticism, living in "charterhouses" in England. *See also* Benedictines, Carmelites, Cistercians, Franciscans, Mendicants.

Carucage: Tax on plowland. *See also* Carucate.

Carucate: From *caruca*, "plow," a measurement of land equivalent to an area that could be plowed by eight oxen in a year's time. *See also* Carucage, Hide.

Cassock: A long, full-length man's coat and fitted sleeves designed for warmth and sometimes lined with fur. Worn especially by priests and other clerics.

Castellan: The warden or governor of a castle or fortification.

Castle: A fortification with a broad-ranging variety of architectural features designed for safety and defense. *See also* Bailey, Bastion, Drawbridge, Keep, Moat.

Casuistry: A system of moral theology which takes full account of the circumstances and intentions of penitents and formulates rules for particular cases.

Catapult: Stone-throwing engine, usually employing torsion. *See also* Ballista, Trebuchet.

Cathars: Members of a heretical sect in southern France during the twelfth and thirteenth centuries, who held a dualistic belief that matter was evil and thus Christ never took human form. *See also* Albigensians.

Cathedral or cathedral church: The central church in a diocese, the seat of a bishop's cathedra, or throne.

Catholic Church: From Greek *catholicos*, meaning "universal," the name was applied by a group of second century Christians to distinguish themselves from other groups, particularly the Gnostic Christians, and came to be applied to the dominant Church in the Middle Ages which adhered to the ancient creeds: Eastern Orthodox, Roman Catholics, and Anglicans.

Cellarer: The monk at a monastery who oversees the food supply and provisions for the community.

Cenobitism: Monastic life in a community as opposed to a monastic life of solitude. *See also* Eremiticism.

Ceorl: In Anglo-Saxon England, a freeman or free tenant of the lowest rank, who might aspire to become a thegn if he could acquire enough land. *See also* Thegn or thane.

Cerevelliere: A globular steel cap worn to protect the head during battle, which evolved by the fourteenth century into the Bascient. *See also* Bascinet.

Cesspits: A form of private latrine, dug in yards behind or even beneath dwellings, built when access to a public latrine was limited or at a distance. When full, their contents would be used as manure or dumped in rivers.

Chamber: The personal quarters or sleeping rooms of a noble or king, overseen by a chamberlain.

Chamberlain: The officer in a royal household responsible for overseeing the king or noble's chamber and private household.

Chancellor: The head of the Chancery, an officer in a royal household, often a bishop familiar with law, who served as the king's secretary and was responsible for domestic and foreign affairs.

Chancery: The part of the English government that issued charters, letters, and writs under the Great Seal of England, functioning as the department of interior and defense and often initiating legal action.

Chantry: An endowment or institution endowed to say masses for the souls of the deceased.

Charter: A document issued by a lord or king, addressed to the public, in which was recorded title to property or, in a charter of franchise, freedom from servitude.

Chasuble: A sleeveless mantle worn by a priest.

Chattels: Goods, such as furniture and other personal effects, that could move with their owner; an interest in land was known as chattels real (compare the modern "real estate").

Chirograph: A record of an agreement or contract between parties, in which the terms were written on one piece of parchment, a wavy line was drawn through the agreement, and then the agreement was cut in half, with one half given to each party. Chirographs prevented forgery by making it clear that two halves of the document were original when it could be demonstrated that their broken lines matched.

Chivalry: The culture and ethic that grew out of the eleventh and twelfth century concept of the noble knight, whose life was devoted to his liege lord, the defense of the weak, and the honor of his lady.

Christendom: Those territories in Europe and beyond occupied primarily by Christians.

Church: When used alone in the context of the Middle Ages, generally capitalized in reference to the universal Catholic Church. Lowercased, a reference to the building or complex that hosted services, including nave, altars, choir, and apse. *See also* Cathedral.

Church courts: The religious court system that enforced canon law and was overseen by the Church. It had jurisdiction over such matters as marriage, annulment, wills, inheritance, offenses against personal character (defamation, slander), and determinations of heresy or breach of faith.

Cinque Ports: Beginning in the eleventh century, five boroughs located on the English Channel whose barons were granted special privileges for providing ships in time of war.

Cistercians: A branch of the Benedictine monks in the twelfth and thirteenth centuries who advocated reform through a strict return to Saint Benedict's rule. *See also* Benedictines.

Clerics or clergy: A general term for all members of the Church, including abbots, monks, priests, friars, bishops, archbishops, cardinals, and others. *See also* Benefit of clergy.

Cloister: The covered walkways surrounding a grassy courtyard, lined with arches and looking in toward the courtyard.

Close: An enclosed field or area.

Close helmet: A round-topped helmet attached to neck armor.

Cluny: Founded in Burgundy in 910, one of the most famous monasteries, which by the eleventh century was the headquarters of a series of monasteries across Europe. Among its more famous denizens was Peter Abelard, Odo of Lagery (Pope Urban II), and William of Saint-Thierry.

Codex: A medieval unprinted (manuscript) book, usually made of leaves of parchment sewn together and bound between parchment, wooden, or leather covers, but also in roll and other forms.

Coif: A defensive covering for the head made out of chain mail.

College: In the Middle Ages, an ecclesiastical body with a distinct legal status, separate from a church or monastery, that had an academic or scholarly mission.

Common law: In England, unwritten laws that developed from judicial decisions made in royal courts, based on custom and precedent; these laws eventually became universal and supplanted local statutes and equities. All law in the United States, with the exception of the state of Louisiana, is based on English common law.

Communitas (*pl.* communitates): Associations or communities such as towns and corporate entities, the basis for corporations.

Commutation: Conversion of labor services into a monetary value.

Constable: From the Latin for "count of the stable," an office, accompanied by a detailed system of wards or constabularies, that evolved in the century following the Norman Conquest, when French invasion of England was feared. Constables' duties included local law enforcement, nightwatch, the securing of town gates, and the right to interrogate suspicious characters.

Convent: *See* Nunnery.

Coroner: An office in England originally charged with keeping track of the Crown's legal actions (pleas) and, only later, to examine dead bodies to determine cause of death.

Corrody: An annual or lifetime provision of food and shelter, and sometimes also money, in return for service, often to laypersons by a religious house or monastery. The social function of a corrody was in some ways similar to that of a pension.

Corvée: The labor that a serf owed to his lord or the landowner on whose land he made his living.

Coterell: A bondman who held a small plot of land. *See also* Bondman.

Cottager, cottar, or cotter: A peasant with a cottage but little or no land, the lowest of the peasant class in England. *See also* Bordar, Serf, Villein.

Council: A meeting of religious leaders; an "ecumenical council" is a meeting of the highest bishops and the pope. *See also* Synod.

Count: From Latin *comes* (companion) and Middle French *comte*, the French or continental equivalent of an earl. The office became a noble title, beneath duke and above baron and knight.

Couter: An elbow guard.

Craft or mistery: A skilled occupation, industry, or trade taught by means of an apprenticeship system whereby the apprentice learned under a master craftsman and worked his way to the top. (The Latin-derived "mistery" referred to mastery.) Craftsmen formed leagues or guilds and were regulated in towns. *See also* Guild, Journeyman.

Creed: A formal statement of belief, often religious or theological, such as the Apostles' Creed and the Nicene Creed.

Crenelation: A battlement at the top of a castle wall or tower formed by crenels (openings) and merlons (solid square or sawtooth parapets between openings), resulting in a notched look. See also Battlement, Parapet.

Crest: The heraldic design on a helmet.

Croft: An enclosed patch of land or garden area adjacent to a cottage and used for pasture or growing crops.

Crop rotation: The agricultural practice, common during the Middle Ages, of dividing land into three strips or areas, of which one was sown with spring crops or grain, one with fall crops or grain, and one left alone, or fallow, to "rejuvenate" soil depleted of its nutrients.

Crusades: The eight military expeditions of Europeans to the Middle East between 1095 and 1271 to defend the Holy Land against Muslim rulers. Derived from the word for "cross," which became a crest worn by the Christian participants. Later commonly used to signify any Christian war not only to defend but also to prosyletize.

Cubit: A medieval unit of length roughly equal to an arm's length (about 0.5 meter, or 18 inches).

Cuisses: Plate armor worn to protect the thighs.

Culverin: A relatively lightweight cannon that was mounted on a portable frame and fired small-calibre lead or bronze bullets; a predecessor of the harquebus (early sixteenth century) and of later handguns.

Curate: A priest who could "cure" souls in a particular parish.

Curia: Any court (Latin *curia*), either ecclesiastical or royal. Often appears with another, definitive word appended, such as "curia regis" (the royal court or king's court).

Curtain wall: A castle wall enclosing a courtyard or an outer wall of a castle, between towers.

Cymru (*pron.* CIHM-ree): The Welsh name for the Welsh.

Cynebot: The atonement to the nation for the killing of the king.

Cyrillic: The Slavic alphabet, used in Bulgaria, Serbia, Macedonia, and Russia, essentially introduced in the ninth century by Saints Cyril and Methodius in the form of its predecessor, Old Church Slavonic.

Czar or tsar: A Slavic emperor, a title first used by the medieval Bulgarians and Serbs.

Danegeld: Literally, "Dane gold" or "Dane money," a tribute in England paid to the Danish rulers and later to other English kings.

Danelaw: The region in England in East Anglia, the East Midlands, Lincolnshire, and Yorkshire that was heavily settled by the Danes in the eighth and ninth centuries and under their jurisdiction.

Daub: *See* Wattle and daub.

Deacon: In the Church, the order below priest, one of the Major Orders. Deacons and archdeacons served the priest in ministering to the parish by helping care for the poor and maintaining the church grounds.

Debenture: A receipt that could be redeemed for money, given for goods or services to the king.

Demesne: In the feudal system, lands reserved solely for the use of the lord or king, unoccupied by tenants, although worked by serfs.

Despot: In the Byzantine Empire, an office second only to emperor, given to a holder of a particular territory.

Devshirme: During the Ottoman (Turkish) Empire, a levy of Christian boys, collected for training and recruitment to serve in various parts of the administration, such as the Janissaries or the emperor's Household. *See also* Janissaries.

Dextrarius (French *destrier*): A warhorse.

Diocese: An administrative district of the Church under a bishop's jurisdiction, which during the early Middle Ages provided a system for political governance in the wake of Roman disintegration.

Dispensation: A license to go outside the law, particularly canon law, which was issued by the pope.

Disseisin: Wrongful dispossession of land.

Distraint: A means of forcing a court appearance by seizing certain of the person's possessions; also, arrest.

Divine Office: The particular religious service recited by priests at a fixed time of day and once during the night. *See also* Canonical hours.

Divine right: The concept that God bestowed the right to rule upon kings.

Doge: A ruler of Venice, from the mid-eighth century to the end of the eighteenth. The doges were powerful leaders during the Middle Ages, since Venice was a free state and central trading city.

Domesday Book: The 1086 census of England ordered by King William after the Norman conquest (1066). It recorded properties and their holders, thus enabling the royal government to provide for itself an adequate and consistent income, since officials knew what revenues could be expected from any piece of land. Two volumes, Great Domesday and Little Domesday, covered much of England, with some notable exceptions (London and a few other centers were not covered, for example).

Dominicans: An order of mendicant friars founded by Saint Dominic and sanctioned by Pope Honorius in 1216. They emphasized scholarship and the defeat of heresy. Sometimes known as Black Friars for the color of their habits. Thomas Aquinas was a Dominican. *See also* Benedictines, Carmelites, Carthusians, Cistercians, Franciscans, Mendicants.

Dongjon: *See* Keep.

Dower: The rights of a bride to property of her husband as a result of their marriage, which was determined either specifically through a gift from the husband after the wedding or by default as a third of the husband's lands. *See also* Dowery, Marriage.

Dowery: Land or a fee provided to a nunnery for a new entrant, or goods and money that were offered by a bride's family to her husband.

Drawbridge: A wooden bridge that could be raised or lowered, often leading to a castle gateway, spanning a moat or trough of water that surrounded the fortification to dissuade entry. *See also* Moat.

Dream vision: A type of allegory in which the narrator or a character falls asleep and dreams a dream that becomes the framed story. Famous medieval dream visions include the thirteenth century *Roman de la Rose*, Dante's *The Divine Comedy* (c. 1320), William Langland's *The Vision of William, Concerning Piers the Plowman* (c. 1362), and Geoffrey Chaucer's *Hous of Fame* (1372-1380) and *Book of the Duchess* (c. 1370). *See also* Allegory.

Dualism: A worldview that has typified several religions (Gnosticism, Manichaeanism, Bogomils, Cathars), holding that the world is divided and controlled by both good and evil, the material and the spiritual.

Duke: From Roman *dux*, a governor, especially of a military jurisdiction; later, a member of nobility who was lord over several counties (headed by "counts"), who could pass his title to offspring.

Dungeon: A jail located in a castle tower.

Ealdorman or ealderman: *See* Alderman.

Earl: Originally an officer who oversaw several shires, with their sheriffs, eventually the most elevated rank of nobility in medieval England that was not of royal blood. *See also* Ealdorman.

Eire: The name for Ireland in Irish.

Emir or amir: The title of an Islamic commander, loosely a prince, referring to high military officers, provincial governors of the Islamic empire, and rulers who, although technically under the the caliph, were essentially independent (such as the Umayyad emirs of Córdoba during the eighth and ninth centuries).

Enfeoffment: Investiture with dignities or possessions.

Eremiticism: A life of solitude, led by hermits or monks, as opposed to a monastic life lived in community. *See also* Cenobitism.

Escheat: The right of a feudal lord to lands held by a vassal or serf, if no heirs exist or if the holder commits a crime, treason, or otherwise gives up his right to hold the land.

Essoin: An acceptable excuse for not attending court.

Estates or Three Orders: The three main sectors of society: the nobility, the clergy, and the bourgeois or merchant class.

Exchequer: Beginning in the twelfth century, the financial department of England's royal government.

Excommunication: The official ousting of a member of the Roman Catholic Church from its membership and/or communion with faithful Christians, one of the worst sentences that could befall a Christian during the Middle Ages both socially and legally.

Fair: A regional market held approximately once or twice a year, where a wide variety of both local and imported goods could be purchased.

Falchion: A short, curved sword with a broad blade.

Farce: From the Latin *farcire*, meaning "to stuff." Originally an insertion into established Church liturgy in the Middle Ages, "farce" later became the term for specifically comic scenes inserted into early liturgical drama. The term has come to refer to any play that evokes laughter by such low-comedy devices as physical humor, rough wit, and ridiculous and improbable situations and characters.

Fatwa: A legal opinion or ruling issued by an Islamic legal scholar, or mufti.

Fealty: The obligation of loyalty a vassal owed to his lord, sworn by oath.

Fief: Also known as a fee or holding, the land a lord granted in return for service.

Feudalism: The system of governance in medieval Europe characterized by a landed nobility who had responsibilities to the king, in return for the use of land (fiefs) exploited with the labor of the peasantry (serfs).

Fletcher: An arrow maker.

Flying buttress: An arch carrying the thrust of a roof from the upper part of a wall to a free-standing support.

Forestel: An assault on the king's highway.

Franchise: *See* Freedom.

Franciscans: A mendicant order of friars, founded by Saint Francis of Assisi, that emphasized preaching and helped establish early universities. They wore gray and therefore also were known as Gray or Grey Friars. *See also* Benedictines, Carmelites, Carthusians, Cistercians, Dominicans, Mendicants.

Frankpledge: In Anglo-Saxon England, a small grouping of people (technically ten, but varying in practice) that formed the lowest administrative jurisdiction of governance, responsible for one another's lawful conduct.

Franks: The Germanic tribe of peoples that settled much of western and central Europe during the sixth and seventh centuries and eventually dominated what is today France, Germany, Switzerland, and northern Italy, giving rise to the Merovingian and Carolingian Dynasties.

Freedom: Rather than the modern concept of personal liberty, a legal status, also called the "franchise" or the "liberty," acquired from a lord that carried with it specified rights, including some personal freedoms. Often these were accorded to townsmen and sometimes to women. "Franchise" or "liberty" could also refer to the region within which these freeman's rights were in effect.

Freehold: An estate held for life and often inheritable.

Freeman: A man granted freedom (or the franchise, or liberty), still owing obligations to a lord. *See also* Freedom.

Freeman of a town: A man who has acquired (by birth, privilege, or payment) membership in a craft guild, allowing him certain rights within the town, such as the free practice of his craft.

Friar: A member of a mendicant (begging) order of preachers, many of which arose during the twelfth and thirteenth centuries. *See also* Benedictines, Carmelites, Carthusians, Cistercians, Dominicans, Franciscans, Mendicants.

Friars Minor: *See* Franciscans.

Fuqaha: An Islamic scholar learned in jurisprudence. *See also* ʿUlama.

Furlong: A measurement of distance, roughly 220 yards (200 meters) in length, which corresponded to the average length of a furrow in most fields.

Fyrd: An Anglo-Saxon militia or army.

Gabelle: A tax on salt, a commodity which could be bought only at royal or ducal depots.

Gael: Celtic inhabitants of Scotland, Ireland, and the Isle of Man, giving rise to the modern word "Gaelic" for the languages spoken by these peoples.

Gambeson: A quilted linen jacket stuffed with flax or rags, worn as a body defense by infantrymen and poor knights.

Garderobe: A latrine or a lavatory located in a castle wall with a chute ending in a pit.

Garth: A piece of enclosed land next to a house, sometimes cloistered.

Geld: Old English for money, payment, tax, or tribute. *See also* Danegeld.

Gentry: A class consisting of knights, squires, and gentlemen.

Gestum: A portion of food or drink appropriate to a guest.

Gild: *See* Guild.

Ghazi: Arabic term for an Islamic warrior against unbelievers.

Goliardic poetry: Satiric poetry, originally aimed at the Church and the pope and written by wandering students and renegade clerics in the Middle Ages, later associated with minstrels and loose living. Some of these works were collected during the nineteenth century as the *Carmina Burana*. In 1884, John Addington compiled a collection titled *Wine, Women, and Song*.

Gore: A wedge of arable land created by irregularity of terrain and plowing in strips.

Gorget: A piece of plate armor that covers the neck and throat.

Gothic: Anything pertaining to Gothic peoples, but more often denoting a style of European architecture between the twelfth and sixteenth centuries characterized by ornateness, strong vertical lines, and pointed arches.

Grange system: A system of agriculture in Europe, established by monks, which existed outside the feudal manorial system.

Great hall: A building or room in a castle used for the main meeting or dining area.

Greaves: Plate armor for the legs, particularly the lower legs.

Greek fire: An explosive compound that was ignited and hurled into the enemy's path or stronghold.

Green: A "common" area of lawn or grassland initially used by villagers to graze animals; evolved into the parklike areas that characterize cities today.

Guild: A fraternity or association of skilled craftsmen, usually in a certain industry or art. In the towns where they formed, guilds became important not only economically but also politically.

Hadith: The collected sayings and deeds of the Prophet Muḥammad, one of the major sources of Islamic law.

Hajj: The pilgrimage to Mecca, required of all Muslims at least once in their lives.

Haketon: A protective leather coat or jacket, reinforced with mail.

Halberd: A polearm with a rear spike and top spike. *See also* Pole-ax.

Half-timber: A type of construction that typified medieval buildings, with main timbers framing the structure and intevening spaces filled with wattle and daub. *See also* Wattle and daub.

Hanse: An Old English term connoting commercial use and, applied to merchant guilds, the fee for becoming a member of such a guild. The term gave rise to the name for the Hanseatic League, the association of mercantile towns of northern Germany established in the mid-twelfth century.

Harem: An Arabic term connoting something forbidden or taboo and eventually applied to holy places in Mecca, Medina, Jerusalem, and elsewhere. Came to be applied to the women's quarters of a residence.

Haubergeon: A coat of mail that was smaller than a hauberk. *See also* Hauberk.

Hauberk: A hooded tunic or shirt made of mail and designed to protect the head, arms, and torso down to the knees.

Heptarchy: The seven pre-Viking kingdoms of England: Wessex, Mercia, Northumbria, Kent, East Anglia, Essex, and Sussex.

Heresy: A belief, religious doctrine, or policy that contradicted the orthodoxy of the Roman Catholic Church, determined by Church authority and, if held and not repented, subject to severe punishment.

Heretic: A person who held or purveyed heresy.

Hesychasm: Based on a movement introduced to Athos by Gregory of Sinai in the early fourteenth century, a mystical approach to spiritual communion with God that later became associated with social and political movements that led to a civil war within the Byzantine state.

Hide: In England, a measure of land necessary to sustain a household, averaging about 120 acres, on which a tax assessment, also called a hide, was based.

Hijra or hegira: The migration of Muḥammad and his followers to Medina (dated in the Western calendar to 622).

Holy orders: *See* Major Orders, Minor Orders.

Homage: The formal ceremony of recognition by a tenant that he held the land of a lord and owed him service for it. *See also* Fealty.

Housbote: A tenant's right to repair his house using wood from the lord's estate.

Household: The royal family, servants, and other officials attending an English king, which eventually gave rise to divisions or departments of government such as the chancery, exchequer, and courts of law.

Humanism: Born in fourteenth century Italy, a worldview that places humankind, human values, and human achievements at the center of the universe, as opposed to supernatural or religious worldviews, which see humanity as inferior or intrinsically depraved. Humanism distinguished Renaissance from medieval thought and eventually led to the Reformation, individualism, and the notion that humankind could triumph over nature. As Humanism blossomed, so did science, revealing physical laws that explained natural phenomena and seemed at odds with biblical and theological explanations of the universe. Humanism also was characterized by a return to classic Greek and Latin (pre-Christian) literature.

Humors: In medieval and Renaissance medicine, the humors were the four bodily fluids—blood, phlegm, yellow bile, and black bile—any excess of which created a distortion or imbalance of personality; by extension, the term came to mean "mood" or "disposition."

Hundred: In Anglo-Saxon England, a subdivision of a shire that theoretically was about one hundred hides. *See also* Hide.

Hussites: Followers of John Hus, regarded as heretical by the Church.

Iconoclasm: The destruction of icons, sacred images of Christ or saints. The Iconoclastic Controversy, which divided the eastern and western Church during the eighth and ninth centuries, concerned the policy of the East to destroy such images as idolatrous; in the West such images were revered.

Imam: An Islamic religious and political leader, one of the titles assumed by the caliph and later particularly of the spiritual leaders of the Shīʿites.

Indulgence: A grant of remission of penance for sins, issued by a bishop or the pope, in exchange for an act or, later, a fee.

Infidel: A non-Christian, particularly a Muslim during the Middle Ages.

Interdict: A sentence imposed by the Church on a territory or jurisdiction, prohibiting the administration of the sacraments in order to force adherence to Church doctrine or authority.

Investiture: The act of formally placing a person, such as a bishop, in office. The Investiture Controversy between Holy Roman Emperor Henry IV and Pope Gregory VII was waged over the secular emperor's right to grant such offices versus that of the pope; it resulted in the compromise established in the Concordat of Worms (1107).

Islam: The religion founded by the Prophet Muḥammad, which after his death in 632 resulted in the rapid spread of Islam from Arabia east through Persia, India, and Southeast Asia and west through Africa and southern Spain. The resulting clash of Islamic and Christian cultures contributed to both intellectual advancement and military conflict, particularly during the Crusades of the eleventh and twelfth centuries. *See also* Muslim.

Jack: A thick, protective leather coat, sometimes reinforced with metal studs or plates.

Janissaries: From the Turkish for "new corps," a corps of troops originally recruited by taking non-Muslim children as slaves of the sultan. The Janissaries played a key role in the rise of the Ottoman Turks during fifteenth century.

Jihad: A holy war waged by Muslims against nonbelievers in Islam, considered in the Middle Ages a duty imposed by holy law.

Jongleur: In medieval France, a wandering minstrel.

Journeyman: A wage worker in a trade guild who has graduated from apprenticeship under a master craftsman and is considered competent in his craft.

Jury: In the Middle Ages, a body of men sworn to give a "true answer" (*veredictum* or verdict) to a question put before them. The institution took many forms for many purposes and evolved into the court juries familiar today.

Justiciar: In England during the late tenth through early thirteenth centuries, a judicial officer and the king's surrogate during his absence.

Jutes: A Germanic people originating on the Continent and settling in southeastern England in the fifth century. *See also* Angles, Saxons.

Keep or dongjon: The part of a castle deemed to be safest, surrounded by the thickest walls or deep within the fortifications, often within a central tower.

Kettle: A type of open-faced helmet worn during the fourteenth and fifteenth centuries.

Khan: Beginning in the tenth century, the title of a Turkish, Central Asian, or Mongol ruler who reigned over a group of tribes or territories. Mongol rulers in Persia were known as il-khans ("sous" or "under" khans who ruled under a sovereign).

King: During the Middle Ages in Europe, a lord who ruled a large region and under whom ruled subordinate lords who were, in the feudal system, his vassals and owed him fealty. Through this system developed larger political entities, such as the Holy Roman Empire and eventually the nation-states of Europe. *See also* Feudalism.

King's peace: A zone of protection around the king, in which conflict was prohibited and violation of which was a felony. When this zone eventually extended to the king's entire realm, all criminal matters came under his jurisdiction or were delegated to local courts under the king's peace.

Knight: A warrior with weapons, armor, and a horse who supported the king; an early professional soldier. Initially not part of the nobility, knights evolved with the rise of chivalry to follow an idealized code of conduct that became associated with their profession. The position of knight became hereditary by the fifteenth century, forming the top rank of the gentry class. *See also* Gentry.

Knights Hospitallers: An order of monks who ministered to the ill during the Crusades.

Knights Templar (or Templars): A religious-military order founded to protect the Holy Land and its pilgrims.

Laity: Unordained (nonclerical) members of the Church.

Lay: A medieval French lyric narrative poem (French *lai*), mostly brief and relating stories of courtly love. The lays of the late twelfth century poet Marie de France are considered the epitome of the form, which was imitated by the author of *Sir Orfeo*, by Geoffrey Chaucer in his "Franklin's Tale," and by Thomas Chestre in his *Sir Launfal*.

Leet court: A lower court with a jurisdiction corresponding to that ot the frankpledge, a "leet" (or ward) being the territory occupied by the frankpledge. Hence, a type of local or town court.

Legate: A representative of the pope.

Leodgeld or leudgeld: *See* Wergeld.

Liberty: *See* Freedom.

Liege or liege lord: The main lord to whom a knight owed allegiance.

Liturgical drama: The term refers to plays performed as part of the liturgy of the Church during the Middle Ages and therefore is not invoked for authored works. The origin of these plays was in the tropes or interpolations into the Latin text of the liturgy, which was chanted by the clergy. These interpolations were expanded and eventually developed into independent performances in the vernacular. The performances gradually moved out of the church proper and were performed by members of the laity. While the plays ceased to be liturgical, they continued to deal with religious themes, particularly drawn from the Old and New Testaments. *See also* Liturgy, Miracle play, Morality play, Mystery play, Passion play.

Liturgy: Church services including public prayers, rituals such as Mass, the Divine Office, and the anointing of kings.

Lollard: A follower of the heretical theology of John Wyclif during the fourteenth century, which emphasized lay preaching of scripture to the masses. Literally meaning "mumbler," the term was later used disparagingly.

Lombards: A "barbarian" tribe that settled in northern Italy and eventually ruled Rome after its fall in 476.

Madrasa: A school for Muslim learning, often but not always attached to a mosque.

Major Orders: The orders of priest, deacon, and subdeacon. *See also* Minor Orders.

Mamlūk: In Islamic countries, literally, "owned," meaning a slave. The term gave its name to a series of sultans of Egypt during the thirteenth, fourteenth, and fifteenth centuries.

Manichaeanism: A dualistic religion, based on the teachings of a Persian named Mani, in which light (good) and darkness (evil) were seen as opposing forces. Considered heretical by Christians, in Europe "Manichee" was a disparaging term. *See also* Dualism.

Manor: A small estate, consisting of roughly 1,000 to 2,000 acres, that was largely self-sufficient and generally held by a knight or other lord, with tenants who worked the land; often included its own manorial court, which regulated land tenure, inheritance, marriage practices, and personal relationships.

Manumission: The process whereby a lord freed a serf.

March: A border area. Barons or lords of such areas became known as "marcher lords," "marquises" (French), or "margraves" (German).

Marriage: A term originally referring to the lands a bride's family gave her upon wedding. This union was regulated by manorial law, requiring a license for which a fee was charged. *See also* Dower, Dowery.

Mayor: The head of a borough, similar to a bailiff except that he was elected by the townsmen and not appointed by the lord of the borough.

Mendicants: Friars and orders of friars, who by virtue of abstaining from owning personal property lived on the charity of others by begging, rather than on land endowments. Dominicans, Franciscans, and Carmelites were mendicant orders of friars. *See also* Friar.

Minor Orders: Any of the four lower orders—porter, lector, exorcist, and acolyte—required for entry into one of the Major Orders. *See also* Major Orders.

Minstrels: Itinerant musicians, jugglers, acrobats, and other entertainers who often traveled in groups, known as *Minnesänger* in Germany and troubadours or *jongleurs* in France.

Miracle play: A religious play dramatizing the lives of the saints and divine miracles. (The term "mystery play" is used to designate plays derived from the Scriptures as opposed to those dealing with saints' lives.) Miracle plays were originally associated with the celebration of saints' feast days and with religious processions (particularly the Corpus Christi festival) and were performed in Latin as part of the liturgical services. Later, these plays were expanded, performed in the vernacular, and moved into the streets. Trade guilds were often responsible for the performance of a particular play, so that in time a series of performances by various guilds would create a cycle of plays. *See also* Liturgical drama, Morality play, Mystery play, Passion play.

Missal: A book containing all parts of the Mass.

Moat or motte: A defensive trench around a castle, sometimes filled with water. *See also* Drawbridge.

Monarchy: *See* National monarchy.

Monastery: A place where monks or nuns lived a religious life, frequently including a chapter house, where meetings occurred, as well as sleeping quarters and various other facilities depending on the work of the monastery.

Mongols: A group of steppe peoples who rose to power in Central and East Asia during the thirteenth century under Genghis Khan and reached their height during the reign of Kublai Khan (r. 1260-1294).

Monks and nuns: Men and women, respectively, who surrendered worldly possessions to live a life of prayer, study, charitable works, celibacy, healing, and often poverty. *See also* Mendicants.

Monophysites: Early Christians who denied that Jesus Christ had human attributes and maintained his unitary divine nature, a doctrine deemed heretical by the Orthodox Church.

Moot: In England, a community gathering incorporating aspects of a town hall meeting and a community or family court.

Morality play: During the late Middle Ages and early Renaissance, a play containing allegorical figures (often virtues and vices) that are typically involved in the struggle over a person's soul. The anonymously written *Everyman* (first extant version 1508) is one of the most famous medieval examples of this form. *See also* Miracle play, Mystery play, Passion play.

Mortmain: Literally, "dead hand." Land held by the Church in perpetuity. The term lent its name to an English statute of 1279 that forbade the transfer of land to the Church without regard for the existence of prior rights and obligations.

Mufti: A specialist in Islamic law, not a public official but a private scholar who functioned as a consultant. *See also* Qadi.

Muslim: A follower of Islam.

Mystery play: The term "mystery play" (derived from the French term *mystère*) is used to designate plays derived from the Scriptures as opposed to those dealing with saints' lives (mystery plays). Trade guilds were often responsible for the performance of a particular play, so that in time a series of performances by various guilds would create a cycle of plays. Some examples of subjects derived from Scripture include Christ's Passion, the Fall of Man, and the story of Noah. This form of dramatic entertainment reached its height in the fifteenth and sixteenth centuries. *See also* Miracle play, Morality play, Passion play.

Mysticism: The practice of many religious faiths, including Christianity and Islam, with an emphasis on the nonrational, spiritual, felt rather than intellectual aspect of religious truth as an emotional or transcendent experience.

National monarchy: A form of government that arose in the thirteenth century in Western Europe; a king and his bureaucracy gained effective control over the loyalty and taxes of their subjects, often at the expense of the church; the most successful medieval national monarchies were those of England and France.

Nobility: Landed lords who had responsibilities to the king, and who in return for the use of land (fiefs) exploited the labor of the peasantry (serfs).

Normans: The northern French people who, led by William the Conqueror, in 1066 conquered the Anglo-Saxon population of England.

Novel disseisin: A writ designed to restore property quickly to an owner recently dispossessed of his land illegally.

Nun: *See* Monks and nuns.

Nunnery: A convent or monastery for women.

Oligarchy: A form of government in which an organized elite, or small group of lords, controls power to its own benefit.

Ordeal: A means of judging the guilt or innocence of a person by trial. Many different types of ordeal existed in the Middle Ages, from the "ordeal by bread and cheese," in which an outcome of choking indicated guilt, to more dangerous ordeals, which threatened life. Ironically, death as a result of undergoing an ordeal in some cases proved the accused's innocence.

Orders: *See* Major Orders, Minor Orders.

Orthodox Church: In the Byzantine Empire and Slavic countries, The form of Christianity that prevailed, headed by the patriarchs of Constantinople.

Ostrogoths: A group of Gothic peoples who eventually settled in northern Italy.

Ottomans: Turkish rulers of the Islamic world who ruled as sultans from roughly 1281 to 1922. Their conquest of the seat of the Byzantine Empire and Eastern Christian Orthodoxy, Constantinople, in 1453 marked their ascendant power.

Oyer and terminer: A commission issued to a panel of justices to hear (oyer) and determine (terminer) individual complaints.

Palatinate: A county or principality ruled by a lord whose rights included those of a king, such as the right to coin money or appoint judges. Also, in Germany, the proper name of a principality during the Middle Ages. The term "palatine" referred to the lord of a palatinate or a resident of the (German) Palatinate.

Palfrey: A riding horse.

Palisade: A strong stake-wood fence built for defense.

Parapet: The wall on top of a fortification or at the outside of a wall walk, designed for defense.

Parchment: A very durable material used, like paper, for writing, made from the skins of sheep or other animals.

Pardoner: A person with a license to sell indulgences (pardons).

Parish: Part of a diocese overseen by a priest, whose residents are termed parishioners. *See also* Diocese.

Parlement: In France, the highest court of appeal, located in Paris near the Palais de Justice. Also, an English variant spelling of "parliament," generically meaning a congress or meeting for the purpose of discussing and determining public matters.

Parson: A rector, or head of a parish church.

Parsonage: The house occupied by a parson, rector, or vicar, and therefore sometimes called a rectory or vicarage. *See also* Rector, Vicar.

Passion play: A play that depicted the life, and particularly the events leading to the death or Passion, of Jesus Christ. Passion plays had their origin in the pagan rites of ancient Egypt and the Near East. In Christian Europe, many medieval plays presented episodes from the life of Christ and are referred to as Passion plays. *See also* Miracle play, Morality play, Mystery play.

Patriarch: A bishop who headed one of the main patriarchates (dioceses): Rome, Constantinople, Alexandria, Antioch, or Jerusalem.

Pauldron: A piece of curved plate armor worn on the rear shoulder.

Paulicians: A Christian sect, considered heretical, that arose in Armenia and eastern Anatolia and suffered at the hands of the Byzantines.

Pavise: A large shield mounted on a hinged frame for use by those, such as archers and crossbowmen, who could not hold a shield in battle.

Pax Dei (Peace or Truce of God): The policy or movement that attempted to protect noncombatants such as women, the clergy, and the poor from injury during war; violations could be punished by excommunication.

Peace of God: *See* Pax Dei.

Peer: An equal in rank or social status.

Pelagianism: A doctrine, condemned at the Synod of Orange in 529 as heresy, that denied the transmission of Original Sin and emphasized human endeavor as a means to salvation.

Petition: A formal request or complaint.

Pilgrimage: A journey to a holy place, including Mecca for Muslims and Jerusalem for Christians. Canterbury, England's holy see, was the destination of Chaucer's pilgrims in *The Canterbury Tales*.

Pluralism: The holding of more than one beneficiary or church office at a time by a single cleric, easily and commonly abused during the later Middle Ages.

Pole-ax: A weapon built on a shaft about five feet long, with an ax at one end and a spike or hammer head at the other.

Poleyn: Plate armor that protected the kneecap.

Pope: The head of the Roman Catholic Church, also known as the Bishop of Rome. The pope not only was the highest officer of the most influential institution in Europe during the Middle Ages but also exercised a dominant role in political affairs until at least the Reformation.

Priest: A man holding a clerical office below that of bishop and above that of deacon.

Primogeniture: The system of inheritance, common in the Middle Ages, whereby a father's estate was passed to his eldest son.

Prior or prioress: Respectively, a male or female head of a priory, a type of monastic house of less importance than a monastery or abbey; also, the second-in-command after an abbot or abbess.

Privy-Seal, Office of the: In England, the office which issued statements and correspondence from the king that were less formal than those that bore the Great Seal and went out of Chancery. *See also* Chancery.

Pronoia: In the Byzantine Empire, Bulgaria, and Serbia a grant or benefict, usually land, in exchange for military service, which reverted to the state upon the recipient's death rather than being handed down to offspring.

Purveyance: The right of a king to require provision of food and other goods in return for payment.

Qadi: A Muslim judge who administered the holy law of Islam. *See also* Mufti.

Quadrivium: The standard advanced subjects of study during the Middle Ages—arithmetic, geometry, astronomy, and music—undertaken after mastery of the trivium. *See also* Trivium.

Quintain: A training machine consisting of a rotating dummy with shield, suspended on a tether from a pole, on which were mounted horizontal poles that rotated. Knights used the dummy for target practice while avoiding the rotating arms.

Ramadan: The month in which the Qur'ān was first revealed, therefore holy to Muslims, who abstain from eating, drinking, and sexual intercourse from daybreak until nightfall during this month every year.

Rebeck: A three-stringed musical instrument played with a bow, a predecessor of the fiddle.

Rector: A cleric who is the head of a rectory.

Rectory: A type of parish.

Reeve: A manorial overseer, either appointed or elected, who was responsible for the collection of dues and rents owed by peasants to the king.

Refectory: A hall where monks took their meals together.

Regalia: Royal rights.

Regular clergy: Monks, canons, friars, and other clergy who lived in communities under a rule, as opposed to secular clergy, who worked in the world.

Relic: An object—such as a piece of clothing, a bone, a book, or another personal item—venerated by the faithful for its close association with Jesus or a saint.

Rents: Yearly dues that freeholders paid to hold manorial lands.

Rerebrace: Plate armor for the upper arm.

Reredos: A carved and painted screen behind the altar in a church.

Ridge-and-furrow agriculture: Farming that uses parallel plowed bands of ridges and furrows year after year.

Romance: Originally, a "romance" was any work written in Old French; the medieval romances were prose or verse stories about courtly and chivalric matters, originally sung by troubadours extolling knightly virtues and courtly love (as opposed to epic or heroic exploits). The story often included the knight's adventures, conflicts in defense of a heroine (women became major and individualized figures in fiction at this time), supernatural beings (dragons, wizards), and sometimes unexplained or magical events. Three subcategories of the medieval romance are the Matter of Britain (including tales of King Arthur and his knights), the Matter of France (Charlemagne), and the Matter of Rome (based on ancient history). *See also* Arthurian romance.

Romanesque: A style of European architecture typical from the tenth to the late twelfth century on the Continent and in Norman England.

Romania: Not the modern southeast European state but rather the post-fifth century Roman Empire from Byzantine times until the mid-fifteenth century, which expanded and contracted based on Islamic and other incursions.

Rūm: Arabic for Rome, which connoted Europe, the Islamic term for the Byzantine Empire, sometimes including European Christians. After the Seljuk Turks invaded Anatolia, the term still was used for the former Byzantine territories, as in Seljuk Rūm.

Sabaton: Plate armor for the foot.

Sacraments: The sacred acts that conferred grace, of which there were in medieval times seven, including celebration of the Mass.

Saga: Originally applied to medieval Icelandic and other Scandinavian stories of heroic exploits and handed down by oral tradition. The term has come to signify any tale of heroic achievement or great adventure.

Salat: The rituals attending the performance of Islamic prayers, the calls to which were made by a muezzin from a minaret or tower near the mosque.

Sallet: A type of helmet worn in the fifteenth century.

Saltpetre: The explosive compound potassium nitrate, used to make gunpowder.

Sanctuary, right of: The right of a fugitive from justice to take refuge in a church for some days or weeks before being forced to flee.

Saxons: A Germanic people who infiltrated and settled in England during the fifth century and assimilated with local tribes to form the Anglo-Saxons. *See also* Angles, Jutes.

Sayyid: An Arabian and later Sufi lord or master.

Scale armor: Armor made of small plates of horn or metal, attached to a cloth or leather coat.

Sceat (*pl.* sceattas): A Saxon silver coin of the late seventh, eighth, and early ninth centuries.

Schism: A formal split in church hierarchy resulting from a procedural disagreement, which during the Middle Ages resulted in the creation of the Greek Orthodox Church (1054) and the Great Schism (1378-1414) or division between those who followed the pope in Rome and those who followed the pope in Avignon.

Scholasticism: Also called Schoolmen, the Scholastics were those philosophers and theologians of the twelfth and thirteenth centuries who wished to bring the thought of classical philosophers such as Aristotle and Plato into alignment with Christian doctrine. Famous Scholastics include Peter Abelard, Saint Albertus Magnus, Saint Thomas Aquinas, and John Duns Scotus.

Scutage: Payment to the king in lieu of personal, usually military, service.

Secular clergy: As opposed to regular clergy, clerics who lived in the world rather than in a monastery under rule. *See also* Regular clergy.

Selion: A strip of arable land in an open field.

Seneschal: The manager or steward of a household or estate, or the chief officer of a lord.

Serf: A peasant, only partly free, bound to work his lord's land and who must pay a fee or service (corvée) to work that portion of the land that supplies his own livelihood. Serfs included cottagers, smallholders, and villeins. In general, this was the lowest rung of society, working about half the week for the lord and generally bound for life to the soil. *See also* Bordar, Corvée, Cottager, Feudalism, Villein.

Seven Deadly Sins: The mortal sins recognized by Christians throughout the Middle Ages and later, varying slightly among sources but primarily Pride, Anger, Envy, Covetousness, Gluttony, Lechery (lust), and Sloth (laziness), capitalized here because they were often portrayed allegorically in medieval morality plays as characters.

Seven liberal arts: The subjects that made up the trivium (grammar, logic, and rhetoric) and the quadrivium (arithmetic, geometry, astronomy, and music), the mastery of which was considered necessary for a solid education during the Middle Ages.

Seven Moral Virtues: Seven Christian virtues recognized throughout the Middle Ages and later, varying slightly among sources but primarily Charity, Abstinence, Chastity, Industry, Generosity, Meekness, and Patience, capitalized here because they were often portrayed allegorically in medieval morality plays as characters.

Shambles: An area of a town where butchers dumped offal and other waste products for consumption by dogs and scavengers. Often near a river, the remains generally drained into the town's water supply.

Shariʿa: Islamic holy law.

Shaykh or sheikh: Arabic for "elder," referring to a tribal and generally any leader.

Sheriff: The head of a shire, who oversaw both administrative and judicial functions. From the combined terms "shire" and "reeve." *See also* Reeve.

Shields: *See* Buckler, Pavise, Targe.

Shīʿites: A faction of Islam that rivals Sunni or orthodox Islam, founded between 657 and 661 by the fourth caliph, ʿAlī ibn Abī Ṭālib, in reaction to fears that Muslims were straying from the original precepts of the Prophet. *See also* Sunni.

Shire: In England, the generic name for a county, headed by a sheriff (shire reeve).

Shogun: A military dictator in Japan from the late twelfth through the late nineteenth century.

Sicilian school: A group of twelfth and thirteenth century Italian poets (not all from Sicily) who created vernacular love poetry and invented *canzones* and sonnets. They included Giacomo da Lentini, Guido delle Colonne, Giacomino Pugliese, and Rinaldo d'Aquino. The impact of their poetry—both in form and in theme—would be felt into the seventeenth century in poets such as William Shakespeare.

Siege: An attack on a town or fortification that generally lasted days, weeks, months, or even years, using tactics to wear down the enemy within the fortification by means of repeated assaults or cutting off the enemy from supplies (starvation).

Simony: The buying and selling of church offices or sacraments, widely abused.

Sipahi or spahi: An Ottoman cavalryman who received a grant called a timar.

Sollerets: Armor for the feet.

Sottie: A form of medieval French farce that presented political, religious, or social satire.

Spaudler: Curved plate armor the shoulder, devised in layers to enable movement.

Squire: An assistant to a knight who might also be in training to become a knight.

Subinfeudation: The process of creating subordinate tenancies out of one landholding, which made it possible for a lord's vassal to develop his own vassals.

Suevi: A barbarian tribe that eventually settled in northern Spain during the fifth century; eventually they were overcome by the Visigoths.

Suffragans: Bishops ordained to conduct services such as ordinations and confirmations but who did not have the power of the bishop over an entire diocese.

Sultan: Beginning in the eleventh century, any political and military ruler of an Islamic state or emirate (as opposed to the caliph, the religious authority of the Islamic state). Used for Ottoman rulers.

Sunnis: Muslims belonging to the dominant or orthodox Islamic majority, thought to have originated in the Prophet Muḥammad's practice of Islam. *See also* Shīʿites.

Surcoat: A long garment worn over armor.

Suzerain: Any feudal lord, including the king.

Synod: A meeting or council of church officials.

Tabard: A loose garment, short, open at the side, with side sleeves, and worn by some knights.

Taille: Any tax levied by the king or other lord, often a property tax.

Tallage: Any of a variety of taxes levied on boroughs, towns, tenants of royal estates, generally of an arbitrary, direct, or occasional nature.

Talmud: The rabbinic writings that together form Judaic law.

Tansy: A bitter medicinal herb and the cakes baked using it, consumed often after Lent to purify the body.

Targe: A shield for an infantryman, either round or oval. *See also* Buckler, Pavise.

Tenure: An interest or a right in land stemming from a lord and often in exchange for military or other service.

Teutonic Knights: A German military order, based in Prussia, Hungary, and Germany, that brought the Baltic region under Catholic control and launched a series of military crusades against peoples who resisted conversion and assimilation.

Thane: *See* Thegn.

Thegn or thane: Especially in Anglo-Saxon England before 1066, a military retainer of the king or landholding member of the nobility.

Three Orders: *See* Estates

Tithe: One-tenth of a person's income or produce, manditorily given to support the Church or local clergy.

Tonsure: The shaving of the head, the rite attendant upon entering the clergy. The ceremony was also generally applied to giving up one's life to holy service.

Tourney: A staged combat between knights for show, which sometimes got out of hand. In 1270, the Statute of Arms attempted to regulate the conduct of tourneys.

Trailbaston: In the fourteenth century, special judicial power granted to put down hoodlums or allow broad license to investigate crimes and corruption in a particular area.

Trebuchet: A large weapon or war machine designed to catapult projectile boulders into walls and battlements during siege warfare.

Trivium: Grammar, rhetoric, and dialectics (logic), the fundamental subjects of study during the Middle Ages. *See also* Quadrivium.

Troubadour: From the eleventh to thirteenth centuries in Provence, Catalonia, and northern Italy, lyric poet-singers who wrote and performed metrically intricate works about courtly love and chivalry. They were very popular, and many became famous. Today they are known chiefly for their role in propagating a concept of love and honor that significantly influence later attitudes toward love and marriage.

Truce of God: *See* Pax Dei.

Tsar: *See* Czar.

ʿUlama: An Islamic scholar, specifically in religious subjects. Also, the class of professional religious scholars nearest to the Muslim clergy.

Ultimogeniture: Inheritance by the youngest son. *See also* Primogeniture.

Usury: Interest charged on a loan, particularly very high interest. The practice was prohibited to Christians, leaving Jews and others exempt from this restriction and opening opportunities for financial services to be offered by those groups.

Vambrace: Plate armor for the forearm.

Vandals: A Germanic tribe that migrated west across southern Europe and settled in northern Africa.

Vassal: A freeman who swears fealty to a lord, pays him homage, and holds land from him, for which he owes military and other services.

Vaulting: An architectural term for the stone arches in a ceiling or roof.

Vicar: A substitute for the parish priest, often distrusted in the Middle Ages as corrupt.

Vices: Faults of character; also, in the allegorical English morality plays, Vice and personifications of particular vices typically appeared as stock characters. *See also* Seven Deadly Sins.

Villefranche: A town with a charter of franchise. *See also* Villeneuve.

Villein: The wealthiest class of peasant, who had rights to cultivate several dozen acres of land, although not necessarily located in the same plots. *See also* Bordar, Cottager, Freeman, Serf.

Villeneuve: A new town established by a franchise. *See also* Villefranche.

Virtues: *See* Cardinal virtues, Seven Moral Virtues.

Visigoths: The Germanic tribe that inflicted the earliest damage on Rome in the late fourth and early fifth centuries; eventually settled in Spain, defeating the Suevi by the late sixth century.

Vows: Promises made by monks and nuns to God, dedicating their lives to Christ. Common vows included vows of chastity, poverty, obedience, and silence.

Waldensians: Followers of Peter Waldo, a twelfth century advocate of the apostolic life and a return to the simple type of Christianity reflected in the Gospels, unencumbered with ecclesiastical organization or hierarchical structure. Considered early Protestants, the Waldensians were excommunicated c. 1175.

Ward: A courtyard or bailey. *See also* Bailey, Keep.

Wattle and daub: A type of construction in which wooden timbers or laths form a frame, between which a mixture of wattles (straw) and daub (mud clay) would be applied as a filling, and sealed over by daub.

Wergeld or wergild: In Anglo-Saxon England, a "blood-price," or fine paid for killing a man. The fine varied by the rank of the homicide, and all men had a blood-price.

White Friars or Monks: *See* Carmelites, Cistercians.

Witan or witenagemot: A council composed of nobles and ecclesiastics which advised the Anglo-Saxon Kings of England. By custom it also "elected" or ratified the successor to the throne. Resembles the commune concilium.

Wormwood: A bitter-tasting plant with white or yellow flowers used as an herb to aid digestion.

Writ: Any letter stating an official command, mandate, or order, usually issued by the king, a lord, or other high official. Writs "patent" were for public, for all to read, and "closed" writs were directed privately to individuals.

Yale: An image of a fantastic animal, often combining parts of several different animals, appearing on heralds and coats of arms.

Zanj or zanji: Used by Arab marine traders to refer to "the land of black people." The people of East Africa. Used loosely to refer to black people in general.

BIBLIOGRAPHY

PRIMARY SOURCES
Single Works 924
Compilations 930

GENERAL STUDIES AND REFERENCE WORKS . . 931

CULTURAL HISTORY BY SUBJECT
Cross-cultural, Diasporic, and General Religious Studies 932
Philosophy and the Arts 933
Science, Technology, and Trade 935
Women in the Middle Ages 936

SOCIOPOLITICAL AND RELIGIOUS HISTORY BY REGION
Africa 937
Americas 937
Asia
East Asia 938
Mongolia and Central Asia 940
South and Southeast Asia 940
Europe
Byzantine Empire and the Balkans 940
Russia and Eastern Europe 941
Scandinavia 942
Western Europe and the British Isles 942
Middle East and Islamic Studies 946

PRIMARY SOURCES

SINGLE WORKS

Abelard, Peter. *Abelard and Heloise: The Story of His Misfortunes and the Personal Letters*. Translated by Betty Radice. London: Folio Society, 1977.

Alfonso X. *Las Siete Partidas*. 5 vols. Translated by Samuel Parsons Scott. Philadelphia: University of Pennsylvania Press, 2001.

Alvares, Francisco. *The Prester John of the Indies*. Translated by Lord Stanley of Alderley, revised and edited with additional material by G. F. Beckingham and G. W. B. Huntingford. Cambridge, England: Hakluyt Society, Cambridge University Press, 1961.

Andreas, Capellanus. *The Art of Courtly Love*. Translated by John Jay Parry. 1941. Reprint. New York: Columbia University Press, 1990.

Angela da Foligno. *Complete Works*. Translated by Paul Lachance. New York: Paulist Press, 1993.

The Anglo-Saxon Chronicle. Edited by Dorothy Whitelock, David C. Douglas, and Susie I. Tucker. 2d ed. New Brunswick, N.J.: Rutgers University Press, 1989.

Anselm, Saint. *The Letters of Saint Anselm of Canterbury*. Translated by Walter Frölich. Kalamazoo, Mich: Cistercian Publications, 1990.

Arnold of Villanova. *Arnaldi de Villanova: Opera Medica Omnia*. 16 vols. Edited by Michael R. McVaugh. Granada, Spain: Seminarium Historiae Medicae Granatensis, 1975.

Ashʿarī, ʿAlī ibn Ismail al-. *Abūl-Ḥasan ʿAlī ibn Ismāīl al-Aš̌ʿarī's Al-Ibānah an ʿuşūl ad-diyānah (The Elucidation of Islām's Foundation)*. 1940. Reprint. Edited and translated by Walter Conrad Klein. New York: Kraus, 1967.

___________. *The Theology of al-Ashʿarī*. Translated by Richard J. McCarthy. Beirut: Imprimerie Catholique, 1953.

Astronomus. *Son of Charlemagne: A Contemporary Life of Louis the Pious*. Translated by Allen Cabaniss. Syracuse, N.Y.: Syracuse University Press, 1961.

Averroës. *Averroës' Middle Commentaries on Aristotle's Categories and "De interpretatione."* Translated by Charles E. Butterworth. Princeton, N.J.: Princeton University Press, 1983.

___________. *Averroës on Plato's "Republic."* Translated by Ralph Lerner. Ithaca, N.Y.: Cornell University Press, 1974.

___________. *On the Harmony of Religion and Philosophy*. Translated by George F. Hourani. London: Luzac, 1961.

___________. *Tahāfut al-tahāfut (Incoherence of the Incoherence)*. Translated by Simon van den Bergh. London: Luzac, 1954.

Avicenna. *The Life of Ibn Sina: A Critical Edition*. Translated by William E. Gohlman. Albany: State University of New York Press, 1974.

Bacon, Roger. *Roger Bacon's Philosophy of Nature: A Critical Edition*, edited by David C. Lindberg. South Bend, Ind.: St. Augustine's Press, 1998.

Bāṇa. *The Harsa-carita*. Translated by E. B. Cowell and F. W. Thomas. London: Royal Asiatic Society, 1897.

Becket, Thomas. *The Correspondence of Thomas Becket: Archbishop of Canterbury, 1162-1170*, edited by Anne J. Duggan. New York: Oxford University Press, 2000.

Bede. *Bede: A History of the English Church and People*. Translated by Leo Sherley-Price. New York: Penguin Books, 1985.

____________. *The Ecclesiastical History of the English People, the Greater Chronicle: Bede's Letter to Egbert*. Edited by Judith McClure and Roger Collins. New York: Oxford University Press, 1999.

____________. *Historical Works*. Translated by J. E. King. 2 vols. Reprint. Cambridge, Mass.: Harvard University Press, 1994-1996.

Benjamin of Tudela. *The Itinerary of Benjamin of Tudela*. Translated with an introduction and notes by Marcus Nathan Adler. London: H. Frowde, 1907.

Bīrūnī, Muḥammad ibn Aḥmad. *The Exhaustive Treatise on Shadows*. Edited and translated by E. S. Kennedy. 2 vols. Aleppo, Syria: Institute for the History of Arabic Science, University of Aleppo, 1976.

Boccaccio, Giovanni. *The Decameron*. Translated by G. H. McWilliam. Harmondsworth, England: Penguin Books, 1972.

Boniface, Saint. *The Letters of Saint Boniface*. Edited and translated by Ephraim Emerton. New York: Columbia University Press, 2000.

Bower, Walter. *Scotichronicon*. Edited by D. E. R. Watt. Edinburgh: Mercat Press, 1987-1997.

Bracciolini, Poggio. *Two Renaissance Book Hunters: The Letters of Poggius Bracciolini to Nicolaus de Niccolis*. Translated by Phyllis Walter Goodhart Gordon. 1974. Reprint. New York: Columbia University Press, 1991.

Bracton, Henry de. *Bracton on the Laws and Customs of England*. Translated by Samuel E. Thorne. 4 vols. Cambridge, Mass.: Harvard University Press, 1968.

Bruni, Leonardo. *The Humanism of Leonardo Bruni: Selected Texts*. Translated and introduced by Gordon Griffiths, James Hankins, and David Thompson. Binghamton, N.Y.: Medieval and Renaissance Texts and Studies in conjunction with the Renaissance Society of America, 1987.

Burtius, Nicolaus. *Musices Opusculum*. Translated by Clement A. Miller. Neuhausen-Stuttgart: Hänssler-Verlag, 1983.

Cambrensis, Giraldus. *Expugnation Hibernica: The Conquest of Ireland*. Edited and translated by A. B. Scott and F. X. Martin. Dublin: Royal Irish Academy, 1978.

Campbell, Alistair, ed. *Encomium Emmae Reginae*. London: Royal Historical Society, 1949. Reprint. New York: Cambridge University Press, 1998.

Cassiodorus. *Cassiodorus: An Explanation of the Psalms*. Translated and annotated by P. G. Walsh. 3 vols. New York: Paulist Press, 1990-1991.

____________. *An Introduction to Divine and Human Readings*. Translated by Leslie Webber Jones. 1946. Reprint. New York: Octagon Books, 1966.

____________. *The "Variae" of Magnus Aurelius Cassiodorus Senator*. Translated with notes and introduction by S. J. B. Barnish. Liverpool, England: Liverpool University Press, 1992.

Castries, Due de. *The Lives of the Kings and Queens of France*. Translated by Anne Dobell. New York: Alfred A. Knopf, 1979.

Catherine of Siena, Saint. *Catherine of Siena: Passion for the Truth, Compassion for Humanity*. Edited, annotated, and introduced by Mary O'Driscoll. New Rochelle, N.Y.: New City Press, 1993.

____________. *The Dialogue: Catherine of Siena*. Translated by Suzanne Noffke. New York: Paulist Press, 1980.

____________. *The Letters of Catherine of Siena*. Translated by Suzanne Noffke. Tempe, Ariz.: Arizona Center for Medieval and Renaissance Studies, 2000.

Cavalcanti, Guido. *The Complete Poems*. Translated and with an introduction by Marc A. Cirigliano. New York: Italica Press, 1992.

Charles d'Orléans. *Charles d'Orléans: Poésies*. Edited by Pierre Champion. 2 vols. Reprint. Paris: Librairie Honore Champion, 1966.

____________. *The English Poems of Charles of Orléans*. Edited by Robert Steele and Mabel Day. Reprint. London: Oxford University Press, 1970.

Charles IV. *Karoli IV Imperatoris Romanorum vita ab eo ipso conscripta; et, Hystoria nova de Sancto Wenceslao Martyre = Autobiography of Emperor Charles IV; and, His Legend of St. Wenceslas*. Edited by Balázs Nagy and Frank Schaer, with an introduction by Ferdinand Seibt. New York: Central European University Press, 2001.

Chartier, Alain. *The Poetical Works of Alain Chartier.* Edited by J. C. Laidlaw. London: Cambridge University Press, 1974.

Chaucer, Geoffrey. *The Riverside Chaucer.* Edited by Larry D. Benson. 3d ed. Boston: Houghton Mifflin, 1987.

Chrétien de Troyes. *Chrétien de Troyes: The Knight with the Lion: Or, Yvain.* Edited and translated by William W. Kibler. New York: Garland, 1986.

Christine de Pizan. *Christine de Pisan: Autobiography of a Medieval Woman (1363-1430).* Translated and annotated by Anil De Silva-Vigler. London: Minerva, 1996.

The Chronicle of Novgorod. Translated by Robert Michell and Nevill Forbes. New York: AMS Press, 1970.

Chu Hsi. *Further Reflections on Things at Hand.* Translated by Allen Wittenburn. Lanham, Md.: University Press of America, 1991.

Chu Hsi and Lu Tsu-ch'ien. *Reflections on Things at Hand: The Neo-Confucian Anthology.* Translated by Wing-tsit Chan. New York: Columbia University Press, 1967.

Clari, Robert de. *The Conquest of Constantinople.* Translated and edited by Edgar Holmes McNeal. 1936. Reprint. Toronto: University of Toronto Press and the Medieval Academy of America, 1996.

The Clear Mirror: A Chronicle of the Japanese Court During the Kamakura Period, 1185-1333. Translated by George W. Perkins. Stanford, Calif.: Stanford University Press, 1998.

Confucius. *The Analects.* Translated by Arthur Waley. New York: Alfred A. Knopf, 2000.

Cross, Samuel Hazzard, and Olgerd P. Sherbowitz-Wetzor, eds. and trans. *The Russian Primary Chronicle.* Cambridge, Mass.: Medieval Academy of America, 1953.

Davidson, L. S., and J. O. Ward, eds. *The Sorcery Trial of Alice Kyteler: A Contemporary Account (1324).* Binghamton: Center for Medieval and Early Renaissance Studies, State University of New York at Binghamton, 1993.

De Crespigny, Rafe, trans. *To Establish Peace: Being the Chronicle of Late Han for the Years 189-220 A.D. as recorded in chapters 59 to 69 of the "Zizhi tongjian" of Sima Guang.* Canberra, Australia: Faculty of Asian Studies, Australian National University, 1996.

De Slane, Baron MacGuckin, ed. and trans. *Ibn Khallikan's Biographical Dictionary.* 1871. Reprint. 4 vols. New York: Johnson Reprint, 1961. Vol.

Dhuoda. *Dhuoda: Handbook for Her Warrior Son.* Translated by Marcelle Thiébaux. New York: Cambridge University Press, 1998.

Dīn, Rashīd al-. *The Successors of Genghis Khan.* Translated by John Andrew Doyle. New York: Columbia University Press, 1971.

Dodge, Bayard, ed. and trans. *The Fihrist of al-Nadīm: A Tenth-Century Survey of Muslim Culture.* 2 vols. New York: Columbia University Press, 1970.

Domesday Book: A Complete Translation. Editedy by Anne Williams and G. H. Martin. New York: Penguin Books, 2002.

Donatello. *Donatello.* Florence: Giunti, 1999.

Du Fu. *The Selected Poems of Du Fu.* Translated by Burton Watson. New York: Columbia University Press, 2002.

Ducas. *Decline and Fall of Byzantium to the Ottoman Turks.* Translated by Harry J. Magoulias. Detroit, Mich.: Wayne State University Press, 1975.

Dudo of St. Quentin. *History of the Normans.* Translated by Eric Christiansen. Rochester, N.Y.: Boydell Press, 1998.

Dušan, Stefan. "The Code of Stephan Dušan." Translated by Malcolm Burr. *Slavonic and East European Review* 28 (1949-1950): 198-217, 516-539.

Einhard. *Charlemagne's Courtier: The Complete Einhard.* Edited and Translated by Paul Edward Dutton. Peterborough, Ont.: Broadview Press, 1998.

Fibonacci, Leonardo. *Fibonacci's "Liber abaci": A Translation into Modern English of Leonardo Pisano's Book of Calculation.* New York: Springer, 2002.

Firdusi. *The Epic of the Kings: Shāh-nāma, the National Epic of Persia, by Ferdowsi.* Translated by Reuben Levy. Chicago: University of Chicago Press, 1967.

____________. *The Tragedy of Sohráb and Rostám: From the Persian National Epic, the Shahname of Abol-Qasem Ferdowsi.* Translated by Jerome W. Clinton. Rev. ed. Seattle: University of Washington Press, 1996.

FitzGerald, Edward. *The Rubáiyát of Omar Khayyám.* 4th ed. London: Bernard Quaritch, 1879.

Francis and Clare: The Complete Works. Translated by Regis J. Armstrong and Ignatius C. Brady. New York: Paulist Press, 1982.

Froissart, Jean. *Chronicles. Selected, Translated, and Edited by Geoffrey Brereton.* Baltimore: Penguin Books, 1968.

Fulbert, Saint. *The Letters and Poems of Fulbert of Chartres*. Translated by Frederick Behrends. Oxford, England: Clarendon Press, 1976.

Geoffrey of Monmouth. *The History of the Kings of Britain*. Translated by Lewis Thorpe. New York: Penguin Books, 1984.

___________. *The Life of Merlin (Vita Merlini)*. Edited and translated by Basil Clarke. Cardiff: University of Wales Press, 1974.

Gesta Stephani. Translated and edited by K. R. Potter and R. H. C. Davis. Oxford, England: Clarendon Press, 1976.

Gregory of Tours. *The History of the Franks*. Translated and edited by O. M. Dalton. 2 vols. Oxford, England: Oxford University Press, 1971.

___________. *Life of the Fathers*. 2d ed. Translated and edited by Edward James. Liverpool, England: Liverpool University Press, 1991.

Gregory the Great. *Life and Miracles of Saint Benedict: Book Two of the Dialogues*. Translated by Odo J. Zimmerman and Benedict R. Avery. Reprint. 1949. Westport, Conn.: Greenwood Press, 1980.

Gregory VII. *The Correspondence of Pope Gregory VII: Selected Letters from the Registrum*. Translated by Ephraim Emerton. 1932. Reprint. New York: Columbia University Press, 1990.

___________. *The Register of Pope Gregory VII, 1073-1085: An English Translation*. New York: Oxford University Press, 2002.

Guido d'Arezzo. *Guido d'Arezzo's "Regule rithmice," "Prologus in antiphonarium," and "Epistola ad michahelem": A Critical Text and Translation with an Introduction, Annotations, Indices, and New Manuscript Inventories*. Edited by Dolores Pesce. Ottawa, Canada: Institute of Mediaeval Music, 1999.

Guy de Chauliac. *The Middle English Translation of Guy de Chauliac's Anatomy, with Guy's Essay on the History of Medicine*. Edited by Bjorn Wallner. Lund, Sweden: CWK Gleerup, 1964.

Hadeda, Yoshito S. *Kūkai, Major Works: Translated with an Account of His Life and a Study of His Thought*. New York: Columbia University Press, 1972.

Hafiz. *The Divan of Hafez: A Bilingual Text, Persian-English*. Translated by Reza Saberi. Lanham, Md.: University Press of America, 2002.

___________. *Hafez: Dance of Life*. Translated by Michael Boylan. Washington, D.C.: Mage, 1988.

Hartmann von Aue. *Hartmann Von Aue: "Gregorius, the Good Sinner."* Translated by Sheema Zeben Buehne. New York: Frederick Ungar, 1966.

Hildegard of Bingen. *Book of Divine Works, with Letters and Songs*. Translated and edited by Matthew Fox. Santa Fe, N.Mex.: Bear, 1987.

___________. *Hildegard von Bingen's "Physica": The Complete English Translation of Her Classic Work on Health and Healing*. Translated by Priscilla Throop. Rochester, Vt.: Healing Arts Press, 1998.

___________. *Illuminations of Hildegard of Bingen*. Edited by Matthew Fox. Santa Fe, N.Mex.: Bear, 1985.

___________. *Scivias*. Translated by Bruce Hozeski. Santa Fe, N.Mex.: Bear, 1986.

Hōnen. *Hōnen's Senchakushu: Passages on the Selection of the Nembutsu in the Original Vow*. Translated by Hirokawa Takatoshi. Honolulu: University of Hawaii Press, 1998.

Ibn Baṭṭūṭah. *Travels of Ibn Battuta*. Translated and edited by H. A. R. Gibb. 4 vols. Cambridge, England: Cambridge University Press, 1958-2000.

Ibn Gabirol. *Selected Poems of Solomon Ibn Gabirol*. Translated by Peter Cole. Princeton, N.J.: Princeton University Press, 2001.

Ibn Khaldūn. *Ibn Khaldūn and Tamerlane: Their Historic Meeting in Damascus, 1401 A.D*. Translated by Walter J. Fischel. Berkeley: University of California Press, 1952.

Isidore of Seville. *History of the Kings of the Goths, Vandals, and Suevi*. Translated by Guido Donini and Gordon B. Ford, Jr. 2d rev. ed. Leiden, the Netherlands: E. J. Brill, 1970.

Jāḥiẓ, al-. *Sobriety and Mirth: A Selection of the Shorter Writings of al-Jāḥiẓ*. Translated by Jim Colville. New York: Kegan Paul, 2002.

James I, the Conqueror. *The Chronicle of James I, King of Aragon, Surnamed the Conqueror.* Translated by John Forster. 1883. Reprint. Farnborough, England: Gregg International, 1968.

Joachim of Fiore. *Liber de concordia Novi ac Veteris Testamenti*. Edited by E. Randolph Daniel. Philadelphia: American Philosophical Society, 1983.

Jones, Thomas. *Brut y Tywysogyon: Or, The Chronicle of the Princes*. 2d ed. Cardiff: University of Wales Press, 1973.

Judah ha-Levi. *Ninety-two Poems and Hymns of Yehuda Halevi*. Edited by Richard A. Cohen. Translated by Thomas Kovach, Eva Jospe, and Gilya Gerda Schmidt. Albany: State University of New York Press, 2000.

Julian of Norwich. *A Book of Showings to the Anchoress Julian of Norwich*. Edited by Edmund Colledge and

James Walsh. 2 vols. Toronto: Pontifical Institute of Mediaeval Studies, 1978.

___________. *Revelations of Divine Love*. Translated by Clifton Wolters. Baltimore: Penguin Books, 1973.

Juzjani, Siraj-i Minhaj. *Tabakat-i Nasiri*. Translated by H. G. Raverty. 2 vols. 1881. Reprint. Calcutta, India: Asiatic Society, 1995.

Kardong, Terrence. *Benedict's Rule: A Translation and Commentary*. Collegeville, Minn.: Liturgical Press, 1996.

Kempe, Margery. *The Book of Margery Kempe: A New Translation, Contexts, Criticism*. Translated and edited by Lynn Staley. New York: Norton, 2001.

Khayyám, Omar. *The Algebra of Omar Khayyám*. Translated by Daoud S. Kasir. 1931. Reprint. New York: AMS Press, 1972.

Kim Pu-sik. *Samguk sagi*. Translated and edited by Yi Pyŏng-do. Seoul: Ŭryu Munhwasa, 1977.

Kitabatake, Chikafusa. *A Chronicle of Gods and Sovereigns: "Jinno shotoki" of Kitabatake Chikafusa*. Translated by H. Paul Varley. New York: Columbia University Press, 1980.

Koryŏsa. Edited by Chŏng Inji, et el. Seoul: Kyŏngin Munhwasa, 1972.

Kritovoulos. *History of Mehmed the Conqueror*. Translated by Charles T. Riggs. Princeton, N.J.: Princeton University Press, 1954.

The Legend and Writings of Saint Clare of Assisi. St. Bonaventure, N.Y.: Franciscan Institute, 1953.

Levi Ben Gershom. *The Wars of the Lord: Book One: The Immortality of the Soul*. Translated by Seymour Feldman. Philadelphia: Jewish Publication Society, 1984.

___________. *The Wars of the Lord: Book Two, Book Three, and Book Four*. Translated by Seymour Feldman. Philadelphia: Jewish Publication Society, 1987.

Li Bo. *Banished Immortal: Visions of Li T'ai-po*. Translated by Sam Hamill. Fredonia, N.Y.: White Pine Press, 1987.

___________. *Li Pai: Two Hundred Selected Poems*. Translated by Rewi Alley. 1980. Reprint. Hongkong: Joint Publishing, 1987.

___________. *The Selected Poems of Li Po*. Translated by David Hinton. New York: New Directions, 1996.

Li Qingzhao. *As Though Dreaming: The Tz'u of Pure Jade*. Translated by Lenore Mayhew and William McNaughton. Berkeley, Calif.: Serendipity Books, 1977.

___________. *Li Ch'ing-chao: Complete Poems*. Translated and edited by Kenneth Rexroth and Ling Chung. New York: New Directions, 1979.

The Life of Cola di Rienzo. Translated by John Wright. Toronto: Pontifical Institute of Mediaeval Studies, 1975.

Liudprand, Bishop of Cremona. *The Embassy to Constantinople and Other Writings*. Translated by F. A. Wright, edited by John Julius Norwich. 1930. Reprint. Rutland, Vt.: Charles E. Tuttle, 1993.

Llull, Ramón. *Doctor Illuminatus: A Ramón Llull Reader*, edited and translated by Anthony Bonner. Princeton, N.J.: Princeton University Press, 1993.

___________. *Selected Works of Ramón Llull, 1232-1316*. Edited and translated by Anthony Bonner. 2 vols. Princeton, N.J.: Princeton University Press, 1985.

Maimonides, Moses. *Rambam: Readings in the Philosophy of Moses Maimonides*. Translated by Lenn Evan Goodman. New York: Viking Press, 1976.

Maitland, F. W., ed. *Bracton's Note Book: A Collection of Cases Decided in the King's Court During the Reign of Henry the Third*. 3 vols. 1887. Reprint. Buffalo, N.Y.: W. S. Hein, 1999.

Maurice. *Maurice's Strategikon: Handbook of Byzantine Military Strategy*. Translated by George T. Dennis. Philadelphia: University of Pennsylvania Press, 1984.

Mi Fei. *Mi Fu on Ink-Stones*. Translated by R. H. van Gulik. Peking: H. Vetch, 1938.

Müneccimbasi, Ahmet ibn Lutfullah. *A History of Sharvan and Darband in the Tenth-Eleventh Centuries*. Translated and edited by V. Minorsky. Cambridge, England: W. Heffer, 1958.

Murasaki Shikibu. *The Diary of Lady Murasaki*. Translated by Richard Bowring. London: Penguin, 1999.

___________. *The Tale of Genji*. Translated by Royall Tyler. 2 vols. New York: Viking, 2001.

Neel, Carol, ed. *Handbook for William: A Carolingian Woman's Counsel for Her Son*. Lincoln: University of Nebraska Press, 1991.

Nichiren. *Nichiren: Selected Writings*. Translated by Laurel R. Rood. Honolulu: University of Hawaii Press, 1980.

Nicholas of Autrecourt. *Nicholas of Autrecourt: His Correspondence with Master Giles and Bernard of Arezzo, a Critical Edition from the Two Parisian Manuscripts*. Introduction, translation, explanatory notes, and indexes by L. M. de Rijk. New York: E. J. Brill, 1994.

Nihongi: Chronicles of Japan from the Earliest Times to A.D. 697. Translated by W. G. Aston. 1896. Reprint. Tokyo: Charles E. Tuttle, 1972.

Nijō. *The Confessions of Lady Nijō*. Translated by Karen Brazell. Stanford, Calif.: Stanford University Press, 1973.

Niẓām al-Mulk. *The Book of Government: Or, Rules for Kings*. Translated by Hubert Darke. Richmond, Surrey, England: Curzon Press, 2002.

Nizāmī Arūzī. *Chahár Maqála (The Four Discourses) of Niẓāmī-i-Arūẓī-i-Samarqandi*. Translated by Edward G. Browne. 1921. Reprint. London: Luzac, 1978.

Ockham, William of. *Guillelmi de Ockham Opera Politica*. Edited by H. S. Offler et al. 3 vols. Manchester, England: Manchester University Press, 1940, 1956, 1963.

___________. *Predestination, God's Foreknowledge, and Future Contingencies*. Translated by Marilyn McCord Adams and Norman Kretzmann. New York: Appleton-Century-Crofts, 1969.

Okagami, the Great Mirror: Fujiwara Michinaga and His Times. Translated by Helen Craig McCullough. Princeton, N.J.: Princeton University Press, 1980.

Ouyang, Xiu. *Love and Time: Poems of Ou-yang Hsiu*. Edited and translated by J. P. Seaton. Port Townsend, Wash.: Copper Canyon Press, 1989.

Paul of Aegina. *The Seven Books of Paulus Aegineta*. Translated by Francis Adams. 3 vols. London: Sydenham Society, 1844-1847.

Paul the Deacon. *History of the Langobards*. Translated by William Dudley Foulke. Philadelphia: University of Pennsylvania Press, 1974.

Pecham, John. *John Pecham and the Science of Optics*. Edited by David C. Lindberg. Madison: University of Wisconsin Press, 1970.

Peregrinus of Maricourt, Petrus. *Epistle of Petrus Peregrinus of Maricourt, to Sygerus of Foucaucourt, Soldier, Concerning the Magnet*. Translated by Silvanus P. Thompson. London: Chiswick Press, 1902.

Petrus, Sarnensis. *The History of the Albigensian Crusade*. Translated by W. A. Sibly and M. D. Sibly. Rochester, N.Y.: Boydell Press, 1998.

Philippi, Donald L., trans. *Kojiki*. Princeton, N. J.: Princeton University Press, 1968.

Polo, Marco. *The Travels of Marco Polo*. Translated by Ronald Latham. 1958. Reprint. New York: Penguin Books, 1996.

Porete, Marguerite. *The Mirror of Simple Souls*. Translated by Ellen Babinsky. New York: Paulist Press, 1993.

Procopius. *History of the Wars of Justinian*. Translated by H. B. Dewing. London: Heinemann, 1928.

___________. *Secret History*. New York: Folio Society, 2000.

Psellus, Michael. *Fourteen Byzantine Rulers: The Chronographia*. Translated by Edgar R. A. Sewter. 1966. Rev. ed. New York: Penguin Books, 1982.

Rūmī, al-. *The Mathnawí of Jalālu'ddin Rūmī*. Translated and edited by Reynold A. Nicholson. Vols. 2, 4, 6. 1926-1934. Reprint. London: Luzac, 1972.

___________. *Mystical Poems of Rūmī, Second Selection*. Translated by Arthur J. Arberry. Chicago: University of Chicago Press 1991.

___________. *The Spiritual Physick of Rhazes*. Translated by Arthur J. Arberry. London: John Murray, 1950.

___________. *Tales from "The Masnavi,"* and *More Tales from "The Masnavi."* Translated by Arthur J. Arberry. 1961-1963. Reprint. Surrey, England: Curzon Press, 1993. Bibliography.

___________. *A Treatise on the Small-Pox and Measles*. Translated by William Alexander Greenhill. London: Sydenham Society, 1848.

Ruysbroek, Willem van. *The Mission of Friar William of Rubruck: His Journey to the Court of the Great Khan Möngke, 1253-1255*. Translated by Peter Jackson. 1900. Reprint. London: Hakluyt Society, 1990.

Saʿdi. *The "Gulistan": Or, Rose Garden of Saʿdi*. Translated by Edward Rehatsek. 1888. Reprint. New York: Putnam, 1965.

___________. *Morals Pointed and Tales Adorned: The "Bustan" of Saʿdi*. Translated by G. M. Wickens. Buffalo, N.Y.: University of Toronto Press, 1974.

Salimbene. *The Chronicle of Salimbene de Adam*. Translated and edited by Joseph L. Baird, Giuseppe Baglivi, and John Robert Kane. Binghamton, N.Y.: Medieval and Renaissance Texts and Studies, 1986.

Sei Shōnagon, *The Pillow Book of Sei Shōnagon*. Translated by Ivan Morris. 1967. Reprint. New York: Columbia University, 1991.

Son-Jara: The Mande Epic. Translated by John William Johnson. 3d ed. Bloomington: Indiana University Press, 2003.

Su Dongpo. *Selected Poems of Su Tung-p'o*. Translated by Burton Watson. Port Townsend, Wash.: Copper Canyon Press, 1994.

Sunjata: Three Mandika Versions. Edited by Gordon Innes. London: University of London, 1974.

Ṭabarī, al-. *Biographies of the Prophet's Companions and Their Successors*. Translated by Ella Landau-Tasseron. Albany: State University of New York Press, 1998.

___________. *The Reign of al-Muʿtasim (833-842).* Translated by Elma Marin. New Haven, Conn.: American Oriental Society, 1951.

The Taiheiki: A Chronicle of Medieval Japan. Translated by Helen Craig McCullough. 1959. Reprint. Tokyo: Charles E. Tuttle, 1979.

A Tale of Flowering Fortunes: Annals of Japanese Aristocratic Life in the Heian Period. 2 vols. Translated by William McCullough and Helen Craig McCullough. Stanford, Calif.: Stanford University Press, 1980.

The Tale of the Heike. Translated by Helen Craig McCullough. Stanford, Calif.: Stanford University Press, 1988.

Theoleptos of Philadelphia. *The Life and Letters of Theoleptos of Philadelphia.* Edited by Angela Constantinides Hero. Brookline, Mass.: Hellenic College Press, 1994.

Theophanes. *The Chronicle of Theophanes Confessor: Byzantine and Near Eastern History, A.D. 284-813.* Translated by Cyril Mango and Roger Scott. New York: Oxford University Press, 1997.

The Trotula: A Medieval Compendium of Women's Medicine. Edited and translated by Monica H. Green. Philadelphia: University of Pennsylvania Press, 2001.

Tursun Beg. *The History of Mehmed the Conqueror.* Edited and translated by Halil Inalcik and Rhoads Murphey. Chicago: Bibliotheca Islamica, 1978.

Utbi, Abdul Nasr Muhammad bin Muhammad al Jabbar al. *Kitāb-i-Yamini.* Translated by James Reynolds. 1858. Reprint. Lahore, Pakistan: Qausain, 1975.

Valla, Lorenzo. *The Treatise of Lorenzo Valla on the Donation of Constantine.* Translated by Christopher B. Coleman. Toronto: University of Toronto Press in association with the Renaissance Society of America, 1993.

Venette, Jean de. *The Chronicle of Jean de Venette.* Translated by Jean Birdsall. Edited by Richard A. Newhall. New York: Columbia University Press, 1953.

Villani, Giovanni. *Villani's "Chronicle": Being Selections from the First Nine Books of the "Chroniche fiorentine" of Giovanni Villani.* Translated by Rose E. Selfe. 2d ed. London: Constable, 1906.

Villehardouin, Geoffroi de, and Jean de Joinville. *Memoirs of the Crusades.* Translated by Sir Frank Marzials. Reprint. Westport, Conn.: Greenwood Press, 1983.

The Vinland Sagas: The Norse Discovery of America. Translated by Magnus Magnusson and Hermann Pálsson. New York: Penguin Books, 1970.

Wadding, Luke, ed. *Annales Minorum seu Trium Ordinum.* 25 vols. Rome: St. Francisco Institutorum, 1731-1886.

Wang Wei. *Laughing Lost in the Mountains: Poems of Wang Wei.* Translated by Tony Barnstone, Willis Barnstone, and Xu Haixin. Hanover, N.H.: University Press of New England, 1991.

___________. *Poems of Wang Wei.* Translated by G. W. Robinson. Baltimore: Penguin Books, 1973.

___________. *The Poetry of Wang Wei: New Translations and Commentary.* Translated by Pauline Yu. Bloomington: Indiana University Press, 1980.

William of Tyre. *A History of Deeds Done Beyond the Sea.* 1941. Reprint. New York: Octagon Books, 1976.

Wu Cheng'en. *The Journey to the West.* 4 vols. Translated by Anthony C. Yu. Chicago: University of Chicago Press, 1977.

Yamagiwa, Joseph K., trans. *The Okagami: A Japanese Historical Tale.* Rutland, Vt.: Charles E. Tuttle, 1966.

Yaqut. *The Introductory Chapters of Yaqut's "Muʿjam al-buldān."* Translated and annotated by Wadie Jwaideh. Leiden, the Netherlands: E. J. Brill, 1959.

Yoshitsune: A Fifteenth-Century Japanese Chronicle. Translated by Helen Craig McCullough. Stanford, Calif.: Stanford University Press, 1966.

Zeami Motokiyo. *Kadensho.* Translated by Sakurai Chuichi, Hayashi Shuseki, Satoi Rokuro, and Miyai Bin. Kyoto: Sumiya Shinobe Publishing Institute, 1968.

___________. *On the Art of the Nō Drama: The Major Treatises of Zeami.* Translated by J. Thomas Rimer and Yamazaki Masakazu. Princeton, N.J.: Princeton University Press, 1984.

COMPILATIONS

Albertson, Clinton, ed. and trans. *Anglo-Saxon Saints and Heroes.* Bronx, N.Y.: Fordham University Press, 1967.

Anderson, Alan Orr, comp. and trans. *Early Sources of Scottish History, A.D. 500 to 1286.* 2 vols. Edinburgh: Oliver and Boyd, 1922.

Andrea, Alfred J, ed. *Contemporary Sources for the Fourth Crusade.* Boston: Brill, 2000.

Armstrong, Regis J., J. A. Wayne Hellman, and William J. Short, eds. *Francis of Assisi: Early Documents.* 3 vols. New York: New City Press, 1999-2001.

Ashdown, Margaret, trans. and ed. *English and Norse Documents Relating to the Reign of Ethelred the Unready.* Cambridge, England: Cambridge University Press, 1930.

Barton, Simon, and Richard Fletcher, trans. and eds. *The World of El Cid: Chronicles of the Spanish Reconquest*. New York: St. Martin's Press, 2000.

Bowie, Fiona, ed. *Beguine Spirituality: Mystical Writings of Mechtild of Magdeburg, Beatrice of Nazareth, and Hadewijch of Brabant*. Translated by Oliver Davies. New York: Crossroad, 1990.

Carlerius, Egidius, Johannes Tinctoris, and Carlo Valguilo. *"That Liberal and Virtuous Art": Three Humanist Treatises on Music*. Edited and translated by J. Donald Cullington. Newtonabbey, Ireland: University of Ulster, 2001.

Carolingian Chronicles: Frankish Royal Annals and Nithard's Histories. Translated by Bernhard W. Scholz and Barbara Rogers. Ann Arbor: University of Michigan Press, 1970.

Chang, Kang-i Sun, and Haun Saussy, eds. *Women Writers of Traditional China: An Anthology of Poetry and Criticism*. Stanford, Calif.: Stanford University Press, 1999.

Crawford, Anne, ed. *The Letters of the Queens of England, 1066-1547*. New ed. Stroud: Sutton, 2002.

Crow, Martin M., and Clair C. Olson, eds. *Chaucer Life-Records*. Austin: University of Texas Press, 1966.

De Bary, William Theodore, et al., comps. *Sources of Japanese Tradition*. Vol. 1. 2d ed. New York: Columbia University Press, 2001.

De Bary, William Theodore, Irene Bloom, and Wing-tsit Chan, comps. *Sources of Chinese Tradition*. 2d ed. New York: Columbia University Press, 1999-2000.

Duichev, Ivan, ed. *Kiril and Methodius, Founders of Slavic Writing: A Collection of Sources and Critical Studies*. Translated by Spass Nikolev. New York: Columbia University Press, 1985.

Ernst, Carl W., trans., and comp. *Teachings of Sufism*. Boston: Shambhala, 1999.

Hakluyt, Richard, comp. *The Texts and Versions of John de Plano Carpini and William de Rubruquis, as Printed for the First Time by Hakluyt in 1598, Together with Some Shorter Pieces*. Edited by C. Raymond Beazley. London: Hakluyt Society, 1903. Reprint. Nendeln/Liechtenstein: Kraus Reprint, 1967.

Head, Thomas, ed. Medieval Hagiography: An Anthology. New York: Garland, 2000.

The Laws of the Earliest English Kings. Edited and translated by F. L. Attenborough. Cambridge, England: Cambridge University Press, 1922.

Lehner, Francis C., ed. *Saint Dominic: Biographical Documents*. Washington, D.C.: Thomist Press, 1964.

McCullough, Helen Craig, comp. and ed. *Classical Japanese Prose: An Anthology*. Stanford, Calif.: Stanford University Press, 1990.

Maitland, F. W., ed. *Select Passages from the Works of Bracton and Azo*. London: B. Quaritch, 1895.

Morillo, Stephen, ed. *The Battle of Hastings: Sources and Interpretations*. Rochester, N.Y.: Boydell Press, 1996.

O'Donovan, Oliver, and Joan Lockwood O'Donovan, eds. *From Irenaeus to Grotius: A Sourcebook in Christian Political Thought, 100-1625*. Grand Rapids, Mich.: William B. Eerdmans, 1999.

Pine, Red, trans. *Poems of the Masters: China's Classic Anthology of T'ang and Sung Dynasty Verse*. Port Townsend, Wash.: Copper Canyon Press, 2003.

Press, Alan R., ed. and trans. *Anthology of Troubadour Lyric Poetry*. Austin: University of Texas Press, 1971.

Rebay, Luciano, ed. *Italian Poetry: A Selection from Saint Francis of Assisi to Salvatore Quasimodo*. New York: Dover Books, 1969.

Robertson, A. J., ed. and trans. *The Laws of the Kings of England from Edmund to Henry I*. Felinfach, Wales: Llanerch, 2000.

Sells, Michael A., ed. and trans. *Early Islamic Mysticism: Sufi, Qurʾān, Mirʿaj, Poetic, and Theological Writings*. New York: Paulist Press, 1996.

Seth, Vikram, trans. *Three Chinese Poets: Translations of Poems by Wang Wei, Li Bai, and Du Fu*. Boston: Faber and Faber, 1992.

Somerville, Robert, and Bruce C. Brasington, trans. and comps. *Prefaces to Canon Law Books in Latin Christianity: Selected Translations, 500-1245*. New Haven, Conn.: Yale University Press, 1998.

Staunton, Michael, trans. *The Lives of Thomas Becket*. New York: Palgrave, 2001.

Thiébaux, Marcelle, ed. and trans. *The Writings of Medieval Women*. 2d ed. New York: Garland, 1994.

Treharne, Reginald F., and I. J. Sanders, eds. *Documents of the Baronial Movement of Reform and Rebellion, 1258-1267*. Oxford, England: Clarendon Press, 1973.

Waddell, Helen, ed. and trans. *Medieval Latin Lyrics*. 1933. Reprint. Baltimore: Penguin Books, 1968.

Walker, Greg, ed. *Medieval Drama: An Anthology*. Malden, Mass.: Blackwell, 2000.

Wilson, Katharina M., ed. *Medieval Women Writers*. Athens: University of Georgia Press, 1984.

GENERAL STUDIES AND REFERENCE WORKS

Backman, Clifford R. *The Worlds of Medieval Europe*. New York: Oxford University Press, 2002.

Bartlett, Robert, ed. *Medieval Panorama*. Los Angeles: J. Paul Getty Museum, 2001.

Beatty, J., and O. Johnson. *Heritage of Western Civilization*. 2 vols. 8th ed. Englewood Cliffs, N.J.: Prentice Hall, 1995.

Cook, William R., and Ronald B. Herzman. *The Medieval World View: An Introduction*. 2d ed. New York: Oxford University Press, 2004.

Evans, G. R. *Fifty Key Medieval Thinkers*. New York: Routledge, 2002.

Frayling, Christopher. *Strange Landscape: A Journey Through the Middle Ages*. London: BBC Books, 1995.

Gyug, Richard F., ed. *Medieval Cultures in Contact*. New York: Fordham University Press, 2003.

Hackett, Jeremiah, ed. *World Eras: Medieval Europe, 814-1350*. Detroit: Gale Group, 2001.

Holmes, George, ed. *The Oxford Illustrated History of Medieval Europe*. New York: Oxford University Press, 2001.

Huizinga, Johan. *The Waning of the Middle Ages*. London: Edward Arnold, 1937. Reprint. Mineola, N.Y.: Dover, 1999.

Jordan, William Chester, ed. *Dictionary of the Middle Ages: Supplement*. New York: Scribner, 2004.

Linehan, Peter, and Janet L. Nelson, eds. *The Medieval World*. New York: Routledge, 2001.

Medieval World. Danbury, Conn.: Grolier Educational, 2001.

The Middle Ages. Vol. 3 in *World History by Era*. San Diego, Calif.: Greenhaven Press, 2001.

Perry, Curtis, ed. *Material Culture and Cultural Materialisms in the Middle Ages and the Renaissance*. Turnhout, Belgium: Brepols, 2001.

Rollo-Koster, Joëlle, ed. *Medieval and Early Modern Ritual: Formalized Behavior in Europe, China, and Japan*. Boston: Brill, 2002.

Rosenwein, Barbara H. *A Short History of the Middle Ages*. Orchard Park, N.Y.: Broadview Press, 2002.

Strayer, Joseph R., ed. *Dictionary of the Middle Ages*. New York: Scribner, 1982-1989.

Vauchez, Andre, Barrie Dobson, and Michael Lapidge, eds. *Encyclopedia of the Middle Ages*. Translated by Adrian Walford. Chicago: Fitzroy Dearborn, 2000.

CULTURAL HISTORY BY SUBJECT

CROSS-CULTURAL, DIASPORIC, AND GENERAL RELIGIOUS STUDIES

Ahituv, Shmuel, ed. *A Historical Atlas of the Jewish People: From the Time of the Patriarchs to the Present*. New York: Continuum, 2003.

Amundsen, Darrel W., ed. *Medicine, Society, and Faith in the Ancient and Medieval Worlds*. Baltimore: The Johns Hopkins University Press, 1996.

Biller, Peter, and Joseph Ziegler. *Religion and Medicine in the Middle Ages*. Suffolk, England: York Medieval Press, 2001.

Blumenfeld-Kosinski, R., D. Robertson, and N. Bradley Warren, eds. *The Vernacular Spirit: Essays on Medieval Religious Literature*. New York: Palgrave, 2002.

Declercq, Georges. *Anno Domini: The Origins of the Christian Era*. Turnhout, Belgium: Brepols, 2000.

Ekelund, Robert B, Jr., et al., eds. *Sacred Trust: The Medieval Church as an Economic Firm*. New York: Oxford University Press, 1996.

England, John C. *The Hidden History of Christianity in Asia*. Delhi: Indian Society for the Promotion of Christian Knowledge, 1996.

Evans, G. R., ed. *The Medieval Theologians*. Malden, Mass.: Blackwell, 2001.

Farmer, David Hugh. *The Oxford Dictionary of Saints*. New York: Oxford University Press, 2003.

Faulkner, Quentin. *Wiser than Despair: The Evolution of Ideas in the Relationship of Music and the Christian Church*. Westport, Conn.: Greenwood Press, 1996.

Finley, Mitch. *The Seeker's Guide to the Christian Story*. Chicago: Loyola Press, 1998.

Fletcher, R. A. *The Barbarian Conversion: From Paganism to Christianity*. Berkeley: University of California Press, 1999.

Hecht, N. S., et al., eds. *An Introduction to the History and Sources of Jewish Law*. New York: Oxford University Press, 1996.

Idel, Moshe, and Mortimer Ostow, eds. *Jewish Mystical Leaders in the Thirteenth Century*. Northvale, N.J.: Jason Aronson, 1998.

Inglis, John, ed. *Medieval Philosophy and the Classical Tradition in Islam, Judaism, and Christianity*. Richmond, Surrey, England: Curzon, 2002.

Irvin, Dale T., and Scott W. Sunquist. *Earliest Christianity to 1453*. Vol. 1 in *History of the World Christian Movement*. Orbis, N.Y.: Maryknoll, 2001.

Ladner, Gerhart B. *God, Cosmos, and Humankind: The World of Early Christian Symbolism*. Translated by

Thomas Dunlap. Berkeley: University of California Press, 1995.

Liu, Xinru. *Silk and Religion: An Exploration of Material Life and the Thought of People, A.D. 600-1200.* New York: Oxford University Press, 1996.

MacMullen, Ramsay. *Christianity and Paganism in the Fourth to Eighth Centuries.* New Haven, Conn.: Yale University Press, 1997.

Margolies, Morris B. *Twenty Twenty: Jewish Visionaries Through Two Thousand Years.* Northvale, N.J.: Jason Aronson, 2000.

Marrone, Steven P. *The Light of Thy Countenance: Science and Knowledge of God in the Thirteenth Century.* 2 vols. Boston: Brill, 2001.

Moffett, Samuel Hugh. *Beginnings to 1500.* Vol. 1 in *A History of Christianity in Asia.* Orbis, N.Y.: Maryknoll, 1998.

Scholem, Gershom G. *Major Trends in Jewish Mysticism.* New York: Schocken Books, 1995.

Seeskin, Kenneth. *Searching for a Distant God: The Legacy of Maimonides.* New York: Oxford University Press, 2000.

Sen, Tansen. *Buddhism, Diplomacy, and Trade: The Realignment of Sino-Indian Relations, 600-1400.* Honolulu: University of Hawaii Press, 2003.

Valantasis, Richard, ed. *Religions of Late Antiquity in Practice.* Princeton, N.J.: Princeton University Press, 2000.

Watkins, Dom Basil, ed. *The Book of Saints: A Comprehensive Biographical Dictionary.* 7th rev. ed. New York: Continuum, 2002.

PHILOSOPHY AND THE ARTS

Anidjar, Gil. *"Our Place in al-Andalus": Kabbalah, Philosophy, Literature in Arab Jewish Letters.* Stanford, Calif.: Stanford University Press, 2002.

Barnhart, Richard M., et al. *Three Thousand Years of Chinese Painting.* New Haven, Conn.: Yale University Press, 1997.

Borchert, Till-Holger. *Age of Van Eyck: The Mediterranean World and Early Netherlandish Painting, 1430-1530.* New York: Thames and Hudson, 2002.

Butterfield, Ardis. *Poetry and Music in Medieval France: From Jean Renart to Guillaume de Machaut.* New York: Cambridge University Press, 2002.

Calkins, Robert G. *Medieval Architecture in Western Europe: From A.D. 300 to 1500.* New York: Oxford University Press, 1998.

Curran, S. Terrie. *English from Cædmon to Chaucer: The Literary Development of English.* Prospect Heights, Ill.: Waveland Press, 2002.

De Hamel, Christopher. *The British Library Guide to Manuscript Illumination: History and Techniques.* Toronto: University of Toronto Press, 2001.

De Vos, Dirk. *The Flemish Primitives: The Masterpieces.* Princeton, N.J.: Princeton University Press, 2002.

Dini, Giuletta Chelazzi, Alessandro Angelini, and Bernardina Sani. *Sienese Painting: From Duccio to the Birth of the Baroque.* New York: H. N. Abrams, 1998.

Echard, Siân. *Arthurian Narrative in the Latin Tradition.* New York: Cambridge University Press, 1998.

Faulkner, Quentin. *Wiser than Despair: The Evolution of Ideas in the Relationship of Music and the Christian Church.* Westport, Conn.: Greenwood Press, 1996.

Flynn, William T. *Medieval Music as Medieval Exegesis.* Lanham, Md.: Scarecrow Press, 1999.

Frankl, Paul, and Paul Crossley. *Gothic Architecture.* Rev. ed. New Haven, Conn.: Yale University Press, 2000.

Fubini, Riccardo. *Humanism and Secularization: From Petrarch to Valla.* Durham, N.C.: Duke University Press, 2003.

Gao, Jianping. *The Expressive Act in Chinese Art: From Calligraphy to Painting.* Stockholm: Almqvist & Wiksell International, 1996.

Hartt, Frederick, and David G. Wilkins. *History of Italian Renaissance Art: Painting, Sculpture, Architecture.* 5th ed. New York: H. N. Abrams, 2003.

Hen, Yitzhak. *The Royal Patronage of Liturgy in Frankish Gaul to the Death of Charles the Bald.* Woodbridge: Boydell Press for the Henry Bradshaw Society, 2001.

Heng, Geraldine. *Empire of Magic: Medieval Romance and the Politics of Cultural Fantasy.* New York: Columbia University Press, 2003.

Horomitsu, Washizuka, et al. *Enlightenment Embodied: The Art of the Japanese Buddhist Sculptor, Seventh to Fourteenth Centuries.* Translated and edited by Reiko Tomii and Kathleen M. Fraiello. New York: Agency for Cultural Affairs, Government of Japan, and Japan Society, 1997.

Ierodiakonou, Katerina, ed. *Byzantine Philosophy and Its Ancient Sources.* New York: Oxford University Press, 2002.

Inglis, John, ed. *Medieval Philosophy and the Classical Tradition in Islam, Judaism and Christianity.* Richmond, Surrey, England: Curzon, 2002.

Jackson, W. H., and S. A. Ranawake, eds. *The Arthur of the Germans: The Arthurian Legend in Medieval German and Dutch Literature*. Cardiff: University of Wales Press, 2000.

Kessler, Herbert L. *Spiritual Seeing: Picturing God's Invisibility in Medieval Art*. Philadelphia: University of Pennsylvania Press, 2000.

Kowalski, Jeff Karl, ed. *Mesoamerican Architecture as a Cultural Symbol*. New York: Oxford University Press, 1999.

Ladis, Andrew, ed. *Franciscanism, the Papacy, and Art in the Age of Giotto*. New York: Garland, 1998.

____________. *Giotto and the World of Early Italian Art: An Anthology of Literature*. New York: Garland, 1998.

Liu Shu-hsien. *Understanding Confucian Philosophy, Classical and Sung-Ming*. Westport, Conn.: Greenwood Press, 1998.

Marenbon, John, ed. *Medieval Philosophy*. New York: Routledge, 1998.

Mayernik, David. *Timeless Cities: An Architect's Reflections on Renaissance Italy*. Boulder, Colo.: Westview Press, 2003.

Menocal, Maria Rosa, Raymond P. Scheindlin, and Michael Sells, eds. *The Literature of Al-Andalus*. New York: Cambridge University Press, 2000.

Murck, Alfreda. *Poetry and Painting in Song China: The Subtle Art of Dissent*. Cambridge, Mass.: Harvard University Press, 2000.

Ortolani, Benito. *The Japanese Theater: From Shamanistic Ritual to Contemporary Pluralism*. Rev. ed. Princeton, N.J.: Princeton University Press, 1995.

Paoletti, John T., and Gary M. Radke. *Art in Renaissance Italy*. 2d ed. Upper Saddle River, N. J.: Harry N. Abrams, 2002.

Paolucci, Antonio. *The Origins of Renaissance Art: The Bapistery Doors, Florence*. Translated by Françoise Pouncey Chiarini. New York: Braziller, 1996.

Pillsbury, Joanne, ed. *Moche Art and Archaeology in Ancient Peru*. Washington, D.C.: National Gallery of Art, 2001.

Pope-Hennessy, John. *Italian Gothic Sculpture*. Vol. 1 in *An Introduction to Italian Sculpture*. 4th ed. London: Phaidon Press, 1996.

Quillen, Carol E. *Rereading the Renaissance: Petrarch, Augustine, and the Language of Humanism*. Ann Arbor: University of Michigan Press, 1998.

Rey, Roger. *Bede, Rhetoric, and the Creation of Christian Latin Culture*. Jarrow, England: St. Paul's Church, 1997.

Robinson, Cynthia. *In Praise of Song: The Making of Courtly Culture in al-Andalus and Provence, 1005-1134 A.D.* Boston: Brill, 2002.

Stanley-Baker, Joan. *Japanese Art*. Rev. ed. New York: Thames and Hudson, 2000.

Stinger, Charles L. *The Renaissance in Rome*. 1985. Reprint. Bloomington: Indiana University Press, 1998.

Stratford, Neil. *Studies in Burgundian Romanesque Sculpture*. 2 vols. London: Pindar Press, 1998.

Strohm, Reinhard, and Bonnie J. Blackburn, eds. *Music as Concept and Practice in the Late Middle Ages*. Vol 3., pt. 1 in *The New Oxford History of Music*. 2d ed. New York: Oxford University Press, 2001.

Sturman, Peter Charles. *Mi Fu: Style and the Art of Calligraphy in Northern Song China*. New Haven, Conn.: Yale University Press, 1997.

Sullivan, Michael. *The Arts of China*. 4th ed. Berkeley: University of California Press, 1999.

____________. *The Three Perfections: Chinese Painting, Poetry, and Calligraphy*. Rev. ed. New York: George Braziller, 1999.

Sullivan, Robert G. *Justice and the Social Context of Early Middle High German Literature*. New York: Routledge, 2001.

Tanenbaum, Adena. *The Contemplative Soul: Hebrew Poetry and Philosophical Theory in Medieval Spain*. Boston: Brill, 2002.

Treitler, Leo. *With Voice and Pen: Coming to Know Medieval Song and How It Was Made*. New York: Oxford University Press, 2003.

Understanding Art: A Reference Guide to Painting, Sculpture, and Architecture in the Romanesque, Gothic, Renaissance, and Baroque Periods. 2 vols. Armonk, N.Y.: Sharpe Reference, 2000.

Walker, Paul Robert. *The Feud that Sparked the Renaissance: How Brunelleschi and Ghiberti Changed the Art World*. New York: William Morrow, 2002.

Warning, Rainer. *The Ambivalences of Medieval Religious Drama*. Translated by Steven Rendall. Stanford, Calif.: Stanford University Press, 2001.

Watt, W. Montgomery. *The Formative Period of Islamic Thought*. Boston: Oneworld, 1998.

____________. *Islamic Philosophy and Theology: An Extended Survey*. 2d ed. Edinburgh: Edinburgh University Press, 1995.

Wippel, John F. *Mediaeval Reactions to the Encounter Between Faith and Reason*. Milwaukee, Wis.: Marquette University Press, 1995.

Witt, Ronald G. *In the Footsteps of the Ancients: The Origins of Humanism from Lovato to Bruni*. Boston: Brill, 2000.

Science, Technology, and Trade

Amundsen, Darrel W., ed. *Medicine, Society, and Faith in the Ancient and Medieval Worlds*. Baltimore: The Johns Hopkins University Press, 1996.

Arrault, Alain, and Catherin Jami, eds. *Science and Technology in East Asia: The Legacy of Joseph Needham*. Turnhout, Belgium: Brepoplis, 2001.

Aveni, Anthony F., ed. *Skywatchers*. Rev. ed. Austin: University of Texas Press, 2001.

Bakar, Osman. *The History and Philosophy of Islamic Science*. Cambridge, England: Islamic Texts Society, 1999.

Bloom, Jonathan M. *Paper Before Print: The History and Impact of Paper on the Islamic World*. New Haven, Conn.: Yale University Press, 2001.

Bovill, E. W. *The Golden Trade of the Moors*. 2d ed., rev. Princeton, N.J.: Marcus Weiner, 1995.

Bradbury, Jim. *The Medieval Archer.* Rochester, N.Y.: Boydell and Brewer, 1999.

Cajori, Florian. *A History of Mathematics*. 1931. 5th ed. Providence, R.I.: AMS Chelsea, 2000.

Cipolla, Carlo M. *Clocks and Culture, 1300-1700*. 1978. Reprint. New York: Norton, 2003.

Favier, Jean. *Gold and Spices: The Rise of Commerce in the Middle Ages*. Translated by Caroline Higgitt. New York: Holmes and Meier, 1998.

Febvre, Lucien, and Henri-Jean Martin. Translated by David Gerard. 1976. Reprint. *The Coming of the Book: The Impact of Printing, 1450-1800*. London: Verso, 1997.

Fleet, Kate. *European and Islamic Trade in the Early Ottoman State: The Merchants of Genoa and Turkey.* New York: Cambridge University Press, 1999.

French, R. K. *Medicine Before Science: The Rational and Learned Doctor from the Middle Ages to the Enlightenment*. New York: Cambridge University Press, 2003.

Friedman, John Block, and Kristen Mossler Figg, eds. *Trade, Travel, and Exploration in the Middle Ages: An Encyclopedia*. New York: Garland, 2000.

García-Ballester, Luís. *Galen and Galenism: Theory and Medical Practice from Antiquity to the European Renaissance*. Burlington, Vt.: Ashgate, 2002.

____________. *Medicine in a Multicultural Society: Christian, Jewish, and Muslim Practitioners in the Spanish Kingdoms, 1222-1610*. Aldershot, England: Ashgate, 2001.

Hardy, Robert. *The Longbow: A Social and Military History.* London: Bois d'Arc Press, 1998.

Hogendijk, Jan P., and Abdelhamid I. Sabra, eds. *The Enterprise of Science in Islam: New Perspectives*. Cambridge, Mass.: MIT Press, 2003.

Huff, Toby E. *The Rise of Early Modern Science: Islam, China, and the West*. 2d ed. New York: Cambridge University Press, 2003.

Joseph, George Gheverghese. *The Crest of the Peacock: The Non-European Roots of Mathematics*. Rev. ed. Princeton, N.J.: Princeton University Press, 2000.

Kennedy, Edward S. *Astronomy and Astrology in the Medieval Islamic World.* Brookfield, Vt.: Ashgate, 1998.

Kotek, Samuel S., and Luís García-Ballester, eds. *Medicine and Medical Ethics in Medieval and Early Modern Spain: An Intercultural Approach*. Jerusalem: Magnes Press, 1996.

Lakshmikantham, V., and S. Leela. *The Origin of Mathematics*. Lanham, Md.: University Press of America, 2000.

Landes, David S. *Revolution in Time: Clocks and the Making of the Modern World.* Rev. ed. Cambridge, Mass.: Harvard University Press, 2000.

Major, John S. *The Silk Route: Seven Thousand Miles of History.* New York: HarperCollins, 1995.

Man, John. *Gutenberg: How One Man Remade the World with Words*. New York: John Wiley & Sons, 2002.

Manzanilla, Linda, ed. *Emergence and Change in Early Urban Societies*. New York: Plenum Press, 1997.

O'Boyle, Cornelius. *The Art of Medicine: Medical Teaching at the University of Paris, 1250-1400*. Boston: Brill, 1998.

Ptak, Roderich. *China and the Asian Seas: Trade, Travel, and Visions of the Others, 1400-1750*. Brookfield, Vt.: Ashgate, 1998.

Rashed, Roshdi, ed. *Encyclopedia of the History of Arabic Science*. 3 vols. New York: Routledge, 1996.

Rawcliffe, Carole. *Medicine and Society in Later Medieval England*. Phoenix Mill, England: Alan Sutton, 1995.

Selin, Helaine, ed. *Mathematics Across Cultures: The History of Non-Western Mathematics*. Boston: Kluwer Academic, 2000.

Sen, Tansen. *Buddhism, Diplomacy, and Trade: The Realignment of Sino-Indian Relations, 600-1400*. Honolulu: University of Hawaii Press, 2003.

Shubao, Luo, ed. *An Illustrated History of Printing in Ancient China*. Kowloon, Hong Kong: City University of Hong Kong Press, 1998.

Sonnenfeld, Albert, Jean-Louis Flandrin, and Massimo Montanari. *Food: A Culinary History From Antiquity to the Present*. Translated by Clarissa Botsford et al. New York: Columbia University Press, 1999.

Spufford, Peter. *Power and Profit: The Merchant in Medieval Europe*. London: Thames & Hudson, 2002.

Stephens, Mitchell. *A History of News*. Fort Worth, Texas: Harcourt Brace, 1997.

Stockwell, Foster. *Westerners in China: A History of Exploration and Trade, Ancient Times Through the Present*. Jefferson, N.C.: McFarland, 2003.

Temple, Robert K. G. *The Genius of China: Three Thousand Years of Science, Discovery, and Invention*. 1986. Reprint. New York: Prion Books, 1999.

Turner, Howard R. *Science in Medieval Islam: An Illustrated Introduction*. Austin: University of Texas Press, 1997.

Weber, Max. *The History of Commercial Partnerships in the Middle Ages*. Translated by Lutz Kaelber. Lanham, Md.: Rowman and Littlefield, 2003.

Wood, Frances. *The Silk Road: Two Thousand Years in the Heart of Asia*. Berkeley: University of California Press, 2002.

Wyatt, James C. Y. *When Silk Was Gold: Central Asian and Chinese Textiles*. New York: Metropolitan Museum of Art, 1997.

WOMEN IN THE MIDDLE AGES

Ardren, Tracy, ed. *Ancient Maya Women*. Walnut Creek, Calif.: AltaMira Press, 2002.

Bornstein, Daniel, and Roberto Rusconi, eds. *Women and Religion in Medieval and Renaissance Italy*. Translated by Margery J. Schneider. Chicago: University of Chicago Press, 1996.

Cass, Victoria Baldwin. *Dangerous Women: Warriors, Grannies, and Geishas of the Ming*. Lanham, Md.: Rowan & Littlefield, 1999.

Conn, Marie A. *Noble Daughters: Unheralded Women in Western Christianity, Thirteenth to Eighteenth Centuries*. Westport, Conn.: Greenwood Press, 2000.

Cosman, Madeleine Pelner. *Women at Work in Medieval Europe*. New York: Facts on File, 2000.

Dor, Juliette, Lesley Johnson, and Jocelyn Wogan-Browne, eds. *New Trends in Feminine Spirituality: The Holy Women of Liège and Their Impact*. Turnhout: Brepols, Belgium, 1999.

Duggan, Anne J., ed. *Queens and Queenship in Medieval Europe*. Rochester, N.Y.: Boydell Press, 1997.

Falk, Nancy, and Rita Gross, eds. *Unspoken Worlds: Women's Religious Lives in Non-Western Cultures*. 3d ed. Belmont, Calif.: Wadsworth/Thomson Learning, 2001.

Furlong, Monica, ed. *Visions and Longings: Medieval Women Mystics*. Boston: Random House, 1996.

Furst, Lilian R., ed. *Women Healers and Physicians: Climbing a Long Hill*. Lexington: University Press of Kentucky, 1997.

Garland, Lynda. *Byzantine Empresses: Women and Power in Byzantium, A.D. 527-1204*. New York: Routledge, 1999.

Green, Monica. *Women's Healthcare in the Medieval West: Texts and Contexts*. Aldershot, England: Ashgate, 2000.

Hambly, Gavin R. G., ed. *Women in the Medieval Islamic World*. New York: St. Martin's Press, 1998.

Heinemann, Evelyn. *Witches: A Psychoanalytic Exploration of the Killing of Women*. New York: Free Association Books, 2000.

Herrin, Judith. *Women in Purple: Rulers of Medieval Byzantium*. Princeton, N.J.: Princeton University Press, 2001.

James, Liz. *Empresses and Power in Early Byzantium*. New York: Leicester University Press, 2001.

Klassen, John M. *Warring Maidens, Captive Wives, and Hussite Queens: Women and Men at War and at Peace in Fifteenth Century Bohemia*. New York: Columbia University Press, 1999.

Kors, Alan Charles, and Edward Peters, eds. *Witchcraft in Europe, 400-1700: A Documentary History*. 1972. Rev. ed. Philadelphia: University of Pennsylvania Press, 2001.

Larsen, Anne R, and Colette H. Winn, eds. *Writings by Pre-Revolutionary French Women: From Marie de France to Elizabeth Vigée-Le Brun*. New York: Garland, 2000.

Levack, Brian P. *The Witch-Hunt in Early Modern Europe*. 2d ed. Harlow, England: Longman, 1995.

Levy, Howard S. *The Lotus Lovers: The Complete History of the Curious Erotic Custom of Footbinding in China*. 1966. Reprint. Buffalo, N.Y.: Prometheus Books, 1992.

McCash, June Hall, ed. *The Cultural Patronage of Medieval Women*. Athens: University of Georgia Press, 1996.

Mooney, Catherine M., ed. *Gendered Voices: Medieval Saints and Their Interpreters*. Philadelphia: University of Pennsylvania Press, 1999.

Ruch, Barbara, ed. *Engendering Faith: Women and Buddhism in Premodern Japan*. Ann Arbor, Mich.: Center for Japanese Studies, University of Michigan, 2002.

Salisbury, Eve, Georgiana Donavin, and Merrall Llewelyn Price, eds. *Domestic Violence in Medieval Texts*. Gainesville: University Press, of Florida, 2002.

Schmitt, Miriam, and Linda Kulzer, eds. *Medieval Women Monastics: Wisdom's Wellsprings*. Collegeville, Minn.: Liturgical Press, 1996.

Smith, Lesley, and Jane H. M. Taylor, eds. *Women, the Book, and the Godly: Selected Proceedings of the St. Hilda's Conference, 1993*. Rochester, N.Y.: D. S. Brewer, 1995.

Smith, Margaret. *Muslim Women Mystics: The Life and Work of Rābiʿa and Other Women Mystics in Islam*. Boston: Oneworld, 2001.

Stevenson, Barbara, and Cynthia Ho, eds. *Crossing the Bridge: Comparative Essays on Medieval European and Heian Japanese Women Writers*. New York: Palgrave, 2000.

Thurston, Robert W. *Witch, Wicce, Mother Goose: The Rise and Fall of the Witch Hunts in Europe and North America*. New York: Longman, 2001.

Venarde, Bruce L. *Women's Monasticism and Medieval Society: Nunneries in France and England, 890-1215*. Ithaca, N.Y.: Cornell University Press, 1997.

Wang, Ping. *Aching for Beauty: Footbinding in China*. Minneapolis: University of Minnesota Press, 2000.

Sociopolitical and Religious History by Region

Africa

Bovill, E. W. *The Golden Trade of the Moors*. 2d ed., rev. Princeton, N.J.: Marcus Weiner, 1995.

Conrad, David C., ed. *Epic Ancestors of the Sunjata Era: Oral Tradition from the Maninka of Guinea*. Illustrated by Mohamed Chejan Kromah and Sidiki Doumbia. Madison, Wis.: African Studies Program, University of Wisconsin, 1999.

Davidson, Basil, ed. *The African Past: Chronicle from Antiquity to Modern Times*. Boston: Little, Brown, 1964.

Fage, J. D. *A History of West Africa: An Introductory Survey*. 4th ed. New York: Cambridge University Press, 1969.

Falola, Toyin, ed. *Africa*. Durham, N.D.: Carolina Academic Press, 2000.

Hamdun, Said, and Noël King, trans. and eds. *Ibn Battuta in Black Africa*. Foreword by Ross Dunn. Princeton, N.J.: M. Wiener, 1994.

Julien, Charles-André. *History of North Africa: Tunisia, Algeria, Morocco*. Translated by John Petrie, edited by C. C. Stewart and Roger Le Tourneau. London: Routledge & Kegan Paul, 1970.

Ki-Zerbo, Joseph, and Djibril Tamsir Niane, eds. *Africa from the Twelfth to the Sixteenth Century*. Berkeley: University of California Press, 1997.

Le Tourneau, Roger. *The Almohad Movement in North Africa in the Twelfth and Thirteenth Centuries*. Princeton, N.J.: Princeton University Press, 1969.

Munro-Hay, Stuart. *Ethiopia, the Unknown Land: A Cultural and Historical Guide*. London: I. B. Tauris, 2002.

Niane, D. T., ed. *Africa from the Twelfth to the Sixteenth Century*. Vol. 4 in *UNESCO General History of Africa*. Berkeley: University of California Press, 1984.

Russell, Peter. *Portugal, Spain, and the African Atlantic, 1343-1490: Chivalry and Crusade from John of Gaunt to Henry the Navigator and Beyond*. Brookfield, Vt.: Variorum, 1995.

Taha, Abdulwahid Dhanun. *The Muslim Conquest of North Africa and Spain*. London & New York: Routledge, 1989.

Trimingham, J. Spencer. *A History of Islam in West Africa*. London: Oxford University Press, 1962.

Americas

Abbott, David R. *Ceramics and Community Organization Among the Hohokam*. Tucson: University of Arizona Press, 2000.

Bauer, Brian S. *The Sacred Landscape of the Inca: The Cusco Ceque System*. Austin: University of Texas Press, 1998.

Carrasco, David, ed. *Aztec Ceremonial Landscapes*. Niwot: University Press of Colorado, 1999.

Carrasco, Pedro. *The Tenochca Empire of Ancient Mexico: The Triple Alliance of Tenochtitlán, Tetzcoco, and Tlacopan*. Norman: University of Oklahoma Press, 1999.

Chappell, Sally A. Kitt. *Cahokia: Mirror of the Cosmos*. Chicago: University of Chicago Press, 2002.

Coe, Michael D. *The Maya*. 6th ed. New York: Thames and Hudson, 1999.

Doyel, David E., Suzanne K. Fish, and Paul R. Fish, eds. *The Hohokam Village Revisited*. Glenwood Springs,

Colo.: American Association for the Advancement of Science, 2000.

Emerson, Thomas E. *Cahokia and the Archaeology of Power.* Tuscaloosa: University of Alabama Press, 1997.

Emerson, Thomas E., and R. Barry Lewis, eds. *Cahokia and the Hinterlands: Middle Mississippian Cultures of the Midwest.* Urbana: University of Illinois Press, 2000.

Fagan, Brian M. *Ancient North America: The Archaeology of a Continent.* 3d ed. New York: Thames and Hudson, 2000.

Francis, Leo, III. *Native Time: An Historical Time Line of Native America.* New York: St. Martin's Press, 1996.

Jones, Lindsay. *Twin City Tales: A Hermeneutical Reassessment of Tula and Chichén Itzá.* Niwot: University Press of Colorado, 1995.

Julien, Catherine. *Reading Inca History.* Iowa City: University of Iowa Press, 2000.

Kearney, Milo, and Manuel Madrano. *Medieval Culture and the Mexican American Borderlands.* College Station: Texas A&M University Press, 2001.

Kimmel, Eric A. *Montezuma and the Fall of the Aztecs.* New York: Holiday House, 2000.

Kolata, Alan L., ed. *Tiwanaku and Its Hinterland: Archaeology and Paleoecology of an Andean Civilization.* 2 vols. Washington, D.C.: Smithsonian Institution Press, 1996.

Kowalski, Jeff Karl, ed. *Mesoamerican Architecture as a Cultural Symbol.* New York: Oxford University Press, 1999.

Mastache, Alba Guadalupe, Robert H. Cobean, and Dan M. Healan. *Ancient Tollan: Tula and the Toltec Heartland.* Boulder: University Press of Colorado, 2002.

Mehrer, Mark. *Cahokia's Countryside: Household Archaeology, Settlement Patterns, and Social Power.* DeKalb: Northern Illinois University Press, 1995.

Meyer, Michael C., William L. Sherman, and Susan M. Deeds. *The Course of Mexican History.* 6th ed. New York: Oxford University Press, 1999.

Milner, George R. *The Cahokia Chiefdom: The Archaeology of a Mississippian Society.* Washington, D.C.: Smithsonian Institution Press, 1998.

Moseley, Michael E. *The Incas and Their Ancestors: The Archaeology of Peru.* Rev. ed. New York: Thames and Hudson, 2001.

O'Connor, Mallory McCane. *Lost Cities of the Ancient Southeast.* Gainesville: University Press of Florida, 1995.

Oswalt, Wendell H. *Eskimos and Explorers.* 2d ed. Lincoln: University of Nebraska Press, 1999.

Pauketat, Timothy R., and Thomas E. Emerson, eds. *Cahokia: Domination and Ideology in the Mississippian World.* Lincoln: University of Nebraska Press, 2000.

Pillsbury, Joanne, ed. *Moche Art and Archaeology in Ancient Peru.* Washington, D.C.: National Gallery of Art, 2001.

Plog, Stephen. *Ancient Peoples of the American Southwest.* London: Thames and Hudson, 1997.

Pritzker, Barry M. *A Native American Encyclopedia: History, Culture, and Peoples.* New York: Oxford University Press, 2000.

Rostworowski de Diez Canseco, María. *History of the Inca Realm.* Translated by Harry B. Iceland. New York: Cambridge University Press, 1999.

Seaver, Kirsten A. *The Frozen Echo: Greenland and the Exploration of North America, circa A.D. 1000-1500.* Stanford, Calif.: Stanford University Press, 1996.

Silverman, Helaine, and William Isbell, eds. *Andean Archaeology I: Variations on Sociopolitical Organization.* New York: Kluwer Academic, 2002.

Stanish, Charles. *Ancient Titicaca: The Evolution of Complex Society in Southern Peru and Northern Bolivia.* Berkeley: University of California Press, 2003.

Sturtevant, William C., ed. *Handbook of North American Indians.* Vol. 13, *Plains*, edited by Raymond J. Demallie. Washington, D.C.: Smithsonian Institution Press, 2001.

Sutton, Mark Q. *An Introduction to Native North America.* Boston: Allyn and Bacon, 2000.

Wahlgren, Erik. *The Vikings and America.* London: Thames and Hudson, 2000.

Wood, W. Raymond, ed. *Archaeology on the Great Plains.* Lawrence: University of Kansas Press, 1998.

Young, Biloine Whiting, and Melvin L. Fowler. *Cahokia: The Great Native American Metropolis.* Urbana: University of Illinois Press, 2000.

ASIA

East Asia

Antony, Robert J. *Like Froth Floating on the Sea: The World of Pirates and Seafarers in Late Imperial South China.* China Research Monographs 56. Berkeley, Calif.: Institute of East Asian Studies, 2003.

Benn, Charles D. *Daily Life in Traditional China: The Tang Dynasty.* Westport, Conn.: Greenwood Press, 2002.

Bentley, John. *Historiographical Trends in Early Japan.* New York: Edwin Mellen Press, 2002.

Brook, Timothy. *The Confusions of Pleasure: Commerce and Culture in Ming China*. Berkeley: University of California Press, 1998.

Chaffee, John W. *Branches of Heaven: A History of the Imperial Clan of Sung China*. Cambridge, Mass.: Harvard University Press, 1999.

Duncan, John. *The Origins of the Chosōn Dynasty*. Seattle: University of Washington Press, 2000.

Ebrey, Patricia B. *The Cambridge Illustrated History of China*. New York: Cambridge University Press, 1996.

Elman, Benjamin A. *A Cultural History of Civil Examinations in Late Imperial China*. Berkeley: University of California Press, 2000.

Farmer, Edward L. *Zhu Yuanzhang and Early Ming Legislation*. Leiden, the Netherlands: E. J. Brill, 1995.

Farris, William. *Population, Disease, and Land in Early Japan, 645-900*. Cambridge, Mass.: Harvard University Press, 1995.

Frank, Herbert, and Hok-lam Chan, eds. *Studies on the Jurchens and the Chin Dynasty*. Brokfield, Vt.: Ashgate, 1997.

Gernet, Jacques. *Buddhism in Chinese Society: An Economic History from the Fifth to the Tenth Centuries*. Translated by Franciscus Verellen. New York: Columbia University Press, 1995.

Graff, David A. *Medieval Chinese Warfare, 300-900*. New York: Routledge, 2002.

Graff, David A., and Robin Higham. *A Military History of China*. Cambridge, England: Westview Press, 2002.

Hansen, Valerie. *The Open Empire: A History of China to 1600*. New York: W. W. Norton, 2000.

Holcombe, Charles. *The Genesis of East Asia: 221 B.C.-A.D. 907*. Honolulu: University of Hawaii Press, 2001.

Keene, Donald. *Seeds in the Heart*. New York: Columbia University Press, 1999.

Lee, Thomas H. C. *Education in Traditional China: A History*. Boston: Brill, 2000.

Levathes, Louise. *When China Ruled the Seas: The Treasure Fleet of the Dragon Throne, 1405-1433*. New York: Oxford University Press, 1996.

Littleton, Scott. *Shintō: Origins, Rituals, Festivals, Spirits, Sacred Places*. New York: Oxford University Press, 2002.

Lopez, Donald, ed. *Religions of China in Practice*. Princeton, N.J.: Princeton University Press, 1996.

Martin, Peter. *The Chrysanthemum Throne: A History of the Emperors of Japan*. Honolulu: University of Hawai'i Press, 1997.

Mass, Jeffrey P., ed. *The Origins of Japan's Medieval World: Courtiers, Clerics, Warriors, and Peasants in the Fourteenth Century*. Stanford, Calif.: Stanford University Press, 1997.

Mote, F. W. *Imperial China 900-1800*. Cambridge, Mass.: Harvard University Press, 1999.

Murphey, Rhoads. *East Asia: A New History*. 2d ed. New York: Longman, 2001.

Paludan, Ann. *Chronicle of the Chinese Emperors: The Reign-by-Reign Record of the Rulers of Imperial China*. London: Thames and Hudson, 1998.

Piggott, Joan R. *The Emergence of Japanese Kingship*. Stanford, Calif.: Stanford University Press, 1997.

Ptak, Roderich. *China and the Asian Seas: Trade, Travel, and Visions of the Others, 1400-1750*. Brookfield, Vt.: Ashgate, 1998.

Pulleyblank, Edwin G. *Essays on Tang and Pre-Tang China*. Burlington, Vt.: Ashgate, 2001.

Ren, Jiyu, ed. *A History of Chinese Daoism*. Beijing: Chinese Social Sciences Press, 2001.

Roberts, J. A. G. *A Concise History of China*. Cambridge, Mass.: Harvard University Press, 2003.

___________. *Prehistory to c. 1800*. Vol. 1 in *A History of China*. New York: St. Martin's, 1996.

Sato, Hiroaki. *Legends of the Samurai*. New York: Overlook Press, 1995.

Schultz, Edward L. *Generals and Scholars: Military Rule in Medieval Korea*. Honolulu: University of Hawaii Press, 2001.

Shively, Donald, ed. *Heian Japan*. Vol. 2 in *The Cambridge History of Japan*. Cambridge, Mass.: Cambridge University Press, 1999.

Souyri, Pierre Francois. *The World Turned Upside Down: Medieval Japanese Society*. Translated by Käthe Roth. New York: Columbia University Press, 2001.

Standaert, Nicolas, ed. *Handbook of Christianity in China: 635-1800*. Leiden, the Netherlands: E. J. Brill, 2001.

Tamura, Yoshio. *Japanese Buddhism: A Cultural History*. Translated by Jeffrey Hunter. Tokyo: Tuttle, 2001.

Tillmann, Hoyt Cleveland, and Stephen H. West, eds. *China Under Jurchen Rule: Essays on Chin Intellectual and Cultural History*. Albany: State University of New York Press, 1995.

Tu Weiming, ed. *Confucian Traditions in East Asian Modernity: Moral Education and Economic Culture in Japan and the Four Mini-Dragons*. Cambridge, Mass.: Harvard University Press, 1996.

Turnbull, Stephen. *The Samurai Sourcebook*. New York: Arms and Armour, 1999.

Varley, H. Paul. *Japanese Culture*. 4th ed. Honolulu: University of Hawaii Press, 2000.

Von Glahn, Richard. *Fountains of Fortune: Money and Monetary Policy in China, Tenth to Seventeenth Centuries*. New York: Cambridge University Press, 1996.

Von Glahn, Richard, and Paul Jakov Smith. *The Song-Yuan-Ming Transition in Chinese History*. Cambridge, Mass.: Harvard University Press, 2003.

Walton, Linda A. *Academies and Society in Southern Sung China*. Honolulu: University of Hawaii Press, 1999.

Zhang, Guangbao. *Inner Alchemical Daoism During Tang and Song Dynasties*. Shanghai: Shanghai Cultural Press, 2001.

Mongolia and Central Asia

Amitai-Preiss, Reuven. *Mongols and Mamlūks: The Mamlūk-Ilkhanid War, 1260-1281*. New York: Cambridge University Press, 1995.

Amitai-Preiss, Reuven, and David O. Morgan, eds. *The Mongol Empire and Its Legacy*. Boston: Brill, 1999.

Bretschneider, E. *Medieval Researches from Eastern Asiatic Sources*. Richmond, England: Curzon, 2002.

Chaliand, Gérard. *Nomadic Empires: From Mongolia to the Danube*. Translated by A. M. Berrett. New Brunswick, N.J.: Transaction, 2004.

Chan, Hok-Lam. *China and the Mongols: History and Legend under the Yuan and Ming*. Brookfield, Vt.: Ashgate, 1999.

Golden, Peter B. *Nomads and Sedentary Societies in Medieval Eurasia*. Washington, D.C.: American Historical Association, 1998.

Komaroff, Linda, and Stefano Carboni, eds. *The Legacy of Genghis Khan: Courtly Art and Culture in Western Asia, 1256-1353*. New Haven, Conn.: Yale University Press, 2002.

Power, Daniel, and Naomi Standen, eds. *Frontiers in Question: Eurasian Borderlands, 700-1700*. New York: St. Martin's Press, 1999.

Reid, Robert W. *A Brief Political and Military Chronology of the Mediaeval Mongols, From the Birth of Chinggis Qan to the Death of Qubilai Qaghan*. Bloomington, Ind.: Mongolia Society, 2002.

Roux, Jean-Paul. *Genghis Khan and the Mongol Empire*. New York: Harry N. Abrams, 2003.

Wood, Frances. *The Silk Road: Two Thousand Years in the Heart of Asia*. Berkeley: University of California Press, 2002.

South and Southeast Asia

Chandra, Satish. *Essays on Medieval Indian History*. New York: Oxford University Press, 2003.

Chattopadhyaya, Brajadulal. *The Making of Early Medieval India*. New York: Oxford University Press, 1997.

Higham, Charles. *The Civilization of Angkor*. Berkeley: University of California Press, 2001.

Holt, John Clifford. *The Religious World of Kirti Sri: Buddhism, Art, and Politics of Late Medieval Sri Lanka*. New York: Oxford University Press, 1996.

Jackson, Peter. *The Delhi Sultanate*. Cambridge, England: Cambridge University Press, 1999.

Mabbett, Ian, and David Chandler. *The Khmers*. Oxford, England: Blackwell, 1995.

Mannikka, Eleanor. *Angkor Wat: Time, Space, and Kingship*. Honolulu: University of Hawaii Press, 2000.

Proceedings of the International Seminar and Colloquium on Fifteen Hundred Years of Aryabhateeyam. Kochi, India: Kerala Sastra Sahitya Parishad, 2002.

Srinivasa Chari, S. M. *The Philosophy of the Upaniśads: A Study Based on the Evaluation of the Comments of Śaṇkara, Rāmānuja, and Madhva*. New Delhi: Munshiram Manoharial, 2002.

Subrahmanyam, S., ed. *Money and the Market in India, 1100-1700*. Delhi: Oxford University Press, 1998.

Thapar, Romila. *Early India: From the Origins to A.D. 1300*. Berkeley: University of California Press, 2002.

Velukutty, K. K. *Heritages to and from Aryabhatta*. Elipara, India: Sahithi, 1997.

EUROPE

Byzantine Empire and the Balkans

Angold, Michael J. *The Byzantine Empire, 1025-1204: A Political History*. 2d ed. New York: Longman, 1997.

Asbridge, Thomas S. *The Creation of the Principality of Antioch, 1098-1130*. Rochester N.Y.: Boydell Press, 2000.

Bartlett, W. B. *An Ungodly War: The Sack of Constantinople and the Fourth Crusade*. Thrupp, Stroud, Gloucestershire: Sutton, 2000.

Bowlus, Charles R. *Franks, Moravians, and Magyars: The Struggle for the Middle Danube, 788-907*. Philadelphia: University of Pennsylvania Press, 1995.

Clari, Robert de. *The Conquest of Constantinople*. Translated and edited by Edgar Holmes McNeal. 1936. Reprint. Toronto: University of Toronto Press and the Medieval Academy of America, 1996.

Cox, John K. *The History of Serbia*. Westport, Conn.: Greenwood Press, 2002.

Crampton, R. J. *A Concise History of Bulgaria*. New York: Cambridge University Press, 1997.

Engel, Pál. *The Realm of St. Stephen: A History of Medieval Hungary, 895-1526*. Translated by Tamás Pálosfalvi. Edited by Andrew Ayton. New York: I. B. Tauris, 2001.

Evans, James Allan. *The Age of Justinian: The Circumstances of Imperial Power*. New York: Routledge, 1996.

Freely, John. *Istanbul: The Imperial City*. New York: Viking, 1996.

Fudge, Thomas A. *The Magnificent Ride: The First Reformation in Hussite Bohemia*. Brookfield, Vt.: Ashgate, 1998.

Goodwin, Jason. *Lords of the Horizons: A History of the Ottoman Empire*. New York: Picador, 2003.

Grant, Michael. *From Rome to Byzantium: The Fifth Century A.D.* New York: Routledge, 1998.

Inalcik, Halil. *The Ottoman Empire: The Classical Age, 1300-1600*. Translated by Norman Itzkowitz and Colin Imber. London: Phoenix Press, 2000.

Kosztolnyik, Z. J. *Hungary Under the Early Árpáds, 890's to 1063*. Boulder, Colo.: East European Monographs, 2002.

Lázár, István. *Hungary: A Brief History*. Translated by Albert Tezla. 6th ed. Budapest: Corvina Press, 2001.

Lendavi, Paul. *The Hungarians: A Thousand Years of Victory in Defeat*. Translated by Ann Major. Princeton, N.J.: Princeton University Press, 2003.

Lev, Yaacov, ed. *The Medieval Mediterranean: Peoples, Economies and Cultures, 400-1453*. Vol. 9 in *War and Society in the Eastern Mediterranean, Seventh-Fifteenth Centuries*. Leiden, the Netherlands: Brill, 1997.

Mango, Cyril, ed. *The Oxford History of Byzantium*. New York: Oxford University Press, 2002.

Norwich, John Julius. *A Short History of Byzantium*. New York: Knopf, 1997.

Obolensky, Dimitri. *Byzantium and Slavic Christianity: Influence of Dialogue?* Berkeley, Calif.: Patriarch Athenagoras Orthodox Institute, 1998.

Parry, Kenneth. *Depicting the Word: Byzantine Iconophile Thought of the Eighth and Ninth Centuries*. New York: E. J. Brill, 1996.

Pavlikianov, Cyril. *The Medieval Aristocracy on Mount Athos: The Philological and Documentary Evidence for the Activity of Byzantine, Georgian, and Slav Aristocrats and Eminent Churchmen in the Monasteries of Mount Athos form the Tenth to the Fifteenth Century*. Sofia, Bulgaria: Center for Slavo-Byzantine Studies, 2001.

Pavlowitch, Stevan K. *Serbia: The History of an Idea*. New York: New York University Press, 2002.

Queller, Donald E., and Thomas F. Madden. *The Fourth Crusade: The Conquest of Constantinople, 1201-1204*. 2d ed. Philadelphia: University of Pennsylvania Press, 1997.

Róna-Tas, András. *Hungarians and Europe in the Early Middle Ages: An Introduction to Early Hungarian History*. New York: Central European University Press, 1999.

Sayer, Derek. *The Coasts of Bohemia*. Princeton, N.J.: Princeton University Press, 1998.

Teich, Mikuláš, ed. *Bohemia in History*. New York: Cambridge University Press, 1998.

Treadgold, Warren. *A History of the Byzantine State and Society*. Stanford, Calif.: Stanford University Press, 1997.

Whittow, Mark. *The Making of Byzantium, 600-1025*. Berkeley: University of California Press, 1996.

Zimbardo, Xavier. *Monks of Dust: The Holy Men of Mount Athos*. New York: Rizzoli, 2001.

Russia and Eastern Europe

Alen, Rupert, and Anna Marie Dahlquist. *Royal Families of Medieval Scandinavia, Flanders, and Kiev*. Kingsburg, Calif.: Kings River, 1997.

Bideleux, Robert, and Ian Jeffries. *A History of Eastern Europe: Crisis and Change*. New York: Routledge, 1998.

Brisbane, Mark, and David Gaimster, eds. *Novgorod: The Archaeology of a Russian Medieval City and Its Hinterland*. London: British Museum, 2001.

Demetz, Peter. *Prague in Black and Gold: Scenes from the Life of a European City*. New York: Hill and Wang, 1997.

Duffy, James P., and Vincent L. Ricci. *Czars: Russia's Rulers for More Than One Thousand Years*. New York: Facts on File, 1995.

Dukes, Paul. *A History of Russia: Medieval, Modern, Contemporary, Circa 882-1996*. 3d ed. Durham, N.C.: Duke University Press, 1998.

Eastmond, Anthony. *Royal Imagery in Medieval Georgia*. Philadelphia: Pennsylvania State University Press, 1998.

Fennell, John. *A History of the Russian Church, to 1448*. London: Longman, 1995.

Franklin, Simon, and Jonathan Shepard. *The Emergence of Rus, 750-1200*. New York: Longman, 1996.

Hartog, Leo de. *Russia and the Mongol Yoke: The History of the Russian Principalities and the Golden Horde, 1221-1502*. New York: British Academic Press, 1996.

Longworth, Philip. *The Making of Eastern Europe: From Prehistory to Postcommunism*. 2d ed. New York: St. Martin's Press, 1997.

Lukowski, Jerzy, and Hubert Zawadski. *A Concise History of Poland*. New York: Cambridge University Press, 2001.

Riasanovsky, Nicholas V. *A History of Russia*. 6th ed. New York: Oxford University Press, 2000.

Rosen, Roger. *Georgia: A Sovereign Country of the Caucasus*. Hong Kong: Odyssey, 1999.

Tachiaos, Anthony-Emil N. *Cyril and Methodius of Thessalonica: The Acculturation of the Slavs*. Crestwood, N.Y.: St. Vladimir's Seminary Press, 2001.

Warnes, David. *Chronicle of the Russian Tsars*. London: Thames and Hudson, 1999.

Scandinavia

Alen, Rupert, and Anna Marie Dahlquist. *Royal Families of Medieval Scandinavia, Flanders, and Kiev*. Kingsburg, Calif.: Kings River, 1997.

Barrett, James H., ed. *Contact, Continuity, and Collapse: The Norse Colonization of the North Atlantic*. Turnhout, Belgium: Brepols, 2003.

Davies, Wendy, ed. *From the Vikings to the Normans*. New York: Oxford University Press, 2003.

Graham-Campbell, James, ed. *The Viking World*. London: Frances Lincoln, 2001.

Hadley, D. M. *The Northern Danelaw: Its Social Structure*. London: Leicester University Press, 2000.

Haywood, John. The Penguin Historical Atlas of the Vikings. New York: Viking Press, 1995.

Konstam, Angus. *Historical Atlas of the Viking World*. New York: Checkmark Books, 2002.

Lausten, Martin Schwarz. *A Church History of Denmark*. Translated by Frederick H. Cryer. Burlington, Vt.: Ashgate, 2002.

Marsden, John. *The Fury of the Northmen: Saints, Shrines and Sea-Raiders in the Viking Age A.D. 793-878*. New York: St. Martin's Press, 1995.

Page, R. I. *The Chronicles of the Vikings*. Toronto: University of Toronto Press, 1995.

Roesdahl, Else. *The Vikings*. 2d ed. Translated by Susan M. Margeson and Kirsten Williams. New York: Penguin Books, 1998.

Ross, Margaret Clunies, ed. *Old Icelandic Literature and Society*. New York: Cambridge University Press, 2000.

Sawyer, Peter, ed. *The Oxford Illustrated History of the Vikings*. New York: Oxford University Press, 2001.

Singleton, Fred. *A Short History of Finland*. 2d ed. Cambridge, England: Cambridge University Press, 1998.

Western Europe and the British Isles

Alcock, Leslie. *Arthur's Britain: History and Archaeology, A.D. 367-634*. New York: Penguin Books, 2001.

Alexander, Michael V. C. *Three Crises in Early English History: Personalities and Politics During the Norman Conquest, the Reign of King John, and the Wars of the Roses*. Lanham, Md.: University Press of America, 1998.

Allmand, Christopher. *War, Government and Power in Late Medieval France*. Liverpool, England: Liverpool University Press, 2000.

Amory, Patrick. *People and Identity in Ostrogothic Italy, 489-554*. New York: Cambridge University Press, 1997.

Bachrach, Bernard S. *Early Carolingian Warfare: Prelude to Empire*. Philadelphia: University of Pennsylvania Press, 2001.

Baker, Denise N. *Inscribing the Hundred Years' War in French and English Cultures*. Albany: State University of New York Press, 2000.

Barrow, G. W. S. *Kingship and Unity: Scotland, 1000-1306*. 2d ed. Edinburgh: Edinburgh University Press, 2003.

Bellitto, Christopher M. *The General Councils: A History of the Twenty-one General Councils from Nicaea to Vatican II*. New York: Paulist Press, 2002.

Berman, Constance Hoffman. *The Cistercian Evolution: The Invention of a Religious Order in Twelfth-century Europe*. Philadelphia: University of Pennsylvania Press, 2000.

Bolton, Brenda. *Studies on Papal Authority and Pastoral Care*. Brookfield, Vt.: Variorum, 1995.

Bower, Walter. *Scotichronicon*. Edited by D. E. R. Watt. Edinburgh: Mercat Press, 1987-1997.

Bremmer, Rolf H., Jr., Kees Dekker, and David F. Johnson, eds. *Rome and the North: The Early Reception of Gregory the Great in Germanic Europe*. Sterling, Va.: Peeters, 2001.

Brooke, Christopher. *The Age of the Cloister: The Story of Monastic Life in the Middle Ages*. Rev. ed. Mahwah, N.J.: HiddenSpring, 2003.

___________. *The Saxon and Norman Kings*. 3d ed. Malden, Mass.: Blackwell, 2001.

Brown, R. Allen. *The Normans*. 2d ed. Woodbridge, England: Boydell & Brewer, 1995.

Brown, Warren. *Unjust Seizure: Conflict, Interest, and Authority in an Early Medieval Society*. Ithaca, N.Y.: Cornell University Press, 2001.

Brucker, Gene A. *Florence, the Golden Age, 1138-1737*. Berkeley: University of California, 1998.

Burl, Aubrey. *God's Heretics: The Albigensian Crusade*. Stroud, England: Sutton, 2002.

Burne, Alfred H. *The Agincourt War: A Military History of the Latter Part of the Hundred Years' War from 1369 to 1453*. Ware, Hertfordshire, England: Wordsworth Editions, 1999.

___________. *The Crécy War: A Military History of the Hundred Years' War from 1337 to the Peace of Bretigny, 1360*. New York: Oxford University Press, 1955.

Byrne, Francis John. *Irish Kings and High-Kings*. Portland, Oreg.: Four Courts Press, 2001.

Chibnall, Marjorie. *The Normans*. Malden, Mass.: Blackwell, 2000.

Christys, Ann. *Christians in Al-Andalus, 711-1000*. Richmond, England: Curzon, 2002.

Coppa, Frank J., ed. *Encyclopedia of the Vatican and Papacy*. Westport, Conn.: Greenwood Press, 1999.

___________. *The Great Popes Through History: An Encyclopedia*. Westport, Conn.: Greenwood Press, 2002.

Coppée, Henry. *History of the Conquest of Spain by the Arab-Moors: With a Sketch of the Civilization Which They Achieved and Imparted to Europe*. 2 vols. Piscataway, N.J.: Georgia Press, 2002.

Courtenay, William J., and Jürgen Miethke, eds. *Universities and Schooling in Medieval Society*. Boston: Brill, 2000.

Cowdrey, H. E. J. *Popes and Church Reform in the Eleventh Century*. Burlington, Vt.: Ashgate/Variorum, 2000.

Crouch, David. *The Normans: The History of a Dynasty*. London: Hambledon and London, 2002.

Curry, Anne. *The Hundred Years' War*. 2d ed. New York: Palgrave Macmillan, 2003.

Danziger, Danny, and John Gillingham. *1215: The Year of Magna Carta*. London: Hodder & Stoughton, 2003.

Davies, John. *The Making of Wales*. Herndon, Va.: Sutton, 1996.

Davies, R. R. *The Age of Conquest: Wales, 1063-1415*. New York: Oxford University Press, 2000.

Davis, Oliver, trans. *Celtic Spirituality*. New York: Paulist Press, 1999.

Duffy, Eamon. *Saints and Sinners: A History of the Popes*. 2d ed. New Haven, Conn.: Yale University Press, 2001.

Duffy, Seán. *Ireland in the Middle Ages*. New York: St. Martin's Press, 1997.

___________, ed. *Robert the Bruce's Irish Wars: The Invasions of Ireland, 1306-1329*. Charleston, S.C.: Tempus, 2002.

Dunbabin, Jean. *France in the Making, 843-1180*. 2d ed. New York: Oxford University Press, 2000.

Dunn, Alastair. *The Great Rising of 1381: The Peasants' Revolt and England's Failed Revolution*. Stroud, Gloucestershire, England: Tempus, 2002.

Dunn, Diana, ed. *War and Society in Medieval and Early Modern Britain*. Liverpool, England: Liverpool University Press, 2000.

Eyck, Frank. *Religion and Politics in German History: From the Beginnings to the French Revolution*. New York: St. Martin's Press, 1998.

Farmer, Sharon, and Barbara H. Rosenwein, eds. *Monks and Nuns, Saints and Outcasts: Religion in Medieval Society*. Ithaca, N.Y.: Cornell University Press, 2000.

Fassler, Margot E., and Rebecca A. Baltzer, eds. *The Divine Office in the Latin Middle Ages: Methodology and Source Studies, Regional Developments, Hagiography*. New York: Oxford University Press, 2000.

Ferzoco, George, and Carolyn Muessig, eds. *Medieval Monastic Education*. New York: Leicester University Press, 2000.

Fleming, Robin. *Domesday Book and the Law: Society and Legal Custom in Early Medieval England*. New York: Cambridge University Press, 1998.

Fletcher, Richard. *Bloodfeud: Murder and Revenge in Anglo-Saxon England*. New York: Allen Lane/Penguin Press, 2002.

Fouracre, Paul. *The Age of Charles Martel*. New York: Longman, 2000.

France, John. *Western Warfare in the Age of the Crusades, 1000-1300*. Ithaca, N.Y.: Cornell University Press, 1999.

Fregosi, Paul. *Jihad in the West: Muslim Conquests from the Seventh to the Twenty-first Centuries*. Amherst, N.Y.: Prometheus Books, 1998.

Fry, Michael. *The Scottish Empire*. East Lothian, Scotland: Tuckwell Press, 2001.

Fryde, E. B. *Peasants and Landlords in Later Medieval England: c. 1380-c. 1525*. New York: St. Martin's Press, 1996.

Fuentes, Carlos. *The Buried Mirror: Reflection on Spain and the New World*. 1992. Reprint. Boston: Houghton Mifflin, 1999.

Geary, Patrick J. *The Myth of Nations: The Medieval Origins of Europe*. Princeton, N.J.: Princeton University Press, 2002.

Gillingham, John. *The Angevin Empire*. 2d ed. New York: Oxford University Press, 2001.

Goodman, Jennifer R. *Chivalry and Exploration, 1298-1630*. Rochester, N.Y.: Boydell Press, 1998.

Gore, Terry L. *Neglected Heroes: Leadership and War in the Early Medieval Period*. Westport, Conn.: Praeger, 1995.

Gracia, Jorge J. E., and Timothy B. Noone, eds. *A Companion to Philosophy in the Middle Ages*. Malden, Mass.: Blackwell, 2003.

Hallam, Elizabeth M., and Judith Everard. *Capetian France, 987-1328*. 2d ed. New York: Longman, 2001.

Hanson, Carl. *Atlantic Emporium: Portugal and the Wider World, 1147-1497*. New Orleans, La.: University Press of the South, 2001.

Heinzelmann, Martin. *Gregory of Tours: History and Society in the Sixth Century*. Translated by Christopher Carroll. New York: Cambridge University Press, 2001.

Hill, David, and Robert Cowie, eds. *Wics: The Early Mediaeval Trading Centres of Northern Europe*. Sheffield, England: Sheffield Academic Press, 2001.

Hillerbrand, Hans J., ed. *The Oxford Encyclopedia of the Reformation*. 4 vols. New York: Oxford University Press, 1996.

Hillgarth, J. N. *Spain and the Mediterranean in the Later Middle Ages: Studies in Political and Intellectual History*. Burlington, Vt.: Ashgate Variorum, 2003.

Hines, John. *Anglo-Saxons from the Migration Period to the Eighth Century: An Ethnographic Perspective*. Rochester, N.Y.: Boydell & Brewer, 1997.

Holmes, George. *Europe, Hierarchy and Revolt, 1320-1450*. 2d ed. Malden, Mass.: Blackwell, 2000.

Howard, Ian. *Swein Forkbeard's Invasions and the Danish Conquest of England, 991-1017*. Rochester, N.Y.: Boydell and Brewer, 2003.

Innes, Matthew. *State and Society in the Early Middle Ages: The Middle Rhine Valley, 400-1000*. New York: Cambridge University Press, 2000.

Jasper, Detlev, and Fuhrmann, Horst. *Papal Letters in the Early Middle Ages: History of Medieval Canon Law*. Washington, D.C.: Catholic University of America Press, 2001.

Jeep, John M., et al., eds. *Medieval Germany: An Encyclopedia*. New York: Garland, 2001.

John, Eric. *Re-assessing Anglo-Saxon England*. New York: Saint Martin's Press, 1997.

Jones, Philip. *The Italian City-State: From Commune to Signoria*. New York: Oxford University Press, 1997.

Jones, Prudence, and Nigel Pennick. *A History of Pagan Europe*. New York: Routledge, 1997.

Jotischky, Andrew. *The Carmelites and Antiquity: Mendicants and Their Pasts in the Middle Ages*. New York: Oxford University Press, 2002.

Kennedy, Hugh. *Muslim Spain and Portugal: A Political History of Al-Andalus*. Menlo Park, Calif.: Addison-Wesley, 1997.

Kennedy, William J. *The Site of Petrarchism: Early Modern National Sentiment in Italy, France, and England*. Baltimore: The Johns Hopkins University Press, 2003.

Klaniczay, Gábor. *Holy Rulers and Blessed Princesses: Dynastic Cults in Medieval Central Europe*. Translated by Éva Pálmai. New York: Cambridge University Press, 2002.

Kooper, Erik, ed. *The Medieval Chronicle: Proceedings of the First International Conference on the Medieval Chronicle*. Atlanta: Rodopi, 1999.

Larner, John. *Marco Polo and the Discovery of the World*. New Haven, Conn.: Yale University Press, 1999.

La Rocca, Cristina, ed. *Italy in the Early Middle Ages, 476-1000*. New York: Oxford University Press, 2002.

Levillain, Philippe, ed. *The Papacy: An Encyclopedia*. New York: Routledge, 2002.

Long, John D. *The Bible in English: John Wycliffe and William Tyndale*. Lanham, Md.: University Press of America, 1998.

Loud, G. A. *The Age of Robert Guiscard: Southern Italy and the Norman Conquest*. New York: Longman, 2000.

Loyn, H. R. *The Vikings in Britain*. Rev. ed. Cambridge, Mass.: Blackwell, 1995.

Lydon, James F. *The Lordship of Ireland in the Middle Ages*. Rev. ed. Dublin: Four Courts Press, 2003.

McBrien, Richard P. *Lives of the Popes: The Pontiffs from Saint Peter to John Paul II*. San Francisco: Harper-SanFrancisco, 1997.

MacDonald, Fiona. *The World in the Time of Charlemagne*. New York: Silver Burdett Press, 1998.

McGinn, Bernard. *The Flowering of Mysticism: Men and Women in the New Mysticism, 1200-1350*. New York: Crossroad, 1998.

McKitterick, Rosamond. *The Frankish Kings and Culture in the Early Middle Ages*. Aldershot, England: Variorum, 1995.

___________, ed. *The New Cambridge Medieval History*. 7 vols. New York: Cambridge University Press, 2000.

Madden, Thomas F. *Enrico Dandolo and the Rise of Venice*. Baltimore: The Johns Hopkins University Press, 2003.

Mann, Nicholas, and Birger Munk Olsen, eds. *Medieval and Renaissance Scholarship: Proceedings of the Second European Science Foundation Workshop on the Classical Tradition in the Middle Ages and the Renaissance*. New York: E. J. Brill, 1997.

Marín, Manuela, and Julio Samsó, eds. *The Formation of al-Andalus*. 2 vols. Brookfield, Vt.: Ashgate, 1998.

Markale, Jean. *Courtly Love: The Path of Sexual Initiation*. Translated by Jon Graham. Rochester, Vt.: Inner Traditions, 2000.

Maxwell-Stuart, P. G. *Chronicle of the Popes: The Reign-by-Reign Record of the Papacy from Saint Peter to the Present*. New York: Thames and Hudson, 1997.

Meddicott, J. A., and D. M. Palliser, eds. *The Medieval State*. Rio Grande, Ohio: Hambledon Press, 2000.

Moody, T. W., and F. X. Martin, eds. *The Course of Irish History*. Rev. ed. Lanham, Md.: Roberts Rhinehart, 2001.

Moore, Robert Ian. *The First European Revolution, c. 970-1215*. Malden, Mass.: Blackwell, 2000.

Moreira, Isabel. *Dreams, Visions, and Spiritual Authority in Merovingian Gaul*. Ithaca, N.Y.: Cornell University Press, 2000.

Muldoon, James. *Canon Law, the Expansion of Europe, and World Order*. Aldershot, England: Ashgate, 1998.

Murray, Alexander Calander, ed. *After Rome's Fall: Narrators and Sources of Early Medieval History*. Buffalo, N.Y.: University of Toronto Press, 1998.

Nederman, Cary J. *Worlds of Difference: European Discourses of Toleration, c. 1100-c. 1550*. University Park: Pennsylvania State University Press, 2000.

Neillands, Robin. *The Hundred Years' War*. Rev. ed. New York: Routledge, 2001.

Nicholas, David. *The Growth of the Medieval City: From Late Antiquity to the Early Fourteenth Century*. New York: Longman, 1997.

___________. *Trade, Urbanisation, and the Family: Studies in the History of Medieval Flanders*. Brookfield, Vt.: Variorum, 1996.

___________. *Urban Europe, 1100-1700*. New York: Palgrave Macmillan, 2003.

O'Callaghan, Joseph F. *Alfonso X, the Cortes, and Government in Medieval Spain*. Brookfield, Vt.: Ashgate, 1998.

___________. *Reconquest and Crusade in Medieval Spain*. Philadelphia: University of Pennsylvania Press, 2002.

Ó Cróinín, Dáibhí. *Early Medieval Ireland, 400-1200*. New York: Longman, 1995.

Penrose, Mary E. *Roots Deep and Strong: Great Men and Women of the Church*. New York: Paulist Press, 1995.

Pollard, A. J. *The Wars of the Roses*. 2d ed. New York: Palgrave, 2001.

Prestwich, Michael. *The Three Edwards: War and State in England, 1272-1377*. New York: Routledge, 2003.

Pullen, Bruce Reed. *Discovering Celtic Christianity: Its Roots, Relationships, and Relevance*. Mystic, Conn.: Twenty-Third/Bayard, 1999.

Raban, Sandra. *England Under Edward I and Edward II, 1259-1327*. Malden, Mass.: Blackwell, 2000.

Reilly, Bernard F. *The Contest of Christian and Muslim Spain: 1031-1157*. Cambridge, Mass.: Blackwell, 1995.

Rey, Roger. *Bede, Rhetoric, and the Creation of Christian Latin Culture*. Jarrow, England: St. Paul's Church, 1997.

Roberts, John L. *Lost Kingdoms: Celtic Scotland and the Middle Ages*. Edinburgh: Edinburgh University Press, 1997.

Robertson, A. J., ed. and trans. *The Laws of the Kings of England from Edmund to Henry I*. Felinfach, Wales: Llanerch, 2000.

Robinson, Cynthia. *In Praise of Song: The Making of Courtly Culture in al-Andalus and Provence, 1005-1134 A.D.* Boston: Brill, 2002.

Roffe, David. *Domesday: The Inquest and the Book*. New York: Oxford University Press, 2000.

Rousselot, Pierre. *The Problem of Love in the Middle Ages: A Historical Contribution*. Translated by Alan Vincelette. Milwaukee, Wis.: Marquette University Press, 2001.

Russell, Jeffrey Burton. *The Devil, Heresy, and Witchcraft in the Middle Ages*. Boston: Brill, 1998.

Russell, Peter. *Portugal, Spain, and the African Atlantic, 1343-1490: Chivalry and Crusade from John of*

Gaunt to Henry the Navigator and Beyond. Brookfield, Vt.: Variorum, 1995.

Saggau, Elise, ed. *True Followers of Justice: Identity, Insertion, and Itinerancy Among the Early Franciscans.* St. Bonaventure, N.Y.: The Franciscan Institute, 2000.

Saul, Nigel, ed. *The Oxford Illustrated History of Medieval England.* New York: Oxford University Press, 1997.

Schutz, Herbert. *The Germanic Realms in Pre-Carolingian Central Europe, 400-750.* New York: P. Lang, 2000.

Seward, Desmond. *A Brief History of the Hundred Years' War: The English in France, 1337-1453.* London: Robinson, 2003.

Shopkow, Leah. *History and Community: Norman Historical Writing in the Eleventh and Twelfth Centuries.* Washington, D.C.: Catholic University of America Press, 1997.

Signer, Michael A., and John van Engen, eds. *Jews and Christians in Twelfth-century Europe.* Notre Dame, Ind.: University of Notre Dame Press, 2001.

Sims-Williams, Patrick. *Britain and Early Christian Europe: Studies in Early Medieval History and Culture.* Brookfield, Vt.: Variorum, 1995.

Smith, Robert, and John S. Moore, eds. *The House of Commons: Seven Hundred Years of British Tradition.* London: Smith's Peerage, 1996.

Staunton, Michael. *The Story of Christian Ireland: From St. Patrick to the Peace Process.* Dublin: Emerald Press, 2001.

Sumption, Jonathan. *The Albigensian Crusade.* Boston: Faber, 1999.

____________. *The Hundred Years War.* 2 vols. Philadelphia: University of Pennsylvania Press, 1999.

Szarmach, Paul E., ed. *Holy Men and Holy Women: Old English Prose Saints' Lives and Their Contexts.* Albany: State University of New York Press, 1996.

Thijssen, J. M. M. H. *Censure and Heresy at the University of Paris, 1200-1400.* Philadelphia: University of Pennsylvania Press, 1998.

Thomson, John A. F. *The Western Church in the Middle Ages.* New York: Arnold, 1998.

Tobin, Stephen. *The Cistercians: Monks and Monasteries of Europe.* Woodstock, N.Y.: Overlook Press, 1995.

Turner, Ralph V. *The English Judiciary in the Age of Glanvill and Bracton, c. 1176-1230.* Holmes Beach, Fla.: Gaunt, 2001.

Turvey, Roger. *The Welsh Princes: The Native Rulers of Wales, 1063-1283.* London: Longman, 2002.

Ullmann, Walter. *A Short History of the Papacy in the Middle Ages.* 1972. Reprint. New York: Routledge, 2003.

Valente, Claire. *The Theory and Practice of Revolt in Medieval England.* Burlington, Vt.: Ashgate, 2003.

Verbruggen, J. F. *The Art of Warfare in Western Europe During the Middle Ages.* Woodbridge, England: Boydell Press, 1997.

Walker, David. *The Normans in Britain.* Oxford, England: Blackwell, 1995.

Warburg, Aby. *The Renewal of Pagan Antiquity: Contributions to the Cultural History of the European Renaissance.* Translated by David Britt. Los Angeles: Getty Research Institute for the History of Art and the Humanities, 1999.

Watson, Fiona J. *Under the Hammer: Edward I and Scotland, 1286-1307.* East Lothian, Scotland: Tuckwell Press, 1998.

Webster, Bruce. *Medieval Scotland: The Making of an Identity.* New York: St. Martin's Press, 1997.

Weiler, Björn K. U., ed. *England and Europe in the Reign of Henry III (1216-1272).* Burlington, Vt.: Ashgate, 2002.

Wells, John. *The House of Lords: From Saxon Wargods to a Modern Senate.* London: Hodder and Stoughton, 1997.

Winius, George D., ed. *Portugal, the Pathfinder: Journeys from the Medieval Toward the Modern World, 1300-circa 1600.* Madison, Wis.: Hispanic Seminary of Medieval Studies, 1995.

Wippel, John F. *Mediaeval Reactions to the Encounter Between Faith and Reason.* Milwaukee, Wis.: Marquette University Press, 1995.

Wolf, Kenneth Baxter. *Making History: The Normans and Their Historians in Eleventh-Century Italy.* Philadelphia: University of Pennsylvania Press, 1995.

Wolfram, Herwig. *The Roman Empire and Its Germanic Peoples.* Translated by Thomas Dunlap. Berkeley: University of California Press, 1997.

Wood, Ian N., ed. *Franks and Alamanni in the Merovingian Period: An Ethnographic Perspective.* Rochester, N.Y.: Boydell Press, 1999.

MIDDLE EAST AND ISLAMIC STUDIES

Boas, Adrian J. *Crusader Archaeology: The Material Culture of the Latin East.* New York: Routledge, 1999.

Bosworth, Clifford Edmund. *The New Islamic Dynasties: A Chronological and Genealogical Manual.* 1967. Rev. ed. New York: Columbia University Press, 1996.

Brockelmann, Carl. *History of the Islamic Peoples.* Translated by Joel Carmichael and Moshe Perlmann. New York: Routledge, 2000.

Cartlidge, Cherese. *The Crusades: Failed Holy Wars.* San Diego, Calif.: Lucent Books, 2002.

Curtis, John, ed. *Mesopotamia and Iran in the Parthian and Sāsānian Periods: Rejection and Revival c. 238 B.C.-A.D. 642.* London: British Museum Press, 2000.

Donner, Fred M. *Narratives of Islamic Origins: The Beginnings of Islamic Historical Writing.* Princeton, N.J.: Darwin Press, 1998.

Encyclopaedia of Islam. Leiden, the Netherlands: Brill 2003.

Esposito, John, ed. *The Oxford History of Islam.* New York: Oxford University Press, 1999.

Folda, Jaroslav. *The Art of the Crusaders in the Holy Land, 1098-1187.* New York: Cambridge University Press, 1995.

Foss, Michael. *People of the First Crusade.* New York: Arcade Publishing, 1997.

Fyzee, Asaf A. A. *Outlines of Muḥammadan Law.* 4th ed. New York: Oxford University Press, 1999.

Hawting, G. R. *The First Dynasty of Islam: The Umayyad Caliphate A.D. 661-750.* New York: Routledge, 2000.

Hitti, Philip K. *History of the Arabs: From the Earliest Times to the Present.* 10th ed. New York: Palgrave, Macmillan, 2002.

Holt, P. M. *Early Mamlūk Diplomacy, 1260-1290: Treaties of Baybars and Qalawun with Christian Rulers.* New York: E. J. Brill, 1995.

Hurvitz, Nimrod. *The Formation of Hanbalism: Piety into Power.* New York: RoutledgeCurzon, 2002.

Kahn, Masood Ali, and S. Ram, eds. *Encyclopaedia of Sufism.* 12 vols. New Delhi: Anmol, 2003.

Kazmi, Hasan Askari. *The Makers of Medieval Muslim Geography: Alberuni.* Delhi, India: Renaissance, 1995.

Knysh, Alexander. *Ibn ʿArabī in the Later Islamic Tradition: The Making of a Polemical Image in Medieval Islam.* Albany: State University of New York Press, 1999.

Madden, Thomas F., ed. *The Crusades: The Essential Readings.* Malden, Mass.: Blackwell, 2002.

Martin, Richard C., Mark R. Woodward, and Dwi S. Atmaja. *Defenders of Reason in Islam: Mutazilism from Medieval School to Modern Symbol.* Boston: Oneworld, 1997.

Meisami, Julie Scott. *Persian Historiography to the End of the Twelfth Century.* Edinburgh: Edinburgh University Press, 1999.

Nasr, Seyyed Hossein. *The Islamic Intellectual Tradition in Persia.* Edited by Mehdi Amin Razavi. Richmond, Surrey, England: Curzon Press, 1996.

Ouyang, Wen-chin. *Literary Criticism in Medieval Arabic-Islamic Culture: The Making of a Tradition.* Edinburgh: Edinburgh University Press, 1997.

Raby, Julian, and Jeremy Johns, eds. *Bayt-al-Maqdis: ʿAbd al-Malik's Jerusalem.* New York: Oxford University Press, for the Board of Faculty of Oriental Studies, 1992-1999.

Reston, James, Jr. *Warriors of God: Richard the Lionheart and Saladin in the Third Crusade.* New York: Knopf, 2002.

Riley-Smith, Jonathan. *The First Crusaders, 1095-1131.* New York: Cambridge University Press, 1997.

____________, ed. *The Oxford History of the Crusades.* New York: Oxford University Press, 1999.

Robinson, Chase F. *Islamic Historiography.* New York: Cambridge University Press, 2003.

Rubin, Uri. *The Eye of the Beholder: The Life of Muḥammad as Viewed by the Early Muslims.* Princeton, N.J.: Darwin Press, 1995.

Schimmel, Annemarie. *As Through a Veil: Mystical Poetry in Islam.* 1982. Reprint. Boston: Oneworld, 2001.

Sicker, Martin. *The Pre-Islamic Middle East.* Westport, Conn.: Praeger, 2000.

Sicker, Michael. *The Islamic World in Ascendancy: From the Arab Conquests to the Siege of Vienna.* Westport, Conn.: Praeger, 2000.

Smith, G. Rex. *Studies in the Medieval History of the Yemen and South Arabia.* Brookfield, Vt.: Ashgate, 1997.

Stroumsa, Sarah. *Freethinkers of Medieval Islam: Ibn al-Rāwandī, Abū Bakr al-Rāzī and Their Impact on Islamic Thought.* Boston: Brill, 1999.

Von Grunebaum, Gustav Edmund. *Classical Islam: A History, 600-1258.* Translated by Katherine Watson. New York: Barnes and Noble Books, 1996.

Watt, W. Montgomery. *The Formative Period of Islamic Thought.* Boston: Oneworld, 1998.

____________. *Islamic Philosophy and Theology: An Extended Survey.* 2d ed. Edinburgh: Edinburgh University Press, 1995.

Wiesehofer, Josef. *Ancient Persia: From 550 B.D. to 650 A.D.* Translated by Azizeh Azodi. New York: I. B. Tauris, 1996.

—*Andy Perry*

WEB SITES

The sites listed below were visited by the editors of Salem Press in March of 2004. Because URLs frequently change or are moved, their accuracy cannot be guaranteed; however, long-standing sites—such as those of university departments, national organizations, and government agencies—generally maintain links when sites move or otherwise may upgrade their offerings and hence remain useful. —Jeffry Jensen

GENERAL

About.com: Medieval History
http://historymedren.about.com/
Created by About.com, this site is made up of original articles on medieval history, as well as "annotated links to selected relevant Internet resources, compiled by a subject specialist, a subject-specific bulletin board, and details of related news and events." Some of the topics included are armor and weaponry, the Crusades, Knightly Orders and the Knights Templar, medieval history organizations, science and technology, and women in the period.

Ancient World Web
http://www.julen.net/ancient/
This site includes annotated lists of Web sites concerning ancient and medieval "history, theory, and scholarship."

Country Studies
http://countrystudies.us/
This site makes it possible to read the online versions of country books previously published through the Country Studies/Area Handbook Series by the Federal Research Division of the Library of Congress. There are more than one hundred countries from around the world covered in the series. Each title has a wealth of information on such topics as history, society, geography, and economy.

Enter the Middle Ages
http://emuseum.mnsu.edu/history/middleages/
Divided into four sections, this site discusses how the Knight's Realm, the Nun's Realm, the Merchants Realm, and the Peasants Realm fit into the society of the Middle Ages.

Eyewitness to the Middle Ages and the Renaissance
http://www.ibiscom.com/mefrm.htm
This site includes first-person accounts of such important events in history as the invasion of England in 1066, the murder of Thomas Becket in 1170, the Crusaders' capture of Jerusalem in 1099, Kublai Khan in battle in 1287, the Black Death of 1348, and much more.

Internet Medieval Sourcebook
http://www.fordham.edu/halsall/sbook.html
This site is the product of Fordham University Center for Medieval Studies and is maintained by Paul Halsall. It has three primary index pages as well as a number of supplementary documents. The first index page, Selected Sources, includes numerous texts that can be used for teaching purposes. The second index page, Full Text Sources, includes the full text of medieval sources. The sources are arranged by type. The third index page, Saints' Lives, includes biographies taken from ancient, medieval, and Byzantine sources. One of the more intriguing supplementary documents is the Medieval Legal History. This section groups together all texts that are relevant to the history of law.

The Labyrinth: A World Wide Web Server for Medieval Studies
http://www.georgetown.edu/labyrinth-home.html
This massive information network provides connections to numerous electronic texts, databases, and services through Georgetown University's WWW server. The national cultures or countries included in the Labyrinth are Anglo-Saxon, Byzantium, Celtic, England (1066-1500), France, Germany, Iberia, Italy, and Scandinavian. Some of the special topics that will be of interest to the casual as well as dedicated medieval researcher are the Crusades, Chivalry, Medieval Women, and Vikings, Runes, and Norse Culture. The site can best be described as a "global information network" that provides "free, organized access to electronic resources in medieval studies."

Medieval Europe
http://history.boisestate.edu/westciv/medieval/
A fine overview of medieval European history that includes such topics of discussion as the Dark Ages, the Carolingian era, the Moors, the Vikings, the Papacy,

and the Black Death. This site is maintained by Boise State University.

MEMDB: Medieval and Early Modern Database
http://www.scc.rutgers.edu/memdb
This data bank was established at Rutgers University. The MEMDB aims to make available to scholars "an expanding library of information in electronic format on the medieval and early modern periods of European history, circa 800-1815 C.E."

Middle Ages by Historylink 101
http://www.historylink101.com/midieval.htm
This site makes available a full range of Middle Ages links, including art, daily life, maps, and biographies.

Multimedia History Tutorials, Applied History Research Group, University of Calgary
http://www.ucalgary.ca/applied_history/tutor/
These multimedia tutorials were created to "work with existing courses taught at colleges and universities throughout Alberta." Some of the topics covered include the End of Europe's Middle Ages, the European Voyages of Exploration, the Islamic World to 1600, and People North America: Population Movements and Migration.

NetSERF: The Internet Connection for Medieval Resources
http://www.netserf.org
This site is sponsored by Catholic University's Department of History and maintained by Beau Harbin. The index makes it possible for a researcher to investigate such categories as archaeology, art, civilizations, culture, literature, people, religion, science and technology, women, history, and law. The civilizations that can be researched include the Anglo-Norman, Anglo-Saxon, Byzantine, English, French, Italian, Viking, and Welsh.

ORB: On-Line Text Materials for Medieval Studies
http://www.the-orb.net
The Online Resource Book for Medieval Studies (ORB) has been put together through the cooperative efforts of various scholars. ORB makes its home at the College of Staten Island, City University of New York, and Kathryn Talarico is its editor. Previously ORB was edited by Carolyn Schriber of Rhodes College. This site is truly an academic site. Medieval scholars and serious students of the Middle Ages will benefit from the care taken by all involved. ORB includes such extraordinary sections as the ORB Encyclopedia, the ORB Textbook Library, What Every Medievalist Should Know, Resources for Teaching, Of General Interest, External Links, E-Texts, and the ORB Reference Shelf. The site has to be considered a work-in-progress. It can only be hoped that the original idea of this site, "to establish an online textbook source for medieval studies on the World-Wide Web," will continue to be the guiding vision for the ORB.

The Proceedings of the Friesian School
http://www.friesian.com/
This extraordinary site is maintained by Kelley L. Ross of the Department of Philosophy, Los Angeles Valley College. It is possible to select the following sections: History of Philosophy, Epistemology, Metaphysics, Philosophy of Science, Value Theory, Political Economy, Philosophy of Religion, Philosophy of History, Dissertations, and Reviews. The site is ever-expanding and covers all periods of history. Most of its many detailed pages provide full-color maps, geneaological charts, and regnal tables. The site also includes an extraordinary guide and index to its lists of rulers.

Ragz International World History Center
http://www.ragz-international.com/
At this site a researcher can locate anything that has to do with world history on the World Wide Web. It is possible to find photographs, paintings, carvings, and quotations. Some of the pages on this site are dedicated to important periods and civilizations in Western history, including Art, Philosophy, Historical Documents, European History, the Middle Ages, the Crusades, the Holy Roman Empire, and the Mongols.

WebChron: Web Chronology Project
http://campus.northpark.edu/history/webchron/
The Web Chronology Project is a program that was started by the History Department of North Park University. It includes a series of "hyperlinked chronologies developed by the instructors and historical articles prepared by students intended for use in history classes." There are chronologies for different regions and for different themes.

AFRICA

Civilizations in Africa
http://www.wsu.edu:8080/~dee/CIVAFRCA/CIVAFRCA.HTM
Maintained by Washington State University, this site includes discussions on various African civilizations

and a glossary of African terms and concepts. There is also an annotated resource list of Africa Web links and African Studies WWW links. Some of the other sections that serious students of Africa can avail themselves of are History, African Art, and Newsgroups. The principal author and designer of the site is Richard Hooker. Paul Brians, of the WSU English Department, has served as the primary editor of the site.

Internet African History Sourcebook
http://www.fordham.edu/halsall/africa/africasbook.html
One of the "sourcebook" products of Fordham University, maintained by Paul Halsall. This site presents "historical sources on the history, of human societies in the continent of Africa."

ART

ICMA: The International Center of Medieval Art
http://www.medievalart.org/resources/
The ICMA was formed in order to "promote and encourage the study, understanding, and appreciation of the visual arts of the Middle Ages produced in Europe, the Mediterranean region, and the Slavic world, during the period between ca. 300 and ca. 1500 C.E." The online resource links are divided into the following topics: Archaeology, architecture, Byzantium, costume, libraries and centers for medieval studies and databases, manuscript/text studies, the Middle East, museums, online grant research, online reference, painting, and sculpture.

Metropolitan Museum of Art: Timeline of Art History
http://www.metmuseum.org/toah/splash.htm
This site provides a "chronological, geographical, and thematic exploration of the history of art from around the world, as illustrated especially by the Metropolitan Museum of Art's collection." Within each time line, a student will find "representative art from the Museum's collection, a chart of time periods, a map of the region, an overview, and a list of key events."

ASIA

Asian Historical Architecture
http://www.orientalarchitecture.com/
This site makes it possible to look at many thousands of photographs of Asian architecture through the links to more than 450 Web sites.

Center for Chinese Studies Library, Berkeley
http://www.lib.berkeley.edu/CCSL/
In addition to including the CCSL's own catalog and bibliography, this site lists many links to sites that focus on Chinese history.

Chinese History and Culture
http://www.cernet.edu.cn/history.html
This informative site includes a time line of the Chinese dynasties, a fine narrative history of China, and much more.

Internet East Asian History Sourcebook
http://www.fordham.edu/halsall/eastasia/eastasiasbook.html
One of the highly-regarded "sourcebook" projects of Fordham University, maintained by Paul Halsall. Through this site, it is possible to find historical and cultural information on China, Japan, Korea, and Vietnam.

Internet Indian History Sourcebook
http://www.fordham.edu/halsall/indiasbook.html
Maintained by Paul Halsall, this site is one of Fordham University's "sourcebook" products. Like its counterparts, this one includes an extraordinary amount of useful historical and cultural information.

BRITAIN

The Camelot Project: Arthurian Texts, Images, Bibliographies, and Basic Information
http://www.lib.rochester.edu/camelot/cphome.stm
Sponsored by the University of Rochester, this site is "designed to make available in electronic format a database of Arthurian texts, images, bibliographies, and basic information." It includes menus of writers, artists, guidebooks, and many related topics. The texts have been prepared by the Consortium for the Teaching of the Middle Ages (TEAM) in association with the University of Rochester. The project was designed by Alan Lupack and Barbara Tepa Lupack.

The Medieval World: British History, 1066-1500
http://www.spartacus.schoolnet.co.uk/Medieval.htm
This encyclopedia was produced by Spartacus, a publishing company organized by teachers. It includes information on such subjects as medieval warfare, monarchs, the Normans, medieval farming, the Anglo-Saxons, and much more. While the majority of articles are brief, this site serves as a wonderful introduction to Britain.

TimeRef
http://www.timeref.org/
This site includes numerous time lines for British events from 800 to 1499. There also are maps that "show the locations of castles, abbeys, and cathedrals in England, Scotland, and Wales." Amazingly "every person and building on this site has its own time line and links to related subjects." As a bonus there is a glossary of terms, architectural information, and three-dimensional images of buildings.

Uniting the Kingdoms?
http://www.pro.gov.uk/pathways/utk/
Sponsored by National Archives of the United Kingdom, this Web exhibition takes a detailed look "at how the governments and people of England, Scotland, Ireland, and Wales, and of England's French territories, interacted in politics, warfare, religion, trade and everyday life" during the Middle Ages. In addition to each separate history being divided into chapters, there is a listing of the monarchs of England, Scotland, and France, as well as numerous relevant maps.

LITERATURE

Luminarium: Anthology of Middle English Literature (1350-1485)
http://www.luminarium.org/medlit
Created by Anniina Jokinen in 1996 and continually updated since, this site includes the literature of Geoffrey Chaucer, John Gower, William Langland, Julian of Norwich, Margery Kempe, Sir Thomas Malory, Everyman, Medieval Plays, and Medieval Lyrics. A fine collection of essays and articles concerning literature of this period and these authors also has been included.

Medieval Drama Links
http://collectorspost.com/Catalogue/medramalinks.htm
An organized collection of links to such topics as drama texts, articles, books, set design, make-up, costumes, dance, music, and musical instruments. Each link is annotated.

Medieval Resources
http://www.umm.maine.edu/faculty/necastro/medieval/index.asp
This site can be best described as a "digital library of full-text resources" as well as a "virtual library of links and a subject guide to its many topics." There are sections on such topics as Geoffrey Chaucer, Medieval and Renaissance Drama, Storybook of the Middle Ages, and Dante.

The Schøyen Collection: Checklist of 222 Manuscripts Spanning 5000 Years
http://www.nb.no/baser/schoyen/
In addition to digital representations of photographs of or from the original manuscripts, this site includes "references to 222 manuscripts from the whole world from the ancient period (starting 3200 bc), the medieval period, and the post-medieval period."

University of California Press eScholarship Editions
http://escholarship.cdlib.org/ucpress/
Hundreds of books published by the University of California Press are included here in full text, including several books from the Middle Ages.

THE MIDDLE EAST

Ancient Near East and the Mediterranean World
http://www.lib.uchicago.edu/e/dl/proj/neh2/
This project was completed by the University of Chicago library and "preserves deteriorated research materials relating to the history, art and archaeology of the ancient Near East and the ancient Mediterranean world." Some of the regions covered at this site are Assyria, Babylonia, Egypt, Nubia, Persia, and Sumer.

Encyclopedia of the Orient
http://i-cias.com/e.o/index.htm
This ready-reference online encyclopedia covers all of the countries of North Africa and the Middle East. The articles are geared toward the high-school and undergraduate student who needs quick and concise information on the people and places of this often neglected region of the world.

Internet Islamic History Sourcebook
http://www.fordham.edu/halsall/islam/islamsbook.html
This site is one of the "sourcebook" products of Fordham University and is maintained by Paul Halsall. Many links to original documents are included as well as links to other online resources.

Internet Jewish History Sourcebook
http://www.fordham.edu/halsall/jewish/jewishsbook.html
One of Fordham University's "sourcebook" products that is maintained by Paul Halsall. As with the other sourcebook sites, this one includes a wealth of relevant information as well as links to other Web resources.

Military History

De Re Militari

http://www.deremilitari.org/

Created by the Society for Medieval Military History, this site provides access to primary sources, book reviews, and bibliographies. There is also information on lectures and conferences relevant to the subject at hand.

History of the Crusades

http://libtext.library.wisc.edu/HistCrusades/

Provided by the University of Wisconsin Libraries, this site provides an online edition of a "six-volume narrative history of medieval Christian military expeditions to the Holy Land." This classic work originally was edited by Kenneth M. Setton and published by the University of Wisconsin Press.

Music

A Guide to Medieval and Renaissance Instruments

http://www.s-hamilton.k12.ia.us/antiqua/instrumt.html

More than thirty musical instruments are discussed at this site. It is possible to find the history, pictures, alternate names, and even sound-wave clips on each of these instruments. Some of the fascinating instruments included are the bagpipe, bladder pipe, dulcimer, harpsichord, hurdy-gurdy, lute, organetto, recorder, shofar, and viol.

Science and Technology

Medieval Science Page

http://members.aol.com/mcnelis/medsci_index.html

This site was created and is maintained by James McNelis, who is the editor-in-chief of Envoi: A Review Journal of Medieval Literature. It attempts to provide a "convenient and comprehensive set of links to all Internet resources worldwide which deal with aspects of medieval science, both in Western and other cultures." The site has been continually updated since 1995. Some of the topics include alchemy, astronomy, botany, cosmology, mathematics, medicine, technology, time, and weights and measures.

Medieval Technology Pages

http://scholar.chem.nyu.edu/technology.html

Maintained by New York University, this site provides information concerning "technological innovation and related subjects in western Europe during the Middle Ages." Some of the topics covered are the horizontal loom, windmills, and agricultural tools.

The Year 1000: A Legacy of Science and Technology

http://www.lindahall.org/events_exhibit/ex_year_1000.shtml

This online exhibit focuses on the technological developments in the year 1000. This year is described as a "turning point towards High Medieval civilization with individuals and societies around the world making contributions to science, technology and culture." The site is edited by Nancy V. Green, a librarian at the Linda Hall Library of Science, Engineering and Technology in Kansas City, Missouri.

Women

Feminae: Medieval Women and Gender Index

http://www.haverford.edu/library/reference/mschaus/mfi/mfi.html

This index includes more than eight thousand records from "journal articles, book reviews, and essays in books about women, sexuality, and gender during the Middle Ages." Margaret Schaus, a Haverford College librarian, is the editor of this "searchable, annotated index."

Monastic Matrix: A Scholarly Resource for the Study of Women's Religious Communities from 400 to 1600 C.E.

http://monasticmatrix.org/

Maintained through the Department of History at the University of Southern California, this site includes information that relates to "women's religious life, activities and patronage." All of the religious communities mentioned are searchable by "name, region, date, and other access points." Primary documents, a bibliography, and a visual library also are included.

Women Writers of the Middle Ages

http://www.lib.rochester.edu/camelot/womenbib.htm

This site is part of the University of Rochester's Camelot Project. It consists of a "bibliography of works by and about women writers of the Middle Ages."

—*Jeffry Jensen*

Great Events from History

The Middle Ages

477 - 1453

Chronological List of Entries

477-600 c.e.

5th or 6th century: Confucianism Arrives in Japan
484: White Huns Raid India
496: Baptism of Clovis
c. 500-1000: Rise of Swahili Cultures
c. 500-1000: Tiwanaku Civilization Flourishes in Andean Highlands
6th-8th centuries: Sogdians Dominate Central Asian Trade
February 2, 506: Alaric II Drafts the *Breviarum Alarici*
524: Imprisonment and Death of Boethius
529-534: Justinian's Code Is Compiled
532-537: Building of Hagia Sophia
538-552: Buddhism Arrives in Japan
563: Silk Worms Are Smuggled to the Byzantine Empire
567-568: Sāsānians and Turks Defeat the White Huns
568-571: Lombard Conquest of Italy
581: Sui Dynasty Reunifies China
590-604: Reforms of Pope Gregory the Great
593-604: Regency of Shōtoku Taishi
595-665: Invention of Decimals and Negative Numbers
596-597: See of Canterbury Is Established
c. 600-950: El Tajín Is Built

601-700 c.e.

7th-8th centuries: Maya Build Astronomical Observatory at Palenque
7th-8th centuries: Papermaking Spreads to Korea, Japan, and Central Asia
7th-13th centuries: Mogollons Establish Agricultural Settlements
605-610: Building of the Grand Canal
606: National University Awards First Doctorate
606-647: Reign of Harṣa of Kanauj
607-839: Japan Sends Embassies to China
c. 610-632: Muḥammad Receives Revelations
c. 611-642: Reign of Pulakeśin II
618: Founding of the Tang Dynasty
627-650: Reign of Songtsen Gampo
629-645: Pilgrimage of Xuanzang
630-668: Reign of Narasiṃhavarman I Mahāmalla
630-711: Islam Expands Throughout North Africa
635-800: Founding of Lindisfarne and Creation of the *Book of Kells*
August 15-20, 636: Battle of Yarmūk
637-657: Islam Expands Throughout the Middle East
645-646: Adoption of *Nengo* System and Taika Reforms
652-c. 1171: Christian Nubia and Muslim Egypt Sign Treaty
668-935: Silla Unification of Korea
October 10, 680: Martyrdom of Prophet's Grandson Ḥusayn
682-1377: Expansion of Śrivijaya
685-691: Building of the Dome of the Rock
690-705: Reign of Empress Wu
c. 700: Bow and Arrow Spread into North America
c. 700-1000: Building of Chichén Itzá
c. 700-1000: Heavy Plow Helps Increase Agricultural Yields
c. 700-1100: Settlement of the South Pacific Islands
c. 700-1253: Confederation of Thai Tribes

701-800 C.E.

8th-14th centuries: Cahokia Becomes the First North American City
8th-15th centuries: Hohokam Adapt to the Desert Southwest
701: Taihō Laws Reform Japanese Government
c. 710: Construction of the Kāilaśanātha Temple
April or May, 711: Ṭārik Crosses into Spain
March 9, 712, and July 1, 720: Writing of *Kojiki* and *Nihon shoki*
713-741: First Newspapers in China
726-843: Iconoclastic Controversy
729: Founding of Nanzhao
730: Rise of the Pratihāras
731: Bede Writes *Ecclesiastical History of the English People*
October 11, 732: Battle of Tours
735: Christianity Is Introduced into Germany
740: Khazars Convert to Judaism
744-840: Uighur Turks Rule Central Asia
c. 750-1240: Rise and Fall of Ghana
751: Battle of Talas River
754: Coronation of Pépin the Short
755-763: Rebellion of An Lushan
763: Tibetans Capture Chang'an
770-810: Reign of Dharmapāla
775-840: Building of Borobuḍur
780: Beginning of the Harem System
780: Rise of the Sailendra Family
781: Alcuin Becomes Adviser to Charlemagne
786-809: Reign of Hārūn al-Rashīd
788-850: Śaṇkara Expounds Advaita Vedānta
791: Buddhism Becomes Tibetan State Religion
792: Rise of the Samurai
June 7, 793: Norse Raid Lindisfarne Monastery
794-1185: Heian Period
c. 800: *Kana* Syllabary Is Developed
c. 800-1350: Mississippian Mound-Building Culture Flourishes

801-900 C.E.

9th-14th centuries: Rise of the Toutswe Kingdom
9th-15th centuries: Plains Village Culture Flourishes
802: Founding of the Khmer Empire
809: First Islamic Public Hospital
812: Paper Money First Used in China
832: Nanzhao Subjugates Pyu
834: Gypsies Expelled from Persia
838-842: Tibetan Empire Dissolves
840-846: Uighur Migrations
843: Treaty of Verdun
845: Suppression of Buddhism
Mid-9th century: Invention of Gunpowder and Guns
c. 850: Development of Slavic Alphabet
850-950: Viking Era
After 850: Foundation of Chan Chan
858: Rise of the Fujiwara Family
863: Nanzhao Captures Hanoi
864: Boris Converts to Christianity
868: First Book Printed
869-883: Zanj Revolt of African Slaves
872-973: Publication of *The History of al-Ṭabarī*
877-889: Indravarman I Conquers the Thai and the Mons
878: Alfred Defeats the Danes
890's: Magyars Invade Italy, Saxony, and Bavaria
893: Beginning of Bulgaria's Golden Age

901-1000 C.E.

Early 10th century: Qarakhanids Convert to Islam
10th century: Cult of Quetzalcóatl Spreads Through Mesoamerica
10th-11th centuries: First Hausa State Established
907-960: Period of Five Dynasties and Ten Kingdoms
915: Parāntaka I Conquers Pāṇḍya
918-936: Foundation of the Koryŏ Dynasty

927: Compilation of the *Engi Shiki*
936: Khitans Settle Near Beijing
939-944: Reign of Ngo Quyen
c. 950: Court of Córdoba Flourishes in Spain
c. 950-1100: Rise of Madrasas
c. 950-1150: Toltecs Build Tula
August 10, 955: Otto I Defeats the Magyars
956: Oğhuz Turks Migrate to Transoxiana
958-1076: Koreans Adopt the Tang Civil Service Model
960: Founding of the Song Dynasty
c. 960: Jews Settle in Bohemia
960-1279: Scholar-Official Class Flourishes Under Song Dynasty
963: Foundation of the Mount Athos Monasteries
969-1171: Reign of the Fāṭimids
972: Building of al-Azhar Mosque
973: Foundation of the Western Cālukya Dynasty
976-1025: Reign of Basil II
982: Le Dai Hanh Invades Champa
c. 985-1014: Reign of Rājarāja I
987: Hugh Capet Is Elected to the French Throne
988: Baptism of Vladimir I
992-1054: Ghana Takes Control of Awdaghust
998-1030: Reign of Maḥmūd of Ghazna
c. 1000: Collapse of the Huari and Tiwanaku Civilizations
c. 1000: Footbinding Develops in Chinese Society
c. 1000: Hindi Becomes India's Dominant Language

1001-1100 C.E.

11th century: Expansion of Sunni Islam in North Africa and Iberia
11th-12th centuries: Building of Romanesque Cathedrals
11th-12th centuries: First European-Native American Contact
11th-15th centuries: Development of the Ife Kingdom and Yoruba Culture
11th-15th centuries: Great Zimbabwe Urbanism and Architecture
After 1000: Development of Miracle and Mystery Plays
c. 1001: Sei Shōnagon Completes *The Pillow Book*
c. 1004: Murasaki Shikibu Writes *The Tale of Genji*
1009: Destruction of the Church of the Holy Sepulchre
1010: Firdusi Composes the *Shahnamah*
c. 1010: Songhai Kingdom Converts to Islam
c. 1010-1015: Avicenna Writes His *Canon of Medicine*
1012: Rice Is Introduced into China
April 23, 1014: Battle of Clontarf
1016: Canute Conquers England
c. 1025: Scholars at Chartres Revive Interest in the Classics
1031: Caliphate of Córdoba Falls
1040-1055: Expansion of the Seljuk Turks
c. 1045: Bi Sheng Develops Movable Earthenware Type
1048: Zīrids Break from Fāṭimid Dynasty and Revive Sunni Islam
1054: Beginning of the Rome-Constantinople Schism
1062-1147: Almoravids Conquer Morocco and Establish the Almoravid Empire
October 14, 1066: Battle of Hastings
1069-1072: Wang Anshi Introduces Bureaucratic Reforms
August 26, 1071: Battle of Manzikert
c. 1075-1086: Hummay Founds the Sefuwa Dynasty
c. 1075-1220: Emergence of Mapungubwe
1076: Almoravids Sack Kumbi
1077: Seljuk Dynasty Is Founded
1086: Domesday Survey
November, 1092-June 15, 1094: El Cid Conquers Valencia
November 27, 1095: Pope Urban II Calls the First Crusade
March 21, 1098: Foundation of the Cistercian Order
c. 1100: Arabic Numerals Are Introduced into Europe
c. 1100: Founding of Timbuktu
c. 1100: Origins of Swahili in Its Written Form
c. 1100: Rise of Courtly Love
1100-1300: European Universities Emerge

1101-1200 C.E.

12th century: Coins Are Minted on the Swahili Coast
12th century: Trading Center of Kilwa Kisiwani Is Founded
12th century: Wang Chongyang Founds Quanzhen Daoism
12th-14th centuries: Social and Political Impact of Leprosy
1115: Foundation of the Jin Dynasty
c. 1120: Order of the Knights Templars Is Founded
1127-1130: Creation of the Kingdom of Sicily
1130: Birth of Zhu Xi
1130: Karakitai Empire Established
1136: Hildegard von Bingen Becomes Abbess
1145: Kim Pu-sik Writes *Samguk Sagi*
c. 1145: Prester John Myth Sweeps Across Europe
1147-1149: Second Crusade
c. 1150: Moors Transmit Classical Philosophy and Medicine to Europe
c. 1150: Refinements in Banking
1150: Venetian Merchants Dominate Trade with the East
c. 1150-1200: Development of Gothic Architecture
c. 1150-1200: Rise of the Hansa Merchant Union
1152: Frederick Barbarossa Is Elected King of Germany
1153: Jin Move Their Capital to Beijing
1154-1204: Angevin Empire Is Established
1155: Charter of Lorris Is Written
September 17, 1156: Austria Emerges as a National Entity
1156-1192: Minamoto Yoritomo Becomes Shogun
1167: Foundation of the Nemanjid Dynasty
1169-1172: Normans Invade Ireland
December 29, 1170: Murder of Thomas Becket
1175: Hōnen Shōnin Founds Pure Land Buddhism
c. 1175: Waldensian Excommunications Usher in Protestant Movement
c. 1180: Chrétien de Troyes Writes *Perceval*
c. 1181-1221: Lalibela Founds the Christian Capital of Ethiopia
1189-1192: Third Crusade
1190: Moses Maimonides Writes *The Guide of the Perplexed*
c. 1190-1279: Ma-Xia School of Painting Flourishes
1193: Turkish Raiders Destroy Buddhist University at Nalanda
1196-1258: Ch'oe Family Takes Power in Korea
c. 1200: Common-Law Tradition Emerges in England
c. 1200: Fairs of Champagne
c. 1200: Scientific Cattle Breeding Developed
c. 1200-1230: Manco Capac Founds the Inca State

1201-1300 C.E.

13th century: Ndiadiane N'diaye Founds the Wolof Empire
1204: Genghis Khan Founds Mongol Empire
1204: Knights of the Fourth Crusade Capture Constantinople
1206-1210: Quṭ al-Dīn Aybak Establishes the Delhi Sultanate
April 16, 1209: Founding of the Franciscans
1209-1229: Albigensian Crusade
1212: Children's Crusade
July 27, 1214: Battle of Bouvines
June 15, 1215: Signing of the Magna Carta
November 11-30, 1215: Fourth Lateran Council
1217-1221: Fifth Crusade
1219-1333: Hōjō Family Dominates Shoguns, Rules Japan
1221-1259: Mai Dunama Dibbalemi Expands Kanem Empire
1225: Tran Thai Tong Establishes Tran Dynasty
1225-1231: Jalāl al-Dīn Expands the Khwārizmian Empire
1227-1230: Frederick II Leads the Sixth Crusade
1228-1231: Teutonic Knights Bring Baltic Region Under Catholic Control
1230: Unification of Castile and León
1230's-1255: Reign of Sundiata of Mali
1233: Papal Inquisition
1236-1240: Reign of Raziya
July 15, 1240: Alexander Nevsky Defends Novgorod from Swedish Invaders
1248-1254: Failure of the Seventh Crusade
Late 13th century: Maoris Hunt Moa to Extinction

c. 1250: Improvements in Shipbuilding and Navigation
c. 1250-1300: Homosexuality Criminalized and Subject to Death Penalty
1258: Provisions of Oxford Are Established
1259: Mangrai Founds the Kingdom of Lan Na
September 3, 1260: Battle of Ain Jālūt
c. 1265-1273: Thomas Aquinas Compiles the *Summa Theologica*
1270-1285: Yekuno Amlak Founds the Solomonid Dynasty
1271-1295: Travels of Marco Polo
1273: Sufi Order of Mawlawīyah Is Established
1275: First Mechanical Clock
1275: Nestorian Archbishopric Is Founded in Beijing
c. 1275: The *Zohar* Is Transcribed
1285: Statute of Winchester
1290-1306: Jews Are Expelled from England, France, and Southern Italy
April, 1291: Fall of Acre, Palestine
1295: Model Parliament
1295: Ramkhamhaeng Conquers the Mekong and Menam Valleys
1299: ʿAlāʾ-ud-Dīn Muḥammad Khaljī Conquers Gujarat

1301-1400 C.E.

July 27, 1302: Battle of Bapheus
November 18, 1302: Boniface VIII Issues the Bull *Unam Sanctam*
1305-1417: Avignon Papacy and the Great Schism
c. 1306-1320: Dante Writes *The Divine Comedy*
c. 1310-1350: William of Ockham Attacks Thomist Ideas
June 23-24, 1314: Battle of Bannockburn
November 15, 1315: Swiss Victory at Morgarten over Habsburg Forces
c. 1320: Origins of the Bubonic Plague
1323-1326: Champa Wins Independence from Dai Viet
August 1, 1323-August 23, 1328: Peasants' Revolt in Flanders
July 2, 1324: Lady Alice Kyteler Is Found Guilty of Witchcraft
1324-1325: Mansa Mūsā's Pilgrimage to Mecca Sparks Interest in Mali Empire
1325-1355: Travels of Ibn Baṭṭūṭah
1325-1519: Aztecs Build Tenochtitlán
1328-1350: Flowering of Late Medieval Physics
November, 1330: Basarab Defeats the Hungarians
1333: Kilwa Kisiwani Begins Economic and Historical Decline
1336-1392: Yoshino Civil Wars
1337-1453: Hundred Years' War
1340: Al-ʿUmarī Writes a History of Africa
August 26, 1346: Battle of Crécy
1347: ʿAlāʾ-ud-Dīn Bahman Shāh Founds the Bahmanī Sultanate
1347-1352: Invasion of the Black Death in Europe
May 20, 1347-October 8, 1354: Cola di Rienzo Leads Popular Uprising in Rome
1350: Ramathibodi I Creates First Thai Legal System
c. 1350-1400: Petrarch and Boccaccio Recover Classical Texts
January 10, 1356, and December 25, 1356: Golden Bull
c. 1360-1440: Kan'ami and Zeami Perfect Nō Drama
1366: Statute of Kilkenny
1368: Establishment of the Ming Dynasty
1368: Tibet Gains Independence from Mongols
1373-1410: Jean Froissart Compiles His *Chronicles*
1377: Ibn Khaldūn Completes His *Muqaddimah*
1377-1378: Condemnation of John Wyclif
c. 1380: Compilation of the Wise Sayings of Lal Ded
September 8, 1380: Battle of Kulikovo
May-June, 1381: Peasants' Revolt in England
1381-1405: Tamerlane's Conquests
1382-1395: Reign of Sthitimalla
c. 1387: Chinese Create the Eight-Legged Essay
1387-1400: Chaucer Writes *The Canterbury Tales*
June 28, 1389: Turkish Conquest of Serbia
c. 1392: Foundation of the Gelugpa Order
July, 1392: Establishment of the Yi Dynasty
1397: Publication of the Laws of Great Ming
June 17, 1397: Kalmar Union Is Formed
1399-1404: Tamerlane Builds the Bibi Khanum Mosque
1400-1500: Foundation of the West African States of Benin

1401-1453 C.E.

1403-1407: *Yonglo Dadian* Encyclopedia Is Compiled
1405-1433: Zheng He's Naval Expeditions
July 15, 1410: Battle of Tannenberg
c. 1410-1440: Florentine School of Art Emerges
1414-1418: Council of Constance
July 6, 1415: Martyrdom of Jan Hus
1415-1460: Prince Henry the Navigator Promotes Portuguese Exploration
1428: Le Loi Establishes Later Le Dynasty
May 4-8, 1429: Joan of Arc's Relief of Orléans
1440: Donation of Constantine Is Exposed
1442-1456: János Hunyadi Defends Hungary Against the Ottomans
1444-1446: Albanian Chieftains Unite Under Prince Skanderbeg
c. 1450: Gutenberg Pioneers the Printing Press
1453: English Are Driven from France
May 29, 1453: Fall of Constantinople

Category Index

List of Categories

Agriculture IX
Architecture IX
Communications IX
Cultural and intellectual history IX
Diplomacy and international relations XI
Economics XI
Education XI
Engineering XI
Environment XI
Expansion and land acquisition XI
Exploration and discovery XII
Government and politics XII
Health and medicine XIV
Historiography XIV
Laws, acts, and legal history XIV
Literature XV
Mathematics XV
Organizations and institutions XV
Philosophy XV
Religion XVI
Science and technology XVII
Social reform XVII
Trade and commerce XVII
Transportation XVIII
Wars, uprisings, and civil unrest XVIII

Agriculture

563: Silk Worms Are Smuggled to the Byzantine Empire, 31
7th-13th cent.: Mogollons Establish Agricultural Settlements, 61
c. 700-1000: Heavy Plow Helps Increase Agricultural Yields, 127
8th-15th cent.: Hohokam Adapt to the Desert Southwest, 137
c. 800-1350: Mississippian Mound-Building Culture Flourishes, 215
9th-14th cent.: Rise of the Toutswe Kingdom, 219
9th-15th cent.: Plains Village Culture Flourishes, 221
1012: Rice Is Introduced into China, 401
c. 1200: Scientific Cattle Breeding Developed, 574

Architecture

532-537: Building of Hagia Sophia, 25
c. 600-950: El Tajín Is Built, 53
685-691: Building of the Dome of the Rock, 116
c. 700-1000: Building of Chichén Itzá, 124
8th-14th cent.: Cahokia Becomes the First North American City, 134
8th-15th cent.: Hohokam Adapt to the Desert Southwest, 137
c. 710: Construction of the Kāilaśanātha Temple, 142
730: Rise of the Pratihāras, 156
775-840: Building of Borobuḍur, 185
After 850: Foundation of Chan Chan, 255
c. 950-1150: Toltecs Build Tula, 313
972: Building of al-Azhar Mosque, 336
c. 1000: Collapse of the Huari and Tiwanaku Civilizations, 360
11th-12th cent.: Building of Romanesque Cathedrals, 370
11th-15th cent.: Great Zimbabwe Urbanism and Architecture, 378
1009: Destruction of the Church of the Holy Sepulchre, 390
c. 1181-1221: Lalibela Founds the Christian Capital of Ethiopia, 554
1325-1519: Aztecs Build Tenochtitlán, 731
1399-1404: Tamerlane Builds the Bibi Khanum Mosque, 822

Communications

7th-8th cent.: Papermaking Spreads to Korea, Japan, and Central Asia, 59
713-741: First Newspapers in China, 149
868: First Book Printed, 265
c. 1000: Hindi Becomes India's Dominant Language, 365
c. 1045: Bi Sheng Develops Movable Earthenware Type, 418
c. 1100: Origins of Swahili in Its Written Form, 464
c. 1450: Gutenberg Pioneers the Printing Press, 861

Cultural and intellectual history

5th or 6th cent.: Confucianism Arrives in Japan, 1
c. 500-1000: Rise of Swahili Cultures, 9
c. 500-c. 1000: Tiwanaku Civilization Flourishes in Andean Highlands, 11

524: Imprisonment and Death of Boethius, 19
538-552: Buddhism Arrives in Japan, 28
595-665: Invention of Decimals and Negative Numbers, 47
7th-early 8th cent.: Maya Build Astronomical Observatory at Palenque, 56
7th-13th cent.: Mogollons Establish Agricultural Settlements, 61
618: Founding of the Tang Dynasty, 79
629-645: Pilgrimage of Xuanzang, 85
630-668: Reign of Narasiṃhavarman I Mahāmalla, 88
635-800: Founding of Lindisfarne and Creation of the *Book of Kells*, 94
668-935: Silla Unification of Korea, 108
c. 700-1000: Building of Chichén Itzá, 124
8th-14th cent.: Cahokia Becomes the First North American City, 134
8th-15th cent.: Hohokam Adapt to the Desert Southwest, 137
713-741: First Newspapers in China, 149
731: Bede Writes *Ecclesiastical History of the English People*, 160
740: Khazars Convert to Judaism, 168
780: Beginning of the Harem System, 188
780: Rise of the Sailendra Family, 191
781: Alcuin Becomes Adviser to Charlemagne, 193
786-809: Reign of Hārūn al-Rashīd, 196
794-1185: Heian Period, 210
c. 800: *Kana* Syllabary Is Developed, 213
9th-15th cent.: Plains Village Culture Flourishes, 221
834: Gypsies Expelled from Persia, 234
840-846: Uighur Migrations, 239
c. 850: Development of Slavic Alphabet, 249
872-973: Publication of *The History of al-Ṭabarī*, 270
890's: Magyars Invade Italy, Saxony, and Bavaria, 279
893: Beginning of Bulgaria's Golden Age, 282
Early 10th cent.: Qarakhanids Convert to Islam, 285
10th cent.: Cult of Quetzalcóatl Spreads Through Mesoamerica, 287
c. 950: Court of Córdoba Flourishes in Spain, 307
c. 950-1100: Rise of Madrasas, 310
c. 950-1150: Toltecs Build Tula, 313
960: Founding of the Song Dynasty, 322
c. 960: Jews Settle in Bohemia, 326
960-1279: Scholar-Official Class Flowers Under Song Dynasty, 327
c. 985-1014: Reign of Rājarāja I, 346
c. 1000: Footbinding Develops in Chinese Society, 362
c. 1000: Hindi Becomes India's Dominant Language, 365
11th-12th cent.: Building of Romanesque Cathedrals, 370
11th-15th cent.: Development of the Ife Kingdom and Yoruba Culture, 376
After 1000: Development of Miracle and Mystery Plays, 381
c. 1001: Sei Shōnagon Completes *The Pillow Book*, 385
c. 1004: Murasaki Shikibu Writes *The Tale of Genji*, 387
1010: Firdusi Composes the *Shahnamah*, 393
c. 1010-1015: Avicenna Writes His *Canon of Medicine*, 397
c. 1025: Scholars at Chartres Revive Interest in the Classics, 409
1031: Caliphate of Córdoba Falls, 412
c. 1045: Bi Sheng Develops Movable Earthenware Type, 418
Oct. 14, 1066: Battle of Hastings, 428
c. 1100: Arabic Numerals Are Introduced into Europe, 458
c. 1100: Founding of Timbuktu, 461
c. 1100: Origins of Swahili in Its Written Form, 464
c. 1100: Rise of Courtly Love, 466
1100-1300: European Universities Emerge, 470
1130: Birth of Zhu Xi, 491
c. 1145: Prester John Myth Sweeps Across Europe, 500
c. 1150: Moors Transmit Classical Philosophy and Medicine to Europe, 507
c. 1150-1200: Development of Gothic Architecture, 516
1175: Hōnen Shōnin Founds Pure Land Buddhism, 547
1190: Moses Maimonides Writes *The Guide of the Perplexed*, 560
c. 1190-1279: Ma-Xia School of Painting Flourishes, 562
c. 1200-1230: Manco Capac Founds the Inca State, 576
Late 13th cent.: Maoris Hunt Moa to Extinction, 645
c. 1250-1300: Homosexuality Criminalized and Subject to Death Penalty, 652
c. 1265-1273: Thomas Aquinas Compiles the *Summa Theologica*, 662
1271-1295: Travels of Marco Polo, 667
1275: Nestorian Archbishopric Is Founded in Beijing, 676
c. 1306-1320: Dante Writes *The Divine Comedy*, 703
c. 1310-1350: William of Ockham Attacks Thomist Ideas, 707

July 2, 1324: Lady Alice Kyteler Is Found Guilty of Witchcraft, 726
1325-1355: Travels of Ibn Baṭṭūṭah, 729
1325-1519: Aztecs Build Tenochtitlán, 731
1340: Al-ʿUmarī Writes a History of Africa, 748
c. 1350-1400: Petrarch and Boccaccio Recover Classical Texts, 764
c. 1360-1440: Kan'ami and Zeami Perfect Nō Drama, 769
1373-1410: Jean Froissart Compiles His *Chronicles*, 780
1377: Ibn Khaldūn Completes His *Muqaddimah*, 783
1387-1400: Chaucer Writes *The Canterbury Tales*, 806
1403-1407: *Yonglo Dadian* Encyclopedia Is Compiled, 827
c. 1410-1440: Florentine School of Art Emerges, 834
1440: Donation of Constantine Is Exposed, 852
c. 1450: Gutenberg Pioneers the Printing Press, 861

Diplomacy and international relations
607-839: Japan Sends Embassies to China, 72
652-c. 1171: Christian Nubia and Muslim Egypt Sign Treaty, 106
843: Treaty of Verdun, 241
June 17, 1397: Kalmar Union Is Formed, 820
1405-1433: Zheng He's Naval Expeditions, 829

Economics
6th-8th cent.: Sogdians Dominate Central Asian Trade, 14
605-610: Building of the Grand Canal, 64
c. 700-1000: Heavy Plow Helps Increase Agricultural Yields, 127
812: Paper Money First Used in China, 229
1086: Domesday Survey, 444
12th cent.: Coins Are Minted on the Swahili Coast, 474
12th cent.: Trading Center of Kilwa Kisiwani Founded, 476
1150: Venetian Merchants Dominate Trade with the East, 513
c. 1150-1200: Rise of the Hansa Merchant Union, 519
1155: Charter of Lorris Is Written, 531
c. 1200: Fairs of Champagne, 571
1333: Kilwa Kisiwani Begins Economic and Historical Decline, 739

Education
606: National University Awards First Doctorate, 66
781: Alcuin Becomes Adviser to Charlemagne, 193
c. 950: Court of Córdoba Flourishes in Spain, 307
c. 950-1100: Rise of Madrasas, 310
972: Building of al-Azhar Mosque, 336
c. 1025: Scholars at Chartres Revive Interest in the Classics, 409
1100-1300: European Universities Emerge, 470
c. 1150: Moors Transmit Classical Philosophy and Medicine to Europe, 507
1193: Turkish Raiders Destroy Buddhist University at Nalanda, 565
c. 1387: Chinese Create the Eight-Legged Essay, 803

Engineering
532-537: Building of Hagia Sophia, 25
605-610: Building of the Grand Canal, 64
685-691: Building of the Dome of the Rock, 116
775-840: Building of Borobuḍur, 185
972: Building of al-Azhar Mosque, 336
11th-12th cent.: Building of Romanesque Cathedrals, 370
11th-15th cent.: Great Zimbabwe Urbanism and Architecture, 378
c. 1250: Improvements in Shipbuilding and Navigation, 648

Environment
c. 700-1000: Heavy Plow Helps Increase Agricultural Yields, 127
8th-14th cent.: Cahokia Becomes the First North American City, 134
c. 1000: Collapse of the Huari and Tiwanaku Civilizations, 360
Late 13th cent.: Maoris Hunt Moa to Extinction, 645
1347-1352: Invasion of the Black Death in Europe, 756

Expansion and land acquisition
484: White Huns Raid India, 3
c. 500-1000: Rise of Swahili Cultures, 9
c. 500-c. 1000: Tiwanaku Civilization Flourishes in Andean Highlands, 11
567-568: Sāsānians and Turks Defeat the White Huns, 33
568-571: Lombard Conquest of Italy, 36
c. 600-950: El Tajín Is Built, 53
c. 611-642: Reign of Pulakeśin II, 77
630-711: Islam Expands Throughout North Africa, 91
637-657: Islam Expands Throughout the Middle East, 101
682-1377: Expansion of Śrivijaya, 113

c. 700-1100: Settlement of the South Pacific Islands, 130
c. 700-1253: Confederation of Thai Tribes, 132
Apr. or May, 711: Ṭārik Crosses into Spain, 144
744-840: Uighur Turks Rule Central Asia, 170
770-810: Reign of Dharmapāla, 183
9th-15th cent.: Plains Village Culture Flourishes, 221
832: Nanzhao Subjugates Pyu, 232
840-846: Uighur Migrations, 239
843: Treaty of Verdun, 241
850-950: Viking Era, 251
877-889: Indravarman I Conquers the Thai and the Mons, 273
878: Alfred Defeats the Danes, 276
890's: Magyars Invade Italy, Saxony, and Bavaria, 279
893: Beginning of Bulgaria's Golden Age, 282
915: Parāntaka I Conquers Pāṇḍya, 294
936: Khitans Settle Near Beijing, 302
c. 950-1150: Toltecs Build Tula, 313
956: Oğhuz Turks Migrate to Transoxiana, 318
969-1171: Reign of the Fāṭimids, 333
c. 985-1014: Reign of Rājarāja I, 346
992-1054: Ghana Takes Control of Awdaghust, 355
998-1030: Reign of Maḥmūd of Ghazna, 357
c. 1000: Collapse of the Huari and Tiwanaku Civilizations, 360
11th cent.: Expansion of Sunni Islam in North Africa and Iberia, 367
11th-12th cent.: First European-Native American Contact, 373
Apr. 23, 1014: Battle of Clontarf, 403
1016: Canute Conquers England, 406
1040-1055: Expansion of the Seljuk Turks, 415
1048: Zīrids Break from Fāṭimid Dynasty and Revive Sunni Islam, 420
1062-1147: Almoravids Conquer Morocco and Establish the Almoravid Empire, 425
1076: Almoravids Sack Kumbi, 440
1077: Seljuk Dynasty Is Founded, 442
1115: Foundation of the Jin Dynasty, 483
1130: Karakitai Empire Established, 493
1153: Jin Move Their Capital to Beijing, 525
1154-1204: Angevin Empire Is Established, 528
1167: Foundation of the Nemanjid Dynasty, 540
1169-1172: Normans Invade Ireland, 542
c. 1200-1230: Manco Capac Founds the Inca State, 576
1204: Genghis Khan Founds Mongol Empire, 581
1206-1210: Quṭ al-Dīn Aybak Establishes the Delhi Sultanate, 587
1221-1259: Mai Dunama Dibbalemi Expands Kanem Empire, 614
1225-1231: Jalāl al-Dīn Expands the Khwārizmian Empire, 618
1228-1231: Teutonic Knights Bring Baltic Region Under Catholic Control, 624
July 15, 1240: Alexander Nevsky Defends Novgorod from Swedish Invaders, 638
1259: Mangrai Founds the Kingdom of Lan Na, 657
1295: Ramkhamhaeng Conquers the Mekong and Menam Valleys, 690
1299: ʿAlāʾ-ud-Dīn Muḥammad Khaljī Conquers Gujarat, 692
Nov. 15, 1315: Swiss Victory at Morgarten over Habsburg Forces, 713
1325-1519: Aztecs Build Tenochtitlán, 731
Nov., 1330: Basarab Defeats the Hungarians, 737
1337-1453: Hundred Years' War, 744
1347: ʿAlāʾ-ud-Dīn Bahman Shāh Founds the Bahmanī Sultanate, 753
Jan. 10, 1356, and December 25, 1356: Golden Bull, 767
1381-1405: Tamerlane's Conquests, 797
June 28, 1389: Turkish Conquest of Serbia, 809

EXPLORATION AND DISCOVERY

c. 700-1100: Settlement of the South Pacific Islands, 130
11th-12th cent.: First European-Native American Contact, 373
c. 1145: Prester John Myth Sweeps Across Europe, 500
1325-1355: Travels of Ibn Baṭṭūṭah, 729
1415-1460: Prince Henry the Navigator Promotes Portuguese Exploration, 844

GOVERNMENT AND POLITICS

496: Baptism of Clovis, 6
Feb. 2, 506: Alaric II Drafts the *Breviarum Alarici*, 17
524: Imprisonment and Death of Boethius, 19
529-534: Justinian's Code Is Compiled, 23
581: Sui Dynasty Reunifies China, 39
593-604: Regency of Shōtoku Taishi, 45
606-647: Reign of Harṣa of Kanauj, 69
c. 611-642: Reign of Pulakeśin II, 77
618: Founding of the Tang Dynasty, 79
627-650: Reign of Songtsen Gampo, 82
630-668: Reign of Narasiṃhavarman I Mahāmalla, 88
645-646: Adoption of *Nengo* System and Taika Reforms, 104

652-c. 1171: Christian Nubia and Muslim Egypt Sign Treaty, 106
668-935: Silla Unification of Korea, 108
682-1377: Expansion of Śrivijaya, 113
690-705: Reign of Empress Wu, 120
c. 700-1253: Confederation of Thai Tribes, 132
729: Founding of Nanzhao, 154
730: Rise of the Pratihāras, 156
744-840: Uighur Turks Rule Central Asia, 170
c. 750-1240: Rise and Fall of Ghana, 172
754: Coronation of Pépin the Short, 176
780: Rise of the Sailendra Family, 191
781: Alcuin Becomes Adviser to Charlemagne, 193
786-809: Reign of Hārūn al-Rashīd, 196
791: Buddhism Becomes Tibetan State Religion, 202
792: Rise of the Samurai, 204
794-1185: Heian Period, 210
9th-14th cent.: Rise of the Toutswe Kingdom, 219
802: Founding of the Khmer Empire, 223
832: Nanzhao Subjugates Pyu, 232
838-842: Tibetan Empire Dissolves, 237
843: Treaty of Verdun, 241
After 850: Foundation of Chan Chan, 255
858: Rise of the Fujiwara Family, 257
864: Boris Converts to Christianity, 262
877-889: Indravarman I Conquers the Thai and the Mons, 273
893: Beginning of Bulgaria's Golden Age, 282
10th-11th cent.: First Hausa State Established, 289
907-960: Period of Five Dynasties and Ten Kingdoms, 291
915: Parāntaka I Conquers Pāṇḍya, 294
918-936: Foundation of the Koryŏ Dynasty, 297
927: Compilation of the *Engi Shiki*, 299
936: Khitans Settle Near Beijing, 302
939-944: Reign of Ngo Quyen, 304
c. 950: Court of Córdoba Flourishes in Spain, 307
958-1076: Koreans Adopt the Tang Civil Service Model, 320
960: Founding of the Song Dynasty, 322
969-1171: Reign of the Fāṭimids, 333
973: Foundation of the Western Cālukya Dynasty, 338
976-1025: Reign of Basil II, 341
c. 985-1014: Reign of Rājarāja I, 346
987: Hugh Capet Is Elected to the French Throne, 349
988: Baptism of Vladimir I, 352
998-1030: Reign of Maḥmūd of Ghazna, 357
c. 1000: Collapse of the Huari and Tiwanaku Civilizations, 360
11th-15th cent.: Development of the Ife Kingdom and Yoruba Culture, 376
11th-15th cent.: Great Zimbabwe Urbanism and Architecture, 378
1031: Caliphate of Córdoba Falls, 412
1048: Zīrids Break from Fāṭimid Dynasty and Revive Sunni Islam, 420
1054: Beginning of the Rome-Constantinople Schism, 422
1069-1072: Wang Anshi Introduces Bureaucratic Reforms, 432
c. 1075-1086: Hummay Founds Sefuwa Dynasty, 436
1075-c. 1220: Emergence of Mapungubwe, 438
1076: Almoravids Sack Kumbi, 440
1077: Seljuk Dynasty Is Founded, 442
1086: Domesday Survey, 444
Nov., 1092-June 15, 1094: El Cid Conquers Valencia, 447
1115: Foundation of the Jin Dynasty, 483
1127-1130: Creation of the Kingdom of Sicily, 488
1130: Karakitai Empire Established, 493
c. 1150-1200: Rise of the Hansa Merchant Union, 519
1152: Frederick Barbarossa Is Elected King of Germany, 522
1153: Jin Move Their Capital to Beijing, 525
1154-1204: Angevin Empire Is Established, 528
1155: Charter of Lorris Is Written, 531
Sept. 17, 1156: Austria Emerges as a National Entity, 534
1156-1192: Minamoto Yoritomo Becomes Shogun, 537
1167: Foundation of the Nemanjid Dynasty, 540
Dec. 29, 1170: Murder of Thomas Becket, 545
c. 1181-1221: Lalibela Founds the Christian Capital of Ethiopia, 554
1196-1258: Ch'oe Family Takes Power in Korea, 567
c. 1200: Common-Law Tradition Emerges in England, 569
c. 1200-1230: Manco Capac Founds the Inca State, 576
13th cent.: Ndiadiane N'diaye Founds the Wolof Empire, 579
1204: Genghis Khan Founds Mongol Empire, 581
1206-1210: Quṭ al-Dīn Aybak Establishes the Delhi Sultanate, 587
1209-1229: Albigensian Crusade, 593
June 15, 1215: Signing of the Magna Carta, 602
1219-1333: Hōjō Family Dominates Shoguns, Rules Japan, 611

1221-1259: Mai Dunama Dibbalemi Expands Kanem Empire, 614
1225: Tran Thai Tong Establishes Tran Dynasty, 616
1225-1231: Jalāl al-Dīn Expands the Khwārizmian Empire, 618
1228-1231: Teutonic Knights Bring Baltic Region Under Catholic Control, 624
1230: Unification of Castile and León, 627
1230's-1255: Reign of Sundiata of Mali, 630
1236-1240: Reign of Raziya, 636
July 15, 1240: Alexander Nevsky Defends Novgorod from Swedish Invaders, 638
1259: Mangrai Founds the Kingdom of Lan Na, 657
1270-1285: Yekuno Amlak Founds the Solomonid Dynasty, 665
1285: Statute of Winchester, 680
1295: Model Parliament, 688
1295: Ramkhamhaeng Conquers the Mekong and Menam Valleys, 690
Nov. 15, 1315: Swiss Victory at Morgarten over Habsburg Forces, 713
1323-1326: Champa Wins Independence from Dai Viet, 718
1324-1325: Mansa Mūsā's Pilgrimage to Mecca Sparks Interest in Mali Empire, 723
Nov., 1330: Basarab Defeats the Hungarians, 737
1336-1392: Yoshino Civil Wars, 741
1347: ʿAlāʾ-ud-Dīn Bahman Shāh Founds the Bahmanī Sultanate, 753
1350: Ramathibodi I Creates First Thai Legal System, 762
Jan. 10, 1356, and December 25, 1356: Golden Bull, 767
1366: Statute of Kilkenny, 772
1368: Establishment of the Ming Dynasty, 775
1368: Tibet Gains Independence from Mongols, 777
1373-1410: Jean Froissart Compiles His *Chronicles*, 780
1377-1378: Condemnation of John Wyclif, 786
May-June, 1381: Peasants' Revolt in England, 794
1382-1395: Reign of Sthitimalla, 801
c. 1392: Foundation of the Gelugpa Order, 812
July, 1392: Establishment of the Yi Dynasty, 815
June 17, 1397: Kalmar Union Is Formed, 820
1400-1500: Foundation of the West African States of Benin, 824
1414-1418: Council of Constance, 837
July 6, 1415: Martyrdom of Jan Hus, 841
1428: Le Loi Establishes Later Le Dynasty, 847
May 4-8, 1429: Joan of Arc's Relief of Orléans, 849
1444-1446: Albanian Chieftains Unite Under Prince Skanderbeg, 858
1453: English Are Driven from France, 864
May 29, 1453: Fall of Constantinople, 869

Health and medicine

809: First Islamic Public Hospital, 226
c. 1000: Footbinding Develops in Chinese Society, 362
c. 1010-1015: Avicenna Writes His *Canon of Medicine*, 397
12th-14th cent.: Social and Political Impact of Leprosy, 480
c. 1150: Moors Transmit Classical Philosophy and Medicine to Europe, 507
c. 1320: Origins of the Bubonic Plague, 716
1347-1352: Invasion of the Black Death in Europe, 756

Historiography

Mar. 9, 712, and July 1, 720: Writing of *Kojiki* and *Nihon shoki*, 147
731: Bede Writes *Ecclesiastical History of the English People*, 160
872-973: Publication of *The History of al-Ṭabarī*, 270
1010: Firdusi Composes the *Shahnamah*, 393
1145: Kim Pu-sik Writes *Samguk Sagi*, 498
1325-1355: Travels of Ibn Baṭṭūṭah, 729
1340: Al-ʿUmarī Writes a History of Africa, 748
1373-1410: Jean Froissart Compiles His *Chronicles*, 780
1377: Ibn Khaldūn Completes His *Muqaddimah*, 783

Laws, acts, and legal history

Feb. 2, 506: Alaric II Drafts the *Breviarum Alarici*, 17
529-534: Justinian's Code Is Compiled, 23
593-604: Regency of Shōtoku Taishi, 45
645-646: Adoption of *Nengo* System and Taika Reforms, 104
701: Taihō Laws Reform Japanese Government, 140
780: Beginning of the Harem System, 188
843: Treaty of Verdun, 241
927: Compilation of the *Engi Shiki*, 299
1086: Domesday Survey, 444
1155: Charter of Lorris Is Written, 531
c. 1200: Common-Law Tradition Emerges in England, 569
June 15, 1215: Signing of the Magna Carta, 602
1233: Papal Inquisition, 632
c. 1250-1300: Homosexuality Criminalized and Subject to Death Penalty, 652
1258: Provisions of Oxford Are Established, 655

1285: Statute of Winchester, 680
1295: Model Parliament, 688
Nov. 18, 1302: Boniface VIII Issues the Bull *Unam Sanctam*, 697
July 2, 1324: Lady Alice Kyteler Is Found Guilty of Witchcraft, 726
1350: Ramathibodi I Creates First Thai Legal System, 762
Jan. 10, 1356, and December 25, 1356: Golden Bull, 767
1366: Statute of Kilkenny, 772
1397: Publication of the Laws of Great Ming, 818
June 17, 1397: Kalmar Union Is Formed, 820

Literature

635-800: Founding of Lindisfarne and Creation of the *Book of Kells*, 94
731: Bede Writes *Ecclesiastical History of the English People*, 160
c. 850: Development of Slavic Alphabet, 249
868: First Book Printed, 265
872-973: Publication of *The History of al-Ṭabarī*, 270
c. 1000: Hindi Becomes India's Dominant Language, 365
After 1000: Development of Miracle and Mystery Plays, 381
c. 1001: Sei Shōnagon Completes *The Pillow Book*, 385
c. 1004: Murasaki Shikibu Writes *The Tale of Genji*, 387
1010: Firdusi Composes the *Shahnamah*, 393
c. 1010-1015: Avicenna Writes His *Canon of Medicine*, 397
c. 1100: Origins of Swahili in Its Written Form, 464
c. 1100: Rise of Courtly Love, 466
1136: Hildegard von Bingen Becomes Abbess, 495
c. 1145: Prester John Myth Sweeps Across Europe, 500
c. 1180: Chrétien de Troyes Writes *Perceval*, 552
1190: Moses Maimonides Writes *The Guide of the Perplexed*, 560
c. 1265-1273: Thomas Aquinas Compiles the *Summa Theologica*, 662
c. 1275: The *Zohar* Is Transcribed, 678
c. 1306-1320: Dante Writes *The Divine Comedy*, 703
c. 1360-1440: Kan'ami and Zeami Perfect Nō Drama, 769
1373-1410: Jean Froissart Compiles His *Chronicles*, 780
1377-1378: Condemnation of John Wyclif, 786
c. 1380: Compilation of the Wise Sayings of Lal Ded, 789
1387-1400: Chaucer Writes *The Canterbury Tales*, 806
1403-1407: *Yonglo Dadian* Encyclopedia Is Compiled, 827
c. 1450: Gutenberg Pioneers the Printing Press, 861

Mathematics

595-665: Invention of Decimals and Negative Numbers, 47
c. 1100: Arabic Numerals Are Introduced into Europe, 458

Organizations and institutions

596-597: See of Canterbury Is Established, 49
809: First Islamic Public Hospital, 226
c. 950-1100: Rise of Madrasas, 310
963: Foundation of the Mount Athos Monasteries, 330
1054: Beginning of the Rome-Constantinople Schism, 422
Mar. 21, 1098: Foundation of the Cistercian Order, 455
1100-1300: European Universities Emerge, 470
c. 1120: Order of the Knights Templar Is Founded, 485
c. 1150-1200: Rise of the Hansa Merchant Union, 519
Apr. 16, 1209: Founding of the Franciscans, 589
1228-1231: Teutonic Knights Bring Baltic Region Under Catholic Control, 624
1285: Statute of Winchester, 680

Philosophy

5th or 6th cent.: Confucianism Arrives in Japan, 1
788-850: Śaṅkara Expounds Advaita Vedānta, 200
872-973: Publication of *The History of al-Ṭabarī*, 270
12th cent.: Wang Chongyang Founds Quanzhen Daoism, 478
1130: Birth of Zhu Xi, 491
c. 1150: Moors Transmit Classical Philosophy and Medicine to Europe, 507
1190: Moses Maimonides Writes *The Guide of the Perplexed*, 560
c. 1190-1279: Ma-Xia School of Painting Flourishes, 562
c. 1265-1273: Thomas Aquinas Compiles the *Summa Theologica*, 662
c. 1275: The *Zohar* Is Transcribed, 678
c. 1380: Compilation of the Wise Sayings of Lal Ded, 789

RELIGION

5th or 6th cent.: Confucianism Arrives in Japan, 1
496: Baptism of Clovis, 6
c. 500-1000: Tiwanaku Civilization Flourishes in Andean Highlands, 11
532-537: Building of Hagia Sophia, 25
538-552: Buddhism Arrives in Japan, 28
590-604: Reforms of Pope Gregory the Great, 42
596-597: See of Canterbury Is Established, 49
c. 610-632: Muḥammad Receives Revelations, 74
627-650: Reign of Songtsen Gampo, 82
629-645: Pilgrimage of Xuanzang, 85
630-711: Islam Expands Throughout North Africa, 91
635-800: Founding of Lindisfarne and Creation of the *Book of Kells*, 94
637-657: Islam Expands Throughout the Middle East, 101
Oct. 10, 680: Martyrdom of Prophet's Grandson Ḥusayn, 111
685-691: Building of the Dome of the Rock, 116
726-843: Iconoclastic Controversy, 151
731: Bede Writes *Ecclesiastical History of the English People*, 160
Oct. 11, 732: Battle of Tours, 162
735: Christianity Is Introduced into Germany, 165
740: Khazars Convert to Judaism, 168
754: Coronation of Pépin the Short, 176
775-840: Building of Borobuḍur, 185
780: Rise of the Sailendra Family, 191
788-850: Śaṅkara Expounds Advaita Vedānta, 200
791: Buddhism Becomes Tibetan State Religion, 202
June 7, 793: Norse Raid Lindisfarne Monastery, 206
838-842: Tibetan Empire Dissolves, 237
845: Suppression of Buddhism, 245
c. 850: Development of Slavic Alphabet, 249
864: Boris Converts to Christianity, 262
872-973: Publication of *The History of al-Ṭabarī*, 270
Early 10th cent.: Qarakhanids Convert to Islam, 285
10th cent.: Cult of Quetzalcóatl Spreads Through Mesoamerica, 287
927: Compilation of the *Engi Shiki*, 299
c. 950: Court of Córdoba Flourishes in Spain, 307
c. 950-1100: Rise of Madrasas, 310
Aug. 10, 955: Otto I Defeats the Magyars, 316
c. 960: Jews Settle in Bohemia, 326
963: Foundation of the Mount Athos Monasteries, 330
969-1171: Reign of the Fāṭimids, 333
972: Building of al-Azhar Mosque, 336
988: Baptism of Vladimir I, 352
11th cent.: Expansion of Sunni Islam in North Africa and Iberia, 367
After 1000: Development of Miracle and Mystery Plays, 381
1009: Destruction of the Church of the Holy Sepulchre, 390
c. 1010: Songhai Kingdom Converts to Islam, 395
1016: Canute Conquers England, 406
c. 1025: Scholars at Chartres Revive Interest in the Classics, 409
1031: Caliphate of Córdoba Falls, 412
1048: Zīrids Break from Fāṭimid Dynasty and Revive Sunni Islam, 420
1054: Beginning of the Rome-Constantinople Schism, 422
1062-1147: Almoravids Conquer Morocco and Establish the Almoravid Empire, 425
c. 1075-1086: Hummay Founds Sefuwa Dynasty, 436
Nov. 27, 1095: Pope Urban II Calls the First Crusade, 450
Mar. 21, 1098: Foundation of the Cistercian Order, 455
1100-1300: European Universities Emerge, 470
12th cent.: Wang Chongyang Founds Quanzhen Daoism, 478
c. 1120: Order of the Knights Templar Is Founded, 485
1136: Hildegard von Bingen Becomes Abbess, 495
c. 1145: Prester John Myth Sweeps Across Europe, 500
1147-1149: Second Crusade, 503
Dec. 29, 1170: Murder of Thomas Becket, 545
1175: Hōnen Shōnin Founds Pure Land Buddhism, 547
c. 1175: Waldensian Excommunications Usher in Protestant Movement, 549
1189-1192: Third Crusade, 557
1190: Moses Maimonides Writes *The Guide of the Perplexed*, 560
1193: Turkish Raiders Destroy Buddhist University at Nalanda, 565
1204: Knights of the Fourth Crusade Capture Constantinople, 584
Apr. 16, 1209: Founding of the Franciscans, 589
1209-1229: Albigensian Crusade, 593
1212: Children's Crusade, 596
Nov. 11-30, 1215: Fourth Lateran Council, 605
1217-1221: Fifth Crusade, 608
1221-1259: Mai Dunama Dibbalemi Expands Kanem Empire, 614
1227-1230: Frederick II Leads the Sixth Crusade, 621
1228-1231: Teutonic Knights Bring Baltic Region Under Catholic Control, 624

1230: Unification of Castile and León, 627
1233: Papal Inquisition, 632
July 15, 1240: Alexander Nevsky Defends Novgorod from Swedish Invaders, 638
1248-1254: Failure of the Seventh Crusade, 641
c. 1250-1300: Homosexuality Criminalized and Subject to Death Penalty, 652
c. 1265-1273: Thomas Aquinas Compiles the *Summa Theologica*, 662
1273: Sufi Order of Mawlawīyah Is Established, 671
1275: Nestorian Archbishopric Is Founded in Beijing, 676
c. 1275: The *Zohar* Is Transcribed, 678
1290-1306: Jews Are Expelled from England, France, and Southern Italy, 683
Apr., 1291: Fall of Acre, 686
Nov. 18, 1302: Boniface VIII Issues the Bull *Unam Sanctam*, 697
1305-1417: Avignon Papacy and the Great Schism, 700
c. 1310-1350: William of Ockham Attacks Thomist Ideas, 707
July 2, 1324: Lady Alice Kyteler Is Found Guilty of Witchcraft, 726
1324-1325: Mansa Mūsā's Pilgrimage to Mecca Sparks Interest in Mali Empire, 723
1325-1519: Aztecs Build Tenochtitlán, 731
Jan. 10, 1356, and December 25, 1356: Golden Bull, 767
1377-1378: Condemnation of John Wyclif, 786
c. 1380: Compilation of the Wise Sayings of Lal Ded, 789
c. 1392: Foundation of the Gelugpa Order, 812
1414-1418: Council of Constance, 837
July 6, 1415: Martyrdom of Jan Hus, 841
May 4-8, 1429: Joan of Arc's Relief of Orléans, 849
1440: Donation of Constantine Is Exposed, 852
May 29, 1453: Fall of Constantinople, 869

Science and technology
563: Silk Worms Are Smuggled to the Byzantine Empire, 31
595-665: Invention of Decimals and Negative Numbers, 47
7th-early 8th cent.: Maya Build Astronomical Observatory at Palenque, 56
7th-8th cent.: Papermaking Spreads to Korea, Japan, and Central Asia, 59
c. 700: Bow and Arrow Spread into North America, 122
c. 700-1000: Heavy Plow Helps Increase Agricultural Yields, 127
8th-15th cent.: Hohokam Adapt to the Desert Southwest, 137
Mid-9th cent.: Invention of Gunpowder and Guns, 247
After 850: Foundation of Chan Chan, 255
c. 1045: Bi Sheng Develops Movable Earthenware Type, 418
c. 1200: Scientific Cattle Breeding Developed, 574
c. 1250: Improvements in Shipbuilding and Navigation, 648
1275: First Mechanical Clock, 673
1328-1350: Flowering of Late Medieval Physics, 734
c. 1450: Gutenberg Pioneers the Printing Press, 861

Social reform
809: First Islamic Public Hospital, 226
1136: Hildegard von Bingen Becomes Abbess, 495
1155: Charter of Lorris Is Written, 531
c. 1175: Waldensian Excommunications Usher in Protestant Movement, 549
June 15, 1215: Signing of the Magna Carta, 602
1233: Papal Inquisition, 632
c. 1250-1300: Homosexuality Criminalized and Subject to Death Penalty, 652
1285: Statute of Winchester, 680
1290-1306: Jews Are Expelled from England, France, and Southern Italy, 683
1295: Model Parliament, 688
Aug. 1, 1323-August 23, 1328: Peasants' Revolt in Flanders, 721
1347-1352: Invasion of the Black Death in Europe, 756
May 20, 1347-October 8, 1354: Cola di Rienzo Leads Popular Uprising in Rome, 759
1366: Statute of Kilkenny, 772
May-June, 1381: Peasants' Revolt in England, 794

Trade and commerce
c. 500-1000: Rise of Swahili Cultures, 9
6th-8th cent.: Sogdians Dominate Central Asian Trade, 14
563: Silk Worms Are Smuggled to the Byzantine Empire, 31
630-711: Islam Expands Throughout North Africa, 91
8th-14th cent.: Cahokia Becomes the First North American City, 134
740: Khazars Convert to Judaism, 168
812: Paper Money First Used in China, 229
c. 950-1150: Toltecs Build Tula, 313

11th-15th cent.: Development of the Ife Kingdom and Yoruba Culture, 376
11th-15th cent.: Great Zimbabwe Urbanism and Architecture, 378
c. 1010: Songhai Kingdom Converts to Islam, 395
1076: Almoravids Sack Kumbi, 440
c. 1100: Founding of Timbuktu, 461
12th cent.: Coins Are Minted on the Swahili Coast, 474
12th cent.: Trading Center of Kilwa Kisiwani Founded, 476
c. 1150: Refinements in Banking, 511
1150: Venetian Merchants Dominate Trade with the East, 513
c. 1150-1200: Rise of the Hansa Merchant Union, 519
c. 1200: Fairs of Champagne, 571
c. 1200: Scientific Cattle Breeding Developed, 574
c. 1250: Improvements in Shipbuilding and Navigation, 648
1271-1295: Travels of Marco Polo, 667
1325-1519: Aztecs Build Tenochtitlán, 731
1333: Kilwa Kisiwani Begins Economic and Historical Decline, 739
June 17, 1397: Kalmar Union Is Formed, 820
1405-1433: Zheng He's Naval Expeditions, 829
1415-1460: Prince Henry the Navigator Promotes Portuguese Exploration, 844

TRANSPORTATION

605-610: Building of the Grand Canal, 64
1150: Venetian Merchants Dominate Trade with the East, 513
c. 1150-1200: Rise of the Hansa Merchant Union, 519
c. 1250: Improvements in Shipbuilding and Navigation, 648

WARS, UPRISINGS, AND CIVIL UNREST

484: White Huns Raid India, 3
567-568: Sāsānians and Turks Defeat the White Huns, 33
568-571: Lombard Conquest of Italy, 36
581: Sui Dynasty Reunifies China, 39
c. 600-950: El Tajín Is Built, 53
630-711: Islam Expands Throughout North Africa, 91
Aug. 15-20, 636: Battle of Yarmūk, 97
637-657: Islam Expands Throughout the Middle East, 101
Oct. 10, 680: Martyrdom of Prophet's Grandson Ḥusayn, 111
Apr. or May, 711: Ṭārik Crosses into Spain, 144
Oct. 11, 732: Battle of Tours, 162
751: Battle of Talas River, 174
755-763: Rebellion of An Lushan, 179
763: Tibetans Capture Chang'an, 181
792: Rise of the Samurai, 204
June 7, 793: Norse Raid Lindisfarne Monastery, 206
834: Gypsies Expelled from Persia, 234
838-842: Tibetan Empire Dissolves, 237
Mid-9th cent.: Invention of Gunpowder and Guns, 247
863: Nanzhao Captures Hanoi, 260
869-883: Zanj Revolt of African Slaves, 267
877-889: Indravarman I Conquers the Thai and the Mons, 273
878: Alfred Defeats the Danes, 276
890's: Magyars Invade Italy, Saxony, and Bavaria, 279
907-960: Period of Five Dynasties and Ten Kingdoms, 291
915: Parāntaka I Conquers Pāṇḍya, 294
939-944: Reign of Ngo Quyen, 304
Aug. 10, 955: Otto I Defeats the Magyars, 316
982: Le Dai Hanh Invades Champa, 344
992-1054: Ghana Takes Control of Awdaghust, 355
998-1030: Reign of Maḥmūd of Ghazna, 357c. 1000: Collapse of the Huari and Tiwanaku Civilizations, 360
11th cent.: Expansion of Sunni Islam in North Africa and Iberia, 367
1009: Destruction of the Church of the Holy Sepulchre, 390
Apr. 23, 1014: Battle of Clontarf, 403
1016: Canute Conquers England, 406
1031: Caliphate of Córdoba Falls, 412
1062-1147: Almoravids Conquer Morocco and Establish the Almoravid Empire, 425
Oct. 14, 1066: Battle of Hastings, 428
Aug. 26, 1071: Battle of Manzikert, 434
Nov., 1092-June 15, 1094: El Cid Conquers Valencia, 447
Nov. 27, 1095: Pope Urban II Calls the First Crusade, 450
1147-1149: Second Crusade, 503
1156-1192: Minamoto Yoritomo Becomes Shogun, 537
1169-1172: Normans Invade Ireland, 542
1189-1192: Third Crusade, 557
1193: Turkish Raiders Destroy Buddhist University at Nalanda, 565
1204: Knights of the Fourth Crusade Capture Constantinople, 584
1209-1229: Albigensian Crusade, 593

July 27, 1214: Battle of Bouvines, 599
1217-1221: Fifth Crusade, 608
1225-1231: Jalāl al-Dīn Expands the Khwārizmian Empire, 618
1227-1230: Frederick II Leads the Sixth Crusade, 621
1228-1231: Teutonic Knights Bring Baltic Region Under Catholic Control, 624
1230's-1255: Reign of Sundiata of Mali, 630
July 15, 1240: Alexander Nevsky Defends Novgorod from Swedish Invaders, 638
1248-1254: Failure of the Seventh Crusade, 641
Sept. 3, 1260: Battle of Ain Jālūt, 659
Apr., 1291: Fall of Acre, 686
1299: ʿAlāʾ-ud-Dīn Muḥammad Khaljī Conquers Gujarat, 692
July 27, 1302: Battle of Bapheus, 695
June 23-24, 1314: Battle of Bannockburn, 709
Nov. 15, 1315: Swiss Victory at Morgarten over Habsburg Forces, 713
1323-1326: Champa Wins Independence from Dai Viet, 718
Aug. 1, 1323-August 23, 1328: Peasants' Revolt in Flanders, 721
Nov., 1330: Basarab Defeats the Hungarians, 737
1336-1392: Yoshino Civil Wars, 741
1337-1453: Hundred Years' War, 744
Aug. 26, 1346: Battle of Crécy, 750
1347: ʿAlāʾ-ud-Dīn Bahman Shāh Founds the Bahmanī Sultanate, 753
May 20, 1347-October 8, 1354: Cola di Rienzo Leads Popular Uprising in Rome, 759
1373-1410: Jean Froissart Compiles His *Chronicles*, 780
Sept. 8, 1380: Battle of Kulikovo, 791
May-June, 1381: Peasants' Revolt in England, 794
1381-1405: Tamerlane's Conquests, 797
June 28, 1389: Turkish Conquest of Serbia, 809
July 15, 1410: Battle of Tannenberg, 831
1428: Le Loi Establishes Later Le Dynasty, 847
May 4-8, 1429: Joan of Arc's Relief of Orléans, 849
1442-1456: János Hunyadi Defends Hungary Against the Ottomans, 854
1444-1446: Albanian Chieftains Unite Under Prince Skanderbeg, 858
1453: English Are Driven from France, 864
May 29, 1453: Fall of Constantinople, 869

GEOGRAPHICAL INDEX

List of Geographical Categories

Africa XXI
Albania XXII
Arabia XXII
Australia XXII
Bohemia XXII
Bulgaria XXII
Byzantine Empire XXII
Central America XXII
Central Asia XXII
China XXIII
Egypt XXIII
England XXIV
Europe (General) XXIV
Flanders XXIV
France XXIV
Germany XXV
Greece XXV
Greenland XXV
Hungary XXV
India XXV
Iran XXV
Iraq XXVI
Ireland XXVI
Israel/Palestine XXVI
Italy XXVI
Japan XXVI
Korea XXVII
Macedonia XXVII
Middle East XXVII
Moravia XXVII
Netherlands XXVII
New Zealand XXVII
North America XXVII
Pacific Islands XXVII
Poland XXVIII
Portugal XXVIII
Romania XXVIII
Russia XXVIII
Scandinavia XXVIII
Scotland XXVIII
Serbia XXVIII
South America XXVIII
Southeast Asia XXVIII
Spain XXVIII
Switzerland XXVIII
Syria XXVIII
Tibet XXIX
Turkey XXIX

AFGHANISTAN. *See* **CENTRAL ASIA**

AFRICA. *See also* **EGYPT**
c. 500-1000: Rise of Swahili Cultures, 9
630-711: Islam Expands Throughout North Africa, 91
637-657: Islam Expands Throughout the Middle East, 101
652-c. 1171: Christian Nubia and Muslim Egypt Sign Treaty, 106
Apr. or May, 711: Ṭārik Crosses into Spain, 144
c. 750-1240: Rise and Fall of Ghana, 172
9th-14th cent.: Rise of the Toutswe Kingdom, 219
10th-11th cent.: First Hausa State Established, 289
992-1054: Ghana Takes Control of Awdaghust, 355
11th cent.: Expansion of Sunni Islam in North Africa and Iberia, 367
11th-15th cent.: Development of the Ife Kingdom and Yoruba Culture, 376
11th-15th cent.: Great Zimbabwe Urbanism and Architecture, 378
c. 1010: Songhai Kingdom Converts to Islam, 395
1048: Zīrids Break from Fāṭimid Dynasty and Revive Sunni Islam, 420
1062-1147: Almoravids Conquer Morocco and Establish the Almoravid Empire, 425
c. 1075-1086: Hummay Founds Sefuwa Dynasty, 436
1075-c. 1220: Emergence of Mapungubwe, 438
1076: Almoravids Sack Kumbi, 440
c. 1100: Founding of Timbuktu, 461
c. 1100: Origins of Swahili in Its Written Form, 464
12th cent.: Coins Are Minted on the Swahili Coast, 474
12th cent.: Trading Center of Kilwa Kisiwani Founded, 476
c. 1145: Prester John Myth Sweeps Across Europe, 500
c. 1181-1221: Lalibela Founds the Christian Capital of Ethiopia, 554
13th cent.: Ndiadiane N'diaye Founds the Wolof Empire, 579
1221-1259: Mai Dunama Dibbalemi Expands Kanem Empire, 614
1230's-1255: Reign of Sundiata of Mali, 630

1270-1285: Yekuno Amlak Founds the Solomonid Dynasty, 665
1324-1325: Mansa Mūsā's Pilgrimage to Mecca Sparks Interest in Mali Empire, 723
1325-1355: Travels of Ibn Baṭṭūṭah, 729
1333: Kilwa Kisiwani Begins Economic and Historical Decline, 739
1340: Al-ʿUmarī Writes a History of Africa, 748
1377: Ibn Khaldūn Completes His *Muqaddimah*, 783
1400-1500: Foundation of the West African States of Benin, 824
1405-1433: Zheng He's Naval Expeditions, 829

ALBANIA
1444-1446: Albanian Chieftains Unite Under Prince Skanderbeg, 858

ALMOHAD EMPIRE. *See* **AFRICA**

ANATOLIA. *See* **TURKEY**

ARABIA. *See also* **IRAN; IRAQ**
c. 610-632: Muḥammad Receives Revelations, 74
637-657: Islam Expands Throughout the Middle East, 101
786-809: Reign of Hārūn al-Rashīd, 196
1325-1355: Travels of Ibn Baṭṭūṭah, 729
1405-1433: Zheng He's Naval Expeditions, 829

ASIA. *See* **CENTRAL ASIA; CHINA; INDIA; JAPAN; KOREA; SOUTHEAST ASIA**

AUSTRALIA
c. 700-1100: Settlement of the South Pacific Islands, 130

BALKAN PENINSULA. *See* **GREECE; MACEDONIA; SERBIA**

BELGIUM. *See* **NETHERLANDS; FLANDERS**

BOHEMIA
c. 960: Jews Settle in Bohemia, 326
July 6, 1415: Martyrdom of Jan Hus, 841

BRITISH ISLES. *See* **ENGLAND; IRELAND; SCOTLAND**

BULGARIA
c. 850: Development of Slavic Alphabet, 249
864: Boris Converts to Christianity, 262
893: Beginning of Bulgaria's Golden Age, 282

BURMA. *See* **SOUTHEAST ASIA**

BYZANTINE EMPIRE
529-534: Justinian's Code Is Compiled, 23
532-537: Building of Hagia Sophia, 25
563: Silk Worms Are Smuggled to the Byzantine Empire, 31
637-657: Islam Expands Throughout the Middle East, 101
726-843: Iconoclastic Controversy, 151
c. 850: Development of Slavic Alphabet, 249
976-1025: Reign of Basil II, 341
1054: Beginning of the Rome-Constantinople Schism, 422
Aug. 26, 1071: Battle of Manzikert, 434
Nov. 27, 1095: Pope Urban II Calls the First Crusade, 450
1147-1149: Second Crusade, 503
1189-1192: Third Crusade, 557
1204: Knights of the Fourth Crusade Capture Constantinople, 584
1217-1221: Fifth Crusade, 608
1227-1230: Frederick II Leads the Sixth Crusade, 621
1248-1254: Failure of the Seventh Crusade, 641
May 29, 1453: Fall of Constantinople, 869

CAMBODIA. *See* **SOUTHEAST ASIA**

CENTRAL AMERICA
c. 600-950: El Tajín Is Built, 53
7th-early 8th cent.: Maya Build Astronomical Observatory at Palenque, 56
7th-13th cent.: Mogollons Establish Agricultural Settlements, 61
c. 700-1000: Building of Chichén Itzá, 124
10th cent.: Cult of Quetzalcóatl Spreads Through Mesoamerica, 287
c. 950-1150: Toltecs Build Tula, 313
1325-1519: Aztecs Build Tenochtitlán, 731

CENTRAL ASIA. *See also* **TIBET**
6th-8th cent.: Sogdians Dominate Central Asian Trade, 14
567-568: Sāsānians and Turks Defeat the White Huns, 33
7th-8th cent.: Papermaking Spreads to Korea, Japan, and Central Asia, 59

629-645: Pilgrimage of Xuanzang, 85
744-840: Uighur Turks Rule Central Asia, 170
751: Battle of Talas River, 174
840-846: Uighur Migrations, 239
Early 10th cent.: Qarakhanids Convert to Islam, 285
956: Oğhuz Turks Migrate to Transoxiana, 318
998-1030: Reign of Maḥmūd of Ghazna, 357
1040-1055: Expansion of the Seljuk Turks, 415
1130: Karakitai Empire Established, 493
c. 1145: Prester John Myth Sweeps Across Europe, 500
1225-1231: Jalāl al-Dīn Expands the Khwārizmian Empire, 618
c. 1320: Origins of the Bubonic Plague, 716
1325-1355: Travels of Ibn Baṭṭūṭah, 729
1381-1405: Tamerlane's Conquests, 797
1399-1404: Tamerlane Builds the Bibi Khanum Mosque, 822

China
581: Sui Dynasty Reunifies China, 39
595-665: Invention of Decimals and Negative Numbers, 47
7th-8th cent.: Papermaking Spreads to Korea, Japan, and Central Asia, 59
605-610: Building of the Grand Canal, 64
606: National University Awards First Doctorate, 66
607-839: Japan Sends Embassies to China, 72
618: Founding of the Tang Dynasty, 79
627-650: Reign of Songtsen Gampo, 82
629-645: Pilgrimage of Xuanzang, 85
690-705: Reign of Empress Wu, 120
c. 700-1253: Confederation of Thai Tribes, 132
713-741: First Newspapers in China, 149
729: Founding of Nanzhao, 154
744-840: Uighur Turks Rule Central Asia, 170
755-763: Rebellion of An Lushan, 179
763: Tibetans Capture Chang'an, 181
791: Buddhism Becomes Tibetan State Religion, 202
812: Paper Money First Used in China, 229
840-846: Uighur Migrations, 239
845: Suppression of Buddhism, 245
Mid-9th cent.: Invention of Gunpowder and Guns, 247
868: First Book Printed, 265
Early 10th cent.: Qarakhanids Convert to Islam, 285
907-960: Period of Five Dynasties and Ten Kingdoms, 291
936: Khitans Settle Near Beijing, 302
960: Founding of the Song Dynasty, 322
960-1279: Scholar-Official Class Flowers Under Song Dynasty, 327
c. 1000: Footbinding Develops in Chinese Society, 362
1012: Rice Is Introduced into China, 401
c. 1045: Bi Sheng Develops Movable Earthenware Type, 418
1069-1072: Wang Anshi Introduces Bureaucratic Reforms, 432
12th cent.: Wang Chongyang Founds Quanzhen Daoism, 478
1115: Foundation of the Jin Dynasty, 483
1130: Birth of Zhu Xi, 491
1130: Karakitai Empire Established, 493
1153: Jin Move Their Capital to Beijing, 525
c. 1190-1279: Ma-Xia School of Painting Flourishes, 562
1204: Genghis Khan Founds Mongol Empire, 581
1225: Tran Thai Tong Establishes Tran Dynasty, 616
1271-1295: Travels of Marco Polo, 667
1275: Nestorian Archbishopric Is Founded in Beijing, 676
c. 1320: Origins of the Bubonic Plague, 716
1325-1355: Travels of Ibn Baṭṭūṭah, 729
1368: Establishment of the Ming Dynasty, 775
c. 1387: Chinese Create the Eight-Legged Essay, 803
1397: Publication of the Laws of Great Ming, 818
1403-1407: *Yonglo Dadian* Encyclopedia Is Compiled, 827
1405-1433: Zheng He's Naval Expeditions, 829
1428: Le Loi Establishes Later Le Dynasty, 847

Czech Republic. *See* **Bohemia; Moravia**

East Asia. *See* **China; Japan; Korea; Southeast Asia**

Egypt
637-657: Islam Expands Throughout the Middle East, 101
652-c. 1171: Christian Nubia and Muslim Egypt Sign Treaty, 106
969-1171: Reign of the Fāṭimids, 333
972: Building of al-Azhar Mosque, 336
1190: Moses Maimonides Writes *The Guide of the Perplexed*, 560
1217-1221: Fifth Crusade, 608
1248-1254: Failure of the Seventh Crusade, 641
c. 1320: Origins of the Bubonic Plague, 716
1325-1355: Travels of Ibn Baṭṭūṭah, 729
1340: Al-ʿUmarī Writes a History of Africa, 748

ENGLAND
596-597: See of Canterbury Is Established, 49
635-800: Founding of Lindisfarne and Creation of the *Book of Kells*, 94
731: Bede Writes *Ecclesiastical History of the English People*, 160
June 7, 793: Norse Raid Lindisfarne Monastery, 206
878: Alfred Defeats the Danes, 276
After 1000: Development of Miracle and Mystery Plays, 381
1016: Canute Conquers England, 406
Oct. 14, 1066: Battle of Hastings, 428
1086: Domesday Survey, 444
1154-1204: Angevin Empire Is Established, 528
Dec. 29, 1170: Murder of Thomas Becket, 545
c. 1200: Common-Law Tradition Emerges in England, 569
June 15, 1215: Signing of the Magna Carta, 602
1258: Provisions of Oxford Are Established, 655
1285: Statute of Winchester, 680
1290-1306: Jews Are Expelled from England, France, and Southern Italy, 683
1295: Model Parliament, 688
1373-1410: Jean Froissart Compiles His *Chronicles*, 780
1377-1378: Condemnation of John Wyclif, 786
May-June, 1381: Peasants' Revolt in England, 794
1387-1400: Chaucer Writes *The Canterbury Tales*, 806

ETHIOPIA. *See* **AFRICA**

EUROPE (GENERAL). *See also* **SPECIFIC COUNTRIES**
c. 700-1000: Heavy Plow Helps Increase Agricultural Yields, 127
726-843: Iconoclastic Controversy, 151
11th-12th cent.: Building of Romanesque Cathedrals, 370
Nov. 27, 1095: Pope Urban II Calls the First Crusade, 450
c. 1100: Arabic Numerals Are Introduced into Europe, 458
1100-1300: European Universities Emerge, 470
12th-14th cent.: Social and Political Impact of Leprosy, 480
c. 1145: Prester John Myth Sweeps Across Europe, 500
1147-1149: Second Crusade, 503
c. 1150: Refinements in Banking, 511
c. 1175: Waldensian Excommunications Usher in Protestant Movement, 549
1189-1192: Third Crusade, 557
c. 1200: Scientific Cattle Breeding Developed, 574
1204: Knights of the Fourth Crusade Capture Constantinople, 584
1217-1221: Fifth Crusade, 608
1227-1230: Frederick II Leads the Sixth Crusade, 621
1248-1254: Failure of the Seventh Crusade, 641
c. 1250: Improvements in Shipbuilding and Navigation, 648
c. 1250-1300: Homosexuality Criminalized and Subject to Death Penalty, 652
1305-1417: Avignon Papacy and the Great Schism, 700
1310-c. 1350: William of Ockham Attacks Thomist Ideas, 707
1328-1350: Flowering of Late Medieval Physics, 734
1347-1352: Invasion of the Black Death in Europe, 756

FLANDERS. *See also* **NETHERLANDS**
July 27, 1214: Battle of Bouvines, 599
Aug. 1, 1323-August 23, 1328: Peasants' Revolt in Flanders, 721
1373-1410: Jean Froissart Compiles His *Chronicles*, 780

FRANCE
496: Baptism of Clovis, 6
Feb. 2, 506: Alaric II Drafts the *Breviarum Alarici*, 17
Oct. 11, 732: Battle of Tours, 162
754: Coronation of Pépin the Short, 176
843: Treaty of Verdun, 241
987: Hugh Capet Is Elected to the French Throne, 349
After 1000: Development of Miracle and Mystery Plays, 381
c. 1025: Scholars at Chartres Revive Interest in the Classics, 409
Nov. 27, 1095: Pope Urban II Calls the First Crusade, 450
Mar. 21, 1098: Foundation of the Cistercian Order, 455
c. 1100: Rise of Courtly Love, 466
c. 1150-1200: Development of Gothic Architecture, 516
1154-1204: Angevin Empire Is Established, 528
1155: Charter of Lorris Is Written, 531
c. 1175: Waldensian Excommunications Usher in Protestant Movement, 549
c. 1180: Chrétien de Troyes Writes *Perceval*, 552
c. 1200: Fairs of Champagne, 571
1209-1229: Albigensian Crusade, 593
1212: Children's Crusade, 596

July 27, 1214: Battle of Bouvines, 599
1233: Papal Inquisition, 632
c. 1265-1273: Thomas Aquinas Compiles the *Summa Theologica*, 662
1275: First Mechanical Clock, 673
1290-1306: Jews Are Expelled from England, France, and Southern Italy, 683
1337-1453: Hundred Years' War, 744
Aug. 26, 1346: Battle of Crécy, 750
c. 1350-1400: Petrarch and Boccaccio Recover Classical Texts, 764
Jan. 10, 1356, and December 25, 1356: Golden Bull, 767
1373-1410: Jean Froissart Compiles His *Chronicles*, 780
May 4-8, 1429: Joan of Arc's Relief of Orléans, 849
1453: English Are Driven from France, 864

Georgia. *See* **Russia**

Germany
735: Christianity Is Introduced into Germany, 165
890's: Magyars Invade Italy, Saxony, and Bavaria, 279
Aug. 10, 955: Otto I Defeats the Magyars, 316
1136: Hildegard von Bingen Becomes Abbess, 495
c. 1150-1200: Rise of the Hansa Merchant Union, 519
1152: Frederick Barbarossa Is Elected King of Germany, 522
Sept. 17, 1156: Austria Emerges as a National Entity, 534
1212: Children's Crusade, 596
1228-1231: Teutonic Knights Bring Baltic Region Under Catholic Control, 624
1233: Papal Inquisition, 632
Jan. 10, 1356, and December 25, 1356: Golden Bull, 767
July 6, 1415: Martyrdom of Jan Hus, 841
c. 1450: Gutenberg Pioneers the Printing Press, 861

Greece. *See also* **Byzantine Empire; Macedonia**
963: Foundation of the Mount Athos Monasteries, 330

Greenland. *See also* **Scandinavia**
11th-12th cent.: First European-Native American Contact, 373

Holy Roman Empire. *See* **Germany**

Hungary
890's: Magyars Invade Italy, Saxony, and Bavaria, 279
1442-1456: János Hunyadi Defends Hungary Against the Ottomans, 854

India
484: White Huns Raid India, 3
595-665: Invention of Decimals and Negative Numbers, 47
606-647: Reign of Harṣa of Kanauj, 69
c. 611-642: Reign of Pulakeśin II, 77
629-645: Pilgrimage of Xuanzang, 85
630-668: Reign of Narasiṃhavarman I Mahāmalla, 88
c. 710: Construction of the Kāilaśanātha Temple, 142
730: Rise of the Pratihāras, 156
770-810: Reign of Dharmapāla, 183
788-850: Śaṅkara Expounds Advaita Vedānta, 200
915: Parāntaka I Conquers Pāṇḍya, 294
973: Foundation of the Western Cālukya Dynasty, 338
c. 985-1014: Reign of Rājarāja I, 346
c. 1000: Hindi Becomes India's Dominant Language, 365
c. 1100: Arabic Numerals Are Introduced into Europe, 458
c. 1145: Prester John Myth Sweeps Across Europe, 500
1193: Turkish Raiders Destroy Buddhist University at Nalanda, 565
1206-1210: Quṭ al-Dīn Aybak Establishes the Delhi Sultanate, 587
1236-1240: Reign of Raziya, 636
1299: ʿAlāʾ-ud-Dīn Muḥammad Khaljī Conquers Gujarat, 692
1325-1355: Travels of Ibn Baṭṭūṭah, 729
1347: ʿAlāʾ-ud-Dīn Bahman Shāh Founds the Bahmanī Sultanate, 753
c. 1380: Compilation of the Wise Sayings of Lal Ded, 789
1382-1395: Reign of Sthitimalla, 801

Indonesia. *See* **Southeast Asia**

Iran
567-568: Sāsānians and Turks Defeat the White Huns, 33
637-657: Islam Expands Throughout the Middle East, 101
809: First Islamic Public Hospital, 226

834: Gypsies Expelled from Persia, 234
c. 950-1100: Rise of Madrasas, 310
1010: Firdusi Composes the *Shahnamah*, 393
c. 1010-1015: Avicenna Writes His *Canon of Medicine*, 397
1040-1055: Expansion of the Seljuk Turks, 415
1225-1231: Jalāl al-Dīn Expands the Khwārizmian Empire, 618
1271-1295: Travels of Marco Polo, 667

IRAQ

637-657: Islam Expands Throughout the Middle East, 101
Oct. 10, 680: Martyrdom of Prophet's Grandson Ḥusayn, 111
780: Beginning of the Harem System, 188
786-809: Reign of Hārūn al-Rashīd, 196
809: First Islamic Public Hospital, 226
869-883: Zanj Revolt of African Slaves, 267
872-973: Publication of *The History of al-Ṭabarī*, 270
c. 950-1100: Rise of Madrasas, 310
1010: Firdusi Composes the *Shahnamah*, 393
1040-1055: Expansion of the Seljuk Turks, 415
1381-1405: Tamerlane's Conquests, 797

IRELAND

635-800: Founding of Lindisfarne and Creation of the *Book of Kells*, 94
Apr. 23, 1014: Battle of Clontarf, 403
1169-1172: Normans Invade Ireland, 542
July 2, 1324: Lady Alice Kyteler Is Found Guilty of Witchcraft, 726
1366: Statute of Kilkenny, 772

ISRAEL/PALESTINE

Aug. 15-20, 636: Battle of Yarmūk, 97
637-657: Islam Expands Throughout the Middle East, 101
685-691: Building of the Dome of the Rock, 116
1009: Destruction of the Church of the Holy Sepulchre, 390
Nov. 27, 1095: Pope Urban II Calls the First Crusade, 450
c. 1120: Order of the Knights Templar Is Founded, 485
1147-1149: Second Crusade, 503
1189-1192: Third Crusade, 557
1204: Knights of the Fourth Crusade Capture Constantinople, 584
1217-1221: Fifth Crusade, 608
1227-1230: Frederick II Leads the Sixth Crusade, 621
1248-1254: Failure of the Seventh Crusade, 641
Sept. 3, 1260: Battle of Ain Jālūt, 659
Apr., 1291: Fall of Acre, 686

ITALY

524: Imprisonment and Death of Boethius, 19
568-571: Lombard Conquest of Italy, 36
590-604: Reforms of Pope Gregory the Great, 42
726-843: Iconoclastic Controversy, 151
781: Alcuin Becomes Adviser to Charlemagne, 193
890's: Magyars Invade Italy, Saxony, and Bavaria, 279
1127-1130: Creation of the Kingdom of Sicily, 488
c. 1150: Refinements in Banking, 511
1150: Venetian Merchants Dominate Trade with the East, 513
c. 1175: Waldensian Excommunications Usher in Protestant Movement, 549
Apr. 16, 1209: Founding of the Franciscans, 589
1212: Children's Crusade, 596
Nov. 11-30, 1215: Fourth Lateran Council, 605
1227-1230: Frederick II Leads the Sixth Crusade, 621
1233: Papal Inquisition, 632
c. 1265-1273: Thomas Aquinas Compiles the *Summa Theologica*, 662
1271-1295: Travels of Marco Polo, 667
1290-1306: Jews Are Expelled from England, France, and Southern Italy, 683
Nov. 18, 1302: Boniface VIII Issues the Bull *Unam Sanctam*, 697
c. 1306-1320: Dante Writes *The Divine Comedy*, 703
May 20, 1347-October 8, 1354: Cola di Rienzo Leads Popular Uprising in Rome, 759
c. 1350-1400: Petrarch and Boccaccio Recover Classical Texts, 764
c. 1410-1440: Florentine School of Art Emerges, 834
1440: Donation of Constantine Is Exposed, 852

JAPAN

5th or 6th cent.: Confucianism Arrives in Japan, 1
538-552: Buddhism Arrives in Japan, 28
593-604: Regency of Shōtoku Taishi, 45
7th-8th cent.: Papermaking Spreads to Korea, Japan, and Central Asia, 59
607-839: Japan Sends Embassies to China, 72
645-646: Adoption of *Nengo* System and Taika Reforms, 104
701: Taihō Laws Reform Japanese Government, 140
Mar. 9, 712, and July 1, 720: Writing of *Kojiki* and *Nihon shoki*, 147

792: Rise of the Samurai, 204
794-1185: Heian Period, 210
c. 800: *Kana* Syllabary Is Developed, 213
858: Rise of the Fujiwara Family, 257
927: Compilation of the *Engi Shiki*, 299
c. 1001: Sei Shōnagon Completes *The Pillow Book*, 385
c. 1004: Murasaki Shikibu Writes *The Tale of Genji*, 387
1156-1192: Minamoto Yoritomo Becomes Shogun, 537
1175: Hōnen Shōnin Founds Pure Land Buddhism, 547
1219-1333: Hōjō Family Dominates Shoguns, Rules Japan, 611
1336-1392: Yoshino Civil Wars, 741
c. 1360-1440: Kan'ami and Zeami Perfect Nō Drama, 769

JERUSALEM. *See* **ISRAEL/PALESTINE**

KAZAKHSTAN. *See* **CENTRAL ASIA**

KHMER. *See* **SOUTHEAST ASIA**

KIEVAN RUS. *See* **RUSSIA**

KOREA
7th-8th cent.: Papermaking Spreads to Korea, Japan, and Central Asia, 59
668-935: Silla Unification of Korea, 108
918-936: Foundation of the Koryŏ Dynasty, 297
958-1076: Koreans Adopt the Tang Civil Service Model, 320
1145: Kim Pu-sik Writes *Samguk Sagi*, 498
1196-1258: Ch'oe Family Takes Power in Korea, 567
July, 1392: Establishment of the Yi Dynasty, 815

MACEDONIA
c. 850: Development of Slavic Alphabet, 249

MALAYSIA. *See* **SOUTHEAST ASIA**

MALI. *See* **AFRICA**

MIDDLE EAST. *See also* **AFRICA; ARABIA; BYZANTINE EMPIRE; EGYPT; IRAN; IRAQ; ISRAEL/PALESTINE; SYRIA; TURKEY**
c. 1145: Prester John Myth Sweeps Across Europe, 500
c. 1250: Improvements in Shipbuilding and Navigation, 648
c. 1320: Origins of the Bubonic Plague, 716

MONGOLIA. *See* **CHINA**

MORAVIA
c. 850: Development of Slavic Alphabet, 249
890's: Magyars Invade Italy, Saxony, and Bavaria, 279

MOROCCO. *See* **AFRICA**

NETHERLANDS. *See also* **FLANDERS**
735: Christianity Is Introduced into Germany, 165

NEW ZEALAND
c. 700-1100: Settlement of the South Pacific Islands, 130
Late 13th cent.: Maoris Hunt Moa to Extinction, 645

NICAEA. *See* **TURKEY**

NORTH AMERICA
7th-13th cent.: Mogollons Establish Agricultural Settlements, 61
c. 700: Bow and Arrow Spread into North America, 122
8th-14th cent.: Cahokia Becomes the First North American City, 134
8th-15th cent.: Hohokam Adapt to the Desert Southwest, 137
c. 800-1350: Mississippian Mound-Building Culture Flourishes, 215
9th-15th cent.: Plains Village Culture Flourishes, 221
850-950: Viking Era, 251
11th-12th cent.: First European-Native American Contact, 373

NORWAY. *See* **SCANDINAVIA**

OCEANIA. *See* **PACIFIC ISLANDS**

OTTOMAN EMPIRE. *See* **TURKEY**

PACIFIC ISLANDS
c. 700-1100: Settlement of the South Pacific Islands, 130

PALESTINE. *See* **ISRAEL/PALESTINE**

PERSIA. *See* **IRAN**

POLAND
July 15, 1410: Battle of Tannenberg, 831

PORTUGAL
1147-1149: Second Crusade, 503
1415-1460: Prince Henry the Navigator Promotes Portuguese Exploration, 844

PRUSSIA. *See* **GERMANY**

ROMANIA
Nov., 1330: Basarab Defeats the Hungarians, 737

RUSSIA
740: Khazars Convert to Judaism, 168
c. 850: Development of Slavic Alphabet, 249
988: Baptism of Vladimir I, 352
July 15, 1240: Alexander Nevsky Defends Novgorod from Swedish Invaders, 638
Sept. 8, 1380: Battle of Kulikovo, 791

SAUDI ARABIA. *See* **ARABIA**

SCANDINAVIA
850-950: Viking Era, 251
June 17, 1397: Kalmar Union Is Formed, 820

SCOTLAND
June 23-24, 1314: Battle of Bannockburn, 709

SCYTHIA. *See* **CENTRAL ASIA**

SERBIA
c. 850: Development of Slavic Alphabet, 249
1167: Foundation of the Nemanjid Dynasty, 540
June 28, 1389: Turkish Conquest of Serbia, 809

SOUTH AMERICA
c. 500-1000: Tiwanaku Civilization Flourishes in Andean Highlands, 11
After 850: Foundation of Chan Chan, 255
c. 1000: Collapse of the Huari and Tiwanaku Civilizations, 360
c. 1200-1230: Manco Capac Founds the Inca State, 576

SOUTHEAST ASIA
682-1377: Expansion of Śrivijaya, 113
c. 700-1253: Confederation of Thai Tribes, 132
775-840: Building of Borobuḍur, 185
780: Rise of the Sailendra Family, 191
802: Founding of the Khmer Empire, 223
832: Nanzhao Subjugates Pyu, 232
863: Nanzhao Captures Hanoi, 260
877-889: Indravarman I Conquers the Thai and the Mons, 273
939-944: Reign of Ngo Quyen, 304
982: Le Dai Hanh Invades Champa, 344
1225: Tran Thai Tong Establishes Tran Dynasty, 616
1259: Mangrai Founds the Kingdom of Lan Na, 657
1295: Ramkhamhaeng Conquers the Mekong and Menam Valleys, 690
1323-1326: Champa Wins Independence from Dai Viet, 718
1325-1355: Travels of Ibn Baṭṭūṭah, 729
1350: Ramathibodi I Creates First Thai Legal System, 762
1405-1433: Zheng He's Naval Expeditions, 829
1428: Le Loi Establishes Later Le Dynasty, 847

SPAIN
Apr. or May, 711: Ṭārik Crosses into Spain, 144
c. 950: Court of Córdoba Flourishes in Spain, 307
1031: Caliphate of Córdoba Falls, 412
Nov., 1092-June 15, 1094: El Cid Conquers Valencia, 447
c. 1150: Moors Transmit Classical Philosophy and Medicine to Europe, 507
1190: Moses Maimonides Writes *The Guide of the Perplexed*, 560
1230: Unification of Castile and León, 627
1233: Papal Inquisition, 632
c. 1275: The *Zohar* Is Transcribed, 678
1325-1355: Travels of Ibn Baṭṭūṭah, 729

SWEDEN. *See* **SCANDINAVIA**

SWITZERLAND
Nov. 15, 1315: Swiss Victory at Morgarten over Habsburg Forces, 713
1414-1418: Council of Constance, 837

SYRIA
Aug. 15-20, 636: Battle of Yarmūk, 97
786-809: Reign of Hārūn al-Rashīd, 196
809: First Islamic Public Hospital, 226
1381-1405: Tamerlane's Conquests, 797

THAILAND. *See* **SOUTHEAST ASIA**

TIBET. *See also* **CHINA**
627-650: Reign of Songtsen Gampo, 82
763: Tibetans Capture Chang'an, 181
791: Buddhism Becomes Tibetan State Religion, 202
838-842: Tibetan Empire Dissolves, 237
1368: Tibet Gains Independence from Mongols, 777
c. 1392: Foundation of the Gelugpa Order, 812

TRANSOXIANA. *See* **CENTRAL ASIA**

TURKEY
529-534: Justinian's Code Is Compiled, 23
532-537: Building of Hagia Sophia, 25
563: Silk Worms Are Smuggled to the Byzantine Empire, 31
637-657: Islam Expands Throughout the Middle East, 101
726-843: Iconoclastic Controversy, 151
786-809: Reign of Hārūn al-Rashīd, 196
976-1025: Reign of Basil II, 341
1054: Beginning of the Rome-Constantinople Schism, 422
Aug. 26, 1071: Battle of Manzikert, 434
1077: Seljuk Dynasty Is Founded, 442
1189-1192: Third Crusade, 557
1204: Knights of the Fourth Crusade Capture Constantinople, 584
1225-1231: Jalāl al-Dīn Expands the Khwārizmian Empire, 618
1271-1295: Travels of Marco Polo, 667
1273: Sufi Order of Mawlawīyah Is Established, 671
July 27, 1302: Battle of Bapheus, 695
May 29, 1453: Fall of Constantinople, 869

TURKISTAN. *See* **CENTRAL ASIA**

UKRAINE. *See* **RUSSIA**

UZBEKISTAN. *See* **RUSSIA**

VIETNAM. *See* **SOUTHEAST ASIA**

PERSONAGES INDEX

Abaoji, 302
ʿAbd al-ʿAtāhiyah, 198
ʿAbd al-Karim. *See* Satuq Bughra Khān
ʿAbd al-Malik, 10, 93, 116
ʿAbd al-Muʾmin, 368
ʿAbd al-Raḥmān I, 307
ʿAbd al-Raḥmān II, 307
ʿAbd al-Raḥmān III al-Nāṣir, 169, 307, 413, 507
ʿAbd al-Rahman (governor), 162
ʿAbd Allāh ibn al-Zubayr, 118
ʿAbd Allāh ibn Saʿd ibn Abī Sarḥ, 91
Abdullah Barshambu, 107
Abdullah ibn Saʿad ibn Abū Sarḥ, 106
Abe no Nakamaro, 73
Abelard, Peter, 470
Abhaya Malla, 801
Abraham ben Azriel, 326
Abraham ben David of Posquieres, 561
Abū al-ʿAbbās (Muslim commander), 269
Abū al-ʿAbbās as-Saffāḥ (ʿAbbāsid caliph), 179
Abū al-Mawāhib, 474, 740
Abū al-Muhajir, 92
Abū al-Nuwās, 198
Abū Āmir al-Manṣūr, 307
Abū Bakr (first Islamic caliph), 74, 98, 101
Abū Bakr ibn ʿUmar (Berber leader), 356, 440
Abū ʿInān Fāris, 730, 783
Abū Mikhnaf, 272
Abū Sālim, 783
Abū Ṭālib, 74
Abū ʿUbaidah, 98
Abū ʿUbayd Abdallāh al-Bakrī, 396
Abū Yaʿqūb Yūsuf, 507
Abū Yazīd, 421
Abū Ziad, 783
Abūʾl-Naṣr Sāmāni, 285
Adalbero of Reims, 350
Adam de la Halle, 383
Adelaide, Saint, 317
Adelard of Bath, 460, 509
Adhémar de Monteil, 452
Āditya I, 295
Adrian IV (pope), 543
Ælle, 277
Æthelbert I, 50
Æthelfrith of Bernicia (Northumbrian king), 95
Æthelred I, 277
Aguda, 303, 483
Ahmed Yesevi, 286
Ahmet Yukneki, 240
Ai Fa, 658
Aidan, Saint, 96
Airlangga, 115
ʿĀʾishah, 102
Aistulf (Lombard king), 176
A-ku-ta. *See* Aguda
ʿAlāʾ al-Dawlah, 398
ʿAlāʾ-ud-Dīn Bahman Shāh, 753-755
ʿAlāʾ-ud-Dīn Muḥammad Khaljī, 692-694
Alain de Lille, 653
Alaric II, 17-19
Alberic, Saint, 456
Albert (king of Sweden), 820
Albert of Saxony, 735
Albertus Magnus, 653, 663
Albinus of Canterbury, 161
Alboin, 36
Alcuin, 193-196, 209
Alexander III (pope), 501, 546
Alexander IV, 655
Alexander V (antipope), 841
Alexander (Byzantine emperor), 283
Alexander Nevsky, Saint, 638-641
Alexius I Comnenus, 424, 452, 514
Alexius III Angelus, 585
Alexius V Ducas Murzuphlus, 585
Alfasi, Isaac, 560
Alfonso I (king of Aragon and Navarre), 628
Alfonso I (king of Asturias), 627
Alfonso V (king of Aragon), 853, 859
Alfonso VI (king of León and Castile), 448, 628
Alfonso VII (king of León and Castile), 628
Alfonso VIII (king of Castile), 628
Alfonso IX (king of León), 628
Alfonso X (king of Castile and León), 509
Alfred the Great, 252, 276-279
ʿAlī (fourth Islamic caliph), 74, 102, 111
ʿAlī bin al-Ḥasan, 474, 476, 739
ʿAlī ibn Muḥammad, 268
ʿAlī ibn Yūsuf, 426
Ali Pasha, 858
Alp Arslan (Gujarat governor), 694
Alp Arslan (Seljuk sultan), 416, 434, 442
Alphonse of Poitiers, 642
Altan Khan, 814
Amade Tseyon, 666
Amalric de Lusignan, 686
Amīn, al-, 198
Amir Khusrau, 693
ʿAmr ibn al-ʿAṣ, 91, 106
An Lushan, 170, 175, 179-181, 526
Anandpal, 358
Anastasius (Byzantine emperor), 8
Anawrahta, 233
Andrew II, 609, 625
Andronicus II Palaeologus, 695
Angelicus, Doctor. *See* Thomas Aquinas
Anna, Princess of the Byzantine Empire, 169, 341, 353
Anthemius of Tralles, 26
Antoku, 537
A-pao-chi. *See* Abaoji
Appar, 88-89
Argyros, 424
Ari Malla, 801
Aristotle, 21, 507, 663, 707, 734

Arjunadeva, 801
Arnaud Amalric, 594
Arnulf, 280
Árpád, 280
Arumoḷivarman. *See* Rājarāja I
Āryabhaṭa the Elder, 47
Ashikaga Takauji, 742
Ashikaga Yoshimitsu, 743, 770
Ashraf Ṣalāḥ al-Dīn Khalīl, al- (Mamlūk sultan), 686
Ashrāf, al- (sultan of Aleppo and Damascus), 619
Aśoka, 459
Asperukh, 262
Asser, 277
Athanasios of Athos, 330
Atsiz, 494
Augustine, Saint, 663
Augustine of Canterbury, 43, 50, 96
Avempace, 507
Averroës, 308, 507, 663, 734
Avicenna, 227, 309, 397-400, 507, 560
Awata no Mahito, 140
Ayyūb, 620

Bacon, Roger, 509
Bādīs ibn al-Mansūr, 420
Bahrām V (Persian king), 234
Bahrām Shāh (Dehli sultan), 637
Bakhtiar Khaljī. *See* Ikhtar-ud-Dīn Muḥammad-ibn-Bakhtiar Khaljī
Bakri, al-, 172
Baldwin I, 586
Baldwin II, 485
Baldwin IV, 481
Baliol, John de, 709
Ball, John, 795
Ballaban Pasha, 860
Ban Muang, 691
Bāṇa, 69
Bang Klang Hao, 133, 691
Baoyi, 171
Bardas Phocas, 341
Bardas Skleros, 341
Barham V, 34
Baroncelli, Francesco, 760
Basarab I, 737-739
Basil I the Macedonian, 263
Basil II, 341-343, 353, 695
Basil Bulgaroktonus. *See* Basil II
Basil the Chamberlain, 341
Bayajidda, 290
Bayan Chor. *See* Moyanchuo
Baybars I, 107, 337, 659
Bayezid I, 810
Becket, Saint Thomas, 545-547
Bede the Venerable, Saint, 96, 160-162, 193
Belknap, Robert, 795
Benedict XII, 700
Benedict XIII (antipope), 701
Benedict Biscop, Saint, 96, 160
Benedict Gaetani. *See* Boniface VIII
Benedict of Nursia, Saint, 43, 128, 455
Berengar II, 317
Berengaria, 558
Berhtwulf (king of Mercia), 277
Bernard (king of Italy), 242
Bernard of Clairvaux, Saint, 456-457, 471, 485, 504, 706
Bertha, 50
Berthold IV of Zähringen, 522
Bhāskara, 48
Bhimdeva II, 693
Bi Sheng, 418-420, 861
Bigod, Hugh, 656
Bijjala Kalacuri, 340
Bilge Kur Kadir, 239
Birger Jarl, 639
Bīrunī, al-, 358
Blanche of Castile, 642
Bo Juyi, 180
Boccaccio, Giovanni, 757, 764-766
Bodel, Jean, 382
Boethius, 19-22
Bohemond I, 424, 452
Bohemond VI, 660
Boniface VIII, 634, 697-700, 705
Boniface, Saint, 165
Boris I of Bulgaria, 262-264, 282
Bradwardine, Thomas, 734
Brahamana Haricandra, 156
Brahmagupta, 48, 459
Brian (king of Ireland), 403
Brodar, 405
Bruce, Robert, 710
Brunelleschi, Filippo, 834
Bsod-nams-rgya-mtsho. *See* Sonam Gyatso
Bügü. *See* Mouyu
Bulan, 168
Bulgar Slayer. *See* Basil II
Buridan, Jean, 735
Buyiruq Khan, 582

Cacciaguida, 704
Ca' da Mosto. *See* Cadamosto, Alvise
Cadamosto, Alvise, 580, 845
Cai Lun, 59, 149
Cai Xi, 261
Canute I the Great, 406-408
Cao Pei. *See* Wendi (Wei emperor)
Capella, Martianus, 409
Capellanus, Andreas, 466
Capestrano, Giovani da. *See* John of Capestrano
Capet, Hugh, 351
Cavalcanti, Guido, 466, 704
Cave, Robert, 795
Caxton, William, 863
Ce Acatl Topiltzin. *See* Quetzalcóatl (god); Topiltzin-Quetzalcóatl
Celestine V, 697
Ceolfrith, 160
Ceolwulf II (king of Mercia), 277
Ceolwulf (Northumbrian king), 160
Cesarini, Julian, 855
Ch'in-tsung. *See* Qinzong (Song emperor)
Chagatai, 822
Chaghrï Beg, 415
Chai Songkhram, 658
Chakrayudha, 184
Chang Panchi. *See* Zhang Bangji
Changchub Gyaltsen, 778
Chao K'uang-yin. *See* Zhao Kuangyin
Charlemagne, 152, 193, 197, 209, 242
Charles I, 685
Charles I (king of Hungary). *See* Charles IV (Holy Roman Emperor)

Charles II the Bald (Holy Roman Emperor), 242
Charles IV (Holy Roman Emperor), 738, 760, 767
Charles IV (king of France), 722, 744
Charles V (king of France), 745, 781
Charles VI (king of France), 746, 780, 849, 865
Charles VII (king of France), 747, 849, 866
Charles Martel, 162, 165
Charles of Anjou, 642
Charles of Lorraine, 242, 350
Charles of Valois, 705
Chaucer, Geoffrey, 756, 765, 806-809
Chauliac, Guy de. *See* Guy de Chauliac
Che Anan, 719
Che Bong Nga, 720
Che Nang, 719
Cheng Hao, 491
Cheng Ho. *See* Zheng He
Cheng Yi, 491
Chen-tsung. *See* Zhenzong (Song emperor, r. 998-1022)
Chenzong. *See* Temür Oljeitu
Che-tsung. *See* Zhezong (Song emperor, r. 1086-1101)
Chichén Itzá, 124-127
Childeric III, 176
Ch'oe Ch'ung-hŏn, 567
Ch'oe Ch'ung-su, 567
Ch'oe Hang, 568
Ch'oe U, 568
Ch'oe Ŭi, 568
Ch'oe Yŏng, 817
Chŏng Chung-bu, 567
Chŏng To-chŏn, 817
Chormaqān, 619
Chou Tun-i. *See* Zhou Dunyi
Chrétien de Troyes, 466, 552-554
Christian II (king of Denmark, Norway, and Sweden), 821
Christian (bishop of Prussia), 624
Chu Chan-chi. *See* Xuande (Ming emperor)
Chu Hsi. *See* Zhu Xi
Chu Kao-chih. *See* Hongxi (Ming emperor)
Chu Ti. *See* Yonglo
Chu Wen. *See* Zhu Wen
Chu Yüan-chang. *See* Zhu Yuanzhang
Chulamanivarmadeva, 115
Chung-tsung. *See* Zhongzong (Tang emperor)
Cibial, Gonzalo, 845
Cid, El, 447-450
Clare, Richard de, 543, 773
Clare of Assisi, Saint, 590
Clement V (pope), 699-700, 759
Clement VI (pope), 700, 760
Clement VII (antipope), 701, 786
Clotilda, Saint, 7
Cloud Serpent. *See* Mixcóatl
Clovis, 6-8, 17
Colman, Saint, 96
Columba, Saint, 95
Confucius, 803
Conrad III, 504, 522, 534
Conrad of Masovia, 624
Constantine I the Great, 390, 422, 852
Constantine V Copronymus, 152
Constantine VI, 152, 196
Constantine VII Porphyrogenitus, 283
Constantine VIII, 341
Constantine IX Monomachus, 391, 423
Constantine X Ducas, 442
Constantine XI Palaeologus, 870
Cordovera, Moses, 679
Cortés, Hernán, 731
Coster, Laurens Janszoon, 862
Cunimund, 36
Cuthbert, Saint, 97, 208
Cyril, Saint, 168, 249, 263

Daigo, 300
Daizong (Tang emperor), 171, 180, 182
Dalai Lama, Third. *See* Sonam Gyatso
Damian, Peter, 652
Damjing, 60
Dandolo, Enrico, 584
Dante, 466, 509, 703-707, 764
Dao Yan, 827
Daqīqī, al-, 393
Dāʾūd bin al-Ḥasan, 740
Deguang, 302
Devagupta, 69
Deval Devi (Rājput queen), 693
Devaladevi (Malla regent queen), 801
Devaraja (god-king), cult of, 225
Dhanga, 158
Dharmapāla, 183-185
Dhruwa, 184
Díaz, Jimena, 448
Díaz de Vivar, Rodrigo. *See* Cid, El
Dibbalemi, Mai Dunama, 437, 614-616
Digunai, 526
Dil Naʿad, 554
Dinh Bo Linh, 306, 344
Dinh Toan, 344
Djanibeg, 717
Dmitry Donskoy, 792
Do Thich, 344
Do Thu Trung, 261
Do Ton Thanh, 260
Dominic, Saint, 607
Donatello, 834
Doncho. *See* Damjing
Dumbleton, John, 735
Dun Mohe, 171
Dunois, Jean, 849
Duong Dien Nghe, 304
Duqaq, 415

Eanflæd, 161
Edmund Ironside, 407
Edmund Rich, 655
Edward I, 570, 680, 684, 688, 709, 773
Edward II, 710, 744
Edward III, 744, 752, 773, 780
Edward the Black Prince, 781
Edward the Confessor, 408, 428
Edwin (Northumbrian king), 95, 160
Egbert, 276

Einhard, 194
El Cid. *See* Cid, El
Eleanor of Aquitaine, 466, 505, 528
Enian Tegin, 239
Ennin, 73
Erik of Pomerania, 820
Erik the Red, 254, 373
Erik Thorvaldson. *See* Erik the Red
Ethelred I (Northumbrian king), 209
Ethelred II, the Unready, 406, 519
Eudo, 162
Eugenius III, 497, 504
Eugenius IV, 839, 853
Euric, 17
Ewedo, 825
Eweka, 824
Ewuare the Great, 825

Faḍl, al-, 197
Falkenberg, Johannes, 839
Fāṭimah, 74
Feng Dao, 266
Feng Tao. *See* Feng Dao
Ferdinand I, 447, 628
Ferdinand II, 628
Ferdinand III, 628
Ferdinand of Naples, 860
Ferdowsi. *See* Firdusi
Ferrand, 599
Ferreus, Hugh, 597
Filangieri, Richard, 622
Firdawsi. *See* Firdusi
Firdusi, 234, 358, 393-395
Fitzgerald, Maurice, 544
Fitzstephen, Robert, 544
Foliot, Gilbert, 545
Francesco di Pietro di Bernardone. *See* Francis of Assisi, Saint
Francis of Assisi, Saint, 589
Frederick I Barbarossa, 471, 519, 522-525, 535, 557, 584
Frederick II, 490, 605, 609, 621-625, 633, 641, 685
Frederick of Rothenburg, 522
Froissart, Jean, 752, 780-782
Fujiwara Akiko, 387
Fujiwara Fuhito, 140
Fujiwara Kamatari, 104
Fujiwara Kanezane, 539
Fujiwara Michinaga, 211
Fujiwara Mototsune, 257, 299
Fujiwara no Kiyokawa, 73
Fujiwara Nobutaka, 387
Fujiwara Shunzei, 389
Fujiwara Tametoki, 387
Fujiwara Teika, 389
Fujiwara Yoshifusa, 257
Fulbert of Chartres, Saint, 409
Fürst, Walter, 713
Fust, Johann, 862

Gao Pian, 261
Gao Xianzhi, 60, 174
Gaozong (Tang emperor), 84, 120
Gaozu (Tang emperor). *See* Li Yuan (Tang emperor)
Gautier de Coincy, 383
Gautier Sans Avoir, 452
Gemmei, 73, 147
Genghis Khan, 325, 484, 501, 581-583, 618, 659, 813
Genshō, 148
Geoffrey IV (count of Anjou), 528
George I (Makurian king), 107
George II (Makurian king), 107
George Brankovich, 811
Gerard of Cremona, 398
Gerbert of Aurillac. *See* Sylvester II (pope)
Gerroni, Giovanni, 760
Ghalib, 413
Ghazzālī, al-, 507
Ghiberti, Lorenzo, 834
Ghiyāṣ-ud-Dīn Maḥmūd, 588
Ghiyāṣ-ud-Dīn Muḥammad, 587
Ghiyāth al-Dīn, 619
Gilbert (earl of Gloucester), 710
Giustiniani, Giovanni, 869
Glanville, Ranulf de, 603
Go-Daigo, 741
Godan Khan, 778, 813
Godfred, 252
Godfrey of Bouillon, 452
Godrum. *See* Guthrum
Gomes, Diogo, 845
Gonçalves, Antao, 845
Gonçalves, John, 844
Gongdi, 40
Gopāla, 183
Go-Shirakawa, 537
Go-Toba, 539, 612
Govinda II, 184
Grahvarman of Kanauj, 69
Gregory II, Saint, 152, 165
Gregory III, 152
Gregory IV, 242
Gregory V, 342
Gregory VIII, 557
Gregory IX, 591, 621, 625, 633, 641
Gregory X, 668
Gregory XI, 700, 787
Gregory of Sinai, 332
Gregory of Tours, 6
Gregory the Great, 42-44, 49, 95, 481; on the qualities of a preacher, 42
Guarnerius. *See* Irnerius
Gucumatz. *See* Quetzalcóatl (god)
Guillaume de Poitiers, 466
Guiraut Riquier, 466
Guli Peiluo, 170
Guo Wei, 293, 322
Guo Zixing, 775
Gustav I Vasa, 821
Gutenberg, Johann, 861-864
Guthrum, 252, 277
Guy de Chauliac, 756
Guy of Provins, 650

Hailing, king of. *See* Xizong (Jin emperor)
Hakam I, al-, 307
Hakam II, al-, 307, 413
Ḥākim, al-, 334, 390
Hákon VI (king of Norway), 820
Hales, Robert, 795
Halfdan, 277
Han Roe, 567
Harivarman II, 345
Harivarman III, 345
Harold II (king of England), 428
Harold Hardrada (king of Norway), 428
Harold Harefoot (king of England), 407
Harṣa, 69-71, 77, 87

Harthacnut, 407
Hārūn al-Rashīd, 196-199, 226
Hārūn Bughra Khān, 286
Ḥasan (Islamic caliph), 111
Ḥasān-e Ṣabbāḥ, 335
Hashang Mahāyāna, 203
Ḥassān (Muslim commander), 93
Hayton, 660
Heinrich von Plauen, 832
Hemp Prince. *See* Kyŏngsun
Henry I (king of England), 528, 569
Henry II (king of England), 519, 528, 542, 545, 569, 680, 773
Henry II de Lusignan, 686
Henry II Jasomirgott, 522, 534
Henry III (king of England), 604, 655
Henry IV (king of England), 481, 502, 746
Henry V (king of England), 746, 864
Henry VI (king of England and France), 746, 849, 865
Henry VII (Holy Roman Emperor), 704
Henry IV (Holy Roman Emperor), 488
Henry the Lion, 520, 522, 534
Henry the Navigator, Prince, 502, 844-847; *map* of expeditions, 846
Henry the Proud, 534
Heraclius, 97
Hermann Balke, 626
Heytesbury, William, 735
Hīdī, al-, 196
Hieda no Are, 147
Higbald, 209
Hilda of Whitby, Saint, 161
Hildegard von Bingen, 495-498
Hishām I, 307
Hishām II, 307, 413
Hōjō Masako, 612
Hōjō Tokimasa, 537
Hōjō Yoshitoki, 612
Hōnen Shōnin, 547-549
Hongwu. *See* Zhu Yuanzhang
Hongxi (Ming emperor), 830
Honorius III, 607, 609, 621
Hsia Kuei. *See* Xia Gui
Hsieh Chin. *See* Xie Jin
Hsieh yü-chia-ssu. *See* Xie Yujiasi
Hsien-tsung. *See* Xianzong (Tang emperor)
Hsi-tsung. *See* Xizong (Jin emperor)
Hsüan-jen. *See* Xuan Ren
Hsüan-tsang (Buddhist monk). *See* Xuanzang (Buddhist monk)
Hsüan-tsung (Tang emperor). *See* Xuanzong (Tang emperor)
Huang Chao, 82, 291
Huang Sheng, 363
Hugh Capet, 349-352
Hugh de Die, 456
Hugues des Payens, 485
Hŭijong, 567
Hui-tsung. *See* Huizong (Song emperor)
Huizong (Song emperor), 484, 525
Hülagü, 642, 659
Humbert of Silva Candida, 423
Hummay, Dunama bin, 436-437, 748
Hung-wu. *See* Zhu Yuanzhang
Hunyadi, János, 811, 854-858
Hur al-Riyahi, 111
Hus, Jan, 551, 838, 841-843
Ḥusayn, 111-113
Huyen Tran, 719
Hyejong, 320

I-Xing, 674
Ibn-Adret, Solomon, 679
Ibn al-Qanātir, 99
Ibn Bajja of Saragossa. *See* Avempace
Ibn Baṭṭūṭah, 474, 476, 725, 729-731, 740
Ibn Faḍl Allāh al-ʿUmarī. *See* ʿUmarī, al-
Ibn Gabirol, 679
Ibn Isḥāq, 272
Ibn Juzayy al-Kalbi, 730
Ibn Khaldūn, 783-785
Ibn Saʿīd, 614
Ibn Tāfrākīn, 783
Ibn Tufayl, 507
Ibn Tūmart, 367
Ibn Yāsīn, 426
I-Ching. *See* Yijing (Buddhist pilgrim)
I-Hsing. *See* I-Xing
Igor, 253, 352
I-tsing. *See* Yijing (Buddhist pilgrim)
I-tsung. *See* Yizong (Tang emperor)
Ikhtar-ud-Dīn Muḥammad-ibn-Bakhtiar Khaljī, 565, 588
Ikhtiar al-Dīn Altuniya, 637
Iltutmish, 589, 636
Imoshun, 155
Indra III, 158
Indravarman I, 273-275
Indravarman IV, 344
Indrayadha, 183
Injong, 498
Innocent III, 471, 584, 590, 594, 596, 605, 608, 621, 633
Innocent IV, 634, 641, 655
Innocent VI, 700, 760
Irene, Saint, 152, 196
Irnerius, 471
Isaac II Angelus, 584
Isaac ben Moses of Vienna, 326
Isabella of France, 744
Isanavaraman, 224
Isidore of Miletus, 26
Isidore the Younger, 27
Ismāʿīl Mukh Afghan. *See* Nāṣir-ud-Dīn Ismāʿīl Shāh
Ivar the Boneless, 277
Iyasus Moa, 666

Jabala bin al-Ayham, 99
Jacques de Molay, 487
Jadwiga, 831
Jaʿfar, 197
Jagadhekamalla I, 339
Jagadhekamalla II, 340
Jagiełło. *See* Władysław II Jagiełło
Jaipal, 357
Jalairtai, 568
Jalāl al-Dīn Mingburnu, 618-620
Jalāl al-Dīn Rūmī, 671
Jalāl-ud-Dīn Fīrūz Khaljī, 693
Jamāl al-Dīn ʿAbd Allāh, 749

Jamāl al-Dīn Yakut, 637
Jamuqa, 581
Jawhar, 336
Jaya Sinhavarman III, 719
Jaya Sinhavarman IV, 719
Jayachandra, 588
Jayadeva Malla, 801
Jayanasa, 114
Jayasimha I, 339
Jayasthiti. *See* Sthitimalla
Jayavarman I, 224
Jayavarman II, 224
Jayavarman VII, 133, 225, 690
Jean de Venette, 757-758
Jehanne la Pucelle. *See* Joan of Arc
Jenson, Nicolaus, 863
Jerome of Prague, 841
Jianwen (Ming emperor), 827
Jibrāʾīl ibn Bukhtishu, 226
Jitō, 147
Joachim of Fiore, 606
Joan of Arc, 746, 849-852, 865
John I (king of Portugal), 502
John I Tzimisces, 330, 342
John II (king of France), 745
John II Comnenus, 515
John XII (pope), 317
John XVI (antipope), 342
John XXII (pope), 700
John XXIII (antipope), 841
John XXIII (pope), 837
John (king of England), 519, 529, 599, 602, 605
John Cantacuzenus, 809
John of Brienne, 609, 621
John of Capestrano, 856
John of Damascus, 152
John of Gaunt, 780, 786, 794
John of Lancaster, 849, 865
John of Namur, 722
John of Salisbury, 543
John Philoponus, 734
John Stratsimir, 810
John the Cappadocian, 23
Joinville, Jean de, 644
Jomei, 72
Joseph (king of Khazaria), 168
Jui-tsung. *See* Ruizong (Tang emperor)
Julian, Count, 145
Julien of Sidon, 660
Justin I, 23, 31
Justin II, 32, 37
Justinian I, 23-25, 31, 37, 471
Jutta von Spanheim, 496
Jyotimalla, 802

Kūkai. *See* Kōbō Daishi
Kāfūr, 693
Kāhina, Damia al-, 93
Kalidurut, 106
Kamala Devi, 693
Kamalaśīla, 203
Kammu, 204
Kan'ami Kiyotsugu, 769
Kangjong, 567
Kanz al-Dawla, 107
Kao Hsien-chih. *See* Gao Xianzhi
Kao P'ien. *See* Gao Pian
Kao-tsu. *See* Li Yuan (Tang emperor)
Kao-tsung. *See* Gaozong (Tang emperor)
Kasila, 92
Kastrioti, George. *See* Skanderbeg
Kastrioti, Hamza, 859
Kastrioti, John, 858
Kasyapa VI, 295
Kavadh I, 34
Kawashima, Prince, 147
Ke Cuncheng, 676
Ker, Abel, 795
Keykubād, 619
Khadija (Maldives queen), 730
Khadīja (Muḥammad's wife), 74
Khālid ibn al-Walīd, 98
Khamfu, 658
Khayzurān, al-, 196
Khosrow I, 31, 34
Khosrow II, 77, 390
Khuc Thua Du, 304
Khwārizmī, al-, 48, 459, 471
Ki no Kiyohito, 148
Ki no Tsurayuki, 213
Kieu Cong Tien, 305
Kim Don-jung, 567
Kim Pu-sik, 498-500
Kimmei, 29
Kirill, 638
Kīrtivarman I, 77
Kitbuqa, 659
Kiyohara Motosuke, 385
Koberger, Anthony, 863
Kōbō Daishi, 30, 212-213
Kojong, 567
Kōkō, 257
Kolofeng, 133, 154, 233
Komparu Zenchiku, 770
Kongmin Wang, 816
Kossoi, 396
Krum, 262
Kublai Khan, 133, 155, 233, 238, 325, 527, 617, 668, 778, 813, 816, 818
Kubrat (semilegendary), 262
Küchlüg, 495, 581
Kudanbes, 107
Kukulcán. *See* Quetzalcóatl (god)
Ku-li p'ei-lo. *See* Guli Peiluo
Kŭmgang, 298
Kung-ye, 110, 297
Kuo Tzu-hsing. *See* Guo Zixing
Kuo Wei. *See* Guo Wei
Kupe (legendary), 131
Kusunoki Masashige, 742
Kusunoki Masatsura, 742
Kutluk. *See* Xie Yujiasi
Kutluk Bilgé Kül. *See* Guli Peiluo
Kūya, 548
Kwangjong, 320
Kyŏn-hwŏn, 297
Kyŏng-ae, 298
Kyŏngjong, 320
Kyŏngsun, 298
Kyriell, Thomas, 866
Kyteler, Lady Alice, 726-729

Ladislas V Posthumous, 856
Lajos. *See* Louis I the Great (king of Hungary)
Lal Ded, 789-791
Lalibela, 554-556, 665
Lalla Arifa. *See* Lal Ded
Lalleshwari. *See* Lal Ded
Lambert of Spoleto, 280
Lang Darma, 237
Langton, Stephen, 529
Lazar I Hrebeljanović, 809
Le Dai Hanh, 344-346, 719
Le Hoan. *See* Le Dai Hanh

Le Loi, 847-849
Ledrede, Richard de, 727
Leif Eriksson, 254, 374
Leo III (Byzantine emperor), 152, 423
Leo III (pope), 152
Leo IV (Byzantine emperor), 152
Leo V (Byzantine emperor), 153
Leo VI (Byzantine emperor), 283, 330
Leo IX (pope), 423, 653
Leonardo of Pisa, 460
Leopold I of Austria, 714
Leopold V, 557
Leopold of Babenberg, 534
Lhalung Palgye Dorje, 238
Li Che. *See* Zhongzong (Tang emperor)
Li Chen (protector general of Annam), 304
Li Cho (protector general of Annam), 260
Li Cunxu (Later Liang general), 293
Li Dang. *See* Ruizong (Tang emperor)
Li Hong (Tang prince), 120
Li Hsien. *See* Li Xian (Tang prince)
Li Hu (protector general of Annam), 261
Li Linfu (Tang minister), 179
Li Tang. *See* Ruizong (Tang emperor)
Li Tang (Song painter), 563
Li Ts'un-hsü. *See* Li Cunxu (Later Liang general)
Li Xian (Tang prince), 120
Li Yu. *See* Suzong (Tang emperor)
Li Yu (Southern Tang emperor), 363
Li Yuan (Tang emperor), 40, 79, 120
Li Zhe. *See* Zhongzong (Tang emperor)
Li Zhi. *See* Gaozong (Tang emperor)
Lionel of Antwerp, 773
Liu Chih-yüan. *See* Liu Zhiyuan
Liu Hongcao, 305
Liu Yan, 304
Liu Zhiyuan, 293
Llywelyn ap Gruffudd, 655
Lo Tai, 692
Lombard, Peter, 472, 663
Longinus, 37
Lorenzo, Nicola di. *See* Rienzo, Cola di
Lothair I (Holy Roman Emperor), 242
Lothair II, 534
Lothair (king of France), 350
Louis I (count of Flanders), 721
Louis I the Great (king of Hungary), 738
Louis I the Pious (Holy Roman Emperor), 242
Louis II the German (king of Germany), 242
Louis IV (king of Germany and Holy Roman Emperor), 708, 767
Louis V (king of France), 350
Louis VI (king of France), 532
Louis VII (king of France), 504, 532, 546, 684
Louis VIII (king of France), 595
Louis IX (king of France), 490, 641
Lu Chiu-yüan. *See* Lu Jiuyuan
Lu Jiuyuan, 324
Lu Tai, 692
Lu Tsu-ch'ien. *See* Lu Zuqian
Lu Zuqian, 491
Lucius III, 551
Lull, Raymond, 651
Luo Shuangshuang, 363
Luria, Isaac ben Solomon, 679
Luu Ky Tong, 345
Luzarches, Robert de, 517
Ly Chieu Hoang, 616
Ly Hue Tong, 616

Ma Yuan, 562
Ma-ŭi T'ae-ja. *See* Kyŏngsun
MacMurrough, Dermot, 543
MacMurrough, Eva, 543
Máel Mórda mac Murchada, 404
Maghan I, Mansa, 725
Magnus II (king of Sweden), 820
Mahāvīra, 48
Mahdī, al-, 196
Mahendrapāla I, 158
Mahendravarman I, 78, 88
Mahendravarman II, 90
Mahendravarman III, 142
Mahipāla, 158
Maḥmūd Kāshgarī, 239, 285
Maḥmūd of Ghazna, 156, 235, 319, 357-359, 393, 416, 565, 692
Maid of Orléans. *See* Joan of Arc
Maimonides, Moses, 308, 509, 560-562
Malik al-Kāmil, al-, 610, 622, 641
Malik Shāh, 434, 442
Mama Ocllo, 577
Mamai, 792
Ma'mūn, al-, 235
Manco Capac, 576-578
Mandeville, Sir John (legendary), 501
Maṇgaleśa, 77
Mangrai, 133, 657-659, 691
Mangu, 659
Manṣūr, Abū ʿĀmir al-, 413
Manṣūr, al-(ʿAbbāsid caliph), 196
Manṣūr, al- (Zīrid ruler), 420
Manuel I Comnenus, 435, 504, 515
Manuel II Comnenus, 501
Mara Tekle Haimanot, 554
Margaret I of Denmark, Norway, and Sweden, 820-822
Margaret of Provence, 642
Marsilius of Padua, 787
Martin V, 839
Martin of Tours, Saint, 7
Masaccio, 834
Masʿūd I, 416
Matilda (English princess), 528
Mayta Capac, 578
Me Agtsom, 181, 202
Mehmed II, 27, 811, 856, 860, 869
Merkurios, 107
Methodius, Saint, 168, 249, 263
Michael I, 152
Michael III, 263
Michael IV, 391
Michael VII Ducas, 443
Michael VIII Palaeologus, 435, 586
Michael Cerularius, 423
Mihira Bhoja, 158
Mihirakula, 4
Milica, 810
Minabuchi no Shōan, 73

Minamoto Noriyori, 538
Minamoto Sanetomo, 612
Minamoto Tameyoshi, 537
Minamoto Yoriie, 612
Minamoto Yorimasa, 537
Minamoto Yoritomo, 537-540, 611
Minamoto Yoshimochi, 770
Minamoto Yoshinaka, 537
Minamoto Yoshitsune, 538
Mircea the Old, 738
Mixcóatl, 313
Miyake no Fujimaro, 148
Moïse Golem, 858
Mo-ch'o. *See* Mochuo
Mochihito, 537
Mochuo, 170
Moctezuma, 733
Montfort, Simon de, 595, 607, 656
Mortimer, Roger, 744
Moses de León, 678-680
Motoshige. *See* On'ami
Mouyu, 171
Mou-yü. *See* Mouyu
Mouzalon, George, 696
Moyanchuo, 170
Mo-yen-ch'o. *See* Moyanchuo
Muʿāwiyah I, 91, 102, 111, 117
Muḥammad I Askia, 396
Muḥammad II (Khwārizm ruler), 495, 618
Muḥammad (the Prophet), 74-76, 97, 101
Muḥammad ibn Ibrāhīm al-Fazārī, 459
Muḥammad ibn Tughluq, 694, 730, 753
Muʾizz, al-, 333, 336
Muʾizz ibn Bādīs, al-, 420
Muʿizz-ud-Dīn Muḥammad, 587, 693
Mularaja II, 587
Müller, Johann, 735
Müneccimbaşi, Ahmed Dede, 286
Munjong, 321
Murad I, 696, 809
Murad II, 854, 858
Murasaki Shikibu, 212, 387-389
Murchad, 404
Mūsā, Mansa, 396, 462, 631, 723-726, 749
Mūsa ibn Nuṣayr, 93, 144
Mushafi, al-, 413
Muʿtaṣim, al-, 587
Muwaffaq, al-, 268
Muẓaffar, al- (chamberlain of), 414
Muẓaffar Shah (sultan of Gujarat), 694
Mwene Mutapa, 380
My (protector general of Annam), 304
Myŏngjong, 567

Naḥmanides, 679
Naʿakuto Laʿab, 555
Nāgabhaṭa I, 157
Nāgabhaṭa II, 184
Naka no Ōe, 104
Namri Songtsen, 82
Narasiṃhavarman I Mahāmalla, 78, 88-90
Narasiṃhavarman II, 142
Narasiṃhavarman II Rājasiṃha, 142
Narses (Byzantine general), 36
Narshakhī, Abū Bakr Muḥammad ibn Jafar, 285
Nāṣir al-Dīn Qabacha, 588
Nāṣir-ud-Dīn Ismāʿīl Shāh, 754
Ndiadiane N'diaye, 579-580
Neckam, Alexander, 650
Nemanja, Stephen I, 540
Nemanja, Stephen II, 540
Ngam Muang, 133, 658, 691
Ngo Quyen, 304-306
Nguyen Trai, 847
Nicephorus I, 153, 197
Nicephorus II Phocas, 330
Nichiren, 30
Nicholas V (antipope), 700
Nicholas Alexander, 738
Nicholas of Cologne, 597
Nicholas of Cusa, 735, 852
Nicholas the Great, 263
Nicholas the Mystic, 283
Nitta Yoshisada, 742
Niẓām al-Mulk, 311, 417, 434, 443
Niẓām-ud-Dīn Awliyā, 754
Nogaret, Guillaume de, 699
Nūḥ ibn Manṣūr, 398
Nusrat Khan, 693

Ō no Yasumaro, 147
Obadiah, 168
Ockham, William of, 707-709
O'Connor, Rory, 543
Oduduwa (legendary), 376, 824
Offa (Mercian king), 209
Ogatai, 484
Olaf II (king of Denmark and Norway), 820
Olaf IV (king of Norway). *See* Olaf II (king of Denmark and Norway)
Oleg, 253, 792
Olga, Saint, 352
Omortag, 262
On'ami, 770
Ong-Khan. *See* Toghrïl
Ono no Imoko, 72
Oranmiyan, 824
Orbais, Jean d', 517
Oresme, Nicholas, 735
Orhan, 696
O'Rourke, Dervorgilla, 543
O'Rourke, Tiernan, 543
Osakabe, Prince, 140
Osman I, 695, 809
Ospak, 405
O-sung, 238
Oswald (Northumbrian king), 95
Otakar II, 326
O'Toole, Laurence, 544
Otto I, 316-318, 423
Otto III, 342, 852
Otto IV, 599
Otto de Grandison, 686
Otto of Freising, 501
Our Prince One Reed. *See* Quetzalcóatl (god)
Outlaw, William, 727
Oye Masahira, 259

Pacal, 56
Pachacuti, 578
Padmasambhava, 202, 237, 812
P'agpa, 813
Panamkarana, 192
Pannartz, Arnold, 863

Pao-i. *See* Baoyi
Paramesvaravarman, 344
Parāntaka I, 294-296
Park Jin-jae, 567
Paschal I, 153
Paul the Deacon, 36, 194
Paulinus (Italian grammarian), 194
Paulinus, Saint, 51, 160
P'ei Shih-ch'ing. *See* Pei Shiqing
Pei Shiqing, 72
Pelagius II, 42
Pelagius of Albano, 610
Pelayo, 627
Pépin I (king of Aquitaine), 242
Pépin III the Short (Frankish mayor), 176-178
Peroz, 34
Peter II (king of Aragon and Catalonia), 551
Peter of Murrone. *See* Celestine V
Peter of Pisa, 194
Peter the Deacon, 43
Peter the Hermit, 452
Peter the Venerable, 509
Petit, John, 839
Petrarch, 467, 702, 764-766
Petronilla of Meath, 728
Peyar, 89
Pha Muang, 691
Philip II (king of France), 529, 557, 594, 596, 599, 684
Philip II the Bold (duke of Burgundy), 780
Philip III (king of France), 684
Philip III the Good (duke of Burgundy), 865
Philip IV the Fair (king of France), 486, 684, 698
Philip VI (king of France), 722, 745, 752
Philip of Swabia, 584
Philippa of Hainaut, 744, 780
Philoponous, John. *See* John Philoponus
Photios, 263
Phra Ramkhamhaeng. *See* Ban Muang
Pi Sheng. *See* Bi Sheng
Pietro II Orseolo, 514
Pilaoko, 133, 154
Pius II, 860
Po Chü-yi. *See* Bo Juyi
Poer, Arnold le, 727
Polo, Maffeo, 668
Polo, Marco, 115, 229, 231, 501, 667-670; *map* of journey, 668
Polo, Niccolò, 668
Porcus, William, 597
Portinari, Beatrice, 704
Poykai, 89
Prabhākaravardhana, 69
Prester John (legendary), 500-503, 555
Pṛithivīrāja, 588
Prola I, 340
Pulakeśin I, 338
Pulakeśin II, 70, 77-79, 88, 338
Pūtān, 89

Qā'im, al-, 417
Qalā'ūn, 686
Qinzong (Song emperor), 484
Qiwan-ud-Dīn Qutlugh Khan, 754
Quetzalcóatl (god), 125, 287-289, 313
Quṭ al-Dīn Aybak, 587-589, 636, 693
Qutlugh Khan. *See* Qiwan-ud-Dīn Qutlugh Khan
Quṭuz, 659

Rabban Sauma, 676
Ragnar Lothbrok, 277
Rāja Karṇadeva II, 693
Rajalladevi, 801
Rājarāja I, 296, 339, 346-348
Rājasiṃha II, 295
Rājendra III, 296
Rājendracōla Deva I, 115, 296, 339, 347
Rājyasrī, 69
Rājyavardhana, 69
Ralpachen, 237
Ramadhipati, 692
Ramakhamhaeng, 133
Ramathibodi I, 762-763
Ramkhamhaeng, 657, 690-692, 762
Raṅgapatākā, 142
Ranna of Kannada, 339
Raymond VI, 594
Raymond VII, 595
Raymond of Peñafort, 663
Raymond of Poitiers, 505
Raymond of Saint-Gilles, 452
Rāzī, al-, 227, 508
Raziya, 636-638
Reginald of Piperno, 663
Regiomontanus. *See* Müller, Johann
Remigius of Reims, 7
Renaud, 599
Richard I, 529, 557
Richard II, 746, 780, 794
Richardis von Sade, 497
Rienzo, Cola di, 759-761
Rinpoche. *See* Padmasambhava
Robert II of Jerusalem, 453
Robert II the Pious (king of France), 351
Robert Guiscard, 488, 514
Robert of Artois, 642
Robert of Cassel, 721
Robert of Losinga, 444
Robert of Molesme, Saint, 455
Roderick (king of the Visigoths), 144, 627
Roger I (conqueror of Sicily), 488
Roger II (king of Sicily), 489, 504
Roger of York, 546
Romanus I Lecapenus, 284
Romanus IV Diogenes, 434, 442
Rosamund, 36
Rotislav, 249
Rudolf IV of Habsburg (duke), 768
Rudolph IV, 235
Rudravarman, 273
Ruizong (Tang emperor), 121
Ruknuddin Firūz Shah, 636
Rūmī. *See* Jalāl al-Dīn Rūmī
Ruprecht of the Rhine, 837
Rurik, 253
Rutebeuf, 383

Sadako, 385
Saichō, 30
Saif-ud-Dīn Ghūri, 754
Saisset, Bernard, 698
Sakya Pandit, 778, 813

Saladin, 107, 335, 337, 502, 557
Sambandar, 89
Samuel (czar of Bulgaria), 341
Samuel ben Judah ibn Tibbon, 561
Sancho II, 447
Sanggrāmadhanañjaya, 192
Sanjar, 494, 501
Sanjaya, 115
Śaṅkara, 200-201
Saray Mulk Khanum, 822
Ṣaṣāṇka, 69, 183
Satuq Bughra Khān, 240, 285
Saṭyaśraya, 339, 346
Sayf bin ʿUmar, 272
Schöffer, Peter, 863
Sei Shōnagon, 385-387
Seiwa, 257
Sejong, 817
Seljuk, 415, 434, 442
Sergius II, 423
Sesshū, 564
Severus Sebokht, 459
Shōshi. *See* Fujiwara Akiko
Shah Melik, 416
Shah Turkan, 636
Shams al-Dawlah, 398
Shams al-Dīn, 671
Shams-ud-din Ilyas, 801
Shen K'ua. *See* Shen Kuo
Shen Kuo, 418
Shen-tsung. *See* Shenzong (Song emperor)
Shenzong (Song emperor), 432
Shi Chaoyi, 171
Shi Jingtang, 293, 302
Shih Ch'ao-I. *See* Shi Chaoyi
Shinran, 30, 548
Shi-tsung. *See* Shizong (Jin emperor)
Shizong (Jin emperor), 526
Shōtoku Taishi, 2, 45-47, 72, 105, 147
Shūbun, 564
Sigismund (king of Hungary and Holy Roman Emperor), 701, 831, 837, 841, 854
Sigurd, 405
Sima Guang, 121, 433
Simhavarman, 88
Simhavishnu, 88
Simon of Sudbury, 787, 795
Sinchi Roca, 577
Sin-gŏm, 298
Sinjong, 567
Sinulo, 132, 154
Siraj-ud-Dīn Junaydi, 754
Sitric Mac-Aulaffe I, 404
Skanda Gupta, 4
Skanderbeg, 856, 858-860
Sŏckch'ŏng, 297
Soga Emishi, 104
Soga Iname, 30, 104
Soga Umako, 30, 45
Somadeva, 366
Someśvara I, 339
Someśvara II, 339
Someśvara III, 339
Someśvara IV, 340
Someśvara V, 340
Sonam Gyatso, 814
Sŏng, 28
Sŏngjong, 321
Songtsen Gampo, 82-85, 202, 237
Sonni ʿAlī, 396
Sophia, 37
Sri Indraditya; *map* of empire, 70. *See also* Bang Klang Hao Hara
Ssu-ma Kuang. *See* Sima Guang
Statius, 706
Stauffacher, Rudolf, 713
Stefan Dušan, 809
Stefan Lazarevich, 810
Sten Sture the Younger, 821
Stephen II (pope), 176
Stephen Harding, Saint, 456
Stephen of Cloyes, 596
Stephen the Younger, Saint, 152
Steuco, Agostino, 853
Sthitimalla, 801-803
Strongbow. *See* Clare, Richard de
Su Song, 674
Subh, 413
Subüktigin, 156, 319
Suger, 517
Suiko, 2, 45, 72, 148
Sulaymān, Mansa, 725, 749
Süleyman (founder of Seljuk Rum), 434, 443
Sulṭān Walad, 671
Sumanguru, 173, 630, 724
Sun Junze, 563
Sundiata, 173, 396, 630-632, 725
Sutoku, 537
Su-tsung. *See* Suzong (Tang emperor)
Suzong (Tang emperor), 180, 182
Svyatoslav I, 169, 352
Sweinheim, Konrad, 863
Sweyn Forkbeard, 406
Swineshead, Richard, 735
Syagrius of Soissons, 17
Sylvester II (pope), 308, 350, 409, 674
Symeon, 282
Symmachus, Quintus Aurelius Memmius, 20
T'aejo, King. *See* Wang Kŏn
T'ai-tsu (Khitan Liao emperor). *See* Abaoji
T'ai-tsu (Song emperor). *See* Zhao Kuangyin
Tai-tsung. *See* Daizong (Tang emperor)
T'ai-tsung (Jin emperor). *See* Taizong (Jin emperor)
T'ai-tsung (Khitan Liao emperor). *See* Deguang
T'ai-tsung (Song emperor). *See* Taizong (Song emperor)
T'ai-tsung (Tang emperor). *See* Taizong (Tang emperor)
T'ien-tsu. *See* Tianzuodi (Khitan Liao emperor)
Ṭabarī, al-, 270, 273
Taiking, 155
Taila II, 338
Taila III, 340
Taimas, 619
Taira Kiyomori, 537
Taizong (Jin emperor), 484
Taizong (Khitan Liao emperor). *See* Deguang
Taizong (Song emperor), 323, 344
Taizong (Tang emperor), 83, 86, 120, 229, 245

Taizu (Khitan Liao emperor). *See* Abaoji
Taizu (Song emperor). *See* Zhao Kuangyin
Tāj-ud-Dīn Yildiz, 588
Takamuko no Kuromaro, 73
Talbot, John, 849, 867
Tamerlane, 784, 797-800, 811, 822-824; *map* of empire, 798
Tao-yen. *See* Dao Yan
Ṭārik ibn-Ziyād, 144-146, 627
Tayang Khan, 581
Tekle Haymanot, 666
Tell, Wilhelm (legendary), 713
Temmu, 147
Tempier, Étienne, 664
Temür Oljeitu, 778
Tesfa Iyesus. *See* Yekuno Amlak
Tezcatlipoca, 315
Theobald (archbishop of Canterbury), 545
Theodora (Byzantine empress), 23, 153
Theodore Studites, 153
Theodore Trithourios, 98
Theodoric the Great, 19
Theodosius II (Byzantine emperor), 18, 23
Theodulf, 194
Theophano, 341
Theophilus, 153
Thibaut V, 684
13 Rabbit, 53
Thomas Aquinas, 472, 509, 652, 662-665, 707
Thomas the Slav, 153
Thorfinn Karlsefni, 374
Thorvald Eriksson, 374
Tianzuodi (Khitan Liao emperor), 483
Tidjani, al-, 615
Ti-ku-nai. *See* Digunai
Tilutane, 172
Timur. *See* Tamerlane
Tō no Shikibu. *See* Murasaki Shikibu
Toghrïl (Kereit ruler), 581
Toghrïl Beg (Seljuk Turk sultan), 415, 434, 442
Toi (legendary), 131
Toktamish, 799
Tö-kuang. *See* Deguang
Tomislav, 284
Toneri, Prince, 148
Topiltzin-Quetzalcóatl, 287
Toqto'a Beki, 582
Toramana, 4
Tounka, 356
Tran Anh Tong, 719
Tran Canh. *See* Tran Thai Tong
Tran Minh Tong, 719
Tran Nhan Tong, 719
Tran Thai Tong, 616-618
Tran Thu Do, 616
Tran Thua, 616
Tribonian, 23
Trilocanapāla, 158
Trisong Detsen, 182, 202, 237
Tristão, Nuno, 845
Ts'ai Hsi. *See* Cai Xi
Ts'ai Lun. *See* Cai Lun
Ts'ao P'ei. *See* Wendi (Wei emperor)
Tsongkhapa, 779
Tsuiling, 155
Tun Mo-ho. *See* Dun Mohe
Turanshah, 107
Tvrtko I, 810
Tyler, Wat, 794; meeting with Richard II, 795

Ubaydullah ibn Ziyad, 111
Uda, 257, 299
Udaya IV, 295
Ughe Tegin, 239
Ŭijong, 567
Ulászló I. *See* Władysław III
Uli, Mansa, 725
Ulrich von Jungingen, 831
Ulugh Khan, 693
ʿUmar I, 98, 101, 116
ʿUmar ibn Saʿad, 111
ʿUmarī, al-, 614, 748-750
ʿUqbah ibn Nāfiʿ, 92
Uqlīdisī, al-, 48
Urban II, 424, 443, 450-454, 514
Urban V, 700
Urban VI, 701
Urraca, 448, 628
ʿUtba bin Abū Sufyān, 91
ʿUthmān. *See* Osman I
ʿUthmān ibn ʿAffān, 91, 102

Vahān, 99
Valdemar II, 624
Valdemar IV (king of Denmark), 820
Valdès, Pierre. *See* Waldo, Peter
Valentinian III, 23
Valla, Lorenzo, 853
Vatsarāja, 157, 183
Venette, Jean de. *See* Jean de Venette
Vergil, 705
Vermundo III (king of León), 628
Vijayālaya, 294, 346
Vikramāditya VI, 339
Vira Ballala I, 340
Vivar, Rodrigo Díaz de. *See* Cid, El
Vladimir I, 169, 249, 341, 352-355
Vladimir (ruler of Bulgaria), 282
Vlado, Pierre. *See* Waldo, Peter
Von Attinghausen, Werner, 713
Von Salza, Hermann, 625
Vytautas, 831

Waldo, Peter, 549
Walīd I, al-, 118
Wallace, William, 709
Walter the Penniless. *See* Gautier Sans Avoir
Walworth, William, 796
Wang Anshi, 323, 432-434
Wang Che. *See* Wang Chongyang
Wang Ch'i. *See* Sŏngjong
Wang Chieh. *See* Wang Jie
Wang Chongyang, 478-480
Wang Ch'ung-yang. *See* Wang Chongyang
Wang Guan, 261
Wang Hae. *See* Injong
Wang Hwi. *See* Munjong
Wang Jie, 265
Wang Kŏn, 110, 297, 320
Wang Shi, 261
Wang So. *See* Kwangjong
Wang Yangming, 492

Wang Yu. *See* Kyŏngjong
Wang Zhe. *See* Wang Chongyang
Wani, 1, 147
Wanyan Liang. *See* Digunai
Wanyan Min. *See* Aguda
Wanyan Sheng. *See* Taizong (Jin emperor)
Wan-yen Min. *See* Aguda
Wāqidī, 272
Welf VI, Count, 522
Wen Huangdi. *See* Yonglo
Wenceslas (king of Germany and Holy Roman Emperor), 831, 837, 841
Wendi (Sui emperor), 39, 64, 67, 79
Wendi (Wei emperor), 66
Wen-huang-ti. *See* Yonglo
Wenzheng, 83
Wiching, Bishop, 249
William, earl of Salisbury, 642
William de Beaujeau, 686
William of Malmesbury, 428
William of Modena, 626
William of Moerbeke, 663
William of Ockham, 787
William of Rubrouck, 677
William of Saint-Thierry, 457
William the Bad (king of Sicily), 489
William the Conqueror, 408, 428, 444, 569, 744
William the Good (king of Sicily), 489
Willibrord, Saint, 165
Winfrid. *See* Boniface, Saint
Witiza, 144
Władysław II Jagiełło, 793, 831, 839
Władysław III, 854
Wolfram von Eschenbach, 502
Wŏnjong, 816
Wu Hou, 120-122
Wu Zetian. *See* Wu Hou
Wu-tsung. *See* Wuzong (Tang emperor)
Wuzong (Tang emperor), 245
Wyclif, John, 786-789, 838, 841
Wynfrith. *See* Boniface, Saint

Xia Gui, 562
Xianzong (Tang emperor), 231
Xiao Baojuan, 363
Xie Jin, 827
Xie Yujiasi, 171
Xizong (Jin emperor), 526
Xuan Ren, 433
Xuande (Ming emperor), 830
Xuanzang, 565
Xuanzang (Buddhist monk), 69, 78, 81, 85-88, 157, 245; *map* of travels, 86
Xuanzong (Tang emperor), 133, 154, 175, 179, 181

Yabghu, 415
Yaḥyā ibn Ibrāhīm, 426
Yaḥyā ibn Khālid al-Barmakī, 196
Yang-gil, 297
Yang Guang. *See* Yangdi
Yang Guifei, 179, 181
Yang Guozhong, 179
Yang Jian. *See* Wendi (Sui emperor)
Yang Kuei-fei. *See* Yang Guifei
Yang Kuo-chung. *See* Yang Guozhong
Yangdi, 40, 64, 67, 72
Yao Guangxiao. *See* Dao Yan
Yao Kuang-hsiao. *See* Dao Yan
Yao Niang. *See* Yaoniang
Yao-ku. *See* Deguang
Yaoniang, 363
Yaroslav Vsevolodovich, 639
Yazdegerd III, 35, 394
Yazīd I, 111
Yejong, 499
Yekuno Amlak, 665-667
Yelü Dashi, 493
Yōmei, 45
Yi Chach'un, 816
Yi Go, 567
Yi Sŏng-gye, 816
Yi T'aejo. *See* Yi Sŏng-gye
Yi Ŭi-bang, 567
Yi Ŭi-min, 567
Yiba, 658
Yijing (Buddhist pilgrim), 114, 191
Yikuno Amlak, 556
Yimrehane-Kristos, 555
Yitbarek, 555, 665
Yizong (Tang emperor), 155
Yonglo, 827, 829, 847
Yōzei, 257
Yumtan, 238
Yung-lo. *See* Yonglo
Yūsuf Buluggīn I ibn Zīrī, 420
Yūsuf ibn Tāshufīn, 367, 426, 448
Yūsuf Khāss Hājib, 239

Zacharias (pope), 176
Ẓafār Khan. *See* ʿAlāʾ-ud-Dīn Bahman Shāh; Muẓaffar (sultan of Gujarat)
Zagan Pasha, 870
Zaharije, 284
Zahrawi, al-, 508
Zbynêk, Zajic, 841
Zeami Motokiyo, 770
Zell, Ulrich, 863
Zera Yacob, 666
Zhang Bangji, 363
Zhao Kuangyin, 293, 303, 322, 327
Zheng He, 829-830
Zhenzong (Song emperor, r. 998-1022), 401
Zhezong (Song emperor, r. 1086-1101), 433
Zhongzong (Tang emperor), 120
Zhou, Madame, 363
Zhou Dunyi, 491
Zhu Di. *See* Yonglo
Zhu Gaozhi. *See* Hongxi (Ming emperor)
Zhu Wen, 292
Zhu Xi, 324, 328, 363, 491-493
Zhu Yuanzhang, 775, 778, 818, 827
Zhu Yunwen. *See* Jianwen (Ming emperor)
Zhu Zhanji. *See* Xuande (Ming emperor)
Zīrī ibn Manad, 420
Zoe Karbonopsina, 283
Zuhayr bnu Qays al-Balawī, 93
Zwentibald, 281

Subject Index

ʿAbbāsid caliphate, 199
ʿAbbāsids, 179, 188, 196-199, 226, 235, 267, 307, 319, 333, 357, 417; *map*, 197
Abbot Suger on the Abbey Church of St. Denis and Its Art Treasures (Suger), 517
Acre, fall of (1291), 686-688
Acre, Siege of (1191), 557
Advaita Vedānta, 200-201
Afghanistan. *See* Geographical Index under Central Asia
Africa; agriculture, 10; architecture, 379, 476, 740; art, 825; iron-smelting, 10; Islam and, 91-94, 367-369, 436, 748; *map*, xliv, lxxx; papermaking, 60; religion, 426, 439; sculpture, 377; slavery, 290, 476, 579; taxation, 477; trade, 9, 290, 356, 377, 395, 437-438, 440, 461, 464, 474, 614, 630, 740, 825. *See also* Geographical Index under Africa; Egypt
Aghlabids, 336
Agincourt, Battle of (1415), 746, 753, 849, 864
Agriculture; Africa, 10; Ayutthaya, 762; cattle breeding, 574-576; China, 80, 401, 432; Cōlas, 295; Europe, 127-130, 571; Greenland, 374; Hohokam, 137; Huari, 360; Mississippian culture, 215; Mogollons, 61-63; Peru, 360; Plains Village culture, 221; Tiwanaku, 11, 360; Uighurs, 240; Vietnam, 617. *See also* Category Index
Ailao, 132, 154
Ain Jālūt, Battle of (1260), 659-662
Aksum, 554
Al-Andalus. *See* Andalusia
Al-Azhar mosque, 333, 336-338
Al Manṣūrah, Battle of (1250), 643
Al-Zallāqah, Battle of (1086), 367, 426
Alans, 696
Albania, 858-860
Albigensian Crusade (1209-1229), 593-596, 607, 632
Albigensians (as heretics), 595
Alchemy, China, 247, 478
Alemanni, 713
Alexandria, Treaty of (642), 91
Alf layla wa-layla. *See Arabian Nights' Entertainments, The*
Algeria. *See* Geographical Index under Africa
Almohad Empire. *See* Geographical Index under Africa
Almohads, 367, 426
Almoravids, 356, 367, 425-427, 440-441, 448
Alodia, 106
Amdo, 82
Americas. *See* Geographical Index under North America, Central America, South America
Americas to c. 1500 (*map*), xlv, lxxxi
An Lushan Rebellion, 170, 175, 179-182, 230
Analects, The (Confucius), 1, 328, 491
Anatolia. *See* Geographical Index under Turkey
Andalusia, 308, 412, 507; architecture, 426
Andes, Central, 11
Angevin Dynasty, 738
Angevin Empire, 528-531, 599, 656, 772; *map*, 529
Angkor Wat, 225, 273
Angkorean period, 225, 273
Anglo-Saxon Chronicle, 278
Anglo-Saxons; Christianity and, 43; end of, 430; Vikings and, 208
Annals of Inisfallen, 404
Annals of Ulster, 403
Annam, 260, 304
Anti-Semitism, 758
Arabia. *See* Geographical Index under Arabia, Iran, Iraq
Arabian Nights' Entertainments, The, 198
Arabs; medicine, 508; Swahili and, 10
Architecture; Africa, 379, 476, 740; Andalusia, 426; Austral Islands, 130; Aztecs, 733; Byzantine, 26; Cālukya, 78; Central Asia, 822; Chartres Cathedral, 409; Chichén Itzá, 125; Chimú Empire, 255; China, 526; Christian, 370-373; Cōlas, 295; El Tajín, 53; Ethiopia, 555; Franks, 195; Gothic, 516-518; Inca, 578; India, 89, 142, 159; Italy, 834; Java, 185; Korea, 109; Mississippian culture, 215; Muslim, 116, 336; Palenque, 56; Peru, 255; Romanesque, 516; Sailendra family, 192; Seljuk Turks, 443; Southeast Asia, 115; Sukhothai, 691; Tiwanaku, 12; Toltec Empire, 315. *See also* Category Index
Arianism, 6; Visigoths, 627
Arithmetic of al-Uqlidisi, The (al-Uqlīdisī), 48
Arms, Assize of (1181), 681
Árpád Dynasty, 738
Arras, Treaty of (1435), 747, 865
Art; Africa, 825; Cōlas, 347; Florence, 834; Ghaznavid Dynasty, 358; Korea, 109; Renaissance, 834; Song Dynasty, 324; Toltec Empire, 315
Aryabhatiya, The (Āryabhaṭa the Elder), 47
Ascalon, Battle of (1123), 514

Ascension of Christ and the Giving of the Keys to Saint Peter (Donatello), 835
Ashikaga pretenders (*table*), 742
Asia. *See* Geographical Index under Central Asia, China, India, Japan, Korea, Southeast Asia
Asia, European exploration of, 667-670
Asia, *maps* of, 16, 86, 114, 323, 582, 668, 717, 798
Assassins, 335
Astrolabe, 650
Astronomy; education, 410; Maya, 56-59; Muslim, 308
Asuka emperors (*table*), 46
Asuka Kiyomihara code, 140
Aśvamedha, 77
Atabetül-hakayik (Ahmet Yukneki), 240
Athos, Mount, 330-332
Austral Islands, 130
Austria, 534-536, 768
Avars, 35, 37, 279, 534
Avignon Papacy (1305-1378), 700-703, 759, 767. *See also* Papacy
Awdaghust, 355-357, 440
Ayudhya. *See* Ayutthaya
Ayuthaya. *See* Ayutthaya
Ayuthia. *See* Ayutthaya
Ayutthaya, 762-763
Ayyūbid Dynasty, 337, 557; fall of, 659
Aztecs, 288, 731-734

Babylonian Captivity of the Church, 699, 702. *See also* Avignon Papacy (1305-1378)
Bach-dang River, Battle of the (938), 305
Bahmanī sultanate, 753-755
Bakufu, 538
Balkan Peninsula. *See* Geographical Index under Greece, Macedonia, Serbia
Ball courts and games; Central America, 55; Hohokam, 138
Baltic (*map*), 626
Baltic region, Christianity, 624-627
Banking, Italy, 511-513
Bannockburn, Battle of (1314), 709-712; *map*, 712
Bantus, 219, 464
Banu Hilal Bedouins, 421
Bapheus, Battle of (1302), 695-697
Barlas, 822
Barmakids, 197
Barons' Crusade. *See* Crusades, First
Basmils, 170
Basra, sack of (871), 269
Bataszek, Battle of (1441), 855
Battle of Clontarf, The, 404
Bavaria, 534; Magyar invasion of, 279-282
Bede the Venerable, Saint, 51
Bedouins; Banū Hilāl, 421; religion, 74
Beijing, 525-527
Bejaïa, 783
Belgium. *See* Geographical Index under Netherlands, Flanders
Benedictine Rule, 455
Benedictines, 128
Benevento, Battle of (1266), 704
Benin, 824-826
Berbers, 91, 172, 333, 355, 367, 395, 420, 425, 440, 447, 461
Bergamo, Council of (1218), 551
Bhakti cults, 89, 200
Bibi Khanum Mosque, 822-824
Bible, Gutenberg, 862
Black Death, 730, 740, 745, 756-758; description, 758; *map*, 717. *See also* Bubonic plague
Bohemia; Jews and, 326-327; martyrdom in, 841-843. *See also* Geographical Index
Bon, 238, 812
Bonpo, 84, 202
Book, first printed, 265-267
Book of Divine Works (Hildegard von Bingen), 496
Book of Government, The (Niẓām al-Mulk), 417, 443
Book of Kells, 94-97
Book of Splendor. See *Zohar*
Books of Opinions of Peter Lombard, The. See *Sentences*
Borobuḍur, 185-187, 192
Bouvines, Battle of (1214), 599-602
Bow and arrow, 122-124, 215
Brahmasphuṭasiddhānta (Brahmagupta), 48
Brétigny, Treaty of (1360), 745, 864
Breviarum Alarici, 17-19
Bṛhadīśvara Temple, 346
British Isles. *See* Geographical Index under England, Ireland, Scotland
Bubonic plague, 716-718; *map*, 717. *See also* Black Death
Buddhism; China, 80, 85, 121, 293, 328; Confucianism and, 492; India, 86, 184; Islam and, 565; Japan, 28-31, 45, 204, 212, 548; Java, 185, 192; Korea, 81, 109, 297; Nestorianism and, 677; persecution of, 238, 245, 566; printing and, 265; Southeast Asia, 113; Sukhothai, 691; suppression of, 245-247; Tibet, 84, 202-203, 237, 777, 812; Vietnam, 617. *See also* Chan Buddhism; Mahāyāna Buddhism; Mādhyamika school; Pure Land Buddhism; Shingon sect; Sŏn Buddhism; Tantric Buddhism; Tendai sect; Theravāda Buddhism; Zen Buddhism
Buddhist Records of the Western World (Xuanzang), 71, 87
Bulgaria, 282-284; Christianity and, 262-264; *map*, 283. *See also* Geographical Index
Bulgarian Empire, Second, 737
Bulgaro-Vlach Empire. *See* Bulgarian Empire, Second
Bulgars, 279, 342, 352
Bulguksa. *See* Pulguksa
Burial mounds (Cahokia), 136

Burma. *See* Pagan Empire; Pyu
Bushidō, 204, 259
Buyid Dynasty, 417
Byzantine Empire, 36, 91, 341-343, 435, 695; Bulgars and, 282; Muslim invasion of, 196, 451; Seljuk Turks and, 442; Serbs and, 540; silk and, 31-33; Turkish invasion of, 869; Venice and, 514. *See also* Geographical Index
Byzantine Empire at Justinian's Death, 565 C.E. (*map*), xl, lxxvi

Cahokia, 134-136, 216
Calendar, Maya solar, 57
Caliphates; ʿAbbāsids, 199; first (*table*), 99
Cālukya Dynasty, 77, 79, 338; *map*, 89; *regional tables*, 78, 340
Cālukya Dynasty, Western. *See* Western Cālukya Dynasty
Cālukyas; Cōla invasion of, 346; Pallavas and, 88
Cambodia. *See* Khmers; Geographical Index under Southeast Asia
Camel, Battle of the (656), 102
Canon of Medicine (Avicenna), 397-400
Cantar de mío Cid, El. *See Poem of the Cid, The*
Canterbury, see of, 49-52
Canterbury Tales, The (Chaucer), 756, 806-809; prologue, 807
Canzoniere (Petrarch), 764
Capetian Dynasty, 349-352, 744
Capuchins, 591
Carolingian Empire, 280, 768-814 C.E. (*map*), xli, lxxvii
Carolingian Renaissance, 193-196
Carolingians, 176; *maps*, 243
Cartography, Portugal, 844
Casa Grande, 138
Caste system; Nepal, 802; Wolof Empire, 579
Castile and León, unification of, 627-629
Castillo (at Chichén Itzá), 126
Castillon, Battle of (1453), 747
Cath Cluana Tarbh. *See Battle of Clontarf, The*
Catharists, 594, 726
Cathedrals, Romanesque, 370-373
Catholic Church. *See* Christianity; Roman Catholic Church
Cattle; breeding, 574-576; Toutswe and, 220; trade in, 380, 438
Celtic Christianity, 95
Cenote of Sacrifice, 126
Central Asia; architecture, 822; papermaking, 60; *maps*, 16, 34, 358, 798. *See also* Geographical Index
Ceuta, conquest of (1415), 844
Champa, 718-720; rice, 401; Vietnamese invasion of, 344-346
Champagne, fairs of, 571-574
Chan Buddhism, 202, 246
Chan Chan, 255-257
Chandelās, 158
Chang'an, Tibetan capture of, 181-183, 237
Chartres Cathedral, school at, 409-412
Chen Dynasty, 39
Chenla, 224
Chi Lang Pass, Battle of (1427), 847
Chiang Mai, 658
Children's Crusade, 596-599
Chimú Empire, 255-257
China; Buddhism, 80, 121, 245; clocks, 674; coinage, 229; education, 67, 491; epidemics in, 716; exploration, 829-830; governmental reforms, 432; influence on Japan, 73, 140; influence on Khitans, 303; influence on Korea, 108, 320; law, 39; *maps*, 81, 323; newspapers in, 149-151; painting, 562; papermaking, 59; printing, 418-420; religion, 478, 676; reunification of, 39; taxation, 39; Tibet and, 202, 238; trade, 80; Vietnam and, 847. *See also* Geographical Index
Chinese Monks in India (Yijing), 191
Chivalry, 468; decline of, 753, 781
Ch'oe family, 567-569
Chosŏn Dynasty. *See* Yi Dynasty
Christianity; Arian and Nicene, 17; Baltic region, 624-627; Bulgaria, 262-264; Celtic, 51, 95; conversion of Franks, 6; England, 43, 49, 94; Ethiopia, 555, 666; France, 600; Germany, 165-167; heresy and, 632; Ireland, 96; Islam and, 100, 106-108, 500; Italy, 590; Kievan Rus, 249, 352-355; Magyars, 317; Northumbria, 51; persecution of, 390; philosophy and, 663; Reformation, 549-552; schisms in, 422-425; Slavs, 249; Spain, 145, 628; Vikings, 278, 407; women and, 495-498
Chronicles (Froissart), 780-782; extract, 752
Chu Dynasty, 292
Church; corruption in, 702; persecution of heretics, 727; power of the, 700
Church of the Holy Sepulchre, 118, 390-392
Church reform, 42-44, 455; England, 786
Church-state relationship; Ethiopia, 666; European, 177, 699
Cibotus, Battle of (1096), 452
Cistercians, 455-458, 574
Civil service examinations. *See* Examinations, Chinese civil service
Civil unrest. *See* Category Index under Wars, uprisings, and civil unrest
Clericis laicos, 698
Clermont, Council of (1095), 451, 453

Clock, first mechanical, 673-675
Clontarf, Battle of (1014), 403-405
Cluniac reform, 455
Code of Maimonides, The (Maimonides), 561
Codex Euricianus, 17
Codex Justinianus, 23
Codex Theodosianus, 18
Cogadh Gaedhel re Gallaibh. See *War of the Gaedhil with the Gail, The*
Coinage; China, 229, 245; Europe, 511, 571; Swahili coast, 474-475
Cōlas, 294-296, 339, 346-348; *regional table*, 295, 347; Śrivijaya and, 115
Colonnas, 697
Commerce. *See* Category Index under Trade and commerce
Communications. *See* Category Index
Compass, 650
Compendium of the Turkic Dialects (Kāshgarī), 239, 286
Complete Perfection (Daoism). *See* Quanzhen Daoism
Confucianism; Chinese revival of, 293; Japan, 1-3, 45, 140, 205; Jurchens, 525; Korea, 81, 499, 817
Conscription, Japan, 204
Consolation of Philosophy, The (Boethius), 19, 21
Constance, Council of (1414-1418), 701, 788, 837-841; *Sacrosancta*, 838
Constance, Peace of (1183), 523
Constantine, Donation of, 786, 852-854
Constantinople; capture of, 584-587; fall of (1453), 811, 869-872
Constantinople, Latin Kingdom of, 695
Constantinople, Siege of (717), 152
Constitutions of Clarendon, 545
Constitutum Constantini. *See* Constantine, Donation of
Conventuals (monastic movement), 591
Cook Islands, 130
Córdoba, 307-309, 412-415; Umayyad rulers (*table*), 307
Coricancha, 578
Corpus juris civilis, 24, 471
Corvée system; Korea, 297; Siam, 762
Council, Frankfurt (794), 152
Courtly love, 466-470, 806; rules of, 466
Courtrai, Battle of (1302), 721
Cravant, Battle of (1423), 746
Crécy, Battle of (1346), 745, 750-753
Crest Jewel of Wisdom, The (Śaṅkara), 200
Cross, Brethren of the, 757
Crossbow, 751
Crusades, 235, 391, 424, 435, 502, 599, 626, 686, 855; First, 335, 443, 450-454; Second, 503-506; Third, 524, 557-559; Fourth, 330, 584-587, 605, 695; Fifth, 606, 608-611; Sixth, 621-624; Seventh, 641-645; cathedral construction and, 370; Childrens', 596, 599; *map*, 643; Peasants', 452; *table*, 450
Cuarte, Battle of (1094), 449
Cultural and intellectual history. *See* Category Index
Czech Republic. *See* Geographical Index under Bohemia, Moravia

Da Xue. *See Great Learning, The*
Dadu. *See* Beijing
Dai Viet, 718-720. *See also* Vietnam
Dai-la. *See* La Thanh
Dál Cais, 404
Dalālat al-Hāʾrīn. *See Guide of the Perplexed, The*
Damianites, 590
Dandāngān Castle, Battle of (1040), 416
Danegeld, 277, 444
Danelaw, 252, 406; *map*, 277
Danes, defeat of, 276-279; *map*, 277
Dannoura, Battle of (1185), 538
Daoism, 246-247, 293; Nestorianism and, 677. *See also* Quanzhen Daoism
Datang xiyouji. See *Buddhist Records of the Western World*
Datang xiyu qiufa gaoseng zhuan. See *Chinese Monks in India*
David (Donatello), 835
Dayunhe. *See* Grand Canal (China)
De concordantia catholica (Nicholas of Cusa), 852
De consolatione philosophiae. See *Consolation of Philosophy, The*
De falso credita et ementita Constantini donatione declamatio. See *Treatise of Lorenzo Valla on the Donation of Constantine, The*
De liber alter de consecratione ecclesiae Sancti Dionysii. See *Abbot Suger on the Abbey Church of St. Denis and Its Art Treasures*
De nuptis philologie et mercurii. See *Marriage of Philology and Mercury*
De operatione Dei. See *Book of Divine Works*
Decameron (Boccaccio), 757, 764
Decimals, development of, 47-49
Delhi sultanate, 587-589, 636-638, 692-694; Khaljī *regional table*, 693; *map*, 637; Slave *regional table*, 588
Denmark, 820. *See* Geographical Index under Scandinavia
Dervish order, 671
Deutsche Orden, Der. *See* Teutonic Knights
Dge-lugs-pa. *See* Gelugpa order
Diamond Sutra, 265
Dibao, 150
Diplomacy and international relations. *See* Category Index

Discovery. *See* Category Index under Exploration and discovery
Divina commedia, La. See *Divine Comedy, The*
Divine Comedy, The (Dante), 703-707
Divisament dou monde. See *Travels of Marco Polo, The*
Division Imperii (817), 242
Dīwān lughāt al-Turk. See *Compendium of the Turkic Dialects*
Djenne. *See* Jenne
Djolof Empire. *See* Wolof Empire
Doctrine of the Mean, The, 491
Dolce stil nuovo, 466, 704
Dome of the Rock, 116-119
Domesday survey, 430, 444-447
Dominicans, 607
Donation of Pépin, 176
Drama. *See* Theater
Druzism, 391
Dublin, Vikings and, 404
Dunhuang, 265

Early Le Dynasty, 306
East Mark, 534
Easter, date of, 96
Eastern Hemisphere c. 800 C.E. (*map*), xxxv, lxxi
Eastern Hemisphere c. 1000 (*map*), xxxvi, lxii
Eastern Hemisphere, 1279 (*map*), xxxvii, lxxiii
Eastern Hemisphere, 1492 (*map*), xxxviii, lxxiv
Eastern Orthodox Church, 151. *See also* Orthodox Church
Ecclesiastical History of the English People (Bede), 96, 160-162
Economics. *See* Category Index
Edessa, fall of (1144), 503
Edington, Battle of. *See* Ethundune, Battle of (878)
Education; China, 66-68, 491, 803-805; classics, 409-412; Europe, 470-473; France, 409; Franks, 193; India, 565; Muslim, 271, 310-313, 337; Vietnam, 617, 848. *See also* Category Index
Egypt, 106-108; Fāṭimid conquest of, 333, 336; Mongol invasion of, 659; Muslim conquest of, 91; trade, 333. *See also* Geographical Index
Eight Canton Federation, 715
El Caracol, 126
El Tajín, 53-55
Encyclopedia, Chinese, 827-828
Engi Shiki, 299-301
Engineering. *See* Category Index
England; Christianity, 43, 49, 94; defeat by France, 864-868; law, 656; literature, 807; *maps*, 277, 529, 866; military, 680; Norman conquest of, 428; Parliament, 689; Viking conquest of, 406-408; Viking raids on, 206-210, 251, 276. *See also* Geographical Index
Environment. *See* Category Index
Ephthalites. *See* White Huns
Erzincan, Battle of (1230), 619
Eşfahān, Battle of (1221), 619
Ethiopia, 554-556; Christianity, 666; Islam, 666. *See also* Geographical Index under Africa
Ethundune, Battle of (878), 278
Europe; clocks, 674; coinage, 511; education, 470-473; *map*, 702; trade, 571. *See also* Geographical Index under Europe and specific countries
Europe at Clovis's Death, 511 C.E. (*map*), xxxix, lxxv
Europe in the Fourteenth Century (*map*), xliii, lxxix
Examinations, Chinese civil service, 39, 66-68, 328, 803-805; Jin Dynasty, 526; Korean adoption of, 320-322; reform of, 432; Song Dynasty, 323
Expansion and land acquisition. *See* Category Index
Exploration; of Asia, 667-670; Chinese, 829-830; Muslim, 729; Portuguese, 844-847; of South Pacific, 131
Exploration and discovery. *See* Category Index
Expulsion of Adam and Eve (Masaccio), 836

Falköping, Battle of (1389), 820
Fāṭimids, 107, 333-336, 390, 420-422; *map*, 334
Feast of Herod (Donatello), 835
Fès, 783
Feudalism; England, 430, 569; Europe, 744, 747; France, 468; Japan, 205, 259; Norman, 528
Field of Blackbirds, Battle of the. *See* Kosovo, Battle of (1389)
Filioque doctrine, 195, 423
Five Dynasties and Ten Kingdoms (China), 175, 291-294, 302, 322, 327, 363, 483; *regional tables*, 292
Flagellants, Brotherhood of the, 757
Flanders. *See* Geographical Index under Flanders, Netherlands
Florentine School of Art, 834-837
Footbinding, 362-364
Former Shu Dynasty, 292
Formigny, Battle of (1450), 747, 866
Forty Amirs, 636
Four Books of Dialogues on the Lives of the Italian Fathers and on the Immortality of Souls, The (Gregory the Great), 43
France; Christianity, 600; *maps*, 747, 866; monasticism, 455; poetry, 467; victory over England, 864-868. *See also* Geographical Index
Franciscans, 589-592, 607
Franks, 176, 713; architecture, 195; conversion to Christianity, 6; education, 193; medicine, 508; theology, 195
Friars Minor of the Regular Observance, 591

Fudoki, 211
Fujigawa, Battle of (1180), 537
Fujiwara family, 211, 257-260, 299; *table*, 258
Funan, 114, 224
Fūshikaden. See *Kadensho*

Gaeta, Treaty of (1451), 859
Gandhavyūha, 186
Ganita sara sangraha (Mahāvīra), 48
Gao, 395, 725
Gaoliang River, Battle of the (979), 303
Gattamelata (Donatello), 835
Gauḍa Dynasty, 183
Gaul, Muslim invasion of, 162
Gelugpa order, 779, 812-815
Geluk-pa. *See* Gelugpa order
Gempei War (1180-1185), 537, 611, 741
Genji. *See* Minamoto
Genji monogatari. See *Tale of Genji, The*
Georgia. *See* Geographical Index under Central Asia, Russia
Gepids, 36
Germany; Magyar invasions of, 316; monasticism, 496; trade, 519-521. *See also* Geographical Index
Ghana (ancient), 172-174, 355-357, 440, 461, 579
Ghassānids, 98
Ghaznavid Dynasty, 156, 319, 357-359; *map*, 358
Ghibellines, 704
Ghūrids, 587, 693
Ghuzz. *See* Oğhuz Turks
Gitanos, 235
Gloucester, Statutes of (1278), 680
Göktürk Empire, 415
Gold; Africa, 476; trade in, 172, 462, 474, 630, 725, 740
Golden Bull of Charles IV (1356), 767-769
Golden Bull of Rimini (1226), 625
Golden Horde, 717
Golden lotus. *See* Footbinding
Gotland, 520
Government and politics. *See* Category Index
Governmental reforms in China, 432
Granada, Fall of (1492), 146
Grand Canal (China), 40, 64-66, 79, 526
Great Lavra, 330
Great Learning, The, 491
Great Ming Code, 818-819
Great Moravia, 249, 280
Great Schism (1378-1417), 700-703, 786, 837; *map*, 702. *See also* Schism, Rome and Constantinople
Great Treatise on the Stages of the Path of Enlightenment, The (Tsongkhapa), 813
Great Wall (Sui Dynasty), 40
Great Zimbabwe, 378-381, 439, 476
Greece. *See* Geographical Index
Greenland; colonization of, 254; Inuit and, 373; Norse settlement of, 374. *See also* Geographical Index under Greenland, Scandinavia
Guelphs, 704
Guide of the Perplexed, The (Maimonides), 560-562
Gujarat, conquest of (1299), 692-694
Gunpowder and guns, invention of, 247-248
Gupta Empire, 4, 69
Gurjara-Pratihāras. *See* Pratihāras
Gypsies, 234-236

Habbakuk (Donatello), 835
Habsburgs, defeat of (1315), 713-715
Hadith, 75
Hagia Sophia, 25-28
Hall of Columns, 53
Ḥammādids, 421
Han Dynasty, Later. *See* Later Han Dynasty
Han Dynasty, Northern. *See* Northern Han Dynasty
Han Dynasty, Southern. *See* Southern Han Dynasty
Han Gou, 64
Hanoi. *See* La Thanh
Hansa, 519-521
Hanseatic League, 820; *map*, 520
Hansen's disease. *See* Leprosy
Harem System, 188-190
Haripunjaya, 658
Harshacharita of Banabhatta, The (Bāṇa), 69
Hastings, Battle of (1066), 428-431
Hausa state, 289-291
Health and medicine. *See* Category Index
Heian period, 210-213, 257, 388, 537; *table*, 211
Heiji disturbance (1159), 537
Heike. *See* Taira
Heling, 191
Hephthalites. *See* White Huns
Heresy; Arian, 6, 627; Church and, 726; death penalty for, 551, 653; definition of, 423; England, 727; Hus, 838, 841; Joan of Arc, 851; Knights Templar, 486; leprosy as punishment for, 481; Nestorianism, 501; papal Inquisition, 632, 683; prosecution of, 606; William of Ockham, 708; Wyclif, 787
Hesychast regimen, 332
Hindi, 365-366
Hinduism, 200; Cōlas, 347; Islam and, 366
Historia ecclesiastica gentis Anglorum. See *Ecclesiastical History of the English People*
Historia Francorum. See *History of the Franks, The*
Historiography; Africa, 748-750; France, 780; Japan, 148; Korea, 498; Muslim, 271. *See also* Category Index
History of al-Ṭabarī, The (al-Ṭabarī), 270-273
History of the Franks, The (Gregory of Tours), 6

Ho Dynasty, 847
Hōgen disturbance (1156), 537
Hohenstaufens, 522, 534
Hohokam, 137-139
Hōjō family, 539, 611-613, 741; *table of regents*, 612
Ho-ling. *See* Heling
Holy Roman Empire, 713, 767; creation of, 317; Venice and, 514
Holy Roman Empire c. 1190 (*map*), xliv, lxxviii
Homosexuality, 652-654
Homs, Battle of (1281), 661
Hospital, Islamic public, 226-229
Hoysaḷas, 340
Huari civilization, 360-362, 576
Humanism, 766
Humors, four, 398
Hundred Years' War (1337-1453), 700, 744-748, 752, 780, 794, 839, 849, 864; *maps*, 747, 866
Hungary, 737-739; Ottoman invasion of, 854-857
Hunnic migrations (*map*), 4
Huns. *See* White Huns
Hunting, Toutswe, 219
Hussites, 838, 842
Hwarang, 108

Iberia, Islam and, 367-369; *map*, 368
Iceland. *See* Geographical Index under Scandinavia
Iceland, Viking invasion of, 254
Ichinotani, Battle of (1184), 538
Iconoclastic Controversy, 151-153, 177, 194, 423
Ife kingdom, 376-378
Ikhshidids, 336
Incas, 576-578
Incoherence of the Incoherence (Averroës), 507
India, 71, 638; architecture, 89, 142, 159; Buddhism, 86, 184; drama, 88; Islam, 358; language in, 365-366; Mahāyāna Buddhism, 200; *maps*, 4, 70, 89, 157, 197, 637; monasticism, 201; Muslim invasions of, 156, 357, 587, 692; philosophy, 200; poetry, 89, 789; religion, 71, 159, 200, 789; Turkish raids on, 565-566; White Hunnic raids on, 3-5; women in, 636. *See also* Geographical Index
Indonesia, 191
Indrapura, 345; fall of (982), 344, 719
Inferno (Dante), 705
Inquisition, 561, 632-635, 685; Spanish, 634, 683
Institutions. *See* Category Index under Organizations and institutions
Intellectual history. *See* Category Index under Cultural and intellectual history
International relations. *See* Category Index under Diplomacy and international relations
Inticancha, 577
Inuit, Thule, 373-375
Iran. *See* Geographical Index
Iraq. *See* Geographical Index
Ireland; Christianity, 96; England and, 773; Norman invasion of, 542-544; Vikings and, 403. *See also* Geographical Index
Iron-smelting in Africa, 10
Irrigation; Hohokam, 137; Huari, 360; Peru, 360; Tiwanaku, 12, 360
Ishibashiyama, Battle of (1180), 537
Islam, 74-76; Africa, 91-94, 367-369, 395, 436, 748; Buddhism and, 565; Christianity and, 100, 106-108; Christians and, 607, 844; Ethiopia, 666; Hausa, 291; Iberia, 367-369; India, 358; influence on Spain, 146; Mali, 631, 724; *maps*, 92, 197, 253, 334; medicine, 198; Middle East, 101-104; Qarakhanids, 285-287; Seljuk Turks, 319, 443; Sicily, 489; spread of, 151; Uighurs, 240. *See also* Ismāʿīlī Shīʿite Islam; Khāijites; Mawlawīyah; Shīʿite Islam; Sufism; Sunni Islam
Islamic Empire, 101
Ismāʿīlī Shīʿite Islam, 333
Israel/Palestine. *See* Geographical Index
Italy, 713; architecture, 834; banking, 511-513; Christianity, 590; Lombard conquest of, 36-39; Magyar invasion of, 279-282; painting, 836; philosophy, 21; poetry, 704, 764; sculpture, 834; theology, 42. *See also* Geographical Index
Ivory, trade in, 462

Jōdo sect. *See* Pure Land Buddhism
Jōdo Shinshū. *See* True Pure Land Buddhism
Jacquerie movement (1358), 781
Jami Masjid, 755
Japan; Buddhism, 45, 548; Confucianism, 1-3, 45; diplomatic missions to China, 72-74; feudalism, 205, 259; historiography, 148; law, 140-142, 210; literature, 213, 385, 389, 743; papermaking, 60; regents, 257-260; *regional tables*, 46, 258; religion, 301; *table of historical periods*, 148; taxation, 204; writing, 213-215. *See also* Geographical Index
Jarrow, Viking raid on, 276
Java, 115; architecture, 185; Buddhism, 185
Jayavarman II, 273
Jayavarman III, 273
Jenne, 395, 462
Jerusalem; Christianity and, 390; fall of (1187), 557; Islam and, 118; Venice and, 514
Jeu de Robin et de Marion, Le. See *Play of Robin and Marion, The*

Jeu de Saint-Nicolas, Le. See *Play of Saint Nicholas of Jean Bodel*
Jews; Bohemia and, 326-327; Christians and, 607; expulsion from England, France, and southern Italy, 683-685; Spain, 146. *See also* Judaism
Jiangnan He, 64
Jihad, 75
Jin Dynasty, 432, 483-485, 493, 498, 525-527; *table*, 484
Jin Dynasty, Jurchen. *See* Jin Dynasty
Jin Dynasty, Later. *See* Later Jin Dynasty
Jin Dynasty, Western. *See* Western Jin Dynasty
Jin gang jing. See *Diamond Sutra*
Jin si lü. See *Reflections on Things at Hand*
Jingnan Dynasty. *See* Nanping Dynasty
Jinshi, 66-68
Jogaila. *See* Władysław II Jagiełło
Jokhang, 84
Jōkyū War (1221), 612
Jolof Empire. *See* Wolof Empire
Journey to the West (Wu), 87
Jubilee (Roman), 698
Judaism, 560, 678; Berbers and, 93; persecution of, 683-685, 757; Russia and, 168-170. *See also* Jews
Jurchen Jin Dynasty. *See* Jin Dynasty
Jurchens, 303, 324, 483-485, 493, 525-527

Kabbalah, 678
Kadam order, 812
Kadensho (Zeami), 771
Kadisiya, Battle of (637). *See* Qadisiyah, Battle of (637)
Kagyu order, 778, 812
Kahuripan kingdom, 115
Kāilaśanātha Temple, 142-144
Kaiyuan tongbao, 229, 245
Kaiyuan zabao, 150
Kākatīyas, 340
Kalish, Peace of (1343), 831
Kalmar Union, 820-822
Kamakura shogunate, 537-540, 612; *table*, 539
Kampyō testament, 258
Kana syllabary, 213-215
Kanauj, 69-71
Kanauj Triangle, *map*, 157
Kanchou Uighurs, 239
Kanem Empire, 436, 614-616, 748
Kanghwa, 568, 815
Kanuri, 614
Karakhoja Uighur Kingdom, 239
Karakitai, 493-495
Karanga, 379
Karbalā᾽, Battle of (680), 111
Kathāsaritsāgara. See *Ocean of Story, The*
Kazakhstan. *See* Geographical Index under Central Asia
Kebra nagast, 666
Kemmu Restoration, 742
Kereits, 581
Khāijites, 103, 111, 420
Khaljī Dynasty, 693, 753; *table*, 693
Kharlukhs, 170
Khazars, 168-170, 280, 352
Khirghiz, 239
Khitan Liao Dynasty, 302, 432, 483, 525
Khitans, 175, 293, 302-304, 323-324, 493, 527
Khmers, 223-225, 273-275. *See also* Geographical Index under Southeast Asia
Khorāsān, 799
Khujand, Battle of (1137), 493
Khwārizmian Empire, 494, 618-620; Mongol invasion of, 619
Kievan Rus, 169; Christianity, 352-355; *map*, 354; religion, 353. *See also* Geographical Index under Russia
Kilkenny, Statute of (1366), 772-774
Kilwa Kisiwani, 474, 476-477, 739-741
Kingozi culture, 9
Kirina, Battle of (1235), 173, 725
Kitāb al-fuṣūl fi al-ḥisāb al-Hindī. See *Arithmetic of al-Uqlidisi, The*
Kitāb al-jabr wa al-muqābalah (al-Khwārizmī), 471
Knights of the Hospital of Saint Mary of the Germans at Jerusalem. *See* Teutonic Knights
Knights Templar, 485-488
Koguryŏ kingdom, Later. *See* Later Koguryŏ kingdom
Kojiki, 147-149, 210
Kokin wakashū, 211, 214
Kokinshū. See *Kokin wakashū*
Koran. *See* Qur᾽ān
Korea; architecture, 109; art, 109; Buddhism, 81; Chinese invasion of, 40, 79; Confucianism, 81; historiography, 498; influence on Japan, 210; law, 321; Mongol invasions of, 568, 815; papermaking, 60; pottery, 109; slavery, 321; writing, 321. *See also* Geographical Index
Koryŏ Dynasty, 110, 297-299, 320, 483, 498-500, 567-569, 815; *regional table*, 298
Kosovo, Battle of (1389), 738, 810
Kosovo, Second Battle of (1448), 856, 859
Koyunhisar. *See* Bapheus
Kufans, 111
Kulikovo, Battle of (1380), 791-794
Kumbi, 172; sack of (1076), 356, 440-441
Kutadgú bilig. See *Wisdom of Royal Glory*
Kyŏngju, 109

La Janda, Battle of (711), 144
La Thanh, capture of, 260-262
Lalitavistara, 186
Lam Ap. *See* Champa
Lamrim Ch'enmo. See *Great Treatise on the Stages of the Path of Enlightenment, The*
Lan Na, 133, 657-659, 691

Land acquisition. *See* Category Index under Expansion and land acquisition
Lao, 132
Las Navas de Tolosa, Battle of (1212), 368
Lastra, Battle of (1304), 705
Later Han Dynasty, 293
Later Jin Dynasty, 293
Later Koguryŏ kingdom, 110, 297
Later Le Dynasty, 847-849
Later Liang Dynasty, 39, 292
Later Paekche Dynasty, 297
Later Shu Dynasty, 292
Later Tang Dynasty, 293
Later Three Kingdoms period (Korea), 297
Later Zhou Dynasty, 293, 322
Lateran Council, Second (1139), 605
Lateran Council, Third (1179), 550, 584, 594, 605, 683
Lateran Council, Fourth (1215), 326, 605-609, 683
Laws and law codes; Byzantine Empire, 23-25; China, 39; Church, 606; common, 569-571; Danish, 252; England, 528, 569-571, 603, 656, 680, 773; France, 533; Ireland, 773; Islamic, 310; Japan, 140-142, 210, 299-301; Korea, 321; labor, 794; Nepal, 802; Roman, 17, 23; Taihō, 140-141; Thai, 762-763; Visigoths, 17. *See also* Category Index under Laws, acts, and legal history
Le Dynasty, Early. *See* Early Le Dynasty
Le Dynasty, Later. *See* Later Le Dynasty
Lechfeld, Battle of (955), 317, 534
Legal history. *See* Laws and law codes; Category Index under Laws, acts, and legal history
León and Castile, unification of. *See* Castile and León, unification of
Leprosy, 480-482
Lex romana Visigothorum. See *Breviarium Alarici*
Lezha, League of, 858
Liang Dynasty, Later. *See* Later Liang Dynasty
Liao Dynasty, 493; *regional tables*, 303
Liao Dynasty, Khitan. *See* Khitan Liao Dynasty
Liao Dynasty, Western; *regional table*, 303. *See also* Western Liao Dynasty
Liber abaci (Leonardo of Pisa), 48, 460
Liber regulae pastoralis. See *Pastoral Care*
Liberal arts, seven, 195
Lindisfarne, 94-97; Viking raid on, 206-210, 251, 276, 406
Lin-yi. *See* Champa
Literature; China, 828; Cōlas, 347; England, 807; Islamic, 198; Japan, 212-213, 385, 389, 743; Kashmir, 789; Mali, 631. *See also* Category Index
Lithuania, 626, 792, 831
Liu Hung-ts'ao
Lives of Saints Peter and Paul (Masaccio), 836
Livonia, 626
Lollards, 787
Lombards, 36-39, 176; *king table*, 38
Longbow, 750
Lorris, Charter of (1155), 531-533; key provisions, 532
Lübeck, 519
Lunyu. See *Analects, The*
Ly Dynasty, 616

Ma-Xia school, 562-564
Macedonia. *See* Geographical Index
Mādhyamika school, 200
Madrasa Nizamiya, 311
Madrasas, 240, 310-313, 337
Maghreb, 421, 426, 783
Magna Carta, 530, 602-605; key provisions, 604
Magomi, 437
Magyars, 279-282, 316-318; *map* of raids, 253
Mahabalipuram, 89
Mahābhārata (Vyāsa), 339
Mahākarmavibhanga, 185
Mahāyāna Buddhism, 85, 186; India, 200
Mahdali Dynasty, 474, 740
Majapahit, 115
Makura no sōshi. See *Pillow Book, The*
Makuria, 106
Malayu, 115
Mālegiti Śivālaya, 78
Mali, 173, 462, 630-632, 723-726, 748; Islam, 724; religion, 396. *See* Geographical Index under Africa
Malikites, 421
Malinke, 630
Malla Dynasty, 801-803
Mamlūks, 587
Mamlūk Dynasty, 659, 687, 748; *map*, 660
Mandinka state. *See* Mali
Manichaeanism, Uighurs and, 171
Manu, 762
Manyōshū, 211
Manzikert, Battle of (1071), 434-435, 442, 452
Maoris, 130, 645-648
Mapungubwe, 438-439
Marica, Battle of (1371), 738, 809
Marriage as a political tool; Angevin Empire, 528; Aztecs, 315; Byzantine Empire, 342, 353; China, 293; Delhi sultanate, 637; England, 773; France, 153, 865; Japan, 45, 211, 259; León and Castile, 628; Lithuania, 831; Thai, 133; Tibet, 83
Marriage of Philology and Mercury (Capella), 409
Martyrdom; Bohemia, 841-843; Islam, 111-113
Masālik al-abṣār fi Mamālik al-am; ār (al-ʿUmarī), 748

Masjid-i Jami. *See* Bibi Khanum Mosque
Masts, Battle of the (655), 102
Mataram, 115
Mathematics; education, 410; India, 48; Muslim, 308. *See also* Category Index
Mathnawī-i ma ʿnawī. *See Mathnawi, The*
Mathnawi, The (Rūmī), 671
Maukhari, 69
Mawlawīyah, 671-673
Maya civilization, 56-59
Meaux, Treaty of (1229), 633
Mecca; Ibn Baṭṭūṭah, 729; Mūsā, Mansa, 396, 723-726; pilgrimages to, 75; Yaḥyā ibn Ibrāhīm, 426; Yūsuf ibn Tāshufīn, 367
Medicine; education, 410; Frankish, 508; Muslim, 198, 226-229, 397, 507-511; Uighurs, 240; Village Plains culture, 222. *See* Category Index under Health and medicine
Meguti Temple, 78
Mencius (Mencius), 491
Mengzi. See *Mencius*
Mercia, Viking settlement of, 278
Merkits, 582
Merovingians, 176. *See also* Carolingians; Franks
Mesoamerica, *map*, 58; religion, 287-289
Mesopotamia. *See* Geographical Index under Iraq
Mevleviye. *See* Mawlawīyah
Mexico. *See* Geographical Index under Central America
Middle East. *See* Geographical Index under Africa, Arabia, Egypt, Iran, Iraq, Israel/Palestine, Middle East, Syria, Turkey
Middle East, Islam and, 101-104
Middle East, *maps* of, 92, 334, 416, 660, 798
Migrations; Chams to Vietnam, 718; Gypsies into the Middle East and Europe, 235; Hausa to Niger, 290; Incas to Acamama, 577; Indians to south India, 5; Kanuri to Kanem, 614; Lombards to Italy, 36; Mississippian culture to Great Plains, 217; Muslims to Egypt, 107; Oğhuz Turks to Transoxiana, 318-320, 415; Ostrogoths to Italy, 20; Polynesian, 131; Pyu north to Pagan, 233; Swahili cultures to Bantu area, 9; Thai to Southeast Asia, 132, 154, 657; Thai tribes to Southeast Asia, 133; Uighurs to Turkistan and China, 239-241; Vikings to England, 207; Wolof to Senegal River region, 579
Military; Aztecs, 732; China, 432; England, 680; Europe, 781
Mimbreno, 62
Min Dynasty, 292
Minamoto family, 212, 537, 612, 741
Ming Dynasty, 775-778, 816, 827; *table*, 776; women, 363
Minggan, 583
Miracle de Théophile, Le. See *Théophilus*
Miracle plays, 381-384
Miracles de Notre-Dame (Gautier de Coincy), 383
Mishneh Torah. See *Code of Maimonides, The*
Mississippian culture, 134, 215-218
Model Parliament, 688-690
Mogadishu, 474
Mogollons, 61-63
Monarchy, England, 602
Monasticism; agriculture and, 574; Buddhism, 245; France, 455; Germany, 496; Greece, 330-332; India, 201; Tibet, 812
Money, paper, 229-232
Mongolia. *See* Geographical Index under China
Mongols, 325, 484, 502, 581-583, 668, 791, 797-800; Champa and, 719; conquest of Nanzhao, 133; invasion of Lan Na, 658; invasion of Nanzhao, 155; *map*, 582; religion, 676; *table of rulers*, 581; Tibet and, 777-779
Monks Mound, 135, 217
Monomane, 771
Mononobe, 1, 29, 45
Monophysite Christianity, 106
Mons, 233, 657; Khmer conquest of, 273-275
Moors, 507-511
Moravia. *See* Great Moravia; Geographical Index
Morgarten, Battle of (1315), 713-715
Morocco. *See* Geographical Index under Africa
Morocco, Almoravid conquest of, 425-427
Mortmain, Statute of (1279), 680
Mound building; Cahokia, 135; Hopewell, 215; *map*, 216
Muangs, 132, 154
Mula Attha, 763
Muqaddimah (Ibn Khaldūn), 783-785
Murābitūn, al-. *See* Almoravids
Murasaki Shikibu, 388
Murasaki Shikibu nikki. See *Murasaki Shikibu: Her Diary and Poetic Memoirs*
Murasaki Shikibu: Her Diary and Poetic Memoirs (Murasaki Shikibu), 387
Muromachi emperors (*table*), 742
Muromachi period, 771
Muscovy, 791
Music; Christian, 497; Cōlas, 347; Gregorian chants, 44; Gypsy, 235; Japan, 770; Kashmir, 790; Mali, 631; Mawlawīyah, 671; Muslim, 198; Pallava, 142; Sogdiana, 14; troubadours, 469; Uighurs, 240
Muslims. *See* Islam
Myoch'ŏng, 498
Mystère d'Adam, 381-382

Mystery plays, 381-384; stage directions, 382
Mysticism, Germany, 496; Judaism, 678

Nahavand, Battle of (642), 102
Naiman, 581
Nakatomi, 1, 29, 104
Nalanda, 86, 565-566
Nam Chieu. *See* Nanzhao
Nanboku-cho. *See* Northern and Southern Courts (Japan)
Nanchao. *See* Nanzhao
Nanping Dynasty, 292
Nanzhao, 132, 154-156, 232-234, 260-262; Mongol conquest of, 133, 657
Nara emperors (*table*), 46
Nara period, 204, 210
Native Americans, European contact with, 373-375
Navigation, 648-652
Near East. *See* Geographical Index under Arabia, Egypt, Iran, Iraq, Israel/Palestine, Middle East, Syria, Turkey
Nemanjid Dynasty, 540-542, 809
Nembutsu, 548
Nengo system, 104-106
Neo-Confucianism, 324, 328, 491; women and, 363
Nepal, 801-803
Nestorianism, 501, 676-678
Netherlands. *See* Geographical Index under Flanders, Netherlands
New Life, The (Dante), 704
New Zealand, 130
Newspapers, first, 149-151
Niani, 748
Nicaea. *See* Geographical Index under Turkey
Nicaea, Council of (787), 152, 423
Nihon shoki, 29, 147-149, 210
Nihongi. See *Nihon shoki*
Nika riots (532), 25
Nishapur, Battle of (1038), 416
Nizaris, 335. *See also* Assassins
Njáls Saga. See *Story of Burnt Njal, The*
Nō drama, 769-772; Zeami's rules, 770
Nobatia, 106
Nocturnal, 651
Nominalism, 708
Norman Conquest (1066), 428, 430
Normandy, Viking settlement in, 252
Normans, 542-544; Venice and, 514
Norsemen, 251. *See also* Vikings
Northern and Southern Courts (Japan), 742
Northern Dynasties (China), 39
Northern Han Dynasty, 292
Northern Song Dynasty, 324, 418; *table*, 324
Northumbria, 95, 160, 207; Christianity, 51
Norway, 820. *See also* Geographical Index under Scandinavia
Norwich, Jews of, 683
Notre Dame, cathedral school at, 471
Novgorod, Swedish invasion of, 638-641
Nubia, 106-108
Numbers, negative, 47-49
Numerals, Arabic, 458-460
Nyingma order, 202, 779, 812

Observants (monastic movement), 591
Observatory (at Chichén Itzá). *See* El Caracol
Ocean navigation. *See* Navigation; Travel by sea
Ocean of Story, The (Somadeva), 366
Oğhuz Turks, 318-320, 415-417, 695
Olmecs, 287
One Hundred, Council of, 704
Opéra-comique, 383
Ordu Balik, 170
Organizations and institutions. *See* Category Index
Orléans, Siege of (1428-1429), 849, 865
Orsini, 697
Orthodox Church; Bulgaria, 284; Byzantine Empire, 332, 584, 869; Ethiopia, 555, 666; Russia, 352, 640, 792; Serbia, 541, 809
Ostrogoths, 20, 36
Ottomans, 671, 697, 809, 870; invasion of Hungary, 854-857
Ouolof Empire. *See* Wolof Empire; Geographical Index under Turkey
Outremer, 504
Oxford, Provisions of (1258), 655-657
Oxford Council (1222), 683

Pacific Islands, South, 130-132
Pacified South. *See* Vietnam
Paekche Dynasty, Later. *See* Later Paekche Dynasty
Paekche kingdom, 28
Pagan Empire, 233
Paganism; Franks, 6; Kievan Rus, 354; Prussia, 624; Vikings, 251
Painting; China, 562; Italy, 836
Pajano, 11
Pālas, 183, 185; Pratihāras and, 158; *table*, 184
Palenque, 56
Pallavas, 88-90, 142, 294; Cālukyans and, 78; *map*, 89; *regional table*, 90
Pāṇḍyas; Cōla conquest of, 294-296; Pallavas and, 88
Papacy; power of, 700; relations with Eastern churches, 43, 263; relations with Holy Roman Empire, 490, 685; role in money lending, 512. *See also* Avignon Papacy
Paper, invention of, 59, 149
Papermaking, 59-61, 174
Paris, Treaty of (1259), 655
Parliament, Model. *See* Model Parliament
Pastoral Care (Gregory the Great), 43
Peasants' Revolt (England, 1381), 746, 781, 787, 794-797

Peasants' Revolt (Flanders, 1323-1328), 721-723; *map*, 722
Pechenegs, 280
Pépin, Donation of. *See* Donation of Pépin
Perceval (Chrétien de Troyes), 552-554
Persia; expulsion of Gypsies, 234-236; poetry, 393. *See also* Geographical Index under Iran
Peru; agriculture, 360; irrigation, 360; religion, 577
Pharmacology, Muslim, 508
Phayao, 133, 658, 691
Philip VI (king of France), 780
Philosophy; China, 324, 328, 492; France, 707; India, 200; Italy, 21; Jewish, 560; Muslim, 507-511. *See* Category Index
Physics, 734-737
Pillars of Islam, five fundamental, 75
Pillow Book, The (Sei Shōnagon), 259, 385-387
Pisa, Council of (1408), 837
Plague, *map*, 717
Plague, bubonic. *See* Black Death; Bubonic plague
Plains Village culture, 221-223
Play of Robin and Marion, The (Adam de la Halle), 383
Play of Saint Nicholas of Jean Bodel (Bodel), 382
Plays. *See* Miracle plays; Mystery plays; Nō drama
Plow, 127-130
Poem of the Cid, The, 447
Poema de mío Cid. See *Poem of the Cid, The*
Poetry; England, 806; France, 467, 553; India, 89, 789; Italy, 704, 764; Muslim, 198; Persia, 393
Poitiers, Battle of (732). *See* Tours, Battle of
Poitiers, Battle of (1356), 745, 753
Poland. *See* Geographical Index
Politics. *See* Category Index under Government and politics
Polynesians, 130-132, 645-648
Poor Clares, 592
Poor Knights of Christ and the Temple of Solomon. *See* Knights Templar
Poor Men of Lyons, 549
Popol Vuh, 288
Portugal, exploration of, 844-847. *See also* Geographical Index
Posada, Battle of (1330), 738
Pottery; Hohokam, 139; Korean, 109; Mogollon, 62
Prague, 326
Pratihāra Dynasty, *table*, 158
Pratihāras, 156-159, 183
Preah Ko, 274
Prester John (legendary), 501
Printing; China, 149, 265-267, 324, 418-420; Germany, 861-864
Protestant Reformation. *See* Reformation
Pueblo cultures, 61
Pulguksa, 109
Pure Land Buddhism, 547-549
Pushyabhutis, 69
Pyramid B (at Tula), 314
Pyramid of the Niches, 53
Pyu, 155; conquest of, 232-234

Qadisiyah, Battle of (637), 35, 101
Qānūn fi al-ṭibb, al-. See *Canon of Medicine*
Qarakhanids, 239, 285-287, 493; Seljuk defeat of, 416
Qatwan, Battle of (1141), 494
Qian Shu Dynasty. *See* Former Shu Dynasty
Qidan. *See* Khitans
Quadrivium, 195
Quanzhen Daoism, 478-480
Quoc hoc Vien, 617
Quoc tu Giam, 848
Qurʾān, 75
Quṭb Mīnār, 588
Quwwat al-Islam, 588
Rājarājeśvara. *See* Bṛhadīśvara Temple
Rājasiṃheśvara Temple. *See* Kāilaśanātha Temple
Rājputs, 693
Rāmāyaṇa (Vālmīki), 802
Rāśṭrakūṭas, 156, 184, 338
Rathas, 89
Reconquista, 307, 447, 504, 628
Records of Ancient Matters. See *Kojiki*
Records of Wind and Earth. See *Fudoki*
Red Head Robbers, 816
Red Turban Rebellion (1351-1356), 775
Reflections on Things at Hand (Zhu Xi), 491
Reformation, 167, 549-552, 707, 853
Regents of Japan, 257-260
Religion; Africa, 426, 439; Aztecs, 732; Bedouins, 74; Cālukyas, 338; Chimú Empire, 256; China, 478; Cōlas, 347; Hausa, 291; Inca, 577; India, 71, 159, 200, 789; Japan, 301; Karakitai, 494; Khazars, 169; Khitans, 303; Khmer, 225; Kievan Rus, 353; Mali, 396; Maya, 57; Mesoamerica, 287-289; Mississippian culture, 216; Mongols, 676; Nepal, 802; Peru, 256, 577; Southeast Asia, 115; Tibet, 84, 237; Tiwanaku, 12; Uighurs, 239-240; Village Plains culture, 222. *See also* Category Index
Rense, Declaration of (1338), 767
Rerum vulgarium fragmenta. See *Canzoniere*
Rhymes. See *Canzoniere*
Riazan, 792
Rice; Champa, 401; China, 401-403
Richard II; meeting with Wat Tyler, 795
Rígomezö, Battle of. *See* Kosovo, Second Battle of (1448)

Riḥlah (Ibn Baṭṭūṭah), 730
Roman Catholic Church, 151; Germany, 167. *See also* Christianity
Roman Empire, Eastern. *See* Byzantine Empire
Roman Empire, Western, 17
Romana mater, 698
Romance (genre), 552
Romanians, 737
Romansh, 713
Rome, popular uprising in, 759-761
Russia; Judaism in, 168-170; *map*, 354; Mongol invasion of, 791. *See also* Kievan Rus; Slavs; Geographical Index

Sacrosancta (Council of Constance), 838
Sailendra family, 115, 185, 191-192, 348
Saint George and the Dragon (Donatello), 835
Sakha Attha, 763
Sakya order, 777, 812
Sallinwerder, Treaty of (1398), 831
Salt trade (Africa), 462
Sāmānid Dynasty, 239, 285, 319, 398
Samarqand, 822; papermaking, 60
Samguk Sagi (Kim), 498-500
Samoans, 130
Samogitia, 831
Samurai, 204-206, 259, 611
Samurai dokoro, 537
Samye, 202, 237, 812
Samye, Council of (792-794), 203
Sanskrit, 365
Sāsānian Empire, 33-36, 97; dynastic table, 35; *map*, 34; silk trade, 31
Saudi Arabia. *See* Geographical Index under Arabia
Saxony, Magyar invasion of, 279-282
Sayf bin Dhī Yazan, 436, 748
Scandinavia. *See* Geographical Index
Schism; Constantinople and Rome, 869; definition of, 423; Rome and Constantinople, 422-425, 451, 584
Scholar-officials, 66, 327-329
Scholasticism, 309, 509, 707
Schwyz, 713
Science and technology. *See* Category Index
Scivias (Hildegard von Bingen), 496
Scotland; English invasion of, 709, 744; *map*, 712. *See also* Geographical Index
Sculpture; Africa, 377; Italy, 834
Scythia. *See* Geographical Index under Central Asia
Sea travel. *See* Travel by sea
Sefuwa Dynasty, 436-437, 614, 748
Selection of the Nembutsu in the Original Vow, The (Hōnen), 548
Seljuk Turks, 415-417, 434, 442-444; Crusades and, 503; *map*, 416
Senchaku hongan nembutsu-shū. See *Selection of the Nembutsu in the Original Vow, The*
Sengoku period. *See* Warring States period (Japan)
Sentences (Lombard), 472, 663
Sententiarum libri IV. See *Sentences*
Serbia; Turkish conquest of, 809-812. *See also* Geographical Index
Serbs, 540
Serfs, 531
Seven liberal arts, 195
Seventeen Article Constitution, 2, 45
Shahnamah (Firdusi), 234, 285, 393-395
Shaivites, 88, 143
Shan, 132
Shanyang Qu, 64
Shih Ching-t'ang, 953
Shīʿite Islam, 103, 112, 333
Shingon sect, 30, 213
Shintō, 29, 211, 300; samurai and, 206
Shipbuilding, 648-652
Shirazi Dynasty, 474, 739
Shishigatani affair (1177), 537
Shōen, 211, 300, 537
Shoguns, Kamakura, 539
Shu Dynasty, Former. *See* Former Shu Dynasty
Shu Dynasty, Later. *See* Later Shu Dynasty
Siberia. *See* Geographical Index under Russia
Sicilian Vespers (1282), 490
Sicily, Kingdom of, 488-490
Silk; Byzantine Empire and, 31-33, 175; payment in, 230; Sogdians and, 16
Silk Road, 14, 31, 168, 175; *map*, 16
Silla Dynasty, United, 108-110, 297; *regional table*, 109
Silla kingdom, 28
Sixteen Prefectures (China), 302
Siyāsat-nāma. See *Book of Government, The*
Skraelings, 374
Slave Dynasty. *See* Delhi sultanate
Slave Investigation Act (956), 321
Slavery; Africa, 267-270, 290, 476, 579; Ayutthaya, 762; Europe, 514; Gypsies, 235; Korea, 321; Muslim, 587; Portugal, 845
Slavs, 249-251, 263; Bulgars and, 282; Vikings and, 252
Sluis, Battle of (1340), 745
Snaketown, 137
Social reform. *See* Category Index
Soga family, 1, 45, 104
Sogdians, 14-17; Uighurs and, 171
Sokkuram hermitage, 109
Solaṅkis, 693
Solomonid Dynasty, 556, 665-667
Somnath, Battle of (1299), 693
Sŏn Buddhism, 110
Song Dynasty, 293, 303, 322-325, 327-329, 432, 483, 525; *map*, 323; newspapers and, 150; *table*, 324; Vietnam and, 344

Song Dynasty, Northern. *See* Northern Song Dynasty
Song Dynasty, Southern. *See* Southern Song Dynasty
Songhai kingdom, 461; Islam and, 395-397
Soninkes, 172, 356
Southeast Asia; architecture, 115; Buddhism, 113; *map*, 114; religion, 115. *See also* Geographical Index
Southern Dynasties (China), 39
Southern Han Dynasty, 292, 304
Southern Song Dynasty, 324, 484; painting, 562; *table*, 324
Southern Tang Dynasty, 292, 363
Spain; Christianity, 145, 628; Islam and, 367; *map*, 368; Muslims and, 144-146, 162, 307, 412, 447, 627; papermaking, 60. *See* Castile and León; Geographical Index
Sparrow parable (Bede), 51
Spirituals (monastic movement), 591
Spurgyal, 82
Sri Harṣacarita. See *Harshacharita of Banabhatta, The*
Sri Lanka, Cōla invasion of, 295
Śrivijaya, 113-116, 192, 296; *map*, 114
Stipend Land Law (976), 321
Stirling Bridge, Battle of (1297), 710
Stockholm Bloodbath (1520), 821
Story of Burnt Njal, The, 404
Strasbourg Oaths, 242, 244
Students, university, 471
Sufism, 671-673
Sui Dynasty, 39-41, 64, 67, 79; Japan and, 72; *regional table*, 40
Sukhothai, 133, 657, 690-692
Sumatra, 115
Summa theologiae. See *Summa Theologica*
Summa Theologica (Thomas Aquinas), 472, 662-665, 707
Sung Dynasty. *See* Song Dynasty
Sunni Islam, 112, 312, 333, 367-369, 420
Susu kingdom, 173, 630, 725
Swahili cultures, 9-11, 464-465, 474-475
Sweden, 820. *See also* Geographical Index under Scandinavia
Sweet new style. *See Dolce stil nuovo*
Swiss Republic, 713-715
Syria. *See* Geographical Index

Tabaristān. *See* Geographical Index under Iran
Taborites, 842
Tabrīz, capture of (1386), 799
Tahāfut at-tahāfut. See *Incoherence of the Incoherence*
Tahitians, 130
Tahuantinsuyo, 577
Taiheiki, The, 743
Taihō code, 73, 140-142, 300
Taika reforms, 46, 73, 104-106, 140
Taira family, 212, 537, 612, 741
Talas River, Battle of (751), 35, 60, 170, 174-176, 179
Tale of Genji, The (Murasaki Shikibu), 212, 214, 259, 385, 387-389
Tang Dynasty, 79-82, 170, 174, 179, 320; education, 67; fall of, 291; Japan and, 210; *map*, 81; military in, 247; Nanzhao and, 132, 154, 233; *regional table*, 80; Sogdians and, 15; Tibet and, 181; Vietnam and, 260; Vietnamese and, 304
Tang Dynasty, Later. *See* Later Tang Dynasty
Tang Dynasty, Southern. *See* Southern Tang Dynasty
Tannenberg, Battle of (1410), 831-833
Tantric Buddhism, 115, 203, 566
Tantrism (Hinduism), 159
Tarain, Battle of (1215/1216), 636
Tarain, First Battle of (1191), 588
Tarain, Second Battle of (1192), 588
Taʾrīkh al-rusul wa al-mulūk. See *History of al-Ṭabarī, The*
Tashkent, 174
Taxation; Africa, 477; China, 39, 230; Church, 698; England, 444, 795; France, 533; Ghana, 355; Japan, 141, 204; of Jews, 683; Khazars, 168; Korea, 297; Tibet, 237
Technology. *See* Category Index under Science and technology
Tekrur, 579
Temple of Kukulcan. *See* Castillo (at Chichén Itzá)
Temple of Quetzalcóatl. *See* Pyramid B (at Tula)
Temple of the Inscriptions, 56
Ten Kingdoms (China). *See* Five Dynasties and Ten Kingdoms (China)
Ten Thousand Leaves, The. *See* Manyōshū
Tendai sect, 30, 300, 547
Tenochtitlán, 731-734
Terminism, 708
Teutonic Knights, 624-627, 831; *map*, 626
Thai, 132-134; Khmer conquest of, 273-275; law, 762-763
Thamanasat, 762
Theater; Christian, 381; India, 88; medieval stage directions, 382; miracle plays, 381-384; mystery plays, 381-384; Nō, 769-772
Theater state, Tiwanaku, 12
Theology; England, 708, 787; France, 708; Franks, 195; Italy, 42
Théophilus (Rutebeuf), 383
Theravāda Buddhism, 133, 691; Lan Na, 658
Thorn, Treaty of (1411), 833
Thousand and One Nights, The. See *Arabian Nights' Entertainments, The*

Three Kingdoms period, Later. *See* Later Three Kingdoms period (Korea)
Tibet, 82-85, 237-239; Buddhism in, 202-203; Mongols and, 777-779; Uighurs and, 171
T'ieh-le. *See* Tiele
Tiele, 170
Timbuktu, 395, 461-463, 725
Tiwanaku civilization, 11-14, 360-362
Toledo, Jews in, 508
Tollán. *See* Tula
Toltec Empire, 125, 287, 313-316
Tongans, 130
Tongji Qu, 64
Tosa Diary, The (Ki no Tsurayuki), 213
Tosa nikki. See *Tosa Diary, The*
Toulouse, Battle of (721), 162
Toulouse, kingdom of, 17
Tours, Battle of (732), 162-164
Tours, Truce of (1444), 747, 866
Toutswe kingdom, 219-221
Towns, rise of, 532
Trade, 33; Africa, 9, 290, 356, 377, 395, 437-438, 440, 461, 464, 474, 476-477, 614, 630, 740, 825; Aztecs, 732; Byzantine Empire, 91; Cahokia, 135; Central Asia, 14-17; Chimú Empire, 256; China, 80, 323, 668; Cōlas, 295, 348; Egypt, 333; Europe, 571, 844; Germany, 519-521; Italy, 511; Khazars, 168; Kilwa Kisiwani, 740; Mogollon civilization, 62; Novgorod, 639; Peru, 256; Venice, 513-515; Vietnam, 617. *See also* Category Index
Tran Dynasty, 616-618, 847
Translations; Arabic to Latin, 309; Greek to Arabic, 226, 507; Sanskrit to Chinese, 87; Sanskrit to Tibetan, 237; Syriac to Arabic, 226
Transoxiana, 318-320. *See also* Geographical Index under Central Asia
Transportation. *See* Category Index
Transubstantiation, 606, 787, 842
Travel by land; al-Bakri, 172; Buddhists, 30; Jean Froissart, 780; Ibn Baṭṭūṭah, 476, 729; Kāshgarī, 240; Mansa Mūsā, 724; Marco Polo, 115, 668; Muslim traders, 356; Silk Road, 14, 182; al-Ṭabarī, 270; al-ʿUmarī, 749; Xuanzang, 78, 85, 245
Travel by sea, 114, 648-652; China, 324; Grand Canal, 41; Polynesians, 131; Thule Inuit, 373; Vikings, 207; Zheng He, 830
Travels of Ibn Battuta. See *Riḥlah*
Travels of Marco Polo, The (Polo), 670
Travels of Sir John Mandeville, 501
Treatise of Lorenzo Valla on the Donation of Constantine, The (Valla), 853
Treatise on Proportions (Bradwardine), 734
Treatise on the Laws and Customs of the Kingdom of England (Glanville), 603
Tribute Money, The (Masaccio), 836
Trivium, 195
Trois, Treaty of (1420), 849
Troubadours, 469
Troyes, Council of (1128), 485
Troyes, Treaty of (1420), 746, 865
True Pure Land Buddhism, 548
Tuḥfat al-nuṣ ār fi gharaʿib al-amsar wa-ʿajaʿib al-asfar; *Riḥlah*, 953
Tuareg, 461
T'u-chüeh. *See* Tuque
Tughluqid Dynasty, 753
Tula, 313-316; similarity to Chichén Itzá, 125
Tuque, 170
Turkey. *See* Geographical Index
Turkish Slave Dynasty. *See* Delhi sultanate
Turkistan. *See* Geographical Index under Central Asia
Turkmenistan. *See* Geographical Index under Central Asia
Turks, 33-36. *See also* Ottomans; Seljuk Turks
Typography; China, 266, 418-420; Germany, 861-864

U, King, 816
ʿUbayd All3h al-Mahdt , 333
Uighurs, 170-172, 239-241; Tang Dynasty and, 182
Ukraine. *See* Geographical Index under Russia
Ulus Chagatai, 797
Umayyad caliphate, 111, 188, 196, 307; fall of, 412-415; Sogdians and, 15; *table*, 307
Unam sanctam (Boniface VIII), 697-699, 705; *extract*, 698
Universities; Chinese, 67; European, 470-473; rules of conduct, 471
Unterwalden, 713
Upper Śivālaya Temple, 78
Uprisings. *See* Category Index under Wars, uprisings, and civil unrest
Urdu. *See* Hindi
Uri, 713
Uzbekistan. *See* Geographical Index under Central Asia

Vajracchedikā-prajñāpāramitā Sūtra. See *Diamond Sutra*
Valencia, conquest of, 447-450
Varangian Guard, 353, 695. *See also* Vikings
Varna, Battle of (1444), 855, 858
Vellur, Battle of (915), 295
Venice; Crusades and, 585; Peace of (1177), 523; shipmaking, 649; trade, 513-515
Verdun, Treaty of (843), 241-244; *map*, 243
Verneuil, Battle of (1424), 746
Verona, Council of (1184), 550, 633

Vietnam, 304-306, 847-849; China and, 81, 617; Nanzhao invasion of, 155; *table of historic periods*, 305. *See also* Geographical Index under Southeast Asia
Vijayanagar, 754
Vikings, 251-255, 406, 648; *map* of raids, 208, 253; migration into England, 207
Villeinage, 796
Vinland, 254, 374
Visigoths, 17, 145, 627
Vita nuova, La. See *New Life, The*
Vivekachudamani. See *Crest Jewel of Wisdom, The*

Wagadu. *See* Ghana
Walachians, 737-739
Waldensians, 549-552, 726, 841
Wales, rebellion against England, 655
War of the Gaedhil with the Gail, The, 403
Wari. *See* Huari civilization
Warring States period (Japan), 743
Wars, uprisings, and civil unrest. *See* Category Index
Welfs, 534
Wends, 504, 534
Western Cālukya Dynasty, 338-340
Western Jin Dynasty, 39
Western Liao Dynasty, 484
Westminster I (1275), 680
Westminster II (1285), 680
Westminster III (1290), 680
Whitby, Synod of (664), 96
White Deer Hollow Academy, 491
White Huns, 3, 69; defeat of, 33-36; *map*, 4
White Monks. *See* Cistercians
Wild Goose Pagoda, 87
Winchester, Statute of (1285), 680-682
Windsor, Treaty of (1175), 544
Winterthur, Battle of (1292), 713
Wisdom of Royal Glory (Yūsuf Khāss Hājib), 239, 286
Witchcraft, 726-729
Wittelsbach Dynasty, 767
Wolof Empire, 579-580
Women; China, 121, 328, 362-364; Christianity and, 495-498; France, 468; India, 636, 789; Japan, 387; Ming Dynasty, 363; Muslim, 188; Neo-Confucianism, 363; Yuan Dynasty, 363
Woodhenge, 135, 217
Writing; El Tajín, 54; India, 366; Japan, 213-215; Korea, 321; Slavs, 249-251; Sogdiana, 14; Swahili, 464; Thai, 691; Tibet, 84; Uighurs, 239
Wu Dynasty, 292
Wu-Yue Dynasty, 292

Xi'an. *See* Chang'an
Xin Tang shu (Ouyang), 191
Xiyouji. See *Journey to the West*
Xylography, 266

Yaloge, 170
Yamini Dynasty, 565
Yarmūk, Battle of (636), 97-100
Yaya-Mama, 11
Yeke Mongol Ulus, 583
Yellow Hat order. *See* Gelugpa order
Yellow Uighurs, 239
Yenjing. *See* Beijing
Yi Dynasty, 815-817; *table*, 816
Yongji Qu, 64
Yonglo Dadian, 827-828
Yōrō code, 141
Yorubas, 376-378
Yoshino Civil Wars (1336-1392), 741-743
Yuan Dynasty, 325, 525, 617, 676, 775, 777, 816, 818; Quanzhen Daoism in, 478; women, 363
Yūgen, 771
Yuzhou. *See* Beijing

Zagwe Dynasty, 554, 665
Zanj revolt (869-883), 267-270
Zen Buddhism, 30; samurai and, 206
Zero, concept of, 47, 458
Zhang-zhung confederacy, 82
Zhong yong. See *Doctrine of the Mean, The*
Zhongdu. *See* Beijing
Zhou Dynasty, Later. *See* Later Zhou Dynasty
Zimbabwe. *See* Great Zimbabwe
Zīrids, 420-422
Zohar (Moses de León), 678-680
Zuihitsu, 386